Human Development

A Cultural Approach

SECOND EDITION

Jeffrey Jensen Arnett
Clark University

Boston   Columbus   Indianapolis   New York   San Francisco   Amsterdam
Cape Town   Dubai   London   Madrid   Milan   Munich   Paris   Montréal   Toronto
Delhi   Mexico City   São Paulo   Sydney   Hong Kong   Seoul   Singapore   Taipei   Tokyo

VP, Product Development: Dickson Musslewhite
Senior Acquisitions Editor: Amber Chow
Editorial Assistant: Luke Robbins
Director of Development: Sharon Geary
Senior Development Editor: Julie Swasey
VP, Director of Marketing: Brandy Dawson
Director, Project Management Services: Lisa Iarkowski
Project Team Lead: Linda Behrens
Project Manager: Barbara Mack
Program Team Lead: Amber Mackey
Program Manager: Diane Szulecki
Director of Field Marketing: Jonathan Cottrell
Senior Product Marketing Manager: Lindsey Prudhomme Gill
Executive Field Marketing Manager: Kate Stewart
Marketing Assistant, Field Marketing: Paige Patunas

Marketing Assistant, Product Marketing: Jessica Warren
Operations Manager: Mary Fischer
Operations Specialist: Diane Peirano
Associate Director of Design: Blair Brown
Interior Design: Kathryn Foot
Cover Art Director: Maria Lange
Cover Design: Pentagram
Cover Art: Cover illustration by Alec Doherty,
  © Pearson Education, Inc.
Digital Media Editor: Christopher Fegan
Digital Media Project Manager: Pamela Weldin
**Full-Service Project Management
  and Composition:** Integra Software Services Pvt. Ltd.
Printer/Binder: RR Donnelley/Roanoke
Cover Printer: Phoenix Color/Hagerstown

Credits and acknowledgments borrowed from other sources and reproduced, with permission,
in this textbook appear on appropriate page within text or on pages C-1–C-4.

Library of Congress Cataloging-in-Publication Data

Arnett, Jeffrey Jensen.
  Human development: a cultural approach/Jeffrey Jensen Arnett.—Second edition.
    pages cm
  Includes bibliographical references and index.
  ISBN 978-0-13-379242-3 (student edition: alk. paper)
  1. Developmental psychology—Cross-cultural studies.   I. Title.
  BF713.A816 2016
  305.2—dc23

                                                    2014039405

10 9 8 7 6 5 4 3 2 1

Student Edition
ISBN-10:   0-13-379242-0
ISBN-13: 978-0-13-379242-3

Books á la Carte
ISBN-10:   0-13-401216-X
ISBN-13: 978-0-13-401216-2

*To my mom, who loved it all,
from start to finish.*

Contents

Preface

Welcome to the second edition of *Human Development: A Cultural Approach!* This edition features updated coverage and current research throughout, as well as an increased focus on the cultural diversity that exists within the United States. During the revision process, I have worked closely with the Pearson team to develop a wide range of interactive features that make the content and cultural approach even more engaging. Throughout the book, you'll see exciting new videos, interactive maps and figures, and self-assessments that will allow students to become more active and enthusiastic learners.

I think you will find that the interactive resources for this edition are unmatched by any other human development textbook. However, what sets this book apart more than anything else is that it presents a portrayal of development that covers the whole amazing range of human cultural diversity. As someone who has taught human development courses for years and was familiar with the available textbooks, I was struck by how narrow all of them seemed to be. They focused on human development in the United States as if it were the typical pattern for people everywhere, with only the occasional mention of people in other parts of the world. If you knew nothing about human development except what you read in a standard textbook, you would conclude that 95% of the human population must reside in the United States. Yet the United States makes up actually less than 5% of the world's population, and there is an immense range of patterns of human development in cultures around the globe, with most of those patterns strikingly different than the mainstream American model. And even within the United States, cultural diversity is much greater than what is found in the typical textbook.

So, in writing this textbook, I decided to take a cultural approach. I set out to portray human development as it takes place across all the different varieties of cultural patterns that people have devised in response to their local conditions and the creative inspiration of their imaginations. My goal was to teach students to *think culturally*, so that when they apply human development to the work they do or to their own lives, they understand that there is, always and everywhere, a cultural basis to development. The cultural approach also includes learning how to critique research for the extent to which it does or does not take the cultural basis of development into account. I provide this kind of critique at numerous points throughout the book, with the intent that students will learn how to do it themselves by the time they reach the end.

I know from my experience as a teacher that students find it fascinating to learn about the different forms that human development takes in various cultures, but there are also practical benefits to the cultural approach. It is more important than ever for students to have knowledge of the wider world because of the increasingly globalized economy and because so many problems, such as disease and climate change, cross borders. Whether they travel the globe or remain in their home towns, in a culturally diverse and globalized world, students will benefit from being able to apply the cultural approach and think culturally about development, whether in social interactions with friends and neighbors, or in their careers, as they may have patients, students, or coworkers who come from different cultures.

Did you notice that the design on the cover is in the shape of a frog? The Chinese have an expression that loosely translates as "the frog in the well knows not of the great ocean," and it is often used as a cautionary reminder to look beyond our own experience and not to assume that what is true for ourselves is true for everyone else as well. I think all of us are like that frog, in a way. We've grown up in a certain cultural context. We've learned to think about life in a certain way. And most of us don't realize how broad and diverse our world really is. My hope is that this book will help more students lift themselves out of the well and appreciate the wonderful diversity of human development.

The cultural approach makes this textbook much different from other life-span textbooks, but there are other features that make this textbook distinct. This is the only major textbook to include a separate chapter on toddlerhood, the second and third years of life. I have always been puzzled by the way other textbooks gloss over toddlerhood, usually including the second year of life as part of "infancy" and the third year of life as part of "early childhood." Yet any parent knows that years 2 and 3 are a lot different from what comes before or after, and I remember this well from my own experience as a father of twins. Infants cannot walk or talk, and once toddlers learn to do both in years 2 and 3, their experience of life—and their parents' experiences—change utterly. Toddlers are also different from older children, in that their ability for emotional self-regulation and their awareness of what is and is not acceptable behavior in their culture is much more limited.

This textbook is also alone among major textbooks in dividing the adult life span into stages of emerging adulthood, young adulthood, middle adulthood, and late adulthood. Emerging adulthood, roughly ages 18–29, is a new life stage that has arisen in developed countries over the past 50 years, as people have entered later into the commitments that structure adult life in most cultures: marriage, parenthood, and stable work. Other textbooks either call the whole period from age 18 through 40 "young adulthood" (which makes little sense, in that for most people in developed countries the ages 18–29 are vastly different than the ages 30–40), or they have an emerging adulthood chapter and then lump young and middle adulthood together as "adulthood" (which also makes little sense, given that it means applying one life stage term to ages 25–60). I originally proposed the theory of emerging adulthood in 2000, and it has now become widely used in the social sciences. I think it is a fascinating and dynamic time of life, and I know students enjoy learning about it, as many of them are in that life stage or have recently passed through it.

This textbook is somewhat shorter than most other texts on human development. There is one chapter devoted to each phase of life, for a total of 13 chapters. Each chapter is divided into three major sections, which correspond to the physical, the cognitive, and the emotional and social domains of development. This is an introductory textbook, and the goal is not to teach students everything there is to know about every aspect of human development, but rather to provide them with a foundation of knowledge on human development that hopefully will inspire them to learn more, in other courses and throughout life.

What's New in the Second Edition?

Broader Emphasis on Cultural Diversity

New "Chapter Introduction" Videos begin each chapter and provide an overview of the developmental stage being covered. The videos feature Americans from diverse backgrounds discussing their lives, experiences, and the role that culture has played in their development.

ACROSS CULTURES, THE TRANSITION FROM EARLY CHILDHOOD TO MIDDLE CHILDHOOD IS RECOGNIZED AS AN IMPORTANT SHIFT IN CHILDREN'S DEVELOPMENT, WHEN THEY BECOME CAPABLE OF GREATER COGNITIVE CHALLENGES AND PERSONAL RESPONSIBILITY (SAMEROFF & HAITH, 1996). In developing countries, middle childhood is often the age when children are first given important family duties, such as taking care of younger siblings, buying or selling goods, maintaining a fire, or caring for domestic animals (Gaskins, 2015; Weisner, 1996). According to Roy D'Andrade (1987), middle childhood is when children first show a grasp of **cultural models**, which are cognitive structures pertaining to common activities, for example buying something at the market, herding cattle, taking care of an infant, making bread, or delivering a message to a relative's house. Children in both developed and developing countries begin formal schooling in middle childhood, which includes cultural models of "listen to the teacher," "wait your turn," and "do your homework." Children begin to grasp cultural models as early as toddlerhood, but during middle childhood their understanding of cultural models acquires greater complexity, so that they become capable of taking on a much broader range of tasks (Gaskins, 2015; Weisner, 1996).

Here as elsewhere in the human life span, how we experience a given stage of life depends greatly on cultural context. Children in all cultures become more capable of useful work in middle childhood, but the nature of their work varies greatly. For many children throughout human history it has been mainly farm work—tending the fields, herding the cows, and feeding the chickens. For today's children, it might be school work or household work in developed countries, and any of a wide range of work in developing countries, from household work to factory work to feeding domestic animals. In this chapter we explore a wide range of cultural variations in children's experiences of middle childhood.

Watch CHAPTER INTRODUCTION: MIDDLE CHILDHOOD

Cultural Focus: Adolescent Conflict with Parents

In traditional cultures, it is rare for parents and adolescents to engage in the kind of frequent conflicts typical of parent–adolescent relationships in Western cultures (Larson et al., 2010). The role of parent carries greater authority in traditional cultures than in the West, and this makes it less likely that adolescents in such cultures will express disagreements and resentments toward their parents (Phinney et al., 2005). Even when they disagree with their parents, they are unlikely to express it because of their feelings of duty and respect (Phinney & Ong, 2002). Outside of the West, interdependence is a higher value than independence, not only during adolescence but throughout adulthood (Markus & Kitayama, 2010; Phinney et al., 2005). Just as a dramatic increase in autonomy during adolescence prepares Western adolescents for adult life in an individualistic culture, learning to submit to the authority of one's parents prepares adolescents in traditional cultures for an adult life in which interdependence is among the highest values and each person has a clearly designated position in a family hierarchy.

In this video, adolescents from a variety of cultures are interviewed as they discuss their changing relationships with their parents as well as with their friends.

Review Question:

The narrator tells us that interdependence is valued in the Mexican village where one of the female teens is from. What are the economic reasons why interdependence might be more adaptive in this Mexican village than in the American family also shown in the video?

Watch ADOLESCENT CONFLICT WITH PARENTS ACROSS CULTURES

Updated "Cultural Focus" Features highlight how culture impacts various aspects of development, such as breast-feeding practices, gross motor development, marriage and family relationships, and work and retirement. Students read an overview of the topic, watch a cross-cultural video with footage from the United States, Mexico, and Botswana, and then answer a review question.

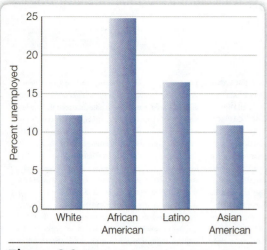

Figure 9.9 U.S. Unemployment Rates for Emerging Adults (Ages 16–24)

What explains the differences among ethnic groups?

SOURCE: Based on Bureau of Labor Statistics (2014)

New Research and Artwork have been incorporated to help students appreciate the diversity that exists within the United States, and understand the role of culture, ethnicity, SES, and other factors in human development.

Increased Attention to Research Methodology

Updated "Research Focus" Features offer a detailed description of a research study, including its premises, methods, results, and limitations. New to this edition, each feature is available in both a traditional narrative format and as a sketch-art style video. Multiple-choice review questions appear at the end of the feature to ensure that students have a solid understanding of the research study and methodology.

Research Focus: Early Child Care and Its Consequences

The "NICHD Study of Early Child Care" began in 1991 with over 1,300 young children (from infancy through early childhood) at 10 sites around the United States.

The children and their families were followed longitudinally for 7 years (NICHD Early Child Care Research Network, 2005). The sample was diverse in socioeconomic (SES) background, ethnicity, and geographical region. Multiple methods were used to assess the children and their families, including observations, interviews, questionnaires, and standardized tests.

Multiple aspects of the care children received were also assessed, including quantity, stability, quality, and type of care. A wide range of children's developmental domains were examined, including physical, social, emotional, cognitive, and language development.

There were many notable and illuminating findings in the study. About three-fourths of the children in the study began nonmaternal child care by the age of 4 months. During infancy and toddlerhood most of this care was provided by relatives, but enrollment in child-care centers increased during toddlerhood, and beyond age 2 most children receiving nonmaternal care were in centers. Infants and toddlers averaged 33 hours a week in nonmaternal care. African American infants and toddlers experienced the highest number of hours per week of nonmaternal care and White infants and toddlers the lowest, with Latinos in between.

For infants and toddlers, the focus of the study was on how child-care arrangements might be related to attachment. The observations measured how sensitive and responsive caregivers were with the children, the two most important determinants of attachment quality according to attachment theory.

As measured by the Strange Situation, attachments to mothers were no different for toddlers receiving nonmaternal care than for toddlers receiving only maternal care. However, insecure attachments were more likely if the nonmaternal care was low in quality, for more than 10 hours per week, or if mothers were low in sensitivity.

This was an impressively ambitious and comprehensive study, but even this study has limitations. Most notably, the children were not randomly assigned into child-care groups. The choices about the care they received and how many hours per week they were in care were made by their parents, not the researchers. Consequently, the outcomes of the children's child-care experiences were interwoven with many other variables, such as parents' income, education, and ethnicity. This is an example of how social scientists are rarely able to create an ideal experimental situation in their research, but must usually take human behavior as they find it and do their best to unravel the daunting complexity of real life.

Review Questions:

1. Which of the following was NOT one of the research methods used in the study?
   a. questionnaires
   b. neurological exams
   c. interviews
   d. observations

2. Which of the following factors was related to insecure attachment in the toddlers?
   a. low-quality non-maternal care
   b. greater than 10 hours a week in non-maternal care
   c. low sensitivity in maternal care
   d. all of the above

Watch RESEARCH FOCUS: EARLY CHILD CARE AND ITS CONSEQUENCES

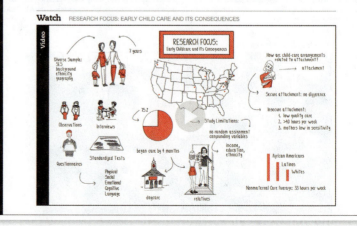

New Opportunities to Apply Knowledge

New "Career Focus" Videos are offered in every chapter, allowing students to learn about a wide variety of career paths. In the videos, career professionals describe their jobs and explain how a knowledge of human development and culture influence their work on a daily basis. Over 30 careers are profiled, including a genetic counselor, a pediatric nurse practitioner, a counselor, a middle school teacher, a community organizer, an advertising executive, and a hospice worker.

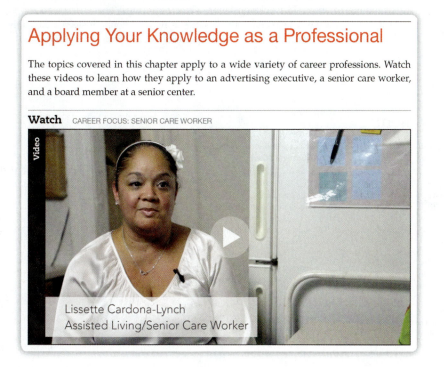

Applying Your Knowledge as a Professional

The topics covered in this chapter apply to a wide variety of career professions. Watch these videos to learn how they apply to an advertising executive, a senior care worker, and a board member at a senior center.

Watch   CAREER FOCUS: SENIOR CARE WORKER

Video

Lissette Cardona-Lynch
Assisted Living/Senior Care Worker

New "Critical Thinking Questions" encourage students to think more deeply and critically about a developmental topic. These questions appear in every major section and often focus on the role of culture in human development.

CRITICAL THINKING QUESTION

How might a culture's values of individualism or collectivism influence toilet-training practices?

Teaching and Learning Aids

Learning Objectives

Learning objectives for each chapter are listed at the start of each section as well as alongside every section heading. Based on Bloom's taxonomy, these numbered objectives help students better organize and understand the material. The end-of-section summary is organized around these same objectives, as are all of the supplements and assessment material.

Neonatal Sleeping Patterns

LO 3.9   Describe neonates' patterns of waking and sleeping, including how and why these patterns differ across cultures.

As discussed in Chapter 2, even in the womb there are cycles of waking and sleeping, beginning at about 28 weeks gestation. Once born, most neonates spend more time asleep than awake. The average for neonates is 16 to 17 hours of sleep a day, although there is great variation, from about 10 hours to about 21 (Peirano et al., 2003).

Summary: Physical Development

LO 5.1   Describe the typical changes in physical growth that take place in toddlerhood and explain the harmful effects of nutritional deficiencies on growth.

Toddlers' physical growth continues at a pace that is slightly reduced from infancy but is nevertheless faster than at any later time of life. Toddlers in developing countries often suffer protein and micronutrient deficiencies that impede their physical and cognitive development.

LO 5.2   Describe the changes in brain development that take place during toddlerhood, and identify the two most common methods of measuring brain activity.

The brain's synaptic density peaks at the end of toddlerhood, followed by many years of synaptic pruning. The two most common methods of measuring brain activity are the EEG and the fMRI.

LO 5.4   Describe the advances in motor development that take place during toddlerhood.

In their gross motor development, toddlers learn to walk, run, climb, and kick a ball. Toddlers in traditional cultures are often restricted in their movements to protect them from danger—especially cooking fires. Advances in fine motor development include holding a cup and building a tower of blocks. In their third year, toddlers may be able to brush their teeth, with some assistance.

LO 5.5   Compare and contrast the process and timing of toilet training in developed countries and traditional cultures.

Children vary widely in the timing of learning toilet training, but most are toilet trained by the end of toddlerhood. In traditional cultures, toddlers usually learn controlled elimination through observing and imitating older children.

Section Summaries

Organized by learning objective, a summary now appears at the end of each major section.

Practice Quizzes and Chapter Quiz

New multiple-choice practice quizzes appear after each section to help students assess their comprehension of the material. A cumulative multiple-choice test appears at the end of every chapter.

Practice Quiz   ANSWERS AVAILABLE IN ANSWER KEY.

1. The heritability of intelligence _____ from childhood to adulthood.
   a. decreases
   b. increases
   c. stays the same
   d. has not been calculated in this area of research

2. The higher the concordance rate, _____.
   a. the more similar the two persons are
   b. the more different the two persons are
   c. the higher the person's chances of having twins
   d. The higher the person's quality of life is likely to be

3. Girls normally begin menstruating around age 11-16, toward the lower end of this range under healthy conditions and toward the higher end when nutrition is insufficient. This is an

4. In recent decades in Western countries, there has been little change in average height, indicating that the populations of these countries have reached the upper boundary of _____ for height.
   a. their concordance rate   c. their reaction range
   b. their heritability   d. their polygenic inheritance

5. A toddler from the Hamer tribe in Ethiopia was adopted by an American couple who described themselves as "non-athletes." This tribe was known for having members who are exceptionally tall. Once she started school, she asked to play in the after-school basketball program, tried out for the team in middle school and high school and eventually went on to earn a scholarship to play in college. This is an example of _____.
   a. polygenic inheritance
   b. incomplete dominance
   c. a self-fulfilling prophecy
   d. niche picking

Chapter Quiz

1. Keisha has inherited one recessive gene for the sickle-cell trait along with one normal dominant gene. As a result of this _____, she is resistant to malaria and does not have sickle-cell anemia.
   a. dominant-recessive inheritance
   b. incomplete dominance
   c. polygenic inheritance
   d. reaction range

2. Who has the greatest risk of developing hemophilia, which is an X-linked recessive disorder?
   a. A female who has one X chromosome that contains the gene for this disorder
   b. A male who has one X chromosome that contains the gene for this disorder
   c. Males and females with one X chromosome that contains the gene for the disorder will have equal risk.
   d. Only Native Americans, due to their unique genetic makeup

6. As a result of the process of crossing over _____.
   a. the risk of Down syndrome is increased
   b. boys are more likely to be born with a learning disability
   c. women are at increased risk for infertility
   d. each child born to a set of parents is genetically unique (with the exception of identical twins)

7. S.J. is most likely to have DZ twins if _____.
   a. she has Asian biological parents
   b. she is in her late teens
   c. she is concerned about gaining too much weight and severely restricts her calorie intake
   d. her mother had DZ twins

8. If Susan learns that her infertility problem is due to a problem with the _____ successfully implanting, something went wrong during the germinal period.
   a. zygote
   b. blastocyst

REVEL™

Experience Designed for the Way Today's Students Read, Think, and Learn

When students are engaged deeply, they learn more effectively and perform better in their courses. This simple fact inspired the creation of REVEL: an immersive learning experience designed for the way today's students read, think, and learn. Built in collaboration with educators and students nationwide, REVEL is the newest, fully digital way to deliver respected Pearson content.

REVEL enlivens course content with media interactives and assessments—integrated directly within the authors' narrative—that provide opportunities for students to read about and practice course material in tandem. This immersive experience boosts student engagement, which leads to better understanding of concepts and improved performance throughout the course.

Learn more about REVEL

http://www.pearsonhighered.com/revel/

In developed countries, too, peer relations expand in toddlerhood, often in the form of some kind of group child care (Rubin et al., 2006). Research observing toddlers in these settings has found that their peer play interactions are more advanced than early studies had reported. One influential early study reported that toddlers engaged exclusively in *solitary play*, all by themselves, or *parallel play*, in which they would take part in the same activity but without acknowledging each other (Parten, 1932). However, more recent studies have found that toddlers engage in not only solitary and parallel play but in *simple social play*, where they talk to each other, smile, and give and receive toys, and even in *cooperative pretend play*, involving a shared fantasy such as pretending to be animals (Howes, 1996; Hughes & Dunn, 2007). Watch the video *Styles of Play* for examples of toddlers engaging in various types of play.

The Second Edition includes integrated videos and media content throughout, allowing students to explore topics more deeply at the point of relevancy.

Watch STYLES OF PLAY

Parallel Play

Revel also offers the ability for students to assess their content mastery by taking multiple-choice quizzes that offer instant feedback and by participating in a variety of writing assignments such as peer-reviewed questions and auto-graded assignments.

MyPsychLab™

MyPsychLab combines proven learning applications with powerful assessment to engage students, assess their learning, and help them succeed.

- **An individualized study plan for each student**, based on performance on chapter pre-tests, helps students focus on the specific topics where they need the most support. The personalized study plan arranges content from less complex thinking—like remembering and understanding—to more complex critical-thinking skills—like applying and analyzing—and is based on Bloom's taxonomy. Every level of the study plan provides a formative assessment quiz.

- **MyVirtualChild and MyVirtualLife.** MyVirtualChild is an interactive simulation that allows students to play the role of a parent and raise their own virtual child. By making decisions about specific scenarios, students can raise their children from birth to age 18 and learn firsthand how their own decisions and other parenting actions affect their child over time. In MyVirtualLife, students make decisions for a virtual version of themselves from emerging adulthood through the end of life.

- **Media assignments** for each chapter—including videos with assignable questions— feed directly into the gradebook, enabling instructors to track student progress automatically.

- **The Pearson eText** lets students access their textbook anytime and anywhere, and any way they want, including listening online.

- **The MyPsychLab Question Library** provides over 2,400 test items in the form of Pre-Tests, Post-Tests, and Chapter Exams. These questions are parallel forms of questions found in the instructor test bank, ensuring that students using MyPsychLab for review and practice will find their tests to be of similar tone and difficulty, while protecting the integrity of the instructor test bank.

With assessment tied to every video, application, and chapter, students get immediate feedback, and instructors can see what their students know with just a few clicks. Instructors can also personalize MyPsychLab to meet the needs of their students.

Teaching and Learning Package

A textbook is but one component of a comprehensive learning package. The author team that prepared the teaching and learning package had as its goal to deliver the most comprehensive and integrated package on the market. All supplements were developed around the textbook's carefully constructed learning objectives. The authors are grateful to reviewers and focus group members who provided invaluable feedback and suggestions for improving various elements of the program.

TEST BANK   Revised by David Hurford (Pittsburg State University), Dorothy Marsil (Kennesaw State University), and Nicole Martin (Kennesaw State University), the Test Bank contains over 4,000 questions, many of which were class-tested in multiple classes at both 2-year and 4-year institutions across the country prior to publication. Item analysis is provided for all class-tested items. All conceptual and applied multiple-choice questions include rationales for each correct answer and the key distracter. The item analysis helps instructors create balanced tests, while the rationales serve both as an added guarantee of quality and as a time-saver when students challenge the keyed answer for a specific item. Each chapter of the test bank includes a Total Assessment Guide, an easy-to-reference grid that organizes all test items by learning objective and question type.

TOTAL ASSESSMENT GUIDE

Chapter 2
Genetics and Prenatal Development

Learning Objectives	Factual (Multiple Choice)	Conceptual (Multiple Choice)	Applied (Multiple Choice)	True/False Questions	Short Answer Questions	Essay Questions
QUICK QUIZ 1	1–3, 5–89, 10	4	9			
QUICK QUIZ 2	1, 3, 5, 6, 8, 9	2, 7, 10	4			
2.1 Distinguish between genotype and phenotype and identify the different forms of genetic inheritance.	1, 3, 12	2, 4, 7, 9, 11	5, 6, 8, 10	1, 2		1
2.2 Describe the sex chromosomes and identify what makes them different from other chromosomes.	13, 18	16	14, 15, 17	3, 4	1	
2.3 Describe how behavior geneticists use heritability estimates and concordance rates in their research.	19–27, 30, 34, 35, 37, 39–43, 46, 49–51	28, 29, 33, 38, 45, 47, 48	31, 32, 36, 44	5–11	2, 3	

The test bank comes with Pearson MyTest, a powerful test generation program that helps instructors easily create and print quizzes and exams. Questions and tests can be authored online, allowing instructors ultimate flexibility and the ability to efficiently manage assessments wherever and whenever they want. Instructors can easily access existing questions and then edit, create, and store using simple drag-and-drop and Word-like controls. Data on each question provides information relevant to difficulty level and page number. In addition, each question maps to the text's major section and learning objective. For more information go to www.PearsonMyTest.com.

ENHANCED LECTURE POWERPOINT SLIDES WITH EMBEDDED VIDEOS Written by Marvin Tobias (St. Charles Community College), the Enhanced Lecture PowerPoints offer detailed outlines of key points for each chapter supported by selected visuals from the textbook, and include the videos from the human development video series featured in the text. Standard Lecture PowerPoints without embedded videos are also available. A separate *Art and Figure* version of these presentations contains all art from the textbook for which Pearson has been granted electronic permissions.

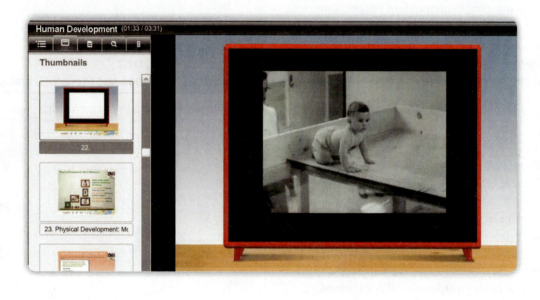

INSTRUCTOR'S MANUAL Written and compiled by Dorothy Marsil (Kennesaw State University), the Instructor's Manual includes suggestions for preparing for the course, sample syllabi, and current trends and strategies for successful teaching. Each chapter offers integrated teaching outlines and a list of the key terms for quick reference, and includes an extensive bank of lecture launchers, handouts, and activities, and suggestions for integrating third-party videos and web resources. Answers to the in-text features are provided. Detailed critical-thinking problems with accompanying rubrics were written by Diana Joy of the Community College of Denver. A set of questions for using MyVirtualChild with the cultural approach, written by Guyla Davis of Ouachita Baptist University, is also included. The electronic format features click-and-view hotlinks that allow instructors to quickly review or print any resource from a particular chapter. This tool saves prep work and helps you maximize your classroom time.

ACCESSING ALL RESOURCES For a list of all student resources available with *Human Development: A Cultural Approach*, Second Edition, go to www.mypearsonstore.com, enter the text ISBN (0133792420) and check out the "Everything That Goes with It" section under the book cover.

For access to all instructor supplements for *Human Development: A Cultural Approach*, Second Edition, go to www.pearsonhighered.com/irc and follow the directions to register (or log in if you already have a Pearson user name and password). Once you have registered and your status as an instructor is verified, you will be e-mailed a log-in name and password. Use your log-in name and password to access the catalog.

You can request hard copies of the supplements through your Pearson sales representative. If you do not know your sales representative, go to www.pearsonhighered.com/replocator and follow the directions. For technical support for any of your Pearson products, you and your students can contact http://247.pearsoned.com.

Acknowledgments

I am grateful to all of the talented and dedicated people who contributed to the second edition. I would especially like to thank Amber Chow, the Senior Acquisitions Editor, who enthusiastically supported my vision for the book and mobilized all the resources necessary to bring it to fruition. Julie Swasey performed superbly as the Senior Development Editor, going over every line of my writing multiple times and repeatedly making it better. Thanks also go to Barbara Mack at Pearson and to Chakira Lane at Integra Software Services for coordinating all aspects of production. Debbie Coniglio, Joshua Johnson, Julie Tondreau, and Veronica Grupico filmed the wonderful new chapter introduction and career videos, under the guidance of Ashley Maynard, as well as producing the new Research Focus videos. Katie Toulmin, Nick Kaufman, Howard Stern, and others at NKP Media, advised by Ashley Maynard and Bianca Dahl, filmed the fabulous Cultural Focus videos. Diane Szulecki, the Program Manager, oversaw all aspects of the program and its supplements package, and Pamela Weldin, the Digital Media Project Manager, produced the MyPsychLab site and coordinated all aspects of digital media production. Lindsey Prudhomme Gill, Senior Product Marketing Manager, handled the marketing of the text and organized focus groups that provided valuable feedback on the Revel eText. Carly Bergey found the photos that do a great job of reflecting the cultural approach of the book. Kathryn Foot created the interior design and Pentagram created the cover design. I'd also like to thank Alec Doherty for the cover illustration, and Luke Robbins for coordinating the reviews and for his assistance with uploading the digital assets for the Revel eText.

Finally, I would like to thank the hundreds of reviewers who reviewed chapters, sections, and other materials in the course of the development of the book. I benefited greatly from their suggestions and corrections, and now instructors and students reading the book will benefit, too.

The Development of Human Development: A Cultural Approach

This textbook is the product of the most extensive development effort this market has ever witnessed. *Human Development: A Cultural Approach* reflects the countless hours and extraordinary efforts of a team of authors, editors, and reviewers that shared a vision for not only a unique human development textbook, but also the most comprehensive and integrated supplements program on the market. Over 250 manuscript reviewers provided invaluable feedback for making this text as accessible and relevant to students as possible. Each chapter was also reviewed by a panel of subject-matter experts to ensure accuracy and currency. Dozens of focus-group participants helped guide every aspect of the program, from content coverage to the art style and design to the configuration of the supplements. In fact, some of those focus-group participants were so invested in the project that they became members of the supplements author team themselves. Dozens of students compared the manuscript to their current textbooks and provided suggestions for improving the prose and design. We thank everyone who participated in ways great and small, and hope that you are as pleased with the finished product as we are!

INSTRUCTORS

Alaska
Karen Gibson, *University of Alaska Anchorage*

Alabama
Sarah Luckadoo, *Jefferson State Community College*
Carroll Tingle, *University of Alabama*

Arizona
Richard Detzel, *Arizona State University* and *Northern Arizona University*
Elaine Groppenbacher, *Chandler Gilbert Community College* and *Western International University*

California
Patricia Bellas, *Irvine Valley College*
Bella DePaulo, *University of California, Santa Barbara*
Ann Englert, *Cal Poly, Pomona*
Lenore Frigo, *Shasta College*
Mary Garcia-Lemus, *Cal Poly San Luis Obispo*
Mary Gauvain, *University of California, Riverside*
Arthur Gonchar, *University of La Verne*
Brian Grossman, *San Jose State University*
Richard Kandus, *Mt. San Jacinto College*
Michelle Pilati, *Rio Hondo College*
Wendy Sanders, *College of the Desert*
Emily Scott-Lowe, *Pepperdine University*
Susan Siaw, *Cal Poly Pomona*

Colorado
Silvia Sara Canetto, *Colorado State University*
Jessica Herrick, *Mesa State College*
Diana Joy, *Community College of Denver*
David MacPhee, *Colorado State University*
Peggy Norwood, *Community College of Aurora*

Connecticut

Carol LaLiberte, *Asnuntuck Community College*

Florida

Maggie Anderson, *Valencia Community College*

Diana Ciesko, *Valencia Community College*

Sorah Dubitsky, *Florida International University*

Shayn Lloyd, *Tallahassee Community College*

Haili Marotti, *Edison State Community College*

Seth Schwartz, *University of Miami*

Anne Van Landingham, *Orlando Tech*

Lois Willoughby, *Miami Dade College*

Georgia

Jennie Dilworth, *Georgia Southern University*

Dorothy Marsil, *Kennesaw State University*

Nicole Rossi, *Augusta State University*

Amy Skinner, *Gordon College*

Sharon Todd, *Southern Crescent Technical College*

Hawaii

Katherine Aumer, *Hawaii Pacific University*

Illinois

Gregory Braswell, *Illinois State University*

Carolyn Fallahi, *Waubonsee Community College*

Lisa Fozio-Thielk, *Waubonsee Community College*

Christine Grela, *McHenry County College*

Lynnel Kiely, *City Colleges of Chicago: Harold Washington College*

Kathy Kufskie, *Southwestern Illinois College*

Mikki Meadows, *Eastern Illinois University*

Michelle Sherwood, *Eastern Illinois University*

Beth Venzke, *Concordia University Chicago*

Indiana

Kimberly Bays, *Ball State University*

Iowa

Shawn Haake, *Iowa Central Community College*

Brenda Lohman, *Iowa State University*

Jennifer Meehan Brennom, *Kirkwood Community College*

James Rodgers, *Hawkeye Community College*

Kari Terzino, *Iowa State University*

Kansas

Joyce Frey, *Pratt Community College*

David P. Hurford, *Pittsburg State University*

Kentucky

Myra Bundy, *Eastern Kentucky University*

Janet Dean, *Asbury University*

Louisiana

Kim Herrington, *Louisiana State University at Alexandria*

Eartha Johnson, *Dillard University*

Maine

Diane Lemay, *University of Maine at Augusta*

Elena Perrello, *The University of Maine* and *Husson University*

Ed Raymaker, *Eastern Maine Community College*

Candace Schulenburg, *Cape Cod Community College*

Maryland

Diane Finley, *University of Maryland University College*

Stacy Fruhling, *Anne Arundel Community College*

Carol Miller, *Anne Arundel Community College*

Gary Popoli, *Harford Community College*

Terry Portis, *Anne Arundel Community College*

Rachelle Tannenbaum, *Anne Arundel Community College*

Nicole Williams, *Anne Arundel Community College*

Massachusetts

Claire Ford, *Bridgewater State University*

Barbara Madden, *Fitchburg State University*

Candace J. Schulenburg, *Cape Cod Community College*

Michigan

Nancy Hartshorne, *Delta College*

H. Russell Searight, *Lake Superior State University*

Minnesota

Jarilyn Gess, *Minnesota State University Moorhead*

Dana Gross, *St. Olaf College*

Rodney Raasch, *Normandale Community College*

Mississippi

Linda Fayard, *Mississippi Gulf Coast Community College*

Donna Carol Gainer, *Mississippi State University*

Linda Morse, *Mississippi State University*

Missouri

Scott Brandhorst, *Southeast Missouri State University*

Sabrina Brinson, *Missouri State University*

Peter J. Green, *Maryville University*

Nebraska

Susan Sarver, *University of Nebraska-Lincoln*

Nevada

Bridget Walsh, *University of Nevada, Reno*

New Jersey

Christine Floether, *Centenary College*

Melissa Sapio, *Montclair State University*

New Mexico

Katherine Demitrakis, *Central New Mexico Community College*

New York

Paul Anderer, *SUNY Canton*

Rachel Annunziato, *Fordham University*

Sybillyn Jennings, *Russell Sage College-The Sage Colleges*

Judith Kuppersmith, *College of Staten Island*

Jonathan Lang, *Borough of Manhattan Community College*

Steven McCloud, *Borough of Manhattan Community College*

Julie McIntyre, *The Sage Colleges*

Elisa Perram, *The Graduate Center, The City University of New York*

North Carolina

Paul Foos, *University of North Carolina, Charlotte*
Donna Henderson, *Wake Forest University*
Amy Holmes, *Davidson County Community College*
Jason McCoy, *Cape Fear Community College*
Andrew Supple, *University of North Carolina at Greensboro*
Maureen Vandermaas-Peeler, *Elon University*

Ohio

Amie Dunstan, *Lorain County Community College*
Jamie Harmount, *Ohio University*
James Jackson, *Clark State Community College*
James Jordan, *Lorain County Community College*
William Kimberlin, *Lorain County Community College*
Jennifer King-Cooper, *Sinclair Community College*
Carol Miller, *Sinclair Community College*
Michelle Slattery, *North Central State College*

Ontario, CA

Lillian Campbell, *Humber College*

Oklahoma

Matthew Brosi, *Oklahoma State University*
Yuthika Kim, *Oklahoma City Community College*
Gregory Parks, *Oklahoma City Community College*
John Phelan, *Western Oklahoma State College*

Oregon

Alishia Huntoon, *Oregon Institute of Technology*

Pennsylvania

Melissa Calderon, *Community College of Allegheny County*
Martin Packer, *Duquesne University*

Rhode Island

Clare Sartori, *University of Rhode Island*

South Carolina

Brantlee Haire, *Florence-Darlington Technical College*
Salvador Macias, *University of South Carolina Sumter*
Megan McIlreavy, *Coastal Carolina University*

Tennessee

Clark McKinney, *Southwest Tennessee Community College*

Texas

Terra Bartee, *Cisco College*
Wanda Clark, *South Plains College*
Trina Cowan, *Northwest Vista College*
Stephanie Ding, *Del Mar College*
Jim Francis, *San Jacinto College-South*
Robert Gates, *Cisco College*
Jerry Green, *Tarrant County College-Northeast Campus*
Heather Hill, *St. Mary's University*
Jean Raniseski, *Alvin Community College*
Darla Rocha, *San Jacinto College*
Victoria Van Wie, *Lone Star College-CyFair*
Kim Wombles, *Cisco College*

Utah

Ann M. Berghout Austin, *Utah State University*
Thomas J. Farrer, *Brigham Young University*
Sam Hardy, *Brigham Young University*
Shirlene Law, *Utah State University*
Volkan Sahin, *Weber State University*
Julie Smart, *Utah State University*

Virginia

Christopher Arra, *Northern Virginia Community College-Woodbridge*
Geri M. Lotze, *Virginia Commonwealth University*
Stephan Prifti, *George Mason University*
Steve Wisecarver, *Lord Fairfax Community College*

Washington

Pamela Costa, *Tacoma Community College*
Dan Ferguson, *Walla Walla Community College*
Amy Kassler, *South Puget Sound Community College*
Staci Simmelink-Johnson, *Walla Walla Community College*

Wyoming

Ruth Doyle, *Casper College*

Australia

Laurie Chapin, *Victoria University*

Canada

Lauren Polvere, *Concordia University*

REVIEWER CONFERENCE PARTICIPANTS

Ann Englert, *California State Polytechnic University, Pomona*
Kathleen Hopkins, *SUNY Rockland Community College*
David P. Hurford, *Pittsburg State University*
Richard Kandus, *Mt. San Jacinto College*
Yuthika Kim, *Oklahoma City Community College*
Dorothy Marsil, *Kennesaw State University*
Julie McIntyre, *The Sage Colleges*
Carol Miller, *Anne Arundel Community College*
Steve Wisecarver, *Lord Fairfax Community College*

TEXT FOCUS GROUPS

Tenelnger Abrom-Johnson, *Prairie View A&M University*
Triin Anton, *University of Arizona*
A. Nayena Blankson, *Valencia Community College*
Gina Brelsford, *Penn State Harrisburg*
Guyla Davis, *Ouachita Baptist University*
Mark Davis, *University of West Alabama*
Ann Englert, *California State Polytechnic University, Pomona*
Jessica Hehman, *University of Redlands*
Diana Joy, *Community College of Denver*
Richard Kandus, *Mt. San Jacinto College*
Yuthika Kim, *Oklahoma City Community College*
Carolyn Lorente, *North Virginia Community College*
Connie Manos-Andrea, *Inver Hills Community College*
Dorothy Marsil, *Kennesaw State University*

Denise McClung, *West Virginia University at Parkersburg*
David F. McGrevy, *San Diego Mesa College and University of San Diego*
Julie McIntyre, *The Sage Colleges*
Robin Montvilo, *Rhode Island College*
Natasha Otto, *Morgan State University*
Rachel M. Petty, *University of the District of Columbia*
Marc Wolpoff, *Riverside City College*
Christine Ziegler, *Kennesaw State University*

SUPPLEMENTS FOCUS GROUP

Darin LaMar Baskin, *Houston Community College*
Trina Cowan, *Northwest Vista College*
Mark Evans, *Tarrant County College*
Jerry Green, *Tarrant County College*

David P. Hurford, *Pittsburg State University*
Diana Joy, *Community College of Denver*
Rose Mary Istre, *San Jacinto College*
Yuthika Kim, *Oklahoma City Community College*
Franz Klutschkowski, *North Central Texas College*
Dorothy Marsil, *Kennesaw State University*
Darla Rocha, *San Jacinto College-North*

STUDENT REVIEWERS

Kacie Farrar
Easha Khanam
Christina Kroder
Heather Lacis
Samantha Piterniak
Kaleigh Sankowski

STUDENT FOCUS GROUP PARTICIPANTS

Krista Anderson
Noelle Armstrong
Tori Bailey
Alaynah Bakosh
Kevin Barnes
Blake Bender
Heather Bennett
Ashlie Bogenschutz
Chelsea Boyd
Bianca Brown
Jasmine Brown
Kelsie Brown
Victor Calderon
Myndi Casey
Flor Cerda
Kolbi Chaffin
Jose Gabriel Checo
Percilla Colley
Nicole Collier
Alexandria Cornell
Brandon Culver
Jayson De Leon
Cody Decker
Tiarra Edwards
Michelle England
Nicole Evans
Emma Fialka-Feldman

Hope Foreback
Bailey Francis
Leslie Frantz
David Garcia
Shannon Gogel
Eric Gould
Che Grippon
Dolly M. Guadalupe
Lucia Guerrero
Daniel Guillen
Cassandra Hagan
Jamie Hall
Ashton Hooper
Antony Karanja
Jesse Klaucke
Joshua Laboy
Ashley Lacy
Abta Laylor
Janella Leach
Julien Lima
Kelsey Love
Erica Lynn
Chelsey Mann
Melissa Methaney
Nick McCommon
Kristie McCormick
Emily McWilliams

Claudia Mendez
Krystle Mercado
Ashley Minning
Paul Mitchell
Sarah Mocherniak
Francisco Moncada
Isaiah Moore
Juan Moreno
Austin Morris
Jodie Mudd
Tia Nguyen
Jacob Nieves
Tiffany Potemra
Veronica Poul
Michelle Richardson
David Riffle
Trey Robb
Kristin Serkowski
Richard Stillman
Amber Thichangthong
Marilyn Toribio
Tugce Tuskan
Kelci Wallace
Edyta Werner
Ashley Williams

About the Author

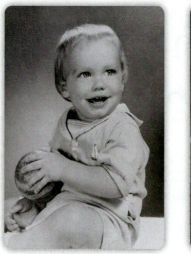

Jeffrey Jensen Arnett is a Research Professor in the Department of Psychology at Clark University in Worcester, Massachusetts. He received his Ph.D. in developmental psychology in 1986 from the University of Virginia, and did 3 years of postdoctoral work at the University of Chicago. From 1992–1998 he was Associate Professor in the Department of Human Development and Family Studies at the University of Missouri, where he taught a 300-student life-span development course every semester. In the fall of 2005, he was a Fulbright Scholar at the University of Copenhagen in Denmark.

His primary scholarly interest for the past 20 years has been in emerging adulthood. He coined the term, and he has conducted research on emerging adults concerning a wide variety of topics, involving several different ethnic groups in American society. He is the Founding President and Executive Director of the Society for the Study of Emerging Adulthood (SSEA; www.ssea.org). From 2005 to 2014 he was the editor of the Journal of Adolescent Research, and currently he is on the Editorial Board of JAR and five other journals. He has published many theoretical and research papers on emerging adulthood in peer-reviewed journals, as well as the books *Adolescence and Emerging Adulthood: A Cultural Approach* (2015, 6th edition, Pearson), and *Emerging Adulthood: The Winding Road from the Late Teens Through the Twenties* (2015, 2nd edition, Oxford University Press).

He lives in Worcester, Massachusetts, with his wife Lene Jensen and their twins, Miles and Paris. For more information on Dr. Arnett and his research, see **www.jeffreyarnett.com**.

Chapter 1
A Cultural Approach to Human Development

THE CHINESE HAVE AN EXPRESSION FOR THE LIMITED WAY ALL OF US LEARN TO SEE THE WORLD: *jing di zhi wa,* meaning "frog in the bottom of a well." The expression comes from a fable about a frog that has lived its entire life in a small well. The frog assumes that its tiny world is all there is, and it has no idea of the true size of the world. It is only when a passing turtle tells the frog of the great ocean to the east that the frog realizes there is much more to the world than it had known.

All of us are like that frog. We grow up as members of a culture and learn, through direct and indirect teaching, to see the world from the perspective that becomes most familiar to us. Because the people around us usually share that perspective, we seldom have cause to question it. Like the frog, we rarely suspect how big and diverse our human species really is.

The goal of this book is to lift you out of the well, by taking a cultural approach to understanding **human development**, the ways people grow and change across the life span. This means that the emphasis of the book is on how persons develop as members of a culture. **Culture** is the total pattern of a group's customs, beliefs, art, and technology. In other words, a culture is a group's common way of life, passed on from one generation to the next. From the day we are born, all of us experience our lives as members of a culture (sometimes more than one), and this profoundly influences how we develop, how we behave, how we see the world, and how we experience life.

Biology is important, too, of course, and at various points we will discuss the interaction between biological and cultural or social influences. However, human beings everywhere have essentially the same biological constitution, yet their paths through the life span are remarkably varied depending on the culture in which their development takes place.

In the course of this book I will be your fellow frog, your guide and companion as we rise together out of the well to gaze at the broad, diverse, fascinating cultural panorama of the human journey. The book will introduce you to many variations in human development and cultural practices you did not know about before, which may lead you to see your own development and your own cultural practices in a new light. We'll also learn to analyze and critique research based on whether it does or does not take culture into account. By the time you finish this book, you should be able to *think culturally.*

In this chapter we set the stage for the rest of the book. The first section provides a broad summary of human life today around the world as well as an examination of how culture developed out of our evolutionary history. In the second section, we look at the history of theoretical conceptions of human development along with a new cultural-developmental theory that will be the framework for this book. Finally, the third section provides an overview of human development as a scientific field.

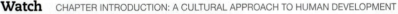

Watch   CHAPTER INTRODUCTION: A CULTURAL APPROACH TO HUMAN DEVELOPMENT

Section 1   Human Development Today and Its Origins

 Learning Objectives

1.1 Describe how the human population has changed over the past 10,000 years and explain why the United States is following a different demographic path from other developed countries.

1.2 Distinguish between the demographic profiles of developed countries and developing countries in terms of cultural values, income, and education.

1.3 Define the term *socioeconomic status* (SES) and explain why SES, gender, and ethnicity are important aspects of human development within countries.

1.4 Explain the process of natural selection and trace the evolutionary origins of the human species.

1.5 Summarize the major changes in human cultures since the Upper Paleolithic period.

1.6 Apply information about human evolution to how human development takes place today.

HUMAN DEVELOPMENT TODAY AND ITS ORIGINS: A Demographic Profile of Humanity Today

Since the goal of this book is to provide you with an understanding of how human development takes place in cultures all around the world, let's begin with a demographic profile of the world's human population in the early 21st century.

Population Growth and Change

LO 1.1   **Describe how the human population has changed over the past 10,000 years and explain why the United States is following a different demographic path from other developed countries.**

human development

ways people grow and change across the life span; includes people's biological, cognitive, psychological, and social functioning

culture

total pattern of a group's customs, beliefs, art, and technology

Perhaps the most striking demographic feature of the human population today is the sheer size of it. For most of history the total human population was under 10 million (McFalls, 2007). Women typically had from four to eight children, but most of the children died in infancy or childhood and never reached reproductive age. The human population began to increase notably around 10,000 years ago, with the development of agriculture and domestication of animals (Diamond, 1992).

Population growth in the millennia that followed was very slow, and it was not until about 400 years ago that the world population reached 500 million persons. Since that time, and especially in the past century, population growth has accelerated at an astonishing rate (see **Figure 1.1**). It took just 150 years for the human population to double

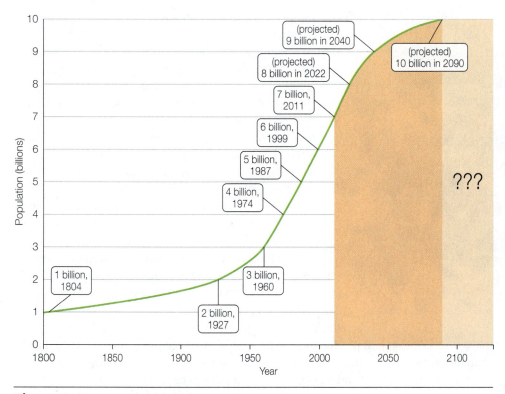

Figure 1.1 World Population Growth

What happened in recent human history to cause population to rise so dramatically?
SOURCE: Based on Population Reference Bureau (2014).

from 500 million to 1 billion, passing that threshold around the year 1800. Then came the medical advances of the 20th century, and the elimination or sharp reduction of deadly diseases like smallpox, typhus, diphtheria, and cholera. Subsequently, the human population reached 2 billion by 1930, then tripled to 6 billion by 1999. The 7-billion threshold was surpassed just 12 years later, in early 2011.

How high will the human population go? This is difficult to say, but most projections indicate it will rise to 10 billion by about 2090 and thereafter stabilize and perhaps slightly decline. This forecast is based on the worldwide decline in birthrates that has taken place in recent years. The **total fertility rate (TFR)** (number of births per woman) worldwide is currently 2.5, which is substantially higher than the rate of 2.1 that is the *replacement rate* of a stable population. However, the TFR has been declining sharply for over a decade and will decline to 2.1 by 2050 if current trends continue (Population Reference Bureau, 2014).

The population increase from now to 2090 will not take place equally around the world. On the contrary, there is a stark "global demographic divide" between the wealthy, economically developed countries that make up less than 20% of the world's population, and the economically developing countries that contain the majority of the world's population (Kent & Haub, 2005). Nearly all the population growth in the decades to come will take place in the economically developing countries. In contrast, nearly all wealthy countries are expected to decline in population during this period and beyond, because they have fertility rates that are well below replacement rate.

For the purposes of this text, we'll use the term **developed countries** to refer to the most affluent countries in the world. Classifications of developed countries vary, but usually this designation includes the United States, Canada, Japan, South Korea, Australia, New Zealand, Chile, and nearly all the countries of Europe (Organization for Economic Cooperation and Development [OECD], 2014). (The term "Western countries" is sometimes used to refer to most developed countries, because they are in the Western hemisphere, except Japan and South Korea, which are considered Eastern countries.) For our discussion, developed countries will be contrasted with **developing countries**,

total fertility rate (TFR)
in a population, the number of births per woman

developed countries
world's most economically developed and affluent countries, with the highest median levels of income and education

developing countries
countries that have lower levels of income and education than developed countries but are experiencing rapid economic growth

which have less wealth than the developed countries but are experiencing rapid economic growth as they join the globalized economy. Many developing countries are changing rapidly today. For example, India is a developing country, and most of its people live on an income of less than two dollars a day (United Nations Development Program [UNDP], 2014). About half of Indian children are underweight and malnourished (World Bank, 2011). Less than half of Indian adolescents complete secondary school. Only about half of adult women are literate, and about three-fourths of adult men. About two-thirds of India's population lives in rural villages, although there is a massive migration occurring from rural to urban areas, led mostly by young people. However, India's economy has been booming for the past 2 decades, lifting hundreds of millions of Indians out of poverty (UNDP, 2014). India is now a world leader in manufacturing, telecommunications, and services. If the economy continues to grow at its present pace India will lead the world in economic production by 2050 (Price Waterhouse Coopers, 2011). Life is changing rapidly for Indians, and children born today are likely to experience much different economic and cultural contexts than their parents or grandparents have known.

Nearly all the world population growth from now to 2050 will take place in developing countries. Pictured here is a busy street in Jodhpur, India.

The current population of developed countries is 1.3 billion, about 18% of the total world population, and the population of developing countries is about 6 billion, about 82% of the world's population (Population Reference Bureau, 2014). Among developed countries, the United States is one of the few likely to gain rather than lose population in the next few decades. Currently there are about 316 million persons in the United States, but by 2050 there will be 400 million. Nearly all the other developed countries are expected to decline in population between now and 2050. The decline will be steepest in Japan, which is projected to drop from a current population of 120 million to just 97 million by 2050, due to a low fertility rate and virtually no immigration (Population Reference Bureau, 2014).

There are two reasons why the United States is following a different demographic path than most other developed countries. First, the United States has a total fertility rate of 1.9, which is slightly below the replacement rate of 2.1 but still higher than the TFR in most other developed countries (Population Reference Bureau, 2014). Second, and more importantly, the United States allows more legal immigration than most other developed countries do, and there are millions of undocumented immigrants as well (Suarez-Orozco, 2015). The increase in population in the United States between now and 2050 will result entirely from immigration (Martin & Midgley, 2010). Both legal and undocumented immigrants to the United States come mainly from Mexico and Latin America, although many also come from Asia and other parts of the world. Consequently, as **Figure 1.2** shows, by 2050 the proportion of the U.S. population that is Latino is projected to rise from 16% to 30%. Canada, the United Kingdom, and Australia also have relatively open immigration policies, so they, too, may avoid the population decline that is projected for most developed countries (DeParle, 2010).

439 million
4%
8%
12%
310 million
30%
2%
5%
12%
16%
46%
65%

☐ Other
☐ Asian American
☐ African American
☐ Latino
☐ White

2010 Actual   2050 Projected

Figure 1.2 Projected Ethnic Changes in the U.S. Population to 2050

Which ethnic group is projected to change the most in the coming decades, and why?

SOURCE: Based on Kaiser Family Foundation (2013).

CRITICAL THINKING QUESTION

What kinds of public policy changes might be necessary in the United States between now and 2050 to adapt to nearly 100 million more immigrants and a rise in the proportion of Latinos to 30%?

Variations Across Countries

LO 1.2   **Distinguish between the demographic profiles of developed countries and developing countries in terms of cultural values, income, and education.**

The demographic contrast of developed countries compared to the rest of the world is stark not only with respect to population but also in other key areas, such as income and education (see **Map 1.1**). With respect to income, about 40% of the world's population lives on less than two dollars per day, and 80% of the world's population lives on a family income of less than $6,000 per year (Population Reference Bureau, 2014). At one extreme are the

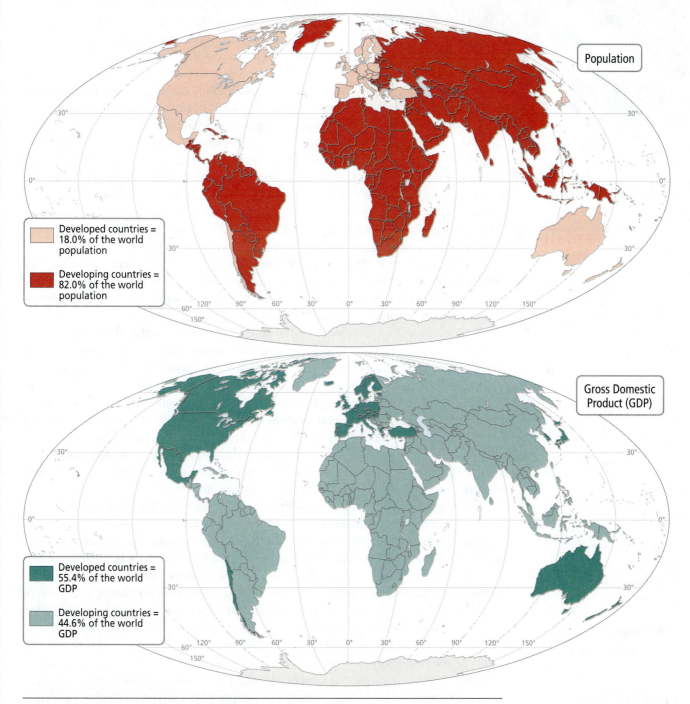

Map 1.1 Worldwide Variations in Population and Income Levels

Developed countries represent only 18% of the world population yet they are much wealthier than developing countries. At what point in its economic development should a developing country be reclassified as a developed country?

By age 10, many children in developing countries are no longer in school. Here, a child in Cameroon helps his mother make flour.

developed countries, where 9 of 10 persons are in the top 20% of the global income distribution, and at the other extreme is southern Africa, where half of the population is in the bottom 20% of global income. Africa's economic growth has been strong for the past decade, but it remains the poorest region in the world (McKinsey Global Institute, 2010; UNDP, 2015).

A similar contrast between rich and poor countries exists regarding education. Your experience as a college student is a rare and privileged status in most of the world. In developed countries, virtually all children obtain primary and secondary education, and about 50% go on to tertiary education (college or other postsecondary training). However, in developing countries about 20% of children do not complete primary school and only about half are enrolled in secondary school (UNDP, 2014). College and other tertiary education is only for the wealthy elite.

There are also some broad cultural differences between developed and developing countries, even though each category is very diverse. One important difference is that the cultures of developed countries tend to be based on **individualistic** values such as independence and self-expression, especially in Western developed countries (Greenfield, 2005). In contrast, developing countries tend to prize **collectivistic** values such as obedience and group harmony (Sullivan & Cottone, 2010). These are not mutually exclusive categories and each country has some balance between individualistic and collectivistic values. Furthermore, most countries contain a variety of cultures, some of which may be relatively individualistic whereas others are relatively collectivistic. Nevertheless, the overall distinction between individualism and collectivism is useful for describing broad differences between human groups.

Within developing countries there is often a sharp divide between rural and urban areas, with people in urban areas having higher incomes and receiving more education and better medical care. Often, the lives of middle-class persons in urban areas of developing countries resemble the lives of people in developed countries in many ways, yet they are much different than people in rural areas of their own countries (UNDP, 2014). In this book, the term **traditional cultures** will be used to refer to people in the rural areas of developing countries, who tend to adhere more closely to the historical traditions of their culture than people in urban areas do. Traditional cultures tend to be more collectivistic than other cultures are, in part because in rural areas close ties with others are often an economic necessity (Sullivan & Cottone, 2010).

This demographic profile of humanity today demonstrates that if you wish to understand human development, it is crucial to understand the lives of people in developing countries, who comprise the majority of the world's population. The tendency in most social science research, especially in psychology, has been to ignore or strip away culture in pursuit of universal principles of development (Jensen, 2011; Rozin, 2006). Most research on human development is on the 18% of the world's population that lives in developed countries—especially the 5% of the world's population that lives in the United States—because research requires money and developed countries can afford more of it than developing countries can (Arnett, 2008). This is changing, and in recent years there has been increasing attention paid in psychology and other social science fields to the cultural context of human development (Jensen, 2015; Shweder, 2011). By now, researchers have presented descriptions of human development in places all over the world, and researchers studying American society have increased their attention to cultures within the United States that are outside of the White middle class.

Expanding our awareness of the other 95% of humanity also has many practical applications. Increasingly the world is approaching the *global village* that the social

individualistic

cultural values such as independence and self-expression

collectivistic

cultural values such as obedience and group harmony

traditional culture

in developing countries, a rural culture that adheres more closely to cultural traditions than people in urban areas do

philosopher Marshall McLuhan (1960) forecast over half a century ago. In recent decades there has been an acceleration in the process of **globalization**, which refers to the increasing connections between different parts of the world in trade, travel, migration, and communication (Arnett, 2002; Jensen et al., 2012; Hermans, 2015). Consequently, wherever you live in the world, in the course of your personal and professional life you are likely to have many contacts with people of other cultures. Those of you going into the nursing profession may one day have patients who have a cultural background in various parts of Asia or South America. Those of you pursuing careers in education will likely teach students whose families emigrated from countries in Africa or Europe. Your coworkers, your neighbors, possibly even your friends and family members may include people from a variety of different cultural backgrounds. Through the Internet you may have contact with people all over the world, via e-mail, Facebook and other social media, YouTube, and new technologies to come. Thus, understanding the cultural approach to human development is likely to be useful in all aspects of life, helping you to communicate with and understand the perspectives of others in a diverse, globalized world.

Variations Within Countries

LO 1.3 **Define the term** *socioeconomic status* **(SES) and explain why SES, gender, and ethnicity are important aspects of human development within countries.**

The contrast between developed countries and developing countries will be used often in this book, as a general way of drawing a contrast between human development in relatively rich and relatively poor countries. However, it should be noted that there is substantial variation within each of these categories. All developed countries are relatively wealthy, but human development in Japan is quite different from human development in France or Canada. All developing countries are less wealthy than developed countries, but human development in China is quite different than human development in Brazil or Nigeria. Throughout the book we will explore variations in human development within the broad categories of developed countries and developing countries.

Not only is there important variation in human development within each category of "developed" and "developing" countries, but there is additional variation within each country. Most countries today have a **majority culture** that sets most of the norms and standards and holds most of the positions of political, economic, intellectual, and media power. In addition, there may be many minority cultures defined by ethnicity, religion, language, or other characteristics.

Variations in human development also occur due to differences within countries in the settings and circumstances of individual lives. The settings and circumstances that contribute to variations in pathways of human development are called **contexts**. Contexts include environmental settings such as family, school, community, media, and culture, all of which will be discussed in this book. Three other important aspects of variation that will be highlighted are socioeconomic status, gender, and ethnicity.

The term **socioeconomic status (SES)** is often used to refer to a person's *social class*, which includes educational level, income level, and occupational status. For children and adolescents, because they have not yet reached the social-class level they will have as adults, SES is usually used in reference to their parents' levels of education, income, and occupation. In most countries, SES is highly important in shaping human development. It influences everything from the risk of infant mortality to the quality and duration of children's education to the kind of work adults do to the likelihood of obtaining health care in late adulthood. Differences in SES are especially sharp in developing countries (UNDP, 2014). In a country such as India or Saudi Arabia or Peru, growing up as a member of the upper-class SES elite is very different from growing up as a member of the relatively poor majority, in terms of access to resources such as health care and education. However, even in developed countries there are important

globalization

increasing connections between different parts of the world in trade, travel, migration, and communication

majority culture

within a country, the cultural group that sets most of the norms and standards and holds most of the positions of political, economic, intellectual, and media power

contexts

settings and circumstances that contribute to variations in pathways of human development, including SES, gender, and ethnicity, as well as family, school, community, media, and culture

socioeconomic status (SES)

person's social class, including educational level, income level, and occupational status

Within each country, SES is an influential context of human development. Here, a low-SES family in the United States.

ethnicity

group identity that may include components such as cultural origin, cultural traditions, race, religion, and language

SES differences in access to resources throughout the course of human development. For example, in the United States infant mortality is higher among low-SES families than among high-SES families, in part because low-SES mothers are less likely to receive prenatal care (Daniels et al., 2006).

Gender is a key factor in development throughout the life span, in every culture (Carroll & Wolpe, 2005; UNDP, 2014). The expectations cultures have for males and females are different from the time they are born (Hatfield & Rapson, 2005). However, the degree of the differences varies greatly among cultures. In most developed countries today, the differences are relatively blurred: Men and women hold many of the same jobs, wear many of the same clothes (e.g., jeans, T-shirts), and enjoy many of the same entertainments. If you have grown up in a developed country, you may be surprised to learn in the chapters to come how deep gender differences go in many other cultures. Nevertheless, gender-specific expectations exist in developed countries, too, as we will see.

Finally, **ethnicity** is a crucial part of human development. Ethnicity may include a variety of components, such as cultural origin, cultural traditions, race, religion, and language. Minority ethnic groups may arise as a consequence of immigration. There are also countries in which ethnic groups have a long-standing presence and may even have arrived before the majority culture. For example, Aboriginal peoples lived in Australia for many generations before the first European settlers arrived. Many African countries were constructed by European colonial powers in the 19th century and consist of people of a variety of ethnicities, each of whom has lived in their region for many generations. Often, ethnic minorities within countries have distinct cultural patterns that are different from those of the majority culture. For example, in the Canadian majority culture, premarital sex is common, but in the large Asian Canadian minority group, female virginity at marriage is still highly valued (Sears, 2012). In many developed countries, most of the ethnic minority groups have values that are less individualistic and more collectivistic than in the majority culture (Suarez-Orozco, 2015).

Practice Quiz   ANSWERS AVAILABLE IN ANSWER KEY.

1. Between now and 2050, the increase in the population of the United States will be nearly entirely caused by what?
   a. Increased life expectancy
   b. Higher majority fertility
   c. Higher minority fertility
   d. Immigration

2. S. is a young girl who lives in a rural area of a developing country. Her family adheres strongly to the historical traditions of their culture. S lives in a(n) _____ culture.
   a. conservative
   b. traditional
   c. archaic
   d. conventional

3. A. and W. are brothers and work together. A. owns a cleaning business, and his brother W helps when the jobs are too big for A. to do alone. These brothers most likely live in a(n) _____ culture.
   a. collectivistic
   b. individualistic
   c. conventional
   d. caste

4. Dr. Wu is conducting research and plans to measure the socioeconomic status (SES) of his participants. His measure of SES will most likely include which of the following?
   a. Income level, education level, and occupational status
   b. Income level, area of education or specialized training, and race
   c. Income level and reputation
   d. Income level and ethnicity

5. Phoebe is very proud of her ability to speak Japanese, her parents' native language, and she has taught herself a number of traditional Japanese dances and songs. Phoebe is proud of her _____.
   a. ethnicity
   b. majority culture
   c. socioeconomic status
   d. caste status

HUMAN DEVELOPMENT TODAY AND ITS ORIGINS: Human Origins and the Birth of Culture

Using a cultural approach to human development, we will see that humans are fabulously diverse in how they live. But how did this diversity arise? Humans are one species, so how did so many different ways of life develop from one biological origin? Before we turn our attention to the development of individuals—called **ontogenetic** development—it is important to understand our **phylogenetic** development, that is, the development of the human species. Let's take a brief tour now of human evolutionary history, as a foundation for understanding the birth of culture and the historical context of individual human development today. For students who hold religious beliefs that may lead them to object to evolutionary theory, I understand that you may find this part of the book challenging, but it is nevertheless important to know about the theory of evolution and the evidence supporting it, as this is the view of human origins accepted by virtually all scientists.

Our Evolutionary Beginnings

LO 1.4   **Explain the process of natural selection and trace the evolutionary origins of the human species.**

To understand human origins it is important to know a few basic principles of the theory of evolution, first proposed by Charles Darwin in 1859 in his book *The Origin of Species*. At the heart of the theory of evolution is the proposition that species change through the process of **natural selection**. In natural selection, the young of any species are born with variations on a wide range of characteristics. Some may be relatively large and others relatively small, some relatively fast and others relatively slow, and so on. Among the young, those who will be most likely to survive until they can reproduce will be the ones whose variations are best adapted to their environment. The video *Natural Selection* has more detail on this process.

ontogenetic
characteristic pattern of individual development in a species

phylogenetic
pertaining to the development of a species

natural selection
evolutionary process in which the offspring best adapted to their environment survive to produce offspring of their own

Watch   NATURAL SELECTION

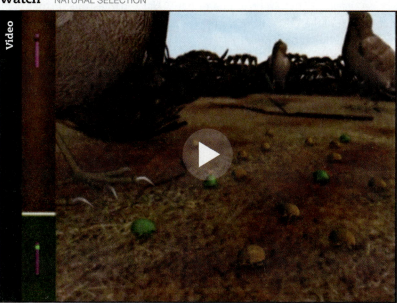

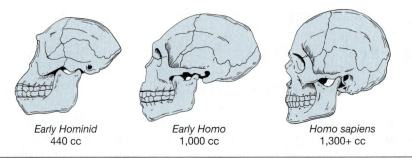

Early Hominid	Early Homo	Homo sapiens
440 cc	1,000 cc	1,300+ cc

Figure 1.3 Changes in Brain Size in Early Humans

The mastery of fire by the early *Homo* species resulted in a sharp increase in brain size.

hominid

evolutionary line that led to modern humans

Homo sapiens

species of modern humans

hunter-gatherer

social and economic system in which economic life is based on hunting (mostly by males) and gathering edible plants (mostly by females)

When did human evolution begin? According to evolutionary biologists, humans, chimpanzees, and gorillas had a common primate ancestor until 6 to 8 million years ago (Shreeve, 2010). At about that time, this common ancestor split into three paths, leading to the development of humans as well as to chimpanzees and gorillas. The evolutionary line that eventually led to humans is known as the **hominid** line. The primate ancestor we share with chimpanzees and gorillas lived in Africa, and so did the early hominids, as chimpanzees and gorillas do today.

By 200,000 years ago the early hominid species had evolved into our species, **Homo sapiens** (Shreve, 2011; Wilson, 2012). During the millions of years of evolution that led to Homo sapiens, several characteristics developed that made us distinct from earlier hominids and from other primates:

1. *Larger brain.* The most striking and important change during this period was the size of early *Homo's* brain, which became over twice as large as the brain of early hominids (see **Figure 1.3**; brain sizes are shown in cubic centimeters [cc]).
2. *Wider pelvis, females.* The female *Homo's* pelvis became wider to allow the birth of bigger-brained babies.
3. *Longer dependency.* The larger brains of early *Homo* babies meant that babies were born less mature than they were for earlier hominids, resulting in a longer period of infant and childhood dependency.
4. *Development of tools.* Creating tools enhanced early *Homo's* success in obtaining food. The earliest tools were apparently made by striking one stone against another to create a sharp edge. The tools may have been used for purposes such as slicing animal meat and whittling wood into sharp sticks for hunting.
5. *Control of fire.* Controlled use of fire enabled our early ancestors to cook food, and because cooked food is used much more efficiently by the body than raw food, this led to another burst in brain size (Wrangham, 2009). At the same time, the size of the teeth and jaws diminished, because cooked food was easier to eat than raw food.

The long period of infant dependency may have made it difficult for early *Homo* mothers to travel for long distances to accompany the males on hunting or scavenging expeditions (Wrangham, 2009). So, a **hunter-gatherer** way of life developed, in which females remained in a relatively stable home base, caring for children and perhaps gathering edible plants in the local area, while males went out to hunt or scavenge.

The Origin of Cultures and Civilizations

LO 1.5 **Summarize the major changes in human cultures since the Upper Paleolithic period.**

Physically, *Homo sapiens* has changed little from 200,000 years ago to the present. However, a dramatic change in the development of the human species took place during the **Upper Paleolithic period** from 40,000 to about 10,000 years ago (Ember et al., 2011; Wilson, 2012) (see **Figure 1.4**).

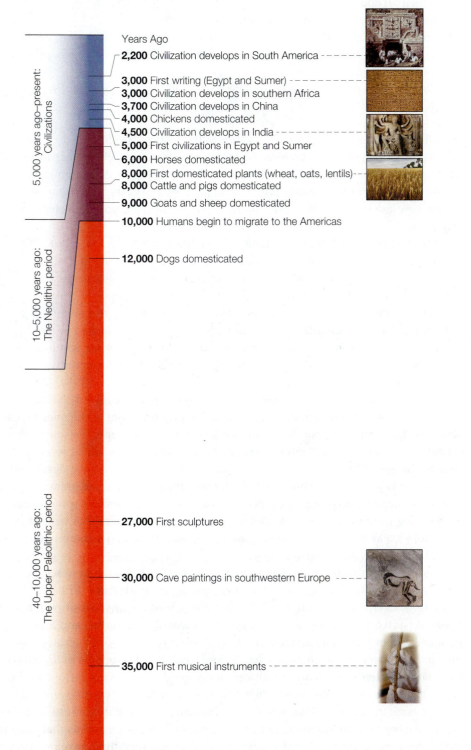

5,000 years ago–present: Civilizations

Years Ago

2,200 Civilization develops in South America

3,000 First writing (Egypt and Sumer)
3,000 Civilization develops in southern Africa
3,700 Civilization develops in China
4,000 Chickens domesticated
4,500 Civilization develops in India
5,000 First civilizations in Egypt and Sumer
6,000 Horses domesticated
8,000 First domesticated plants (wheat, oats, lentils)
8,000 Cattle and pigs domesticated
9,000 Goats and sheep domesticated
10,000 Humans begin to migrate to the Americas

10–5,000 years ago: The Neolithic period

12,000 Dogs domesticated

40–10,000 years ago: The Upper Paleolithic period

27,000 First sculptures

30,000 Cave paintings in southwestern Europe

35,000 First musical instruments

40,000 Humans first reach Australia

Figure 1.4 Key Changes in Human Species Development, Past 40,000 Years

Upper Paleolithic period

period of human history from 40,000 to 10,000 years ago, when distinct human cultures first developed

For the first time, art appeared: musical instruments; paintings on cave walls; small ivory beads attached to clothes; decorative objects made from bone, antler, or shell; and human and animal figures carved from ivory or sculpted from clay.

Several other important changes mark the Upper Paleolithic, in addition to the sudden burst of artistic production:

- Humans began to bury their dead, sometimes including art objects in the graves.
- For the first time cultural differences developed between human groups, as reflected in their art and tools.
- Trade took place between human groups.
- There was a rapid acceleration in the development of tools, including the bow and arrow, a spear thrower that could launch a spear at an animal (or perhaps at human enemies), and the harpoon.
- The first boats were invented, allowing humans to reach and populate Australia and New Guinea.

Why this sudden burst of changes during the Upper Paleolithic, when there is no evidence for changes in the brain or body? Some researchers believe that this is when language first appeared (Diamond, 1992; Leakey, 1994). However, anatomical evidence of a capacity for spoken language is evident at least 300,000 years ago (Wrangham, 2009). So, for now the origin of the revolutionary changes of the Upper Paleolithic remains a mystery.

The next period of dramatic change, from 10,000 years ago to about 5,000 years ago, is known as the **Neolithic period** (Johnson, 2005). During this time, humans broadened their food sources by cultivating plants and domesticating animals. The key contributor to this advance was climate change. The Upper Paleolithic was the time of the last Ice Age, when average global temperatures were about 10 degrees Celsius (50 degrees Fahrenheit) below today's temperatures. Glaciers covered Europe as far south as present-day Berlin, and in North America, as far south as what is now Chicago. By the Neolithic period the climate was much warmer, resembling our climate today.

As the climate became warmer and wetter, new plants evolved that were good human food sources, and humans began to try to produce more of the ones they liked best. The huge animals that had been hunted during the Upper Paleolithic became extinct, perhaps from overhunting, perhaps because the animals failed to adapt to the climate changes (Diamond, 1992). Domestication of animals may have developed as a food source to replace the extinct animals. Along with agriculture and animal care came new tools: mortars and pestles for processing plants into food, and the spindle and loom for weaving cotton and wool into clothing. Larger, sturdier dwellings were built (and furniture such as beds and tables) because people stayed in settled communities longer to tend their plants and animals.

The final major historical change that provides the basis for how we live today began around 5,000 years ago with the development of **civilization** (Ridley, 2010). The characteristics that mark civilization include cities, writing, specialization into different kinds of work, differences among people in wealth and status, and a centralized political system known as a **state**. The first civilizations developed around the same time in Egypt and Sumer (part of what is now Iraq). Because people in these civilizations kept written records and produced many goods, we have a lot of information about how they lived. We know they had laws and sewer systems, and that their social classes included priests, soldiers, craftsmen, government workers, and slaves. We know they built monuments to their leaders, such as the pyramids that still stand today in Egypt. They produced a vast range of goods including jewelry, sculpture,

Neolithic period

era of human history from 10,000 to 5,000 years ago, when animals and plants were first domesticated

civilization

form of human social life, beginning about 5,000 years ago, that includes cities, writing, occupational specialization, and states

state

centralized political system that is an essential feature of a civilization

sailboats, wheeled wagons, and swords. Later civilizations developed in India (around 4,500 years ago), China (around 3,700 years ago), southern Africa (around 3,000 years ago), the Mediterranean area (Greece and Rome, around 2,700 years ago), and South America (around 2,200 years ago).

Why did civilizations and states arise? As agricultural production became more efficient, especially after the invention of irrigation, not everyone in a cultural group had to work on food production. This allowed some members of the group to be concentrated in cities, away from food-production areas, where they could specialize as merchants, artists, musicians, bureaucrats, and religious and political leaders. Furthermore, as the use of irrigation expanded there was a need for a state to build and oversee the system, and as trade expanded there was a need for a state to build infrastructure such as roadways. Trade also connected people in larger cultural groups that could be united into a common state (Ridley, 2010).

Human Evolution and Human Development Today

LO 1.6 **Apply information about human evolution to how human development takes place today.**

What does this history of our development as a species tell us about human development today? First, it is important to recognize that how we develop today is based partly on our evolutionary history. We still share many characteristics with our hominid relatives and ancestors, such as a large brain compared to our body size, a relatively long period of childhood dependence on adults before reaching maturity, and cooperative living in social groups. Researchers working in the field of **evolutionary psychology** claim that many other characteristics of human development are influenced by our evolutionary history, such as aggressiveness and mate selection (Crawford & Krebs, 2008). We will examine their claims in the course of the book.

A second important fact to note about our evolutionary history is that biologically we have changed little since the origin of *Homo sapiens* about 200,000 years ago, yet how we live has changed in astonishing ways (Ridley, 2010; Wilson, 2012). Although we are a species that originated in the grasslands and forests of Africa, now we live in every environment on earth, from mountains to deserts, from tropical jungles to the Arctic. Although we are a species that evolved to live in small groups of a few dozen persons, now most of us live in cities with millions of other people. Although human females are capable of giving birth to at least eight children in the course of their reproductive lives, and probably did so through most of history, now most women have one, two, or three children—or perhaps none at all.

It is remarkable that an animal like us, which evolved in Africa adapted through natural selection to a hunting-and-gathering way of life, could have developed over the past 40,000 years an astonishing array of cultures, most of which bear little resemblance to our hunter-gatherer origins. Once we developed the large brain that is the most distinctive characteristic of our species, we became capable of altering our environments, so that it was no longer natural selection alone that would determine how we would live, but the cultures we created. As far as we can tell from the fossil record, all early hominids lived in the same way (Shreeve, 2010). Even different groups of early *Homo sapiens* seem to have lived more or less alike before the Upper Paleolithic period, as hunters and gatherers in small groups.

Today there are hundreds of different cultures around the world, all part of the human community but each with its distinctive way of life. There are wide cultural variations in how we live, such as how we care for infants, what we expect from children, how we respond to the changes of puberty, and how we regard the elderly. As members of the

evolutionary psychology
branch of psychology that examines how patterns of human functioning and behavior have resulted from adaptations to evolutionary conditions

species *Homo sapiens* we all share a similar biology, but cultures shape the raw material of biology into widely different paths through the life span.

It is also culture that makes us unique as a species. Other animals have evolved in ways that are adaptive for a particular set of environmental conditions. They can learn in the course of their lifetimes, certainly, but the scope of their learning is limited. When their environment changes, if their species is to survive it will do so not by learning new skills required by a new environment but through a process of natural selection that will enable those best-suited *genetically* to the new environmental conditions to survive long enough to reproduce, while the others do not.

In contrast, once humans developed the large brain we have now, it enabled us to survive in any environment by inventing and learning new skills and methods of survival, and then passing them along to others as part of a cultural way of life. We can survive and thrive even in conditions that are vastly different from our environment of evolutionary adaptation, because our capacity for cultural learning is so large and, compared to other animals, there is relatively little about us that is fixed by instinct.

Practice Quiz   ANSWERS AVAILABLE IN ANSWER KEY.

1. Unlike earlier hominids, *Homo sapiens* had _____.
   a. much heavier and thicker bones
   √ b. smaller teeth and jaws
   c. a slightly smaller brain
   d. a narrower pelvis among females and a larger pelvis among males

2. Which of the following statements best describes the effects of natural selection?
   a. Species are eliminated, or "selected," one-by-one over thousands of years, and no new species are developed.
   √ b. Species change little by little with each generation, and over a long period of time they can develop into new species.
   c. New species are naturally developed only every 2,000 years, and all previously existing species die out.
   d. Species change over short periods of time, and this change occurs roughly every 1,000 years.

3. The dramatic change in the development of the human species that took place during the Upper Paleolithic period was that, for the first time, _____.

   a. brains got larger
   b. tools were created
   √ c. art appeared
   d. jaws got larger to eat a wider variety of plants

4. Dr. Jenks is interested in how mate selection is shaped by our evolutionary history. She most likely considers herself a(n) _____.
   a. biopsychologist
   b. developmental psychologist
   √ c. evolutionary psychologist
   d. social archeologist

5. Which of the following is TRUE?
   √ a. The development of larger brains allowed our species to be capable of altering our environment.
   b. Biologically, humans have changed drastically since the origin of Homo sapiens.
   c. There are fewer than 10 cultures around the world today.
   d. We are a species that originated in south Asia.

Summary: Human Development Today and Its Origins

LO 1.1   **Describe how the human population has changed over the past 10,000 years and explain why the United States is following a different demographic path from other developed countries.**

The total human population was under 10 million for most of history, but it rose from 2 billion in 1930 to 7 billion in 2011, and is expected to increase to 10 billion by 2090. Unlike most developed countries, the United States is projected to increase in population during the 21st century, due primarily to immigration.

LO 1.2   **Distinguish between the demographic profiles of developed countries and developing countries in terms of cultural values, income, and education.**

In general, cultural values are more individualistic in developed countries and more collectivistic in developing countries. Most people in developing countries are poor and live in rural areas, but these countries are experiencing rapid economic development and a massive migration to urban areas. Also, young people are receiving increasing levels of education as their countries become wealthier and enter the global economy.

LO 1.3 **Define the term** *socioeconomic status* **(SES) and explain why SES, gender, and ethnicity are important aspects of human development within countries.**

SES includes educational level, income level, and occupational status. It influences access to resources such as education and health care. Gender shapes expectations and opportunities in most cultures throughout life. Ethnicity often includes a distinct cultural identity.

LO 1.4 **Explain the process of natural selection and trace the evolutionary origins of the human species.**

Natural selection results in species change because the young who are best adapted to the environment will be most likely to survive and reproduce. Humans arose from earlier hominids and developed distinctive characteristics such as large brains, long infancy, tool use, and control of fire. Our species, *Homo sapiens*, first appeared about 200,000 years ago.

LO 1.5 **Summarize the major changes in human cultures since the Upper Paleolithic period.**

The Upper Paleolithic period (40,000–10,000 years ago) is the first time human cultures became distinct from one another in their art and tools. During the Neolithic period (10,000–5,000 years ago), humans first domesticated plants and animals. The first civilizations around 5,000 years ago marked the origin of writing, specialized work, and a centralized state.

LO 1.6 **Apply information about human evolution to how human development takes place today.**

Humans are one species, but since the birth of culture, human groups have developed remarkably diverse ways of life. Our exceptionally large brain has allowed us to create cultural practices that enable us to live in a wide range of environments.

Section 2 Theories of Human Development

⌄ Learning Objectives

1.7 Compare and contrast three ancient conceptions of development through the life span.

1.8 Summarize Freud's psychosexual theory of human development and describe its main limitations.

1.9 Describe the eight stages of Erikson's psychosocial theory of human development.

1.10 Define the five systems of Bronfenbrenner's ecological theory and explain how it differs from stage theories.

1.11 Outline the cultural-developmental model that will be the structure of this book and describe the new life stage of emerging adulthood.

THEORIES OF HUMAN DEVELOPMENT: Ancient Conceptions

LO 1.7 **Compare and contrast three ancient conceptions of development through the life span.**

Although human development is young as an area of the social sciences, people have been thinking for a long time about how we change with age throughout life. In this section we examine three ancient ways of conceptualizing human development (see **Figure 1.5**). As you read these conceptions, observe that all three were written by and for men only. The absence of women from these conceptions of human development reflects the fact that in most cultures throughout history, men have held most of the power and have often kept women excluded from areas such as religious leadership and philosophy that inspired life-stage conceptions.

Probably the oldest known conception of the life course is in the *Dharmashastras*, the sacred law books of the Hindu religion, first written about 3,000 years ago (Kakar, 1998; Rose, 2004). In this conception there are four stages of a man's life, each lasting about 25 years in an ideal life span of 100 years.

> Apprentice, ages 0–25
> Householder, ages 26–50
> Forest dweller, ages 51–75
> Renunciant, ages 75–100

The apprentice stage comprises childhood and adolescence. This is the stage in which a boy is dependent on his parents, as he grows up and learns the skills necessary for adult life. In the householder stage, the young man has married and is in charge of his own household. This is a time of many responsibilities, ranging from providing for a wife and family to taking care of elderly parents to engaging in productive work.

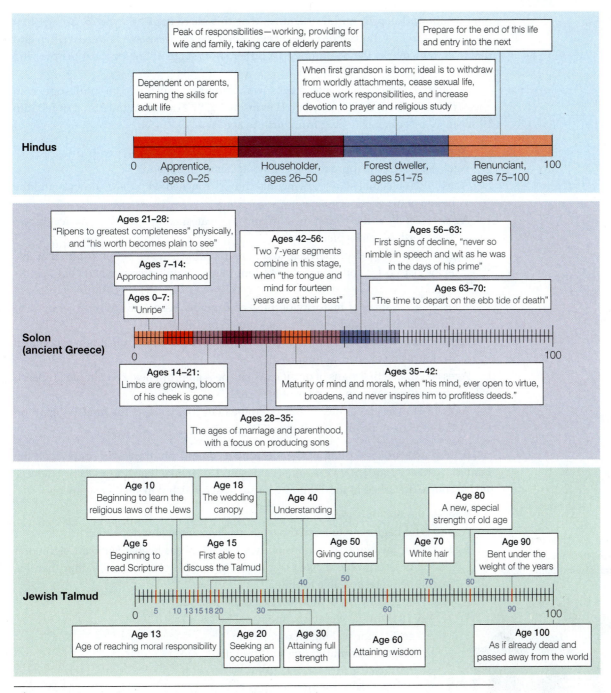

Figure 1.5 The Life Course in Three Traditions

The third stage, forest dweller, begins when a man's first grandson is born. The religious ideal in this stage is for a man to withdraw from the world and literally live in the forest, devoting himself to prayer and religious study, and cultivating patience and compassion. Few Hindus ever actually withdraw to the forest, but even those who remain within society are supposed to begin to withdraw from worldly attachments. This means an end to sexual life, a decline in work responsibilities, and the beginning of a transfer of household responsibilities to the sons of the family.

The final stage of life is that of renunciant. The renunciant goes even further than the forest dweller in rejecting worldly attachments. The purpose of life in this stage is simply to prepare for the end of this life and entry into the next (Hindus believe in reincarnation). Keep in mind, of course, that this stage *begins* at age 75, an age that few people reached thousands of years ago when the *Dharmashastras* were written and that even now marks the beginning of a rather short stage of life for most people who reach it.

Another conception of life stages was proposed by Solon, a philosopher in ancient Greece about 2,500 years ago (Levinson, 1978). For Solon, the life span fell into 10 seven-year segments lasting from birth to age 70.

Ages 0–7: A stage of being "unripe."

Ages 7–14: Signs of approaching manhood "show in the bud."

Ages 14–21: His limbs are growing, his chin is "touched with fleecy down," and the bloom of his cheek is gone.

Ages 21–28: Now the young man "ripens to greatest completeness" physically, and "his worth becomes plain to see."

Ages 28–35: The ages of marriage and parenthood, when "he bethinks him that this is the season for courting, bethinks him that sons will preserve and continue his line."

Ages 35–42: A stage of maturity of mind and morals, when "his mind, ever open to virtue, broadens, and never inspires him to profitless deeds."

Ages 42–56: Two 7-year segments combine in this stage, when "the tongue and mind for fourteen years are at their best."

Ages 56–63: The first signs of decline, when "he is able, but never so nimble in speech and wit as he was in the days of his prime."

Ages 63–70: The end of life. At this point the man "has come to the time to depart on the ebb tide of death." (Levinson, 1976, p. 326)

A third ancient conception of the life course comes from the Jewish holy book the Talmud, written about 1,500 years ago (Levinson, 1978). Like the Hindu *Dharmashastras*, the life course described in the Talmud goes up to age 100, but in smaller segments.

Age 5 is the age for beginning to read Scripture.

Age 10 is for beginning to learn the religious laws of the Jewish people.

Age 13 is the age of moral responsibility, when a boy has his Bar Mitzvah, signifying that he is responsible for keeping the religious commandments, rather than his parents being responsible for him.

Age 15 is for first being able to discuss the Talmud.

Age 18 is for the wedding canopy.

Age 20 is for seeking an occupation.

Age 30 is for attaining full strength.

Age 40 is for understanding.

Age 50 is for giving counsel.

Age 60 is for becoming an elder and attaining wisdom.

Age 70 is for white hair.

Age 80 is for reaching a new, special strength of old age.

Age 90 is for being bent under the weight of the years.

Age 100 is for being as if already dead and passed away from the world.

In the life course according to the Jewish holy book the Talmud, 13 is the age of moral responsibility.

Although the three conceptions of human development just presented were written in widely different places and times, they share certain similarities. All are ideal conceptions, a view of how we develop if all goes well: Preparation for life is made in youth, skills and expertise are gained in adulthood, and wisdom and peace are the fruits of old age. Furthermore, all view youth as a time of immaturity, adulthood as a time of great responsibilities and peak productivity, and the final stages of life as a preparation for death. These conceptions are also ideals in the sense that they assume that a person will live to old age, which is not something that most people could realistically expect until very recently.

One important difference among the three ancient conceptions of human development is that they have very different ways of dividing up the life span, from just four stages in the *Dharmashastras* to 14 in the Talmud. This is a useful reminder that for humans the life span is not really divided into clear and definite biologically based stages, the way an insect has stages of larva, juvenile, and adult. Instead, conceptions of human development are only partly biological—infants everywhere cannot walk or talk, adolescents everywhere experience puberty—and are also culturally and socially based.

Practice Quiz   ANSWERS AVAILABLE IN ANSWER KEY.

1. The *Dharmashastras* are the sacred law books of the _____ religion that describe four stages of a man's life.
   a. Christian
   b. Hindu
   c. Jewish
   d. Buddhist

2. According to the Jewish holy book, _____ is the age of moral responsibility.
   a. 8   **c.** 13
   b. 10   **d.** 18

3. The *Dharmashastras*, the Talmud, and the conception of life proposed by Solon _____.
   a. were written within a year of one another
   b. were written by men
   c. each divide the life span into 5-year periods
   d. are all sacred law books of the Hindu religion

THEORIES OF HUMAN DEVELOPMENT: Scientific Conceptions

The scientific study of human development has been around for a relatively short time, only about 120 years. During that time there have been three major ways of conceptualizing human development: the psychosexual approach, the psychosocial approach, and the ecological approach.

Freud's Psychosexual Theory

LO 1.8   **Summarize Freud's psychosexual theory of human development and describe its main limitations.**

The earliest scientific theory of human development was devised by Sigmund Freud (1856–1939), who was a physician in Vienna, Austria, in the late 19th century (Breger, 2000). Working with persons suffering from various mental health problems, Freud concluded that a consistent theme across patients was that they seemed to have experienced some kind of traumatic event in childhood. The trauma then became buried in their unconscious minds, or *repressed*, and continued thereafter to shape their personality and their mental functioning even though they could no longer remember it.

In an effort to address their problems, Freud developed the first method of psychotherapy, which he called *psychoanalysis*. The purpose of psychoanalysis was to bring patients' repressed memories from the unconscious into consciousness, through having them discuss their dreams and their childhood experiences while guided by the psychoanalyst. According to Freud, just making the repressed memories conscious would be enough to heal the patient.

Freud's experiences as a psychoanalyst were the basis of his **psychosexual theory**. He believed that sexual desire was the driving force behind human development. Sexual desire arises from a part of the mind Freud called the *id*, and operates on the basis of the *pleasure principle*, meaning that it constantly seeks immediate and unrestrained satisfaction. However, from early in childhood, adults in the environment teach the child to develop a conscience, or *superego*, that restricts the satisfaction of desires and makes the child feel guilty for disobeying. At the same time as the superego develops, an *ego* also develops that serves as a mediator between id and superego. The ego operates on the *reality principle*, allowing the child to seek satisfaction within the constraints imposed by the superego.

For Freud, everything important in development happens before adulthood. In fact, Freud viewed the personality as complete by age 6. Although sexual desire is the driving force behind human development throughout life in Freud's theory, the locus of the sexual drive shifts around the body during the course of early development (see **Table 1.1**). Infancy is the *oral stage*, when sexual sensations are concentrated in the mouth. Infants derive pleasure from sucking, chewing, and biting. The next stage, beginning at about a year and a half, is the *anal stage*, when sexual sensations are concentrated in the anus. Toddlers derive their greatest pleasure from the act of elimination and are fascinated by feces. The *phallic stage*, from about age 3 to 6, is the most important stage of all in Freud's theory. In this stage sexual sensations become located in the genitals, but the child's sexual desires are focused particularly on the other-sex parent. Freud proposed that all children experience an *Oedipus complex* in which they desire to displace their same-sex parent and enjoy sexual access to the other-sex parent, as Oedipus did in the famous Greek myth.

According to Freud, the Oedipus complex is resolved when the child, fearing that the same-sex parent will punish his or her incestuous desires, gives up those desires and instead identifies with the same-sex parent, seeking to become more similar to that parent. In Freud's theory this leads to the fourth stage of psychosexual development, the *latency stage*, lasting from about age 6 until puberty. During this period the child represses sexual desires and focuses the energy from those desires on learning social and intellectual skills.

The fifth and last stage in Freud's theory is the *genital stage*, from puberty onward. The sexual drive reemerges, but this time in a way approved by the superego, directed toward persons outside the family.

psychosexual theory
Freud's theory proposing that sexual desire is the driving force behind human development

Table 1.1 Freud's Psychosexual Stages

Age period	Psychosexual stage	Main features
Infancy	Oral	Sexual sensations centered on the mouth; pleasure derived from sucking, chewing, biting
Toddlerhood	Anal	Sexual sensations centered on the anus; high interest in feces; pleasure derived from elimination
Early childhood	Phallic	Sexual sensations move to genitals; sexual desire for other-sex parent and fear of same-sex parent
Middle childhood	Latency	Sexual desires repressed; focus on developing social and cognitive skills
Adolescence	Genital	Reemergence of sexual desire, now directed outside the family

From our perspective today, it's easy to see plenty of gaping holes in psychosexual theory (Breger, 2000). Sexuality is certainly an important part of human development, but human behavior is complex and cannot be reduced to a single motive. Also, although his theory emphasizes the crucial importance of the first 6 years of life, Freud never studied children. His view of childhood was based on the retrospective accounts of patients who came to him for psychoanalysis, mainly upper-class women in Vienna. (Yet, ironically, his psychosexual theory emphasized boys' development and virtually ignored girls.) Nevertheless, Freud's psychosexual theory was the dominant view of human development throughout the first half of the 20th century (Robins et al., 1999). Today, few people who study human development adhere to Freud's psychosexual theory, even among psychoanalysts (Grunbaum, 2006).

Erikson's Psychosocial Theory

LO 1.9   Describe the eight stages of Erikson's psychosocial theory of human development.

Even though Freud's theory was dominant in psychology for over a half century, from the beginning many people objected to what they regarded as an excessive emphasis on the sexual drive as the basis for all development. Among the skeptics was Erik Erikson (1902–1994). Although he was trained as a psychoanalyst in Freud's circle in Vienna, he doubted the validity of Freud's psychosexual theory. Instead, Erikson proposed a theory of development with two crucial differences from Freud's theory. First, it was a **psychosocial theory**, in which the driving force behind development was not sexuality but the need to become integrated into the social and cultural environment. Second, Erikson viewed development as continuing throughout the life span, not as determined solely by the early years as in Freud's theory.

Erikson (1950) proposed a sequence of eight stages of development (see **Figure 1.6** on the next page). Each stage is characterized by a distinctive developmental challenge or "crisis" that the person must resolve. A successful resolution of the crisis prepares the person well for the next stage of development. However, a person who has difficulty with the crisis in one stage enters the next stage at high risk for being unsuccessful at that crisis as well. The stages build on each other, for better and for worse.

In the first stage of life, during infancy, the developmental challenge is *trust versus mistrust*. If the infant is loved and cared for, a sense of basic trust develops that the world is a good place and need not be feared. If not well-loved in infancy, the child learns to mistrust others and to doubt that life will be rewarding.

In the second stage, during toddlerhood, the developmental challenge is *autonomy versus shame and doubt*. During this stage the child develops a sense of self distinct from others. If the child is allowed some scope for making choices, a healthy sense of autonomy develops, but if there is excessive restraint or punishment, the child experiences shame and doubt.

In the third stage, during early childhood, the developmental challenge is *initiative versus guilt*. In this stage the child becomes capable of planning activities in a purposeful way. With encouragement of this new ability a sense of initiative develops, but if the child is discouraged and treated harshly then guilt is experienced.

The fourth stage, during middle to late childhood, is *industry versus inferiority*. In this stage children move out more into the world and begin to learn the knowledge and skills required by their culture. If a child is encouraged and taught well, a sense of industry develops that includes enthusiasm for learning and confidence in mastering the skills required. However, a child who is unsuccessful at learning what is demanded is likely to experience inferiority.

The fifth stage is adolescence, with the challenge of *identity versus identity confusion*. Adolescents must develop an awareness of who they are, what their capacities are, and

psychosocial theory
Erikson's theory that human development is driven by the need to become integrated into the social and cultural environment

Erik Erikson was the first to propose a life span theory of human development.

Infancy:
Trust vs. mistrust
Main developmental challenge is to establish bond with trusted caregiver

Toddlerhood:
Autonomy vs. shame and doubt
Main developmental challenge is to develop a healthy sense of self as distinct from others

Early Childhood:
Initiative vs. guilt
Main developmental challenge is to initiate activities in a purposeful way

Middle Childhood:
Industry vs. inferiority
Main developmental challenge is to begin to learn knowledge and skills of culture

Adolescence:
Identity vs. identity confusion
Main developmental challenge is to develop a secure and coherent identity

Early Adulthood:
Intimacy vs. isolation
Main developmental challenge is to establish a committed, long-term love relationship

Middle Adulthood:
Generativity vs. stagnation
Main developmental challenge is to care for others and contribute to well-being of the young

Late Adulthood:
Ego integrity vs. despair
Main developmental challenge is to evaluate lifetime, accept it as it is

Figure 1.6 Erikson's Eight Stages of Psychosocial Development

what their place is within their culture. For those who are unable to achieve this, identity confusion results.

The sixth stage, *intimacy versus isolation,* takes place in early adulthood. In this stage, the challenge for young adults is to risk their newly formed identity by entering a committed intimate relationship, usually marriage. Those who are unable or unwilling to make themselves vulnerable end up isolated, without an intimate relationship.

The seventh stage, in middle adulthood, involves the challenge of *generativity versus stagnation.* The generative person in middle adulthood is focused on how to contribute to the well-being of the next generation, through providing for and caring for others. Persons who focus instead on their own needs at midlife end up in a state of stagnation.

Finally, in the eighth stage, late adulthood, the challenge is *ego integrity versus despair.* This is a stage of looking back and reflecting on how one's life has been experienced. The person who accepts what life has provided, good and bad parts alike, and concludes that it was a life well spent can be considered to have ego integrity. In contrast, the person who is filled with regrets and resentments at this stage of life experiences despair.

Erikson's psychosocial theory has endured better than Freud's psychosexual theory. Today, nearly all researchers who study human development would agree that development is lifelong, with important changes taking place at every phase of the life span (Baltes, 2006; Lerner, 2006; Jensen, 2015). Similarly, nearly all researchers on human development today would agree with Erikson's emphasis on the social and cultural basis of development. However, not all of Erikson's proposed life stages have been accepted as valid or valuable. It is mainly his ideas about identity in adolescence and generativity in midlife that have inspired substantial interest and attention among researchers (Clark, 2010).

CRITICAL THINKING QUESTION

Based on your own experiences, which theory of human development do you consider more valid, Erikson's or Freud's?

Bronfenbrenner's Ecological Theory

LO 1.10 Define the five systems of Bronfenbrenner's ecological theory and explain how it differs from stage theories.

An important recent theory of human development is Urie Bronfenbrenner's **ecological theory** (Bronfenbrenner, 1980; 1998; 2000; 2005). Unlike the theories proposed by Freud and Erikson, Bronfenbrenner's is not a stage theory of human development. Instead, his theory focuses on the multiple influences that shape human development in the social environment.

Bronfenbrenner presented his theory as a reaction to what he viewed as an overemphasis in developmental psychology on the immediate environment, especially the mother–child relationship. The immediate environment is important, Bronfenbrenner

ecological theory
Bronfenbrenner's theory that human development is shaped by five interrelated systems in the social environment

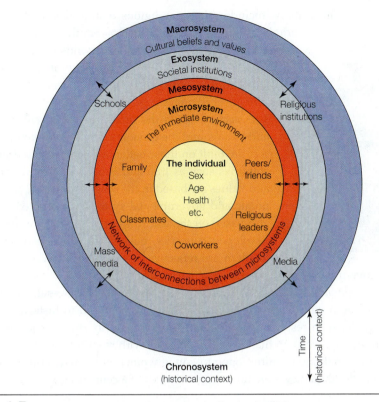

Figure 1.7 The Systems in Bronfenbrenner's Ecological Theory

How does this theory of human development differ from Freud's and Erikson's?

acknowledged, but much more than this is involved in children's development. Bronfenbrenner's theory was intended to draw attention to the broader cultural environment that people experience as they develop, and to the ways the different levels of a person's environment interact. In later writings (Bronfenbrenner, 2000, 2005; Bronfenbrenner & Morris, 1998), Bronfenbrenner added a biological dimension to his framework and it is now sometimes called a *bioecological theory*, but the distinctive contribution of the theory remains its portrayal of the cultural environment.

According to Bronfenbrenner, there are five key levels or *systems* that play a part in human development (see **Figure 1.7**):

1. The *microsystem* is Bronfenbrenner's term for the immediate environment, the settings where people experience their daily lives. Microsystems in most cultures include relationships with each parent, with siblings, and perhaps with extended family; with peers and friends; with teachers; and with other adults (such as coaches, religious leaders, and employers). Bronfenbrenner emphasizes that the child is an *active* agent in the microsystems. For example, children are affected by their parents but children's behavior affects their parents as well; children are affected by their friends but they also make choices about whom to have as friends. The microsystem is where most research in developmental psychology has focused. Today, however, most developmental psychologists use the term *context* rather than microsystem to refer to immediate environmental settings and relationships.

2. The *mesosystem* is the network of interconnections between the various microsystems. For example, a child who is experiencing abusive treatment from parents may become difficult to handle in relationships with teachers; or, if a parent's employer demands longer hours in the workplace the parent's relationship with the child may be affected.

3. The *exosystem* refers to the societal institutions that have indirect but potentially important influences on development. In Bronfenbrenner's theory, these

In countries such as Iran, the macrosystem is based on Islam, which influences all aspects of life.

institutions include schools, religious institutions, and media. For example, in Asian countries such as South Korea, competition to get into college is intense and depends chiefly on adolescents' performance on a national exam at the end of high school; consequently, the high school years are a period of extreme academic stress.

4. The *macrosystem* is the broad system of cultural beliefs and values, and the economic and governmental systems that are built on those beliefs and values. For example, in countries such as Iran and Saudi Arabia, cultural beliefs and values are based in the religion of Islam, and the economic and governmental systems of those countries are also based on the teachings of Islam. In contrast, in most developed countries, beliefs in the value of individual freedom are reflected in a free-market economic system and in governmental systems of representative democracy.

5. Finally, the *chronosystem* refers to changes that occur in developmental circumstances over time, both with respect to individual development and to historical changes. For example, with respect to individual development, losing your job is a much different experience at 15 than it would be at 45; with respect to historical changes, the occupational opportunities open to young women in many countries today are much broader than they were for young women half a century ago.

There are many characteristics of Bronfenbrenner's ecological theory that make it important and useful for the approach that will be taken in this book. His theory recognizes the importance of historical contexts as influences on development, as we will in this book. Also, Bronfenbrenner emphasized that children and adolescents are active participants in their development, not merely the passive recipients of external influences, and that will be stressed throughout this book as well.

A Cultural-Developmental Model for This Book

LO 1.11 Outline the cultural-developmental model that will be the structure of this book and describe the new life stage of emerging adulthood.

The structure of this textbook combines elements of Erikson's and Bronfenbrenner's approaches and goes beyond them. Today there is a widespread consensus among researchers and theorists that human development is lifelong and that important changes take place throughout the life span, as Erikson proposed (Baltes, 2006). There is also a consensus in favor of Bronfenbrenner's view that it is not just the immediate family environment that is important in human development but multiple contexts interacting in multiple ways (Lerner, 2006).

However, neither Erikson nor Bronfenbrenner recognized sufficiently the essential importance of culture in shaping human development through the life span. The framework for this book will be the *cultural-developmental approach* to human development (Jensen, 2008, 2011, 2015). According to this approach, it is crucial to recognize that throughout the life span, people live within cultural communities where they continuously interact and negotiate with others who convey cultural beliefs, skills, and knowledge. In the course of their development, people learn and respond to the ways of their culture, and become participants in shaping the culture's future. The biological basis of development is important in many ways, but it is culture that determines what we learn, what we aspire to become, and how we see ourselves in relation to the world. This is why, according to the cultural-developmental approach, it is necessary to study development across diverse cultures in order to have a full understanding of it. The approach also highlights that in today's globalizing world, cultural change can be quite rapid, and it is not uncommon for individuals to identify with more than one culture.

In this book, the stages of human development will be divided as follows:

- Prenatal development, from conception until birth
- Infancy, birth to age 12 months
- Toddlerhood, the 2nd and 3rd years of life, ages 12–36 months
- Early childhood, ages 3–6
- Middle childhood, ages 6–9
- Adolescence
- Emerging adulthood
- Young adulthood
- Middle adulthood
- Late adulthood

People in developed countries often continue their education into their twenties.

You are probably familiar with all these stage terms, with the possible exception of *emerging adulthood*. **Emerging adulthood** is a new stage of life between adolescence and young adulthood that has appeared in recent decades, primarily in developed countries (Arnett, 2000, 2011, 2014, 2015). The rise of this new life stage reflects the fact that most people in developed countries now continue their education into their twenties and enter marriage and parenthood in their late twenties or early thirties, rather than in their late teens or early twenties as was true half a century ago. Emerging adulthood is a life stage in which most people are not as dependent on their parents as they were in childhood and adolescence but have not yet made commitments to the stable roles in love and work that structure adult life for most people. This new life stage exists mainly in developed countries, because for most people in developing countries, education still ends in adolescence and marriage and parenthood begin in the late teens or early twenties (Arnett, 2015). However, emerging adulthood is becoming steadily more common in developing countries (Jensen et al., 2012).

Age ranges can be specified for the early stages, but the age ranges of later stages are more ambiguous and variable. Adolescence begins with the first evidence of puberty, but puberty may begin as early as age 9 or 10 or as late as age 15 or 16, depending on cultural conditions. Emerging adulthood exists in some cultures and not others, and consequently, young-adult responsibilities such as marriage and stable work may be taken on as early as the teens or as late as the early thirties. Middle adulthood and late adulthood are also variable and depend on the typical life expectancy in a particular culture.

Stages are a useful way of conceptualizing human development because they draw our attention to the distinctive features of each age period, which helps us understand how people change over time (Arnett & Tanner, 2009). However, it should be kept in mind that for the most part, there are no sharp breaks between the stages. For example, toddlerhood is different from early childhood in many important ways, but the typical 34-month-old is not sharply different than the typical 37-month-old; nothing magical or dramatic occurs at 36 months to mark the end of one stage and the beginning of the next. Similarly, nothing definite happens at a specific age to mark the end of young adulthood and the beginning of middle adulthood. To put it another way, scholars of human development generally regard development as *continuous* rather than *discontinuous* (Baltes, 2006).

emerging adulthood

new life stage in developed countries, lasting from the late teens through the twenties, in which people are gradually making their way toward taking on adult responsibilities in love and work

Practice Quiz ANSWERS AVAILABLE IN ANSWER KEY.

1. According to Freud _____.
   a. the root of mental health problems in his patients was that they seemed to have experienced some type of traumatic event during the transition to young adulthood
   b. children experience the anal stage that leads them to want to have sexual access to their opposite-sex parents
   ✓ c. everything important in development happened before adulthood
   d. the oral stage lasts from about ages 3 to 6

2. One critique of Freud's theory is that _____.
   a. it reduced human behavior to only one motive: the need to be integrated into the social environment
   ✓ b. Freud never studied children
   c. it was derived from studying his own patients, most of whom were middle-class men
   d. he focused on culture much more than other aspects of development

3. Bram does not ever want to get married. The idea of a lifetime commitment makes him anxious and uncomfortable, and any time a girlfriend brings up the subject of marriage, he breaks up with her. According to Erikson, Bram will not successfully resolve the _____ crisis.

   a. autonomy versus commitment
   b. identity versus identity confusion
   c. generativity versus stagnation
   ✓ d. intimacy versus isolation

4. Belinda's parents are divorced, but they work together to be sure that they have open lines of communication with their daughter's teacher and attend as many school functions as possible. The strong interconnection between Belinda's parents and the various aspects of her school is an example of the _____.
   a. microsystem   ✓ c. mesosystem
   b. macrosystem   d. exosystem

5. Which statement concerning the developmental period known as **emerging adulthood** is *most accurate* according to Arnett?
   ✓ a. It is a life stage in which most people have not yet made commitments to the stable roles of love and work that structure adult life for most people.
   b. Compared to emerging adults of past generations, today's emerging adults are more dependent upon their romantic partners.
   c. Emerging adulthood is a period that replaces middle age.
   d. It is more common in developing countries than in developed countries.

Summary: Theories of Human Development

LO 1.7   Compare and contrast three ancient conceptions of development through the life span.

Stage conceptions of the life span were developed thousands of years ago in the Hindu, Greek, and Jewish cultures. There were four stages in the Hindu conception, 10 in the Greek, and 14 in the Jewish. All three conceptions concerned only men and ignored women's development.

All three ancient conceptions are ideals in that they assume that life will go well and will continue into old age. All view youth as a time of preparation and immaturity, adulthood as a time of great responsibilities and peak achievements, and the final stages of life as a preparation for death.

LO 1.8   Summarize Freud's psychosexual theory of human development and describe its main limitations.

Freud's psychosexual theory of development emphasized the sexual drive as the primary motivator of human behavior. He proposed five stages of psychosexual development, but believed that the early stages were crucial and that most of later development was determined by age 6.

LO 1.9   Describe the eight stages of Erikson's psychosocial theory of human development.

Erikson proposed a psychosocial theory of development that emphasized social and cultural influences and proposed that important changes take place throughout the life span. In his theory of eight stages throughout the life span, each stage is characterized by a distinctive "crisis" with two possible resolutions, one healthy and one unhealthy.

LO 1.10   Define the five systems of Bronfenbrenner's ecological theory and explain how it differs from stage theories.

Bronfenbrenner's ecological theory emphasizes the different systems that interact in a person's development, including microsystems, the mesosystem, the exosystem, the macrosystem, and the chronosystem. It is not a stage theory and instead emphasizes the multiple influences that shape human development in the social environment throughout life.

LO 1.11   Outline the cultural-developmental model that will be the structure of this book and describe the new life stage of emerging adulthood.

In this book the life span is divided into 10 stages, from prenatal development to late adulthood. Most of the stages occur in all cultures, but emerging adulthood is a new life stage between adolescence and young adulthood that has become typical mainly in developed countries, although it is growing more common in developing countries. During emerging adulthood most people are less dependent on their parents but have not yet made commitments to the stable roles in love and work that structure adult life for most people.

Section 3   How We Study Human Development

∨ Learning Objectives

1.12 Recall the five steps of the scientific method and the meanings and functions of hypotheses, sampling, and procedure in scientific research.

1.13 Describe some ethical standards for human development research.

1.14 Summarize the main methods used in research on human development.

1.15 Describe the major types of research designs used in human development research.

HOW WE STUDY HUMAN DEVELOPMENT: The Scientific Method

The field of human development is based on scientific research, and to understand the research presented in this book it is important for you to know the essential elements of how the scientific process works. Here we look at this process and how it is applied to the study of human development.

The Five Steps of the Scientific Method

LO 1.12 **Recall the five steps of the scientific method and the meanings and functions of hypotheses, sampling, and procedure in scientific research.**

In its classic form, the **scientific method** involves five basic steps: (1) identifying a question to be investigated, (2) forming a hypothesis, (3) choosing a research method and a research design, (4) collecting data to test the hypothesis, and (5) drawing conclusions that lead to new questions and new hypotheses. **Figure 1.8** on the next page summarizes these steps.

STEP 1: IDENTIFY A QUESTION OF SCIENTIFIC INTEREST Every scientific study begins with an idea (Machado & Silva, 2007). A researcher wants to find an answer to a question that can be addressed using scientific methods. For example, in research on human development the question might be "How do infants who breast-feed differ in their physical and social development from infants who bottle-feed?" or "How does the marriage relationship between young couples change when they have their first baby?" or "What are the most important determinants of physical and mental health in late adulthood?" The question of interest may be generated by a theory or previous research, or it may be something the researcher has noticed from personal observation or experience.

STEP 2: FORM A HYPOTHESIS In seeking to answer the question generated in Step 1, the researcher proposes one or more hypotheses. A **hypothesis** is the researcher's idea about one possible answer to the question of interest. For example, a researcher may be interested in the question "What happens to parents' marital satisfaction when their youngest child leaves home?" and propose the hypothesis "Marital satisfaction tends to improve because parents now have more time and energy for the marital relationship."

scientific method

process of scientific investigation, involving a series of steps from identifying a research question through forming a hypothesis, selecting research methods and designs, collecting and analyzing data, and drawing conclusions

hypothesis

in the scientific process, a researcher's idea about one possible answer to the question proposed for investigation

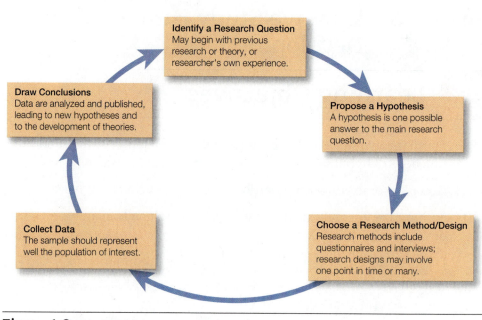

Figure 1.8 The Steps of the Scientific Method

The researcher would then design a study to test that hypothesis. The hypotheses of a study are crucial, because they influence the sampling, research methods, research design, data analysis, and interpretation that follow.

STEP 3: CHOOSE A RESEARCH METHOD AND A RESEARCH DESIGN Once the hypothesis is proposed, the investigator must choose a research method and a research design (Salkind, 2011). The **research method** is the approach to investigating the hypothesis. For example, in human development research two common research methods are questionnaires and interviews. The **research design** is the plan for when and how to collect the data for the study, for example the decision of whether to collect data at one time point or at more than one point. More detail on research methods and designs will be presented shortly.

STEP 4: COLLECT DATA TO TEST THE HYPOTHESIS After forming a hypothesis and choosing a research method and design, researchers who study human development seek to obtain a **sample**, which is a group of people who participate in a research study. The sample should represent the **population**, which is the entire category of people the sample represents. Suppose, for example, a researcher wants to study adolescents' attitudes toward contraception. Adolescents are the population, and the specific adolescents who participate in the study comprise the sample.

The goal in finding a sample is to seek out a sample that will be *representative* of the population of interest (Goodwin, 1995). To continue the example of a study of adolescents' attitudes toward contraceptive use, the waiting room of a clinic offering contraceptive services would probably not be a good place to look for a sample, because the adolescents coming to such a clinic would be quite likely to have more favorable attitudes toward contraception than adolescents in general; otherwise, why would they be in a place that offers contraceptive services? If the population of interest is adolescents in general, it would be better to sample them through schools or through a telephone survey that selects households randomly from the community.

On the other hand, if a researcher is particularly interested in attitudes toward contraception among the population of adolescents who are already using or planning to use contraception, then a clinic offering contraceptive services would be a good place to find a sample. It depends on the population the researcher wishes to study and on the questions the researcher wishes to address. Again, the sample should be *representative* of the

research method

in the scientific process, the approach to investigating the hypothesis

research design

plan for when and how to collect the data for a study

sample

subset of a population for which data are collected in a scientific study

population

in research, the entire category of people represented by a sample

population of interest. If it is, then the findings from the sample will be *generalizable* to the population. In other words, the findings from the sample will make it possible to draw conclusions about not just the sample itself, but the larger population of people that the sample is intended to represent.

The **procedure** of the study is the way the study is conducted and the data are collected. One aspect of the procedure is the circumstances of the data collection. Researchers try to collect data in a way that will not be biased. For example, they must be careful not to phrase questions in an interview or questionnaire in a way that seems to lead people toward a desired response. They must also assure participants that their responses will be confidential, especially if the study concerns a sensitive topic such as sexual behavior or drug use.

STEP 5: DRAW CONCLUSIONS AND FORM NEW QUESTIONS AND HYPOTHESES

Once the data for a study have been collected, statistical analyses are usually conducted to examine relationships between different parts of the data. Often, the analyses are determined by the hypotheses that generated the study. For example, a researcher studying relationships with parents in middle childhood may hypothesize, based on a theory or on past research, that children in this stage are closer to their mothers than to their fathers. The scientist will then test that hypothesis with a statistical analysis comparing the quality of children's relationships with mothers and with fathers.

Once the data are analyzed they must be interpreted. When scientists write up the results of their research for publication in a scientific journal, they interpret the results of the study in light of relevant theories and previous research. After researchers write an article describing the methods used, the results of the statistical analyses, and the interpretation of the results, they typically submit the manuscript for the article to a professional journal. The editor of the journal then sends the manuscript out for review by other researchers. In other words, the manuscript is **peer reviewed** for its scientific accuracy and credibility and for the importance of its contribution to the field. The editor typically relies on the reviews by the researchers' peers in deciding whether or not to accept the manuscript for publication. If the editor determines that the manuscript has passed the peer-review process successfully, the article is published in the journal. In addition to research articles, most journals publish occasional theoretical articles and review articles that integrate the findings from numerous other studies. Researchers studying human development also publish the results of their investigations in books, and often these books go through the peer-review process.

The results of research often lead to the development or modification of theories. A good **theory** is a framework that presents a set of interconnected ideas in an original way and inspires further research. Theories and research are intrinsically connected: A theory generates hypotheses that can be tested in research, and research leads to modifications of the theory, which generate further hypotheses and further research. There is no separate chapter on theories in this book, because theories and research are intrinsically connected and should be presented together. Theories are presented in every chapter in relation to the research they have generated and the questions they have raised for future research.

Ethics in Human Development Research

LO 1.13 Describe some ethical standards for human development research.

Imagine that you were a human development researcher who was interested in language development, and you hypothesized that the number of words spoken to a toddler would influence the size of the toddler's vocabulary a year later. So, you designed a study in which families with toddlers were randomly assigned to two groups: In one

If a sample of adolescents is obtained from a birth control clinic, what population does it represent?

procedure

the way a study is conducted and the data are collected

peer-review

in scientific research, the system of having other scientists review a manuscript to judge its merits and worthiness for publication

theory

framework that presents a set of interconnected ideas in an original way and inspires further research

group parents were trained to speak frequently to their toddlers, whereas in the other group the parents were given no instructions. Is this research design ethical?

Imagine that you were a human development researcher interested in the question of what makes marriages last or not. So, you proposed a study in which you invited couples in their 30s to come into a laboratory situation, where they were provided with a list of possible secrets that partners might keep from each other and asked to pick one of them to discuss, while being filmed by the researchers. Is this research design ethical?

Imagine that you were a human development researcher who was working to develop a drug to prevent memory loss in late adulthood. In experiments with rats the drug had been shown to enhance memory, in that after receiving the drug, the rats had increased success in running mazes they had run before. However, the rats receiving the drug also died earlier than the rats in the control group. Would it be ethical to conduct a study on humans in late adulthood in which one group received the drug and another group did not?

These are the kinds of ethical issues that arise in the course of research on human development. To prevent ethical violations, most institutions that sponsor research, such as universities and research institutes, require proposals for research to be approved by an *institutional review board (IRB)*. IRBs are usually comprised of people who have research experience themselves and therefore can judge whether the research being proposed follows reasonable ethical guidelines. In addition to IRBs, professional organizations such as the Society for Research on Child Development (SRCD) often have a set of ethical guidelines for researchers.

The requirements of IRBs and the ethical guidelines of professional organizations usually include the following components (Fisher, 2003; Rosnow & Rosenthal, 2005; Salkind, 2011):

1. *Protection from physical and psychological harm.* The most important consideration in human development research is that the persons participating in the research will not be harmed by it.

2. *Informed consent prior to participation.* One standard ethical requirement of human development research is **informed consent**. Participants in any scientific study are supposed to be presented with a *consent form* before they participate. Consent forms typically include information about who is conducting the study, what the purposes of the study are, what participation in the study involves, what risks (if any) are involved in participating, and what the person can expect to receive in return for participation. Consent forms also usually include a statement indicating that participation in the study is voluntary, and that persons may withdraw from participation in the study at any time. For persons under age 18, the consent of one of their parents is also usually required as part of a study's procedures.

3. *Confidentiality.* Researchers are ethically required to take steps to ensure that all information provided by participants in human development research is confidential, meaning that it will not be shared with anyone outside the immediate research group and any results from the research will not identify any of the participants by name.

4. *Deception and debriefing.* Sometimes human development research involves deception. For example, a study might involve having children play a game but fix the game to ensure that they will lose, because the objective of the study is to examine how children respond to losing a game. IRBs require researchers to show that the deception in the proposed study will cause no harm. Also, ethical guidelines require that participants in a study that involves deception must be *debriefed,* which means that following their participation they must be told the true purpose of the study and the reason for the deception.

informed consent

standard procedure in social scientific studies that entails informing potential participants of what their participation would involve, including any possible risks, and giving them the opportunity to agree to participate or not

---

CRITICAL THINKING QUESTION

Of the three hypothetical studies described here, which do you think would be likely to receive IRB approval and which not?

Practice Quiz

1. Dr. Kim decided to conduct interviews with middle school children rather than administering questionnaires because she wanted to hear from them in their own words. Her use of interviews is an example of _____.

   a. an unbiased sample   **c.** a theory

   b. confidential responses   **d.** the research method

2. Even though Dr. Hernandez is not administering drugs, but merely asking adolescents questions about various drugs, she still needs to submit her proposal to the _____ to prevent potential ethical violations.

   a. Grants and Standards Board

   b. Institutional Review Board

   c. International Standards Board

   d. University Research Screening

3. Hypotheses refer to _____.

   a. developing a research design

   b. creating unbiased questions on a questionnaire

   c. forming a possible answer to a research question

   d. choosing a research method

4. When Dr. McIntyre conducted her research with elementary and middle schools students, rather than having a space for a name, students were asked to come up with a password and write it on the top of their questionnaire packet. This was done to ensure _____.

   a. debriefing of participants   **c.** confidentiality

   b. informed consent   **d.** generalizability of the findings

5. Shaleen is a student in an Introductory Psychology class and is participating in a study at her university. Which of the following is likely to happen first?

   a. Her demographic data will be analyzed.

   b. She will be debriefed so that she can decide whether she wants to participate.

   c. She will sign a consent form.

   d. She will answer questions in a questionnaire booklet.

HOW WE STUDY HUMAN DEVELOPMENT: Research Methods and Designs

Although all investigators of human development follow the scientific method in some form, there are many different ways of investigating research questions. Studies vary in the methods used and in their research designs.

Research Methods

LO 1.14 Summarize the main methods used in research on human development.

Researchers study human development in a variety of academic disciplines, including psychology, sociology, anthropology, education, social work, family studies, and medicine. They use various methods in their investigations, each of which has both strengths and limitations. We'll examine each of the major research methods next, then consider an issue that is important across methods, the question of reliability and validity.

QUESTIONNAIRES The most commonly used method in social science research is the questionnaire (Salkind, 2011). Usually, questionnaires have a *closed-question* format, which means that participants are provided with specific responses to choose from (Shaughnessy et al., 2011). Sometimes the questions have an *open-ended question* format, which means that participants are allowed to state their response following the question. One advantage of closed questions is that they make it possible to collect and analyze responses from a large number of people in a relatively short time. Everyone responds to the same questions with the same response options. For this reason, closed questions have often been used in large-scale surveys.

Although questionnaires are the dominant type of method used in the study of human development, the use of questionnaires has certain limitations (Arnett, 2005). When a closed-question format is used, the range of possible responses is already specified, and the participant must choose from the responses provided. The researcher tries to include the responses that seem most plausible and most likely, but it is impossible in a few brief response options to do justice to the depth and diversity of human experience. For example, if a questionnaire contains an item such as "How close are you to your spouse? A. very close; B. somewhat close; C. not very close; D. not at all close," it is probably true that people who choose "very close" really are closer to their marriage partners than people who choose "not at all close." But this alone does not begin to capture the complexity of the marriage relationship.

INTERVIEWS Interviews are intended to provide the kind of individuality and complexity that questionnaires usually lack. An interview allows a researcher to hear people describe their lives in their own words, with all the uniqueness and richness that such descriptions make possible. Interviews also enable a researcher to know the whole person and see how the various parts of the person's life are intertwined. For example, an interview on an adolescent's family relationships might reveal how the adolescent's relationship with her mother is affected by her relationship with her father, and how the whole family has been affected by certain events—perhaps a family member's loss of a job, psychological problems, medical problems, or substance abuse.

Interviews provide **qualitative** data, as contrasted with the **quantitative** (numerical) data of questionnaires, and qualitative data can be interesting and informative. (Qualitative data are nonnumerical and include not only interview data but also data from other nonnumerical methods such as descriptive observations, video recordings, or photographs.) However, like questionnaires, interviews have limitations (Shaughnessy et al., 2011). Because interviews do not typically provide a range of specific responses the way questionnaires do, interview responses have to be coded according to some plan of classification. For example, if you asked emerging adults the interview question "What do you think makes a person an adult?" you might get a fascinating range of responses. However, to make sense of the data and present them in a scientific format, at some point you would have to code the responses into categories—legal markers, biological markers, character qualities, and so on. Only in this way would you be able to say something about the pattern of responses in your sample. Coding interview data takes time, effort, and money. This is one of the reasons far more studies are conducted using questionnaires than interviews.

OBSERVATIONS Another way researchers learn about human development is through *observations*. Studies using this method involve observing people and recording their behavior either on video or through written records. In some studies the observations take place in the natural environment. For example, a study of aggressive behavior in children might involve observations on a school playground. In other studies the observations take place in a laboratory setting. For example, many laboratory studies of attachments between toddlers and their parents have been conducted in which the parent leaves the room briefly and the toddler's behavior is observed while the parent is absent and when the parent returns. Whether in the natural environment or the laboratory, after the observations are completed the data are coded and analyzed.

Observational methods have an advantage over questionnaires and interviews in that they involve actual behavior rather than self-reports of behavior. However, the disadvantage of observations

qualitative

data that is collected in nonnumerical form

quantitative

data that is collected in numerical form

Observations allow researchers to assess behavior directly rather than through self-report. Here, an infant's cognitive development is assessed.

is that the people being observed may be aware of the observer and this awareness may make their behavior different than it would be under normal conditions. For example, parents being observed in a laboratory setting with their children may be nicer to them than they would be at home.

ETHNOGRAPHIC RESEARCH Researchers have also learned about human development through **ethnographic research** (Jessor et al., 1996). In this method researchers spend a considerable amount of time with the people they wish to study, often by actually living among them. Information gained in ethnographic research typically comes from researchers' observations, experiences, and informal conversations with the people they are studying. Ethnographic research is commonly used by anthropologists, usually in studying non-Western cultures. Anthropologists usually report the results of their research in an *ethnography,* which is a book that presents an anthropologist's observations of what life is like in a particular

Ethnographic research entails living among the people in the culture of interest. Here, the renowned anthropologist Margaret Mead talks to a mother in the Manus culture of Papua New Guinea.

culture. Ethnographic research is also used by some social scientists today to study a particular aspect of their own culture (e.g., Douglass, 2005).

The main advantage of the ethnographic method is that it allows the researcher to learn how people behave in their daily lives. Other methods capture only a slice or summary of people's lives, but the ethnographic method provides insights into the whole span of daily experience. The main disadvantage of the ethnographic method is that it requires a great deal of time, commitment, and sacrifice by the researcher. It means that researchers must give up their own lives for a period of time, from a few weeks to years, in order to live among the people whose lives they wish to understand. Also, an ethnographic researcher is likely to form relationships with the people being studied, which may bias the interpretation of the results.

CASE STUDIES The case study method entails the detailed examination of the life of one person or a small number of persons. For more on this method, and an illustration from a famous study, see the *Research Focus: Darwin's Diary, A Case Study* feature on the next page.

BIOLOGICAL MEASUREMENTS Biological changes are a central part of human development, so research may include biological measures in areas such as hormonal functioning, brain functioning, and the genetic basis of development. Some of this research involves assessing biological characteristics, such as hormone levels, and relating the results to data using other methods, such as questionnaires on aggressive behavior. Research on brain functioning often involves measuring brain activity during different kinds of behavior, like listening to music or solving a math problem. Research on genetics increasingly involves directly examining the structure of genes.

Biological methods have the advantage of providing precise measurements of many aspects of human functioning. They allow researchers to gain knowledge into how biological aspects of development are related to cognitive, social, and emotional functioning. However, biological methods tend to rely on expensive equipment. Also, although biological measurements can be precise, their relation to other aspects of functioning is often far from exact. For example, if levels of a certain hormone are positively associated with aggressive behavior, it may be that the hormone causes the aggressive behavior, or it could be that aggressive behavior causes levels of the hormone to rise. Methods in brain research yield data from monitoring the brain's electrical activity or recording images of the brain while it is engaged in various activities, but those data can be difficult to interpret (Gergen, 2011).

ethnographic research

research method that involves spending extensive time among the people being studied

Research Focus: Darwin's Diary, A Case Study

The case study method entails the detailed examination of the life of one person or a small number of persons. The advantage of a case study is in the detail and richness that is possible when only one or a few persons are being described. The disadvantage of the case study is that it is especially difficult to generalize the results to larger groups of people on the basis of only one or a few people's experiences.

Some of the most influential studies in the history of human development research were case studies. For example, Jean Piaget initially based his ideas about infants' cognitive development on his detailed observations of his own three children. Also, Charles Darwin recorded an extensive case study of the early years of his son Doddy.

Darwin is best known for his 1859 book *The Origin of Species*, which laid out his theory of evolution and dramatically changed how humans view themselves in relation to nature. However, twenty years before he published *The Origin of Species*, Darwin embarked on a different project.

He decided to keep a diary record of the development of his first child, Doddy. Already Darwin was intensely interested in how and why animal species differ from one another. By keeping a careful record of Doddy's development, Darwin hoped to find evidence toward answering questions such as: "What is innate and what is learned?" "What skills emerge in the first years of a child's life, and at what ages?" and "How are human children different from other young primates?"

In his diary, Darwin recorded observations and insights concerning Doddy's cognitive, language, social, and moral development.

In observing Doddy's cognitive development, Darwin noted that it was at about 4 months of age that Doddy first became able to coordinate simple actions:

> Took my finger to his mouth & as usual could not get it back in, on account of his own hand being in the way; then he slipped his own back & so got my finger in. —This was not chance & therefore a kind of reasoning (p. 12).

Beginning to coordinate actions in this way was later recognized by psychological researchers as an important marker of early cognitive development.

With regard to social development, Darwin observed, as later researchers would, that Doddy's first smiles were the expression of internal states rather than being intended as communication. "When little under five weeks old, smiled but certainly not from pleasure" (p. 3). Over the course of the next months Darwin recorded how smiling changed from an expression of internal feelings to a social act directed toward others.

Darwin also noted Doddy's aggressive behavior. On one occasion when Doddy was 13 months old, he became angry when his nurse tried to take a piece of cake away from him: "He tried to slap her face, went scarlet, screamed & shook his head" (p. 29). Because Doddy had never been physically punished, Darwin concluded that this act of aggression must have been instinctive rather than learned.

Today the case study method is sometimes used in mental health research to describe a case that is unusual or that portrays the characteristics of a mental health issue in an especially vivid way. It is also used in combination with other methods, as a way of providing a sense of the whole of a person's life.

Watch RESEARCH FOCUS: DARWIN'S DIARY, A CASE STUDY

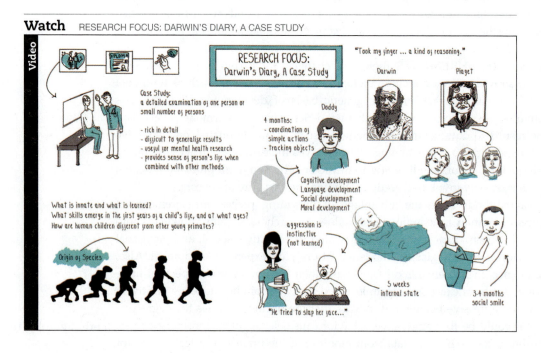

Review Questions:

1. Which of these was one of Darwin's goals in keeping a diary of his son Doddy's development?
   a. To see whether he preferred breast-feeding or bottle-feeding.
   b. To see how he responded to the family pets.
   ✓ c. To identify what was innate and what was learned.
   d. To give parents guidelines on how to soothe their crying children.

2. Which of these emotions did Doddy display vividly at age 13 months, according to Darwin's diary?
   ✓ a. Anger
   b. Sadness
   c. Curiosity
   d. Fear

EXPERIMENTAL RESEARCH An approach used in many kinds of scientific research is the **experimental research method**. In the simplest form of this design, participants in the study are randomly assigned to either the *experimental group,* which receives a treatment of some kind, or the *control group,* which receives no treatment (Goodwin, 2009). Because participants were randomly assigned to either the experimental group or the control group, it can be reasonably assumed that the two groups did not differ prior to the experiment.

In an experiment there are independent variables and dependent variables. The **independent variable** is the variable that is different for the experimental group than for the control group. The **dependent variable** is the outcome that is measured to calculate the results of the experiment. For example, in one classic experiment by Albert Bandura and his colleagues (1961), children in the experimental group were shown a film that involved aggressive behavior by an adult, and children in the control group were shown a film that did not portray aggressive behavior. The independent variable was the content of the film each group was shown. In a play session that followed, children in the treatment group were more aggressive toward an inflated doll ("Bobo") than children in the control group. The dependent variable was the children's aggressiveness.

Another area of human development research for which the experimental research method is commonly used is for **interventions**. Interventions are programs intended to change the attitudes or behavior of the participants. For example, a variety of programs have been developed to prevent adolescents from starting to smoke cigarettes, by promoting critical thinking about cigarette advertising or by attempting to change attitudes associating smoking with peer acceptance (e.g., Horn et al., 2005). The adolescents participating in such a study are randomly assigned to either the experimental group receiving the intervention or the control group that does not receive the intervention. After the intervention, the two groups are assessed for their attitudes and behavior regarding smoking. If the intervention worked, the attitudes and/or behavior of the experimental group should be less favorable toward smoking than those of the control group.

The advantage of the experimental method is that it allows the researcher a high degree of control over participants' behavior. Rather than monitoring behavior that occurs naturally, the researcher attempts to change the normal patterns of behavior by assigning some persons to an experimental group and some to a control group. This allows for a clearer and more definite measure of the effect of the experimental manipulation than is possible in normal life. However, the disadvantage of the experimental method is the flip side of the advantage: Because participants' behavior has been altered through experimental manipulation, it is difficult to say if the results would apply in normal life.

experimental research method

research method that entails comparing an *experimental group* that receives a treatment of some kind to a *control group* that receives no treatment

independent variable

in an experiment, the variable that is different for the experimental group than for the control group

dependent variable

in an experiment, the outcome that is measured to calculate the results of the experiment by comparing the experimental group to the control group

intervention

program intended to change the attitudes or behavior of the participants

Intervention programs are one type of experimental research. Here, adolescents participate in an anti-drug use program.

NATURAL EXPERIMENTS A **natural experiment** is a situation that exists naturally—in other words, the researcher does not control it—but that provides interesting scientific information to the perceptive observer (Goodwin, 2009). One natural experiment used frequently in human development research is adoption. Unlike in most families, children in adoptive families are raised by adults with whom they have no genetic relationship. Because one set of parents provide the child's genes and a different set of parents provide the environment, it is possible to examine the relative contributions of genes and environment to the child's development. Similarities between adoptive parents and adopted children are likely to be due to the environment provided by the parents, because the parents and children are biologically unrelated. Similarities between adopted children and their biological parents are likely to be due to genetics, because the environment the children grew up in was not provided by the biological parents.

Natural experiments provide the advantage of allowing for exceptional insights into the relation between genes and the environment. However, they have disadvantages as well. Families who adopt children are not selected randomly but volunteer and go through an extensive screening process, which makes adoption studies difficult to generalize to biological families. Also, natural experiments tend to be rare and to occur unpredictably, and consequently such studies can only provide answers to a limited range of questions.

RELIABILITY AND VALIDITY In scientific research it is important that research methods have *reliability* and *validity*. **Reliability** refers to the consistency of measurements (Salkind, 2011). There are a variety of types of reliability, but in general, a method has high reliability if it obtains similar results on different occasions. For example, if a questionnaire asked girls in their senior year of high school to recall when their first menstrual period occurred, the questionnaire would be considered reliable if most of the girls answered the same on one occasion as they did when asked the question again 6 months later. Or, if people in late adulthood were interviewed about the quality of their relationships with their grandchildren, the measure would be reliable if the adults' answers were the same in response to two different interviewers (Goodwin, 1995).

Validity refers to the truthfulness of a method (Shaughnessy et al., 2011). A method is valid if it *measures what it claims to measure*. For example, IQ tests are purported to measure intellectual abilities, but as we shall see in Chapter 7, this claim is controversial. Critics claim that IQ tests are not valid (i.e., that they do not measure what they claim to measure). Notice that a measure is not necessarily valid even if it is reliable. It is widely agreed that IQ tests are reliable—people generally score about the same on one occasion as they do on another—but the validity of the tests is disputed. In general, validity is more difficult to establish than reliability. We will examine questions of reliability and validity throughout the book.

Take a moment to review **Table 1.2**, which lists the advantages and limitations of each of the research methods we have discussed.

natural experiment

situation that exists naturally but provides interesting scientific information

reliability

in scientific research, the consistency of measurements across different occasions

validity

in scientific research, the extent to which a research method measures what it claims to measure

Table 1.2 Research Methods: Advantages and Limitations

Methods	Advantages	Limitations
Questionnaire	Large sample, quick data collection	Preset responses, no depth
Interview	Individuality and complexity	Time and effort of coding
Observations	Actual behavior, not self-report	Observation may affect behavior
Ethnographic research	Entire span of daily life	Researcher must live among participants; possible bias
Case studies	Rich, detailed data	Difficult to generalize results
Biological measurements	Precise data	Expensive; relation to behavior may not be clear
Experiment	Control, identification of cause and effect	May not reflect real life
Natural experiment	Illuminate gene–environment relations	Unusual circumstances; rare

Research Designs

LO 1.15 **Describe the major types of research designs used in human development research.**

In addition to choosing a research method, researchers must also choose a design for their study. Common research designs in the study of human development include cross-sectional and longitudinal designs (see **Table 1.3**).

CROSS-SECTIONAL RESEARCH The most common type of research design in the study of human development is **cross-sectional research**. In cross-sectional research, data are collected on a single occasion (Goodwin, 2009). Then, the researcher examines potential relations between variables in the data, based on the hypotheses of the study. For example, researchers may ask a sample of persons in middle adulthood to fill out a questionnaire reporting their physical health and how much they exercise, based on the hypothesis that exercising promotes better physical health. They then analyze the data to see if the amount of exercise is related to physical health (see **Figure 1.9** for a hypothetical illustration of this relationship).

Cross-sectional research has both strengths and weaknesses. The main strength is that these studies can be completed quickly and inexpensively. Data collection is done on one occasion, and the study is finished. This simplicity explains why cross-sectional research is so widely used among researchers.

However, there are weaknesses as well in the cross-sectional research design. Most importantly, cross-sectional research yields a *correlation* between variables, and correlations can be difficult to interpret. A **correlation** is a statistical relationship between two variables, such that knowing one of the variables makes it possible to predict the other. A *positive correlation* means that when one variable increases or decreases the other variable changes in the same direction; a *negative correlation* means that when one variable increases the other decreases. In the example just provided, the researcher may find a positive correlation between exercising and physical health. But does this mean that exercising causes better physical health, or that people with better physical health are more inclined to exercise? Based on cross-sectional research alone, there is no way to tell.

It is a basic statistical principle of scientific research that *correlation does not imply causation*, meaning that when two variables are correlated it is not possible to tell whether one variable caused the other. Nevertheless, this principle is frequently overlooked in research on human development. For example, there are hundreds of studies showing a correlation between parenting behaviors and children's functioning. Frequently this correlation has been interpreted as causation—parenting behaviors *cause* children to function in certain ways—but in fact the correlation alone does not show this (Pinker, 2002). It could be that children's characteristics cause parents to behave in certain ways, or it could be that the behavior of both parents and children is due to a third variable, such as SES or cultural context. We will explore this issue and other *correlation versus causation* questions in later chapters.

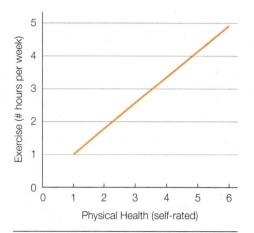

Figure 1.9 Physical Health and Exercise Are Correlated—But Which Causes Which?

cross-sectional research
research design that involves collecting data on a single occasion

correlation
statistical relationship between two variables such that knowing one of the variables makes it possible to predict the other

Table 1.3 Research Designs: Advantages and Limitations

Method	Definition	Advantages	Limitations
Cross-sectional	Data collected at one time point	Quick and inexpensive	Correlations difficult to interpret
Longitudinal	Data collected at two or more time points	Monitors change over time	Time, expense, attrition

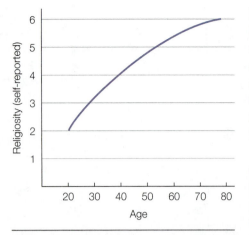

Figure 1.10 Religiosity Changes with Age—But Is It an Age Effect or a Cohort Effect?

longitudinal research

research design in which the same persons are followed over time and data are collected on two or more occasions

cohort effect

in scientific research, an explanation of group differences among people of different ages based on the fact that they grew up in different *cohorts* or historical periods

LONGITUDINAL RESEARCH The limitations of cross-sectional research have led some researchers to use a **longitudinal research** design, in which the same persons are followed over time and data are collected on two or more occasions. The length of longitudinal research designs varies widely, from a few weeks or months to years or even decades. Most longitudinal studies take place over a relatively short period, a year or less, but some studies have followed their samples over an entire lifetime, from infancy to old age (e.g., Frieman & Martin, 2011).

The great advantage of the longitudinal research design is that it allows researchers on human development to examine the question that is at the heart of the study of human development: "How do people change over time?" In addition, the longitudinal research design allows researchers to gain more insight into the question of correlation versus causation. For example, suppose a cross-sectional study of people in young, middle, and late adulthood shows a correlation between age and religiosity: The older people are, the more religious they report themselves to be (see **Figure 1.10** for a hypothetical illustration of this pattern). Does this mean that growing older causes people to become more religious? From a cross-sectional study, there is no way to tell; it could be that the culture has changed over the years, and that the older adults grew up in a more religious era than the younger adults did. This kind of explanation for age differences is called a **cohort effect**; people of different ages vary because they grew up in different *cohorts* or historical periods. However, if you could follow the younger adults into late adulthood using a longitudinal research design, you could see if they became more religious as they grew older. You could then draw more definite conclusions about whether or not aging leads to higher religiosity.

Longitudinal research designs have disadvantages as well. Most importantly, they take a great deal more time, money, and patience than a cross-sectional research design does. Researchers do not learn the outcome to the investigation of their hypothesis until weeks, months, or years later. Over time, it is inevitable that some people will drop out of a longitudinal study, for one reason or another—a process called *attrition*. Consequently, the sample the researcher has at Time 1 is likely to be different than the sample that remains at Time 2, 3, or 4, which limits the conclusions that can be drawn. In most studies, dropout is highest among people from low-SES groups, which means that the longer a longitudinal study goes on, the less likely it is to represent the SES range of the entire population.

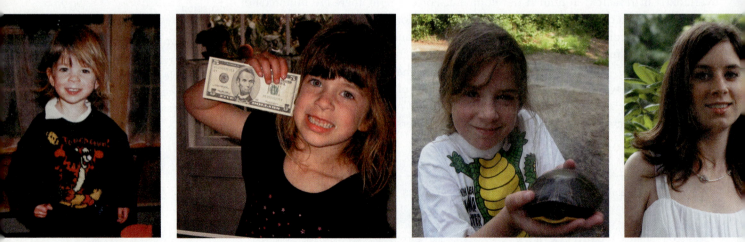

Longitudinal studies follow the same persons over time. Here, an American girl is pictured in toddlerhood, early childhood, middle childhood, and adolescence.

Throughout this book, studies using a wide variety of research methods and research designs will be presented. For now, the methods and designs just described will provide you with an introduction to the approaches used most often.

Practice Quiz   ANSWERS AVAILABLE IN ANSWER KEY.

1. For his post-doctorate research, Yani plans to study human development among indigenous cultures in the mountains of Peru. He plans to move to Peru to integrate with his study subjects, make social connections with them, and observe their daily life up close. Which type of research method is he using?

  a. An intervention

  b. Ethnographic research

  c. An experiment

  d. A quasi-experiment

2. Which of the following is **TRUE** regarding research methods?

  a. The most commonly used method in social science research is the open-ended interview.

  b. The main drawback of the experimental method is that the findings may not generalize in real-life settings.

  c. The strength of the case study approach is the ability to generalize the findings.

  d. The main advantage of gathering non-numerical data from interviews is that coding is relatively quick and inexpensive.

3. Bernice is planning to conduct a cross-sectional study for her dissertation. Which of the following is a limitation that she and her advisor discuss before she begins to collect her data?

  a. Subjects are likely to drop out of the study.

  b. It tends to be more time-consuming than longitudinal research.

  c. Differences may be due to cohort differences.

  d. Because of a rigorous peer-review process, cross-sectional studies are unlikely to be accepted for publication.

4. You are interested in studying the potential changes in intelligence over the lifespan. You have selected 250 people who are currently two years old and you plan to assess them every five years for 40 years. What type of study are you planning on conducting?

  a. Quasi-experimental

  b. Ethnographic

  c. Longitudinal

  d. Cross-sectional

5. What type of correlation describes the situation in which the more hours spent sitting or in sedentary activity on the job, the higher the person's body mass index (BMI)?

  a. A positive correlation

  b. A negative correlation

  c. No correlation

  d. A curved correlation

Summary: How We Study Human Development

LO 1.12 **Recall the five steps of the scientific method and the meanings and functions of hypotheses, sampling, and procedure in scientific research.**

The scientific method entails five main steps: (1) identifying a research question, (2) forming a hypothesis, (3) choosing a research method and a research design, (4) collecting data, and (5) drawing conclusions that lead to new questions and new hypotheses.

LO 1.13 **Describe some ethical standards for human development research.**

Research on human development is required to follow ethical guidelines, which are laid out by professional organizations and enforced by IRBs. The main guidelines include protecting participants from physical or psychological harm, informed consent prior to participation, confidentiality, and debriefing after participation if deception was used.

LO 1.14 **Summarize the main methods used in research on human development.**

A variety of specific methods for data collection are used in the study of human development, ranging from questionnaires and interviews to ethnographic research to experiments. Each method has both strengths and weaknesses. Two important qualities in research methods are reliability (consistency of measurement) and validity (the accuracy of measurement in reflecting real life).

LO 1.15 **Describe the major types of research designs used in human development research.**

Common research designs include cross-sectional and longitudinal. Each design has both strengths and weaknesses.

Applying Your Knowledge as a Professional

The topics covered in this chapter apply to a wide variety of career professions. Watch these videos to learn how they apply to a developmental and evolutionary psychologist and professors of psychology and biology.

Watch CAREER FOCUS: PROFESSOR OF PSYCHOLOGY

LeaAnn Lucas, Ph.D.
Associate Professor, Psychology
Sinclair Community College

Chapter Quiz

1. The United States _____.
   a. is the developed country that will experience the steepest decline in population between now and 2050
   ✓ b. is one of the few developed countries that will experience an increase in population, due largely to immigration
   c. is expected to have approximately the same proportion of Latinos by 2050, but far fewer African Americans
   d. has a total fertility rate that is lower than most developed countries due to the availability of birth control

2. If a researcher wanted to measure the socioeconomic status (SES) of her adult participants, she would need to ask them about which of the following?
   ✓ a. Educational level
   b. Number of children
   c. Religion
   d. Ethnicity

3. Unlike early hominids, *Homo sapiens* had _____.
   a. a narrower pelvis
   b. a shorter period of dependency
   c. a slightly smaller brain
   ✓ d. smaller jaws

4. Which of the following occurred during the Neolithic period?
   a. The climate got much colder.
   b. Humans began to bury their dead for the first time.
   ✓ c. The domestication of animals developed.
   d. Humans reached Australia for the first time.

5. Which of the following best represents the impact of evolution on human development?
   a. Biologically, humans have changed drastically since the origin of *Homo sapiens*.
   b. Our development of bipedal locomotion is the most distinctive characteristic of our species.
   ✓ c. Cultures shape the raw material of biology into widely different paths throughout the life span.
   d. Instincts reduce humans' capacity for cultural learning more than they reduce animals' capacity for cultural learning.

6. The *Dharmashastras*, the sacred law books of the Hindu religion, describe _____ stages of a person's life.
   a. ten
   b. two
   ✓ c. four
   d. twelve

7. The three traditional conceptions of life (in the *Dharmashastras*, the Talmud, and as proposed by Solon) differ _____.

   a. in that only one is a view of how we develop if all goes well

   ✓ b. in the way that they divide the life span

   c. in the level of maturity they attribute to youth

   d. in the stage of life when wisdom is evident

8. According to Freud, _____ is the driving force behind human development.

   a. attachment to one's mother

   ✓ b. sexual desire

   c. cognitive development

   d. trust

9. Although Shanamae makes a good salary in sales, she is questioning whether her work in the retail industry is making a meaningful contribution to society. She is thinking of going back to school to train to be a nurse, so that she can give back to society by helping others. According to Erikson, she is in the stage of _____.

   a. ego integrity versus despair

   b. industry versus inferiority

   ✓ c. generativity versus stagnation

   d. industry versus stagnation

10. The United States' belief in the value of individual freedom, as demonstrated in its capitalist economic system and its governmental system of representative democracy, reflects which system of Bronfenbrenner's theory?

    a. Exosystem

    b. Chronosystem

    c. Microsystem

    ✓ d. Macrosystem

11. Where does the developmental life stage of emerging adulthood usually appear?

    ✓ a. In developed countries

    b. In traditional cultures

    c. In collectivistic cultures

    d. In developing countries

12. _____ generates hypotheses that can be tested in research.

    a. An unbiased sample

    ✓ b. A theory

    c. The research design

    d. The research method

13. In the famous case of Henrietta Lacks, an African American woman's cancer cells were removed from her cervix without her knowledge by a surgeon right before her death in 1951. Researchers wanted to study these cells to learn about the genes that cause cancer and those that suppress it. The ethical requirement of _____ would protect against this happening today.

    ✓ a. informed consent

    b. deception

    c. confidentiality

    d. generalizability of the findings

14. Which of the following statements is true regarding research methods?

    a. Qualitative data is considered unscientific among most researchers in the field of psychology.

    b. The strength of the case study approach is the ability to generalize the findings.

    ✓ c. The ethnographic method allows the researcher to learn how people behave in their daily lives.

    d. The most commonly used method in social science research is the open-ended interview.

15. Which of the following is a problem with cross-sectional research?

    ✓ a. Participants tend to drop out of the study.

    b. It tends to be more expensive to conduct than longitudinal research.

    c. It tends to be more time-consuming than longitudinal research.

    d. It yields a correlation, which may be difficult to interpret.

Chapter 2
Genetics and Prenatal Development

FOR MOTHERS-TO-BE WORLDWIDE, PREGNANCY IS OFTEN EXPERIENCED WITH A COMBINATION OF JOY, HOPE, AND FEAR. Yet here as in other aspects of development, the experience differs substantially depending on the economic and cultural context. For most women in rural areas of developing countries, there is little in the way of technology or medical care to promote the healthy development of the fetus. Instead, pregnant women often rely on folk beliefs, a midwife's years of experience, and social support from the extended family. For most women in developed countries, medical care and technological aids are available throughout pregnancy. Yet prospective mothers and fathers face formidable challenges in altering their lives to make room for the demands of raising a small child while continuing to pursue their careers.

Pregnancy is experienced in many different ways around the world, but everywhere it is a momentous event. In this chapter we examine the process of prenatal development, from its genetic beginnings until the final months of pregnancy. The first section of the chapter covers the basics of genetics and how a new human life begins. In the next section we examine prenatal development and prenatal care for both mother and baby to enhance the likelihood that all will go well. Sometimes problems arise in the course of pregnancy or in becoming pregnant in the first place, so the final section of the chapter addresses prenatal complications and infertility.

Watch CHAPTER INTRODUCTION: GENETICS AND PRENATAL DEVELOPMENT

Section 1 Genetic Influences on Development

∨ Learning Objectives

2.1 Distinguish between genotype and phenotype and identify the different forms of genetic inheritance.

2.2 Describe the sex chromosomes and identify what makes them different from other chromosomes.

2.3 Explain how behavior geneticists use heritability estimates and concordance rates in their research.

2.4 Describe how the concept of epigenesis frames gene–environment interactions, and connect epigenesis to the concept of reaction range.

2.5 Explain how the theory of genotype → environment effects casts new light on the old nature–nurture debate.

2.6 Outline the process of meiosis in the formation of reproductive cells and specify how the process differs for males and females.

2.7 Describe the process of fertilization and conception.

chromosome

sausage-shaped structure in the nucleus of cells, containing genes, which are paired, except in reproductive cells

DNA (deoxyriboynucleic acid)

long strand of cell material that stores and transfers genetic information in all life forms

gene

segment of DNA containing coded instructions for the growth and functioning of the organism

genome

entire store of an organism's hereditary information

genotype

organism's unique genetic inheritance

phenotype

organism's actual characteristics, derived from its genotype

GENETIC INFLUENCES ON DEVELOPMENT: Genetic Basics

In all organisms, humans included, individual development has a genetic beginning. To understand the role of genetics in human development, it is important to have a basic foundation of knowledge about genes and how they function.

Genotype and Phenotype

LO 2.1 **Distinguish between genotype and phenotype and identify the different forms of genetic inheritance.**

Nearly all cells in the human body contain 46 **chromosomes** in 23 pairs, with one chromosome in each pair inherited from the mother and the other inherited from the father (see **Figure 2.1**). The chromosomes are composed of complex molecules known as **DNA (deoxyribonucleic acid)** (see **Figure 2.2**). The DNA in the chromosomes is organized into segments called **genes**, which are the basic units of hereditary information. Genes contain paired sequences of chemicals called *nucleotides*, and these sequences comprise instructions for the functioning and replication of the cells. There are about 23,000 genes in our 46 chromosomes, the total human **genome**, with all together about 3 billion nucleotide pairs (International Human Genome Sequencing Consortium, 2004).

Not all 23,000 genes are expressed in the course of development. The totality of an individual's genes is the **genotype**, and the person's actual characteristics are called the **phenotype**. In part, the difference between genotype and phenotype is a consequence of the person's environment. For example, if you were born with a genotype that included exceptional musical ability, this talent might never be developed if your environment

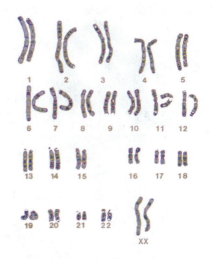

Figure 2.1 The Human Genome

The 46 chromosomes in the human genome are organized into 23 pairs. This is the genome of a female; in a male the 23rd pair would be XY rather than XX.

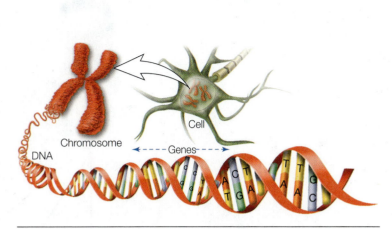

Figure 2.2 The Chemical Structure of DNA

DNA is composed of nucleotide pairs.

provided no access to musical instruments or musical instruction. Consequently, the musical ability present in your genotype would not be apparent in your phenotype.

Another aspect of genetic functioning that influences the relation between genotype and phenotype is **dominant–recessive inheritance** (Jones, 2006). On every pair of chromosomes there are two forms of each gene, one on the chromosome inherited from the mother and one on the chromosome inherited from the father. Each form of the gene is called an **allele**. On many of these pairs of alleles, dominant–recessive inheritance occurs. This means that only one of the two genes—the *dominant gene*—influences the phenotype, whereas the *recessive gene* does not, even though it is part of the genotype. For example, if you inherited a gene for curly hair from one parent and a gene for straight hair from the other, you would have curly hair, because curly hair is dominant and straight hair is recessive. Recessive genes are expressed in the phenotype only when they are paired with another recessive gene. A clear pattern of dominant–recessive inheritance is evident only for traits determined by a single gene, which is not true of most traits, as we will see shortly. Some other examples of dominant and recessive characteristics are shown in **Table 2.1**.

The table shows clear-cut examples of dominant and recessive genes, but sometimes there is **incomplete dominance**, in which the phenotype is influenced primarily, but not exclusively, by the dominant gene. One example of incomplete dominance involves the sickle-cell trait that is common among black Africans and their descendants such as

dominant–recessive inheritance

pattern of inheritance in which a pair of chromosomes contains one dominant and one recessive gene, but only the dominant gene is expressed in the phenotype

allele

on a pair of chromosomes, each of two forms of a gene

incomplete dominance

form of dominant–recessive inheritance in which the phenotype is influenced primarily by the dominant gene but also to some extent by the recessive gene

Table 2.1 Traits with Single-Gene Dominant–Recessive Inheritance

Dominant	Recessive
Curly hair	Straight hair
Dark hair	Blonde hair
Facial dimples	No dimples
Normal hearing	Deafness (some forms)
Normal vision	Nearsighted vision
Freckles	No freckles
Unattached ear lobe	Attached ear lobe
Can roll tongue in U-shape	Cannot roll tongue in U-shape

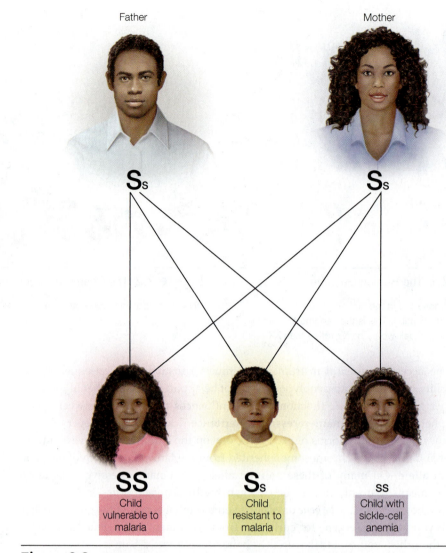

Father   Mother

SS   SS

SS   Ss   ss

| Child vulnerable to malaria | Child resistant to malaria | Child with sickle-cell anemia |

Figure 2.3 Incomplete Dominance in Sickle-Cell Inheritance

Two recessive genes for the sickle-cell trait results in sickle-cell anemia, but having one dominant and one recessive gene provides protection against malaria.

African Americans (see **Figure 2.3**). Most blood cells are shaped like a disk, but when a person inherits two recessive genes for the sickle-cell trait the blood cells become hook-shaped, like the blade of a sickle. This results in a condition called *sickle-cell anemia,* in which the sickle-shaped blood cells clog up the blood vessels and cause pain, susceptibility to disease, and early death. About 1 in 500 Africans (and African Americans) have this disorder, and it also occurs (less commonly) in people whose ancestors are from India or the Mediterranean region (Quinn et al., 2004).

However, if a person inherits only one recessive gene for the sickle-cell trait, along with a normal dominant gene, the dominance is incomplete, and a portion—but not all—of the person's blood cells will be sickle shaped. This portion is not large enough to cause sickle-cell anemia, but it is large enough to make the person resistant to malaria, a blood disease that is spread by mosquitoes. Malaria is often fatal, and even when it is not it can cause brain damage and other enduring health problems. It occurs worldwide in developing countries but is especially common in Africa, killing over a million people a year. In many central African countries over 50% of children are affected (WHO, 2013).

This explains why the sickle-cell trait evolved especially among Africans. Because the effects of contracting malaria are so severe, in evolutionary terms it is an advantage genetically to have the sickle-cell trait to protect against malaria, even if it also raises the risk of sickle-cell anemia.

Most characteristics in human development are not determined solely by a single pair of genes. Despite what you may have heard about the supposed existence of a "gay gene" or "religion gene" or "crime gene," no such genes have been found, nor are they likely to be (Pinker, 2004; "Special report on the human genome," 2010). Although single gene pairs sometimes play a crucial role in development, as in the case of sickle-cell anemia, more commonly the influence of genes is a consequence of **polygenic inheritance**, the interaction of multiple genes rather than just one (Lewis, 2005). This is true for physical characteristics such as height, weight, and skin color, as well as for characteristics such as intelligence, personality, and susceptibility to various diseases (Hoh & Ott, 2003; Karlsson, 2006; Rucker & McGuffin, 2010).

The Sex Chromosomes

LO 2.2   **Describe the sex chromosomes and identify what makes them different from other chromosomes.**

Of the 23 pairs of chromosomes, one pair is different from the rest. These are the **sex chromosomes**, which determine whether the person will be male or female (Jones, 2006). In the female this pair is called XX; in the male, XY. The Y chromosome is notably smaller than other chromosomes and contains only one-third the genetic material. All eggs in the mother contain an X chromosome but sperm may carry either an X or a Y chromosome. So, it is the father's sperm that determines what the sex of the child will be. Ironically, many cultures mistakenly believe that the woman is responsible for the child's sex, and blame her if she fails to have sons (DeLoache & Gottlieb, 2000; Levine et al., 1994).

Many cultures also have beliefs about how to predict the baby's sex (DeLoache & Gottlieb, 2000). According to ancient Mayan beliefs, sex can be predicted from the mother's age and the month of conception; if both are even or odd, it's a girl, but if one is odd and one even, it's a boy. In Chinese tradition there is a similar calculation, also based on the mother's age and the month of conception. In the West today many people believe that if the mother is "carrying high"—the fetus feels high in the uterus—a girl is on the way, but if the mother is "carrying low" it's a boy. Another belief is that if the mother craves sweet foods, the baby will be a girl, but if she craves sour or salty foods she will soon have a boy. And in some countries it is believed that if the mother-to-be's right breast is larger than the left she will have a boy, but if the left breast is largest she will have a girl. None of these beliefs has the slightest scientific basis, but they demonstrate how important gender is to a child's future in most cultures, even before birth.

Many cultures have a bias in favor of boys, and the use of sex-selective abortion to achieve this is resulting in gender ratios skewed toward boys, especially in Asian cultures where this bias is especially pronounced (Abrejo et al., 2009). For more information on this, watch the video *A Preference for Sons* on the next page.

The sex of the developing organism also has biological consequences for prenatal development. Having only one X chromosome makes males more vulnerable than females to a variety of recessive disorders that are linked to the X chromosome (Narayanan et al., 2006). The reason for this is that if a female has one X chromosome that contains the recessive gene for a disorder, the disorder will not show up in her phenotype because the dominant gene on her other X chromosome will prevent it from being expressed. She will be a carrier of the disorder to the next generation but will not have the disorder herself. In contrast, if a male receives one X chromosome containing the recessive gene for a disorder, he will definitely have the disorder because he has no other X chromosome that may contain a dominant gene to block its expression. His Y chromosome cannot serve this function. An example of this pattern of **X-linked inheritance** is

polygenic inheritance
expression of phenotypic characteristics due to the interaction of multiple genes

sex chromosomes
chromosomes that determine whether an organism is male (XY) or female (XX)

X-linked inheritance
pattern of inheritance in which a recessive characteristic is expressed because it is carried on the male's X chromosome

Watch A PREFERENCE FOR SONS

shown in **Figure 2.4** for hemophilia, a disorder in which the blood does not clot properly and the person may bleed to death from even a minor injury. Because of X-linked inheritance, males are at greater risk for a wide variety of genetically based problems, including learning disabilities and intellectual disability (Halpern, 2000; James et al., 2006).

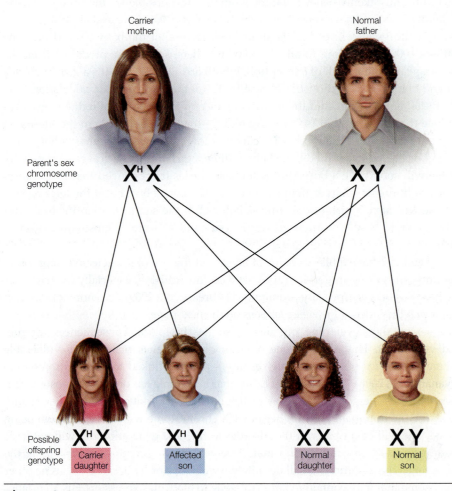

Figure 2.4 X-Linked Inheritance in Hemophilia

Why are males more vulnerable to recessive disorders carried on the X chromosome?

Practice Quiz   ANSWERS AVAILABLE IN ANSWER KEY.

1. Enrico's biological parents were both musicians, so he was born with a(n) _____ that included exceptional musical ability, but because he was never exposed to musical instruments or instruction when he was adopted, he never developed his musical ability.

   a. allele   ✓ **c.** phenotype

   b. genotype   **d.** heritability

2. Errol's father carries two recessive genes for sickle-cell anemia, and Errol's mother carries two normal dominant genes. Therefore, Errol has inherited _____ from his parents.

   a. anemia   **c.** Sickle-cell anemia

   ✓ **b.** A resistance to malaria   **d.** Huntington's chorea

3. Individuals of _____ descent are most likely to have sickle-cell anemia.

   a. Asian   ✓ **c.** African

   b. Hispanic   **d.** Native American

4. Sadie carries the recessive gene for hemophilia, a disorder in which the blood does not clot properly. If Sadie had two children, a boy and a girl, and passed the recessive gene for the disorder to both children, which of her children would develop hemophilia if the father does not have hemophilia himself?

   a. Neither of the two children

   b. Both children

   ✓ **c.** The boy

   d. The girl

5. Which of the following is TRUE?

   ✓ **a.** All eggs in the mother contain an X chromosome.

   b. All sperm carry a Y chromosome.

   c. The Y chromosome is larger than the X chromosome.

   d. The X chromosome and Y chromosome carry the same amount of genetic material.

GENETIC INFLUENCES ON DEVELOPMENT: Genes and the Environment

There is no doubt that genes have some influence on human development, but how much? Scholars have long debated the relative importance of genes and the environment in human development. In this **nature–nurture debate**, some scholars have claimed that development can be explained by genes (nature) and that environment matters little, whereas others have claimed that development depends mainly on environmental factors (nurture) (compare Baumrind, 1993; Scarr, 1993). In recent years, most scholars have reached a consensus that both genes and environment play key roles in human development, although the relative strength of nature and nurture continues to be debated (Dodge, 2007; Lerner, 2006; Pinker, 2004).

Principles of Behavior Genetics

LO 2.3   **Explain how behavior geneticists use heritability estimates and concordance rates in their research.**

The question of how much genes influence human development is at the heart of the field of **behavior genetics** (Gottesman, 2004; Plomin, 2009). Researchers who work in behavior genetics estimate the influence of genes on development by comparing people who share different amounts of their genes, mainly through twin studies and adoption studies. Identical or **monozygotic (MZ) twins** have 100% of their genes in common. Fraternal or **dizygotic (DZ) twins** and siblings have 40–60% of their genes in common. Consequently, when MZ twins are more similar than DZ twins or siblings, this indicates that genetics play a strong role. Adoptive children have no genetic resemblance to their adoptive families. Consequently, adoption studies allow a researcher to study whether certain behaviors or traits of adoptive children are more similar to those of their biological parents (indicating a stronger genetic influence) or their adoptive families (indicating a stronger environmental influence).

By comparing these different groups, behavior geneticists are able to calculate a statistic called **heritability**. Heritability is an estimate of the extent to which genes are

nature–nurture debate

debate among scholars as to whether human development is influenced mainly by genes (nature) or environment (nurture)

behavior genetics

field in the study of human development that aims to identify the extent to which genes influence behavior, primarily by comparing persons who share different amounts of their genes

monozygotic (MZ) twins

twins who have exactly the same genotype; also called identical twins

dizygotic (DZ) twins

twins that result when two ova are released by a female instead of one, and both are fertilized by sperm; also called fraternal twins

heritability

statistical estimate of the extent to which genes are responsible for the differences among persons within a specific population, with values ranging from 0 to 1.00

MZ twins have the same genotype.

responsible for the differences among persons within a specific population. The value of the heritability estimate ranges from 0 to 1.00. The higher the heritability, the more the characteristic is believed to be influenced by genetics.

Behavior genetics has flourished in the past 2 decades, and heritability estimates have been calculated for a wide range of characteristics. For intelligence, heritability estimates for children and adolescents have been found to be about .50, meaning that about half the variation in their IQ scores has been attributed to genetic influences (Turkheimer et al., 2009). With regard to personality characteristics, heritability estimates range from .40 to .50 for a wide array of characteristics such as sociability, activity level, and even religiosity (Bouchard & McGue, 2003).

Heritability estimates have been criticized for giving a misleading impression of the influence of genetics on development (Collins et al., 2000; Rutter, 2002). According to the critics, to state that a trait is heritable implies that we know with precision how much genes contribute to its development, but this is not so. Heritability estimates are simply estimates based on comparisons of persons with different amounts of genetic material in common, not direct measures of the activity of genes. Heritability estimates are a measure not just of genetic influence but of *how much the environment allows the genes to be expressed*. In other words, heritability estimates measure phenotype rather than genotype.

This can be seen in the studies finding that heritability of intelligence increases from childhood to adulthood (McGue & Christensen, 2002). Obviously genes do not change during this time, but the environment changes to allow greater expression of genetic potentials, as children grow into adolescence and become increasingly able to choose their own environments (e.g., whom they will have as friends). Other studies find that heritability of intelligence is higher in middle-class families than in poor families (McCartney & Berry, 2009; Turkheimer et al., 2009). This is not because middle-class families have different kinds of genes than poor families do, but because the greater economic resources of middle-class families make it more likely that children's genotypic potential for intelligence will be expressed in their phenotype.

Another statistic of genetic influence used in behavior genetics is **concordance rate**. This is a percentage that indicates the degree of similarity in phenotype among pairs of family members. Concordance rates range from 0% to 100%. The higher the concordance rate, the more similar the two persons are.

In many studies, comparisons of concordance rates are made between MZ and DZ twins. When concordance rates are higher among MZ than DZ twins, this indicates that the basis for the trait is partly genetic. For example, concordance rates for schizophrenia, a severe mental disorder involving hallucinations and disordered patterns of thinking and behavior, are 50% for MZ twins and 18% for DZ twins (Insel, 2010). This means that when one MZ twin has schizophrenia, 50% of the time the other twin has schizophrenia as well. For DZ twins, when one twin has schizophrenia, the other twin has the disorder only 18% of the time. Adoption studies also sometimes use this statistic, comparing concordance rates between parents and adopted children, parents and biological children, and adoptive or biological siblings.

concordance rate

degree of similarity in phenotype among pairs of family members, expressed as a percentage

epigenesis

in development, the continuous bidirectional interactions between genes and environment

Gene–Environment Interactions: Epigenesis and Reaction Ranges

LO 2.4   **Describe how the concept of epigenesis frames gene–environment interactions, and connect epigenesis to the concept of reaction range.**

Studies of heritability show not only that genes influence development but also that the environment influences how genes are expressed. A related idea is **epigenesis**, which means that development results from the bidirectional interactions between genotype and environment (Gottlieb, 2004; Gottlieb et al., 2007). According to epigenetic theory, genetic activity responds constantly to environmental influences. Development is influenced by genes but not purely determined by them (Moffitt et al., 2006).

Here is an example of epigenesis. Girls normally begin menstruating around age 11–16, toward the lower end of this range under healthy conditions and toward the higher end when nutrition is insufficient or the girl is suffering from medical problems (Neberich et al., 2010). Clearly it is part of the human-female genotype for menstruation to be initiated somewhere in this age range, with the timing influenced by environmental conditions. Furthermore, when girls' environmental conditions change, their menstrual patterns may also change. Girls who experience severe weight loss often stop menstruating (Roberto et al., 2008). If their nutritional intake improves, they begin menstruating again. This demonstrates a continuous interaction between genotype and environment, with menstruation being "turned on" genetically as part of puberty but "turned off" if environmental conditions are dire, then turned on again once the nutritional environment improves.

As this example illustrates, often when genes influence human development it is by establishing boundaries for environmental influences rather than specifying a precise characteristic. In other words, genes establish a **reaction range** of potential expression, and environment determines where a person's phenotype will fall within that range (McCartney & Berry, 2009). To take another example, height is known to be influenced by genes. You can probably tell this just by looking at your own height in relation to other members of your family. However, the genes for height simply establish the reaction range's upper and lower boundaries, and where a person's actual height ends up—the phenotype—is determined by environmental influences such as nutrition and disease.

Evidence for this is clear from the pattern of changes in height in societies around the world over the past century. In most Western countries, average height rose steadily in the first half of the 20th century as nutrition and health care improved (Freedman et al., 2006). The genes of their populations could not have changed in just a generation or two; instead, the improving environment allowed them to reach a higher point in their genetic reaction range for height. In other countries, such as China and South Korea, improvements in nutrition and health care came later, in the second half of the 20th century, so increases in height in those countries have taken place only recently (Wang et al., 2010). However, people are unlikely ever to grow to be 10 or 20 feet tall. In recent decades in Western countries there has been little change in average height, indicating that the populations of these countries have reached the upper boundary of their reaction range for height.

Genes establish a reaction range for height, and environment determines where a person's height falls within that range. Here, sisters of the Hamer tribe in Ethiopia, a tribe known for being exceptionally tall.

The Theory of Genotype → Environment Effects

LO 2.5 Explain how the theory of genotype → environment effects casts new light on the old nature–nurture debate.

One influential theory of behavior genetics is the **theory of genotype → environment effects** proposed by Sandra Scarr and Kathleen McCartney (Plomin, 2009; Scarr, 1993; Scarr & McCartney, 1983). According to this theory, both genotype and environment make essential contributions to human development. However, the relative strengths of genetics and the environment are difficult to unravel because our genes actually influence the kind of environment we experience. That is the reason for the arrow in the term *genotype → environment effects.* Based on our genotypes, we *create our own environments,* to a considerable extent.

reaction range

range of possible developmental paths established by genes; environment determines where development takes place within that range

theory of genotype → environment effects

theory proposing that genes influence the kind of environment we experience

When parents and children are similar, is the similarity due to genetics or environment?

THE THREE FORMS OF GENOTYPE → ENVIRONMENT EFFECTS These genotype → environment effects take three forms: passive, evocative, and active.

- **Passive genotype → environment effects** occur in biological families because *parents provide both genes and environment for their children.* This may seem obvious, but it has profound implications for how we think about development. Take this father–daughter example. Dad has been good at drawing things ever since he was a boy, and now he makes a living as a graphic artist. One of the first birthday presents he gives to his little girl is a set of crayons and colored pencils for drawing. As she grows up, he also teaches her a number of drawing skills as she seems ready to learn them. She goes to college and majors in architecture, then goes on to become an architect. It is easy to see how she became so good at drawing, given an environment that stimulated her drawing abilities so much—right?

Not so fast. It is true that Dad provided her with a stimulating environment, but he also provided her with half her genes. If there are any genes that contribute to drawing ability—such as genes for spatial reasoning and fine motor coordination—she may well have received those from Dad, too. The point is that in a biological family, it is very difficult to separate genetic influences from environmental influences because *parents provide both,* and they are likely to provide an environment that reinforces the tendencies they have provided to their children through their genes.

So, you should be skeptical when you read studies that claim that parents' behavior is the cause of the characteristics of their biological children. Remember from Chapter 1: Correlation does not imply causation! Just because there is a *correlation* between the behavior of parents and the characteristics of their children does not mean the parents' behavior *caused* the children to have those characteristics. Maybe causation was involved, but in biological families it is difficult to tell. One good way to unravel this tangle is through adoption studies. These studies avoid the problem of passive genotype → environment effects because one set of parents provided the children's genes but a different set of parents provided the environment. We'll look at an extraordinary case of adoption in the *Research Focus: Twin Studies: The Story of Oskar and Jack* feature.

passive genotype → environment effects

in the theory of genotype → environment effects, the type that results from the fact that in a biological family, parents provide both genes and environment to their children

evocative genotype → environment effects

in the theory of genotype → environment effects, the type that results when a person's inherited characteristics evoke responses from others in the environment

active genotype → environment effects

in the theory of genotype → environment effects, the type that results when people seek out environments that correspond to their genotypic characteristics

- **Evocative genotype → environment effects** occur when a person's inherited characteristics evoke responses from others in their environment. If you had a son who started reading at age 3 and seemed to love it, you might buy him more books. If you had a daughter who could sink 20-foot jump shots at age 12, you might arrange to send her to basketball camp. Did you ever baby-sit or work in a setting where there were many children? If so, you probably found that children differ in how sociable, cooperative, and obedient they are. In turn, you may have found that you responded differently to them, depending on their characteristics. This is what is meant by evocative genotype → environment effects—with the crucial addition of the assumption that characteristics such as reading ability, athletic ability, and sociability are at least partly based in genetics.

- **Active genotype → environment effects** occur when people seek out environments that correspond to their genotypic characteristics, a process called *niche-picking.* The child who is faster than her peers may be motivated to try out for a sports team; the adolescent with an ear for music may ask for piano lessons; the emerging adult for whom reading has always been slow and difficult may prefer to begin working full-time after high school rather than going to a college or university; in young adulthood a highly sociable person may seek a career that involves being around other people all day. The idea here is that people are drawn to environments that match their inherited abilities.

Research Focus: Twin Studies: The Story of Oskar and Jack

The interplay between genes and the environment is one of the most important, complex, and fascinating topics in the study of human development. One approach that has been helpful in unraveling these interactions is twin studies, especially research on twins separated early in life and raised in different environments. Studies of twins reared apart provide a good example of a natural experiment, which is something that occurs without the intervention of a researcher but can provide valuable scientific information.

The Minnesota Study of Twins Reared Apart, led by Thomas J. Bouchard, Jr., of the University of Minnesota, has been studying separated twins since 1979, and the results have been groundbreaking and sometimes astounding.

Among the most remarkable cases in the Minnesota study is the story of identical twins Oskar and Jack. They were born in Trinidad in 1933, but within 6 months their parents split up.

Oskar left for Germany with his Catholic mother, while Jack remained in Trinidad in the care of his Jewish father. Thus, unlike most separated twins, who at least remain within the same culture and country, Oskar and Jack grew up with the same genotype but with different cultures, different countries, and different religions.

Furthermore, Oskar migrated with his mother to Germany in 1933, the year the Nazis rose to power. And Jack was raised as a Jew, at a time when Jews were targeted for extermination by the Nazis.

In some ways, the twins' childhood family environments were similar—as in similarly miserable. Oskar's mother soon moved to Italy and left him in Germany in the care of his grandmother, who was stern and harsh. Jack's father alternated between ignoring him and beating him. Despite these similarities, their cultures were about as different as could be. Oskar was an enthusiastic member of the Hitler Youth, and he learned to despise Jews and to keep his own half-Jewish background hidden. Jack was raised as a Jew and at 16 was sent by his father to Israel to join the navy, where he met and married an American Jew. At age 21 he and his wife moved to the United States.

What were the results of this extraordinary natural experiment in the two men's adult development? The extensive data collected by the Minnesota team, which included a week of tests and interviews with the men as well as interviews with their family members and others close to them, indicated that they had highly similar adult personalities.

Both were described by themselves and others as short tempered, demanding, and absent minded. In addition, they shared a remarkable range of unusual, quirky personal habits. Both read books from back to front, sneezed loudly in elevators, liked to wear rubber bands on their wrists, and wrapped tape around pens and pencils to get a better grip.

However, their cultural identities and worldviews were as far apart as one might imagine, given the vastly different cultures

Watch   RESEARCH FOCUS: TWIN STUDIES: THE STORY OF OSKAR AND JACK

they grew up in. Oskar repented his membership in the Hitler Youth as an adult, and lamented the Holocaust that had taken millions of Jewish lives under the Nazis—but he considered himself very German, and he and Jack disagreed vehemently over the responsibility and justification for bombings and other acts of war conducted during World War II.

Thus, despite all their similarities in personality, because of their different cultural environments they ultimately had very different identities—starkly separate understandings of who they are and how they fit into the world around them. As Oskar told Jack when they met again in adulthood, "If we had been switched, I would have been the Jew and you would have been the Nazi."

Review Questions:

1. Studies of twins raised apart provide a good example of:
   a. Reliability but not validity
   b. Validity but not reliability
   c. Experimental research
   d. A natural experiment

2. Which of the following is NOT one of the ways that Oskar and Jack were similar?
   a. Both were absent-minded
   b. Both were short tempered
   c. Both had a strong Jewish faith
   d. Both read books from back to front

GENOTYPE → ENVIRONMENT EFFECTS OVER TIME The three types of genotype → environment effects operate throughout childhood, adolescence, and adulthood, but their relative balance changes over time (Scarr, 1993). In childhood, passive genotype → environment effects are especially pronounced, and active genotype → environment effects are relatively weak. This is because the younger a child is, the more parents control the daily environment the child experiences and the less autonomy the child has to seek out environmental influences outside the family.

However, the balance changes as children move through adolescence and into adulthood (Plomin, 2009). Parental control diminishes, so passive genotype → environment effects also diminish. Autonomy increases, so active genotype → environment effects also increase. In adulthood, passive genotype → environment effects fade entirely (except in cultures where persons continue to live with their parents even in adulthood), and active genotype → environment effects move to the forefront. Evocative genotype → environment effects remain relatively stable from childhood through adulthood.

CRITICAL THINKING QUESTION

Think of one of your abilities and describe how the various types of genotype → environment effects may have been involved in your development of that ability.

Practice Quiz   ANSWERS AVAILABLE IN ANSWER KEY.

1. The heritability of intelligence _____ from childhood to adulthood.
   a. decreases
   b. increases
   c. stays the same
   d. has not been calculated in this area of research

2. The higher the concordance rate, _____.
   a. the more similar the two persons are
   b. the more different the two persons are
   c. the higher the person's chances of having twins
   d. The higher the person's quality of life is likely to be

3. Girls normally begin menstruating around age 11-16, toward the lower end of this range under healthy conditions and toward the higher end when nutrition is insufficient. This is an example of _____.
   a. a high concordance rate   c. epigenesis
   b. a low concordance rate   d. heritability

4. In recent decades in Western countries, there has been little change in average height, indicating that the populations of these countries have reached the upper boundary of _____ for height.
   a. their concordance rate   c. their reaction range
   b. their heritability   d. their polygenic inheritance

5. A toddler from the Hamer tribe in Ethiopia was adopted by an American couple who described themselves as "non-athletes." This tribe was known for having members who are exceptionally tall. Once she started school, she asked to play in the after-school basketball program, tried out for the team in middle school and high school and eventually went on to earn a scholarship to play in college. This is an example of _____.
   a. polygenic inheritance
   b. incomplete dominance
   c. a self-fulfilling prophecy
   d. niche picking

GENETIC INFLUENCES ON DEVELOPMENT: Genes and Individual Development

When does individual human development begin? The answer may surprise you. The process of forming a new human being actually begins long before sperm and egg are joined. Sperm and eggs themselves go through a process of development. In this section we look at the genetic basis of prenatal development, beginning with sperm and egg formation.

Sperm and Egg Formation

LO 2.6   **Outline the process of meiosis in the formation of reproductive cells and specify how the process differs for males and females.**

The only cells in the human body that do not contain 46 chromosomes are the reproductive cells or **gametes**: the sperm in the male and the egg or **ovum** (plural, *ova*) in the female. Gametes form in the testes of the male and the ovaries of the female through a process called **meiosis** (see **Figure 2.5**). Meiosis is a variation of **mitosis**, the normal process of cell replication in which the chromosomes duplicate themselves and the cell divides to become two cells, each containing the same number of chromosomes as the original cell (Pankow, 2008). In meiosis, cells that begin with 23 pairs of chromosomes first split into 46 single chromosomes, then replicate themselves and split into two cells, each with 23 pairs of chromosomes like the original cell. So far the process is just like mitosis. But then the pairs separate into single chromosomes and split again, this time into gametes that have 23 unpaired chromosomes instead of the original 46. So, at the end of the process of meiosis, from the original cell in the testes or ovaries, four new cells have been created, each with 23 chromosomes.

There are some important sex differences in the process of meiosis (Jones, 2006). In males meiosis is completed before sperm are released, but in females the final stage of meiosis only takes place when and if the ovum is fertilized by a sperm (more on this shortly). Also, in males the outcome of meiosis is four viable sperm, whereas in females meiosis produces only one viable ovum along with three *polar bodies* that are not functional. The ovum hoards for itself a large quantity of **cytoplasm**, the fluid that will be the main source of nutrients in the early days after conception, whereas the polar bodies are left with little.

Did you ever think about why you are different from your brothers or sisters, even though both of you have 23 chromosomes each from mom and dad? I know I am constantly amazed at how different my twins are. Here's the explanation for sibling diversity. Something fascinating and remarkable happens at the outset of the process of meiosis. After the chromosomes first split and replicate but before the cell divides, pieces of genetic material are exchanged between the alleles in each pair, a process called **crossing over** (refer again to Figure 2.5). Crossing over mixes the combinations of genes in the chromosomes, so that genetic material that originated from the mother and father is rearranged in a virtually infinite number of ways (Pankow, 2008). Your parents could have had

gametes

cells, distinctive to each sex, that are involved in reproduction (egg cells in the ovaries of the female and sperm in the testes of the male)

ovum

mature egg that develops in ovaries, about every 28 days in human females

meiosis

process by which gametes are generated, through separation and duplication of chromosome pairs, ending in four new gametes from the original cell, each with half the number of chromosomes of the original cell

mitosis

process of cell replication in which the chromosomes duplicate themselves and the cell divides into two cells, each with the same number of chromosomes as the original cell

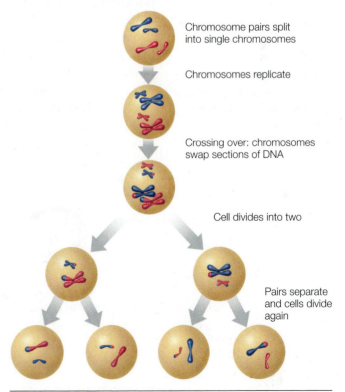

Chromosome pairs split into single chromosomes

Chromosomes replicate

Crossing over: chromosomes swap sections of DNA

Cell divides into two

Pairs separate and cells divide again

Figure 2.5 The Creation of Gametes Through Meiosis

How does meiosis differ from mitosis?

dozens, hundreds, even millions of children together (hypothetically!), and none of them would be exactly like you genetically (unless you have an identical twin).

Here is another interesting fact about the production of gametes. Upon reaching puberty, males begin producing millions of sperm each day. There are 100 to 300 million sperm in the typical male ejaculation (Johnson, 2008). In contrast, females have already produced all the ova they will ever have *while they are still in their own mothers' womb*. Because crossing over begins when ova are created, this means that the development of a unique genotype for each individual begins before the individual's mother is born!

Females are born with about 1 million ova, but this number diminishes to about 40,000 by the time they reach puberty, and about 400 of these will mature during a woman's childbearing years (Johnson, 2008; Moore & Persaud, 2003). Most women run out of ova sometime in their 40s, but men produce sperm throughout their adult lives (although the quantity and quality of the sperm may decline with age) (Finn, 2001).

Conception

LO 2.7 Describe the process of fertilization and conception.

When sexual intercourse takes place between a man and a woman, many millions of sperm from the man begin making their way through the woman's reproductive organs—first into the vagina, then through the cervix, through the uterus, and up the fallopian tubes toward the ovaries. Hundreds of millions of sperm may seem like more than enough, but keep in mind that sperm are composed of a single cell, not much more than 23 chromosomes and a tail, so they are not exactly skilled at navigation. The distance from the vagina to the ovaries is vast for such a small object as a sperm. Furthermore, the woman's body responds to sperm as a foreign substance and begins killing them off immediately. Usually only a few hundred sperm make it up the fallopian tubes to where fertilization can take place (Jones, 2006).

Within the woman, there are two ovaries that release an ovum in alternating months. During the early part of the woman's cycle the ovum is maturing into a **follicle**. The follicle consists of the ovum plus other cells that surround it and provide nutrients. About 14 days into a woman's cycle, the mature follicle bursts and *ovulation* takes place as the ovum is released into the fallopian tube (see **Figure 2.6**). The ovum is 2,000 times larger than a sperm because it contains so much cytoplasm (Johnson, 2008). The cytoplasm will provide nutrients for the first 2 weeks of growth if the ovum is fertilized, until it reaches the uterus and begins drawing nutrients from the mother.

It is only during the first 24 hours after the ovum enters the fallopian tube that fertilization can occur. It takes sperm from a few hours to a whole day to travel up the

cytoplasm

in an ovum, fluid that provides nutrients for the first 2 weeks of growth if the ovum is fertilized, until it reaches the uterus and begins drawing nutrients from the mother

crossing over

at the outset of meiosis, the exchange of genetic material between paired chromosomes

follicle

during the female reproductive cycle, the ovum plus other cells that surround the ovum and provide nutrients

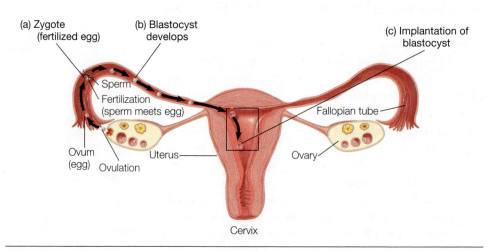

Figure 2.6 Ovulation Process

The two ovaries alternate ovulation in each monthly cycle.

fallopian tubes, so fertilization is most likely to take place if intercourse occurs on the day of ovulation or the two previous days (Wilcox et al., 1995). Sperm can live up to 5 days after entering the woman's body, but most do not last more than 2 days (Johnson, 2008).

When sperm reach the ovum they begin to penetrate the surface of the cell, aided by a chemical on the tip of the sperm that dissolves the ovum's membrane. Once the sperm penetrates the ovum's membrane, the head of the sperm detaches from the tail and continues toward the nucleus of the cell while the tail remains outside. The moment a sperm breaks through, a chemical change takes place in the membrane of the ovum that prevents any other sperm from getting in.

When the sperm head reaches the nucleus of the ovum, the final phase of meiosis is triggered in the ovum (Johnson, 2008). Fertilization takes place as the 23 chromosomes from the ovum pair up with the 23 chromosomes from the sperm and a new cell, the **zygote**, is formed from the two gametes. The zygote's 46 paired chromosomes constitute the new organism's unique genotype, set once and for all at the moment of conception.

Although this is how conception usually takes place, there are occasional variations. One of the most common variations is that two ova are released by the woman instead of one, and both are fertilized by sperm, resulting in DZ twins (recall that DZ stands for *dizygotic*—two zygotes). This takes place overall about once in every 60 births, although there are substantial ethnic variations, ranging from 1 in every 25 births in Nigeria to 1 in every 700 births in Japan (Gall, 1996). In general, Asians have the lowest rates of DZ twins and Africans the highest (Mange & Mange, 1998). In addition to ethnic background, some of the factors that increase the likelihood of DZ twins are a family history of twins, age (older women are more likely to release two eggs at once), and nutrition (women with healthy diets are more likely to have DZ twins) (Bortolus et al., 1999). Today, another common cause of DZ twins is infertility treatments, which we will discuss in more detail later in the chapter.

Twins can also result when a zygote that has just begun the process of cell division splits into two separate clusters of cells, creating MZ twins (recall that MZ stands for *monozygotic*—one zygote). MZ twins are less common than DZ twins, occurring about 1 in every 285 births (Zach et al., 2001). In contrast to DZ twins, MZ twins are not more common in some ethnic groups than others. They take place at the same frequency all around the world. Also unlike DZ twins, MZ twins do not run in families and are not predicted by age or nutrition.

Fertilization can take place only in the first 24 hours after the ovum enters the fallopian tube.

zygote
following fertilization, the new cell formed from the union of sperm and ovum

Practice Quiz   ANSWERS AVAILABLE IN ANSWER KEY.

1. At what age do most women run out of ova?
   a. In their late 20's
   b. Some time in their 30's
   c. In their late 30's
   d. Some time in their 40's

2. As a result of the process of crossing over _____.
   a. the risk of sickle-cell anemia decreases
   b. boys are more likely to be born with a learning disability
   c. the genetic material that originated from the mother and father is rearranged
   d. women are at increased risk for infertility

3. _____ is formed when the ovum and sperm unite and fertilization takes place.
   a. The blastula
   b. The blastocyst
   c. The zygote
   d. The embryo

4. Fertilization can take place only _____.
   a. within three days after the ovum enters the fallopian tube
   b. in the first 24 hours after the ovum enters the fallopian tube
   c. in the first 2 hours after the ovum enters the fallopian tube
   d. if intercourse occurs on the day of ovulation

5. In general, _____ have the highest rates of DZ twins.
   a. African Americans
   b. European Americans
   c. Asian Americans
   d. Hispanic Americans

Summary: Genetic Influences on Development

LO 2.1 Distinguish between genotype and phenotype and identify the different forms of genetic inheritance.

There are 46 chromosomes in the human genome, organized into 23 pairs. The totality of an individual's genes is the genotype, and the person's actual characteristics are called the phenotype. Genotype and phenotype may be different, due to dominant–recessive inheritance, incomplete dominance, and environmental influences. Most human characteristics are polygenic, meaning that they are influenced by multiple genes rather than just one.

LO 2.2 Describe the sex chromosomes and identify what makes them different from other chromosomes.

The sex chromosomes determine whether the person will be male or female. In the female this pair is called XX; in the male, XY. Having only one X chromosome makes males more vulnerable than females to a variety of recessive disorders that are linked to the X chromosome.

LO 2.3 Explain how behavior geneticists use heritability estimates and concordance rates in their research.

Heritability estimates indicate the degree to which a characteristic is believed to be influenced by genes within a specific population. Concordance rates indicate the degree of similarity between people with different amounts of their genes in common, for example MZ and DZ twins.

LO 2.4 Describe how the concept of epigenesis frames gene–environment interactions, and connect epigenesis to the concept of reaction range.

Epigenesis is the concept that development results from bidirectional interactions between genotype and environment. The concept of reaction range also involves gene-environment interactions, because it means that genes set a range for development and environment determines where development falls within that range.

LO 2.5 Explain how the theory of genotype → environment effects casts new light on the old nature–nurture debate.

Rather than viewing nature and nurture as separate forces, this theory proposes that genes influence environments through three types of genotype → environment effects: passive (parents provide both genes and environment to their children); evocative (children evoke responses from those who care for them); and active (children seek out an environment that corresponds to their genotype). The three types of effects operate throughout the life span but their relative balance changes with time.

LO 2.6 Outline the process of meiosis in the formation of reproductive cells and specify how the process differs for males and females.

In meiosis, cells that begin with 23 pairs of chromosomes split and replicate repeatedly until they form four gametes, each with 23 individual chromosomes. In males the outcome of meiosis is four viable sperm, but in females meiosis produces only one viable ovum. Also, males produce millions of sperm daily beginning in puberty, whereas females produce all the eggs they will ever have while still in their mother's womb.

LO 2.7 Describe the process of fertilization and conception.

About 14 days into a woman's cycle an ovum is released into the fallopian tube. For the next 24 hours, fertilization can occur in which the 23 chromosomes from the ovum pair up with the 23 chromosomes from the sperm and a new cell, the zygote, is formed from the two gametes. The zygote's 46 paired chromosomes constitute the new organism's unique genotype, set once and for all at the moment of conception.

Section 2 Prenatal Development and Prenatal Care

Learning Objectives

2.8 Describe the structures that form during the germinal period, and identify when implantation takes place.

2.9 Outline the major milestones of the embryonic period and identify when they take place.

2.10 Describe the major milestones of the fetal period and identify when viability occurs.

2.11 Compare and contrast prenatal care in traditional cultures and developed countries.

2.12 Identify the major teratogens in developing countries and developed countries.

PRENATAL DEVELOPMENT AND PRENATAL CARE: Prenatal Development

When sperm and ovum unite to become a zygote, a remarkable process is set in motion. If all goes well, about 9 months later a fully formed human being will be born. Now we look closely at this process, from conception to birth (summarized in **Figure 2.7**).

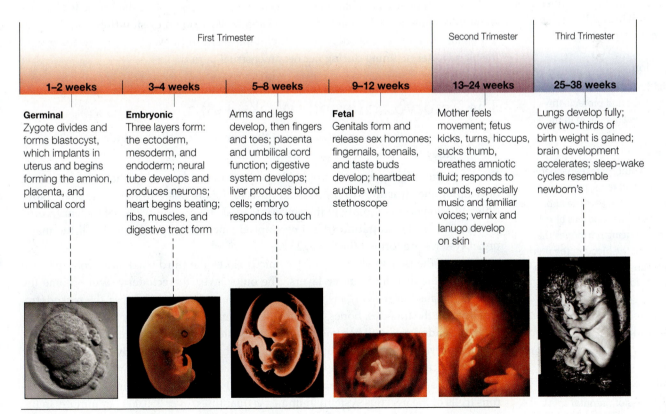

First Trimester				Second Trimester	Third Trimester
1–2 weeks	**3–4 weeks**	**5–8 weeks**	**9–12 weeks**	**13–24 weeks**	**25–38 weeks**
Germinal Zygote divides and forms blastocyst, which implants in uterus and begins forming the amnion, placenta, and umbilical cord	**Embryonic** Three layers form: the ectoderm, mesoderm, and endoderm; neural tube develops and produces neurons; heart begins beating; ribs, muscles, and digestive tract form	Arms and legs develop, then fingers and toes; placenta and umbilical cord function; digestive system develops; liver produces blood cells; embryo responds to touch	**Fetal** Genitals form and release sex hormones; fingernails, toenails, and taste buds develop; heartbeat audible with stethoscope	Mother feels movement; fetus kicks, turns, hiccups, sucks thumb, breathes amniotic fluid; responds to sounds, especially music and familiar voices; vernix and lanugo develop on skin	Lungs develop fully; over two-thirds of birth weight is gained; brain development accelerates; sleep-wake cycles resemble newborn's

Figure 2.7 Milestones of Prenatal Development

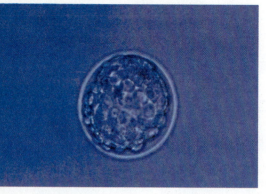

Cell division begins about 30 hours after conception.

germinal period

first 2 weeks after conception

blastocyst

ball of about 100 cells formed by about 1 week following conception

trophoblast

in the blastocyst, the outer layer of cells, which will go on to form structures that provide protection and nourishment to the embryo

embryonic disk

in the blastocyst, the inner layer of cells, which will go on to form the embryo

amnion

fluid-filled membrane that surrounds and protects the developing organism in the womb

placenta

in the womb, gatekeeper between mother and fetus, protecting the fetus from bacteria and wastes in the mother's blood, and producing hormones that maintain the blood in the uterine lining and cause the mother's breasts to produce milk

umbilical cord

structure connecting the placenta to the mother's uterus

embryonic period

weeks 3–8 of prenatal development

The Germinal Period (First 2 Weeks)

LO 2.8 **Describe the structures that form during the germinal period, and identify when implantation takes place.**

The first 2 weeks after fertilization are called the **germinal period** (Jones, 2006). This is the period when the zygote travels down the fallopian tubes to the uterus and implants in the uterine wall. As it travels, it begins cell division and differentiation. The first cell division does not occur until 30 hours after conception, but after that, cell division takes place at a faster rate. By 1 week following conception there is a ball of about 100 cells known as a **blastocyst**. The blastocyst is divided into two layers. The outer layer of cells, called the **trophoblast**, will form the structures that provide protection and nourishment. The inner layer of cells, the **embryonic disk**, will become the embryo of the new organism.

During the second week after conception, implantation occurs as the blastocyst becomes firmly embedded into the lining of the uterus. Since the ovum was released from the ovary, the follicle from which it was released has been generating hormones that have caused the uterus to build up a bloody lining in preparation for receiving the blastocyst. Now the blastocyst is nourished by this blood.

The trophoblast begins to differentiate into several structures during this second week. Part of it forms a membrane, the **amnion**, which surrounds the developing organism and fills with fluid, helping to keep a steady temperature for the organism and protect it against the friction of the mother's movements (Johnson, 2008). In between the uterine wall and the embryonic disk a round structure, the **placenta**, begins to develop. The placenta will allow nutrients to pass from the mother to the developing organism and permit wastes to be removed. It also acts as a gatekeeper, protecting the developing organism from bacteria and wastes in the mother's blood, and it produces hormones that maintain the blood in the uterine lining and cause the mother's breasts to produce milk. An **umbilical cord** also begins to develop, connecting the placenta to the mother's uterus.

Implantation is the outcome of the germinal period if all goes well. However, it is estimated that over half of blastocysts never implant successfully, usually due to chromosomal problems that have caused cell division to slow down or stop (Johnson, 2008). If implantation fails, the blastocyst will be eliminated from the woman's body along with the bloody uterine lining during her next menstrual period.

The Embryonic Period (Weeks 3–8)

LO 2.9 **Outline the major milestones of the embryonic period and identify when they take place.**

During the germinal period the trophoblast differentiated faster than the embryonic disk, developing the structures to protect and nurture the organism during pregnancy. Now, differentiation occurs rapidly in the embryonic disk. Over the 6 weeks of the **embryonic period**, 3–8 weeks' **gestation** (the time elapsed since conception), nearly all the major organ systems are formed (Fleming, 2006).

During the first week of the embryonic period—the third week after conception—the embryonic disk forms three layers. The outer layer, the **ectoderm**, will become the skin, hair, nails, sensory organs, and nervous system. The middle layer, the **mesoderm**, will become the muscles, bones, reproductive system, and circulatory system. The inner layer, the **endoderm**, will become the digestive system and the respiratory system.

The nervous system develops first and fastest (Johnson, 2008). By the end of Week 3 (since conception), part of the ectoderm forms the **neural tube**, which will eventually become the spinal cord and brain. Once formed, the neural tube begins producing **neurons** (cells of the nervous system) in immense quantities, over 250,000 per minute. In the fourth week the shape of the head becomes apparent, and the eyes, nose, mouth, and ears begin to form. The heart begins to beat during this week, and the ribs, muscles, and digestive tract appear. By the end of the fourth week the embryo is only one-quarter-inch long but already remarkably differentiated. Nevertheless, even an expert embryologist would have trouble at this point judging whether the embryo was to become a fish, a bird, or a mammal.

During Weeks 5–8, growth continues its rapid pace. Buds that will become the arms and legs appear in Week 5, developing webbed fingers and toes that lose their webbing by Week 8. The placenta and the umbilical cord become fully functional (Jones, 2006). The digestive system develops, and the liver begins producing blood cells. The heart develops separate chambers. The top of the neural tube continues to develop into the brain, but the bottom of it looks like a tail in Week 5, gradually shrinking to look more like a spinal cord by Week 8.

By the end of the eighth week, the embryo is just 1 inch (2½ centimeters) long and 1/30 of an ounce (1 g) in weight. Yet all the main body parts have formed, as have all of the main organs except the sex organs. Furthermore, the tiny embryo responds to touch, especially around its mouth, and it can move (Moore & Persaud, 2003). Now the embryo looks distinctly human (Johnson, 2008).

The Fetal Period (Week 9–Birth)

LO 2.10 **Describe the major milestones of the fetal period and identify when viability occurs.**

During the **fetal period**, lasting from 9 weeks after conception until birth, the organs continue to develop, and there is tremendous growth in sheer size, from 1/30 of an ounce in weight and 1 inch long at the beginning of the fetal period to an average (in developed countries) of 7½ pounds (3.4 kg) and 20 inches (51 cm) by birth.

By the end of the third month the genitals have formed. After forming, the genitals release hormones that influence the rest of prenatal development, including brain organization, body size, and activity level, with boys becoming on average somewhat larger and more active (Cameron, 2001; DiPietro et al., 2004). Also during the third month, fingernails, toenails, and taste buds begin to develop. The heart has developed enough so that the heartbeat can now be heard through a stethoscope.

After 3 months, the typical fetus weighs about 3 ounces and is 3 inches long. A good way to remember this is as "three times three"—3 months, 3 ounces, 3 inches. Or, you can think of it as 100 days, 100 grams, 100 millimeters. Prenatal development is divided into three 3-month periods called **trimesters**, and the end of the third month marks the end of the first trimester.

During the second trimester, the fetus becomes active and begins to respond to its environment (Henrichs et al., 2010). By the end of the fourth month the fetus's movements can be felt by the mother. Gradually over the course of the second trimester the activity of the fetus becomes more diverse. By the end of the second trimester it breathes amniotic fluid in and out; it kicks, turns, and hiccups; it even sucks its thumb. It also responds to sounds, including voices and music, showing a preference (indicated by increased heart rate) for familiar voices, especially the voice of the mother. A slimy white substance called **vernix** covers the skin, to protect it from chapping due to the amniotic fluid, and downy hair called *lanugo* helps the vernix stick to the skin. By birth the fetus usually sheds its lanugo, although sometimes babies are born with lanugo still on, then shed it in the early weeks of life.

By the end of the second trimester, 6 months after conception, the typical fetus is about 14 inches long (36 cm) and weighs about 2 pounds (0.9 kg). Although it seems well-developed in many aspects of its behavior, it is still questionable in its *viability*, meaning its ability to survive outside of the womb. Babies born before 22 weeks rarely survive, even with the most advanced technological assistance. Even at 26 weeks, near

gestation

in prenatal development, elapsed time since conception

ectoderm

in the embryonic period, the outer layer of cells, which will eventually become the skin, hair, nails, sensory organs, and nervous system (brain and spinal cord)

mesoderm

in the embryonic period, the middle of the three cell layers, which will become the muscles, bones, reproductive system, and circulatory system

endoderm

in the embryonic period, the inner layer of cells, which will become the digestive system and the respiratory system

neural tube

in the embryonic period, the part of the ectoderm that will become the spinal cord and brain

neuron

cell of the nervous system

fetal period

in prenatal development, the period from Week 9 until birth

trimester

one of the three 3-month periods of prenatal development

vernix

at birth, babies are covered with this oily, cheesy substance, which protects their skin from chapping in the womb

the end of the second trimester, the survival rate is only 50%, and the survivors often have disabilities—14% have severe mental disabilities and 12% have cerebral palsy, which entails extensive physical and neurological disabilities (Lorenz et al., 1998). And this survival rate is only for babies that happen to be born in developed countries or in a wealthy family in a developing country. In most of the world, babies born before the end of the second trimester have no access to advanced medical care and will not survive (OECD, 2009).

The main obstacle to viability at the beginning of the third trimester is the immaturity of the lungs. The lungs are the last major organ to become viable, and even a baby born in the seventh or early eighth month may need a respirator to breathe properly. Weight gain is also important. During the last trimester the typical fetus gains over 5 pounds, and this additional weight helps it sustain life. Babies born weighing less than 5.5 pounds are at risk for a wide range of problems, as we will see in detail in Chapter 3.

The brain is even less mature than the lungs in the third trimester, but its immaturity does not represent an obstacle to viability. As described in Chapter 1, in humans, early brain immaturity was an adaptation that occurred in the course of our evolutionary development to enable us to have an exceptionally large brain yet still fit through the birth canal. More than any other animal, humans are born with immature brains, which is why human babies are vulnerable and need parental care longer than other animals do. Nevertheless, more brain development occurs in the last 2 months of prenatal development than in any previous months. Neurons are created in vast numbers, up to 500,000 per minute, and the connections between them become increasingly elaborate (Gross, 2008).

By the third trimester, brain development has progressed to the point where, at 28 weeks, the sleep-wake cycles of the fetus are similar to those of a newborn infant. The fetus becomes increasingly aware of the external environment, especially in its ability to hear and remember sounds (James, 2010). In one study, mothers were asked to read Dr. Seuss's *The Cat in the Hat* to their fetuses every day during the last 6 weeks of pregnancy (DeCasper & Spence, 1986). After birth, the babies showed a preference for a recording of their mother reading *The Cat in the Hat*, by sucking on a plastic nipple in order to turn it on. They sucked harder to hear *The Cat and the Hat* than they did for recordings of their mothers reading similar rhyming stories they had not heard before. Fetuses respond to their internal environment as well. When the mother is highly stressed, the fetus's heart beats faster and its body movements increase (DiPietro et al., 2002).

Practice Quiz   ANSWERS AVAILABLE IN ANSWER KEY.

1. After fertilization, the first 2 weeks of pregnancy is called _____.
   a. the germinal period
   b. the embryonic period
   c. the fetal period
   d. the first trimester

2. The blastocyst forms during the _____.
   a. germinal period
   b. embryonic period
   c. fetal period
   d. second trimester

3. The _____ form from the outer layer of the embryonic disk.
   a. digestive and respiratory systems
   b. brain and spinal cord
   c. skin, hair, nails, sensory organs, and nervous system
   d. lungs and heart

4. During the _____ period of prenatal development nearly all the major organs are formed.
   a. germinal
   b. zygotic
   c. embryonic
   d. fetal

5. Maddox, a baby born 6 weeks prematurely, is more at risk of not surviving than his sister, Shekia, who was born full term because Maddox's _____ is/are still immature.
   a. heart
   b. intestines
   c. lungs
   d. pancreas

PRENATAL DEVELOPMENT AND PRENATAL CARE: Prenatal Care

Because prenatal development carries risks for both mother and fetus, all cultures have developed customs and practices to try to promote a healthy outcome. First we look at some of the practices of prenatal care in traditional cultures, then we look at the scientific approach to prenatal care that has developed recently.

Variations in Prenatal Care

LO 2.11 Compare and contrast prenatal care in traditional cultures and developed countries.

All cultures have a store of advice about what a woman should and should not do during pregnancy (DeLoache & Gottlieb, 2000). What kind of guidelines or advice have you heard? You might ask your mother, your grandmother, and other mothers you know what advice they followed and where they obtained it.

Sometimes pregnancy advice seems practical and sensible. The practical advice reflects the collected wisdom that women pass down to each other over generations, based on their own experiences. Other times the advice may seem odd, especially to someone outside the given culture. Customs that seem peculiar to an outsider may arise because pregnancy is often perilous to both mother and fetus. Cultures sometimes develop their prenatal customs out of the intense desire to ensure that pregnancy will proceed successfully, but without the scientific knowledge that would make such control possible.

Here are a few examples. Among the Beng people of the West African nation of Ivory Coast, pregnant women are advised to avoid drinking palm wine during the early months of pregnancy (Gottlieb, 2000). This is wise practical advice drawn from the experience of women who drank alcohol during pregnancy, with unfortunate results. On the other hand, the mother-to-be is also advised to avoid eating meat from the bushbuck antelope while pregnant, and warned that if she does eat it, her baby may emerge from the womb striped like the antelope.

Thousands of miles away, on the Indonesian island of Bali, "hot" foods are to be avoided during pregnancy, including eggplant, mango, and octopus (Diener, 2000). Also, a pregnant mother should not accept food from someone who is viewed as spiritually impure, such as a menstruating woman or someone who has recently had a death in the family. Witches are believed to be especially attracted to the blood of a pregnant woman and her unborn child, so pregnant women are advised to obtain a magic charm and wear it on their belt or hang it on the gate of their yard, for protection.

Some of the examples of prenatal customs just provided may strike you as strange, but they are understandable as a human attempt to control events that are highly important but also mysterious.

Even in developed countries, which have a long scientific tradition, not much was known about prenatal care from a scientific perspective until recent decades. As recently as the middle of the 20th century, women in developed countries were being advised by their doctors to limit their weight gain during pregnancy to no more than 15 pounds (Eisenberg et al., 2011). By now, scientific studies have shown that women should typically gain 25–35 pounds during pregnancy, and women who gain less than 20 pounds are at risk for having babies who are preterm and low birth weight (Ehrenberg et al., 2003).

In other areas, too, an extensive body of scientific knowledge has accumulated on prenatal care in recent decades. One key conclusion of this research is that pregnant women should receive regular evaluations from a skilled health care worker,

Cultural Focus: Pregnancy and Prenatal Care Across Cultures

Although many cultures have folk beliefs about pregnancy that have no scientific or practical basis, most also have customs that provide genuine relief to pregnant women. One helpful method of prenatal care common in many traditional cultures is massage (Field, 2010; Jordan, 1994). The prenatal massage is usually performed by a **midwife** (a person who assists women in pregnancy and childbirth) in the course of her visits to the pregnant woman. While the massage is taking place, the midwife asks the woman various questions about how the pregnancy is going. As part of the massage, the midwife probes to determine the fetus's position in the uterus. If the fetus is turned in an unfavorable position, so that it would be likely to come out feet first rather than head first, the midwife will attempt an *inversion* to turn the fetus's head toward the vaginal opening. This is sometimes painful, but as we will see in Chapter 3, a head-first birth is much safer than a feet-first birth, for both baby and mother.

Prenatal massage has a long history in many cultures (Jordan, 1994). In recent years, it has also begun to be used by midwives, nurses, and physicians in developed countries. By now, a substantial amount of research has accumulated to support the benefits of massage for mother and fetus. Benefits to the mother include lower likelihood of back pain, less swelling of the joints, and better sleep (Field, 2004, 2010). Babies whose mothers received prenatal massage score higher on scales of their physical and social functioning in the early weeks of life (Field et al., 2006).

In this video expectant mothers from various countries are interviewed regarding their pregnancy experiences. There is also an interview with a Mayan midwife regarding her role in prenatal care. It includes her prenatal massage of a pregnant woman.

Watch PREGNANCY AND PRENATAL CARE ACROSS CULTURES

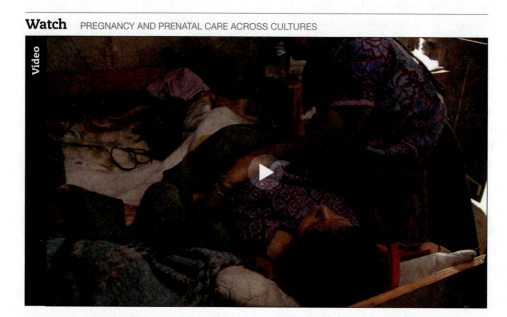

Review Question:

What are the advantages of using a doctor or of using a midwife, as described in this video clip? What others can you think of?

beginning as soon as possible after conception, to monitor the health of mother and fetus and ensure that the pregnancy is proceeding well. Most women in developed countries have access to physicians, nurses, or certified midwives who can provide good prenatal care. However, some poor women may not have access to such care, especially in the United States. The percentage of women in the United States who begin prenatal care in their first trimester varies greatly based on ethnicity and SES, as shown in **Map 2.1**.

Pregnant women in developing countries are much less likely than those in developed countries to receive prenatal care from a skilled health care worker. The World Health Organization's *Making Pregnancy Safer* program has focused on working with governments to set up programs that provide pregnant women with such care (World

midwife

person who assists in pregnant women's prenatal care and the birth process

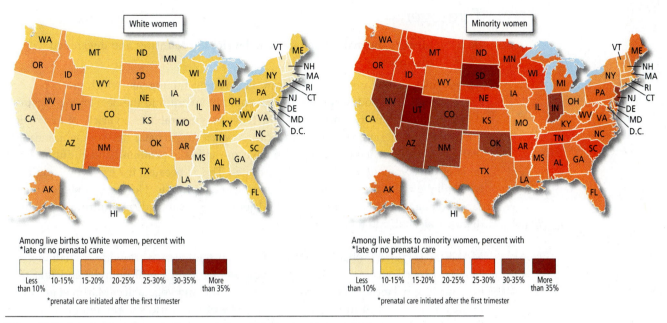

Map 2.1 Ethnic Variations in Prenatal Care Within the United States

How does prenatal care differ for White women compared with other ethnic groups? What economic factors might account for these variations?

Health Organization [WHO], 2009). Currently 99% of maternal and infant deaths occur in developing countries—only 1% occur in developed countries—and the WHO program is focused on the 70 countries with the highest death rates, mostly in Africa and South Asia.

Guidelines for prenatal care focus mostly on three key areas: diet, exercise, and avoidance of potentially harmful influences called teratogens (see **Table 2.2**; WHO, 2009).

CRITICAL THINKING QUESTION

Are there any beliefs in your culture about what a woman should eat or should avoid eating before or during pregnancy? Do the same beliefs apply to men during any point of the conception and gestation continuum?

Moderate exercise is part of good prenatal care.

Table 2.2 Essentials of Prenatal Care

Before Pregnancy

- Have a medical examination to ensure there are no diseases that may affect prenatal development. If not fully vaccinated, obtain vaccinations for diseases, such as rubella, that can damage prenatal development. (Vaccinations may be unsafe during pregnancy.)
- Avoid tobacco, alcohol, and other drugs, which may make it more difficult to become pregnant and are damaging to prenatal development.

During Pregnancy

- *Diet.* Maintain a balanced diet, including protein, grains, fruits, and vegetables. Avoid excessive fats and sugars and obtain sufficient iron and iodine. Gain 25–35 pounds in total; avoid dieting as well as excessive weight gain. Women should also drink more fluids during pregnancy than they normally do, as the fetus needs fluids for healthy development and a pregnant woman's body also requires more.
- *Exercise.* Engage in mild to moderate exercise regularly, including aerobic exercise, to stimulate circulatory system and muscles, as well as Kegel exercises to strengthen vaginal muscles. *Aerobic exercise,* such as walking, jogging, or swimming, stimulates the circulatory and muscular systems of a woman's body (Schmidt et al., 2006). However, it is important to avoid strenuous exercise and high-risk sports, such as long-distance running, contact sports, downhill skiing, waterskiing, and horseback riding.
- *Teratogens.* Avoid tobacco, alcohol, and other drugs. Avoid exposure to X-rays, hazardous chemicals, and infectious diseases.

Teratogens

LO 2.12 Identify the major teratogens in developing countries and developed countries.

An essential part of good prenatal care is avoiding **teratogens**, which are behaviors, environments, and bodily conditions that could be harmful to the developing organism (Haffner, 2007). Both the embryo and the fetus are vulnerable to a variety of teratogens. The embryonic period, especially, is a *critical period* for prenatal development, meaning that it is a period when teratogens can have an especially profound and enduring effect on later development, as **Figure 2.8** illustrates. This is because the embryonic period is when all the major organ systems are forming at a rapid rate. However, some teratogens can do damage during the fetal period. Major teratogens include malnutrition, infectious diseases, alcohol, and tobacco.

MALNUTRITION Probably the most common teratogen worldwide is malnutrition. Medical experts recommend that pregnant women gain 25–30 pounds, and that they eat a healthy, balanced diet of proteins, grains, fruit, and vegetables (Martin et al., 2002). However, if you recall from Chapter 1 that 40% of the world's population lives on less than two dollars a day, you can imagine that most mothers who are part of that 40% receive a prenatal diet that falls far short of the ideal.

Furthermore, about half the world's population is rural, and the diet of people in rural areas often varies substantially depending on the time of year. They may eat fairly well during summer and fall when their crops provide food, but less well during winter and spring when fresh food is unavailable. Consequently, prenatal health may depend greatly on when the child was conceived.

Dramatic evidence of this effect has been shown in recent decades in China (Berry et al., 1999). In the 1980s China had the highest incidence in the world of two serious prenatal disorders, *anencephaly,* in which parts of the brain are missing or malformed, and *spina bifida,* which is an extreme distortion in the shape of the spinal column. It was discovered that in both of these disorders the main cause is a deficiency of folic acid, a nutrient found especially in fruits and vegetables. Furthermore, researchers observed that the traditional marriage period in China is January and February, and most couples

teratogen

behavior, environment, or bodily condition that can have damaging influence on prenatal development

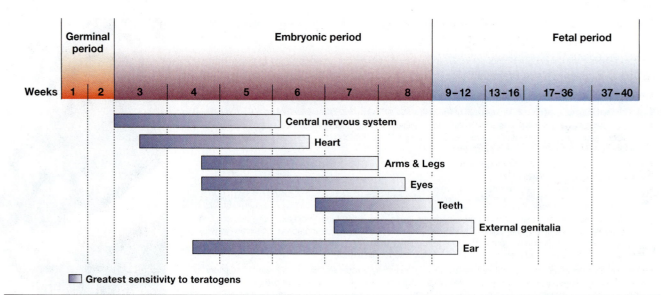

Greatest sensitivity to teratogens

Figure 2.8 Timing of Teratogens

Vulnerability to teratogens is greatest in the embryonic period.
SOURCE: Based on Moore, 1974

try to conceive a child as soon after marriage as possible. Consequently, the early months of pregnancy typically take place in winter and early spring, when rural women are least likely to have fruits and vegetables as part of their diet. After this pattern was discovered, the Chinese government established a nationwide program to provide mothers with supplements of folic acid, and since that time the incidence of anencephaly and spina bifida has been sharply reduced (Centers for Disease Control and Prevention [CDC], 2011).

Many other countries have also taken steps to reduce folic-acid deficiencies in pregnant mothers. After research established that folic acid was the key to preventing anencephaly and spina bifida, governments in many countries passed laws requiring folic acid to be added to grain products such as cereals, bread, pasta, flour, and rice. Almost immediately, the incidence of both disorders fell sharply (Honein et al., 2001). Medical authorities now recommend that women begin taking folic acid supplements and eating plenty of fruits and vegetables even when they are trying to become pregnant, because the damage from lack of folic acid can take place in the early weeks of pregnancy, before the woman knows for sure that she is pregnant (de Villarreal et al., 2006).

Two other common nutritional deficiencies during pregnancy are iron and iodine. Iron-rich foods such as beef, duck, potatoes (including skin), spinach, and dried fruits are important for building the blood supply of mother and fetus. The WHO estimates that nearly one-half of women worldwide are deficient in iron, placing them at risk for having preterm and low-birth-weight babies (WHO, 2009). Even with a healthy diet including iron-rich foods, health authorities recommend an iron supplement from the 12th week of pregnancy onward.

Iodine is also crucial, because low-iodine intake during pregnancy increases the risks of miscarriage, stillbirth, and abnormalities in fetal brain development. In developed countries salt has been iodized since the 1920s, so women receive adequate iodine as part of a normal diet. However, in developing countries most women do not use iodized salt and consequently they often experience iodine deficiencies. The WHO and other major health organizations have made a strong push recently to make iodine supplements available in developing countries, as will be explained in more detail in Chapter 3.

Malnutrition is a common teratogen in developing countries. Pictured here is a pregnant woman in rural Zambia.

INFECTIOUS DISEASES Infectious diseases are far more prevalent in developing countries than in developed countries (WHO, 2009). Many of these diseases influence prenatal development. One of the most prevalent and serious is *rubella* (also known as *German measles*). The embryonic period is a critical period for exposure to rubella. Over half of infants whose mothers contract the illness during this period have severe problems including blindness, deafness, intellectual disability, and abnormalities of the heart, genitals, or intestinal system (Eberhart-Phillips et al., 1993). During the fetal period effects of rubella are less severe, but can include low birth weight, hearing problems, and skeletal defects (Brown & Susser, 2002). Since the late 1960s a vaccine given to children has made rubella rare in developed countries—girls retain the immunity into adulthood, when they become pregnant—but it remains widespread in developing countries where children are less likely to receive the vaccine (Plotkin et al., 1999; WHO, 2009).

Another common infectious disease of prenatal development is **AIDS (acquired immune deficiency syndrome)**, a sexually transmitted infection (STI) caused by the human immunodeficiency virus (HIV), which damages the immune system. HIV/AIDS can be transmitted from mother to child during prenatal development through the blood, during birth, or through breast milk. HIV/AIDS damages brain development prenatally, and infants with HIV are unlikely to survive to adulthood unless they receive an expensive "cocktail" of medications rarely available in the developing countries where AIDS is most common. In developing countries mother–child transmission of

AIDS (acquired immune deficiency syndrome)
sexually transmitted infection caused by HIV, resulting in damage to the immune system

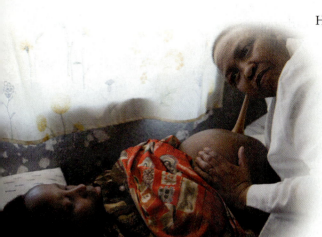

Pregnant women in developing countries who have AIDS rarely receive adequate medical treatment. Here, a woman is being treated at a clinic for HIV/AIDS patients in Lesotho.

HIV/AIDS has been dramatically reduced in recent years through three strategies: (1) effective medicines given to mothers prior to birth; (2) cesarean sections for AIDS-infected mothers; and (3) the use of infant formula in place of breast-feeding (WHO, 2010). However, 95% of all HIV infections take place in Africa, and few African mothers or infants have access to the three strategies that are effective against HIV/AIDS.

ALCOHOL In developed countries, the teratogen that causes the most widespread damage to prenatal development is alcohol (Mattson et al., 2010; Sokol et al., 2003). Although it used to be believed that moderate alcohol use would cause no harm during pregnancy, recent research has shown that the only safe amount of alcohol for a pregnant woman is *none at all*. Even one or two drinks a few days a week puts the developing child at risk for lower height, weight, and head size at birth, and for lower intelligence and higher aggressiveness during childhood (Willford et al., 2004).

When mothers drink heavily during pregnancy, their infants are at risk for **fetal alcohol spectrum disorder (FASD)**, which includes facial deformities, heart problems, misshapen limbs, and a variety of cognitive problems such as intellectual disability and attention and memory deficits (Mattson et al., 2010). Infants born with FASD face a lifetime of trouble, and the more alcohol their mothers drank during pregnancy, the worse their problems are likely to be (Barr & Streissguth, 2001). In childhood and adolescence, their cognitive deficits make it difficult for them to succeed academically or socially in school (Korkman et al., 2003). In adolescence, FASD raises the risk of delinquency, alcohol and drug abuse, and depression and other mental health problems (Baer et al., 2003; Mattson et al., 2010). Rates of FASD are especially alarming, as high as 10%, in some Native American and Canadian First Nations communities where alcoholism is prevalent (Caetano et al., 2006; Tough et al., 2007).

TOBACCO Maternal cigarette smoking has a wide range of damaging effects on prenatal development. Women who smoke during pregnancy are at higher risk for miscarriage and premature birth, and smoking is the leading cause of low birth weight in developed countries (Espy et al., 2011). Maternal smoking raises the risks of health problems in infants, such as impaired heart functioning, difficulty breathing, and even death (Jaakkola & Gissler, 2004). Prenatal exposure to smoking predicts problems in childhood and adolescence, including poorer language skills, problems with attention and memory, and behavior problems (Cornelius et al., 2011; Sawnani et al., 2004).

Fathers' smoking is also a peril to prenatal development. The **secondhand smoke** from fathers' smoking leads to higher risks of low birth weight and childhood cancer (Ruckinger et al., 2010). Rates of smoking are generally higher in developed countries than in developing countries, but they are rising rapidly in developing countries around the world as their economies grow (WHO, 2011).

fetal alcohol spectrum disorder (FASD)

set of problems that occur as a consequence of high maternal alcohol use during pregnancy, including facial deformities, heart problems, misshapen limbs, and a variety of cognitive problems

secondhand smoke

smoke from a cigarette inhaled by those near the smoker

OTHER TERATOGENS Malnutrition and infectious diseases are the most common teratogens in developing countries, with alcohol and tobacco most common in developed countries. However, there are many other potential teratogens. Maternal use of drugs such as cocaine, heroin, and marijuana causes physical, cognitive, and behavioral problems in infants (Messinger & Lester, 2008; National Institute on Drug Abuse, 2001). Certain prescription drugs can also cause harm. For example, Accutane, a drug used to treat severe acne, can cause devastating damage to major organs such as the brain and heart during embryonic development (Honein et al., 2001). Even nonprescription drugs such as cold medicines can be damaging to prenatal development, so women who are pregnant or seeking to become pregnant should always check with their doctors about any medications they may be taking (Morgan et al., 2010). Certain kinds of work are best avoided during pregnancy if they involve exposure to teratogens such as X-rays, hazardous chemicals, or infectious diseases. Other potential teratogens include environmental pollution, radiation, and severe maternal stress.

Practice Quiz   ANSWERS AVAILABLE IN ANSWER KEY.

1. Melinda is a healthy woman who just found out she was pregnant and went for her first prenatal visit. Which of the following pieces of advice is she most likely to receive from her physician?
   a. Avoid even mild exercise.
   b. Avoid Kegel exercises.
   c. Drink slightly less fluids than usual.
   √ d. Eat foods with sufficient iodine.

2. Your sister is pregnant. She has always been health-conscious and exercises regularly. She is planning on engaging in aerobic exercise by continuing to go to her exercise classes. According to most physicians, she should _____.
   a. be very careful as this type of exercise during pregnancy could lower muscle mass
   √ b. exercise regularly as she will stimulate the circulatory system and muscles
   c. exercise regularly because it lowers the chances of teratogens reaching the fetus
   d. avoid aerobic exercise as it has been shown to dangerously increase fetal heart rate

3. The most common teratogen worldwide is _____.
   √ a. malnutrition   c. alcohol
   b. rubella   d. tobacco

4. Marie is a heavy drinker and managed to stop drinking for most of her pregnancy. If she drank alcohol during the _____ period, her baby would be most at risk of structural damage.
   a. prenatal   c. germinal
   √ b. embryonic   d. blastula

5. It is January 1989 in Beijing, China, and Huang and Jiao have just married. They want to conceive a child as soon as possible, as most newly married Chinese couples do. Considering it is the middle of winter, and fruits and vegetables are not readily available, what important nutrient in Huang's prenatal diet is likely to be missing, potentially causing her child to be born with spina bifida?
   √ a. Folic acid   c. Calcium
   b. Potassium   d. Vitamin D

Summary: Prenatal Development and Prenatal Care

LO 2.8   Describe the structures that form during the germinal period, and identify when implantation takes place.

During the germinal period a ball of cells called the blastocyst forms and implants in the lining of the uterus. The blastocyst has two layers, the embryonic disk that will become the embryo of the new organism and the trophoblast that will form the supporting structures of the amnion, placenta, and umbilical cord.

LO 2.9   Outline the major milestones of the embryonic period and identify when they take place.

During the embryonic period (3–8 weeks after conception) all the major organ systems are initially formed, except the sex organs. Rapid development of organs during this period makes it a critical period for the effects of teratogens.

LO 2.10   Describe the major milestones of the fetal period and identify when viability occurs.

During the fetal period (Week 9–birth) organ systems continue to develop and there is immense growth in size. Viability is rare before the third trimester because of the immaturity of the lungs. By 28 weeks the fetus has sleep-wake cycles similar to a newborn baby's and can remember and respond to sound, taste, and the mother's movements.

LO 2.11   Compare and contrast prenatal care in traditional cultures and developed countries.

In traditional cultures prenatal care often includes massage as well as folk knowledge that may or may not have practical consequences. For instance, many cultures advise pregnant women to avoid certain types of food. Essential elements of scientifically-based prenatal care include regular evaluations by a health care professional and guidelines concerning diet, exercise, and avoiding teratogens. Pregnant women are advised to gain 25–30 pounds in the course of pregnancy, and light to moderate exercise is encouraged.

LO 2.12   Identify the major teratogens in developing countries and developed countries.

The major teratogens are malnutrition and infectious diseases in developing countries and alcohol and tobacco in developed countries. The embryonic period is a critical period for prenatal development since all the major organ systems are forming at a rapid rate. However, some teratogens can do damage during the fetal period as well.

Section 3   Pregnancy Problems

Learning Objectives

2.13 Explain how chromosomal disorders occur.

2.14 Describe the three main techniques of prenatal diagnosis, and explain who is likely to seek genetic counseling and for what purposes.

2.15 List the major causes of infertility for both men and women, and describe current treatments.

2.16 Compare rates of infertility worldwide, and contrast the views of infertility in developed and developing countries.

PREGNANCY PROBLEMS: Prenatal Problems

Most pregnancies proceed without major problems and end with the birth of a healthy infant. However, many things can go wrong in the course of prenatal development. In this section, we'll look at some common chromosomal disorders and then examine methods of prenatal monitoring and genetic counseling.

Chromosomal Disorders

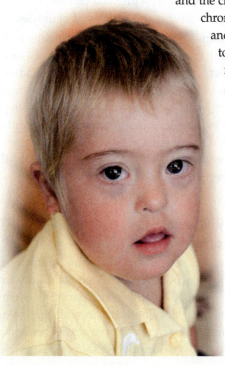

Persons with Down syndrome typically face a wide range of physical and cognitive problems.

LO 2.13 Explain how chromosomal disorders occur.

In the course of the formation of the gametes during meiosis, sometimes errors take place and the chromosomes fail to divide properly. Consequently, instead of ending up with 46 chromosomes in each cell, the person has 45 or 47 (or even, in rare cases, 48 or 49), and problems occur. It is estimated that as many as half of all conceptions involve too many or too few chromosomes, but most of the zygotes that result either never begin to develop or are spontaneously aborted early in the pregnancy (Borgoankar, 1997; Johnson, 2008). In 1 out of 200 live births, the child has a chromosomal disorder. There are two main types of chromosomal disorders: (1) those that involve the sex chromosomes and (2) those that take place on the 21st pair of chromosomes, resulting in a condition known as Down syndrome.

SEX CHROMOSOME DISORDERS The sex chromosomes are especially likely to be involved in chromosomal disorders. A person may have an extra X chromosome (resulting in XXX or XXY), or an extra Y chromosome (XYY), or may have only an X and no second sex chromosome. About 1 in every 500 infants has some type of sex chromosome disorder.

There are two common consequences of sex chromosome disorders (Batzer & Rovitsky, 2009). One is that the person has some type of cognitive deficit, such as intellectual disability (ranging from mild to severe), a learning disorder, or speech impairments. The other kind of problem is that the person has some abnormality in the development of the reproductive system at puberty, such as underdeveloped testes and penis in boys or no ovulation in girls. One of the functions of the sex chromosomes is to direct the production of the sex hormones, and having too few or too many sex chromosomes disrupts this process. However, treatment with hormone supplements is often effective in correcting the problem.

DOWN SYNDROME When there is an extra chromosome on the 21st pair, the condition is known as **Down syndrome**, or *trisomy-21*. Persons with Down syndrome have distinct physical features, including a short, stocky build, an unusually flat face, a large tongue, and an extra fold of skin on the eyelids. They also have cognitive deficits, including intellectual disability and speech problems (Pennington et al., 2003). Many also have problems in their physical development, such as hearing impairments and heart defects.

Their social development varies widely. Some children with Down syndrome smile less readily than other persons and have difficulty making eye contact, but others are exceptionally happy and loving. Supportive and encouraging parents help children with Down syndrome develop more favorably (Hodapp et al., 2012; Sigman, 1999). Intervention programs in infancy and preschool have been shown to enhance their social, emotional, and motor skills (Carr, 2002; Hodapp et al., 2012). In adulthood, with adequate support many are able to hold a job that is highly structured and involves simple tasks.

People with Down syndrome age faster than other people (Berney, 2009). Their total brain volume begins to decrease as early as their 20s. Various physical ailments that may develop for other people in late adulthood begin to afflict people with Down syndrome in their 30s and 40s, including leukemia, cancer, Alzheimer's disease, and heart disease (Hassold & Patterson, 1999). As a result, their life expectancy is considerably lower than in the general population. However, with medical treatment most are able to live into at least their 50s or 60s (Hodapp et al., 2012).

PARENTAL AGE AND CHROMOSOMAL DISORDERS Children with chromosomal problems are almost always born to parents who have no disorder (Batzer & Ravitsky, 2009). Chromosomal problems occur not because the parents have an inherited problem that they pass on to their children, but usually because of the age of the parents, especially the mother. For example, the risk of Down syndrome rises with maternal age, from 1 in 1,900 births at age 20 to 1 in 30 births at age 45 (Meyers et al., 1997). The risk of chromosomal disorders is very low for mothers in their 20s and rises only slightly in the 30s, but rises steeply after age 40 (see **Figure 2.9**; Umrigar et al., 2014).

Recall that a woman's gamete production takes place while she is still in the womb of her own mother. The older she gets, the longer the eggs have been in her ovaries. When conception takes place and the last part of meiosis is completed in the ovum, the older the woman, the greater the likelihood that the chromosomes will not separate properly because they have been suspended in that final stage of meiosis for so long. The father's sperm is the cause of the chromosomal disorder in 5–10% of cases, but it is unclear if the risk increases with the father's age (Crow, 2003; Fisch et al., 2003; Muller et al., 2000).

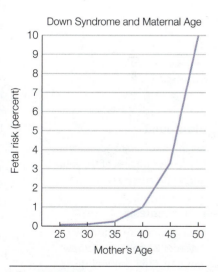

Down Syndrome and Maternal Age

Fetal risk (percent) — *Mother's Age*

Figure 2.9 Down Syndrome and Maternal Age

Why does the risk rise so steeply after age 40?

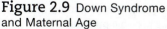
SOURCE: Based on Umrigar et al. (2014).

Prenatal Diagnosis

LO 2.14 Describe the three main techniques of prenatal diagnosis, and explain who is likely to seek genetic counseling and for what purposes.

Various technologies are used to monitor the course of prenatal development. Even before pregnancy, some couples who are at risk for potential problems seek prenatal genetic counseling in order to inform themselves about the nature and degree of the risks they face.

Down syndrome

genetic disorder due to carrying an extra chromosome on the 21st pair

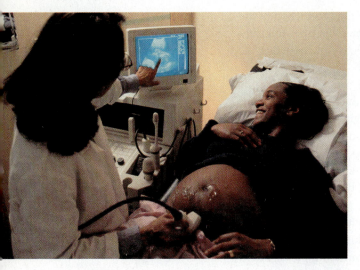

Ultrasound allows medical professionals and parents to monitor prenatal development.

ultrasound

machine that uses sound waves to produce images of the fetus during pregnancy

amniocentesis

prenatal procedure in which a needle is used to withdraw amniotic fluid containing fetal cells from the placenta, allowing possible prenatal problems to be detected

chorionic villus sampling (CVS)

prenatal technique for diagnosing genetic problems, involving taking a sample of cells at 5–10 weeks gestation by inserting a tube into the uterus

TECHNIQUES OF PRENATAL MONITORING In developed countries, a variety of techniques are available to monitor the growth and health of the fetus and detect prenatal problems. Common methods include ultrasound, amniocentesis, and chorionic villus sampling (CVS).

Ultrasound. In **ultrasound**, high-frequency sound waves are directed toward the uterus, and as they bounce off the fetus they are converted by computer into an image that can be viewed on a screen. Ultrasound technology has improved in recent years and the 3D/4D images are distinct enough to make it possible to measure the fetus's size and shape and to monitor its activities (Merz & Abramowicz, 2012). Studies have also found that viewing ultrasound images helps promote a feeling of parental involvement and attachment even before birth (Righetti et al., 2005). I remember well the thrill of seeing my twins on the ultrasound monitor and marveling as they grew from two clumps of cells to full-grown fetuses.

Ultrasound is sometimes used to screen for Down syndrome, which can be detected 13 weeks into prenatal development (Reddy & Mennui, 2006). It is also used for pregnancies that involve multiple fetuses, because these are high-risk pregnancies in which it is common for some of the fetuses to be developing less favorably than others. However, increasingly, ultrasound is used for normal pregnancies in developed countries, not just for those that are high risk (Merz & Abramowicz, 2012). It is cheap, easy, and safe, and it allows doctors to monitor fetal growth and gives parents the enjoyment of seeing the fetus as it is developing in the womb. It also allows parents to learn the sex of the child before birth, if they wish.

Amniocentesis. In **amniocentesis**, a long hollow needle is inserted into the pregnant woman's abdomen and, using the ultrasound image for guidance, a sample of the amniotic fluid is withdrawn from the placenta surrounding the fetus. This fluid contains fetal cells sloughed off in the course of prenatal development, and the cells can be examined for information on the fetus's genotype. Amniocentesis is conducted 15–20 weeks into pregnancy. It is used only for women who are at risk for prenatal problems due to family history or age (35 or older) because it carries a small risk of triggering miscarriage. It can detect 40 different defects in fetal development with 100% accuracy (Brambati & Tului, 2005).

Chorionic villus sampling (CVS). Like amniocentesis, **chorionic villus sampling (CVS)** entails sampling and analyzing cells early in development to detect possible genetic problems. CVS takes place at 5–10 weeks into the pregnancy; the sample is obtained from the cells that are beginning to form the umbilical cord. Guided by ultrasound, a tube is inserted through the vagina and into the uterus to obtain the cell sample. CVS entails a slight but genuine risk of miscarriage or damage to the fetus, so it is used only when there is a family history of genetic abnormalities or the woman is age 35 or over (Brambati & Tului, 2005). It is 99% accurate in diagnosing genetic problems.

GENETIC COUNSELING Even before pregnancy, couples whose family history places them at risk for having children with genetic disorders may seek *genetic counseling,* which involves analyzing the family history and genotypes of prospective parents to identify possible risks (Coughlin, 2009). Those with risks that merit genetic counseling include persons who have an inherited genetic condition or a close relative who has one; couples with a history of miscarriages or infertility; and older couples (women over 35 and men over 40) (Fransen et al., 2006). The decision to obtain genetic counseling may be difficult, because the results may require the couple to make the choice between trying to become pregnant and risking that the child will have a genetic disorder, or deciding not to pursue pregnancy. However, the knowledge obtained from genetic counseling enables people to make an informed decision.

In the first step of genetic counseling, the counselor takes a comprehensive family history from each prospective parent, seeking to identify patterns that may indicate problematic recessive or X-linked genes. Then each partner provides a blood, skin, or urine sample that can be used to analyze their chromosomes to identify possible problems. With the information obtained from genetic counseling, the couple can then decide whether or not they wish to attempt pregnancy (Coughlin, 2009).

Practice Quiz   ANSWERS AVAILABLE IN ANSWER KEY.

1. Julie was a 47-year-old college professor who was shocked to find out she was pregnant. Although she was elated at the idea of having another child, she was worried about having a child with _____ as the chances increase dramatically after age 45.
   a. anencephaly
   b. spina bifida
   c. cystic fibrosis
   d. Down syndrome

2. There are two main types of chromosomal disorders, those that take place on the 21st pair of chromosomes and those _____.
   a. that take place on the 20th pair
   b. that take place on the 22nd pair
   c. that involve the sex chromosomes
   d. that involve rapidly developing chromosomes

3. Which of the following is safest in terms of risk of miscarriage?
   a. Chorionic villus sampling
   b. Amniocentesis
   c. Ultrasound
   d. They all carry about the same level of risk for miscarriage.

4. Which of the following is TRUE regarding people with Down syndrome?
   a. They are at increased risk for an abnormality in the development of the reproductive system.
   b. Their total brain volume tends to increase in their twenties.
   c. They age faster than other people.
   d. With advances in medical treatment, their life expectancy is now about the same as in the general population.

5. Carissa has a family history of Down syndrome and is in her 5th week of pregnancy. She decides that she would like to find out as early as possible whether her unborn child has Down syndrome or any other genetic abnormality. What test is she likely to get?
   a. Chorionic villus sampling
   b. Amniocentesis
   c. Sonogram
   d. Echocardiogram

PREGNANCY PROBLEMS: Infertility

Most women of reproductive age (roughly age 15–40) who have sexual intercourse on a regular basis will become pregnant within a year or two. However, for some couples becoming pregnant is more problematic.

Causes and Treatments

LO 2.15 **List the major causes of infertility for both men and women, and describe current treatments.**

Infertility is defined as the inability to attain pregnancy after at least a year of regular sexual intercourse without contraception. Rates of infertility in the United States have been remarkably consistent over the past century at about 10–15% of couples (Johnson, 2008; Marsh & Ronner, 1996).

SOURCES OF INFERTILITY About half the time the source of infertility is in the male reproductive system and about half the time in the female reproductive system (Jones, 2006). Among men, there are three main sources of infertility (Jequier, 2011): (1) too few sperm may be produced; (2) the quality of the sperm may be poor, due to disease or defects in the sperm manufacturing process in the testicles; or, (3) the sperm

infertility

inability to attain pregnancy after at least a year of regular sexual intercourse

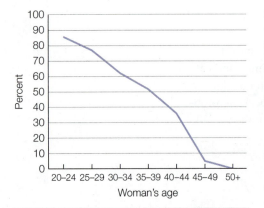

Figure 2.10 Fertility and Maternal Age

Why does fertility decline after the mid-20s?

may be low in *motility* (movement) and therefore unable to make it all the way up the fallopian tubes. These problems may be genetic or they may be caused by behavior such as drug abuse, alcohol abuse, or cigarette smoking. Or, they may be due simply to age—it takes three times longer for men over 40 to impregnate a partner than it does for men under 25, because the quantity and quality of sperm production decreases with age (Patel, 2010).

Among women, infertility is most often caused by problems in ovulation (National Women's Health Information Center, 2011). Inability to ovulate can be caused by disease, or it can be due to drug abuse, alcohol abuse, or cigarette smoking, or to being extremely underweight or overweight. However, age is the most common cause of inability to ovulate (Maheshwari et al., 2008). As you learned early in the chapter, females are born with all the eggs they will ever have in their ovaries, and the quality of those eggs deteriorates gradually after puberty. Fertility decreases for women throughout their 20s and 30s but especially drops after age 40, when they become more likely to have menstrual cycles with no ovulation at all (see **Figure 2.10**).

INFERTILITY TREATMENTS We now know that men and women contribute equally to infertility. However, this knowledge is very recent, coming only in about the past 50 years. For most of human history in most cultures, infertility has been regarded almost exclusively as a female problem, and women suffering from it were described not as infertile but as "barren" (Marsh & Ronner, 1996). In the West, for over 2,000 years, from about the 4th century BCE to the 1800s, the reigning explanation for infertility was based on a theory that both women and men must produce a seed in order for conception to occur, and that the seed was released through orgasm. Because men generally reach orgasm a whole lot easier than women do, the main advice given to infertile couples was for the husband to give more attention to bringing sexual pleasure to his wife. As one advice writer stated in 1708, "The womb must be in a state of delight" or sex would be fruitless (Marsh & Ronner, 1996, p. 15). This theory was wrong, but at least it did no harm. Other treatments for infertility were not just ineffective but damaging to women's health, including surgery on the woman's reproductive anatomy and bloodletting (which is pretty much what it sounds like: making a cut in a blood vessel in the arm and letting blood run out until the alleged imbalance was restored).

During the course of the 20th century, treatments for infertility became more scientifically based and technologically advanced. Today there are a variety of approaches. These methods are used by infertile couples as well as by gay and lesbian couples and by single women. A variety of related methods for overcoming infertility are grouped under the term **assisted reproductive technologies (ART)**, including artificial insemination, fertility drugs, and in vitro fertilization (IVF). ART methods are used in response to a wide variety of infertility problems in either the male or female reproductive system, or both (CDC, 2011).

The oldest effective treatment for infertility is **artificial insemination**, which involves injecting the man's sperm directly into the woman's uterus, timed to coincide with her ovulation (Schoolcraft, 2010). It was first developed in the 19th century when physicians believed the primary cause of infertility was a too-tight cervix (the opening between the vagina and the uterus). Today, artificial insemination most often occurs as *donor insemination,* in which a man other than the woman's husband or partner provides the sperm. Most often this approach is due to problems in the husband or partner's sperm production, but increasingly this procedure is chosen by lesbian couples or single women who wish to have a child. Artificial insemination is the simplest and most effective reproductive technology, with a success rate of over 70% per trial (Wright et al., 2004).

assisted reproductive technologies (ART)

methods for overcoming infertility that include artificial insemination, fertility drugs, and IVF

artificial insemination

procedure of injecting sperm directly into the uterus

If the primary problem is that the woman cannot ovulate properly, the most common approach is to stimulate ovulation through fertility drugs. The drugs mimic the activity of the hormones that normally provoke ovulation. Usually fertility drugs stimulate both the quality and the quantity of follicles in each cycle. Over half of the women who take the drugs become pregnant within six cycles (Schoolcraft, 2010).

Fertility drugs work for many women, but they also carry serious risks, including blood clots, kidney damage, and damage to the ovaries (Lauersen & Bouchez, 2000). The purpose of the drugs is to stimulate the development of follicles in the ovaries, but often more than one follicle develops, resulting in the release of two, three, or more ova. Consequently, use of fertility drugs produces high rates of multiple births, about 10–25% depending on the drug (Schoolcraft, 2010). Usually this means twins, but there is also the possibility of triplets or more. You may have seen magazine stories or television shows about multiple births of six, seven, or eight infants and how

Multiple births often receive extensive media attention, but the consequences of such births are often tragic, with higher risks of miscarriages, premature birth, and serious developmental difficulties.

adorable they are, but the consequences of multiple births are often tragic. The more babies conceived at once, the higher the risk for miscarriages, premature birth, and serious developmental difficulties.

If fertility drugs are unsuccessful in achieving pregnancy, the next step in the ART method is **in vitro fertilization (IVF)**. In IVF, after fertility drugs are used to stimulate the growth of numerous follicles in the woman's ovaries, the ripe ova are then removed and combined with the man's sperm so that fertilization will take place. After a few days it is possible to tell which of the zygotes have developed and which have not, so the most promising two or three are placed into the woman's uterus in the hope that one will continue to develop. In vitro fertilization success rates have steadily improved in recent years, and are currently about 40% per attempt for women under age 35 (Society for Assisted Reproductive Technology [SART], 2014). However, the success rate declines with age to 22% for women ages 38-40 and just 4% for women ages 42 and older.

CRITICAL THINKING QUESTION

Because fertility drugs frequently result in multiple births, should there be legal restrictions on how they can be used?

Infertility Worldwide

LO 2.16 **Compare rates of infertility worldwide, and contrast the views of infertility in developed and developing countries.**

Across cultures, most people wish to have children and infertility is experienced as a source of frustration and distress (Balen & Inhorn, 2002). However, there are definite cultural differences in how seriously infertility is viewed and how it is framed socially. In the individualistic West, infertile couples often experience a sense of sadness and loss. In one Swedish study, couples seeking infertility treatments felt frustration over missing out on a major focus of life, and they experienced a negative effect on their sexual relationship (Hjelmstedt et al., 1999). They felt that they were unable to live up to social and personal expectations for having a child. Other studies have found that infertility often creates strains in the marital relationship; but in the long run, about half of couples report that the experience of infertility made their relationship closer and stronger (Schmidt et al., 2005).

in vitro fertilization (IVF)
form of infertility treatment that involves using drugs to stimulate the growth of multiple follicles in the ovaries, removing the follicles and combining them with sperm, then transferring the most promising zygotes to the uterus

When the first IVF baby was born in 1978 there were concerns that babies conceived in this way might be abnormal in some way. However, by now many of these babies have grown to adulthood without any problems. Today IVF is the basis of thousands of pregnancies per year, almost entirely in developed countries because of the technology and expense it requires.

Outside the West, cultures tend to be more collectivistic, and the social consequences of infertility are even more profound. Infertility is often deeply stigmatized. This is especially true for women, who are usually blamed for the problem and for whom motherhood is essential to their identity and their place within the social world (Inhorn & Balen, 2002; Sembuya, 2010). In many cultures, infertility means much more than that the couple will miss out on the joys of raising a child. It may mean that there will be no one to continue the family tradition of remembering and worshipping the ancestors, a responsibility that often falls on the oldest son, especially in Asian and African cultures. It may also mean that the status of the wife is lowered in relation to her husband, her in-laws, and the community, because infertility is viewed more as her failure than his. Even if she has a daughter, she may still be seen as inadequate if she fails to produce a son. This is misguided since, as we discussed earlier in the chapter, biologically it is the father and not the mother who determines the sex of the child.

Few people in developing countries have access to reproductive technologies like fertility drugs and IVF. Women may try herbal remedies provided by a midwife. Others may seek supernatural remedies. For example, in Ghana women often consult a shaman (religious leader believed to have special powers), who focuses on trying to appease the wrath of the gods believed to be inflicting infertility on the woman as a punishment (Leonard, 2002).

If infertility persists, it is viewed in many cultures as grounds for the husband to divorce his wife or take another wife. For example, in Vietnam it is generally accepted that if a man's wife is infertile he will attempt to have a child with another "wife," even though having more than one wife is actually illegal (Pashigian, 2002). In Cameroon, if a couple cannot conceive a child, the husband's family may encourage him to obtain a divorce and seek the return of the "bridewealth" his family paid to the wife's family when they married (Felman-Savelsberg, 2002).

Practice Quiz   ANSWERS AVAILABLE IN ANSWER KEY.

1. Shonda and Trinity have been a couple for eight years, and they are now excited to take the leap into parenthood together. Because they are both women, they have decided to use _____, which would involve injecting a donor's sperm into Shonda's uterus while she is ovulating.
   a. epidurals
   b. artificial insemination
   c. in vitro fertilization
   d. chorionic villus sampling

2. _____ is the most common cause of inability to ovulate.
   a. Age
   b. Cigarette smoking
   c. Alcohol abuse
   d. Being extremely overweight

3. If the primary problem is that the woman cannot ovulate properly, the most common fertility treatment is _____.
   a. chorionic villus treatment
   b. artificial insemination
   c. fertility drugs
   d. in vitro fertilization

4. In collectivistic cultures infertility is often _____.
   a. accepted
   b. less common
   c. stigmatized
   d. blamed on both parents

Summary: Pregnancy Problems

LO 2.13 Explain how chromosomal disorders occur.

Chromosomal disorders occur when the chromosomes fail to divide properly during meiosis. These disorders may involve the sex chromosomes or may take place on the 21st pair of chromosomes, resulting in a condition known as Down syndrome. Risks of chromosomal disorders rise with parental age.

LO 2.14 Describe the three main techniques of prenatal diagnosis, and explain who is likely to seek genetic counseling and for what purposes.

Prenatal diagnosis may include ultrasound, amniocentesis, and chorionic villus sampling (CVS). Couples who may be at high risk for genetic disorders sometimes seek genetic counseling prior to attempting pregnancy.

LO 2.15 List the major causes of infertility for both men and women, and describe current treatments.

Male infertility may be caused by too few sperm, poor quality of sperm, or low motility of sperm. Female infertility is most often caused by problems in ovulation. Infertility in both men and women is often due to age, but it can also be genetic or caused by behavior such as drug abuse, alcohol abuse, or cigarette smoking.

Treatments for infertility are termed *assisted reproductive technologies* (ART) and include artificial insemination, fertility drugs, and IVF.

LO 2.16 Compare rates of fertility worldwide, and contrast views of infertility in developed and developing countries.

Although worldwide the average infertility rate is about 10–15%, there is variation among countries. In developed countries, infertility often results in frustration and sadness, and presents a challenge to the couple's relationship, although it may ultimately make the relationship stronger. In developing countries, the woman is usually blamed for the infertility, and her social status is damaged.

Applying Your Knowledge as a Professional

The topics covered in this chapter apply to a wide variety of career professions. Watch these videos to learn how they apply to a reproductive endocrinologist, a genetic counselor, and a professor of microbiology.

Watch   CAREER FOCUS: GENETIC COUNSELOR

Video

Elsa Reich, M.S.
Genetic Counselor
NYU Langone Medical Center

444444444444444444

Chapter Quiz

1. Keisha has inherited one recessive gene for the sickle-cell trait along with one normal dominant gene. As a result of this _____, she is resistant to malaria and does not have sickle-cell anemia.
   a. dominant-recessive inheritance
   b. incomplete dominance
   c. polygenic inheritance
   d. reaction range

2. Who has the greatest risk of developing hemophilia, which is an X-linked recessive disorder?
   a. A female who has one X chromosome that contains the gene for this disorder
   b. A male who has one X chromosome that contains the gene for this disorder
   c. Males and females with one X chromosome that contains the gene for the disorder will have equal risk.
   d. Only Native Americans, due to their unique genetic makeup

3. Which of the following questions would a behavior geneticist be most likely to ask?
   a. "Why are children in the same family so different from one another?"
   b. "Are preterm babies more likely to have learning difficulties during the school years?"
   c. "How can prenatal tests be used to detect Down syndrome?"
   d. "What effects does alcohol have on the developing organism?"

4. Why has there been little change in the average height in Western countries over the last few decades?
   a. The population has become overweight or obese, which negatively affects height.
   b. People in Western countries have been exposed to more diseases.
   c. People have reached the upper boundary of their reaction range for height.
   d. Evolutionary influences are causing all populations to decrease in height.

5. John is short for his age and is very coordinated. Although exposed to a variety of activities, none has particularly interested him. His father, who used to wrestle when he was younger, signs John up for wrestling thinking this could be the perfect sport. He convinces John to give it a try and John goes on to become a champion wrestler. This is an example of _____.
   a. passive genotype → environment effects
   b. evocative genotype → environment effects
   c. active genotype → environment effects
   d. heritability

6. As a result of the process of crossing over _____.
   a. the risk of Down syndrome is increased
   b. boys are more likely to be born with a learning disability
   c. women are at increased risk for infertility
   d. each child born to a set of parents is genetically unique (with the exception of identical twins)

7. S.J. is most likely to have DZ twins if _____.
   a. she has Asian biological parents
   b. she is in her late teens
   c. she is concerned about gaining too much weight and severely restricts her calorie intake
   d. her mother had DZ twins

8. If Susan learns that her infertility problem is due to a problem with the _____ successfully implanting, something went wrong during the germinal period.
   a. zygote
   b. blastocyst
   c. fetus
   d. trophoblast

9. During the embryonic period _____.
   a. the blastocyst forms
   b. the zygote is created
   c. the zygote attaches to the uterine wall
   d. the major organs develop

10. Saad, a baby born 6 weeks prematurely, is more at risk of not surviving than Nona, a baby who is full term, because Saad's _____ is/are still immature.
    a. small intestines
    b. heart
    c. lungs
    d. spleen

11. In traditional cultures, prenatal massage _____.
    a. is usually done only when there is reason to believe that the fetus is not developing properly
    b. is usually considered dangerous
    c. has beneficial effects for both mother and fetus
    d. is almost exclusively performed by the pregnant mother herself in complete isolation

12. Which is the following is true of good prenatal care?
    a. Exercise should be avoided.
    b. Tobacco, alcohol, and other drugs should be avoided.
    c. Women should drink fewer fluids than before pregnancy.
    d. Forty to sixty pounds should be gained.

13. K.L.'s baby was born blind, deaf, and with intellectual disability. It is most likely that during her pregnancy she _____.

    a. contracted AIDS

    b. had rubella

    c. had a severe nutritional deficiency

    d. ate foods that were too high in folic acid

14. A child who has an X0 chromosomal makeup (where 0 denotes a missing chromosome where there is supposed to be a 23rd pair) will most likely _____.

    a. be a male with Down syndrome

    b. be a female who will later experience problems in the development of the reproductive system

    c. be a typical female who will not experience cognitive or physical problems

    d. not survive past the age of 3

15. Carissa has a family history of Down syndrome and is in her 5th week of pregnancy. She decides that she would like to find out as early as possible whether her unborn child has Down syndrome or any genetic abnormality. What test is she most likely to get?

    a. Fetal monitoring

    b. Ultrasound

    c. Amniocentesis

    d. Chorionic villus sampling

16. In the United States, about _____ of couples are infertile.

    a. 1–2%

    b. 4–5%

    c. 10–15%

    d. 14–27%

17. Fertility drugs _____.

    a. lead to pregnancy in virtually all women if they take them long enough

    b. decrease a woman's chances of having DZ twins

    c. are also known in the medical community as in vitro fertilization

    d. carry risks such as blood clots and kidney damage

18. A married woman from a non-Western, collectivistic culture has been unable to have a child for over 3 years. Which of the following is most likely?

    a. She will have a higher status relative to her husband.

    b. She will get a lot of social support from her mother-in-law and father-in-law.

    c. She will try IVF.

    d. She will be blamed for this "problem."

Chapter 3
Birth and the Newborn Child

ACROSS CULTURES, THE BIRTH OF A NEW HUMAN BEING IS REGARDED AS A JOYFUL EVENT, WORTHY OF CELEBRATION. At the same time, it is often a physically challenging and potentially perilous process, for both mother and child, especially when modern medical assistance is not available. In this chapter we will look at the birth process, followed by cultural variations in birth beliefs, then at the history of birth in the West and birth variations today around the world. We will then move on to care of the newborn, before ending with the characteristics of the newborn child.

Watch CHAPTER INTRODUCTION: BIRTH AND THE NEWBORN CHILD

Video

Section 1   Birth and Its Cultural Context

∨   Learning Objectives

3.1 Describe the three stages of the birth process and methods for easing its discomfort.

3.2 Name two common types of birth complications and explain how they can be overcome by cesarean delivery.

3.3 Summarize the history of birth in the West from the 15th century to today.

3.4 Describe cultural variations in birth beliefs and identify who may assist with the birth.

3.5 Compare and contrast cultural practices and medical methods for easing the birth process.

3.6 Describe the differences in maternal and neonatal mortality both within and between developed countries and developing countries.

BIRTH AND ITS CULTURAL CONTEXT: The Birth Process

Toward the end of pregnancy, hormonal changes take place that trigger the beginning of the birth process. Most importantly, the hormone **oxytocin** is released from the woman's pituitary gland. When the amount of oxytocin in the expectant mother's blood reaches a certain threshold level, her uterus begins to contract on a frequent and regular basis, and the birth process begins.

Stages of the Birth Process

LO 3.1   **Describe the three stages of the birth process and methods for easing its discomfort.**

The birth process is generally divided into three stages: labor, delivery of the baby, and delivery of the placenta and umbilical cord, as shown in **Figure 3.1** (Mayo Clinic Staff, 2011). There is immense variability among women in the length and difficulty of this process, depending mostly on the size of the woman and the size of the baby, but in general it is longer and more difficult for women giving birth to their first child.

THE FIRST STAGE: LABOR The first stage of the birth process, **labor**, is the longest and most taxing stage, averaging about 12 hours for first births and 6 hours for subsequent births (Lyons, 2007). During labor, contractions of the muscles in the uterus cause the woman's cervix to dilate (open) in preparation for the baby's exit. By the end of labor, the cervix has opened to about 10 centimeters (4½ inches). Labor is painful because the contractions of the muscles of the uterus must occur with increasing intensity, frequency, and duration in order to dilate the cervix and move the fetus down the neck of the uterus and through the vagina. The contractions of the uterus are painful in the same way (and for the same reason) a cramp is painful—pain results when muscles contract intensely for an extended period. At their peak duration, contractions last 60-90 seconds.

oxytocin

hormone released by pituitary gland that causes labor to begin

labor

first stage of the birth process, in which the cervix dilates and the muscles of the uterus contract to push the fetus into the vagina toward the cervix

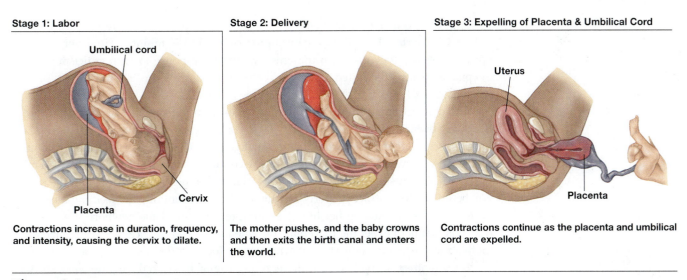

Stage 1: Labor

Umbilical cord

Placenta

Cervix

Contractions increase in duration, frequency, and intensity, causing the cervix to dilate.

Stage 2: Delivery

The mother pushes, and the baby crowns and then exits the birth canal and enters the world.

Stage 3: Expelling of Placenta & Umbilical Cord

Uterus

Placenta

Contractions continue as the placenta and umbilical cord are expelled.

Figure 3.1 The Three Stages of the Birth Process

Which stage is longest and most difficult?

In the early part of labor, as the cervix opens, there may be a thick, stringy, bloody discharge from the vagina known as *bloody show*. Women often experience severe back pain as labor continues. Nausea and trembling of the legs are also common.

Emotional support is crucial to the woman's experience during labor (daMotta et al., 2006). In developed countries she may have her husband present, whereas he would usually be excluded from the birth in developing countries (DeLoache & Gottlieb, 2000). She may have her mother present, or her mother-in-law, and one or more sisters. There may also be a midwife, especially in developing countries, and health personnel, especially in developed countries. These caregivers may assist the woman with not only emotional support but methods to ease her discomfort (to be described later in the chapter).

THE SECOND AND THIRD STAGES: DELIVERY AND EXPELLING THE PLACENTA AND UMBILICAL CORD The second stage of the birth process, **delivery**, usually takes a half hour to an hour, but again there is wide variation (Murkoff & Mazel, 2008). So far in the birth process there has been not much the expectant mother could do to influence it, other than bear the pain and discomfort as well as possible. Now, however, her efforts to push will help move the fetus through the cervix and out of the uterus. Contractions continue to help, too, but for most women the contractions are now less frequent, although they remain 60–90 seconds long. Usually the woman feels a tremendous urge to push during her contractions.

At last *crowning* occurs, meaning that the baby's head appears at the outer opening of the vagina. The woman often experiences a tingling or burning sensation at her vaginal opening as the baby crowns. At this point, if she is giving birth in a hospital she may be given an **episiotomy**, which is an incision to make the vaginal opening larger. The purpose of the

delivery

second stage of the birth process, during which the fetus is pushed out of the cervix and through the birth canal

episiotomy

incision to make the vaginal opening larger during birth process

In developed countries, the husband or other family members often assist with strategies to ease the birth process.

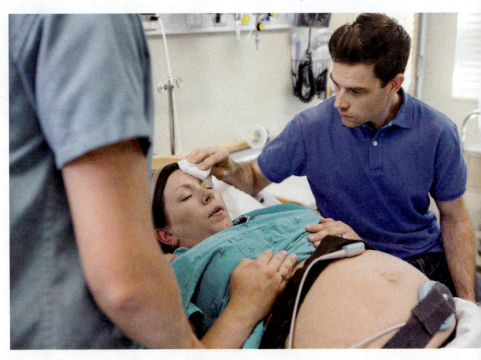

episiotomy is to make the mother's vagina less likely to tear as the fetus's head comes out, and to shorten this part of the birth process by 15 to 30 minutes. However, critics of episiotomies say they are often unnecessary, and in response to such criticism the rate of episiotomies in the United States declined from about 90% in 1970 to just 16% in 2010 (Cassidy, 2006; Frankman et al., 2009; Leapfrog Group, 2014).

The delivery stage ends as the baby emerges from the vagina, but the birth process is not yet over. In this third and final stage, contractions continue as the placenta and umbilical cord are expelled from the uterus (Lyons, 2007). This process usually happens within a few minutes, at most a half hour. The contractions are mild and last about a minute each. Care must be taken that the entire placenta comes out. If it does not, the uterus will be unable to contract properly and the mother will continue to bleed, perhaps even to the point of threatening her life. Beginning to breast-feed the newborn triggers contractions that help expel the placenta, and when advanced medical care is available the mother may be given an injection of synthetic oxytocin for the same purpose.

If the mother has had an episiotomy or her vagina has torn during delivery, she will be stitched up at this time. At this point, too, the umbilical cord must be cut and tied. There are many interesting cultural beliefs surrounding the cutting of the umbilical cord and the disposal of the placenta, as we will see later in the chapter.

The video *Labor and Delivery* shows excerpts from the delivery stage and the expelling of the placenta and umbilical cord, from a real birth.

Watch LABOR AND DELIVERY

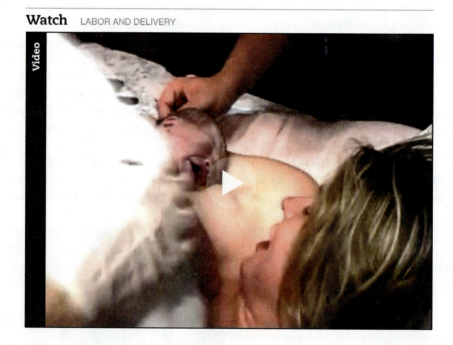

Birth Complications

LO 3.2 Name two common types of birth complications and explain how they can be overcome by cesarean delivery.

We have just examined the birth process as it occurs if all goes well, but of course there are many times when all does not go well. Two of the most common birth complications are *failure to progress* and the *breech presentation* of the fetus.

FAILURE TO PROGRESS AND BREECH PRESENTATION "Failure to progress" means that the woman has begun the birth process but it is taking longer than normal. The woman may stimulate progress by walking around, taking a nap, or having an enema. She may also be given herbal medicines or synthetic oxytocin to stimulate her contractions.

Breech presentation is when the fetus is turned around so that the feet or buttocks are positioned to come first out of the birth canal, rather than the head. About 4% of fetuses present in the breech position (Martin et al., 2005). Breech births are dangerous to the baby because coming out feet- or buttocks-first can cause the umbilical cord to be constricted during delivery, potentially leading to insufficient oxygen and brain damage within minutes. Consequently, attempts are usually made to avoid a breech presentation. Midwives have long used their skills to massage the expectant mother's abdomen and turn the fetus from breech presentation to headfirst (as described in Chapter 2), but it must be done with extreme care to avoid tearing the placenta from the uterine wall. Today physicians in hospitals also seek to turn breech fetuses at about the 37th week of pregnancy. Doctors often use drugs to relax the muscles of the uterus as they attempt to turn the fetus with the massage (Hofmeyr, 2002).

CESAREAN DELIVERY If failure to progress takes place during delivery, or if a fetus in breech position cannot be turned successfully, or if other problems arise in the birth process, the woman may be given a **cesarean delivery**, or **c-section**. The c-section involves cutting open the mother's abdomen and retrieving the baby directly from the uterus. The c-section has been around for a long time—according to legend it is named for the Roman emperor Julius Caesar, who supposedly was born by this method about 2,000 years ago—but until recent decades mothers nearly always died from it, even as the baby was saved. Today, with the standardization of sterile procedures and the use of antibiotics, it is very safe, although it takes women longer to heal from a cesarean than from a vaginal birth (Connolly & Sullivan, 2004). C-sections are generally safe for infants as well, and if the mother has a sexually transmitted infection, such as HIV or genital herpes, it is safer than a vaginal birth because it protects the infant from the risk of contracting the disease during the birth process. As **Map 3.1** shows, rates of c-sections vary widely among countries and do not seem to be related to world region or level of economic development (World Health Organization [WHO], 2014). The World Health Organization recommends that no country's c-section rate should exceed 15% (WHO, 2009), but many countries exceed that rate, including the United States.

breech presentation

positioning of the fetus so that feet or buttocks, rather than the head, are positioned to come first out of the birth canal

cesarean delivery, or **c-section**

type of birth in which mother's abdomen is cut open and fetus is retrieved directly from the uterus

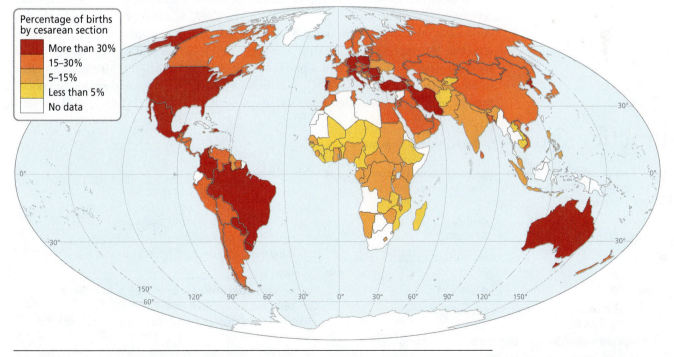

Map 3.1 Cesarean Section Rates, Selected Countries

Which countries have the highest rates of cesarean sections? What determines whether a country has high or low rates?

SOURCE: Based on WHO (2014)

Critics of high c-section rates claim that they are performed far more than is necessary, and that they are often performed not so much to protect the mother and baby as to enrich doctors (c-sections are a type of surgery and thus cost far more than a vaginal birth). However, c-section rates are not substantially higher in countries that rely mostly on private medical insurance and where doctors get paid more for doing more c-sections (like the United States) than in countries like China, Italy, and Canada that have a national health care system that does not pay doctors per c-section (WHO, 2014). More likely, high rates of c-sections result from extreme caution by doctors seeking to avoid disaster during births.

Some of the countries that have the lowest rates of c-sections also have very low rates of birth complications, which seems to indicate that many c-sections performed in other countries are unnecessary (WHO, 2014). Specifically, the countries that have the lowest rates of birth problems as well as the lowest rates of c-sections are the countries of northern Europe, where doctors and mothers alike share a cultural belief that birth should be natural and that technological intervention should take place only when absolutely necessary (Ravn, 2005). However, rates of c-sections are also low in countries like India and in most of Africa, where many people lack access to hospital facilities that could provide c-sections when necessary (WHO, 2014).

For women who have had a c-section, there is a possibility of having a vaginal birth with the next baby, a procedure known as a VBAC (*vaginal birth after cesarean section*; Shorten, 2010). As part of a more general movement in developed countries toward natural, less technological birth experiences, rates of VBAC rose in the 1980s and 1990s, and by the late 1990s about one fourth of American women who had their first baby by c-section had a VBAC with their next baby (Roberts et al., 2007). However, evidence began to indicate that having a VBAC raised birth risks in several ways in comparison to repeat c-sections, most notably the risk of uterine rupture. This occurred rarely, in only about 1% of VBACs, but when it did it sometimes resulted in death of both mother and fetus from the mother's loss of blood (WebMD, 2011). Consequently, the American College of Obstetricians and Gynecologists issued guidelines advocating that an emergency c-section be available for every woman attempting VBAC, and rates of VBACs among American women plummeted, to just 10% a decade later (Shorten, 2010). After an National Institutes of Health (NIH) panel reviewed the evidence in 2010 and declared that a VBAC is safe for nearly all women, the American College of Obstetricians and Gynecologists revised their guidelines in July 2010 to state that "Attempting a vaginal birth after cesarean (VBAC) is a safe and appropriate choice for most women who have had a prior cesarean delivery" (WebMD, 2011, p. 2). In other developed countries as well, VBAC guidelines are in flux as professional groups and policy makers respond to new evidence and shifting views (Foureur et al., 2010).

Practice Quiz ANSWERS AVAILABLE IN ANSWER KEY.

1. Anita is experiencing a burning sensation in the vaginal opening as the top of the baby's head is just starting to show, so she is in the _____ stage of the birth process.
   a. first
   b. second
   c. third
   d. fourth

2. The longest stage of the birth process is _____.
   a. Stage 1
   b. Stage 2
   c. Stage 3
   d. Stage 4

3. Sharice is pregnant and her pituitary gland has released oxytocin. As a result _____.
   a. she will experience relief from the pain of cramping
   b. she will experience a euphoric feeling and relief from anxiety
   c. she will experience failure to progress and is more likely to need a caesarian section
   d. her uterus will begin regular contractions

4. A breech birth _____.
   a. is also known as failure to progress
   b. is considered dangerous because oxygen may be constricted during the birth process
   c. refers to the fetus being in a head first position
   d. is the most common birth position and the safest

5. C-sections _____.
   a. are performed at equally small rates around the world because they are seen as a last resort
   b. can only be performed successfully if the mother is full term
   c. require the same recovery time as a vaginal birth if they are performed correctly
   d. are often performed when the baby is in the breech position

BIRTH AND ITS CULTURAL CONTEXT:
Historical and Cultural Variations

Around 9 months after conception, if survival has been sustained through the amazing, dramatic, and sometimes hazardous events of the germinal, embryonic, and fetal periods, a child is born. Even for the child who has made it through those 9 months, the hazards are far from over. Birth inspires especially intense beliefs in every culture because it is often difficult and sometimes fatal, to mother or child or both. The difficulties and dangers of birth are unique to the human species (Cassidy, 2006). Polar bear mothers, who weigh an average of 500 pounds, give birth to cubs whose heads are smaller than the heads of newborn humans. Even gorillas, one of our closest primate relatives, have babies who average only 2% of their mother's weight at birth, compared to 6% for humans.

Recall from Chapter 1 that over the course of human evolutionary history, the size of the brain more than tripled. Yet the rest of the female body did not grow three times larger, nor did the female pelvis triple in size. Consequently, birth became more problematic among humans than for any other animal, as it became increasingly difficult for the large-brained, big-headed fetus to make it through the birth canal out into the world.

Humans responded to this danger by developing cultural beliefs and practices intended to explain why labor is difficult and to alleviate the pain and enhance the safety of mother and child. Some of these beliefs and practices were surely helpful; others were indisputably harmful. Some of the most harmful beliefs and practices were developed not in traditional cultures but in the West, through the interventions of the medical profession from the 18th to the mid-20th century. It is only in the past 50 years that scientifically-based medical knowledge has led to methods that are genuinely helpful to mothers and babies in the birthing process.

The Peculiar History of Birth in the West

LO 3.3 **Summarize the history of birth in the West from the 15th century to today.**

Given the perils of birth throughout human history one might assume that once modern scientific medicine developed, mothers and babies were safer than in the superstitious past. However, this is not quite how the story goes. On the contrary, as birth became "medical" the dangers for mothers and babies grew worse, not better, for *over a century*.

EARLY HISTORY: FROM MIDWIVES TO DOCTORS In the West as in other cultures, most births throughout most of history were administered by midwives (Ehrenreich, 2010). The role of midwife was widely valued and respected. Most did their work for little or no pay, although families would often present them with a gift after the birth.

This began to change in the 15th century, as a witch-hunting fervor swept over Europe. In 1486 an influential witch-hunting manual was published by two monks, declaring that "No one does more harm to the Catholic faith than midwives" (Cassidy, 2006, p. 33). Midwives became widely suspected of being witches, and many of them were put to death. After the witch-hunting fervor passed, midwifery revived, but to keep out any remaining witches midwives were required to have licenses, issued by the Catholic church.

In the early 18th century a new challenge arose to the status of midwives. Medical schools were established throughout Europe, and the care and assistance of expectant mothers became a distinct field within medicine called **obstetrics**. By the 19th century it became increasingly common for doctors in the West to be called upon to assist in births. Unfortunately, medical training at the time often included virtually nothing about childbirth. All the doctors-to-be were men, and in many medical schools it was considered

obstetrics

field of medicine that focuses on prenatal care and birth

improper for a man to see a woman's genitals under any circumstances. Consequently, medical students learned about assisting a birth only from reading books and attending lectures (Cassidy, 2006).

Doctors developed new methods of assisting births, such as using **forceps**, a pair of tongs used to extract the baby's head from the womb. By the end of the 19th century, half of all American births involved the use of forceps (Ehrenreich, 2010). Forceps were sometimes useful in the hands of an experienced, well-trained doctor—and still are, in rare cases—but doctors of the time were rarely experienced or well trained. Consequently, the use of forceps frequently resulted in damage to the baby or the mother. In the course of the 20th century, as the damage done by forceps was increasingly recognized, their use diminished. By the early 21st century they were used in only 4% of American births (Cassidy, 2006).

Even worse than the pervasive and unnecessary use of forceps in doctor-assisted births in the 19th century was the spread of disease. At the time, no one understood that it was necessary for doctors to wash their hands before examining a patient to avoid spreading infection. Consequently, hospitals became disease factories. Vast numbers of women died following childbirth from what was called *childbed fever* or *puerperal sepsis*. Records show that in many European and American hospitals in the 19th century about 1 in 20 mothers died from childbed fever, and during occasional epidemics the rates were much higher (Nuland, 2003). Records from one Boston hospital in 1883 showed that 75% of mothers giving birth suffered from childbed fever, and 20% died from it (Cassidy, 2006).

In the early 20th century midwives still assisted at about 50% of births, but by 1930 this proportion had dwindled to 15%, and by 1973 to just 1% (Cassidy, 2006). In recent decades midwifery has seen a revival, and currently about 10% of births in the United States are assisted by midwives (MacDorman et al., 2010). Many now receive formal training and are certified and licensed as nurse-midwives, rather than simply learning their skills from an older midwife as in the past. In Europe, midwives are much more common than in the United States, especially in northern Europe. In Norway, for example, 96% of births are assisted by midwives (Cosminsky, 2003).

THE 20TH CENTURY: SLOW PROGRESS In obstetrics as in other branches of medicine, a more scientific basis of knowledge, care, and treatment developed during the 20th century. However, progress was slow. In the early decades of the 20th century medical training remained inadequate. Childbed fever remained a persistent problem. Although hand washing became standard among doctors by the early 20th century, inadequate washing still caused many deaths. It was not until the 1940s that childbed fever was finally vanquished in the United States and Europe as it became standard for obstetricians to wash their hands and also wear rubber gloves in examining women. The development of antibiotics at this time cured the cases of childbed fever that did occur (Carter & Carter, 2005).

In some ways, obstetrical care of women grew still worse in the early 20th century. Episiotomies became more prevalent, when some medical authorities claimed (without evidence) that the procedure made birth safer for mothers and babies. Doctors increasingly used drugs to relieve mothers' pain during birth. In the 19th century physicians had developed drugs to relieve pain during birth, first using ether, and later, chloroform. However, these drugs could be used only just before the birth, because if used earlier they might interfere with the woman's contractions. In addition, these drugs had dangerous side effects that could cause maternal hemorrhage and breathing difficulties in babies.

In the early 20th century a new drug method was developed that resulted in a condition that became known as *Twilight Sleep* (Cassidy, 2008). After being injected with narcotics (mainly morphine), a woman giving birth in Twilight Sleep became less inhibited, which helped her relax

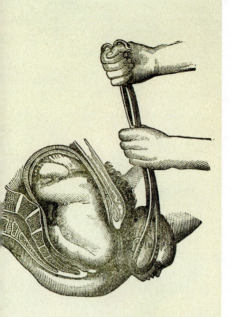

19th-century illustration of use of forceps

forceps

pair of tongs used to extract the baby's head from the womb during delivery

In the mid-20th century birth in developed countries often took place in a condition of "Twilight Sleep," in which the mother was heavily medicated. Shown here is a 1946 photo of a new mother under sedation after giving birth in a London hospital.

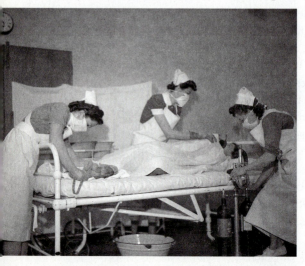

during her contractions and promoted dilation of her cervix, making the use of forceps less likely. Women still felt pain—in fact, screaming and thrashing were so common in Twilight Sleep that women were often strapped in helmets and handcuffed to the birth bed—but afterward they remembered none of it, so as far as they were concerned, the birth had been painless and problem free. From the 1930s through the 1960s use of Twilight Sleep and other drug methods was standard practice in hospitals in Western countries, and women nearly always gave birth while heavily medicated (Cassidy, 2006). If you live in a Western country, ask your grandmother about it.

During the late 1960s a backlash began to develop against the medicalization of birth (Lyon, 2009). Critics claimed that medical procedures such as forceps, episiotomies, and drugs were unnecessary and had been created by the medical profession mainly to make childbirth more profitable. These critics advocated **natural childbirth** as an alternative. Although this term was first proposed in the 1930s, it was only in the 1960s and the decades that followed that a variety of drug- and technology-free approaches to birth became popular, as part of more general trends toward greater rights for women, a greater push for consumer rights, and a growing interest in natural health practices (Thompson, 2005). Natural childbirth methods vary in their details, but all reject medical technologies and interventions as unhelpful to the birth process or even harmful. The premise is that a substantial amount of the pain women experience in childbirth is based on the anxiety created by fear of medical technologies and lack of understanding of the birth process. Consequently, natural childbirth includes classes in which the parents-to-be learn about the birth process. The remainder of the pain experienced in childbirth can be managed by relaxation and breathing techniques. Another important component of natural childbirth approaches is for the expectant mother to have the physical and emotional support of her husband or partner or others who could assist with the relaxation and breathing techniques.

No differences have been found in maternal and neonatal health outcomes between natural childbirth and medical methods, as long as the birth takes place in a health facility where medical intervention is available if necessary (Bergstrom et al., 2009). Most participants in natural childbirth methods report that it lowered their anxiety about the birth and made them feel that they were more knowledgeable about and more in control of the birth process (Westfall & Benoit, 2004). Natural childbirth methods remain popular today, especially in northern Europe (Ravn, 2005).

Although natural childbirth can enhance the birth experience for mothers, some studies have shown much higher rates of poor or fatal outcomes for women who have a "home birth." One large study of 13 million births in the United States found that the neonatal mortality rate (first four weeks) for babies born at home was 10 times higher than for babies born in a hospital setting (Grünebaum et al., 2014). Another analysis with the same sample concluded that babies born at home were 10 times as likely to have difficulty breathing shortly after birth, making them vulnerable to permanent brain damage (Grünebaum et al., 2013). As we have seen, babies' big heads in relation to the size of their mothers' pelvis makes birth in humans more perilous than it is in other species, so medical interventions can be necessary and may be life-saving. Home births are not recommended for women with high-risk pregnancies or pre-existing medical conditions, and women are advised to have a plan for transfer to a medical facility, should complications arise. In African and south Asia, only about half of births take place in a health facility, and this is one reason for the high rates of neonatal mortality in these regions (UNICEF, 2014). Worldwide, rates of neonatal mortality have declined steeply in recent decades, as more regions gain access to modern medical technologies.

In developed countries today, the birth process is better than it has ever been before, for both mothers and babies. The natural childbirth movement has had many positive

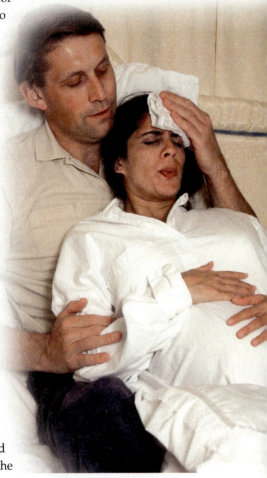

In natural childbirth, husbands or partners often assist with breathing techniques designed to manage the pain.

natural childbirth
approach to childbirth that avoids medical technologies and interventions

effects on how birth is assisted in mainstream medicine. Although most births in developed countries still take place in a hospital, birth has become less like an operation performed by a physician and more of a collaboration between doctors, nurses (often including nurse-midwives), and mothers. Some parents also choose to enlist the help of a doula, an experienced mentor and coach who provides physical, emotional, and informational support to the mother (Chen & Xu, 2013).

Fathers, partners, and other family members and friends are now often involved, too. Prior to the 1960s fathers were totally excluded from the birth, but by the late 1970s the majority of fathers in developed countries were present when their wives gave birth (Simkin, 2007). In general, the father's presence seems to benefit the mother during birth (Kainz et al., 2010). When fathers are present, mothers experience slightly shorter labor and express greater satisfaction with the birth experience (Hodnett et al., 2007). For fathers, being present at the birth evokes intense feelings of wonder and love (Erlandsson & Lindgren, 2009). However, some fathers also experience intense fears for the health and well-being of the mother and baby (Eriksson et al., 2007).

CRITICAL THINKING QUESTION

If you were pregnant or the partner of a pregnant woman, how "natural" would you want the childbirth to be, and why?

Cultural Variations in Birth Beliefs and Practices

LO 3.4 **Describe cultural variations in birth beliefs and identify who may assist with the birth.**

Cultural beliefs about birth are sometimes designed to protect mother and baby, and sometimes designed to isolate them and protect others. In most cultures, older women take the lead in assisting the birth, especially those designated as midwives.

BELIEFS AND RITUALS SURROUNDING BIRTH As noted at the outset of the chapter, across cultures a successful birth is marked with a joyful celebration (Newton & Newton, 2003). For example, among the Ila people of Zimbabwe, women attending the birth will shower praise upon the woman having the baby. After the birth, her husband comes in to congratulate her, and other male relations also enter the hut to clasp her hand and provide her with gifts.

However, there are also cultural practices that frame birth and its aftermath with some degree of fear and wariness. Perhaps because birth is often dangerous, many traditional cultures have developed beliefs that giving birth puts a woman in a state of being spiritually unclean (Newton & Newton, 2003). In some cultures, birth must take place away from where most people reside, so that others will not be contaminated by it. For example, among the Arapesh of New Guinea, birth is allowed to take place only at the outskirts of the village, in a place reserved for other contaminating activities such as excretion and menstruation.

Many cultures have beliefs that the mother remains unclean long after the birth and must be kept away from others, for her own sake as well as theirs (Newton & Newton, 2003). In traditional Vietnam (but not today), the mother was to avoid going out for at least 30 days after birth, in order not to contaminate the rest of the village or endanger herself or her infant; even her husband could not enter her room but could only speak to her from outside the door. Some cultures have rituals for women to purify themselves after birth, and not just non-Western cultures. In the Bible, the twelfth chapter of the book of Leviticus is devoted to ritual purification of women after childbirth, and until recent decades the Catholic church had a special ritual for new mothers to purify themselves.

Why would such beliefs develop? A frequent motivation for the development of cultural beliefs appears to be the desire for control (Jones & Kay, 2003). Birth is often fraught with pain and peril. Humans, faced with this unpleasant prospect, develop beliefs they hope will enable them to avoid, or at least minimize, the pain and peril. It is a comfort to believe that if certain rituals are performed, the mother, the baby, and everyone else will make it through the process unscathed.

The placenta is a component of the birth process that has often carried its own special cultural beliefs. Perhaps because delivery of the placenta is potentially dangerous, many cultures have developed beliefs that the placenta itself is potentially dangerous and must be disposed of properly so that no unpleasant consequences will result (Jones & Kay, 2003). Failure to do so is believed to carry consequences as minor as pimples on the baby or as major as the baby's death.

In some cultures the methods for disposing of the placenta are clear and simple: burial, burning, or throwing it in a river, or keeping it in a special place reserved for placentas. For example, among the Navajo, a Native American culture, the custom was to bury the placenta in a sacred place to underscore the baby's bonds to the ancestral land (Selander, 2011). In other cultures, the traditions surrounding the placenta are more elaborate and involve beliefs that the placenta has a spirit or soul of its own. In these cultures, the placenta is not simply thrown away but given a proper burial similar to that given to a person. For example, in several parts of the world, including Ghana, Malaysia, and Indonesia, the placenta is treated as the baby's semihuman sibling (Cassidy, 2006). Following delivery, the midwife washes the placenta and buries it as she would a stillborn infant. In some cultures the burial includes prayers to the placenta imploring it not to harm the newborn child or the mother.

In developed countries the placenta is recognized as having special value as a source of hormones and nutrients. Hospitals give their placentas to researchers, or to cosmetic manufacturers who use them to make products such as hair conditioner (Jones & Kay, 2003). Some people in Western countries even advocate consuming part of the placenta, on top of "placenta pizza" or blended into a "placenta cocktail" (Weekley, 2007)! Maybe this explains why the word "placenta" is derived from the Latin word for "cake"?

Well, probably not. More likely, this (rare) practice is inspired by the fact that many other mammalian mothers, from mice to monkeys, eat the placenta. The placenta is full of nutrients that can provide a boost to an exhausted new mother about to begin nursing. It also contains the hormone oxytocin, which helps prevent postpartum hemorrhage. Few human cultures have been found to have a custom of eating the placenta, although in some parts of the Philippines midwives add placental blood to a porridge intended to strengthen the new mother (Cassidy, 2006). Also, in traditional Chinese medicine dried placenta is sometimes used to stimulate maternal milk production (Tierra & Tierra, 1998).

WHO HELPS? Although there is great cultural variation in beliefs about birth, there is relatively little variation among traditional cultures in who assists with the birth. Almost always, the main assistants are older women (Bel & Bel, 2007). In one early study of birth practices in 60 traditional cultures, elderly women assisted in 58 of them (Ford, 1945). Rarely, men have been found to be the main birth attendants, such as in some parts of Mexico and the Philippines. More typically, all men are forbidden from even being present during birth, much less serving as the central helper (Newton & Newton, 2003). However, sometimes fathers assist by holding up the mother as she leans, stands, or squats to deliver the baby.

Although a variety of women are typically present with the mother at birth, especially her relatives, the women who are charged with managing the birth process usually have a special status as midwives. Midwives tend to be older women who have had children themselves but are now beyond childbearing age. They have direct experience with childbirth but no longer have young children to care for, so that they are available and able when called to duty.

There are a variety of ways a woman may become a midwife (Cosminsky, 2003). In some cultures, such as in Guatemala and the Ojibwa tribe of Native Americans, she receives what she believes to be a supernatural calling in a dream or vision. In other cultures, the position of midwife is inherited from mother to daughter. Still other cultures allow women to volunteer to be midwives. Regardless of how she comes to the position, typically the woman who is to be a midwife spends several years in apprenticeship to a more experienced midwife before taking the lead in assisting with a birth. Through apprenticeship she learns basic principles of hygiene, methods to ease the birth, and practices for prenatal and postnatal care.

Cultures have varied widely in how they regard midwives. Most often, the midwife has a respected status in her culture, and is held in high regard for her knowledge and skills. However, in some cultures midwives have been regarded with contempt or fear. In India, for example, midwives come from the *castes* (social status groups) that have the lowest status (Cosminsky, 2003). Birth is believed to be unclean and polluting, so only the lowest castes are deemed fit to be involved in it. As we've seen, in Western cultures, from the 15th through the 17th centuries, midwives were frequently accused of being witches and many of them were executed (Cassidy, 2006).

Today, in developed countries and increasingly in developing countries, birth usually takes place in a medical setting and is overseen by medical personnel, including an obstetrician and one or more nurses or nurse-midwives. In addition, the birth mother's husband or partner, mother, mother-in-law, or sisters may be present, but as sources of emotional support, not as assistants in the birth (daMotta et al., 2006).

Cultural Variations in Methods for Easing the Birth

LO 3.5   **Compare and contrast cultural practices and medical methods for easing the birth process.**

As described earlier in the chapter, scientifically-based medical assistance in the birth process is a recent development, historically, and is still not universally available. Consequently, cultures have devised many traditional methods of attempting to ease the birth process. The methods vary, but there are certain common themes. For example, the strategies begin long before birth. As noted in Chapter 2, often the role of midwife includes prenatal visits every few weeks beginning in about the fourth month of pregnancy. When visiting the prospective mother, the midwife typically gives her an abdominal massage. This is believed to make the birth easier, and it also allows the midwife to determine the position of the fetus. If the fetus is in the breech position, she may attempt to turn it.

In addition to massaging the pregnant woman's abdomen, the midwife often gives the mother herbal tea, intended to prevent miscarriage and promote healthy development of the fetus. She also gives the mother advice on diet and exercise. In many cultures in Asia and South America, foods are classified as "hot" or "cold" (a cultural definition, not on the basis of whether they are actually hot or cold), and the mother is forbidden from eating "hot" foods (Cosminsky, 2003). These food classifications have no scientific basis, but they may help to reassure the expectant mother and enhance her confidence going into the birth process.

When the woman begins to go into labor, the midwife is called, and the expectant mother's female relatives gather around her. Sometimes the midwife gives the mother-to-be medicine intended to ease the pain of labor and birth. Many cultures have used herbal medicines, but in the Ukraine,

Midwives are usually the main birth assistants in rural areas of developing countries. Here, a midwife attends to a pregnant woman in her Cambodian village home.

traditionally the first act of the midwife upon arriving at the home of a woman in labor was to give her a generous glass of whiskey (Newton & Newton, 2003). Expectant mothers may be fed special foods to strengthen them for the labor to come. In some cultures women are urged to lie quietly between contractions, but in others they are encouraged to walk around or even to exercise.

During the early part of labor, the midwife may use the intervals between contractions to explain to the expectant mother what is to come—how the contractions will occur more and more frequently, how the woman will eventually have to push the baby out, and what the woman's position should be during the birth (Bel & Bel, 2007). Sometimes the other women present add to the midwife's advice, describing or even demonstrating their own positioning when giving birth. As labor continues, often the midwife and other women present with the mother will urge her on during contractions with "birth talk," calling out encouragement and instructions, and sometimes even scolding her if she screams too loud or complains too much (Bergstrom et al., 2009, 2010).

The longer the labor, the more exhausted the mother and the greater the potential danger to mother and child. Consequently, cultures have created a wide variety of practices intended to speed it up. The most widespread approach, appearing in cultures in all parts of the world, is to use some kind of imagery or metaphor associated with opening up or expulsion (Bates & Turner, 2003). For example, in the Philippines a key (for "opening" the cervix) and a comb (for "untangling" the umbilical cord) are placed under the laboring woman's pillow. In other cultures, ropes are unknotted, bottles are uncorked, or animals are let out of their pens.

In some traditional cultures, the midwife calls on spiritual assistance from a *shaman*, a religious leader believed to have special powers and knowledge of the spirit world. Among the Cuna Indians, for example, according to traditional beliefs, difficult births are caused by the spirit of the womb, Muu, who may, for no apparent reason, decide to hold on to the fetus and prevent it from coming out (Levi-Strauss, 1967). The shaman's job is to invoke magic that will release the fetus from Muu's grip, by singing a song that sends a spirit inside the womb to wage combat against Muu.

Do any of these traditional practices do any good to the woman suffering a difficult labor? Medically, obviously not, but be careful before you dismiss the effects of the shaman's song too easily. There is abundant evidence of the *placebo effect,* which means that sometimes if people believe something affects them, it does, just by virtue of the power of their belief. In the classic example, if people are given a sugar pill containing no medicine and told it is a pain reliever, many of them will report experiencing reduced pain (Balodis et al., 2011). It was not the sugar pill that reduced their pain but their belief that the pill would reduce their pain. In the case of the shaman assisting the birth, the mother may feel genuine relief, not only because of her belief in the shaman's song but because of the emotional and social support the shaman's presence represents (Bates & Turner, 2003).

Emotional and social support help ease the birth for women in developed countries as well (daMott et al., 2006). Here are some nonmedical strategies recommended by health professionals to ease the woman's discomfort during labor (Mayo Clinic Staff, 2011):

- Rock in a rocking chair.
- Breathe in a steady rhythm, fast or slow, depending on what is most comfortable.
- Take a warm shower or bath.
- Place a cool, damp cloth on the forehead.
- Take a walk, stopping to breathe through contractions.
- Have a massage between contractions.

Medical interventions are also common today in developed countries. Women in labor often receive an **epidural**, which involves the injection of an anesthetic drug into the spinal fluid to help them manage the pain while remaining alert (Vallejo et al., 2007). If administered in the correct dosage, an epidural allows enough feeling to remain so

epidural

during birth process, injection of an anesthetic drug into the spinal fluid to help the mother manage the pain while also remaining alert that the woman can push when the time comes, but sometimes synthetic oxytocin has to be administered because the epidural causes contractions to become sluggish. Rates of receiving epidurals for women having a vaginal birth vary widely in developed countries, for example 76% in the United States, 52% in Sweden, 45% in Canada, and 24% in New Zealand (Lane, 2009). The reasons for these variations are not clear.

Several technological developments have made the birth process safer for both mother and baby. The "vacuum," a cup attached to the head of the fetus and linked to an extracting machine that uses vacuum power to pull firmly but steadily, serves the same function as forceps but with less likelihood of damage to either mother or baby (WHO, 2011). **Electronic fetal monitoring (EFM)** tracks the fetus's heartbeat, either externally through the mother's abdomen or directly by running a wire through the cervix and placing a sensor on the fetus's scalp. In the United States, about 85% of births include EFM (Martin et al., 2005). Changes in the fetal heart rate may indicate distress and call for intervention. However, heart rate changes are not easy to interpret and do not necessarily indicate distress, so use of EFM may increase the rate of unnecessary c-sections (Thaker & Stroup, 2003). EFM is most useful in preterm or other high-risk deliveries, when fetal distress is most likely to occur.

An important part of the strategy for easing the birth in many cultures is the physical position of the mother. In nearly all cultures some kind of upright position is used, most commonly kneeling or sitting, followed in prevalence by squatting or standing (Newton & Newton, 2003). Often a woman will lean back on a hammock or bed between contractions, but take a more upright position as birth becomes imminent. Lying flat was the most prevalent delivery position in developed countries during the 20th century, but it is rarely used in traditional cultures, as it makes delivery more difficult by failing to make use of gravity. Today in developed countries many hospitals use a semisitting, half-reclining position (Eisenberg et al., 2011).

After birth, typically the baby is laid on the mother's abdomen until the placenta and umbilical cord are expelled from her uterus. Although there is often great joy and relief at the birth of the baby, the attention of the birth attendants and the mother is immediately directed toward delivering the placenta. A variety of strategies are used to promote the process, such as massage, medication, rituals involving opening or expelling, or attempts to make the woman sneeze or vomit (Cosminsky, 2003). Most common across cultures is the use of herbal medicines, administered as a tea or a douche (a liquid substance placed into the vagina). In developed countries, synthetic oxytocin may be used to promote contractions that will expel the placenta.

After the placenta is expelled, the umbilical cord is cut. Usually the cord is tied with thread, string, or plant fiber. In traditional cultures, some of the customs involved in cutting or treating the cord are unwittingly hazardous to the baby (Cosminsky, 2003). Tools used to cut the cord include bamboo, shell, broken glass, sickles, and razors, and they may not be clean, resulting in transmission of disease to the baby. Methods for treating the cut cord include, in one part of northern India, ash from burned cow dung mixed with dirt, which is now known to increase sharply the baby's risk of tetanus.

Cultural Variations in Neonatal and Maternal Mortality

electronic fetal monitoring (EFM)

method that tracks the fetus's heartbeat, either externally through the mother's abdomen or directly by running a wire through the cervix and placing a sensor on the fetus's scalp

LO 3.6 Describe the differences in maternal and neonatal mortality both within and between developed countries and developing countries.

As you can see from **Map 3.2**, rates of infant and maternal mortality are vastly higher in developing countries than in developed countries. In much of the world, birth remains fraught with risk. However, there are some hopeful signs. Maternal mortality has decreased substantially in developing countries over the past 30 years, due to improvements in nutrition and access to health care (Hogan et al., 2010; UNICEF, 2014).

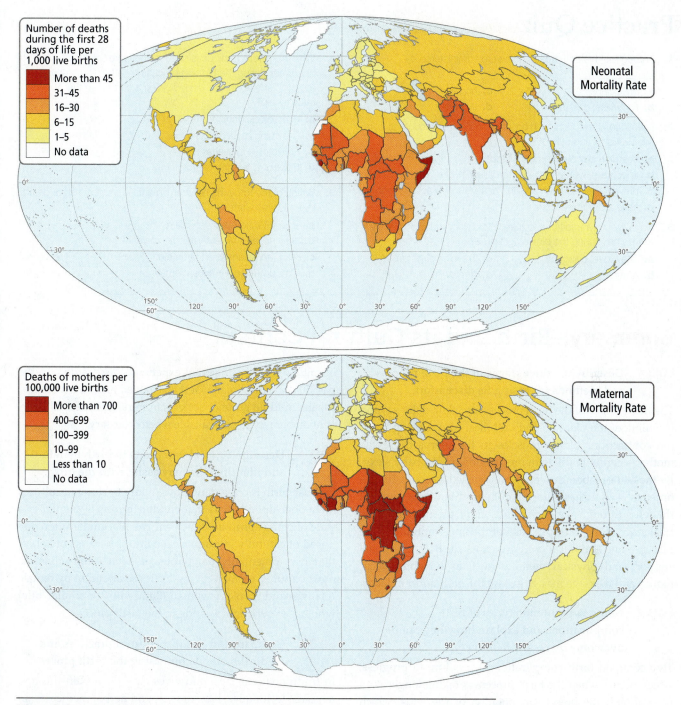

Map 3.2 Neonatal and Maternal Mortality Worldwide

How do neonatal and maternal mortality rates compare? What factors might explain why mortality rates are higher in developing countries than in developed countries?

SOURCE: (top) Based on UNICEF (2014); (bottom) Based on WHO (2014)

There is also substantial variation in neonatal and maternal mortality within developed countries, especially within the United States (UNICEF, 2014). Neonatal mortality is over twice as high for African Americans as for Whites, due primarily to greater poverty and lower access to high-quality medical care among African Americans (CDC, 2014). However, neonatal mortality has dropped steeply across ethnic groups in the United States since 1980, by nearly half. Current rates among Latinos and Asian Americans are similar to those for Whites (CDC, 2014). In contrast, maternal mortality has been rising steadily since 1980, for reasons that are not clear (U.S. Bureau of the Census, 2010). Like neonatal mortality, maternal mortality is much higher among African Americans than in other ethnic groups.

Practice Quiz ANSWERS AVAILABLE IN ANSWER KEY.

1. Throughout history, most births were administered by
   _____.
   a. physicians
   c. nurses
   b. midwives
   d. shamans

2. It was standard practice in hospitals in Western countries from the 1930s through the 1960s to _____.
   a. heavily medicate women in labor
   b. encourage women in labor to deliver at home
   c. prevent women from entering hospitals until active labor
   d. have a drug-free labor

3. Nona lives in a traditional culture. Which individual most likely assists her during the birthing process?
   a. The oldest daughter
   c. The biological father
   b. A nurse
   d. A midwife

4. What medical technique is used to measure the fetus' heartbeat during the birthing process by attaching a device on the mother's abdomen or by placing a sensor on the fetus' scalp?
   a. Forceps delivery
   b. Crowning monitoring
   c. Episiotomy deliveries
   d. Electronic fetal monitoring

5. Which of the following newborn infants is most at risk of death in the United States?
   a. Eric, a White American male.
   b. Jerome, an African-American male.
   c. Alan, an Asian-American male.
   d. Kim, an Asian-American female.

Summary: Birth and Its Cultural Context

LO 3.1 **Describe the three stages of the birth process and methods for easing its discomfort.**

The three stages of the birth process are labor, delivery, and expelling of the placenta and umbilical cord. During labor, the contractions of the muscles in the uterus cause the mother's cervix to dilate in preparation for the baby's exit. By the end of labor, the cervix has opened to about 10 centimeters (4 ½ inches). During delivery, the woman pushes the fetus through the cervix and out of the uterus. In the final stage of the birth process, contractions continue as the placenta and umbilical cord are expelled. Both emotional support and physical methods such as breathing techniques and massage may help ease the discomfort of labor.

LO 3.2 **Name two common types of birth complications and explain how they can be overcome by cesarean delivery.**

Two common birth complications are failure to progress, which occurs when the birth process is taking longer than normal, and the breech presentation of the fetus, which means the fetus is turned around so that the feet or buttocks are positioned to come first out of the birth canal. Both complications can be overcome through the use of a c-section, which today is generally safe for mothers and infants.

LO 3.3 **Summarize the history of birth in the West from the 15th century to today.**

Midwives have assisted in most births historically, but during the 15th century many were accused of being witches and were put to death. In the 18th and 19th centuries, birth became increasingly medical, but deadly infections were often spread to mothers by doctors with unclean hands. In the early 20th century the attempts to make birth safer were overzealous and overly medical, as birth was taken over by doctors and

hospitals, with the maternal experience disregarded. In the past 50 years most of the West has moved toward a more reasonable middle ground, seeking to minimize medical intervention but making it available when necessary.

LO 3.4 **Describe cultural variations in birth beliefs and identify who may assist with the birth.**

Because birth is often dangerous, many traditional cultures have developed beliefs that childbirth puts a woman in a state of being spiritually unclean. The placenta is often disposed of carefully in traditional cultures because of beliefs that it is potentially dangerous or even semihuman. In most cultures, women giving birth are attended by female relatives and an older woman ("midwife" or similar title) who has experience assisting in the birth process.

LO 3.5 **Compare and contrast cultural practices and medical methods for easing the birth process.**

In traditional cultures, midwives ease birth pain through massage techniques, reassurance, and herbal medicines. In developed countries, an anesthetic drug called an epidural is often injected into a woman's spinal fluid to help manage the pain.

LO 3.6 **Describe the differences in maternal and neonatal mortality both within and between developed countries and developing countries.**

In recent decades birth has become routinely safe and humane in developed countries, although there is considerable variation based on SES and ethnicity. Childbirth remains highly dangerous in developing countries where little medical intervention is available, although mortality rates are decreasing due to recent improvements in nutrition and access to health care.

Section 2 The Neonate

Learning Objectives

3.7 Identify the features of the two major scales most often used to assess neonatal health.

3.8 Identify the neonatal classifications for low birth weight and describe the consequences and major treatments.

3.9 Describe neonates' patterns of waking and sleeping, including how and why these patterns differ across cultures.

3.10 Describe the neonatal reflexes, including those that have a functional purpose and those that do not.

3.11 Describe the neonate's sensory abilities with respect to touch, taste and smell, hearing, and sight.

THE NEONATE: The Neonate's Health

Out comes baby at last, after 9 months or so inside the womb. If you were expecting cuddly and cute from the beginning, you may be in for a surprise. The baby may be covered with fine, fuzzy hair called lanugo, a vestige of our hairy primate ancestors. This hair will be shed after a few days, fortunately. The skin may also be coated all over with an oily, cheesy substance called *vernix*, which protected the skin from chapping while in the womb. When my twins were born I was amazed to see that they were covered with this white substance, which I had never known about until that moment.

The head may be a bit misshapen as a consequence of being squeezed through the birth canal. One evolutionary solution to the problem of getting large-brained human fetuses out of the womb is that the skull of the infant's head is not yet fused into one bone. Instead, it is composed of several loosely joined pieces that can move around as necessary during the birth process. In between the pieces are two soft spots called **fontanels**, one on top and one toward the back of the head. It will take about 18 months before the pieces of the skull are firmly joined and the fontanels have disappeared.

It was only 9 months ago that sperm and ovum united to make a single cell, but by birth the newborn baby has 10 trillion cells! The typical newborn child, or **neonate**, is about 20 inches (50 centimeters) long and weighs about 7.5 pounds (3.4 kilograms). (The first four weeks of life comprise the *neonatal period*.) Neonates tend to lose about 10% of their weight in their first few days, because they lose fluids and do not eat much (Verma et al., 2009). By the fifth day they start to regain this weight, and by the end of the second week most are back up to their birth weight.

About half of all neonates have a yellowish look to their skin and eyeballs in the first few days of life. This condition, known as **neonatal jaundice**, is due to the immaturity of the liver (Madlon-Kay, 2002). In most cases, neonatal jaundice disappears after a few days as the liver begins to function normally,

fontanels

soft spots on the skull between loosely joined pieces of the skull that shift during the birth process to assist passage through the birth canal

neonate

newborn baby, up to 4 weeks old

neonatal jaundice

yellowish pallor common in the first few days of life due to immaturity of the liver

At birth, babies are covered with vernix, which protects their skin.

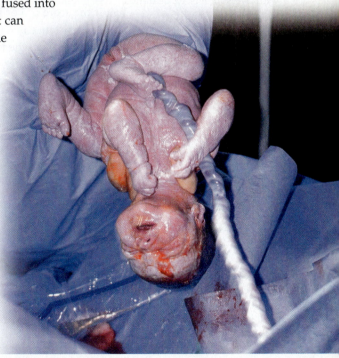

but if it lasts more than a few days it should be treated, or it can result in brain damage (American Academy of Pediatrics [AAP] Committee on Quality Improvement, 2002). The most effective treatment is a simple one, *phototherapy*, which involves exposing the neonate to colored light; blue works best (AAP, 2009).

Measuring Neonatal Health

LO 3.7   **Identify the features of the two major scales most often used to assess neonatal health.**

In the transition from the fetal environment to the outside world, the first few minutes are crucial. Especially important is for neonates to begin to breathe on their own, after months of obtaining their oxygen through their mothers' umbilical cord. Most neonates begin to breathe as soon as they are exposed to air, even before the umbilical cord is cut. However, if they do not, the consequences can become severe very quickly. Deprivation of oxygen, a condition known as **anoxia**, results in swift and massive death of brain cells. If a neonate suffers anoxia for even a few minutes, the result can be permanent cognitive damage.

Because the transition from the fetal environment is crucial and occasionally problematic, methods have been developed for assessing neonatal health. In Western countries, two of the most widely used methods are the Apgar scale and the Brazelton Neonatal Behavioral Assessment Scale (NBAS).

THE APGAR SCALE The **Apgar scale** is named after its creator, the pediatrician Virginia Apgar (1953). The letters *APGAR* also correspond to the five subtests that comprise the scale: Appearance (color), Pulse (heart rate), Grimace (reflex irritability), Activity (muscle tone), and Respiration (breathing). The neonate is rated on each of these five subscales, receiving a score of 0, 1, or 2 (see **Table 3.1**), with the overall score ranging from 0–10. Neonates are rated twice, first about a minute after birth and then after 5 minutes, because sometimes a neonate's condition can change quickly during this time, for better or worse.

A score of 7 to 10 means the neonate is in good to excellent condition. Scores in this range are received by over 98% of American babies (Martin et al., 2003). If the score is from 4 to 6, anoxia is likely and the neonate is in need of assistance to begin breathing. If the score is 3 or below, the neonate is in life-threatening danger and immediate medical assistance is required. In addition to their usefulness immediately after birth, Apgar scores predict the neonate's risk of death in the first month of life, which can alert physicians that careful monitoring is necessary (Casey et al., 2003).

anoxia

deprivation of oxygen during birth process and soon after that can result in serious neurological damage within minutes

Apgar scale

neonatal assessment scale with five subtests: Appearance (color), Pulse (heart rate), Grimace (reflex irritability), Activity (muscle tone), and Respiration (breathing)

Table 3.1 The Apgar Scale

Total Score: 7–10 = Good to excellent condition; 4–6 = Requires assistance to breathe; 3 or below = Life-threatening danger

Subtest	0	1	2
Appearance (Body color)	Blue and pale	Body pink, but extremities blue	Entire body pink
Pulse (Heart rate)	Absent	Slow—less than 100 beats per minute	Fast—100–140 beats per minute
Grimace (Reflex irritability)	No response	Grimace	Coughing, sneezing, and crying
Activity (Muscle tone)	Limp and flaccid	Weak, inactive, but some flexion of extremities	Strong, active motion
Respiration (Breathing)	No breathing for more than 1 minute	Irregular and slow	Good breathing with normal crying

SOURCE: Based on Apgar (1953).

THE BRAZELTON SCALE Another widely used scale of neonatal functioning is the **Brazelton Neonatal Behavioral Assessment Scale (NBAS)**. The NBAS contains 27 items assessing *reflexes* (such as blinking), *physical states* (such as irritability and excitability), *responses to social stimulation*, and *central nervous system instability* (indicated by symptoms such as tremors). Based on these 27 items, the neonate receives an overall rating of "worrisome," "normal," or "superior" (Nugent & Brazelton, 2000; Nugent et al., 2009).

In contrast to the Apgar scale, which is administered immediately after birth, the NBAS is usually performed about a day after birth but can be given any time in the first 2 months. The NBAS most effectively predicts future development if it is given a day after birth and then about a week later. Neonates who are rated normal or superior at both points or who show a "recovery curve" from worrisome to normal or superior have good prospects for development over the next several years, whereas neonates who are worrisome at both points or go down from normal or superior to worrisome are at risk for early developmental problems (Ohgi et al., 2003).

For at-risk neonates as well as others, the NBAS can promote the development of the relationship between parents and their infants. In one study of Brazilian mothers, those who took part in an NBAS-guided discussion of their infants a few days after birth were more likely to smile, vocalize, and establish eye contact with their infants a month later, compared to mothers in a control group who received only general health care information (Wendland-Carro et al., 1999). In an American study of full-term and preterm neonates, parents in both groups who participated in an NBAS program interacted more confidently with their babies than parents who did not take part in the program (Eiden & Reifman, 1996).

The NBAS has also been used in research to examine differences among neonates across cultures and how those differences interact with parenting practices (Nugent et al., 2009). For example, studies comparing Asian and White American neonates on the NBAS have found that the Asian neonates tend to be calmer and less irritable (Muret-Wagstaff & Moore, 1989). This difference may be partly biological, but it also appears to be related to parenting differences. Asian mothers tended to respond quickly to neonates' distress and attempt to soothe them, whereas White mothers were more likely to let the neonates fuss for awhile before tending to them. In another study, in Zambia, many of the neonates were born with low birth weights and were rated worrisome on the NBAS a day after birth (Brazelton et al., 1976). However, a week later most of the worrisome neonates had become normal or superior on the NBAS. The researchers attributed this change to the Zambian mothers' custom of carrying the baby close to their bodies during most of the day, providing soothing comfort as well as sensory stimulation.

Low Birth Weight

LO 3.8 Identify the neonatal classifications for low birth weight and describe the consequences and major treatments.

The weight of a baby at birth is one of the most important indicators of its prospects for survival and healthy development. Neonates are considered to have **low birth weight** if they are born weighing less than 5.5 pounds (2,500 grams). Some neonates with low birth weights are **preterm**, meaning that they were born 3 or more weeks earlier than the optimal 40 weeks after conception. Other low-birth-weight neonates are **small for date**, meaning that they weigh less than 90% of the average for other neonates who were born at the same *gestational age* (number of weeks since conception). Small-for-date neonates are especially at risk, with an infant death rate four times higher than preterm infants (Arcangeli et al., 2012).

Rates of low-birth-weight neonates vary widely among world regions (UNICEF, 2014). As **Map 3.3** on the next page shows, the overall rate worldwide is 15%. Asia and Africa have the highest rates, and Europe the lowest. The current rates in the United

Brazelton Neonatal Behavioral Assessment Scale (NBAS)

27-item scale of neonatal functioning with overall ratings "worrisome," "normal," and "superior"

low birth weight

term for neonates weighing less than 5.5 pounds (2,500 grams)

preterm

babies born at 37 weeks gestation or less

small for date

term applied to neonates who weigh less than 90% of other neonates who were born at the same gestational age

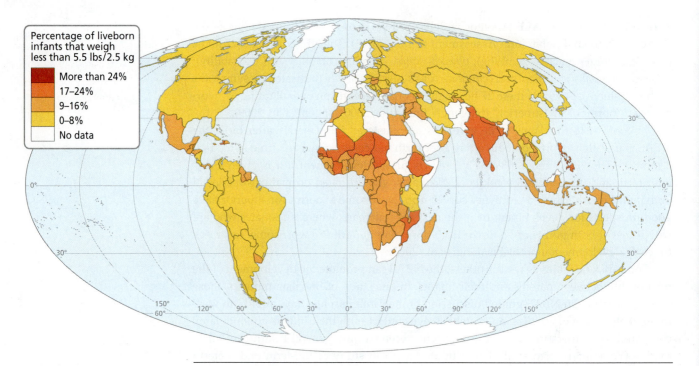

Map 3.3 Rates of Low Birth Weight Around the World

Why are rates so high in developing countries?
SOURCE: Based on UNICEF (2014).

States (8%) and Canada (6%) are lower than in developing regions of the world but higher than in Europe. Within the United States, rates of low birth weight are about twice as high among African Americans as among other ethnic groups, for reasons that may include lower likelihood of good prenatal care and higher levels of stress (Casey Foundation, 2010; Giscombe & Lovel, 2005).

The causes of low birth weight also vary widely among world regions. In developing countries, the main cause is that mothers are frequently malnourished, in poor health, and receive little or no prenatal care. In developed countries, the primary cause of low birth weight is the mother's cigarette smoking (Rückinger et al., 2010). Other contributors to low birth weight are multiple births (the more babies in the womb at once, the lower their birth weights), use of alcohol or other drugs during pregnancy, and young or old maternal age (under 17 or over 40) (Gavin et al., 2011).

CONSEQUENCES OF LOW BIRTH WEIGHT Low-birth-weight babies are at high risk of death in their first year of life. Even in developed countries with advanced medical care, low birth weight is the second most common cause of death in infancy, next to genetic birth defects (Martin et al., 2005). **Very low-birth-weight** neonates, who weigh less than 3.3 pounds (1,500 grams) at birth, and **extremely low-birth-weight** neonates, who weigh less than 2.2 pounds (1,000 grams) at birth, are at especially high risk for early death (Tamaru et al., 2011). Even in the United States, which has the most advanced medical technology in the world, 24% of neonates who weigh less than 3.3 pounds die during their first year, compared to just 1% of those born at 3.3 to 5.5 pounds (Child Trends, 2014). In developing countries, where low birth weight is most common, deaths due to low birth weight contribute to higher overall rates of neonatal mortality.

Why are low-birth-weight neonates at such high risk for death? If they were small for date at birth, it was likely due to factors that interfered with their prenatal development, such as poor maternal nutrition, maternal illness or disease, or exposure to teratogens such as nicotine or alcohol (see Chapter 2). Consequently, they were already less healthy than other neonates when they were born, compounding their risk.

very low birth weight

term for neonates who weigh less than 3.3 pounds (1,500 grams) at birth

extremely low birth weight

term for neonates who weigh less than 2.2 pounds (1,000 grams) at birth

In most cases, low-birth-weight neonates are born many weeks before full term. For preterm neonates, their physical systems are inadequately developed at birth. Their immune systems are immature, leaving them vulnerable to infection (Stoll et al., 2004). Their central nervous systems are also immature, making it difficult for them to perform basic functions such as sucking to obtain nourishment. Their little bodies do not have enough fat to insulate them, so they are at risk of dying from insufficient body heat. Most importantly, their lungs are immature, so they are in danger of dying from being unable to breathe properly. The lungs of a mature neonate are coated with a substance called **surfactant** that helps them breathe and keeps the air sacs in the lungs from collapsing, but preterm infants often have not yet developed surfactant, a deficiency with potentially fatal consequences (Porath et al., 2011). Where advanced medical care is available, mainly in developed countries, preterm neonates are often given surfactant at birth (via a breathing tube), making their survival much more likely (Mugford, 2006).

Babies born with low birth weights are at risk for multiple problems. Unlike this neonate in Uganda, most low-birth-weight neonates in developing countries do not have access to advanced medical care.

TREATMENT FOR LOW-BIRTH-WEIGHT BABIES What else can be done for low-birth-weight babies? In developing countries, where few of them receive medical treatment, traditional methods of infant care are helpful. In many traditional cultures, young infants are strapped close to their mother's body for most of the time as she goes about her daily life (Small, 1998). In the West, this has been studied as a method called **kangaroo care**, in which mothers or fathers are advised to place their preterm newborns skin-to-skin on their chests for 2–3 hours a day during the early weeks of life (Warnock et al., 2010).

Research has shown that kangaroo care has highly beneficial effects on neonatal functioning. It helps newborns stabilize and regulate bodily functions such as heart rate, breathing, body temperature, and sleep–wake cycles (Ludington-Hoe, 2013; Reid, 2004). Preterm infants who receive kangaroo care are more likely to survive their first year, and they have longer periods of sleep, cry less, and gain weight faster than other preterm infants (Charpak et al., 2005; Kostandy et al., 2008). Mothers benefit as well. Kangaroo care gives them more confidence in caring for their tiny, vulnerable baby, which leads to more success in breast-feeding (Feldman et al., 2003; Ludington-Hoe, 2013). The effects of kangaroo care on low-birth-weight babies are so well established that now it is used in over three-fourths of neonatal intensive care units in the United States, and nearly always with preterm neonates in northern Europe (Ludington-Hoe, 2013). An Italian study found that kangaroo care was practiced in two-thirds of the neonatal intensive care units (de Vonderweid & Leonessa, 2009).

The other traditional method of infant care that is helpful for low-birth-weight babies is *infant massage*. This is a widespread custom in Asia, India, and Africa, not just for vulnerable babies but for all of them (McClure, 2000). In the West, infant massage developed because low-birth-weight babies are often placed in an *isolette*, a covered, sterile chamber that provides oxygen and a controlled temperature. The isolette protects neonates from infection but also cuts them off from sensory and social stimulation. Infant massage, pioneered in the West by Tiffany Field and her colleagues (Field, 1998; Field et al., 2010), was intended to relieve the neonate's isolation.

Research has now established the effectiveness of massage in promoting the healthy development of low-birth-weight babies. Preterm neonates who receive three 15-minute massages a day in their first days of life gain weight faster than other preterm babies,

surfactant
substance in lungs that promotes breathing and keeps the air sacs in the lungs from collapsing

kangaroo care
recommended care for preterm and low-birth-weight neonates, in which mothers or fathers are advised to place the baby skin-to-skin on their chests for 2–3 hours a day for the early weeks of life

Kangaroo care has many benefits for low-birth-weight babies.

and they are more active and alert (Field, 2001; Field et al., 2010). The massages work by triggering the release of hormones that promote weight gain, muscle development, and neurological development (Dieter et al., 2003; Ferber et al., 2002; Field et al., 2010). In the United States, 38% of hospitals practice massage in their neonatal intensive care units (Field et al., 2010).

Although kangaroo care and massage can be helpful, low-birth-weight babies are at risk for a variety of problems throughout childhood, adolescence, and adulthood. In childhood, low birth weight predicts physical problems such as asthma and cognitive problems that include language delays and poor school performance (Davis, 2003; Marlow et al., 2005). In adolescence, low birth weight predicts relatively low intelligence-test scores and greater likelihood of repeating a grade (Martin et al., 2008). In adulthood, low birth weight predicts brain abnormalities, attention deficits, and low educational attainment (Fearon et al., 2004; Hofman et al., 2004; Strang-Karlsson et al., 2008).

The lower the birth weight, the worse the problems. Most neonates who weigh 3.3 to 5.5 pounds (1,500 to 2,500 grams) are likely to show no major impairments after a few years as long as they receive adequate nutrition and medical care, but neonates weighing less than 3.3 pounds, the very low-birth-weight and extremely low-birth-weight babies, are likely to have enduring problems in multiple respects (Child Trends, 2014; Davis, 2003). With an unusually healthy and enriched environment, some of the negative consequences of low birth weight can be avoided, even for very low-birth-weight babies (Doyle et al., 2004; Martin et al., 2008). However, in developed countries as well as in developing countries, low-birth-weight babies are most likely to be born to parents who have the fewest resources (UNICEF, 2014; WHO, 2011).

Practice Quiz   ANSWERS AVAILABLE IN ANSWER KEY.

1. What Apgar score indicates that the newborn is in good to excellent condition?

  a. 2   **c.** 10

  b. 5   **d.** 20

2. Approximately when is the Brazelton NBAS administered?

  a. A day after birth or any time in the first 2 months

  b. A day prior to birth

  c. At one year

  d. Between one and two years

3. When individuals who were born with low birth weight become adolescents, they are more likely to _____.

  a. be obese and have poor muscle tone

  b. have low IQ scores and repeat a grade

  c. suffer from clinical depression

  d. have delayed development of secondary sex characteristics

4. Marina and Paolo's preterm baby boy was born weighing only 5 pounds. To stabilize their baby's heart rate, breathing, body temperature, and sleep-wake cycles, Marina and Paolo have been placing the baby on their chests, skin-to-skin, for 2 to 3 hours a day. This well-known, scientifically proven method for stimulating neonatal functioning is called _____.

  a. massage care   **c.** koala care

  b. contact comfort   **d.** kangaroo care

5. Pre-term babies who get massaged three times a day for 15 minutes at a time in their first days of life _____ compared to those who do not.

  a. produce more surfactant

  b. are more coordinated later in life

  c. are less likely to develop jaundice

  d. gain more weight

THE NEONATE: Physical Functioning of the Neonate

Physical functioning in the first few weeks of life is different in some important ways when compared to the rest of life. Neonates sleep more and have a wider range of reflexes than the rest of us do. Their senses are mostly well developed at birth, although hearing and especially sight take some weeks to mature.

Neonatal Sleeping Patterns

LO 3.9 Describe neonates' patterns of waking and sleeping, including how and why these patterns differ across cultures.

As discussed in Chapter 2, even in the womb there are cycles of waking and sleeping, beginning at about 28 weeks gestation. Once born, most neonates spend more time asleep than awake. The average for neonates is 16 to 17 hours of sleep a day, although there is great variation, from about 10 hours to about 21 (Peirano et al., 2003).

Neonates not only sleep much of the time, the pattern and quality of their sleep is different than it will be later in infancy and beyond. Rather than sleeping 16–17 hours straight, they sleep for a few hours, wake up for awhile, sleep a few more hours, and wake up again. Their sleep–wake patterns are governed by when they get hungry, not whether it is light or dark outside (Davis et al., 2004). Of course, neonates' sleep–wake patterns do not fit very well with how most adults prefer to sleep, so parents are often sleep-deprived in the early weeks of their children's lives (Burnham et al., 2002). By about 4 months of age most infants have begun to sleep for longer periods, usually about 6 hours in a row at night, and their total sleep has declined to about 14 hours a day.

Another way that neonates' sleep is distinctive is that they spend an especially high proportion of their sleep in **rapid eye movement (REM) sleep**, so called because during this kind of sleep a person's eyes move back and forth rapidly under the eyelids. A person in REM sleep experiences other physiological changes as well, such as irregular heart rate and breathing and (in males) an erection. Adults spend about 20% of their sleep time in REM sleep, but neonates are in REM sleep about one half the time they are sleeping (Burnham et al., 2002). Furthermore, adults do not enter REM until about an hour after falling asleep, but neonates enter it almost immediately. By about 3 months of age, time spent in REM sleep has fallen to 40%, and infants no longer begin their sleep cycle with it.

In adults, REM sleep is the time when dreams take place. Are neonates dreaming during their extensive REM sleep periods? It is difficult to say, of course—they're not telling—but researchers in this area have generally concluded that the answer is no. Neonate's brain-wave patterns during REM sleep are different from the patterns of adults. For adults, REM brain waves look similar to waking brain waves, but for infants the REM brain waves are different than during either waking or non-REM sleep (Arditi-Babchuck et al., 2009). Researchers believe that for neonates, REM sleep stimulates brain development (McNamara & Sullivan, 2000). This seems to be supported by research showing that the percentage of REM sleep is even greater in fetuses than in neonates, and greater in preterm than in full-term neonates (Arditi-Babchuck et al., 2009; de Weerd & van den Bossche, 2003).

In addition to neonates' distinctive sleep patterns, they have a variety of other states of arousal that change frequently. When they are not sleeping, they may be alert but they may also be drowsy, dazed, fussing, or in a sleep–wake transition.

So far this description of neonates' sleep–wake patterns has been based on research in Western countries, but baby care is an area for which there is wide cultural variation that may influence sleep–wake patterns. In many traditional cultures, neonates and young infants are in physical contact with their mothers almost constantly, and this has important effects on the babies' states of arousal and sleep–wake patterns. For example, among the Kipsigis of Kenya, mothers strap their babies to their backs in the early months of life as they go about their daily work and social activities (Anders & Taylor, 1994; Super & Harkness, 2009). Swaddled cozily on Mom's back, the babies spend more time napping and dozing during the day than a baby in

rapid eye movement (REM) sleep

phase of the sleep cycle in which a person's eyes move back and forth rapidly under the eyelids; persons in REM sleep experience other physiological changes as well

Most neonates sleep 16–17 hours a day.

Table 3.2 Neonatal Reflexes

Reflex	Stimulation	Response	Disappears by...
Stepping	Hold baby under arms with feet touching floor	Makes stepping motions	2 months
Moro	Dip downward suddenly, or loud sound	Arch back, extend arms and legs outward, bring arms together swiftly	3 months
Babkin	Press and stroke both palms	Mouth opens, eyes close, head tilts forward	3 months
Sucking	Object or substance in mouth	Sucking	4 months
Rooting	Touch on cheek or mouth	Turn toward touch	4 months
Grasping	Object placed in palm	Hold tightly	4 months
Swimming	Baby is immersed in water	Holds breath, swims with arms and legs	4 months
Babinski	Stroke sole of foot	Foot twists in, toes fan out	8 months

a developed country would. At night, Kipsigis babies are not placed in a separate room but sleep right alongside their mothers, so they are able to feed whenever they wish. Consequently, for the first year of life they rarely sleep more than 3 hours straight, day or night. In contrast, by 8 months of age American babies typically sleep about 8 hours at night without waking.

Neonatal Reflexes

LO 3.10 Describe the neonatal reflexes, including those that have a functional purpose and those that do not.

Looking at a newborn baby, you might think that it will be many months before it can do much, other than just lie there. Actually, though, neonates have a remarkable range of **reflexes**, which are automatic responses to certain kinds of stimulation. A total of 27 reflexes are present at birth or shortly after (Futagi et al., 2009). Some examples are shown in **Table 3.2** and in the video *Reflexes*.

Watch REFLEXES

Sucking

reflex

automatic response to certain kinds of stimulation

rooting reflex

reflex that causes the neonate to turn its head and open its mouth when it is touched on the cheek or the side of the mouth; helps the neonate find the breast

Some reflexes have clear survival value. Sucking and swallowing reflexes allow the neonate to obtain nourishment from the mother's breast. The **rooting reflex** helps neonates find the breast, because it causes them to turn their heads and open their mouths when touched on the cheek or the side of the mouth. The grasping reflex helps neonates hang on when something is placed in their palms. The **Moro reflex** serves a similar function, causing neonates to arch their backs, fling out their arms, and then bring their arms quickly together in an embrace, in response to a sensation of falling backward or a loud sound. Reflexes for coughing, gagging, sneezing, blinking, and shivering regulate neonates' sensory systems and help them avoid things in the environment that may be unhealthy.

Some reflexes are precursors of voluntary movements that will develop later. The stepping reflex can be observed about a month after birth, by holding an infant under the arms at a height that allows its feet to just touch the floor. Stepping disappears after about two months, but will reappear as voluntary movement later in the first year when the infant starts walking. The swimming reflex is one of the most surprising and remarkable. At about 1 month old, an infant placed face down in water will automatically hold its breath and begin making coordinated swimming movements. After 4 months this reflex has disappeared, and will become voluntary swimming movements only many years later.

Other reflexes have no apparent purpose, other than their obvious entertainment value. With the *Babkin reflex*, a neonate whose palms are firmly stroked will open its mouth, close its eyes, and tilt its head forward. With the *Babinski reflex*, when the sole of the neonate's foot is stroked, it will respond by twisting its foot inward as it fans out its toes (Singerman & Lee, 2008).

Most neonatal reflexes fade away after a few months, as they are replaced by voluntary behavior. However, in the early weeks of life, reflexes serve as important indicators of normal development and healthy functioning (Schott & Rossor, 2003). Both the Apgar and the NBAS include items on reflex responses as an indirect measure of the neonate's neurological development.

The Moro reflex is present at birth, but disappears by 3 months of age.

Neonatal Senses

LO 3.11 Describe the neonate's sensory abilities with respect to touch, taste and smell, hearing, and sight.

The neonate's senses vary widely in how well developed they are at birth. Touch and taste are well developed, even in the womb, but sight does not mature until several months after birth. Let's look at each of the neonate's senses, from the most to the least developed.

TOUCH Touch is the earliest sense to develop. Even as early as 2 months gestation, the rooting reflex is present. By 7 months gestation, 2 months before a full-term birth, all the fetus's body parts respond to touch (Tyano et al., 2010). Most neonatal reflexes involve responses to touch.

Given that touch develops so early and is so advanced at birth, it is surprising that until recent decades, most physicians believed that neonates could not experience pain (Noia et al., 2008). In fact, surgery on neonates was usually performed without anesthetics. Physicians believed that even if neonates felt pain, they felt it only briefly, and they believed that the pain was less important than the danger of giving anesthetic medication to such a young child. This belief may have developed because neonates who experience pain (for example, boys who are circumcised) often either recover quickly and

Moro reflex

reflex in response to a sensation of falling backward or to a loud sound, in which the neonate arches its back, flings out its arms, and then brings its arms quickly together in an embrace

behave normally shortly afterward, or fall into a deep sleep immediately afterward, as a protective mechanism. Also, in response to some types of pain, such as being pricked on the heel, neonates take longer to respond (by several seconds) than they will a few months later (Tyano et al., 2010).

In recent years, research has established clearly that neonates feel pain. Their physiological reactions to pain are much like the reactions of people at other ages: their heart rates and blood pressure increase, their palms sweat, their muscles tense, and their pupils dilate (Warnock & Sandrin, 2004; Williams et al., 2009). They even have a specific kind of high-pitched, intense cry that indicates pain (Simons et al., 2003). Evidence also indicates that neonates who experience intense pain release stress hormones that interfere with sleep and feeding and heighten their sensitivity to later pain (Mitchell & Boss, 2002). For these reasons, physicians' organizations now recommend pain relief for neonates undergoing painful medical procedures (Noia et al., 2008). To minimize the dangers of anesthetics, nonmedical methods such as drinking sugar water can be used, or local rather than general anesthesia (Holsti & Grunau, 2010).

TASTE AND SMELL Like touch, taste is well developed even in the womb. The amniotic fluid that the fetus floats in has the flavor of whatever the mother has recently eaten, and neonates show a preference for the tastes and smells that were distinctive in the mother's diet in the days before birth (Schaal et al., 2000). In one study, when women drank carrot juice during pregnancy, their neonates were more likely to prefer the smell of carrots (Menella, 2000). Neonates exposed to the smell of their mother's amniotic fluid and another woman's amniotic fluid orient their attention to their mother's fluid (Marlier et al., 1998). In fact, neonates find the smell of their mother's amniotic fluid soothing, and cry less when it is present (Varendi et al., 1998).

In addition to showing an early preference for whatever is familiar from the womb, neonates have a variety of innate responses to tastes and smells. Like most children and adults, neonates prefer sweet tastes and smells over bitter or sour ones (Booth et al., 2010). If they smell or taste something bitter or sour, their noses crinkle up, their foreheads wrinkle, and their mouths show a displeased expression (Bartoshuk & Beauchamp, 1994). The video *Taste* shows neonates reacting to various tastes.

Watch   TASTE

Preference for sweet tastes is present before birth. When an artificial sweetener is added to amniotic fluid, fetuses' swallowing becomes more frequent (Booth et al., 2010). After birth, preference for sweet tastes is demonstrated with a facial expression that looks like pleasure, and with a desire to consume more. As just noted, tasting something sweet can have a calming effect on neonates who are in pain. Preference for sweet tastes may be adaptive, because breast milk is slightly sweet (Porges et al., 1993). Enjoying the sweet taste of breast milk may make neonates more likely to nurse successfully.

In addition to their innate preferences, neonates quickly begin to discriminate smells after birth. At 2 days after birth, breast-feeding neonates show no difference in response between their mother's breast smell and the breast smell of another lactating mother, but by 4 days they orient more toward their mother's smell (Porter & Reiser, 2005).

HEARING Hearing is another sense that is quite well developed before birth. As noted in Chapter 2, fetuses become familiar with their mother's voice and other sounds. After birth, they recognize distinctive sounds they heard in the womb.

Neonates have an innate sensitivity to human speech that is apparent from birth (Vouloumanos & Werker, 2004). Studies on this topic typically assess neonates' preferences by how vigorously they suck on a plastic nipple; the more frequently they suck, the stronger their preference for or attention to the sound. Using this method, studies have found that neonates prefer their mother's voice to other women's voices, and their mother's language to foreign languages (Vouloumanos et al., 2010). However, they show no preference for their father's voice over other male voices (Kisilevsky et al., 2003). This may be partly because they heard his voice less while in the womb, and partly because neonates generally prefer high-pitched voices over low-pitched voices.

Neonates can distinguish small changes in speech sounds. In one study, neonates were given a special nipple that would produce a sound of a person saying "ba" every time they sucked on it (Aldridge et al., 2001). They sucked with enthusiasm for a minute or so, then their sucking pace slowed as they got used to the sound and perhaps bored with it. But when the sound changed to "ga," their sucking pace picked up, showing that they recognized the subtle change in the sound and responded to the novelty of it. Changes in neonate's sucking patterns show they also recognize the difference between two-syllable and three-syllable words, and between changes in emphasis such as when ma-*ma* changes to *ma*-ma (Sansavini et al., 1997).

In addition to their language sensitivity, neonates show a very early sensitivity to music (Levitin, 2007). At only a few days old, they respond when a series of musical notes changes from ascending to descending order (Trehub, 2001). After a few months, infants respond to a change in one note of a six-note melody, and to changes in musical keys (Trehub et al., 1985). One study even found that neonates preferred classical music over rock music (Spence & DeCasper, 1987).

Like language awareness, musical awareness begins prenatally. Neonates prefer songs their mother's sang to them during pregnancy to songs their mother sang to them for the first time after birth (Kisilevsky et al., 2003). Neonates' musical responses may simply reflect their familiarity with sounds they heard before birth, but it could also indicate an innate human responsiveness to music (Levitin, 2007). Music is frequently a part of human cultural rituals, and innate responsiveness to music may have served to enhance cohesiveness within human cultural groups.

Although neonates hear quite well in many respects, there are also some limitations to their hearing abilities that will improve over the first 2 years of life (Tharpe & Ashmead, 2001). One reason for these limitations is that it takes awhile after birth for the amniotic fluid to drain out of their ears. Another reason is that their hearing system is not physiologically mature until they are about 2 years old.

Neonates are unable to hear some very soft sounds that adults can hear (Watkin, 2011). Overall, their hearing is better for high-pitched sounds than for midrange or

Neonates and infants prefer sweet tastes to sour ones.

low-pitched sounds (Aslin et al., 1998; Werner & Marean, 1996). They also have difficulty with **sound localization**, that is, with telling where a sound is coming from (Litovsky & Ashmead, 1997). In fact, their abilities for sound localization actually become worse for the first 2 months of life, but then improve rapidly and reach adult levels by 1 year old (Watkin, 2011).

SIGHT Sight is the least developed of the neonate's senses (Atkinson, 2000). Several key structures of the eye are still immature at birth, specifically, (1) the muscles of the *lens*, which adjust the eyes' focus depending on the distance from the object; (2) the cells of the *retina*, the membrane in the back of the eye that collects visual information and converts it into a form that can be sent to the brain; (3) *cones*, which identify colors, and (4) the *optic nerve*, which transmits visual information from the retina to the brain.

At birth, neonates' vision is estimated to range from 20/200 to 20/600, which means that the clarity and accuracy of their perception of an object 20 feet away is comparable to a person with normal 20/20 vision looking at the same object from 200 to 600 feet away (Cavallini et al., 2002). Their visual acuity is best at a distance of 8–14 inches. Vision improves steadily as their eyes mature, and reaches 20/20 sometime in the second half of the first year. Their capacity for *binocular vision*, combining information from both eyes for perceiving depth and motion, is also limited at birth but matures quickly, by about 3–4 months old (Atkinson, 2000). Color vision matures at about the same pace. Neonates can distinguish between red and white but not between white and other colors, probably because the cones are immature (Kellman & Arterberry, 2006). By 4 months old, infants are similar to adults in their perception of colors (Alexander & Hines, 2002; Dobson, 2000).

Just as with taste and hearing, neonates show innate visual preferences (Columbo & Mitchell, 2009). ("Preference" is measured by how long they look at one visual stimulus compared to another. The longer they look, the more they are presumed to prefer the stimulus.) Even shortly after birth they prefer patterns to random designs, curved over straight lines, three-dimensional rather than two-dimensional objects, and colored over gray patterns. Above all, they prefer human faces over any other pattern (Pascalis & Kelly, 2009). This indicates that they are born with cells that are specialized to detect and prefer certain kinds of visual patterns (Csibra et al., 2000).

CRITICAL THINKING QUESTION

sound localization

perceptual ability for telling where a sound is coming from

Given what you have learned here about neonate's sight preferences, how would you design a mobile for a newborn's room?

....

Practice Quiz   ANSWERS AVAILABLE IN ANSWER KEY.

1. Which of the following is TRUE regarding infants' sleep?
  a. Infants spend a greater proportion of time in REM than do adults.
  b. Infants in different cultures have very similar sleep patterns suggesting that the environment plays no role in the sleep wake cycle.
  c. The average newborn sleeps 16-17 hours per day.
  d. On average, male infants sleep longer than their female counterparts.

2. While being held by her grandmother, newborn baby, Juliette, starts to turn toward her grandmother's body and open her mouth. She is demonstrating the _____ reflex.
  a. Babinski
  b. Babkin
  c. Moro
  d. rooting

3. Which of the following is LEAST LIKELY to have survival value?
  a. The Moro reflex
  b. The swimming reflex
  c. The rooting reflex
  d. The Babkin reflex

4. What sense(s) is (are) the first to develop in neonates?
  a. sight
  b. hearing
  c. taste and smell
  d. touch

5. At birth, the least developed of a neonate's senses is _____.
  a. smell
  b. sight
  c. taste
  d. hearing

Summary: The Neonate

LO 3.7 Identify the features of the two major scales most often used to assess neonatal health.

Two of the most widely used methods of assessing neonatal health are the Apgar scale and the Brazelton Neonatal Behavioral Assessment Scale (NBAS). The Apgar scale, which is administered immediately after birth, assesses infants on five subtests with a total rating of 1–10. The NBAS, which is administered any time in the first 2 months, assigns infants an overall rating of "worrisome," "normal," or "superior."

LO 3.8 Identify the neonatal classifications for low birth weight and describe the consequences and major treatments.

Low-birth-weight neonates weigh less than 5.5 pounds and very low-birth-weight neonates weigh less than 3.3 pounds; extremely low-birth-weight babies weigh less than 2.2 pounds. Low birth weight is related to a variety of physical, cognitive, and behavioral problems, not just in infancy but throughout life. Close physical contact and infant massage can help ameliorate the problems.

LO 3.9 Describe neonates' patterns of waking and sleeping, including how and why these patterns differ across cultures.

Neonates sleep an average of 16 to 17 hours a day (in segments of a few hours each), about 50% of it in REM sleep.

By 4 months old the typical infant sleeps for 14 of every 24 hours, including about 6 hours straight at night, and the proportion of REM sleep declines to 40%. These patterns may vary across cultures due to differences in parenting practices such as how much time mothers spend holding their babies.

LO 3.10 Describe the neonatal reflexes, including those that have a functional purpose and those that do not.

There are 27 reflexes present at birth or shortly after, including some related to early survival (such as sucking and rooting) and others that have no apparent function (such as the *Babkin* and *Babinski* reflexes).

LO 3.11 Describe the neonate's sensory abilities with respect to touch, taste and smell, hearing, and sight.

Touch and taste develop prenatally to a large extent, and neonates' abilities are similar to adults'. Neonates quickly begin to discriminate smells after birth, showing a preference for the smell of their mother's breast. Hearing is also quite mature at birth, although neonates hear high-pitched sounds better than other sounds and their ability to localize sound does not mature until about one year old. Sight is the least developed of the senses at birth, due to the physiological immaturity of the visual system, but it reaches maturity by the end of the first year.

Section 3   Caring for the Neonate

∨   Learning Objectives

3.12 Describe the cultural customs surrounding breast-feeding across cultures and history.

3.13 Identify the advantages of breast-feeding and where those advantages are largest.

3.14 Describe neonates' types of crying and how crying patterns and soothing methods vary across cultures.

3.15 Describe the extent to which human mothers "bond" with their neonates and the extent to which this claim has been exaggerated.

3.16 Describe the reasons for postpartum depression and its consequences for children.

CARING FOR THE NEONATE:
Nutrition: Is Breast Best?

One of the most heavily researched topics regarding neonates is the question of how they should be fed. Specifically, attention has focused on whether breast-feeding should be recommended for all children, and if so, for how long. Here we examine the evolutionary and historical basis of breast-feeding, the evidence for its benefits, and the efforts to promote breast-feeding in developing countries.

Historical and Cultural Perspectives on Breast-Feeding

LO 3.12 Describe the cultural customs surrounding breast-feeding across cultures and history.

Both mother and baby are biologically prepared for breast-feeding. In the mother, the preparation begins well before birth. Early in pregnancy the **mammary glands** in her breasts expand greatly in size as milk-producing cells multiply and mature. By 4 months gestation the breasts are ready to produce milk. At birth, the mother's **let-down reflex** in her breasts causes milk to be released to the tip of her nipples whenever she hears the sound of her infant's cry, sees its open mouth, or even thinks about breast-feeding (Walshaw, 2010).

Our closest primate relatives, chimpanzees, breast-feed for about 4 years. In the human past, archaeological and historical evidence indicate that in most cultures infants were fed breast milk as their primary food for 2–3 years, followed by 2–3 more years of occasional nursing. There are also indications that breast feeding in the human past took place at frequent intervals. Among the !Kung San of Central Africa, a modern hunter-gatherer culture, infants feed about every 13 minutes, on average, during their first year of life (Sellen, 2001). In traditional cultures it is typical for infants to be bound to or close to their mothers almost constantly, day and night, allowing for frequent feeding. This has led anthropologists to conclude that this was probably the pattern for 99% of human history (Small, 1998).

mammary glands

in females, the glands that produce milk to nourish babies

let-down reflex

in females, a reflex that causes milk to be released to the tip of the nipples in response to the sound of an infant's cry, seeing its open mouth, or even thinking about breast-feeding

wet nursing

cultural practice, common in human history, of hiring a lactating woman other than the mother to feed the infant

Such frequent feeding is, of course, very demanding on the mother, and many cultures have developed ways of easing this responsibility. One common way has been substituting mothers' milk with milk from other species, especially cows or goats, two species that are domesticated in many cultures and so readily available. Another way is **wet nursing**, which means hiring a lactating woman other than the mother to feed the infant. Wet nursing is a widespread custom as old as recorded human history. European records indicate that by the 1700s in some countries a majority of women employed a wet nurse to breast-feed their babies (Fildes, 1995).

In the late 1800s, manufactured substitutes such as condensed milk and evaporated milk began to be developed and marketed in the West by large corporations such as Borden and Nestlé (Bryder, 2009). The corporations claimed that these milk substitutes were not only more convenient than breast milk but also cleaner and safer. Doctors were persuaded—thanks in part to generous payments from the corporations—and they in turn persuaded new mothers to use the milk substitutes. By the 1940s only 20–30% of babies in the United States were breast-fed, and the percentage stayed in this range until the 1970s (Small, 1998). By then, scientific evidence was accumulating that breast milk was far better than any substitute, and health organizations such as UNICEF and the World Health Organization (WHO) began to wage worldwide campaigns to promote breast-feeding.

In recent years, rates of breast-feeding have risen to over 70% in the United States and Canada due to government-sponsored campaigns touting the health benefits, and breast-feeding has become nearly universal in northern Europe (CDC, 2014; Ryan et al., 2006). In developed countries, the higher the mother's age, educational level, and socioeconomic status, the more likely she is to breast-feed her infant (Schulze & Carlisle, 2010). Within the United States, rates of breast-feeding are higher among Latinos (80%) and Whites (75%) than among African Americans (58%), but rates have risen across all ethnic groups in recent years (CDC, 2013, 2014). It should be noted that these rates are for *any duration* of breast-feeding; across ethnic groups, less than half the neonates who breast-feed initially are still breast-feeding at age 6 months. Worldwide only about half of all infants are breast-fed even for a short time (UNICEF, 2014).

Wet nursing has a long history in Europe. Here, a wet nurse is pictured with a baby in France in 1895.

Cultural Focus: Breast-Feeding Practices Across Cultures

For nearly all of human history, until recent decades, breast-feeding has been practiced in all cultures as the method of delivering nourishment in the early months of life. Neonates are ready for breast-feeding as soon as they are born. The sucking and rooting reflexes are at their strongest 30 minutes after birth (Bryder, 2009). As noted earlier in this chapter, within a few days neonates recognize their mother's smell and the sound of her voice, which helps orient them for feeding.

Breast-feeding not only provides nourishment, it soothes babies when they are distressed. Babies derive comfort from sucking on their mothers' breasts and from the closeness and warmth they experience during breast-feeding, even when they are not hungry. Watch this video to see how mothers and expectant mothers in three countries view breast-feeding.

Watch BREAST-FEEDING PRACTICES ACROSS CULTURES

Review Question:

Were you surprised to see that many of the women interviewed have similar reasons for breast-feeding (regardless of their culture)? What are some of the benefits of breast-feeding that they mentioned?

Benefits of Breast-Feeding

LO 3.13 **Identify the advantages of breast-feeding and where those advantages are largest.**

What benefits of breast-feeding have been demonstrated by scientific research in recent decades? The list is a long one, and includes:

Disease protection. Breast milk contains antibodies and other substances that strengthen the baby's immune system, and breast-feeding has been found to reduce the risk of a wide range of illnesses and diseases, such as diphtheria, pneumonia, ear infections, asthma, and diarrhea, among many others (American Academy of Pediatrics [AAP] Section on Breastfeeding, 2005; Godfrey et al., 2009).

Cognitive development. Breast-fed infants tend to score higher than bottle-fed infants on measures of cognitive functioning, perhaps because the nutrients in breast milk promote early brain development (Kramer et al., 2008). This finding holds up even after controlling for many other factors such as parents' intelligence and education (Feldman & Eidelman, 2003). The benefits are mainly for infants who are preterm or low birth weight and consequently are at risk for cognitive difficulties (Ip et al., 2007; Schulze & Carlisle, 2010).

Reduced obesity. Breast-feeding for at least 6 months reduces the likelihood of obesity in childhood (AAP Section on Breast-feeding, 2005; Shields et al., 2010). This is especially important in developed countries, where rates of obesity have risen dramatically in recent decades.

Better health in childhood and adulthood. In addition to protection from illnesses and disease early in life, breast-feeding promotes long-term health in a variety of ways, such as promoting bone density, enhancing vision, and improving cardiovascular functioning (Gibson et al., 2000; Owen et al., 2002).

Mothers also benefit from breast-feeding (Godfrey & Meyers, 2009). In the days following birth, breast-feeding triggers the release of the hormone oxytocin, which reduces bleeding in the uterus and causes the uterus to return to its original size. Nursing the neonate also helps mothers return to their pre-pregnancy weight, because it burns 500–1,000 calories per day. Nursing has long-term effects as well on mothers' health, strengthening their bones, and reducing their risk of ovarian and breast cancer even many years later (Ip et al., 2007). However, breast-feeding has no influence on the emotional development of the infant or the social relationship between infant and mother (Schulze & Carlisle, 2010).

How long should mothers breast-feed their infants? The World Health Organization (WHO) recommends breast-feeding for 2 years, with solid foods introduced to supplement breast milk at 6 months of age. Few women today breast-feed for the recommended time (see **Map 3.4**).

However, even breast-feeding for only a few days after birth provides important benefits for infants. The first milk the mother produces is **colostrum**, a thick, yellowish liquid that is extremely rich in protein and antibodies that strengthen the neonate's immune system (Napier & Meister, 2000). Colostrum is especially important for neonates to receive, but it lasts only a few days. Perhaps because of its odd appearance, colostrum is erroneously believed in many cultures to be bad for babies. For example, in India many mothers

colostrum

thick, yellowish liquid produced by mammalian mothers during the first days following birth, extremely rich in protein and antibodies that strengthen the baby's immune system

The benefits of breast-feeding are especially important in developing countries, where risks to early development are higher. Here, a mother from the Desia Kondh tribe in India nurses her baby.

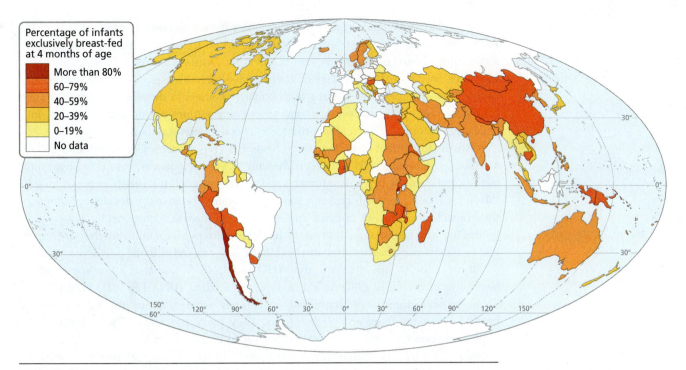

Map 3.4 Percentage of Infants Exclusively Breast-Fed at 4 Months of Age

avoid giving colostrum to their babies, substituting it with a mix of butter and honey they believe is healthier (Small, 1998).

Even in developed countries, where good health care is widely available, breast-feeding provides advantages for infants and mothers. However, in developed countries the advantages of breast-feeding are relatively small (Colen & Ramey, 2014), as we will see in the *Research Focus: Breast-Feeding Benefits: Separating Correlation and Causation* feature on the next page. In contrast, breast-feeding is crucial in developing countries, where risks of many diseases are higher and infants may not receive the vaccinations that are routine in developed countries. In developed countries, breast-feeding helps infants avoid illnesses such as gastrointestinal infections, but in developing countries breast-feeding can be literally a matter of life and death. UNICEF estimates that 1.5 million babies die each year in developing countries because they are bottle-fed rather than breast-fed (UNICEF, 2011). This is not only due to losing the advantages of breast-feeding but to making infant formula with unsafe water, as we will soon see in more detail.

If breast-feeding is so important to infants' health, why don't more mothers nurse in the early months of their children's lives? Some women have difficulty with breast-feeding, either because their infant cannot latch on properly (often a problem with low-birth-weight babies) or because they produce insufficient breast milk (Bryder, 2009). However, there are a number of practical obstacles as well. In developed countries, many mothers are employed outside the home, which makes breast-feeding more difficult (but not impossible; some use a breast pump to make milk available in their absence). Breast-feeding also makes it more difficult for fathers to take part in feeding (except via the pumped breast milk) and more challenging for fathers and mothers to share the care of the baby more or less equally, as many couples in developed countries would prefer (Gennesoni & Tallandini, 2009; Wolf, 2007). One of my most cherished memories of early fatherhood is of the nights when I would get up to do the 3 a.m. feeding and it would be just me and the twins, the whole world silent and sleeping around us, including my exhausted wife. When fathers are able to feed the neonate it helps mothers recover from the physical strain of giving birth (Simkin, 2007).

In developing countries, sometimes mothers have infectious diseases such as HIV/AIDS, tuberculosis, or West Nile virus that could be transmitted through breast milk, so they are advised not to breast-feed (Centers for Disease Control & Prevention, 2002). However, only a small percentage of women have such diseases. A much larger contributor to low rates of breast-feeding is that many mothers in developing countries have been deceived, by the marketing campaigns of corporations selling infant formula, into believing the formula is actually better for infants than breast milk is.

This is false. Infant formula today is better than the condensed or evaporated milk of a century ago, because it is fortified with many of the components that make breast milk healthy, but even the best infant formula today is not as good for infants as breast milk is. Worse yet, infant formula is typically mixed with water, and in many developing countries the available water is not purified and may contain disease. Consequently, not only do infants fed with formula miss out on the health benefits of breast milk, but they are imperiled by the diseases that may be contained in the water mixed with the powdered formula.

In response to this situation, the WHO and UNICEF initiated a worldwide effort beginning in the early 1990s to promote breast-feeding (UNICEF, 2011; WHO, 2000). These organizations have attempted to educate women about the advantages of breast-feeding for them and their infants. They have also worked with hospitals to implement programs to get breast-feeding off to a good start in the first days of the neonate's life. In this "Baby-Friendly Hospital Initiative," hospital personnel educate mothers about breast-feeding prior to the birth, help them with the first feeding shortly after birth, show them how to maintain lactation (milk flow), and organize them into breast-feeding support groups (Merewood et al., 2005; Merten et al., 2005).

The WHO/UNICEF initiative has been successful, with rates of breast-feeding increasing wherever it has been implemented (UNICEF, 2011). However, because most births in developing countries today take place in homes, most mothers are unlikely to come into contact with the Baby-Friendly Hospital Initiative. With only half of infants worldwide breast-fed for even a short time, clearly there remains much room for improvement.

CRITICAL THINKING QUESTION

Given that the benefits of breast-feeding in developed countries are genuine but small, should public policies encourage or discourage more women to breast-feed for longer? Consider the arguments that breast-feeding makes returning to the workplace difficult for women and makes it hard for mothers and fathers to share the infant care equally.

Research Focus: Breast-Feeding Benefits: Separating Correlation and Causation

Numerous studies have found benefits of breast-feeding for children and mothers alike across a wide range of areas. In developing countries, breast-feeding is crucial to infant health, because these populations receive little in the way of vaccines and other medical care to protect them from widespread diseases. But what about in developed countries? How much difference does breast-feeding make to the long-term development of children?

In the most comprehensive summary analysis (also known as a meta-analysis) of breast-feeding studies yet conducted, Stanley Ip and colleagues (2007) screened over 9,000 studies and selected nearly 500 that met their criteria for valid research methods and design. The conclusions of their analysis of the results of the 500 studies generally support the conclusions

stated in this chapter, that breast-feeding is associated with a wide variety of benefits for infants and mothers.

However, the authors also warned that readers should not infer causality. Why not? Because most studies of breast-feeding benefits find a correlation between breast-feeding and benefits, but correlation does not imply causation.

One reason to be skeptical of causation claims in studies of breast-feeding is that breast-feeding status is based on self-selection, meaning that women choose to breast-feed (or not), and those who choose to breast-feed tend to be different in many ways than women who do not.

Most notably, the authors observed, women who breast-feed generally have more education and higher IQs.

Consequently, the differences between the two groups that are attributed to breast-feeding may actually be due to their differences in education and IQ.

Education also tends to be connected to a lot of other aspects of mothers' lives, such as attention to prenatal care, access to health care resources, likelihood of having a stable partner, likelihood of smoking, and household income, among others. The correlation between breast-feeding and babies' development could be explained by any combination of these differences.

So what can be done to find out accurately how much difference breast-feeding makes in babies' and mothers' outcomes? Ethical standards would prohibit assigning new mothers into breast-feeding and non-breast-feeding groups. However, one study that was conducted by Canadian researcher Michael Kramer and his colleagues in Belarus in Eastern Europe approximated this design. The researchers gained the cooperation of thirty-one maternity hospitals and clinics and the study involved over 17,000 women who—note carefully—stated their intention to breast-feed.

Kramer and colleagues randomly assigned the women into two groups, with one group receiving an intervention designed to promote and support breast-feeding by providing women with advice, information, and instruction, whereas the women in the control group received no intervention.

The women and their babies were then followed up by Kramer and colleagues for the next seven years (so far). Over the course of the first year, women in the intervention group were more likely to exclusively breast-feed and babies in this group were less likely to have gastrointestinal infections. At age 6, the children in the intervention group had significantly higher IQs, by 6 points. This is especially notable because most studies on the cognitive effects of breast-feeding find that no effects remain after controlling for education and other confounding variables, unless the children were born preterm or low birth weight. The result found by Kramer and colleagues seems to indicate a small but clear positive effect of breast-feeding on children's cognitive development. Crucially, it shows causation rather than merely causation, because moms and babies were randomly assigned to the two groups, and thus it can be assumed that they were more or less similar in all ways except their group assignment.

Review Questions:

1. Which of the following is NOT one of the characteristics that have been found to distinguish moms who breast-feed from moms who do not, according to research studies summarized by Stanley Ip?
   a. Higher IQs
   b. More physically active during pregnancy
   c. More likely to have a stable partner
   d. More likely to receive prenatal care

2. What was the main finding of the Kramer study that separated moms into an intervention group provided with breast-feeding advice and instruction and a control group who did not receive the intervention, when the children were age 6?
   a. Children in the intervention group had more frequent illnesses.
   b. Children in the intervention group had closer attachments to their moms.
   c. Children in the intervention group had IQs that averaged 6 points higher.
   d. Children in the intervention group had IQs that averaged 16 points higher.

Watch   RESEARCH FOCUS: BREAST-FEEDING BENEFITS: SEPARATING CORRELATION AND CAUSATION

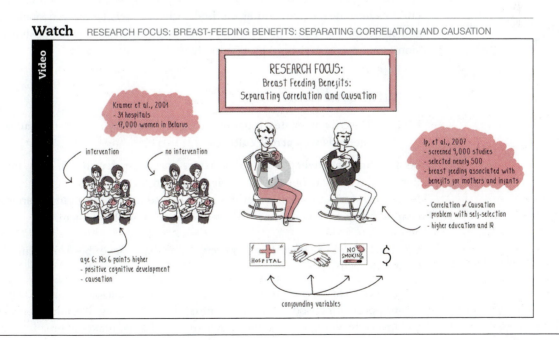

Practice Quiz

1. Your great, great grandmother who had her babies in the late 1800s was probably told by her physician to give her infants _____.
   a. goat's milk or cow's milk
   b. a multivitamin
   c. condensed or evaporated milk
   d. only breast milk

2. In the United States, breast feeding _____.
   a. is more common among women from low socioeconomic status groups because it is less expensive than formula
   b. increased in popularity as formulas came on to the market because people worried about their safety
   c. rates have stayed about the same since the 1940s
   d. rates vary among people of different ethnic backgrounds

3. When would mothers in developing countries be advised not to breast feed?
   a. If they have an infectious disease, such as HIV/AIDS.
   b. If they are very poor.
   c. If their baby is born prematurely and is more likely to have trouble latching on.
   d. If they have small breasts.

4. Which of the following is linked to a reduced likelihood of obesity in childhood?
   a. Introducing solid foods as early as possible
   b. Introducing skim milk by 1 year
   c. Supplementing breast milk with formula in the first six months
   d. Breast feeding for six months

5. How long does the World Health Organization (WHO) recommend that women breast feed?
   a. 6 months
   b. 1 year
   c. 2 years
   d. The recommendation differs depending upon where the woman lives.

CARING FOR THE NEONATE: Social and Emotional Aspects of Neonatal Care

There are few events that change the life of an adult more than having a baby! My wife and I had our twins relatively late—I was 42 and she was 33—and by then we had been together as a couple for over ten years. We were used to late and long dinners, and to lazy weekends waking up late, reading for hours, and taking long walks. All that went out the window when the twins were born. In the early weeks it seemed like all we did all day long—and half the night—was feed them, change them, dress them, walk them, and adore them.

Neonates not only need protection and nutrition, they need social and emotional care as well. Here we look at neonates' crying patterns and the soothing methods that cultures have developed, and at the first social contacts between neonates and others, sometimes called "bonding." In closing the chapter we examine the postpartum depression sometimes experienced by new mothers.

Crying and Soothing

LO 3.14 Describe neonates' types of crying and how crying patterns and soothing methods vary across cultures.

Because human newborns are so immature and dependent in the early months of life, they need some way of signaling their needs to those who care for them, and their most frequent and effective signal is crying. Adults tend to find the crying of an infant hard to bear, so they have developed many creative ways of soothing them.

CRYING Three distinct kinds of crying signals have been identified (Wood & Gustafson, 2001):

Fussing: This is a kind of warm-up cry, when babies are mildly distressed. If no response comes soon, it develops into full-blown crying. It is fairly soft in volume, an unsteady whimper punctuated by pauses and long intakes of breath.

Anger cry: A cry that expels a large volume of air through the vocal cords.

Pain cry: Sudden onset, with no fussing to herald it. Baby takes a large intake of breath and holds it, then lets loose.

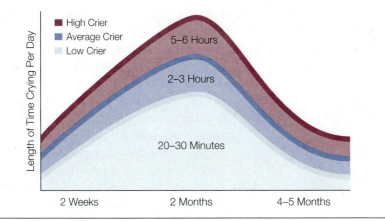
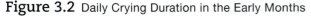

Figure 3.2 Daily Crying Duration in the Early Months

In their first months of life, infants often cry for no apparent reason.
SOURCE: Barr, 2009.

Most parents can tell the difference between an anger cry and a pain cry by the time the infant is about a month old (Zeskind et al., 1992). However, there are lots of other reasons an infant may cry, without a distinctive cry to go with them: hungry, lonely, wet or soiled diaper, tired, uncomfortable, too warm, too cold, or any other kind of frustration. Crying that falls into this general category is usually referred to as a *basic cry* or *frustration cry* (Wood & Gustafson, 2001).

Across a variety of cultures with different infant-care practices, crying frequency follows what is known as the "crying curve" (Barr, 2009): stable for the first 3 weeks of life, rising steadily and reaching a peak by the end of the second month, then declining. **Figure 3.2** shows the pattern for American infants. Sometimes crying has a clear source, but there is a lot of crying in the early months for no particular reason. This is important for parents to remember, because distress in neonates often triggers distress in those around them (Out et al., 2010). **Table 3.3** presents a way to remember the normal features of crying in the first 3 months of life.

SOOTHING AND RESPONDING TO CRIES Although daily crying in the early months of life is consistent across cultures, there is wide variation in the *duration* and *intensity* of crying in infancy. Crying episodes are longer and more intense in cultures where infants are left on their own a lot and have relatively little time when they are being carried around. Four out of five American infants have daily crying episodes in the early months of life of at least 15 minutes that do not have any apparent cause

Table 3.3 Period of PURPLE Crying in the Early Months

A crying baby is difficult for others to bear, especially when the crying is frequent and does not appear to take place for an evident reason. Here is a way to remind parents and others of the normal features of crying in the early months of life.

P	Peak pattern	Crying peaks around age 2 months and then declines
U	Unpredictable	Crying in the early months often comes and goes unpredictably, for no apparent reason
R	Resistant to soothing	Crying may continue despite parents' best soothing efforts
P	Pain-like face	Crying babies may look like they are in pain even though they are not
L	Long lasting	Babies cry for longer in the early months, sometimes 30–40 minutes or more
E	Evening crying	Babies usually cry most in the afternoon and evening

The word *Period* means that the crying has a beginning and an end.

SOURCE: Barr, 2009 [see http://www.purplecrying.info/sections/index.php?sct=1&]

Crying spells are longer and more intense in cultures where neonates are left alone for a substantial part of the day.

swaddling

practice of infant care that involves wrapping an infant tightly in cloths or blankets

Swaddling babies to reduce crying spells is a long tradition in many cultures. Here, a Navajo baby in Arizona is swaddled to a traditional backboard.

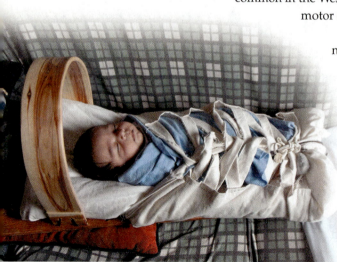

(Eisenberg et al., 2011). In contrast, infants in cultures where babies are held or carried around much of the day rarely have prolonged episodes of crying. For example, in a study comparing infants in South Korea and the United States, the American infants cried for much longer periods, and this appeared to be explained by differences in parenting (Small, 1998). Korean infants spent much less of their time alone than American infants did, Korean mothers carried their infants twice as long per day as the American mothers did, and Korean mothers responded immediately to their infants' cries whereas American mothers often let the infant cry it out.

The relation between parenting and infant crying has also been demonstrated experimentally. In one study, researchers divided American mothers and their newborns into two equal groups (Hunziker & Barr, 1986). The mothers in Group A were asked to carry their babies for at least 3 hours a day, and mothers in Group B were not given any special instructions. Infants' mothers in both groups kept diaries of when and how long their babies cried. When the infants were 8 weeks old, the frequency of crying was the same in both groups, but the duration of crying was only about half as long for Group A, the babies who were held more often, as it was for Group B.

In traditional cultures babies are typically held for most of the day, either by their mothers or by another adult woman or an older sister. When neonates in traditional cultures cry, two common responses are breast-feeding and swaddling (DeLoache & Gottlieb, 2000). Crying often signals hunger, so offering the breast soothes the baby, but even if babies are not hungry they can find consolation in suckling, in the same way that babies in developed countries are soothed by a pacifier.

In **swaddling**, babies are wrapped tightly in cloths so that their arms and legs cannot move. Often the baby is laid on a cradle board and the cloths are wrapped around the board as well as around the baby. Swaddling is an ancient practice, with evidence of it going back 6,000 years (DeMeo, 2006). Swaddling has long been widely used in many cultures, from China to Turkey to South America, in the belief that neonates find it soothing and that it helps them sleep and ensures that their limbs grow properly (van Sleuwen et al., 2007). It fell out of favor in Western cultures in the 17th century, when it became regarded as cruel and unnatural. However, swaddling has recently become more common in the West as studies have indicated that it reduces crying and does not inhibit motor development (Thach, 2009).

What else can parents and other caregivers do to soothe a crying neonate? First, of course, any apparent needs should be addressed, in case the baby is hungry, cold, tired, uncomfortable, injured, or needs a diaper change. For crying that has no apparent source, parents have devised a wide range of methods, such as (Eisenberg et al., 2011):

- Lifting baby up and holding to the shoulder
- Soothing repetitive movements such as rocking gently back and forth or riding in a car or stroller
- Soothing sounds such as singing, a fan or vacuum cleaner, or recordings of nature sounds like waves breaking on a beach
- A warm-water bath
- A pacifier or a finger to suck on
- Distraction, with some new sight or sound

The common theme of these methods appears to be offering a new source of sensory stimulation, especially something gently repetitive. When my twins were neonates we usually tried to soothe them by holding them to the shoulder or singing to them, but if those methods did not work their crying was almost always soothed by the gentle movements of the battery-operated infant seat we called their "wiggly chair." Parents with a crying neonate will often go to great lengths to make the crying stop, so there are many such items on the market today that promise to help parents achieve this goal. The video *Soothing Methods* shows some of the techniques used by parents and caregivers.

Watch SOOTHING METHODS

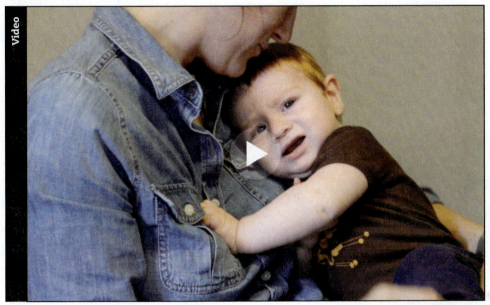

There is also the option of not responding to crying, until the infant stops. For decades, developmental psychologists have debated whether ignoring crying is a good or bad idea. Some argue that ignoring it is a good idea (unless of course the infant has a clear need for food or other care), because parents who respond will reinforce the infant's crying and thus make crying more likely the next time the infant wants attention (Crncec et al., 2010; Gewirtz, 1977; van Ijzendoorn & Hubbard, 2000). Others argue that ignoring it is a bad idea, because infants whose cries are ignored will cry even more in order to get the attention they need (Bell & Ainsworth, 1972; Lohaus et al., 2004). Different studies have reported different findings, so all that can be concluded at this point is that responses to crying do not appear to be strongly related to infants' development (Alvarez, 2004; Hiscock & Jordan, 2004; Lewis & Ramsay, 1999).

About 1 in 10 Western babies have crying patterns of extreme duration, a condition known as **colic**. Babies are considered to be colicky if they fit the "rule of threes" (Barr, 2009): the crying goes on for more than 3 hours a day over more than 3 days at a time for more than 3 weeks. Colic usually begins in the second or third week of life and reaches its peak at 6 weeks, thereafter declining until it disappears at about 3 months of age (Barr & Gunnar, 2000; St. James-Roberts et al., 2003).

The causes of colic are unknown, but it exists primarily in Western cultures, where infants receive relatively little carrying time (Richman et al., 2010). Remedies for colic are also unknown. Babies with colic are inconsolable. None of the soothing methods described above work with them. Fortunately, there appear to be no long-term effects of colic, in babies' physical, emotional, or social development (Barr, 2009; Eisenberg et al., 1996). However, this may be of little comfort to parents who must endure the persistent crying of an inconsolable infant for many weeks. Colic is a risk factor for parents'

colic
infant crying pattern in which the crying goes on for more than 3 hours a day over more than 3 days at a time for more than 3 weeks

maltreatment of their babies (Zeskind & Lester, 2001), so it is important for parents to seek help and support if they feel themselves reaching the breaking point.

Bonding: Myth and Truth

LO 3.15 Describe the extent to which human mothers "bond" with their neonates and the extent to which this claim has been exaggerated.

In some species, especially among birds such as geese, the first minutes after birth are a critical period for relations between mother and offspring. Geese form an instant and enduring bond to the first moving object they see, a phenomenon known as **imprinting**. Usually this first object is their mother, of course, and imprinting quickly to her promotes their survival because they will follow her everywhere she goes when they begin waddling around soon after birth. Konrad Lorenz (1957), who first identified the imprinting process, showed that geese would imprint to any moving object they saw soon after birth (including him—see photo).

Some physicians, learning of this research, applied it to humans and asserted that in humans, too, the first few minutes and hours after birth are critical to mother–infant **bonding** (Klaus & Kennell, 1976). Without contact with the mother shortly after birth, these physicians claimed, the baby's future development is jeopardized. However, when systematic research was done to test this hypothesis, it turned out not to be true (Lamb, 1994; Redshaw, 1997; Weinberg, 2004). Humans are not birds, and they are not at risk for later emotional and social problems if they do not bond with a caregiver in the first minutes, hours, or days after birth.

Nevertheless, this is a rare example of a false idea having good effects. As described earlier in the chapter, in developing countries the birth process had become overly medical by the 1950s and 1960s. Although bonding claims were false, the possibility that they were true led hospitals all over the world to reexamine their policies of sedating the mother and separating mother and child immediately after birth (Lamb, 1994). Subsequently, during the 1970s and after, hospital policies changed so that mother, child, and even father could all be in close contact after the birth. This may not be necessary for the baby's successful later development, but there is no reason not to allow it, and it does alleviate parents' anxieties and promotes feelings of warmth and confidence in caring for their newborn child (Bergstrom et al., 2009). More on the development of the parent-infant relationship will be presented in Chapters 4, 5, and 10.

Goslings will imprint to the first moving object they see, which is usually—but not always—the mother goose. Here, the biologist Konrad Lorenz leads three goslings on a swim.

imprinting
instant and enduring bond to the first moving object seen after birth; common in birds

bonding
concept that in humans the first few minutes and hours after birth are critical to mother–infant relationships

Postpartum Depression

LO 3.16 Describe the reasons for postpartum depression and its consequences for children.

Although the birth of a child is generally greeted with joy, some parents experience a difficult time emotionally in the early months of their baby's life. In one study of new mothers in 11 countries, **postpartum depression** was found at similar rates in all of them, about 10% (Oates et al., 2004). In Western countries this condition was often seen as an illness requiring possible intervention of health professionals, whereas in non-Western countries social support from family members was relied upon for making it through. Studies in the United States and the United Kingdom report that about 4% of fathers also experience postpartum depression in the months following the birth of their child (Dennis, 2004; Ramchandani et al., 2005).

Low emotional states in mothers following birth may be due to rapid hormonal changes, as the high concentrations of estrogen and progesterone in the mother's body return to normal levels. However, postpartum depression is deeper and more enduring. Feelings of sadness and anxiety become so intense that they interfere with the ability to carry out simple daily tasks. Other symptoms include extreme changes in appetite and difficulty sleeping. Postpartum depression often peaks about 4 weeks after childbirth—long after the mother's hormones would have returned to normal levels—and in 25–50% of mothers who experience postpartum depression it lasts 6 months or longer (Beck, 2002; Clay & Seehusen, 2004).

Why do some women and not others develop postpartum depression? Women are more at risk for postpartum depression if they have had previous episodes of major depression or if they have close family members who have experienced major depression (Bloch et al., 2006). This suggests that for postpartum depression, as for other forms of depression, some people may have a genetic vulnerability to becoming depressed when they experience intense life stresses. Women are also more likely to experience postpartum depression if they lack social support from a husband or partner (Iles et al., 2011). Thus even if a mother has a genetic vulnerability to depression, it is unlikely to be expressed unless she also experiences a social and cultural context in which social support is lacking. For fathers, postpartum depression may result from the challenges of reconciling their personal and work-related needs with the demands of being a father (Genesoni & Tallandini, 2009; Ramchandani et al., 2005).

Mothers' and fathers' postpartum depression is related to children's developmental problems in infancy and beyond. Numerous studies of mothers with postpartum depression have found that their infants are more likely than other infants to be irritable, to have problems eating and sleeping, and to have difficulty forming attachments (Herrera et al., 2004; Martins & Griffin, 2000). In later development, the children are at risk for being withdrawn or displaying antisocial behavior (Nylen et al., 2006). Children of fathers with postpartum depression have been found to have similar risks for their development (Kane & Garber, 2004; Ramchandani et al., 2005).

Of course, all of these studies are subject to the research design problem we discussed in Chapter 2, of passive and evocative genotype → environment effects. That is, the children in these studies received not only their environment from their parents but also their genes, and it is difficult to tell whether the relation between their problems and their parents' depression is due to genetics or environment (the problem of passive genotype → environment effects). Also, the studies usually assume that the mother's depression affected the child, but it could also be that the mothers became depressed in part because their infant was especially irritable and difficult (evocative genotype → environment effects). However, observational studies of mothers with postpartum depression have found that they talk to and look at their infant less than other mothers, and that they also touch them less and smile less often at them (Righetti-Veltema et al., 2002). This suggests that the behavior of depressed mothers is different in ways that may affect infants, even if passive and evocative genotype → environment effects are also involved.

Across countries, about 10% of new mothers experience postpartum depression.

postpartum depression

in parents with a new baby, feelings of sadness and anxiety so intense as to interfere with the ability to carry out simple daily tasks

Practice Quiz   ANSWERS AVAILABLE IN ANSWER KEY.

1. Newborn baby, Kiev, lives in a traditional culture. What is most likely to happen when he cries?

   a. He will be ignored until he either self-soothes or cries himself to sleep.

   b. He will be picked up and rocked.

   c. His mother will sing him a lullaby.

   d. He will be breast fed and swaddled.

2. An infant who cries for more than three hours a day, over more than three days at a time, and for more than three weeks is considered _____.

   a. colicky

   b. to have a difficult temperament

   c. at risk for depression later in development

   d. to have a developmental disability

3. Melia had heard that if she did not hold her baby immediately after birth and lie with her on her chest for hours that she and her baby would never _____. Luckily for Melia, research proved this claim to be false because her infant needed immediate medical attention after she was born.

   a. imprint

   b. be properly affiliated

   c. be properly bonded

   d. develop milestones on time

4. Which of the following is TRUE?

   a. There has been a trend in hospital policies in the last decade to keep babies and mothers separate in the first hours after birth to prevent infection.

   b. Imprinting is another name for the Moro reflex.

   c. Lorenz showed that following the first moving object after birth has survival value for geese.

   d. In humans, if there is no contact with the mother shortly after birth, the baby's future development is at risk.

5. Postpartum depression _____.

   a. is experienced by men as well as by women

   b. has been observed only in the United States

   c. is less common among women who have had previous episodes of major depression because they tend to seek preventative treatment

   d. has not been linked with developmental outcomes for babies

Summary: Caring for the Neonate

LO 3.12   Describe the cultural customs surrounding breast-feeding across cultures and history.

In the human past, evidence indicates that in most cultures children were fed breast milk as their primary food for 2 to 3 years. To ease the burden of frequent feedings, the custom of wet nursing (hiring a lactating woman other than the mother to feed the infant) is a widespread custom as old as recorded human history. Using animal substitutes (cow's or goat's milk) also has a long history.

LO 3.13   Identify the advantages conferred by breast-feeding and where those advantages are largest.

Breast-feeding is associated with protection from disease in infancy and better health in childhood and adulthood, healthy cognitive development, and reduced obesity. For mothers, breast-feeding helps their bodies return to normal after pregnancy. The advantages are especially pronounced in developing countries. Nevertheless, worldwide only about half of all infants are breast-fed even for a short time.

LO 3.14   Describe neonates' types of crying and how crying patterns and soothing methods vary across cultures.

Three distinct kinds of crying signals have been identified: fussing, anger, and pain. Crying frequency rises steadily

beginning at 3 weeks of age and reaches a peak by the end of the second month, then declines. This pattern is similar across cultures, but duration and intensity of crying are lower in cultures where babies are held or carried throughout much of the day and night.

LO 3.15   Describe the extent to which human mothers "bond" with their neonates and the extent to which this claim has been exaggerated.

Some physicians have claimed on the basis of animal studies that the first few minutes and hours after birth are critical to mother–infant "bonding." This has now been shown to be false, but the claims had the beneficial effect of changing hospital policies to allow more contact between mothers, fathers, and neonates.

LO 3.16   Describe the reasons for postpartum depression and its consequences for children.

Many mothers experience mood fluctuations in the days following birth as their hormones return to normal levels, but some mothers experience an extended period of postpartum depression, as do some fathers. The basis of postpartum depression appears to be a combination of genetic vulnerability to depression and a social and cultural context that does not provide enough social support.

Applying Your Knowledge as a Professional

The topics covered in this chapter apply to a wide variety of career professions. Watch these videos to learn how they apply to a birth doula and an instructor of maternity nursing.

Watch CAREER FOCUS: BIRTH DOULA

Samantha Huggins
Doula
Carriage House Birth

Chapter Quiz

1. Juanita's cervix is 10 centimeters dilated, so she _____.
   a. is just beginning the labor stage
   b. requires an episiotomy.
   c. has completed labor and is ready to deliver the baby ✓
   d. requires a C-section

2. C-sections _____.
   a. are performed when the baby is in the breech position and attempts to turn the baby into a head-first position have not been successful ✓
   b. require the same recovery time as a vaginal birth if they are performed correctly
   c. have only been proven safe in the cases where there is a failure to progress
   d. are performed at equally small rates around the world because they are seen as a last resort

3. In most cultures, _____ take the lead in assisting the birth.
   a. older men
   b. younger women
   c. older women ✓
   d. religious figures

4. Surita is a midwife in a traditional culture. She is most likely to _____.
   a. have spent time as an apprentice to a more experienced midwife ✓
   b. be childless, so that she is able to devote more time to this work
   c. be a young woman because she will be able to practice midwifery for longer than her older counterparts
   d. exclude other relatives from being present to reduce possible contamination

5. Which of the following is true about birthing practices?
   a. Recently, midwifery has seen a revival, and about 50% of births in the United States are assisted by midwifes.
   b. In the early 1900s, the intervention of doctors often made the birth process less dangerous because they now had better expertise and medical equipment.
   c. In the 1960s, doctors began administering drugs such as ether and chloroform, which offered pain relief without any side effects.
   d. Twilight Sleep was a drug method used in the early 20th century that promoted dilation of the cervix and resulted in mothers forgetting the events of birth. ✓

6. In developing countries _____.
   a. most pregnant women now have access to modern medical technology
   b. giving birth is relatively free of risks because of modernization and globalization
   c. maternal mortality has decreased over the past 30 years ✓
   d. rates of infant mortality are lower than in developed countries because of more holistic and natural approaches to childbirth

7. The five characteristics that are evaluated in the Apgar scale are _____.
   a. the Babinski, Moro, stepping, swimming, and grasping reflexes
   b. color, heart rate, reflex irritability, muscle tone, and breathing ✓
   c. reaction to cuddling, startling, intelligence, vocal response, and visual response.
   d. sucking reflex, responses to social stimulation, and disease symptoms

8. Preterm babies are considered at risk because _____.
   a. their immune systems are immature ✓
   b. they have too much surfactant in their lungs
   c. their bodies generate too much heat
   d. their gestational age is 40 weeks and that is still too early to perform basic functions, such as sucking

9. Compared to adults, neonates _____.
   a. spend a lower proportion of their sleep in REM
   b. enter REM sooner after falling asleep ✓
   c. spend less time sleeping
   d. do not experience eye movements under the eyelids or brain-wave changes during REM sleep

10. Which of the following reflexes has no apparent survival value?
    a. Rooting reflex
    b. Moro reflex
    c. Babinski reflex ✓
    d. Grasping reflex

11. The earliest sense to develop is _____.
    a. taste
    b. touch ✓
    c. vision
    d. hearing

12. Breast feeding _____.

    a. is more common among women from low socioeconomic status groups

    b. increased in popularity as formulas came on to the market because the formulas were very expensive and women worried about product quality

    c. is something both mother and baby are biologically prepared to do

    d. rates have stayed about the same in the United States since the 1940s

13. Which of the following statements about breast feeding is most accurate?

    a. Babies in developing countries are more at risk for health problems if their mothers do not breast feed them than are babies in developed countries.

    b. Breast feeding promotes better health in childhood, but does not have any influence on long-term health.

    c. Breast-fed babies are more likely than bottle-fed babies to become obese in childhood because they are used to eating on demand.

    d. The colostrum that mothers produce in the first weeks after birth can be dangerous to babies, so doctors advise using formula until the mother begins producing milk.

14. American infants _____.

    a. are less likely to experience colic than are babies in non-Western cultures

    b. typically experience colic until they are about a year of age

    c. show the same frequency, intensity, and duration of crying as babies from all over the world

    d. have been found to cry more than babies from cultures where they are held or carried for much of the day

15. Which of the following statements about bonding is most accurate?

    a. There is a critical period for mother–child relations in all species.

    b. Imprinting is another name for the stepping reflex.

    c. In humans, if there is no contact with the mother shortly after birth, the baby's future development is at risk.

    d. Konrad Lorenz showed that following the first moving object after birth has survival value for geese.

16. Postpartum depression _____.

    a. is less common among women who have had previous episodes of major depression because they tend to seek preventive treatment

    b. is experienced by men as well as by women

    c. has a genetic component, and therefore has not been correlated with levels of social support

    d. has been linked with developmental outcomes for babies, but only among male babies

Chapter 4
Infancy

MORE THAN IN OTHER LIFE STAGES, THE DAILY LIFE OF INFANTS IS SIMILAR EVERYWHERE IN SOME WAYS. In all cultures, infants have limited mobility and do not yet use language (the word *infant* means literally "without speech"), although they have a variety of ways of communicating. In all cultures, infants cannot do much for themselves and rely heavily on others for care and protection. However, even in infancy cultural variations are vast. In some cultures infants are carried around for most of the day and breast-feed often, whereas in others, they lay by themselves for a substantial proportion of the day—and night. In this chapter we will explore both cultural similarities and variations in infants' development. Beginning in this chapter and throughout the rest of the book (until the final chapter), the chapters will be divided into three major sections: physical development, cognitive development, and emotional and social development.

Watch   CHAPTER INTRODUCTION: INFANCY

Video

Section 1 Physical Development

∨ Learning Objectives

4.1 Describe how the infant's body changes in the first year, and explain the two basic principles of physical growth.

4.2 Identify the different parts of the brain and describe how the brain changes in the first few years of life.

4.3 Describe how infant sleep changes in the course of the first year and evaluate the risk factors for SIDS, including the research evidence regarding cosleeping.

4.4 Describe how infants' nutritional needs change during the first year of life and identify the reasons for and consequences of malnutrition in infancy.

4.5 List the major causes and preventive methods of infant mortality and describe some cultural approaches to protecting infants.

4.6 Describe the major changes during infancy in gross and fine motor development.

4.7 Describe when and how infants develop depth perception and intermodal perception.

PHYSICAL DEVELOPMENT: Growth and Change in Infancy

We begin this section by examining physical growth (height and weight), the emergence of the first teeth, and infant brain development. Then we'll examine changes in sleeping patterns, the dangers of SIDS, and cultural variations in where infants sleep (and with whom).

Growth Patterns

LO 4.1 **Describe how the infant's body changes in the first year, and explain the two basic principles of physical growth.**

Babies grow at a faster rate in their first year than at any later time of life (Adolph & Berger, 2005). Birth weight doubles by the time the infant is 5 months old, and triples by the end of the first year, to about 22 pounds (10 kilograms) on average. If this rate of growth continued for the next 3 years, the average 4-year-old would weigh 600 pounds! But the rate of weight gain decreases steeply after the first year.

Babies especially accumulate fat in the early months, which helps them maintain a constant body temperature. At 6 months, a well-nourished baby looks on the plump side, but by 1 year children lose much of their "baby fat," and the trend toward a lower ratio of fat to body weight continues until puberty (Fomon & Nelson, 2002).

Height also increases dramatically in the first year, from about 20 inches (50 centimeters) to about 30 inches (75 cm), at the rate of about an inch per month. Unlike weight,

cephalocaudal principle
principle of biological development that growth tends to begin at the top, with the head, and then proceeds downward to the rest of the body

proximodistal principle
principle of biological development that growth proceeds from the middle of the body outward

teething
period of discomfort and pain experienced by infants as their new teeth break through their gums

growth in height in the first year is uneven, occurring in spurts rather than steadily. Studies that have monitored height closely have found that infants may grow very little for several days or even weeks, then spurt a half inch in just a day or two (Lampl et al., 2001). Girls tend to be shorter and lighter than boys, at birth and throughout childhood, until puberty when they briefly surpass boys in height (Geary, 2010).

Another way growth is uneven in infancy is that it tends to begin at the top, with the head, and then proceed downward to the rest of the body (Adolph & Berger, 2005). This is called the **cephalocaudal principle** (*cephalocaudal* is Latin for "head to tail"). So, for example, the head is one-quarter of the neonate's body length, but only one-eighth of an adult's (see **Figure 4.1**). In addition, growth proceeds from the middle of the body outward, which is the **proximodistal principle** (*proximodistal* is Latin for "near to far"). So, for example, the trunk and arms grow faster than the hands and fingers.

Other physical changes take place during infancy as well, including the growth of teeth. For most infants the first tooth appears between 5 and 9 months of age and causes discomfort and pain called **teething**. There is a vast range of variability in teething among infants, from constant pain to no discomfort at all. The first teeth and the molars tend to be especially painful.

Babies often seize the opportunity for something to bite when teething, including their own hands if nothing else is available, because the counterpressure of the bite relieves the pain (Trajanovska et al., 2010). Watch your fingers! You may be surprised how strong a teething baby's bite can be.

Not many of us become more cheerful when in pain, at any age, so it is not surprising that teething babies also tend to become irritable. Some may be reluctant to breast- or bottle-feed (fortunately, most can also eat solid foods by the time they begin teething). And, of course, they become more likely to wake up at night with teething pain. Parents who celebrated when their child began "sleeping through the night" at about 4 months old often find that this was a temporary rather than permanent transition, as the baby now wakes up and cries for relief from teething (Sarrell et al., 2005).

Fortunately, there is a range of strategies to help relieve the infant's teething pain (Trajanovska et al., 2010). Something to bite or chew on, such as a cold wet washcloth

Most babies are plump and have large heads in proportion to their bodies.

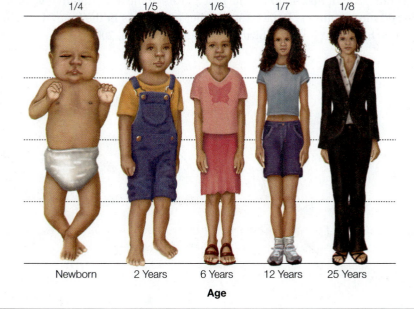

| 1/4 | 1/5 | 1/6 | 1/7 | 1/8 |

| Newborn | 2 Years | 6 Years | 12 Years | 25 Years |

Age

Figure 4.1 The Cephalocaudal Principle of Body Growth

Growth begins with the head and then continues downward to the rest of the body.

Teething is often uncomfortable and painful.

neurotransmitter

chemical that enables neurons to communicate across synapses

axon

part of a neuron that transmits electric impulses and releases neurotransmitters

dendrite

part of the neuron that receives neurotransmitters

or a "teething ring," can provide the counterpressure on the gums that helps relieve the pain. Topical pain relievers rubbed on the gums can also be effective.

Brain Development

LO 4.2 **Identify the different parts of the brain and describe how the brain changes in the first few years of life.**

Recall from Chapter 3 that humans have relatively large brains at birth compared to other animals, thus making the birth process more painful and dangerous. But even though the human brain is relatively large at birth, it is also relatively immature (Johnson, 2001). We come out when we do because if we waited any longer, our brains would be too big for us ever to make it through the birth canal. Consequently, much of the basic brain development that takes place prenatally for other animals takes place in the first year for humans. Note, for example, that other animals are mobile at birth or within a few days or weeks, but humans cannot even crawl for about 6 months and cannot walk until the end of their first year.

Here we will look first at basics of infant brain growth, then at the specialized functions of different parts of the brain. Then we'll explore the special sensitivity of brain development during infancy.

BRAIN GROWTH As you learned in Chapter 2, during the second trimester of prenatal development neurons are produced at the astonishing rate of 250,000 per minute. The pace then slows considerably in the third trimester, as the focus of development shifts to other organs and to overall size. After birth, the brain resumes its explosive growth. The neonate's brain is about 25% the size of an adult's brain, but by age 2 it will reach 70%.

There are about 100–200 billion brain cells, or *neurons,* in the average infant brain (Kostovic et al., 2009). Neurons differ from other cells in the body in that they are not directly connected to each other. Instead, they are separated by tiny gaps called *synapses.* Neurons communicate across the synapses by releasing chemicals called **neurotransmitters**. The **axon** of the neuron releases neurotransmitters, and the **dendrites** receive them (see **Figure 4.2**).

The brain growth that occurs in the first 2 years of life does not involve production of more and more neurons. In fact, the number of neurons in the brain drops by age 2 to about one half what it was at birth (de Haan & Johnson, 2003). There are two other

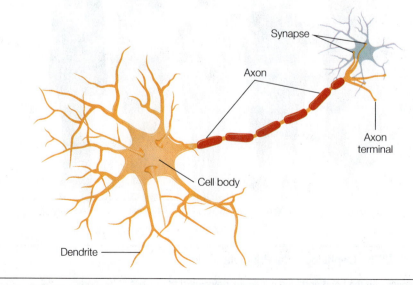

Figure 4.2 The Synapse

ways that brain growth takes place during infancy. First, the dendritic connections between neurons multiply vastly, a process known as **overproduction** or **exuberance** (Kostovic et al., 2009). At birth the neurons have few interconnections, but by age 2 each neuron is connected to hundreds or even thousands of other cells. The greatest density of connections appears in toddlerhood, as we'll see in Chapter 5. The second way the brain grows in infancy is through **myelination**, the process by which the axons become encased in a *myelin sheath,* an envelope of fatty material that increases the speed of communication between neurons (Gale et al., 2004). Myelination is especially active in the early years of life but continues at a slower rate until about age 30 (Taylor, 2006).

As neurons create vast networks of dendrites to connect to other neurons, a process begins that enhances the precision and efficiency of the connections. "Use it or lose it" is the principle that applies, as dendritic connections that are used become stronger and faster and those that are unused wither away, in a process called **synaptic pruning** (Kostovic et al., 2009). If you were growing carrots in a backyard garden and you had planted thousands of seeds, how would you ensure that they would thrive? The best way would be to prune or pluck out the weaker shoots to allow the stronger ones more room and resources to grow on. This is what the brain does with synaptic pruning. Through synaptic pruning, the brain eliminates about one third of its synapses between early childhood and adolescence (Giedd et al., 2010).

BRAIN SPECIALIZATION Although the entire brain is composed of neurons, the neurons in different parts of the brain have specialized functions. Overall, the brain is divided into three major regions, the *hindbrain,* the *midbrain,* and the *forebrain.* Early in prenatal development, the neurons in these three regions begin to specialize. The hindbrain and midbrain mature earliest and perform the basic biological functions necessary to life. They keep your lungs breathing, your heart beating, and your bodily movements balanced.

The forebrain is divided into two main parts, the *limbic system* and the *cerebral cortex.* The structures of the limbic system include the *hypothalamus,* the *thalamus,* and the *hippocampus.* The hypothalamus is small, about the size of a peanut, but plays a key role in monitoring and regulating our basic animal functions, including hunger, thirst, body temperature, sexual desire, and hormonal levels. The thalamus acts as a receiving and transfer center for sensory information from the body to the rest of the brain. The hippocampus is crucial in memory, especially the transfer of information from short-term to long-term memory.

The most distinctively human part of the brain is the outermost part of the forebrain, the **cerebral cortex**. This part of the human brain is far larger than in other animals. For example, adult humans weigh about as much as adult chimpanzees, but have a cerebral cortex three to four times larger (Wrangham, 2009). It accounts for 85% of the brain's total weight, and it is here that most of the brain's growth takes place after birth. The cerebral cortex is the basis of our distinctively human abilities, including the ability to speak and understand language, to solve complex problems, and to think in terms of concepts, ideas, and symbols.

The different parts of the cerebral cortex are specialized in two ways. First, the cerebral cortex is divided into two hemispheres, left and right, which are connected by a band of neural fibers called the *corpus callosum* that allows them to communicate. **Lateralization** is the term for the specialization of the two hemispheres. In general, the left hemisphere is specialized for language and for processing information in a sequential, step-by-step way (Harnad, 2012). The right hemisphere is specialized for spatial reasoning and for processing information in a holistic, integrative way. However, the specialization of the hemispheres should not be exaggerated, because they work together in most aspects of language, emotion, and behavior. No one is mainly a "left-brain" or "right-brain" thinker.

overproduction/exuberance
burst in the production of dendritic connections between neurons

myelination
process of the growth of the myelin sheath around the axon of a neuron

synaptic pruning
process in brain development in which dendritic connections that are used become stronger and faster and those that are unused whither away

cerebral cortex
outer portion of the brain, containing four regions with distinct functions

lateralization
specialization of functions in the two hemispheres of the brain

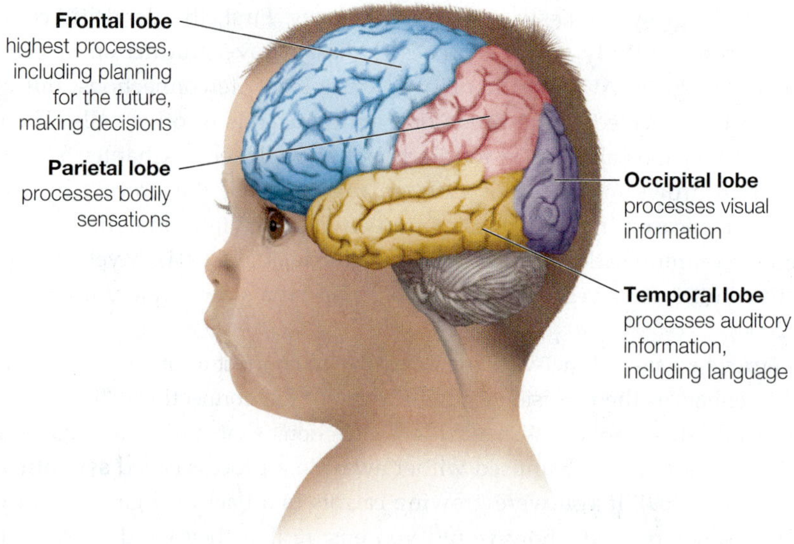

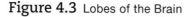

Frontal lobe
highest processes,
including planning
for the future,
making decisions

Parietal lobe
processes bodily
sensations

Occipital lobe
processes visual
information

Temporal lobe
processes auditory
information,
including language

Figure 4.3 Lobes of the Brain

What are the distinct functions of each lobe?

The cerebral cortex is also specialized in that each hemisphere has four regions or lobes with distinct functions (see **Figure 4.3**). The *occipital lobes* at the rear of each hemisphere process visual information. The *temporal lobes* at the lower side of each hemisphere are involved in processing auditory information, including understanding spoken language. The *parietal lobes* above the temporal lobes process information from bodily sensations. The *frontal lobes* behind the forehead are the center of the most advanced human brain processes, including producing spoken language, planning for the future, and making decisions. With the lobes as with the hemispheres, it is important not to exaggerate the degree of specialization, as more than one part of the brain is involved in most brain functions (Harnad, 2012; Knect et al., 2003).

plasticicty

degree to which development can be influenced by environmental circumstances

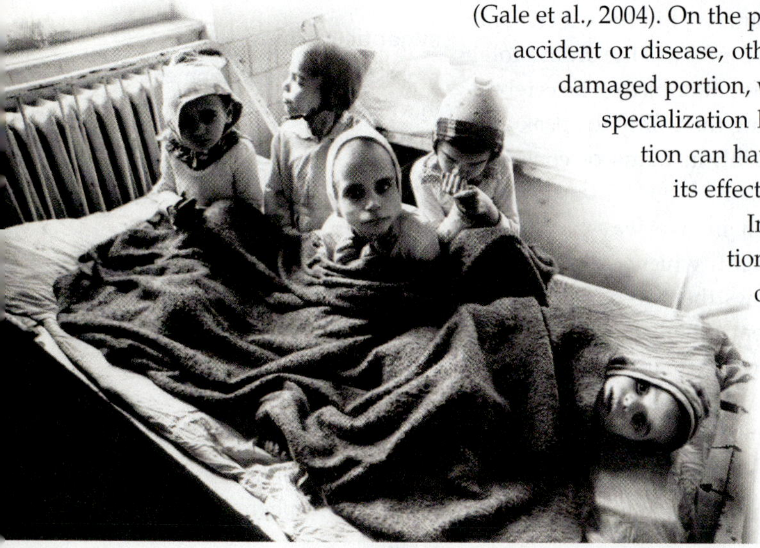

The cognitive recovery of adopted Romanian orphans depended greatly on the age at which they were adopted.

THE PLASTICITY OF THE INFANT BRAIN Even before birth, the brain is well on its way toward specialization in the ways just described. However, in many ways the cerebral cortex of the neonate and the infant is still immature. Because the infant's brain is not as specialized as it will be later in development, it is high in **plasticity**, meaning that it is highly responsive to environmental circumstances.

The high plasticity of the infant brain makes it adaptable but also vulnerable (Gale et al., 2004). On the plus side, if a part of the brain is damaged in infancy due to an accident or disease, other parts of the brain can often take over the functions of the damaged portion, whereas this is less possible later in development once greater specialization has taken place. On the minus side, environmental deprivation can have permanent effects if it takes place in infancy, whereas later its effects would not be as profound or long lasting.

Imagine that, starting tomorrow, for 3 years you lived in conditions of great deprivation, with little food, little interaction with others, and nothing interesting to do. At the end of it, you might be very hungry and not very happy, but it is likely your weight would soon return to normal and your intellectual skills and abilities would be unaffected in the long run. This is what has usually happened to prisoners of war who have been subject to such grim conditions (Moore, 2010).

If the same kind of deprivation had happened to you in the first 3 years of your life, the effects would have been much worse and more enduring. One demonstration of this comes from a horrible natural experiment that took place in Romania about 20 years ago. In the early 1990s, after Communist regimes fell in Eastern European countries, Western visitors to Romania were shocked at the conditions in the country's orphanages. Infants and young children in the orphanages had been given little in the way of nutrition and even less love, attention, and cognitive stimulation. They were kept in large, dim, bare rooms, attended by a small number of indifferent caregivers. In response to widespread outrage, the orphanages were soon closed and the children were adopted into homes in other countries, mostly in Canada and Great Britain.

The children had all been deprived, but they were adopted at different ages. Over the course of the next several years, it was possible to see how much difference the age at adoption made in their cognitive development (O'Connor et al., 2000; Rutter et al., 2004).

Age at adoption made an enormous difference. All the children recovered dramatically in physical size after a year or two in their new homes, but cognitive recovery depended strongly on age at adoption. As shown in **Figure 4.4**, by age 6 the Romanian children who had been adopted when less than 6 months old were no different in their rate of cognitive impairment than British children adopted at the same age (Beckett et al., 2006). However, Romanian children adopted at 6–24 months old had cognitive abilities significantly lower than the Romanian or British children adopted earlier, and Romanian children adopted at age 24–42 months had cognitive abilities that were lower still. This indicates that after about 6 months of age, the damage to the brain due to early deprivation often could not be entirely undone even by years of exposure to a more stimulating environment. Plasticity of the infant brain is high but diminishes steeply over the first few years of life.

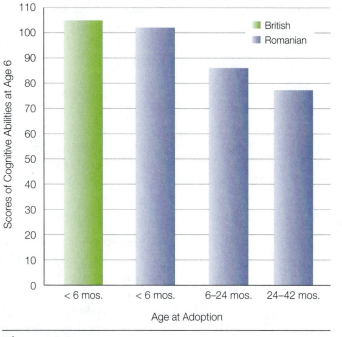

Figure 4.4 Romanian Adoptees' Cognitive Abilities, by Age of Adoption

The later the age of adoption, the lower their cognitive abilities.
SOURCE: Based on Beckett et al., 2006.

Sleep Changes

LO 4.3 Describe how infant sleep changes in the course of the first year and evaluate the risk factors for SIDS, including the research evidence regarding cosleeping.

As described in Chapter 3, neonates sleep for 16–17 hours a day in periods of a few hours, and are in REM sleep about half this time. By 3–4 months old, infants sleep for longer periods, up to 6–7 hours in a row at night, and REM sleep has declined to about 40%. By age 6 months, cultural practices influence how much infants sleep. American infants sleep about 14 hours a day at this age, including daytime naps (Murkoff et al., 2009). However, among the Kipsigis people of Kenya studied by Charles Super and Sara Harkness (1986), infants slept only about 12 hours a day at 6 months of age, perhaps because they spent much of the day strapped to their mothers or an older sibling, and so expended less energy than American infants do. Super and colleagues (1996) also studied infants in the Netherlands and compared their sleep patterns to American infants. The Dutch infants slept about 16 hours a day at 6 months, 2 hours more than the Americans, due to Dutch cultural beliefs emphasizing rest and early bedtimes for young children.

Two important issues of sleep in infancy are the risk of dying during sleep and the issue of whom infants should sleep with. For both issues, there are important cultural variations.

SUDDEN INFANT DEATH SYNDROME (SIDS) When infants are 2–4 months of age, they are at highest risk for **sudden infant death syndrome (SIDS)**. Infants who die of SIDS do not have any apparent illness or disorder, they simply fall asleep and never wake up. SIDS is the leading cause of death for infants 1–12 months of age in developed countries (OECD, 2014). Infants of Asian descent are less likely to die of SIDS than those of European or African descent, and African American and Native American infants are at especially high risk, with rates 4–6 times higher than White Americans (Pickett et al., 2005). The higher rates of SIDS among African Americans and Native Americans are part of a larger pattern than begins with poorer prenatal care and continues with greater vulnerability in the first year of life.

Although deaths from SIDS have no clear cause, there are several factors known to put infants at risk (AAP Task Force on Sudden Infant Death Syndrome, 2011; Kinney & Thach, 2009), including:

- sleeping stomach-down instead of flat on the back;
- low birth weight and low Apgar score;
- having a mother who smoked during pregnancy, or being around smoke during infancy;
- soft bedding, sleeping in an overheated room, or wearing two or more layers of clothing during sleep (most SIDS deaths take place in autumn and winter).

One theory is that babies' vulnerability to SIDS at 2–4 months old reflects the transition from reflex behavior to intentional behavior (Lipsitt, 2003). For their first 2 months of life, when infants' breathing is blocked, a reflex causes them to shake their heads, bring their hands to their face, and push away the cause of the obstruction. After 2 months of age, once the reflex disappears, most babies are able to do this as intentional, learned behavior, but some are unable to make the transition, perhaps due in part to respiratory and muscular vulnerabilities. When these infants experience breathing difficulties during sleep, instead of being able to shake off the difficulty, they die.

One thing that is certain is that sleeping on the back instead of the stomach makes an enormous difference in lowering the risk of SIDS. In 1994, in response to growing research evidence of the risks of stomach-sleeping, pediatricians in the United States launched a major "BACK to Sleep" campaign to inform parents and health professionals of the importance of putting infants to sleep on their backs. Over the next decade, the prevalence of stomach-sleeping among American infants declined from 70% to 20% and SIDS deaths declined by nearly one half (AAP Task Force on Sudden Infant Death Syndrome, 2011; National Center for Health Statistics, 2005). In response to similar campaigns in other countries, SIDS declined by 90% in the United Kingdom and by over 50% in many other developed countries (see **Figure 4.5**; National Sudden and Unexpected Infant/Child Death & Pregnancy Loss Resource Center, 2010).

sudden infant death syndrome (SIDS)

death within the first year of life due to unknown reasons, with no apparent illness or disorder

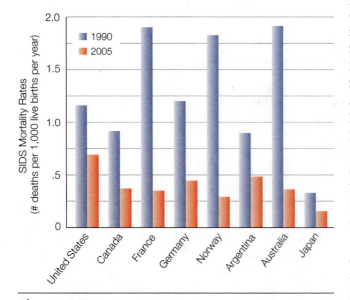

Figure 4.5 The Impact of Prevention Campaigns on SIDS Rates

Why did rates of SIDS decline so much over this period?

COSLEEPING: HELPFUL OR HARMFUL TO BABIES? With whom should infants sleep? Should they sleep by themselves, in a crib or even a room of their own, or should they sleep alongside a parent or a sibling?

If you are a member of a Western culture, you may assume that it is better for infants to have their own crib and room within a few weeks after birth, so that they can learn to be independent and the parents can enjoy their marital intimacy without disruption (or without as much disruption, at least). Prominent pediatricians and health authorities in the United States and other Western countries warn against **cosleeping**, in which the infant sleeps in the same bed as the parents, arguing that it leads to excessive dependence by infants and can endanger the emotional health of infants or even lead to SIDS (American Academy of Pediatrics [AAP] Task Force on Infant Positioning and SIDS, 2000; AAP Task Force on Sudden Infant Death Syndrome, 2011; Spock & Needleman, 2004).

However, this is one of many issues in this book where what is normal and seems healthy and "natural" in Western countries is actually extremely unusual worldwide. Outside of the West, nearly all cultures have some form of cosleeping during infancy (Small, 2005). Many of the parents in these cultures view the Western practice of nightly isolation of infants as "a form of child neglect or worse" (DeLoache & Gottlieb, 2000, pp. 16–17). They believe infants are highly vulnerable to injury, illness, and death, and that sleeping beside the mother is necessary to protect them. This arrangement also makes it easy for the infant to breast-feed when necessary during the night, without disturbing others and arousing the mother only slightly. Typically a child sleeps beside the mother until the next child is born, which is usually when the child is 2–4 years old.

In a study comparing sleeping arrangements among Guatemalan Maya and White Americans, all the Mayan mothers coslept with their infants until the next child was born, whereupon the child would cosleep with the father or in a bed alongside the mother and the new baby (Morelli et al., 1992). The mothers explained that cosleeping helped promote a close parent–child attachment, highly valued in their collectivistic culture. The Mayan mothers were appalled when they learned that American infants typically sleep alone, and regarded this practice as cold and cruel. In contrast, few of the American mothers coslept with their infants, explaining that they wanted the child to become independent and that cosleeping would foster a degree of dependency that would be emotionally unhealthy.

But it is not just in traditional cultures like the Guatemalan Maya that cosleeping is the norm. In Japan and South Korea, two of the most technologically advanced countries in the world, almost all infants cosleep with their mothers, and children continue to sleep with or near their mothers until puberty (Mindell et al., 2010). Like the Mayan mothers, Asian mothers justify their cosleeping practices on the basis of collectivistic values, explaining that this is one way for children to learn from a very early age that they are closely tied to others in bonds of interdependence and mutual obligation.

Cultural customs regarding infant sleeping arrangements are a good example of a **custom complex**, that is, a distinctive cultural pattern of behavior that is based on underlying cultural beliefs. Cosleeping tends to reflect collectivistic beliefs, that members of the culture are closely bound to one another (Small, 1998). In contrast, having infants sleep alone tends to reflect an individualistic belief that each person should learn to be self-sufficient and not rely on others any more than necessary.

Parents in an individualistic culture may fear that cosleeping will make infants and children too dependent. However, children who cosleep with their parents in infancy are actually more self-reliant (e.g., able to dress themselves) and more socially independent (e.g., can make friends by themselves) than other children are (Keller & Goldbert, 2004).

What about the danger of SIDS? Don't cultures where cosleeping is the norm have high rates of SIDS, if cosleeping is a risk factor for SIDS as most American pediatricians believe? On the contrary, SIDS is almost unknown in cultures where cosleeping is the norm (Hewlett & Roulette, 2014). In the United States, however, where most parents do not cosleep, rates of SIDS are among the highest in the world.

There appear to be several reasons for this pattern (McKenna & McDade, 2005). First, most parents and infants in cosleeping cultures sleep on relatively hard surfaces such as a mat on the floor or a futon, thus avoiding the soft bedding that is sometimes implicated in SIDS. Second, infants who cosleep breast-feed more often and longer than infants who do not, and these frequent episodes of arousal in the course of the night make SIDS

In most cultures, mothers and infants cosleep.

cosleeping
cultural practice in which infants and sometimes older children sleep with one or both parents

custom complex
distinctive cultural pattern of behavior that reflects underlying cultural beliefs

less likely. Third, cosleeping mothers tend to lay their infants on their backs to make the mother's breast more easily accessible for breast feeding. Thus back-sleeping developed as a widespread cultural practice for practical reasons long before research showed that it lessened the risk of SIDS.

Some cultures within the United States have a long tradition of infant cosleeping, as shown in the video *Cosleeping*. It is a common practice among African Americans and Latinos (Barajas et al., 2011; Milan et al., 2007). In the rural culture of the Appalachian Mountains children typically sleep alongside their parents for the first 2 years of life (Abbott, 1992). In many developed countries, the prevalence of cosleeping in infancy has grown in recent years as research has shown that it causes no emotional harm and may even be protective against SIDS (Mindell et al., 2010; Willinger et al., 2003). Cosleeping infants may be at risk for SIDS if their parents are obese or consume alcohol or other drugs before sleeping, but otherwise cosleeping is more often a protective factor than a risk factor for SIDS (McKenna & McDade, 2005).

Watch COSLEEPING

CRITICAL THINKING QUESTION

What might cosleeping indicate about expectations for marital relations in a culture that practices it?

Practice Quiz   ANSWERS AVAILABLE IN ANSWER KEY.

1. Atika's trunk and arms grow faster than his hands and fingers. This progression of motor development is called the _____.
   a. cephalocaudal principle
   b. phalange-metatarsal principle
   c. dynamic movement principle
   d. proximodistal principle

2. Errol was adopted from a Romanian orphanage nine years ago. He was physically and emotionally deprived until a couple adopted him at age 2½. It is most likely that Errol _____.
   a. had more cognitive impairment than he would have had if he had been adopted before 6 months of age
   b. will have greater brain plasticity than his counterparts who were not raised in impoverished conditions

   c. will show no signs of cognitive impairment because of overproduction of neurons
   d. stayed overweight for most of his life once he was no longer deprived of food

3. It was discovered at birth that there was significant cell death in Brittany's _____. Her parents were worried that she would be born blind because this part of the brain processes visual information. Luckily, this was not the case because other parts of her brain compensated for this cell loss.
   a. temporal lobe
   b. frontal lobe
   c. parietal lobe
   d. occipital lobe

4. Research has shown that _____ is a risk factor for SIDS.

   a. sleeping on the right side
   b. sleeping on the back
   c. sleeping on the stomach
   d. sleeping on the left side

5. SIDS is almost unknown in cultures _____.

   a. where babies sleep in cribs in a separate room from their parents
   b. where infants and children sleep on soft mattresses
   c. where cosleeping is the norm
   d. where most mothers do not breastfeed their babies

PHYSICAL DEVELOPMENT: Infant Health

Infants' health depends a great deal on where they happened to be born, that is, on their cultural, economic, and social context. Here we look first at how nutritional needs change over the first year, then at the prevalence and effects of malnutrition. This will be followed by an examination of infant mortality rates and causes, immunizations, and cultural beliefs and practices to protect babies.

Nutritional Needs

LO 4.4   **Describe how infants' nutritional needs change during the first year of life and identify the reasons for and consequences of malnutrition in infancy.**

Infants need a lot of food, and they need it often. In fact, during the first year of life nutritional energy needs are greater than at any other time of life, per pound of body weight (Vlaardingerbroek et al., 2009). Infants also need more fat in their diets than at any later point in life, to fuel the growth of their bodies and (especially) their brains.

INTRODUCTION OF SOLID FOODS As noted in Chapter 3, the best way to obtain good high-fat nutrition during infancy is through breast milk. Infants also start eating some solid foods during the first year of life. Cultures vary widely in when they introduce solid food to infants, ranging from those that introduce it after just a few weeks of life to those that wait until the second half of the first year. Age 4–5 months is common, in part because that is an age when infants can sit up with support and also the age when they often begin to show an interest in what others are eating (Small, 2005).

At 4–5 months old infants still have a gag reflex that causes them to spit out any solid item that enters their mouths. Consequently, at first more food ends up on them than in them! The ability to chew and swallow does not develop until the second half of the first year (Napier & Meister, 2000).

In the West, pediatricians generally recommend introducing solid food during the fifth or sixth month of life (Seach et al., 2010). Usually the first solid food is rice cereal mixed with breast milk or formula, made thin when first introduced and gradually thickened as the baby becomes used to eating it (National Center for Education in Maternal and Child Health, 2002). A wider range of foods is introduced in the second half of the first year, but always soft foods that babies can easily eat and digest, such as pureed carrots or applesauce.

In traditional cultures, the first foods to be introduced have been mashed, pureed, or prechewed. For example, among the Balinese in Indonesia, even in the first weeks of life mothers give their babies soft prechewed foods such as bananas to supplement breast milk (Deiner, 2000). In the course of the first year, the range of foods provided to the baby widens, but the mother typically chews the food first.

MALNUTRITION IN INFANCY Because infants have such great nutritional needs, and because their brains and bodies are growing at a faster rate than at any later time of life, the effects of malnutrition in infancy are especially severe and enduring. Infants are capable of thriving mainly on breast milk, along with a little solid food after the early months, so malnutrition in infancy is usually due to the mother being unable or unwilling to breast-feed. Often the problem is that the mother is so ill or malnourished herself that she is unable to produce an adequate supply of breast milk. Or, she may have a disease that can be communicated through breast milk, such as tuberculosis or HIV, and she has been advised not to breast-feed. She may also have been misled to believe that infant formula is better for her baby than breast milk (see Chapter 3), so she has stopped breast-feeding and instead gives her infant the formula substitute, which may not be available in sufficient quantity. If the infant's mother has died—not unusual in the areas of the world where infant malnutrition is most common—there may be no one else who can breast-feed the baby or otherwise provide adequate nutrition.

Malnourished infants are at risk for **marasmus**, a disease in which the body wastes away from lack of nutrients. The body stops growing, the muscles atrophy, the baby becomes increasingly lethargic, and eventually death results. Even among infants who survive, malnutrition impairs normal development for years to come (Galler et al., 2010; Nolan et al., 2002). However, studies in Guatemala and several other countries have found that nutritional supplements for infants in poor families have enduring beneficial effects on their physical, cognitive, and social development (Pollitt et al., 1996).

Infants with marasmus waste away from lack of nourishment.

Infant Mortality

LO 4.5 List the major causes and preventive methods of infant mortality and describe some cultural approaches to protecting infants.

The first year of life has always been a perilous period for the human species. Human females typically have a reproductive span of at least 20 years, from the late teens through the late 30s, and with regular sexual intercourse most would have at least three to seven children during that span. Yet, as we saw in Chapter 1, until recently in human history there was little increase in the total human population. This means that many children died before reaching reproductive age, and based on current patterns it seems likely that many of them died in infancy. Even now, worldwide, the first year of life has the highest risk of death of any period in the entire life span (UNICEF, 2014).

CAUSES AND PREVENTION OF INFANT MORTALITY As noted in Chapter 3, most infant mortality is in fact neonatal mortality. That is, it takes place during the first month of life and is usually due to severe birth defects or low birth weight, or is an indirect consequence of the death of the mother during childbirth (UNICEF, 2014). As with neonatal mortality, rates of infant mortality are much higher in developing countries than in developed countries (see **Map 4.1**).

With regard to deaths beyond the first month but within the first year, in addition to deaths due to malnutrition, diseases are another major cause of infant mortality worldwide. Malaria, a blood disease spread by mosquitoes (see Chapter 2), is a major killer of infants, responsible for about 1 million infant deaths per year, mainly in Africa (Finkel, 2007). Dysentery, an illness of the digestive system, is also one of the top sources of infant mortality, especially in tropical regions where dysentery bacteria thrive.

Overall, the number-one cause of infant mortality beyond the first month but within the first year is diarrhea (UNICEF, 2014). Infants with diarrhea lose fluids and eventually die from dehydration if untreated. Diarrhea may be caused by a range of digestive illnesses, and is often a consequence of bottle-feeding in unsanitary conditions. In developing countries, infants who bottle-feed have a mortality rate five times higher than those who breast-feed (Lamberti, et al. 2010), and many of the deaths are due to diarrhea caused by mixing formula powder with unclean water.

marasmus

disease in which the body wastes away from lack of nutrients

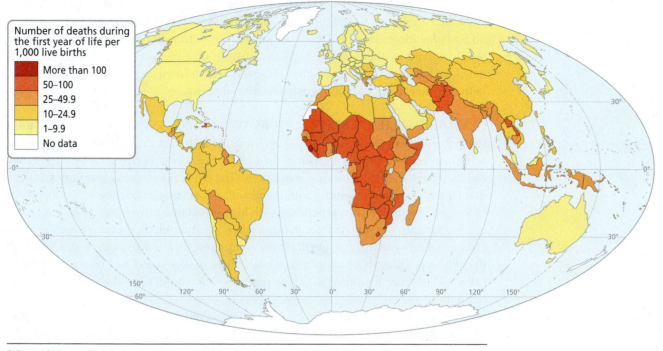

Number of deaths during
the first year of life per
1,000 live births

- More than 100
- 50–100
- 25–49.9
- 10–24.9
- 1–9.9
- No data

Map 4.1 Infant Mortality Rates Worldwide

How do infant mortality rates compare with neonatal mortality rates (as shown in Map 3.2)? What are
some potential causes of the high infant mortality rates in developing countries?
SOURCE: Based on UNICEF (2014).

Diarrhea can be cured easily through simple, inexpensive **oral rehydration therapy (ORT)**. ORT involves having infants with diarrhea drink a solution of salt and glucose mixed with (clean) water. Since 1980 the World Health Organization (WHO) has led an international effort to reduce infant deaths through providing ORT, and the effort has reduced the worldwide rate of infant deaths due to diarrhea from 4.5 million per year to less than 2 million (Boschi-Pinto et al., 2009). However, the reason the rate is still as high as 2 million per year is that even now, in the parts of the world where infant diarrhea is most common, this simple, inexpensive remedy is often unavailable.

Although millions of infants worldwide die yearly from lack of adequate nutrition and medical care, in the past half century many diseases that formerly killed infants and young children have been reduced or even eliminated due to vaccines that provide immunization. Smallpox has been eradicated, measles and polio have been eliminated in large regions of the world, and diphtheria, tetanus, and yellow fever have been greatly reduced in prevalence, all due to immunization programs (Population Reference Bureau, 2014).

Typically, children receive vaccinations for these diseases in the first or second year of life. However, there is a great deal of variability worldwide in how likely children are to be vaccinated. As of 2013, coverage for the major infant vaccines was about 70% in Africa and South Asia, and over 90% in Europe and the Americas (UNICEF, 2013). In recent years, a major effort to provide immunization to all children has been made by the WHO, UNICEF, and private foundations, and the rate of immunization has been increasing, especially in Africa (UNICEF, 2013).

oral rehydration therapy (ORT)

treatment for infant diarrhea
that involves drinking a
solution of salt and glucose
mixed with clean water

Increased prevalence of vaccinations in infancy has greatly reduced infant mortality worldwide. Here, an infant receives a vaccination in southern Sudan.

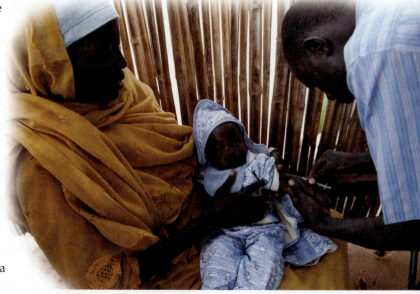

Although rumors have circulated that some vaccinations may actually cause harm to children, for example by triggering autism or causing SIDS, scientific studies have found no basis for these claims (CDC, 2010; Rodier, 2009). Unfortunately, some parents have been deceived by these claims and consequently refused to have their children vaccinated, which, ironically—and sadly—exposes their children and other people's children to the genuine danger of contracting infectious diseases.

CULTURAL BELIEFS AND PRACTICES TO PROTECT INFANTS Perhaps the most striking feature of the infant's social environment in traditional cultures is the parents' acute awareness of infants' vulnerability and their resulting motive to do whatever they can to make the infant's survival most likely. The cultural practices of secluding infants in their early weeks, cosleeping with them, and constantly carrying them developed out of long and painful human experience with high infant mortality.

Historically, parents had no immunizations or other medical care for their infants, but they often went to great lengths to try and protect their babies from death. Although they knew nothing about the physiological causes of illness and had no effective medical remedies, they attempted to devise practices that would allow their infants to avoid harm. In medieval Europe, for example, where an estimated one of every three babies died before their first birthday, a popular belief was that teething was a common cause of death (Fontanel & d'Hartcourt, 1997). This is a case of the common human tendency, discussed in Chapter 1, to confuse correlation and causation. Teething often takes place about midway through the first year. When their infants began suffering symptoms such as fevers and diarrhea after teething began, the parents concluded that teething was the cause, having no idea that the real source of the symptoms was a disease such as malaria, typhus, or cholera. So, they addressed the illness by placing a charm or amulet around the child's neck, or by placing leeches on the baby's gums, sadly to no good effect (Reese, 2000).

Today, too, in cultures where medical remedies for infant illness are scarce, parents often resort to magical practices intended to protect their babies from disease and death. Observations today in places with little access to medical care offer many poignant examples of the cultural practices that have developed to try to protect infants. For example, the people of Bali, in Indonesia, believe that infants should be treated like gods, since they have just arrived from the spirit world, where the gods dwell (Diener, 2000). Consequently, infants should be held constantly and should never touch the ground, out of respect for their godly status. If an infant dies, this is often interpreted as indicating that the infant was not shown the proper respect and so decided to return to the spirit world.

Many cultures resort to magic in an effort to protect their babies. Here, a baby from the Hamer Tribe of Ethiopia wears jewelry the mother has adorned her with to ward off disease.

The Fulani people of West Africa believe that a sharp knife should always be kept near the baby to ward off the witches and evil spirits that may try to take its soul (Johnson, 2000). Compliments to the baby should be avoided at all costs, as this may only make the baby seem more valuable and beautiful and so all the more attractive to the evil spirits. Instead, the Fulani people believe parents should give the infant an unattractive nickname like "Cow Turd," so that the evil spirits will think the baby is not worth taking.

Finally, the Ifalaluk of Micronesia believe that neonates should be covered with cloths in the weeks after birth to encourage sweating, which they believe helps babies grow properly (Le, 2000). Babies should be washed three times a day, morning, noon, and afternoon, but not in the evening, because evil spirits are out then. Any time babies are outside they should be covered with a cloth so that they will not be spied by evil spirits.

Practice Quiz ANSWERS AVAILABLE IN ANSWER KEY.

1. _____ is a disease that occurs in malnourished infants in which their bodies stop growing, muscles atrophy, and they become lethargic.
   a. Failure to thrive
   b. Cerebral palsy
   c. Marasmus
   d. Progeria

2. Kateri, an American infant who lives in the Northeast part of the United States, has become used to eating pureed fruits and vegetables, and just recently she began eating pureed meats. Her parents get excited to see her reactions to each new food they have introduced. She is probably _____ month(s) of age.
   a. 2   **c.** 1
   b. 4–5   **d.** 8–10

3. Biruk is a two-month old infant. He _____.
   a. needs more fat in his diet than at any other time of life
   b. does not eat as often as he will when he is a toddler
   c. has nutritional energy needs that are less than they will be at any other time in life
   d. will probably be introduced to solid foods at about the same age regardless of the culture in which he is raised

4. Sharon is a pediatrician working in a developing country. She would likely use oral rehydration therapy to treat _____.
   a. smallpox
   b. diarrhea
   c. malaria
   d. yellow fever

5. S. is from a traditional culture where medical remedies for infant illness are scarce. He wants to do anything possible to protect his infant son, so he would be LEAST LIKELY to _____.
   a. keep a knife near the baby to warn the witches and evil spirits
   b. hold him as much as possible so that he never touches the ground
   c. cover him with cloth while outside so the spirits are unaware that he is there
   d. adore the baby and give him a nickname such as "king"

PHYSICAL DEVELOPMENT: Motor and Sensory Development

One of the most striking features of human neonates is how little they are able to move around. Even if you hold neonates up, their heads flop to one side because their neck muscles are not yet strong enough to support their large heads. But over the course of the first year they develop from immobile to highly mobile, a dramatic change not just in their lives but in the lives of those who care for them. Sensory development in the first year is more subtle, but advances take place, especially in the sense of sight.

Motor Development

LO 4.6 **Describe the major changes during infancy in gross and fine motor development.**

Over the first year of life remarkable advances take place in motor development. The changes occur in **gross motor development**, which includes balance and posture as well as whole-body movements such as crawling, and in **fine motor development**, which entails more finely tuned movements of the hands such as grasping and manipulating objects.

GROSS MOTOR DEVELOPMENT Ask a parent of an infant what's new, and it's quite likely you'll hear about some new milestone of gross motor development that has recently been achieved. "Emma can now sit up on her own without falling over!" or "Juan is suddenly crawling all over the house!" or "Maru took her first steps yesterday!" There are many achievements of gross motor development over the first year, including holding the head up without support, rolling over, sitting without support, crawling,

gross motor development
development of motor abilities including balance and posture as well as whole-body movements such as crawling

fine motor development
development of motor abilities involving finely tuned movements of the hands such as grasping and manipulating objects

standing, cruising (walking while holding on to something), and (for some) walking. Most children achieve these skills in this sequence, although sometimes the order of skills varies and sometimes children skip steps in the sequence. There is more variability in the timing of each milestone of gross motor development than in the sequence. As you can see in the video *Milestones of Gross Motor Development in Infancy*, for each milestone there is a normal range of variation of several months. Infants could reach the milestones anywhere within those ranges and still be developing normally.

Watch   MILESTONES OF GROSS MOTOR DEVELOPMENT IN INFANCY

In many traditional cultures infants are strapped to their mothers' backs for most of the day. Here, a mother and infant are pictured in rural Vietnam.

How much of infants' gross motor development is *ontogenetic*—meaning that it takes place due to an inborn, genetically based, individual timetable—and how much of it is due to experience and learning? As with most aspects of development, both genetics and environment are involved. Certainly the highly consistent sequence of gross motor milestones suggests an ontogenetic timetable. There is also evidence for genetic group differences, with infants of African heritage reaching most motor milestones earlier than other infants (Kelly et al., 2006). However, most developmental psychologists view gross motor development in infancy as a combination of the genetic timetable, the maturation of the brain, support and assistance from adults for developing the skill, and the child's own efforts to practice the skill (Adolf & Berger, 2006; Thelen, 2001).

Looking at infant gross motor development across cultures provides a vivid picture of how genetics and environment interact. In many traditional cultures it is a common practice for infants to be strapped onto their mothers' backs for most of the day, as the mothers go about their daily business of tending crops, preparing food, and other kinds of work (Pretorious et al., 2002; Super & Harkness, 2015). In some cultures a common infant-care practice in the first few months of life is swaddling, which was discussed in Chapter 3. If infants are strapped to their mothers' backs or swaddled for most of the day, they receive little practice in developing gross motor skills. These restrictive practices are partly to free the mother to work, but cultures that swaddle infants also believe that swaddling protects the infant from sickness and other threats to health (DeLoache & Gottlieb, 2000).

Even after they learn to crawl at about 6 months old and walk at about one year, infants in traditional cultures are restricted in their exercise of these new motor skills. If they are allowed to crawl around and explore they might wander into the cooking fire, or be trampled by livestock, or tumble off a cliff, or any number of other bad things, so it is viewed as best to keep them in someone's arms at all times. For example, among infants in the Gusii culture in Kenya, infants are held or carried 80% of the time their first 6 months, and 60% from 6-12 months, gradually declining to less than 10% by the end of the second year (LeVine et al., 1994).

In contrast, some cultures actively promote infants' gross motor development. For example, the Kipsigis people of Kenya begin encouraging gross motor skills from early on (Super & Harkness, 2009). When only 2–3 months old, infants are placed in shallow holes and kept upright by rolled blankets, months before they would be able to sit on their own. At about the same age, parents start encouraging their infants to practice walking by holding them up and bouncing their feet on the ground. Similarly, in Jamaica mothers massage and stretch their babies' arms and legs beginning in early infancy to promote strength and growth, and like the Kipsigis, beginning at 2–3 months of age they help their babies practice walking (Hopkins & Westra, 1990). In some Western countries, pediatricians now recommend "tummy time" for infants, that is, placing them on their stomachs for a short period each day to encourage them to learn to push up, roll over, sit up, and stand (Ianelli, 2007). Tummy time is viewed as more important now than it was in the past because infants are now supposed to sleep on their backs to reduce the risk of SIDS, and so spend less time on their stomachs.

How much does it matter, ultimately, if cultural practices hinder or promote infants' gross motor development? A little in the short run, perhaps, but not much in the long run. For the most part, infants in cultures where they are strapped to the mother's back or swaddled learn to crawl and walk at about the same age as infants in cultures that neither bind their infants nor make special efforts to support gross motor development (Adolph et al., 2010). One exception is the Ache people, a South American Indian culture (Kaplan & Dove, 1987). Ache mothers have extremely close contact with their infants, strapping, carrying, or holding them 93% of the time during the day and 100% of the night hours. Consequently, Ache children do not typically begin walking until about age two, a year later than the norm across cultures. However, this appears to be partly because Ache infants enjoy being carried around so much that they often refuse to walk even after they are able! In any case, there is no difference in gross motor development by age 6 between Ache children and children in less restrictive cultures.

Infants in cultures where gross motor development is actively stimulated may develop slightly earlier than in cultures where parents make no special efforts. In a study comparing Jamaican immigrant infants in England with native-born English mothers, the Jamaican immigrant infants walked slightly earlier, evidently because their mothers encouraged them to walk and practiced with them, but the two groups were no different in when crawling began (Hopkins & Westra, 1990). In some African cultures that actively stimulate gross motor development, infants walk a few weeks earlier than children in the West (Adolph et al., 2010). Here again, however, by age 6 there are no differences in gross motor development between children in the cultures that promote early motor achievement and cultures that do not. Thus it appears that cultural practices can slightly speed up or slow down the ontogenetic timetable for gross motor development in infancy, but the influence of the environment is relatively small and transient for this particular area of development.

FINE MOTOR DEVELOPMENT One of the evolutionary developments that makes humans anatomically distinctive among animals is the **opposable thumb**, that is, the position of our thumbs opposite our fingers. (Place your thumb now against your fingers and you will see what I mean.) The opposable thumb is the basis of fine motor development, the deft movements of our hands that enable us to make a tool, pick up a small object, or thread a needle. During the first year of life fine motor skills make considerable progress.

opposable thumb
position of the thumb apart from the fingers, unique to humans, that makes possible fine motor movements

By 9–12 months infants are able to grasp small objects.

The principal milestones of fine motor development in infancy are reaching and grasping. Oddly, infants are better at reaching during the first month of life than they are at 2 months of age (Spencer et al., 2000). Neonates will extend their arms awkwardly toward an interesting object, an action called *prereaching,* although it is more like a swipe or a swing than a well-coordinated reach. By 2 months, however, prereaching no longer takes place (Lee et al., 2008). Prereaching is a reflex that occurs in response to an object, and like many reflexes it disappears within the first months of life.

At about 3 months of age, reaching reappears, but in a more coordinated and accurate way than in the neonate. Reaching continues to develop over the course of the first year, becoming smoother, more direct, and more capable of adjusting to changes in the movement and position of the object (Berthier & Carrico, 2010).

Grasping is also a neonatal reflex, and this means it is not under intentional control (Schott & Rossor, 2003). Neonates will automatically grasp whatever is placed in their hands. Like reaching, grasping becomes smoother and more accurate during the first year, as infants learn to adjust the positions of their fingers and thumbs even before their hand reaches the object, and to adjust further once they grasp the object, in response to its size, shape, and weight (Daum & Prinz, 2011). By the end of the first year, infants are able to grasp a spoon well enough to begin to feed themselves.

At the same time as infants' abilities for reaching and grasping are advancing, they are learning to coordinate the two. They use the combination to help them explore the environment around them. By 5 months of age, once they reach and grasp an object, they might hold it with one hand as they explore it with the other, or transfer it from one hand to the other (Keen, 2005).

Learning to coordinate reaching and grasping is the basis of further development of fine motor skills, and an essential part of human motor functioning. However, during infancy it can also be a dangerous ability to have. Beginning at about 4 to 5 months, what is the first thing infants do with an object after reaching and grasping it? They put it in their mouths, of course—whether it is edible or not. (How this tendency somehow

Cultural Focus: Infant Fine Motor Development Across Cultures

Fine motor development in infancy mainly involves learning how to reach and how to grasp, and then how to coordinate the two. Infants everywhere need to learn how to perform these simple but essential activities, and as you will see in this video, infants across countries show similarities in the development of their fine motor skills.

Review Question:

Can you think of any related skills that the pincer grasp might be a precursor for? What about skills related to grasping? In what ways would these primitive skills be important across cultures?

Watch INFANT FINE MOTOR DEVELOPMENT ACROSS CULTURES

survived natural selection is a good question.) At this age they can mainly grasp objects that pose no danger, because their grasping ability is not yet fine enough to enable them to grasp objects they could choke on. However, by 9–12 months of age infants learn the "pincer grasp" that allows them to hold a small object between their thumb and forefinger, such as a marble, a coin, or a crayon stub (Murkoff et al., 2003). This allows them to begin feeding themselves small pieces of food, but the tendency to taste even the untasteable remains at this age, so others have to be especially vigilant in monitoring what infants reach, grasp, and place in their mouths.

Sensory Development

LO 4.7   **Describe when and how infants develop depth perception and intermodal perception.**

As described in Chapter 3, the senses vary in how developed they are at birth. Taste and touch are nearly mature, hearing is well-developed in most respects, and sight is the least mature of the senses.

DEPTH PERCEPTION One important aspect of vision that develops during infancy is **depth perception**, the ability to discern the relative distance of objects in the environment (Kavsec, 2003). The key to depth perception is **binocular vision**, the ability to combine the images of each eye into one image. Because our two eyes are slightly apart on our faces, they have slightly different angles on the visual field before them, and combining these two angles into one image provides a perception of the depth or distance of the object. That is, it indicates the location of the object in relation to the observer and in relation to other objects in the visual field. Binocular vision begins to develop by about 3 months of age (Brown & Miracle, 2003; Slater et al., 2002).

Depth perception becomes especially important once babies become mobile. Prior to that time, their lack of depth perception is harmless, but once they begin to crawl and then walk they may run into things or fall off the edge of surfaces unless they can use depth perception to anticipate hazards.

This was first demonstrated in a classic experiment by Eleanor Gibson and James Walk (1960). Gibson's inspiration for the experiment was a recent trip to the Grand Canyon, where her fear that her young children would tumble over the edge inspired her to wonder when children develop an awareness of depth that allows them to avoid such mishaps. Back in the lab, she and Walk designed a clever experiment. They made a glass-covered table with a checkered pattern below the glass, but on one half of the table the checkered pattern was just below the surface whereas on the other half it was about two feet below, giving the appearance of a "visual cliff" in the middle of the table (see **Figure 4.6**).

depth perception
ability to discern the relative distance of objects in the environment

binocular vision
ability to combine the images of the two eyes into one image

Figure 4.6 The Visual Cliff Experiment

Infants' reluctance to cross the "visual cliff" shows their ability for depth perception.

The infants in the study (ages 6–14 months) were happy to crawl around on the "shallow" side of the cliff, but most would not cross over to the "deep" side, even when their mothers stood on the other side of it and beckoned them encouragingly. This showed that they had learned depth perception.

INTERMODAL PERCEPTION Studies of infants' sensory abilities typically try to isolate a single sense so that it can be studied without interference from the others, but of course this is not how the senses function in real life. Shake a rattle in front of 6-month-old baby and she sees it, hears it, reaches out and touches it, then tastes it, effortlessly coordinating all her senses at once.

The integration and coordination of sensory information is called **intermodal perception** (Lewkowitz & Lickliter, 2013). Even neonates possess a rudimentary form of this ability. When they hear a sound they look in the direction it came from, indicating coordination of auditory and visual responses. Over the course of the first year intermodal perception develops further. One-month-old infants recognize objects they have put in their mouths but have not seen before, indicating integration of touch and sight (Schweinle & Wilcox, 2004). Four-month-old infants look longer at a video of a puppet jumping up and down in time with music than at the same puppet when the jumping does not match the music, suggesting that the correspondence of visual and auditory stimuli appeals to them (Spelke, 1979). By 8 months, infants can even match an unfamiliar person's face with the correct voice when the faces and voices vary on the basis of age and gender, indicating a developing ability to coordinate visual and auditory information (Patterson & Werker, 2002). Thus the early development of intermodal perception helps infants learn about their physical and social world (Lewkowitz & Lickliter, 2013).

intermodal perception

integration and coordination of information from the various senses

Practice Quiz   ANSWERS AVAILABLE IN ANSWER KEY.

1. A typical 1-year-old infant _____.
   a. is able to hold an object with one hand, but can't transfer it from one hand to the other
   b. uses prereaching to get an object of interest
   c. can grasp a utensil to feed himself
   d. will not be able to hold small objects.

2. Mahori was strapped to his mother's back for the first year of his life. Which of the following is LEAST LIKELY?
   a. He will have some muscle atrophy that will cause him to be delayed in walking by a few years.
   b. Mahori's motor development will be similar to an American child if they are compared during kindergarten.
   c. The sequence of his motor development will be the same as that of babies in cultures where walking during infancy is actively encouraged.
   d. Both genes and environment play a role in his motor development.

3. When motor development of infants is compared among cultures, it is clear that environment has _____.
   a. no effect on gross motor development
   b. a large effect on gross motor development
   c. a relatively small effect on gross motor development
   d. more of an effect on males than on females

4. Without _____ babies would not have depth perception.
   a. color vision   c. binocular vision
   b. 20/20 vision   d. intermodal perception

5. Four-month-olds look longer at a video of a puppet jumping up and down in time with music than at the same puppet when the jumping does not match the music. This is evidence of _____.
   a. habituation   c. intermodal perception
   b. the A-not-B-error   d. assimilation

Summary: Physical Development

LO 4.1 **Describe how the infant's body changes in the first year, and explain the two basic principles of physical growth.**

The physical developments of infancy include a tripling of weight and an inch-per-month growth in height. The cephalocaudal principle means that physical growth tends to begin at the top, with the head, and then proceeds downward to the rest of the body. The proximodistal principle means that growth proceeds from the middle of the body outward.

For most infants the first tooth appears between 5 and 9 months of age. Teething pain can be soothed with something to bite or chew on or something cold to drink or eat, or by using topical medications.

LO 4.2 **Identify the different parts of the brain and describe how the brain changes in the first few years of life.**

The brain is separated into two hemispheres connected by the corpus callosum, and each hemisphere has four lobes with distinct functions. Brain development in infancy is concentrated in the expansion of dendritic connections and myelination. Studies of infants and children exposed to extreme deprivation indicate that the brain is especially vulnerable in the first year of life.

LO 4.3 **Describe how infant sleep changes in the course of the first year and evaluate the risk factors for SIDS, including the research evidence regarding cosleeping.**

Sleep needs decline during the first year. SIDS is most common at age 2–4 months. Sleeping on the back rather than the stomach greatly reduces the risk of SIDS. In cultures where infants sleep alongside their mothers on a firm surface the risk of SIDS is very low. Historically and worldwide today, mother–infant cosleeping is far more common than putting babies to sleep in a room of their own.

LO 4.4 **Describe how infants' nutritional needs change during the first year of life and identify the reasons for and consequences of malnutrition in infancy.**

The best way to obtain good high-fat nutrition during infancy is through breast milk. The timing of the introduction of solid food varies among cultures, from the first weeks of life to sometime in the second half of the first year. Malnutrition in infancy is usually due mainly to the mother being unable or unwilling to breast-feed.

LO 4.5 **List the major causes and preventive methods of infant mortality and describe some cultural approaches to protecting infants.**

Malnutrition is a common source of infant mortality, but the most common source is diarrhea. Diarrhea can be cured by oral rehydration therapy (ORT), though access to clean water makes this treatment unavailable in some parts of the world. The cultural practices of secluding infants in their early weeks, cosleeping with them, and constantly carrying them developed out of long and painful human experience with high infant mortality.

LO 4.6 **Describe the major changes during infancy in gross and fine motor development.**

Achievements in gross motor development in infancy include rolling over, crawling, and standing. Cultural practices restricting or encouraging gross motor development make a slight difference in the timing of gross motor achievements, but little difference in the long run. Reaching and grasping are two of the fine motor milestones of the first year.

LO 4.7 **Describe when and how infants develop depth perception and intermodal perception.**

Increased adeptness at binocular vision around 3 months of age enables infants to develop depth perception during the first year. Infants also become better at intermodal perception or coordinating their senses.

Section 2   Cognitive Development

⌄ Learning Objectives

4.8 Describe the meaning of maturation, schemes, assimilation, and accommodation.

4.9 Describe the first four sensorimotor substages and explain how object permanence develops over the course of the first year.

4.10 Summarize the major critiques of Piaget's sensorimotor theory.

4.11 Describe the elements of the information processing model of cognitive functioning.

4.12 Explain how attention and habituation change during infancy.

4.13 Explain how short-term and long-term memory expand during infancy.

4.14 Describe the major scales used in measuring infant development and explain how habituation assessments are used to predict later intelligence.

4.15 Evaluate the claim that educational media enhance infants' cognitive development.

4.16 Describe the course of language development over the first year of life.

4.17 Describe how cultures vary in their stimulation of language development.

COGNITIVE DEVELOPMENT: Piaget's Theory of Cognitive Development

mental structure

in Piaget's theory of cognitive development, the cognitive systems that organize thinking into coherent patterns so that all thinking takes place on the same level of cognitive functioning

cognitive-developmental approach

focus on how cognitive abilities change with age in stage sequence of development, pioneered by Piaget and since taken up by other researchers

Unquestionably, the most influential theory of cognitive development from infancy through adolescence is the one developed by the Swiss psychologist Jean Piaget (pee-ah-JAY), who lived from 1896 to 1980. Piaget's observations convinced him that children of different ages think differently, and that changes in cognitive development proceed in distinct stages (Piaget, 1954).

LO 4.8   **Describe the meaning of maturation, schemes, assimilation, and accommodation.**

Each stage of Piaget's theory involves a different way of thinking about the world. The idea of cognitive stages means that each person's cognitive abilities are organized into coherent **mental structures**; a person who thinks within a particular stage in one aspect of life should think within that stage in all other aspects of life as well, because all thinking is part of the same mental structure (Keating, 1991). Because Piaget focused on how cognition changes with age, his approach (and the approach of those who have followed in his tradition) is known as the **cognitive-developmental approach**.

According to Piaget, the driving force behind development from one stage to the next is **maturation**, a biologically driven program of developmental change (Inhelder & Piaget, 1958; Piaget, 2002). Each of us has within our genotype a prescription for cognitive development that prepares us for certain changes at certain ages. A reasonably normal environment is necessary for cognitive development to occur, but the effect of the environment is limited. You cannot teach a 1-year-old something that only a 4-year-old can learn, no matter how sophisticated your teaching techniques are. By the time the 1-year-old reaches age 4, the biological processes of maturation will make it easy to understand the world as a typical child of 4 understands it, and no special teaching will be required.

Along with maturation, Piaget emphasized that cognitive development is driven by the child's efforts to understand and influence the surrounding environment (Demetriou & Ratopoulos, 2004; Piaget, 2002). Children actively construct their understanding of the world, rather than being merely the passive recipients of environmental influences. Piaget's view was in sharp contrast to the behaviorists (the leading theorists prior to Piaget), who viewed the environment as acting on the child through rewards and punishments rather than seeing the child as an active agent.

Piaget proposed that the child's construction of reality takes place through the use of **schemes**, which are cognitive structures for processing, organizing, and interpreting information. For infants, schemes are based on sensory and motor processes such as sucking and grasping, but after infancy, schemes become symbolic and representational, as words, ideas, and concepts. For example, all nouns are schemes—*tree, chair, dog*—because thinking of these words evokes a cognitive structure that allows you to process, organize, and interpret information.

The two processes involved in the use of schemes are **assimilation and accommodation**. Assimilation occurs when *new information is altered to fit an existing scheme*. In contrast, accommodation entails *changing the scheme to adapt to the new information*. Assimilation and accommodation usually take place together in varying degrees; they are "two sides of the same cognitive coin" (Flavell et al., 2002, p. 5). For example, an infant who has been breast-feeding may use mostly assimilation and a slight degree of accommodation when learning to suck from the nipple on a bottle, but if sucking on a brush handle or a parent's finger the infant would be able to use assimilation less and need to use accommodation more. The video *Assimilation and Accommodation* shows examples of each process.

maturation
concept that an innate, biologically based program is the driving force behind development

schemes
cognitive structures for processing, organizing, and interpreting information.

assimilation
cognitive process of altering new information to fit an existing scheme

accommodation
cognitive process of changing a scheme to adapt to new information

---

Watch   ASSIMILATION AND ACCOMMODATION

People of other ages, too, use both assimilation and accommodation whenever they are processing cognitive information. One example is right in front of you. In the course of reading this textbook, you will read things that sound familiar to you from your own experience, so that you can easily assimilate them to what you already know. Other information, especially the information from cultures other than your own, will be contrary to the schemes you have developed from living in your culture and will require you to use accommodation in order to expand your knowledge and understanding of human development across the life span.

CRITICAL THINKING QUESTION

Provide an example of something a 4-year-old could learn easily but a 1-year-old could not learn even with special teaching.

The Sensorimotor Stage

LO 4.9 **Describe the first four sensorimotor substages and explain how object permanence develops over the course of the first year.**

Based on his own research and his collaborations with his colleague Barbel Inhelder, Piaget devised a theory of cognitive development to describe the stages that children's thinking passes through during their early years (Inhelder & Piaget, 1958; Piaget, 1972; see **Table 4.1**). The first 2 years of life Piaget termed the **sensorimotor stage**. Cognitive development in this stage involves learning how to coordinate the activities of the senses (such as watching an object as it moves across your field of vision) with motor activities (such as reaching out to grasp the object). During infancy, the two major cognitive achievements are the advance in sensorimotor development from reflex behavior to intentional action and the attainment of object permanence.

SENSORIMOTOR SUBSTAGES According to Piaget, the sensorimotor stage can be divided into six substages (Piaget, 1952, 1954). The first four substages take place during the first year of life and will be described here. The last two sensorimotor stages develop in the second year and will be covered in Chapter 5, on toddlerhood.

> **Substage 1: Simple reflexes (0–1 month).** In this substage, cognitive activity is based mainly on the neonatal reflexes described in Chapter 3, such as sucking, rooting, and grasping. Reflexes are a type of scheme, because they are a way of processing and organizing information. However, unlike most schemes, for which there is a balance of assimilation and accommodation, reflex schemes are weighted heavily toward assimilation, because they do not adapt much in response to the environment.

> **Substage 2: First habits and primary circular reactions (1–4 months).** In this substage, infants' activities in relation to the world become based less on reflexes and

sensorimotor stage

in Piaget's theory, the first 2 years of cognitive development, which involves learning how to coordinate the activities of the senses with motor activities

Table 4.1 Stages of Cognitive Development in Piaget's Theory

Ages	Stage	Characteristics
0–2	Sensorimotor	Capable of coordinating the activities of the senses with motor activities
2–7	Preoperational	Capable of symbolic representation, such as in language, but with limited ability to use mental operations
7–11	Concrete operations	Capable of using mental operations, but only in concrete, immediate experience; difficulty thinking hypothetically
11–15 and up	Formal operations	Capable of thinking logically and abstractly; capable of formulating hypotheses and testing them systematically; thinking is more complex; and can think about thinking (metacognition)

more on the infants' purposeful behavior. Specifically, infants in this substage learn to repeat bodily movements that occurred initially by chance. For example, infants often discover how tasty their hands and fingers can be in this substage. While moving their hands around randomly one ends up in their mouth and they begin sucking on it. Finding this sensation pleasurable, they repeat the movement, now intentionally. The movement is *primary* because it focuses on the infant's own body, and *circular* because once it is discovered it is repeated intentionally.

Substage 3: Secondary circular reactions (4–8 months). Like primary circular reactions, secondary circular reactions entail the repetition of movements that originally occurred by chance. The difference is that primary circular reactions involve activity that is restricted to the infant's own body, whereas secondary circular reactions involve activity in relation to the external world. For example, Piaget recorded how his daughter Lucienne accidentally kicked a mobile hanging over her crib. Delighted at the effect, she now repeated the behavior intentionally, over and over, each time squealing with laughter (Crain, 2000).

Substage 4: Coordination of secondary schemes (8–12 months). In this substage, for the first time the baby's actions begin not as accidents but as intentional, goal-directed behavior. Furthermore, rather than exercising one scheme at a time, the infant can now coordinate schemes. For example, at this age Piaget's son Laurent was able to move an object (Piaget's hand) out of the way in order to reach another object (a matchbox), thus coordinating three schemes: moving something aside, reaching, and grasping.

OBJECT PERMANENCE Another important cognitive advance in infancy is the initial understanding of **object permanence**. This is the awareness that objects (including people) continue to exist even when we are not in direct sensory or motor contact with them.

From his observations and simple experiments, Piaget concluded that infants have little understanding of object permanence for much of the first year of life (Piaget, 1952). When infants under 4 months drop an object, they do not look to see where it went. Piaget interpreted this as indicating that, to the infants, the object ceased to exist once they could not see or touch it. From 4 to 8 months, infants who drop an object will look briefly to see where it has gone, but only briefly, which Piaget interpreted as indicating that they are unsure whether the object still exists. If infants at this age are shown an interesting object—Piaget liked to use his pocket watch—and then the object is placed under a blanket, they will not lift up the blanket to look for it.

It is only at 8–12 months that infants begin to show a developing awareness of object permanence. Now, when shown an interesting object that then disappears under a blanket, they will pick up the blanket to find it. However, their grasp of object permanence at this age is still rudimentary, as Piaget showed by making the task slightly more complicated. After an 8–12-month-old successfully solved the object-under-the-blanket task several times, Piaget introduced a second blanket next to the first, showed the infant the object, and this time placed it under the second blanket. Infants at this age then looked for the object—but not under the second blanket, where they had just seen it hidden, but under the first blanket, where they had found it before!

Piaget called this the *A-not-B error*. The infants were used to finding the object under blanket A, so they continued to look under blanket A, not blanket B, even after they had seen the object hidden under blanket B. To Piaget, this error indicated that the infants believed that their own action of looking under blanket A was what had caused the object to reappear. They did not understand that the object continued to exist irrespective of their actions, so they did not yet fully grasp object permanence.

Limited understanding of object permanence could explain why infants love the game "peek-a-boo," in which adults cover their face with their hands or an object (such

object permanence
awareness that objects (including people) continue to exist even when we are not in direct sensory or motor contact with them

Cultural Focus: Object Permanence Across Cultures

Like the development of fine motor skills, the knowledge of object permanence is something that all young children need to learn in order to function in the world. In this video we see demonstrations of children at various ages being tested to see if they grasp the concept of object permanence or not. The children from many different cultures indicate that this is a universal concept.

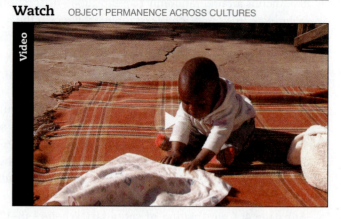

Watch   OBJECT PERMANENCE ACROSS CULTURES

Review Question:

According to this video, object permanence is universal across cultures. Why would this be such an important concept for children to acquire?

as a cloth), then suddenly reveal it. One study found that this game was played by adults and infants across a diverse range of cultures, including Brazil, Greece, India, Iran, Indonesia, South Korea, and South Africa (Fernald & O'Neill, 1993). Infants everywhere delighted in the game, and across cultures there were developmental changes. In the early months, infants enjoyed the game but responded only when the other person's face reappeared. Beginning at about 5 months, babies would begin to smile and laugh even before the other person reappeared, indicating that they were anticipating the event. By 12 months old, infants would initiate the game themselves by holding a cloth up to the adult's face or putting it over their own. Perhaps infants everywhere love "peek-a-boo" because to them, given their limited understanding of object permanence, the other person's face seems to disappear when it is obscured, then suddenly, magically reappears.

Evaluating Piaget's Sensorimotor Theory

LO 4.10   Summarize the major critiques of Piaget's sensorimotor theory.

You may have noticed that some of the examples discussed previously involved Piaget's children. Actually, Piaget initially based his theory of sensorimotor development on his careful observations and experiments with his own three children, Laurent, Lucienne, and Jacqueline. It is remarkable—and it is a testimony to Piaget's brilliance—that a theory based on just three children within the same Swiss family became the reigning theory of infant cognitive development.

Even today, over 70 years after he first proposed it, Piaget's theory of infant cognitive development remains influential. Like all good theories, it has inspired a wealth of research to test its assertions and implications. And, like even the best theories, it has been modified and altered on the basis of research (Morra et al., 2008).

In recent decades, methods of testing infants' cognitive abilities have become much more technologically advanced. Studies using these methods have generally concluded that Piaget's theory was correct in its overall description of infant cognitive development (Marcovitch et al., 2003). However, some critics argue that the theory may have underestimated infants' cognitive abilities, especially with regard to object permanence.

MOTOR COORDINATION AND MEMORY IN OBJECT PERMANENCE Infants' motor development occurs along with their cognitive development, so when they fail to look under a blanket for a hidden object, could it be they lack the motor coordination to search for the object rather than that they believe it is has disappeared? One line of research by Renee Baillargeon and colleagues has tested this hypothesis by using the "violation of expectations method." This method is based on the assumption that infants will look longer at an event that has violated their expectations, and if they look longer at an event violating the rule of object permanence this indicates some understanding of object permanence, without requiring any motor movements. For example, at age 5–6 months, infants will look longer when a toy they have seen hidden at one spot in a sandbox emerges from a different spot (Baillargeon, 2008; Newcombe & Huttenlocher, 2006). This seems to indicate an expectation that it should have emerged from the same spot, as a permanent object would. Even at 2–3 months infants look longer at events that are physically impossible (Wang et al., 2005), perhaps showing a more advanced understanding of objects than Piaget would have predicted.

Some critics of Piaget's sensorimotor theory argue that mistakes regarding object permanence may reflect memory development rather than a failure to understand the properties of objects. For example, with respect to the A-not-B error, the longer the delay between hiding the object under blanket B and the infant's attempts to find it, the higher the likelihood of making the error, suggesting that with a longer delay the infant may simply have forgotten where it was placed (Diamond, 1985).

CULTURE AND OBJECT PERMANENCE Another criticism of Piaget's sensorimotor theory is cultural (Maynard, 2008). The theory was originally based on his own three Swiss children, and nearly all subsequent research has been on children in the West (Mistry & Saraswathi, 2003). However, one of the few non-Western studies, of infants in Ivory Coast, found that infants there reached the milestones of the sensorimotor stages earlier than Piaget had described (Dasen et al., 1978), perhaps because their parents encouraged them to develop motor skills.

Overall, however, Piaget's sensorimotor theory has held up well over many decades. Many parts of it have been supported by research, and so far no other comprehensive theory has come along to replace it. However, the information processing approach described next views infant cognitive development quite differently.

Practice Quiz   ANSWERS AVAILABLE IN ANSWER KEY.

1. Which of the following best describes the Piagetian term of "schemes"?

 a. When new information is altered to fit existing information

 b. When a person's self-concept is changed to adapt to new information

 c. Cognitive structures for processing, organizing, and interpreting information

 d. When a mental structure is changed to adapt to new information

2. Seena likes to suck on a pacifier during naptime at her daycare. One day, her mother forgets to pack the pacifier, so her teachers offer her a plastic toy to suck on instead. In learning to suck on this toy, Seena relies heavily on _____.

 a. accommodation

 b. assimilation

 c. object permanence

 d. maturation

3. Troy is 12 months old and loves to eat goldfish crackers. While sitting in the kitchen he sees a bag of goldfish. When his actions become intentional and goal directed, and he actively moves, reaches for, and grasps the bag of crackers, it is clear that he is in the sensorimotor substage _____.

 a. 4: coordination of secondary schemes

 b. 3: secondary circular reactions

 c. 2: first habits and primary circular reactions

 d. 1: simple reflexes

4. Schaffer loves it when his mother puts a towel over her face and then quickly pulls it down. His big belly laugh at this game of peek-a-boo indicates that _____.

 a. he is assimilating rather than accommodating

 b. he has made the A-not-B error

 c. he has a limited understanding of object permanence

 d. he lacks intermodal perception

5. Which of the following is a critique of Piaget's sensorimotor theory?

 a. His tests of object permanence required motor ability.

 b. It may have overestimated infants' cognitive abilities.

 c. It describes the cognitive abilities of girls more accurately than boys.

 d. His theory was based mostly on children from non-Western cultures.

COGNITIVE DEVELOPMENT:
Information Processing in Infancy

Piaget's theory and the research it inspired focuses on how thinking changes with age. To Piaget, we do not simply expand our cognitive capacity as we develop, we actually think differently at each life stage.

The Information Processing Approach

LO 4.11 Describe the elements of the information processing model of cognitive functioning.

The **information processing approach** to understanding cognitive development is quite different. Rather than viewing cognitive development as *discontinuous,* that is, as separated into distinct stages, the way Piaget did, the information processing approach views cognitive change as *continuous,* meaning gradual and steady. In this view, cognitive processes remain essentially the same over time (Halford, 2005). The focus is not on how mental structures and ways of thinking change with age but on the thinking processes that exist at all ages. Nevertheless, some studies of information processing compare people of various ages to show how thinking capacities change developmentally.

The original model for the information processing approach was the computer (Hunt, 1989). Information processing researchers and theorists have tried to break down human thinking into separate parts in the same way the functions of a computer are separated into capacities for *attention, processing,* and *memory.* In the case of object permanence, for example, someone taking the information processing approach would examine how infants draw their attention to the most relevant aspects of the problem, process the results of each trial, remember the results, and retrieve the results from previous trials to compare to the most recent trial. In this way the information processing approach is a *componential approach* (Sternberg, 1983), because it involves breaking down the thinking process into its various components.

Recent models of information processing have moved away from a simple computer analogy and recognize that the brain is more complex than any computer (Ashcraft, 2009). Rather than occurring in a step-by-step fashion as in a computer, in humans the different components of thinking operate simultaneously, as **Figure 4.7** illustrates. Nevertheless, the focus of information processing remains on the components of the thinking process, especially attention and memory. Let's look next at how attention and memory develop during infancy.

Attention

LO 4.12 Explain how attention and habituation change during infancy.

Information processing begins with stimulus information that enters the senses, but much of what you see, hear, and touch is processed no further. For example, as you

information processing approach

approach to understanding cognitive functioning that focuses on cognitive processes that exist at all ages, rather than on viewing cognitive development in terms of discontinuous stages

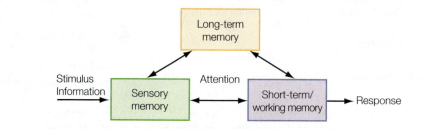

Figure 4.7 Information Processing Model

The components of the model operate simultaneously.

read this, there may be sounds in the environment, other sights in your visual field, and the feeling of your body in the seat where you are reading, but if you are focusing on what you are reading most of this information goes no further than sensory memory. The only information you proceed to process is the information on which you focus your attention.

In infants the study of attention has focused on **habituation**, which is the gradual decrease in attention to a stimulus after repeated presentations. For example, infants will look longer at a toy the first time it is presented than the fourth or fifth time. A complementary concept, **dishabituation**, is the revival of attention when a new stimulus is presented following several presentations of a previous stimulus. For example, if you show infants a picture of the same face several times in a row, then show a new face, they will generally dishabituate to the new face, that is, they will pay more attention to it than to the "old" face. Habituation and dishabituation can be studied by monitoring infants' looking behavior, but infants rarely lay still for long even if they are paying attention to something, so two other methods have been frequently used: heart rate and sucking rate. Heart rate declines when a new stimulus is presented and gradually rises as habituation takes place. Infants suck on a pacifier more frequently when a new stimulus is presented and gradually decline in their sucking rate with habituation.

During the course of the first year of life, it takes less and less time for habituation to occur. When presented with a visual stimulus, neonates may take several minutes before they show signs of habituating (by changing their looking time, heart rate, or sucking rate). By 4–5 months old, habituation in a similar experiment takes only about 10 seconds, and by 7–8 months only a few seconds (Domsch et al., 2010; Kavsek & Bornstein, 2010). This appears to occur because infants become more efficient at perceiving and processing a stimulus.

Joint attention develops by the end of the first year.

Even when they are a few months old, infants of the same age vary in their rates of habituation, and these individual differences tend to be stable over time. Some infants are more efficient than others at processing information; consequently, they habituate more quickly. Infants who habituate relatively slowly appear to do so not because they are especially good at sustaining their attention but because they seem to get stuck on the stimulus and have difficulty disengaging from it. Speed of habituation predicts memory ability on other tasks in infancy, as well as later performance on intelligence tests (Courage et al., 2004; Rose et al., 2005).

In the second half of the first year, infants' patterns of attention become increasingly social. They direct their attention not just to whatever sensations are most stimulating but to what the people around them are attending to, engaging in *joint attention*. By the end of the first year they often notice what important people around them are paying attention to, and will look or point in the same direction. One experiment showed that 10-month-old infants were less likely to look or point in the direction an adult was faced if the adult's eyes were closed or blindfolded, indicating that the infants were aware of the adults' attentional patterns and matched their own to them (Brooks & Meltzoff, 2005).

Joint attention is the basis not just of infants' information processing development but of language and emotional communication (Van Hecke et al., 2007). This makes sense; one way infants and children learn new words is to observe what another person is doing or looking at when they use a word. Often this takes place during social interactions between infants and others, but it can also take place from infants observing where the attention of another person is directed. As we will see in more detail later in the chapter, not all cultures encourage verbal interactions with infants. A cultural analysis of this issue showed that in cultures where verbal interactions with adults are limited, infants and young children learn a great deal of their language by observing adults' language use and "listening in," that is, using joint attention to discern the meaning of words (Akhtar, 2005).

habituation

gradual decrease in attention to a stimulus after repeated presentations

dishabituation

following habituation, the revival of attention when a new stimulus is presented

Memory

LO 4.13 **Explain how short-term and long-term memory expand during infancy.**

Infants' memory abilities expand greatly during the first year of life, both for short-term and for long-term memory. One reflection of the development of short-term memory is their improvement in the object permanence task. As noted earlier, object permanence is a test of short-term memory as well as a test of knowledge of the properties of objects. Memory studies using object permanence tasks show that the number of locations infants can remember and search to look for a hidden object increases sharply in the second half of the first year (Morra et al., 2008).

Long-term memory also improves notably over the course of the first year. In one experiment, researchers tied a string to the foot of infants 2 to 6 months old and taught them to move a mobile hanging above their cribs by kicking their foot (Rovee-Collier, 1999). The 2-month-olds forgot the training within a week—they no longer kicked to make the mobile move when the string was tied to their legs—but the 6-month-olds remembered it for about three weeks, demonstrating better long-term memories.

Further experiments showed an interesting distinction between *recognition memory* and *recall memory* (Hildreth et al., 2003). After the mobile-kicking trick appeared to be lost from the infants' memories, the researchers gave the infants a hint by making the mobile move. The infants *recognized* this clue and began kicking again to make the mobile move, up to a month later, even though they had been unable to *recall* the memory before being prompted. The older the infant was, the more effective the prompting. From infancy onward, recognition memory comes easier to us than recall memory (Flavell et al., 2002).

Infants and young children clearly learn a great deal, so why is it that later in our development we recall so little of what happened in our early years? Some researchers have proposed that long-term memories require language and a sense of self, but other animals also show this "infantile amnesia," so this cannot be the main explanation. Recently, memory researchers have proposed that the answer lies in the development of the hippocampus, part of the lower brain (Josselyn & Frankland, 2012). The hippocampus is immature at birth and adds neurons at a high rate in the early years of development. The addition of so many new neurons may interfere with the existing memory circuits, so that long-term memories cannot be formed until the production of neurons in the hippocampus declines in early childhood, as it becomes more fully developed.

Practice Quiz   ANSWERS AVAILABLE IN ANSWER KEY.

1. Which of the following is analogous to, and was the model for, the information processing approach?
   a. The circuits of a radio
   b. The computer
   c. The human brain
   d. The animal brain

2. You and your brother are babysitting your infant cousin. Initially, he is very interested in a puppet that you were using, but seems to not be very interested in it after a few minutes. Your brother thinks that he might not have a very long attention span. You tell your brother that your cousin is actually displaying _____.
   a. habituation
   b. dishabituation
   c. insensitivity to stimuli
   d. the A-not-B error

3. You are watching your next-door neighbor's 8-month-old infant. You notice that she is getting increasingly social. She directs her attention not just to whatever sensations are most

   stimulating, but to what the people around her are doing. She is _____.
   a. showing the A-not-B error
   b. displaying object permanence
   c. engaging in joint attention
   d. showing recognition

4. Researchers have proposed that the immaturity of the _____ at birth is why humans show infantile amnesia.
   a. cingulate gyrus
   b. hippocampus
   c. frontal lobe
   d. temporal lobe

5. One reflection of the development of infants' short-term memory is their improvement _____.
   a. at the task of object permanence
   b. in their fine motor skills
   c. in their gross motor skills
   d. in their language skills

COGNITIVE DEVELOPMENT:
Assessing Infant Development

Given the many remarkable changes in development that happen over the course of the first year, researchers have long been interested in evaluating infants to see if they are developing normally. There have also been efforts to improve infants' cognitive development through media stimulation.

Approaches to Assessing Development

LO 4.14 Describe the major scales used in measuring infant development and explain how habituation assessments are used to predict later intelligence.

There are a variety of methods used to measure infant development, including the scales approach of Gesell and Bayley. More recently, assessments of infants' cognitive development have focused on information processing, especially habituation.

THE BAYLEY SCALES One approach to assessing infant development was pioneered by Arnold Gesell (1934, 1946). Gesell constructed an assessment of infant development that included four subscales: motor skills (such as sitting), language use, adaptive behavior (such as exploring a new object), and personal–social behavior (such as using a spoon). Following the model of intelligence tests, which produce an *intelligence quotient (IQ)* as an overall measure of mental abilities, Gesell combined the results of his assessment into a **developmental quotient (DQ)** as an overall measure of infants' developmental progress.

Gesell's scale for infants is no longer used, but his approach was continued by Nancy Bayley, who produced the **Bayley Scales of Infant Development**, now in their third edition, the Bayley-III (Bayley, 2005). The Bayley-III can assess development from age 3 months to age 3½ years. There are three main scales on the Bayley-III:

1. *Cognitive Scale*. This scale measures mental abilities such as attention and exploration. For example, at 6 months it assesses whether the baby looks at pictures in a book; at 23–25 months it assesses whether a child can match similar pictures.
2. *Language Scale*. This scale measures use and understanding of language. For example, at 17–19 months it assesses whether the child can identify objects in a picture, and at 38–42 months it assesses whether the child can name four colors.
3. *Motor Scale*. This scale measures fine and gross motor abilities, such as sitting alone for 30 seconds at 6 months, or hopping twice on one foot at 38–42 months.

As with Gesell's scales, the Bayley scales produce an overall DQ.

However, the Bayley scales do not predict later IQ or school performance well (Hack et al., 2005). If you look closely at the examples above, this should not be surprising, as the Bayley scales measure quite different kinds of abilities than the verbal and spatial abilities that later IQ tests measure and that school work requires. (Let's face it, hopping on one foot is not likely to be predictive of school performance or any kind of work you are likely to do as an adult, unless you become a ballet dancer.) The only exception to this is at the lower extreme. An infant who scores very low on the Bayley scales may have serious developmental problems. Consequently, the Bayley scales are used mainly as a screening tool, to identify infants who have serious problems in need of immediate attention, rather than as predictors of later development for children within the normal range.

INFORMATION PROCESSING APPROACHES TO INFANT ASSESSMENT Efforts to predict later intelligence using information-processing approaches have shown

developmental quotient (DQ)

in assessments of infant development, the overall score indicating developmental progress

Bayley Scales of Infant Development

widely used assessment of infant development from age 3 months to 3½ years

Educational media products for infants have not been demonstrated to enhance cognitive development.

greater promise. The focus of these approaches has been on habituation. As noted earlier, infants vary in how long it takes them to habituate to a new stimulus, such as a sight or a sound. Some are "short-lookers" who habituate quickly, others are "long-lookers" who take more time and more presentations of the stimulus before they habituate. The shorter the habituation time, the more efficient the infant's information processing abilities. They look for a shorter length of time because it takes them less time to take in and process information about the stimulus.

Longitudinal studies have found that short-lookers in infancy tend to have higher IQ scores later in development than long-lookers do (Cuevas & Bell, 2014; Kavsek, 2004; Rose et al., 2005). In one study, short-lookers in infancy had higher IQs and higher educational achievement when they were followed up 20 years later, in emerging adulthood (Fagan et al., 2007). Habituation assessments in infancy have also been found to be useful for identifying infants who have developmental problems (Kavsek & Bornstein, 2008). Furthermore, habituation assessments tend to be more reliable than assessments of DQ using the Bayley scales, that is, they are more likely to be consistent when measured across more than one occasion (Cuevas & Bell, 2014; Kavsek, 2004). The most recent version of the Bayley scales now includes a measure of habituation (Bayley, 2005), which may improve reliability and predictive validity above previous versions of the scale.

Can Media Enhance Cognitive Development? The Myth of "Baby Einstein"

LO 4.15 Evaluate the claim that educational media enhance infants' cognitive development.

In addition to efforts to assess infants' cognitive development, efforts have also been made to enhance it. One effort of this kind that has become popular in some developed countries is educational media products for infants.

In the early 1990s a study was published claiming that listening to the music of Mozart enhanced cognitive functioning (Rauscher et al., 1993). The study was conducted with university students, not babies, and the "effect" lasted only 10 minutes, and subsequent studies failed to replicate even a 10-minute effect (Rauscher, 2003). Nevertheless, the study received worldwide attention and inspired the creation of a vast range of educational media products claiming to promote infants' cognitive development.

Do they work? The answer appears to be no. Many studies investigating this question have concluded that educational media products have no effect on infants' cognitive development. In fact, one study of 8- to 16-month-olds found that for every hour of "educational" DVDs viewed per day, the DVD viewers understood 8 to 16 *fewer* words than babies who watched no DVDs (Guernsey, 2007). The authors interpreted this surprising finding as due to the fact that the DVD viewers may have spent less time interacting with the people around them. That is, they were watching DVDs instead of interacting socially, and the DVD watching did not compensate for the deficit in social interaction. Similar results were found in another study (DeLoache et al., 2010). Fortunately, national studies have found that only 10% of babies in the United States use educational media products (Rideout, 2013). Watch the video *Media Use in Infancy* to see examples from various families.

These findings suggest that Piaget was right that children's cognitive maturity has its own innate timetable and that it is fruitless (and perhaps even detrimental) to

Watch MEDIA USE IN INFANCY

Video

try to hurry it along. So what can you do to promote infants' healthy cognitive development? Talk to them, read to them, respond to them—and be patient. They will grow up soon enough.

Practice Quiz ANSWERS AVAILABLE IN ANSWER KEY.

1. According to the text, infants who score extremely low on the Bayley scales _____.
   a. are predicted to do extremely well on IQ tests
   b. may have serious developmental problems and may require intervention
   c. are predicted to do poorly in school due to low motivation and boredom despite high IQ scores
   d. score above normal development milestones and tests of object permanence

2. Your brother is concerned that your nephew is not going to be a very good student when he goes to school because whenever he shows him something new, your nephew only looks at it for a short time. According to the text, is your brother correct?
   a. No, infants who are short-lookers tend to have a higher IQ and higher educational achievement than long-lookers later.
   b. No, infants who are short-lookers tend to have higher IQs in elementary school, but their scores decrease more later in development compared to long-lookers.

   c. Yes, infants who are short-lookers have a lower IQ and lower educational achievement later.
   d. Yes, infants who are short-lookers have a lower IQ, but they work harder than long-lookers.

3. The three main scales on the Bayley–III are the cognitive scale, language scale, and _____ scale.
   a. temperament
   b. personality
   c. attachment
   d. motor

4. Based on the research, do media products created for infants enhance their cognitive functioning?
   a. Yes. Studies show that infants who watch or listen to media products have enhanced cognitive functioning.
   b. Yes, but they only show beneficial effects if used since birth.
   c. No. Studies have concluded that educational media products have no effect on infants' cognitive development.
   d. Yes, but the beneficial effects are only for language development.

COGNITIVE DEVELOPMENT:
The Beginnings of Language

According to the traditional beliefs of the Beng people of Ivory Coast (in Africa), in the spirit world all people understand all languages (Gottlieb, 2000). Babies have just come from the spirit world when they are born, so they understand whatever is said in any language. However, during the first year, memory of all other languages fades and

Table 4.2 Milestones of Infant Language Development

Age	Milestone
2 months	Cooing (preverbal and gurgling sounds)
4–10 months	Babbling (repetitive consonant–vowel combinations)
8–10 months	First gestures (such as "bye-bye")
10–12 months	Comprehension of words and simple sentences
12 months	First spoken word

NOTE: For each milestone there is a normal range, and babies who are somewhat later in reaching the milestones may nevertheless have normal language development.

babies come to understand only the language they hear around them. This is actually a pretty accurate summary of how babies' language development takes place in the course of the first year of life, as we will learn next. (See **Table 4.2** for the milestones of infant language development.)

First Sounds and Words

LO 4.16 **Describe the course of language development over the first year of life.**

Very early on, babies begin to make the sounds that will eventually develop into language (Waxman & Lidz, 2006). The video *Language Development* provides an overview of the progression of sounds. First is **cooing**, the "oo-ing" and "ah-ing" and gurgling sounds babies make beginning at about 2 months old. Often cooing takes place in interactions with others, but sometimes it takes place without interactions, as if babies are discovering their vocal apparatus and trying out the sounds it can make.

Watch LANGUAGE DEVELOPMENT

Video

cooing

prelanguage "oo-ing" and "ah-ing," and gurgling sounds babies make beginning at about 2 months old

babbling

repetitive prelanguage consonant–vowel combinations such as "ba-ba-ba" or "do-do-do-do," made by infants universally beginning at about 6 months old

By about 4-6 months old, cooing develops into **babbling**, repetitive consonant–vowel combinations such as "ba-ba-ba" or "do-do-do-do." When my son Miles was 4 months old he repeated the sounds "ah-gee" so often that for awhile we called him "Mr. Ah-Gee." Babbling appears to be universal among infants. In fact, babies the world over appear to babble with the same sounds initially, regardless of the language of their culture (Lee at al., 2010). Deaf infants exposed to sign language have a form of babbling, too, using their hands instead of sounds (van Beinum, 2008). However, after a couple of months, infants begin to babble in the sounds distinctive to their culture and cease to babble in sounds they have not heard used by the people around them. By the time infants are about 9 months old, untrained listeners can distinguish whether a recording of babbling is from an infant raised amidst French, Arabic, or Chinese (Oller et al., 1997).

By around 8–10 months, infants begin to use gestures to communicate (Goldin-Meadow, 2009). They may lift their arms up to indicate they wish to be picked up, or point to an object they would like to have brought to them, or hold out an object to offer it to someone else, or wave bye-bye. Using gestures is a way of evoking behavior from others (for example, being picked up after lifting their arms in request), and also a way of evoking verbal responses from others (such as a spoken "bye-bye" in response to the infant's gestured bye-bye), at a time when infants still cannot produce words of their own.

Infants' first words usually are spoken a month or two before or after their first birthday. Typical first words include important people ("Mama," "Dada"), familiar animals ("dog"), moving objects ("car"), foods ("milk"), and greetings or farewells ("hi," "bye-bye") (Waxman & Lidz, 2006).

Most infants can speak only a few words, at most, by the end of their first year, but they understand many more words than they can speak. In fact, at all ages, language *comprehension* (the words we understand) exceeds language *production* (the words we use), but the difference is especially striking and notable during infancy. Even as early as 4 months old infants can recognize their own name (Mandel et al., 1995). By their first birthday, although infants can speak only a word or two they understand about 50 words (Menyuk et al., 1995).

The foundations of language comprehension are evident very early, in the abilities of infants to recognize changes in language sounds (Werker & Fennell, 2009). To test this ability, researchers play a spoken sound repeatedly for an infant (for example, "ba, ba, ba, ba"), then change it slightly ("pa, pa, pa, pa"). If an infant looks in the direction of the sound when it changes, this is taken to indicate awareness of the change. Even when only a few weeks old, infants show this awareness (Saffran et al., 2006).

Furthermore, like babbling, discrimination of simple sounds appears to be universal at first, but becomes more specialized toward the end of the first year to the language of the infant's culture. In one study, American and Japanese infants were compared at 6 and 12 months (Iverson et al., 2003). At 6 months, the American and Japanese infants were equally responsive to the distinction between "ra" and "la," even though there are no "r" or "l" sounds in the Japanese language, so the Japanese infants would not have heard this distinction before. However, by 12 months old the American infants could still recognize the "r" versus "l" distinction but the Japanese infants could not, as their language skills were now more specialized to their own language.

Infant-Directed (ID) Speech

LO 4.17 **Describe how cultures vary in their stimulation of language development.**

Suppose you were to say to an adult, "Would you like something to eat?" How would you say it? Now imagine saying the same thing to an infant. Would you change how you said it?

In many cultures, people speak in a special way to infants, called **infant-directed (ID) speech** (Bryant & Barrett, 2007). In ID speech, the pitch of the voice becomes higher than in normal speech, and the intonation is exaggerated. Grammar is simplified, and words and phrases are more likely to be repeated than in normal speech. Topics of ID speech often pertain to objects

infant-directed (ID) speech special form of speech that adults in many cultures direct toward infants, in which the pitch of the voice becomes higher than in normal speech, the intonation is exaggerated, and words and phrases are repeated

Adults in many cultures use infant-directed speech, with high pitch and exaggerated intonation.

("Look at the birdie! See the birdie?") or emotional communication ("What a good girl! You ate your applesauce!").

Why do people often use ID speech with infants? One reason is that the infants seem to like it. Even when ID speech is in a language they do not understand, infants show a preference for it by the time they are 4 months old, as indicated by paying greater attention to ID speech in an unfamiliar language than to non-ID speech in the same language (Singh, 2009). The video *Infant-Directed Speech* provides examples of parents using ID speech with their infants.

Watch INFANT-DIRECTED SPEECH

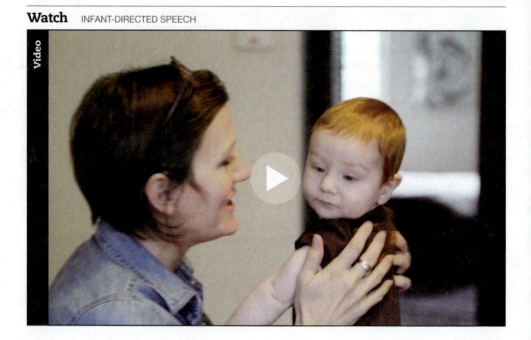

And why do infants like ID speech? One theory is that infants prefer it because it is more emotionally charged than other speech (Trainor et al., 2000). Also, at a time when language is still new to them, ID speech helps infants unravel language's mysteries. The exaggeration and repetition of words gives infants cues to their meaning (Soderstrom, 2007). By exaggerating the sounds used in making words, ID speech provides infants with information about the building blocks of speech they will use in the language of their culture (Kuhl, 2004). The exaggerations of ID speech also separate speech into specific words and phrases more clearly than normal speech does (Thiessen et al., 2005).

ID speech is common in Western cultures (Bryant & Barrett, 2007). Japanese studies have also found that ID speech is common (Mazuka et al., 2008). Outside the developed countries, however, there is more variability. Some traditional cultures use ID speech, such as the Fulani of West Africa, who say single words and phrases to their infants from their very first days of life in an effort to stimulate their language development (Johnson, 2000). However, in other traditional cultures parents do not use ID speech and make no special effort to speak to infants. For example, among the Gusii of Kenya, parents speak to infants substantially less than American parents do (Levine, 1994; Richman et al., 2010). The Gusii, like people in many traditional cultures, carry their infants around almost constantly and have a great deal of physical contact with them, including cosleeping at night, but they do not view it as necessary or useful to speak to infants. Similarly, the Ifaluk people of Micronesia believe there is no point in speaking to infants because they cannot understand what you say (Le, 2000). Nevertheless, despite receiving no ID speech, children in these cultures learn their language fluently within a few years, just as children in cultures with ID speech do.

Does this mean you do not need to speak to your own infants, in your culture? Definitely not. In cultures such as the Gusii and the Ifaluk parents may not speak directly to their infants very often, but infants are part of a language-rich environment all day long. Although no one speaks to infants directly, they are surrounded by conversation from their mother, sister, and other relatives. Instead of spending the day with one parent and perhaps a sibling, as infants do in cultures where ID speech is common, infants in traditional cultures typically have many adults and children around them in the course of the day. Families are bigger, extended family members live either in the same household or nearby, and interactions with other community members are more common (Akhtar & Tomasello, 2000). Perhaps ID speech developed because, in the small nuclear families that are typical of developed countries today, without ID speech infants may have very little other language stimulation. The success of children in traditional cultures in learning their languages despite having no ID speech shows that listening to others' conversations in a language-rich environment is also an effective way of acquiring a language (Akhtar, 2005).

By the end of their first year infants have laid an important foundation for language and can comprehend many words, but their language production is still very limited. The real explosion in language development comes in the second year, so in the next chapter we will examine the origins and growth of language in greater detail.

Practice Quiz   ANSWERS AVAILABLE IN ANSWER KEY.

1. Patrice is 6 months old and is quite talkative. She is now using repetitive consonant-vowel combinations, and her favorite appears to be ba-ba-ba-ba. Patrice has reached the _____ milestone in language development.

  a. cooing
  b. babbling
  c. gurgling
  d. infant-directed speech

2. Babbling _____.

  a. occurs only if the infant can hear
  b. is found only in infants from the Western Hemisphere
  c. is universal
  d. is the stage immediately before cooing

3. Cressida talks to her 5-month-old baby in a sweet, high-pitched, exaggerated manner and says things like, "Good girl, you ate your sweet potatoes! You're a good girl, yes you are!" This special way of speaking to infants is called _____.

  a. speech praise
  b. simplified speech
  c. infant-directed speech
  d. intimate speech

4. The Gusii of Kenya, like people in many traditional cultures, are in physical contact with their children nearly constantly. How do they view talking to children?

  a. They speak only to the upper caste infants.
  b. They speak to the male infants directly, but hardly ever to the females.
  c. They do not think that it is necessary or useful to speak to infants.
  d. They speak to them much more than in Western cultures.

5. Use of infant directed speech _____.

  a. leads to slower development of language than the more sophisticated style of language typically spoken with adults
  b. varies from culture to culture outside the West
  c. involves speaking in a low tone that infants are better able to hear
  d. has been shown to be less interesting to babies than normal speech; a reason why many parents do not use this "baby talk"

Summary: Cognitive Development

LO 4.8   Describe the meaning of maturation, schemes, assimilation, and accommodation.

Maturation is the biologically-based program of development. Piaget proposed that the child's construction of reality takes place through the use of schemes, which are cognitive structures for processing, organizing, and interpreting information. The two processes involved in the use of schemes are assimilation and accommodation. Assimilation occurs when new information is altered to fit an existing scheme. In contrast, accommodation entails changing the scheme to adapt to the new information.

LO 4.9   Describe the first four sensorimotor substages and explain how object permanence develops over the course of the first year.

Substage 1 is based on neonatal reflexes; 2 is based more on purposeful behavior; 3 entails the repetition of movements that first occurred by chance; and 4 is based on intentional, goal-directed behavior. Object permanence has begun to develop by the end of infancy, but it is not complete until the end of the second year.

LO 4.10 Summarize the major critiques of Piaget's sensorimotor theory.

Some critics argue that the theory may have underestimated infants' cognitive abilities. Another criticism of Piaget is cultural, because nearly all research has been on children in the West.

LO 4.11 Describe the elements of the information processing model of cognitive functioning.

In contrast to the cognitive-developmental approach initiated by Piaget, which divides cognitive development into distinct stages, the information-processing approach investigates the processes of cognitive functioning that occur at all ages. The focus is on the components of cognitive functioning, especially attention and memory.

LO 4.12 Explain how attention and habituation change during infancy.

Infants pay more attention to a stimulus they have not seen before. Habituation develops more quickly during the course of the first year, and at any given age, quickness of habituation is positively related to later cognitive achievements. Increasingly during the first year, infants learn through joint attention with others.

LO 4.13 Explain how short-term and long-term memory expand during infancy.

Both short-term and long-term memory improve notably over the course of the first year, though recognition memory comes easier than recall memory, as it does at later ages.

LO 4.14 Describe the major scales used in measuring infant development and explain how habituation assessments are used to predict later intelligence.

The Bayley scales are widely used to measure infants' development, but scores on the Bayley do not predict later cognitive development except for infants with serious deficits. Efforts to predict later intelligence using information processing approaches have shown greater promise. These assessments measure habituation by distinguishing between "short-lookers" and "long-lookers," with short-lookers higher in later intelligence.

LO 4.15 Evaluate the claim that educational media enhance infants' cognitive development.

Many studies investigating this question have concluded that educational media products have no effect on infants' cognitive development and may even be detrimental.

LO 4.16 Describe the course of language development over the first year of life.

Infants begin cooing when about 2 months old. When they first begin to babble at about 6 months, infants use a wide range of sounds, but within a few months they more often make the sounds from the main language they hear around them. First words are usually spoken around the end of the first year; infants can already understand about 50 words by this time.

LO 4.17 Describe how cultures vary in their stimulation of language development.

Many cultures use infant-directed (ID) speech, and babies appear to enjoy hearing it. However, even in cultures that do not use ID speech children become adept users of language by the time they are a few years old.

Section 3 Emotional And Social Development

Learning Objectives

4.18 Define infant temperament and its main dimensions.

4.19 Explain how the idea of goodness-of-fit pertains to temperament on both a family level and a cultural level.

4.20 Identify the primary emotions and describe how they develop during infancy.

4.21 Describe infants' emotional perceptions and how their emotions become increasingly social over the first year.

4.22 List the main features of infants' social worlds across cultures.

4.23 Compare and contrast the two major theories of infants' social development.

EMOTIONAL AND SOCIAL DEVELOPMENT: Temperament

Have you had any experience in caring for infants, perhaps as a baby-sitter, older sibling, or parent? If so, you have probably observed that they differ from early on in how they respond to you and to the environment. As a parent I have certainly observed this in my twins, who have had virtually the same environment all their lives and yet are very different in their emotional responses and expressions. Ask any parents of more than one child, and they will probably tell a similar tale (Reiss et al., 2006).

In the study of human development, these kinds of differences in emotionality are viewed as indicators of **temperament**. Temperament includes qualities such as activity level, soothability, emotionality, and sociability. You can think of temperament as the biologically based raw material of personality (Goldsmith, 2009; Rothbart et al., 2000).

temperament
innate responses to the physical and social environment, including qualities of activity level, irritability, soothability, emotional reactivity, and sociability

Conceptualizing Temperament

LO 4.18 Define infant temperament and its main dimensions.

Researchers on temperament believe that all infants are born with certain tendencies toward behavior and personality development, and the environment then shapes those tendencies in the course of development. Let's look at ways of conceptualizing temperament, then at some of the challenges involved in measuring and studying it (see **Table 4.3** for a summary).

Temperament was originally proposed as a psychological concept by Alexander Thomas and Stella Chess,

Table 4.3 Dimensions of Temperament

Dimension	Description
Activity level	Frequency and intensity of gross motor activity
Attention span	Duration of attention to a single activity
Emotionality	Frequency and intensity of positive and negative emotional expression
Soothability	Responsiveness to attempts to soothe when distressed
Sociability	Degree of interest in others, positive or negative responses to social interactions
Adaptability	Adjustment to changes in routine
Quality of mood	General level of happy versus unhappy mood

who in 1956 began the New York Longitudinal Study (NYLS). They asked parents to evaluate their babies on the basis of dimensions such as activity level and adaptability, then classified the babies into three categories: easy, difficult, and slow-to-warm-up.

1. *Easy* babies (40% of the sample) were those whose moods were generally positive. They adapted well to new situations and were generally moderate rather than extreme in their emotional reactions.
2. *Difficult* babies (10%) did not adapt well to new situations, and their moods were intensely negative more frequently than other babies.
3. *Slow-to-warm-up* babies (15%) were notably low in activity level, reacted negatively to new situations, and had fewer positive or negative emotional extremes than other babies.

By following these babies into adulthood in their longitudinal study, Thomas and Chess were able to show that temperament in infancy predicted later development in some respects (Chess & Thomas, 1984; Ramos et al., 2005; Thomas et al., 1968). The difficult babies in their study were at high risk for problems in childhood, such as aggressive behavior, anxiety, and social withdrawal. Slow-to-warm-up babies rarely seemed to have problems in early childhood, but once they entered school they were sometimes fearful and had problems academically and with peers because of their relatively slow responsiveness.

Perhaps you noticed that the three categories in the classic Thomas and Chess study only added up to 65% of the infants they studied. The other 35% could not be classified as easy, difficult, or slow-to-warm-up. It is clearly a problem to exclude 35% of infants, so other temperament researchers have avoided categories, instead rating all infants on the basis of temperamental traits.

Mary Rothbart and her colleagues have kept some of the Thomas and Chess temperament qualities, such as activity level and attention span, but they added several aspects of emotionality, measuring frequency and intensity of positive and negative emotions (Rothbart, 2004; Rothbart et al., 2009). Similarly, David Buss and Robert Plomin (1984) include some Thomas and Chess dimensions in their model, but add *sociability*, which refers to positive or negative responses to social interactions. Both models have been moderately successful in predicting children's later functioning from infant temperament (Buss, 1995; Rothbart & Bates, 2006). All three models of temperament face measurement challenges, as the *Research Focus: Measuring Temperament* feature shows, because infants' emotional states change so frequently.

Temperament is difficult to assess in a research setting because infants' emotional states fluctuate so much.

Research Focus: Measuring Temperament

In 1956 Alexander Thomas and Stella Chess began the New York Longitudinal Study (NYLS), which assessed infant temperament by judging qualities such as activity level, adaptability, intensity of reactions, and quality of mood. The goal of the study was to see how infants' innate tendencies would be shaped into personality in the course of development through childhood and adolescence.

When Thomas and Chess began studying temperament, no biological measurements were available, so they used parents' reports of infants' behavior as the source of their temperament classifications. Even today, most studies of infant temperament are based on parents' reports.

There are some clear advantages to using parents' reports. After all, parents see their infants in many different situations on a daily basis over a long period of time. In contrast, a researcher who assesses temperament on the basis of the infants' performance on tasks administered in the laboratory sees the infant only on that one occasion. Because infants' states change so frequently, the researcher may assess infants as having a "difficult" temperament when in fact the infant is simply in a temporary state of distress—hungry, perhaps, or tired, or cold, or hot, or in need of a diaper change.

However, parents are not always accurate appraisers of their infants' behavior. For example, mothers who are depressed are more likely to rate their infants' temperament negatively, mothers' and fathers' ratings of their infants' temperament show only low to moderate levels of agreement, and parents tend to rate their twins or other siblings as less similar in temperament than researchers do, which suggests that parents may exaggerate the differences between their children.

Watch   RESEARCH FOCUS: MEASURING TEMPERAMENT

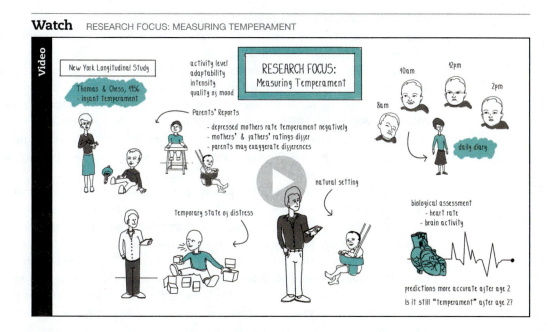

What are the options besides parents' reports? Thomas and Chess recommend that researchers observe infants' behavior in naturalistic settings (such as at home, or at the park) on several occasions, to avoid the problem of observing on just one occasion when the infant may have been in an unusually bad or good mood. Of course, this takes considerably more time and money than a simple parental questionnaire, and even a series of observations may not be as valid as the experiences parents accumulate over months of caring for their infants.

Another approach has been to have parents keep daily diaries of their infants' behavior (recording when they're sleeping, fussing, or crying). Reports using this method have been shown to correlate well with temperament ratings based on parental reports or performance on laboratory tasks.

Biological assessments of temperament are also useful since temperament is regarded as biologically based. One simple but effective biological measure of infant temperament is heart rate. Extremely shy children tend to have consistently high heart rates, and heart rates that show a greater increase in response to new stimulation such as new toys, new smells, or new people; compared to other children. Other biological assessments of temperament have been developed, including measures of brain activity.

Although infant temperament can predict later development to some extent, predictions are more accurate when assessments of temperament are made after age 2. Fussing, crying, and rapid changes in states are common in infancy across a wide range of infants. It is only after age 2 that children's moods and behavior settle into more stable patterns that predict later development. But can temperament still be assumed to be innate and biologically-based once the environment has been experienced for two years or more?

Review Questions:

1. Although parents' reports are often used to evaluate infant temperament, a drawback of using parents' reports is that:
   a. Mothers' and fathers' reports are often inconsistent
   b. Parents tend to exaggerate the differences between their children
   c. Depressed mothers tend to rate their infants' temperaments more negatively
   d. All of the above

2. The most simple and effective biological measure of temperament is:
   a. Blood pressure
   b. Heart rate
   c. Brain-wave intensity
   d. Hormonal stability

Goodness-of-Fit

LO 4.19 **Explain how the idea of goodness-of-fit pertains to temperament on both a family level and a cultural level.**

All approaches to measuring temperament view it as the raw material of personality, which is then shaped by the environment. Thomas and Chess (1977) proposed the concept of **goodness-of-fit**, meaning that children develop best if there is a good fit between

goodness-of-fit

theoretical principle that children develop best if there is a good fit between the temperament of the child and environmental demands

the temperament of the child and environmental demands. In their view, difficult and slow-to-warm-up babies need parents who are aware of their temperaments and willing to be especially patient and nurturing.

Subsequent studies have provided support for the idea of goodness-of-fit, finding that babies with negative temperamental qualities were able to learn to control their emotional reactions better by age 3 if their parents were understanding and tolerant (Warren & Simmens, 2005). Other research has shown that parents who respond to an infant's difficult temperament with anger and frustration are likely to find that the infant becomes a child who is defiant and disobedient, leading to further conflict and frustration for both parents and children (Calkins, 2002).

There may also be something like a cultural goodness-of-fit, given that different cultures have different views of the value of personality traits such as activity level and emotional expressiveness. In general, Asian babies have been found to be less active and irritable than babies in the United States and Canada, and appear to learn to regulate their emotionality earlier and more easily (Chen et al., 2005; Lewis et al., 1993). This temperamental difference may be, in part, the basis for differences later in childhood, such as Asian children being more likely to be shy. However, in contrast to the North American view of shyness as a problem to be overcome, in Asian cultures, shyness is viewed more positively. The child—and the adult—who listens rather than speaks is respected and admired. Consequently, studies of Chinese children have shown that shyness is associated with academic success and being well liked by peers (Chen et al., 1995). Now that China is changing so rapidly, both culturally and economically, there is some evidence that shyness is becoming less valued and related to poor rather than favorable adjustment in childhood (Chen, 2011; Chen et al., 2005). We'll cover more on this in later chapters.

Practice Quiz   ANSWERS AVAILABLE IN ANSWER KEY.

1. Which statement is true about temperament?
   a. It has only been a topic of study in the last decade; before this, psychologists thought that infants were similar in emotionality.
   b. It has only been assessed using cross-sectional methods.
   c. It is considered to have a biological basis.
   d. It has been defined by the same dimensions and measured the same way by various researchers.

2. In Chess and Thomas' (1984) longitudinal study, they classified the infants into their three categories and then followed these infants as they developed into adulthood. What did they find?
   a. Temperament in infancy predicted later development in some respects.
   b. Infant temperament was only predictive of the later development of middle- and high- socioeconomic status individuals.
   c. Infant temperament was only predictive of the later development of the 35% who were not able to be classified into one of the three groups.
   d. It was impossible to predict later development from infant temperament.

3. The most common classification for the babies in Thomas and Chess' original study was _____.
   a. easy   c. moderate
   b. difficult   d. slow-to-warm-up

4. Based on research, if Ru Fong, an infant with a difficult temperament, were to be adopted by parents that show a lot of anger and frustration we might predict which of the following outcomes?
   a. A child who is outgoing
   b. A child who is high in self-confidence but low in sociability
   c. A child who is defiant and disobedient
   d. An easy going child who is good at self-regulating

5. Which of the following best illustrates a good fit between caregiver and child?
   a. A slow-to-warm up baby whose parents are patient and understanding
   b. An irritable baby who is reared by parents who are rigid and intolerant
   c. A "difficult" infant whose parents love their child, but respond with anger
   d. A shy and often fussy child whose parents try to overcome this by encouraging face-to-face interactions with others

EMOTIONAL AND SOCIAL DEVELOPMENT: Infants' Emotions

Expressing and understanding emotions goes deep into our biological nature. As Charles Darwin observed in 1872 in *The Expression of Emotions in Man and Animals*, the strong similarity between emotional expressions in humans and other mammals indicates that human emotional expressions are part of a long evolutionary history. Tigers snarl, wolves growl, chimpanzees—and humans, too—bare their teeth and scream. Darwin also observed that emotional expressions were highly similar among humans in different cultures. Recent researchers have confirmed that people in various cultures can easily identify the emotions expressed in photographs of people from outside their culture (Ekman, 2003).

Primary Emotions

LO 4.20 **Identify the primary emotions and describe how they develop during infancy.**

Infants are born with a limited range of emotions that become differentiated into a wider range in the course of the early years of life. Studies of emotional development distinguish between two broad classes of emotion (Lewis, 2008). **Primary emotions** are the most basic emotions, the ones we share with animals, such as anger, sadness, fear, disgust, surprise, and happiness. Primary emotions are all evident within the first year of life. **Secondary emotions** are emotions that require social learning, such as embarrassment, shame, and guilt. Secondary emotions are also called *sociomoral emotions*, because infants are not born knowing what is embarrassing or shameful but have to learn this from their social environment. Secondary emotions develop mostly in the second year of life, so we will look at the development of primary emotions here and secondary emotions in Chapter 5.

Three primary emotions are evident in the early weeks of life: distress, interest, and pleasure (Lewis, 2008; 2002). Distress is evident in crying, of course, and we have seen in this chapter how infants' interest can be assessed from the first days of life by where they turn their attention. We have also seen, in Chapter 3, that neonates show a facial expression of pleasure when tasting a sweet substance. Gradually in the first months of life these three emotions become differentiated into other primary emotions: distress into anger, sadness, and fear; interest into surprise; and pleasure into happiness. (Disgust also appears early, but unlike distress, interest, and pleasure, it does not develop more complex forms.) Let's look at how each of the other primary emotions develops over the first year.

primary emotions basic emotions, such as anger, sadness, fear, disgust, surprise, and happiness

secondary emotions emotions that require social learning, such as embarrassment, shame, and guilt; also called sociomoral emotions

Infants universally exhibit the primary emotions. Can you tell which primary emotion is represented in each photograph?

Anger is expressed early in the form of a distinctive anger cry, as described in Chapter 3, but as an emotional expression separate from crying it shows development over the course of the first year (Dodge et al., 2006; Lewis, 2010). In one study of infants at 1, 4, and 7 months of age, the babies' responses were observed as their forearms were held down so that they could not move them for a few minutes, a condition none of them liked much (Oster et al., 1992). The 1-month-old infants showed clear distress, but raters (who did not know the hypotheses of the study) did not classify their distress responses as anger. The 4-month-old infants were also distressed, but about half of them showed their distress in facial expressions that could be clearly identified as anger. By 7 months, nearly all the infants showed a definite anger response. Another study also observed the clear expression of anger in 7-month-olds, in response to having an attractive object taken away (Stenberg et al., 1983). As infants become capable of intentional behavior in the second half of the first year, their expressions of anger often occur when their intentions are thwarted (Izard & Ackerman, 2000).

Sadness is rare in the first year of life, except for infants with depressed mothers. When mothers are depressed, by the time infants are 2–3 months old they, too, show facial expressions of sadness (Herrera et al., 2004). Could this be a case of passive genotype → environment interactions? Perhaps both infants and mothers have a genetic predisposition toward sadness in such families. This is something to consider, but in one study nondepressed mothers were instructed to look depressed in a 3-minute interaction with their infants (Cohn & Tronick, 1983). The infants responded with distress, suggesting that sad infants with depressed mothers are responding to their mothers' sadness rather than being genetically predisposed to sad emotional expressions.

Fear develops by 6 months of age (Gartstein et al., 2010). By then infants show facial expressions of fear, for example in response to a toy that moves toward them suddenly and unexpectedly (Buss & Goldsmith, 1998). Fear also becomes social at this age, as infants begin to show *stranger anxiety* in response to unfamiliar adults (Grossman et al., 2005). Stranger anxiety is a sign that the infant has begun to develop attachments to familiar persons, a topic we will discuss in detail in Chapter 5.

Surprise, indicated by an open mouth and raised eyebrows, is first evident about halfway through the first year (Camras et al., 1996). It is most often elicited by something in the infant's perceptual world that violates expectations. For example, a toy such as a jack-in-the-box might elicit surprise, especially the first time the jack pops out.

Finally, the development of happiness is evident in changes in infants' smiles and laughter that take place during the early months. After a few weeks, infants begin to smile in response to certain kinds of sensory stimulation—after feeding, or while urinating, or while having their cheeks stroked (Murkoff et al., 2003). However, it is not until the second or third month of life that the first **social smile** appears, an expression of happiness in response to interacting with others (Fogel et al., 2006). The first laughs occur about a month after the first smiles (Nwokah et al., 1999). Beginning at this age, about 4 months old, both smiles and laughs can be elicited by social interactions or by sensory or perceptual events, such as tickling or kisses or games such as peek-a-boo (Fogel et al., 2006). By the end of the first year, infants have several different kinds of smiles that they show in response to different people and in different situations (Bolzani et al., 2002).

Infants' Emotional Perceptions

LO 4.21 Describe infants' emotional perceptions and how their emotions become increasingly social over the first year.

Infants not only communicate emotions from the first days of life, they also perceive others' emotions. At just a few days old, neonates who hear another neonate cry often begin crying themselves, a phenomenon called **emotional contagion** (Geangu et al.,

social smile

expression of happiness in response to interacting with others, first appearing at age 2–3 months

emotional contagion

in infants, crying in response to hearing another infant cry, evident beginning at just a few days old

2010). This response shows that they recognize and respond to the cry as a signal of distress (Gazzaniga, 2009). Furthermore, they are more likely to cry in response to the cry of a fellow neonate than in response to an older infant's cry, a chimpanzee's cry, or a recording of their own cry, showing that they are remarkably perceptive at discriminating among cries.

At first, infants are better at perceiving emotions by hearing than by seeing. Remember, their auditory system is more developed than their visual system in the early weeks of life. When shown faces in the early weeks, neonates tend to look mainly at the boundaries and edges rather than at the internal features such as mouth and eyes that are most likely to express emotion. By 2–3 months old, infants' eyesight has improved substantially and they have begun to be able to discriminate between happy, sad, and angry faces (Haan et al., 2009; Hunnius et al., 2011). To test this, researchers often use a habituation method, in which infants are presented with the same photograph of the same facial expression repeatedly until they no longer show any interest, that is, they become habituated. Then they are shown the same face with a different facial expression, and if they look longer at the new facial expression this is taken to indicate that they have noticed the difference.

Another interesting way of showing that infants perceive emotions is to show no emotion at all. By age 2–3 months, when parents interacting with their infants are told by researchers to show no emotion for a time, the infants respond with distress (Adamson & Frick, 2003; Tronick, 2007). This method, known as the *still-face paradigm*, shows that infants quickly learn to expect certain emotional reactions from others, especially others who are familiar and important to them (Mesman et al., 2009).

More generally, infants' responses to the still-face paradigm demonstrate that from early on emotions are experienced through relations with others rather than originating only within the individual (Tronick, 2007). In the early weeks of life infants have smiles that are stimulated by internal states and cries that may be due to being hungry, tired, or cold, but infants soon learn to discern others' emotions and adjust their own emotions in response. By the time they are just 2–3 months old, when infants vocalize or smile they expect the others they know and trust to respond in familiar ways, as they have in the past, which is why the still-face paradigm disturbs infants so much.

Another indicator of the development of emotional perception during the first year is in infants' abilities to match auditory and visual emotion. In studies on this topic, infants are shown two photographs with markedly different emotions, such as happiness and sadness. Then a vocal recording is played, matching one of the facial emotions but not the other, and the infants' attention is monitored. By the time they are 7 months old, infants look more at the face that matches the emotion of the voice, showing that they expect the two to go together (Kahana-Kalman & Walker-Andrews, 2001; Soken & Pick, 1999).

Gradually over the first year, infants become more adept at observing others' emotional responses to ambiguous and uncertain situations and using that information to shape their own emotional responses. Known as **social referencing**, this is an important way that infants learn about the world around them. In studies testing social referencing abilities, typically a mother and infant in a laboratory situation are given an unfamiliar toy to play with, and the mother is instructed by the researchers to show positive or negative emotion in relation to the toy. Subsequently, the infant will generally play with the toy if the mother showed positive emotion toward it but avoid it if the mother's emotion was negative. This response appears by the time infants are about 9–10 months old (Schmitow & Stenberg, 2013). One recent study proposed that social referencing is the basis of the development of a sense of humor, which also first develops in the second half of the first year (Mireault et al., 2014). When parents smiled or laughed at an unexpected event, infants did, too.

social referencing

term for process of becoming more adept at observing others' emotional responses to ambiguous and uncertain situations, and using that information to shape one's own emotional responses

Practice Quiz

1. Arman is showing intense fear of a large dog that is approaching his stroller. Fear is an example of a _____.
   a. tertiary emotion
   b. sociomoral emotion
   c. primary emotion
   d. secondary emotion

2. Social smiles first appear _____.
   a. within the first two weeks after birth
   b. in the second or third month
   c. later in the first year
   d. after 18 months

3. Of the emotions listed below, _____ is the emotion an infant would likely display later in development than the others.
   a. fear
   b. shame
   c. disgust
   d. anger

4. While on a walk with her mother, Sofia comes across a dog. She notices that her mother is smiling at the dog, so Sofia also shows a positive reaction to it. Sofia's reaction illustrates _____.
   a. habituation
   b. emotional contagion
   c. social referencing
   d. infant-directed emotion

5. When Lola went back to the nursery after her mother had fed her, she started crying when she heard several of the other neonates crying. This is an example of _____.
   a. social referencing
   b. a difficult temperament
   c. secondary emotions
   d. emotional contagion

EMOTIONAL AND SOCIAL DEVELOPMENT: The Social World of the Infant

The social world of the infant is a crucial part of understanding infant development, because it affects every aspect of development, from physical and motor development to cognitive, emotional, and, of course, social development. Humans are built for social interactions and social relationships from day one. We have seen many examples of this here and in Chapter 3. Human infants recognize the smell and voice of their mother from the first few days of life. When they cry it is often some kind of social interaction that soothes them. They learn about the world through joint attention and social referencing. And so on.

Humans' social environments grow gradually more complex in the course of development as they enter new contexts such as school, community, and workplace. During infancy, social experience and social development occurs within a relatively small circle, a group of persons who are part of the infant's daily environment, and usually there is one person who provides the most love and care—typically, but not always, the mother. Here, let's look first at the broad cultural pattern of the infant's social world, then at two theories of infant social development.

Cultural Themes of Infant Social Life

LO 4.22 List the main features of infants' social worlds across cultures.

Although cultures vary in their customs of infant care, there are several themes that occur frequently across cultures. If we combine what scholars have learned from observing infants in a variety of different cultures today, along with what other scholars have learned from studying human evolutionary history and the history of human societies, a common picture of the social world of the infant emerges (DeLoache & Gottlieb, 2000;

Friedlmeier et al., 2015; Leakey, 1994; Levine, 1977; Levine et al., 1994; Richman et al., 2010; Small, 2005), characterized by the following features:

1. *Infants are with their mothers almost constantly during the early months of life*. Nearly all cultures have a period (usually 1–6 months) following birth when mother and infant do little but rest and recover from the birth together. After this rest period is over, the infant is typically strapped to the mother's back with a cloth as she goes back to her daily duties.

2. *After about 6 months, most daily infant care is done by older girls rather than the mother*. Once infants reach about 6 months old their care is delegated to older girls (usually 6 to 10 years old) so that the mother can devote her energy and attention to her work. Most often the girl is an older sister, but it could be any of a range of other people such as an older brother, cousin, grandmother, aunt, or a girl hired from outside the family. However, at night the infant sleeps with the mother.

3. *Infants are among many other people in the course of a day*. In addition to the mother and the caregiver who takes over at about age 6 months, infants are around many other people in the course of a day, such as siblings, aunts, cousins, grandparents, and neighbors.

4. *Infants are held or carried almost constantly*. In many traditional cultures, infants rarely touch the ground during their early months of life. This practice comes out of the belief that infants are highly vulnerable and must be shielded from dangers. Holding them close is a way of protecting them, and also a way of keeping them comforted, quiet, and manageable.

5. *Fathers are usually remote or absent during the first year*. As we saw in Chapter 3, in most cultures only women are allowed to observe and assist at birth, and this exclusion of men often continues during the first year. Fathers are rarely involved in the direct care of infants, partly because mothers breast-feed their infants frequently but also because care of infants is typically believed to be part of a woman's role but not a man's.

These features are still the dominant worldwide pattern in developing countries (Richman et al., 2010; Small, 2005), but the pattern in developed countries has become quite different over the past two centuries, especially in Western countries. The typical social environment for infants in developed countries is the "nuclear family" consisting of a mother, father (perhaps), and (perhaps) one sibling. Most infants in Western developed countries sleep in a separate room from the time they are born (Goldberg & Keller, 2007). Mother and infant are alone together for much of the time, and the infant may be left in a crib, stroller, or infant seat for a substantial proportion of the day (Baildum et al., 2000). Fathers in developed countries today are more involved than ever in infant care, although still not usually as much as mothers are (Hawkins et al., 2008; Lewis et al., 2009).

Nevertheless, like infants in developing countries, infants in developed countries nearly always grow up to be capable of functioning well socially in their culture. They develop friendships with peers, they find adults outside the family with whom they form relationships, such as teachers, and they grow to adulthood and form work relationships and intimate relationships with persons outside the family, with most eventually starting a new family of their own. Clearly infants can develop well socially in a variety of cultural contexts. What seems to be crucial to infants' social development across cultures is to have at least one social relationship with someone who is devoted to their care, as we will see next.

Infants in many cultures are surrounded by adults all day, but cultures vary in how much the adults interact with infants. Here, two mothers and their babies are with other family members and friends in the Samburu culture of Kenya.

Of the five features of the infant's social world described here, how many are similar to and how many are different from the culture you are from? What do you think explains the differences?

The Foundation of Social Development: Two Theories

LO 4.23 Compare and contrast the two major theories of infants' social development.

trust-versus-mistrust

in Erikson's psychosocial theory, the first stage of development, during infancy, in which the central crisis is the need to establish a stable attachment to a loving and nurturing caregiver

attachment theory

Bowlby's theory of emotional and social development, focusing on the crucial importance of the infant's relationship with the primary caregiver

Both Erikson and Bowlby viewed the first attachment relationship as crucial to future emotional and social development.

The two most influential theories of infants' social development are by Erik Erikson and John Bowlby. As introduced in Chapter 1, Erikson proposed an eight-stage theory of the life span, with a specific developmental challenge or "crisis" for each stage. For infancy, the central crisis in Erikson's theory is **trust versus mistrust** (Erikson, 1950). Erikson recognized how dependent infants are on others for their survival, and this dependence is at the heart of the idea of trust versus mistrust. Because they require others to provide for their needs, they must have someone who can be trusted to care for them and to be a reliable source of nourishment, warmth, love, and protection. Usually this caregiver is the mother, in most cultures, but it could also be a father, grandmother, older sister, or anyone else who provided love and care on a consistent basis. It is not the biological tie that is important but the emotional and social bond.

When infants have a caregiver who provides for them in these ways, they develop a basic trust in their social world. They come to believe that others will be trustworthy, and to believe that they themselves are worthy of love. However, if adequate love and care are lacking in the first year, infants may come to mistrust not only their first caregiver but others in their social world. They learn that they cannot count on the goodwill of others, and they may shrink from social relations in a world that seems harsh and unfriendly. This basic trust or mistrust lasts long beyond infancy. Remember, in Erikson's theory each stage builds on previous stages, for better or worse. Developing trust in infancy provides a strong foundation for all future social development, whereas developing mistrust is likely to be problematic not only in infancy but in future life stages.

A similar theory of infant social development was proposed by John Bowlby (1967). Like Erikson's theory, Bowlby's **attachment theory** focused on the crucial importance of the infant's relationship with the primary caregiver. Like Erikson, Bowlby believed that the quality of this first important social relationship influenced emotional and social development not only in infancy but in later stages of development as well. Like Erikson, Bowlby viewed trust as the key issue in the infant's first attachment to another person. In Bowlby's terms, if the primary caregiver is *sensitive* and *responsive* in caring for the infant, the infant will learn that others, too, can be trusted in social relationships. However, if these qualities are lacking in the primary caregiver, the infant will come to expect—in infancy and in later development—that others, too, may not be reliable social partners.

There are also important differences between the two theories. As we learned in Chapter 1, Erikson's psychosocial theory was a deliberate contrast to Freud's psychosexual theory. However, Bowlby's theory had quite different origins, in evolutionary theory and in research on mother–offspring relationships in animal species. Also, Bowlby's theory inspired methods for evaluating the infant–caregiver relationship that led to a research literature that now comprises thousands of studies (Cassidy & Shaver, 2008; Grossman et al., 2005; Morelli, 2015). Most of this research has been on toddlers rather than infants, so we will save a detailed analysis of Bowlby's theory and the research it generated for the next chapter.

Practice Quiz

1. Across cultures _____.
   a. infants are cared for by their older brothers so that the mother can devote time and energy to her work
   b. infants are usually relatively isolated during the course of the day to decrease the chance of infection
   c. infants are hardly ever carried out of concern that they may become spoiled
   d. fathers are usually remote or absent during the first year

2. Combining what scholars have learned from observing infants in a variety of different cultures today, along with what other scholars have learned from studying human evolutionary history and the history of human societies, what is one of the things that infants' social worlds have in common across most cultures?
   a. Infants are with their mothers almost constantly during the early months of life.
   b. Infants see few people other than their own mother for the first year.
   c. Fathers are very hands on with infants, especially during the first year.
   d. Infants are put down in a quiet space for most of the day while the rest of the family goes about its daily routines.

3. Baby Hibiki feels safe and secure with his mother and knows that she will feed him, keep him warm, and love him. Because of the solid emotional foundation he has at home, Hibiki will come to believe that he can count on others in his social world and that they too are worthy of love. Hibiki will successfully resolve what Erik Erikson called the _____ crisis.
   a. ego integrity versus despair
   b. industry versus inferiority
   c. trust versus mistrust
   d. intimacy versus isolation

4. The origins of Bowlby's theory were in _____ theory.
   a. information processing
   b. Piagetian
   c. behaviorist
   d. evolutionary

5. Both Erikson and Bowlby viewed _____ as crucial to future emotional and social development.
   a. language ability
   b. the first attachment relationship
   c. an easy or slow-to-warm-up temperament
   d. one's biological makeup

Summary: Social and Emotional Development

LO 4.18 Define infant temperament and its main dimensions.

Temperament includes qualities such as activity level, attention span, and emotionality. Thomas and Chess conceptualized temperament by classifying infants as easy, difficult, and slow-to-warm-up. Other theorists rate temperament on the basis of dimensions rather than categories. However, in all cases infant temperament is difficult to measure, due to the frequent changes in infants' states.

LO 4.19 Explain how the idea of goodness-of-fit pertains to temperament on both a family level and a cultural level.

Goodness-of-fit means that children develop best if there is a "good fit" between the temperament of the child and environmental demands. It varies culturally, given that different cultures have different views of the value of personality traits such as emotional expressiveness.

LO 4.20 Identify the primary emotions and describe how they develop during infancy.

The original primary emotions of distress, interest, and pleasure develop into anger, fear, surprise, and happiness within a few months after birth, but sadness tends to appear after infancy.

LO 4.21 Describe infants' emotional perceptions and how their emotions become increasingly social over the first year.

Infants are socially aware of others' emotions from the first days of life, and respond with distress to the distress of others. Toward the end of the first year they draw emotional cues from how others respond to ambiguous situations a process called social referencing.

LO 4.22 List the main features of infants' social worlds across cultures.

Infants are typically cared for by their mothers (in early months) and then by older siblings. They are surrounded by other people and held or carried often. In Western developed countries infants have a smaller social world and more time alone, but they also learn to function socially.

LO 4.23 Compare and contrast the two major theories of infants' social development.

The key to healthy social development, according to Erikson and Bowlby, is a strong, reliable attachment to a primary caregiver. The theories differ in their origins and Bowlby's theory has inspired thousands of studies.

Applying Your Knowledge as a Professional

The topics covered in this chapter apply to a wide variety of career professions. Watch these videos to learn how they apply to a pediatric nurse practitioner and a nanny.

Watch CAREER FOCUS: PEDIATRIC NURSE PRACTITIONER

Video

Melinda Lando
Pediatric Nurse Practitioner

Chapter Quiz

1. Dayle goes to the doctor and expresses concern that her infant's head is too big for his body. The doctor tells her that this is normal because of _____.

   a. the fact that head size varies widely

   b. the cephalocaudal principle

   c. the proximodistal principle

   d. the fact that after infancy, growth slows down considerably

2. If Salma is typical of most infants, his first tooth will appear at _____ of age.

   a. 2 months

   b. 5 to 9 months

   c. 10 to 11 months

   d. 15 months

3. Tara and Paul adopted their baby daughter, Yet Kwai, from a Chinese orphanage 5 years ago. She was physically and emotionally deprived until they adopted her at age 2½. It is most likely that Yet Kwai _____.

   a. stayed underweight for much of her life

   b. had more cognitive impairment than she would have had if she had been adopted before 6 months of age

   c. will have greater brain plasticity later in development because of her nurturing environment

   d. will show no signs of cognitive impairment due to synaptic pruning

4. Sudden infant death syndrome (SIDS) is almost unknown in cultures where cosleeping is the norm because _____.

   a. babies tend to sleep with their parents on relatively hard surfaces

   b. parents tend to put cloth on both sides of their babies so they remain on their sides

   c. babies are less likely to be breast-fed and therefore parents are less likely to roll over on them

   d. babies are less likely to be aroused during the night in these quieter settings

5. Marasmus is _____.

   a. a disease common among malnourished women with HIV

   b. most common during childhood and contracted through breast milk

   c. an infant disease characterized by muscle atrophy and abnormal drowsiness

   d. a deadly disease resulting from contaminated water being used to dilute formula

6. If you were a pediatrician working in a developing country, you would likely use oral rehydration therapy to treat _____.

   a. dysentery   **c.** smallpox and malaria

   b. diarrhea   **d.** yellow fever

7. Mahori was strapped to his mother's back for the first year of his life. Which of the following statements is true?

a. Mahori's parents gave him extra "tummy time" to develop his muscles.

b. Mahori's motor development will be similar to an American child if they are compared during kindergarten.

c. The sequence of his motor development will be different from that of babies in cultures where walking during infancy is actively encouraged.

d. When it comes to Mahori's motor development, environment plays a stronger role than genetics.

8. The key to depth perception is _____.

a. the development of the pincer grasp

b. the development of intermodal perception

c. being able to walk

d. binocular vision

9. Little Rupert goes to the market with his mother and calls all men he sees "Dada." This is an example of _____.

a. a secondary circular reaction

b. the A-not-B error

c. assimilation

d. coordination of secondary schemes

10. Maha begins rooting while being held by her mother's friend, who quickly passes Maha back to her mother to be breast-fed. Based on Piaget's sensorimotor substages, how old is Maha?

a. 0–1 months

b. 1–4 months

c. 4–8 months

d. 8–12 months

11. Critics of Piaget's sensorimotor theory argue that the likelihood of making the A-not-B error depends on the _____.

a. sex of the child

b. time of day the child is tested

c. delay between hiding and searching

d. color of the object

12. Speed of _____ is a good predictor of later memory and intelligence.

a. habituation

b. making the A-not-B error

c. accommodation

d. secondary circular reactions

13. From infancy onward, _____ memory comes easier to us than _____ memory.

a. social, recognition

b. recall, recognition

c. recognition, recall

d. infantile amnesia, recall

14. Scores on the Bayley Scales of Infant Development _____.

a. are useful as a screening tool because those who score very low may have developmental problems

b. are predictive of later IQ or school performance

c. are no longer used because they are considered out of date

d. are calculated for use with children ages 3 months to 9 years

15. Based on research, it would appear that educational media products _____.

a. greatly accelerate the cognitive development of infants

b. are used by almost 50% of babies in the United States

c. have no effect on infants' cognitive development

d. develop better attention spans in babies

16. Babbling _____.

a. is found only in infants from the Western Hemisphere

b. occurs only if the infant can hear

c. develops before cooing

d. is universal

17. Use of infant-directed speech _____.

a. is less common outside the developed countries

b. leads to slower development of language than the style of language typically spoken with adults

c. involves speaking in a lower than normal tone and using less repetition than in normal speech

d. has been shown to be less interesting to babies than normal speech; a reason why many parents do not use this type of "baby talk"

18. Temperament _____.

a. has been measured using the same nineteen components across various studies

b. has only been assessed using cross-sectional methods

c. is considered to have a biological basis

d. has no bearing whatsoever on later development

19. Which of the following best illustrates a good fit between caregiver and child?

a. An irritable baby who is reared by parents who are rigid and intolerant

b. A "difficult" infant whose parents respond with anger and frustration

c. A slow-to-warm-up baby whose parents are understanding and tolerant

d. A baby with a tendency toward negative emotions whose parents try to overcome this by encouraging face-to-face interactions with others

20. The emotion that an infant would most likely display latest in development is _____.

a. fear

b. shame

c. disgust

d. anger

21. When mothers show negative emotions in relation to a toy in the laboratory, infants will avoid the toy, which illustrates _____.

a. habituation

b. social referencing

c. the still-face paradigm

d. goodness of fit

22. Which of the following is a common feature of infant social life in most cultures throughout history?

a. Infants spend a lot of their day in the company of their fathers.

b. Infants are cared for exclusively by the mothers until they become old enough to walk.

c. Infants are often kept away from older adults so that they will be less vulnerable to the spread of disease.

d. Infants are surrounded by others and carried or held almost constantly.

23. Erikson and Bowlby both view _____ as the key issue in an infant's attachment to others.

a. nourishment

b. trust

c. age

d. personality

Chapter 5
Toddlerhood

DEVELOPMENT DURING TODDLERHOOD, THE SECOND AND THIRD YEARS OF LIFE, RIVALS DEVELOPMENT DURING INFANCY FOR EVENTS OF DRAMA AND IMPORTANCE. On their first birthday most infants are barely able to walk without support; by their third birthday toddlers can run, jump, and climb stairs. On their first birthday infants speak only a handful of words; by their third birthday toddlers have achieved remarkable fluency in the language of their culture and are able to understand and speak about nearly any topic under the sun. On their first birthday infants have little in the way of emotional regulation, and show their anger and their exuberance with equal unrestraint; by their third birthday, toddlers have begun to grasp well the moral worldview of their culture, and they exhibit the sociomoral emotions of guilt, embarrassment, and shame. On their first birthday the social world of most infants is limited to parents, siblings, and perhaps some extended family members; but by their third birthday toddlers' social world has greatly expanded. Anthropologist Margaret Mead (1930/2001) described the change from infancy to toddlerhood as going from being a "lap child," in almost constant physical contact with the mother, to being a "knee child" who is attached to the mother but also spends a lot of time in a wider social circle—especially with siblings and older children as part of a mixed-age play group.

Watch CHAPTER INTRODUCTION: TODDLERHOOD

Video

Section 1   Physical Development

⌄ Learning Objectives

5.1 Describe the typical changes in physical growth that take place in toddlerhood and explain the harmful effects of nutritional deficiencies on growth.

5.2 Describe the changes in brain development that take place during toddlerhood, and identify the two most common methods of measuring brain activity.

5.3 Describe the changes in sleeping patterns and sleeping arrangements that take place during toddlerhood.

5.4 Describe the advances in motor development that take place during toddlerhood.

5.5 Compare and contrast the process and timing of toilet training in developed countries and traditional cultures.

5.6 Distinguish the weaning process early in infancy from weaning later in toddlerhood.

PHYSICAL DEVELOPMENT: Growth and Change in Years 2 and 3

During the second and third years of life, physical growth slows down from its blazing pace of the first year, but it remains more rapid than it will be at any later time of life. This is true for bodily growth as well as for brain development. Sleep patterns change substantially, too, in years 2 and 3. Toddlerhood is also a time of dramatic advances in both gross and fine motor development.

Bodily Growth

LO 5.1 Describe the typical changes in physical growth that take place in toddlerhood and explain the harmful effects of nutritional deficiencies on growth.

The growth of the body is swift and steady during the toddler years. **Figure 5.1** shows the changes in height and weight from birth to age 5, based on an international sample including children from Brazil, Ghana, India, Norway, Oman, and the United States (World Health Organization, 2006). Notice how growth is extremely rapid in the first year, then slows in pace during the toddler years and beyond. Throughout childhood the average boy is slightly taller and heavier than the average girl.

During toddlerhood, children lose the "baby fat" of infancy and become leaner as they become longer (Fomon & Nelson, 2002). They no longer need as much fat to keep their bodies at a constant temperature. Also, the head, which was one fourth of the neonate's length, is one fifth of the 2-year-old's height. The rest of the body will continue to grow faster than the head, and by adulthood the head will be one eighth the size of the whole body.

Toddlers in developing countries often do not grow as rapidly as toddlers in developed countries. Typically, at birth and for the first 6 months of life, rates of growth are similar in developed countries and developing countries (Levine et al., 1994), because during the early months infants in most cultures rely mainly on breast milk or infant formula and eat little solid food. However, starting around 6 months of age, when they begin eating solid food as a larger part of their diet, children in developing countries receive less protein and begin to lag in their growth. According to the World Health Organization (WHO, 2010), about one fourth of children worldwide have diets that are deficient in protein, nearly all of them in developing countries. By the time they reach their first birthday, the height and weight of average children in developing countries are comparable to the bottom 5% of children in developed countries, and this pattern continues through childhood into adulthood.

Protein deficiency not only limits the growth of children in developing countries but it makes them vulnerable to disease and early death. One outcome specific to toddlerhood is **kwashiorkor**, in which protein deficiency leads to a range of symptoms such as lethargy, irritability, and thinning hair (Medline, 2008). Often the body swells with water, especially the belly. Toddlers with kwashiorkor may be getting enough food in the form of starches such as rice, bread, or potatoes, but not enough protein. Kwashiorkor lowers the effectiveness of the immune system, making toddlers more vulnerable to disease, and over time can lead to coma followed by death. Improved protein intake can

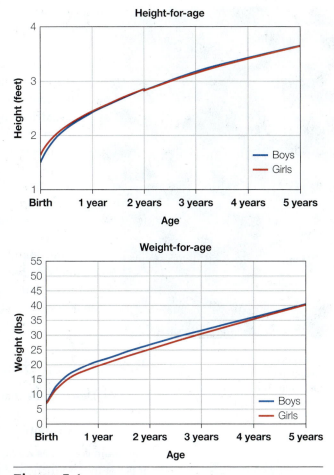

Figure 5.1 Growth Chart from Birth Through Age 5

Growth slows from infancy to toddlerhood but remains rapid.
SOURCE: Based on World Health Organization (2006)

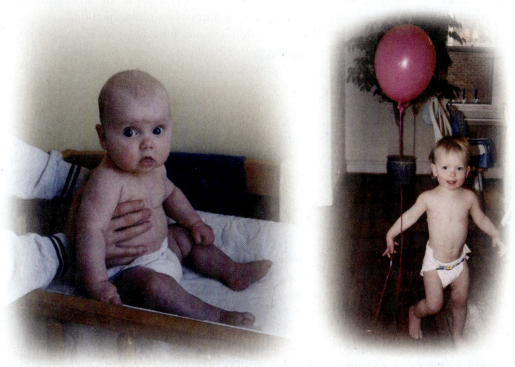

Toddlers lose a lot of their "baby fat" and often become leaner as they grow longer. This is my daughter Paris at 4 months and 18 months.

kwashiorkor

protein deficiency in childhood, leading to symptoms such as lethargy, irritability, thinning hair, and swollen body, which may be fatal if not treated

relieve the symptoms of kwashiorkor, but the damage to physical and cognitive development is likely to be permanent.

In addition to protein, toddlers need a diet that contains **micronutrients** such as iron, zinc, and vitamins A, B12, C, and D. Perhaps the most crucial micronutrient deficiency worldwide is iodine. About one-third of the world's population has a dietary deficiency of iodine, especially in Africa and South Asia (Zimmermann et al., 2008). In young children a lack of iodine inhibits cognitive development, resulting in an estimated IQ (intelligence quotient) deficiency of 10 to 15 points, a substantial margin. Fortunately, adding iodine to a diet is simple—through iodized salt—and cheap, costing only a few cents per person per year. Unfortunately, one third of the world's children still lack this simple micronutrient. Some children in developed countries also lack sufficient micronutrients. One national study of toddlers in the United States found that iron deficiency prevalence rates were about 7% overall and were twice as high among Latino toddlers (12%) as among White or African American toddlers (both 6%; Brotanek et al., 2007). Iron deficiency makes toddlers tired and irritable.

Toddlers who do not receive enough protein in their diets sometimes suffer from kwashiorkor, as in this boy in Uganda.

Brain Development

LO 5.2   **Describe the changes in brain development that take place during toddlerhood, and identify the two most common methods of measuring brain activity.**

The brain continues its rapid growth during the toddler years. As noted in Chapter 4, it is not the production of new brain cells that marks early brain development. In fact, the brain has only about one half as many neurons at age 2 as it did at birth. What most distinguishes early brain development is the steep increase in **synaptic density**, the number of synaptic connections among neurons (Huttenlocher, 2003). These connections multiply immensely in the first 3 years, and toddlerhood is when peak production of new synapses is reached in the frontal lobes, the part of our brain that is the location of many of our most distinctively human cognitive qualities, such as reasoning, planning, and creativity. During toddlerhood new synapses in the frontal cortex are produced at the mind-boggling rate of 2 million per second, reaching a total by age 2 of more than 100 trillion (see **Figure 5.2**; Hill et al., 2010). The peak of synaptic density comes right at the end of toddlerhood, around the third birthday (Thompson & Nelson, 2001).

After the peak of synaptic density, a long process of **synaptic pruning** begins. In synaptic pruning, the connections between neurons become fewer but more efficient, with the synapses that are used becoming more developed, while unused synapses wither away (see Chapter 4). Synaptic pruning will remove about one third of synapses in the frontal cortex from early childhood to adolescence, and after a new burst of synaptic density in early adolescence the process of synaptic pruning will continue at a slower rate through adolescence and into adulthood (Blakemore, 2008; Thompson, 2001).

Methods of assessing brain activity provide evidence of the rapid growth of the toddler brain. One widely used method, the **EEG (electroencephalogram)**, measures the electrical activity of the cerebral cortex. Every time a synapse fires it emits a tiny burst of electricity, which allows researchers to measure the overall activity of the cerebral cortex as well as activation of specific parts of it. EEG research on toddlers has found a sharp increase in overall cortical activity from 18 to 24 months (Bell & Wolfe, 2008), reflecting important advances in cognitive and language development that we will examine later in

micronutrients
dietary ingredients essential to optimal physical growth, including iodine, iron, zinc, and vitamins A, B12, C, and D

synaptic density
density of synapses among neurons in the brain; peaks around age 3

synaptic pruning
Process of reducing number of connections between neurons so that they become more efficient.

EEG (electroencephalogram)
device that measures the electrical activity of the cerebral cortex, allowing researchers to measure overall activity of the cerebral cortex as well as activation of specific parts

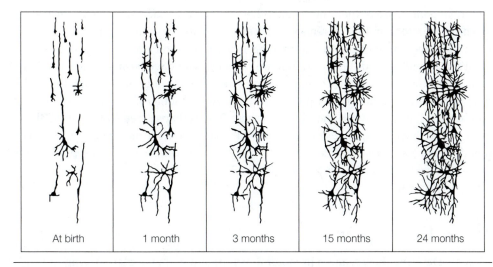

Figure 5.2 Changes in Synaptic Density From Birth to Age 2

Synaptic connections increase throughout the first 2 years, with the greatest density occurring at the end of toddlerhood.

SOURCE: Based on Conel (1930/1963)

this chapter. Another common method, **fMRI (functional magnetic resonance imaging)**, requires a person to lie still inside a machine that uses a magnetic field to record changes in blood flow and oxygen use in the brain in response to different kinds of stimulation, such as music. Unlike the EEG, an fMRI can detect activity in any part of the brain, not just the cerebral cortex. The fMRI method is not often used with toddlers, perhaps because they are too wiggly and incapable of restraining their movements. However, one study solved this problem by assessing toddlers (age 21 months) and 3-year-olds as they slept, and found that toddlers showed greater frontal lobe activity in response to speech than the older children did, reflecting the brain's readiness for rapid language acquisition during the toddler period (Redcay et al., 2008).

Changes in Sleep

LO 5.3   **Describe the changes in sleeping patterns and sleeping arrangements that take place during toddlerhood.**

Sleep declines from 16 to 18 hours a day in the neonate to about 15 hours a day by the first birthday, and further to about 12 to 13 hours by the second birthday. The toddler not only sleeps less than the infant but also has more of a night-sleeping, day-waking arousal schedule. Most toddlers take only one nap during the day by the time they reach 18 months old, compared to the two or more naps a day typical of infants (Iglowstein et al., 2003).

However, this does not mean that toddlers consistently sleep through the night. In fact, one study of toddlers in Israel, England, and Australia found that episodes of waking in the night increased in frequency from 1½ to 2 years of age (Scher et al., 2004). There are two reasons why waking at night often increases during this time. First, there is a resurgence of teething between 13 and 19 months of age (Bong et al., 2008). This time it is the molars—the large teeth in the back of the mouth—which are bigger and more painful as they emerge than were the teeth that emerged in infancy. Second, toddlers develop

fMRI (functional magnetic resonance imaging)

method of monitoring brain activity in which a person lies inside a machine that uses a magnetic field to record changes in blood flow and oxygen use in the brain in response to different kinds of stimulation

It is not until after toddlerhood that most children can lie still long enough to have an fMRI.

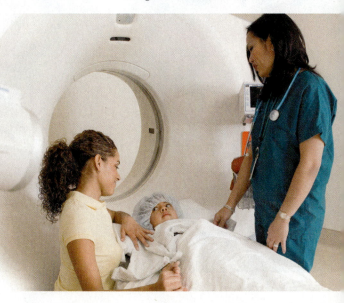

a more definite sense of themselves and others as they approach age 2, and if they sleep in a bed separate from their parents they become more aware of this separation and more intentional about relieving it by summoning a parent or going into the parents' room.

What about the toddlers in traditional cultures, who have been sleeping alongside their mothers through infancy? This sleeping arrangement continues through the beginning of toddlerhood, but it will not last forever. When mothers become pregnant with another child, usually when the toddler reaches 2 or perhaps 3 years old, the toddler is ousted from that cozy spot beside her at night to make room for the new baby. However, this does not mean that toddlers now sleep alone. Instead, they now sleep alongside older siblings, or perhaps the father (Owens, 2004). Throughout life, sleeping alone is rare in traditional cultures.

Motor Development

LO 5.4   **Describe the advances in motor development that take place during toddlerhood.**

Toddlerhood is a time of dramatic advances in motor development. There are few physical advances more life changing than going from barely standing to walking, running, climbing, and jumping—and all this progress in gross motor development takes place during the toddler years. With regard to fine motor development, toddlers go from being able to place a small object inside a large object to holding a cup and building a tower of blocks.

GROSS MOTOR DEVELOPMENT: FROM TODDLING TO RUNNING, JUMPING, AND CLIMBING Next time you see a child about a year old trying to walk, observe closely. When children first begin to walk they spread their feet apart and take small, stiff-legged steps, shifting their weight from one leg to the other. In short, they toddle! This is, in fact, where the word *toddler* comes from, in reference to their tentative, unsteady, wide-stance steps.

At 12–18 months many toddlers can barely walk, but by their third year they can run and jump.

On average, children begin to walk without support at about 11 months old, just as they are about to enter toddlerhood; but there is a wide range of normal variation around this average, from about 9 to 17 months (Adolph & Berger, 2006; Bayley, 2005). Children who walk at 9 months are no more likely than children who walk at 17 months to become Olympic athletes some day, they simply have different biological time lines for learning to walk.

By 15 months most toddlers can stand (briefly) on one leg and have begun to climb, although once they have climbed onto something, they are much less skilled at climbing down. For example, most can climb up stairs at this age but not (safely) down. By 18 months most can run, although at first they run with the same stiff-legged, wide-stance posture as they use for walking. By 24 months they can kick a ball or throw a small object, and their running has become more flexible and fluid. At this age they can now go down the stairs that they earlier learned to climb up, and more: They can squat for minutes at a time, stand on tiptoes, and jump up and down. Small wonder toddlers move around so much, with so many new abilities to try out!

Through the third year, toddlers' gross motor skills continue to develop as they gain more flexibility and balance. They become better at using visual information to adjust their walking and running in response to changes in surfaces, so they become less likely to stumble and fall (Berger et al., 2005). **Table 5.1** summarizes the major milestones in gross motor development during toddlerhood.

FINE MOTOR DEVELOPMENT: FROM SCRIBBLING TO BUILDING WITH BLOCKS Toddler gains in fine motor development are not as revolutionary as their gains in gross motor development, but they are certainly substantial. Already at 12 months they have come a long way in the course of infancy, and can hold an object in one hand while performing an action on it with the other; for example, they can hold a container with the right hand while placing rocks into it with the left hand (Chen et al., 2010). At

Table 5.1 Milestones of Gross Motor Development in Toddlerhood

Age (Months)	Milestone
9–16	Stand alone
9–17	Walk without support
11–19	Stand on one leg
11–21	Climb onto chairs, beds, up stairs, etc.
13–17	Walk backward
14–22	Run
17–30	Jump in place
16–30	Walk on tiptoes
22–36	Walk up and down stairs

SOURCE: Based on Adolph & Berger (2006); Bayley (2005); Coovadia & Wittenberg (2004); Frankenburg et al. (1992); Murkoff et al. (2006).

NOTE: The range shown is the age period at which 90% of toddlers achieve the milestone.

Cultural Focus: Gross Motor Development Across Cultures

The research just described is based on Western, mostly American toddlers. What about toddlers in traditional cultures? As you will recall from Chapter 4, infants in traditional cultures are held or carried most of the time to keep them safe and secure. Toddlers in traditional cultures are allowed slightly more mobility—it is much harder to keep a toddler still than an infant—but they continue to be held and carried for about half their waking hours (Levine, 1977; Morelli, 2015).

Nevertheless, they are equal to toddlers in developed countries in their gross motor skills (Greenfield, 2003). In fact, toddlers in Africa (as well as African Americans) tend to reach gross motor milestones earlier than toddlers of European backgrounds (Kelly et al., 2006).

The reason for restricting toddlers' movements is the same as for infants: to keep them safe and away from harm. In rural areas of traditional cultures fire is especially a danger, as families often have a cooking fire burning perpetually—during the day for cooking meals, during the night for warmth. Other common potential dangers are falling off a cliff, falling into a lake or river, or being trampled by livestock. Holding and carrying toddlers for much of their waking hours makes mishaps less likely.

For similar safety reasons, parents in developed countries "baby proof" their homes once their children become mobile, removing sharp objects and other potential sources of harm (McKenzie, 2004). Parents of toddlers often place gates at the top of stairs to prevent the child from falling, add locks to cabinets containing sharp objects and household chemicals, install

Watch   GROSS MOTOR DEVELOPMENT ACROSS CULTURES

outlet covers to prevent electrocution, and take other measures to protect against potential sources of harm or injury (Eisenberg et al., 2008).

To see how toddlers' gross motor development varies across and within cultures, watch the *Gross Motor Development Across Cultures* video.

Review Question:

Should parents be concerned if their child takes longer than other children to achieve a gross motor milestone, such as learning to walk? Why or why not?

Table 5.2 Milestones of Fine Motor Development in Toddlerhood

Age (Months)	Milestone
7–15	Hold writing instrument (e.g., pencil, crayon)
8–16	Coordinate actions of both hands
10–19	Build tower of two blocks
10–21	Scribble vigorously
12–18	Feed self with spoon
15–23	Build tower of three to four blocks
20–28	Draw straight line on paper
24–32	Brush teeth
26–34	Build tower of 8–10 blocks
29–37	Copy circle

SOURCE: Based on Adolph & Berger (2006); Bayley (2005); Coovadia & Wittenberg (2004); Frankenburg et al. (1992); Murkoff (2011).

NOTE: The range shown is the age period at which 90% of toddlers achieve the milestone.

Toddlers become capable of eating with a spoon and show a right- or left-hand preference for self-feeding.

12 months most have come to show a definite right- or left-hand preference for self-feeding, and over the next 6 months they try a variety of grips on their spoons until they find a grip they will use consistently (McCarty et al., 2001). During the first year of toddlerhood they also learn to hold a cup, scribble with a pencil or crayon, build a tower of three to four blocks, and turn the pages of a book (Murkoff, 2011).

The second year of toddlerhood, from the second to the third birthday, is marked by fewer major advances and more by extending the advances of the previous year. The block tower rises to 8 to 10 blocks, the scribbling becomes skillful enough to draw a semistraight line, and an attempt to copy a circle may result in something that actually looks somewhat like a circle (Chen et al., 2010). Toddlers in their third year of life can even begin to brush their teeth, with a little assistance. **Table 5.2** summarizes the major milestones in fine motor development during toddlerhood.

Practice Quiz ANSWERS AVAILABLE IN ANSWER KEY.

1. _____ is a condition specific to toddlerhood in which protein deficiencies lead to varied symptoms such as swollen bellies and feet, hair loss, and lack of energy.

a. Marasmus **c.** Kwashiorkor
b. SIDS **d.** Hydrocephalus

2. What most distinguishes early brain development in toddlerhood is _____.

a. the steep increase in the density of synaptic connections among neurons
b. Increased activity in the amygdala
c. the formation of the cerebral cortex
d. the production of new brain cells, most notably in the temporal lobe

3. Which statement best represents sleep during toddlerhood?

a. The increased sense of self results in most toddlers wanting to sleep alone.
b. Children sleep consistently through the night.
c. Increased activity results in children sleeping more than they did in infancy.
d. Sleeping alone is rare in traditional cultures.

4. Last week, your neighbors told you their 18-month-old son has been sleeping through the night for the past two months. They were very happy about this new development and were looking forward to many more months of a good night's sleep. This week, however, they say their son has started waking up at night and has been pretty fussy during the day. What is the likely reason for this waking and fussing?

a. He has been drinking too much before bedtime.

b. His increased activity makes it harder for him to slow down and soothe himself.

c. His molars are coming in, and he is teething.

d. He is going through a growth spurt.

5. Garret is approaching toddlerhood. During the next year he should be able to _____.

a. hold a cup and scribble with crayons

b. use a fork and knife with coordination

c. walk up and down stairs without holding on to anything

d. be able to brush his teeth

PHYSICAL DEVELOPMENT: Socializing Physical Functions: Toilet Training and Weaning

Eating and eliminating wastes are two physical functions that humans share with other animals, but for humans these functions become socialized from an early age. Here we look at how toddlers become toilet trained and weaned.

Toilet Training

LO 5.5 **Compare and contrast the process and timing of toilet training in developed countries and traditional cultures.**

The toddler years are when most children first learn to control their urination and defecation and become "toilet trained." Expectations for exactly when during the toddler years this should happen have changed substantially over the past half century in the United States (Blum et al., 2004). During the mid-20th century, pediatricians advocated early toilet training—the earlier the better—and in 1957 a study reported that 92% of American toddlers were toilet trained by the time they were 18 months old (Goode, 1999). Gradually, pediatricians and parents concluded there was little reason to require toilet training so early, and in more recent studies only about 25% of toddlers were toilet trained by 18 months old and only about 60% by their third birthday (Barone et al., 2009; Schum et al., 2001). However, there are variations by social class. The more education parents have, the later their kids tend to be toilet trained (Horn et al., 2006).

Today, most American pediatricians believe it is best to be patient with toddlers' progress toward toilet training, and to time it according to when the toddler seems ready (American Academy of Pediatrics [AAP], 2001). Most toddlers show signs of readiness sometime between 18 and 30 months of age. Some key signs are

- staying "dry" for an hour or two during the day;
- regular bowel movements, occurring at about the same time each day;
- increased anticipation of the event, expressed through looks or words;
- directly asking to use the toilet or to wear underwear instead of a diaper.

Although toilet training usually begins during the toddler years, it rarely happens overnight. Typically it is a process that continues over several weeks, months, or even years. The earlier toilet training begins, the longer it takes to complete it (Blum et al., 2003). After children are generally able to control urination and defecation, they may occasionally have an "accident" when they are especially tired, excited, or stressed (Murkoff, 2011). Even after children have ceased having accidents during the day, they may not have consistent control at night. For this reason, it is common for children to wear "training pants"—in between diapers and underwear—for a period after learning toilet training. Even at age 5, about one fourth of children have an occasional accident, usually at night (Fritz & Rockney, 2004).

Approaches to toilet training have changed in recent decades with experts now recommending a "child-centered" approach.

Toddlers in developed countries usually have this process guided and supervised by parents, but for toddlers in traditional cultures, older siblings and other older children are often the guides. *Toilet training* is probably not the right term to use to refer to this process in traditional cultures, because they rarely have toilets—so let's call it "controlled elimination." By age 2 or 3 most toddlers in traditional cultures spend the majority of their waking hours in groups with children of mixed ages, and they learn controlled elimination from watching and imitating other children (Edwards et al., 2015; LeVine, 1994). Parents may be involved as well. For example, among the Ifaluk people on the Pacific Ocean islands of Micronesia, when toddlers reach about age 2 their parents encourage them to relieve themselves in the nearby lagoon, not in or near the house, and reprimand them if they fail to comply (Le, 2000).

CRITICAL THINKING QUESTION

How might a culture's values of individualism or collectivism influence toilet-training practices?

Weaning

LO 5.6 **Distinguish the weaning process early in infancy from weaning later in toddlerhood.**

As mentioned in Chapter 3, cultures vary widely in whether and how long mothers breast-feed their children. However, based on what we know of human history and of practices today in traditional cultures, it is clear that breast-feeding for 2 to 3 years has been the most typical human custom, until recently (Small, 1998).

weaning
cessation of breast-feeding

Toddlers in traditional cultures often breast-feed until they are about 2 years old. Here, a mother of a hill tribe in a village near Luang Prabang, Laos nurses her toddler.

If breast-feeding takes place for only a few weeks or months during infancy, the transition from breast to bottle usually takes place fairly smoothly, especially if the bottle is introduced gradually (Murkoff et al., 2008). However, the longer breast-feeding continues into toddlerhood, the more challenging **weaning** becomes when the mother decides the time has come for the child to stop drinking breast milk. As we will see in more detail later in the chapter, the toddler is much more socially aware than the infant, and much more capable of exercising intentional behavior. The toddler can also speak up, in a way the infant cannot, to make demands and protest prohibitions.

Consequently, most traditional cultures have customary practices for weaning toddlers from the breast. Often, the approach is gentle and gradual at first, but becomes harsher if the toddler resists. For example, in Bali (an island that is part of Indonesia) parents feed their babies some solid food from the first few days of life, and attempt gradual weaning beginning at about age 2. However, if the gradual approach does not work, mothers coat their breasts with bitter-tasting herbs (Deiner, 2000). Similarly, toddlers in rural villages in Turkey are weaned at about age 2, but if they persist in trying to breast-feed, the mother coats her breasts with tomato paste. The child usually cries and protests, but the method works without fail (Delaney, 2000).

Other cultures separate mother and toddler during weaning, so that the toddler will have no choice but to get used to life without breast-feeding. Among the Fulani people of West Africa, toddlers are sent to their grandmother's household during weaning. If the toddler complains about not breast-feeding, the grandmother may offer her own breast, but the toddler quickly loses interest upon discovering that there is no milk in it (Johnson, 2000).

Practice Quiz

1. Which of the following variables has been shown to be correlated with the timing of toilet training in the United States?

    a. Number of children in the family

    b. Location of the toilet within the house

    c. Education level of the parents

    d. Marital status of the primary caregiver

2. In Western cultures _____.

    a. most children show signs of readiness for toilet training by their first birthday

    b. a sign of being ready to begin toilet training is when the child can stay "dry" for an hour or two during the day

    c. views about toilet training have stayed the same over the last several decades

    d. children are toilet trained in a nearly identical way as their counterparts in traditional cultures

3. You have been trying to toilet train your son, but you are not having much luck. Based on the research, what is most likely to be holding up the process?

    a. Some children simply take months or potentially years to become fully toilet trained.

    b. You are not rewarding him consistently enough when he shows interest.

    c. There must be a physical difficulty that will require a medical exam.

    d. Most females learn to potty train in a week, but almost all boys take several months.

4. You are interested in weaning your toddler. Why is it more of a challenge to wean a toddler than an infant?

    a. Breast feeding a toddler is more socially acceptable in many cultures.

    b. The toddler has developed teeth and might unconsciously resist with biting behaviors.

    c. Toddlers have a stronger bond with the mother than infants because they have been with them longer.

    d. The toddler is more socially aware and has a greater capacity to exercise intentional behavior.

5. Nandranie is a toddler from a traditional culture; she would likely _____.

    a. have experienced some customary practice for being weaned

    b. be abruptly weaned at age 1

    c. be given formula instead of breast milk

    d. still be breast feeding at age 5

Summary: Physical Development

LO 5.1 **Describe the typical changes in physical growth that take place in toddlerhood and explain the harmful effects of nutritional deficiencies on growth.**

Toddlers' physical growth continues at a pace that is slightly reduced from infancy but is nevertheless faster than at any later time of life. Toddlers in developing countries often suffer protein and micronutrient deficiencies that impede their physical and cognitive development.

LO 5.2 **Describe the changes in brain development that take place during toddlerhood, and identify the two most common methods of measuring brain activity.**

The brain's synaptic density peaks at the end of toddlerhood, followed by many years of synaptic pruning. The two most common methods of measuring brain activity are the EEG and the fMRI.

LO 5.3 **Describe the changes in sleeping patterns and sleeping arrangements that take place during toddlerhood.**

Toddlers' episodes of night-waking increase from 18 to 24 months of age, in part due to teething of molars. In traditional cultures, toddlers sleep with their mothers until the next child is born, after which they sleep with other family members.

LO 5.4 **Describe the advances in motor development that take place during toddlerhood.**

In their gross motor development, toddlers learn to walk, run, climb, and kick a ball. Toddlers in traditional cultures are often restricted in their movements to protect them from danger—especially cooking fires. Advances in fine motor development include holding a cup and building a tower of blocks. In their third year, toddlers may be able to brush their teeth, with some assistance.

LO 5.5 **Compare and contrast the process and timing of toilet training in developed countries and traditional cultures.**

Children vary widely in the timing of learning toilet training, but most are toilet trained by the end of toddlerhood. In traditional cultures, toddlers usually learn controlled elimination through observing and imitating older children.

LO 5.6 **Distinguish the weaning process early in infancy from weaning later in toddlerhood.**

When weaning takes place in the second or third year of life, toddlers often resist. Customs in traditional cultures for promoting weaning include sending the toddler to a relative's household for awhile or coating the mother's breast with an unpleasant substance.

Section 2   Cognitive Development

∨ Learning Objectives

5.7 Outline the cognitive achievements of toddlerhood in Piaget's theory.

5.8 Explain Vygotsky's sociocultural theory of cognitive development and contrast it with Piaget's theory.

5.9 Summarize the evidence for the biological and evolutionary bases of language.

5.10 Describe the milestones in language development that take place during the toddler years.

5.11 Identify how parents' stimulation of toddlers' language varies across cultures and evaluate how these variations relate to language development.

COGNITIVE DEVELOPMENT: Cognitive Development Theories

You have already been introduced to Piaget and his theory of infant cognitive development (see Chapter 4). Here his theory continues into toddlerhood. Also, a more cultural perspective on children's cognitive development is presented, in the theory of Lev Vygotsky.

Cognitive Development in Toddlerhood: Piaget's Theory

LO 5.7   **Outline the cognitive achievements of toddlerhood in Piaget's theory.**

Piaget proposed that cognitive development during the first 2 years of life follows a sequence of six sensorimotor stages. As we saw in Chapter 4, during infancy the primary cognitive advance of the first four stages of sensorimotor development is from simple reflexes to intentional, coordinated behavior. Neonates have a wide range of reflexes and little intentional control over their behavior, but by the end of the first year infants have lost most of their reflexes and can perform intentional actions that combine schemes, such as moving one object aside in order to reach another. In the second year of life—during toddlerhood—the final two stages of sensorimotor development are completed.

SENSORIMOTOR STAGE 5: TERTIARY CIRCULAR REACTIONS Piaget called the fifth stage of sensorimotor development *tertiary circular reactions* (age 12–18 months). In this stage, toddlers intentionally try out different behaviors to see what the effects will be. In the previous stage, *secondary circular reactions,* the action first occurs by accident and then is intentionally repeated, but in tertiary circular reactions the action is intentional from the beginning. Like secondary circular reactions, tertiary circular reactions are circular because they are performed repeatedly.

For example, at 17 months my twins discovered how to flush the toilet, and one day they flushed and flushed and flushed until the flushing system broke and the water began overflowing. I discovered this as I sat downstairs reading the newspaper and suddenly observed water whooshing out of the vents in the ceiling! I ran upstairs and there they were, standing in 3 inches of water, giggling with glee, absolutely delighted. I don't recall thinking of Piaget at that moment, but I'll bet he would have been pleased. To Piaget, in this stage toddlers become like little scientists, experimenting on the objects around them in order to learn more about how the world works. My twins certainly learned that day about what happens when you flush a toilet repeatedly.

SENSORIMOTOR STAGE 6: MENTAL REPRESENTATIONS The final stage of sensorimotor development, from 18 to 24 months, is the stage of **mental representations**. Now, instead of trying out a range of actions as in tertiary circular reactions, toddlers first think about the possibilities and select the action most likely to achieve the desired outcome. Piaget gave the example of his daughter Lucienne, who sought to obtain a small chain from inside the matchbox where her father had placed it. First she turned the box upside down; then she tried to jam her finger into it, but neither of these methods worked. She paused for a moment, holding the matchbox and considering it intently. Then she opened and closed her mouth, and suddenly slid back the cover of the matchbox to reveal the chain (Crain, 2000). To Piaget, opening and closing her mouth showed that she was pondering potential solutions, then mimicking the solution that had occurred to her.

Mental representation is a crucial milestone in cognitive development, because it is the basis of the most important and most distinctly human cognitive abilities, including language. The words we use are mental representations of objects, people, actions, and ideas.

OBJECT PERMANENCE IN TODDLERHOOD Object permanence also develops further during toddlerhood. As described in Chapter 4, by their first birthday infants will look for an object that they observe being hidden behind or under another object. However, even at 12 months they still make the "A-not-B error." That is, if they find an object under blanket A, and then a second blanket B is added and they observe the object being hidden under blanket B, they nevertheless tend to look under blanket A, where they found the object the first time.

Toddlers learn to avoid the A-not-B error and search for the object where they last saw it hidden. However, even though the A-not-B error is less common in toddlerhood than in infancy, search errors happen occasionally on this task in toddlerhood and even into early childhood, up to ages 4 and 5 (Hood et al., 2003; Newcombe & Huttenlocher, 2006). But we can say with some confidence that toddlers have attained object permanence once they generally avoid the A-not-B error.

Object permanence is a major advance of cognitive development in toddlerhood, but it is not a distinctly human achievement. In fact, chimpanzees and human toddlers have equal success on object permanence tasks at age 2 (Call, 2001; Collier-Baker & Suddendorf, 2006). Understanding the permanence of the physical world is crucial to being able to function in that world, so it is not surprising that humans and nonhuman primates would share this fundamental ability (Brownell & Kopp, 2007).

DEFERRED IMITATION The ability for mental representation of actions also makes possible **deferred imitation**, which is the ability to repeat actions observed at an earlier time. Piaget's favorite example of deferred imitation involved his daughter Jacqueline, who witnessed another child exploding into an elaborate public tantrum and then repeated the tantrum herself at home the next day (Crain, 2000). Deferred imitation is a crucial ability for learning because it means that when we observe something important to know, we can repeat it later ourselves. Deferred imitation is a frequent part of toddlers' pretend play, as they observe the actions of other children or adults—making a meal, feeding a baby, digging a hole—and then imitate those actions later in their play (Lillard, 2007).

mental representations
Piaget's final stage of sensorimotor development in which toddlers first think about the range of possibilities and then select the action most likely to achieve the desired outcome

deferred imitation
ability to repeat actions observed at an earlier time

Piaget proposed that deferred imitation begins at about 18 months, but subsequent research has shown that it develops much earlier than he had thought (Bauer, 2006). Deferred imitation of facial expressions has been reported as early as 6 weeks of age, when infants exposed to an unusual facial expression from an unfamiliar adult imitated it when the same adult appeared before them the next day (Meltzoff & Moore, 1994). At 6 months of age, infants can imitate a simple sequence of events a day later, such as taking off a puppet's glove and shaking it to ring a bell inside the glove (Barr et al., 2003).

However, if there is a longer delay, toddlers are more proficient at deferred imitation than infants are. In a series of studies, children 9, 13, and 20 months old were shown two-step sequences of events such as placing a car on a track to make a light go on, then pushing a rod to make the car run down a ramp (Bauer et al., 2000; 2001; 2003). After a 1-month interval, shown the same materials, fewer than half of the 9-month-olds could imitate the steps they had seen previously, compared with about two-thirds of the 13-month-olds and nearly all the 20-month-olds. Other studies have shown that better deferred imitation among toddlers than among infants may be due principally to advances in the maturity of the brain. Specifically, the *hippocampus,* that part of the brain especially important in long-term memory encoding and recall, is still in a highly immature state of development during infancy but matures substantially during toddlerhood (Bauer et al., 2010; Liston & Kagan, 2002).

CATEGORIZATION Piaget also believed that mental representation in toddlerhood is the basis of categorization. Once we are able to represent an image of a house mentally, for example, we can understand the category "house" and understand that different houses are all part of that category. These categories, in turn, become the basis for language, because each noun and verb represents a category (Waxman, 2003). The word *truck* represents the category "truck" containing every possible variety of truck; the word *run* represents the category "run" containing all varieties of running, and so on.

Here, too, recent experiments seem to indicate that Piaget underestimated children's early abilities. Infants and toddlers are able to do more than he had thought. Even infants as young as a few months old have been shown to have a rudimentary understanding of categories. This can be demonstrated by their patterns of looking at a series of images. As we have seen, infants tend to look longer at images that are new or unfamiliar, and their attention to images is often used in research to infer what they know and do not know. In one study, 3- and 4-month-old infants were shown photographs of cats (Quinn et al., 1993). After a series of cat photos, the infants were shown two new photos, one of a cat and one of a dog. They looked longer at the dog photo, indicating that they had been using a category for "cat" and looked longer at the dog photo because it did not fit.

However, research has generally confirmed Piaget's insight that categorization becomes more advanced during toddlerhood (Bornstein & Arterberry, 2010). For example, one study compared children who were 9, 12, and 18 months old (Gopnik et al., 1999). The children were given four different toy horses and four different pencils. At 9 months, they played with the objects but made no effort to separate them into categories. At 12 months, some of the children would place the objects into categories

Toddlers' play is often based on deferred imitation. Here, a toddler in Peru offers a bottle to her doll.

and some would not. By 18 months, nearly all the children would systematically and deliberately separate the objects into a "horse" category and a "pencil" category.

By the time they are 2 years old, toddlers can go beyond the appearance of objects to categorize them on the basis of their functions or qualities. In a study demonstrating this ability, 2-year-olds were shown a machine and a collection of blocks that appeared to be identical (Gopnik et al., 1999). Then they were shown that two of the blocks made the machine light up when placed on it, whereas others did not. The researcher picked up one of the blocks that had made the machine light up and said, "This is a blicket. Can you show me the other blicket?" The 2-year-olds were able to choose the other block that had made the machine light go on, even though it looked the same as the blocks that had not had that effect. Although *blicket* was a non-sense word the toddlers had not heard before, they were able to understand that the category "blicket" was defined by causing the machine to light up. Can you see how this experiment also provides a good demonstration of how categorization is the basis of language?

Vygotsky's Cultural Theory of Cognitive Development

LO 5.8 **Explain Vygotsky's sociocultural theory of cognitive development and contrast it with Piaget's theory.**

Although most studies of toddlers' cognitive development pay little attention to cultural context, one cultural approach to cognition has gained increased attention from scholars of human development. This approach is founded on the ideas of the Russian psychologist Lev Vygotsky (1896–1934). Vygotsky died of tuberculosis when he was just 37, and it took decades before his ideas about cognitive development were translated and recognized by scholars outside Russia. It is only in recent decades that his work has been widely influential among Western scholars, but his influence is increasing as interest in understanding the cultural basis of development continues to grow (Gauvain & Nicolaides, 2015; Maynard & Martini, 2005).

Vygotsky's theory is often referred to as a *sociocultural theory*, because in his view cognitive development is always both a social and a cultural process (Daniels et al., 2007). It is social, because children learn through interactions with others and require assistance from others in order to learn what they need to know. It is cultural, because what children need to know is determined by the culture they live in. Vygotsky recognized that there are distinct cultural differences in the knowledge children must acquire—from agricultural skills in rural Asia, to caring for cattle in eastern Africa, to the verbal and scientific reasoning skills taught in Western schools. This is very different from Piaget's theory described earlier, which emphasizes the child's solitary interactions with the physical environment and views cognitive development as essentially the same across cultures.

THE ZONE OF PROXIMAL DEVELOPMENT Two of Vygotsky's most influential ideas are the zone of proximal development and scaffolding (Gauvain & Nicolaides, 2015). The **zone of proximal development** is the distance between skills or tasks that children can accomplish alone and those they are capable of performing if guided by an adult or a more competent peer. According to Vygotsky, children learn best if the instruction they are provided is within the zone of proximal development, so that they need assistance at first but gradually become capable of performing the task on their own. For example, children learning a musical instrument may be lost or overwhelmed if learning entirely on their own, but can make progress if guided by someone who already knows how to play the instrument. Watch the video *Zone of Promixal Development* on the next page to learn more.

zone of proximal development

difference between skills or tasks that children can accomplish alone and those they are capable of performing if guided by an adult or a more competent peer

Watch   ZONE OF PROMIXAL DEVELOPMENT

Video

private speech

in Vygotsky's theory, self-guiding and self-directing comments children make to themselves as they learn in the zone of proximal development

scaffolding

degree of assistance provided to the learner in the zone of proximal development, gradually decreasing as the learner's skills develop

In Vygotsky's theory, children's cognitive development is always both social and cultural. Here, a father in the Middle Eastern country of Oman shows his son how to weave a basket.

As they learn in the zone of proximal development and have conversations with those guiding them, children begin to speak to themselves in a self-guiding and self-directing way, first aloud and then internally. Vygotsky called this **private speech** (Winsler, 2009). As children become more competent in what they are learning, they internalize their private speech and gradually decrease its use. Toddlerhood and early childhood are crucial periods in Vygotsky's theory, because it is during these life stages that children are most likely to use private speech and make the transition from using it aloud to using it internally (Feigenbaum, 2002). However, private speech continues throughout life. In fact, Vygotsky believed that private speech was necessary to all higher order cognitive functioning. In recent years, studies have shown that adolescents and adults use private speech when solving tasks of diverse kinds (Medina et al., 2009).

Another key idea in Vygotsky's theory is **scaffolding**, which is the degree of assistance provided to children in the zone of proximal development. According to Vygotsky, scaffolding should gradually decrease as children become more competent at a task. When children begin learning a task, they require substantial instruction and involvement from an adult or more capable peer; but as they gain knowledge and skill, the teacher should gradually scale back the amount of direct instruction provided. For example, young children require their parents' help to get dressed, but with age and experience they become capable of doing more and more of it themselves, and eventually they can do it on their own. Scaffolding can occur at any age, whenever there is someone who is learning a skill or gaining knowledge from someone else.

Scaffolding and the zone of proximal development underscore the social nature of learning in Vygotsky's theory. In his view, learning always takes place via a social process, through the interactions between someone who possesses knowledge and someone who is in the process of obtaining knowledge. The ideas of the zone of proximal development and scaffolding have been applied to older children's learning as well, and will be explored further in later chapters.

GUIDED PARTICIPATION One scholar who has been important in extending Vygotsky's theory is Barbara Rogoff (1990; 1995; 1998; 2003). Her idea of **guided participation** refers to the interaction between two people (often an adult and a child) as they participate in a culturally valued activity. The guidance is "the direction offered by cultural and social values, as well as social partners" (Rogoff, 1995, p. 142) as learning takes place. As an example of guided participation, Rogoff (2003) describes a toddler and caregiver in Taiwan "playing school" together. As part of the game, the caregiver teaches the toddler to stand up and bow down to the teacher at the beginning and end of class, thereby teaching not only the routine of the classroom but the cultural value of respect for teachers' authority. The teaching in guided participation may also be indirect. For example, from her research with the Mayan people of Guatemala, Rogoff (2003) describes how toddlers observe their mothers making tortillas and attempt to imitate them. Mothers give them a small piece of dough and help their efforts along by rolling the dough into a ball and starting the flattening process but otherwise do not provide explicit teaching, instead allowing toddlers to learn through observing and then attempting to imitate their mother's actions.

guided participation
teaching interaction between two people (often an adult and a child) as they participate in a culturally valued activity

Practice Quiz   ANSWERS AVAILABLE IN ANSWER KEY.

1. Shareef's parents bought him a high chair and he intentionally tipped over his water in the tray over and over again. According to Piaget, Shareef is at the _____ stage.
  a. simple reflexes
  b. primary circular reactions
  c. secondary circular reactions
  d. tertiary circular reactions

2. Eighteen-month-old Omar saw his father stirring a pot on the stove and the next day, picks up his toy bowl and spoon and begins "stirring" an imaginary substance. This is an example of _____.
  a. deferred imitation
  b. sorting objects into categories
  c. tertiary circular reactions
  d. the A-not-B error

3. When children generally avoid making the A-not-B error, they _____.
  a. show the ability to categorize
  b. have attained object permanence
  c. are in the stage of tertiary circular reactions
  d. understand scaffolding

4. According to Vygotsky, _____ is required for cognitive development.
  a. formal education
  b. a strong caregiver-child attachment
  c. social interaction
  d. a good genetic background

5. According to Vygotsky, children learn best if the instruction they are provided is _____.
  a. within the zone of proximal development
  b. concrete in nature
  c. a good fit with their learning style
  d. developed by an educational specialist

COGNITIVE DEVELOPMENT:
Language Development

Of all the qualities that distinguish humans from other animals, language may be the most important. Other species of animals have their own ways of communicating, but language allows humans to communicate about a vastly broader range of topics. Using language, humans can communicate about not just what is observable in the present, the way other animals might communicate about food or predators in their immediate environment, but about an infinite range of things beyond the present moment. With language we can also communicate not just about things that exist but about things that might exist, things that we imagine. As linguist Derrick Bickerton remarks, "Only language could have broken through the prison of immediate experience in which every other creature is locked, releasing us into infinite freedoms of space and time" (Leakey, 1994, p. 119).

In Chapter 4 we looked at the beginnings of language in infancy. However, by the end of infancy most children can only speak a few words. It is during toddlerhood that language development has its most rapid and important advances. Toddlers go from speaking a few words at their first birthday to being fluent users of language by their third birthday. Let's examine the course of this remarkable achievement, looking first at the biological and evolutionary bases of language, then at specific language milestones of toddlerhood, and finally, at the cultural and social context of toddlers' language use.

The Biological and Evolutionary Bases of Language

LO 5.9   **Summarize the evidence for the biological and evolutionary bases of language.**

You may have heard that some primates have learned how to use language. Attempts to teach language to apes have a long history in the social sciences, going back over a half century. In the earliest attempts, researchers treated baby chimpanzees as closely as possible to how a human infant would be treated, having the chimpanzees live in the researcher's household as part of the family and making daily efforts to teach the chimps how to speak. Years of these efforts yielded nothing but the single word "mama"—and a badly disordered household. It turned out that chimpanzees, like other nonhuman primates, lack the vocal apparatus that makes human speech possible.

In the 1960s, researchers hit upon the clever idea of teaching apes sign language. These attempts were much more successful. One famous chimpanzee, Washoe, learned to use about 100 signs, mostly involving requests for food (Small, 2001). She even learned to lie and to make jokes. However, she never learned to make original combinations of signs (with one possible exception, when she saw a duck for the first time and signed "water bird"). Mostly, Washoe and other primates who have learned sign language simply mimic the signs they have been taught by their human teachers. They lack the most important and distinctive feature of human language, which is **infinite generativity**, the ability to take the word symbols of a language and combine them in a virtually infinite number of new ways.

A variety of human biological characteristics indicate that we are a species built for language (Kenneally, 2007). First, humans have a unique vocal apparatus. We are able to make a much wider range of sounds than the other primates because, for us, the larynx is located lower in the throat, which creates a large sound chamber, the pharynx, above the vocal cords. We also have a relatively small and mobile tongue that can push the air coming past the larynx in various ways to make different sounds, and lips that are flexible enough to stop and start the passage of air.

Second, two areas in the left hemisphere of the human brain are specifically devoted to language functions (Nakano & Blumstein, 2004; Pizzamiglio et al., 2005). **Broca's area**

infinite generativity

ability to take the word symbols of a language and combine them in a virtually infinite number of new ways

Chimpanzees can learn to use some sign language in a limited way, but they lack the infinite generativity of human language.

in the left frontal lobe is specialized for language production, and **Wernicke's area** in the left temporal lobe is specialized for language comprehension (see **Figure 5.3**). If damage to one of these areas occurs in adulthood the specialized language function of the area is also damaged; but if damage takes place in childhood, other areas of the brain can compensate—with compensation being greater the younger the brain injury takes place (Akshoomoff et al., 2002; Huttenlocher, 2002). In addition to Broca's and Wernicke's areas, many other regions of the brain contribute to language use (Dick et al., 2004). In fact, some linguists argue that the extraordinary size of the human brain in comparison to other species is due mainly to the evolution of language (Pinker, 2004).

Third, genes for language development have recently been identified (Gazzaniga, 2008; Pinker, 2004). Because Broca's and Wernicke's areas have long been known to be part of normal brain anatomy, the genetic basis of language was clear. However, identifying the specific genes for language strengthens our knowledge of how deeply language is embedded in human phylogenetic (species) development.

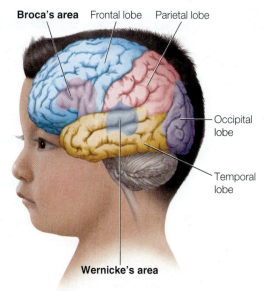

Figure 5.3 Brain Lobes Showing Broca's Area and Wernicke's Area

Although modern humans are biologically equipped for language, our earliest ancestors were not. Early hominids (see Chapter 1) had a larynx similar in placement to modern nonhuman primates, and so must have been incapable of language (Leakey, 1994). The placement of the larynx became notably lower beginning nearly 2 million years ago, and the earliest *Homo sapiens* 200,000 years ago had a vocal apparatus that was not much different from yours. Undoubtedly the development of language gave humans a substantial evolutionary advantage (Small, 2001). Language would have made it easier to communicate about the location of food sources and about how to make tools, which would in turn enhance survival. If your clan could craft a better spear, you would have a better chance of killing the prey that would provide the necessary nourishment. If your group could construct a boat, you could potentially travel to new food sources if the local ones became depleted.

Many evolutionary biologists believe that language also conferred an evolutionary advantage because of its social function. During the course of human evolution, the size of human groups gradually increased (Leakey, 1994), leading to an increased need for communication that would allow them to function effectively. Because language abilities improved the efficiency of group functioning, groups that excelled in language would have been more likely than other groups to survive and reproduce. Within groups, too, using language effectively would have conferred an advantage in obtaining mates, food, and status, so natural selection would have favored language abilities in the course of human evolutionary history (Pinker, 2004).

The marvelous ability that young children have to learn the rules of their language is one more indication of the biological, evolutionary basis of language. A half century ago, at a time when many psychologists were arguing that language has no biological origin and children learn it solely through imitation and parents' reinforcement, linguist Noam Chomsky (1957, 1969) protested that language is too complex to be learned in this way. Observing that all children learn the basic rules of grammar of their language at about the same age, 2 to 3 years old, Chomsky proposed that children are born with a **language acquisition device (LAD)** that enables them to perceive and grasp quickly the grammatical rules in the language around them. Today language researchers generally agree that language development is a biological potential that is then nurtured by social interaction, although there is still a lively debate about the nature of the biological foundation of language and the kinds of social stimulation needed to develop it (Hoff, 2009).

Broca's area

portion of the left frontal lobe of the human brain that is specialized for language production

Wernicke's area

portion of the left temporal lobe of the human brain that is specialized for language comprehension

language acquisition device (LAD)

according to Chomsky, innate feature of the brain that enables children to perceive and grasp quickly the grammatical rules in the language around them

How, specifically, would language have conferred an evolutionary advantage to early humans in obtaining mates, food, and status?

Milestones of Toddler Language: From First Words to Fluency

LO 5.10 Describe the milestones in language development that take place during the toddler years.

Toddlers' advances in language begin slowly but then rise sharply, so that in less than 2 years they go from speaking a few words to being highly adept language users. Especially notable is the amazing burst of language development that occurs at 18 to 24 months.

TWELVE MONTHS TO 18 MONTHS: SLOW EXPANSION For the first 6 months of toddlerhood, language develops at a steady but slow pace. From 12 to 18 months old, toddlers learn to speak one to three new words a week, reaching a total of 10 words by 15 months old and 50 words by about 18 months old, on average, in American studies (Bloom, 1998). There is a wide range of variability around these averages. Toddlers may speak their 10th word anywhere from 13 to 19 months old, and their 50th word anywhere from 14 to 24 months old, and still be considered within the normal range. Just as the timing of taking first steps has no relation to later athletic ability, timing of speaking the first, 10th, or 50th word has no relation to later verbal ability.

The first 50 words tend to be words that are part of toddlers' daily routines (Waxman & Lidz, 2006), and include:

- important people ("Mama," "Dada"),
- familiar animals ("dog," "kitty"),
- body parts ("hair," "tummy"),
- moving objects ("car," "truck"),
- foods ("milk," "cookie"),
- actions ("eat," "bath"),
- household items ("cup," "chair"),
- toys ("ball," "bear"),
- greetings or farewells ("hi," "bye-bye").

Toddlers first learn words they need to use in practical ways to communicate with the people around them, usually as part of shared activities (Newman, 2007). Often at this age they speak in partial words, for example "bah" for bird, "meh" for milk, or "na-na" for banana.

From 12 to 18 months most toddlers use one word at a time, but a single word can have varied meanings. Toddler's single words are called **holophrases**, meaning that for them a single word can be used to represent different forms of whole sentences (Flavell et al., 2002). For example, "cup" could mean "Fill my *cup* with juice," or "I dropped the *cup* on the floor," or "Hand me my *cup,* I can't reach it," or "Here, take this *cup*," depending on when and how and to whom it is said.

Another way toddlers make the most of their limited vocabulary is to have a single word represent a variety of related objects. This is called **overextension** (Bloom, 2000). For example, when the son of two language researchers learned the name of the furry family dog, Nunu, he applied it not only to the original Nunu but to all dogs, as well as to other fuzzy objects such as slippers, and even to a salad with a large black olive that apparently reminded him of Nunu's nose (de Villiers & de Villiers, 1978).

Toddlers also exhibit **underextension**, applying a general word to a specific object (Woodward & Markman, 1998). When I was a child, my family had a cat named Kitty,

holophrase

single word that is used to represent a whole sentence

overextension

use of a single word to represent a variety of related objects

underextension

applying a general word to a specific object

who received that name because my brother was told that it was "the kitty," and began calling it Kitty, and the name stuck. He did not realize that *kitty* was the (slang) name for the larger category, "cats," but mistook it for the proper name of that particular cat. Underextension often occurs in this way, with a toddler first applying a new word to a specific object, then learning later to apply it to a category of objects.

Here, as at all ages, *production* (speaking) lags behind *comprehension* (understanding) in language development. Although toddlers do not reach the 50-word milestone in production until about 18 months old, they usually achieve 50-word comprehension by about 13 months old (Menyuk et al., 1995). During toddlerhood, comprehension is a better predictor of later verbal intelligence than production is (Reznick et al., 1997).

EIGHTEEN MONTHS TO 24 MONTHS: THE NAMING EXPLOSION

After learning to speak words at a slow rate for the first half of their second year, toddlers' word production suddenly takes off from 18 to 24 months. The pace of learning new words doubles, from one to three words per week to five or six words per week (Kopp, 2003). This is known as the *naming explosion* or *vocabulary spurt* (Bloom et al., 1985; Goldfield & Reznick, 1990). After just one time of being told what an object is called, toddlers this age will learn it and remember it, a process called **fast mapping** (Gopnik et al., 1999; Markman & Jaswal, 2004). Fast mapping is due not just to memory but to toddlers' ability to quickly infer the meaning of words based on how the word is used in a sentence and how it seems to be related to words they already know (Dixon et al., 2006). By their second birthday, toddlers have an average vocabulary of about 200 words (Dale & Goodman, 2004). This rapid pace of learning and remembering words will continue for years, but it is especially striking at 18 to 24 months because this is when it begins (Ganger & Brent, 2004). Girls' vocabulary increases faster than boys' vocabulary during this period, initiating a gender difference in verbal abilities that will persist throughout childhood (Lovas, 2011).

Toddlers exhibit overextension when they use a single word (such as "raspberry") to represent a variety of related objects (such as strawberries and other red berries).

Two of the most notable words toddlers learn during this period are *gone* and *no*. Using "gone" reflects their growing awareness of object permanence, as it signifies that something has disappeared from view but still exists somewhere (Gopnik et al., 1999). Using "no" reflects their budding sense of self ("me," "my," and "mine" also begin to be used at this age). Saying "no" can be short for "You may want me to do to that, but I don't want to do it!" Of course, they also begin to hear "No!" more often around this age, as their mobility and curiosity leads them to behavior that the adults around them may regard as dangerous or destructive (Kopp, 2003). During this 18- to 24-month period they also learn to name one or two colors, at least six body parts, and emotional states like "tired" and "mad" (Eisenberg et al., 1996; Kopp, 2003).

Toward the end of the 18- to 24-month period, toddlers begin to combine spoken words for the first time. Their first word combinations are usually two words, in what is called **telegraphic speech** (Bloom, 1998; Brown, 1973; Edmonds, 2011). Telegraphic speech takes similar forms in a variety of languages, from English to German to Finnish to Samoan: "See doggie," "Big car," "My ball," "More cookie," or "Mommy gone" (Bochner & Jones, 2003; Slobin, 1972). Like a telegram in the old days, telegraphic speech strips away connecting words like *the* and *and*, getting right to the point with nouns, verbs, and modifiers.

An interesting feature of telegraphic speech is that it already shows an initial knowledge of syntax (word order). Toddlers say "See doggie," not "Doggie see"; they say "My ball," not "Ball my." Similar to the one-word holophrases used earlier, telegraphic speech implies more understanding of language than it states explicitly: "Big car" means "Look at the big car," "My ball" means "This is my ball," and so on.

Verbal production is the most striking advance of the 18- to 24-month period, but comprehension also advances notably as toddlers become faster and more efficient in

fast mapping

learning and remembering a word for an object after just one time of being told what the object is called

telegraphic speech

two-word phrases that strip away connecting words, such as *the* and *and*

processing words. In one series of experiments, toddlers 15 to 24 months old were shown pictures of two objects at a time while a recorded voice said "Where's the _____?" and named one of the objects (Fernald et al., 2006). At 15 months, toddlers waited until the whole word had been spoken before looking at the object the word referred to, but by 24 months they would shift their gaze even before the word had been completely spoken, for example looking at the shoe as soon as they heard the "sh" part spoken.

TWENTY-FOUR MONTHS TO 36 MONTHS: BECOMING ADEPT AT LANGUAGE
During the third year, toddlers continue to expand their speaking vocabulary at the same rapid pace that began at 18 to 24 months. They learn to use prepositions such as *under, over,* and *through* (Eisenberg et al., 1996). They also use words that reflect a more complex understanding of categories. For example, they understand that a bear is not only a bear but also an animal (Kopp, 2003).

They continue to exhibit overextension and underextension, but with diminishing frequency as their vocabulary expands. They continue to use telegraphic speech as well, but now in three- and four-word statements ("Ball under bed!") rather than two words. Increasingly during the third year they begin to speak in short, complete sentences. At this age my son Miles would point to the moon and protest, "It's too high!" then look at us as if he expected us to do something about it.

By the end of the third year most toddlers are remarkably skilled language users (Maratsos, 1998). They can communicate with others about a wide range of topics. They can speak about events that are happening in the present as well as about past and future events. Toddlers raised in homes where Chinese is spoken have learned that raising or lowering the pitch of a word changes its meaning. French toddlers have learned how to make nasal sounds and say "Voilà!" and !Kung San toddlers in Botswana have learned how to click their tongues against various parts of their mouths to make the words of their language (Small, 2001). Although their pronunciation of words is not as precise as it will become later, by the time they reach age 3 most toddlers can speak clearly enough to make themselves understood about nearly anything they wish.

Furthermore, without any explicit instruction, by the end of the third year toddlers have learned the rules of their language, no matter how complex those rules may seem to someone who does not speak it. Consider this example (Slobin, 1982, 2014). In Turkish, the rules of syntax (word order) are different from English. In English, "The girl fed the dog" has quite a different meaning from "The dog fed the girl." The *subject* (girl) is supposed to go first, followed by the *verb* (fed) and then the *object* (dog). However, in Turkish the object is indicated not by the syntax but by attaching the suffix *u*. So, "The girl fed the dog-u" means the same as "The dog-u fed the girl." Turkish toddlers use the *u* rule correctly by their third year, just as English-speaking children learn the correct use of English syntax by their third year.

Toddlers' language mastery is evident not only in how well they use the rules of their language but in the mistakes they make. As they learn the grammar of their language, they make mistakes that reflect **overregularization**, which means applying grammatical rules even to words that are exceptions to the rule.

Here are two examples from English that illustrate overregularization. First, the plural of most English nouns can be obtained by adding *s* to the singular form, but there are irregular exceptions, such as "mice" as the plural of "mouse," and "feet" as the plural of "foot." In the third year, toddlers sometimes make mistakes with these kinds of words, saying "mouses" instead of "mice" and "foots" instead of "feet." Second, the rule for the past tense of an English verb is to add *ed* to the end, but there are irregular exceptions, such as "went" as the past tense of "go" and "threw" as the past tense of "throw." In the third year toddlers sometimes make mistakes with these exceptions, saying "Mommy *goed* to the store" or "I *throwed* the ball." However, it is a testament to toddlers' language mastery that even by the third year, mistakes of this kind are rare (Bochner & Jones, 2003).

overregularization

applying grammatical rules even to words that are exceptions to the rule

Learning Language in a Social and Cultural Context

LO 5.11 Identify how parents' stimulation of toddlers' language varies across cultures and evaluate how these variations relate to language development.

Humans are biologically built for learning language, but not for learning any specific language. There are over 60,000 different human languages in the world (Small, 2001), but none of them come preinscribed on our brains. Whatever language we learn must come from our social and cultural environment.

This was first shown in a bizarre experiment conducted about 800 years ago. Frederick II, the Holy Roman Emperor (1194–1250), decided he wanted to find out what language infants would speak "naturally," if they were left to their own resources. He chose a group of neonates in an orphanage and instructed their caregivers never to speak in their presence. What language would the babies begin to speak spontaneously, on their own? Would it be Latin, the language of scholars at that time? Would it be German, Frederick's own language, or (God forbid) French, the language of his chief rivals?

The answer turned out to be, as you may have guessed, none of the above. Tragically, all of the infants died. This is a poignant illustration of how we are poised for language to be part of the human social environment, and of how humans need language to develop properly, not just in their language development but in their social development.

What kind of social environment do toddlers need in order to develop their language skills? In American research, the focus has been on how parents foster language development in young children. In the United States and other developed countries, parents often read to their infants and toddlers, explaining the meaning of the words as they go along (Fitneva et al., 2015). This is a way of preparing children for an economic future in which the ability to apprehend and use information will be crucial. Parents in the majority culture are more likely than parents in ethnic minority cultures to read to their toddlers, promoting an early advantage in verbal development that continues through the school years (Driessen et al., 2010).

Several studies have examined social-class differences in parents' language stimulation and how this is related to the pace of toddlers' language development. The higher the social class of the parents, the more likely they are to read to their toddlers (Fitneva et al., 2015). Social class status is also correlated with how much parents speak to their young children. For example, one study videotaped parent–child interactions in the homes of low-, middle-, and high-income families on several occasions, beginning when the children were 7 to 9 months old and continuing until they were about 30 months old (Hart & Risley, 1999). There were striking differences in how many words were spoken to children of different income levels. Parents in high-income families talked the most to their children, averaging about 35 words a minute; parents in middle-income families talked to their children an average of about 20 words a minute; and parents of low-income families provided the least language stimulation, just 10 words per minute. By 30 months old there were substantial differences in the toddlers' vocabularies, averaging 766 words in the high-income families and just 357 words in the low-income families. A more recent study reached similar conclusions (Weisleder & Fernald, 2013).

Of course, there is a research design problem in studies like this, because parents provide not only the environment to their children but their genes; this is known as passive

Toddlers in traditional cultures often experience a language-rich environment. Here, a Mongolian family shares a meal and conversation.

genotype–environment effects (see Chapter 2). In studies of parents and children in biological families, genes and environment are *confounded,* which means they are closely related and difficult to separate. However, in early childhood and beyond, the influence of teachers' language use on children's language development provides more definite evidence of an environmental effect, because teachers and children have no genetic relationship (Huttenlocher et al., 2002).

Cultural Focus: Language Development Across Cultures

Although language development clearly has a biological basis, culture plays an important role as well. Because most research on language development is conducted in developed Western countries, an assumption of this research is that most toddler language use takes place in a parent–toddler dyad—just the two of them. This assumption may be true for the families being studied in developed countries, but the social environment that most toddlers experience worldwide is much different from this, and consequently their language environment differs as well.

Once they learn to walk and begin to talk, toddlers in most cultures spend most of their days not with their parents but in mixed-age groups of other children, including an older girl, often an older sister, who is mainly responsible for caring for them (Edwards et al., 2015). When toddlers are with their parents, usually many other people are around as well, such as siblings, extended-family members, and neighbors. This makes for a language-rich environment, because there is talking going on around them almost constantly, with so many people present. However, relatively little of this talk may be directed specifically at the toddler, because there are so many other people around and because others may not see it as necessary to speak directly to toddlers in order to stimulate their language development (Fitneva et al., 2015).

In fact, the others in a toddler's social environment may even see it as bad parenting to speak often with toddlers. The Gusii people of Kenya believe that encouraging young children to speak is a mistake, because it makes it more likely that they will grow up to be selfish and disobedient (Levine et al., 1994). Their children learn the Gusii language as proficiently as American children learn English, but they learn it from being frequently in social groups where adults and older children are using language, not from having their language development stimulated directly in frequent daily interactions with their parents.

It is not only in rural cultures in developing countries that this approach to toddlers' language development is found, but in developed countries that emphasize collectivistic rather than individualistic cultural beliefs. One study compared Japanese mothers and Canadian mothers in their interactions with their young children (Minami & McCabe, 1995). In Japanese culture, being talkative is considered impolite and undesirable, especially for males, because the Japanese believe it is better to blend in harmoniously with the group than to call attention to yourself (Markus & Kitayama, 2003; Rothbaum et al., 2001). Consequently, the Japanese mothers in the study often discouraged their children from talking, especially their boys. In contrast, the Canadian mothers encouraged their children to talk more, by asking them questions and suggesting they provide more details. This approach was interpreted by the researchers as being based on a belief system favoring individualism and self-expression.

Watch the *Language Development Across Cultures* video to see how parents from different cultural backgrounds communicate with their infants and toddlers and what parents do, if anything, to foster their child's language development.

Watch   LANGUAGE DEVELOPMENT ACROSS CULTURES

Review Question:

Discuss the three factors mentioned in the clip that influence toddler language development. What are some additional factors that might also impact toddler language development?

Practice Quiz

1. When it comes to learning what we consider language, the most significant difference between apes and humans is _____.

  a. the inability of apes to make requests

  b. the inability of apes to generate word symbols in an infinite number of ways

  c. the inability of apes to learn motor movements and signs from humans

  d. the faster pace of humans' sign language

2. Nona was in a serious car accident and suffered damage to her Broca's area. Which of the following is likely to result?

  a. She will have difficulty producing speech.

  b. She will show no emotion.

  c. She will have difficulty with speech comprehension.

  d. She will no longer be able to form short-term memories.

3. Which is an example of overextension?

  a. A child saying, "Mommy goed to the store."

  b. A child saying "The sun is smiling at me."

  c. A child calling all men "Dada."

  d. A child saying, "Mommy gone!"

4. Joquain was thirsty, so he looked at his mother and pointed to the glass on the counter and said, "juice." This is an example of _____.

  a. fast mapping

  b. underextension

  c. overregularization

  d. a holophrase

5. Research has shown that _____.

  a. direct stimulation of language development is discouraged in some cultures

  b. language development is dependent upon the environment rather than genes or biology

  c. in the United States, language development occurs at the same rate across children from different socioeconomic statuses

  d. maternal responsiveness to American children's vocalizations had no impact on when children reached language milestones

Summary: Cognitive Development

LO 5.7 Outline the cognitive achievements of toddlerhood in Piaget's theory.

According to Piaget, the ability for mental representations develops in the second half of the second year and is the basis for important aspects of later cognitive functioning, including problem solving and language. Object permanence also reaches near-completion during this period. Deferred imitation and categorization also require mental representation.

LO 5.8 Explain Vygotsky's sociocultural theory of cognitive development and contrast it with Piaget's theory.

Unlike Piaget and most other cognitive theorists and researchers, Vygotsky emphasized the cultural basis of cognitive development in childhood. He proposed concepts such as scaffolding and the zone of proximal development to describe how children obtain cultural knowledge from adults.

LO 5.9 Summarize the evidence for the biological and evolutionary bases of language.

In humans the larynx is lower in the throat than it is in other primates, making spoken language possible. Humans also have areas in the brain specifically devoted to language functions. Anatomically the capacity for language appears to have first developed in early hominids 2 million years ago.

LO 5.10 Describe the milestones in language development that take place during the toddler years.

At 18 months, most toddlers speak about 50 words, usually in holophrases. By 24 months, most speak about 200 words and combine some words in telegraphic speech. By their third birthdays, most can easily use the language of their culture in full sentences.

LO 5.11 Identify how parents' stimulation of toddlers' language varies across cultures and evaluate how these variations relate to language development.

Cultures vary widely in how much they encourage toddlers' language development, from stimulating language use through direct interactions, to allowing toddlers to be present among conversing adults but otherwise not speaking to them much, to actually discouraging them from talking. Regardless of cultural practices, toddlers generally learn to use their language well by the time they reach age 3.

Section 3 Emotional and Social Development

Learning Objectives

5.12 Describe how emotional development advances during toddlerhood and identify the impact of culture on these changes.

5.13 Describe the changes in self-development that take place during toddlerhood.

5.14 Distinguish between *sex* and *gender* and summarize the evidence for the biological basis of gender development.

5.15 Describe the essential features of attachment theory and identify the four classifications of attachment.

5.16 Identify the key factors influencing the quality of toddlers' attachment to their mothers, and explain what effect attachment quality has on development.

5.17 Compare and contrast the typical patterns of father involvement with infants and toddlers in traditional cultures and developed countries.

5.18 Describe relationships with siblings, peers, and friends during toddlerhood.

5.19 Identify the characteristics of autism and recognize how autism affects prospects for children as they grow to adulthood.

5.20 Identify the typical rates of television use in toddlerhood and explain some consequences of toddlers' TV watching.

EMOTIONAL AND SOCIAL DEVELOPMENT: Emotional Development in Toddlerhood

Toddlerhood is the stage of life when we first learn how to regulate our emotions. As part of this process we learn emotions such as shame and guilt that reflect our responses to the expectations and requirements of others.

Toddlers' Emotions

LO 5.12 Describe how emotional development advances during toddlerhood and identify the impact of culture on these changes.

As toddlers become more self-aware, they learn that the people in their cultural environment regard some behaviors as good and others as bad, some as right and some as wrong, and they learn to feel negative emotions when they do something defined as bad or wrong. They also begin to learn how to regulate their emotions.

EMOTIONAL SELF-REGULATION From the early months of life, infants tend to show how they feel. Happy or sad, hungry or mad, they let you know. Gradually during the first year, infants develop the rudiments of emotional regulation. They learn to turn their attention away from unpleasant stimulation (Axia et al., 1999). The people around them soothe their distress with the kinds of strategies we discussed in Chapter 4, such as cuddling and distraction. In many cultures, frequent breast-feeding is used as an emotional regulator, to quiet babies whenever they begin to fuss (DeLoache & Gottlieb, 2000; Levine et al., 1994).

During toddlerhood, emotional self-regulation advances in four ways (Kopp, 1989; Miller, 2014; Thompson & Goodvin, 2007).

1. First, toddlers develop *behaviors* that can help them regulate their emotions. For example, toddlers who are frightened may run to a trusted adult or older sibling, or cling to a comforting blanket or stuffed animal.

2. Second, toddlers use *language* to promote emotional self-regulation. As noted earlier in the chapter, from about 18 months old toddlers begin to use words to identify and talk about their emotions. Throughout toddlerhood and beyond, talking about feelings with others enhances children's understanding of their own and others' emotions, which in turn promotes their emotional self-regulation (Bugental & Grusec, 2006; Parke & Buriel, 2006).

3. Third, *external requirements* by others extend toddlers' capacities for emotional self-regulation. In toddlerhood, parents begin to convey and enforce rules that require emotional self-regulation: no hitting others no matter how angry you are, no jumping on the table no matter how happy you are, and so on (Calkins, 2007). Cultures vary in their requirements for emotional self-regulation, with collectivistic cultures such as China and Japan tending toward stiffer requirements than the more individualistic cultures of the West (Bornstein, 2006; Laible, 2004; Shweder et al., 2006).

4. Fourth and finally, emotional self-regulation in toddlerhood is promoted by the development of the *sociomoral emotions* (Brownell & Kopp, 2010). Becoming capable of guilt, shame, and embarrassment motivates toddlers to avoid these unpleasant emotional states. Because they may be admonished by others for expressing primary emotions too strongly (e.g., yelling angrily in a grocery store) or in the wrong context (e.g., laughing loudly in a quiet restaurant), they learn emotional self-regulation as part of an effort to win approval from others and avoid their disapproval.

If emotional self-regulation increases from infancy to toddlerhood, why is it toddlerhood that is associated with tantrums—and why is age 2 popularly known in some cultures as the "terrible twos"? Perhaps it is that for toddlers, abilities for emotional self-regulation increase but so do expectations for emotional control. Consequently, when they have the brief but intense outburst of anger, crying, and distress that constitutes a tantrum it is more noticed than the more frequent outbursts of infants (Calkins, 2007). Perhaps it is also that toddlers have a more developed sense of self, including the ability to protest with a tantrum when they don't get their way (Grolnick et al., 2006).

There is a cultural explanation as well. It is interesting to observe that in Western countries, such as the United States and the United Kingdom, it is widely accepted that toddlerhood tantrums are normal and even inevitable (Potegal & Davidson, 2003). One popular American advice book for parents of toddlers asserts that "Tantrums are a fact of toddler life, a behavior that's virtually universal … turning little cherubs into little monsters" (Murkoff et al., 2003, p. 336). Yet outside the West, toddler tantrums are rarely mentioned, and toddlerhood is not seen as an age of "terrible" behavior. In African and Asian cultures, by the time toddlerhood is reached, children have already learned that they are expected to control their emotions and their behavior, and they exercise the control required of them (Holodynski, 2009; Miller, 2014; Miller & Fung, 2010). It appears that tantrums and the allegedly terrible twos are not "universal" after all, but a consequence of Western cultural beliefs in the value of self-expression, which children have already learned well by toddlerhood.

LEARNING THE SOCIOMORAL EMOTIONS As described in Chapter 4, infants across cultures display a range of recognizable *primary emotions* from early in life, including anger, fear, and happiness. In toddlerhood new emotions appear, including guilt, shame, embarrassment, envy, and pride. These are known as *secondary emotions* because they develop later than the primary emotions and they are based on what toddlers experience in their social environment (Cummings et al., 2010). All toddlers have a capacity for developing secondary emotions, as indicated by the fact that these emotions appear across a wide range of cultures and are accompanied by characteristic body postures such as, for shame, lowering their eyes, bowing their heads, or covering their faces with their hands (Barrett & Nelson-Goens, 1997). However, what evokes the secondary emotions depends on what toddlers have been taught in their social and cultural environment.

The secondary emotions are called **sociomoral emotions** because they are evoked based on what the toddler has learned about culturally based standards of right and wrong (Brownell & Kopp, 2010; Mascolo & Fischer, 2007). When toddlers experience guilt, shame, or embarrassment, it is not just because they have made the cognitive comparison between what they have done and what others have expected of them. It is also because they have begun to learn to feel good when they conform to the expected standard and bad when they do not. Thus by age 2 most toddlers have begun to develop a conscience, an internalized set of moral standards that guides their behavior and emotions (Kochanska, 2002; Thompson, 2006).

Another important sociomoral emotion that first develops in toddlerhood is **empathy**, the ability to understand and respond helpfully to another person's distress. Even neonates have an early form of empathy, as indicated by crying when they hear the cry of another infant. Throughout the first year, infants respond to the distress of others with distress of their own. However, true empathy requires an understanding of the self as separate from others, so it develops along with self-awareness in toddlerhood (Gopnik et al., 1999). It is only in the second and especially the third year that toddlers have enough of a developed self to understand the distress of others and respond, not by becoming distressed themselves but by helping other persons relieve their distress (Brownell et al., 2009). In one study, toddlers responded to a researcher's feigned distress by offering a hug, a comforting remark, or a favorite stuffed animal or blanket (Hoffman, 2000). This demonstrates the beginning of **prosocial behavior**, which is behavior intended to help or benefit others (Svetlova et al., 2010).

Although the triggers of the sociomoral emotions are learned from the social environment, there are probably some that are universal. Children everywhere seem to be taught not to hurt the people around them and not to damage or destroy things (Rogoff, 2003). However, even in toddlerhood there are cultural differences in how the sociomoral emotions are shaped. Cultural differences are especially sharp regarding the emotions of pride and shame, that is, in how good a person should feel about individual accomplishments and how quickly, easily, and often shame should be evoked. In Western countries, especially in the United States, pride is often viewed positively (Bellah et al., 1985; Twenge, 2006). Children are praised and encouraged to feel good about themselves for accomplishments such as hitting a ball, dancing in a show, or learning something new. Everybody on the soccer team gets a trophy, win or lose. Shame, in contrast, is applied

Toddlers become capable of sociomoral emotions such as shame.

sociomoral emotions

emotions evoked based on learned, culturally based standards of right and wrong; also called *secondary emotions*

empathy

ability to understand and respond helpfully to another person's distress

prosocial behavior

behavior intended to help or benefit others, including kindness, friendliness, and sharing

with hesitation, as parents and others worry that shame may harm the development of children's self-esteem.

In most non-Western cultures, however, pride is seen as a greater danger than shame. In Japanese and Chinese cultures, for example, children are taught from early on not to call attention to themselves and not to display pride in response to personal success (Akimoto & Sanbonmatsu, 1999; Miller, 2014). For example, in one study of mothers' and 2½-year-olds' conversations about misbehavior in China and the United States, American mothers tended to frame the misbehavior as an emotionally positive learning experience—"Now you know not to do that next time, don't you?"—in order to preserve their toddlers' self-esteem. In contrast, Chinese mothers cultivated shame in their toddlers by emphasizing the negative consequences and negative feelings of others that resulted from the misbehavior (Miller et al., 1997). To the Chinese mothers, teaching their toddlers shame was a way of teaching them to be considerate of others, and a way of preparing them to grow up in a collectivistic culture that emphasizes the value of consideration for others.

The Birth of the Self

LO 5.13 Describe the changes in self-development that take place during toddlerhood.

Even in the early weeks of life there is evidence that infants have the beginnings of a sense of self, a sense of being distinct from the external environment. Many of the topics introduced in Chapter 4 on infancy can be interpreted as reflecting the beginnings of self-awareness. Infants recognize the smell of their mother's breast and the sound of her voice after just a few days of life, indicating an awareness of a difference between their own smells and sounds and those of others. In the first month they display a stronger rooting reflex in response to another person touching their cheek than in response to their own hand performing the same movement (Rochat & Hespos, 1997). After a month or two they begin responding in interactions with others by smiling, moving, and vocalizing, thus showing an awareness of themselves and others as distinct social partners. By the middle of the first year they recognize and respond to their own name when it is spoken by others, indicating the beginning of a name-based identity. By the end of the first year, they search for hidden objects and examine objects and put them in their mouths, all behaviors showing an awareness of the distinction between themselves and the external world (Harter, 2006; Thompson, 2006).

Although self-awareness begins to develop during infancy, it advances in important ways during toddlerhood. It is during the second and third years of life that children first demonstrate **self-recognition**. This was demonstrated in a classic experiment in which toddlers were secretly dabbed on the nose with a red spot, then placed in front of a mirror (Lewis & Brooks-Gunn, 1979). Upon seeing the child with the red nose in the mirror, 9- and 12-month-old infants would reach out to touch the reflection as if it were someone else, but by 18 months most toddlers rubbed their own nose, recognizing the image as themselves.

About the same time self-recognition first appears (as indicated in the red-nose test) toddlers also begin to use personal pronouns for the first time ("I," "me," "mine"), and they begin to refer to themselves by their own names (Lewis & Ramsay, 2004; Pipp et al., 1987). These developments show that by the second half of their second year toddlers have the beginnings of **self-reflection**, the capacity to think about themselves as they would think about other persons and objects. Self-reflection enables toddlers to develop the sociomoral emotions described earlier. As toddlers become more self-aware, they learn that the people in their cultural environment have expectations for how to behave and they learn to feel negative emotions when they do something defined as bad or wrong.

self-recognition
ability to recognize one's image in the mirror as one's self

self-reflection
capacity to think about one's self as one would think about other persons and objects

Gender Identity and the Biology of Gender Development

LO 5.14 Distinguish between *sex* and *gender* and summarize the evidence for the biological basis of gender development.

Another aspect of self-development that begins in toddlerhood is the formation of a **gender identity**. Between 18 and 30 months of age is when children first identify themselves and others as male or female (Kapadia & Gala, 2015). At age 2 they also apply gender terms like *boy* and *girl, woman* and *man* to others (Campbell et al., 2004; Raag, 2003).

Before proceeding further, let's clarify the difference between *sex* and *gender.* In general, social scientists use the term **sex** to refer to the biological status of being male or female. **Gender**, in contrast, refers to the cultural categories of "male" and "female" (Tobach, 2004). Use of the term *sex* implies that the characteristics of males and females have a biological basis. Use of the term *gender* implies that characteristics of males and females may be due to cultural and social beliefs, influences, and perceptions. For example, the fact that males are somewhat larger than females throughout life is a sex difference. However, the fact that girls in many cultures have longer hair than boys is a gender difference. The distinction between a sex difference and a gender difference is not always as clear as in these examples, as we will see in this and other chapters. The degree to which differences between males and females are biological or cultural is a subject of great importance and heated debate in the social sciences.

Even before toddlerhood, in all cultures people communicate gender expectations to boys and girls by dressing them differently, talking to them differently, and playing with them differently (Hatfield & Rapson, 2006). In a classic experimental study (Sidorowicz & Lunney, 1980), adults were asked to play with a 10-month-old infant they did not know. All adults played with the same infant, but some were told it was a girl, some were told it was a boy, and some were given no information about its sex. There were three toys to play with: a rubber football, a doll, and a teething ring. When the adults thought the child was male, 50% of the men and 80% of the women played with the child using the football. When they thought the child was female, 89% of the men and 73% of the women used the doll in play.

In the early years, it is mainly parents who convey cultural gender messages (Kapadia & Gala, 2015; Ruble et al., 2006). They give their children names, and usually the names are distinctively male or female. They dress boys differently from girls and provide them with different toys to play with (Bandura & Bussey, 2004). Toys are gender-specific *custom complexes,* representing distinctive cultural patterns of behavior that are based on underlying cultural beliefs (see Chapter 4). Toys for boys—such as guns, cars, and balls for playing sports—reflect the expectation that boys will be active, aggressive, and competitive. Toys for girls—such as dolls, jewelry, and playhouses—reflect the expectation that girls will be nurturing, cooperative, and attractive in appearance. Children readily learn cultural messages about gender roles in toddlerhood, and by early childhood they help enforce these roles with other children. However, gender development has a biological basis as well; *sex* and *gender* are intertwined. Let's look at the biological basis of gender development here, and then explore gender socialization in depth in Chapter 6.

GENDER AND BIOLOGY The cultural and social basis of gender development is well-substantiated. However, there is also a biological basis to gender development. To put this in terms of the distinction between sex and gender just described, sex differences sometimes

gender identity

awareness of one's self as male or female

sex

biological status of being male or female

gender

cultural categories of "male" and "female"

Gender socialization begins early in all cultures.

underlie gender differences—but not always, as we shall see. There are three elements to the biological basis of gender development: evolutionary, ethological, and hormonal.

In the evolutionary view, males and females develop differently because over the course of many millennia of human evolution, different characteristics promoted survival for the two sexes (Buss, 2004). For males, survival was promoted by aggressiveness, competitiveness, and dominance. Males with these characteristics were more likely than their peers to outfight other males for scarce resources and more likely to gain sexual access to females. Consequently, they were more likely to reproduce, and through the process of natural selection, gradually these characteristics became a standard part of a male human being. The aggressiveness and competitiveness of boys in early childhood is an outcome of a long evolutionary history.

For human females, in contrast, over the course of many millennia of evolution, survival was promoted by being nurturing, cooperative, and emotionally responsive to others. Females with these characteristics were more likely than their peers to attract males who would protect them and provide for them. They needed males to protect them from other males, because they would frequently be pregnant or caring for young children. Females with these qualities were also more likely to be effective at caring for children through the long period of vulnerability and dependency that is characteristic of the young of the human species. Consequently, their offspring were more likely to survive to reproductive age, and through natural selection, gradually these qualities became genetically, biologically based tendencies of the human female. The cooperativeness and emotional responsiveness of girls in early childhood is an outcome of a long evolutionary history.

Ethology, the study of animal behavior, also provides evidence of the biological basis of human gender differences. Many of the differences that exist among male and female humans are also true of our closest primate and mammalian relatives (Diamond, 1992; Pinker, 2004). Like human males, the males in those species closely related to us are also more aggressive, competitive, and dominant than females; and males who are highest in these qualities gain greater sexual access to females. Like human females, females in closely related species also are more nurturing and cooperative than males are, and they have primary responsibility for caring for young children. Like human children, the young of closely related species also play in same-sex groups. The similarity of sex-specific behavior across related species is strong evidence for a biological basis for human gender differences.

Hormonal evidence also supports the biological basis of human gender differences. Throughout life, beginning even prenatally, males and females differ in their hormonal balances, with males having more androgens and females more estrogens. In fact, males must receive a burst of androgens in their third month of prenatal development in order to develop into males. These hormonal differences influence human development and behavior. The strongest evidence for this is in studies of children who have hormonal abnormalities. Girls who were exposed to high levels of androgens in the womb are more likely than their peers to show male play behavior in early childhood, including playing with "male" toys like trucks and a preference for male playmates (Hines, 2004). Boys who were exposed to high levels of estrogens in the womb are more likely than their peers to show female play behavior in early childhood, including playing with "female" toys like dolls and a preference for female playmates (Knickmeyer & Baron-Cohen, 2006). In animal studies, too, females whose levels of prenatal androgen are increased experimentally show increased aggression and more active play than their animal peers, and less interest in caring for their offspring (Maccoby, 2002).

CRITICAL THINKING QUESTION

How is the case of children with hormonal abnormalities an example of a natural experiment? Are there any limitations to its validity as a natural experiment?

ethology

study of animal behavior

THE LIMITS OF BIOLOGY Taken together, the evidence from evolutionary theory, ethological research, and research on hormonal abnormalities makes a strong case for the biological basis of human gender differences. There is little doubt that gender differences are accentuated and reinforced by the socialization environment, in every culture. At the same time, there is little doubt that human males and females are biologically different and that these differences are evident in their development in toddlerhood and beyond, in all cultures.

However, there is good reason to be skeptical and wary of attributing all human gender differences mainly to biology (Kapadia & Gala, 2015). In the course of human history, especially in the last century, gender roles have changed dramatically, even though biologically we have not changed (Brumberg, 1997). It was only 100 years ago that women were excluded from higher education and from virtually all professions. It was widely believed, even among scientists—who were all male—that women were biologically incapable of strenuous intellectual work.

Today, women exceed men in university participation in most countries and are close to or equal to men in obtaining graduate degrees in medicine, law, business, and other fields (Arnett, 2015). That fact should give us pause before we assert that the biological basis of children's gender differences today is indisputable. The changes in women's roles over the past century demonstrate the enormous influence that culture can have on the raw material of biology in human development. As cultures change, gender roles can change, even though the underlying biology of human development remains the same. Many male-female distinctions that were widely thought to be sex differences have turned out to be gender differences after all.

The other issue worth mentioning here is that when we speak of gender differences, we are comparing one-half of the human species to the other, over $3\frac{1}{2}$ billion persons to the other $3\frac{1}{2}$ billion persons. Even where there are gender differences, in early childhood and beyond, there are also many exceptions. To put it another way, the variability within each gender is usually much greater than the differences between the two genders, for most characteristics. Consequently, we should be careful not to let our perceptions of gender differences prejudge our estimations of the qualities or abilities of individual boys and girls or men and women.

Practice Quiz   ANSWERS AVAILABLE IN ANSWER KEY.

1. Which of the following is a sociomoral emotion?
   a. anger
   b. guilt
   c. fear
   d. happiness

2. S. was playing in a group of children and showed pride in his ability to fit the right shape piece into the container. This display of pride would most likely be discouraged by parents in _____.
   a. the United States
   b. Canada
   c. China
   d. New Zealand

3. Researchers secretly dabbed a red spot on the nose of babies of different ages and then placed them in front of a mirror. They were testing _____.
   a. expressive language ability
   b. short-term memory
   c. self-recognition
   d. gender identity

4. Gender identity _____.
   a. refers to the biological status of being male or female
   b. develops much more quickly in females than males
   c. refers to the ability of children to identify themselves as male or female
   d. develops around age 5

5. Which of the following statements about gender is TRUE?
   a. Before toddlerhood, it is only in Western cultures that people communicate gender expectations to boys and girls.
   b. In the early years, it is mainly siblings who convey cultural gender messages.
   c. Gender development has a biological basis, as well as an environmental basis.
   d. Many of the differences that exist among male and female humans are not true of our closest primate and mammalian relatives.

EMOTIONAL AND SOCIAL DEVELOPMENT: Attachment Theory and Research

From infancy to toddlerhood, the social world expands. Across these two life stages, what remains crucial to social development is the relationship with one special person, usually but not always the mother, who provides love and care reliably. In the field of human development the study of this relationship in infancy and toddlerhood has focused on attachment theory and research based on this theory.

Attachment Theory

LO 5.15 **Describe the essential features of attachment theory and identify the four classifications of attachment.**

Because the long dependency of children is such a distinctive characteristic of our species, the question of how the attachments between human children and adults develop has long been of great interest to human development scholars. Attachment theory was first introduced in our discussion of infant social development (see Chapter 4). Here we examine the features of attachment theory in more detail, including ways of evaluating the quality of parent–child attachment and critiques of attachment theory.

BOWLBY'S THEORY Through most of the 20th century there was strong consensus that human infants become attached to their mothers because mothers provide them with food. Hunger is a distressing physical state, especially for babies, who are growing rapidly and need to be fed often. Mothers relieve this distressing state and provide the pleasure of feeding. Over time, infants come to associate the mother with the relief of distress and the experience of pleasure. This association becomes the basis for the love that infants feel for their mothers. This was the dominant view in psychology in the first half of the 20th century. However, around the middle of the 20th century, the British scholar John Bowlby (1969) began to observe that many research findings were inconsistent with this consensus.

There were three findings that were especially notable to Bowlby. First, French psychiatrist René Spitz (1946) reported that infants raised in institutions suffered in their physical and emotional development, even if they were fed well. Spitz studied infants who entered an orphanage when they were 3 to 12 months old. Despite adequate physical care, the babies lost weight and seemed listless and passive, a condition Spitz called *anaclitic depression*. Spitz attributed the infants' condition to the fact that one nurse had to care for seven infants and spent little time with each except for feeding them and changing their diapers. (Anaclitic means "leaning upon," and Spitz chose this term because the infants had no one to lean upon.) The infants showed no sign of developing positive feelings toward the nurse, even though the nurse provided them with nourishment. Other studies of institutionalized infants reported similar results (Rutter, 1996).

The second set of findings that called feeding into question as the basis of the infant–mother bond involved primates, specifically rhesus monkeys. In a classic study, Harry Harlow (1958) placed baby monkeys in a cage with two kinds of artificial "mothers." One of the mothers was made of wire mesh, the other of soft terry cloth. Harlow found that even when he placed the feeding bottle in the wire mother, the baby monkeys spent almost all their time on the cloth mother, going to the wire mother only to feed. Again, a simple link between feeding and emotional bonds seemed called into question.

The third set of findings noted by Bowlby proved the most important for his thinking. These findings came from the field of *ethology*, which, as we have noted, is the study of

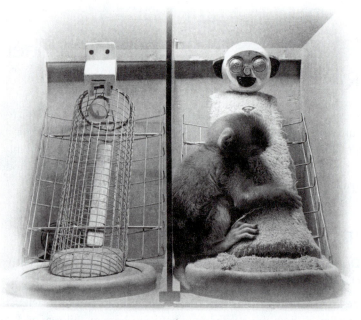

Harlow's studies showed that attachments were not based on nourishment. As shown here, the monkeys preferred the cloth "mother" even though the wire "mother" provided nourishment.

animal behavior. Ethologists reported that for some animals, the bond between newborns and their mothers was instantaneous and occurred immediately after birth. Konrad Lorenz (1965), a German ethologist, showed that newborn goslings would bond to the first moving object they saw after hatching and follow it closely, a phenomenon he called *imprinting* (see Chapter 3). To Lorenz and other ethologists, the foundation of the bond between the young of the species and their mothers was not nourishment but protection. Imprinting to the mother would cause the young to stay close to her and thereby be protected from harm.

Considering these three sets of findings, Bowlby concluded that the emotional tie between children and their mothers was based on children's need for protection and care for many years. Thus, as Bowlby described it, the *attachment* that develops between children and caring adults is an emotional bond that promotes the protection and survival of children during the years they are most vulnerable. The child's **primary attachment figure** is the person who is sought out when the child experiences some kind of distress or threat in the environment, such as hunger, pain, an unfamiliar person, or an unfamiliar setting. Usually the primary attachment figure is a parent, and is most often the mother because in nearly all cultures mothers are primarily the ones who are most involved in the care of infants. However, the primary attachment figure could also be the father, a grandparent, an older sister, or anyone else who is most involved in the infant's care. Separation from the primary attachment figure is experienced by the child as especially threatening, and the loss of the primary attachment figure is a catastrophe for children's development (Bowlby, 1980).

primary attachment figure
person who is sought out when a child experiences some kind of distress or threat in the environment

stranger anxiety
fear in response to unfamiliar persons, usually evident in infants by age 6 months

Cultural Focus: Stranger Anxiety Across Cultures

Although infants can discriminate among the smells and voices of different people in their environment from early on, in their first months they can be held and cared for by a wide range of people, familiar as well as unfamiliar, without protesting. However, by about the middle of the first year of life, this begins to change. Gradually they become more selective, developing stronger preferences for familiar others who have cared for them, and **stranger anxiety** emerges in response to being approached, held, or even smiled at by people they do not recognize and trust. Stranger anxiety exists in a wide range of cultures beginning at about age 6 months and grows stronger in the months that follow (Super & Harkness, 1976). So, if an infant or toddler turns away, frowns, or bursts into tears in response to your friendly overtures, don't take it personally!

Watch STRANGER ANXIETY ACROSS CULTURES

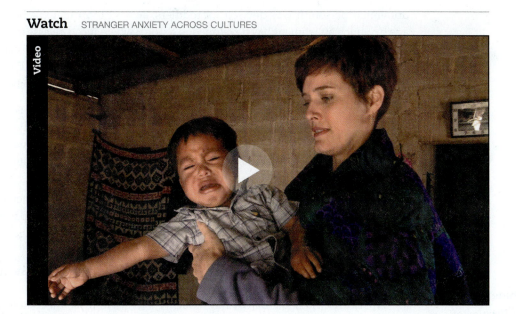

According to Bowlby (1967), there is an evolutionary basis for the development of stranger anxiety at about age 6 months. This is the age when infants first become mobile, and learning to crawl allows them to begin to explore the environment but also carries the risk that they may crawl themselves into big trouble. Learning to stay close to familiar persons and avoid unfamiliar persons helps infants stay near those who will protect them and keep them safe. Consequently, stranger anxiety peaks at the outset of toddlerhood (about 12 months of age) across cultures (Kagan et al., 1978), although the degree of stranger anxiety varies depending on how much toddlers have experienced diverse caregivers.

Watch the *Stranger Anxiety Across Cultures* video to observe how children at different ages and from various cultures react to being approached by strangers and separated from their primary caregivers.

Review Question:

The clip here shows examples of separation and stranger anxiety. Discuss the difference between pure separation anxiety and the impact that including a stranger can have on a child's reaction.

Although it promotes survival for children to stay close to caring adults, it also promotes survival for children to learn about the world around them. Consequently, under normal conditions young children use their primary attachment figure as a **secure base** from which to explore the surrounding environment (Bowlby, 1969). If a threat appears in the environment, attachment behavior is activated and children seek direct physical contact with their attachment figure.

According to Bowlby, attachment develops gradually over the first 2 years of life, culminating in a *goal-corrected partnership* in which both persons use language to communicate about the child's needs and the primary attachment figure's responses. Over time, the child becomes steadily less dependent on the care and protection of the primary attachment figure. However, even into adulthood, people seek out their primary attachment figure for comfort during times of crisis.

secure base

role of primary attachment figure, allows child to explore world while seeking comfort when threats arise

Strange Situation

laboratory assessment of attachment entailing a series of introductions, separations, and reunions involving the child, the mother, and an unfamiliar person

VARIETIES OF ATTACHMENT: THE STRANGE SITUATION Bowlby was a theorist, not a researcher, and he did not conduct studies to test his theory directly. Research on attachment was pioneered by Mary Ainsworth (Ainsworth & Bell, 1969; Ainsworth et al., 1978). Ainsworth followed Bowlby's theory in viewing the child's attachment as being most evident in the response to separation from the primary attachment figure. To evoke children's attachment behavior, Ainsworth devised a laboratory procedure she called the **Strange Situation** (Ainsworth et al., 1978). The Strange Situation is a series of introductions, separations, and reunions involving the child, the mother, and an unfamiliar person. It was devised for toddlers, ages 12 to 24 months, because this is an age by which attachment has developed to a point where it can be assessed.

On the basis of toddlers' responses to the Strange Situation, four classifications of attachment were developed (Ainsworth et al., 1978; Ammaniti et al., 2005). The first three were proposed by Ainsworth, and the fourth was added by later researchers.

Secure attachment. Toddlers in this category use the mother as a secure base from which to explore, in the first part of the Strange Situation when only the mother and toddler are present. Upon separation, securely attached toddlers usually cry or vocalize in protest. When the mother returns, they greet her happily by smiling and going to her to be hugged and held.

Insecure–avoidant attachment. These toddlers show little or no interaction with the mother when she is present, and no response to the mother's departure or return. When these toddlers are picked up in the last episode of the Strange Situation, they may immediately seek to get down.

Insecure–resistant attachment. Toddlers classified as insecure–resistant are less likely than others to explore the toys when the mother is present, and they show greater distress when she leaves the room. When she returns, they show ambivalence, running to greet the mother in seeming relief but then pushing her away when she attempts to comfort or pick them up.

Disorganized–disoriented attachment. Toddlers in this category show extremely unusual behavior in response to the Strange Situation (Ammaniti et al., 2005; van IJzendoorn et al., 1999; Padrón, Carlson, & Sroufe, 2014). They may seem dazed and detached when the mother leaves the room, but with outbursts of anger, and when the mother returns they may seem fearful. Some freeze their movements suddenly in odd postures. This kind of attachment is especially shown by toddlers who show other signs of serious problems, such as autism or Down syndrome, and also by those who have suffered severe abuse or neglect.

Although attachment classification is based on behavior throughout the Strange Situation, Ainsworth viewed the toddler's reunion behavior as the best indicator of the quality of attachment (Ainsworth et al., 1978). Toddlers with secure attachments seemed delighted to see their mothers again after a separation and often sought physical contact with her, whereas toddlers with insecure attachments either responded little to her return (avoidant) or seemed both relieved and angry at her (resistant).

Quality of Attachment

LO 5.16 Identify the key factors influencing the quality of toddlers' attachment to their mothers, and explain what effect attachment quality has on development.

If toddlers differ in the quality of their attachments, what determines those differences? And what implications does attachment quality in toddlerhood have for later development?

DETERMINANTS OF ATTACHMENT QUALITY Ainsworth's early research indicated that about two-thirds of toddlers had secure attachments to their mothers, with the remaining one third either insecure–avoidant or insecure–resistant (Ainsworth et al., 1978). Many other studies of American and European children since then have found similar results (NICHD Early Child Care Research Network, 2006; van IJzendoorn & Sagi, 2010). Disorganized–disoriented attachment is rare.

But what determines the quality of toddlers' attachments to their mothers? In her early research, Ainsworth and her colleagues observed families in their homes, including the same mother–child pairs they later observed in the laboratory in the Strange Situation (Ainsworth, 1977). The home observations were extensive: every 3 weeks for 4 hours, from when the children were 3 weeks old to just past their first birthdays.

secure attachment

healthiest classification of parent–child attachment, in which the child uses the parent as a secure base from which to explore, protests when separated from parent, and is happy when the parent returns

insecure–avoidant attachment

classification of parent–child attachment in which there is relatively little interaction between them and the child shows little response to the parent's absence and may resist being picked up when the parent returns

insecure–resistant attachment

classification of parent–child attachment in which the child shows little exploratory behavior when the parent is present, great distress when the parent leaves the room, and ambivalence upon the parent's return

disorganized–disoriented attachment

classification of parent–child attachment in which the child seems dazed and detached, with possible outbursts of anger, when the parent leaves the room, and exhibits fear upon parent's return

When considering the mother–child interactions in the home in relation to their behavior as observed in the Strange Situation, Ainsworth concluded that the quality of attachment was based mainly on how sensitive and responsive the mother was. To be *sensitive* means to be good at judging what the child needs at any given time. For example, sensitive mothers could tell when their children had had enough to eat, whereas others seemed to stop feeding while the children were still hungry or tried to keep feeding them after they seemed full. To be *responsive* means to be quick to assist or soothe the children when they need it. For example, responsive mothers would hug or pick up or talk soothingly when their children were distressed, whereas others would let them cry for awhile before going to their assistance.

According to attachment theory, based on the degree of their mothers' sensitive and responsive behavior over the first year of life, children develop an *internal working model* of what to expect about her availability and supportiveness during times of need (Bowlby, 1969, 1980; Bretherton & Munholland, 1999). Children with secure attachments have developed an internal working model of the mother as someone they can rely upon to provide help and protection. Children with insecure attachments are unsure that the mother will come through when they need her. They have an internal working model of her as someone who is unpredictable and cannot always be trusted. One reason the Strange Situation is first assessed in toddlerhood rather than infancy is that it is only by toddlerhood that children are cognitively mature enough to have developed an internal working model of their primary attachment figure (Ainsworth et al., 1978; Bowlby, 1969).

Attachment behavior is especially activated if the toddler is distressed.

ATTACHMENT QUALITY AND LATER DEVELOPMENT According to Bowlby (1969), the internal working model of the primary caregiver formed in infancy and toddlerhood is later applied to other relationships. Consequently, the attachment to the primary caregiver established in the first 2 years shapes expectations and interactions in relationships with others throughout life, from friends to teachers to romantic partners to one's own future children. Securely attached children are able to love and trust others because they could love and trust their primary caregiver in their early years. Insecurely attached children display hostility, indifference, or overdependence on others in later relationships, because they find it difficult to believe others will be worthy of their love and trust (Thompson, 1998).

This is a bold and intriguing claim. How well does it hold up in research? A number of longitudinal studies on attachment have by now followed samples from toddlerhood through adolescence or emerging adulthood, and they provide mixed support for the predictions of attachment theory. Some longitudinal studies show a relationship between attachment quality assessed in toddlerhood and later emotional and social development, but other studies do not (Egeland & Carlson, 2004; Fraley et al., 2013). The current view is that attachment quality in infancy and toddlerhood establishes tendencies and expectations that may then be modified by later experiences in childhood, adolescence, and beyond (McCarthy & Maughan, 2010; Thompson, 2008). To put this in terms of the theory, the internal working model established early may be modified substantially by later experiences. Only disorganized–disoriented attachment is highly predictive of later problems (Ammaniti et al., 2005; van IJzendoorn et al., 1999; Vondra & Barnett, 1999). Toddlers with this attachment classification exhibit high hostility and aggression in early and middle childhood, and are likely to have cognitive problems as well (Weinfield et al., 2004). In adolescence and beyond, toddlers who had been classified as disorganized–disoriented are at higher risk for behavior problems and psychopathology (van IJzendoorn et al., 1999). However, this type of attachment is believed to be due to underlying biologically-based problems in neurological development, not to the behavior of the primary caregiver (Barnett et al., 1999; Macfie et al., 2001). Since Ainsworth's classic studies, researchers have also investigated toddlers' attachments to fathers and other nonmaternal caregivers. We examine one such study in the *Research Focus: Early Child Care and Its Consequences* feature on the next page.

Research Focus: Early Child Care and Its Consequences

The "NICHD Study of Early Child Care" began in 1991 with over 1,300 young children (from infancy through early childhood) at 10 sites around the United States.

The children and their families were followed longitudinally for 7 years (NICHD Early Child Care Research Network, 2005). The sample was diverse in socioeconomic (SES) background, ethnicity, and geographical region.Multiple methods were used to assess the children and their families, including observations, interviews, questionnaires, and standardized tests.

Multiple aspects of the care children received were also assessed, including quantity, stability, quality, and type of care. A wide range of children's developmental domains were examined, including physical, social, emotional, cognitive, and language development.

There were many notable and illuminating findings in the study. About three-fourths of the children in the study began nonmaternal child care by the age of 4 months. During infancy and toddlerhood most of this care was provided by relatives, but enrollment in child-care centers increased during toddlerhood, and beyond age 2 most children receiving nonmaternal care were in centers. Infants and toddlers averaged 33 hours a week in nonmaternal care. African American infants and toddlers experienced the highest number of hours per week of nonmaternal care and White infants and toddlers the lowest, with Latinos in between.

For infants and toddlers, the focus of the study was on how child-care arrangements might be related to attachment. The observations measured how sensitive and responsive caregivers were with the children, the two most important determinants of attachment quality according to attachment theory.

As measured by the Strange Situation, attachments to mothers were no different for toddlers receiving nonmaternal care than for toddlers receiving only maternal care. However, insecure attachments were more likely if the nonmaternal care was low in quality, for more than 10 hours per week, or if mothers were low in sensitivity.

This was an impressively ambitious and comprehensive study, but even this study has limitations. Most notably, the children were not randomly assigned into child-care groups. The choices about the care they received and how many hours per week they were in care were made by their parents, not the researchers. Consequently, the outcomes of the children's child-care experiences were interwoven with many other variables, such as parents' income, education, and ethnicity. This is an example of how social scientists are rarely able to create an ideal experimental situation in their research, but must usually take human behavior as they find it and do their best to unravel the daunting complexity of real life.

Review Questions:

1. Which of the following was NOT one of the research methods used in the study?
   a. questionnaires
   b. neurological exams
   c. interviews
   d. observations

2. Which of the following factors was related to insecure attachment in the toddlers?
   a. low-quality non-maternal care
   b. greater than 10 hours a week in non-maternal care
   c. low sensitivity in maternal care
   d. all of the above

Watch RESEARCH FOCUS: EARLY CHILD CARE AND ITS CONSEQUENCES

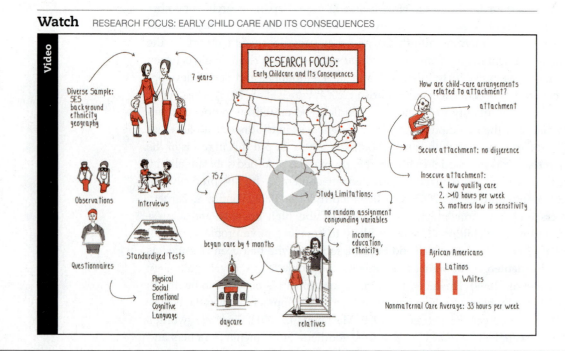

CRITIQUES OF ATTACHMENT THEORY Attachment theory is undoubtedly one of the most influential theories of human development. It has generated hundreds of studies since Bowlby first articulated it over 40 years ago (Atkinson & Goldberg, 2004; Cassidy & Shaver, 2010; Sroufe et al., 2005). However, it has also generated critiques that have pointed to limitations of the theory.

The "child effect" is one of the most common critiques of attachment theory. It claims the theory overstates the mother's influence and understates the child's influence on quality of attachment, in two related ways. First, it fails to recognize that children are born with different temperaments (see Chapter 4; Bakermans-Kranenburg et al., 2004). If, in the Strange Situation, a toddler is highly anxious when the mother leaves the room, then behaves aggressively by pushing her away when she returns, it could be due to a difficult temperament, not to the mother's failure to be sufficiently sensitive and responsive (Atkinson et al., 1999; van IJzendoorn et al., 2004).

Second, in attachment theory the direction of influence is one-way, from parents to children, but increasingly in recent decades researchers of human development have emphasized that parent–child relations are *reciprocal* or *bidirectional*. Parents influence their children, but children also influence their parents. For example, mothers of toddlers with a disorganized–disoriented attachment classification have been found to behave differently in the Strange Situation than other mothers. They may fail to respond when their toddlers become distressed, and may hold them at arm's length when picking them up, rather than comforting them by holding them close (Lyons-Ruth et al., 1999; van IJzendoorn et al., 1999). These mothers sometimes appear confused, frustrated, or impatient. This could be a failure to be sensitive and responsive, but it is also possible that the mothers are responding to the toddler's behavioral difficulties (Barnett et al., 1999). Most likely is that the mothers and disorganized–disoriented toddlers are influencing each other in a negative bidirectional cycle (Lyons-Ruth et al., 1999; Symons, 2001).

The other major critique of Bowlby's theory is cultural. In the decades of research since Bowlby proposed his theory, some researchers have concluded that children's attachments are "recognizably the same" across cultures (Cassidy & Shaver, 2010, p. xiii). However, other researchers have pointed to possible cultural biases in the theory.

Some aspects of attachment may be universal. In all cultures, infants and toddlers develop attachments to the people around them who provide loving, protective care (van IJzendoorn & Sagi, 2010). There is evidence that parents in many cultures have a common view of what constitutes a securely attached child. One study involved mothers of toddlers in six cultures: China, Columbia, Germany, Israel, Japan, and the United States (Posada et al., 1995). Across cultures, mothers described an "ideally secure" child in similar ways, as relying on the mother in times of need but also being willing to explore the surrounding world—in short, using her as a secure base from which to explore, much as described in attachment theory. Other studies involving multiple cultures have found that secure attachment is the most common classification in all cultures studied so far (van IJzendoorn & Sagi, 2010).

However, cultural variations have also been found (Morelli, 2015). One study compared Strange Situation results for toddlers in the United States, Japan, and several northern European countries (van IJzendoorn & Kroonenberg, 1988). In all countries, the majority of toddlers were found to be securely attached (see **Figure 5.4** on the next page). However, the U.S. and northern European toddlers were more likely than Japanese toddlers to be classified as insecure–avoidant. In contrast, insecure–resistant attachment was especially common among the Japanese toddlers, compared to toddlers in the other countries. These differences were attributed to cultural differences in typical patterns of care. Specifically, a

Toddlers in high-quality child-care centers are as likely as children in home care to have secure attachments.

Is early attachment the basis of all future love relationships?

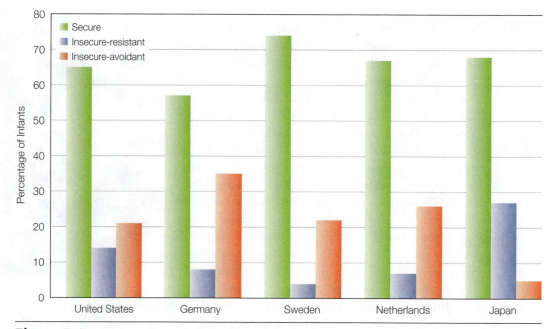

Figure 5.4 Cultural Variations in the Strange Situation

Across cultures, most toddlers exhibit secure attachment in response to the Strange Situation. In this study toddlers in Japan were more likely to be classified as insecure-resistant and less likely to be classified as insecure-avoidant than toddlers in other countries.

SOURCE: Based on van IJzendoorn & Kroonenberg (1988)

U.S. and northern European cultural emphasis on early independence was deemed to make insecure–avoidant attachment more likely, whereas in Japan mothers are rarely apart from their children and encourage a high degree of dependency in children. Consequently, their toddlers may have found the Strange Situation more stressful than the European or American toddlers did, making the insecure–resistant attachment classification more likely.

In traditional cultures, any kind of insecure attachment is probably rare (Morelli, 2015). Infants are soothed immediately at the first sign of distress, often with breastfeeding. Toddlers are typically cared for by an older sister and also have frequent contact with the mother. However, as we have seen, weaning can be a major event in the lives of toddlers in traditional cultures, and it may have an influence on the security of attachment. In one of Ainsworth's (1977) earliest studies, on mother–child attachments in Uganda, she observed that toddlers in Uganda often changed in attachment after weaning, suddenly showing a sharp increase in insecurity, including "a remarkable increase in their fear of strangers" (p. 143).

In general, the traditional, non-Western norm of maternal care emphasizes interdependence and collectivism to a greater extent than is found in attachment theory (Morelli & Rothbaum, 2007; Rothbaum et al., 2000; Rothbaum & Morelli, 2005). Attachment theorists emphasize that sensitive and responsive maternal care should provide love and care while also encouraging self-expression and independence, but this is not an ideal found in all or even most cultures. For example, Rothbaum and colleagues (2007) describe the Japanese concept of *amae* (ah-may-uh), which is a very close, physical, indulgent relationship between the mother and her young child. This is the ideal in Japan, but to some attachment researchers it fits the description of the kind of mothering that promotes insecure–resistant attachment (George & Solomon, 1999). Also, attachment researchers describe how

Mothers and children in Japan often have very close relationships.

toddlers with secure attachments grow up to be children who are self-reliant, socially assertive, and have high self-esteem, but these traits are not viewed as virtues in all cultures (Rothbaum et al., 2000; Sullivan & Cottone, 2010).

Practice Quiz   ANSWERS AVAILABLE IN ANSWER KEY.

1. Secure attachment is characterized by _____.
    a. the child looking to the mother for approval of gender appropriate behavior
    b. a willingness of the child to use the caregiver as a secure base to explore the environment
    c. the child acting both relieved and angry at the caregiver after seeing her again after separation
    d. the child not crying when the mother leaves the room because she or he knows she will return

2. Which of the following best describes Morton, a toddler who is considered securely attached based on the strange situation test?
    a. The toddler usually cries upon separation, but when the mother returns he greets her happily and begins to smile.
    b. The toddler shows little or no interaction with the mother when she is present and no response when she departs.
    c. The toddler is less likely than others to explore the room and pushes the mother away when she attempts to comfort the child or pick her up.
    d. The toddler seems dazed and detached when the mother leaves the room and remains fearful upon her return.

3. In elementary and secondary school Brice showed problems, such as hostility and cognitive deficits. Later on in college he was diagnosed with various types of psychopathology. Based on the research he most likely had a _____ attachment classification.
    a. insecure-avoidant   c. disorganized-disoriented
    b. insecure-resistant   d. difficult

4. When it comes to attachment _____.
    a. children develop an internal working model of what to expect about their mother's availability and supportiveness in times of need based on how sensitive and responsive she was over the first year of life
    b. Ainsworth's early research found that the majority of toddlers had insecure-resistant attachments to their mothers
    c. studies involving multiple cultures have found that insecure-avoidant attachment is the most common classification
    d. studies using the Strange Situation have found no differences in attachment status among children from the United States and Japan

5. In traditional cultures such as Uganda, _____ can be a major event in the lives of toddlers and it may have an influence on the security of attachment.
    a. learning to sleep alone
    b. weaning
    c. experiencing war
    d. being away from siblings who are working or at school

EMOTIONAL AND SOCIAL DEVELOPMENT: The Social World of the Toddler

In toddlerhood as in infancy, the social world includes ties to family, especially mothers and fathers. However, in toddlerhood relations with siblings, peers, and friends become more prominent. Toddlerhood is also when autism first appears for some children, a serious disruption in their social development. Media use continues to be important in toddlerhood, especially television.

The Role of Fathers

LO 5.17 Compare and contrast the typical patterns of father involvement with infants and toddlers in traditional cultures and developed countries.

In nearly all cultures, mothers play a central role in the care of infants and toddlers (Shwalb & Shwalb, 2015). As we have seen, fathers in traditional cultures are often excluded entirely from the birth process; in the weeks after birth, the mother and neonate are usually together constantly, whereas the father may or may not be involved in early care. There are two reasons that mothers have historically been the primary caretakers of infants and toddlers. The first reason is biological. Because breast milk has usually been the main form of nourishment for human infants during the first half year, the mother tends to be the one who cares for the infant, more than anyone else. Consequently, by toddlerhood mothers are usually the primary attachment figure (Bowlby, 1969; Cassidy & Shaver, 2010).

The second reason has a cultural basis. In most cultures through nearly all of human history, male and female gender roles have been separate and distinct (Gilmore, 1990; Hatfield & Rapson, 1996; Kapadia & Gala, 2015). In their adult roles, women have been expected to run the household and care for children, whereas men have been expected to protect and provide for the family (Arnett, 1998). In their leisure time women relax with children and other women, and men relax with other men (Gilmore, 1990). Consequently, in most cultures, historically, fathers have been on the periphery of the emotional lives of children.

FATHERS IN TRADITIONAL CULTURES Although fathers are rarely involved in daily child care in traditional cultures, they are part of the child's social environment in other ways. For example, in China the father's traditional role is provider and disciplinarian (Ho, 1987). Care and nurturance is left to the mother. In Latin America, too, the tradition is that the father provides for the family and has unquestioned authority over his children, although in many Latin American cultures this role coexists with warm, affectionate relations with his children (Halgunseth et al., 2006). Many cultures in Africa have a tradition of **polygyny**, meaning that men often have more than one wife (Westoff, 2003). (*Polygamy* is a more general term referring to having two or more spouses, regardless of whether they are wives or husbands.) Households are composed of each wife and her children, with the father either living separately or rotating among them. Here, too, his role is that of provider and disciplinarian, and the children are not usually emotionally close to him (Nsamenang, 1992). Polygyny has become less common in recent decades, but still occurs in about one-third of marriages in sub-Saharan Africa (Riley Bove, 2009).

Although the most common cultural pattern worldwide is that fathers serve as providers but are otherwise remote from the emotional lives of infants and toddlers, there are some notable exceptions. Among the Manus people of New Guinea studied by Margaret Mead (1930/2001), during the first year of life the infant and mother are together almost constantly, and the father is involved only occasionally. However, once the child enters toddlerhood and begins to walk the father takes over most child care. The toddler sleeps with the father, plays with him, rides on his back, and goes along on his daily fishing expeditions. Later in childhood, if the parents quarrel and separate, the children often choose to stay with the father, indicating that by then he has become the primary attachment figure.

FATHERS IN DEVELOPED COUNTRIES In some ways, the role of fathers in developed countries today is in line with the pattern historically and in traditional societies. Across developed countries, fathers interact less with their infants and toddlers than mothers do, and provide less care such as bathing, feeding, dressing, and soothing (Chuang et al., 2004; Lamb & Lewis, 2010; Shwalb & Shwalb, 2015). In the United States, about one third of toddlers live with single mothers; nonresident fathers are less involved in care of their toddlers than fathers who live in the household, although involvement is greater among nonresident fathers who are African American or Latino than among Whites (Cabrera et al., 2008). When fathers do interact with their infants and toddlers, it tends to be in play rather than care, especially in physical, highly stimulating, rough-and-tumble play (Lamb & Lewis, 2010; Paquette, 2004). Dad is the one throwing the kids in the air and catching them, or wrestling with them, but usually he has not been the one feeding them applesauce or changing their diapers.

However, there is a definite trend toward greater father involvement, as gender roles have become more flexible and egalitarian in developed countries (Pleck, 2010). American fathers have been found to spend about 85% as much time as mothers do in caring for their young children, and Canadian fathers about

polygyny
cultural tradition in which men have more than one wife

Fathers in modern developed countries do more child care than they did in the past, but still not as much as mothers do.

75% (Lamb, 2010). Fathers are more likely to provide near-equal care for young children when the mother and father work similar numbers of hours outside the home, and when marital satisfaction is high (Lamb & Lewis, 2010; NICHD Early Child Care Network, 2000). Like the example of the Manus people, the findings of recent changes in fathers' care for young children in developed countries show that parenting is to a large extent a learned rather than innate behavioral pattern that can change as a culture changes.

The Wider Social World: Siblings, Peers, and Friends

LO 5.18 Describe relationships with siblings, peers, and friends during toddlerhood.

In studies of social development in toddlerhood, the focus has been on relations with parents, especially attachments to mothers. However, among the many ways toddlerhood is distinct from infancy is that the toddler's social world broadens to include a wider range of people, including siblings, peers, and friends.

SIBLINGS: YOUNGER AND OLDER We have seen already how important sibling relationships are for toddlers in traditional cultures, where an older sibling, usually a sister, often takes over the main responsibility for child care from the mother. Toddlers in these cultures most certainly develop an attachment to the older siblings who care for them, but from the limited evidence available, it appears to be a secondary attachment rather than the primary attachment (Ainsworth, 1977; Levine et al., 1994). That is, under most conditions toddlers are content to be under the care of older siblings, but in times of crisis they want the care and comfort of their mothers.

In developed countries, too, studies show that toddlers have attachments to siblings (Shumaker et al., 2011). One study used an adaptation of the Strange Situation to examine American toddlers' attachments to older siblings (Samuels, 1980). Two-year-old toddlers and their mothers were asked to come to the backyard of an unfamiliar home, sometimes with—and sometimes without—a 4-year-old sibling present. When no older sibling was present, the toddlers mostly responded to the mother's departure with distress and to her return with great relief, much as they do in the standard Strange Situation. However, when the older sibling was there along with the toddler, the toddler rarely showed distress when the mother left the backyard. The older sibling provided the emotional comfort and security of an attachment figure, making this outdoor Strange Situation less strange and intimidating.

A substantial amount of research on toddlers' relations with siblings has focused on how they respond to the birth of a younger sibling. Overall, their reaction tends to be negative (Boer et al., 2013). Often, following the birth of a younger sibling, toddlers' attachment to the mother changes from secure to insecure, as they feel threatened by all the attention given to the new baby (Teti et al., 1996). Some toddlers display problems such as increased aggressiveness toward others, or become increasingly whiny, demanding, and disobedient (Hughes & Dunn, 2007). They may regress in their progress toward toilet training or self-feeding. Sometimes mothers become less patient and responsive with their toddlers, under the stress of caring for both a toddler and a new baby (Dunn & Kendrick, 1982).

What can parents do to ease the transition for toddlers? Studies indicate that if mothers pay special attention to the toddler before the new baby arrives and explain the feelings and needs of the baby after the birth, toddlers respond more positively to their new sibling (Boer et al., 2013; Howe et al., 2001; Hughes & Dunn, 2007). However, the reality is that across cultures, conflict is more common with siblings than in any other relationship throughout childhood and adolescence, as we will see in more detail in Chapter 6.

What if the toddler is the younger sibling rather than the older sibling? Here there is both an upside and a downside. The upside is that once younger siblings are

Toddlers often react negatively to the birth of a younger sibling.

no longer infants but toddlers, and develop the ability to talk, walk, and share in pretend play, older siblings show less resentment and become much more interested in playing with them (Hughes & Dunn, 2007). By their second year of life, toddlers often imitate their older siblings and look to them for cues on what to do and how to do it (Barr & Hayne, 2003).

The downside is that conflict rises as toddlers become increasingly capable of asserting their own interests and desires. In one study that followed toddlers and their older siblings from when the toddlers were 14 months old to when they were 24 months old, home observations showed that conflict increased steadily during this period and became more physical (Dunn & Munn, 1985). In another study, 15- to 23-month-old toddlers showed remarkably advanced abilities for annoying their older siblings (Dunn, 1988). For example, one toddler left a fight with an older sibling to go and destroy an object the older sibling cherished; another toddler ran to find a toy spider and pushed it in his older sibling's face, knowing the older sibling was afraid of spiders!

PEERS AND...FRIENDS? In most cultures, toddlerhood is a time of forming the first social relations outside the family. In traditional cultures, this usually means being part of a peer play group that may include siblings and cousins as well as other children (Gaskins, 2015). These play groups usually include children of a variety of ages, but toddlerhood is when children first come into the group after having been cared for during infancy mainly by the mother.

In developed countries, too, peer relations expand in toddlerhood, often in the form of some kind of group child care (Rubin et al., 2006). Research observing toddlers in these settings has found that their peer play interactions are more advanced than early studies had reported. One influential early study reported that toddlers engaged exclusively in *solitary play*, all by themselves, or *parallel play*, in which they would take part in the same activity but without acknowledging each other (Parten, 1932). However, more recent studies have found that toddlers engage in not only solitary and parallel play but in *simple social play*, where they talk to each other, smile, and give and receive toys, and even in *cooperative pretend play*, involving a shared fantasy such as pretending to be animals (Howes, 1996; Hughes & Dunn, 2007). Watch the video *Styles of Play* for examples of toddlers engaging in various types of play.

Toddlers in developed countries engage in advanced forms of play with their friends.

Watch STYLES OF PLAY

Parallel Play

Furthermore, toddlers who know each other well tend to engage in more advanced forms of play than unacquainted toddlers do. In one study of toddlers attending the same child-care center, even young toddlers (16–17 months old) engaged in simple social play (Howes, 1985). By 24 months, half of the toddlers engaged in cooperative pretend play, and this kind of play was observed in all the toddlers between 30 and 36 months old. This is a striking contrast to studies of social relations among unacquainted toddlers, which had found mainly solitary and parallel play, with cooperative pretend play not appearing until at least age 3 (Howes, 1996; Hughes & Dunn, 2007).

Toddler friends smile and laugh more with each other than they do with nonfriends. Here, three boys in South Africa share a laugh.

Clearly toddlers are capable of playing with each other in a variety of ways, but do they really form friendships? A substantial and growing body of research suggests they do (Goldman & Buysse, 2007). Their friendships appear to have many of the same features of friendships at other ages, such as companionship, mutual affection, and emotional closeness (Rubin et al., 2006). Even shortly after their first birthday, toddlers prefer some of their child-care or play-group peers over others and seek them out as companions when they are together (Shonkoff & Phillips, 2000). Like older children and even adults, toddlers choose each other as friends based partly on similarities, such as activity level and social skills (Rubin et al., 2006). Toddlers who become friends develop favorite games they play when together (Howes, 1996). Toddler friends share emotions more frequently with each other than they do with nonfriends. They smile and laugh more, but also have more conflicts, although conflicts between toddler friends are milder and more quickly resolved than among nonfriends (Ross & Lollis, 1989). Friendships do change in quality with age, as we will see in the chapters to come, but even in toddlerhood many of the features of friendship are evident.

Autism: A Disruption in Social Development

LO 5.19 **Identify the characteristics of autism and recognize how autism affects prospects for children as they grow to adulthood.**

In 1938, a well-known child psychiatrist received a visit from parents concerned about their little boy, Donald (Donovan & Zucker, 2010). According to the parents, even as a baby Donald had displayed "no apparent affection" (p. 85) for his parents, and still did not. He never cried when separated from them or wished to be comforted by them. Nor did he seem interested in other adults or children, appearing to "live within himself" (p. 85) with no need for social relations. Furthermore, Donald's use of language was peculiar. He was often unresponsive to his parents' instructions and requests, and did not even react to his own name. Yet certain unusual words captivated him and he would repeat them over and over again: *trumpet vine, business, chrysanthemum.* He enjoyed repetition not only of words but of behaviors, such as spinning round objects.

This description was the basis of the initial diagnosis of what became known as **autism**, and the main features of the diagnosis are the same today as they were for Donald: (1) lack of interest in social relations, (2) abnormal language development, and (3) repetitive behavior (American Psychiatric Association, 2013). Many children with autism also prefer to have highly predictable routines and hate to have them disrupted. Some also have exceptional, isolated mental skills—Donald, for example, could multiply large numbers instantly in his head—but this is rare. The majority of children with autism are low in intelligence and exhibit some degree of intellectual disability (Lord & Bishop, 2010). The video *Against Odds: Children with Autism* on the next page provides more information about this disorder.

autism

developmental disorder marked by a lack of interest in social relations, abnormal language development, and repetitive behavior

Video

Watch AGAINST ODDS: CHILDREN WITH AUTISM

In the United States, 1 in 68 children fit the diagnostic criteria for *autistic spectrum disorder* (ASD), meaning that they exhibit repetitive behavior and serious deficits in language development and social behavior (Centers for Disease Control and Prevention [CDC], 2014). These rates are consistent across Asia, Europe, and North America, with some variation based on diagnostic criteria used (CDC, 2010). The origins of the disorder are unclear. It is believed to have a genetic basis, as evidence of abnormal brain development is present in the unusually large brains of children who will later develop autism (Hadjikhani et al., 2004). Various environmental causes for autism have been proposed, from dietary contributors to toddlerhood vaccines, but none of them has been supported by research. Rates of autism have increased in recent decades in developed countries, but there is no consensus on the reasons for the increase (CDC, 2010). It may be that disorders once diagnosed as schizophrenia or mental retardation are now diagnosed as autism due to increased awareness of the disorder (Donovan & Zucker, 2010). Physicians in many countries now routinely screen toddlers for the disorder, whereas they did not in the past (CDC, 2010).

Toddlers with autism have deficits in their social and language development. Here, a boy plays alone at a school for children with autism in Beijing, China.

Usually the diagnosis of autism or ASD is made during toddlerhood, between 18 and 30 months of age (American Psychiatric Association, 2013). However, studies analyzing home videos of infants later diagnosed with autism indicate that signs of the disorder are already present in infancy (Dawson et al., 1998; Werner et al., 2000). Even at 8 to 10 months old, infants with autism show little or no evidence of normal social behaviors. They do not engage in joint attention with parents, or point to objects to show to others, or look at others, or respond to their own name. During infancy some of this behavior could be attributed to differences in temperament, but the diagnosis of autism becomes more definite in toddlerhood with the failure to develop language skills during a period that is normally a time of dramatic advances. About half of children with autism never develop language skills well enough to communicate about even basic needs, and the half who do develop some language skills are nevertheless impaired in their ability to communicate with others (Hale & Tager-Flusberg, 2005). Their social deficits compound their language deficits: Their lack of interest in others and lack of ability to understand others' perspectives makes it difficult for them to engage in the normal exchange of conversation that other people perform without effort, even in toddlerhood.

What happens to children with autism when they grow up? Eighty-five percent of them continue to live with parents, siblings, or other relatives (Donovan & Zucker, 2010). Some live in government-sponsored group homes, and in rare cases they are able to function at a high enough level to live alone, as Donald (now in his 70s) does. In some ways autism becomes more problematic in adulthood than in childhood, because adults with autism often lack emotional regulation as children with autism do but are bigger and can cause more disruption. They also develop sexual desires, without the social knowledge of the appropriate expression of those desires. There is no cure for autism and few effective treatments, but with help, many children and adults with autism can learn some skills for daily living, such as wearing clean clothes, asking for directions (and then following them), and keeping track of money.

Media Use in Toddlerhood

LO 5.20 **Identify the typical rates of television use in toddlerhood and explain some consequences of toddlers' TV watching.**

Media use, especially watching television, is a typical part of daily life in most countries, even during toddlerhood. According to a national study in the United States, 58% of children under 3 watch TV every day, and 30% even have a TV in their bedroom (Rideout & Hamel, 2006). African American and Latino toddlers watch more TV than toddlers in other ethnic groups, initiating a pattern of ethnic differences that will continue throughout life (Anand et al., 2005). Television dominates at all ages, but digital devices are increasingly popular, even among toddlers. A national survey in 2013 found that 38% of 2-year-olds in the United States had used digital devices such as iPhones or tablets (Rideout et al., 2013). There is now a vast range of "apps" (digital programs) for babies and toddlers, including educational apps, game apps, and art and music apps.

Most research on the effects of media use focus on television. Already in the second year of life, toddlers have begun to understand that the images on the TV screen are not real. In one study, 9-month-old infants and 14- and 19-month-old toddlers were shown a video in which a woman demonstrated how to play with a variety of toys for young children (Pierroutsakos & Troseth, 2003). The infants reached out to the screen and attempted to grasp, hit, or rub the toys, but the toddlers did not. However, other studies have shown that toddlers sometimes interact with televised images by talking to them, which suggests that for toddlers the television/reality boundary is not completely clear (Garrison & Christakis, 2005).

How does TV-watching influence toddlers? Surveys indicate that a majority of American parents fear that TV may harm their young children (Rideout et al., 2003; Woodward & Gridina, 2000). However, with television, as with other media we will examine in future chapters, the effects depend very much on the media content. In one American study, one group of 2-year-olds was shown the TV show *Barney and Friends*, featuring a large, purple, talking dinosaur who encourages prosocial behavior such as kindness and sharing. This group was then compared in free play to another group of 2-year-olds who had not seen the show (Singer & Singer, 1998). The toddlers in the *Barney* group showed more prosocial behavior and less aggressiveness, along with a greater tendency to engage in symbolic play. In a national (American) study, 70% of parents of children under age 3 reported that their toddlers had imitated positive behavior they had seen on television, such as sharing or helping, whereas only 27% had imitated aggressive behavior such as hitting or kicking (Rideout & Hamel, 2006).

Television shows with prosocial themes can inspire prosocial behavior in toddlers.

displacement effect

in media research, term for how media use occupies time that may have been spent on other activities

With regard to the effects of TV-watching on cognitive development, evidence is mixed, with some studies indicating that watching TV helps toddlers expand their vocabularies and others reporting that it may be detrimental to language development (Courage & Setliff, 2009). Again, content matters. One study had parents report toddlers' TV-viewing patterns every 3 months from age 6–30 months, then assessed the toddlers' language development at 30 months (Linebarger & Walker, 2005). Watching educational programs such as *Dora the Explorer* resulted in greater vocabularies and higher expressive language scores than watching other programs did. Other studies have found that TV can inspire imaginative play among toddlers (Weber, 2006). I remember this well from when my twins were toddlers, how they would watch a TV show or a video and then invent their own elaborate games pretending to be characters they had watched, such as the *Teletubbies* or *Peter Pan*. We even bought them Teletubbies dolls to facilitate the games.

Even if TV sometimes inspires prosocial or creative behavior, a persistent concern about television use from toddlerhood onward is the **displacement effect**; that is, the fact that time spent watching TV is time not spent doing other activities such as reading or playing with other children (Weber, 2006). In 2001, the American Academy of Pediatrics recommended that children under 2 years old should not watch television at all, and children 2 years and older should be limited to no more than 2 hours of TV a day (American Academy of Pediatrics Committee on Public Education, 2001). The basis for this recommendation was not that television content is damaging but that young children would benefit more from active learning through experiences such as play and conversations with others (Kirkorian et al., 2008). It should be added that in many households the television is on nearly all the time, and consequently even toddlers are exposed to TV content that is a long way from *Barney* (Rideout & Hamel, 2006).

Practice Quiz   ANSWERS AVAILABLE IN ANSWER KEY.

1. Josh is a toddler who lives in New Zealand. His father would most likely be observed in which of the following activities with him?
   a. Bathing him
   b. Feeding him
   c. Teaching him to read
   d. Playing with him

2. During toddlerhood _____.
   a. those who know each other well usually engage in solitary play rather than other forms of play
   b. friendships seem to have many of the same features of friendships at other ages
   c. there seems to be no preference for play partners; they play equally with whatever children are present
   d. children are not yet capable of engaging in simply social play or cooperative pretend play

3. Research on sibling relationships during the toddler years has found that _____.
   a. they tend to have a positive reaction to the birth of a younger sibling
   b. in developed countries, but not in traditional cultures, toddlers have attachments to their siblings
   c. toddlers' attachments to their siblings tend to be secondary attachments rather than primary attachments

   d. only in individualistic cultures is conflict more common with siblings than in any other relationship throughout childhood and adolescence

4. Marcelle was diagnosed with autism at the age of 3. Which behavior would you be most likely to see if you observed him in his day care classroom?
   a. A preoccupation with talking to adults
   b. A preoccupation with repetitive movements
   c. A preoccupation with staring at faces because that is what most interests them
   d. A tendency to interrupt others until they look at him and include him in the conversation

5. Research has shown that _____.
   a. children are only able to learn to model aggressive behaviors during toddlerhood because prosocial behaviors require more advanced cognitive development
   b. in the United States it is rare to have a TV in a young child's room
   c. the displacement effect is no longer considered a problem because of all the media options available
   d. the effects of television and other media depend on the content

Summary: Emotional and Social Development

LO 5.12 Describe how emotional development advances during toddlerhood and identify the impact of culture on these changes.

Sociomoral emotions developing in toddlerhood include guilt, shame, embarrassment, envy, and pride. They are called sociomoral emotions because they indicate that toddlers have begun to learn the moral standards of their culture. Toddlers in Western cultures have occasional tantrums, perhaps because they have a more developed sense of intentionality than infants do and so are more likely to protest when thwarted. However, tantrums are rare outside the West where cultures place less emphasis on self-expression.

LO 5.13 Describe the changes in self-development that take place during toddlerhood.

The birth of the self in toddlerhood is indicated in the development of self-recognition and self-reflection. Toddlers begin to use personal pronouns such as "I" and "me" and to refer to themselves by name.

LO 5.14 Distinguish between *sex* and *gender* and summarize the evidence for the biological basis of gender development.

Sex is the biological status of being male or female, whereas *gender* refers to the cultural categories of "male" and "female." Gender identity first develops during toddlerhood, as children begin to identify themselves and others as male or female. The biological basis of gender is indicated in evolutionary theory, ethological studies, and hormonal studies. However, changes in male and female roles in recent times have shown that these roles can change dramatically over a relatively short time and therefore biological assumptions about gender should be viewed with skepticism.

LO 5.15 Describe the essential features of attachment theory and identify the four classifications of attachment.

In formulating attachment theory, Bowlby emphasized the evolutionary need for a person who would provide protection and care during the vulnerable early years of life. Ainsworth developed the Strange Situation to assess attachment quality, and concluded that it showed three distinct types of attachment: secure, insecure–avoidant, and insecure–resistant. Disorganized–disoriented is a fourth classification, added by later researchers.

LO 5.16 Identify the key factors influencing the quality of toddlers' attachment to their mothers, and explain what effect attachment quality has on development.

The quality of attachment is based mainly on how sensitive and responsive a mother is toward her child. Research indicates some relation between attachment quality in toddlerhood and later development, but also shows that the internal working model established in toddlerhood can be modified by later experiences. Attachment quality is also influenced by infant temperament, and by reciprocal or bidirectional influences between parent and child.

LO 5.17 Compare and contrast the typical patterns of father involvement with infants and toddlers in traditional cultures and developed countries.

Fathers in traditional cultures usually serve as family providers but are remote from toddlers' emotional lives, although there are exceptions. Across cultures, fathers tend to provide less physical and emotional care than mothers, but this is changing as gender roles and work responsibilities change.

LO 5.18 Describe relationships with siblings, peers, and friends during toddlerhood.

Across cultures, toddlers often react negatively to the birth of a younger sibling. When toddlers themselves are the younger siblings, their older siblings enjoy playing with them more than when they were infants, but conflict tends to rise as toddlers become more capable of asserting their own desires. With friends, toddler play takes a variety of forms, including solitary play, parallel play, simple social play, and cooperative pretend play. Toddlers' friendships often have qualities similar to friendships at older ages, including companionship, mutual affection, and emotional closeness.

LO 5.19 Identify the characteristics of autism and recognize how autism affects prospects for children as they grow to adulthood.

Autism is a developmental disorder marked by a lack of interest in social relations, abnormal language development, and repetitive behavior. The social and language deficits of autism make social and cognitive development problematic in childhood and beyond.

LO 5.20 Identify the typical rates of television use in toddlerhood and explain some consequences of toddlers' TV watching.

Toddlers in many countries watch TV every day. Television watching in toddlerhood may promote prosocial behavior if the TV content is prosocial, but there are concerns about the displacement effect, especially for children under 2 years old.

Applying Your Knowledge as a Professional

The topics covered in this chapter apply to a wide variety of career professions. Watch these videos to learn how they apply to a family dentist, a state legislator, and the director of a childcare and resource agency.

Watch CAREER FOCUS: FAMILY DENTIST

Sarah Hubert, DDS
Family Dentist
Williamsburg Dental Arts

Chapter Quiz

1. _____ is a potentially fatal condition specific to toddlerhood in which protein deficiency leads to varied symptoms such as swollen bellies, thinning hair, and lethargy.
  a. Marasmus
  b. Dysentery
  c. Sudden infant death syndrome
  d. Kwashiorkor

2. What most characterizes early brain development in toddlerhood is _____.
  a. the formation of the cerebral cortex
  b. the steep increase in synaptic density
  c. activity in the amygdala
  d. the production of new brain cells

3. During toddlerhood, _____.
  a. sleeping alone is rare in traditional cultures
  b. children sleep more than they did in infancy, because they are much more active
  c. naps are no longer needed
  d. children sleep consistently throughout the night

4. Toddlers _____.
  a. who do not walk by 1 year are likely to have a gross motor problem
  b. in traditional cultures are equal to toddlers from Western cultures in the development of their gross motor skills
  c. can usually run before they can stand briefly on one leg
  d. show the same pace of gross motor development as fine motor development

5. In the West, _____.
  a. most children show signs of readiness for toilet training by their first birthday
  b. views on toilet training have remained the same over the last several decades
  c. children are toilet trained in a way that is nearly identical to their counterparts in traditional cultures
  d. a sign of being ready to begin toilet training is when the child can stay "dry" for an hour or two during the day

6. A toddler from a traditional culture would likely _____.
  a. experience some customary practice for being weaned
  b. be abruptly be weaned at age 1
  c. be given formula instead of breast milk
  d. still be breast feeding at age 5

7. When children generally avoid making the A-not-B error, they _____.
  a. show the ability to categorize
  b. have attained object permanence
  c. understand scaffolding
  d. use tertiary circular reactions

8. According to Vygotsky, _____ is required for cognitive development.
  a. social interaction
  b. formal education
  c. strong parent–child attachment
  d. emotional self-regulation

9. When it comes to learning language, the most significant difference between apes and humans is _____.
   a. the inability for apes to learn more than a few signs
   b. the faster pace of humans' sign language
   c. the inability of apes to generate word symbols in an infinite number of ways
   d. the inability of apes to make requests

10. Which is an example of overextension?
    a. A child saying, "He hitted me with a stick"
    b. A child saying, "The moon looks happy tonight"
    c. A child calling all dogs "Spot"
    d. A child saying "I no like peas"

11. Research on language development has shown that _____.
    a. social class status is correlated with how much parents speak to their young children
    b. genetics plays very little role in verbal ability
    c. language development in American children is not linked to income level of parents
    d. maternal responsiveness to American children's verbalizations has no impact on when children reach language milestones

12. Which emotion doesn't appear until toddlerhood?
    a. Anger   c. Fear
    b. Pride   d. Happiness

13. The capacity of toddlers to think about themselves as they would about other people and objects is _____.
    a. gender identity   c. stranger anxiety
    b. sex roles   d. self-reflection

14. When children can identify themselves and others as either male or female, they have developed _____.
    a. custom complexes   c. gender stereotypes
    b. gender identity   d. gender expectations

15. Which of the following best characterizes insecure-resistant attachment?
    a. a willingness to use the caregiver as a secure base to explore the environment
    b. a tendency to be self-centered
    c. acting both relieved and angry at a caregiver after seeing him or her again after separation
    d. a dependency on the mother for approval of all activities

16. Research has shown that a child with a(n) _____ attachment is most likely to have later problems such as hostility, psychopathology, and cognitive deficits.
    a. insecure–resistant   c. disorganized–disoriented
    b. insecure–avoidant   d. goal–corrected

17. Which of the following best describes attachment across cultures?
    a. Autonomy and independence are encouraged from an early age across cultures.
    b. In all cultures, infants and toddlers develop attachments to the people around them who provide loving, protective care.
    c. Insecure–resistant attachment is the most common classification in all cultures because many children find the Strange Situation to be very stressful.
    d. Children from the United States and Japan tend to be classified the same way in studies employing the Strange Situation paradigm.

18. In developed countries, fathers would most likely be observed in which of the following activities with their infants or toddlers?
    a. Bathing
    b. Feeding
    c. Soothing
    d. Playing

19. During toddlerhood, _____.
    a. those who know each other well usually engage in solitary play rather than other forms of play
    b. friendships are based on companionship, mutual affection, and emotional closeness
    c. there seems to be no preference for play partners; they play equally with whatever children are present
    d. children are not yet capable of engaging in simply social play or cooperative pretend play

20. Which behavior would be most characteristic of a child who has been diagnosed with autism?
    a. Preoccupation with talking to strangers
    b. Preoccupation with repetitive movements
    c. Preoccupation with looking at faces
    d. Preoccupation with pointing at objects until others look at them

21. Research on media has shown that _____.
    a. in the United States, it is rare to have a TV in a young child's bedroom
    b. children are only able to learn to model aggressive behaviors at this age because prosocial behaviors require more advanced cognitive development
    c. TV can inspire imaginative play among toddlers
    d. the displacement effect is no longer considered a major problem because of all the media options available

Chapter 6
Early Childhood

IT IS MORNING IN A DAY CARE CENTER IN AALBORG, DENMARK, AND LARS OLSEN, AGE 4, IS EXCITED TO SEE HIS FRIENDS AS HIS MOTHER DROPS HIM OFF ON THE WAY TO WORK. There will be lots of games to play, and their teacher will read them a story and begin teaching the children to recognize letters.

In the afternoon Lars's mother picks him up on the way from her job at an accounting firm, and the two of them go home. Soon his father arrives home from work, too, and Lars watches television while his parents prepare dinner.

After dinner, Lars watches more TV as his parents clean up, then he and his father play a board game. Bedtime comes at 8 p.m. sharp. His mother puts him to bed, reading him a story before giving him a kiss and wishing him good night.

Meanwhile, an ocean away in a Mayan village in Guatemala, 5-year-old Maricela helps her mother make the day's tortillas. Mari flattens a ball of dough into a tortilla as her mother cooks. Afterward, Mari watches her younger brother Roberto, age 2, and plays with him as her mother goes about the day's work. Later she will help her mother fetch water and firewood. Her older siblings will return from school, and her father from work, and the family will share a meal around the fire within their simple dwelling.

In the evening, the family gathers around the ever-smoldering fire, and Mari sits on her father's lap.

Before long Mari is asleep, and the next morning she will have no memory of being passed from her father to her older sister, or of falling asleep by her sister's side next to the fire.

As we have seen in the previous two chapters, from birth onward children's development can be very different depending on their culture. In early childhood the cultural contexts of development expand in several important ways, as the stories of Lars and Mari show. Children begin to learn culturally specific skills, through participation in daily tasks with their parents and siblings in some cultures, as in Mari's case, or through participation in group care and preschool in other cultures, as for Lars. Their play comes to include pretend play, and the materials of their fantasy games are drawn from their cultural environment—toys and games for Lars, tortillas for Mari. They become increasingly aware of their culture's differential gender expectations for boys and girls. And they develop an awareness of their culture's values and moral order. By sleeping alone in his bedroom, Lars is learning the cultural value of individualism; by sleeping alongside others, Mari is learning that she is always intertwined with others in bonds of mutual support and obligation.

We will explore all of these areas in the course of this chapter. First, we examine the changes in physical and motor development that occur in early childhood.

Watch CHAPTER INTRODUCTION: EARLY CHILDHOOD

Section 1 Physical Development

⌄ Learning Objectives

6.1 Describe the physical growth and change that takes place during early childhood.

6.2 Describe the changes in brain development that take place during early childhood and the aspects of brain development that explain "infantile" amnesia.

6.3 Identify the main nutritional deficiencies and the primary sources of injury, illness, and mortality during early childhood in developed and developing countries.

6.4 Describe changes in gross and fine motor abilities during early childhood.

6.5 Describe the development of handedness and identify the consequences and cultural views of left-handedness.

PHYSICAL DEVELOPMENT: Growth from Age 3 to 6

The pace of bodily growth continues to decline in the period from toddlerhood to early childhood, as it did from infancy to toddlerhood. A variety of parts of the brain make crucial strides forward, although brain development still has a long way to go. Optimal growth in the body and the brain require adequate health and nutrition, which are lacking in much of the world during early childhood.

Bodily Growth

LO 6.1 **Describe the physical growth and change that takes place during early childhood.**

From ages 3 to 6 the typical American child grows 2–3 inches per year (5–7 ½ cm) and adds 5 to 7 pounds (2.3–3.2 kg). The typical 3-year-old is about 35 inches tall (89 cm) and weighs about 30 pounds (13.6 kg); the typical 6-year-old is about 45 inches tall (114 cm) and weighs about 45 pounds (20.4 kg). Throughout this period, boys are slightly taller and heavier than girls, although the average differences are small. Both boys and girls gain more in weight than in height during early childhood, but most add more muscle than fat. From toddlerhood to early childhood, most children lose their remaining "baby fat" and their bodily proportions become similar to those of adults.

In developing countries, average heights and weights in early childhood are considerably lower, due to poorer nutrition and higher likelihood of childhood diseases. For example, the average 6-year-old in Bangladesh is only as tall as the average 4-year-old in Sweden (Leathers & Foster, 2004).

Within developing countries, too, differences in socioeconomic status influence gains in height and weight in early childhood. As noted in earlier chapters, economic differences tend to be large in developing countries; most have a relatively small middle and upper class and a large population of low-income people. Wealthier people have more access to nutritional foods, so their children are taller and weigh more than poorer children of the same age (UNICEF, 2014). Given roughly equal levels of nutrition and health care, individual differences in height and weight gains during childhood are due to genetics (Chambers et al., 2001).

By their third birthday, most children have a full set of 20 teeth (Eisenberg et al., 1996). These are their *primary* or "baby" teeth that will be replaced by 32 permanent teeth in the course of childhood, beginning at about age 6. However, this replacement process takes place slowly, lasting until about age 14, so children use their baby teeth for up to 10 years and have to learn how to take care of them to prevent tooth decay.

In developed countries, children usually have their first visit to the dentist around age 3 (Bottenberg et al., 2008; Chi et al., 2011). Most children learn how to brush their teeth in early childhood, and in developed countries it is increasingly common for children's dental care to include fluoride rinses and sealants (plastic tooth coatings). Some countries and local areas also add fluoride to the water system, which greatly reduces children's rates of tooth decay. Nevertheless, about 40% of North American children have at least one dental cavity by age 5 (World Health Organization [WHO], 2008), primarily due to inconsistent dental care and to diets that are heavy in sugars and starches that cause cavities. Children in developing countries are less likely to have diets loaded with sugars and starches, but they are also less likely to have fluoride in their water systems and less likely to have access to regular dental care that would provide fluoride rinses and sealants. Overall, children in most developing countries have more tooth decay in early and middle childhood than children in developed countries do (WHO, 2008).

Young children in developing countries are often relatively small in stature, such as this child in Uganda.

Brain Development and "Infantile" Amnesia

LO 6.2 **Describe the changes in brain development that take place during early childhood and the aspects of brain development that explain "infantile" amnesia.**

The size of the brain continues to increase gradually during early childhood. At age 3 the brain is about 70% of its adult weight, and at age 6, about 90% (Bauer et al., 2009). In contrast, the average 6-year-old's body weight is less than 30% what it will be in adulthood, so the growth of the brain outpaces the rest of the body (Nihart, 1993).

The frontal lobes grow faster than the rest of the cerebral cortex during early childhood (Anderson et al., 2008; Blumenthal et al., 1999). Growth in the frontal lobes underlies the advances in emotional regulation, foresight, and planned behavior that take place during the preschool years (Diamond, 2004). Throughout the cerebral cortex, growth from age 3 to 15 takes place not gradually but in spurts within the different lobes, followed by periods of vigorous synaptic pruning (Hill et al., 2010).

During early childhood the number of neurons continues the decline that began in toddlerhood via synaptic pruning. The increase in brain size and weight during early childhood is due to an increase in dendritic connections between neurons and to myelination (see Chapter 4 if you need to refresh your memory about myelination). Four parts of the brain are especially notable for their myelination during early childhood (see **Figure 6.1** on the next page).

In the **corpus callosum**, the band of neural fibers connecting the right and left hemispheres of the cerebral cortex, myelination peaks during early childhood, although it continues at a slower pace through adolescence. The corpus callosum allows for coordination of activity between the two hemispheres, so increased myelination of this area of the brain enhances the speed of functioning throughout the cerebral cortex.

corpus callosum

band of neural fibers connecting the two hemispheres of the brain

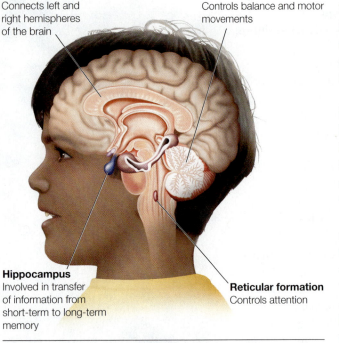

Corpus callosum
Connects left and right hemispheres of the brain

Cerebellum
Controls balance and motor movements

Hippocampus
Involved in transfer of information from short-term to long-term memory

Reticular formation
Controls attention

Figure 6.1 Brain Development in Early Childhood

In which structures is myelination completed by age 5?

cerebellum

structure at the base of the brain involved in balance and motor movements

reticular formation

part of the lower brain, involved in attention

hippocampus

structure involved in transfer of information from short-term to long-term memory

infantile amnesia

inability to remember anything that happened prior to age 2

Substantial myelination also takes place in early childhood in the **cerebellum**, a structure at the base of the brain involved in balance and motor movements. Increased myelination enhances connections between the cerebellum and the cerebral cortex. This change underlies the child's increasing abilities to jump, run, climb, and throw a ball.

In the **reticular formation**, a part of the brain involved in attention, myelination is completed by age 5, which helps explain the increase in attention span that takes place in the course of early childhood. For example, by age 4 or 5 most children could easily sit for 10–15 minutes in preschool while a story is read aloud, whereas most toddlers would be unable to sit still and pay attention for so long.

Similarly, myelination in the **hippocampus** is completed by age 5. The hippocampus is involved in the transfer of information from short-term to long-term memory, so the completion of myelination by age 5 may explain why *autobiographical memory* (memory for personal events and experiences) is limited prior to this age (Rolls, 2000). However, myelination in the hippocampus is gradual, and most adults can remember some autobiographical events that happened before age 5 (Howe et al., 2009). For example, in one study children who had been hospitalized for a medical emergency at age 2–3 were interviewed 5 years later (Peterson & Whalen, 2001). Even the children who were only 2 years old at the time of the injury recalled the main features of their hospital experience accurately 5 years later, although memory for details of the experience improved with age.

Other studies have found that many children and adults have autobiographical memories for events and experiences that happened as early as age 2, but remember little or nothing prior to this age (Courage & Cowan, 2009). The inability to remember anything prior to age 2 is known as **infantile amnesia**. One theory proposes that autobiographical memory before age 2 is limited because the awareness of self becomes stable at about 2 years of age and serves as a new organizer around which events can be encoded, stored, and retrieved in memory as personal, that is, as having happened "to me" (Howe et al., 2009). Another perspective proposes that the encoding of memories is promoted by language development, because language allows us to tell ourselves a narrative of events and experiences; consequently, most autobiographical memory is encoded only after language development accelerates at age 2 (Newcombe et al., 2007).

Autobiographical memory may also be partly cultural. In a study comparing adults' autobiographical memories, British and (White) American adults remembered more events prior to age 5 than Chinese adults did, and their earliest memory was 6 months earlier on average (Wang et al., 2009). The interpretation proposed by the authors was that the greater individualism of British and American cultures promotes greater attention to individual experiences and consequently more and earlier autobiographical memories.

Health and Safety in Early Childhood

LO 6.3 **Identify the main nutritional deficiencies and the primary sources of injury, illness, and mortality during early childhood in developed and developing countries.**

By early childhood, children are not as vulnerable to health threats as they were in infancy and toddlerhood (UNICEF, 2014). Nevertheless, there are many health and safety concerns associated with this period. Proper nutrition is essential to a child's healthy development, yet in developing countries the rates of malnutrition are alarmingly high. Children in developing countries remain vulnerable to some illnesses and diseases, and children worldwide are subject to high rates of injuries compared to other periods of the life course.

NUTRITION AND MALNUTRITION As the rate of physical growth slows down in early childhood, food consumption diminishes as well. Children may have some meals, or even some whole days, where they eat little. This can be alarming to parents, but it is nothing to worry about as long as it does not happen over an extended period and is not accompanied by symptoms that may indicate illness or disease. Appetites vary a lot from day to day in early childhood, and the 5-year-old who barely touched dinner one night may eat nearly as much as Mom and Dad the next night (Hursti, 1999).

Children generally learn to like whatever foods the adults in their environment like and provide for them. In India kids eat rice with spicy sauces, in Japan kids eat sushi, in Mexico kids eat chili peppers. Nevertheless, a myth persists among many North American parents that kids in early childhood will only eat a small range of foods high in fat and sugar content, such as hamburgers, hot dogs, fried chicken, and macaroni and cheese (Zehle et al., 2007). This false belief then becomes a self-fulfilling prophecy, as children who eat foods high in sugar and fat lose their taste for healthier foods (Black et al., 2002). The assumption that young children like only foods high in fat and sugar also leads parents to bribe their children to eat healthier foods—"If you eat three more bites of carrots, then you can have some ice cream"—which leads the children to view healthy foods as a trial and unhealthy foods as a reward (Birch et al., 2003). These cultural beliefs contribute to high rates of childhood obesity in many developed countries, as we will see in more detail in Chapter 7.

Because young children in developed countries often eat too much of unhealthy foods and too little of healthy foods, many of them have specific nutritional deficiencies despite living in cultures where food is abundant. Calcium is the most common nutritional deficiency in the United States, with one third of American 3-year-olds consuming less than the amount recommended by health authorities (Wagner & Greer, 2008). Calcium is especially important for the growth of bones and teeth, and is found in foods such as beans, peas, broccoli, and dairy products (for example yogurt, milk, and cheese). Over the past 30 years, as children have consumed less milk and more soft drinks, calcium deficiencies in early childhood have become more common (Thacher et al., 2010).

In developing countries, malnutrition is the norm rather than the exception. The World Health Organization estimates that about 80% of children in developing countries lack sufficient food or essential nutrients (Van de Poel et al., 2008). The two most common types of nutritional deficiencies involve protein and iron. Lack of protein is experienced by about 25% of children under age 5 worldwide, and can result in two fatal diseases described in Chapters 4 and 5, marasmus (in infancy) and kwashiorkor (in toddlerhood and early childhood). Iron deficiency, known as **anemia**, is experienced by the majority of children under age 5 in developing countries (WHO, 2008). Anemia causes fatigue, irritability, and difficulty sustaining attention, which in turn lead to problems in cognitive and social development (Kaplan et al., 2007; Rao & Georgieff, 2001). Foods rich in iron include most meats, as well as vegetables such as potatoes, peas, and beets, and grains such as oatmeal and brown rice. As noted in Chapter 5, young children in developed countries may also experience anemia if they do not eat enough healthy foods (Brotanek et al., 2007).

anemia

dietary deficiency of iron that causes problems such as fatigue, irritability, and attention difficulties

Many children in developed countries have nutritional deficiencies despite an abundance of food. Here, a child in London eats a fast-food meal that is high in fat and sugar.

CRITICAL THINKING QUESTION

Consider the foods that you typically see on the "Kid's Menu" in restaurants. How do these menus reflect cultural beliefs about food?

ILLNESS AND DISEASE In developing countries, the causes of death in early childhood are usually illnesses and diseases, especially pneumonia, malaria, and measles (UNICEF, 2008). Malnutrition is believed to be indirectly responsible for about half of early childhood deaths, because a lack of sufficient food reduces the effectiveness of the body's immune system.

However, remarkable progress has been made in recent decades in reducing mortality in children under age 5. From 1960 to 2006, the number of deaths worldwide of children under age 5 declined from 20 million to under 10 million, even though the world's population more than doubled during that time (UNICEF, 2008). Progress has continued in recent years. As **Figure 6.2** illustrates, in many of the poorest countries in the world, under-5 mortality rates fell by more than half from 1990 to 2012 (Economist, 2014). The decline is due to a variety of factors, especially improved food production in developing countries and increased prevalence of childhood vaccinations.

In developed countries, where most children receive vaccinations and have access to adequate food and medical care, life-threatening illnesses are rare but minor illnesses are common in early childhood, with most children experiencing seven to ten per year (Kesson, 2007). Minor illnesses help build up the immune system, so that children experience them less frequently with age.

INJURIES Do you remember becoming injured at all in early childhood? If you do, you are in good company. Most young children—and their parents—can count on spending a portion of their childhood nursing an injury; a minor "boo-boo" if they're lucky, but in some cases something more serious.

Young children have high activity levels and their motor development is advanced enough for them to be able to run, jump, and climb, but their cognitive development is not yet advanced enough for them to anticipate situations that might be dangerous. This combination leads to high rates of injuries in early childhood. In the United States each

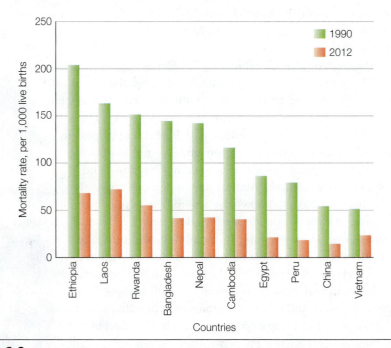

Figure 6.2 Reduction in Early Childhood Mortality Rates, Select Countries

SOURCE: Based on data from WHO; UN estimates

year, one third of children under 10 become injured badly enough to receive medical attention (Field & Behrman, 2003). Boys are more likely than girls to become injured in early childhood, because their play tends to be rougher and more physically active. However, in developed countries, most of the injuries and deaths that take place in early childhood are due not to high activity levels but to motor vehicle accidents (National Highway Traffic Safety Administration [NHTSA], 2014; Safe Kids Worldwide, 2013). Other common causes of injury and death in early childhood are drowning, falls, fire, and choking.

You might think that rates of injury and death due to accidents in early childhood would be lower in developing countries than in developed countries, since people in developing countries are less likely to own the cars that are the predominant source of early childhood injury and death in developed countries. However, rates of early childhood injury and death due to accidents are actually higher in developing countries (WHO, 2008). For example, rates of unintentional injury among 1- to 14-year-olds in South Africa are 5 times higher than in developed countries; in Vietnam, rates are 4 times higher, and in China 3 times higher. This is due to more stringent safety codes in developed countries, such as requiring child seats in cars, strict building codes to prevent fires, and lifeguards in public swimming areas where drowning is a potential danger. An organization called Safe Kids Worldwide (2009) is working to advocate safety measures for young children in both developed and developing countries. It currently has chapters in 16 countries, including China, Brazil, India, and Canada, and is expanding steadily.

Despite the high rates of accidental injury among young children in developing countries, disease is a far greater danger. Only 3% of deaths of children under 5 in developing countries are due to injuries, and virtually all the other 97% are due to illness and disease (UNICEF, 2008). In contrast, even though rates of accidental injuries are much lower in developed countries than in developing countries, accidental injuries are the leading cause of death for young children in developed countries because so few of them die from illness or disease.

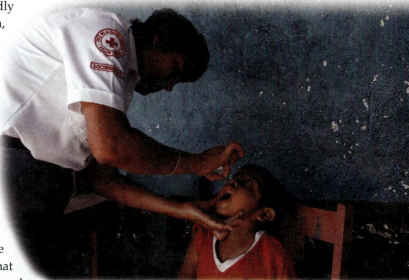

Deaths worldwide among children age 5 and under have declined by over half in the past 50 years, largely due to increased childhood vaccinations. Here, a Red Cross volunteer in El Salvador gives an oral vaccination to a 6-year-old boy.

Practice Quiz   ANSWERS AVAILABLE IN ANSWER KEY.

1. During early childhood _____.
   a. the amount of tooth decay is similar between children in developing and developed countries
   b. girls are slightly taller and heavier than boys
   c. physical development occurs at a more rapid pace than it did in the first three years
   d. most children become more like adults in terms of their body proportions

2. Your cousin has a five-year-old son and a three-year-old daughter. He has been taking them to story time at the library, but his daughter is having a very difficult time sitting still, even for 10 minutes. His son is able to sit through the entire story time because his _____ is more fully developed than his sister's.
   a. reticular formation   c. corpus callosum
   b. hippocampus   d. cerebellum

3. Limited autobiographical memory prior to age 5 is probably due to incomplete myelination of the _____.
   a. reticular formation   c. corpus callosum
   b. hippocampus   d. Broca's area

4. Walter is a 5-year-old boy who lives in the United States. Based on the research, if he has a nutritional problem it is most likely to be _____.
   a. marasmus   c. calcium deficiency
   b. kwashiorkor   d. protein deficiency

5. Accidental injury among young children _____.
   a. is less of a danger than disease in developing countries
   b. happens at a greater rate in developed countries than in developing countries
   c. is equally common among boys and girls
   d. is extremely rare in the United States because of increased awareness and better technology; rates are under 5%

PHYSICAL DEVELOPMENT: Motor Development

One thing for certain about motor activity in early childhood is that there is a lot of it. Children of this age are frequently on the move, enjoying and extending the development of their new motor abilities.

Gross and Fine Motor Skills

LO 6.4   Describe changes in gross and fine motor abilities during early childhood.

In many ways, gross motor development in early childhood extends abilities that first appeared in toddlerhood. Toddlers can hop a step or two with both feet, but from age 3 to 6 young children learn to make more hops in a row and to hop on one foot. Toddlers can jump, but from age 3 to 6 children learn to jump farther from a standing position and to make a running jump. Toddlers begin to climb stairs, but age 3 to 6 is when children learn to climb stairs without support, alternating their feet. Toddlers can throw a ball, but from age 3 to 6, children learn to throw a ball farther and more accurately, and they become better at catching a ball, too. They also increase their running speed and their ability to stop suddenly or change direction. The video *Gross Motor Development in Early Childhood* provides more information on this topic. Gender differences in gross motor development appear in early childhood, with boys generally becoming better at skills emphasizing strength or size, such as jumping and throwing a ball, and girls becoming better at body-coordination skills, such as balancing on one foot (Cratty, 1986; Lung et al., 2011).

Watch   GROSS MOTOR DEVELOPMENT IN EARLY CHILDHOOD

Fine motor development in early childhood involves a similar extension of skills that arose in toddlerhood, along with some new skills. As toddlers they could already pick up a small object using two fingers, but now they learn to do it more quickly and precisely. They could already hold a crayon and scribble on a piece of paper, but in early childhood they learn to draw something that is recognizable to others, such as a person, animal, or building. By age 6 they can even draw shapes such as a circle or triangle, and their first letters and some short words, perhaps including their own name. New fine motor skills learned in early childhood include putting on and removing their clothes, using scissors, and using a knife to cut soft food (Cratty, 1986; Piek et al., 2008). Their growing fine motor abilities allows children to learn to do many things their parents had been doing for them, such as putting on a coat or shoes, and brushing their teeth.

Handedness

LO 6.5 **Describe the development of handedness and identify the consequences and cultural views of left-handedness.**

Once children begin drawing or writing in early childhood, they show a clear preference for using their right or left hand, but **handedness** appears long before early childhood. In fact, even prenatally, fetuses show a definite preference for sucking the thumb of their right or left hand, with 90% preferring the right thumb (Hepper et al., 2005). The same 90% proportion of right-handers continues into childhood and throughout adulthood in most cultures (Hinojosa et al., 2003).

Gross motor skills advance from toddlerhood to early childhood.

If handedness appears so early, that must mean it is determined genetically, right? Actually, the evidence is mixed on this issue. Adopted children are more likely to resemble their biological parents than their adoptive parents in their handedness, suggesting a genetic origin (Carter-Salzman, 1980). On the other hand (pun intended), identical twins are more likely than ordinary siblings to *differ* in handedness, even though identical twins share 100% of their genotype and other siblings only about 50% (Derom et al., 1996). This appears to be due to the fact that twins usually lie in opposite ways within the uterus, whereas most singletons lie toward the left. Lying toward one side allows for greater movement and hence greater development of the hand on the other side, so most twins end up with one being right-handed and one being left-handed, while most singletons end up right-handed.

Nevertheless, as usual, culture is also a big part of the picture. Historically, many cultures have viewed left-handedness as dangerous and evil and have suppressed its development in children (Grimshaw & Wilson, 2013). In Western languages, the word *sinister* is derived from a Latin word meaning "on the left," and many paintings in Western art depict the devil as left-handed. In many Asian and Middle Eastern cultures, only the left hand is supposed to be used for wiping up after defecation, and all other activities are supposed to be done mainly with the right hand. In Africa, even today, using the left hand is suppressed in many cultures from childhood onward, and the prevalence of left-handedness in some African countries is as low as 1%, far lower than the 10% figure in cultures where left-handedness is tolerated (Provins, 1997).

Why do so many cultures regard left-handedness with such fear and contempt? Perhaps negative cultural beliefs about left-handedness developed because people noticed that left-handedness was associated with a greater likelihood of various problems. Left-handed infants are more likely to be born prematurely or to experience an unusually difficult birth, and there is evidence that brain damage prenatally or during birth can contribute to left-handedness (Powls et al., 1996). In early and middle childhood, left-handers are more likely to have problems learning to read and to have other verbal learning disabilities (Natsopoulos et al., 1998). This may have something to do

handedness
preference for using either the right or left hand in gross and fine motor activities

Why have so many cultures regarded being left-handed as evil or dangerous?

with the fact that about one fourth of left-handers process language in both hemispheres rather than primarily in the left hemisphere (Knecht et al., 2000). In adulthood, people who are left-handed have lower life expectancy and are more likely to die in accidents (Grimshaw & Wilson, 2013).

However, this explanation is not entirely convincing because left-handedness is associated not only with greater likelihood of some types of problems but with excellence and even genius in certain fields. Left-handed children are more likely to show exceptional verbal and math abilities (Bower, 1985; Flannery & Leiderman, 1995). Left-handers are especially likely to have strong visual–spatial abilities, and consequently they are more likely than right-handers to become architects or artists (Grimshaw & Wilson, 2013). Some of the greatest artists in the Western tradition have been left-handed, including Leonardo da Vinci, Michelangelo, and Pablo Picasso (Schacter & Ransil, 1996). It is worth keeping in mind that the majority of left-handers are in the normal range in their cognitive development, and show neither unusual problems nor unusual gifts. Hence the widespread cultural prejudice against left-handers remains mysterious.

Practice Quiz   ANSWERS AVAILABLE IN ANSWER KEY.

1. In early childhood (from ages 3–6) _____.
   a. fine motor skills are refined, but gross motor skills remain the same as they were in toddlerhood
   b. children from high socioeconomic status tend to have better gross motor skills than their counterparts from lower socioeconomic backgrounds
   c. girls and boys are equally skilled at body-coordination skills, such as balancing on one foot
   d. gender differences in gross motor development appear.

2. Imagine that you have just walked into a kindergarten classroom during art time and all the children in this particular class are 5 years old. What would you most likely see?
   a. Most of the children drawing something that is recognizable, such as a person or animal
   b. Most of the children scribbling on a piece of paper
   c. Most of the children showing depth and realistic detail in their artwork
   d. Most of the girls getting frustrated because they can't hold a crayon or paintbrush

3. A child who is left-handed _____.
   a. likely first developed this tendency during the preschool years
   b. is often praised for their uniqueness in non-Western cultures
   c. will be more likely to learn to be right handed in an Asian or African culture than in the United States
   d. will always have a left-handed twin if they are monozygotic (MZ) twins

4. One can see a preference for the use of a particular hand, handedness, over another as early as _____.
   a. the prenatal period   c. toddlerhood
   b. infancy   d. age 5

5. Which of the following is **TRUE** regarding handedness?
   a. A premature birth is more common among left-handed infants.
   b. Left-handed people are less likely to have problems learning to read than right- handed people.
   c. Children do not show hand preference until the middle of kindergarten when they are learning to write.
   d. Left-handed people tend to have poorer verbal and math ability than right-handed people.

Summary: Physical Development

LO 6.1 **Describe the physical growth and change that takes place during early childhood.**

The pace of physical development slows in early childhood. From ages 3 to 6 the typical American child grows 2–3 inches per year and adds 5–7 pounds. Average heights and weights in early childhood are considerably lower in developing countries, due to inadequate nutrition and higher likelihood of childhood diseases.

LO 6.2 **Describe the changes in brain development that take place during early childhood and the aspects of brain development that explain "infantile" amnesia.**

The most notable changes in brain development during early childhood take place in the connections between neurons and in myelination. Most people experience infantile amnesia (the inability to remember anything prior to age 2) and have limited memory for personal events that happened before age 5, due mainly to the immaturity of the hippocampus.

LO 6.3 **Identify the main nutritional deficiencies and the primary sources of injury, illness, and mortality during early childhood in developed and developing countries.**

About 80% of children in developing countries experience nutritional deficiencies, but a surprisingly high percentage of children in developed countries experience them as well. Calcium is the most common nutritional deficiency in the United States, whereas the two most common types of malnutrition in developing countries are lack of protein and lack of iron. Mortality rates in early childhood are much higher in developing countries than in developed countries, due mainly to the greater prevalence of infectious diseases, but have declined substantially in recent years. In developed countries, the most common cause of injury and death by far in early childhood is motor vehicle accidents.

LO 6.4 **Describe changes in gross and fine motor abilities during early childhood.**

From age 3 to 6, young children learn to: make more hops in a row and hop on one foot; jump farther from a standing position and make a running jump; climb stairs without support, alternating their feet; throw a ball farther and more accurately; become better at catching a ball; and increase their running speed and their ability to stop suddenly or change direction. In their fine motor development, children learn to pick up small objects more quickly and precisely, draw something that is recognizable to others, write their first letters and some short words, put on and remove their clothes, use scissors, and use a knife to cut soft food.

LO 6.5 **Describe the development of handedness and identify the consequences and cultural views of left-handedness.**

About 10% of children are left-handed. Handedness is due primarily to the direction in which fetuses lie in the womb, although there is also a small genetic influence. Being left-handed has been stigmatized in many cultures, perhaps due to its association with higher risk of developmental problems, but it is also associated with exceptional abilities.

Section 2 Cognitive Development

⌄ Learning Objectives

6.6 Explain the features of Piaget's preoperational stage of cognitive development.

6.7 Explain what "theory of mind" is and the evidence for how it develops during early childhood.

6.8 Identify the ways that cultural learning takes place in early childhood.

6.9 Identify the features that are most important in preschool quality and explain how they reflect cultural values.

6.10 Describe the distinctive practices of Japanese preschools and how they reflect cultural values.

6.11 Describe early intervention programs and their outcomes.

6.12 Explain how advances in vocabulary and grammar occur in early childhood.

6.13 Describe how children learn pragmatics in early childhood, and identify to what extent these social rules are culturally based.

COGNITIVE DEVELOPMENT: Theories of Cognitive Development

In the course of early childhood, children make many remarkable advances in their cognitive development. Several theories shed light on these developments, including Piaget's preoperational stage; "theory of mind," which examines how children think about the thoughts of others; and theories of cultural learning that emphasize the ways that young children gain the knowledge and skills of their culture. These theories complement each other to provide a comprehensive picture of cognitive development in early childhood.

Piaget's Preoperational Stage of Cognitive Development

LO 6.6 **Explain the features of Piaget's preoperational stage of cognitive development.**

In Piaget's theory, early childhood is a crucial turning point in children's cognitive development because this is when thinking becomes *representational* (Piaget, 1952). During the first 2 years of life, the sensorimotor stage, thinking takes place primarily in association with sensorimotor activities such as reaching and grasping. Gradually toward the end of the sensorimotor period, in the second half of the second year, children begin to internalize the images of their sensorimotor activities, marking the beginning of representational thought.

However, it is during the latter part of toddlerhood and especially in early childhood that we become truly representational thinkers. Language requires the ability to represent the world symbolically, through words, and this is when language skills develop most dramatically. Once we can represent the world through language, we are freed from our momentary sensorimotor experience. With language we can represent not only the present but the past and the future, not only the world as we see it before us but the world as we previously experienced it and the world as it will be—the coming cold (or warm) season, a decline in the availability of food or water, and so on. We can even represent the world as it has never been, through mentally combining ideas—flying monkeys, talking trees, and people who have superhuman powers.

These are marvelous cognitive achievements, and yet early childhood fascinated Piaget not only for what children of this age are able to do cognitively but also for the kinds of mistakes they make. In fact, Piaget termed the age period from 2 to 7 the **preoperational stage**, emphasizing that children of this age were not yet able to perform mental *operations,* that is, cognitive procedures that follow certain logical rules. Piaget specified a number of areas of preoperational cognitive mistakes that are characteristic of early childhood, including conservation, egocentrism, and classification.

CONSERVATION According to Piaget, children in early childhood lack the ability to understand **conservation**, the principle that the amount of a physical substance remains the same even if its physical appearance changes. In his best known demonstration of this mistake, Piaget showed young children two identical glasses holding equal amounts of water and asked them if the two amounts of water were equal. The children typically answered "yes"—they were capable of understanding that much. Then Piaget poured the contents from one of the glasses into a taller, thinner glass, and asked the children again if the two amounts of water were equal. Now most of the children answered "no," failing to understand that the *amount* of water remained the same even though the *appearance* of the water changed. Piaget also demonstrated that children made this error with other substances besides water, as shown in the video *Conservation Tasks.*

Watch CONSERVATION TASKS

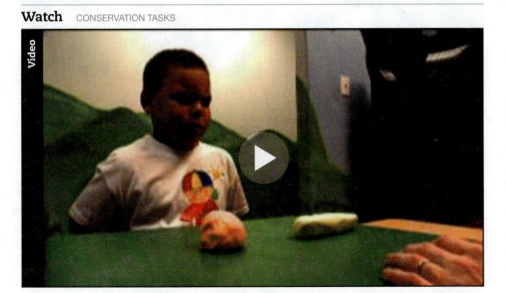

Piaget interpreted children's mistakes on conservation tasks as indicating two kinds of cognitive deficiencies. The first is **centration**, meaning that young children's thinking is *centered,* or focused, on one noticeable aspect of a cognitive problem to the exclusion of other important aspects. In the conservation-of-liquid task, they notice the change in height as the water is poured into the taller glass but neglect to observe the change in width that takes place simultaneously.

preoperational stage

cognitive stage from age 2 to 7 during which the child becomes capable of representing the world symbolically—for example, through the use of language—but is still very limited in ability to use mental operations

conservation

mental ability to understand that the quantity of a substance or material remains the same even if its appearance changes

centration

Piaget's term for young children's thinking as being centered, or focused, on one noticeable aspect of a cognitive problem to the exclusion of other important aspects

View 1   View 2

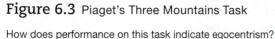

Figure 6.3 Piaget's Three Mountains Task

How does performance on this task indicate egocentrism?

Second, young children lack **reversibility**, the ability to reverse an action mentally. When the water is poured from the original glass to the taller glass in the conservation task, anyone who can reverse that action mentally can see that the amount of water would be the same. Young children cannot perform the mental operation of reversibility, so they mistakenly believe the amount of water has changed.

EGOCENTRISM Another cognitive limitation of the preoperational stage, in Piaget's view, is **egocentrism**, the inability to distinguish between your own perspective and another person's perspective. To demonstrate egocentrism, Piaget and his colleague Barbel Inhelder (1969) devised what they called the "three mountains task" (see **Figure 6.3**). In this task a child is shown a clay model of three different mountains of varying sizes, one with snow on top, one with a red cross, and one with a house. The child walks around the table to see what the mountain looks like from each side, then sits down while the experimenter moves a doll to different points around the table. At each of the doll's locations, the child is shown a series of photographs and asked which one indicates the doll's point of view. In the early years of the preoperational stage, children tend to pick the photo that matches their own perspective, not the doll's. Watch the video *Egocentrism Task* for another example of a research study on this topic.

Watch EGOCENTRISM TASK

reversibility

ability to reverse an action mentally

egocentrism

cognitive inability to distinguish between one's own perspective and another person's perspective

animism

tendency to attribute human thoughts and feelings to inanimate objects and forces

One aspect of egocentrism is **animism**, the tendency to attribute human thoughts and feelings to inanimate objects and forces. According to Piaget, when young children believe that the thunder is angry or the moon is following them, it reflects their animistic thinking. It also reflects their egocentrism, in that they are attributing the thoughts and feelings that they might have themselves to things that are inanimate.

Children's play with stuffed animals and dolls is a good example of animistic thinking. When they play with these toys, children frequently attribute human thoughts and feelings to them, often the thoughts and feelings they might have themselves. This is play, but it is a kind of play they take seriously. At age 5, my daughter Paris would sometimes "find" a stuffed puppy or kitten on our porch that she would treat as if it were a live animal that would now be her pet. If you humorously suggested that this might be an especially easy pet to care for, being stuffed—as I made the mistake of doing one day—she took great offense and insisted it was a real animal. To her, at that moment, it was.

CLASSIFICATION Preoperational children also lack the capacity for **classification**, according to Piaget, meaning that they have difficulty understanding that objects can be simultaneously part of more than one "class" or group. He demonstrated this by showing children a drawing of 4 blue flowers and 12 yellow flowers and asking them, "Are there more yellow flowers, or more flowers?" In early childhood, children would typically answer "More yellow flowers," because they did not understand that yellow flowers could be part of the class "yellow flowers" and simultaneously part of the class "flowers."

Here, as with conservation, the cognitive limitations of centration and lack of reversibility are at the root of the error, in Piaget's view. Young children center on the fact that the yellow flowers are yellow, which leads them to overlook that the yellow flowers are also flowers. They also lack reversibility in that they cannot perform the mental operation of placing the yellow and blue flowers together into the "flowers" class and then moving them back into the "yellow flowers" and "blue flowers" classes, respectively.

EVALUATING PIAGET'S THEORY Piaget's theory of preoperational thought in early childhood has been challenged in the decades since he proposed it. The criticisms focus on two issues: claims that he underestimated children's cognitive capabilities, and claims that development is more continuous and less stagelike than he proposed.

Many studies over the past several decades have shown that children ages 2–7 are cognitively capable of more than Piaget recognized. For example, regarding egocentrism, when the three mountains task is modified so that familiar objects are used instead of the three-mountain model, children give less egocentric responses (Newcombe & Huttenlocher, 1992). Studies using other methods also show that 2- to 7-year-old children are less egocentric than Piaget thought. As described in Chapter 5, even toddlers show the beginnings of an ability to take others' perspectives, when they discern what they can do to annoy a sibling (Dunn, 1988). By age 4, children switch to shorter, simpler sentences when talking to toddlers or babies, showing a distinctly un-egocentric ability to take the perspective of the younger children (Bryant & Barrett, 2007).

Regarding Piaget's stage claims, research has shown that the development of cognitive skills in childhood is less stagelike and more continuous than Piaget believed (Bibok et al., 2009). Remember, Piaget's stage theory asserts that movement from one stage to another represents a wholesale cognitive shift, a change not just in specific cognitive skills but in how children think. In this view, children ages 2–7 are incapable of performing mental operations, and then in the next stage they become able to do so. However, research has generally shown that the ability to perform mental operations changes gradually over the course of childhood (Case, 1999).

How does animism reflect young children's egocentrism?

Understanding Thinking: The Development of "Theory of Mind"

LO 6.7 **Explain what "theory of mind" is and the evidence for how it develops during early childhood.**

Current research on cognitive development in early childhood has moved beyond Piaget's theories. One popular area of research in recent years is **theory of mind**, the ability to understand thinking processes in one's self and others.

Understanding how others think is a challenge even for adults, but the beginnings of theory of mind appear very early, in infancy. Through behavior such as joint attention

classification

ability to understand that objects can be part of more than one cognitive group, for example an object can be classified with red objects as well as with round objects

theory of mind

ability to understand thinking processes in one's self and others

and the use of prelanguage vocalizations, infants show that they understand that others have mental states such as intentionality (Tomasello & Rakoczy, 2003). By age 2, as they begin to use language more, children show increasing recognition that others have thoughts and emotions that can be contrasted with their own (e.g., "That man is mad!" or "I like applesauce. Brother no like applesauce."). At age 2, children begin to use words that refer to mental processes, such as "think," "remember," and "pretend" (Flavell et al., 2002). By age 3, children know it is possible for them and others to imagine something that is not physically present (such as an ice cream cone). They can respond to an imaginary event as if it has really happened, and they realize that others can do the same (Andrews et al., 2003). This understanding becomes the basis of pretend play for many years to come.

However, there are limits to 3-year-olds' theory of mind, and crucial changes take place in the course of early childhood. They are better than 2-year-olds at understanding that others have thoughts and feelings that are different than their own, but they find it difficult to take others' perspectives. Perspective-taking ability advances considerably from age 3 to 6 (Callahan et al., 2005).

This change is vividly demonstrated in research involving *false-belief tasks.* In one experiment testing understanding of false beliefs, children are shown a doll named Maxi who places chocolate in a cabinet and then leaves the room (Amsterlaw & Wellman, 2006). Next another doll, his mother, enters the room and moves the chocolate to a different place. Children are then asked, "Where will Maxi look for the chocolate when he returns?" Most 3-year-old children answer erroneously that Maxi will look for the chocolate in the new place, where his mother stored it. In contrast, by age 4 most children recognize that Maxi will believe falsely that the chocolate is in the cabinet where he left it. The proportion of children who understand this correctly rises even higher by age 5.

Cultural Focus: Theory of Mind Across Cultures

In another false belief task, children are shown a box that appears to contain a kind of candy called "Smarties" and asked what they think is in the box (Gopnik & Astington, 1988). After they answer "candy" or "Smarties" they are shown that the box in fact contains pencils. Then they are asked what another person, who has not been shown the contents, will think is in the box. "Candy" or "Smarties" is the correct answer, showing theory of mind; "pencils" is incorrect. Most children in developed countries pass the test by the time they are 4 or 5 years old.

Watch THEORY OF MIND ACROSS CULTURES

By age 6, nearly all children in developed countries solve false-belief tasks easily. In the video shown here, you will see that American children make errors in the false belief task at age 3 but answer correctly by age 5. However, in Mexico and Botswana, children continue to make mistakes at age 7. This could be because children in these cultures have not had pre-school experiences that involved similar tasks. What other explanations could there be? What hypothesis would you propose, and how would you test it?

Review Question:

Can you think of any social interactions that may help or hinder a child in developing a theory of mind?

Cultural Learning in Early Childhood

LO 6.8   **Identify the ways that cultural learning takes place in early childhood.**

In Piaget's depiction of cognitive development, the young child is like a solitary little scientist gradually mastering the concepts of conservation and classification and overcoming the errors of egocentrism and animism. Vygotsky's sociocultural theory of learning takes a much different approach, viewing cognitive development as a social and cultural process (see Chapter 5). Children learn not through their individual interactions with the environment but through the social process of guided participation, as they interact with a more knowledgeable member of the culture (often an older sibling or parent) in the course of daily activities.

Early childhood is a period when this kind of cultural learning comes to the fore (Gauvain & Nicolaides, 2015). More than in toddlerhood, young children have the capacity for learning culturally specific skills. The Mayan example that began this chapter provides one illustration. A 5-year-old can readily learn the skills involved in making tortillas, whereas a 2-year-old would not have the necessary learning abilities, motor skills, or impulse control (Rogoff, 2003). In many cultures, the end of early childhood, ages 5–6, is the time when children are first given important responsibilities in the family for food preparation, child care, and animal care (LeVine & New, 2008). During early childhood they acquire the cultural learning necessary for these duties, sometimes through direct instruction but more often through observing and participating in adults' activities.

How is cultural learning taking place here?

It is not only in traditional cultures that cultural learning takes place via guided participation. For example, a child in an economically developed country might help his parents prepare a grocery shopping list, and in the course of this process learn culturally valued skills such as reading, using lists as tools for organization and planning, and calculating sums of money (Rogoff, 2003). Children in Western countries are also encouraged to speak up and hold conversations. For example, over dinner American parents often ask their young children a series of questions ("What songs did you sing at preschool? What did you have for a snack?"), thereby preparing them for the question-and-answer structure of formal schooling they will enter in middle childhood (Martini, 1996). This is in contrast to cultures from Asia to northern Canada in which silence is valued, especially in children, and children who talk frequently are viewed as immature and low in intelligence (Rogoff, 2003).

Two factors make cultural learning in developed countries different from cultural learning in traditional cultures. One is that children in developed countries are often apart from their families for a substantial part of the day, in a preschool or another group-care setting. Cultural learning takes place in the preschool setting, of course—recall the example of Lars that began this chapter—but it is mostly a more direct kind of instruction (e.g., learning letters) rather than the cultural learning that takes place through guided participation in daily activities within the family. Second, the activities of adults in a complex economy are less accessible to children's learning than the activities that children learn through guided participation in traditional cultures, such as child care, tending animals, and food preparation. Most jobs in a complex economy require advanced skills of reading, analyzing information, and using technology, so there is a limit to which children can learn these skills through guided participation, especially in early childhood.

Practice Quiz   ANSWERS AVAILABLE IN ANSWER KEY.

1. In Piagetian terms, which of the following is the principle that the amount of a physical substance remains the same even if its physical appearance changes?
   a. Physical stability
   b. Reversibility
   c. Centration
   d. Conservation

2. Five-year-old Marco draws a picture of a train with a smiley face and sunglasses. This is an example of _____.
   a. animism
   b. sensorimotor thought
   c. centration
   d. reversibility

3. Which of the following is TRUE regarding theory of mind?
   a. It refers to the independence and stubbornness characteristic of toddlers as they develop a sense of self.
   b. It develops the same way in all cultures with spoken language.
   c. It begins to develop around age 5.
   d. It is measured with false-belief tasks.

4. According to your text, what is one of the factors that make cultural learning in developed countries different from cultural learning in traditional cultures?

   a. Children in developed countries are often apart from their families for a substantial part of the day, so they don't have as much guided participation in daily activities within the family as children in traditional cultures do.
   b. Parents in developed countries have assimilated into the culture and are not as interested in teaching their children skills or traditions as parents in traditional cultures are.
   c. Children in developed countries aren't interested in guided participation in daily activities the way children in traditional cultures are.
   d. Parents in developed countries believe that their children should learn independently.

5. Learning to be able to set the table in a developed country, such as the United States, or to help prepare food in a nontraditional culture, such as Botswana, are examples of cultural learning. According to Vygotsky, these skills _____.
   a. develop as part of a social process
   b. must be learned in the sensorimotor stage first or they never fully develop
   c. develop best if they take place in a formal setting
   d. are usually first taught in toddlerhood

COGNITIVE DEVELOPMENT: Early Childhood Education

Traditionally in many cultures, formal schooling has started at about age 7. This is the age at which children have been viewed as first capable of learning the skills of reading, writing, and math. However, because the need to learn how to use words and numbers is so strong in the modern information-based economy, in many countries school now begins earlier than ever. In developed countries about three-fourths of 3- to 5-year-old children are enrolled in group child care, preschool, or kindergarten (OECD, 2013). In developing countries, the percentages are lower but rising. In the United States, about half of American states now fund some type of preschool programs for 4-year-old children, usually focusing on children from low-income families. Nevertheless, preschool participation in the United States lags behind nearly all other developed countries (OECD, 2013).

The Importance of Preschool Quality

LO 6.9   **Identify the features that are most important in preschool quality and explain how they reflect cultural values.**

What are the cognitive and social effects of attending preschool? For the most part, attending preschool is beneficial for young children (Campbell et al., 2002). Cognitive benefits of attending preschool include higher verbal skills and stronger performance on measures of memory and listening comprehension (Clarke-Stewart & Allhusen, 2002). Children from low-income families especially benefit cognitively from preschool (Love et al., 2013). They perform better on tests of school-readiness than children of similar backgrounds who did not attend preschool.

There are also social benefits to attending preschool. Children who attend preschool are generally more independent and socially confident than children who remain home (National Institute of Child Health and Human Development [NICHD] Early Child Care Research Network, 2006). However, there appear to be social costs as well. Children attending preschool have been observed to be less compliant, less respectful toward adults, and more aggressive than other children (Jennings & Reingle, 2013). Furthermore, these negative social effects may endure long past preschool age. In one large national (U.S.) longitudinal study, children who attended preschool for more than 10 hours per week were more disruptive in class once they entered school, in follow-ups extending through 6th grade (NICHD Early Child Care Research Network, 2006).

Yet these findings concerning the overall positive or negative outcomes associated with preschool can be misleading. Preschool programs vary vastly in quality, and many studies have found that the quality of preschool child care is more important than simply the fact of whether children are in preschool or not (Clarke-Stewart & Allhusen, 2002; Maccoby & Lewis, 2003; NICHD Early Child Care Research Network, 2006). Also, cultural context matters. A recent national study in Norway found no relation between hours in preschool and aggression (Zachrisson et al., 2013).

What factors should parents consider when searching for a high-quality preschool experience for their children? There is a broad consensus among scholars of early childhood development that the most important features include the following (Lavzer & Goodson, 2006; National Association for the Education of Young Children [NAEYC], 2010; Vandell et al, 2005):

- *Education and training of teachers.* Unlike teachers at higher grade levels, preschool teachers often are not required to have education or credentials specific to early childhood education. Preschool teachers who have training in early childhood education provide a better social and cognitive environment.
- *Class size and child–teacher ratio.* Experts recommend no more than 20 children in a classroom, and a ratio of children to preschool teachers no higher than five to ten 3-year-olds per teacher or seven to ten 4-year-olds per teacher.
- *Age-appropriate materials and activities.* In early childhood, children learn more through active engagement with materials rather than through formal lessons or rote learning.
- *Teacher–child interactions.* Teachers should spend most of their time in interactions with the children rather than with each other. They should circulate among the children, asking questions, offering suggestions, and assisting them when necessary.

Notice that the criteria for high-quality preschools do not include intense academic instruction. Here again there is a broad consensus among early childhood scholars that preschool teaching should be based on *developmentally appropriate educational practice* (NAEYC, 2010). At the preschool age, this means that learning should involve exploring and discovering through relatively unstructured, hands-on experiences—learning about the physical world through playing in a water or sand area, for example, or learning new words through songs and nursery rhymes.

One of the preschool programs best known for high quality and developmentally appropriate practice is the Montessori program. Research by developmental psychologist Angeline Lillard (2008; Lillard & Else-Quest, 2006) has demonstrated the effectiveness of the Montessori approach. Lillard compared two groups of 3- to 6-year-old children. One group of children had attended a Montessori preschool, and the other

Japanese preschools emphasize group play and cooperation.

group attended other types of preschools. All the children in the non-Montessori group had originally applied to Montessori schools but were not able to enter due to space limitations, with admission determined by a random lottery. This was a crucial aspect of the study design; do you see why? If the researchers had simply compared children in Montessori schools with children in non-Montessori schools, any differences would have been difficult to interpret, because there may have been many other differences between the families of children in the two types of schools (e.g., children in Montessori schools may have more-educated parents). Because the families of children in the non-Montessori schools had also applied to get their children into the Montessori schools, and selection among them was random via a lottery, it can be assumed that the family backgrounds of the children in the two groups were similar.

The children who attended Montessori preschools were more advanced in both cognitive and social development than the children who attended the other preschools. Cognitively, the Montessori children scored higher on tests of reading and math skills than the other children. Socially, in playground observations the Montessori children engaged more in cooperative play and less in rough, chaotic play such as wrestling. In sum, the Montessori approach appears to provide children with a setting that encourages self-initiated, active learning and thereby enhances cognitive and social development.

Although attending preschool has become a typical experience among children in developed countries, there is great variation in how countries structure preschool and what they wish young children to learn. In most countries, parents hope for social benefits from preschool, but there is variation among countries in expectations of cognitive and academic benefits. In some countries, such as China and the United States, learning basic academic skills is one of the primary goals of having children attend preschool (Johnson et al., 2003; Tobin et al., 2009). In other countries, such as Japan and most European countries, learning academic skills is a low priority in preschool (Hayashi et al., 2009). Rather, preschool is mainly a time for learning social skills such as how to function as a member of a group.

Japan is of particular interest in this area, because Japanese students have long been at or near the top of international comparisons in reading, math, and science from middle childhood through high school (NCES, 2014). You might expect, then, that one reason for this success is that they begin academic instruction earlier than in other countries, but just the opposite turns out to be true. In one study of Japanese and American parents and preschool teachers, only 2% of the Japanese listed "to give children a good start academically" as one of the top three reasons for young children to attend preschool (Tobin et al., 2009). In contrast, over half the Americans named this as one of the top three reasons. There was a similarly sharp contrast in response to the item "to give children the experience of being a member of the group." Sixty percent of Japanese endorsed this reason for preschool, compared to just 20% of the Americans.

Preschools in Japan teach nothing about reading and numbers. Instead, the focus is on group play, so that children will learn the values of cooperation and sharing. Preschool children wear identical uniforms, with different colors to indicate their classroom membership. They each have the same equipment, which they keep in identical drawers. Through being introduced to these cultural practices in preschool, children also learn collectivistic Japanese values.

Preschool as a Cognitive Intervention

LO 6.10 Describe early intervention programs and their outcomes.

One type of preschool experience that focuses intensively on cognitive development is the **early intervention program**. These are programs directed at young children who are at risk for later school problems because they come from low-income families. The goal of early intervention programs is to give these children extra cognitive stimulation in early childhood so that they will have a better opportunity to succeed once they enter school.

By far the largest early intervention program in the United States is Project Head Start. The program began in 1965 and is still going strong, with about 1 million American children enrolled each year (Head Start Bureau, 2010). The program provides 1 or 2 years of preschool, but it also includes other services. Children in the program receive free meals and health care. Parents receive health care as well as job-training services. Parents are also directly involved in the Head Start program, serving on councils that make policies for the centers and sometimes serving as teachers in the classroom. Canada has a similar program focusing on First Nations minority children who are often at risk for later school problems.

Do these programs work? The answer is not simple. The main goal of Head Start originally was to raise the intelligence of children from low-income backgrounds so that their academic performance would be enhanced once they entered school. Children in Head Start show a boost in IQ and academic achievement after their participation in the program, compared to children from similar backgrounds who did not take part, so in this respect, yes, the program worked. However, a consistent pattern in Head Start and many other early intervention programs is that the IQ and achievement gains fade within 2 or 3 years of entering elementary school (Barnett & Hustedt, 2005). This is not surprising in view of the fact that children in the program typically enter poorly funded, low-quality public schools after their Head Start experience, but nevertheless the fading of the initial gains was unexpected and fell short of the original goals of the program.

However, there have been some favorable results from the Head Start program, too (Brooks-Gunn, 2003; Resnick, 2010). Children who have participated in Head Start are less likely to be placed in special education or to repeat a grade. It should be kept in mind that Head Start is a program with a million children in tens of thousands of programs, and inevitably the programs vary in quality (Resnick, 2010; Zigler & Styfco, 2004). The more the mother is involved in the program, the more her child demonstrates benefits in terms of academic and social skills (Marcon, 1999).

Head Start was designed to serve children ages 4–6 and give them a "head start" in school readiness, but in the 1990s a new program, Early Head Start (ESH), was initiated for low-income families and their children from infancy up to age 3 (Raikes et al., 2010). The goal of this program was to see if greater effects on cognitive and social development could be obtained by beginning the intervention at an earlier age. Research has shown that by age 5 the ESH children exhibited better attention and fewer behavioral problems than children from similar families who were in a control group (Love et al., 2013). EHS moms benefitted, too, in their mental health and likelihood of employment. However, for children, being in EHS did not affect their early school achievement unless it was followed by preschool programs at age 3–4.

Some small-scale, intensive early intervention programs have shown a broader range of enduring effects. One of the best known is the High Scope Preschool Project, a full-day, 2-year preschool program for children from low-income families (Schweinhart et al., 2004). The High Scope children showed the familiar pattern of an initial gain in IQ and academic achievement followed by a decline, but they demonstrated many other benefits of the program, compared to a control group. In adolescence, the girls

early intervention program
program directed at young children who are at risk for later problems, intended to prevent problems from developing

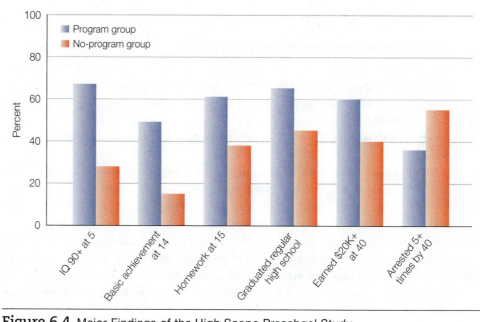

Figure 6.4 Major Findings of the High Scope Preschool Study

High Scope participants showed better academic performance, IQ scores, and earning potential and were less likely to be arrested later in life than other children.
SOURCE: Based on Schweinhart et al., 2005.

were less likely to become pregnant and the boys were less likely to be arrested, and both boys and girls were more likely to graduate from high school and attend college (see **Figure 6.4**). At age 27, the High Scope participants were more likely to be married and to own their home, less likely to have spent time in prison, and their monthly income was higher. At age 40, High Scope participants still displayed benefits of the program in a wide range of areas, including income and family stability. This program shows that an intensive, high-quality early intervention program can have profound and lasting benefits.

Practice Quiz   ANSWERS AVAILABLE IN ANSWER KEY.

1. As a parent of a three-year-old, you have visited several preschool programs to determine the one that will provide the highest quality experience. Which of the following should **NOT** be heavily weighted in your decision about which preschool to pick?

   a. Whether the teachers have been formally trained and have educational credentials

   b. Whether they make good use of time by providing worksheets and flashcards to practice numbers and letters

   c. Whether the teachers spend a lot of time interacting with the children, rather than with each other

   d. Whether there is a small class size

2. For the Japanese _____.

   a. preschool is mainly a time for learning social skills and gaining experience being a member of a group

   b. learning academic skills is the number one goal of having their children attend preschool

   c. the same top reasons for young children to attend preschool are listed by parents and preschool teachers as their counterparts in the United States

   d. individuality is stressed from the time children enter preschool as a way to encourage children to reach their full potential

3. There is a broad consensus among early childhood scholars that preschool teaching should be based on _____.

   a. repetition and rote learning to ensure the mastery of core concepts

   b. building skills for science, technology, engineering, and math (STEM)

   c. whole language learning

   d. unstructured, hands-on experiences

4. Compared to low-income children who did not participate in High Scope Preschool Project, children who did
_____.

    a. were more likely to be married and own their own home by
age 27

    b. had lower incomes at age 27, but were more likely to enjoy
their work

    c. were just as likely to drop out of high school because of the
need to help support their families

    d. were just as likely to be arrested and go to prison, but to
have shorter prison sentences

5. Compared to a comparison group of children with low socioeconomic status who did not attend Head Start, those children
who did _____.

    a. showed a boost in IQ and achievement from elementary
school until the end of high school

    b. had higher grades, but lower self-esteem because of the
pressure to achieve

    c. were less likely to be placed in special education classes

    d. improved their academic performance, but were still more
likely to repeat at least one grade

COGNITIVE DEVELOPMENT:
Language Development

As we saw in Chapter 5, by age 3 children are remarkably adept at using language. Nevertheless, their language development from age 3 to 6 continues at a remarkable pace, in areas including vocabulary, grammar, and pragmatics.

Advances in Vocabulary and Grammar

**LO 6.11 Explain how advances in vocabulary and grammar occur
in early childhood.**

Perhaps the most amazing advance in early childhood language is the growth in children's vocabulary. The average 3-year-old has a vocabulary of about 1,000 words; by age 6, the average vocabulary has increased to over 2,500 words (Bloom, 1998). This means they are adding words nearly every day (Clark, 1995).

How do they do it? Clearly children's brains are built for learning language, as noted in the previous chapter, and early childhood is a **sensitive period** for language development, when the capacity for learning new words is especially pronounced (Pinker, 1994). As we learned in Chapter 5, young children add new words to their vocabulary through a process known as *fast mapping* (Ganger & Brent, 2004; Swingley, 2010). This means that as young children learn new words they begin to form a mental map of interconnected sets of word categories. When they hear a word the first time they instantly connect it to one of these categories based on how the word is used in a sentence and how it seems to be related to words they already know, to help discern its meaning.

The kinds of words children fast-map earliest depend partly on the language. Children learning Eastern languages such as Chinese, Japanese, and Korean tend to learn more verbs than nouns at first, because sentences often emphasize verbs but only imply the nouns without speaking them (Kim et al., 2000). In contrast, children learning English and other Western languages fast-map nouns earlier than verbs, because nouns are prominent in these languages. In both Eastern and Western languages, modifiers (such as large, narrow, pretty, low) are added more slowly than nouns and verbs (Mintz, 2005).

As young children add new words to their vocabulary, they also continue to learn **grammar**, which is a language's distinctive system of rules. Some examples of rules include single/plural forms; past, present, and future tense; word order; and use of

sensitive period
in the course of development, a period when the capacity for learning in a specific area is especially pronounced

grammar
a language's distinctive system of rules

This is a fup.

Now there is another one.
There are two of them.
There are two _____ .

Figure 6.5 Berko's
Language Study

This scenario is similar to the one posed to children in Berko's study. How do the results of Berko's study show young children's grasp of grammar?
SOURCE: Adapted from Berko, 1958.

pragmatics
social and cultural context of language that guides people as to what is appropriate to say and not to say in a given social situation

How might the language used in this kind of play demonstrate a grasp of pragmatics?

articles (such as "a" and "the") and prepositions (such as "under" and "by"). Without any formal training, young children grasp the grammatical rules of their language with few errors simply by hearing and using the language in daily interactions. By age 4, it is estimated that children use correct grammar in 90% of their statements (Guasti, 2000; Pinker, 1994).

But how do we know they have really learned the rules of their language? Couldn't they simply be repeating what they hear older children and adults say? In a classic study investigating this question, Jean Berko (1958) had young children respond to questions involving nonsense words such as "wug" (see **Figure 6.5** for a similar example). Although they had never heard the words before—Berko had made them up—the children were able to apply the grammar of English and use nouns in plural and possessive forms. As noted in Chapter 5, the readiness with which children learn grammar indicates that they possess what Chomsky (1969) called a language acquisition device, which is an innate capacity for quickly grasping a language's rules.

Pragmatics: Social and Cultural Rules of Language

LO 6.12 **Describe how children learn pragmatics in early childhood, and identify to what extent these social rules are culturally based.**

In order to use language effectively, children must learn not only vocabulary and grammar but the social rules or **pragmatics** for using language in interaction with others. Pragmatics guide us in knowing what to say—and what not to say—in a given social situation. For example, children learn to say "please" when asking for something and "thank you" when they receive something.

Children begin learning pragmatics even before they begin speaking, through gestures, for example when they wave "bye-bye" to someone when leaving. By the age of 2, they know the pragmatics of a basic conversation, including taking turns speaking (Pan & Snow, 1999). However, at this age they have not yet grasped the pragmatics of sustaining a conversation on one topic, and they tend to change topics rapidly as new things occur to them, without much awareness of the other person's perspective.

By age 4, children are more sensitive to the characteristics of their conversational partner and will adjust their speech accordingly. In one study using hand puppets, 4-year-olds used different kinds of speech when acting out different puppet roles (Anderson, 2000). When playing a socially dominant role such as teacher or doctor they used commands frequently, whereas when playing subordinate roles such as student or patient they spoke more politely.

The use of pragmatics represents not only social understanding but cultural knowledge. All cultures have their own rules for what kinds of speech can be used in what kinds of situations. For example, some cultures require children to address adults with respectful titles, such as "Mr." for adult men. Many cultures have words that are classified as "bad words" that are not supposed to be spoken, especially by children.

These are the kinds of pragmatics children learn in the course of early childhood, but while they are learning them there can be some embarrassing (and hilarious) moments for parents along the way. One day, when she was about 3 years old, my daughter Paris and I were going through the check-out line in the grocery store, and she said to the clerk, apropos of nothing, "When I grow to a mommy, I'm going to have a baby in my tummy!" On another occasion, my son Miles was talking about how he planned to live to be 100 years old and asked me if I would still be around by then. "Probably not," I said. "You're only 4 years old, and I'm 46." "Ooohhh," he said with genuine concern in his voice, "then you don't have many years left!" Adults understand intuitively that young children lack a sense of pragmatics, so they tend to find such moments amusing rather than offensive. By middle childhood, most children learn when it is culturally appropriate to speak and when it is best to keep your thoughts to yourself.

CRITICAL THINKING QUESTION

Can you think of examples of how pragmatics have changed in your culture, compared to a century ago?

Practice Quiz   ANSWERS AVAILABLE IN ANSWER KEY.

1. While learning language, children who learn English and other Western languages have been shown to fast-map _____ first.
  a. verbs
  b. nouns
  c. adjectives
  d. possessives

2. Which of the following is TRUE?
  a. Children learning English fast-map nouns earlier than verbs.
  b. Japanese and Korean children tend to learn nouns before verbs.
  c. In both Eastern and Western languages, modifiers are added before nouns and verbs.
  d. Vocabulary growth slows down in toddlerhood and then speeds up again by around age 5.

3. In Berko's (1958) classic experiment, she showed young children a picture of a figure called a "wug" and then showed them two of these figures. She then asked them to respond to the following question: "Now there are two _____." Berko was measuring children's understanding of what?
  a. overextension
  b. possessives
  c. pragmatics
  d. grammar

4. Four-year-old Nicco uses infant-directed speech when talking to his neighbor's new baby; this demonstrates _____.
  a. overregularization
  b. fast mapping
  c. pragmatics
  d. existence of the language acquisition device

Summary: Cognitive Development

LO 6.6   Explain the features of Piaget's preoperational stage of cognitive development.

Piaget viewed the preoperational stage of cognitive development (ages 2–7) as prone to a variety of errors, including centration, lack of reversibility, egocentrism, and animism. In this stage they make mistakes in tasks of conservation and classification. Research has shown that Piaget underestimated the cognitive abilities of early childhood.

LO 6.7   Explain what "theory of mind" is and the evidence for how it develops during early childhood.

Theory of mind is the ability to understand thinking processes in one's self and others. By age 2, as they begin to use language more, children show increasing recognition that others have thoughts and emotions that can be contrasted with their own. By age 3, children know it is possible for them and others to imagine something that is not physically present, an understanding that becomes the basis of pretend play for many years to come. While 3-year-olds are better than 2-year-olds at understanding that others have thoughts and feelings that are different from their own, they still find it difficult to take others' perspectives. Perspective-taking ability advances considerably from age 3 to 6, as demonstrated by performance on false-belief tasks.

LO 6.8   Identify the ways that cultural learning takes place in early childhood.

A great deal of cultural learning takes place in early childhood through observing and working alongside parents or siblings, and in many cultures children begin to make important work contributions to the family during this stage. In developed countries, children also gain cultural learning in the preschool setting.

LO 6.9 Identify the features that are most important in preschool quality and explain how they reflect cultural values.

Children generally benefit cognitively from attending preschool, but the social effects of preschool are more mixed and in some ways negative. Key dimensions of high-quality preschool programs include education and training of teachers, class size and child–teacher ratio, age-appropriate materials and activities, and quality of teacher–child interactions.

American and Chinese preschools often include academic preparation, but preschools in Japan focus more on group play, so that collectivistic Japanese values, such as cooperation and sharing, are reinforced.

LO 6.10 Describe early intervention programs and their outcomes.

Early intervention programs have often resulted in a rise in IQ that fades after a few years. Some early interventions via preschool have had long-term positive effects on children's development, but the effects depend greatly on the quality of the program.

LO 6.11 Explain how advances in vocabulary and grammar occur in early childhood.

Children's vocabularies expand immensely in early childhood, from about 1,000 words at age 3 to about 2,500 words at age 6, and they readily grasp the grammatical rules of their culture with few errors by age 4.

LO 6.12 Describe how children learn pragmatics in early childhood, and identify to what extent these social rules are culturally based.

Pragmatics guide us in knowing what to say—and what not to say—in a given social situation, and by age 4, children are sensitive to the characteristics of their conversational partner and will adjust their speech accordingly. All cultures have their own rules for what kinds of speech can be used in what kinds of situations.

Section 3 Emotional and Social Development

 Learning Objectives

6.13 Identify advances in emotional understanding and self-regulation during early childhood.

6.14 Describe moral development in early childhood, including empathy, modeling, and morality as cultural learning.

6.15 Describe the roles that parents and peers play in gender socialization, and explain how gender schemas lead to self-socialization.

6.16 Describe the four types of parenting "styles" and identify the cultural limitations of this model.

6.17 Describe the main cultural variations in how parents discipline young children, and explain how cultural context influences children's responses to discipline.

6.18 Explain the meanings of Mead's social stages from infancy through early childhood.

6.19 Identify the most common features of sibling relationships worldwide, and describe how children with no siblings differ from other children.

6.20 Explain how the quality of friendships changes from toddlerhood to early childhood, and describe the role of play and aggression in young children's friendships.

6.21 Identify the rates and consequences of media use in early childhood.

EMOTIONAL AND SOCIAL DEVELOPMENT: Emotional Regulation and Gender Socialization

After the emotional volatility and intensity of the toddler years, children make great advances in emotional self-regulation in early childhood. Also notable in their emotional development during this time is increasing empathy and a greater grasp of the moral system of their culture, learned in part by modeling their behavior after the behavior of others who are important in their lives. With regard to gender development, early childhood is a life stage of great importance, with children gaining a fuller understanding of the gender roles and expectations of their culture and beginning to enforce those gender roles on others as well on themselves.

Emotional Regulation

LO 6.13 Identify advances in emotional understanding and self-regulation during early childhood.

Early childhood is a time of great advances in emotional development, specifically in emotional understanding and self-regulation. With respect to emotional understanding, in the course of early childhood children become adept at understanding the sources of other people's expressed emotions (Eisenberg & Fabes, 2006). In studies that show children cards depicting expressed emotions, by age 5 children are usually accurate in explaining the emotions of the situation (e.g., "She's happy because she got a present," or "He's sad because his mom scolded him"). They are also adept at understanding how emotional states are the basis of subsequent actions; for example, an angry child is more likely to hit someone (Kagan & Hershkowitz, 2005).

Young children become more adept not only at understanding others' emotions but at controlling their own. In fact, **emotional self-regulation** is considered to be one of the major developmental tasks of early childhood (Grolnick et al., 2006). Developing emotional self-regulation is crucial to social relations, because maintaining harmonious social relations often requires us to restrain our immediate impulses—to wait in line, to let others go first in a game or a conversation, or to take fewer pieces of candy than we really want. Across cultures, early childhood is a time when expectations for emotional self-regulation increase (Whiting & Edwards, 1988). From age 2 to 6, extremes of emotional expression such as temper tantrums, crying, and physical aggression decrease (Alink et al., 2006; Carlson, 2003). In the brain, the development of the frontal cortex promotes this process, because this is the part of the brain most involved in emotional self-regulation (Bell & Wolfe, 2007).

Another key reason why emotional outbursts decline during early childhood is that children learn strategies for regulating their emotions (Grolnick et al., 2006). Experimental studies have identified the strategies that young children use when presented with an emotionally challenging situation, such as being given a disappointing prize after being led to expect a very attractive prize (Eisenberg & Fabes, 2007). Some of the most effective strategies are leaving the situation; talking to themselves; redirecting their attention to a different activity; and seeking comfort from an attachment figure. These strategies are part of what researchers call *effortful control,* when children focus their attention on managing their emotions (Cipriano & Stifter, 2010). Parents can help young children develop effortful control, by providing emotional and physical comfort when their children are upset, by suggesting possible strategies for managing emotions, and by modeling effortful control themselves (Katz & Windecker-Nelson, 2004).

Children vary in their success at achieving emotional self-regulation in early childhood, depending both on their temperament and on the socialization provided by parents and others. Children who have problems of **undercontrol** in early childhood have inadequately developed emotional self-regulation. These children are at risk for **externalizing problems**, such as aggression and conflict with others, in early childhood and beyond (Cole et al., 2003). However, developing **overcontrol**, an excessive degree of self-regulation of emotions, is also problematic. This can lead to **internalizing problems**, such as anxiety and depression, in early childhood and beyond (Grolnick et al., 2006). Throughout life, internalizing problems are more common among females and externalizing problems are more common among males (Frick & Kimonis, 2008; Ollendick et al., 2008).

Successful emotional regulation means developing a level of effortful control that is between the two extremes. As Erikson (1950) noted in proposing that early childhood is the stage of **initiative vs. guilt**, children need to learn emotional control but without

Extreme expressions of emotion decrease in the course of early childhood, as effortful control develops.

emotional self-regulation
ability to exercise control over one's emotions

undercontrol
trait of having inadequate emotional self-regulation

externalizing problems
problems that involve others, such as aggression

overcontrol
trait of having excessive emotional self-regulation

internalizing problems
problems that entail turning distress inward, toward the self, such as depression and anxiety

being so tightly regulated that they feel excess guilt and their ability to initiate activities is undermined. But different cultures have different views of what the optimal level of emotional control is (Chen et al., 2007). Behavior that looks like undercontrol in one culture could be valued as a healthy expression of assertiveness in another culture, at least for boys (Levine & New, 2008). Behavior that looks like overcontrol in one culture could be valued as the virtue of reticence in another culture (Chen et al., 2011; Rogoff, 2003).

Moral Development

LO 6.14 **Describe moral development in early childhood, including empathy, modeling, and morality as cultural learning.**

As described in Chapter 5, toddlerhood is when the sociomoral emotions first appear, such as guilt, shame, embarrassment, and pride. Even in toddlerhood, the sociomoral emotions are shaped by cultural standards. Toddlers feel guilt, shame, or embarrassment when they violate the expected standards for behavior in their social environment, and pride when they comply.

One sociomoral emotion that is especially important to moral development in early childhood is empathy. As we have seen, toddlers and even infants show indications of empathy, but the capacity for empathy develops further in early childhood (Eisenberg & Valiente, 2004). Children become better at perspective-taking, and being able to understand how others think and feel makes them more empathic. Empathy promotes prosocial behavior such as being generous or helpful. It contributes to the moral understanding of principles such as avoiding harm and being fair, because through empathy children understand how their behavior would make another person feel. As empathy increases, prosocial behavior increases over the course of early childhood (Eisenberg et al., 2006).

In early childhood, moral development advances further as children gain a more detailed and complex understanding of the rules and expectations of their culture (Jensen, 2015). Toddlers know when others approve or disapprove of something they have done, and they usually respond with the appropriate sociomoral emotion. However, in early childhood there is greater awareness of the rule or expectation that evoked the approval or disapproval. Also, young children are more capable than toddlers of anticipating the potential consequences of their actions and avoiding behaviors that would be morally disapproved (Grolnick et al., 2006).

Young children do not inherently know the rules and expectations of their culture and must learn them, sometimes by unknowingly violating them and then observing the consequences in the responses of their parents and others. For example, one day when our twins were about 4 years old, they got into the laundry room in the basement and took cups of liquid detergent and spread it all over the basement furniture—sofa, table, loveseat, CD player—all of which were ruined! I don't think they had any intention or awareness of doing something wrong, although after we found out what they had done they knew from our response they should never do it again. And they never did.

A good example of cultural learning of morality can be found in the research of Richard Shweder, who has compared children, adolescents, and adults in India and the United States (2009; Shweder et al., 1990). Shweder has found that by about age 5, children already grasp the moral standards of their culture, and their views change little from childhood to adolescence to adulthood.

Shweder found that there are some similarities in moral views in early childhood in India and the United States, but also many differences. At age 5, children in both countries have learned that it is wrong to take others' property ("steal flowers from a neighbor's garden") or to inflict harm intentionally ("kick a dog sleeping on the side of the road"). However, young children also view many issues with a different moral perspective depending on whether they live in India or the United States. Young children in the United States view it as acceptable to eat beef, but young children in India view it as wrong. Young children in India view it as acceptable for more of a father's inheritance

initiative vs. guilt

in Erikson's lifespan theory, the early childhood stage in which the alternatives are learning to plan activities in a purposeful way, or being afflicted with excess guilt that undermines initiative

Moral lessons are often communicated through stories. Here, a village elder tells children stories in Tanzania.

to go to his son than to his daughter, but young children in the United States view it as wrong. Young children in both cultures have the ability to understand their culture's moral rules, even though the moral rules they have learned by early childhood are quite different.

How do children learn moral rules so early in life? There are several ways. Sometimes moral rules are taught explicitly. The Ten Commandments of the Jewish and Christian religions are a good example of this. Sometimes morality is taught through stories. Barbara Rogoff (2003) gives examples of storytelling as moral instruction in a variety of cultures, including Canadian First Nations people, Native Americans, and the Xhosa people of South Africa. Among the Xhosa (pronounced ZO-sa), it is usually the elders who tell the stories, but the stories have been told many times before, and even young children soon learn the stories and participate in the narrative.

CRITICAL THINKING QUESTION

Describe a childhood story or fairy tale told in your culture that communicates a moral lesson.

Young children also learn morality through custom complexes (see Chapter 4). Remember, the essence of the custom complex is that every customary practice of a culture contains not just the customary practice itself but the underlying cultural beliefs, often including moral beliefs. Shweder (Shweder et al., 1990) gives an example of this kind of moral learning in India. Like people in many cultures, Indians believe that a woman's menstrual blood has potentially dangerous powers. Consequently, a menstruating woman is not supposed to cook food or sleep in the same bed as her husband. By the end of early childhood, Indian children have learned not just that a menstruating woman does not cook food or sleep with her husband (the cultural practice) but that it would be *wrong* for her to do so (the moral belief).

A variation on the custom complex can be found in American research on *modeling*. Research extending over more than 30 years has shown that young children tend to model their behavior after the behavior of others they observe (Bandura, 1977; Bussey & Bandura, 2004). Most of this research has been experimental, involving situations where children observe other children or adults behaving aggressively or kindly, selfishly or generously; then children's own behavior in a similar experimental situation is observed. Children are especially likely to model their behavior after another person if the other person's behavior is rewarded. Also, they are more likely to model their behavior after adults who are warm and responsive or who are viewed as having authority or prestige. According to modeling theory, after observing multiple occasions of others' behavior being rewarded or punished, children conclude that the rewarded behavior is morally desirable and the punished behavior is forbidden (Bandura, 2002). So, by observing behavior (and its consequences), they learn their culture's principles of moral conduct. As in the custom complex, culturally-patterned behavior implies underlying moral beliefs.

In addition to grasping early their culture's moral principles, young children begin to display the rudiments of moral reasoning. By the age of 3 or 4, children are capable of making moral judgments that involve considerations of justice and fairness (Helwig, 2008). By age 4 they understand the difference between telling the truth and lying, and they believe it is wrong to tell lies even when the liar is not caught (Bussey, 1992). However, their moral reasoning tends to be rigid at this age. They are more likely than older children to state that stealing and lying are always wrong, without regard to the circumstances (Lourenco, 2003). Also, their moral judgments tend to be based more on fear of punishment than is the case for older children and adults (Gibbs, 2003). Their moral reasoning will become more complex with age, as we will see in later chapters.

Teaching moral rules is a large part of parenting young children. Sometimes the hardest part is keeping a straight face. My wife and I bought a nice leather chair for our living room when our twins turned 4 years old, thinking that by now they were old enough to know they should be gentle with a nice piece of furniture. Wrong! Within 2 weeks they had put several large scratches in it. When confronted, they confessed at first, but then retracted their confession and looked for an alibi. "We didn't do it, Daddy," claimed Paris, lawyer for the defense. "Well, then who did?" I demanded. She cast her eyes down, as if it were painful for her to reveal the true offender. "Santa Claus," she confessed.

Gender Development

LO 6.15 **Describe the roles that parents and peers play in gender socialization, and explain how gender schemas lead to self-socialization.**

In all cultures, gender is a fundamental organizing principle of social life. All cultures distinguish different roles and expectations for males and females, although the strictness of those roles and expectations varies widely. Of course, many other animals, including all our mammal relatives and certainly our primate cousins, have male–female differences in their typical patterns of behavior and development. What makes humans distinctive is that, unlike other animals, we require culture to tell us how males and females are supposed to behave.

GENDER IDENTITY AND GENDER SOCIALIZATION Early childhood is an especially important period with respect to gender development. Recall from Chapter 5 that even earlier, at age 2, children attain *gender identity*, that is, they understand themselves as being either male or female (Ruble et al., 2006). However, in early childhood, gender issues intensify, as shown in the video *Gender Socialization*. By age 3–4, children associate a variety of things with either males or females, including toys, games, clothes, household items, occupations, and even colors (Kapadia & Gala, 2015).

Watch GENDER SOCIALIZATION

Furthermore, they are often adamant and rigid in their perceptions of maleness and femaleness, denying, for example, that it would be possible for a boy to wear a ponytail and still remain a boy, or for a girl to play roughly and still remain a girl (Blakemore,

2003)! One reason for their insistence on strict gender roles at this age may be cognitive. It is not until age 6 or 7 that children attain **gender constancy**, the understanding that maleness and femaleness are biological and cannot change (Ruble et al., 2006). Earlier, children may be so insistent about maintaining **gender roles** because they believe that changing external features like clothes or hair styles could result in a change in gender.

The similarity of children's gender roles and gender behavior across cultures is striking, and there is a biological basis to some gender differences, as we saw in Chapter 5. However, children in all cultures are also subject to gender socialization.

GENDER SOCIALIZATION As we learned in Chapter 5, parents play an active role in delivering cultural gender messages to their children (Liben et al., 2013; Ruble et al., 2006). They may give their children distinctively male or female names, dress them in gender-specific colors and styles, and provide them with cars or dolls to play with (Bandura & Bussey, 2004).

Parents' important role in gender socialization continues in early childhood. They continue to give their children the clothes and toys they believe are gender appropriate. They express approval when their children behave in gender-appropriate ways, and disapproval when their children violate gender expectations (Kapadia & Gala, 2015). In conversations, parents sometimes communicate gender expectations directly (e.g., "Don't cry, you're not a little girl, are you?"). They also communicate indirectly, by approving or not contradicting their children's gender statements. ("Only boys can be doctors, Mommy.") Parents also provide models, through their own behavior, language, and appearance, of how males and females are supposed to be different in their culture (Bandura & Bussey, 2004).

Fathers become especially important to gender socialization in early childhood and beyond. They tend to be more insistent about conformity to gender roles than mothers are, especially for boys (Lamb, 2010). They may not want their daughters to play rough-and-tumble games, but they are adamant that their boys not be "wimps." As we will see in later chapters, males' greater fear of violations of gender roles is something that continues throughout life in many cultures.

Peers also become a major source of gender socialization in early childhood. Once children learn gender roles and expectations, they apply them not only to themselves but to each other. They reinforce each other for gender-appropriate behavior, and reject peers who violate gender roles (Matlin, 2004; Ruble et al., 2006). Here, too, the expectations are stricter for boys than for girls (Liben et al., 2013). Boys who cry easily or who like to play with girls and engage in girls' games are likely to be ostracized by other boys (David et al., 2004).

GENDER SCHEMAS AND SELF-SOCIALIZATION As a result of gender socialization, from early childhood onward children use **gender schemas** as a way of understanding and interpreting the world around them. Recall from Chapter 4 that *scheme* is Piaget's term for a cognitive structure for organizing and processing information. (*Scheme* and *schema* are used interchangeably in psychology.) A gender schema is a gender-based cognitive structure for organizing and processing information (Martin & Ruble, 2004).

According to gender-schema theory, gender is one of our most important schemas from early childhood onward. By the time we reach the end of early childhood, on the basis of our socialization we have learned to categorize a wide range of activities, objects, and personality characteristics as "female" or "male." This includes not just the obvious—vaginas are female, penises are male—but many things that have no inherent "femaleness" or "maleness" but are nevertheless taught as possessing gender. Examples include the moon as "female" and the sun as "male" in traditional Chinese culture, or blue as a "boy color" and pink as a "girl color" (in Korea, pink is a "boy color," which illustrates how cultural these designations are).

gender constancy
understanding that maleness and femaleness are biological and cannot change

gender roles
cultural expectations for appearance and behavior specific to males or females

gender schema
gender-based cognitive structure for organizing and processing information, comprising expectations for males' and females' appearance and behavior

Fathers tend to promote conformity to gender roles more than mothers do.

Gender schemas influence how we interpret the behavior of others and what we expect from them (Frawley, 2008). This well-known story provides an example: "A little boy and his father were in a terrible automobile accident. The father died, but the boy was rushed to the hospital. As the boy was rushed into surgery, the doctor looked down at him and said, 'I cannot operate on this boy—he is my son!'"

How could the boy be the doctor's son, if the father died in the accident? The answer, of course, is that the doctor is the boy's *mother*. But people reading this story are often puzzled by it because their gender schemas have led them to assume the doctor was male. (This story is less effective than it used to be, because so many women are physicians today! Try it on someone.)

In early childhood, children tend to believe that their own preferences are true for everyone in their gender (Liben et al., 2013). For example, a boy who dislikes peas may justify it by claiming "boys don't like peas." Young children also tend to remember in ways that reflect their gender schemas. In one study (Liben & Signorella, 1993), children who were shown pictures that violated typical gender roles (e.g., a woman driving a truck) tended to remember them in accordance with their gender schemas (a man, not a woman, driving the truck). Throughout life, we tend to notice information that fits within our gender schemas and ignore or dismiss information that is inconsistent with them (David et al., 2004).

Once young children possess gender schemas, they seek to maintain consistency between their schemas and their behavior, a process called **self-socialization**. Boys become quite insistent about doing things they regard as boy things and avoiding things that girls do; girls become equally intent on avoiding boy things and doing things they regard as appropriate for girls (Bandura & Bussey, 2004; Tobin et al., 2010). In this way, according to a prominent gender scholar, "cultural myths become self-fulfilling prophesies" (Bem, 1981, p. 355). By the end of early childhood, gender roles are enforced not only by socialization from others but by self-socialization, as children strive to conform to the gender expectations they perceive in the culture around them.

Once children learn the gender roles of their culture, they may strive to conform to them. Here, girls in Cambodia attend a dance class.

self-socialization

process by which people seek to maintain consistency between their gender schemas and their behavior

Practice Quiz ANSWERS AVAILABLE IN ANSWER KEY.

1. Which of the following is TRUE regarding emotional regulation?
   a. The development of the temporal lobe promotes self-regulation.
   b. Self-regulation develops earlier in boys than in girls.
   c. Temper tantrums and crying decrease from age 2 to 6.
   d. Different cultures have similar views about what the optimal level of control is.

2. In early childhood _____.
   a. moral judgments tend to be based more on fear of punishment than is the case for older children
   b. children are not yet able to experience empathy
   c. children from different cultures learn the same moral rules
   d. children have more difficulty with perspective taking than they did earlier in development because of their stronger sense of self

3. Gender identity _____.
   a. develops much more quickly in females than males
   b. includes an understanding that maleness and femaleness are biological

   c. refers to the ability of children to identify themselves as male and female
   d. develops around age 5

4. The way we organize and process information in terms of gender-based categories is referred to as _____.
   a. gender stereotyping
   b. gender constancy
   c. gender schemas
   d. self-socialization

5. Chris realized that even though the teacher dressed up like Michael Jackson for Halloween, she is still a female. Based on this information, one would expect that Chris _____.
   a. has not yet attained gender identity, but knows the gender identity of the teacher
   b. uses gender schemas, but does not yet understand gender constancy
   c. is a 4-year-old boy
   d. is a 7-year- old boy

EMOTIONAL AND SOCIAL DEVELOPMENT: Parenting

Parents are a key part of children's lives everywhere, but how parents view their role and their approaches to discipline and punishment vary widely. First, we look at an influential model of parenting "styles" based on American parenting, then at more culturally based views of parenting.

Parenting "Styles"

LO 6.16 Describe the four types of parenting "styles" and identify the cultural limitations of this model.

Have you heard the joke about the man who, before he had any children, had five theories about how they should be raised? Ten years later he had five children and no theories.

Well, jokes aside, most parents do have ideas about how best to raise children, even after they have had children for awhile (Harkness et al., 2015; Tamis-Lamonda et al., 2008). In research, the investigation of this topic has often involved the study of **parenting styles**, that is, the practices that parents exhibit in relation to their children and their beliefs about those practices. This research originated in the United States and has involved mainly American children and their parents, although it has now been applied in some other countries as well.

For over 50 years, American scholars have engaged in research on this topic, and the results have been quite consistent (Bornstein & Bradley, 2014; Collins & Laursen, 2004; Maccoby & Martin, 1983). Virtually all of the prominent scholars who have studied parenting have described it in terms of two dimensions: demandingness and responsiveness (also known by other terms such as *control* and *warmth*). Parental **demandingness** is the degree to which parents set down rules and expectations for behavior and require their children to comply with them. Parental **responsiveness** is the degree to which parents are sensitive to their children's needs and express love, warmth, and concern for them.

Various scholars have combined these two dimensions to describe different kinds of parenting styles. For many years, the best known and most widely used conception of parenting styles was the one articulated by Diana Baumrind (1968, 1971, 1991a, 1991b). Her research on middle-class White American families, along with the research of other scholars inspired by her ideas, has identified four distinct parenting styles (Collins & Laursen, 2004; Maccoby & Martin, 1983; Steinberg, 2000; see **Table 6.1**).

Authoritative parents are high in demandingness and high in responsiveness. They set clear rules and expectations for their children. Furthermore, they make clear what the consequences will be if their children do not comply, and they make those consequences stick if necessary. However, authoritative parents do not simply "lay down the law" and then enforce it rigidly. A distinctive feature of authoritative parents is that they *explain* the reasons for their rules and expectations to their children, and they willingly engage in discussion with their children over issues of discipline, sometimes leading to negotiation and compromise. For example, a child who wants to eat a whole bag of candy would not simply be told "No!" by an authoritative parent but something like, "No, it wouldn't be healthy and it would be bad for your teeth." Authoritative parents are also loving and warm toward their children, and they respond to what their children need and desire.

Authoritarian parents are high in demandingness but low in responsiveness. They require obedience from their children, and they punish

---

parenting styles

practices that parents exhibit in relation to their children and their beliefs about those practices

demandingness

degree to which parents set down rules and expectations for behavior and require their children to comply with them

responsiveness

degree to which parents are sensitive to their children's needs and express love, warmth, and concern for them

authoritative parents

in classifications of parenting styles, parents who are high in demandingness and high in responsiveness

authoritarian parents

in classifications of parenting styles, parents who are high in demandingness but low in responsiveness

---

Table 6.1 Parenting Styles and the Two Dimensions of Parenting

		Demandingness	
		High	Low
Responsiveness	High	Authoritative	Permissive
	Low	Authoritarian	Disengaged

disobedience without compromise. None of the verbal give-and-take common with authoritative parents is allowed by authoritarian parents. They expect their commands to be followed without dispute or dissent. To continue with the candy example, the authoritarian parent would respond to the child's request for a bag of candy simply by saying "No!" with no explanation. Also, authoritarian parents show little in the way of love or warmth toward their children. Their demandingness takes place without responsiveness, in a way that shows little emotional attachment and may even be hostile.

Permissive parents are low in demandingness and high in responsiveness. They have few clear expectations for their children's behavior, and they rarely discipline them. Instead, their emphasis is on responsiveness. They believe that children need love that is truly "unconditional." They may see discipline and control as having the potential to damage their children's healthy tendencies for developing creativity and expressing themselves however they wish. They provide their children with love and warmth and give them a great deal of freedom to do as they please.

Disengaged parents are low in both demandingness and responsiveness. Their goal may be to minimize the amount of time and emotion they devote to parenting. Thus, they require little of their children and rarely bother to correct their behavior or place clear limits on what they are allowed to do. They also express little in the way of love or concern for their children. They may seem to have little emotional attachment to them.

THE EFFECTS OF PARENTING STYLES ON CHILDREN A great deal of research has been conducted on how parenting styles influence children's development. A summary of the results is shown in **Table 6.2**. In general, authoritative parenting is associated with the most favorable outcomes, at least by American standards. Children who have authoritative parents tend to be independent, self-assured, creative, and socially skilled (Baumrind, 1991a, 1991b; Collins & Larsen, 2004; Steinberg, 2000; Williams et al., 2009). They also tend to do well in school and to get along well with their peers and with adults (Hastings et al., 2007; Spera, 2005). Authoritative parenting helps children develop characteristics such as optimism and self-regulation that in turn have positive effects on a wide range of behaviors (Jackson et al., 2005; Purdie et al., 2004).

All the other parenting styles are associated with some negative outcomes, although the type of negative outcome varies depending on the specific parenting style (Baumrind, 1991a, 1991b; Snyder et al., 2005). Children with authoritarian parents tend to be less self-assured, less creative, and less socially adept than other children. Boys with authoritarian parents are more often aggressive and unruly, whereas girls are more often anxious and unhappy (Bornstein & Bradley, 2014; Russell et al., 2003). Children with permissive parents tend to be immature and lack self-control. Because they lack self-control, they have difficulty getting along with peers and teachers (Linver et al., 2002). Children with disengaged parents also tend to be impulsive. Partly as a consequence of their impulsiveness, and partly because disengaged parents do little to monitor their activities, children with disengaged parents tend to have higher rates of behavior problems (Pelaez et al., 2008).

A MORE COMPLEX PICTURE OF PARENTING EFFECTS Although parents undoubtedly affect their children profoundly by their parenting, the process is not nearly

permissive parents
in classifications of parenting styles, parents who are low in demandingness and high in responsiveness

disengaged parents
in classifications of parenting styles, parents who are low in both demandingness and responsiveness

Table 6.2 Outcomes Associated with Parenting Styles in White Middle-Class Families

Authoritative	Authoritarian	Permissive	Disengaged
Independent	Dependent	Irresponsible	Impulsive
Creative	Passive	Conforming	Behavior problems
Self-assured	Conforming	Immature	Early sex, drugs
Socially skilled			

How does the idea of reciprocal effects complicate claims of the effects of parenting styles?

reciprocal or **bidirectional effects**

in relations between two persons, the principle that each of them affects the other

filial piety

belief that children should respect, obey, and revere their parents throughout life; common in Asian cultures

as simple as the cause-and-effect model just described. Sometimes discussions of parenting make it sound as though Parenting Style A automatically and inevitably produces Child Type X. However, enough research has taken place by now to indicate that the relationship between parenting styles and children's development is considerably more complex than that (Bornstein & Bradley, 2014; Lamb & Lewis, 2005; Parke & Buriel, 2006). Not only are children affected by their parents, but parents are affected by their children. This principle is referred to by scholars as **reciprocal or bidirectional effects** between parents and children (Combs-Ronto et al., 2009).

Recall our discussion of evocative genotype → environment effects in Chapter 2. Children are not like billiard balls that head predictably in the direction they are propelled. They have personalities and desires of their own that they bring to the parent–child relationship. Thus, children may evoke certain behaviors from their parents. An especially aggressive child may evoke authoritarian parenting; perhaps the parents find that authoritative explanations of the rules are simply ignored, and their responsiveness diminishes as a result of the child's repeated disobedience and disruptiveness. An especially mild-tempered child may evoke permissive parenting, because parents may see no point in laying down specific rules for a child who has no inclination to do anything wrong anyway.

Does this research discredit the claim that parenting styles influence children? No, but it does modify it. Parents certainly have beliefs about what is best for their children, and they try to express those beliefs through their parenting behavior (Alwin, 1988; Harkness et al., 2015; Way et al., 2007). However, parents' actual behavior is affected not only by what they believe is best but also by how their children behave toward them and respond to their parenting. Being an authoritative parent is easier if your child responds to your demandingness and responsiveness with compliance and love, and not so easy if your love is rejected and your rules and the reasons you provide for them are rejected. Parents whose efforts to persuade their children through reasoning and discussion fall on deaf ears may be tempted either to demand compliance (and become more authoritarian) or to give up trying (and become permissive or disengaged).

PARENTING STYLES IN OTHER CULTURES So far we have looked at the parenting styles research based mainly on White middle-class American families. What does research in other cultures indicate about parenting and its effects in early childhood?

One important observation is how rare the authoritative parenting style is in non-Western cultures (Bornstein & Bradley, 2014; Harkness et al., 2015). Remember, a distinctive feature of authoritative parents is that they do not rely on the authority of the parental role to ensure that children comply with their commands and instructions. They do not simply declare the rules and expect to be obeyed. On the contrary, authoritative parents explain the reasons for what they want children to do and engage in discussion over the guidelines for their children's behavior (Baumrind, 1971, 1991a; Steinberg & Levine, 1997).

Outside of the West, however, this is an extremely rare way of parenting. In traditional cultures, parents expect that their authority will be obeyed, without question and without requiring an explanation (LeVine et al., 2008). This is true not only in nearly all developing countries but also in developed countries outside the West, most notably Asian countries such as Japan and South Korea (Tseng, 2004; Zhang & Fuligni, 2006). Asian cultures have a tradition of **filial piety**, meaning that children are expected to respect, obey, and revere their parents throughout life (Lieber et al., 2004). The role of parent carries greater inherent authority than it does in the West. Parents are not supposed to provide reasons why they should be respected and obeyed. The simple fact that they are parents and their children are children is viewed as sufficient justification for their authority.

In Latin American cultures, too, the authority of parents is viewed as paramount. The Latino cultural belief system places a premium on the idea of *respeto,* which emphasizes respect for and obedience to parents and elders, especially the father (Cabrera & Garcia-Coll, 2004; Halgunseth et al., 2006; Harwood et al. 2002). The role of the parent is considered to be enough to command authority, without requiring that the parents explain their rules to their children. Another pillar of Latino cultural beliefs is **familismo**, which emphasizes the love, closeness, and mutual obligations of Latino family life (Halgunseth et al., 2006; Harwood et al., 2002).

Does this mean that the typical parenting style in non-Western cultures is authoritarian? No, although sometimes scholars have come to this erroneous conclusion. It would be more accurate to state that the parenting-styles model is a cultural model, rooted in the American majority culture, and does not apply well to most other cultures. Of course, children everywhere need to have parents or other caregivers provide care for them in early childhood and beyond, and across cultures parents provide some combination of warmth and control. However, "responsiveness" is a distinctly American kind of warmth, emphasizing praise and physical affection, and "demandingness" is a distinctly American kind of control, emphasizing explanation and negotiation rather than the assertion of parental authority. Other cultures have their own culturally based forms of warmth and control, but across cultures, warmth rarely takes the American form of praise, and control rarely takes the American form of explanation and negotiation (Matsumoto & Yoo, 2006; Miller, 2004; Wang & Tamis-Lamonda, 2003).

Even within American society, the authoritative style is mainly dominant among White, middle-class families (Bornstein & Bradley, 2014). Most American minority cultures, including African Americans, Latinos, and Asian Americans, have been classified by researchers as "authoritarian," but this is inaccurate and results from applying to them a model that was based on the White majority culture (Chao & Tseng, 2002). Each minority culture has its own distinctive form of warmth, but all tend to emphasize obeying parental authority rather than encouraging explanation and negotiation. Hence the American model of parenting styles cannot really be applied to them.

Within cultures, parenting varies depending on the personalities of the parents, their goals for their children, and the characteristics of the children that evoke particular parenting responses. Overall, however, the dominant approach to parenting in a culture reflects certain things about the underlying cultural beliefs, such as the value of interdependence versus independence and the status of parental authority over children (Harkness et al., 2015; Giles-Sims & Lockhart, 2005; Hulei et al., 2006). The cultural context of parenting is so crucial that what looks like the same parental behavior in two different cultures can have two very different effects, as we will see in the next section.

In most cultures, parents expect to be respected and obeyed without justifying their actions. Here, a mother and daughter in Japan.

Discipline and Punishment

LO 6.17 Describe the main cultural variations in how parents discipline young children, and explain how cultural context influences children's responses to discipline.

In many cultures, early childhood is when issues of discipline for disapproved of behavior first arise. As we have seen, it is common for cultures to be indulgent of infants and toddlers, because they are seen to be too young to exercise much judgment or self-control. However, by early childhood children become more capable of emotional and behavioral self-regulation, and when they disobey or defy the authority of others they are believed

familismo

cultural belief among Latinos that emphasizes the love, closeness, and mutual obligations among family members

to have enough understanding to know what they were doing and to be responsible for the consequences. For this reason, early childhood is usually the age when children are first disciplined for not following expectations or not doing what is required of them.

CULTURAL VARIATIONS IN DISCIPLINE All cultures require children to learn and follow cultural rules and expectations, and all cultures have some system of discipline for misbehavior. However, cultures vary widely in the nature of the discipline, and the consequences of discipline vary depending on the cultural beliefs that underlie the approach.

In Western cultures the approach to discipline in early childhood tends to emphasize the authoritative style of explaining the consequences of misbehavior and the reasons for discipline (Huang et al., 2009; Tamis-Lamonda et al., 2008). ("Michael, if you don't stop banging that toy against the floor I'm going to take it away! Okay, now I'm going to take it away until you can learn to play with it nicely.") Western parents also tend to use a lot of praise for compliant and obedient behavior, which is notable because the use of praise is very rare in other cultures (LeVine et al., 2008; Whiting & Edwards, 1988). Discipline for misbehavior may involve taking away privileges or a **time out**, in which the child is required to sit still in a designated place for a brief period, usually only a few minutes (Morawska & Sanders, 2011). Little research has been conducted on the effectiveness of the time out under normal family circumstances, but it has been shown to be effective with young children who have behavioral problems (Everett et al., 2007; Fabiano et al., 2004).

In addition to using time out, parenting researchers recommend (1) explaining the reasons for discipline; (2) being consistent so that the consequences will be predictable to the child (and hence avoidable); and (3) exercising discipline at the time of the misbehavior (not later on) so that the connection will be clear (Klass et al., 2008). One popular approach suggests that if a parent's request to a young child is ignored or disobeyed, the parent counts a warning: "One-two-*three*," and if the request is not obeyed by "three" the child is then put in time out, 1 minute for each year of their age (Phelan, 2010). I can tell you, my wife and I found that this worked like magic with our twins in early childhood; we almost never got to "three."

Other cultures have different approaches to discipline. Japan provides an interesting example of a culture where shame and withdrawal of love is the core of discipline in early childhood. Recall that *amae*, introduced in Chapter 5, is a Japanese word that describes the close attachment between mother and child (Rothbaum et al., 2007). During infancy, *amae* takes the form of an emotionally indulgent and physically close relationship between the Japanese mother and her baby. However, in toddlerhood and early childhood, a new element, shame and withdrawal of love, is added. Japanese mothers rarely respond to their children's misbehavior with loud reprimands or physical punishment. Instead, they express disappointment and withdraw their love temporarily. The child feels shame, which is a powerful inducement not to disobey again.

This system of early childhood socialization seems to work well in Japan. Japanese children have low rates of behavioral problems, and high rates of academic achievement (Takahashi & Takeuchi, 2007). They grow up to be Japanese adults who have low rates of crime and social problems and high levels of economic productivity, making Japan one of the most stable and economically successful societies in the world.

However, the same parental behaviors appear to have a different, more negative effect in Western countries. Among American researchers, parenting that uses shame and withdrawal of love has been described using the term **psychological control** (Barber, 2002). This kind of parenting has been found in American studies to be related to

"Time out" is a popular discipline strategy among middle-class American parents.

time out

disciplinary strategy in which the child is required to sit still in a designated place for a brief period

negative outcomes in early childhood and beyond, including anxious, withdrawn, and aggressive behavior, as well as problems with peers (Barber et al., 2005; Silk et al., 2003). In Finland, too, a longitudinal study that began in early childhood found psychological control to predict negative outcomes in later childhood and adolescence, especially when psychological control was combined with physical affection, as it is in *amae* (Aunola & Nurmi, 2004).

What explains this difference? Why does *amae* appear to work well in Japan but not in the West? It is difficult to say, since this question has not been researched directly. However, the answer may be some kind of interaction between the parents' behavior and the cultural belief system. In Japan, *amae* fits neatly into a larger system of cultural beliefs about duty and obligations to others, especially to family. In the West, psychological control contrasts and perhaps collides with cultural beliefs about the value of thinking and behaving independently. It may be this friction between the parental practices and the cultural beliefs that results in negative outcomes, not the parental practices in themselves.

PHYSICAL PUNISHMENT AND ITS CONSEQUENCES Research on physical punishment (also known as **corporal punishment**) suggests a similar kind of interaction between parenting practices and cultural beliefs. Physical punishment of young children is common in most parts of the world (Curran et al., 2001; Levine & New, 2008). This approach to punishment has a long history. Most adults in most countries around the world remember experiencing physical punishment as children. Although most countries still allow parents to spank their young children, nearly all outlaw beatings and other harsh forms of physical punishment, which the historical record shows to have been quite common until about 100 years ago (Straus, 1994).

Is physical punishment damaging to young children, or is it a form of instruction that teaches them to respect and obey adults? Here, as with *amae*, the answer appears to be very different depending on the cultural context. Many studies in the United States and Europe have been conducted on physical punishment of young children, and these studies have found a correlation between physical punishment and a wide range of antisocial behaviors in children, including telling lies, fighting with peers, and disobeying parents (Alaggia & Vine, 2006; Kazdin & Benjet, 2003). Furthermore, several longitudinal studies have reported that physical punishment in early childhood increases the likelihood of bullying and delinquency in adolescence and aggressive behavior (including spousal abuse) in adulthood (Ferguson, 2013). On the basis of these studies, some scholars have concluded that physical punishment in early childhood increases children's compliance in the short run but damages their moral and mental health in the long run (Amato & Fowler, 2002; Gershoff, 2002).

However, studies that cast a wider cultural net report considerably more complicated findings. In one longitudinal study, White and African American families were studied when the children were in early childhood and then 12 years later, when the children were in adolescence (Lansford et al., 2004). The White children showed the familiar pattern: physical punishment in early childhood predicted aggressive and antisocial behavior in adolescence. However, for African American children, physical punishment in early childhood was related to becoming less aggressive and antisocial in adolescence. Other studies have reported similar findings of the generally beneficial results of early childhood physical punishment among African Americans (Bluestone & Tamis-Lamonda, 1999; Brody & Flor, 1998; Steele et al., 2005). Similarly, studies of traditional cultures have found that many of the parents in these cultures use physical punishment on young children, and the children nevertheless grow up to be well-behaved, productive, mentally healthy adults (Levine et al., 2008; Whiting & Edwards, 1988).

Like the findings regarding *amae*, the findings on physical punishment show the crucial role of cultural context in how young children respond to their parents' behavior. In White American and European cultures, physical punishment is generally

psychological control

parenting strategy that uses shame and withdrawal of love to influence children's behavior

corporal punishment

physical punishment of children

disapproved and not widely or frequently used (Bornstein & Bradley, 2014). In these cultures, physical punishment is likely to be combined with anger (Ferguson, 2013). In contrast, among African Americans, and in traditional cultures, the use of physical punishment in early childhood is widespread (Ispa & Halgunseth, 2004; Simons et al., 2013). Usually, it is mild in degree and is delivered not in an angry rage but calmly and sternly, as part of a "no-nonsense" parenting style (Brody & Flor, 1998). Physical punishment is often combined with parental warmth, so that children understand their parents' behavior not as a frightening and threatening loss of parental control but as a practice intended to teach them right from wrong and the importance of obeying their parents (Gunnoe & Mariner, 1997; Mosby et al., 1999). This cultural context makes the meaning and the consequences of physical punishment much different than it is in White American and European cultures.

CHILD ABUSE AND NEGLECT Although there are wide cultural variations in discipline and punishment of young children, today there is a widespread view across cultures that children should not be physically harmed and that parents have a responsibility to provide for their children's physical and emotional needs (UNICEF, 2011). However, there are all kinds of parents in the world, and in all cultures there are some who fail to meet these basic requirements. **Child maltreatment** includes both the abuse and neglect of children, specifically:

- *Physical abuse,* which entails causing physical harm to a child, through hitting, kicking, biting, burning, or shaking the child;
- *Emotional abuse,* including ridicule and humiliation as well as behavior causing emotional trauma to children, such as locking them in a dark closet;
- *Sexual abuse,* meaning any kind of sexual contact with a minor; and
- *Neglect,* which is failure to meet children's basic needs of food, shelter, clothing, medical attention, and supervision.

Most research on the maltreatment of young children has focused on physical abuse. A variety of risk factors for physical abuse have been identified, involving characteristics of children as well as characteristics of parents. Young children are at risk for physical abuse if they are temperamentally difficult or if they are unusually aggressive or active and hence more difficult for parents to control (Li et al., 2010). Parental risk factors for physical abuse of children include poverty, unemployment, and single motherhood, all of which contribute to stress, which may in turn trigger abuse (Geeraert et al., 2004; Zielinski, 2009). Stepfathers are more likely to be abusive than biological fathers are, and child abuse is correlated with spouse abuse, suggesting that the abuser has a problem with anger management and self-control that is expressed in multiple ways (Asawa et al., 2008). Abusive parents often view their children as somehow deserving the abuse because of disobedience or because they are "no good" and will not respond to anything else (Bugental & Happaney, 2004). Parents who abuse their children were abused by their own parents in about one third of cases (Cicchetti & Toth, 1998).

Physical abuse is destructive to young children in a wide variety of ways. It impairs emotional self-development, including self-regulation, empathy, and self-concept (Haugaard & Hazen, 2004). It is damaging to the development of friendships and social skills, because abused children find it difficult to trust others (Elliott et al., 2005). It also interferes with school performance, as abused children are often low in academic motivation and have behavior problems in the classroom (Boden et al., 2007). Furthermore, children who are abused are at risk for later emotional, social, and academic problems in adolescence and beyond (Fergusson et al., 2008; Herrenkohl et al., 2004).

What can be done to help abused children? In most cultures, there is some kind of system that removes children from their parents' care when the parents are abusive. In traditional cultures, the system tends to be informal. Children with abusive parents may go to live with relatives with whom they have a more positive, less conflictual

child maltreatment

abuse or neglect of children, including physical, emotional, or sexual abuse

relationship (LeVine et al., 2008). In Western countries, it is more often the formal legal system that intervenes in cases of child abuse. A state agency investigates reports of abuse, and if the report is verified the child is removed from the home.

The agency may then place the child in **foster care**, in which adults approved by the agency take over the care of the child (Pew Commission on Foster Care, 2004). In the United States, about one fourth of children in foster care are placed with relatives through the formal system (Child Welfare Information Gateway, 2013). In addition, three times as many children are estimated to live with nonparental relatives without the intervention of an agency, similar to the informal system of traditional cultures. Sometimes children in foster care return home after a period, sometimes they are adopted by their foster family, and sometimes they "age out" of foster care when they turn age 18 (Smith, 2011). Children in foster care are at high risk for academic, social, and behavioral problems, especially if they experience multiple foster-home placements (Crum, 2010; Plant & Siegel, 2008; Vig et al., 2005).

Another alternative is for children to live in a *group home* staffed by the state agency that oversees child abuse and neglect cases (Dunn et al., 2010). I worked in a group home when I was an emerging adult, years ago. I still remember many of the kids vividly, especially one boy who had scars all over his back from where his parents had beaten and burned him. Group homes are usually a temporary alternative until the child can be placed in foster care or with relatives (DeSena et al., 2005).

Programs have also been developed to prevent child maltreatment. In the United States, one notable program is the *Nurse–Family Partnership* (NFP), with sites in 22 states (DHHS, 2005). In this program, expectant mothers who have many of the risk factors for abuse receive regular home visits by a trained nurse for 2 years. The nurse provides information and advice about how to handle crises, how to manage children's behavior without physical punishment, and how to access community agencies that provide services for families (Olds, 2010). In a 15-year follow-up comparing families who participated in the NFP to other families with similar risks, the NFP group showed a 79% reduction in child abuse and neglect (Eckenrode et al., 2001).

foster care

for maltreated children, approach in which adults approved by a state agency take over the care of the child

Practice Quiz   ANSWERS AVAILABLE IN ANSWER KEY.

1. Research on parenting has found that _____.

   a. the two main dimensions of parenting are demandingness and strictness

   b. children of permissive parents tend to do better in school than children of other parenting styles because they learn to think for themselves

   c. there are bidirectional effects between parents and their children

   d. the outcomes for children of authoritative parents are virtually identical to outcomes for children of permissive parents

2. If parents listen receptively to opinions from their children, their parenting style is considered to be _____.

   a. authoritative

   b. authoritarian

   c. child-centered

   d. autocratic

3. The dimension of parenting known as responsiveness is also known as _____.

   a. setting limits

   b. psychological control

   c. warmth

   d. disengaged

4. The use of shame as a punishment _____.

   a. is referred to as psychological control among American researchers

   b. has been related to positive outcomes in both Western and traditional cultures

   c. is associated with high rates of behavior problems in Japanese children

   d. is universally accepted as the best method of discipline because it does not include physical punishment

5. Which of the following is the most accurate statement based on existing research?

   a. Western parents tend to use a lot of praise for compliant behavior.

   b. Not all cultures have some system of discipline for misbehavior; some feel that children are inherently good and do not need discipline.

   c. Permissive parenting would be most likely in cultures that have a tradition of filial piety.

   d. Japanese mothers usually respond to their children's misbehavior with loud reprimands and physical punishment.

EMOTIONAL AND SOCIAL DEVELOPMENT: The Child's Expanding Social World

Across cultures, the social world expands considerably in early childhood. Infants and toddlers need a great deal of care, nurturance, and supervision. And, as we have seen in the previous two chapters, infants and toddlers are usually kept in close proximity to someone who will provide this for them, usually the mother, sometimes in collaboration with a father, grandmother, aunt, or older sibling. However, in early childhood, children move further into the wider world.

Mead's Classifications of Childhood Social Stages

LO 6.18 Explain the meanings of Mead's social stages from infancy through early childhood.

When they reach early childhood, children still need a considerable amount of care, but they no longer need to be constantly watched by others. The anthropologist Margaret Mead (1935) proposed a general scheme many decades ago that still applies well to how most of the world's children experience the social changes of childhood (see **Table 6.3**). Recall from Chapter 5 that Mead designated children ages 0–2 with the term *lap child,* to denote their near-constant dependence on the care and monitoring of others. For early childhood, Mead proposed two terms. At ages 3–4 is the *knee child,* who is still cared for mainly by the mother but also spends time with other children, especially of the same gender. At ages 5–6 is the *yard child,* who is given more scope to venture beyond the immediate family area and into the "yard," that is, into a social world where parents are nearby but not always directly present.

Margaret Mead's scheme was the basis of a classic study of young children across cultures conducted by anthropologists Beatrice Whiting and Carolyn Edwards (1988). Whiting and Edwards studied children ages 2–10 in twelve different places around the world, including Africa, Asia, South America, and the United States. Their goal was to see what kinds of similarities and differences exist in the social worlds of children across cultures.

They found substantial similarities worldwide in how cultures socialize young children and structure their social environments. From lap children to knee children to yard children, there is a gradual lessening of dependence on the mother and a gradual move into the social orbit of peers and older children. Like lap children, knee children receive a great deal of nurturance from mothers and from older children. However, more is required of knee children than of lap children. Knee children are expected to stop breast-feeding and to have less bodily contact with the mother. Parents and older children expect knee children to be toilet trained, to have basic manners (such as waiting their turn), and to perform minor chores. Older children exercise more dominance over knee children than over lap children, because knee children are perceived as better able to understand and follow commands.

Table 6.3 Mead's Classifications of Childhood Social Stages

Age	Term	Features
0–2	Lap child	Needs constant care; doted on by others
3–4	Knee child	Still cared for mainly by mothers, but spends more time with other children
5–6	Yard child	More time spent with same-sex peers; sometimes unsupervised

Yard children are allowed more freedom than knee children. Yard children spend most of their time close to home, as knee children do, but 20% of the time they are outside of their immediate home area doing errands or playing. However, most cultures share a view that children cannot reason very well until about age 6, and this limits how far a yard child can be away from home or supervision.

The cultures studied by Mead and by Whiting and Edwards were mostly in developing countries, but many of the same patterns apply in developed countries. Across countries and cultures, the social world expands in early childhood to include more time and more interactions with siblings, peers, and friends. In developed countries the media world expands as well, as children not only watch TV as they have from infancy, but many also begin to play electronic games as well.

Across cultures, children are given more autonomy and more responsibility in the course of early childhood. Here, a girl washes dishes outside her Guatemalan home.

Siblings and "Only Children"

LO 6.19 **Identify the most common features of sibling relationships worldwide, and describe how children with no siblings differ from other children.**

A gap of 2–4 years between children is common worldwide, traditionally. In developing countries, especially in rural areas, breast-feeding often lasts at least 2 years, and breast-feeding acts as a natural contraceptive by suppressing the mother's ovulation (although it is not 100% effective). In economically developed countries, parents often choose to space their children by 2–4 years (maybe it takes them that long to forget how much work it is to take care of an infant!). Consequently, it is often in early childhood that children experience the birth of a younger sibling.

How do young children respond to a baby brother or sister? As we learned in Chapter 5, jealousy is the predominant emotion, initially. In their study of 12 cultures, Whiting and Edwards (1988) found a great deal of variability on most issues, but in all 12 cultures jealousy was recognized as a common response to the birth of a younger sibling. Nevertheless, there was great variability in how parents responded to the jealousy of young children, from physical punishment in Africa to trying to comfort and reassure the jealous child in the United States. From the outset, young children expressed love as well as jealousy toward their younger siblings. Like people of other ages, they enjoyed doting on the lap child. More recent American studies show this same pattern of ambivalence toward younger siblings. Aggressive and hostile behavior is common, but so is helping, sharing, and teaching (Kramer & Kowal, 2005; Martin & Ross, 2005; Natsuaki et al., 2009).

Ambivalence continues with age, when there is a younger sibling in early childhood and an older sibling in middle childhood. Middle-childhood siblings care for and teach their younger siblings, but also command and dominate them, and sometimes physically punish them (Howe & Recchia, 2009; Pike et al., 2005; Volling, 2003). Younger siblings admire their older siblings and model their behavior after them, trying to learn to do what their older siblings can do, although sometimes resenting their authority. But even conflict between siblings can have positive effects. Studies indicate that young children with older siblings possess more advanced theory of mind understanding than children who have no older sibling (McAlister & Peterson, 2007; Randell & Peterson, 2009). One explanation of this is that, as siblings argue, compete, and cooperate they learn better how to understand the thinking of others and accept that others have a point of view that may be different than their own.

What about children who have no siblings? This has become an increasingly common condition over the past half century, as birthrates have fallen worldwide. In the United States, about 20% of children have no siblings. In some parts of Europe and Asia birthrates are just 1.1–1.4 children per woman, meaning that there are more children who do not have a sibling than do have one (Population Reference Bureau, 2014). What is it like to be an **only child**?

Having siblings is a mixed blessing, and having no siblings has mixed effects as well. In general, "only children" fare at least as well as children with siblings (Brody, 2004). Their self-esteem, social maturity, and intelligence tend to be somewhat higher than children with siblings, perhaps because they have more interactions with adults (Dunn, 2004). However, in American studies they are somewhat less successful in social relations with peers, perhaps because children with siblings gain peer-like practice in social relations (Kitzmann et al., 2002).

Only children have been especially common in China in recent decades. Beginning in 1978, in response to fears of overpopulation, the Chinese government instituted a "one-child policy," making it illegal for parents to have more than one child without special government approval. There were fears that this policy would create a generation of "little emperors and empresses" who were overindulged and selfish, but those fears appear to be unfounded. Like only children in the United States, only children in China demonstrate several advantages over children with siblings, including higher cognitive development, higher emotional security, and higher likeability (Jiao et al.,1996; Wang & Fong, 2009; Yang et al., 1995). Unlike their American counterparts, Chinese only children show no deficits in social skills or peer acceptance (Hart et al., 2003). One unexpected benefit of the one-child policy is that girls, who in Chinese tradition have been less favored than boys, have more opportunities in education than they did when they had to compete with brothers for family resources (Fong, 2002). China has recently loosened its one-child policy, due to concerns that if the birthrate remains low the population may become too heavily weighted toward older people who are no longer working.

Because of its "one-child" policy, China today has many children without siblings.

Peers and Friends

LO 6.20 Explain how the quality of friendships changes from toddlerhood to early childhood, and describe the role of play and aggression in young children's friendships.

As described in Chapter 5, even toddlers are capable of forming friendships (Rubin et al., 2005). They delight in each other's company, they enjoy favorite shared activities, and they provide each other with companionship and emotional support. In early childhood, friendships also have these qualities, but by this age children are more capable than toddlers of understanding and describing what a friendship entails. They regard a friend as someone you like and who likes you, and as someone who plays with you and shares toys with you (Hartup & Abecassis, 2004). By age 5 or 6, they also understand that friendship is characterized by mutual trust and support, and that a friend is someone you can rely on over time (Bagwell & Schmidt, 2013).

only child
child who has no siblings

Before proceeding further, it is important to distinguish between friends and peers. Friends, as you know, are people with whom you develop a valued, mutual relationship. **Peers** are persons who share some aspect of their status in common, such as age. So, in social science research on human development, a child's peers are the same-age children who are part of the daily environment, such as the other children in the child's class at school. Some of those children may become the child's friends, others may not; a child's friends are usually peers, but not all peers become friends.

Across cultures, relations with both peers and friends tend to become more segregated by gender in the course of early childhood. Boys tend to have other boys as their peers and friends, and the social world of girls is populated mostly by other females. However, cultures differ substantially in the mix of ages in peer groups. A striking difference in early childhood peer relations between traditional cultures and Western cultures is that in the West, mixed-age peer play groups are relatively rare. By age 3 or 4, most children are in some kind of preschool setting for at least part of their typical week, and preschool classes are grouped by age. In contrast, children in traditional cultures often play in mixed-age groups that may include children in toddlerhood, early childhood, and middle childhood (LeVine and New, 2008).

Two of the most researched topics concerning peers and friends in early childhood are play and aggression.

PLAY IN EARLY CHILDHOOD As mentioned in Chapter 5, in toddlerhood and early childhood there are several distinct types of play, including solitary play, parallel play, simple social play, and cooperative pretend play. From toddlerhood through early childhood, solitary play and parallel play decline somewhat while simple social play and cooperative pretend play increase (Hughes & Dunn, 2007). Cooperative pretend play becomes more complex in the course of early childhood, as children's imaginations bloom and they become more creative and adept at using symbols, for example using a stick to represent a sword and a blanket over two chairs to represent a castle (Dyer & Moneta, 2006). Like toddlers, most young children display a variety of types of play, engaging in cooperative play for awhile and then making a transition to solitary play or parallel play (Robinson et al., 2003). The video *Development of Play Styles in Early Childhood* provides more on this topic.

peers
persons who share some aspect of their status in common, such as age

Watch   DEVELOPMENT OF PLAY STYLES IN EARLY CHILDHOOD

Video

In most cultures, the proportion of same-gender play rises during early childhood. Here, young girls in India play a clapping game together.

In the course of early childhood and beyond, children become more sex-segregated in their play (Gaskins, 2015). In the 12-cultures study by Whiting and Edwards (1988), across cultures children played in same-sex groups 30–40% of the time at ages 2–3, rising to over 90% of the time by age 11.

American studies report similar results (Fabes et al., 2003). In one observational study, the percent of time playing in same-sex groups was 45% for 4-year-old children and 73% for 6-year-old children (Martin & Fabes, 2001). Furthermore, numerous studies have found that boys generally engage in high-activity, aggressive, competitive, "rough-and-tumble" play in their groups, whereas girls' play tends to be quieter, more cooperative, and more likely to involve fantasy and role playing (Ruble et al., 2006).

Children vary in their levels of sociability from infancy onward, and by early childhood there are distinct differences among children in how successful they are at using the social skills required for play in a group setting. Preschool social life rewards the bold, and children who are temperamentally inhibited spend a lot of their preschool time watching others play without taking part themselves (Coplan et al., 2004; Rubin et al., 2002). However, for some children it simply takes time to become accustomed to the preschool social environment. The more preschool experience children have, the more successful they are at taking part in social play (Dyer & Moneta, 2006). Sometimes children observe other children's play as a prelude to entering the play themselves (Lindsey & Colwell, 2003). Also, some children simply enjoy playing by themselves. They may spend more time than others in solitary play, but this could be an indication of an unusually lively and creative imagination rather than a sign of being withdrawn or rejected (Coplan et al., 2004). There are also cultural differences in how shyness in early childhood is regarded by peers, as you will see in the *Research Focus: Shyness in China and Canada: Cultural Interpretations* feature.

Research Focus: Shyness in China and Canada: Cultural Interpretations

In studies of young children in the West, shyness has long been associated with negative characteristics such as anxiety, insecurity, and social incompetence. Shy children have been found to experience problems in their relations with peers and to be prone to negative self-perceptions and depression. Shyness in young children has been viewed by Western researchers as a problem to be cured.

But what about in other cultural contexts? Xinyin Chen, a developmental psychologist who grew up in China and now lives in Canada, hypothesized that shyness would have a different meaning in the Chinese cultural context, and set out to compare the consequences of shyness among Chinese and Canadian children (Chen et al., 2006).

In one study conducted by Chen and his colleagues, 4-year-old children in China and Canada were invited into a laboratory setting in groups of four and observed in two 15-minute free-play interactions.

Shy children were identified as those who spent the most time in onlooker behavior (watching the activities of others) or unoccupied behavior (wandering around the room alone or sitting alone doing nothing). Through this process, 50 of 200 Chinese children and 45 of 180 Canadian children were classified as shy. Although the proportion of shy children to non-shy children was identical in the two countries, the responses shy children received from their peers were very different. When shy Canadian children made attempts to interact with their peers, the peers often reacted negatively (for instance, saying "No!" or "I won't do it") and rarely reacted positively with encouragement and support.

In contrast, peers of shy children in China responded much more positively when shy children initiated contact, often inviting them to play or allowing them to join a game. Overall, peers in Canada tended to be antagonistic or nonresponsive toward shy children, whereas in China, peers of shy children were more often supportive and cooperative.

However, Chen and his colleagues have been conducting research in China for over 20 years now, and they have recorded striking shifts in the social implications of shyness for young Chinese children over that time. Recent decades have been a period of dramatic social change in China, as the country has moved rapidly from a state-controlled Communist economy to a free-market economy. This transition has resulted in changes in values as well, with a decline in the traditional Chinese collectivistic values of duty, respect, and obligation, and a rise in individualistic values of self-assertion and independence.

The change in values has been reflected in Chen's research on peers' responses to shy Chinese children. In the 1990 sample Chen studied, shyness was positively associated with a variety of favorable aspects of adjustment, including peer acceptance, leadership, and academic achievement. However, by the time Chen repeated the study in 2002, the correlation had flipped.

Now shyness was associated with negative adjustment, including peer rejection and depression. In just a 12-year period, the cultural meaning of shyness had reversed. As Chen observed, "the extensive change toward the capitalistic system in the economic reform and the introduction of Western ideologies may have led to the decline in the adaptive value of shyness."

Review Quiz:

1. Studies of young Chinese children in the 1990s and a decade later showed that over that time period:
   a. prevalence of shyness increased due to economic upheaval.
   b. prevalence of aggressiveness increased during the transition to a market economy.
   c. shyness became less culturally valued.
   d. aggressiveness among girls rose substantially.

Watch   RESEARCH FOCUS: SHYNESS IN CHINA AND CANADA: CULTURAL INTERPRETATIONS

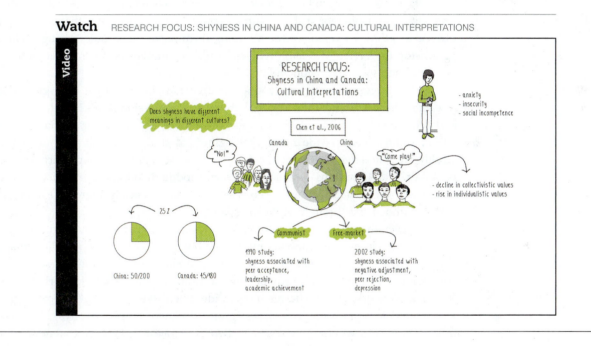

Play in early childhood is widespread across cultures, especially in the first years of this life stage (Gaskins, 2015). In one study comparing four cultural groups, in all four groups the 3-year-old children spent more time in play than in any other activity (Tudge et al., 2006). However, anthropologists have observed some cultures where play is rare even in early childhood, such as the Maya of Guatemala (Gaskins, 2000). In general, the more work parents have to do, the earlier they involve children in work and the less time children have for play (Rogoff, 2003). Nevertheless, in general, children in traditional cultures have some time for play. Often their play is structured and directed by the older children in the mixed-age peer group. Outside of the West, it is rare for children to play with adults (LeVine et al., 2008).

Sometimes children's play involves imitations of adult activity, such as going to the market (Rogoff, 2003; Roopnarine et al., 1994). Other times, play is purely for fun. For example, in India, young girls play a game that involves clapping hands in time to a song. They clap against each other's hands in a complex pattern as they sing, going faster and faster as the song proceeds. The song goes through 11 verses that describe a girl's likely course through life at each age, ending with turning into a spirit. In early childhood, girls learn first by observing and listening as the older girls play, then by gradually taking part in the clapping song themselves.

AGGRESSION Early childhood is an important time for the development of aggression. As young children move more into the world of peers, they encounter more competition for resources—toys, play companions, adult attention, the last cookie—and this competition sometimes leads to conflict and aggression (Rubin & Pepler, 2013).

Scholars distinguish between several different types of aggression (Underwood, 2003). **Instrumental aggression** is involved when a child wants something (toys, food, attention) and uses aggressive behavior or words to get it. A child may also exhibit signs of anger and intend to inflict pain or harm on others. This is known as **hostile aggression**. Instrumental and hostile aggression can each be expressed in several ways. *Physical aggression* includes hitting, kicking, pushing, or striking with an object. *Verbal aggression* is the use of words to hurt others, through yelling at them, calling them names, or hostile teasing. **Relational aggression** (or *social aggression*) involves damaging another person's reputation among peers through social exclusion and malicious gossip.

Physical aggression among young children has been a target of a great deal of research. There is abundant evidence that physical aggression peaks in toddlerhood and early childhood (Alink et al., 2006). One top aggression researcher, Richard Tremblay (2004), summarized a wide range of longitudinal studies extending from infancy to adulthood, across many countries, and found a common pattern that physical aggression peaks at 24 to 42 months—the second year of toddlerhood and the first year of early childhood—then declines. Boys are consistently more physically aggressive than girls, in early childhood and throughout the life span.

However, there is a great deal of variation around this average pattern. Not all boys are aggressive in early childhood, and not all boys and girls show a decline in aggression after age 3. One national study in the United States followed the course of physical aggression in a longitudinal study of children from age 2 to 9 (NICHD Early Childhood Research Network, 2004). The researchers identified five different "trajectory groups" with regard to aggression. The largest group declined steeply in physical aggression from age 2 to 9. However, there were also two "low trajectory" groups that never showed much physical aggression, one "moderate trajectory" group that remained moderate, and one "high trajectory" group that remained high.

In general, individual differences in physical aggression remain stable across time. That is, children who rarely display physical aggression in early childhood are unlikely to display it in middle childhood and adolescence, and children who are especially aggressive in early childhood tend to be more aggressive than their peers in later periods as well (Brame et al., 2001; Lansford et al., 2006; Schaeffer et al., 2003; Vaillancourt et al., 2003). However, longitudinal studies show that parents who are especially patient, sensitive, and involved can reduce high aggression in early childhood to moderate aggression by middle childhood (NICHD Early Childhood Research Network, 2004; Rubin & Pepler, 2013). Early childhood is a crucial time for socializing physical aggression, because when aggression is still high at the end of early childhood it is a strong predictor of later aggressive behavior in adolescence and adulthood (Loeber et al., 2005; Tremblay & Nagin, 2005).

Across cultures, aggression is frequently part of children's play in early and middle childhood, especially for boys (Edwards, 2005; Gaskins, 2015). Physical "rough-and-tumble" play such as wrestling is common among boys of the same age when they are brought together in school and playground settings (Scott & Panksepp, 2003).

Physical aggression peaks in early childhood.

instrumental aggression
type of aggression when a child wants something and uses aggressive behavior or words to get it

hostile aggression
type of aggression that entails signs of anger and intent to inflict pain or harm on others

relational aggression
type of aggression that involves damaging another person's reputation among peers through social exclusion and malicious gossip

This aggressive play occurs in other mammals as well, and is a way of establishing a dominance hierarchy (Hassett et al., 2008). Aggressive play establishes who is on top and who is not, and in this way serves to avoid more serious aggression.

In contrast to physical aggression, verbal aggression rises across early childhood, at least in the Western countries where this research has been done (Dodge et al., 2006; Underwood, 2003). As children become more adept at using words, they grow capable of applying their verbal abilities to a wide range of purposes, including aggression. Also, verbal aggression becomes substituted for physical aggression across the years of early childhood as children learn that adults regard physical aggression toward peers as unacceptable and as children become more capable of restraining their physically aggressive impulses (Tremblay, 2000, 2004; Tremblay & Nagin, 2005).

Relational aggression also becomes more common in the course of early childhood (Crick et al., 2006). Like the increase in verbal aggression, the increase in relational aggression reflects children's growing cognitive and social understanding. They become more capable of understanding the complexities of social relationships, and more aware of the ways that social weapons can be used to hurt others and gain social status. They learn that a punch on the shoulder does not hurt nearly as much, or last nearly as long, as the pain of being the only one not invited to a birthday party or being the subject of a nasty rumor (Murray-Close et al., 2007; Nelson et al., 2005). Verbal and relational aggression are slightly more common among girls than among boys in early childhood, but the differences are minor—much smaller than the gap between boys and girls in physical aggression (Underwood, 2003).

Media Use in Early Childhood

LO 6.21   **Identify the rates and consequences of media use in early childhood.**

Early childhood is a period when children's media world expands greatly, especially in developed countries. Many types of media use increase from toddlerhood to early childhood (Lemish, 2007). Do you remember how old you were when you first started to watch TV? How about using a computer? Or playing a game on a handheld device? In 2011, a national sample of American families were asked how old their children where when they first used different kinds of media in the household (Rideout, 2013). Results showed that:

- 89% had watched TV by 9 months
- 85% had watched DVDs or videotapes by 11 months
- 59% had used a computer by 3 ½ years
- 51% had played a game on a console by 3 years and 11 months
- 44% had played a game on a handheld device by 3 years and 11 months.

Total daily time devoted to media use is about 2 hours for American children ages 2–8. The major types of media used in early childhood are television, electronic games, and recorded music.

THE NEGATIVE IMPACTS OF TELEVISION USE: VIOLENCE AND ADVERTISING
Television is popular with people all over the world, including young children. In early childhood, TV-viewing time per day varies from about 1 hour in the United States, Sweden, and Germany to about 3 hours in Hungary and Turkey (Hasebrink, 2007a; Rideout, 2013). In the United States, over 40% of children ages 2–8 have a TV set in their bedroom (Rideout, 2013). The most popular shows among young children are the ones made especially for them, such as cartoons and educational shows like *Sesame Street* (Lemish, 2007; Rideout, 2013).

Although television is embraced everywhere for its entertainment value, many people have concerns about the effects of television, especially on children and especially with respect to violence. Content analyses have found that children's programs are even more violent than programs for adults. One study found that two-thirds of all children's programs contained violence, and about half the violence took place in cartoons (Aikat, 2007). Violence was portrayed as funny about two-thirds of the time, and in most cases the victims were not shown experiencing pain and the perpetrator of the violence was not punished.

What are the effects of witnessing so much TV violence on young children's development? More than 5 decades of research, including more than 300 studies using a variety of methods, has led to a strong consensus among scholars that watching TV violence increases children's aggression (Bushman & Chandler, 2007). The more aggressive children are, the more they like to watch TV violence, but TV violence inspires aggressive thoughts and behavior even in children who are not usually aggressive (Bushman & Huesmann, 2001). Experimental studies indicate that causation is involved, not just correlation. For example, in one early study, children in a preschool were randomly assigned to two groups (Steur et al., 1971). Over 11 days, one group watched violent cartoons, whereas the other group saw the same cartoons but with the violence removed. During playground observations following this 11-day experiment, children who had seen the violent cartoons were more likely than children in the nonviolent cartoon group to kick and hit their peers.

Young children ages 3–6 are believed to be especially vulnerable to the effects of TV violence (Bushman & Chandler, 2003). They are more likely than younger or older children to model their behavior after the behavior of others, including TV characters. Also, they are less likely than older children to have a clear understanding of the boundary between fantasy and reality, and so more likely to believe that what they witness on TV is real.

Another important effect of TV watching in early childhood concerns advertising. In the United States, the average child sees about 40,000 TV commercials each year, mostly for toys, cereal, candy, and fast food (Scheibe, 2007). Young children are especially susceptible to advertising, as they are less aware of advertising intent than older children are. Most do not perceive a distinction between a program and an advertisement until about age 5 (Jennings, 2007). The more TV young children watch, the more they attempt to influence their parents to buy the advertised products (Valkenburg & Buijzen, 2007). Because most of the products children see advertised are unhealthy foods, concern has grown that TV advertising is one influence behind the growing international epidemic of obesity in children (Bergstrom, 2007a).

THE BENEFICIAL EFFECTS OF EDUCATIONAL TELEVISION TV has also been found to have some beneficial effects on young children. In recent decades, educational programs have been developed that are highly popular among young children. Perhaps most notable is the *Sesame Street* program, which is broadcast in 120 countries worldwide (Truglio, 2007). The content of the program is based on knowledge from developmental psychology of what will be most appealing to young children and most effective at teaching them the academic skills that will prepare them for school (Bergstrom, 2007b). Content is adapted to the culture in which the program is shown, for example addressing the stigma of AIDS in South Africa and promoting cross-cultural respect and understanding among children in the Middle East (Truglio, 2007).

Studies of *Sesame Street* and other programs have shown impressive positive effects on young children's development. In one study, viewing *Sesame Street* at ages 2 and 3 predicted higher scores at age 5 on tests of language development and math skills, even controlling for parents' education and income (Scantlin, 2007). In another study, children who viewed *Sesame Street* at age 5 were recontacted at ages 15 and 19 and were found to have higher grades in English, math, and science than children in the comparison group (Anderson et al., 2001). Studies of *Sesame Street* and other educational programs have shown the programs to have other positive effects as well, such as promoting imaginative play (Scantlin, 2007) and prosocial behavior such as cooperation (Bergstrom, 2007b).

ELECTRONIC GAMES AND MUSIC Although the focus of most media research concerning young children has been on television, other media are also important in their lives, notably electronic games and recorded music.

Television is now nearly universal, but playing electronic games usually depends on access to a computer, and computer access is much more variable across countries. In one international study, over 60% of households in developed countries reported having a computer, but this percentage was much lower in other regions, including eastern Europe (25%), Latin America (about 10%), and Africa (about 5%) (Hasebrink, 2007b). In U.S. studies, 91% of 5- to 8-year-olds have used a computer, and average daily time playing electronic games is 9 minutes (Rideout, 2013). Boys play electronic games more than girls do, overall, and the kinds of games they prefer differ, with boys preferring fighting and sports games and girls preferring adventure and learning games (Kubisch, 2007). These gender differences endure through childhood and adolescence, as we will see in later chapters. Electronic games can also be played on handheld devices and mobile phones, but access to these media tends to come in middle childhood and beyond.

Listening to recorded music is also part of the daily media diet of most children in developed countries. Over half of parents of young children report singing to or playing music for them each day (Kinnally, 2007). On average, children ages 2–8 listen to music for about 16 minutes per day. Children ages 3–5 listen mostly to children's songs, but by age 6 children pay more attention to popular music and start to recognize and prefer the latest "hit songs" of the day.

Music evokes a positive response even from infants, but early childhood is an especially important time for the development of responses to music (Kinnally, 2007). It is during early childhood that children first connect musical sounds with specific emotions, for example recognizing songs in major keys as happy and songs in minor keys as sad. By age 5, children show distinct preferences for music that is harmonious rather than dissonant and has a steady rather than erratic beat. There is little research on the effects of music on young children. Research on music's effects is concentrated on adolescence because of concerns about the effects of violent music on adolescent development, as we will see later in the book.

Listening to recorded music is a common part of children's lives in developed countries.

Practice Quiz   ANSWERS AVAILABLE IN ANSWER KEY.

1. Lucien is still cared for mainly by his mother, who just recently stopped breast feeding. He also spends a lot of time with his older siblings and the older children who live nearby. When he is distressed, the older children comfort him if the mother is not in the vicinity. Using Mead's classification, Lucien would be considered a _____.
   a. knee child
   b. yard child
   c. lap child
   d. neighborhood child

2. Hyejin is an only child from China. Which of the following is most likely true?
   a. She has higher cognitive development than her counterparts with siblings.
   b. She scores lower on likeability than her counterparts with siblings who have had to share and negotiate.

   c. She would be considered overindulged and selfish.
   d. She has poorer social skills, but is considered more assertive than her counterparts with siblings.

3. Based on the research, which of the following is most likely true of Sebastian, a four-year-old American male?
   a. If he is especially physically aggressive at this time in development, he is unlikely to be more aggressive than his peers later on.
   b. He is less likely to be physically aggressive than girls at this age.
   c. He engages in rough-and-tumble play at recess when he is around other boys of the same age.
   d. He is much more likely than female peers his age to use relational and verbal aggression.

4. Which of the following would you most likely to see five-year-olds doing on a playground in a Western culture?
   a. Girls playing catch with the boys
   b. Boys playing a game to see who could throw a ball the farthest
   c. Boys engaging in cooperative, fantasy play
   d. Children playing in mixed-age groups
5. Which of the following is TRUE regarding media use in early childhood?

a. Children are able to connect musical sounds with specific emotions.
b. Most of the research on the effects of music has focused on very young children.
c. Girls are more likely than boys to prefer violent video games because they are striving to achieve an independent and assertive identity.
d. Boys and girls spend equal amounts of time playing electronic games.

Summary: Emotional and Social Development

LO 6.13   Identify advances in emotional understanding and self-regulation during early childhood.

Early childhood is a key time for the development of emotional self-regulation, as children improve at effortful control. Children also improve in their ability to understand the sources of others' emotions.

LO 6.14   Describe moral development in early childhood, including empathy, modeling, and morality as cultural learning.

The capacity for empathy increases in early childhood, which leads in turn to an increase in prosocial behavior. Children learn morality in part through modeling, i.e., observing the behavior of others and its consequences. Early childhood is also a time when children begin to show a capacity for moral reasoning, and demonstrate that they have learned the moral beliefs of their culture.

LO 6.15   Describe the roles that parents and peers play in gender socialization, and explain how gender schemas lead to self-socialization.

Children learn gender identity by age 2, but do not learn gender constancy until age 6 or 7. During early childhood they often become rigid in their views of gender roles. Parents are key agents of gender socialization, especially fathers, and conformity to gender roles is enforced by peers as well. Once young children possess gender schemas, they seek to maintain consistency between their schemas and their behavior, a process called self-socialization.

LO 6.16   Describe the four types of parenting "styles" and identify the cultural limitations of this model.

American parenting research has emphasized the dimensions of demandingness and responsiveness, in combinations resulting in four categories of "parenting styles": authoritative, authoritarian, permissive, and disengaged. By American standards, authoritative parenting is associated with the most favorable outcomes. However, the relationship between parenting styles and children's development is complex due to reciprocal effects between parents and children.

The effects of parenting on young children depend substantially on cultural context. The authoritative parenting style is very rare in non-Western cultures because parents expect that their authority will be obeyed without question and without requiring an explanation.

LO 6.17   Describe the main cultural variations in how parents discipline young children, and explain how cultural context influences children's responses to discipline.

In Western cultures the approach to discipline in early childhood tends to emphasize the authoritative approach of explaining the consequences of misbehavior and the reasons for discipline, whereas outside of the West, the parental role has more authority and children are expected to obey. Physical punishment and "psychological control" have quite different effects on children depending on the cultural context.

LO 6.18   Explain the meanings of Mead's social stages from infancy through early childhood.

According to Margaret Mead, across cultures, early childhood often entails a progression from "knee child" at ages 3–4 to "yard child" at ages 5–6, with children allowed more unsupervised play with peers as they become older.

LO 6.19   Identify the most common features of sibling relationships worldwide, and describe how children with no siblings differ from other children.

A combination of conflict along with helping and sharing between siblings is very common worldwide in early childhood. "Only children" fare very well compared to children with siblings, even in China, where there has been concern about the social effects of the government's "one-child" population policy.

LO 6.20 **Explain how the quality of friendships changes from toddlerhood to early childhood, and describe the role of play and aggression in young children's friendships.**

Children engage in cooperative pretend play more in early childhood than in toddlerhood. Physical aggression peaks in toddlerhood and the first year of early childhood, then declines as verbal aggression rises.

LO 6.21 **Identify the rates and consequences of media use in early childhood.**

In early childhood, TV-viewing time per day varies from about 1 to 3 hours across developed countries. Abundant evidence shows that violent television promotes aggressive behavior in young children. Boys most often play electronic games involving fighting and sports, whereas girls prefer adventure and learning games. Early childhood is an especially important time for the development of responses to music, as children learn to connect musical sounds with specific emotions.

Applying Your Knowledge as a Professional

The topics covered in this chapter apply to a wide variety of career professions. Watch these videos to learn how they apply to a paramedic and a dance instructor.

Watch   CAREER FOCUS: DANCE INSTRUCTOR

Sanoe Garcia
Dance Instructor

Chapter Quiz

1. Which of the following best describes the physical changes that take place during early childhood?

   a. Both boys and girls gain more in weight than in height, but most add more muscle than fat.

   b. Physical development occurs at a more rapid pace than it did in the first 3 years.

   c. Girls are slightly taller and heavier than boys.

   d. Cross-cultural comparisons have shown that only genetics play a role in individual differences in height and weight.

2. The limited memory for personal events and experiences prior to age 5 is probably due to incomplete myelination of the _____.

   a. reticular formation   **c.** cerebellum

   b. corpus callosum   **d.** hippocampus

3. The two most common types of nutritional deficiencies in developing countries are a lack of protein and _____.

   a. marasmus   **c.** iron

   b. kwashiorkor   **d.** calcium

4. How does motor development change between ages 3 and 6?

   a. Children's fine motor skills become refined, but their gross motor skills remain the same as they were in toddlerhood.

   b. Children's fine motor skills have been found to develop at the same rate all over the world.

   c. Children develop the same motor skills at the same pace, regardless of gender.

   d. Fine motor skill development allows children to become more independent by doing things, such as putting on a coat and using a knife to cut soft food.

5. Which of the following statements about handedness is most accurate?

   a. The prevalence of left-handedness in some African countries is as low as 1% because using the left hand is suppressed.

   b. Children first develop this tendency during the preschool years.

   c. Children who are left-handed are often praised for their uniqueness in non-Western cultures.

   d. There is no genetic component to handedness; it is based purely on one's environment.

6. A 5-year-old child draws a yellow sun in the upper corner of her paper complete with a smiley face and sunglasses. This is an example of _____.

   a. sensorimotor thought

   b. animism

   c. gross motor skill refinement

   d. centered thinking

7. Which of the following is true regarding theory of mind?

   a. Children show a decrease in this ability from 4 to 6 years of age because they are becoming more independent.

   b. It develops the same way in all cultures with spoken language.

   c. It begins to develop, in rudimentary form, sometime in infancy.

   d. A child who demonstrates theory of mind is not yet able to think about thinking.

8. Cultural learning skills, such as learning to set the table in a developed country or to help prepare food in a traditional culture, _____.

   a. develop as part of a social and cultural process, according to Vygotsky

   b. must be learned in the sensorimotor stage first or they never fully develop

   c. cannot be appropriately acquired until early adolescence

   d. usually develop best if they take place in a formal setting

9. As a parent of a 3-year-old, you have visited several preschool programs to determine the one that will provide the highest-quality experience. Which of the following should be important in your decision about which preschool to pick, according to research?

   a. The presence of formal lesson plans rather than play materials

   b. Formal classrooms where the teacher sits in front and answers questions

   c. No more than 10 students per teacher

   d. A strong emphasis on rote learning

10. In Japan, _____.

   a. learning academic skills is the number one goal of having children attend preschool

   b. preschool is mainly a time for learning social skills

   c. parents and preschool teachers list the same top reasons for young children to attend preschool as do their counterparts in the United States

   d. individuality is stressed from the time children enter preschool as a way to encourage children to reach their full potential

11. A consistent pattern in early intervention programs such as Head Start is that the early gains in IQ and achievement _____.

   a. fade within 2 or 3 years of entering elementary school

   b. continue to increase throughout middle school

   c. continue, but only for females

   d. continue throughout the lifespan

12. Young children's use of grammar _____.

   a. is entirely dependent on formal instruction in preschool

   b. develops more slowly in traditional cultures

   c. develops simply by hearing and using the language in daily interactions

   d. is mostly incorrect until age 6

13. When a 4-year-old uses infant-directed speech when talking to her neighbor's new baby, this demonstrates _____.

   a. a sensitive period

   b. fast mapping

   c. classification

   d. pragmatics

14. A key reason why emotional outbursts decline in early childhood is that children _____.

   a. learn strategies for regulating their emotions, in a practice known as effortful control

   b. have a more sophisticated theory of mind at this age

   c. at this age are no longer at risk for externalizing problems

   d. have learned the skill of over-controlling their emotions

15. Which of the following statements accurately describes moral development in early childhood?

   a. Children at this age are not yet able to experience empathy.

   b. Socioemotional emotions such as shame and pride first appear.

   c. Perspective taking and being able to understand how others think and feel make children more empathic at this age.

   d. Young children inherently know the rules and expectations of their culture without needing to be taught.

16. The process by which people seek to maintain consistency between their gender schemas and their behavior is referred to as _____.

   a. gender identity

   b. gender constancy

   c. self-socialization

   d. self-regulation

17. Research on parenting has found that _____.

    a. the two main dimensions of parenting are demandingness and strictness

    b. children of permissive parents tend to do better in school than children of other parenting styles because they learn to think for themselves

    c. there are bidirectional effects between parents and their children

    d. the outcomes for children of authoritative parents are virtually identical to outcomes for children of permissive parents

18. Which of the following is the most accurate statement based on existing research?

    a. The typical parenting style in non-Western cultures is authoritarian.

    b. The American model of parenting does not apply well to most other cultures.

    c. Providing explanations to their children is most common among non-Western parents who spend more time with their children than do American parents.

    d. Permissive parenting would be most likely in cultures that have a tradition of filial piety.

19. The use of shame as a form of discipline _____.

    a. has resulted in positive outcomes in both the United States and Finland

    b. is referred to as psychological control by American researchers

    c. is associated with high rates of behavior problems in Japanese children

    d. is universally accepted as the best method of discipline because it does not include physical punishment

20. Which of the following is true regarding siblings?

    a. A gap of 4 to 8 years between children is common in many cultures across the world.

    b. "Only children" are maladjusted, meaning they are more prone to depressive behavior disorders.

    c. Jealousy is a common response to the birth of a younger sibling across cultures.

    d. Research has shown that young children with older siblings have a more advanced theory of mind than those who are only children.

21. If you were a researcher observing play among 5-year-old children in the United States, what would you be most likely to observe?

    a. Boys playing with children from other kindergarten classes, rather than older boys

    b. Girls playing kickball with the boys (with the girls serving as referees to make sure the boys follow the rules)

    c. Boys engaging in cooperative, fantasy play

    d. The boys challenging the girls to a wrestling match

22. Watching TV during young childhood _____.

    a. has not been associated with any positive effects on development

    b. is a popular leisure activity all over the world

    c. has been correlated with aggressive thoughts and behaviors, but only among males who were already extremely aggressive before viewing

    d. has not been studied experimentally, and therefore no conclusions about causation can be made

Chapter 7
Middle Childhood

ACROSS CULTURES, THE TRANSITION FROM EARLY CHILDHOOD TO MIDDLE CHILDHOOD IS RECOGNIZED AS AN IMPORTANT SHIFT IN CHILDREN'S DEVELOPMENT, WHEN THEY BECOME CAPABLE OF GREATER COGNITIVE CHALLENGES AND PERSONAL RESPONSIBILITY (SAMEROFF & HAITH, 1996). In developing countries, middle childhood is often the age when children are first given important family duties, such as taking care of younger siblings, buying or selling goods, maintaining a fire, or caring for domestic animals (Gaskins, 2015; Weisner, 1996). According to Roy D'Andrade (1987), middle childhood is when children first show a grasp of **cultural models**, which are cognitive structures pertaining to common activities, for example buying something at the market, herding cattle, taking care of an infant, making bread, or delivering a message to a relative's house. Children in both developed and developing countries begin formal schooling in middle childhood, which includes cultural models of "listen to the teacher," "wait your turn," and "do your homework." Children begin to grasp cultural models as early as toddlerhood, but during middle childhood their understanding of cultural models acquires greater complexity, so that they become capable of taking on a much broader range of tasks (Gaskins, 2015; Weisner, 1996).

Here as elsewhere in the human life span, how we experience a given stage of life depends greatly on cultural context. Children in all cultures become more capable of useful work in middle childhood, but the nature of their work varies greatly. For many children throughout human history it has been mainly farm work—tending the fields, herding the cows, and feeding the chickens. For today's children, it might be school work or household work in developed countries, and any of a wide range of work in developing countries, from household work to factory work to feeding domestic animals. In this chapter we explore a wide range of cultural variations in children's experiences of middle childhood.

Watch CHAPTER INTRODUCTION: MIDDLE CHILDHOOD

Section 1   Physical Development

∨   Learning Objectives

7.1 Identify the changes in physical and sensory development that take place during middle childhood.

7.2 Explain how motor development advances in middle childhood and how these advancements are related to new skills and participation in games and sports.

7.3 Describe the negative effects of both malnutrition and obesity on development, and identify the causes of obesity.

7.4 Explain why rates of illness and injury are relatively low in middle childhood, and why rates of asthma have risen.

PHYSICAL DEVELOPMENT:
Growth in Middle Childhood

cultural models

cognitive structures pertaining to common cultural activities

body mass index (BMI)

measure of the ratio of weight to height

Middle childhood growth is not as rapid as at earlier ages, but children continue to add height and weight. Some children become near-sighted during these years and need to start wearing glasses.

Physical Growth and Sensory Development

Middle childhood is the time of life when people are most likely to be slim.

LO 7.1   Identify the changes in physical and sensory development that take place during middle childhood.

In middle childhood, physical growth continues at a slow but steady pace, about 2–3 inches (5–8 cm) per year in height and about 5–7 pounds (2½–3 kg) per year in weight. Boys continue to be slightly taller and to weigh slightly more than girls, on average. For both boys and girls, middle childhood is the time of life when they are mostly likely to be slim. Of all age groups in the life span, 6- to 10-year-olds have the lowest **body mass index (BMI)**, a measure of the ratio of weight to height (Gillaume & Lissau, 2002). Boys continue to have somewhat more muscle than girls do in middle childhood, and girls continue to have somewhat more body fat, so the average boy is stronger than the average girl. However, both boys and girls grow stronger during this stage. For example, the average 10-year-old can throw a ball twice as far as the average

6-year-old. Children run faster and longer, too, over the course of middle childhood, as lung capacity expands (Malina et al., 2004).

From age 6 to 12, children lose all 20 of their "primary teeth" and new, permanent teeth replace them. The two top front teeth are usually the first to go. The permanent teeth are adult-sized teeth that do not grow much once they come in, giving children in middle childhood a toothy smile that sometimes looks a little too big for their mouths.

Sight and hearing both change in middle childhood, hearing usually for the better, sight more likely for the worse. Hearing often improves because the tube in the inner ear that is the site of ear infections in toddlerhood and early childhood has now matured and is longer and narrower than it was before (Bluestone, 2007). This structural change makes it less likely for fluid containing bacteria to flow from the mouth to the ear, which in turn makes inner ear infections less likely.

With regard to sight, the incidence of **myopia**, also known as being *nearsighted*, rises sharply in middle childhood. This is a problem that is more likely to occur in developed countries than in developing countries. The more children read, write, and use computers, the more likely they are to develop myopia (Feldkamper & Schaeffel, 2003; Saw et al., 2002). Consequently, rates of myopia are highest in the developed countries where children are mostly likely to have access to books and computers. Myopia is also partly genetic, as MZ twins have a higher concordance rate (see Chapter 1) than DZ twins do (Pacella et al., 1999). About one fourth of children in developed countries need glasses by the end of middle childhood (Mutti et al., 2002).

Motor Development

LO 7.2 Explain how motor development advances in middle childhood and how these advancements are related to new skills and participation in games and sports.

Children advance in both gross and fine motor development during middle childhood, nearly reaching maturity in their fine motor abilities. Children become stronger and more agile, and as their gross motor skills develop, they spend more of their days in active play and organized sports. They also become capable of complex fine motor activities such as writing.

GROSS MOTOR DEVELOPMENT AND PHYSICAL ACTIVITY Watch a group of children on the playground of an elementary school, and you will see lots of activity. In one corner, a group of girls practices a dance routine one of them has learned from watching a TV show. In another, boys play four square, bouncing a ball into each other's square and attempting to defend their own by knocking the ball to someone else's square. In the middle, a group of boys and girls play tag, the perennial favorite.

In a variety of ways, gross motor development advances from early to middle childhood. Children's *balance* improves, allowing them to stay steady on a bike without training wheels or walk on a board across a river. They become *stronger*, so that they can jump higher and throw a ball farther. Their *coordination* advances so that they can perform movements in activities such as swimming and skating that require the synchronization of different body parts. They have greater *agility* so that they can move more quickly and precisely, for example when changing directions while playing soccer. Finally, their *reaction time* becomes faster, allowing them to respond rapidly to changing information, for example when hitting a tennis ball over the net or when catching or hitting a baseball (Kail, 2003). Increasing myelination of the *corpus callosum* connecting

myopia
visual condition of being unable to see distant objects clearly; also known as being nearsighted

the two hemispheres of the brain (see Chapter 6) accelerates reaction time in middle childhood for both gross motor and fine motor tasks (Roeder et al., 2008). The video *Gross Motor Development in Middle Childhood* shows examples of these advances.

Watch GROSS MOTOR DEVELOPMENT IN MIDDLE CHILDHOOD

As their gross motor development advances, children can enjoy a wide range of games and sports. All over the world, middle childhood is a time of playing physically active games with siblings and friends, from tag and hide-and-seek to soccer, cricket, baseball, and basketball. Most of their play is informal, and takes place on the street or in a park or in the school yard when a few kids gather and decide to start a game (Kirchner, 2000). However, middle childhood is also the time when children are most likely to be involved in organized sports. For example, Little League baseball is played in 75 countries around the world during the middle childhood years. In the United States, 66% of boys and 52% of girls are involved in organized sports at least once between the ages of 5 and 18 (Statistic Brain, 2014). Although boys are slightly more likely than girls to play on sports teams in middle childhood, the rate of participation among girls has risen worldwide in recent decades, especially in sports such as soccer, swimming, gymnastics, and basketball.

Middle childhood is when children are most likely to be involved in organized sports.

Nevertheless, in the view of public health advocates, children do not get nearly as much gross motor activity as they should, leading to high rates of obesity, as we will see shortly. Middle childhood may be a time of great advancements in gross motor abilities, but physically active games and sports compete today with the electronic allurements of TV and computer games (Anderson & Butcher, 2006). In some places, schools are less likely than in the past to be a setting for physical activity. In the United States, the percentage of children involved in daily "physical education" programs during middle childhood decreased from 80% in 1969 to just 8% by 2005 (Centers for Disease Control and Prevention [CDC], 2006). Health authorities recommend 60 minutes of physical activity a day for children ages 6–17, but few American children get that much (see **http://www.cdc.gov/physicalactivity/everyone/guidelines/index.html**).

FINE MOTOR DEVELOPMENT Fine motor development also makes great advances from early childhood to middle childhood. Not many 3- or 4-year-olds can tie their shoes successfully, but nearly all 8- to 9-year-olds can. In Asian cultures, only about half of 4-year-olds can use chopsticks well enough to eat with them, but for children 6 years old and up it comes easily (Wong et al., 2002). In many developing countries, children become valuable as factory workers in middle childhood because of their abilities to perform intricate fine motor tasks such as weaving rugs (International Labor Organization [ILO], 2013).

Across cultures, advances in fine motor development are especially evident in two areas, drawing and writing. In early childhood, drawing skills are limited to crude depictions of two-dimensional figures. However, in the course of middle childhood children learn to indicate three-dimensional depth by overlapping objects and making near objects smaller than distant ones (Braine et al., 1993). They also learn to draw objects in greater detail and to adjust the size and relation of objects in a drawing so that they fit together into one coherent whole (see **Figure 7.1**; Case & Okamoto, 1996).

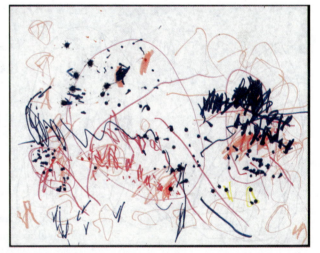

With regard to writing, in early childhood most children learn to write a few letters and numbers in rough form. In middle childhood, their skills greatly advance (Berninger et al., 2006). Even by age 6 most children are able to write the letters of the alphabet, their own names, and numbers from 1 to 10. In the course of the next several years, as their fine motor abilities develop, they are able to make their letters smaller and neater with more consistent height and spacing. By age 8 or 9 most children can learn to write in cursive. By the end of middle childhood their fine motor abilities have nearly reached adult maturity, whereas gross motor development will continue to advance for many years to come.

Figure 7.1 Change in Drawing Abilities from Early to Middle Childhood

Drawings become more realistic as fine motor development advances during middle childhood. Here are drawings that my daughter, Paris, made at ages 3 (top), 5 (left), and 7 (right).

Practice Quiz ANSWERS AVAILABLE IN ANSWER KEY.

1. During middle childhood _____.
   a. girls are usually taller and heavier than boys
   b. girls and boys are more likely to be slim than at any other time
   c. the incidence of myopia decreases
   d. ear infections are more likely than they were earlier in the lifespan because of more exposure to germs during the school years

2. During middle childhood, _____.
   a. bodies are pudgier than they were in toddlerhood with a higher body mass index
   b. children run longer and faster because of expanded lung capacity
   c. the proportion of body fat is identical for girls and boys
   d. growth continues at the same rate as in infancy

3. During middle childhood, there is an increase in myelination of the _____ that accelerates the reaction time for both boys and girls.

   a. Broca's area
   b. Wernicke's area
   c. corpus callosum
   d. pituitary gland

4. For 6-year-old Emannuel, which of the following fine motor tasks is developmentally appropriate?
   a. Writing complete sentences and spelling multi-syllable words, such as "hippopotamus"
   b. Running a 4-minute mile, jumping over hurdles, and dribbling a basketball
   c. Writing the letters of the alphabet, writing his name, and writing numbers from 1 to 10
   d. Writing in cursive

5. By the time Shawna has reached the end of middle childhood, what abilities are close to adult maturity?
   a. Fine motor abilities
   b. Gross motor abilities
   c. Eye-hand coordination
   d. Psycho-motor skills

PHYSICAL DEVELOPMENT: Health Issues

Middle childhood is an exceptionally healthy time of life. In this life stage, children become less vulnerable to the effects of malnutrition, and it is the time of life when they are least likely to be obese. However, obesity has become more prevalent in recent decades in developed countries, even in middle childhood.

Malnutrition and Obesity

LO 7.3 **Describe the negative effects of both malnutrition and obesity on development, and identify the causes of obesity.**

By middle childhood, children have grown large enough that they are less vulnerable to the effects of malnutrition than they were earlier. Even if they are deprived of food for a period of time, their bodies have enough resources to weather the deprivation without the effects being as severe as in earlier life stages. Nevertheless, malnutrition can have enduring negative effects in middle childhood. Obesity also becomes a problem for many children in middle childhood, especially those in developed countries.

MALNUTRITION As we have seen in previous chapters, malnutrition in early development often results in illness, disease, or death. In middle childhood, bodies are stronger and more resilient, and immune systems are better developed. Nevertheless, malnutrition has effects in middle childhood as well. Even for children who survive early malnutrition, the damage to their physical and cognitive development accumulates by middle childhood (Liu et al., 2003).

A longitudinal study in Guatemala showed how nutrition in the early years contributes to cognitive and social functioning in middle childhood (Barrett & Frank, 1987). Children who were classified in early childhood as having "high nutrient levels" were more likely than children with "low nutrient levels" to explore new environments in middle childhood and to persist in a frustrating situation. They were also more energetic, less anxious, and showed more positive emotion. A more recent study, in Ghana, reported similar results, with children who experienced mild-to-moderate malnutrition in their early years demonstrating lower levels of cognitive development in middle childhood on standardized tests and in teacher ratings, compared to children who were not malnourished (Appoh & Krekling, 2004). The malnourished children were also more likely to be rated by teachers as anxious, sad, and withdrawn (Appoh, 2004).

Other studies in other countries have found similar results, with better-nourished children scoring higher than malnourished children on a wide range of cognitive and social measures in middle childhood (Grigorenko, 2003; Kitsao-Wekulo et al., 2013). However, there is a consensus that the sensitive period for long-term effects of malnutrition is from the second trimester of pregnancy through age 3 (Galler et al., 2005). Malnutrition that begins after age 3 does not appear to result in permanent cognitive or behavioral deficits.

OBESITY Children in developed countries have a different kind of nutritional problem: not too few calories but too many. Across countries, rates of **overweight** and **obesity** are highest in the most affluent regions (North America and Europe) and lowest in the poorest regions (Africa and Southeast Asia) (Wang & Lobstein, 2006). Rates across the United States are higher than in most other developed countries and are especially high in the least affluent ethnic minority groups, including African Americans and Latinos, as shown in **Figure 7.2** (Ogden et al., 2014). Rates of overweight and obesity have risen sharply worldwide in recent decades. **Figure 7.3** shows the increase in childhood obesity within the United States since the 1970s.

A variety of changes have contributed to the rise in childhood obesity (Ogden et al., 2014). Most important is the change in diets. Over recent decades people have become less likely to prepare meals at home and more likely to buy meals away from home, especially "fast foods" like hamburgers, french fries, and pizza that are high in fat content, and then they wash it down with soft drinks high in sugar content. This change reflects other social changes: Parents are less likely to prepare meals at home because they are more likely than in the past to be single parents or to be part of a dual-earner couple. Rates of overweight and obesity are rising in the populations of developing countries in part because their diets are becoming more like the diets of people in developed countries (Gu et al., 2005; Popkin, 2010).

Another contributor is television. Most children in most developed countries watch at least 2 hours of television a day (Rideout, 2013). In a longitudinal study that followed a sample of American children from age 4 to 11, TV watching predicted gains in body fat (Proctor et al., 2003). Specifically, children who watched at least 3 hours of TV a day gained 40% more body fat over the course of the study than children who watched less than 1½ hours a day. Other studies have shown that the more time children watch TV the less time they spend in physical exercise (Institute of Medicine, 2005; Williams, 2005). Watching TV also exposes children to numerous advertisements for high-fat, high-sugar foods, which they then lobby their parents to buy (Kelly et al., 2010). Rates of overweight and obesity are especially high among African American and Latino children in part because those are also the children that tend to watch the most TV per day (Rideout, 2013). The allure of the Internet and electronic games gives children additional reasons to stay inside rather than getting outside and playing active physical games (Anderson & Butcher, 2006).

Genetics also make a contribution to obesity. Concordance rates for obesity are higher among MZ twins than

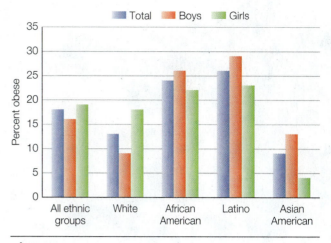

Figure 7.2 Childhood Obesity Rates in the United States, by Ethnicity

SOURCE: Based on Ogden et al. (2014).

overweight

in children, defined as having a BMI exceeding 18

obesity

in children, defined as having a BMI exceeding 21

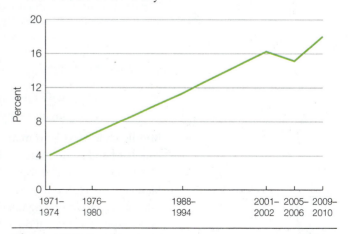

Figure 7.3 The Rise in Childhood Obesity, United States, Children Ages 6-11

SOURCE: Based on Fryar et al. (2012).

Rates of obesity are rising in developing countries as diets become more like those in the developed world. This photo was taken in Mexico, which has one of the highest child obesity rates in the world.

DZ twins. Adopted children tend to have BMIs that are closer to their biological parents than to their adoptive parents (Whitaker et al., 1997). Research has even identified a specific gene, called FTO, that sharply increases children's risk for obesity (Frayling et al., 2007). However, genetics cannot explain recent rises in obesity rates. Genetics provide only a risk for overweight and obesity, not a definite destiny.

A compelling demonstration of this comes from a naturalistic study of the Pima Indians in Arizona and Mexico (Gladwell, 1998). The Pima of Mexico live in a remote region and still maintain their traditional ways, including a traditional cultural diet that is high in vegetables and low in fats and sugars. In contrast, the Pima of Arizona have changed in recent decades and their diets have become more like the American mainstream. Consequently, they have an average BMI that is 50% higher than their counterparts in Mexico, even though the two groups are very similar genetically.

Obesity has both social and physical consequences for children. Being obese increases the likelihood that a child will be socially excluded and the object of ridicule by peers (Janssen et al., 2004; Puhl et al., 2010). Other children tend to associate obesity with undesirable traits such as being lazy, sloppy, ugly, and stupid (Tiggemann & Anesbury, 2000). By middle childhood obesity is a risk factor for a variety of emotional and behavioral problems (Puhl et al., 2010).

Physically, the consequences of obesity are equally serious. Even in middle childhood, obesity can result in diabetes, which can eventually lead to problems such as blindness, kidney failure, and stroke (Hannon et al., 2005; Ramchamdani, 2004). Obesity also proves hard to shake from childhood to adulthood. About 80% of obese children remain overweight as adults (Ogden et al., 2014; Oken & Lightdale, 2000). For adults, the range of health problems resulting from obesity is even greater—including high blood pressure, heart attack, and cancer—and more likely to be fatal (Ng et al., 2014).

What can be done to reverse the sharp increase in childhood obesity? One step is recognizing the problem. Perhaps because obese children tend to have obese parents, studies indicate that fewer than half of parents of obese children view their children as overweight (Jeffrey, 2004; Young-Hyman et al., 2003). Public policies have begun to address the problem of childhood obesity. In the United States, school lunches have been notoriously unhealthy for decades, but national standards have been recently revised to provide healthier school lunches that are lower in fats and sugars (Jalonick, 2010).

CRITICAL THINKING QUESTION

Why do you think overweight and obesity are most common among low-income American ethnic groups even though, internationally, overweight and obesity are highest in the highest income countries?

Illness and Injuries

LO 7.4 **Explain why rates of illness and injury are relatively low in middle childhood, and why rates of asthma have risen.**

Middle childhood is in many ways the safest, healthiest time of life. In both developed countries and developing countries, death rates are lower during middle childhood than at any other period of the life span (Hyder & Lunnen, 2009; National Center for Health Statistics [NCHS], 2009). In developed countries, by middle childhood nearly all children have been vaccinated against the diseases that may have been fatal in earlier eras, such as smallpox, typhus, and diphtheria. In developing countries, an increasing proportion of children receive vaccinations in infancy, toddlerhood, and early childhood (World Health Organization [WHO], 2010). Even children who do not receive vaccinations are less susceptible to fatal diseases in middle childhood than they were earlier in their development. Their natural immune systems have become stronger, and their bodies are bigger, stronger, and more resilient.

In developed countries, even rates of minor illnesses have declined in middle childhood in recent decades, due to public health policies. Over time, food production has become cleaner and safer, and food content more closely regulated by government agencies. The air and water have become cleaner in developed countries due to laws and restrictions by governments. For example, according to national U.S. studies, in 1978 nearly 30% of children ages 5–10 had dangerously elevated levels of lead in their blood, which can cause brain damage; by 2001, the rate had fallen to 1% (Morbidity and Mortality Weekly Report [MMWR], 2005). This decline reflects government policies that eliminated lead from gasoline and household paint.

One exception to this trend toward healthier development in middle childhood is **asthma**, a chronic illness of the lungs characterized by wheezing, coughing, and shortness of breath. A person with asthma has periodic "asthma attacks" in which breathing is especially difficult (Israel, 2005). An asthma attack can be triggered by cold weather, exercise, illnesses, allergies, emotional stress, or for no clear reason (Akinbami & Schoendorf, 2002). Asthma attacks can be reduced through the use of medical injections and inhalers (Glauber et al., 2001; Yoos et al., 2006).

Middle childhood is when rates of asthma are highest. This Indian girl is using an inhaler to relieve the symptoms.

Rates of asthma are highest in middle childhood, and are increasing worldwide (Greenwood, 2011). Boys are at higher risk than girls, for reasons that are not clear (Federico & Liu, 2003). Other risk factors are low birth weight, having a parent who smokes, living in poverty, and obesity (Saha et al., 2005). Susceptibility to asthma is also transmitted genetically (Bosse & Hudson, 2007).

Why are rates of asthma higher now than in the past? The answer appears to be different for developed countries than for developing countries. In developed countries, common features of today's family households contribute to asthma, including carpets, hairy pets, and airtight windows (Tamay et al., 2007). There is also a "hygiene hypothesis" suggesting that high standards of cleanliness and sanitation expose children to fewer viruses and bacteria, and consequently they have fewer illnesses in their early years that would strengthen their immune systems and make them less susceptible to asthma (Tedeschi & Airaghi, 2006). In developing countries, air pollution has become worse as a result of increased industrialization, and air pollution can trigger asthma. One study in Mongolia compared people in rural and urban areas and found substantially higher rates of asthma in urban areas, due mainly to poorer air quality (Vinanen et al., 2007).

Rates of asthma are especially high among African American children, because they often live in urban neighborhoods where the air quality is poor (Pearlman et al., 2006). African Americans also have especially high rates of risk factors for asthma such as low birth weight and obesity. However, one study found that among children with asthma, the families of African American children were more likely than White families to take steps to change the environment in order to reduce risk factors that can trigger asthma attacks, with steps including use of mattress covers, use of pillow covers, cigarette smoke avoidance, pet avoidance, and carpet removal (Roy & Wisnivesky, 2010).

Like illness rates, injury rates are relatively low in middle childhood (Hyder & Lunnen, 2011; U.S. Department of Health and Human Services, 2005). Children in middle childhood are more agile than younger children and better at anticipating situations that may cause injury; compared to older children, they are kept closer to home and so are less likely to become involved in risky situations. The most common cause of injury in middle childhood is automobile accidents, followed by bicycle accidents (Safe Kids Worldwide, 2013). The use of bicycle helmets has become common in middle childhood in recent decades, and this practice has led to a sharp decrease in the number of head injuries experienced during these years (Miller et al., 2012).

asthma
chronic illness of the lungs characterized by wheezing, coughing, and shortness of breath

Practice Quiz ANSWERS AVAILABLE IN ANSWER KEY.

1. What is the current understanding of how genetics influence obesity?
   a. Genetics is a good explanation for recent rises in obesity rates during childhood; however it does little to explain the rates of obesity for adulthood.
   b. Genetics only explains obesity with regard to females.
   c. Obesity is more likely to be caused by genetics than the environment.
   d. Genetics cannot explain recent rises in obesity rates, but rather, genetics provides only a risk for overweight and obesity.

2. Rates of childhood obesity _____.
   a. are higher in the United States than in most other developed countries
   b. are equally high in different parts of the United States
   c. have stayed relatively stable in the last decade
   d. are highest among Americans from economically advantaged backgrounds who have access to more foods

3. Your neighbors eat out quite a bit, and most of it is fast food. Their 8-year-old daughter is obese with a BMI of 24. Which of the following statements is most accurate?
   a. They should not be concerned because most children outgrow their obesity.
   b. As long as they emphasize that "beauty is from within," they should not be concerned about emotional problems.
   c. They should be concerned because she is at heightened risk for kidney failure and blindness.
   d. They should be concerned because of an increased chance of ADHD correlated with the stress of being obese.

4. In developed countries,_____.
   a. lead poisoning continues to be one of the top causes of death during middle childhood
   b. middle childhood is the least safe time of life because of an increased need for independence at this period in development
   c. even children who do not receive vaccinations are less susceptible to fatal diseases in middle childhood than they were earlier in their development
   d. rates of minor illnesses have increased during recent decades, even though rates of more serious illnesses have declined

5. Which of the following is a risk factor for asthma?
   a. Being male
   b. Living in the Western part of the United States
   c. Having French ancestry
   d. Being underweight

Summary: Physical Development

LO 7.1 Identify the changes in physical and sensory development that take place during middle childhood.

In middle childhood physical growth continues at a slow but steady pace, about 2–3 inches (5–8 cm) per year in height and about 5–7 pounds (2½–3 kg) per year in weight. Children lose all 20 primary teeth and their permanent teeth begin to grow in. Ear health improves, but one-fourth of children become nearsighted during middle childhood.

LO 7.2 Explain how motor development advances in middle childhood and how these advancements are related to new skills and participation in games and sports.

Children's gross motor skills improve in middle childhood due to improved balance, increased strength, better coordination, greater agility, and faster reaction time. As their gross motor development advances, children improve their performance in a wide range of games and sports, and many of them participate in organized sports. Fine motor development reaches nearly an adult level at this age, and across cultures, advances are especially evident in two areas: drawing and writing.

LO 7.3 Describe the negative effects of both malnutrition and obesity on development, and identify the causes of obesity.

Studies have shown that better-nourished children are more energetic, less anxious, show more positive emotion, and score higher than malnourished children on a wide range of cognitive measures in middle childhood. Across countries, rates of overweight and obesity are highest in the most affluent regions (North America and Europe) and lowest in the poorest regions (Africa and Southeast Asia). Obesity is a cultural phenomenon, and a variety of social and cultural changes have contributed to this problem, including diets with more fast food and high rates of television viewing. Genetics also make a contribution. Socially, being obese increases the likelihood that a child will be excluded and the object of ridicule by peers. Physically, obesity can result in diabetes in middle childhood, which eventually can lead to problems such as blindness, kidney failure, and stroke.

LO 7.4 Explain why rates of illness and injury are relatively low in middle childhood, and why rates of asthma have risen.

In both developed and developing countries, middle childhood is a time of unusually high physical well-being, with low rates of illnesses and diseases due to stronger immune systems, and the health of children has improved in recent years because of increased immunization rates and better public health policies. Rates of asthma have risen in developed countries due to carpets, pets, and airtight windows, and in developing countries due to worsening air pollution. Compared to younger children, children in middle childhood are more agile and better at anticipating situations that may cause injury.

Section 2 Cognitive Development

∨ Learning Objectives

7.5 Explain the major cognitive advances that occur during Piaget's concrete operations stage.

7.6 Describe how attention and memory change from early childhood to middle childhood, and identify the characteristics of children who have ADHD.

7.7 Describe the main features and critiques of intelligence tests, and compare and contrast Gardner's and Sternberg's approaches to conceptualizing intelligence.

7.8 Identify the advances in vocabulary, grammar, and pragmatics during middle childhood.

7.9 Explain the consequences for cognitive development of growing up bilingual.

7.10 Summarize the variations worldwide in school enrollment, socialization practices, and academic achievement during middle childhood.

7.11 Describe how reading and math skills develop from early childhood to middle childhood and the variations in approaches to teaching these skills.

COGNITIVE DEVELOPMENT: Theories of Cognitive Development

As we have seen in previous chapters, Piaget's approach and the information processing approach offer two different but complementary ways of understanding cognitive development. First we examine Piaget's ideas about concrete operations, then we discuss information processing advances in attention and memory.

Concrete Operations

LO 7.5 **Explain the major cognitive advances that occur during Piaget's concrete operations stage.**

If you grew up in a Western country, perhaps you believed in Santa Claus when you were a young child. According to the story, Santa Claus rides a sleigh borne by flying reindeer around the world on Christmas Eve, and at each house he comes down the chimney and delivers toys to all the good girls and boys. Do you remember when you stopped believing it? For most children, the story starts to seem far-fetched once they get to be 7 or 8 years old (Sameroff & Haith, 1996). How could one person make it all the way around the world in one night, even with flying reindeer? How could a large man make it down a narrow chimney, dragging a sack full of toys? And what if you don't have a chimney? The loss of belief in this myth reflects gains in cognitive development, as children develop a more true-to-life understanding of the world.

Middle childhood is when children develop a better grasp of what the physical world is really like and what is and is not possible. Recall from Chapter 6 that according to Piaget's theory of cognitive development, early childhood is the preoperational stage. In Piaget's view, children ages 2–6 are most notable cognitively for what they *cannot* do—they cannot perform mental operations—and for the kinds of mistakes they make.

Around age 7, children make an important cognitive advance toward becoming more systematic, planful, and logical thinkers. Piaget termed the cognitive stage from age 7 to 11 **concrete operations**. During this stage children become capable of using mental operations, which allow them to organize and manipulate information mentally instead of relying on physical and sensory associations. According to Piaget, the advances of concrete operations are evident in new abilities for performing tasks of conservation, classification, and seriation.

ADVANCES IN CONCRETE OPERATIONS As described in Chapter 6, prior to age 7 children usually make mistakes when performing tasks requiring an understanding of *conservation* (refer back to Learning Objective 6.6). Conservation is a key milestone of cognitive development because it enables the child to perceive regularities and principles in the natural world, which is the basis of being able to think logically about how the world works.

A second important cognitive achievement of concrete operations is *classification*. Although in early childhood young children can sort objects or events that share common characteristics into the same class—*red, round, sweet, dog,* for example—and can also combine classes into more general categories—elephants and rabbits are both part of the larger class "animals"—they run into difficulty when a classification problem requires a mental operation. For example, in one experiment, Piaget showed a 5-year-old boy a drawing of 12 girls and 2 boys, and this exchange followed (Piaget, 1965, p. 167):

Piaget: Are there more girls or more children?
Boy: More girls.
Piaget: But aren't the girls children?
Boy: Yes.
Piaget: Then are there more children or more girls?
Boy: More girls.

Amusing, no doubt, at your age, but if you think about it, answering this question requires a fairly challenging mental operation, at least for a 5-year-old. He must separate the girls and boys in the drawing into two classes (girls and boys), add them to form a larger class (children), and understand that the larger class (children) can be broken down again into each of its subclasses (girls and boys). Crucially, this must be done *mentally*. The number of girls can be compared to the number of boys visually, but comparing the number of children to the number of girls cannot, because girls are part of both categories. For this reason the 5-year-old trips up on the problem, but by age 8 or 9 most children perform this mental operation easily. In another experiment, Piaget interviewed a 9-year-old boy, showing him a drawing of 12 yellow tulips, 3 red tulips, and 6 daisies:

concrete operations

in Piaget's theory, the cognitive stage in which children become capable of using mental operations

Piaget: Which would make a bigger bunch, all the tulips or the yellow tulips?
Boy: All the tulips, of course. You'd be taking the yellow tulips as well.
Piaget: And which would be bigger, all the tulips or all the flowers?
Boy: All the flowers. If you take all the flowers, you take all the tulips, too.

(Adapted from Ginsburg & Opper, 1979, p. 123)

seriation

ability to arrange things in a logical order, such as shortest to longest, thinnest to thickest, or lightest to darkest

Seriation, the third achievement of concrete operations emphasized by Piaget, is the ability to arrange things in a logical order (e.g., shortest to longest, thinnest to thickest, lightest to darkest). Piaget found that preoperational children have an incomplete grasp of concepts such as *longer than* or *smaller than*. For example, when asked to arrange a set of sticks from shortest to longest, children in the preoperational age period would typically start with a short stick, then pick a long stick—but then pick another short stick, then another long stick, and so on. However, by age 7 most children can accurately arrange six to eight sticks by length. The video *Seriation* provides more examples of this.

Watch SERIATION

This kind of seriation task can be done visually—that is, it does not require a mental operation—but Piaget also found that during concrete operations children developed the ability to seriate mentally. Take this problem, for example. If Julia is taller than Anna and Anna is taller than Lynn, is Julia taller than Lynn? To get this right, the child has to be able to order the heights mentally from tallest to shortest: Julia, Anna, Lynn. Piaget considered the achievement of this skill of performing mental operations to be a key part of learning to think logically and systematically.

EVALUATING PIAGET'S THEORY As mentioned in Chapter 6, research testing Piaget's theory has found that, for concrete operations as for the preoperational stage, children are capable of performing some tasks at an earlier age than Piaget had claimed (Marti & Rodriguez, 2012; Vilette, 2002). However, for Piaget it was not enough for a child to grasp *some* aspects of conservation, classification, and seriation in order to be considered a concrete operational thinker; the child had to have *complete* mastery of the tasks associated with the stage (Piaget, 1965). Thus, the difference between Piaget and his critics on this issue is more a matter of definition—"What qualifies a child as a concrete operational thinker?"—than of research findings. Piaget also claimed that teaching children the principles of concrete operations would not work because their grasp of the principles of the stage has to occur naturally as part of their interaction with their environment (Piaget, 1965). Here his critics appear to be right, with many studies showing that with training and instruction, children under age 7 can learn to perform the tasks of concrete operations and also understand the underlying principles well enough to apply them to new tasks (Marti & Rodriguez, 2012; Parameswaran, 2003).

Transporting Piaget's tasks across cultures shows that acquiring an understanding of concrete operations depends on exposure to similar tasks and materials. For example, in one study of 4- to 13-year-old children in the Maya culture of Mexico and in Los Angeles, the children in Los Angeles performed better than the Mayan children on standard tests of concrete operations, whereas the Mayan children performed better on similar concrete operations tasks that involved materials used in weaving, because these materials were familiar from their daily lives (Maynard & Greenfield, 2003).

Information Processing

LO 7.6 Describe how attention and memory change from early childhood to middle childhood, and identify the characteristics of children who have ADHD.

Ever try to play a board game with a 3-year-old? If you do, it better be short and simple. But by middle childhood, children can play a wide variety of board games that adults enjoy, too, because their powers of attention and memory have advanced. This is one reflection of how information processing improves during middle childhood. Due to increased myelination in the brain, especially of the corpus callosum connecting the two hemispheres, speed of processing information increases (Roeder et al., 2008). Consequently, the amount of time required to perform various tasks decreases in the course of middle childhood. Advances are also made in the two key areas of information processing: attention and memory.

ATTENTION AND ADHD In middle childhood, children become more capable of focusing their attention on relevant information and disregarding what is irrelevant, an ability termed **selective attention** (Goldberg et al., 2001; Janssen et al., 2014). For example, in one line of research, children of various ages were shown a series of cards, each containing one animal and one household item, and told to try and remember where the animal on each card was located (Hagen & Hale, 1973). Nothing was mentioned about the household items. Afterward, when asked about the location of the animals on each card, older children performed better than younger children. However, when asked how many of the household items they could remember, younger children performed better than older children. The older children were capable of focusing on the information they were told would be relevant, the location of the animals, and capable of ignoring the household items as irrelevant. In contrast, the poorer performance of the younger children in identifying the locations of the animals was partly due to being distracted by the household items.

Being able to maintain attention becomes especially important once children enter school at about age 6 or 7, because the school setting requires children to pay attention to their teachers' instructions. Children with especially notable difficulties in maintaining attention may be diagnosed with **attention-deficit/hyperactivity disorder (ADHD)**, which includes problems of inattention, hyperactivity, and impulsiveness. Children with ADHD have difficulty following instructions and waiting their turn. In the United States, it is estimated that 7% of children ages 4–10 are diagnosed with ADHD (National Resource Center on ADHD, 2014). Boys are over twice as likely as girls to have ADHD. The diagnosis is usually made by a pediatrician after evaluation of the child and consultation with parents and teachers (Sax & Kautz, 2003). Watch the video *A Boy Talks About Having ADHD* for a child's perspective on the disorder.

In the United States, nearly 9 of 10 children and adolescents diagnosed with ADHD receive Ritalin or other medications to suppress their hyperactivity and help them concentrate better (Kaplan et al., 2004). Medications are often effective in controlling the symptoms of ADHD, with 70% of children showing improvements in academic performance and peer relations (Prasad et al. 2013). However, there are concerns about side effects, including slower physical growth and higher risk of depression (Reeves & Schweitzer, 2004). Behavioral therapies are also effective, and the combination of medication and behavioral therapy is more effective than either treatment alone (American Academy of Pediatrics, 2005; Hoza et al., 2008).

Although most research on ADHD has taken place in the United States, one large study of ADHD was completed in Europe, involving over 1,500 children and adolescents (ages 6–18) in 10 countries (Rotheberger et al., 2006). In this Attention-deficit/hyperactivity Disorder Observational Research in Europe (ADORE) study, pediatricians and child psychiatrists across Europe collected observational data on children and adolescents at

selective attention

ability to focus attention on relevant information and disregard what is irrelevant

attention-deficit/ hyperactivity disorder (ADHD)

diagnosis that includes problems of inattention, hyperactivity, and impulsiveness

Watch A BOY TALKS ABOUT HAVING ADHD

seven time points over 2 years, with data including diagnosis, treatment, and outcomes. Parents also participated, and their assessments showed high agreement with the assessments of the pediatricians and child psychiatrists.

Like the American studies, ADORE found higher rates of ADHD among boys than among girls, but the ratios varied widely among countries, from 3:1 to 16:1 (Novik et al., 2006). Symptoms of ADHD were similar among boys and girls, but girls with ADHD were more likely than boys to have additional emotional problems and to be bullied by their peers, whereas ADHD boys were more likely than girls to have conduct problems. For both boys and girls, having ADHD resulted in frequent problems in their relations with peers, teachers, and parents (Coghill et al., 2006). Parents reported frequent stresses and strains due to children's ADHD behavior, including disruptions of family activities and worries about the future (Riley et al., 2006). In contrast to the American approach of relying heavily on Ritalin and other medications, the European approaches to treatment were diverse: medications (25%), psychotherapy (19%), combination of medications and psychotherapy (25%), other therapy (10%), and no treatment (21%) (Preuss et al., 2006).

MEMORY In early childhood, memory is often fleeting, as any parent can attest who has ever asked a 4-year-old what happened to those nice new mittens he wore out to play that morning. Mittens? What mittens?

In middle childhood the capacity of working memory enlarges. On memory tests for sequences of numbers, the length of the sequence recalled is just 4 numbers for the typical 7-year-old, but for the typical 12-year-old it has increased to 7, equal to adults (Kail, 2003). More importantly, middle childhood is the period when children first learn to use **mnemonics** (memory strategies) such as rehearsal, organization, and elaboration.

Rehearsal, which involves repeating the information over and over, is a simple but effective mnemonic. You probably use it yourself, for example, when someone tells you a phone number and you are trying to remember it between the time you hear it and the time you use it. In a classic study, John Flavell and his

mnemonics

memory strategies, such as rehearsal, organization, and elaboration

rehearsal

mnemonic that involves repeating the same information over and over

ADHD is usually first diagnosed in middle childhood, when children are required to sit still for long periods in school.

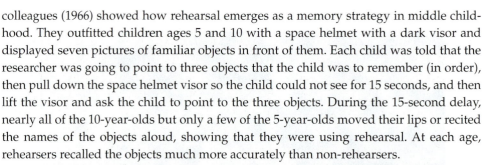

colleagues (1966) showed how rehearsal emerges as a memory strategy in middle childhood. They outfitted children ages 5 and 10 with a space helmet with a dark visor and displayed seven pictures of familiar objects in front of them. Each child was told that the researcher was going to point to three objects that the child was to remember (in order), then pull down the space helmet visor so the child could not see for 15 seconds, and then lift the visor and ask the child to point to the three objects. During the 15-second delay, nearly all of the 10-year-olds but only a few of the 5-year-olds moved their lips or recited the names of the objects aloud, showing that they were using rehearsal. At each age, rehearsers recalled the objects much more accurately than non-rehearsers.

Organization—placing things into meaningful categories—is another effective memory strategy that is used more commonly in the course of middle childhood (Schneider, 2002). Studies typically test this ability by giving people a list of items to remember, for example, shoes, zebra, baseball, cow, tennis racket, dress, raccoon, soccer goal, hat. Numerous studies have shown that if children are given a list of items to remember, they are more likely to group them into categories—clothes, animals, sports items—in middle childhood than in early childhood (Sang et al., 2002). Organization is a highly effective memory strategy, because each category serves as a *retrieval cue* for the items within the category, so that if the category can be remembered, all the items within the category are likely to be remembered as well (Schneider, 2002).

A third mnemonic that comes into greater use in middle childhood is **elaboration**, which involves transforming bits of information in a way that connects them and hence makes them easier to remember (Terry, 2003). One example of this is the standard way of teaching children the lines of the treble clef in music, EGBDF: *Every Good Boy Does Fine.* Or, if you were going to the grocery store and wanted to remember to buy butter, lettuce, apples, and milk, you could arrange the first letters of each of the items into one word, *BLAM.* The word *BLAM* serves as a retrieval cue for the items represented by each letter of the word.

Although children are more likely to use organization and elaboration in middle childhood than in early childhood, even in middle childhood and beyond, relatively few people use memory strategies on a regular basis. Instead, they rely on more concrete, practical methods. In one study, children in kindergarten and 1st, 3rd, and 5th grade were asked how they would remember to bring their ice skates to a party the next day (Kreutzer et al., 1975). At all three ages, children came up with sensible approaches such as putting the skates where they would be easy to see, writing themselves a note, and tying a string to their finger.

Another reason why memory improves from early childhood to middle childhood is that children's knowledge base expands, and the more you know, the easier it is to remember new information that is related to what you know. In a classic study illustrating this, 10-year-old chess masters and college student novice chess players were compared in their ability to remember configurations of pieces on a chess board (Chi, 1978). The 10-year-old chess masters performed far better than the college student novices, even though the college students were better at recalling a series of random numbers. In another study, 9- and 10-year-olds were separated into two groups, soccer "experts" and soccer "novices," and asked to try to remember lists of soccer items and non-soccer items (Schneider & Bjorklund, 1992). The soccer experts remembered more items on the soccer list than on the non-soccer list.

Middle childhood is not only a time of advances in memory abilities but of advances in understanding how memory works, or **metamemory**. Even by age 5 or 6, most children have some grasp of metamemory (Kvavilashvili & Ford, 2014). They recognize that it is easier to remember something that happened yesterday than something that happened long ago. They understand

organization

mnemonic that involves placing things mentally into meaningful categories

elaboration

mnemonic that involves transforming bits of information in a way that connects them and hence makes them easier to remember

metamemory

understanding of how memory works

Why do young chess masters remember chess configurations better than older novices do?

that short lists are easier to remember than long lists, and that familiar items are more easily remembered than unfamiliar items. However, their appraisal of their own memory abilities tends to be inflated. When children in early childhood and middle childhood were shown a series of 10 pictures and asked if they could remember all of them, more than half of the younger children but only a few older children claimed they could (none of them actually could!) (Flavell et al., 1970). In the course of middle childhood, children develop more accurate assessments of their memory abilities (Schneider & Pressley, 1997).

Intelligence and Intelligence Tests

LO 7.7   **Describe the main features and critiques of intelligence tests, and compare and contrast Gardner's and Sternberg's approaches to conceptualizing intelligence.**

Both the Piagetian approach and the information-processing approach describe general patterns of cognitive development and functioning, intended to apply to all children. However, at any given age there are also *individual differences* among children in their cognitive functioning. Within any group of same-age children, some will perform relatively high in their cognitive functioning and some relatively low. Even in infancy, toddlerhood, and early childhood, individual differences in cognitive development are evident, as children reach various cognitive milestones at different times, such as saying their first word. However, individual differences become more evident and more important in middle childhood, when children enter formal schooling and begin to be tested and evaluated on a regular basis.

In the study of human development, the examination of individual differences in cognitive development has focused mainly on measurements of **intelligence**. Definitions of intelligence vary, but it is generally understood to be a person's capacity for acquiring knowledge, reasoning, and solving problems (Sternberg, 2004). Intelligence tests usually provide an overall score of general intelligence as well as several subscores that reflect different aspects of intelligence.

Let us begin by looking at the characteristics of one of the most widely used intelligence tests, and follow with an exploration of the genetic and environmental sources of individual differences in intelligence. Then, we will consider two alternative ways of conceptualizing and measuring intelligence.

THE WECHSLER INTELLIGENCE TESTS   The most widely used intelligence tests are the Wechsler scales, including the *Wechsler Intelligence Scale for Children (WISC-IV)* for ages 6 to 16 and the *Wechsler Adult Intelligence Scale (WAIS-IV)* for ages 16 and up.

The Wechsler scales consist of 11 subtests, of which 6 are Verbal subtests and 5 are Performance subtests. The results provide an overall **intelligence quotient,** or **IQ** score, which is calculated relative to the performance of other people of the same age, with 100 as the **median** score. The overall IQ can be broken down into a Verbal IQ score, a Performance IQ score, and scores for each of the 11 subtests. More detail on each of the subscales of the WISC-IV is provided in **Table 7.1** on the next page, so you can get an idea of what IQ tests really measure.

How accurate are the Wechsler IQ tests? IQ tests were originally developed to test children's abilities as they entered school, and IQ has proven to be a good predictor of children's school performance. One study of children in 46 countries found that across countries, IQ scores and school achievement scores were highly correlated (Lynn & Mikk, 2007). IQ scores are also quite good predictors of success in adulthood, as Chapter 10 will explore in more detail (Benbow & Lubinski, 2009).

However, IQ tests have been criticized on a variety of grounds. Critics have complained that IQ tests assess only a narrow range of abilities, and miss some of the most

intelligence

capacity for acquiring knowledge, reasoning, and solving problems

intelligence quotient (IQ)

score of mental ability as assessed by intelligence tests, calculated relative to the performance of other people the same age

median

in a distribution of data, the score that is precisely in the middle, with half the distribution lying above and half below

Table 7.1 The WISC-IV: Sample Items

Verbal Subtests	
Information	General knowledge questions, for example, "Who wrote Huckleberry Finn?"
Vocabulary	Give definitions, for example, "What does formulate mean?"
Similarities	Describe relationship between two things, for example, "In what ways are an apple and an orange alike?" and "In what ways are a book and a movie alike?"
Arithmetic	Verbal arithmetic problems, for example, "How many hours does it take to drive 140 miles at a rate of 30 miles per hour?"
Comprehension	Practical knowledge, for example, "Why is it important to use zip codes when you mail letters?"
Digit Span	Short-term memory test. Sequences of numbers of increasing length are recited, and the person is required to repeat them.
Performance Subtests	
	For all the performance tests, scores are based on speed as well as accuracy of response.
Picture arrangement	Cards depicting various activities are provided, and the person is required to place them in an order that tells a coherent story.
Picture completion	Cards are provided depicting an object or scene with something missing, and the person is required to point out what is missing (for example, a dog is shown with only three legs).
Matrix reasoning	Patterns are shown with one piece missing. The person chooses from five options the one that will fill in the missing piece accurately.
Block design	Blocks are provided with two sides all white, two sides all red, and two sides half red and half white. A card is shown with a geometrical pattern, and the person must arrange the blocks so that they match the pattern on the card.
Digit symbol	At top of sheet, numbers are shown with matching symbols. Below, sequences of symbols are given with an empty box below each symbol. The person must place the matching number in the box below each symbol.

important aspects of intelligence, such as creativity. IQ tests have also been attacked as culturally biased, because some of the vocabulary and general knowledge items would be more familiar to someone who was part of the middle-class culture (Ogbu, 2002). However, attempts to develop "culture-fair" tests have found the same kinds of group differences as standard IQ tests have found (Johnson et al., 2008). It may not be possible to develop a culture-fair or culture-free IQ test, because by the time people are able to take the tests (age 6) their cognitive development has already been shaped by living in a particular cultural and social environment. Although IQ tests aspire to test raw intellectual abilities, this would not really be possible unless everyone was exposed to essentially the same environment in the years before taking the test, which is obviously not the case. However, new approaches to studying intelligence have provided important insights into the relation between genetics and environment in performance on IQ tests, as we will discuss next.

INFLUENCES ON INTELLIGENCE IQ scores for a population-based sample usually fall into a **normal distribution**, or *bell curve,* in which most people are near the middle of the distribution and the proportions decrease at the low and high extremes, as shown in **Figure 7.4**. Persons with IQs below 70 are classified as having **intellectual disability**, and those with IQs above 130 are classified as **gifted**. But what determines whether a person's score is low, high, or somewhere in the middle? Is intelligence mainly an inherited trait, or is it shaped mainly by the environment?

As noted in Chapter 2, social scientists increasingly regard the old nature–nurture debates as sterile and obsolete. Nearly all accept that both genetics and environment are involved in development, including in the development of intelligence. A variety of new findings presented in the past 20 years provide insights into how genetics and environments interact and how both contribute to intelligence. Most of these studies use the

normal distribution

typical distribution of characteristics of a population, resembling a bell curve in which most cases fall near the middle and the proportions decrease at the low and high extremes

intellectual disability

level of cognitive abilities of persons who score 70 or below on IQ tests

gifted

in IQ test performance, persons who score 130 or above

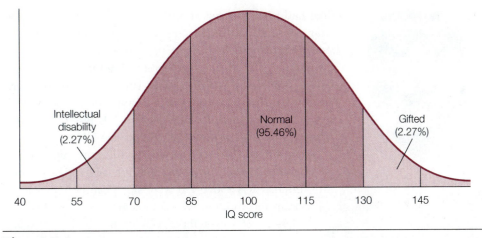

Figure 7.4 Bell Curve for Intelligence

IQ scores for a population-based sample usually fall into this kind of pattern.

natural experiments of adoption studies or twin studies in order to avoid the problem of passive genotype → environment effects. When parents provide both genetics and environment, as they do in most families, it is very difficult to judge the relative contribution of each. Adoption and twin studies help unravel that tangle.

One important conclusion from adoption and twin studies is that the more two people in a family are alike genetically, the higher the correlation in their IQs (Brant et al., 2009). As shown in **Figure 7.5**, adopted siblings, who have none of their genotype in common, have a relatively low correlation for IQ, about .24. The environmental influence is apparent—ordinarily, the correlation between two genetically unrelated children would be zero—but limited. Parents and their biological children, who share half of their genotype in common, are correlated for IQ at about .40, slightly higher if they live together than if they live apart. The correlation for biological siblings is higher, about .50, and slightly higher still for DZ twins. Biological siblings and DZ twins share the same proportion of their genotype in common as parents and biological children do (again, about half), so the greater IQ similarity in DZ twins must be due to greater environmental similarity, from the womb onward. The highest IQ correlation of all, about .85, is among MZ twins, who have exactly the same genotype. Even when they are adopted by separate families and raised apart, the correlation in IQ scores of MZ twins is about .75 (Brant et al., 2009).

The results of these studies leave little doubt that genetics contribute strongly to IQ scores. It is especially striking that the correlation in IQ is much lower for adopted siblings, who have grown up in the same family and neighborhood and attended the same schools, than it is for MZ twins who have been raised separately and have never even known each other.

However, other adoption studies show that both environment and genetics have a strong influence on intelligence. In one study, researchers recruited a sample of adopted children whose biological mothers were at two extremes, either IQ under 95 or above 120 (remember, 100 is the median population IQ) (Loehlin et al., 1997). All the

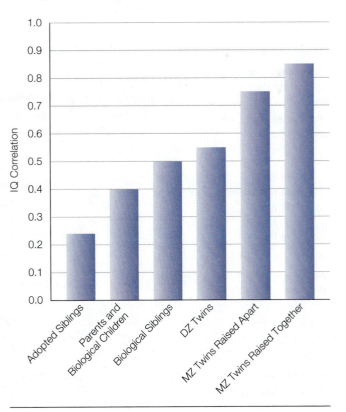

Figure 7.5 IQ and Genetics

The closer the genetic relationship, the higher the correlation in IQ.
SOURCE: Based on Brant et al. (2009).

Identical twins have similar IQs, even when reared apart. Here, 6-year-old MZ twin sisters in Thailand smile for the camera.

children had been adopted at birth by parents who were above average in education and income. When tested in middle childhood, children in both groups were above average in IQ. If we can assume that the high-education, high-income adoptive parents provided a healthy, stable, stimulating environment, this shows a strong influence of the environment for the children whose biological mothers all had IQs less than 95. On average they were above 100, due to the advantages of an environment provided by high-education, high-income parents. However, the children whose biological mothers had IQs above 120 were significantly higher in IQ than the children whose biological mothers had IQs less than 95, even though children in both groups had an advantaged environment, which showed the substantial influence of genetics.

Taken together, the adoption and twin IQ studies show that both genetics and environment contribute to the development of intelligence. Specifically, every child has a genetically based *reaction range* for intelligence, meaning a range of possible developmental paths (refer back to Learning Objective 2.4). With a healthy, stimulating environment, children reach the top of their reaction range for intelligence; with a poor, unhealthy, or chaotic environment, children are likely to develop a level of intelligence toward the bottom of the reaction range. There is both an upper and a lower limit to the reaction range. Even with an optimal environment, children with relatively low intellectual abilities are unlikely to develop superior intelligence; even with a subnormal environment, children with relatively high intellectual abilities are unlikely to end up well below average in IQ.

Recent research has revealed new insights into the intricate relations between genetics and environment in the development of intelligence. Specifically, research indicates that the influence of the environment on IQ is stronger for poor children than for children of affluent families (Nesbitt, 2009; Turkheimer et al., 2009). The less stimulating the environment, the less genetics influence IQ, because children's potentials are suppressed in an unstimulating environment. In contrast, an affluent environment generally allows children to receive the cognitive stimulation necessary to reach the top of their reaction range for IQ.

Flynn effect

steep rise in the median IQ score in Western countries during the 20th century, named after James Flynn, who first identified it

One other highly important finding that attests to the importance of environmental influences on intelligence is that the median IQ score in Western countries rose dramatically in the course of the 20th century, a phenomenon known as the **Flynn effect**, named for the scholar who first noted it, James Flynn (1999, 2012). From 1932 to 1997 the median IQ score among children in the United States rose by 20 points (Howard, 2001). This is a huge difference. It means that a child whose IQ was average in 1932 would be way below average by today's standard. It means that half of children today would have scored at least 120 by 1932 scoring, placing them in the "superior intelligence" range, and about one fourth of children today would be considered by 1932 standards to have "very superior intelligence"—a classification actually held by only 3% of children in 1932 (Horton, 2001). As shown in **Figure 7.6**, similar results have been found in other countries as well (Flynn, 1999, 2012).

What explains the Flynn effect? The causes must be environmental, rather than genetic; the genes of the human

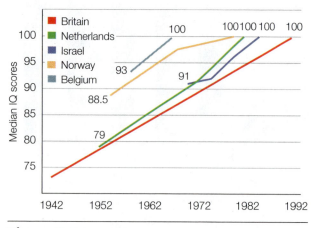

Figure 7.6 Flynn Effect

IQ scores rose across developed countries in the late 20th century.

SOURCE: Flynn (1999)

population could not have changed so dramatically in such a short time. But what about the environment improved so much in the course of the 20th century that would explain such a dramatic rise in median IQ scores? Several possibilities have been identified (Rodgers & Wanstrom, 2007). Prenatal care is better now than in the early 20th century, and better prenatal care leads to better intellectual development, including higher IQs. Families are generally smaller now than in the early 20th century, and in general the fewer children in a family, the higher their IQs. Far more children attend preschool now than was true in 1932, and preschool enhances young children's intellectual development. It has even been suggested that the invention of television may be one of the sources of the Flynn effect. Although television and other media are often blamed for societal ills, there is good evidence that watching educational television enhances young children's intellectual development (Scantlin, 2007).

An especially persuasive explanation has recently been proposed: the decline of infectious diseases (Eppig et al., 2010). Christopher Eppig and his colleagues note that the brain requires a great deal of the body's physical energy—87% in newborns, nearly half in 5-year-olds, and 25% in adults. Infectious diseases compete for this energy by activating the body's immune system and interfering with the body's processing of food during years when the brain is growing and developing rapidly. If this explanation is true, there should be an inverse relationship between IQ and infectious disease rates, and this pattern was evident in the researchers' analysis of data from 113 countries (as shown in **Figure 7.7**). The higher a country's infectious disease burden, the lower the country's median IQ. Thus the Flynn effect may have been primarily due to the elimination of major infectious diseases in developed countries. A Flynn effect of the future may be awaiting developing countries as they reduce and eliminate infectious diseases.

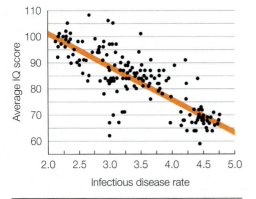

Figure 7.7 Inverse Relation Between IQ and Disease

Could this explain the Flynn effect?
SOURCE: Eppig et al. (2010)

OTHER CONCEPTIONS OF INTELLIGENCE: GARDNER'S AND STERNBERG'S THEORIES IQ testing has dominated research on children's intellectual development for nearly a century. However, in recent decades alternative theories of intelligence have been proposed. These theories have sought to present a conception of intelligence that is much broader than the traditional one. Two of the most influential alternative theories of intelligence have been presented by Howard Gardner and Robert Sternberg.

Gardner's (1983, 2004) **theory of multiple intelligences** includes eight types of intelligence (see **Table 7.2**). In Gardner's view only two of them, *linguistic* and *logical–mathematical* intelligences, are evaluated by intelligence tests. The other intelligences are *spatial* (the ability to think three-dimensionally); *musical; bodily–kinesthetic* (the kind that athletes and dancers excel in); *naturalist* (ability for understanding natural phenomena); *interpersonal* (ability for understanding and interacting with others); and *intrapersonal*

theory of multiple intelligences

Gardner's theory that there are eight distinct types of intelligence

Table 7.2 Gardner's Theory of Multiple Intelligences

Type of Intelligence	Description
Linguistic	Ability to use language
Musical	Ability to compose and/or perform music
Logical/mathematical	Ability to think logically and to solve mathematical problems
Spatial	Ability to understand how objects are oriented in space
Bodily-kinesthetic	Speed, agility, and gross motor control.
Interpersonal	Sensitivity to others and understanding motivation of others
Intrapersonal	Understanding of one's emotions and how they guide actions
Naturalist	Ability to recognize the patterns found in nature

(self-understanding). As evidence for the existence of these different types of intelligence, Gardner argues that each involves distinct cognitive skills, that each can be destroyed by damage to a particular part of the brain, and that each appears in extremes in geniuses as well as in *idiots savant* (the French term for people who are low in general intelligence but possess an extraordinary ability in one specialized area).

Gardner argues that schools should give more attention to the development of all eight kinds of intelligence and design programs that would be tailored to each child's individual profile of intelligences. He has proposed methods for assessing different intelligences, such as measuring musical intelligence by having people attempt to sing a song, play an instrument, or orchestrate a melody (Gardner, 1999, 2011). However, thus far neither Gardner nor others have developed reliable and valid methods for analyzing the intelligences he proposes. Gardner has also been criticized for extending the boundaries of intelligence too widely. When an adolescent displays exceptional musical ability, is this an indication of musical "intelligence" or simply of musical talent? Gardner himself has been critical of the concept of "emotional intelligence" proposed by Daniel Goleman and others (Goleman, 1997), arguing that the capacity to empathize and cooperate with others is better viewed as "emotional sensitivity" rather than intelligence (Gardner, 1999). However, Gardner is vulnerable to a similar criticism for proposing "interpersonal" and "intrapersonal" intelligences. Gardner (2011) is continuing to develop his theory and methods to assess it.

triarchic theory of intelligence

Sternberg's theory that there are three distinct but related forms of intelligence

Is musical ability a type of intelligence?

CRITICAL THINKING QUESTION

Do you agree that all the mental abilities described by Gardner are different types of intelligence? If not, which types would you remove? Are there other types you would add?

Sternberg's (1983, 1988, 2002, 2003, 2005) **triarchic theory of intelligence** includes three distinct but related forms of intelligence. *Analytical intelligence* is Sternberg's term for the kind of intelligence that IQ tests measure, which involves acquiring, storing, analyzing, and retrieving information. *Creative intelligence* involves the ability to combine information in original ways to produce new insights, ideas, and problem-solving strategies. *Practical intelligence* is the ability to apply information to the kinds of problems faced in everyday life, including the capacity to evaluate social situations. Sternberg has conducted extensive research to develop tests of intelligence that measure the three types of intelligence he proposes. These tests involve solving problems, applying knowledge, and developing creative strategies. Sternberg's research on Americans has demonstrated that each person has a different profile on the three intelligences that can be assessed (Sternberg, 2005, 2007). He proposes that the three components are universal and contribute to intelligent performance in all cultures (Sternberg, 2005), but so far the theory has been tested little outside the United States. Neither Sternberg's nor Gardner's tests are widely used among psychologists, in part because they take longer to administer and score than standard IQ tests do.

The underlying issue in judging alternative theories of intelligence is the question of how intelligence should be defined. If intelligence is defined simply as the mental abilities required to succeed in school, the traditional approach to conceptualizing and measuring intelligence is generally successful. However, if one wishes to define intelligence more broadly, as the entire range of human mental abilities, the traditional approach may be seen as too narrow, and an approach such as Gardner's or Sternberg's may be preferred. For a thoughtful perspective on how differently cultures may conceptualize intelligence, see the video *Robert Sternberg on Cultural Influences*.

Watch ROBERT STERNBERG ON CULTURAL INFLUENCES

Video

Practice Quiz ANSWERS AVAILABLE IN ANSWER KEY.

1. Maurice is 8 years old and is shown two round balls of clay that are equal in size. He watches as the experimenter rolls one ball into a long sausage shape. When asked, "Which has more clay?" he will likely reply _____.

   a. the ball

   b. the long one that looks like a sausage

   c. I'm not sure; I'll need to weigh them

   d. they're both the same

2. Marina is 9 years old and is capable of concrete operational thought. Like most other children her age, she should _____.

   a. fail the three mountain task, but pass the abstract thinking task

   b. still have great difficulty with seriation tasks, such as arranging items from shortest to longest

   c. be able to organize and manipulate information mentally

   d. think in terms of hypotheticals

3. Research on ADHD _____.

   a. has found similar treatments utilized across the various countries that have been studied

   b. has found that less than half of children diagnosed with this disorder in the United States receive medication

   c. has shown that like the American studies, studies in other countries found higher rates among boys than among girls

   d. has shown that two of the most common side effects of medication are weight gain and stuttering

4. Selective attention _____.

   a. refers to the placement of things into meaningful categories

   b. refers to thinking about thinking

   c. refers to focusing on the relevant stimuli, while ignoring what is irrelevant

   d. is a common measure of intelligence

5. Both Gardner's and Sternberg's theory of intelligence propose _____.

   a. that there are multiple components of intelligence

   b. that there are three different types of intelligence

   c. that creativity is genetically determined

   d. an IQ score that allows comparisons among individuals

COGNITIVE DEVELOPMENT:
Language Development

In middle childhood, advances in language development may not be as noticeable as in the earliest years of life, but they are nevertheless dramatic. There are important advances in vocabulary, grammar, and pragmatics. Bilingual children face special challenges in language development but also benefit in some ways.

Vocabulary, Grammar, and Pragmatics

LO 7.8 **Identify the advances in vocabulary, grammar, and pragmatics during middle childhood.**

Once they enter formal school at age 5–7 and begin reading, children's vocabulary expands as never before, as they pick up new words not just from conversations but from books. At age 6 the average child knows about 10,000 words, but by age 10 or 11 this sum has increased fourfold, to about 40,000 (Fitneva & Matsui, 2015). Part of this growth comes from children's growing abilities to understand the different forms words can take. A child who learns the meaning of *calculate* will also now understand *calculating, calculated, calculation*, and *miscalculate* (Anglin, 1993).

The grammar of children's language use becomes more complex in middle childhood. For example, they are more likely than younger children to use *conditional sentences* such as "If you let me play with that toy, I'll share my lunch with you."

Another important aspect of language that improves in middle childhood is *pragmatics*, the social context and conventions of language. As noted in Chapter 6, even in early childhood children have begun to understand pragmatics. For example, they realize that what people say is not always just what they mean, and that interpretation is required. They understand that "How many times do I have to tell you not to feed the dog off your plate?" is not really a math question. However, in middle childhood the understanding of pragmatics grows substantially (Ishihara, 2014). This can be seen vividly in children's use of humor. A substantial amount of humor in middle childhood involves violating the expectations set by pragmatics. For example, here is an old joke that made my son Miles howl with laughter when he first learned it at age 8:

Man: "Waiter, what's that fly doing in my soup?"
Waiter: "I believe he's doing the backstroke, sir."

For this to be funny, you have to understand pragmatics. Specifically, you have to understand that by asking "What's that fly doing in my soup?" the man means "What are you going to do about that disgusting fly?" The waiter, a bit slow on his pragmatics, interprets the man to mean, "What activity is that fly engaged in?" What makes it funny is that your understanding of pragmatics leads you to expect the first response, and the second response comes as a surprise. By substituting the expected pragmatic meaning of the question with an unexpected meaning, the joke creates a humorous effect (at least if you are 8 years old).

Pragmatics are always culturally grounded, which is one reason why jokes don't travel well between cultures. To know the pragmatics of a language, you have to know well the culture of the people using the language. For example, many languages have two forms of the word "you," one form used when there is a close attachment (such as with family and close friends) and the other used with unfamiliar persons and persons with whom there is a professional but not personal relationship (such as employers or students). Knowing when and with whom to use each form of "you" requires extensive familiarity not just with the language but with the cultural norms for using the two forms in the appropriate social contexts.

Bilingualism

LO 7.9 **Explain the consequences for cognitive development of growing up bilingual.**

A rising number of children around the world grow up knowing two languages; that is, they are **bilingual**. There are two main reasons for this trend. First, with increased migration between countries, children are more likely to be exposed early to two languages, one spoken at home and one spoken with friends, teachers, and others outside the home.

bilingual

capable of using two languages

Second, school systems increasingly seek to teach children a second language to enhance their ability to participate in the global economy. Because the United States is the most influential country in the world economy, English is the most common second language for children around the world. For example, in China all children now begin learning English in primary school (Chang, 2008). There are many bilingual families living within the United States as well, due to the large number of immigrants that have come to the United States in recent decades, and they speak a variety of languages (see **Map 7.1**).

As we have seen in previous chapters, children are marvelously well-suited to learning a language. But what happens when they try to learn two languages? Does learning two languages enhance their language development or impede it?

For the most part, becoming bilingual is favorable to language development. When children learn two languages, they usually become adept at using both (Baker, 2011; Ishihara, 2014). Learning a secondary language does not interfere with mastering the primary language (Lessow-Hurley, 2005). One minor problem that does arise is that in early childhood there is sometimes a tendency to intermix the syntax of the two languages. For example, in Spanish dropping the subject in a sentence is grammatically correct, as in *no quiero ir.* However, if a child who is bilingual in Spanish applies this rule to English it comes out as *no want go,* which is not correct. By middle childhood, children can easily keep their two languages separate, although they may intentionally import some words from one language when speaking in the other, to create "Spanglish" (a blend of Spanish and English) or "Chinglish" (a blend of Chinese and English), for example.

When children learn their second language after already becoming fluent in a first language, it takes longer to master the second language, usually 3–5 years (Baker, 2011; Hakuta, 1999). Even so, learning a second language comes much easier in early and middle childhood than it does at later ages. For example, in one study, adults who had immigrated to the United States from China or Korea at various ages were tested on their grammatical knowledge of English (Johnson & Newport, 1991). The participants who had arrived in the United States in early or middle childhood scored as well on the test as native English speakers, but beyond middle childhood, the older the age at immigration,

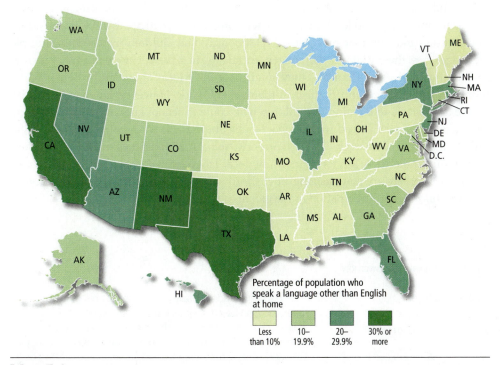

Percentage of population who speak a language other than English at home

Less than 10% | 10–19.9% | 20–29.9% | 30% or more

Map 7.1 Bilingualism in the United States

Which states have the highest percentage of bilingual families? How might this relate to the ethnic diversity that exists within these states?

Many Indian children learn several languages.

the less the person's grammatical knowledge. Other studies have shown that beyond the age of about 12 it is difficult for people to learn to speak a new language without a noticeable accent (Birdsong, 2006). Clearly, children have a biological readiness for learning a new language that adults lack, but the decline in this ability is gradual and steady from childhood to adulthood.

Becoming bilingual has a variety of benefits. Children who are bilingual have better **metalinguistic skills** than single-language children, meaning that they have greater awareness of the underlying structure of language (Schwartz et al., 2008). In one early study (Oren, 1981), researchers compared bilingual and single-language children ages 4–5 on metalanguage skills by instructing them to use nonsense words for familiar objects (e.g., *dimp* for dog, *wug* for car) and by asking them questions about the implications of changing object labels (if we call a dog a cow, does it give milk?). The bilingual children were consistently better than the single-language children in metalanguage understanding. Specifically, they were better at applying grammatical rules to nonsense words (one *wug,* two *wugs*) and at understanding that words are symbols for objects (calling a dog a cow won't make it give milk). Other studies have confirmed that bilingual children are better than single-language children at detecting mistakes in grammar and meaning (Baker, 2011; Bialystok, 1993, 1997). Bilingual children also score higher on more general measures of cognitive ability, such as analytical reasoning, cognitive flexibility, and cognitive complexity, indicating that becoming bilingual also has general cognitive benefits (Bialystok, 1999, 2001; Swanson et al., 2004).

In some countries, such as India, many children are not just bilingual but **multilingual**. Indian children first learn their local language, of which there are over a thousand across India (MacKenzie, 2009). Then they learn Hindi, which is the official national language, and many also learn English as well, in order to participate in the global economy. Studies indicate that by middle childhood, Indian children exposed to multiple languages use their different languages effectively in different contexts (Bhargava & Mendiratta, 2007). For example, they might use their local language at home, Hindi with friends at school, and English in their school work. However, language diversity can be an obstacle to learning for children who come to school knowing only their local language and are then faced with a school curriculum that is entirely in a new and unfamiliar language (MacKenzie, 2009). Currently, some Indian schools are changing their curriculum in the early school years to the local language before introducing Hindi or English, but others are emphasizing English from the outset of schooling in an effort to prepare children for participation in the global economy.

metalinguistic skills

in the understanding of language, skills that reflect awareness of the underlying structure of language

multilingual

capable of using three or more languages

Practice Quiz   ANSWERS AVAILABLE IN ANSWER KEY.

1. Compared to her brother in first grade, Fari, a 9-year-old in fourth grade, will be MORE likely to _____.

  a. have trouble understanding jokes because children take everything literally at this age

  b. use fewer conditional sentences because children are aware that others may misinterpret them

  c. realize that what people say is not always what they mean

  d. use longer sentences, but with less complex grammar

2. After his mother accidentally put the peanut butter in the refrigerator, Carl heard his father say to his mother, "Well, that was smart." Carl understood that his father was not giving her a compliment and it did not mean his mother was especially intelligent. This is an example of increased understanding of _____.

  a. pragmatics   **c.** the past imperfect tense

  b. conditional sentences   **d.** decentering

3. Children who are bilingual _____.

    a. are usually behind their single-language counterparts in meta-linguistic skills

    b. take longer to master the second language when they learn it after already becoming fluent in the first language

    c. learn the second language better after age 12 because they have a more sophisticated understanding of syntax by this point in development

    d. score lower on tests of metalinguistic skills, but higher on IQ tests

4. S. grew up in Shanghai, China; one cousin grew up in Japan, and another grew up in Italy. It is most likely that all three learned _____ as their second language.

    a. French

    b. German

    c. English

    d. Spanish

COGNITIVE DEVELOPMENT: School in Middle Childhood

In most of the world today, the daily lives of children in middle childhood are oriented around school. School is where they begin to gain the cognitive skills, especially in reading and math, that will enable them to participate economically in adult life.

School Experiences and Achievement

LO 7.10 **Summarize the variations worldwide in school enrollment, socialization practices, and academic achievement during middle childhood.**

For people who have grown up in a place where going to school is a routine part of children's development in middle childhood, it is easy to assume that this has always been the case. Indeed, many developmental psychologists refer to children in middle childhood as "school-age children," as if going to school is a natural, universal, and inevitable part of children's development once they reach the age of 6 or 7. However, attending school has been a typical part of children's lives in most countries only for less than 200 years. In the United States, for example, it is estimated that prior to 1800 only about half of children attended school, and even for those who did, it lasted only a few years (Rogoff et al., 2005). Enrollment increased steadily over the 19th century, as industrialization created jobs that required literacy and people migrated from farms to urban areas, and by 1900 most children completed several years of schooling. The school year remained quite short in the late 19th century, taking place mostly during the winter months, when children's labor was not needed on the farm. In 1870, the average child enrolled in school attended for only 78 days per year. Classrooms often mixed children of a wide range of ages.

Today, going to school has become a typical part of middle childhood, but it still is not universal, as **Figure 7.8** shows (UNICEF, 2014). In most developing countries, about 18% of children ages 6–10 do not attend primary school, and in sub-Saharan Africa, 23% of boys and 21% of girls ages 6–10 do not attend. However, in all developing countries, primary school enrollment has risen steeply in recent decades.

In many developing countries, the change to a school-oriented daily life in middle childhood has been

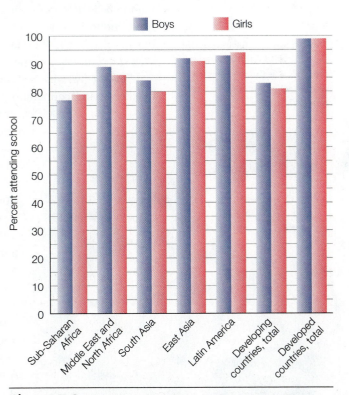

Figure 7.8 Primary School Attendance in World Regions

Attending primary school is common but not universal, worldwide.

SOURCE: Based on UNICEF (2014)

Table 7.3 From Work to School in One Generation: Guatemalan Children and Parents

	Parents %	Children %
Girls learn weaving	87	0
Boys learn to care for younger children	53	7
Boys do farm work	57	36
Expect education beyond Grade 6 (boys)	7	71
Expect education beyond Grade 6 (girls)	3	76
Expect to weave as adults (girls)	43	15
Expect to do farm work as adults (boys)	77	22

SOURCE: Based on Rogoff et al. (2005)

swift (Gaskins, 2015). For example, in Guatemala, Barbara Rogoff has been conducting ethnographic research in the same village for over 30 years. Over the course of just one generation, children's experiences were transformed (see **Table 7.3**; Rogoff et al., 2005). For example, not a single village girl today has learned weaving, even though nearly all of their mothers weaved as girls. For boys, the percentage who helped care for younger children dropped from 53% to 7% in just one generation. The percentage of boys helping with farm work also dropped from the parents' generation to the current generation. Because they now spend most of the day in school, girls no longer learn weaving, and boys are no longer available for farm work.

The change in children's focus from work to school was reflected in the change in their aspirations. In the parents' generation, few expected as children to continue education past Grade 6; for today's children, about three-fourths expect to go beyond Grade 6, and over half expect to go beyond Grade 12. Both boys and girls today envisioned a wider range of future occupations than their parents could have imagined, including accountant, teacher, pastor, and doctor.

A great deal of research has focused on comparisons between schools in the United States and in Asian countries such as Japan, China, and South Korea. These Asian countries have cultural traditions going back over 2 millennia emphasizing the importance and value of education, and the traditions remain strong today. High standards are applied to all children, as people in these countries believe that educational success is derived mainly from hard work and any child can succeed who tries hard enough (Stevenson et al., 2000; Sun et al., 2013). The same beliefs are characteristic of Asian American families (Fuligni et al., 2005). In contrast, most other Americans tend to believe that educational success is due mainly to innate ability, so when a child does poorly they tend to believe there is not much that can be done. Another difference is that Asian children tend to view academic striving as something they do not just for themselves but as a moral obligation to their families (Sun et al., 2013). In contrast, American children tend to view academic achievement as a mark of individual success.

Several features of Asian schools reflect collectivistic cultural beliefs emphasizing obedience and cooperation. Children are required to wear uniforms, a classic *custom complex* (see Chapter 1) underscoring diminished individuality and emphasizing conformity to the group. Children are also required to help to maintain the cleanliness and order of the school, emphasizing the collectivistic cultural value of contributing to the well-being of the community. Furthermore, children often work in groups, with students who have mastered a concept instructing those who have yet to grasp it (Shapiro & Azuma, 2004). In contrast, children in American schools typically do not wear uniforms (except in some private schools), are not required to help with school maintenance, and spend more time working alone (Stevenson & Zusho, 2002).

There are other important differences between the United States and Asian countries in the structure of the school day and year. Asian children spend more time on a typical school day learning academic subjects than American children do; Americans spend only about half as much of their school time in academic activities as children in China and Japan do, and spend more school time in art, music, and sports (Shapiro & Azuma, 2004). Both the school day and the school year are

Children in many Asian countries are required to wear school uniforms. How is the requirement of wearing school uniforms a custom complex?

longer in Asian countries. The school year in the United States is 180 days, compared to 220 in South Korea and 245 in China (Luckie, 2010).

How are these differences in school socialization and structure related to children's academic performance? In recent years, several excellent cross-national studies of academic performance have been conducted at regular intervals, including the Progress in International Reading Literacy Study (PIRLS) and the Trends in International Mathematics and Science Study (TIMSS). On the basis of these results, it appears that academic performance in 4th grade is related mainly to countries' economic development rather than to differences in cultural beliefs and (consequently) in educational practices (NCES, 2013). The highest-performing countries have widely varying educational approaches, but they all have high levels of economic development. As a result, they are most able to afford the resources that contribute to high academic performance, from good prenatal care to high-quality preschools to well-funded primary schools.

Within countries as well, the economic background of the family makes a great difference in children's academic performance. This is especially true in the United States, where schools are funded mostly on the basis of local property taxes rather than by the national government. As a result, the rich get richer, and the poor get poorer: schools in the poorest areas have the least amount of resources to provide for children coming from

Cultural Focus: School and Education in Middle Childhood Across Cultures

Attending primary school has become a near-universal experience of middle childhood. However, in some countries there are many children who attend for only a few years, because their labor is desperately needed by their families for economic survival.

All primary schools teach children reading, writing, and math, but there are many variations in how children are taught and in what is expected of them, as you will see in this video.

Until recently, boys were more likely than girls to attend primary school. School attendance requires school fees in many countries, and some poor families would use their extremely limited resources for the boys' education. Girls were often kept home because it was believed that boys' education would be of greater benefit to the family. However, in recent years this gender difference has disappeared, and boys and girls are now equally likely to obtain primary education (UNICEF, 2014). In this video, a Mexican girl observes that in her village, girls are more likely than boys to attend schools, because boys are more often required to work to help the family.

Review Question:

What common educational themes do you see among the individuals in this video?

Watch SCHOOL AND EDUCATION IN MIDDLE CHILDHOOD ACROSS CULTURES

poor families, whereas schools in the most affluent areas have the most resources, and the children attending those schools, who are mainly from affluent families, reap the benefits. Not surprisingly, given this system, children from low-income families generally score worse than children from high-income families on tests of academic achievement (NCES, 2013). Similarly, the wealthiest American states have the highest school achievement test scores, and the poorest states have the lowest scores.

Learning the Cognitive Skills of School: Reading and Mathematics

LO 7.11 **Describe how reading and math skills develop from early childhood to middle childhood and the variations in approaches to teaching these skills.**

In most cultures, middle childhood is when children first learn how to read and how to do math. However, there are variations in the timing and methods of teaching these skills, both within and between cultures.

APPROACHES TO READING Children learn language with remarkable proficiency without being explicitly taught or instructed, just from being around others who use the language and interacting with them. However, when they reach middle childhood, children must learn a whole new way of processing language, via reading, and for most children learning to read takes direct instruction. Learning to read is a relatively new development in human history. Until about 200 years ago, most people were illiterate all their lives. For example, in the United States in 1800, only about half of army recruits were even able to sign their own names on the enlistment documents (Rogoff et al., 2005). Because most human economic activity involved simple agriculture or hunting or fishing, learning to read was unnecessary for most people. They could learn what they needed to know from observing others and working alongside them, through guided participation. Today, of course, in a globalized, information-based economy, learning to read is an essential skill for most economic activity, across cultures. Consequently, children almost everywhere learn to read, usually beginning around age 6 or 7, when they enter school.

Think for a moment about the cognitive skills reading requires, so that you can appreciate how complex and challenging it is. In order to read, you have to recognize that letters are symbols of sounds, and then match a speech sound to each letter or letter combination. You have to know the meanings of whole words—one or two at first, then dozens, then hundreds, and eventually many thousands. As you read a sentence, you have to keep the meanings of individual words or combinations of words in working memory while you continue to read the rest of the sentence. At the end of the sentence, you must put all the word and phrase meanings together into a coherent meaning for the sentence as a whole. Then you have to combine sentences into paragraphs and derive meanings of paragraphs from the relations between the sentences; then combine paragraphs for still larger meanings; and so on.

By now this process no doubt comes naturally to you, after so many years of reading. We perform the complex cognitive tasks of reading automatically after reading for some years, without thinking about the components that go into it. But what is the best way to teach children who are first learning to read? Two major approaches have emerged in educational research over the years. The **phonics approach** advocates teaching children by breaking down words into their component sounds, called phonics, then putting the phonics together into words (Gray et al., 2007). Reading in this approach involves learning gradually more complex units: phonics, then single words, then short sentences, then somewhat longer sentences, and so on. After mastering their phonics and being able to read simple words and sentences, children begin to read longer materials such as poems and stories.

phonics approach

method of teaching reading that advocates breaking down words into their component sounds, called phonics, then putting the phonics together into words

The other major approach to teaching reading is the **whole-language approach** (Donat, 2006). In this view, the emphasis should be on the meaning of written language in whole passages, rather than breaking down each word into its smallest components. This approach advocates teaching children to read using complete written material, such as poems, stories, and lists of related items. Children are encouraged to guess at the meaning of words they do not know, based on the context of the word within the written material. In this view, if the material is coherent and interesting, children will be motivated to learn and remember the meanings of words they do not know.

Which approach works best? Each side has advocates, but evidence is substantial that the phonics approach is more effective at teaching children who are first learning to read (Beck & Beck, 2012). Children who have fallen behind in their reading progress using other methods improve substantially when taught with the phonics approach (Shawitz et al., 2004; Xue & Meisels, 2004). However, once children have begun to read they can also benefit from supplementing phonics instruction with the whole-language approach, with its emphasis on the larger meanings of written language and on using material from school subjects such as history and science to teach reading as well (Pressley et al., 2002; Silva & Martins, 2003).

Although learning to read is cognitively challenging, most children become able readers by Grade 3 (Popp, 2005). However, some children find learning to read unusually difficult. One condition that interferes with learning to read is **dyslexia**, which includes difficulty sounding out letters, difficulty learning to spell words, and a tendency to misperceive the order of letters in words (Snowling, 2004; Spafford & Grosser, 2005). Dyslexia is one of the most common types of **learning disabilities**, which are cognitive disorders that impede the development of learning a specific skill such as reading or math. As with other learning disabilities, children with dyslexia are not necessarily any less intelligent than other children; their cognitive problem is specific to the skill of reading. The causes of dyslexia are not known, but boys are about 3 times as likely as girls to have the disability, suggesting a genetic link to the Y chromosome (Hensler et al., 2010; Vidyasagar, 2004).

LEARNING MATH SKILLS There has been far more research on the development of reading than on the development of math skills (Berch & Mazzocco, 2007). Nevertheless, some interesting aspects of math development have been discovered. One is that even some nonhuman animals have a primitive awareness of **numeracy**, which means understanding the meaning of numbers, just as *literacy* means understanding the meaning of written words (Posner & Rothbart, 2007). Rats can be taught to discriminate between a two-tone and an eight-tone sequence, even when the sequences are matched in total duration. Monkeys can learn that the numbers 0 through 9 represent different quantities of rewards. In human infants the beginning of numeracy appears surprisingly early. When they are just 6 weeks old, if they are shown a toy behind a screen and see a second toy added, when the screen is then lowered they look longer and appear more surprised if one or three toys are revealed rather than the two toys they expected.

From toddlerhood through middle childhood, the development of math skills follows a path parallel to the development of language and readings skills (Doherty & Landells, 2006). Children begin to count around age 2, the same age at which their language development accelerates dramatically. They begin to be able to do simple addition and subtraction around age 5, about the same age they often learn to read their first words. In the course of middle childhood, as they become more adept readers, they typically advance in their math skills, moving from addition and subtraction to multiplication and division, and increasing their speed of processing in response to math problems (Posner & Rothbart, 2007). Children who have problems learning to read frequently have problems mastering early math skills as well.

Cultures vary in their timing and approach to teaching math skills to children, with consequences for the pace of children's learning. One study compared 5-year-old children

whole-language approach
method of teaching reading in which the emphasis is on the meaning of written language in whole passages, rather than breaking down words into their smallest components

dyslexia
learning disability that includes difficulty sounding out letters, difficulty learning to spell words, and a tendency to misperceive the order of letters in words

learning disability
cognitive disorder that impedes the development of learning a specific skill such as reading or math

numeracy
understanding of the meaning of numbers

Street children may learn math from the transactions involving the objects they sell. Here, a boy sells candy in a park in Rio de Janeiro, Brazil.

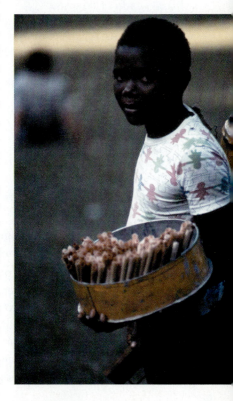

in China, Finland, and England (Aunio et al., 2008). The children in China scored highest, with children in Finland second, and the English children third. The authors related these variations to cultural differences in how math is taught and promoted. Children in China learn math beginning in preschool, and there is a strong cultural emphasis on math as an important basis of future learning and success. In contrast, English preschools usually make little attempt to teach children math skills, in the belief that they are not ready to learn math until they enter formal schooling.

Most children learn math skills within school, but sometimes math skills can be learned effectively in a practical setting. In a study of Brazilian street children, Geoffrey Saxe (2002) found that in selling candy they worked out complex calculations of prices and profits. Some had attended school and some had not, and the ones who had been to school were more advanced in some math skills but not in the skills necessary for them to succeed in their candy selling on the street.

Practice Quiz ANSWERS AVAILABLE IN ANSWER KEY.

1. Which statement best describes the history of education in the United States?

  a. During the late 19th century, children went to school mostly during the spring and summer because it was too expensive to heat the schoolhouse in other times of the year.

  b. Enrollment in school decreased throughout much of the 19th century.

  c. In the late 19th century, classrooms were segregated by gender and age.

  d. Prior to 1800, about half of children did not attend school.

2. Which of the following is one of several features of Asian schools that reflect collectivistic cultural beliefs?

  a. Children are required to help maintain the cleanliness and order of the school.

  b. Children are required to go to school fewer days than children in Western cultures.

  c. Rather than wearing a school uniform, parents decide how their children will dress.

  d. Children often work alone so they can master difficult skills as quickly as possible.

3. Zarena would have both the **shortest** school day and school year if she lived in _____.

  a. South Korea **c.** Japan

  b. China **d.** The United States

4. Research on reading and math skills has shown that _____.

  a. children who have trouble learning to read often have trouble mastering early math skills as well

  b. in the last two decades, girls are more likely to be diagnosed with dyslexia than are boys

  c. only humans have any awareness of numeracy

  d. all approaches to reading are equally effective when children are first learning to read

5. When first learning to read, Kara was taught using the phonics approach and Yolanda was taught with the whole-language approach. Which of the following outcomes is most likely based on existing research?

  a. Kara will learn to read faster than Yolanda.

  b. Yolanda will learn to read faster than Kara.

  c. Both of them will learn to read equally well.

  d. Kara is more at risk of developing dyslexia because of the confusion between the sound and appearance of letters linked to the phonics approach.

Summary: Cognitive Development

LO 7.5 **Explain the major cognitive advances that occur during Piaget's concrete operations stage.**

According to Piaget, children progress from the preoperational stage to the stage of concrete operations during middle childhood, as they learn to think more systematically and scientifically about how the world works and avoid cognitive errors. Cognitive advances during this stage include the ability to understand conservation, improved classification skills, and the understanding of seriation.

LO 7.6 **Describe how attention and memory change from early childhood to middle childhood, and identify the characteristics of children who have ADHD.**

In middle childhood, children become more capable of focusing their attention on relevant information and disregarding what is irrelevant. Children with especially notable difficulties in maintaining attention may be diagnosed with attention-deficit/hyperactivity disorder (ADHD), which includes problems of inattention, hyperactivity, and impulsiveness. Middle childhood is the period when children first learn to use memory strategies such as rehearsal, organization, and elaboration.

LO 7.7 Describe the main features and critiques of intelligence tests, and compare and contrast Gardner's and Sternberg's approaches to conceptualizing intelligence.

Intelligence testing first becomes a reliable predictor of later development in middle childhood. Critics have complained, however, that IQ tests assess only a narrow range of abilities, and miss some of the most important aspects of intelligence, such as creativity. Average IQ scores have risen substantially over the 20th century. In recent decades, alternative theories of intelligence have sought to present a conception of intelligence that is much broader than the traditional one. These include Howard Gardner's theory of multiple intelligences and Robert Sternberg's triarchic theory of intelligence. In Gardner's theory there are eight types of intelligence, whereas Sternberg proposes three, but neither theorist has been able to develop an effective way of assessing the intelligences they proposed.

LO 7.8 Identify the advances in vocabulary, grammar, and pragmatics during middle childhood.

Language development continues apace with massive additions to children's vocabularies once they learn to read. There is a fourfold increase in children's vocabularies between the ages of 6 and 10 or 11, and the grammar of children's language use becomes more complex. Their understanding of pragmatics also grows substantially during middle childhood, which can be seen vividly in children's use and appreciation of humor.

LO 7.9 Explain the consequences for cognitive development of growing up bilingual.

Becoming bilingual is beneficial, most notably in the development of metalinguistic knowledge. The difficulty of learning a second language increases with age.

LO 7.10 Summarize the variations worldwide in school enrollment, socialization practices, and academic achievement during middle childhood.

Attending school is a relatively recent historical development in children's lives, and even today 18% of children in developing countries do not attend primary school. School has important influences on children's social development because it separates children from the world of adults and places them among same-age peers. It also makes them less of an economic asset to their parents. Schools vary widely around the world depending on cultural beliefs about how children should learn, but it is economic development, not school philosophy, that mainly determines children's performance on international tests of academic performance.

LO 7.11 Describe how reading and math skills develop from early childhood to middle childhood and the variations in approaches to teaching these skills.

In middle childhood, children must learn a new way of processing language, via reading, and for most children learning to read takes direct instruction. Phonics appears to be the most effective approach to teaching children to read. Most children learn math skills within school, but sometimes math skills can be learned effectively in a practical setting.

Section 3 Emotional and Social Development

Learning Objectives

7.12 Describe the main features of emotional self-regulation and understanding in middle childhood and how other life stages compare.

7.13 Explain how different ways of thinking about the self are rooted in cultural beliefs, and summarize how self-concept and self-esteem change in middle childhood.

7.14 Describe how beliefs and behavior regarding gender change in middle childhood, including cultural variations.

7.15 Explain the distinctive features of family relations in middle childhood, and describe the consequences of parental divorce and remarriage.

7.16 Explain the main basis of friendships in middle childhood, and describe the four categories of peer social status and the dynamics between bullies and victims.

7.17 Describe the kinds of work children do in middle childhood, and explain why work patterns differ between developed and developing countries.

7.18 Summarize the rates of daily TV-watching among children worldwide, and describe the positive and negative effects of television, especially the hazards related to TV violence.

EMOTIONAL AND SOCIAL DEVELOPMENT: Emotional and Self-Development

Children advance in their emotional self-regulation in middle childhood and experience relatively few emotional extremes. They grow in their self-understanding, and their self-esteem is generally high, although it depends on cultural context. They grow in their understanding of gender roles, too, but in some respects they become more rigid about those roles.

Smooth Sailing: Advances in Emotional Self-Regulation

LO 7.12 Describe the main features of emotional self-regulation and understanding in middle childhood and how other life stages compare.

Middle childhood is in some ways a golden age emotionally, a time of high well-being and relatively low volatility. In infancy, toddlerhood, and even early childhood, there are many emotional highs, but plenty of emotional lows, too. Outbursts of crying and anger are fairly frequent in the early years of life, but by middle childhood the frequency of such negative emotions has declined substantially (Shipman et al., 2003). Negative emotions will rise again in adolescence, as we will see in Chapter 8, but during middle childhood most days are free of any negative emotional extremes.

One valuable source of information about emotions in middle childhood is research using the **Experience Sampling Method (ESM)** pioneered by Reed Larson and his colleagues (Larson & Richards, 1994; Larson et al., 2002; Richards et al., 2002). The ESM involves having people wear wristwatch beepers that randomly beep during the day so that people can record their thoughts, feelings, and behavior. Each time they are "beeped," participants rate the degree to which they currently feel happy to unhappy, cheerful to irritable, and friendly to angry, as well as how hurried, tired, and competitive they are feeling. The focus of Larson's research has been on adolescence, so we'll discuss the ESM method in more detail in Chapter 8, but some of his research has included middle childhood in order to chart the emotional changes that take place from middle childhood to adolescence.

The overall conclusion of ESM research with regard to middle childhood is that it is time of remarkable contentment and emotional stability (Larson & Richards, 1994). When beeped, children in middle childhood report being "very happy" 28% of the time, a far higher percentage than for adolescents or adults. Children at this age mostly have "quite enjoyable lives" in which they "bask in a kind of naïve happiness" (Larson & Richards, 1994, p. 85). Sure, they are sad or angry occasionally, but it is almost always due to something concrete and immediate such as getting scolded by a parent or losing a game, "events that pass quickly and are forgotten" (p. 85).

Emotional self-regulation improves from early childhood to middle childhood in part because the environment requires it (Geldhof et al., 2010). Middle childhood is often a time of moving into new contexts: primary school, civic organizations (such as the Boy Scouts and Girl Scouts), sports teams, and music groups. All of these contexts make demands for emotional self-regulation. Children are required to do what they are told (whether they feel like it or not), to wait their turn, and to cooperate with others. Expressions of emotional extremes are disruptive to the functioning of the group and are discouraged. Most children are capable of meeting these demands by middle childhood.

Emotional understanding also advances from early to middle childhood. Children become better able to understand both their own and others' emotions. They become aware that they can experience two contradictory emotions at once, an emotional state known as **ambivalence**; for example being both happy (because my team won the game) and sad (because my best friend was on the losing team) (Pons et al., 2003). They also learn how to conceal their emotions intentionally (Saarni, 1999). This allows them to show a socially acceptable emotion such as gratitude when, for example, they open a birthday present they didn't really want. In Asian cultures, children in middle childhood learn the concept of "face," which means showing to others the appropriate and expected emotion regardless of how you actually feel (Han, 2011).

In the same way that children become able to suppress or conceal their own true emotions, they come to understand that other people may display emotional expressions that do not indicate what they actually feel (Saarni, 1999). Children's understanding of others' emotions is also reflected in increased capacity for empathy (Goldstein & Winner, 2012; Hoffman, 2000). By middle childhood, children become better cognitively at perspective-taking, and the ability to understand how others view events fosters the ability to understand how they feel, too.

Middle childhood is an exceptionally happy time of life.

Experience Sampling Method (ESM)

research method that involves having people wear beepers, usually for a period of 1 week; when they are beeped at random times during the day, they record a variety of characteristics of their experience at that moment

ambivalence

emotional state of experiencing two contradictory emotions at once

Self-Understanding

LO 7.13 Explain how different ways of thinking about the self are rooted in cultural beliefs, and summarize how self-concept and self-esteem change in middle childhood.

self-concept

person's perception and evaluation of him- or herself

social comparison

how persons view themselves in relation to others with regard to status, abilities, or achievements

In middle childhood, children become more accurate in comparing themselves to others.

Sociologist George Herbert Mead (1934) made a distinction between what he called the *I-self* (how we believe others view us) and the *me-self* (how we view ourselves). Both the I-self and the me-self change in important ways in middle childhood. We discuss the me-self first, then the I-self, and then we look at the cultural basis of conceptions of the self.

SELF-CONCEPT Our **self-concept**, that is, how we view and evaluate ourselves, changes during middle childhood from the external to the internal and from the physical to the psychological (Lerner et al., 2005; Marsh & Ayotte, 2003; Rosenberg, 1979). Up until the age of 7 or 8, most children describe themselves mainly in terms of external, concrete, physical characteristics. ("My name is Mona. I'm 7 years old. I have brown eyes and short black hair. I have two little brothers.") They may mention specific possessions ("I have a red bicycle.") and activities they enjoy ("I like to dance." "I like to play sports.").

In the course of middle childhood, they add more internal, psychological, personality-related traits to their self-descriptions ("I'm shy." "I'm friendly." "I try to be helpful."). They may also mention characteristics that are *not me* ("I don't like art." "I'm not very good at math."). Toward the end of middle childhood their descriptions become more complex, as they recognize that they may be different on different occasions (Harter, 2003) ("Mostly I'm easy to get along with, but sometimes I lose my temper.").

Another important change in self-concept in middle childhood is that children engage in more accurate **social comparison**, in which they compare themselves to others (Guest, 2007). A 6-year-old might describe himself by saying, "I'm really good at math," whereas a 9-year-old might say "I'm better than most kids at math, although there are a couple of kids in my class who are a little better." These social comparisons reflect advances in the cognitive ability of seriation, discussed earlier in the chapter. In the same way that children learn how to arrange sticks accurately from shortest to tallest in middle childhood, they also learn to rank themselves more accurately in abilities relative to other children. The age grading of schools promotes social comparisons, as it places children in a setting where they spend most of a typical day around other children their age. Teachers compare them to one another by giving them grades, and they notice who is relatively good and relatively not so good at reading, math, and so on.

Self-concept can be influenced not only by age but by social context. In a multicultural society like the United States, the views of the majority culture can influence how children in minority cultures think about themselves. One classic study in the 1940s found that when African American and White children in middle childhood were given a choice of two dolls to play with, one White and one Black, even most of the Black children chose the White doll (Clark & Clark, 1947). Furthermore, children of both groups tended to choose the White doll as the "good" doll and the Black doll as the "bad" doll. Even recent studies continue to show that children often view dark skin as "bad" and white skin as "good" (Byrd, 2012).

SELF-ESTEEM **Self-esteem** is a person's overall sense of worth and well-being. A great deal has been written and discussed about self-esteem in American society in the past 50 years. Even among Western countries, Americans value high self-esteem to a greater extent than people in other countries, and the gap between Americans and non-Western countries in this respect is especially great. For example, in traditional Japanese culture, self-criticism is a virtue and high self-esteem is a character problem (Heine et al., 1999). The belief in the value of high self-esteem is part of American individualism (Bellah et al., 1985; Rychlak, 2003).

Self-esteem declines slightly in the transition from early childhood to middle childhood, as children enter a school environment in which social comparisons are a daily experience (Lerner et al., 2005; Wigfield et al., 1997). The decline is mild, and simply reflects children's more realistic appraisal of their abilities as they compare themselves to others and are rated by teachers. For the rest of middle childhood, overall self-esteem is high for most children, reflecting the generally positive emotional states mentioned earlier. In Western countries, having low self-esteem in middle childhood is related to anxiety, depression, and antisocial behavior (Robins et al., 2001).

An important change in self-esteem in middle childhood is that it becomes more differentiated. In addition to overall self-esteem, children have self-concepts for several specific areas, including academic competence, social competence, athletic competence, and physical appearance (Harter, 2012; Marsh & Ayotte, 2003). Within each of these areas, self-concept is differentiated into sub-areas. For example, children may see themselves as good at baseball but not basketball, while also having an overall high or low evaluation of their athletic competence.

Children combine their different areas of self-concept into an overall level of self-esteem. For most children and adolescents, physical appearance is the strongest contributor to overall self-esteem (Harter, 2012; Klomsten et al., 2004). However, in other areas, children's self-concept contributes to overall self-esteem only if they value doing well in that area. For example, a child may be no good at sports but not care about sports, in which case low athletic self-concept would have no effect on overall self-esteem.

CULTURE AND THE SELF The conception of the self that children have by middle childhood varies substantially among cultures. In discussing cultural differences in conceptions of the self scholars typically distinguish between the *independent self* promoted by individualistic cultures and the *interdependent self* promoted by collectivistic cultures (Cross & Gore, 2003; Markus & Kitayama, 1991; Shweder et al., 2006). Cultures that promote an independent, individualistic self also promote and encourage reflection about the self. In such cultures it is seen as a good thing to think about yourself, to consider who you are as an independent person, and to think highly of yourself (within certain limits, of course—no culture values selfishness or egocentrism). Americans are especially known for their individualism and their focus on self-oriented issues. It was an American who first invented the term *self-esteem* (William James, in the late 19th century), and the United States continues to be known to the rest of the world as a place where the independent self is valued and promoted (Green et al., 2005; Triandis, 1995).

However, not all cultures look at the self in this way or value the self to the same extent. In collectivistic cultures, an interdependent conception of the self prevails

self-esteem

person's overall sense of worth and well-being

(Markus & Kitayama 2010). In these cultures, the interests of the group—the family, the kinship group, the ethnic group, the nation, the religious institution—are supposed to come first, before the needs of the individual. This means that it is not necessarily a good thing, in these cultures, to think highly of yourself. People who think highly of themselves, who possess a high level of self-esteem, threaten the harmony of the group because they may be inclined to pursue their personal interests regardless of the interests of the groups to which they belong.

Cultural variations in views of the self influence approaches to parenting. Parents in most places and times have been more worried that their children would become too selfish than that they would have low self-esteem. As a result, parents have discouraged self-inflation as part of family socialization (Harkness et al., 2015; LeVine et al., 2008). However, this kind of parenting works differently if it is part of a cultural norm rather than an exception within a culture. For example, children from Asian cultures are discouraged from valuing the self highly, yet they generally have high levels of academic performance and low levels of psychological problems (Markus & Kitayama, 2010). In contrast, children within the American majority culture who are exposed to parenting that is critical and negative show negative effects such as depression and poor academic performance (Bender et al., 2007; DeHart et al., 2006). It may be that children in Asian cultures learn to expect criticism if they show signs of high self-esteem, and they see this as normal in comparison to other children, whereas American children learn to expect frequent praise, and hence they suffer more if their parents are more critical than the parents of their peers (Rudy & Grusec, 2006).

It should be added that most cultures are not purely either independent or interdependent in their conceptions of the self, but have elements of each (Killen & Wainryb, 2000). Also, with globalization, many cultures that have a tradition of interdependence are changing toward a more independent view of the self (Arnett, 2002, 2011).

Gender Development

LO 7.14 Describe how beliefs and behavior regarding gender change in middle childhood, including cultural variations.

As described in Chapter 6, cultural beliefs about gender become well established by the end of early childhood. Gender roles become even more sharply divided during middle childhood. In traditional cultures, the daily activities of men and women are very different, and the activities of boys and girls become more differentiated in middle childhood as they begin to take part in their parents' work. In the human past, men have been responsible for hunting, fishing, caring for domestic animals, and fighting off animal and human attackers (Gilmore, 1990). Women have been responsible for caring for young children, tending the crops, food preparation, and running the household (Shlegel & Barry, 1991). This pattern still prevails in many developing countries (Gaskins, 2015). During middle childhood, boys increasingly learn to do what men do and girls increasingly learn to do what women do.

Boys and girls not only learn gender-specific tasks in middle childhood, they are also socialized to develop personality characteristics that enhance performance on those tasks: independence and toughness, for boys, and nurturance and compliance for girls. In an early study of 110 traditional cultures, boys and girls were socialized to develop these gender-specific traits in virtually all cultures (Barry et al., 1957). More recent analyses of gender socialization in traditional cultures have found that these patterns persist (Banerjee, 2005; Kapadia & Gala, 2015; LeVine, 2008).

In developing countries, the kinds of work children and adults do is often divided strictly by gender. Here, a girl in Mozambique helps prepare cassava, a local food.

In modern developed countries, too, children's gender attitudes and behavior become more stereotyped in middle childhood. Children increasingly view personality traits as associated with one gender or the other rather than both. Traits such as "gentle" and "dependent" become increasingly viewed as feminine, and traits such as "ambitious" and "dominant" become increasingly viewed as masculine (Best, 2001; Heyman & Legare, 2004). Both boys and girls come to see occupations they associate with men (such as firefighter or astronomer) as having higher status than occupations they associate with women (such as nurse or librarian) (Liben et al., 2001; Weisgram et al., 2010). Furthermore, children increasingly perceive some school subjects as boys' areas (such as math and science) and others as girls' areas (such as reading and art) (Guay et al., 2010). Teachers may bring gender biases into the classroom, perhaps unknowingly, in ways that influence children's perceptions of what areas are gender-appropriate for them (Sadker & Sadker, 1994). Accordingly, boys come to feel more competent than girls at math and science and girls come to feel more competent than boys at verbal skills—even when they have equal abilities in these areas (Hong et al., 2003).

Socially, children become even more gender-segregated in their play groups in middle childhood than they were in early childhood. In traditional cultures, gender-segregated play is a consequence of the gender-specific work boys and girls are doing by middle childhood. In the 12-culture analysis by Whiting and Edwards (1988; see Chapter 6), same-gender play groups rose from a proportion of 30–40% at age 2–3 to over 90% by age 8–11. However, the same pattern is true in developed countries, where boys and girls are in the same schools engaged in the same daily activities (McHale et al., 2003). When boys' and girls' play groups do interact in middle childhood, it tends to be in a manner that is at once quasi-romantic and antagonistic, such as playing a game in which the girls chase the boys, or tossing mild insults at each other, like the one my daughter Paris came home chanting one day at age 7:

GIRLS go to COllege to get more KNOWledge.
BOYS go to JUpiter to get more STUpider.

Thorne (1986) calls this kind of gender play "border work" and sees its function as clarifying gender boundaries during middle childhood. It can also be seen as the first tentative step toward the romantic relations that will develop in adolescence.

In terms of their gender self-perceptions, boys and girls head in different directions in middle childhood (Banerjee, 2005; Kapadia & Gala, 2015). Boys increasingly describe themselves in terms of "masculine" traits. They become more likely to avoid activities that might be considered feminine, because their peers become increasingly intolerant of anything that threatens to cross gender boundaries (Blakemore, 2003). In contrast, girls become more likely to attribute "masculine" characteristics such as "forceful" and "self-reliant" to themselves in the course of middle childhood. They do not become less likely to describe themselves as having "feminine" traits such as "warm" and "compassionate," but they add "masculine" traits to their self-perceptions. Similarly, they become more likely during middle childhood to consider future occupations usually associated with men, whereas boys become less likely to consider future occupations associated with women (Gaskins, 2015; Liben & Bigler, 2002).

Why are interactions between boys and girls often quasi-romantic and antagonistic in middle childhood?

Practice Quiz ANSWERS AVAILABLE IN ANSWER KEY.

1. During middle childhood _____.
   a. children are less content than in adolescence mostly because they do not have the social skills required to manage peer conflict
   b. it is harder for children to hide their emotions than in early childhood because they become so much more intense at this period of development
   c. children are aware that they can experience two contradictory emotions at once
   d. the ability to self-regulate decreases from early childhood, mostly because of the many different contexts they experience

2. Dr. Marinello is using the Experience Sampling Method (ESM) method for her research. She is mostly likely measuring _____.
   a. emotions
   b. self-esteem
   c. self-concept
   d. meta-cognitive awareness

3. Nine-year-old Xinyin is a boy from China, a collectivistic culture. He would be more likely than his counterpart in the United States to answer the fill-in-the-blank question, "I am _____" with the following,

   a. one of the smartest kids in my class
   b. a boy with brown hair
   c. a son
   d. good at soccer and tennis

4. When compared to her 6-year-old sister, Isabelle, an 8th grader, is more likely to describe herself in terms of _____ characteristics
   a. physical
   b. concrete
   c. psychological
   d. external

5. During middle childhood _____.
   a. both boys and girls come to see occupations they associate with men as having higher status than occupations they associate with women
   b. gender segregation is unique to play groups in the United States
   c. boys feel less competent than their female counterparts in math and science even when they have equal abilities in these areas based on their grades
   d. play groups in traditional cultures become less gender-segregated than they were in early childhood

EMOTIONAL AND SOCIAL DEVELOPMENT: The Social and Cultural Contexts of Middle Childhood

There is both continuity and change in social contexts from early to middle childhood. Nearly all children remain within a family context, although the composition of the family may change in some cultures due to parents' divorce or remarriage. A new social context is added, as children in nearly all cultures begin formal schooling when they enter this life stage. For children in developing countries today, middle childhood may also mean entering a work setting such as a factory. In all countries, media have become an important socialization context, especially television.

Family Relations

LO 7.15 Explain the distinctive features of family relations in middle childhood, and describe the consequences of parental divorce and remarriage.

Middle childhood represents a key turning point in family relations. Up until that time, children in all cultures need, and receive, a great deal of care and supervision, from parents and older siblings and sometimes from extended family members. They lack sufficient emotional and behavioral self-regulation to be on their own for even a short period of time. However, in middle childhood they become much more capable of going about their daily activities without constant monitoring and control by others. From early childhood to middle childhood, parents and children move away from direct parental control and toward **coregulation**, in which parents provide broad guidelines for behavior but children are capable of a substantial amount of independent, self-directed behavior (Calkins, 2012; Maccoby, 1984; McHale et al., 2003). Parents continue to provide assistance and instruction, and they continue to know where their children are and what they are doing nearly all the time, but there is less need for direct, moment-to-moment monitoring.

This pattern applies across cultures. In developed countries, studies have shown that children spend substantially less time with their parents in middle childhood than in early childhood (Parke, 2004). Children respond more to parents' rules and reasoning, due to advances in cognitive development and self-regulation, and parents in turn use more explanation and less physical punishment (Collins et al., 2002; Parke, 2004). Parents begin to give their children simple daily chores such as making their own beds in the morning and setting the table for dinner.

In traditional cultures, parents and children also move toward coregulation in middle childhood. Children have learned family rules and routines by middle childhood and will often carry out their family duties without having to be told or urged by their parents (Gaskins, 2015; Weisner, 1996). Also, children are allowed to play and explore further from home once they reach middle childhood (Whiting & Edwards, 1988). Boys are allowed more of this freedom than girls are, in part because girls are assigned more daily responsibilities in middle childhood. However, girls are also allowed more scope for independent activity in middle childhood. For example, in the Mexican village described by Beverly Chinas (1992), when they reach middle childhood girls have responsibility for going to the village market each day to sell the tortillas they and their mothers have made that morning. By middle childhood they are capable of going to the market without an adult to monitor them, and they are also capable of making the monetary calculations required in selling the tortillas and providing change.

Sibling relationships also change in middle childhood (Bryant, 2014). Children with an older sibling often benefit from the sibling's help with academic, peer, and parent issues (Brody, 2004). Both older and young siblings benefit from mutual companionship and assistance. However, the sibling rivalry and jealousy mentioned in Chapter 6 continues in middle childhood. In fact, sibling conflict peaks in middle childhood (Cole & Kerns, 2001). In one study that recorded episodes of conflict between siblings, the average frequency of conflict was once every 20 minutes they were together (Kramer et al., 1999). The most common source of conflict is personal possessions (McGuire et al., 2000). Sibling conflict is especially high when one sibling perceives the other as receiving more affection and material resources from the parents (Dunn, 2004). Other factors contributing to sibling conflict are family financial stress and parents' marital conflict (Jenkins et al., 2003).

DIVERSE FAMILY FORMS Children worldwide grow up in a wide variety of family environments. Some children have parents who are married while others are in single-parent, divorced, or stepfamilies; some children are raised by heterosexual parents while others are raised by gay or lesbian parents; and still others live with extended family members or in multigenerational families. Some are adopted or live with relatives other than their parents. In the United States, only 59% of children live with both biological parents through middle childhood (Childstats.gov, 2013). Of the rest, about 24% live with a single mom, 5% live with a biological parent and stepparent, and 12% live in other family forms, such as with a grandmother or with adoptive parents.

coregulation
relationship between parents and children in which parents provide broad guidelines for behavior but children are capable of a substantial amount of independent, self-directed behavior

Siblings often benefit from having each other as companions.

Gay couples are now allowed to adopt children in some American states and some European countries, and lesbian couples often adopt children or become artificially inseminated. In the latest U.S. census, over 20% of gay couples and one third of lesbian couples were living with children, a dramatic increase over the past 20 years (U.S. Bureau of the Census, 2010). The video *A Family with Two Fathers* describes the adoption process for one such family. Studies of the children of gay and lesbian couples have found that they are highly similar to other children (Goldberg, 2010; Patterson, 2002). In adolescence nearly all are heterosexual, despite the homosexual model their parents provide (Hyde & DeLamater, 2005).

Watch A FAMILY WITH TWO FATHERS

Over the past 50 years, it has become increasingly common in some countries for children to be born to a single mother. The United States is one of the countries where the increase has been greatest. Single motherhood has increased among both Whites and African Americans, but is highest among African Americans; over 70% of African American children are born to a single mother (U.S. Bureau of the Census, 2010). Rates of single motherhood are also high in northern Europe (Ruggeri & Bird, 2014). However, it is more likely in northern Europe than in the United States for the father to be in the home as well, even though the mother and father may not be married. If we combine those children born to single mothers with those living with a single parent as a result of divorce, fewer than half of American children live with both biological parents throughout their entire childhood.

Poverty is common in single-parent families.

What are the consequences of growing up with in a single-parent household? Because there is only one parent to carry out household responsibilities such as cooking and cleaning, children in single-parent households often contribute a great deal to the functioning of the family, much like children in traditional cultures. However, the most important consequence of growing up in a single-parent family is that it greatly increases the likelihood of growing up in poverty, and growing up in poverty, in turn, has a range of negative effects on children (Harvey & Fine, 2004). Children in single-parent families generally are at higher risk for behavior problems and low school achievement when compared to their peers in two-parent families (Ricciuti, 2004).

Single-parent families are diverse, and many children who grow up in single-parent families function very well. When the mother makes enough money so the family is not in poverty, children in single-parent families function as well as children in two-parent families (Lipman et al., 2002). Single-father families are relatively rare, but children with a single father are no different than their peers in middle childhood in regard to social and academic functioning (Amato, 2000). It should also be noted that having a single parent does not always mean there is only one adult in the household. In many African American families the grandmother is highly involved and provides child care, household help, and financial support to the single mother (Crowther & Rodrigues, 2003). In about one fourth of families with an African American single mother, the grandmother also lives in the household (Kelch-Oliver, 2011).

CHILDREN'S RESPONSES TO DIVORCE Rates of divorce have risen dramatically over the past half century in the United States, Canada, and northern Europe. Currently, close to half of children in many of these countries experience their parents' divorce by the time they reach middle childhood. In contrast, divorce remains rare in southern Europe and in non-Western countries.

How do children respond to their parents' divorce? A wealth of American and European research has addressed this question, including several excellent longitudinal studies. Overall, children respond negatively in a variety of ways, especially boys and especially in the first 2 years following divorce (Amato & Anthony, 2014). Children display increases in both externalizing problems (such as unruly behavior and conflict with mothers, siblings, peers, and teachers) and internalizing problems (such as depressed mood, anxieties, phobias, and sleep disturbances) (Clarke-Stewart & Brentano, 2006). Their school performance also declines (Amato & Boyd, 2013). If the divorce takes place during early childhood, children often blame themselves, but by middle childhood most children are less egocentric and more capable of understanding that their parents may have reasons for divorcing that have nothing to do with them (Hetherington & Kelly, 2002). In the video *Pam: Divorced Mother of Nine-Year-Old*, a woman describes the impact that her divorce has had on her daughter.

Watch PAM: DIVORCED MOTHER OF NINE-YEAR-OLD

In one renowned longitudinal study of divorces that took place when the children were in middle childhood, the researchers classified 25% of the children in divorced families as having severe emotional or behavioral problems, compared to 10% of children in two-parent nondivorced families (Hetherington & Kelly, 2002). The low point for most children came 1 year after divorce. After that point, most children gradually improved in functioning, and by 2 years post-divorce, girls were mostly back to normal. However, boys' problems were still evident even 5 years after divorce. Problems continue for some children into adolescence, and new consequences appear, as we shall see in Chapter 8.

Not all children react negatively to divorce. Even if 25% have severe problems, that leaves 75% who do not. What factors influence how a divorce will affect children? Increasingly researchers have focused on **family process**, that is, the quality of the relationships between family members before, during, and after the divorce. In all families, whether divorced or not, parental conflict is linked to children's emotional and behavioral problems (Kelly & Emery, 2003). When parents divorce with minimal conflict, or when parents are able to keep their conflicts private, children show far fewer problems (Amato & Anthony, 2014). If divorce results in a transition from a high-conflict household to a low-conflict household, children's functioning often improves rather than deteriorates (Davies et al., 2002).

Another aspect of family process is children's relationship to the mother after divorce. Mothers often struggle in numerous ways following divorce (Wallerstein & Johnson-Reitz, 2004). In addition to the emotional stress of the divorce and conflict with ex-husbands, they now have full responsibility for household tasks and child care. There is increased financial stress, with the father's income no longer coming directly into the household. Most countries have laws requiring fathers to contribute to the care of their children after leaving the household, but despite these laws mothers often receive less than full child support from their ex-husbands (Children's Defense Fund, 2005; Statistics Canada, 2010). Given this pile-up of stresses, it is not surprising that the mother's parenting often takes a turn for the worse in the aftermath of divorce, becoming less warm, less consistent, and more punitive (Hetherington & Kelly, 2002).

Relationships between boys and their mothers are especially likely to go downhill after divorce. Mothers and boys sometimes become sucked into a **coercive cycle** following divorce, in which boys' less compliant behavior evokes harsh responses from mothers, which in turn makes boys even more resistant to their mothers' control, evoking even harsher responses, and so on (Patterson, 2002). However, when the mother is able to maintain a healthy balance of warmth and control despite the stresses, her children's response to divorce is likely to be less severe (Leon, 2003).

Family processes involving fathers are also important in the aftermath of divorce. In about 90% of cases (across countries) mothers retain custody of the children, so the father leaves the household and the children no longer see him on a daily basis. They may stay with him every weekend or every other weekend, and perhaps see him one evening during the week, in addition to talking to him on the phone. Now fathers must get used to taking care of the children on their own, without mothers present, and children must get used to two households that may have different sets of rules. For most children, contact with the father diminishes over time, and only 35–40% of children in mother-custody families still have at least weekly contact with their fathers within a few years of the divorce (Kelly, 2003). When the father remarries, as most do, his contact with children from the first marriage declines steeply (Dunn, 2002). However, when fathers remain involved and loving, children have fewer post-divorce problems (Dunn et al., 2004; Finley & Schwartz, 2010).

In recent decades, **divorce mediation** has developed as a way of minimizing the damage to children that may take place due to heightened parental conflict during and after divorce (Emery et al., 2005; Sbarra & Emery, 2008). In divorce mediation, a professional

Relationships between mothers and sons sometimes go downhill following divorce.

family process

quality of the relationships between family members

coercive cycle

pattern in relations between parents and children in which children's disobedient behavior evokes harsh responses from parents, which in turn makes children even more resistant to parental control, evoking even harsher responses

divorce mediation

arrangement in which a professional mediator meets with divorcing parents to help them negotiate an agreement that both will find acceptable

mediator meets with divorcing parents to help them negotiate an agreement that both will find acceptable. Research has shown that mediation can settle a large percentage of cases otherwise headed for court and lead to better functioning in children following divorce, and to improved relationships between divorced parents and their children, even 12 years after the settlement (Emery et al., 2005).

OUT OF THE FRYING PAN: CHILDREN'S RESPONSES TO REMARRIAGE Most adults who divorce remarry. Consequently, most children who experience their parents' divorce spend part of their childhood in a stepfamily. Because mothers retain custody of the children in about 90% of divorces, most stepfamilies involve the entrance of a stepfather into the family.

You might expect that the entrance of a stepfather would be a positive development in most cases, given the problems that face mother-headed families following divorce. Low income is a problem, and when the stepfather comes into the family this usually means a rise in overall family income. Mothers' stress over handling all the household and child care responsibilities is a problem, and after a stepfather enters the family he can share some of the load. Mothers' emotional well-being is a problem, and her well-being is typically enhanced by remarriage, at least initially (Visher et al., 2003). If mothers' lives improve in all these ways, their children's lives must improve, too, right?

Unfortunately, no. Frequently, children take a turn for the worse once a stepfather enters the family. Compared to children in nondivorced families, children in stepfamilies have lower academic achievement, lower self-esteem, and greater behavioral problems (Coleman et al., 2000; Nicholson et al., 2008). According to one estimate, about 20% of children in stepfamilies have serious problems in at least one aspect of functioning in middle childhood, compared to 10% of their peers in nondivorced families (Hetherington & Kelly, 2002). Girls respond more negatively than boys to remarriage, a reversal of their responses to divorce (Bray, 1999). If the stepfather also has children of his own that he brings into the household, making a *blended stepfamily*, the outcomes for children are even worse than in other stepfamilies (Becker et al., 2013).

There are a number of reasons for children's negative responses to remarriage. First, remarriage represents another disruption that requires adjustment, usually at a point when the family had begun to stabilize following the earlier disruption of divorce (Hetherington & Stanley-Hagan, 2002). Second, stepfathers may be perceived by children as coming in between them and their mothers, especially by girls, who may have become closer to their mothers following divorce (Bray, 1999). Third, and perhaps most importantly, children may resent and resist their stepfathers' attempts to exercise authority and discipline (Robertson, 2008). Stepfathers may be attempting to support the mother in parenting and to fulfill the family role of father, but children may refuse to regard him as a "real" father and may in fact regard him as taking their biological father's rightful place (Weaver & Coleman, 2010). When asked to draw their families, many children in stepfamilies literally leave their stepfathers out of the picture (Stafford, 2004).

However, it is important to add that here, as elsewhere, family process counts for as much as family structure. Many stepfathers and stepchildren form harmonious, close relationships (Becker et al., 2013; Coleman et al., 2000). The likelihood of this outcome is enhanced if the stepfather is warm and open to his stepchildren and does not immediately try to assert authority (Visher et al., 2003). Also, the younger the children are, the more open they tend to be to accepting the stepfather (Jeynes, 2007). The likelihood of conflict between stepfathers and stepchildren increases with the children's age, from early childhood to middle childhood and again from middle childhood to adolescence (Hetherington & Kelly, 2002).

Friends and Peers

LO 7.16 Explain the main basis of friendships in middle childhood, and describe the four categories of peer social status and the dynamics between bullies and victims.

Friends rise in importance from early childhood to middle childhood, as greater freedom of movement allows children to visit and play with friends. Also, the entrance into formal schooling takes children away from the family social environment and places them in an environment where they spend a substantial amount of most days around many other children of similar age. Daily contact between children makes it possible for them to develop close friendships.

In this discussion of friends and peers we will first examine the characteristics of friendships in middle childhood, and then look at popularity and bullying in peer groups.

MAKING FRIENDS Why do children become friends with some peers but not others? An abundance of research over several decades has shown that the main basis of friendship is similarity, not just during middle childhood but at all ages (Rubin et al., 2008). People tend to prefer being around others who are like themselves, a principle called **selective association** (Popp et al., 2008). We have already seen how gender is an especially important basis of selective association in middle childhood. Boys tend to play with boys and girls with girls, more than at either younger or older ages. Other important criteria for selective association in middle childhood are sociability, aggression, and academic orientation (Hartup, 1996). Sociable kids are attracted to each other as friends, as are shy kids; aggressive kids tend to form friendships with each other, as do kids who refrain from aggression; kids who care a lot about school tend to become friends, and so do kids who dislike school.

In middle childhood, shared activities are still an important part of friendships, but now trust, too, becomes important. Children name fewer of their peers as friends, and friendships last longer, often several years (Rose & Asher, 1999). Your friends are kids who not only like to do things you like to do, but also whom you can rely on to be nice to you almost all the time, and whom you can trust with information you would not reveal to just anyone. In one study of children in Grades 3 to 6, the expectation that a friend would keep a secret increased from 25% to 72% across that age span among girls; among boys the increase came later and did not rise as high (Azmitia et al., 1998). This finding reflects a more general gender difference found in many other studies, that girls prize trust in middle childhood friendships more than boys do, and that boys' friendships focus more on shared activities, although for both genders trust is more important in middle childhood than in early childhood (Rubin et al., 2008). As trust becomes more important to friendships in middle childhood, breaches of trust (such as breaking a promise or failing to provide help when needed) also become the main reason for ending friendships (Hartup & Abecassis, 2004).

PLAYING WITH FRIENDS Even though trust becomes a more important part of friendship in middle childhood, friends continue to enjoy playing together in shared activities. Recall from Chapter 6 that play in early childhood most often takes the form of simple social play or cooperative pretend play. These types of play continue in middle childhood. For example, children might play with dolls or action figures together, or they might pretend to be superheroes or animals.

selective association

in social relations, the principle that people tend to prefer being around others who are like themselves

Trust becomes more important to friendships in middle childhood.

What is new about play in middle childhood is that it becomes more complex and more rule-based. Children in early childhood may play with action figures, but in middle childhood there may be elaborate rules about the powers and limitations of the characters. For example, in the early 21st century, Japanese games involving Pokemon action figures became popular in middle childhood play worldwide, especially among boys (Ogletree et al., 2004; Simmons, 2014). These games involve characters with an elaborate range of powers and provide children with the enjoyment of competition and mastering complex information and rules. In early childhood the information about the characters would be too abundant and the rules too complex for children to follow, but by middle childhood this cognitive challenge is exciting and pleasurable.

In addition to games such as Pokemon, many of the games with rules that children play in middle childhood are more cognitively challenging than the games younger children play. Card games and board games become popular, and often these games require children to count, remember, and plan strategies. Middle childhood is also a time when many children develop an interest in hobbies such as collecting certain types of objects (e.g., coins, dolls) or constructing and building things (such as with LEGO toys, a Danish invention that is popular around the world in middle childhood). These hobbies also provide enjoyable cognitive challenges of organizing and planning (McHale et al., 2001). Recently, electronic games have become a highly popular type of game in middle childhood, and these games also present substantial cognitive challenges (Olson et al., 2008).

Although the complexity and cognitive challenges of play in middle childhood distinguish it from play in early childhood, children continue to enjoy simple games as well (Manning, 1998). According to cross-cultural studies, games such as tag and hide-and-seek are popular all over the world in middle childhood (Edwards, 2000). Children also play simple games that are drawn from their local environment, such as the herding games played by boys in Kenya in the course of caring for cattle.

Middle childhood games also reflect children's advances in gross motor development. As children develop greater physical agility and skill in middle childhood, their games with rules include various sports that require greater physical challenges than their early childhood games did. As noted earlier in the chapter, in many countries middle childhood is the time when children first join organized teams to play sports such as soccer, baseball, or basketball. Many children also play sports in games they organize themselves, often including discussions of the rules of the game (Davies, 2004).

POPULARITY AND UNPOPULARITY In addition to having friendships, children are also part of a larger social world of peers, especially once they enter primary school. Schools are usually **age graded**, which means that students at a given grade level tend to be the same age. When children are in a social environment with children of different ages, age is a key determinant of **social status**, in that older children tend to have more authority than younger children. However, when all children are about the same age, they find other ways of establishing who is high in social status and who is low. Based on children's ratings of who they like or dislike among their peers, researchers have described four categories of social status (Cillessen & Mayeux, 2004; Rubin et al., 2008):

- *Popular children* are the ones who are most often rated as "liked" and rarely rated as "disliked."
- *Rejected children* are most often disliked and rarely liked by other children. Usually, rejected children are disliked mainly for being overly aggressive, but in about 10–20% of cases rejected children are shy and withdrawn (Hymel et al., 2004; Sandstrom & Zakriski, 2004). Boys are more likely than girls to be rejected.
- *Neglected children* are rarely mentioned as either liked or disliked; other children have trouble remembering who they are. Girls are more likely than boys to be neglected.
- *Controversial children* are liked by some children but disliked by others. They may be aggressive at times but friendly at other times.

age graded

social organization based on grouping persons of similar ages

social status

within a group, the degree of power, authority, and influence that each person has in the view of the others

About two-thirds of children in American samples fall into one of these categories in middle childhood, according to most studies (Wentzel, 2003). The rest are rated in mixed ways by other children and are classified by researchers as "average."

What characteristics determine a child's social status? Abundant research indicates that the strongest influence on popularity is **social skills** such as being friendly, helpful, cooperative, and considerate (Caravita & Cillessen, 2012; Chan et al., 2000). Children with social skills are good at perspective-taking; consequently they are good at understanding and responding to other children's needs and interests (Cassidy et al., 2003). Other important influences on popularity are intelligence, physical appearance, and (for boys) athletic ability (McHale et al., 2003). Despite the stereotype of the "nerd" or "geek" as a kid who is unpopular for being smart, in general, intelligence enhances popularity in middle childhood (in adolescence it becomes a bit more complicated, as we will see in Chapter 8). "Nerds" and "geeks" are unpopular because they lack social skills, not because of their intelligence.

Rejected children are usually more aggressive than other children, and their aggressiveness leads to conflicts (Coie, 2004). They tend to be impulsive and have difficulty controlling their emotional reactions, which disrupts group activities, to the annoyance of their peers. In addition to this lack of self-control, their lack of social skills and social understanding leads to conflict with others. According to Kenneth Dodge (2008), who has done decades of research on this topic, rejected children often fail in their **social information processing (SIP)**. That is, they tend to interpret their peers' behavior as hostile even when it is not, and they tend to blame others when there is conflict.

For rejected children who are withdrawn rather than aggressive, the basis of their rejection is less clear. They may be shy and even fearful of other children, but these characteristics are also found often in neglected children. What distinguishes between rejected-withdrawn and neglected children? Rejected-withdrawn children are more likely to have internalizing problems such as low self-esteem and anxiety. In contrast, neglected children are usually quite well-adjusted (Wentzel, 2003). They may not engage in social interactions with peers as frequently as other children do, but they usually have social skills equal to average children, are not unhappy, and report having friends.

Controversial children often have good social skills, as popular children do, but they are also high in aggressiveness, like rejected children (DeRosier & Thomas, 2003). Their social skills make them popular with some children, and their aggressiveness makes them unpopular with others. They may be adept at forming alliances with some children and excluding others. Sometimes they defy adult authority in ways their peers admire but do not dare to emulate (Vaillancourt & Hymel, 2006).

Social status is related to other aspects of children's development, in middle childhood and beyond, especially for rejected children. Because other children exclude them from their play and they have few or no friends, rejected children often feel lonely and they dislike going to school (Buhs & Ladd, 2001). Their aggressiveness and impulsiveness cause problems in their other social relationships, not just with peers, and they have higher rates of conflict with parents and teachers than other children do (Coie, 2004). According to longitudinal studies, being rejected in middle childhood is predictive of later conduct problems in adolescence and emerging adulthood (Caravita & Cillessen, 2012; Miller-Johnson et al., 2003). This does not necessarily mean that being rejected causes later problems; rather, it may indicate that the aggressiveness that inspires rejection from peers in middle childhood often continues at later ages and causes problems that take other forms. Nevertheless, being rejected by peers makes it more difficult for children to develop the social skills that would allow them to overcome a tendency toward aggressiveness.

Because rejected children are at risk for a downward spiral of problems in their social relationships, psychologists have developed interventions to try to ameliorate

social skills

behaviors that include being friendly, helpful, cooperative, and considerate

social information processing (SIP)

in social encounters, evaluations of others' intentions, motivations, and behavior

their low social status. Some of these interventions focus on social skills, training rejected children how to initiate friendly interactions with their peers (Asher & Rose, 1997). Other programs focus on social information processing, and seek to teach rejected children to avoid jumping to the conclusion that their peers' intentions toward them are negative (Li et al., 2013). As part of the intervention, rejected children may be asked to role play hypothetical situations with peers, or watch a videotape of peer interactions with an instructor and talk about why the peers in the video acted as they did (Ladd et al., 2004). These programs have often shown success in the short term, improving rejected children's social understanding and the quality of their peer interactions, but it is unknown whether the gains from the programs are deep enough to result in enduring improvements in rejected children's peer relations.

The prevalence of bullying rises through middle childhood across countries.

CRITICAL THINKING QUESTION

Which of these categories of social status do you believe applied best to you in middle childhood: popular, rejected, neglected, controversial, or average? Do you believe your social status at that life stage has influenced your later development, or not?

BULLIES AND VICTIMS An extreme form of peer rejection in adolescence is **bullying**. Bullying is defined by researchers as having three components (Olweus, 2000; Wolak et al., 2007): *aggression* (physical or verbal); *repetition* (not just one incident but a pattern over time); and *power imbalance* (the bully has higher peer status than the victim). The prevalence of bullying rises through middle childhood and peaks in early adolescence, then declines substantially by late adolescence (Pepler et al., 2006). Bullying is an international phenomenon, observed in many countries in Europe (Dijkstra et al., 2008; Eslea et al., 2004; Gini et al., 2008), Asia (Ando et al., 2005; Hokoda et al., 2006; Kanetsuna et al., 2006), and North America (Espelage & Swearer, 2004; Pepler et al., 2008; Volk et al., 2006). Estimates vary depending on age and country, but overall about 20% of children are victims of bullies at some point during middle childhood. Boys are more often bullies as well as victims (Berger, 2007). Boys bully using both physical and verbal aggression, but girls can be bullies, too, most often using verbal methods (Pepler et al., 2004; Rigby, 2004).

There are two general types of bullies in middle childhood. Some are rejected children who are bully-victims, that is, they are bullied by children who are higher in status and they in turn look for lower-status victims to bully (Kochenderfer-Ladd, 2003). Bully-victims often come from families where the parents are harsh or even physically abusive (Schwartz et al., 2001). Other bullies are controversial children who may have high peer status for their physical appearance, athletic abilities, or social skills, but who are also resented and feared for their bullying behavior toward some children (Vaillancourt et al., 2003). Bullies of both types tend to have a problem controlling their aggressive behavior toward others, not just toward peers but in their other relationships, during middle childhood and beyond (Olweus, 2000). Bullies are also at higher risk than other children for depression (Fekkes et al., 2004; Ireland & Archer, 2004).

Victims of bullying are most often rejected-withdrawn children who are low in self-esteem and social skills (Champion et al., 2003). Because they have few friends, they often have no allies when bullies begin victimizing them (Goldbaum et al., 2003). They cry easily in response to bullying, which makes other children regard them as weak and vulnerable and deepens their rejection. Compared to other children, victims of bullying are more likely to be depressed and lonely (Baldry & Farrington, 2004; Rigby, 2004). Their low moods and loneliness may be partly a response to being bullied, but these are also characteristics that may make bullies regard them as easy targets.

bullying

pattern of maltreatment of peers, including aggression; repetition; and power imbalance

Cultural Focus: Friendships and Peer Relationships in Middle Childhood Across Cultures

Although selective association is an important basis of friendship at all ages, over the course of childhood friendships change in other ways. An important change from early to middle childhood is in the relative balance of activities and trust (Rubin et al., 2008). Friendships in early childhood are based mainly on shared activities. Your friends are the kids who like to do the same things you like to do. Consequently, young children usually claim they have lots of friends, and their friends are more or less interchangeable. If you like to ride bikes, whoever is available to ride bikes

with you is your friend. When they describe their friends, young children talk mainly about their shared activities (Damon, 1983; Rubin et al., 2008). In this video, children in three cultures talk about their friendships.

Review Question:

Many of those interviewed discuss how friendships in middle childhood are often same gender. Why do you feel this self-segregation takes place?

Watch FRIENDSHIPS AND PEER RELATIONSHIPS IN MIDDLE CHILDHOOD ACROSS CULTURES

Video

How do other children respond when they witness one of their peers being bullied? One study observed American children in Grades 1–6 on playgrounds and recorded bullying episodes (Hawkins et al., 2001). Other children intervened to help a victim about half the time, and when they did the bullies usually backed off. However, a study in Finland found that in 20–30% of bullying episodes, peers actually encouraged bullies and sometimes even joined in against the victim (Salmivalli & Voeten, 2004).

Work

LO 7.17 **Describe the kinds of work children do in middle childhood, and explain why work patterns differ between developed and developing countries.**

Increasingly in the course of middle childhood, my twins came up with ways to put themselves to work and earn money, especially my daughter Paris. For example, when she was 7 years old, she invented a drink she called "Raspberry Ramble," made of apple juice, spiced tea, and crushed raspberries. She claimed we could sell large quantities of it and make a fortune. That same year, on a trip to Denmark, she collected dozens of rocks on the beach and announced she was opening a "rock museum" on her bed that we could enjoy for a very reasonable price. Erik Erikson (1950), whose life span theory we have been discussing in each chapter (see Chapter 1), called middle childhood the stage of **industry versus inferiority**, when children become capable of doing useful work as well as their own self-directed projects, unless the adults around them are too critical of their efforts, leading them to develop a sense of inferiority instead. This part of Erikson's theory has received little research. However, it is possible to see some verification of it in the way children across cultures are regarded as more capable than they were in early childhood and in the way they are often given important work responsibilities (Gaskins, 2015; Rogoff, 2003).

Children in developing countries often work long hours in poor conditions by middle childhood. Here, a young boy works in a factory in Bangladesh.

In developing countries, the work that children do in middle childhood is often not merely a form of play, as it was for my daughter, but a serious and sometimes perilous contribution to the family. In most developed countries, it is illegal to employ children in middle childhood (United Nations Development Programme [UNDP], 2010). However, in a large proportion of the world, middle childhood is the time when productive work begins. Children who do not attend school are usually working, often for their families on a farm or family business, but sometimes in industrial settings. With the globalization of the world economy, many large companies have moved much of their manufacturing to developing countries, where labor costs are cheaper. Cheapest of all is the labor of children. Before middle childhood, children are too immature and lacking in self-regulation to be useful in manufacturing. Their gross and fine motor skills are limited, their attention wanders too much, and they are too erratic in their behavior and their emotions. However, by age 6 or 7 children have the motor skills, the cognitive skills, and the emotional and behavioral self-regulation to be excellent workers at many jobs.

The International Labor Organization (ILO) has estimated that about 73 million children ages 5–11 are employed worldwide, which is about 9% of the total population of children in that age group, and 95% of working children are in developing countries (ILO, 2013). A substantial proportion of children work in Latin America, Asia, and the Middle East/North Africa, but the greatest number of child workers is found in sub-Saharan Africa. Agricultural work is the most common form of child employment, usually on commercial farms or plantations, often working alongside parents but for only one third to one half the pay (ILO, 2013). Children can quickly master the skills needed to plant, tend, and harvest agricultural products.

In addition, many children in these countries work in factories and shops where they perform labor such as weaving carpets, sewing clothes, gluing shoes, curing leather, and polishing gems. The working conditions are often miserable—crowded garment factories where the doors are locked and children (and adults) work 14-hour shifts, small poorly-lit huts where they sit at a loom weaving carpets for hours on end, glass factories where the temperatures are unbearably hot and children carry rods of molten glass from one station to another (ILO, 2004). Other children work in cities in a wide variety of jobs, including in domestic service, at grocery shops, in tea stalls, and delivering messages and packages.

industry versus inferiority
Erikson's middle childhood stage, in which the alternatives are to learn to work effectively with cultural materials or, if adults are too critical, develop a sense of being incapable of working effectively

If children's work is so often difficult and dangerous, why do parents allow their children to work, and why do governments not outlaw child labor? For parents, the simple answer is that they need the money. As we have seen in Chapter 1, billions of people worldwide are very poor. Poor families in developing countries often depend on children's contributions to the family income for basic necessities such as food and clothing. Children's work may be difficult and dangerous, but so is the work of adults;

often, parents and children work in the same factories. As for governments, nearly all countries do have laws prohibiting child labor, but some developing countries do not enforce them, because of bribes from the companies employing the children or because they do not wish to incur the wrath of parents who need their children's income (Chaudary & Sharma, 2007).

Although the exploitation of children's labor in developing countries is widespread and often harsh, signs of positive changes can be seen. According to the International Labor Organization, the number of child laborers ages 5–11 is rapidly declining (ILO, 2013). This decline has taken place because the issue of child and adolescent labor has received increased attention from the world media, governments, and international organizations such as the ILO and the United Nations Children's Fund (UNICEF). Furthermore, legislative action has been taken in many countries to raise the number of years children are legally required to attend school and to enforce the often-ignored laws against employing children younger than their mid-teens. Amid such signs of progress, it remains true that millions of children work in unhealthy conditions all around the world (ILO, 2013).

Media Use

LO 7.18 **Summarize the rates of daily TV-watching among children worldwide, and describe the positive and negative effects of television, especially the hazards related to TV violence.**

Media use is a part of daily life for most children even in early childhood, as we saw Chapter 6. Rates of media use remain about the same from early to middle childhood, except that time playing electronic games daily goes up, as shown in **Figure 7.9** (Rideout, 2013). Although many new media forms have appeared in the past decade, such as social media, television remains the most-used media form among children, at about an hour a day. By middle childhood about one fourth of children's media use involves **media multitasking**, the simultaneous use of more than one media form, such as playing an electronic game while watching TV (Warren, 2007).

As noted in Chapters 5 and 6, media forms and media content within each form are highly diverse, so it would be a mistake to characterize media use in childhood as solely

media multitasking

simultaneous use of more than one media form, such as playing an electronic game while watching TV

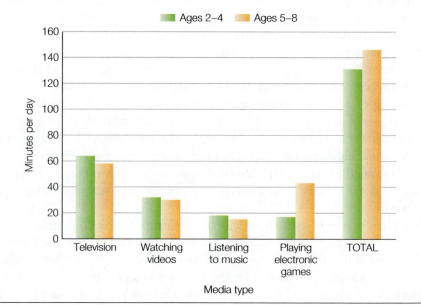

Figure 7.9 Media Use in Early and Middle Childhood

SOURCE: Based on Rideout (2013).

positive or negative. There is a big difference between watching *Clifford the Big Red Dog* on TV and watching a highly violent movie or TV show; children who play on prosocial websites like *Webkinz* or *Club Penguin* can be expected to respond differently than children who play violent electronic games like *Quake* or *Mortal Kombat*.

In general, media research on middle childhood has focused on the question of negative effects, as it has at other ages, but positive effects have also been noted. With regard to television, one analysis of 34 studies found that prosocial content in children's television shows had positive effects on four areas of children's functioning: altruism, positive social interactions, self-control, and combating negative stereotypes (Kotler, 2007). Furthermore, the positive effect of prosocial content was found to be equal to or greater than the negative effects of violent content. The Internet has been shown to be a valuable resource for children to learn about a wide range of topics, in school projects or just for enjoyment (Foehr, 2007; Van Evra, 2007). Much of children's media use is simply harmless fun, such as listening to music, playing nonviolent electronic games, and watching children's television shows.

The consequences of media use depend partly on whether children are light, moderate, or heavy media users (Van Evra, 2007). Light to moderate media use is generally harmless and can even be positive, especially if the media content is educational, prosocial, or at least nonviolent. In contrast, heavy media use is associated with a variety of problems in middle childhood, including obesity, anxiety, poor school performance, and social isolation. It is difficult to tell whether heavy media use is a cause or consequence of these problems; perhaps it is both.

Of all the problems associated with media use in middle childhood, aggression has been studied most extensively, specifically the effects of violent television on children's aggressiveness. As noted in Chapter 6, violence is common in the content of television shows. It is estimated that the average child in the United States witnesses 200,000 acts of violence on television by age 18, including 16,000 murders (Aikat, 2007). The violence is not just on adults' programs that children watch along with their parents. On the contrary, an analysis of programming for children ages 5–10 on eight TV networks found that the programs depicted an average of eight acts of violence per hour, *higher* than the rate on shows for adults (Fyfe, 2006).

With such high rates of violence in the television shows that children watch most, many parents and scholars have expressed concern about the possibility that television violence causes aggression in children. Although early childhood is considered to be the life stage of greatest vulnerability to the effects of media violence, some of the most important studies linking media violence to children's aggression have focused on middle childhood. The key studies have included field experiments, longitudinal studies, and natural experiments.

In field experiments, children's social behavior has been observed following exposure to violent television. For example, in one field experiment, there were two groups of boys at a summer camp (Bushman & Chandler, 2007). One group was shown violent films every evening for five nights; the other group watched nonviolent films during this period. Subsequently, observations of the boys' social behavior showed that the boys who watched the violent films were more likely than the boys in the nonviolent film group to display physical and verbal aggression.

Several longitudinal studies by Rowell Huesmann and colleagues have shown that watching high amounts of violent television in middle childhood predicts aggressive behavior at later life stages (Coyne, 2007; Huesmann et al., 2003). One study involved boys and girls in five countries: Australia, Finland, Israel, Poland, and the United States. The children's TV-watching patterns and aggressive behavior were assessed at age 6 and then 5 years later at age 11. High levels of exposure to TV violence at age 6 predicted aggressive behavior at age 11 across countries, even controlling statistically for initial aggressiveness at age 6. Studies by other researchers in South Africa and the Netherlands have reported similar results (Coyne, 2007).

Huesmann's longitudinal study in the United States extends even further into the life span (Huesmann et al., 1984; Huesmann et al., 2003). Television-viewing patterns and aggressive behavior were assessed in middle childhood (age 8) and again at ages 19 and 30. A correlation was found at age 8 between aggressiveness and watching violent TV, not surprisingly. But watching violent TV at age 8 also predicted aggressive behavior in boys at age 19, and by age 30 the men who had watched high amounts of violent TV at age 8 were more likely to be arrested, more likely to have traffic violations, and more likely to abuse their children. As in the other longitudinal studies by Huesmann and colleagues, the results predicting aggressive behavior at ages 19 and 30 were sustained even when aggressiveness at age 8 was controlled statistically. So, it was not simply that aggressive persons liked to watch violent television at all three ages, but that aggressive 8-year-olds who watched high levels of TV violence were more likely to be aggressive at later ages than similarly aggressive 8-year-olds who watched lower levels of TV violence.

Perhaps the most persuasive evidence that watching television causes aggression in children comes from a natural experiment in a Canadian town. This natural experiment is the subject of the *Research Focus: TV or Not TV?* feature.

In sum, there is good reason for concern about the effects of violent media content in middle childhood. However, it should be kept in mind that media can have positive effects as well. The focus of media research is generally on the negative effects, in middle childhood as in other life stages; but with nonviolent content, and if used in moderation, media use can be a positive and enjoyable part of childhood (Van Evra, 2007).

Research Focus: TV or Not TV?

Researchers on human development are limited in the methods they can use, because they have to take into account ethical issues concerning the rights and well-being of the people they involve in their studies. For instance, the environments of human beings cannot be changed and manipulated in the same way as those of animals, especially if the change would involve a condition that is potentially unhealthy or dangerous.

One way that researchers can obtain information about human development despite this restriction is to look for opportunities for a natural experiment. A natural experiment is a condition that takes place without the researcher's manipulation or involvement, but that nevertheless provides important information to the perceptive observer.

One human development topic for which natural experiments have been available is the effect of television on children's behavior. Television use spread all over the world with remarkable speed after it was invented in the 1940s, but there are still parts of the world that do not have television or have received it only recently.

In the early 1980s, a group of Canadian researchers, led by Tannis MacBeth, observed that there were areas of Canada that still did not have TV, although it was spreading rapidly. They decided to take advantage of this natural experiment to observe children's behavior before and after the introduction of TV.

Three towns were included in the study: "Notel" (as the researchers dubbed it), which had no television at the beginning of the study, "Unitel," which had one television channel, and "Multitel," with multiple channels. The focus of the study was on middle childhood, grades 1–5. In each grade, 5 boys and 5 girls were randomly selected in each town for participation in the study.

Each child's behavior was recorded by a trained observer for 21 one-minute periods over a period of 2 weeks across different times of day and different settings (for instance, school and home). The observers focused on aggressive behavior, using a checklist of 14 physically aggressive behaviors (such as hits, pushes, bites) and 9 verbally aggressive behaviors (such as mocking, curses, and threats). Neither children, nor parents, nor teachers were aware that the study focused on aggressive behavior or television.

In addition to the observations, the researchers obtained peer and teacher ratings of children's aggressiveness.

The ratings and observations took place just before the introduction of TV to Notel and then 2 years later, after Notel had obtained TV reception. The same children were included in the study at Time 1 and Time 2.

The results of the study showed clearly that the introduction of television caused children in Notel to become more aggressive. Children in Notel increased their rates of both physical and verbal aggression from Time 1 to Time 2, whereas there was no change for children in Unitel or Multitel. The increase in aggression in Notel occurred for both boys and girls. In all three towns at Time 2, the more TV children watched, the more aggressive they were.

This natural experiment provides persuasive evidence that the relation between TV watching and aggressiveness in children involves not only correlation but causation. It would not be ethical to place children into a "TV" condition and a "Not TV" condition—especially with what we now know about TV's potential effects—but making use of the natural experiment taking place in Notel, Unitel, and Multitel allowed the researchers to obtain important results about the effects of television on children's behavior.

Review Question:

1. The finding of greater aggression in Notel after the introduction of TV can best be interpreted as:
   a. Correlation but not causation
   b. Causation, because levels of aggression were assessed before and after the introduction of TV
   c. Neither correlation nor causation, because children's behavior in Notel did not change once TV was introduced
   d. None of the above

Watch RESEARCH FOCUS: TV OR NOT TV?

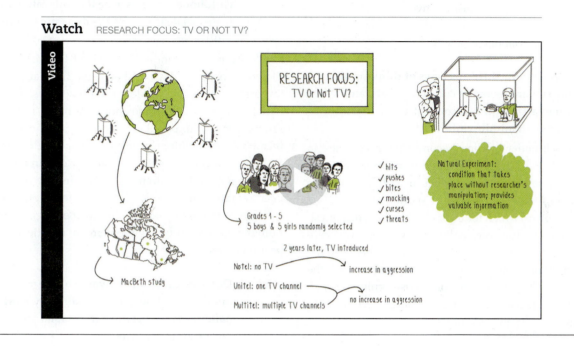

Practice Quiz   ANSWERS AVAILABLE IN ANSWER KEY.

1. Which of the following best illustrates coregulation?
   a. A child makes her bed without being asked because she knows that her parents expect the house to stay clean.
   b. Siblings both run to their mother to tell her what the other did to get that child in trouble.
   c. A parent tells her child how disappointed she is in her behavior.
   d. A child speaks for her younger, nonverbal sibling.

2. Which of the following statements about families is TRUE?
   a. Most children of gay and lesbian couples are heterosexual.
   b. In an effort to escape poverty, children of single-parent families have higher achievement in school than their counterparts from two-parent families.
   c. Single motherhood is highest among Hispanic-Americans.
   d. Compared to other countries, rates of single motherhood are lowest in Northern Europe.

3. In middle childhood, _____ becomes the main reason for children ending friendships.
   a. having less leisure time as a result of more homework
   b. different religious backgrounds
   c. violating trust
   d. increased competitiveness

4. Around the world, child labor _____.
   a. is most likely to involve working in service industries, such as cleaning
   b. is highest in Germany and Spain
   c. has been declining as a result of greater attention to the problem of exploitation
   d. is no longer a problem as a result of an increase in the number of years children are required to go to school

5. Marin, an 8-year-old boy, watches high amounts of violence on the television in his room and his parents are usually not around to monitor the content or enforce time limits on his viewing. Which of the following is most accurate based on research?
   a. He is more likely to be aggressive in adulthood.
   b. He is no more likely to be aggressive in adulthood than his counterparts who watch either little or no violence.
   c. He is less likely to be aggressive in adulthood than his counterparts who watch either little or no violence because he was able to work out his frustrations vicariously through watching others.
   d. No longitudinal research has examined this question.

Summary: Emotional and Social Development

LO 7.12 **Describe the main features of emotional self-regulation and understanding in middle childhood and how other life stages compare.**

Emotionally, middle childhood is generally a time of exceptional stability and contentment as emotional self-regulation becomes firmly established and emotional understanding advances. Increased involvement in contexts outside the family, such as school and sports teams, requires higher levels of emotional self-regulation.

LO 7.13 **Explain how different ways of thinking about the self are rooted in cultural beliefs, and summarize how self-concept and self-esteem change in middle childhood.**

Children's self-understanding becomes more complex in middle childhood, and they engage in more social comparison once they enter school. Their overall self-concepts are based on their self-concepts in specific areas that are important to them, which for most children includes physical appearance. In discussing cultural differences in conceptions of the self scholars typically distinguish between the *independent self* promoted by individualistic cultures and the *interdependent self* promoted by collectivistic cultures. High self-esteem is encouraged in individualistic cultures but discouraged in collectivistic cultures.

LO 7.14 **Describe how beliefs and behavior regarding gender change in middle childhood, including cultural variations.**

Children's tasks and play become more gender-segregated in middle childhood, and their views of gender roles become more sharply defined. In traditional cultures boys and girls do separate kinds of work in middle childhood, but playing in gender-specific groups takes place across cultures.

LO 7.15 **Explain the distinctive features of family relations in middle childhood, and describe the consequences of parental divorce and remarriage.**

Children become more independent during middle childhood as they and their parents move toward coregulation rather than parental dominance and control. Conflict with siblings peaks at this age. Divorce has become increasingly common in developed countries, and children (especially boys) respond negatively to divorce, particularly when it includes high conflict between parents. Parents' remarriage is also experienced negatively in middle childhood, even though it often improves the family's economic situation.

LO 7.16 **Explain the main basis of friendships in middle childhood, and describe the four categories of peer social status and the dynamics between bullies and victims.**

Similarity is important as the basis of friendship in middle childhood, as it is at other ages. Trust also becomes important in middle childhood friendships. Children's play becomes more complex and rule-based in this stage. Popularity and unpopularity become prominent in peer relations once children develop the capacity for seriation and spend a considerable part of their day in age-graded schools. Rejected children have the greatest problems in peer relations and the poorest long-term prospects for social development, mainly due to their aggressiveness. Bullying is a worldwide problem in middle childhood peer relations.

LO 7.17 **Describe the kinds of work children do in middle childhood, and explain why work patterns differ between developed and developing countries.**

About 73 million children in developing countries perform paid work by the time they reach middle childhood, in a wide variety of jobs ranging from agricultural work to factory work. Children in developing countries work more than children in developed countries in middle childhood because their contribution to the family income is needed.

LO 7.18 **Summarize the rates of daily TV-watching among children worldwide, and describe the positive and negative effects of television, especially the hazards related to TV violence.**

Children's media use stays about the same from early childhood to middle childhood, except for a rise in time playing electronic games. A causal link between media violence and aggression in middle childhood has been established through field studies, longitudinal studies, and natural experiments. Prosocial TV content promotes qualities such as altruism and self-control.

Applying Your Knowledge as a Professional

The topics covered in this chapter apply to a wide variety of career professions. Watch these videos to learn how they apply to a counselor, a zoo director, and a court appointed special advocate for children.

Watch   CAREER FOCUS: ZOO DIRECTOR

Video

Thane Maynard
Director of Cincinnati Zoo & Botanical Garden

Chapter Quiz

1. Which best describes sensory changes during middle childhood?

    a. Hearing problems increase due to higher rates of ear infections.

    b. The incidence of myopia increases.

    c. Vision and hearing both improve dramatically.

    d. Rates of farsightedness increase while myopia decreases.

2. Rates of overweight and obesity _____.

    a. are rising worldwide

    b. are lowest among African American females compared to all other ethnic groups in the United States

    c. are lower among Latinos and Native Americans than among European Americans

    d. are lowest in the most affluent regions of the world, such as North America and Europe

3. In developed countries _____.

    a. rates of lead poisoning in children have fallen over the last several decades

    b. middle childhood is one of the least safe and healthy times of life because of children's increased need for independence

    c. the most common cause of injury is poisoning

    d. asthma rates are at their lowest point in decades

4. In middle childhood, _____.

    a. girls are more likely than their male counterparts to be on a sports team because they are more collaborative

    b. children are more likely to be involved in organized sports than they were when they were younger

    c. children are less coordinated than they were in early childhood because they are going through an awkward phase

    d. children have a slower reaction time than they did early in childhood because they are less impulsive

5. By the end of middle childhood _____.

   a. fine motor development has nearly reached adult maturity

   b. children's drawings look about the same as they did in early childhood in terms of level of detail

   c. improvements in fine motor skills are seen primarily among children who were educated in a formal school setting

   d. most children are just beginning to learn to tie their shoes

6. When capable of concrete operational thought, children _____.

   a. still have great difficulty with seriation tasks, such as arranging items from shortest to longest

   b. can organize and manipulate information mentally

   c. can reason about abstractions

   d. are likely to be misled by appearances

7. In the United States, about _____ of children between ages 4 and 10 are diagnosed with ADHD.

   a. 1%

   b. 4%

   c. 7%

   d. 15%

8. The Wechsler Intelligence Scale for Children (WISC-IV) _____.

   a. is the most widely used intelligence test for children

   b. has been criticized for focusing too much on creativity and not enough on core skills of reading and writing

   c. has both math and performance subtests

   d. has only been predictive of the future outcomes of gifted children

9. Research on reading and math skills _____.

   a. has only been conducted in the United States and Canada

   b. has shown that girls are more likely to be diagnosed with dyslexia than are boys

   c. has shown that the whole-language approach is more effective than the phonics approach for children who are first learning to read

   d. has found that even some nonhuman animals have a primitive awareness of numeracy

10. Compared to younger children, those in middle childhood _____.

   a. use less complex grammar, but longer sentences

   b. are more serious and therefore have more difficulty understanding the punch lines in jokes

   c. are more likely to realize that what people say is not always what they mean

   d. are less likely to use conditional sentences (e.g., If you do this, I will do that....) because they know that it may be interpreted negatively

11. Compared to single-language children, those who are bilingual _____.

   a. are behind in metalinguistic skills

   b. have better metalinguistic skills

   c. are worse at detecting mistakes in grammar

   d. score lower on general measures of cognitive ability

12. Compared to Asian students, American schoolchildren _____.

   a. spend more time studying art and music

   b. work in groups and help teach one another difficult concepts

   c. have a longer school year

   d. care about the maintenance of their schools

13. During middle childhood, _____.

   a. children learn how to conceal their emotions and show socially acceptable emotions

   b. children tend to be less happy than they were in early childhood because they engage in more social comparison

   c. children experience less emotional stability than they did at early stages in development because they are changing social contexts more often

   d. children's emotions become more intense, so they are not yet able to conceal their true feelings

14. A 9-year-old boy from a collectivistic culture, such as Japan, would be most likely to describe himself as _____.

   a. really good at math

   b. shy

   c. a son

   d. funny as can be

15. In terms of gender development, during middle childhood
_____.

   a. children increasingly view personality traits as associated with one gender or the other

   b. play groups become less gender-segregated than they were in early childhood

   c. gender roles become less rigid than earlier in life

   d. play groups become less gender-segregated in developed countries only

16. Which of the following best illustrates coregulation?

   a. Siblings negotiate a conflict without resorting to physical aggression.

   b. A child is able to prepare himself breakfast, provided that he follow his parents' rules and not use the stove.

   c. A child counts to three and tells himself to calm down after getting angry at his brother.

   d. A child describes himself in relation to others.

17. Sam is unpopular and has trouble making friends. He is aggressive and just last week started a fight by punching a boy who disagreed with him. Which of the following is most likely the case? Sam is a(n) _____ child.

   a. neglected   **c.** controversial

   b. rejected   **d.** average

18. Child labor _____.

   a. has declined worldwide in the last decade

   b. is most common in Mexico and Hawaii

   c. is considered legal in most countries

   d. is difficult to monitor because no international labor organizations exist

19. Media use in middle childhood _____.

   a. has not been associated with any positive outcomes

   b. has only been studied with male participants

   c. has been associated with a number of negative outcomes later in development

   d. has been linked with aggression only in the United States

Chapter 8
Adolescence

ADOLESCENCE IS A TIME OF DRAMATIC CHANGES. THE PHYSICAL CHANGES ARE THE MOST OBVIOUS, AS THE BODY GOES THROUGH PUBERTY. However, there are other dramatic changes as well, in family relations, peer relations, sexuality, and media use. Adolescents also change in how they think and talk about the world around them.

Adolescence is a cultural construction, not simply a biological phenomenon or an age range. *Puberty*—the set of biological changes involved in reaching physical and sexual maturity—is universal, and the same biological changes take place in puberty for young people everywhere, although with differences in timing and in cultural meanings, as we shall see. But adolescence is more than the events and processes of puberty. **Adolescence** is a period of the life span between the time puberty begins and the time adult status is approached, when young people are preparing to take on the roles and responsibilities of adulthood in their culture. To say that adolescence is culturally constructed means that cultures vary in how they define adult status and in the content of the adult roles and responsibilities adolescents are learning to fulfill. Almost all cultures have some kind of adolescence, but the length, content, and daily experiences of adolescence vary greatly among cultures (Larson et al., 2010). There is no definite age when adolescence begins or ends, but it usually begins after age 10 and ends by age 20, so it comprises most of the second decade of life.

There are two broad cultural forms that adolescence takes today. In developed countries, adolescents begin puberty early in the second decade of life, usually around age 10 or 11. They spend most of their days in school with their peers. Outside of school, too, they spend most of their leisure time with other persons their age—friends and romantic partners. A substantial proportion of their daily lives involves media use, including mobile phones, electronic games, television, and recorded music.

But there is another cultural form of adolescence that is prevalent in most of the developing world, including Africa, Asia, and South America. In this kind of adolescence, a typical day is spent not mostly with peers in school but with family members, working (Schlegel, 2010; Schlegel & Barry, 2015). Girls spend most of their time with their mothers and other adult women, learning the skills and knowledge necessary to fulfill the roles for women in their culture. Boys spend most of their time with adult men, learning to do what men in their culture are required to do, but they are allowed more time with friends than adolescent girls are. Some adolescent boys and girls in developing countries go to school, but for others school is something they left behind by the end of childhood.

We will discuss both of these forms of adolescence in the course of this chapter, and the many variations that exist within each form. We will also discuss the ways that the traditional cultural forms of adolescence are changing with exposure to industrialization and globalization.

Watch CHAPTER INTRODUCTION: ADOLESCENCE

Section 1   Physical Development

⌄   Learning Objectives

8.1 List the physical changes that begin puberty and summarize the surprising changes in brain development during adolescence.

8.2 Describe the normative timing of pubertal events, cultural variations, and how being early or late influences emotional and social development.

8.3 Identify the main gender differences in puberty rituals worldwide.

8.4 Describe the prevalence, symptoms, and treatment of eating disorders.

8.5 Classify adolescent substance use into four categories.

adolescence

period of the life span between the time puberty begins and the time adult status is approached, when young people are preparing to take on the roles and responsibilities of adulthood in their culture

puberty

changes in physiology, anatomy, and physical functioning that develop a person into a mature adult biologically and prepare the body for sexual reproduction

estrogens

sex hormones that have especially high levels in females from puberty onward and are mostly responsible for female primary and secondary sex characteristics

androgens

sex hormones that have especially high levels in males from puberty onward and are mostly responsible for male primary and secondary sex characteristics

estradiol

the estrogen most important in pubertal development among girls

testosterone

the androgen most important in pubertal development among boys

PHYSICAL DEVELOPMENT: The Metamorphosis: Biological Changes of Puberty

Adolescence begins with the first notable changes of puberty, and in the course of puberty the body is transformed in many ways and reaches the capacity for sexual reproduction. Many changes take place, and they are often dramatic. After growing at a more or less steady rate through childhood, at some time early in the second decade of life children begin a remarkable metamorphosis that includes a growth spurt, the appearance of pubic hair and underarm hair, changes in body shape, breast development and menstruation in girls, the appearance of facial hair in boys, and much more. The changes can be exciting and joyful, but adolescents experience them with other emotions as well—fear, surprise, annoyance, and anxiety. New research reveals some surprising findings in brain development, too, as we will see.

The Physical Changes of Puberty

LO 8.1   List the physical changes that begin puberty and summarize the surprising changes in brain development during adolescence.

The word *puberty* is derived from the Latin word *pubescere*, which means "to grow hairy." This fits; during puberty hair sprouts in a lot of places where it had not been before! But adolescents do a lot more during puberty than grow hairy. **Puberty** entails a biological revolution that dramatically changes the adolescent's anatomy, physiology, and physical appearance. By the time adolescents reach the end of their second decade of life they look much different than before puberty, their bodies function much differently, and they are biologically prepared for sexual reproduction.

HORMONAL CHANGES During middle childhood the proportion of fat in the body gradually increases, and once a threshold level is reached a series of chemical events is triggered beginning in the *hypothalamus* (refer back to Chapter 4, L.O. 4.2), a bean-sized structure located in the lower part of the brain (Shalatin & Philip, 2003). These events

Puberty transforms physical appearance. These photos show the same boy at age 11 and age 15.

primary sex characteristics

production of eggs (ova) and sperm and the development of the sex organs

secondary sex characteristics

bodily changes of puberty not directly related to reproduction

menarche

first menstrual period

spermarche

beginning of development of sperm in boys' testicles at puberty

lead the ovaries (in girls) and testes (in boys) to increase their production of the sex hormones. There are two classes of sex hormones, the **estrogens** and the **androgens**. With respect to pubertal development, the most important estrogen is **estradiol** and the most important androgen is **testosterone** (Shirtcliff et al., 2009).

Estradiol and testosterone are produced in both males and females, and throughout childhood the levels of these hormones are about the same in boys and girls (Money, 1980). However, once puberty begins, the balance changes dramatically (see **Figure 8.1**).

By the mid-teens, estradiol production is about 8 times as high in females as it was before puberty, but only about twice as high in males (Susman & Rogol, 2004). In contrast, testosterone production in males is about 20 times as high by the mid-teens as it was before puberty, but in females it is only about 4 times as high. These hormonal increases lead to the other bodily changes of puberty, the primary and secondary sex characteristics.

PRIMARY AND SECONDARY SEX CHARACTERISTICS Two kinds of changes take place in the body in response to increased sex hormones during puberty. **Primary sex characteristics** are directly related to reproduction: specifically, the production of ova (eggs) in females and sperm in males. **Secondary sex characteristics** are the other bodily changes resulting from the rise in sex hormones during puberty, not including the changes related directly to reproduction.

The development of ova and sperm takes place quite differently (refer to Chapter 2). Females are born with all the eggs they will ever have, and they have about 40,000 eggs in their ovaries at the time they reach puberty. Once a girl reaches **menarche** (her first menstrual period) and begins having menstrual cycles, one egg develops into a mature egg, or *ovum*, every 28 days or so. Females release about 400 ova in the course of their reproductive lives.

In contrast, males have no sperm in their testes when they are born, and they do not produce any until they reach puberty. However, beginning with their first ejaculation (called **spermarche**), males produce sperm in astonishing quantities. There are between 100 and 300 million sperm in the typical male ejaculation, which means that the average male produces millions of sperm every day. If you are a man, you will probably produce over a million sperm during the time you read this chapter—even if you are a fast reader!

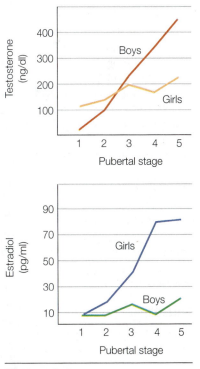

Figure 8.1 Hormonal Changes in Puberty

Girls and boys follow very different hormonal paths at this life stage.

SOURCE: Nottelmann et al. (1987)

Figure 8.2 Timing of the Physical Changes of Puberty
SOURCE: Based on Goldstein (1976); Chumlea et al. (2003)

The secondary sex characteristics are many and varied, ranging from the growth of pubic hair to a lowering of the voice to increased production of skin oils and sweat. A summary of the major secondary sex characteristics and when they develop is shown in **Figure 8.2**.

BRAIN DEVELOPMENT In addition to the hormonal changes and development of primary and secondary sex characteristics, there are important neurological changes taking place during adolescence. In recent years, there has been a surge of research on neurological development in adolescence and emerging adulthood (Casey et al., 2008; Giedd, 2008; Taber-Thomas & Perez-Edgar, 2015). Some of the findings from this new research have been surprising and have overturned previous views of brain development in adolescence.

It has long been known that by age 6 the brain is already 95% of its adult size. However, when it comes to brain development, size is not everything. Equally if not more important are the synaptic connections between the neurons (refer back to Chapter 4). Now scientists have learned that a sharp increase in synaptic connections occurs around the time puberty begins, ages 10–12, a process called *overproduction* or *exuberance*. Earlier studies had shown that overproduction occurs during prenatal development and through the first three years of life, but now it turns out that overproduction occurs in early adolescence as well (Giedd, 2008). Overproduction of synaptic connections occurs in many parts of the brain during adolescence but is especially concentrated in the frontal lobes (Keating, 2004). The frontal lobes are involved in most of the higher functions of the brain, such as planning ahead, solving problems, and making moral judgments.

The findings about overproduction in early adolescence are surprising and fascinating, but equally fascinating is what follows. Overproduction peaks at about age 11 or 12, but obviously that is not when our cognitive abilities peak. In the years that follow a massive amount of *synaptic pruning* takes place, in which the overproduction of synapses is whittled down considerably—synapses that are used remain, whereas those that are not used wither away (see Chapter 4). In fact, between the ages of 12 and 20 the average brain loses 7% to 10% of its volume through synaptic pruning (Giedd et al., 2012). Research using fMRI methods (refer to Chapter 5) shows that synaptic pruning is especially rapid in adolescents with high intelligence (Shaw et al., 2006). Synaptic pruning allows the brain to work more efficiently, as brain pathways become more specialized. However, as the brain specializes in this way it also becomes less flexible and less amenable to change.

Myelination is another important process of neurological growth in adolescence (refer again to Chapter 4). Myelin is a blanket of fat wrapped around the main part of the neuron, and it serves the function of keeping the brain's electrical signals on one path and increases their speed. Like overproduction, myelination was previously thought to be finished prior to puberty but has now been found to continue through the teens (Giedd, 2008; Sowell et al., 2002). This is another indication of how brain functioning is becoming faster and more efficient during adolescence. However, like synaptic pruning, myelination also makes brain functioning less flexible and changeable.

Finally, one last recent surprise for researchers studying brain development in adolescence has been the growth of the cerebellum (refer back to Chapter 6). This is perhaps the biggest surprise of all, because the cerebellum is part of the lower brain, well beneath the cortex, and has long been thought to be involved only in basic functions such as movement. Now, however, research shows that the cerebellum is important for many higher functions as well, such as mathematics, music, decision making, and even social skills and understanding humor. It also turns out that the cerebellum continues to grow through adolescence and well into emerging adulthood, suggesting that the potential for these functions continues to grow as well (Strauch, 2003). In fact, it is the last structure of the brain to stop growing, not completing its phase of overproduction and pruning until the mid-twenties (Taber-Thomas & Perez-Edgar, 2015).

The Timing of Puberty

LO 8.2 **Describe the normative timing of pubertal events, cultural variations, and how being early or late influences emotional and social development.**

A great deal of variability exists among individuals in the timing of the development of primary and secondary sex characteristics (refer back to Figure 8.2). For example, among girls, underarm hair could begin to appear as early as age 10 or as late as age 16; among boys, the change in voice could begin as early as age 11 or as late as age 15. Overall, girls begin puberty 2 years earlier than boys, on average (Archibald et al., 2003).

The norms in Figure 8.2 are for White American and British adolescents, who have been studied extensively in this area for many decades, but three studies demonstrate the variations that may exist in other groups. Among the Kikuyu, a culture in Kenya, boys show the first physical changes of puberty *before* their female peers, a reversal of the Western pattern (Worthman, 1987). In a study of Chinese girls, researchers found that pubic hair began to develop in most girls about 2 years after the development of breast buds, and only a few months before menarche, whereas in the Western pattern girls develop pubic hair much earlier (Lee et al., 1963). Also, in an American study (Herman-Giddens et al., 1997; Herman-Giddens et al., 2001), many African American girls were found to begin developing breast buds and pubic hair considerably earlier than White girls. At age 8, nearly 50% of the African American girls had begun to develop breasts or pubic hair or both, compared with just 15% of the White girls. This was true even though African American and White girls were similar in their ages of menarche. Similarly, pubic hair and genital development began earlier for African American boys than

Boys in Kenya reach puberty before girls do, contrary to the pattern in the West.

for White boys. Studies such as these indicate that it is important to investigate further cultural differences in the rates, timing, and order of pubertal events.

Given a similar cultural environment, variation in the order and timing of pubertal events among adolescents appears to be due to genetics. The more similar two people are genetically, the more similar they tend to be in the timing of their pubertal events, with identical twins the most similar of all (Ge et al., 2007; Marshall, 1978). However, when cultural environments vary, the timing of puberty also varies, as we shall see next.

CULTURE AND THE TIMING OF PUBERTY Culture includes a group's technologies, and technologies include food production and medical care. The age at which puberty begins is strongly influenced by the extent to which food production provides adequate nutrition and medical care protects health, throughout childhood (Alsaker & Flammer, 2006; Eveleth & Tanner, 1990).

Persuasive evidence for the influence of technologies on pubertal timing comes from historical records showing a steady decrease in the average age of menarche in Western countries from the mid-19th to the late-20th century, as shown in **Figure 8.3**. This downward pattern in the age of menarche, known as a **secular trend**, has occurred in every Western country for which records exist (Sørensen et al., 2012). Menarche is not a perfect indicator of the initiation of puberty—the first outward signs of puberty appear much earlier for most girls, and of course menarche does not apply to boys. However, menarche is a good indicator of when other events have begun in girls, and it is a reasonable assumption that if the downward trend in the age of puberty has occurred for girls, it has occurred for boys as well. Menarche is also the only aspect of pubertal development for which we have records going back so many decades. Scholars believe that the downward trend in the age of menarche is due to improvements in nutrition and medical care that have taken place during the past 150 years (Archibald et al., 2003; Bullough, 1981). As the inset to Figure 8.3 shows, age of menarche has been unchanged since about 1970, as access to adequate nutrition and medical care have become widespread in developed countries.

Further evidence of the role of nutrition and medical care in pubertal timing comes from cultural comparisons in the present. The average age of menarche is lowest in developed countries (currently about 12.5 years old), where adequacy of nutrition and medical care is highest (Eveleth & Tanner, 1990; McDowell et al., 2007; Sørensen et al., 2012). In contrast, menarche takes place at an average age as high as 15 in developing countries, where nutrition may be limited and medical care is often rare or nonexistent

secular trend

change in the characteristics of a population over time

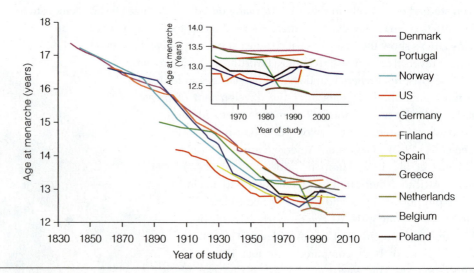

Figure 8.3 The Secular Trend in Age of Menarche

Why did age of reaching menarche decline?

SOURCE: Sørensen et al (2012)

(Eveleth & Tanner, 1990). In countries that have undergone rapid economic development in recent decades, such as China and South Korea, a corresponding decline in the average age of menarche has been recorded (Graham et al., 1999; Park et al., 1999).

SOCIAL AND PERSONAL RESPONSES TO PUBERTAL TIMING Think back for a moment to when you were passing through puberty. What were your most memorable pubertal events? How did you respond to those events—and how did the people around you respond? I loved to sing at that age, and I distinctly remember going from soprano at age 13—the only boy in a sea of girls—to 2nd bass by age 15. I reached puberty quite a bit later than most of my peers.

Social and personal responses to puberty are intertwined, because how adolescents respond to reaching puberty depends in part on how others respond to them. In developed countries, social and personal responses may depend on whether adolescents reach puberty relatively early or relatively late compared with their peers. When adolescents spend time in school on most days, surrounded by peers, they become acutely aware of how their maturation compares to others'.

A great deal of research has been conducted on early versus late maturation among adolescents in the West, especially in the United States, extending back over a half century. The results are complex: They differ depending on gender, and the short-term effects of maturing early or late appear to differ from the long-term effects.

Research consistently shows that the effects of early maturation are usually negative for girls. Findings from a variety of Western countries concur that early-maturing girls are at risk for numerous problems, including depressed mood, negative body image, eating disorders, substance use, delinquency, aggressive behavior, school problems, and conflict with parents (Harden & Mendle, 2012; Lynne et al., 2007; Westling et al., 2008). Early maturation is a problem for girls in part because it leads to a shorter and heavier appearance, which is a disadvantage in cultures that value slimness in females. It can also be troublesome because their early physical development draws the attention of older boys, who then introduce them to an older group of friends and to substance use, delinquency, and early sexual activity (Lynne et al., 2007; Westling et al., 2008). Studies of the long-term effects of early maturation for girls are mixed, with some finding that the effects diminish by the late teens and others finding negative effects well into emerging adulthood (Graber et al., 2004; Posner, 2006; Weichold et al., 2003).

In contrast to girls, the effects of early maturation for boys are positive in some ways and negative in others (Mendle & Ferrero, 2012). Early-maturing boys tend to have more favorable body images and higher popularity than other boys (Graber et al., 1997; Weichold et al., 2003). The earlier development of facial hair, lowered voice, and other secondary sex characteristics may make early-maturing boys more attractive to girls. Early-maturing boys may also have a long-term advantage. One study that followed early-maturing adolescent boys 40 years later found that they had achieved greater success in their careers and had higher marital satisfaction than later-maturing boys (Taga et al., 2006). However, not everything about being an early-maturing boy is favorable. Like their female counterparts, early-maturing boys tend to become involved earlier in delinquency, sex, and substance use (Westling et al., 2008).

Early-maturing girls are at high risk for problems, in part because they attract the interest of older boys.

Late-maturing boys also show evidence of problems. Compared to boys who mature "on time," late-maturing boys have higher rates of alcohol use and delinquency (Mendle & Ferrero, 2012). They also have lower grades in school (Weichold et al., 2003). There is some evidence that late-maturing boys have elevated levels of substance use and deviant behavior well into emerging adulthood (Biehl et al., 2007; Graber et al., 2004). Late-maturing girls have relatively few problems (Weichold et al., 2003).

Cultural Responses: Puberty Rituals

LO 8.3   **Identify the main gender differences in puberty rituals worldwide.**

Does your culture have any formal way of marking the entrance from childhood to adolescence? Have you ever participated in or witnessed a bar mitzvah or bat mitzvah, the Catholic ritual of confirmation, or the *quinciñeara* that takes place at age 15 for girls in Latin American cultures? These are examples of **puberty rituals** that have developed in many cultures to mark the departure from childhood and the entrance into adolescence. Puberty rituals are especially common in traditional cultures. Alice Schlegel and Herbert Barry (1991) analyzed information on adolescent development across 186 traditional cultures and reported that 68% had a puberty ritual for boys, 79% for girls (Schlegel & Barry, 1991).

For girls, menarche is the pubertal event that is most often marked by ritual (Schlegel & Barry, 2015). In fact, in many cultures menarche initiates a monthly ritual related to menstruation that lasts throughout a woman's reproductive life. It is remarkably common for cultures to have strong beliefs concerning the power of menstrual blood. Such beliefs are not universal, but they have been common in all parts of the world, in a wide variety of cultures. Menstrual blood is often believed to present a danger to the growth and life of crops, to the health of livestock, to the likelihood of success among hunters, and to the health and well-being of other people, particularly the menstruating woman's husband (Buckley & Gottlieb, 1988; Marvan & Trujillo, 2010). Consequently, the behavior and movement of menstruating women are often restricted in many domains, including food preparation and consumption, social activities, religious practices, bathing, school attendance, and sexual activities (Crumbley, 2006; Mensch et al., 1998). Menarche is often believed to possess special power, perhaps because it is a girl's first menstruation, so the restrictions imposed may be even more elaborate and extensive (Yeung & Tang, 2005).

Traditional puberty rituals for males do not focus on a particular biological event comparable to menarche for females, but the rites for males nevertheless share some common characteristics. Typically, they require the young man to display courage, strength, and endurance (Gilmore, 1990; Schlegel & Barry, 2015). Daily life in traditional cultures often demands these capacities from young men in warfare, hunting, fishing, and other tasks. Thus the rituals could be interpreted as letting them know what will be required of them as adult men and testing whether they will be up to adulthood's challenges.

In the past, rituals for boys were often violent, requiring boys to submit to and sometimes engage in bloodletting of various kinds. For example, among the Amhara of Ethiopia, boys were forced to take part in whipping contests in which they faced off and lacerated each other's faces and bodies (LeVine, 1966).

puberty ritual

formal custom developed in many cultures to mark the departure from childhood and the entrance into adolescence

Public circumcision for boys at puberty is still practiced in some African cultures. Here, three Masai adolescents from Tanzania celebrate their successful completion of the ritual.

Although these rituals may sound cruel if you have grown up in the West, adults of these cultures believed that the rituals were necessary for boys to make the passage out of childhood toward manhood and to be ready to face life's challenges. In all these cultures, however, the rituals have declined in frequency or disappeared altogether in recent decades as a consequence of globalization (Schlegel, 2010; Schlegel & Barry, 2015). Because traditional cultures are changing rapidly in response to globalization, the traditional puberty rituals no longer seem relevant to the futures that young people anticipate. However, public circumcision for boys is still maintained as a puberty ritual in many African cultures (Vincent, 2008).

Female circumcision in adolescence, which involves cutting or altering the genitals, also remains common in Africa, with rates of over 70% in many countries and above 90% in Mali, Egypt, Somalia, and Djibouti (Baron & Denmark,

2006; Chibber et al., 2011). The physical consequences of circumcision are much more severe for girls than for boys. Typically, a great deal of bleeding occurs, and the possibility of infection is high. Afterward many girls have chronic pain whenever they menstruate or urinate, and their risks of urinary infections and childbirth complications are heightened (Eldin, 2009). Critics have termed it *female genital mutilation* (FGM) and have waged an international campaign against it (Odeku et al., 2009). Nevertheless, it remains viewed in many African cultures as necessary in order for a young woman to be an acceptable marriage partner (Baron & Denmark, 2006).

CRITICAL THINKING QUESTION

Are there any rituals in Western cultures that are comparable to the puberty rituals in traditional cultures? Should people in Western cultures recognize and mark the attainment of puberty more than they do now? If so, why, and how?

Practice Quiz ANSWERS AVAILABLE IN ANSWER KEY.

1. Estradiol _____.
   a. is produced only in females
   b. increases in females by the mid-teens
   c. is an androgen important in pubertal development
   d. is a sex hormone that is regulated by the amygdala

2. Which of the following is a secondary sex characteristic?
   a. Fallopian tubes   c. Breasts
   b. Ova   d. Vagina

3. In regards to the onset/timing of puberty, who of the following is more at risk for substance use and delinquency?
   a. Late maturing boys   c. Early-maturing girls
   b. On-time maturing boys   d. Late-maturing girls

4. Tran is an 8-year-old girl who lives in a Western country in an urban area. If one were to compare the timing of puberty for Tran to the timing of puberty for her ancestral female lineage, one would expect that Tran will experience puberty _____ others did in her family's history.
   a. similar to when   c. slightly older than
   b. younger than   d. significantly older than

5. In many traditional cultures, young men are required to demonstrate courage, strength, and endurance in their coming-of-age rituals because _____.
   a. daily life often requires these capacities
   b. it is a way to show off for the young women observing
   c. they want to assert their power over women
   d. they are required by national law

PHYSICAL DEVELOPMENT: Health Issues in Adolescence

Like middle childhood, adolescence is a life stage when physical health is generally good. The immune system functions more effectively in middle childhood and adolescence than earlier in development, so susceptibility to infectious diseases is lower. Diseases that will become more common later in adulthood, such as heart disease and cancer, are very rare during adolescence. However, unlike middle childhood, adolescence is a time when problems arise not from physical functioning but from behavior. Two common problems of adolescence are eating disorders and substance use. (Automobile accidents are the number one cause of mortality in adolescence, but this topic will be discussed in Chapter 9.)

Eating Disorders

LO 8.4 **Describe the prevalence, symptoms, and treatment of eating disorders.**

For many adolescents, changes in the way they think about their bodies are accompanied by changes in the way they think about food. Girls, in particular, pay more attention to the food they eat once they reach adolescence, and worry more about eating too much

Young women with anorexia nervosa often see themselves as too fat even when they are so thin their lives are at risk.

and getting fat (Nichter, 2001). Sixty percent of American adolescent girls and 30% of boys believe they weigh too much, even though only 15% of girls and 16% of boys are actually overweight by medical standards (Centers for Disease Control and Prevention [CDC], 2008). This dissatisfaction exists far more often among girls than among boys (Gray et al., 2011). Boys are much less likely to believe they are overweight, and much more likely to be satisfied with their bodies.

These perceptions can lead adolescents to exhibit eating disordered behavior, including fasting for 24 hours or more, use of diet products, purging, and use of laxatives to control weight. According to a national U.S. study, about 20% of American adolescent girls and 10% of boys in Grades 9–12 report engaging in eating disordered behavior in the past 30 days (CDC, 2008). Similar findings have been reported in other Western countries. In a national study of German 11- to 17-year-olds, one third of girls and 15% of boys reported symptoms of eating disorders (Herpetz-Dahlmann et al., 2008). In Finland, a large study of 14- to 15-year-olds found eating disordered behavior among 24% of girls and 16% of boys (Hautala et al., 2008).

The two most common eating disorders are **anorexia nervosa** (intentional self-starvation) and **bulimia** (binge eating combined with purging [intentional vomiting]). About 0.3% of American adolescents have anorexia nervosa and about 0.9% have bulimia (Swanson et al., 2011). Nearly all (90%) of eating disorders occur among females. Most cases of eating disorders have their onset among females in their teens and early 20s (Smink et al., 2012).

Anorexia is characterized by four primary symptoms:

1. inability to maintain body weight at least 85% of normal for height;
2. fear of weight gain;
3. lack of menstruation; and
4. distorted body image.

One of the most striking symptoms of anorexia is the cognitive distortion of body image (Striegel-Moore & Franko, 2006). Young women with anorexia sincerely believe themselves to be too fat, even when they have become so thin that their lives are threatened. Standing in front of a mirror with them and pointing out how emaciated they look does no good—the person with anorexia looks in the mirror and sees a fat person, no matter how thin she is. The video *Anorexia Nervosa: Tamora* provides an example of this.

anorexia nervosa

eating disorder characterized by intentional self-starvation

bulimia

eating disorder characterized by episodes of binge eating followed by purging (self-induced vomiting)

Watch ANOREXIA NERVOSA: TAMORA

Like those with anorexia, persons with bulimia have strong fears that their bodies will become big and fat (Bowers et al., 2003). They engage in binge eating, which means eating a large amount of food in a short time. Then they purge themselves; that is, they use laxatives or induce vomiting to get rid of the food they have just eaten during a binge episode. People with bulimia often suffer damage to their teeth from repeated vomiting (because stomach acids erode tooth enamel). Unlike those with anorexia, persons with bulimia typically maintain a normal weight, because they have more or less normal eating patterns in between their episodes of bingeing and purging (Striegel-Moore & Franko, 2006). Another difference from anorexia is that persons with bulimia do not regard their eating patterns as normal. They view themselves as having a problem and often hate themselves in the aftermath of their binge episodes.

Self-starvation among young women has a long history in Western countries (Vandereycken & van Deth, 1994). Today, eating disorders are most common in cultures that emphasize slimness as part of the female physical ideal, especially Western countries (Latzer, Merrick, & Stein, 2011; Walcott et al., 2003). Presented with a cultural ideal that portrays the ideal female body as slim, at a time when their bodies are biologically tending to become less slim and more rounded, many adolescent girls feel distressed at the changes taking place in their body shape, and they attempt to resist or at least modify those changes. Young women who have an eating disorder are at higher risk for other internalizing disorders, such as depression and anxiety disorders (Swanson et al., 2011; Swinbourne & Touyz, 2007). Eating disordered behavior is also related to substance use, especially cigarette smoking and binge drinking (Pisetsky et al., 2008). Within the United States, eating disorders are more common among White women than among women of other ethnic groups, probably due to a greater cultural value on female slimness.

Although mainly a Western problem, eating disorders are increasing in parts of the world that are becoming more Westernized. For example, on the island nation of Fiji, traditionally the ideal body type for women was round and curvy. However, television was first introduced in 1995, mostly with programming from the United States and other Western countries, and subsequently the incidence of eating disorders rose substantially (Becker et al., 2007). Interviews with adolescent girls on Fiji showed that they admired the Western television characters and wanted to look like them, and that this goal in turn led to higher incidence of negative body image, preoccupation with weight, and purging behavior to control weight (Becker, 2004).

The success of treating anorexia and bulimia through hospitalization, medication, or psychotherapy is limited (Bulik et al., 2007; Grilo & Mitchell, 2010). About two-thirds of people treated for anorexia in hospital programs improve, but one third remain chronically ill despite treatment (Steinhausen et al., 2003). Similarly, although treatments for bulimia are successful in about 50% of cases, there are repeated relapses in the other 50% of cases, and recovery is often slow (Smink et al., 2012). Adolescents and emerging adults with a history of eating disorders often continue to show significant impairments in mental and physical health, self-image, and social functioning even after their eating disorder has faded (Berkman et al., 2007; Striegel-Moore et al., 2003). About 10% of those with anorexia eventually die from starvation or from physical problems caused by their weight loss, one of the highest mortality rates of any psychiatric disorder (Smink et al., 2012).

Substance Use

LO 8.5 Classify adolescent substance use into four categories.

In American society, substance use is rare before adolescence but fairly common by the end of secondary school (Johnston et al., 2014). In 2013, according to national Monitoring the Future (MTF) data, 39% of American high school seniors used alcohol and 26% reported binge drinking—consuming five or more alcoholic drinks in a row— at least once in the past month. Cigarette use (at least once in the past 30 days) was reported by 16% of high school seniors in 2013. Rates of marijuana use were actually higher than for cigarette smoking: 23% of high school seniors reported using marijuana in the past month in the 2013 MTF survey. In general, substance use in adolescence is highest among Native Americans, followed by White and Latino adolescents, with African American and Asian American adolescents lowest (Shih et al., 2010). Other than alcohol, cigarettes, and marijuana, substance use is uncommon among American adolescents.

How do the current rates of substance use in adolescence and emerging adulthood compare with previous decades? Because the MTF studies go back to 1975, there are excellent data on this question for American adolescents over more than three decades (Johnston et al., 2014). Rates of most types of substance use (past month) among adolescents in 12th grade declined from the late 1970s to the early 1990s, rose through the rest of the 1990s, then declined further over the past decade. Alcohol use declined from about 70% in 1975 to 39% in 2013. Cigarette smoking declined from nearly 40% in 1975 to 16% in 2013. Marijuana use declined from a peak of 37% in 1978 to 23% in 2013. Use of amphetamines peaked at 15% in 1981 and declined to 4% by 2013. During this period, an increasing proportion of young people defined themselves as "straight-edge," meaning that they abstain from all substance use (Kuhn, 2010). The reasons for this shift away from substance use are not clear, but it is likely that an intensive government-funded public campaign against teenage substance use during this period contributed to the decline.

Rates of substance use in adolescence vary across Western countries. A study by the World Health Organization (WHO) investigated use of alcohol and cigarettes among 15-year-olds in 41 Western countries (WHO, 2013). A summary of the results is shown in **Figure 8.4**.

Rates of cigarette smoking are lower among adolescents in the United States and Canada than in Europe, most likely because governments in the United States and Canada have waged large-scale public health campaigns against smoking, whereas European countries have not. Cigarette smoking among young people is of particular concern, because in the long run smoking is the source of more illness and mortality than all illegal drugs combined, and because the majority of persons who smoke begin in their early teens (Johnston et al., 2014).

Young people use substances for a variety of purposes, which can be classified as experimental, social, medicinal, and addictive (Weiner, 1992). Young people who take part in *experimental substance use* try a substance once or perhaps a few times out of curiosity and then do not use it again. *Social substance use* involves the use of substances during social activities with one or more friends. Parties and dances are common settings for social substance use in adolescence and emerging adulthood. *Medicinal substance use* is undertaken to relieve an unpleasant emotional state such as sadness, anxiety, stress, or loneliness. Using substances for these purposes has been described as a kind of **self-medication** (Reimuller et al., 2011). Young people who use substances

self-medication

use of substances to relieve unpleasant emotional states

Rates of smoking in adolescence are higher in Europe than in the United States and Canada. Here, young adolescents in Germany light up.

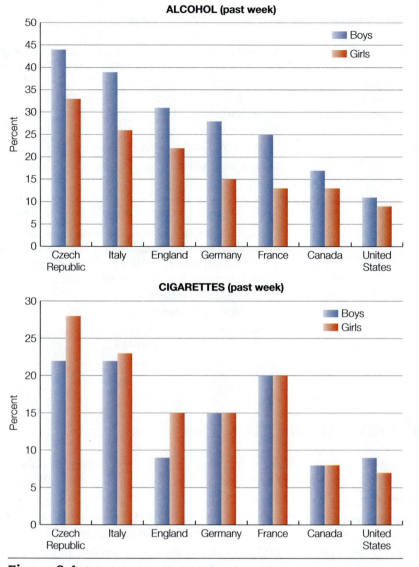

Figure 8.4 Substance Use in Western Countries

Why are rates of alcohol and cigarette use low in the United States and Canada?

SOURCE: Based on WHO (2013)

for self-medication tend to use them more frequently than those whose purposes are mainly social or experimental. Finally, *addictive substance use* takes place when a person has come to depend on regular use of substances to feel good physically or psychologically. People who are addicted to a substance experience withdrawal symptoms such as high anxiety and tremors when they stop taking the substance. Addictive substance use involves the most regular and frequent substance use of the four categories described here.

All substance use in adolescence and emerging adulthood is considered "problem behavior" in the sense that it is something that adults generally view as a problem if young people engage in it. However, the four categories described here indicate that young people may use substances in diverse ways, with diverse implications for their development. We'll explore substance use and abuse in further detail when we cover emerging adulthood in Chapter 9.

Practice Quiz ANSWERS AVAILABLE IN ANSWER KEY.

1. Which of the following statements about eating disorders is most accurate?

   a. People with bulimia are usually slightly underweight.

   b. Bulimia is slightly more common than anorexia nervosa.

   c. Over the past decade, anorexia nervosa has become more common in males than in females.

   d. Persons with bulimia do not view themselves as having a problem and regard their eating patterns as normal.

2. Vanessa is terrified of becoming fat. Her weight is normal, and most of the time she has normal eating habits, but sometimes she loses control and "binges" on large amounts of food. In an effort to avoid becoming fat, Vanessa makes herself throw up after these binges. Vanessa is exhibiting symptoms of _____.

   a. bulimia

   b. anorexia nervosa

   c. pica

   d. the secular trend

3. Based on the most recent statistics, which of the following American adolescents is LEAST likely to use substances such as alcohol, cigarettes, or marijuana?

   a. John, who is White

   b. Loreto, who is Latino

   c. James, who is Chinese American

   d. Jerome, who is Native American

4. Which of the following adolescents is LEAST likely to smoke cigarettes?

   a. Michael, from Canada   **c.** Jon, from Switzerland

   b. Marcelle, from France   **d.** Marc, from Italy

5. Rather than turning to other coping strategies, such as talking about his problems or even taking a walk to burn off steam, John smokes pot to reduce stress, anxiety or sadness. This pattern of substance use is referred to as _____.

   a. medicinal substance use

   b. addictive substance use

   c. social substance use

   d. experimental substance use

Summary: Physical Development

LO 8.1   List the physical changes that begin puberty and summarize the surprising changes in brain development during adolescence.

Increases in sex hormones lead to the development of primary and secondary sex characteristics. Recent findings in brain research show that the adolescent brain develops in some surprising ways, including a burst of overproduction (followed by synaptic pruning) and increased myelination.

LO 8.2   Describe the normative timing of pubertal events, cultural variations, and how being early or late influences emotional and social development.

The timing of pubertal events is determined partly by genes, but puberty generally begins earlier in cultures with adequate nutrition and medical care. Early maturing girls are at risk for a wide variety of problems, in part because they draw the attention of older boys.

LO 8.3   Identify the main gender differences in puberty rituals worldwide.

Most traditional cultures mark puberty with a community ritual. For boys, puberty rituals often entail tests of strength and endurance, whereas for girls puberty rituals center around menarche.

LO 8.4   Describe the prevalence, symptoms, and treatment of eating disorders.

Eating disorders are most prevalent in adolescence and emerging adulthood, and occur mainly among females. Prevalence of symptoms is higher than full-blown disorders; in some Western countries one third of girls report eating disordered behavior such as fasting for more than 24 hours and using laxatives to control weight. Treatments for eating disorders have had limited success.

LO 8.5   Classify adolescent substance use into four categories.

Adolescents' substance use can be classified as experimental, social, medicinal, or addictive. Adolescents whose substance use is addictive experience withdrawal symptoms when they reduce or stop their use of the substance.

Section 2   Cognitive Development

∨   Learning Objectives

8.6 Explain the features of hypothetical-deductive reasoning and identify critiques of Piaget's theory of formal operations.

8.7 Summarize the major changes in attention and memory that take place from middle childhood to adolescence.

8.8 Define the imaginary audience and the personal fable and explain how they reflect egocentrism in adolescence.

8.9 Produce an example of the zone of proximal development and scaffolding involving adolescents.

8.10 Compare and contrast the secondary education systems and academic performance of developed countries and developing countries.

8.11 Summarize the typical forms of adolescent work in developing countries and developed countries, and name the features of apprenticeships in Europe.

COGNITIVE DEVELOPMENT:
Adolescent Cognition

In adolescence, as at earlier life stages, Piaget's theory of cognitive development has been influential but has also been questioned and critiqued. Research using the information-processing approach documents the advances in memory and attention that occur in adolescence. Cognitive approaches have also been applied to social topics, investigating how adolescents view themselves and others.

Piaget's Theory of Formal Operations

LO 8.6   **Explain the features of hypothetical-deductive reasoning and identify critiques of Piaget's theory of formal operations.**

According to Piaget (1972), the stage of **formal operations** begins at about age 11 and reaches completion somewhere between ages 15 and 20. Children in concrete operations can perform simple tasks that require logical and systematic thinking, but formal operations allows adolescents to reason about complex tasks and problems involving multiple variables. It also includes the development of abstract thinking, which allows adolescents to think about abstract ideas such as justice and time and gives them the ability to imagine a wide range of possible solutions to a problem, even if they have had no direct experience with the problem.

HYPOTHETICAL-DEDUCTIVE REASONING The stage of formal operations involves the development of **hypothetical-deductive reasoning**, which is the ability to think scientifically and apply the rigor of the scientific method to cognitive tasks. To demonstrate this new ability, let us look at one of the tasks Piaget used to test whether

formal operations

in Piaget's theory, cognitive stage beginning at age 11 in which people learn to think systematically about possibilities and hypotheses

hypothetical-deductive reasoning

Piaget's term for the process of applying scientific thinking to cognitive tasks

Figure 8.5 Pendulum Problem

How does performance on this task test formal operations?

a child has progressed from concrete to formal operations, the *pendulum problem* (Inhelder & Piaget, 1958). In this task, illustrated in **Figure 8.5**, children and adolescents are shown a pendulum (consisting of a weight hanging from a string and then set in motion) and asked to try to figure out what determines the speed at which the pendulum sways from side to side. Is it the heaviness of the weight? The length of the string? The height from which the weight is dropped? The force with which it is dropped? They are given various weights and various lengths of string to use in their deliberations.

Children in concrete operations tend to approach the problem with random attempts, often changing more than one variable at a time. They may try the heaviest weight on the longest string dropped from medium height with medium force, then a medium weight on the smallest string dropped from medium height with less force. When the speed of the pendulum changes, it remains difficult for them to say what caused the change, because they altered more than one variable at a time. If they happen to arrive at the right answer—it's the length of the string—they find it difficult to explain why. This is crucial, for Piaget. Cognitive advances at each stage are reflected not just in the answers children devise for problems, but in their explanations for how they arrived at the solution.

It is only with formal operations that we become able to find the right answer to a problem like this and to understand and explain why it is the right answer. The formal operational thinker approaches the pendulum problem by utilizing the kind of hypothetical thinking involved in a scientific experiment. "Let's see, it could be weight; let me try changing the weight while keeping everything else the same. No, that's not it; same speed. Maybe it's length; if I change the length while keeping everything else the same, that seems to make a difference; it goes faster with a shorter string. But let me try height, too; no change; then force; no change there, either. So it's length, and only length, that makes the difference." Thus, the formal operational thinker changes one variable while holding the others constant and tests the different possibilities systematically. Through this process the formal operational thinker arrives at an answer that not only is correct but can also be defended and explained.

CRITIQUES OF PIAGET'S THEORY OF FORMAL OPERATIONS Formal operations is the part of Piaget's theory that has been critiqued the most and that has been found to require the most modifications (Keating, 2004; Marti & Rodriguez, 2012). The limitations of Piaget's theory of formal operations fall into two related categories: individual differences in the attainment of formal operations, and the cultural basis of adolescent cognitive development.

As noted in Chapter 4, Piaget asserted that people develop through the same stages at about the same ages (Inhelder & Piaget, 1958). Every 8-year-old is in the stage of concrete operations; every 15-year-old should be a formal operational thinker. Furthermore, Piaget's idea of stages means that 15-year-olds should reason in formal operations in all aspects of their lives, because the same mental structure should be applied no matter what the nature of the problem (Keating, 2004).

Abundant research indicates decisively that these claims were inaccurate, especially for formal operations (Kuhn, 2008). In adolescence and even in adulthood, a great range of individual differences exists in the extent to which people use formal operations. Some adolescents and adults use formal operations over a wide range of situations; others use it selectively; still others appear to use it rarely or not at all. On any given Piagetian task of formal operations, the success rate among late adolescents and adults is only 40–60%, depending on the task and on individual factors such as educational background (Keating, 2004; Lawson & Wollman, 2003). Furthermore, even people who demonstrate the capacity for formal operations tend to use it selectively, for problems and situations in which they have the most experience and knowledge (Flavell et al., 1993). For example, an adolescent with experience working on cars may find it easy to apply principles of formal operations in that area but have difficulty performing classroom tasks that require formal operations. Adolescents who have had courses in math and science are more likely than other adolescents to exhibit formal operational thought (Keating, 2004; Lawson & Wollman, 2003).

Questions have also been raised about the extent to which cultures differ in whether their members reach formal operations at all. By the early 1970s numerous studies indicated that cultures varied widely in the prevalence with which their members displayed an understanding of formal operations on the kinds of tasks that Piaget and others had used to measure it, and many researchers concluded that in some cultures formal operational thought does not develop, particularly in cultures that do not have formal schooling that includes training in the scientific method (Cole, 1996). More recent research suggests that people in many cultures use reasoning that could be called formal operational, provided that they are using materials and tasks familiar to them and relevant to their daily lives (Matusov, 2000). There is widespread support among scholars for the view that the stage of formal operations constitutes a universal human potential but it takes different forms across cultures depending on the kinds of problems people encounter in their daily lives (Cole, 1996).

In what ways might hunting seals require formal operations?

For example, adolescent boys in the Inuit culture of the Canadian Arctic traditionally learn how to hunt seals (Condon, 1990; Grigorenko et al., 2004). To become successful, a boy would have to think through the components involved in a hunt and test his knowledge of hunting through experience. If he were unsuccessful on a particular outing, he would have to ask himself why. Was it because of the location he chose? The equipment he took along? The tracking method he used? Or were there other causes? On the next hunt he might alter one or more of these factors to see if his success improved. This would be hypothetical-deductive reasoning, altering and testing different variables to arrive at the solution to a problem. However, in every culture there is likely to be considerable variation in the extent to which adolescents and adults display formal operational thought, from persons who display it in a wide variety of circumstances to persons who display it little or not at all.

Piaget's theory of formal operations has inspired a great deal of research on adolescents' cognitive development. However, information processing research shows other types of gains in cognitive development from childhood to adolescence.

Information Processing: Selective Attention and Advances in Memory

LO 8.7 Summarize the major changes in attention and memory that take place from middle childhood to adolescence.

As noted in previous chapters, attention and memory are the two keys to cognition in the information processing approach, and in both areas distinctive forms of cognitive development sprout in adolescence. Adolescents become more proficient at both selective and divided attention, and they become better at using memory strategies.

Are you able to read a textbook while someone else in the same room is watching television? Are you able to have a conversation at a party where music and other conversations are blaring loudly all around you? These are tasks that require *selective attention,* the ability to focus on relevant information while screening out information that is irrelevant (refer back to Chapter 7; Hahn et al., 2009). Adolescents tend to be better than younger children at tasks that require selective attention, and emerging adults are generally better than adolescents (Sinha & Goel, 2012). Adolescents are also more adept than younger children at tasks that require **divided attention**—reading a book and listening to music at the same time, for example—but even for adolescents, divided attention may result in less efficient learning than if attention were focused entirely on one thing. One study found that watching TV interfered with adolescents' homework performance but listening to music did not (Pool et al., 2003).

Memory also improves in adolescence, especially long-term memory. Adolescents are more likely than younger children to use *mnemonic devices* (memory strategies; refer to Chapter 7, L.O. 7.6), such as organizing information into coherent patterns (Schneider, 2010). Think of what you do, for example, when you sit down to read a textbook chapter. You probably have various organizational strategies you have developed over the years (if you do not, you would be wise to develop some), such as writing a chapter outline, organizing information into categories, focusing on key terms, and so on. By planning your reading in these ways, you remember (and learn) more effectively.

Another way long-term memory improves in adolescence is that adolescents have more experience and more knowledge than children do, and these advantages enhance the effectiveness of long-term memory (Keating, 1990; Keating, 2004). Having more knowledge helps you learn new information and store it in long-term memory. This is a key difference between short-term and long-term memory. The capacity of short-term memory is limited, so the more information you have in there already, the less effectively you can add new information to it. With long-term memory, however, the capacity is essentially unlimited, and the more you know the easier it is to learn new information because you can relate it to what you already know.

Social Cognition: The Imaginary Audience and the Personal Fable

LO 8.8 **Define the imaginary audience and the personal fable and explain how they reflect egocentrism in adolescence.**

Cognitive development in adolescence includes the development of **metacognition**, which is the capacity to think about thinking. This advance includes the ability to think about not only your own thoughts but also the thoughts of others. Adolescents are generally better at metacognition than younger children are. However, when their metacognitive abilities first develop, adolescents may have difficulty distinguishing their thinking about their own thoughts from their thinking about the thoughts of others, resulting in a distinctive kind of **adolescent egocentrism**. Ideas about adolescent egocentrism were first put forward by Piaget (1967) and were developed further by David Elkind (1967, 1985; Alberts et al., 2007). According to Elkind, adolescent egocentrism has two aspects, the imaginary audience and the personal fable.

THE IMAGINARY AUDIENCE The **imaginary audience** results from adolescents' limited capacity to distinguish between their thinking about themselves and their thinking about the thoughts of others. Because they think about themselves so much and are so acutely aware of how they might appear to others, they conclude that others must also be thinking about them a great deal. Because they exaggerate the extent to which others think about them, they imagine a rapt audience for their appearance and behavior.

divided attention

ability to focus on more than one task at a time

metacognition

capacity to think about thinking

adolescent egocentrism

type of egocentrism in which adolescents have difficulty distinguishing their thinking about their own thoughts from their thinking about the thoughts of others

imaginary audience

belief that others are acutely aware of and attentive to one's appearance and behavior

The imaginary audience makes adolescents much more self-conscious than they were in middle childhood, as shown in the video *Imaginary Audience*. Do you remember waking up in 7th or 8th grade with a pimple on your forehead, or discovering a mustard stain on your pants and wondering how long it had been there, or saying something in class that made everybody laugh (even though you didn't intend it to be funny)? Of course, experiences like these are not much fun as an adult, either. But they tend to be worse in adolescence, because the imaginary audience makes it seem as though "everybody" knows about your humiliation and will remember it for a long, long time.

Watch IMAGINARY AUDIENCE

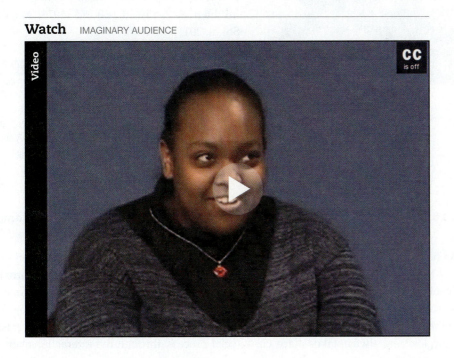

The imaginary audience is not something that simply disappears when adolescence ends. Adults are egocentric, too, to some extent. Adults, too, imagine (and sometimes exaggerate) an audience for their behavior. It is just that this tendency is stronger in adolescence, when the capacity for distinguishing between our own perspective and the perspective of others is less developed (Alberts et al., 2007).

THE PERSONAL FABLE According to Elkind (1967, 1985), the belief in an imaginary audience that is highly conscious of how you look and act leads to the belief that there must be something special, something unique, about you. Adolescents' belief in the uniqueness of their personal experiences and their personal destiny is known as the **personal fable**.

The personal fable can be the source of adolescent anguish, when it makes them feel that "no one understands me" because no one can share their unique experience (Elkind, 1978). It can be the source of high hopes, too, as adolescents imagine their unique personal destiny leading to the fulfillment of their dreams to be a rock musician, a professional athlete, a famous actor, or simply successful in the field of their choice. It can also contribute to risky behavior by adolescents whose sense of uniqueness leads them to believe that adverse consequences from behavior such as unprotected sex or drunk driving "won't happen to me." According to research by Elkind and his colleagues, personal fable scores increase from early to mid-adolescence and are correlated with participation in risk behaviors (Alberts et al., 2007).

personal fable
belief in one's personal uniqueness, often including a sense of invulnerability to the consequences of taking risks

The personal fable can lead adolescents to believe that negative consequences from taking risks "won't happen to me."

Like the imaginary audience, the personal fable diminishes with age, but it never disappears entirely for most of us. Even most adults like to think there is something special, if not unique, about their personal experiences and their personal destiny. But the personal fable tends to be stronger in adolescence than at later ages, because with age our experiences and conversations with others lead us to an awareness that our thoughts and feelings are not as exceptional as we once might have believed (Elkind, 1978; Martin & Sokol, 2011).

CRITICAL THINKING QUESTION

Do you think most people your age have outgrown adolescent egocentrism? Give examples of the imaginary audience and the personal fable that you have witnessed among your peers or experienced yourself.

Culture and Cognition

LO 8.9 Produce an example of the zone of proximal development and scaffolding involving adolescents.

As noted in previous chapters, two of Vygotsky's most influential ideas are scaffolding and the zone of proximal development (see Chapter 5, L.O. 5.8). The zone of proximal development is the difference between skills or tasks a person can accomplish alone and those they are capable of doing if guided by a more experienced person. Scaffolding refers to the degree of assistance provided in the zone of proximal development. In Vygotsky's view, learning always takes place via a social process, through the interactions between someone who possesses knowledge and someone who is in the process of obtaining it.

Scaffolding and the zone of proximal development continue to apply during adolescence, when the skills necessary for adult work are being learned. An example can be found in research on weaving skills among male adolescents in the Dioula culture in Ivory Coast, on the western coast of Africa (Tanon, 1994). An important part of the Dioula economy is making and selling large handmade cloths with elaborate designs. The training of weavers begins when they are age 10–12 and continues for several years. Boys grow up watching their fathers weave, but it is in early adolescence that they begin learning weaving skills themselves. Teaching takes place through scaffolding: The boy attempts a simple weaving pattern, the father corrects his mistakes, the boy tries again. When the boy gets it right, the father gives him a more complex pattern, thus raising the upper boundary of the zone of proximal development so that the boy continues to be challenged and his skills continue to improve. As the boy becomes more competent at weaving, the scaffolding provided by the father diminishes. Eventually the boy gets his own loom, but he continues to consult with his father for several years before he can weave entirely by himself.

As this example illustrates, learning in adolescence is always a cultural process, in which adolescents are acquiring the skills and knowledge that will be useful in their culture. Increasingly, the skills and knowledge of the global economy involve the ability to use information technology such as computers and the Internet. In most countries, the highest paying jobs require these kinds of skills. However, as the example of the Dioula illustrates, in developing countries the most necessary skills and knowledge are often those involved in making things the family can use or that other people will want to buy (Larson et al., 2010).

Practice Quiz

1. You recently were watching your nephew, who is 13 years old, try to figure out why his bike's gears won't work. You were fascinated by the systematic problem-solving strategies that he used. You remember just a few months ago he would not have been able to perform at this level of hypothesis testing, but would have most likely tried random solutions haphazardly. According to Piaget, what type of reasoning is he using?

a. Brainstorming
b. Hypothetical-deductive reasoning
c. Working backwards
d. Seriation

2. Which of the following statements is the **most accurate** based on research on formal operational thinking?

a. Adolescents who have had courses in the language arts and music are more likely than other adolescents to exhibit formal operational thought.
b. The way that formal operational thinking is manifested is likely different across different cultures.
c. Once people obtain formal operational thinking skills, they use them consistently across all tasks and situations.
d. People tend to use formal operations for problems and situations in which they have less experience and knowledge.

3. What is the capacity of long-term memory?

a. It has a limit of 7 plus or minus 1 item.
b. It has a limit of 7 plus or minus 2 items.
c. It is essentially unlimited.
d. It is limited neurologically to 4 billion engrams.

4. Jace thinks he's a really good driver. He often speeds on long stretches of highway and doesn't usually slow down on the curves in the road despite what the signs say. He brags to his friends in the car that he can drive fast because he knows what he's doing. He goes on to say that only bad drivers get themselves in accidents. His way of thinking demonstrates _____.

a. selective attention
b. the imaginary audience
c. the personal fable
d. hypothetical-deductive reasoning

5. When learning to weave, boys in the Dioula culture start by watching their fathers weave, and then learn to weave themselves in early adolescence. The boy starts off working on his own to complete a simple pattern and gets help when he makes mistakes. He moves on to more complex patterns and continues to consult with his father for several years until he can weave completely on his own. This is an example of _____.

a. scaffolding
b. hypothetical-deductive reasoning
c. divided attention
d. accommodation

COGNITIVE DEVELOPMENT:
Education and Work

Their cognitive advances prepare adolescents for new forms of school and work, especially as they enter secondary school, where the demands are greater and the social environment is often less supportive. In developing countries, young people often engage in adult work by adolescence, and in developed countries they may take part-time jobs or apprenticeships that introduce them to the adult world of work.

Schools: Secondary Education

LO 8.10 Compare and contrast the secondary education systems and academic performance of developed countries and developing countries.

The transition to secondary school is challenging for adolescents. It usually means moving from a small, personalized classroom setting to a larger setting where a student has not one teacher but five or six or more. It also means moving into a setting where the academic work is at a higher level and grades are suddenly viewed as a more serious measure of academic attainment than they may have been in primary school.

These changes in school experience can add to early adolescents' anxieties and school-related stress. A longitudinal study of over 1,500 adolescents found a steady decline from the beginning of 6th grade to the end of 8th grade in students' perceptions of teacher support, autonomy in the classroom, and clarity of school rules and regulations (Way et al., 2007). These declines were in turn related to declines in psychological well-being and increases in behavior problems. However, there were also benefits from the transition to secondary school. One study found that 7th-grade adolescents made more positive than negative comments about the transition to middle school, with positive comments about

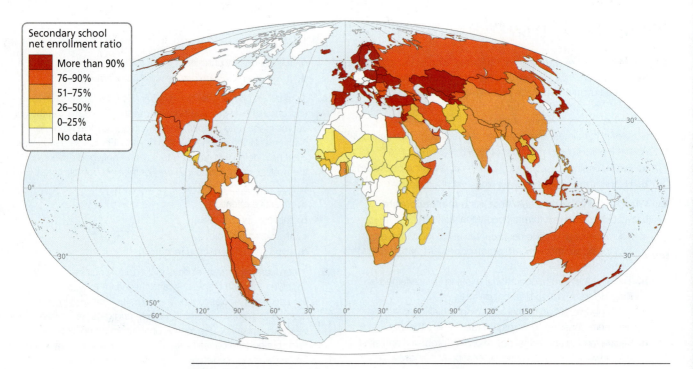

Map 8.1 Secondary School Enrollment Worldwide

Which countries have the highest enrollment rates for secondary education? Which are the lowest? What cultural and economic factors might explain these variations?

topics such as peer relationships (more people to "hang around" with), academics (greater diversity of classes available), and independence (Berndt & Mekos, 1995).

There is a great deal of diversity worldwide in the kinds of **secondary schools** (middle schools and high schools) that adolescents attend. World regions also vary in how likely adolescents are to attend secondary school at all. There is an especially sharp contrast between developed countries and developing countries. Virtually all adolescents are enrolled in secondary school in developed countries. In contrast, in many developing countries only about 50% of adolescents attend secondary school (UNESCO, 2014; see **Map 8.1**). It should be added that if you are a member of an ethnic minority in a developed country and your family has a low income, your chances of finishing secondary school may be substantially lower than in the majority culture (NCES, 2014). In the United States, high school graduation rates vary widely by ethnic group, as **Figure 8.6** shows (NCES, 2014).

secondary school

school attended during adolescence, after primary school

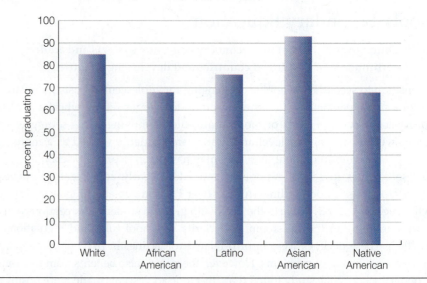

Figure 8.6 U.S. High School Completion Rate by Ethnic Group
SOURCE: Based on NCES (2014)

INTERNATIONAL VARIATIONS IN SECONDARY SYSTEMS The United States is unusual in having only one institution—the "comprehensive" school—as the source of secondary education. Canada and Japan also have comprehensive secondary schools as the norm, but most other countries have several different kinds of schools that adolescents may attend. European countries usually have three types of secondary schools (Hamilton & Hamilton, 2006). About half of adolescents attend a *college-preparatory school* that offers a variety of academic courses. The goal is general education rather than training for any specific profession. About one fourth of adolescents attend a *vocational school,* where they learn the skills involved in a specific occupation such as plumbing or auto mechanics. Some European countries also have a third type of secondary school, a *professional school,* devoted to teacher training, the arts, or some other specific purpose. About one fourth of European adolescents usually attend this type of school.

Pressure for academic performance is high in Asian countries because the stakes are high.

One consequence of the European system is that adolescents must decide at a relatively early age what direction to pursue for their education and occupation. At age 15 or 16 adolescents choose which type of secondary school they will enter, and this is a decision that is likely to have an enormous impact on the rest of their lives. Usually the decision is made by adolescents in conference with their parents and teachers, based on adolescents' interests as well as on their school performance (Motola et al., 1998). Although adolescents sometimes change schools after a year or two, and adolescents who attend a vocational school sometimes attend university, these switches are rare.

In contrast to developed countries, where attending secondary school is virtually universal for adolescents and the schools are well funded, in developing countries secondary education is often difficult to obtain and relatively few adolescents stay in school until graduation. A number of common themes recur in accounts of secondary education in developing countries (Lloyd, 2005; Lloyd et al., 2008). All developing countries have seen rising rates of enrollment in recent decades (UNESCO, 2014). That's about where the good news ends. Many of the schools are poorly funded and overcrowded. Many countries have too few teachers, and the teachers are insufficiently trained. Often families have to pay for secondary education, a cost they find difficult to afford, and families may have to pay for books and other educational supplies as well. There tends to be one education for the elite—in exclusive private schools and well-funded universities—and a much inferior education for everyone else.

Education is, in all parts of the world, the basis of many of the good things in life, from income level to physical and mental health (Lloyd, 2005; Lloyd et al., 2008; Stromquist, 2007). Yet for the majority of the world's adolescents and emerging adults, their educational fate was already largely determined at birth, simply on the basis of where they were born.

INTERNATIONAL COMPARISONS IN ACADEMIC PERFORMANCE For about 30 years, there have been international studies that compare adolescents on academic performance. **Figure 8.7** on the next page shows the most recent performance of adolescents in various countries around the world on 8th-grade achievement tests. The pattern of results is similar across reading and math. In both areas, the pattern is the same as in middle childhood (discussed in Chapter 7): the affluent developed countries tend to perform better than the developing countries.

In math and science, Japan and South Korea are consistently at the top. In adolescence as at earlier ages, Eastern schools focus almost exclusively on **rote learning** (memorizing information through repetition), whereas Western schools place more emphasis on promoting critical thinking and creativity (Kember & Watkins, 2010).

rote learning

learning by memorization and repetition

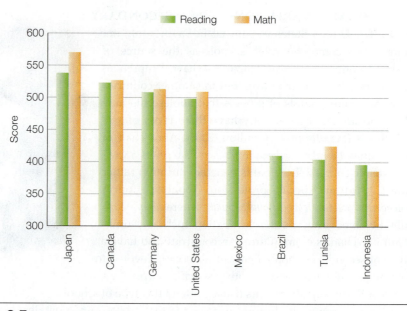

Figure 8.7 International Performance in Reading and Math, 8th Grade

What explains why Japan scores highest?

SOURCE: Based on NCES (2014)

Another crucial difference is that in the East the consequences of school performance in adolescence are much more serious and enduring. Adolescents in Japan and South Korea have to take entrance exams for both high school and college. These two exams have a great influence on young people's occupational fate for the rest of their lives, because in Asian countries, obtaining a job is based primarily on the status of the schools a person has attended. To prepare for the entrance exams, adolescents in Eastern countries are pressed by parents and teachers to apply themselves seriously at school and in their homework. In addition, from middle childhood through adolescence many of them attend "cram schools" after school or receive instruction from private tutors (Takahashi & Takeuchi, 2007).

With longer school days, a longer school year, cram schools, and private tutors, Eastern adolescents have far less time for after-school leisure and informal socializing with friends than American adolescents do (Chaudhary & Sharma, 2012). In recent decades some Asian countries have reduced the length of the school day and cut the number of school days per week from six to five, but the average school day remains long and cram schools remain the norm (Takahashi & Takeuchi, 2007).

Work

LO 8.11 Summarize the typical forms of adolescent work in developing countries and developed countries, and name the features of apprenticeships in Europe.

Adolescents' new physical, cognitive, and social abilities make them valuable as potential workers all around the world. However, the kind of work they do varies sharply between developing countries and developed countries.

ADOLESCENT WORK IN DEVELOPING COUNTRIES As we have seen in previous chapters, for children in developing countries, work often begins long before adolescence. Within the family, from early childhood onward, children begin to contribute to the work required in daily life, helping with tasks such as cleaning, cooking, gathering firewood, and caring for younger siblings. By middle childhood, many of them work in factory settings, where they do jobs such as weaving rugs and polishing gems (International Labor Organization [ILO], 2013). They also work on farms and in domestic service, and some sell goods on the street.

Adolescents in developing countries often do the same types of difficult, dangerous, and poorly paid work as younger children do, as described in Chapter 7, but one type of work that usually begins in adolescence is prostitution. Estimates of the number of adolescent sex workers in developing countries vary, but it is widely agreed that adolescent prostitution is a pervasive problem, especially in Asia, and within Asia especially in Thailand (Basu & Chau, 2007; ILO, 2002). Of course, adolescent sex workers exist in developed countries as well, but the problem is much more widespread in developing countries.

Adolescent girls in these countries become sex workers in several ways. Some are kidnapped and taken to a separate country. Isolated in a country where they are not citizens and where they do not know the language, they are highly vulnerable and dependent on their kidnappers. Some are rural adolescent girls who are promised jobs in restaurants or domestic service, then forced to become prostitutes once the recruiter takes them to their urban destination. Sometimes parents sell the girls into prostitution, out of desperate poverty or simply out of the desire for more consumer goods (ILO, 2004). A large proportion of the customers in Asian brothels are Western tourists, leading the United States and several European countries to pass laws permitting prosecution of their citizens for sexually exploiting young adolescent girls in other countries.

ADOLESCENT WORK IN DEVELOPED COUNTRIES What do you remember about your jobs in adolescence, if you worked at that time? I still remember a lot about mine, even though they were mostly forgettable. Like many adolescents, I mostly worked in low-paying restaurant jobs, mainly washing dishes and cooking hamburgers, French fries, and other greasy items. I usually didn't last long on these jobs. On one of my dishwashing jobs, the third day of work a friend and I discovered that creative use of the sprayers intended to rinse the dishes could quickly turn our boring dishwashing task into an exciting game of Spray Wars. Of course, we were fired immediately.

But what did we care? There were plenty of other jobs around, and for us not much depended on working except how much money would be available for having fun on the weekend. For adolescents in developed countries, work is usually not done as part of contributing to family survival but as a way of supporting an active leisure life. About 80% of adolescents in the United States and Canada hold at least one part-time job by the end of high school (Lee & Staff, 2007). Very little of the money they earn goes to their family's living expenses or saving for their future education (although adolescents in ethnic minority groups are more likely to contribute to their families; Fuligni, 2011; Mortimer, 2003). For the most part, the money goes toward purchases for themselves, here and now: stylish clothes, music, car payments and gas, concert tickets, movies, eating out—and alcohol, cigarettes, and other drugs (Greenberger & Steinberg, 1986; Mortimer, 2013).

Unlike in developing countries, the work done by adolescents in developed countries does little to prepare them for the kind of work they are likely to be doing as adults. For example, the majority of jobs held by American and Canadian adolescents in high school involve restaurant work or retail sales (Mortimer, 2013; Staff et al., 2004). Consequently, few adolescents see their high school jobs as the basis for a future career (Mortimer et al., 2008).

Not only does working part-time appear to do adolescents little good in developed countries, it can be harmful to their development in a variety of ways. The amount of time worked per week is a crucial variable. Most studies find that up to 10 hours a week working at a part-time job has little effect on adolescents' development. However, beyond 10 hours a week problems arise, and beyond 20 hours a week the problems become considerably worse.

Apprenticeships are common in Europe. These adolescents are apprenticing at a German power plant company.

Beyond 10 hours a week, the more adolescents work the lower their grades, the less time they spend on homework, the more they cut class, the more they cheat on their schoolwork, the less committed they are to school, and the lower their educational aspirations (Marsh & Kleitman, 2005). Similarly, reports of psychological symptoms jump sharply for adolescents working more than 10 hours a week and continue to rise among adolescents working 20 hours a week or more (Lee & Staff, 2007; Mortimer, 2013). Canadian research reports that when adolescents take on demanding jobs, they reduce their sleep by an hour per night and eliminate nearly all sports activities (Sears et al., 2006). Adolescents who work are also more likely to use alcohol, cigarettes, and other drugs, especially if they work more than 10 hours a week (Bachman et al., 2003; Longest & Shanahan, 2007; Wu et al., 2003). A national study of adolescents in Finland also found numerous negative effects of working more than 20 hours a week (Kuovonen & Kivivuori, 2001).

Although working part-time is related to a variety of negative outcomes, a case can also be made in favor of adolescent work, as long as it is 10 hours a week or less. Adolescents see many benefits from their work, such as learning responsibility, how to manage money, social skills, and how to organize their time (Aronson et al., 1996; Mortimer, 2013). Over 40% believe that their jobs have helped them develop new occupational skills, in contrast to the portrayal of adolescent work as involving nothing but dreary tasks (although we might note that 40%, while substantial, is still a minority).

APPRENTICESHIPS IN EUROPE Although most employment in adolescence in the United States and Canada has little relation to later jobs, many European countries have a long tradition of apprenticeships that provides excellent preparation for adult occupations. In an **apprenticeship**, an adolescent "novice" serves under contract to a "master" who has substantial experience in a profession, and through working under the master the novice learns the skills required (Hamilton & Hamilton, 2000; Hamilton & Hamilton, 2006; Vazsonyi & Snider, 2008). Although apprenticeships originally began centuries ago in craft professions such as carpentry and blacksmithing, today they are undertaken to prepare for a wide range of professions, from auto mechanics and carpenters to police officers, computer technicians, and child-care workers (Fuller et al., 2005). Apprenticeships are especially common in central and northern Europe. For example, over 60% of adolescents in Germany and Switzerland participate in apprenticeships (Dolphin & Lanning, 2011).

Common features of apprenticeship programs are (Hamilton & Hamilton, 2006):

- entry at age 16, with the apprenticeship lasting 2 to 3 years;
- continued part-time schooling while in the apprenticeship, with the school curriculum closely connected to the training received in the apprenticeship;
- training that takes place in the workplace, under real working conditions; and
- preparation for a career in a respected profession that provides an adequate income.

apprenticeship

an arrangement, common in Europe, in which an adolescent "novice" serves under contract to a "master" who has substantial experience in a profession, and through working under the master, learns the skills required to enter the profession

This kind of program requires close coordination between schools and employers, so that what adolescents learn at school will complement and reinforce what is being learned in their apprenticeship. This means that schools consult employers with respect to the skills required in the workplace, and employers make opportunities available for adolescent apprentices. In Europe, the employers see this as worth their trouble because apprenticeships provide them with a reliable supply of well-qualified entry-level employees (Dustmann & Schoenberg, 2008).

Practice Quiz

1. Students from _____ usually have three types of secondary schools.

a. Japan   **c.** the United States

b. Europe   **d.** Canada

2. Compared to their peers in the United States, adolescents in Asian countries _____.

a. have a shorter school day

b. have a shorter school year

c. have to take entrance exams for both high school and college

d. are taught with an emphasis on critical thinking and creativity

3. In math and science, students from _____ consistently score at the top.

a. the United States and China   **c.** Russia and China

b. Japan and South Korea   **d.** China and Wales

4. If you are an adolescent living in _____ you are most likely to be participating in an apprenticeship program.

a. the United States

b. New Zealand

c. Germany

d. Canada

5. Which of the following is **TRUE** about work during adolescence?

a. Few American adolescents see their high school jobs as the basis for a future career.

b. Most are likely to work answering phones and doing clerical work in an office setting.

c. Less than half of adolescents in the United States and Canada have held at least one part-time job by the end of high school.

d. The United States is the only country where part-time work is associated with problem behavior.

Summary: Cognitive Development

LO 8.6 **Explain the features of hypothetical-deductive reasoning and identify critiques of Piaget's theory of formal operations.**

Hypothetical-deductive reasoning entails the ability to test solutions to a problem systematically, altering one variable while holding the others constant. The pendulum problem is one way Piaget tested the attainment of formal operations.

Piaget proposed that when adolescents reach formal operations they use it for all cognitive activities; however, research has shown that both adolescents and adults tend to use formal operations in some areas of their lives but not in others. Piaget also proposed that formal operations is a universal stage of cognitive development, but its prevalence appears to vary across cultures as measured by standard tasks, although it may be used in the course of culturally specific daily activities.

LO 8.7 **Summarize the major changes in attention and memory that take place from middle childhood to adolescence.**

Information processing abilities improve in adolescence, with the notable additions of selective attention, divided attention, and use of mnemonic devices.

LO 8.8 **Define the imaginary audience and the personal fable and explain how they reflect egocentrism in adolescence.**

The imaginary audience is the exaggerated belief that others are paying intense attention to one's appearance and behavior. The personal fable is the belief that there is something special and unique about one's personal destiny. The imaginary audience results from adolescents' egocentric inability to distinguish their thoughts about themselves from their thoughts about others' thoughts.

LO 8.9 **Produce an example of the zone of proximal development and scaffolding involving adolescents.**

Scaffolding and the zone of proximal development are evident in adolescence, when the skills necessary for adult work are being learned. For example, male adolescents in the Dioula culture in Ivory Coast are first taught simple weaving patterns but learn increasingly complex patterns as their skills improve in response to correction and instruction by their fathers, until they can weave entirely by themselves.

LO 8.10 **Compare and contrast the secondary education systems and academic performance of developed countries and developing countries.**

The United States, Canada, and Japan have a comprehensive high school, but most other countries have at least three different types of secondary school. Academic performance is generally higher in developed countries than in developing countries, but highest of all in Asian developed countries, where pressure to excel is high.

LO 8.11 **Summarize the typical forms of adolescent work in developing countries and developed countries, and describe the features of apprenticeships in Europe.**

Adolescents' work is often hard and perilous in developing countries, and in some countries adolescent girls are forced into prostitution. In developed countries, working more than 10 hours per week interferes with adolescents' school performance, sleep, and psychological health. In some European countries, apprenticeships are available, in which adolescents spend part of their time in school and part of their time in the workplace receiving direct occupational training.

Section 3 Emotional and Social Development

Learning Objectives

8.12 Summarize the results of the ESM studies with respect to adolescent emotionality.

8.13 Describe how self-understanding, self-concept, and self-esteem change during adolescence.

8.14 Discriminate between Kohlberg's theory of moral development and Jensen's worldviews theory.

8.15 Describe the cultural variations in religious beliefs during adolescence as well as the sources and outcomes of religiosity within cultures.

8.16 Summarize the cultural variations in adolescents' relationships with parents, siblings, and extended family.

8.17 Describe cultural variations in adolescents' relationships with friends, and characterize their interactions with peers.

8.18 Identify cultural variations in adolescent love and sexuality, including variations in pregnancy and contraceptive use.

8.19 Explain the function of media use in adolescents' lives and apply the Media Practice Model to the playing of electronic games.

8.20 Summarize the explanations for why age and crime are so strongly correlated, and describe the multisystemic approach to combating delinquency.

8.21 Identify the different types and rates of depression and summarize the most effective treatments.

8.22 Define resilience and name the protective factors that are related to resilience in adolescence.

EMOTIONAL AND SOCIAL DEVELOPMENT: Emotional and Self-Development

Adolescence has long been regarded as a time of emotional volatility, and here we'll look at the history of views on this topic as well as current research. Issues of self-concept and self-esteem are also at the forefront of adolescent development, partly due to advances in cognitive development. Gender issues are prominent as well, because adolescence involves reaching sexual maturity.

Emotionality in Adolescence: Storm and Stress?

LO 8.12 Summarize the results of the ESM studies with respect to adolescent emotionality.

One of the most ancient and enduring observations of adolescence is that it is a time of heightened emotions (Arnett, 1999). Over 2,000 years ago, the Greek philosopher Aristotle observed that youth "are heated by Nature as drunken men by wine." About 250 years ago, the French philosopher Jean-Jacques Rousseau made a similar observation: "As the roaring of the waves precedes the tempest, so the murmur of rising passions announces the tumultuous change" of puberty and adolescence. Around the same time that Rousseau was writing, a type of German literature was developing that became known as *"sturm und drang"* literature—German for "storm and stress." In these stories, young people in their teens and early twenties experienced extreme emotions of angst, sadness, and romantic passion.

What does contemporary research tell us about the validity of these historical and popular views of adolescent emotionality? Probably the best source of data on this question is research using the Experience Sampling Method (ESM), which involves having people wear wristwatch beepers and then beeping them randomly during the day so that they can record their thoughts, feelings, and behavior (refer back to Chapter 7) (Csikszentmihalyi & Larson, 1984; Larson & Csikszentmihalyi, 2014; Schneider, 2006). ESM studies have also been conducted on younger children and adults, so if we compare the patterns of emotions reported by the different groups, we can get a good sense of whether adolescence is a stage of more extremes of emotions than middle childhood or adulthood.

The results indicate that adolescence in the United States is often a time of emotional volatility (Larson & Csikszentmihalyi, 2014; Larson et al., 1980; Larson & Richards, 1994). American adolescents report feeling "self-conscious" and "embarrassed" two to three times more often than their parents and are also more likely than their parents to feel awkward, lonely, nervous, and ignored. Adolescents are also moodier when compared to younger children. Comparing preadolescent 5th graders to adolescent 8th graders, Reed Larson and Maryse Richards (1994) describe the emotional "fall from grace" that occurs during that time, as the proportion of time experienced as "very happy" declines by 50%, and similar declines take place in reports of feeling "great," "proud," and "in control." The result is an overall "deflation of childhood happiness" (p. 85) as childhood ends and adolescence begins.

How do emotional states change during the course of adolescence? Larson and Richards assessed their original ESM sample of 5th to 8th graders 4 years later, in 9th to 12th grades (Larson et al., 2002). As **Figure 8.8** shows, they found that there was a decline in average emotional states with age.

What about other cultures? Is adolescent emotionality especially an American phenomenon, or does it take place in other cultures as well? There is limited evidence to answer this question. However, in one study ESM was used with adolescents and their parents in India (Verma & Larson, 1999). The results indicated that, in India as in the United States, adolescents reported more extremes of emotion than their parents did.

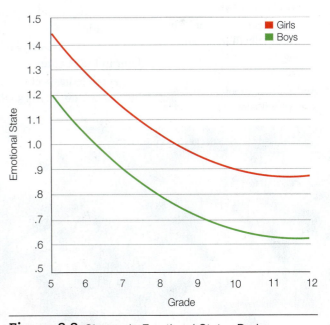

Figure 8.8 Change in Emotional States During Adolescence

Average emotional state becomes steadily more negative in the course of adolescence.

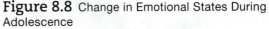
SOURCE: Larson et al. (2002)

Self-Development in Adolescence

LO 8.13 Describe how self-understanding, self-concept, and self-esteem change during adolescence.

Self-conceptions become more complex in adolescence, due to advances in cognitive development. Self-esteem also becomes more complex, but overall self-esteem declines in early adolescence before rising in late adolescence and emerging adulthood.

actual self

person's perception of the self as it is, contrasted with the possible self

possible self

person's conceptions of the self as it potentially may be; may include both an ideal self and a feared self

ideal self

person one would like to be

feared self

person one imagines it is possible to become but dreads becoming

false self

self a person may present to others while realizing that it does not represent what he or she is actually thinking and feeling

Adolescents are most likely to use a false self with dating partners.

SELF-UNDERSTANDING AND SELF-CONCEPT Self-conceptions in adolescence become more complex and more abstract. One aspect of the complexity of adolescents' self-conceptions is that they can distinguish between an **actual self** and **possible selves** (Markus & Nurius, 1986; Oyserman & Fryberg, 2006; Whitty, 2002). The actual self is your self-conception, and possible selves are the different people you imagine you could become in the future depending on your choices and experiences. Scholars distinguish two kinds of possible selves, an ideal self and a feared self (Chalk et al., 2005). The **ideal self** is the person the adolescent would like to be (for example, an adolescent may have an ideal of becoming highly popular with peers or highly successful in athletics or music). The **feared self** is the person the adolescent dreads becoming (for example, an adolescent might fear becoming an alcoholic, or fear becoming like a disgraced relative or friend). Both kinds of possible selves require adolescents to think abstractly. That is, possible selves exist only as abstractions, as *ideas* in the adolescent's mind.

The capacity for thinking about an actual, an ideal, and a feared self is a cognitive achievement, but this capacity may be troubling in some respects. If you can imagine an ideal self, you can also become aware of the discrepancy between your actual self and your ideal self, between what you are and what you wish you were. If the discrepancy is large enough, it can result in feelings of failure, inadequacy, and depression. Studies have found that the size of the discrepancy between the actual and ideal self is related to depressed mood in both adolescents and emerging adults (Moretti & Wiebe, 1999; Papadakis et al., 2006). Furthermore, the discrepancy between the actual and the ideal self is greater in mid-adolescence than in either early or late adolescence (Ferguson et al., 2010). This helps explain why rates of depressed mood rise from early adolescence to mid-adolescence, as we will see in more detail later in the chapter.

A related aspect of the increasing complexity of self-conceptions is that adolescents become aware of times when they are exhibiting a **false self**, which is a self they present to others while realizing that it does not represent what they are actually thinking and feeling (Harter et al., 1997; Weir et al., 2010). With whom would you think adolescents would be most likely to exhibit their false selves—friends, parents, or potential romantic partners? Research indicates that adolescents are most likely to put on their false selves with potential romantic partners, and least likely with their close friends; parents are in between (Harter, 2006; Sippola et al., 2007). Most adolescents indicate that they sometimes dislike putting on a false self, but many also say that some degree of false self behavior is acceptable and even desirable, to impress someone or to conceal aspects of the self they do not want others to see.

SELF-ESTEEM Several longitudinal studies show that self-esteem declines in early adolescence, then rises through late adolescence and emerging

adulthood (Harter, 2012; Robins & Trzesniewski, 2005). There are a number of reasons why self-esteem might follow this developmental pattern. The "imaginary audience" that we have discussed as part of adolescents' cognitive development can make them self-conscious in a way that decreases their self-esteem (Elkind, 1967, 1985). That is, as adolescents develop the capacity to imagine that others are especially conscious of how they look and what they say and how they act, they may suspect or fear that others are judging them harshly.

And they may be right. Adolescents in Western cultures tend to value the opinion of their peers highly, especially on day-to-day issues such as how they are dressed and what they say in social situations (Berndt, 1996). Also, their peers have developed new cognitive capacities for sarcasm and ridicule, which tend to be dispensed freely toward any peer who seems odd or awkward or uncool (Eder, 1995; Rosenblum & Way, 2004). So, the combination of greater self-consciousness about evaluations by peers and peers' potentially harsh evaluations contributes to declines in self-esteem in early adolescence. Self-esteem rises in late adolescence and emerging adulthood as peers' evaluations become less important (Berndt, 1986; Robins & Trzesniewski, 2005).

As scholars have studied self-esteem, they have concluded that it has many aspects in addition to overall self-esteem. Multiple aspects of adolescent self-esteem have been investigated by Susan Harter (1990a, 1990b, 2006, 2012). Her *Self-Perception Profile for Adolescents* distinguishes the following eight domains of adolescent self-concept:

- Scholastic competence
- Social acceptance
- Athletic competence
- Physical appearance
- Job competence
- Romantic appeal
- Behavioral conduct
- Close friendship

In addition to the eight subscales on specific domains of self-concept, Harter's scale also contains a subscale for global (overall) self-esteem. Her research indicates that adolescents do not need to have a positive self-image in all domains to have high global self-esteem. Each domain of self-concept influences global self-esteem only to the extent that the adolescent views that domain as important. For example, some adolescents may view themselves as having low scholastic competence, but that would only influence their global self-esteem if it was important to them to do well in school.

Nevertheless, some domains of self-concept are more important than others to most adolescents. Research by Harter and others has found that physical appearance is most strongly related to global self-esteem, followed by social acceptance from peers (DuBois et al., 1996; Harter, 2012; Shapka & Keating, 2005). Adolescent girls are more likely than boys to emphasize physical appearance as a basis for self-esteem. Because girls tend to evaluate their physical appearance negatively, and because physical appearance is at the heart of their global self-esteem, girls' self-esteem tends to be lower than boys' during adolescence (Robins & Trzesniewski, 2005; Shapka & Keating, 2005).

GENDER INTENSIFICATION IN ADOLESCENCE Gender is related not only to self-esteem but to many other aspects of self-development in adolescence. Psychologists John Hill and Mary Ellen Lynch (1983; Lynch 1991) proposed that adolescence is a particularly important time in gender socialization, especially for girls. According to their **gender-intensification hypothesis**, psychological and behavioral differences between males and females become more pronounced in the transition from childhood to adolescence because of intensified socialization pressures to conform to culturally prescribed gender roles. Hill and Lynch (1983) believe that it is this intensified socialization pressure, rather than the biological changes of puberty, that results in increased differences

gender-intensification hypothesis

hypothesis that psychological and behavioral differences between males and females become more pronounced at adolescence because of intensified socialization pressures to conform to culturally prescribed gender roles between males and females as adolescence progresses. Furthermore, they argue that the intensity of gender socialization in adolescence is greater for females than for males, and that this is reflected in a variety of ways in adolescent girls' development. For an illustration of how girls in the United States respond to gender intensification, view the *Body Image in Adolescent Girls* video.

Watch   BODY IMAGE IN ADOLESCENT GIRLS

Since Hill and Lynch (1983) proposed this hypothesis, other studies have been presented that support it (Galambos, 2004; Shanahan et al., 2007; Priess & Lindberg, 2014). In one study, boys and girls filled out a questionnaire on gender identity each year in 6th, 7th, and 8th grades (Galambos et al., 1990). Over this 2-year period, girls' self-descriptions became more "feminine" (e.g., gentle, affectionate) and boys' self-descriptions became more "masculine" (e.g., tough, aggressive). However, in contrast to Hill and Lynch's (1983) claim that gender intensification is strongest for girls, the pattern in this study was especially strong for boys and masculinity. A more recent study found that gender stereotypes were embraced more by adolescents than by younger children, for both boys and girls (Rowley et al., 2007). Another study found that increased conformity to gender roles during early adolescence took place primarily for adolescents whose parents valued traditional gender roles (Crouter et al., 1995).

Gender intensification is often considerably stronger in traditional cultures than in the West. One striking difference in gender expectations in traditional cultures is that for boys manhood is something that has to be *achieved*, whereas girls reach womanhood inevitably, mainly through their biological changes (Leavitt, 1998; Lindsay & Miescher, 2003). It is true that girls are required to demonstrate various skills and character qualities before they can be said to have reached womanhood. However, in most traditional cultures womanhood is seen as something that girls attain naturally during adolescence, and their readiness for womanhood is viewed as indisputably marked when they reach menarche. Adolescent boys have no comparable biological marker of readiness for manhood. For them, the attainment of manhood is often fraught with peril and carries a definite and formidable possibility of failure.

So, what must an adolescent boy in traditional cultures do to achieve manhood and escape the stigma of being viewed as a failed man? The anthropologist David Gilmore

(1990) examined this question in traditional cultures around the world and concluded that an adolescent boy must demonstrate three capacities before he can be considered a man: *provide, protect,* and *procreate.* He must *provide* in the sense that he must demonstrate that he has developed skills that are economically useful and that will enable him to support the wife and children he is likely to have as an adult man. For example, if what adult men mainly do is fish, the adolescent boy must demonstrate that he has learned the skills involved in fishing adequately enough to provide for a family.

Second, he must *protect,* in the sense that he must show that he can contribute to the protection of his family, kinship group, tribe, and other groups to which he belongs, from attacks by human enemies or animal predators. He learns this by acquiring the skills of warfare and the capacity to use weapons. Conflict between human groups has been a fact of life in most cultures throughout human history, so this is a pervasive requirement. Finally, he must learn to *procreate,* in the sense that he must gain some degree of sexual experience before marriage. This is not so he can demonstrate his sexual attractiveness but simply so that he can demonstrate that in marriage he will be able to perform sexually well enough to produce children.

Learning to provide for a family economically is a traditional part of the male gender role. Here, an Egyptian father and son fish together on the Nile River.

Practice Quiz ANSWERS AVAILABLE IN ANSWER KEY.

1. Dr. Rose often uses the Experience Sampling Method (ESM) in her research. Which of the following is most likely to be the topic of her work?
   a. Gender differences in academic interests
   b. Changes in emotions between childhood and adolescence
   c. The effects of different lighting conditions on mating behavior in crayfish
   d. The part-time work experiences of adolescents from different countries.

2. Larson and Richards (1994) compared preadolescent 5th-graders to adolescent 8th-graders and found that the percent of time experienced as "very happy" _____.
   a. increased slightly
   b. increased dramatically
   c. stayed the same
   d. decreased

3. When comparing the emotions experienced by American adolescents with those experienced by their parents, researchers found that the adolescents reported feeling _____ more often.
   a. self-conscious
   b. bored
   c. happy
   d. proud

4. Kerry loves and respects her mother; however, her mother works in a job that she hates in the deli at a local grocery store. Kerry knows that she wants better for herself and wants to earn a college degree and have a teaching career. Kerry has a positive outlook on life and has strong self-esteem; her future seems bright. There are many selves described in this scenario—which of the following best describes Kerry's trepidation about working in a dissatisfying career?
   a. Real self
   b. False self
   c. Feared self
   d. Realistic self

5. Research has shown that during adolescence, _____ is most strongly related to global self-esteem.
   a. physical appearance
   b. scholastic competence
   c. athletic competence
   d. social acceptance

6. Charlotte is a typical American girl. Based on the research, one would expect her self-esteem to be lowest in _____.
   a. the late elementary school years
   b. early adolescence
   c. late adolescence
   d. emerging adulthood

EMOTIONAL AND SOCIAL DEVELOPMENT: Cultural Beliefs: Morality and Religion

As we have seen earlier in the chapter, cognitive development in adolescence entails a greater capacity for abstract and complex thinking. This capacity is applied not only to scientific and practical problems but also to cultural beliefs, most notably in the areas of moral and religious development.

Moral Development

LO 8.14 Discriminate between Kohlberg's theory of moral development and Jensen's worldviews theory.

For most of the past half century, moral development was viewed as following a universal pattern, grounded in cognitive development. However, more recently, moral development has been argued to be fundamentally rooted in cultural beliefs. First we look at a theory of universal moral development, then at a cultural theory.

KOHLBERG'S THEORY OF MORAL DEVELOPMENT Lawrence Kohlberg (1958) presented an influential theory of moral development that dominated research on this topic for several decades. Kohlberg viewed moral development as based on cognitive development, and believed that moral thinking changes in predictable ways as cognitive abilities develop, regardless of culture. He presented people with hypothetical moral dilemmas and had them indicate what behavior they believed was right or wrong in that situation, and why.

Kohlberg began his research by studying the moral judgments of 72 boys ages 10, 13, and 16 from middle-class and working-class families in the Chicago area (Kohlberg, 1958). He presented the boys with a series of fictional dilemmas, each of which was constructed to elicit their moral reasoning. For example, in one dilemma, a man must decide whether or not to steal a drug he cannot afford, to save his dying wife.

To Kohlberg, what was crucial for understanding the level of people's moral development was not whether they concluded that the actions of the persons in the dilemma were right or wrong but how they explained their conclusions; his focus was on adolescents' *moral reasoning,* not moral evaluations of right and wrong or their moral behavior. Kohlberg (1976) developed a system for classifying moral reasoning into three levels of moral development, as follows:

Level 1: **Preconventional reasoning**. At this level, moral reasoning is based on perceptions of the likelihood of external rewards and punishments. What is right is what avoids punishment or results in rewards.

Level 2: **Conventional reasoning**. At this level, moral reasoning is less egocentric and the person advocates the value of conforming to the moral expectations of others. What is right is whatever agrees with the rules established by tradition and by authorities.

Level 3: **Postconventional reasoning**. Moral reasoning at this level is based on the person's own independent judgments rather than on what others view as wrong or right. What is right is derived from the person's perception of objective, universal principles rather than being based on the needs of the individual (as in Level 1) or the standards of the group (as in Level 2).

---

preconventional reasoning
first level in Kohlberg's theory of moral development, in which moral reasoning is based on perceptions of the likelihood of external rewards and punishments

conventional reasoning
second level in Kohlberg's theory of moral development, in which moral reasoning is based on the expectations of others

postconventional reasoning
third level in Kohlberg's theory of moral development, in which moral reasoning is based on the individual's own independent judgments rather than on what others view as wrong or right

Kohlberg followed his initial group of adolescent boys over the next 20 years (Colby et al., 1983), interviewing them every 3 or 4 years, and he and his colleagues also conducted numerous other studies on moral reasoning in adolescence and adulthood. The results verified Kohlberg's theory of moral development in two ways:

• The stage of moral reasoning tended to increase with age. However, even after 20 years, when all of the original participants were in their 30s, few of them had proceeded to Level 3 (Colby et al., 1983).

• Moral development proceeded in the predicted way, in the sense that the participants did not drop from a higher level to a lower level but proceeded from one level to the next highest over time.

Kohlberg's goal was to propose a universal theory of moral development, a theory that would apply to people in all cultures. One reason he used hypothetical moral dilemmas rather than having people talk about moral issues they had confronted in real life was that he believed that the culture-specific and person-specific *content* of moral reasoning is not important to understanding moral development. According to Kohlberg, what matters is the *structure* of moral reasoning, not the content. In other words, what matters is *how* people make their moral judgments, not whether they view certain acts as right or wrong.

CULTURE AND MORAL DEVELOPMENT: THE WORLDVIEWS THEORY Does Kohlberg's theory of moral development apply universally, as he intended? Research based on Kohlberg's theory has included cross-cultural studies in countries all over the world, such as Turkey, Japan, Taiwan, Kenya, Israel, and India (Gibbs et al., 2007; Snarey, 1985). Many of these studies have focused on moral development in adolescence and emerging adulthood. In general, the studies confirm Kohlberg's hypothesis that moral development as classified by his coding system progresses with age. Also, as in the American studies, participants in longitudinal studies in other cultures have rarely been found to regress to an earlier stage.

worldview
set of cultural beliefs that explain what it means to be human, how human relations should be conducted, and how human problems should be addressed

Nevertheless, Kohlberg's claims of a universal theory of moral development have been challenged, most notably by cultural psychologist Richard Shweder (2003; Shweder et al., 1990; Shweder et al., 2006). Shweder argued that it is impossible to understand moral development unless you understand the cultural worldview that underlies it. In contrast to Kohlberg, Shweder proposed that the *content* of people's moral reasoning, including their views of right and wrong, is at the heart of moral development and cannot simply be ignored.

Shweder and his colleagues have presented an alternative to Kohlberg's theory of moral development (Shweder et al., 1997). The new theory has been developed mostly by a former student of Shweder's, Lene Jensen (1997a, 1997b, 2008, 2011, 2015). According to Jensen, the ultimate basis of morality is a person's **worldview**. A worldview is a set of cultural beliefs that explain what it means to be human, how human relations should be conducted, and how human problems should be addressed. Worldviews provide the basis for *moral reasoning* (explanations for why a behavior is right or wrong). The outcome of moral reasoning is *moral evaluations* (judgments as to whether a behavior is right or wrong), which in turn prescribe *moral behaviors*. Moral behaviors reinforce worldviews. An illustration of the worldviews theory is shown in **Figure 8.9**.

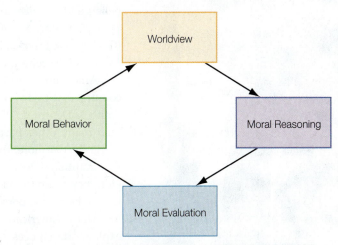

Figure 8.9 Worldviews Theory

How is this theory different from Kohlberg's?
SOURCE: Based on Jensen (2008)

In her research, Jensen codes people's responses to moral issues according to three types of "ethics" based on different worldviews.

- The *Ethic of Autonomy* defines the individual as the primary moral authority. Individuals are viewed as having a right to do as they wish so long as their behavior does not harm others.
- The *Ethic of Community* defines individuals as members of social groups to which they have commitments and obligations. In this ethic, the responsibilities of roles in the family, community, and other groups are the basis of one's moral judgments.
- The *Ethic of Divinity* defines the individual as a spiritual entity, subject to the prescriptions of a divine authority. This ethic includes moral views based on traditional religious authorities and religious texts (e.g., the Bible, the Koran).

Several recent studies using the three ethics have focused on adolescents. For example, a study in India found that adolescents used more Autonomy than their parents did, whereas the parents used Community more; use of Divinity was rare in both groups (Kapadia & Bhangaokar, 2015). An American study compared children, adolescents, and adults, and found that adolescents as well as adults used less Autonomy and more Community than children did (Jensen, 2015). A study in Finland found that most adolescents used a combination of Autonomy and Community in their moral reasoning, but for conservatively religious adolescents, Divinity was used most often (Vainio, 2015). Research using the three ethics has only begun, and it remains to be seen how their use changes in different cultures throughout the life span (Jensen, 2011).

secular

based on nonreligious beliefs and values

African American adolescents are often highly religious.

Religious Beliefs

LO 8.15 Describe the cultural variations in religious beliefs during adolescence as well as the sources and outcomes of religiosity within cultures.

Like moral development, the development of religious beliefs reaches a critical point in adolescence, because adolescence is a time when the abstract ideas involved in religious beliefs can first be fully grasped. In general, adolescents and emerging adults in developed countries are less religious than their counterparts in developing countries. Developed countries tend to be highly **secular**, which means based on nonreligious beliefs and values. In every developed country, religion has gradually faded in its influence over the past two centuries (Bellah et al., 1985; Watson, 2014). Religious beliefs and practices are especially low among adolescents in Europe. For example, in Belgium only 8% of 18-year-olds attend religious services at least once a month (Goossens & Luyckx, 2006). In Spain, traditionally a highly Catholic country, only 18% of adolescents attend church regularly (Gibbons & Stiles, 2004).

Americans are more religious than people in virtually any other developed country, and this is reflected in the lives of American adolescents (see **Table 8.1**; Smith & Denton, 2005). However, religion has a lower priority for most of them than many other parts of their lives, including school, friendships, media, and work. Furthermore, the religious beliefs of American adolescents tend not to follow traditional doctrines, and they often know little about the doctrine of the religion they claim to follow. Instead, they tend to believe that religious faith is about how to be a good person and feel happy (Smith & Denton, 2005).

Many American adolescents are religious, but many others are not. What explains differences among adolescents in their religiosity? Family characteristics are one important influence (Smith & Denton, 2005). Adolescents are more likely to embrace the importance of religion when their parents talk about religious issues and participate in religious activities (King et al., 2002; Layton et al., 2011). Adolescents are less likely to be religious when their parents disagree with each other about religious beliefs, and when their parents are divorced (Smith & Denton, 2005). Ethnicity is another factor. In American society religious faith and religious practices tend to be stronger among African Americans than among Whites (Chatters et al., 2008).

The relatively high rate of religiosity among African American adolescents helps explain why they have such low rates of alcohol and drug use (Stevens-Watkins et al., 2010). However, it is not only among minority groups that religiosity is associated with favorable adolescent outcomes. Across American cultural groups, adolescents who are more religious report less depression and lower rates of premarital sex, drug use, and delinquent behavior (Kerestes et al., 2004; Smith & Denton, 2005). The protective value of religious involvement is especially strong for adolescents living in the worst neighborhoods (Bridges & Moore, 2002). Religious adolescents tend to have better relationships with their parents (Smith & Denton, 2005; Wilcox, 2008). Also, adolescents who value religion are more likely than other adolescents to perform volunteer service in their community (Hart & Atkins, 2004; Youniss et al., 1999). In other cultures, too, religious involvement has been found to be related to a variety of positive outcomes, for example among Indonesian Muslim adolescents (French et al., 2008).

Table 8.1 Religious Beliefs of American Adolescents

Believe in God or a universal spirit	84%
Pray at least once a week	65%
Religion important in daily life	51%
Believe in the existence of angels	63%
Attend religious services at least twice a month	52%
Involved in a church youth group	38%

SOURCE: Based on Smith & Denton (2005)

Practice Quiz   ANSWERS AVAILABLE IN ANSWER KEY.

1. Kohlberg's proposition of a universal theory of moral development has been challenged by Shweder and his student, Jensen, who believe that it is impossible to understand moral development unless you understand an individual's _____.
   a. social context
   b. cultural worldview
   c. personality factors
   d. intellectual abilities

2. Research on Kohlberg's stages of moral development _____.
   a. was originally conducted with a large sample of males and females
   b. showed that the stages tended to increase with age, but that few proceeded to Level 3
   c. is based on the premise that what matters is the content of moral reasoning, not the structure
   d. showed that more than half of participants slipped to a lower level over time

3. Religious faith and practices _____.
   a. tend to be weaker among African Americans than among Whites in the United States
   b. are highest among adolescents in Europe compared to adolescents in other countries
   c. are associated with lower rates of drug use and delinquent behavior
   d. are as central to the lives of adolescents from divorced families as they are from non-divorced families

4. Adolescents who are more religious _____.
   a. are more likely to attend college
   b. are less likely to be held back in school
   c. report less depression
   d. have more conflict with their parents because they openly discuss their views

EMOTIONAL AND SOCIAL DEVELOPMENT: The Social and Cultural Contexts of Adolescence

Like younger children, adolescents typically remain within the family, and most of them also attend school. However, social contexts of peers, romantic relations, work, and media often have greater prominence in adolescence than previously. Also, for some adolescents certain types of problems develop that were rare in previous life stages.

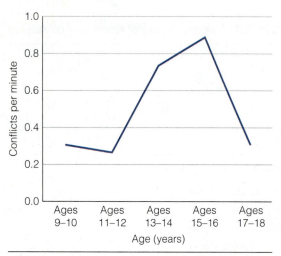

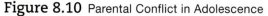

Figure 8.10 Parental Conflict in Adolescence

Why does conflict peak in the mid-teens?
SOURCE: Granic et al. (2003)

autonomy

quality of being independent and self-sufficient, capable of thinking for one's self

Why does conflict with parents rise from middle childhood to adolescence?

Family Relationships

LO 8.16 Summarize the cultural variations in adolescents' relationships with parents, siblings, and extended family.

The family is a key part of the daily social context of adolescents in all cultures, but in most cultures there are also profound changes in family relations from middle childhood to adolescence. Perhaps the most notable change is the decline in the amount of time spent with family members, as described in the *Research Focus: The Daily Rhythms of Adolescents' Family Lives* feature on page 388. When adolescents do spend time with their parents, conflict is more frequent than in middle childhood, as we will see next.

CONFLICT WITH PARENTS   Numerous studies have shown that adolescents and their parents agree on many of their beliefs and values, and typically they have a great deal of love and respect for one another (Kağitçibaşi & Yalin, 2015; Moore et al., 2002; Smetana, 2005). Nevertheless, studies in Western countries also indicate that conflict with parents increases sharply in early adolescence, compared with middle childhood, and remains high for several years before declining in late adolescence (Dworkin & Larson, 2001; Kağitçibaşi & Yalin, 2015; Laursen et al., 1998).

Figure 8.10 shows the increase in conflict from middle childhood to adolescence, from a longitudinal study that observed American mothers and sons in videotaped interactions on five occasions over 8 years (Granic et al., 2003). A Canadian study found that 40% of adolescents reported arguments with their parents at least once a week (Sears et al., 2006). Conflict in adolescence is especially frequent and intense between mothers and daughters (Collins & Laursen, 2004). By mid-adolescence, conflict with parents tends to become somewhat less frequent but more intense before declining substantially in late adolescence (Laursen et al., 1998).

There are several reasons why conflict with parents often rises during adolescence. First, adolescence entails reaching sexual maturity, which means that sexual issues may be a source of conflict in a way they would not have been in childhood (Arnett, 1999). Early-maturing adolescents tend to have more conflict with parents than adolescents who mature "on time," perhaps because sexual issues arise earlier (Collins & Laursen, 2004). Second, advances in cognitive development make it possible for adolescents to rebut their parents' reasoning about rules and restrictions more effectively than they could have earlier. Third, and most importantly, in many cultures adolescence is a time of gaining greater independence from the family. Although parents and adolescents in these cultures usually share the same goal that the adolescent will eventually become a self-sufficient adult, they often disagree about the pace of adolescents' growing **autonomy** (Daddis & Smetana, 2006; Smetana, 2005). Parents may have concerns about adolescents' safety with respect to sexuality, automobile driving, and substance use, and so restrict adolescents' behavior in an effort to protect them from risks (Arnett, 1999). Adolescents expect to be able to make their own decisions in these areas and resent their parents' restrictions, so conflict results.

However, not all cultures value and encourage increased autonomy in adolescence, as you will see in the *Cultural Focus: Adolescent Conflict with Parents* feature.

SIBLING AND EXTENDED-FAMILY RELATIONS For about 80% of American adolescents, and similar proportions in other developed countries, the family system also includes relationships with at least one sibling (U.S. Bureau of the Census, 2009). The proportion of families with siblings is even higher in developing countries, where birthrates tend to be higher and families with only one child are rare (Population Reference Bureau, 2014).

How did you get along with your siblings when you were in adolescence? My older brother Mike and I fought constantly during my adolescence, with me mostly on the losing end (until I hit my growth spurt and grew to be six foot three; he seemed to lose interest in fighting with me after that). Relations with siblings in adolescence often involve conflict. In studies that compare adolescents' relationships with siblings to relationships with parents, grandparents, teachers, and friends, adolescents report more frequent

Cultural Focus: Adolescent Conflict with Parents

In traditional cultures, it is rare for parents and adolescents to engage in the kind of frequent conflicts typical of parent–adolescent relationships in Western cultures (Larson et al., 2010). The role of parent carries greater authority in traditional cultures than in the West, and this makes it less likely that adolescents in such cultures will express disagreements and resentments toward their parents (Phinney et al., 2005). Even when they disagree with their parents, they are unlikely to express it because of their feelings of duty and respect (Phinney & Ong, 2002). Outside of the West, interdependence is a higher value than independence, not only during adolescence but throughout adulthood (Markus & Kitayama, 2010; Phinney et al., 2005). Just as a dramatic increase in autonomy during adolescence prepares Western adolescents for adult life in an individualistic culture, learning to submit to the

authority of one's parents prepares adolescents in traditional cultures for an adult life in which interdependence is among the highest values and each person has a clearly designated position in a family hierarchy.

In this video, adolescents from a variety of cultures are interviewed as they discuss their changing relationships with their parents as well as with their friends.

Review Question:

The narrator tells us that interdependence is valued in the Mexican village where one of the female teens is from. What are the economic reasons why interdependence might be more adaptive in this Mexican village than in the American family also shown in the video?

Watch   ADOLESCENT CONFLICT WITH PARENTS ACROSS CULTURES

Research Focus: The Daily Rhythms of Adolescents' Family Lives

Adolescent researchers have found the Experience Sampling Method (ESM) to be a helpful source of information on adolescents' social lives. The ESM involves having people wear beeper watches that randomly beep during the day so that people can record their thoughts, feelings, and behavior as events take place. Reed Larson and Maryse Richards are the two scholars who have done the most to apply the ESM to adolescents and their families.

In their classic book *Divergent Realities: The Emotional Lives of Mothers, Fathers, and Adolescents* (Larson & Richards, 1994), they described the results of their research on a sample of 483 American adolescents in fifth through twelfth grades, and another sample of 55 fifth through eighth graders and their parents. All were two-parent, White families. In each family, three family members (adolescent, mother, and father) were beeped at the same times, about 30 times per day between 7:30 in the morning and 9:30 at night, during the week of the study.

When beeped, adolescents and their parents paused from whatever they were doing and recorded a variety of information about where they were, whom they were with, what they were doing, and how they were feeling.

One striking finding of the study was that adolescents and their parents averaged only about an hour a day spent in shared activities, and their most common shared activity was watching television. The amount of time adolescents spent with their families dropped sharply between fifth and twelfth grades. In turn, there was an increase from fifth to ninth grade in the amount of time adolescents spent alone in their bedrooms.

The study also revealed some interesting differences in mothers' and fathers' relationships with adolescents. The majority of mother–adolescent interactions were rated positively by both of them, especially experiences such as talking together, going out together, and sharing a meal.

However, adolescents' negative feelings toward their mothers increased sharply from fifth to ninth grade, and their feelings of closeness to mothers decreased.

As for fathers, they tended to be only tenuously involved in their adolescents' lives. For most of the time they spent with their adolescents, the mother was there as well, and the mother tended to be more directly involved. Fathers averaged only 12 minutes per day alone with their adolescents, and 40% of this time was spent watching TV together.

The study showed that parents are often important influences on adolescents' emotional states. Adolescents brought home to the family their emotions from the rest of the day. If their parents were responsive and caring, adolescents' moods improved and their negative emotions were relieved. In contrast, if adolescents felt their parents were unavailable or unresponsive, their negative feelings became even worse. Even though adolescents spend less time with the parents than when they were younger, parents remain powerful influences in their lives.

Review Questions:

1. In the ESM studies of adolescents and their parents, adolescents have been found to have the most positive feelings when with _____ and the most negative feelings toward _____.
   a. Mothers; fathers
   b. Mothers; mothers
   c. Fathers; mothers
   d. Fathers; fathers

Watch RESEARCH FOCUS: THE DAILY RHYTHMS OF ADOLESCENTS' FAMILY LIVES

conflicts with their siblings than with anyone else (Campione-Barr & Smetana, 2010). Common sources of conflict include teasing, possessions (e.g., borrowing a sibling's clothes without permission), responsibility for chores, name-calling, invasions of privacy, and perceived unequal treatment by parents (Noller, 2005; Updegraff et al., 2005). However, even though adolescents tend to have more conflicts with siblings than in their other relationships, conflict with siblings is lower in adolescence than at younger ages (Brody, 2004; Noller, 2005). From childhood to adolescence, relationships with siblings become less emotionally intense, mainly because adolescents gradually spend less time with their siblings (Hetherington et al., 1999).

As noted in previous chapters, by middle childhood, children in traditional cultures often have responsibility for caring for young siblings, and for many this responsibility continues into adolescence. In Schlegel and Barry's (1991) analysis of adolescence in traditional cultures, over 80% of adolescent boys and girls had frequent responsibility for caring for younger siblings. This responsibility promotes conflict between siblings, but also close attachments. Time together, and closeness, is especially high between siblings of the same gender, mainly because in traditional cultures, daily activities are often separated by gender. Close relationships between siblings are also common in African American families, in part because many African American families are headed by single mothers who rely on older siblings to help with child care (Brody et al., 2003).

Adolescents in traditional cultures also tend to be close to their extended family members. In these cultures children often grow up in a household that includes not only their parents and siblings but also grandparents, and often uncles, aunts, and cousins as well. These living arrangements promote closeness between adolescents and their extended family. In Schlegel and Barry's (1991) cross-cultural analysis, daily contact was as high with grandparents as with parents for adolescents in traditional cultures, and adolescents were usually even closer to their grandparents than to their parents. Perhaps this is because parents typically exercise authority over adolescents, which may add ambivalence to adolescents' relationships with their parents, whereas grandparents are less likely to exercise authority and may focus more on nurturing and supporting adolescents.

Extended family members are also important figures in the lives of adolescents in Western majority cultures. About 80% of American adolescents list at least one member of their extended family among the people most important to them, and closeness to grandparents is positively related to adolescents' well-being (Ruiz & Silverstein, 2007). However, in the American majority culture adolescents' contact with extended family members is relatively infrequent, in part because extended family members often live many miles away. When extended family members live within the household or nearby, as is often the case in African American, Latino, and Asian American families, adolescents' closeness to them tends to resemble the pattern in traditional cultures (Fuligni et al., 1999; Suarez-Orozco & Suarez-Orozco, 1996; Oberlander et al., 2007).

Peers and Friends

LO 8.17 Describe cultural variations in adolescents' relationships with friends, and characterize their interactions with peers.

As time spent with family decreases from middle childhood to adolescence, time spent with friends increases, in most cultures. Friends also become increasingly important in adolescents' emotional lives. In adolescence, as at other ages, friends choose one another primarily due to similarities in characteristics such as age, gender, ethnic group, personality, and leisure interests (Popp et al., 2008). As shown in the video *Peer Pressure: Tim* on the next page, adolescence is also a time of increasing peer pressure.

Watch PEER PRESSURE: TIM

FRIENDSHIPS: CULTURAL THEMES AND VARIATIONS Although family ties remain important in the lives of adolescents, friends become preferred in some ways. Adolescents indicate that they depend more on friends than on their parents or siblings for companionship and intimacy (French et al., 2001; Nickerson & Nagle, 2005; Updegraff et al., 2002). Friends become the source of adolescents' happiest experiences, the people with whom they feel most comfortable, and the persons they feel they can talk to most openly (French, 2015; Richards et al., 2002; Youniss & Smollar, 1985).

European studies comparing relationships with parents and friends show a pattern similar to American studies. For example, a study of Dutch adolescents (ages 15 to 19) asked them who they rely on to communicate about themselves, including their personal feelings, sorrows, and secrets (Bois-Reymond & Ravesloot, 1996). Nearly half of the adolescents named their best friend or their romantic partner, whereas just 20% named one or both parents (only 3% their fathers). Another Dutch study found that 82% of adolescents named spending free time with friends as their favorite activity (Meeus, 2006).

Adolescents in Western cultures tend to be happiest when with friends.

Studies in other European countries confirm that adolescents tend to be happiest when with their friends and that they tend to turn to their friends for advice and information on social relationships and leisure, although they come to parents for advice about education and career plans (Hurrelmann, 1996).

As noted earlier in the chapter, adolescence in traditional cultures often entails less involvement with family and greater involvement with peers for boys but not for girls. However, for boys as well as girls, the social and emotional balance between friends and family remains tilted more toward family for adolescents in developing countries than it does in the West. For example, in India, adolescents tend to spend their leisure time with family rather than friends, not because they are required to do so but because of collectivistic Indian cultural values and because they enjoy their time with family (Chaudhary & Sharma, 2012; Larson et al., 2000). Among Brazilian adolescents, emotional support is higher from parents than friends (Van Horn & Cunegatto Marques, 2000). In a study comparing adolescents in Indonesia and the United States, Indonesian adolescents rated their family members higher and their friends lower on companionship and enjoyment, compared to American adolescents (French et al., 2001). Nevertheless, friends were the primary source of intimacy in both countries. Thus, it may be that adolescents in developing countries remain close to their families even as they also develop greater closeness to their friends during adolescence, whereas in the West closeness to family diminishes as closeness to friends grows.

THE IMPORTANCE OF INTIMACY Probably the most important feature of adolescent friendships is intimacy. **Intimacy** is the degree to which two people share personal knowledge, thoughts, and feelings. Adolescent friends confide hopes and fears, and help each other understand what is going on with their parents, their teachers, and peers to a far greater degree than younger children do.

When adolescents are asked what they would want a friend to be like or how they can tell that someone is their friend, they tend to mention intimate features of the relationship (Berndt, 1996; Radmacher & Azmitia, 2006). They state, for example, that a friend is someone who understands you, someone you can share your problems with, someone who will listen when you have something important to say (Bauminger et al., 2008; Way, 2004). Younger children are less likely to mention these kinds of features and more likely to stress shared activities—we both like to play basketball, we ride bikes together, we play computer games, and so on. There are consistent gender differences in the intimacy of adolescent friendships, with girls tending to have more intimate friendships than boys do (Bauminger et al., 2008). Girls spend more time than boys talking to their friends, and they place a higher value on talking together as a component of their friendships (Apter, 1990; Youniss & Smollar, 1985). Girls also rate their friendships as higher in affection, helpfulness, and nurturance, compared with boys' ratings of their friendships (Bokhorst et al., 2010). And girls are more likely than boys to say they trust and feel close to their friends (Shulman et al., 1997). In contrast, even in adolescence, boys are more likely to emphasize shared activities as the basis of friendship, such as sports or hobbies (Radmacher & Azmitia, 2006).

Nevertheless, intimacy does become more important to boys' friendships in adolescence, even if not to the same extent as for girls. In one study of African American, Latino, and Asian American boys from poor and working-class families, Niobe Way (2004) reported themes of intimacy that involved sharing secrets, protecting one another physically and emotionally, and disclosing feelings about family and friends.

CLIQUES AND CROWDS So far we have focused on close friendships. Now we turn to larger groups of friends and peers. Scholars generally make a distinction between two types of adolescent social groups, cliques and crowds. **Cliques** are small groups of friends who know each other well, do things together, and form a regular social group (Brown & Braun, 2013). Cliques have no precise size—3 to 12 is a rough range—but they are small enough so that all the members of the clique feel they know each other well and they think of themselves as a cohesive group. Sometimes cliques are defined by distinctive shared activities—for example, working on cars, playing music, playing basketball—and sometimes simply by shared friendship (a group of friends who eat lunch together every day, for example).

intimacy
degree to which two people share personal knowledge, thoughts, and feelings

clique
small group of friends who know each other well, do things together, and form a regular social group

Cliques are often formed around shared activities. Here, South African adolescents enjoy a game of soccer.

Crowds, in contrast, are larger, reputation-based groups of adolescents who are not necessarily friends and may not spend much time together (Brown et al., 2008; Brown & Braun, 2013; Horn, 2003). A review of 44 studies on adolescent crowds concluded that five major types of crowds are found in many schools (Susman et al., 2007):

- Elites (a.k.a. Populars, Preppies). The crowd recognized as having the highest social status in the school.
- Athletes (a.k.a. Jocks). Sports-oriented students, usually members of at least one sports team.
- Academics (a.k.a. Brains, Nerds, Geeks). Known for striving for good grades and for being socially inept.
- Deviants (a.k.a. Druggies, Burnouts). Alienated from the school social environment, suspected by other students of using illicit drugs and engaging in other risky activities.
- Others (a.k.a. Normals, Nobodies). Students who do not stand out in any particular way, neither positively nor negatively; mostly ignored by other students.

Crowds mainly serve the function of helping adolescents to locate themselves and others within the secondary school social structure. In other words, crowds help adolescents to define their own identities and the identities of others. Knowing that others think of you as a "Brain" has implications for your identity—it means you are the kind of person who likes school, does well in school, and perhaps has more success in school than in social situations. Thinking of someone else as a "Druggie" tells you something about that person (whether it is accurate or not)—he or she uses drugs, of course, probably dresses unconventionally, and does not seem to care much about school.

BULLYING At the age of 15, Phoebe Prince immigrated to the United States from Ireland with her family. She liked her new school at first and made friends, but then a popular boy took an interest in her, and she dated him a few times. Other girls who were interested in the boy began to harass her aggressively, calling her names in school and sending vicious e-mail messages spreading false rumors about her. Friendless and persecuted in and out of school, she sank deeper and deeper into despair and finally committed suicide, to the horror of her family and her community.

This shocking true-life example shows how serious the consequences of bullying in adolescence can be. As noted in Chapter 7, bullying is common in middle childhood, but the prevalence of bullying rises through middle childhood and peaks in early adolescence, then declines substantially by late adolescence (Pepler et al., 2006). Bullying is an international phenomenon, observed in many countries in Europe (Dijkstra et al., 2008; Gini et al., 2008), Asia (Ando et al., 2005; Hokoda et al., 2006), and North America (Pepler et al., 2008; Volk et al., 2006). In a landmark study of bullying among over 100,000 adolescents ages 11–15 in 28 countries around the world, self-reported prevalence rates of being a victim of bullying ranged from 6% among girls in Sweden to 41% among boys in Lithuania, with rates in most countries in the 10–20% range (Due et al., 2005). Across countries, in this study and many others, boys are consistently more likely than girls to be bullies as well as victims.

Bullying has a variety of negative effects on adolescents' development. In the 28-country study of adolescent bullying just mentioned, victims of bullying reported higher rates of a wide range of problems, including physical symptoms such as headaches, backaches, and difficulty sleeping, as well as psychological symptoms such as loneliness, helplessness, anxiety, and unhappiness (Due et al., 2005). Not only victims but also bullies are at high risk for problems (Klomek et al., 2007). A Canadian study of bullying that surveyed adolescents for 7 years beginning at ages 10–14 found that bullies reported more psychological problems and more problems in their relationships with parents and peers than non-bullies did (Pepler et al., 2008).

A recent variation on bullying is **cyberbullying** (also called electronic bullying), which involves bullying behavior via social media (such as Facebook), e-mail, or mobile

crowd

large, reputation-based group of adolescents

cyberbullying

bullying via electronic means, mainly through the Internet

phones (Kowalski et al., 2012; Valkenberg & Peter, 2011). A Swedish study of 12- to 20-year-olds found an age pattern of cyberbullying similar to what has been found in studies of "traditional" bullying, with the highest rates in early adolescence and a decline through late adolescence and emerging adulthood (Slonje & Smith, 2008). In a study of nearly 4,000 adolescents in Grades 6–8 in the United States, 11% reported being victims of a cyberbullying incident at least once in the past 2 months; 7% indicated that they had been cyberbullies as well as victims during this time period; and 4% reported committing a cyberbullying incident (Kowalski & Limber, 2007). Notably, half of the victims did not know the bully's identity, a key difference between cyberbullying and other bullying. However, cyberbullying usually involves only a single incident, so it does not involve the repetition required in the standard definition of traditional bullying (refer to Chapter 7), and might be better termed *online harassment* (Wolak et al., 2007).

Love and Sexuality

LO 8.18 Identify cultural variations in adolescent love and sexuality, including variations in adolescent pregnancy and contraceptive use.

Puberty means reaching sexual maturity. Consequently, adolescence is when sexual feelings begin to stir and—in many cultures, but not all—sexual behavior is initiated. First we look at love, then at sex.

FALLING IN LOVE The prevalence of involvement in romantic relationships increases gradually over the course of adolescence. According to a study in the United States called the National Study of Adolescent Health, the percentage of adolescents reporting a current romantic relationship rises from 17% in 7th grade to 32% in 9th grade to 44% in 11th grade (Furman & Hand, 2006). By 11th grade, 80% of adolescents had experienced a romantic relationship at some point, even if they did not have one currently. Adolescents with an Asian cultural background tend to have their first romantic relationship later than adolescents with a European, African American, or Latino cultural background, because of Asian cultural beliefs that discourage early involvement in romantic relationships and encourage minimal or no sexual involvement before marriage (Connolly & McIsaac, 2011; Regan et al., 2004).

In the West most adolescents have a romantic partner at some point in their teens.

It is not only in the West, and not only in developed countries, that adolescents experience romantic love. On the contrary, feelings of passion appear to be virtually universal among young people. One study investigated this issue systematically by analyzing the *Standard Cross-Cultural Sample*, a collection of data provided by anthropologists on 186 traditional cultures representing six distinct geographical regions around the world (Jankowiak & Fischer, 1992). The researchers concluded that there was evidence that young people fell passionately in love in *all but one* of the 186 cultures studied. Across cultures, young lovers experienced the delight and despair of passionate love, told stories about famous lovers, and sang love songs.

However, this does not mean that young people in all cultures are allowed to act on their feelings of love. On the contrary, romantic love as the basis for marriage is a fairly new cultural idea (Hatfield & Rapson, 2005). As we will see in detail in Chapter 10, in most cultures throughout most of history, marriages have been arranged by parents, with little regard for the passionate desires of their children.

CULTURAL VARIATIONS IN ADOLESCENT SEXUALITY Even though adolescents in all cultures go through similar biological processes in reaching sexual maturity, cultures vary enormously in how they view adolescent sexuality. Variations among countries in sexual behavior during adolescence is due primarily to variations in cultural beliefs about the acceptability (or not) of premarital sex. The best framework for understanding this variation among countries remains a book that is now over 60 years old, *Patterns of Sexual Behavior,* by Clellan Ford and Frank Beach (1951). These two anthropologists compiled information about sexuality from over 200 cultures. On the basis of their analysis they described three types of cultural approaches to adolescent sexuality: *permissive, semirestrictive,* and *restrictive.*

Permissive cultures tolerate and even encourage adolescent sexuality. Most of the countries of northern Europe today would fall into this category. Adolescents in these countries usually begin an active sexual life in their late teens, and parents often allow them to have a boyfriend or girlfriend spend the night (Trost, 2012).

Semirestrictive cultures have prohibitions on premarital adolescent sex. However, in these cultures the formal prohibitions are not strongly enforced and are easily evaded. Adults in these cultures tend to ignore evidence of premarital sexual behavior as long as young people are fairly discreet. Most developed countries today would fall into this category, including the United States, Canada, and most of Europe (Regnerus, 2011).

Restrictive cultures place strong prohibitions on adolescent sexual activity before marriage. The prohibition on premarital sex is enforced through strong social norms and by keeping boys and girls separated through adolescence. Young people in Asia and South America tend to disapprove strongly of premarital sex, reflecting the view they have been taught by their cultures (Regan et al., 2004).

In some countries, the restrictiveness of the taboo on premarital sex even includes the threat of physical punishment and public shaming. A number of Middle Eastern countries take this approach, including Algeria, Syria, and Saudi Arabia. Premarital female virginity is a matter of not only the girl's honor but the honor of her family, and if she is known to lose her virginity before marriage, the males of her family may punish her, beat her, or even kill her (Dorjee et al., 2013). Although many cultures also value male premarital chastity, no culture punishes male premarital sex with such severity.

permissive culture

culture that encourages and expects sexual activity from their adolescents

semirestrictive culture

culture that has prohibitions on premarital adolescent sex, but the prohibitions are not strongly enforced and are easily evaded

restrictive culture

culture that places strong prohibitions on adolescent sexual activity before marriage

Why are rates of adolescent pregnancy especially high in the United States?

CRITICAL THINKING QUESTION

Is there a gender double standard for adolescent sexuality in your culture? Provide some examples to support your answer.

ADOLESCENT PREGNANCY AND CONTRACEPTIVE USE Although cultures vary in how they view adolescent sex, nearly everywhere in the world premarital pregnancy in adolescence is viewed as undesirable. Two types of countries have low rates of premarital pregnancy: those that are permissive about adolescent sex and those that are restrictive. Northern European countries such as Denmark, Sweden, and the Netherlands have low rates of adolescent pregnancy because they are permissive about adolescent sex (Avery & Lazdane, 2008). There are explicit safe-sex campaigns in the media. Adolescents have easy access to all types of contraception. Parents accept that their children will become sexually active by their late teens (Trost, 2012).

At the other end of the spectrum, restrictive countries such as Japan, South Korea, and Morocco strictly forbid adolescent sex (Davis & Davis, 2012; Dorjee et al., 2013; Hatfield & Rapson, 2005). Adolescents in these countries are strongly discouraged even from dating until they are well into emerging adulthood and are seriously looking for a marriage partner. It is rare for an adolescent boy and girl even to spend time alone together, much less have sex. Some adolescents follow the call of nature anyway and violate the taboo, but violations are rare because the taboo is so strong and the shame of being exposed for breaking it is so great.

The United States has a higher rate of teenage pregnancy than any other developed country, as **Figure 8.11** illustrates. The main reason American adolescents have high rates of teenage pregnancy may be that there is no clear cultural message regarding adolescent sexuality (Males, 2011). The semirestrictive view of adolescent sexuality prevails: Adolescent sex is not strictly forbidden, but neither is it widely accepted. As a consequence, most American adolescents have sexual intercourse at some time before they reach the end of their teens, but often those who are sexually active are not comfortable enough with their sexuality to acknowledge that they are having sex and to prepare for it responsibly by obtaining and using contraception. Watch the video *Teen Pregnancy* to hear one adolescent's experience with pregnancy. However, rates of teen pregnancy in the United States have declined steeply in the past 2 decades, especially among African Americans (Males, 2011). This may be because the threat of HIV/AIDS has made it more acceptable in the United States to talk to adolescents about sex and contraception and to provide them with sex education through the schools.

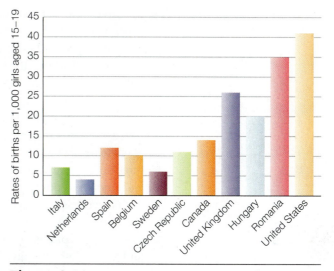

Figure 8.11 Teenage Pregnancy Rates in Developed Countries

Why are rates so high in the United States?
SOURCE: Based on WHO (2010)

Watch TEEN PREGNANCY

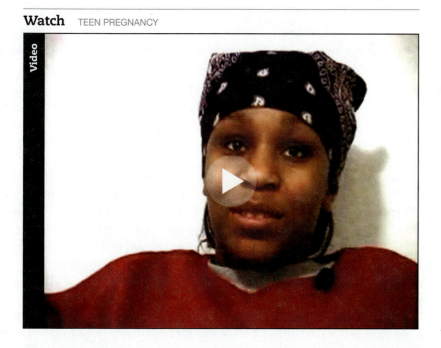

SEXUAL ORIENTATION Adolescence is when most people first become fully aware of their **sexual orientation**, meaning their tendencies of sexual attraction. In American society, 2% of adolescents self-identify as lesbian, gay, or bisexual (LGB) (Savin-Williams & Joyner, 2014). In the past in Western cultures, and still today in many of the world's cultures, most people would keep this knowledge to themselves all their lives because they would be stigmatized and persecuted if they disclosed the truth. Today in most Western cultures, however, LGBs commonly engage in a process of **coming out**, which involves a person's recognizing his or her own sexual identity and then disclosing the truth to friends, family, and others (Flowers & Buston, 2001; Savin-Williams, 2001). Awareness of an LGB sexual identity usually begins in early adolescence, with disclosure to others coming in late adolescence or emerging adulthood (Floyd & Bakeman, 2006).

sexual orientation

a person's tendencies of sexual attraction

coming out

for homosexuals, the process of acknowledging their homosexuality and then disclosing the truth to their friends, family, and others

Given the pervasiveness of **homophobia** (fear and hatred of homosexuals) that exists in many societies, coming to the realization of an LGB identity can be traumatic for many adolescents. Lesbian, gay, or bisexual adolescents are often the targets of bullying when peers learn of their sexual identity (Mishna et al., 2009). Many parents respond with dismay or even anger when they learn that their adolescents are lesbian, gay, or bisexual. When parents reject LGB adolescents after learning of their sexual identity, the consequences are dire. One study found that LGB adolescents who experienced parental rejection were eight times more likely to report having attempted suicide, six times more likely to report high levels of depression, three times more likely to use illegal drugs, and three times more likely to have had unprotected sex than LGB adolescents whose parents were more accepting of their sexual orientation (Ryan, 2009).

Nevertheless, in recent years there has been a noticeable change in Western attitudes toward LGBs, constituting "a dramatic cultural shift" toward more favorable and tolerant perceptions, according to Ritch Savin-Williams (2005), a prominent researcher on LGB adolescents. Savin-Williams notes changes in popular culture, such as favorable portrayals of LGBs in television, movies, and popular songs. Notably, the average age of coming out has declined in recent decades, from 21 in the 1970s to 16 in the present, perhaps because of growing acceptance of homosexuality (Savin-Williams & Joyner, 2014). Several European countries and most American states now allow same-sex marriages, another sign that people in the West are becoming more accepting of variations in sexual orientation.

Media Use

LO 8.19 Explain the function of media use in adolescents' lives and apply the Media Practice Model to the playing of electronic games.

Now that my twins are 15 years old, media use has become an important part of their daily lives. My son Miles loves his iPad, and uses it daily for everything from researching school assignments to playing electronic games to monitoring the latest sports news. For my daughter Paris, recorded music is her primary media use. She loves to sing along with everything from Taylor Swift to opera.

No account of adolescent development would be complete without a description of the media they use. Recorded music, television, movies, magazines, electronic games, mobile phones, and the Internet are part of the daily environment for nearly all adolescents currently growing up in developed countries (and increasingly in developing countries as well). There is a dramatic increase in media use from middle childhood to early adolescence, especially in TV and electronic games. A national American study found that adolescents use media for about 8 hours a day (Rideout et al., 2010). About one fourth of their media use involves multiple media—listening to music while playing an electronic game, for example, or reading a magazine while watching TV. Despite the rise of social media, it is the old-fashioned television that still dominates adolescents' media use, at nearly 5 hours per day. This is true in Europe as well (Rey-López et al., 2010).

A MODEL OF ADOLESCENTS' MEDIA USES Spending 8 hours a day on anything means that it is a big part of your life, and many concerns have been expressed about adolescents' media use (Arnett, 2007). Although claims are often made about the harmful effects of media on adolescents, their media use is more complex than simple cause and effect. A helpful model of the functions media play in the lives of adolescents has been presented by Jane Brown and her colleagues (Brown, 2006; Brown et al., 2002; Steele, 2006). An illustration of their *Media Practice Model* is shown in **Figure 8.12**.

As the figure shows, the model proposes that adolescents' media use is active in a number of ways. Adolescents do not all have the same media preferences. Rather, each adolescent's identity motivates the *selection* of media products. Paying attention to certain media products leads to *interaction* with those products, meaning that the products

homophobia

fear and hatred of homosexuals

are evaluated and interpreted. Then adolescents engage in *application* of the media content they have chosen. They may incorporate this content into their identities—for example, adolescents who respond to cigarette advertisements by taking up smoking—or they may resist the content—for example, adolescents who respond to cigarette advertisements by rejecting them as false and misleading. Their developing identity then motivates new media selections, and so on. This model reminds us that adolescents actively select the media they use, and they respond to media content in diverse ways depending on how they interpret it and how it relates to them personally.

Adolescents use media for many different purposes, but as with younger children, the focus of research has been on negative effects. In the following discussion, we examine electronic games, which have been the target of some of these concerns. (Chapter 9 will cover the use of mobile phones and social media such as Facebook.)

ELECTRONIC GAMES A relatively new type of media use among adolescents is electronic games, usually played on a computer or a handheld device. This form of media use has quickly become popular among adolescents, especially boys (Rideout et al., 2013). In a study of middle school students in the United States (Olson et al., 2007), 94% reported having played electronic games during the preceding 6 months. Of those who played electronic games, one third of boys and 11% of girls said they played nearly every day.

The majority of adolescents' favorite electronic games involve violence (Gentile, 2011). Many studies have examined the relation between violent electronic games and aggressiveness (Anderson et al., 2007; Brake, 2006; Funk et al., 2005; Gentile, 2011). One study asked boys themselves about the effects of playing violent electronic games (Olson et al., 2008). The interviews showed that the boys (ages 12–14) used electronic games to experience fantasies of power and fame, and to explore what they perceived to be exciting new situations. The boys enjoyed the social aspect of electronic game playing, in playing with friends and talking about the games with friends. The boys also said they used electronic games to work through feelings of anger or stress, and that playing the games had a cathartic effect on these negative feelings. They did not believe that playing violent electronic games affected them negatively.

It seems likely that with electronic games, as with other violent media, there is a wide range of individual differences in responses, with young people who are already at risk for violent behavior being most likely to be affected by the games, as well as most likely to be attracted to them (Funk, 2003; Slater et al., 2003; Unsworth et al., 2007). With electronic games as with television, violent content may rarely provoke violent behavior, but it more often influences social attitudes. For example, playing violent electronic games has been found to lower empathy and raise the acceptability of violent responses to social situations (Anderson, 2004; Funk, 2005; Funk et al., 2005; Gentile, 2011).

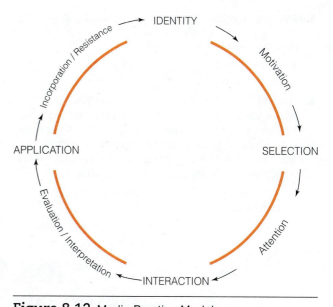

Figure 8.12 Media Practice Model

In this model, identity is the main motivator of media use.
SOURCE: Brown et al. (2002), p. 9

Practice Quiz ANSWERS AVAILABLE IN ANSWER KEY.

1. In the United States, conflict in adolescence _____.

  a. is most intense between fathers and sons

  b. steadily increases until the end of emerging adulthood

  c. is more frequent between early-maturing adolescents and their parents compared to "on-time" adolescents and their parents

  d. is similar in frequency to that observed in traditional cultures

2. Sanjay is part of a small group of friends, also known as a _____, who eat lunch together at school every day and socialize with each other on the weekends.

  a. clique

  b. crowd

  c. faction

  d. subgroup

3. Menna is an adolescent from a Western culture. When asked about the most important feature of her friendships, she is most likely to mention _____.

   a. similar interests   **c.** intimacy

   b. similar future goals   **d.** the popularity of the person

4. Niels, 17, is in a sexual relationship with his girlfriend, Henriette. Niels's parents are well-aware that he and Henriette are having sex, and, like most other parents in his country, not only are they fine with it, but they also have no problem with Henriette spending the night in Niels's bedroom. Niels and his family are most likely living in a(n) _____ culture.

   a. restrictive   **c.** semirestrictive

   b. permissive   **d.** open

5. Research on adolescents' media use has found that _____.

   a. males did not report enjoying the social aspect of gaming

   b. American adolescents use media for about two hours every day and a bit less during the school week

   c. more boys than girls report playing electronic games nearly every day

   d. it makes people more empathic as they often identify with the victim

EMOTIONAL AND SOCIAL DEVELOPMENT: Problems and Resilience

After the relatively calm period of middle childhood, a variety of types of problems rise in prevalence during adolescence, including crime and delinquency and depressed mood. (Automobile accidents will be covered in Chapter 9.) However, most adolescents make it through this life stage without serious problems, and many adolescents exhibit resilience in the face of difficult conditions.

Crime and Delinquency

LO 8.20 Summarize the explanations for why age and crime are so strongly correlated, and describe the multisystemic approach to combating delinquency.

Rates of crime begin rising in the mid-teens and peak at about age 18, then decline steadily. The great majority of crimes are committed by young people—mostly males—who are between the ages of 12 and 25 (Craig & Piquero, 2015). In the West, this finding is remarkably consistent over a period of greater than 150 years. **Figure 8.13** shows the age–crime relationship at two points, one in the 1840s and one relatively recent. At any point before, after, or in between these times, in most countries, the pattern would look very similar (Craig & Piquero, 2015; Wilson & Herrnstein, 1985). Adolescents and emerging adults are not only more likely than children or adults to commit crimes but also more likely to be the victims of crimes.

What explains the strong and consistent relationship between age and crime? One theory suggests that the key to explaining the age–crime relationship is that adolescents and emerging adults combine increased independence from parents and other adult authorities with increased time with peers and increased orientation toward peers (Wilson & Herrnstein, 1985). A consistent finding of research on crime is that crimes committed by young people in their teens and early 20s usually take place in a group, in contrast to the solitary crimes typical of adult offenders (Dishion & Dodge, 2005). Crime is an activity that in some adolescent cliques is encouraged and admired (Dishion et al., 1999). However, this theory does not explain why it is mainly boys who commit crimes, and why girls, who also become more independent from parents and more peer-oriented in adolescence, rarely do.

Most surveys find that over three-fourths of adolescent boys commit at least one criminal act sometime before the age of 20 (Loebert & Burke, 2011; Moffitt, 2003). However, there are obvious differences between committing one or two acts of minor

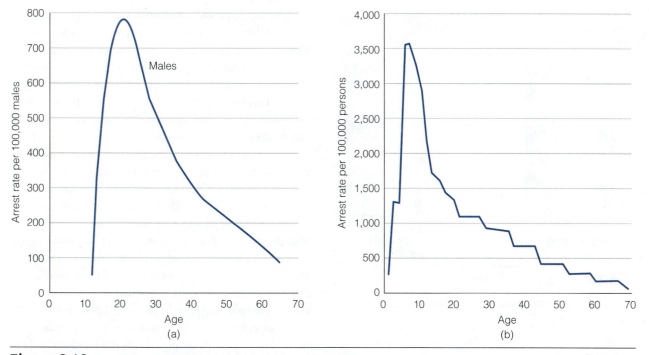

Figure 8.13 Age–Crime Relationship in (a) 1842 and (b) 1992

Why does crime peak in the late teens?

SOURCE: Gottfredson & Hirschi (1990), p. 125; Osgood (2009)

crime—vandalism or underage drinking, for example—and committing crimes frequently over a long period, including more serious crimes such as rape and assault. Ten percent of young men commit over two-thirds of all offenses (Craig & Piquero, 2015). What are the differences between adolescents who commit an occasional minor violation of the law and adolescents who are at risk for more serious, long-term criminal behavior?

Terrie Moffitt (2003, 2007) has proposed a provocative theory in which she distinguishes between *adolescence-limited* delinquency and *life-course-persistent* delinquency. In Moffitt's view, these are two distinct types of delinquency, each with different motivations and different sources. However, the two types may be hard to distinguish from one another in adolescence, when criminal offenses are more common than in childhood or adulthood. The way to tell them apart, according to Moffitt, is to look at behavior before adolescence.

Life-course-persistent delinquents (LCPDs) show a pattern of problems from birth onward. Moffitt believes their problems originate in neuropsychological deficits that are evident in a difficult temperament in infancy and a high likelihood of attention-deficit/hyperactivity disorder (ADHD) and learning disabilities in childhood; all of these are more common among boys than girls. Children with these problems are also more likely than other children to grow up in a high-risk environment (e.g., low-income family, single parent), with parents who have a variety of problems of their own. Consequently, their neurological deficits tend to be made worse rather than better by their environments. When they reach adolescence, children with the combination of neurological deficits and a high-risk environment are highly prone to engage in criminal activity. Furthermore, they tend to continue their criminal activity long after adolescence has ended, well into adulthood.

The **adolescence-limited delinquents (ALDs)** follow a much different pattern. They show no signs of problems in infancy or childhood, and few of them engage in any criminal activity after their mid-20s. It is just during adolescence—actually, adolescence and emerging adulthood, ages 12 to 25—that they have a period of occasional criminal activity, breaking the law with behavior such as vandalism, theft, and use of illegal drugs.

life-course-persistent delinquent (LCPD)

delinquent who shows a pattern of problems from birth onward and whose problems continue into adulthood

adolescent-limited delinquent (ALD)

delinquent who shows no evidence of problems prior to adolescence and whose delinquent behavior in adolescence is temporary

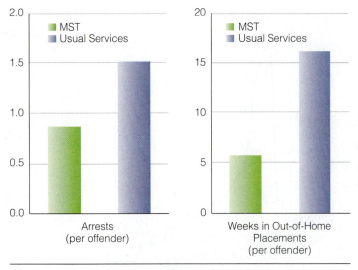

Figure 8.14 Multisystemic Approach to Delinquency

Why is MST more effective than other types of interventions for delinquency?
SOURCE: Alexander (2001), p. 42

As we have seen earlier in the chapter, the brain is still a long way from maturity during adolescence. Does the immaturity of the brain help explain why rates of delinquency and some other types of risky behavior are higher in adolescence than at younger ages? This theory has been proposed by researchers who claim that neurological studies show that the brain's frontal lobe areas in charge of judgment and impulse control are not mature until at least the mid-20s; consequently, during adolescence behavior is governed more by emotions and less by reason than in later years (Steinberg, 2010). However, other researchers dispute this conclusion. Some studies have found that the brain development of adolescents who engage in risky behavior is actually *more* mature in some ways than in their less-risk-prone peers (Engelmann et al., 2011). Others point out that rates of most types of risky behavior continue to increase into the early 20s; brain development also advances during this time, so immaturity of the brain cannot explain the increase in risky behavior during these years (Males, 2010). It should also be noted that boys and girls are highly similar in brain development during adolescence, yet boys commit far more crimes.

Delinquency has often proven to be resistant to change in adolescence, but one successful approach has been to intervene at several levels, including the home, the school, and the neighborhood. This is known as the *multisystemic approach* (Borduin et al., 2003; Henggeler, 2011). Programs based on this approach include parent training, job training and vocational counseling, and the development of neighborhood activities such as youth centers and athletic leagues. The goal is to direct the energy of delinquents into more socially constructive directions. The multisystemic approach has now been adopted by youth agencies all over the world (Henggeler, 2011; Schoenwald et al., 2008). As **Figure 8.14** illustrates, programs using this approach have been shown to be effective in reducing arrests and out-of-home placements among delinquents (Henggeler et al., 2007; Ogden & Amlund, 2006). Furthermore, multisystemic programs have been found to be cheaper than other programs, primarily because they reduce the amount of time that delinquent adolescents spend in foster homes and detention centers (Alexander, 2001).

Depression

LO 8.21 Identify the different types and rates of depression and summarize the most effective treatments.

Do you remember feeling sad at times during your teen years? As we have seen earlier in the chapter, studies of adolescents' emotional lives have found that they experience sadness and other negative emotions much more frequently than younger children or adults do.

Psychologists make distinctions between different levels of depression. **Depressed mood** is a term for a temporary period of sadness, without any related symptoms. The most serious form of depression is **major depressive disorder**, which includes a more enduring period of sadness along with other symptoms such as frequent crying, fatigue, feelings of worthlessness, and feeling guilty, lonely, or worried. Major depressive disorder may also include symptoms such as difficulty sleeping and changes in appetite (American Psychiatric Association [APA], 2013).

Rates of major depressive disorder among adolescents range in various studies from 3% to 7% (Cheung et al., 2005; Compas et al., 1993; Thapar et al., 2012), which is about the

depressed mood

enduring period of sadness, without any other related symptoms of depression

major depressive disorder

clinical diagnosis that includes a range of specific symptoms such as depressed mood, appetite disturbances, sleeping disturbances, and fatigue

same rate found in studies of adults. However, rates of depressed mood are substantially higher. For example, one longitudinal study found that the rate of depressed mood for Dutch adolescents at age 11 was 27% for girls and 21% for boys, rising by age 19 to 37% for girls and 23% for boys (Bennik et al., 2013). The most common causes of depressed mood tend to be common experiences among adolescents: conflict with friends or family members, disappointment or rejection in love, and poor performance in school (Costello et al., 2008; Larson & Richards, 1994).

One of the strongest risk factors for all types of depression in adolescence and beyond is simply being female (Thapar et al., 2012). A variety of explanations have been proposed. Some scholars have suggested that body image concerns provoke depression. There is substantial evidence that adolescent girls who have a poor body image are more likely than other girls to be depressed (Graber et al., 2007; Marcotte et al., 2002; Wichstrom et al., 1999). Also, when faced with the beginning of a depressed mood, boys (and men) are more likely to distract themselves (and forget about it), whereas girls (and women) have a greater tendency to **ruminate** on their depressed feelings and thereby amplify them (Jose & Brown, 2008; Nolen-Hoeksema et al., 2008). Adolescent girls are more likely than adolescent boys to devote their thoughts and feelings to their personal relationships, and these relationships can be a source of distress and sadness (Bakker et al., 2010; Conway et al., 2011).

For adolescents, as for adults, the two main types of treatment for depression are antidepressant medications and psychotherapy. Recent studies indicate that newly developed antidepressants such as Prozac are highly effective in treating adolescent depression (Bostic et al., 2005; Brent, 2004; Cohen et al., 2004; Thapar et al., 2012). The combination of the newest medications and psychotherapy appear to be the most effective approach to treating adolescent depression. In one recent major study of 12- to 17-year-olds at 13 sites across the United States who had been diagnosed with major depression, 71% of the adolescents who received both Prozac and psychotherapy experienced an improvement in their symptoms (Treatment for Adolescents with Depression Study Team, 2004, 2007). Improvement rates for the other groups were 61% for Prozac alone, 43% for psychotherapy alone, and 35% for the placebo group. However, some research has raised concerns that use of antidepressants with adolescents may provoke suicidal thoughts and behavior (Bridge et al., 2007). Other research contradicts this finding, so currently it is advised that adolescents who are on antidepressant medications should be monitored closely (Thapar et al., 2012).

Resilience in Adolescence

LO 8.22 Define resilience and name the protective factors that are related to resilience in adolescence.

When adolescents develop problems, the source of the problems can often be traced to risk factors, such as poverty, poor family relationships, abusive or neglectful parenting, and inadequate schools. However, there are also many adolescents who face dire conditions yet manage to adapt and function well. **Resilience** is the term for this phenomenon, defined as "good outcomes in spite of serious threats to adaptation and development" (Masten, 2001, p. 228). Sometimes "good outcomes" are measured as notable academic or social achievements, sometimes as psychological traits such as high well-being or self-esteem, and sometimes as the absence of notable problems. Young people who are resilient are not necessarily high achievers who have some kind of extraordinary ability. More often they display what resilience researcher Ann Masten calls the "ordinary magic" of being able to function reasonably well despite being faced with unusually difficult circumstances (Masten, 2001, p. 227).

Resilience is promoted by **protective factors** that enable adolescents to overcome the risk factors in their lives (Rafaelli & Iturbide, 2015). Some of the most important

ruminate
to think persistently about bad feelings and experiences

resilience
overcoming adverse environmental circumstances and achieving healthy development despite those circumstances

protective factors
characteristics of young people that are related to lower likelihood of problems despite experiencing high-risk circumstances

A mentor can be a source of resilience for adolescents at risk for problems. Here, an adolescent girl and her mentor discuss homework together at an after school mentoring program in New Orleans.

protective factors identified in resilience research are high intelligence, physical attractiveness, parenting that provides an effective balance of warmth and control, and a caring adult "mentor" outside the family. For example, high intelligence may allow an adolescent to perform well academically despite going to a low-quality school and living in a disorderly household (Masten et al., 2006). Effective parenting may help an adolescent have a positive self-image and avoid antisocial behavior despite growing up in poverty and living in a rough neighborhood (Brody & Flor, 1998). A mentor may foster high academic goals and good future planning in an adolescent whose family life is characterized by abuse or neglect (Rhodes & DuBois, 2008).

One classic study followed a group of infants from birth through adolescence (Werner & Smith, 1982, 1992, 2001). It is known as the Kauai (KOW-ee) study, after the Hawaiian island where the study took place. The Kauai study focused on a high-risk group of children who had four or more risk factors by age 2, such as problems in physical development, parents' marital conflict, parental drug abuse, low maternal education, and poverty. Out of this group, there was a resilient subgroup that showed good social and academic functioning and few behavior problems by ages 10–18. Compared with their less resilient peers, adolescents in the resilient group were found to benefit from several protective factors, including one well-functioning parent, higher intelligence, and higher physical attractiveness.

More recent studies have supported the Kauai findings but also broadened the range of protective factors (Masten, 2007, 2014). *Religiosity* has become recognized as an especially important protective factor. Adolescents who have a strong religious faith are less likely to have problems such as substance abuse, even when they have grown up in a high-risk environment (Howard et al., 2007; Wallace et al., 2007).

Practice Quiz ANSWERS AVAILABLE IN ANSWER KEY.

1. Theo is an adolescent boy who has gotten in trouble for a number of delinquent acts such as underage drinking, vandalizing on Halloween, and trespassing. Researchers who take a biological approach would explain this behavior as being caused by an immature _____.
   a. frontal lobe
   b. occipital lobe
   c. hypothalamus
   d. pituitary gland

2. During high school, Joe was a popular kid who got into trouble when hanging around a group of older friends. One time he even climbed through the window of a convenience store to steal beer when they'd run out at a party. Eventually, Joe got a steady job, got married, and had children. He mentioned at his reunion that he regretted the poor choices he had made. According to Moffitt, Joe would be considered a(n) _____.
   a. adolescent-limited delinquent
   b. conduct disorder-persistent delinquent
   c. sporadic delinquent
   d. time specific delinquent

3. Fifteen-year-old Sadreana has been diagnosed with major depressive disorder. Her treatment is most likely to include _____.

   a. systematic desensitization and aversion therapy
   b. equine therapy and electroconvulsive therapy
   c. psychotherapy and antidepressant medications
   d. psychoanalytic therapy and electroconvulsive therapy

4. Which of the following statements about depression is TRUE?
   a. Over 90% of individuals eventually get a diagnosis of major depressive disorder in adolescence.
   b. Depressed mood includes symptoms such as difficulty sleeping and changes in appetite.
   c. Rates of depressed mood rise notably from middle childhood to adolescence.
   d. Girls tend to use distraction more than boys when faced with the beginning of a depressed mood.

5. Which of the following is one of the most important protective factors identified in resilience research, enabling adolescents to overcome the risk factors in their lives?
   a. Being tall and mature looking for their age
   b. Athletic ability
   c. Artistic talent and high scores on measures of creativity
   d. A caring mentor outside the family

Summary: Emotional and Social Development

LO 8.12 Summarize the results of the ESM studies with respect to adolescent emotionality.

Experience Sampling Method (ESM) studies show greater mood swings in adolescence than in middle childhood or adulthood. Also, there is a decline in overall emotional state from 5th grade through 12th grade.

LO 8.13 Describe how self-understanding, self-concept, and self-esteem change during adolescence.

Self-development in adolescence is complex and may include an ideal self, a possible self, a feared self, and a false self along with an actual self. Overall self-esteem often declines in early adolescence, especially for girls. Self-concept includes a variety of aspects in adolescence, but overall self-concept is strongly influenced by self-perceptions of physical attractiveness. Adolescence is a time of gender intensification, as young people become more aware of the gender expectations of their culture. Boys in many cultures risk becoming a failed man unless they learn to provide, protect, and procreate. Girls are generally believed to reach womanhood when they reach menarche.

LO 8.14 Discriminate between Kohlberg's theory of moral development and Jensen's worldviews theory.

Kohlberg proposed three universal levels of moral reasoning: preconventional, conventional, and postconventional. According to Jensen, morality develops in culturally-diverse ways based on Ethics of Autonomy, Community, and Divinity.

LO 8.15 Describe the cultural variations in religious beliefs during adolescence as well as the sources and outcomes of religiosity within cultures.

American adolescents are more religious than adolescents in other developed countries. In general, higher religiosity is related to a variety of positive features of adolescents' development, such as better relationships with parents and lower rates of substance use.

LO 8.16 Summarize the cultural variations in adolescents' relationships with parents, siblings, and extended family.

Adolescence is a time of increased conflict with parents in cultures that promote autonomy. Sibling conflict is not as high in adolescence as in earlier life stages, but adolescents have more conflict with siblings than in any of their other relationships. Relations with grandparents tend to be close and positive worldwide.

LO 8.17 Describe cultural variations in adolescents' relationships with friends, and characterize their interactions with peers.

In most cultures, adolescents spend less time with family and more time with friends than they did in middle childhood. Intimacy is more important in adolescent friendships than at earlier ages. Adolescents also have groups of friends, or "cliques," and see their peers as falling into "crowds." Bullying is more common in adolescence than at other ages.

LO 8.18 Identify cultural variations in adolescent love and sexuality, including variations in adolescent pregnancy and contraceptive use.

Cultures vary widely in their tolerance of adolescent sexuality, from permissive to semi-restrictive to restrictive. Rates of adolescent pregnancy are lowest in cultures that are highly accepting of adolescent sexuality and in those that strictly forbid it. American adolescents have high rates of adolescent pregnancy, due mainly to the mixed cultural messages they receive about adolescent sexuality.

LO 8.19 Explain the function of media use in adolescents' lives and apply the Media Practice Model to the playing of electronic games.

Adolescents are avid users of a wide range of media, from television and music to electronic games. Concern has been expressed about the potential negative effects of playing electronic games, mainly focusing on aggressive behavior and attitudes, but positive effects have been found in areas such as mood regulation.

LO 8.20 Summarize the explanations for why age and crime are so strongly correlated, and describe the multisystemic approach to combating delinquency.

According to one theory, age and crime are highly correlated because adolescents are more independent from parents than at earlier ages and also more peer-oriented. The multisystemic approach entails intervening at several levels, including home, school, and neighborhood.

LO 8.21 Identify the different types and rates of depression and summarize the most effective treatments.

Depressed mood involves a relatively brief period of sadness, whereas major depression entails a more enduring period of sadness combined with a variety of other symptoms, such as disruptions in patterns of sleeping and eating. Although major depression is rare in adolescence, depressed mood is common, especially among adolescent girls. The most effective approach to treating adolescent depression combines the newest medications and psychotherapy.

LO 8.22 Define resilience and name the protective factors that are related to resilience in adolescence.

Resilience means functioning well despite adverse circumstances. Some of the protective factors promoting resilience in adolescence are high intelligence, a good relationship with a parent or mentor, and physical attractiveness.

Applying Your Knowledge as a Professional

The topics covered in this chapter apply to a wide variety of career professions. Watch these videos to learn how they apply to a middle school teacher, a high school teacher and coach, a family court judge, and the head of a residential facility for teenage mothers.

Watch   CAREER FOCUS: MIDDLE SCHOOL TEACHER

Terra Spears
Middle school teacher

Chapter Quiz

1. The most important estrogen is estradiol and the most important androgen is _____.

   a. human growth hormone   **c.** leptin

   b. testosterone   **d.** insulin

2. Which of the following best describes pubertal timing?

   a. The average age of menarche is much later today than it was in earlier generations.

   b. Menarche takes place as late as age 15 in some developing countries, due to lack of proper nutrition and medical care.

   c. The timing of puberty has no effect on adolescent boys.

   d. The effects of early maturation are generally positive for girls.

3. Puberty rituals _____.

   a. developed to mark the departure from adolescence into emerging adulthood

   b. are only carried out for females and are most often related to menstruation

   c. are declining in many cultures as a consequence of globalization

   d. focus on a particular biological event across all cultures

4. In the United States, girls _____.

   a. who have an eating disorder are also more likely than other females to be depressed

   b. with bulimia are usually about 20% overweight

   c. who are Asian American are more likely to have eating disorders than are those in other ethnic groups

   d. are more likely than boys to be satisfied with their bodies

5. The substance use of an adolescent who drinks alcohol to relieve feelings of sadness and loneliness would be classified as _____.

   a. social substance use   **c.** experimental substance use

   b. medicinal substance use   **d.** addictive substance use

6. Compared to the concrete thinking abilities displayed in childhood, the ability to reason in adolescence _____.

   a. utilizes the hypothetical thinking involved in a scientific experiment

   b. involves more random attempts at problem solving as they persist longer

   c. differs quantitatively, but not qualitatively

   d. is not significantly different

7. Which of the following best represents the research on formal operational thinking across cultures?

   a. Formal operational thinking takes the same form, regardless of culture.

   b. Individuals in collectivisitic cultures take much longer to develop formal operations.

   c. Formal operational thinking only exists in developed countries.

   d. The way that formal operational thinking is manifested is likely different across different cultures.

8. Compared to his 7-year-old brother, a 14-year-old will have an easier time reading a book and listening to music at the same time because he's more adept at _____.

   a. using mnemonic devices consistently

   b. tasks that require divided attention

c. tasks that require transfer of information from sensory memory to short-term memory

d. maximizing his metamemory

9. Compared to his brother in college, Jonah is more likely to think that if he starts smoking marijuana, he will be able to quit when he wants to and nothing bad will happen. This way of thinking demonstrates _____.

a. the personal fable   c. selective attention

b. the imaginary audience d. hypothetical reasoning

10. After learning to knit a simple scarf with her grandmother's guidance, Alexis began to knit a sweater while on break from college. She went over to her grandmother's once when she had a question. By the time Alexis had to go back to school, she had nearly finished the sweater. She finished the sweater a few weeks later while she was back at college, needing only one Skype session to help her. After finishing the sweater, her grandmother mailed her a pattern so she can knit a handbag. This illustrates _____.

a. selective attention   c. scaffolding

b. synaptic pruning   d. hypothetical-deductive reasoning

11. Compared to schools in the United States, those in Eastern countries _____.

a. have a shorter school day

b. are all sex-segregated

c. focus almost exclusively on rote learning

d. place a greater emphasis on creativity

12. Adolescents in developed countries who work part-time _____.

a. are less likely to use drugs and alcohol than their nonworking counterparts

b. have higher grades in school than other students

c. usually contribute the majority of their earnings to support the household income

d. do not typically see their high school jobs as the basis for a future career

13. A developmental psychologist would most likely use the Experience Sampling Method (ESM) to _____.

a. evaluate the strength of cohort differences

b. examine changes in emotions at various time points

c. examine how different environmental experiences affect brain development

d. determine whether behavioral differences between males and females become more pronounced in the transition from childhood to adolescence

14. Adolescents are most likely to exhibit their false selves with _____.

a. close friends   c. acquaintances

b. dating partners   d. parents

15. In traditional cultures, girls reach womanhood mainly through _____.

a. their achievments

b. the same means that males reach manhood

c. their biological changes

d. protecting their young

16. Research on Kohlberg's stages of moral development has shown that _____.

a. the stage of moral reasoning achieved tends to increase with age

b. over time, people regress to an earlier stage of moral reasoning

c. people often skip stages and advance to the highest stage in adulthood

d. the majority of people reach Stage 5: community right and individual rights orientation

17. Religiosity in adolescence is _____.

a. usually lowest among African Americans

b. associated with lower rates of delinquency

c. highest in European and Asian countries

d. the same regardless of if adolscents' parents are married or divorced

18. In Western countries, conflict with parents _____.

a. remains constant during adolescence

b. steadily increases until the end of emerging adulthood

c. declines in late adolescence

d. is highest during middle childhood

19. Who comprises the source of adolescents' happiest experiences?

a. Friends   c. Extended family

b. Parents   d. Siblings

20. On the basis of anthropological evidence, the United States would be considered a(n) _____ culture in terms of its cultural beliefs about the acceptability (or not) of premarital sex.

a. permissive   c. semirestrictive

b. authoritarian   d. restrictive

21. Research on the media use of adolescents _____.

a. has found that only females report that they enjoy the social aspect of gaming

b. has found that adolescents in industrialized countries use media for about 2 hours every day

c. has focused primarily on the benefits, such as increasing problem-solving ability and strategizing

d. has shown that the content of electronic games is related to their emotional responses

22. Which of the following best describes the relationships between age and crime?

a. Adolescents are less likely than adults to commit crimes because they do not have enough opportunity to do so.

b. Adolescents are less likely to be the victims of crime than are children or adults.

c. Adolescents are likely to commit crimes alone because they worry about their reputation if they get caught.

d. A small percentage of adolescents commit the majority of crimes.

23. Which of the following statements about depression is most accurate?

a. Rates of major depressive disorder are higher among adolescents than rates of depressed mood.

b. Psychotherapy alone was as effective in treating adolescent depression as psychotherapy combined with medication.

c. Rates of depressed mood rise substantially from middle childhood to adolescence.

d. Boys are more likely than girls to show increases in depressed mood during adolescence.

24. Research on resilience has shown that _____.

a. bouncing back from adversity requires a high level of achievement and extraordinary abilities

b. high intelligence characterizes many individuals who are considered resilient

c. as a group, girls are more resilient than boys

d. parenting has no influence on resilience

Chapter 9
Emerging Adulthood

ANDY, AGE 21, LIVES WITH HIS GIRLFRIEND IN A MODEST ONE-BEDROOM APARTMENT IN CENTRAL MISSOURI. He went to college but dropped out after 2 years, partly because he missed home and partly because he was not sure what he wanted to study. He does not know what he would like to do next, so he is working for a landscaping firm, mowing lawns and trimming shrubs for now. He is also uncertain about love. Although he lives with his girlfriend, he moved in with her mainly for financial reasons and does not see her as part of his future. He is thinking of moving to San Francisco in a few months to make a new start in a new place.

Chunming, age 19, recently left the small Chinese village where she grew up and migrated to Guangdong, one of China's booming industrial cities. Her parents objected, but Chunming felt there was no future for her in the village, and left anyway. In Guangdong, a cousin helped her get a job in a factory making athletic shoes. Chunming lives in a factory dormitory, where she shares a room with nine other young women who work in the factory. They work on the assembly line 10½ hours a day, 5 days a week, plus a half day on Saturday, for a salary of about 72 U.S. dollars a month. Nevertheless, she feels lucky. She dreams of finding a sweet and handsome husband, and perhaps starting a small business with him, or at least finding a job outside the factory.

The lives of Andy and Chunming are very different. However, one thing they have in common is that their lives are vastly different than what their parents or grandparents experienced at a similar age. The lives of young people all over the world have changed dramatically over the past half century. This chapter is about the new life stage of *emerging adulthood* that has developed as a consequence of those changes.

Watch CHAPTER INTRODUCTION: EMERGING ADULTHOOD

Section 1   Physical Development

∨   Learning Objectives

9.1 Name the five developmental features distinctive to emerging adulthood.

9.2 Describe some of the ways emerging adulthood varies among cultures, with specific reference to European and Asian countries.

9.3 Name the indicators that emerging adulthood is a period of peak physical functioning.

9.4 Summarize college students' sleep patterns and the main elements of sleep hygiene.

9.5 Explain why young drivers have the highest rates of crashes, and name the most effective approach to reducing those rates.

9.6 Explain why rates of substance use peak in the early 20s and then decline.

PHYSICAL DEVELOPMENT:
The Emergence of Emerging Adulthood

Before we examine the changes in physical development that occur in emerging adulthood, let's begin with a closer look at the origins of this new life stage. Traditionally, theories of human development described a stage of adolescence followed by a stage of young adulthood (Erikson, 1950). The transition to young adulthood was assumed to be marked by entry to adult roles, specifically marriage, parenthood, and stable work. For most people, entry into these roles took place around the age of 20 or shortly thereafter. By their early 20s, most people had formed the stable structure of an adult life.

However, traditional stage models no longer fit the pattern of development that most people experience, especially in developed countries. The 20s are not a time of settling into a stable occupational path but a time of exceptional instability in work, as the completion of education and training is followed by multiple job changes, for most people. Similarly, most people marry and become parents in their late 20s or early 30s rather than in their early 20s.

As a consequence of these changes, it is increasingly recognized among scholars in human development that a new life stage has developed between adolescence and young adulthood. Rather than making the transition from adolescence to young adulthood quickly at around age 20, most people in developed countries experience a stage of *emerging adulthood* from their late teens to at least their mid-20s, before entering a more stable young adulthood at around age 30 (Arnett, 2004; Arnett, 2007; Arnett, 2011). "Thirty is the new 20," as a popular American saying puts it.

Five Features

LO 9.1   **Name the five developmental features distinctive to emerging adulthood.**

Perhaps the most obvious indicator of the emergence of emerging adulthood as a normative life stage in developed countries is the rise in the ages of entering marriage and parenthood. As recently as 1960 the median age of marriage in most developed countries was in the very early 20s, around 21 for women and 23 for men (Douglass, 2005). Now the median age of marriage is 27 in the United States (as **Figure 9.1** shows), and close to 30 in most other developed countries (Arnett, 2015). Age at entering parenthood followed a similar rise.

But why the dramatic rise in the typical ages of entering marriage and parenthood? Four revolutionary changes took place in the 1960s and '70s that laid the foundation for the new life stage of emerging adulthood: the Technology Revolution, the Sexual Revolution, the Women's Movement, and the Youth Movement (Arnett, 2015).

By the Technology Revolution, I do not mean iPads and iPhones, but rather the manufacturing technologies that transformed the American economy. In the past half century, the United States and other developed countries have shifted from a manufacturing economy to a service economy requiring information and technology skills. Within the United States, participation in *tertiary education* (any education or training past high school) varies by ethnic group, but it has risen in all groups in recent decades, as **Figure 9.2** shows (Arnett, 2011). Most young people wait until they have finished school before they start thinking seriously about making adult commitments such as marriage and parenthood, and for many of them this means postponing those commitments until at least their late 20s.

The Sexual Revolution, sparked by the invention of the birth control pill in 1964, was another important contributor. Widespread use of "the Pill," in combination with less stringent standards of sexual morality after the sexual revolution of the 1960s and early 1970s, meant that young people no longer had to enter marriage in order to have a stable sexual relationship (Arnett, 2015). Now most young people have a series of sexual relationships before entering marriage, and there is widespread tolerance for premarital sex in the context of a committed, loving relationship.

The Women's Movement of the 1960s and '70s vastly expanded the opportunities available to young women (Arnett, 2015). Women's roles have changed in ways that make an early entry into adult obligations less desirable for them now compared to 50 years ago. The young women of the 1950s and early 1960s were under a great deal of social pressure to find a husband. Being a single woman was simply not a viable social status for a woman after her early 20s. Relatively few women attended college, and those who did were often there for the purpose of meeting their future husbands. The range of occupations open to young women was severely restricted, as it had been traditionally—secretary, waitress, teacher, nurse, perhaps a few others. Even these occupations were supposed to be temporary for young women. What they were really supposed to be focusing on was finding a husband and having children.

For the young women of the 21st century, all this has changed. In nearly every developed country, at every level of education from grade school through graduate school, girls now excel over boys. Young women's occupational possibilities are now virtually unlimited, and although men still dominate in engineering and some sciences, women are equal to men in obtaining law, business, and medical degrees. With so many options open to them, and with so little pressure on them to marry in their early 20s, the lives of young women in developed countries today have changed almost beyond recognition from what they were 50 years ago. Like young men, they typically spend the years from the late teens through at least the mid-20s trying out various possible options before making definite choices.

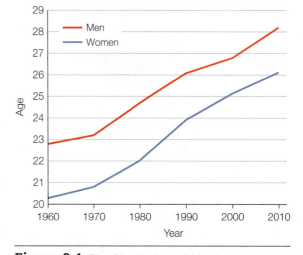

Figure 9.1 The Rise in Age of Marriage Since 1960, United States

SOURCE: Based on U.S. Bureau of the Census (2004, 2010).

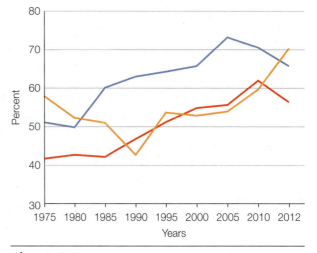

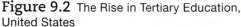

Figure 9.2 The Rise in Tertiary Education, United States

Today in developed countries, young women exceed young men in educational attainment and have a wide range of opportunities in the workplace that they did not have before.

The fourth major change of the 1960s and '70s was the Youth Movement, which denigrated adulthood and exalted being, acting, and feeling young. As a consequence of the Youth Movement, there has been a profound change in how young people view the meaning and value of becoming an adult and entering adult roles of spouse, parent, and employee. Young people of the 1950s were eager to enter adulthood and "settle down" (Modell, 1989). Perhaps because they grew up during the upheavals of the Great Depression and World War II, achieving the stability of a secure job, marriage, home, and children seemed like a great achievement to them. Also, because many of them planned to have three, four, or even five or more children, they had good reason to get started early in order to have all the children they wanted and space them out at reasonable intervals.

The young people of today, in contrast, see adulthood and its obligations in quite a different light. In their late teens and early 20s, marriage, home, and children are seen by most of them not as achievements to be pursued but as perils to be avoided (Arnett, 2015). It is not that they reject the prospect of marriage, home, and (one or two) children—eventually. It is just that, in their late teens and early 20s, they ponder these obligations and think, "yes, but *not yet.*" Adulthood and its commitments offer security and stability, but also represent a closing of doors—the end of independence, the end of spontaneity, the end of a sense of wide-open possibility.

What are the main features of emerging adulthood? What makes it distinct from the adolescence that precedes it and the young adulthood that follows it? There are five characteristics that distinguish emerging adulthood from other age periods (Arnett, 2004; Arnett, 2006; Arnett, 2015; Reifman et al., 2006). Emerging adulthood is

1. the age of identity explorations;
2. the age of instability;
3. the self-focused age;
4. the age of feeling in-between; and
5. the age of possibilities.

All of these features begin to develop before emerging adulthood and continue to develop afterward, but it is during emerging adulthood that they reach their peak (Reifman et al., 2006).

Perhaps the most distinctive characteristic of emerging adulthood is that it is the *age of identity explorations.* This means that it is an age when people explore various possibilities in love and work as they move toward making enduring choices. Through trying out these different possibilities they develop a more definite identity, that is, an understanding of who they are, what their capabilities and limitations are, what their beliefs and values are, and how they fit into the society around them. Erik Erikson (1950), who was the first to develop the idea of identity (see Chapter 1), asserted that it is mainly an issue in adolescence, but that was over 50 years ago, and today it is mainly in emerging adulthood that identity explorations take place (Arnett, 2000; Arnett, 2004; Arnett, 2005b; Arnett, 2015; Schwartz et al., 2005).

The explorations of emerging adulthood also make it the *age of instability.* As they explore different possibilities in love and work, emerging adults' lives are often unstable. A good illustration of this is in how often they move from one residence to another. As **Figure 9.3** shows, rates of residential change in American society are much higher at

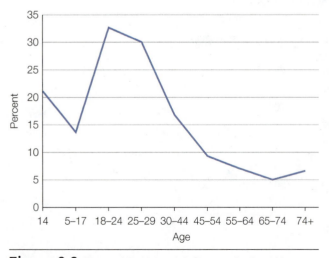

Figure 9.3 Rate of Residential Change in Past Year, United States

Why does the rate of residential change peak in emerging adulthood?

SOURCE: U.S. Bureau of the Census (2011)

ages 18–29 than at any other period of life. This is a reflection of the explorations going on in emerging adults' lives. Some move out of their parents' household for the first time in their late teens to attend a residential college, others move out simply to be independent (Goldscheider & Goldscheider, 1999). They may move again when they drop out of college or when they graduate. They may cohabit with a romantic partner, then move out when the relationship ends. Some move to another part of the country or the world to study or work. For nearly half of American emerging adults, their residential changes include moving back in with their parents at least once (Sassler et al., 2008). In countries where emerging adults remain home rather than moving out, such as in most of southern Europe, they may nevertheless experience instability in education, work, and love relationships (Douglass, 2005; Douglass, 2007; Iacovou, 2011).

Emerging adulthood is also a *self-focused age*, a time in between adolescents' reliance on parents and young adults' long-term commitments in love and work. During these years, emerging adults focus on themselves as they develop the knowledge, skills, and self-understanding they will need for adult life. In the course of emerging adulthood they learn to make independent decisions small and large, about everything from what to have for dinner to whether or not to marry their current partner.

Being self-focused does not mean being selfish, and emerging adults are generally less egocentric than adolescents and more capable of taking the perspectives of others (Arnett, 2004; Lapsley & Woodbury, 2015). The goal of being self-focused is learning to stand alone as a self-sufficient person, but emerging adults do not see self-sufficiency as a permanent state. Rather, they view it as a necessary step before committing themselves to lasting relationships with others, in love and work.

Another distinctive feature of emerging adulthood is that it is an *age of feeling in-between*, no longer an adolescent but not fully an adult. When asked, "Do you feel that you have reached adulthood?" the majority of emerging adults respond neither "yes" nor "no" but with the ambiguous "in some ways yes, in some ways no" (Arnett, 1997; Arnett, 1998; Arnett, 2001; Arnett, 2003; Arnett, 2004; Arnett & Schwab, 2012; Nelson & Luster, 2015). As **Figure 9.4** shows, it is only when people reach their late 20s that a clear majority feel they have reached adulthood. Most emerging adults have the subjective feeling of being in a transitional period of life, on the way to adulthood but not there yet. This "in-between" feeling in emerging adulthood has been found in a wide range of countries, including Argentina (Facio & Micocci, 2003), Israel (Mayseless & Scharf, 2003), the Czech Republic (Macek et al., 2007), China (Nelson et al., 2004), and Austria (Sirsch et al., 2009).

Finally, emerging adulthood is the *age of possibilities*, when many different futures remain possible, when little about a person's direction in life has been decided for certain. It tends to be an age of high hopes, in part because few of their dreams have been tested in the fires of real life. In one national survey of 18- to 29-year-olds in the United States, nearly all—89%—agreed with the statement "I am confident that eventually I will get to where I want to be in life" (Arnett & Schwab, 2012). This optimism in emerging adulthood has been found in other countries as well, such as China (Nelson & Chen, 2007).

Emerging adulthood is also the age of possibilities because it is a time that holds the potential for dramatic changes. For those who have come from a troubled family, this is their chance to try to straighten the parts of themselves that have become twisted. No longer dependent on their parents, no longer subject to their parents' problems on a daily basis, they may be able to make independent decisions—perhaps to move

The 20s are the decade of life when people are most likely to change residence.

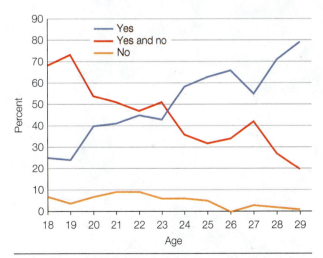

Figure 9.4 Do You Feel You Have Reached Adulthood?

Emerging adults often feel adult in some ways but not others.
SOURCE: Based on Arnett (2015).

to a different area or go to college—that turn their lives in a dramatically different direction (Arnett, 2004; Masten et al., 2006). Even for those who have come from families that are relatively happy and healthy, emerging adulthood is an opportunity to transform themselves so that they are not merely made in their parents' images but have made independent decisions about what kind of person they wish to be and how they wish to live. For this limited window of time—7, perhaps 10 years—the fulfillment of all their hopes seems possible, because for most people the range of their choices for how to live is greater than it has ever been before and greater than it will ever be again.

The Cultural Context of Emerging Adulthood

LO 9.2 **Describe some of the ways emerging adulthood varies among cultures, with specific reference to European and Asian countries.**

Emerging adulthood exists as a life stage across developed countries, but the forms it takes vary by world region (Arnett, 2011). Europe is the region where emerging adulthood is longest and most leisurely. The median age of entering marriage and parenthood is around 30 in most European countries (Douglass, 2007; Moreno Mínguez et al., 2012). Europe today is the location of the most affluent, generous, egalitarian societies in the world—in fact, in human history (Arnett, 2007). Governments pay for tertiary education, assist young people in finding jobs, and provide generous unemployment benefits for those who cannot find work. In northern Europe, many governments also provide housing support. Emerging adults in European societies make the most of these advantages.

In Asian countries such as Japan, emerging adults feel an obligation to take care of their parents.

The experience of emerging adulthood in Asian developed countries is markedly different than in Europe. Europe has a long history of individualism, dating back at least 500 years, and today's emerging adults represent that legacy in their focus on self-development and leisure. In contrast, Asian cultures have a shared history emphasizing collectivism and family obligations. Although Asian cultures have become more individualistic in recent decades as a consequence of globalization, the legacy of collectivism persists in the lives of emerging adults. They pursue identity explorations and self-development during emerging adulthood, like their American and European counterparts, but within narrower boundaries set by their sense of obligations to others, especially their parents (Phinney & Baldelomar, 2011). For example, in their views of the most important criteria for becoming an adult, emerging adults in the United States and Europe consistently rank *financial independence* among the most important markers of adulthood. In contrast, emerging adults with an Asian cultural background especially emphasize *capable of supporting parents financially* as among the most important criteria (Arnett, 2003; Nelson et al., 2004; Zhong & Arnett, 2014). This sense of family obligation may curtail their identity explorations in emerging adulthood to some extent, as they pay more heed to their parents' wishes about what they should study and what job they should take and where they should live than emerging adults do in the West.

Within countries as well as between countries, emerging adulthood takes many different forms, just as we have seen for adolescence and childhood. About half of emerging adults in developed countries obtain tertiary education and training, but that leaves half who do not, and their experience of emerging adulthood is much different. Specifically, they are likely to have a much more difficult time finding a decent job in an economy that rewards educational credentials. There are other important differences across countries and cultures, such as in the degree of tolerance for premarital sex and cohabitation, as we will see later in the chapter. Thus there is not just one emerging adulthood that is experienced worldwide, but many emerging adulthoods with distinctive cultural characteristics (Arnett, 2011).

Currently in developing countries, there tends to be a split between urban and rural areas in whether emerging adulthood is experienced at all. Young people in urban areas of countries such as China and India are more likely to experience emerging adulthood, because they marry later, have children later, obtain more education, and have a greater range of occupational and recreational opportunities than young people in rural areas have (Nelson & Chen, 2007; Zhong & Arnett, 2014). In contrast, young people in rural areas of developing countries often receive minimal schooling, marry early, and have little choice of occupation aside from agricultural work.

However, emerging adulthood is likely to become more pervasive worldwide in the decades to come, with the increasing globalization of the world economy (Arnett, 2011). Participation in tertiary education is rising in developing countries, as are median marriage ages, especially in the urban middle class. These changes open up the possibility for the spread of emerging adulthood in developing countries. It seems possible that by the end of the 21st century emerging adulthood will be a normative period for young people worldwide, although it is likely to continue to vary in length and content both within and between countries.

Cultural Focus: The Features of Emerging Adulthood

Emerging adulthood is not a universal period of human development but a period that exists under certain conditions that have occurred only quite recently and only in some cultures. As we have seen, what is mainly required for emerging adulthood to exist is a relatively high median age of entering marriage and parenthood, in the late 20s or beyond. Postponing marriage and parenthood until the late 20s allows the late teens and most of the 20s to be devoted to other activities, such as the identity explorations just described. So, emerging adulthood exists today mainly in developed countries, including Europe, the United States, Canada, Australia, and New Zealand, along with Asian countries such as Japan and South Korea (Arnett, 2011).

This video shows interviews with individuals from various cultures regarding the features of emerging adulthood.

Watch THE FEATURES OF EMERGING ADULTHOOD

Review Question:

Emerging adulthood is described as an "unstable" time in one's life. Based on this video, why would this be an accurate description?

Practice Quiz

1. In the United States, nearly all 18- to 29-years olds (89%) agreed with the statement _____.
   a. "I have chosen a career path that brings satisfaction and stability to my life."
   b. "I am confident that eventually I will get to where I want to be in life."
   c. "I am who I am and that is never going to change."
   d. "It's a relief to finally be financially independent."

2. According to Arnett, four revolutionary changes took place in the _____ that laid the foundation for the new life stage of emerging adulthood.
   a. 1960's and '70's
   b. 1980's and '90's
   c. 1990's and 2000's
   d. last decade

3. An emerging adult answered the question "What is the most important criterion for becoming an adult?" with the response of "becoming capable of supporting my parents financially." This person is most likely from _____.

   a. Germany
   b. France
   c. the United States
   d. Japan

4. When asked about the most important criteria for becoming an adult, an emerging adult from the United States is most likely to say _____.
   a. getting married
   b. having a child
   c. being financially independent
   d. moving out of the house

5. Research has shown that in developing countries, _____ are more likely to experience emerging adulthood.
   a. young people in urban areas
   b. females
   c. young people from divorced families
   d. young people who are true to their traditional heritage

PHYSICAL DEVELOPMENT: Physical Changes of Emerging Adulthood

Physical maturity is reached in many ways by the end of adolescence. By age 18, people reach their full height. Puberty is over, and a degree of sexual maturity has been attained that is sufficient to allow for reproduction. However, strength and endurance continue to grow into the 20s for most people, and illness rates are especially low as the immune system reaches peak effectiveness. On the other hand, health risks continue to loom in some areas, most notably automobile accidents and substance abuse.

The Peak of Physical Functioning

LO 9.3 **Name the indicators that emerging adulthood is a period of peak physical functioning.**

Do you enjoy watching the Olympics? I don't watch much TV, but the Olympics is one show I watch for many hours every two years. It's fun to marvel at the amazing physical feats performed by the athletes in events ranging from speed skating and snowboarding in the Winter Olympics to the pole vault and the 1500 meter run in the Summer Olympics. The competition exhibits human athletic performance at its highest.

Have you noticed that nearly all the athletes in the Olympics are ages 18–29? Emerging adulthood is the life stage of peak physical functioning, when the body is at its zenith of health, strength, and vigor. Physical stamina is often measured in terms of *maximum oxygen uptake*, or **VO2 max**, which reflects the ability of the body to take in oxygen and transport it to various organs. VO2 max peaks in the early 20s (Whaley, 2007). Similarly, **cardiac output**, the quantity of blood flow from the heart, peaks at age 25 (Lakatta, 1990; Parker et al., 2007). Reaction time is also faster in the early 20s than at any other time of life. Studies of grip strength among men show the same pattern, with a peak in the 20s followed by a steady decline (Aldwin & Spiro, 2006). The strength of the bones increases during this time as well. Even after maximum height

VO2 max

ability of the body to take in oxygen and transport it to various organs; also called maximum oxygen update

cardiac output

quantity of blood flow from the heart

is attained in the late teens, the bones continue to grow in density, and peak bone mass is reached in the 20s (Zumwalt, 2008).

It is not only the Olympics that demonstrate that emerging adulthood is a stage of exceptional physical functioning in terms of peak performances in athletic activity. Several studies have been conducted to determine the ages when athletes produce their best performances (Ericsson, 1990; Schultz & Curnow, 1988; Stones & Kozma, 1996; Tanaka & Seals, 2003). The peak ages have been found to vary depending on the sport, with swimmers youngest (the late teens) and golfers oldest (the early 30s). However, for most sports the peak age of performance comes during the 20s.

Emerging adulthood is also the period of the life span with the least susceptibility to physical illnesses (Braveman et al., 2011; Gans, 1990). This is especially true in modern times, when vaccines and medical treatments have dramatically lowered the risk of diseases such as polio that used to strike mainly during these years. Emerging adults are no longer vulnerable to the illnesses and diseases of childhood, and with rare exceptions they are not yet vulnerable to diseases such as cancer and heart disease that rise in prevalence later in adulthood. Because the immune system is at its most effective during emerging adulthood, the late teens and early 20s are the years of fewest hospital stays and fewest days spent sick in bed at home.

In many ways, then, emerging adulthood is an exceptionally healthy time of life. However, this is not the whole story. The lifestyles of many emerging adults often include a variety of factors that undermine health, such as poor nutrition, lack of sleep, and the high stress of trying to juggle school and work or multiple jobs (Braveman et al., 2011; Ma et al., 2002; Steptoe & Wardle, 2001). Longitudinal studies in the United States and Finland have found that physical activity, sports participation, and exercise decline from adolescence through emerging adulthood (Gordon-Larsen et al., 2004; Telama et al., 2005). These lifestyle factors often make emerging adults feel tired, weak, and depleted, despite their bodies' potential for optimal health. Furthermore, in many countries the late teens and early 20s are the years of highest incidence of a variety of types of injury, death, and disease due to behavior (Arnett, 2015). The areas of heightened risk in emerging adulthood include automobile accidents and substance abuse, as we'll see shortly. The risks associated with sexual activity, including sexually transmitted infections (STIs), will be explored later in the chapter.

Emerging adulthood is a time of peak physical functioning. The swimmer Michael Phelps won a record seven gold medals at the 2008 Olympic games, at the age of 23, but has found it difficult to stay on top as he approaches age 30.

Sleep Patterns and Deficits

LO 9.4 **Summarize college students' sleep patterns and the main elements of sleep hygiene.**

How are you sleeping these days? If you are reading this, you are probably a college student, and if you are a college student your sleep pattern is probably not ideal—far from it. Nearly all research on sleep in emerging adulthood has focused on college students in developed countries. According to this research, college students' sleep patterns are distinctive in ways that undermine their cognitive functioning and their emotional well-being. College students are more than twice as likely as other adults to report the symptoms of *delayed sleep phase syndrome* (Brown et al., 2002). This syndrome entails a pattern of sleeping far longer on weekends and holidays than on school or work days, which leads to poor academic and job performance as well as excessive sleepiness during school and work days. College students tend to accumulate a *sleep debt* during the week as they sleep less than they need, then they try to make up their lost sleep when they have time off, with negative consequences for their cognitive and emotional functioning (Regestein et al., 2010).

Most emerging adults tend toward eveningness, not morningness.

College students' self-reports of their sleep patterns indicate that problems are common. Two-thirds of students report occasional sleep problems and about one fourth report frequent severe sleep disturbances such as insomnia (Buboltz et al., 2002). Sleep disturbances are in turn related to a wide variety of problems, such as depression and anxiety (Millman, 2005). Poor sleeping habits also cause cognitive deficits in attention, memory, and critical thinking.

One reason college students and other emerging adults often have sleep problems is that the daily routines of their lives are set mostly by older adults who are likely to have different sleep preferences than they do. Sleep researchers have established that people vary in their **morningness** and **eveningness**, that is, their preference for either going to bed early and waking up early (morningness) or going to bed late and waking up late (eveningness). Furthermore, these preferences change with age, due to hormonal changes that are part of normal physical development, specifically, levels of *growth hormone*. One massive study of over 55,000 Europeans from childhood through late adulthood concluded that children tend toward morningness, but in the course of adolescence and the early part of emerging adulthood the balance shifts toward eveningness, with the peak of eveningness coming at about age 20–21 (slightly earlier for women than for men) (Roenneberg et al., 2007). After age 20–21, the balance shifts again toward morningness for the remainder of the life span. Other studies have found similar relations between age and sleep preferences (Brown et al., 2002). So, your 60-year-old professors may schedule their classes for 8:00 or 8:30 a.m., because that is a time of day when they feel alert and ready to go, whereas if you are in your early 20s that may well be a time of day when you feel like something scraped off the bottom of the garbage can.

However, it is not just physiological changes that contribute to college students' sleep disturbances, but also lifestyle factors, such as partying until late at night or waiting until the day before an exam to begin studying seriously. Have you ever stayed up all night long to study for an exam or to complete a paper due the next day? Among American college students this feat, known as an "all-nighter," is quite common. In one study of students at a 4-year liberal arts college, 60% had pulled at least one all-nighter since coming to college (Thacher, 2008). Those who had pulled an all-nighter tended to have a greater preference for eveningness and had poorer overall academic achievement. Another study of all-nighters found that students who stayed up all night before exams self-rated their exam performance as better than students who slept 8 hours, but their actual performance turned out to be much worse (Pilcher & Waters, 1997).

Sleep experts recommend the following practices to promote *sleep hygiene* (Brown et al., 2002; Horne, 2014):

- waking at the same time each day;
- getting regular exercise;
- taking late-afternoon naps;
- limiting caffeine intake;
- avoiding excessive alcohol intake.

morningness

preference for going to bed early and waking up early

eveningness

preference for going to bed late and waking up late

This may seem like common sense advice, but the actual behavior of many students contradicts these suggestions. Many drink coffee frequently during the day to stay alert, not realizing that frequent caffeine use will make it more difficult for them to sleep that night. Many believe that they can compensate for getting little sleep during the week by making it up during weekends and holidays, but this is precisely the delayed sleep phase syndrome, just discussed, that constitutes disrupted sleep. And of course, many drink alcohol excessively, with sleep hygiene the last thing on their minds.

Practice Quiz

1. Grip strength, cardiac output, maximum oxygen uptake, and bone density all peak during what time period?

   a. The early teen years

   b. The 20s

   c. The 30s

   d. The 40s

2. Which of the following statements about the health of emerging adults is most accurate?

   a. Most emerging adults experience an increased susceptibility to physical illness due to the increased stressors associated with this developmental period

   b. Exercise tends to decline from adolescence through emerging adulthood, but overall this is a healthy stage of life.

   c. Emerging adults are at a high risk of getting cancer and heart disease.

   d. The immune system is least effective during emerging adulthood.

3. According to research (Brown et al., 2002), college students are more than twice as likely as other adults to report _____.

   a. taking naps

   b. insomnia

   c. delayed sleep phase syndrome

   d. restless leg syndrome

4. Which of the following statements best summarizes the current research on sleep patterns of emerging adults?

   a. Preference for being a morning person versus a night person changes with age due to increased levels of cortisol.

   b. Students who stayed up all night before exams thought they did worse than their peers who got a full night's sleep.

   c. The peak of eveningness comes at around age 20-21.

   d. Research showing delayed sleep phase syndrome and sleep debt is based mostly on emerging adults who work full time, rather than those who attend college, because their lives are so hectic.

5. Which of the following statements best summarizes the current research on college students' sleep patterns?

   a. Although they cause a number of ailments, sleep problems are relatively rare among college students.

   b. Preferences for morningness and eveningness change with age.

   c. Although incurring a sleep debt can result in changes in mood, it does not affect cognitive functioning.

   d. Most emerging adults tend toward morningness after their first year of college.

PHYSICAL DEVELOPMENT: Risk Behavior and Health Issues

When I was 21 years old, during the summer between my junior and senior years of college, I was hungry for adventure, so I decided to take a hitchhiking trip across the United States. I stuck out my thumb down the street from my house in Michigan and proceeded to hitchhike 8,000 miles, from Michigan west to Seattle, down to Los Angeles, then all the way home again via Las Vegas. It was an adventure, all right, and in most ways a good one. For decades afterward I kept in touch with an elderly couple I met on that trip, who were remarkably kind to me.

It strikes me today, looking back on it, that my hitchhiking trip was probably not a very good idea—to say the least—but the risks I took in emerging adulthood are not unique. Emerging adulthood is a time of life when many types of risk behavior reach their peak prevalence (Arnett, 2000, 2015). Unlike children and adolescents, emerging adults do not have their parents monitoring their behavior and setting rules for them, at least not nearly to the same extent. Unlike older adults, many emerging adults do not have the daily responsibilities of long-term commitments to a partner and children and to a long-term employer to restrain their behavior. Because emerging adulthood is the low point of **social control**—the restraints on behavior imposed by social obligations and relationships—individuals are more likely to take certain kinds of risks (Arnett, 2005; Hirschi, 2002). (Nobody could stop me from taking that hitchhiking trip, although my mom certainly tried.) Not all emerging adults take risks of course, but risk behavior of some kinds is more common at this time than at other age periods. Here we examine automobile driving and substance use.

social control

restraints on behavior imposed by social obligations and relationships

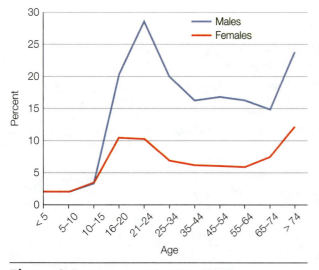

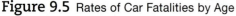

Figure 9.5 Rates of Car Fatalities by Age

Why are rates so high at ages 16–24?
SOURCE: Based on NHTSA (2014)

Injuries and Fatalities: Automobile Accidents

LO 9.5 **Explain why young drivers have the highest rates of crashes, and name the most effective approach to reducing those rates.**

Across developed countries, the most serious threat to the lives and health of adolescents and emerging adults comes from automobile driving (Patton et al., 2009). In the United States, young people ages 16 to 24 have the highest rates of automobile accidents, injuries, and fatalities of any age group (see **Figure 9.5**; National Highway Traffic Safety Administration [NHTSA], 2014). In other developed countries, a higher minimum driving age (usually 18) and less access to automobiles have made rates of accidents and fatalities among young people substantially lower than in the United States, but motor vehicle injuries are the leading cause of death during emerging adulthood in those countries as well (Pan et al., 2007; Twisk & Stacey, 2007).

What is responsible for these grim statistics? Is it young drivers' inexperience or their risky driving behavior? Inexperience certainly plays a large role. Rates of accidents and fatalities are extremely high in the early months of driving, but fall dramatically by 1 year after licensure (McNight & Peck, 2002; Valentine & Williams, 2013). Studies that have attempted to disentangle experience and age in young drivers have generally concluded that inexperience is partly responsible for young drivers' accidents and fatalities.

However, studies have also concluded that inexperience is not the only factor involved. Equally important is the way young people drive and the kinds of risks they take (Valentine & Williams, 2013). Compared to older drivers, young drivers (especially males) are more likely to drive at excessive speeds, follow other vehicles too closely, violate traffic signs and signals, take more risks in lane changing and passing other vehicles, allow too little time to merge, and fail to yield to pedestrians (Bina et al., 2006; Williams & Ferguson, 2002). They are also more likely than older drivers to report driving under the influence of alcohol. Drivers ages 21 to 24 involved in fatal accidents are more likely to have been intoxicated at the time of the accident than persons in any other age group (NHTSA, 2014). Nearly half of American college students report driving while intoxicated within the past year (Clapp et al., 2005; Glassman et al., 2010). Young people are also less likely than older drivers to wear seat belts, and in serious car crashes, occupants not wearing seat belts are twice as likely to be killed and three times as likely to be injured, compared to those wearing seat belts (NHTSA, 2011).

> 💬 I love to drive fast, but after awhile driving fast just wasn't doing it any more. So I started driving without the lights on [at night], going about ninety on country roads. I even got a friend to do it. We'd go cruising down country roads, turn off the lights, and just fly. It was incredible. We'd go as fast as we could, [and] at night, with no lights it feels like you're just flying."
>
> —Nick, age 23 (in Arnett, 1996, p. 79)

What else leads to crashes among young drivers? Young drivers are more likely than older drivers to believe their friends would approve of risky driving behavior such as speeding, closely following another vehicle, and passing another car in risky circumstances (Chen et al., 2007; U.S. Department of Transportation, 1995). Driver characteristics matter, too. Personality characteristics such as sensation seeking and aggressiveness promote risky driving and subsequent crashes, and these characteristics tend to be highest in young male drivers (Shope & Bingham, 2008).

What can be done to reduce the rates of automobile accidents and fatalities among young drivers? Parental involvement and monitoring of adolescents' driving behavior has been shown to be especially important in the early months of driving, and interventions to increase parental involvement can be effective (Simons-Morton et al., 2002; Simons-Morton et al., 2006; Simons-Morton, 2007; Simons-Morton et al., 2008). However, by far the most effective approach is a program of restricted driving privileges called **graduated driver licensing (GDL)**. GDL is a government program in which young people obtain driving privileges gradually, contingent on a safe driving record, rather than all at once. GDL programs allow young people to obtain driving experience under conditions that limit the likelihood of crashes by restricting the circumstances under which novices can drive (Foss, 2007; Williams et al., 2012).

graduated driver licensing (GDL)

government program in which young people obtain driving privileges gradually, contingent on a safe driving record, rather than all at once

Research Focus: Graduated Driver Licensing

Automobile accidents are a major source of injuries and fatalities worldwide, especially for young people, but in recent years effective public policies have been developed to reduce the number of deaths.

Graduated driver licensing (GDL) is a government program in which young people obtain driving privileges gradually, contingent on a safe driving record, rather than all at once. These programs typically include three stages. The learning license is the stage in which the young person obtains driving experience under the supervision of an experienced driver. For example, the GDL program in California requires young people to complete learning-license driver training of 50 hours under the supervision of a parent, of which 10 hours must take place at night.

The second stage is a period of restricted license driving. In this stage young drivers are allowed to drive unsupervised, but with tighter restrictions than those that apply to adults. The restrictions are based on research revealing the factors that are most likely to place young drivers at risk for crashes.

For example, in some states GDL programs include driving curfews, which prohibit young drivers from driving late at night except for a specific purpose such as going to and from work. There are also prohibitions against driving with teenage passengers when no adults are present, requirements for seat belt use, and a "zero tolerance" rule for alcohol use. Recently, most American states have also passed laws against any cell phone use for novice drivers, including both calling and texting.

In the restricted stage, any violations of these restrictions may result in a suspended license. It is only after the GDL period has passed—usually no more than one year—that a young person obtains a full license and has the same driving privileges as adults.

What have research studies shown regarding the effectiveness of GDL programs? Numerous studies in the past decade have shown GDL programs to be the most effective way to reduce automobile accidents among young drivers. One summary review (or meta-analysis) of 21 studies conducted by Jean Shope in 2007 concluded that GDL programs consistently

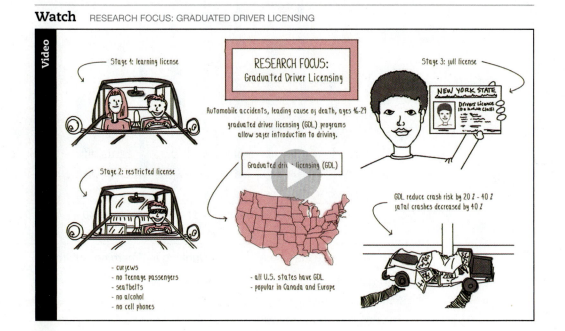

Watch RESEARCH FOCUS: GRADUATED DRIVER LICENSING

reduce young drivers' crash risk by 20% to 40%. Driving curfews in particular have been found to reduce young people's crash involvement dramatically. Fatal crashes among 16-year-old drivers in the United States decreased by 40% in the past decade, and this improvement is attributed mainly to GDL programs.

Legislators in many states have responded to this evidence by passing more of these programs. All 50 American states now have some kind of GDL program, a dramatic rise over the past 20 years. Graduated driver license programs have also been instituted in Canada and are becoming more common in European countries. Research indicates that these laws work in part by making it easier for parents to enforce restrictions on their adolescents' driving behavior. Across developed countries, automobile accidents remain the number-one cause of death in the teens and 20s, but effective GDL programs have dramatically reduced the number of deaths in recent decades.

Review Questions:

1. Which of the following is NOT one of the typical components of a GDL program?
   a. Driving curfew
   b. No more than 2 teenage passengers
   c. Mandatory seat belt use
   d. Zero tolerance for alcohol

2. Which of the following has been the consequence of widespread adoption of GDL programs?
   a. Injuries among teens have declined, but not fatalities
   b. Most teens have found ways to avoid the regulations
   c. Auto fatalities among 16-year-olds have sharply declined
   d. Girls' driving habits have changed but boys' have not

Substance Use and Abuse

LO 9.6 **Explain why rates of substance use peak in the early 20s and then decline.**

binge drinking

consuming five or more drinks in a row for men, four in a row for women

Many types of substance use reach their peak in emerging adulthood. The national Monitoring the Future study, which has followed up several American cohorts from high school through middle age, shows that substance use of all kinds rises through the late teens and peaks in the early 20s before declining in the late 20s. **Figure 9.6** shows the pattern for marijuana use and **binge drinking** (consuming five or more drinks in

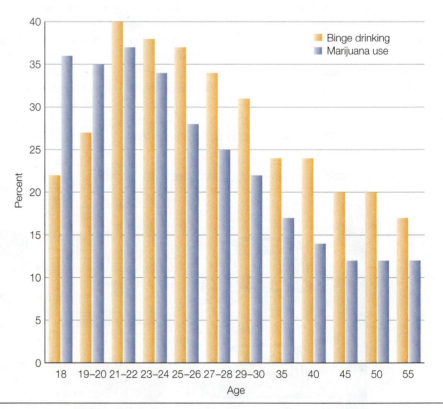

Figure 9.6 Marijuana Use and Binge Drinking in Emerging Adulthood

Rates of most kinds of substance use peak in the early 20s.

SOURCE: Based on Johnston et al. (2014)

a row for men, four in a row for women) (Bachman et al., 2008). Substance use, especially alcohol use, is higher among college students than among emerging adults who do not attend college (Core Institute, 2013). It also tends to be somewhat higher among men than among women.

Some evidence shows that substance use is also high among emerging adults in other developed countries. A study of Spanish adults reported that among 18- to 24-year-olds, rates of binge drinking in the past 30 days were 31% for men and 18% for women, far higher than in any other age group (Valencia-Martín et al., 2007). A peak in binge drinking in emerging adulthood has been found in other European countries as well (Kuntsche et al., 2004). Among female college students in Scotland, most regarded binge drinking as "harmless fun" (Guise & Gill, 2007). However, binge drinking and other types of substance use in emerging adulthood are related to a wide variety of negative consequences, from fatal car crashes to unintended pregnancy to criminal activity to physical fights, in both Europe and the United States (Jochman & Fromme, 2010; Plant et al., 2010).

What explains the higher rates of substance use among emerging adults? Wayne Osgood has proposed a useful answer to this question. Osgood (2009; Osgood et al., 2005; Osgood et al., 1996) borrows from a sociological theory that explains all deviance on the basis of *propensity* and *opportunity*. People behave deviantly when they have a combination of sufficient propensity (that is, motivation for behaving deviantly) along with sufficient opportunity. In his explanation, Osgood especially focuses on the high degree of opportunity that emerging adults have for engaging in substance use and other deviant behavior, as a result of spending a high proportion of their time in unstructured socializing.

Osgood uses the term **unstructured socializing** to include behavior such as riding around in a car for fun, going to parties, visiting friends informally, and going out with friends. Unstructured socializing is highest in the late teens and early 20s and, emerging adults who are highest in unstructured socializing are also highest in use of alcohol and marijuana (Osgood et al., 2005; Osgood et al., 1996). Rates of most types of substance use are especially high among emerging adults who are college students because they have so many opportunities for unstructured socializing.

Osgood and others have found that the relationship between unstructured socializing and deviance holds not only for substance use but for other types of risk behavior such as crime and dangerous driving (Haynie & Osgood, 2005; Maimon & Browning, 2010). Furthermore, the relationship between unstructured socializing and deviance holds for both genders, a variety of ethnic groups, and across a wide range of developed and developing countries. Research also shows that substance use and other types of risk behavior decline in the mid- to late 20s, as role transitions such as marriage, parenthood, and full-time work cause a sharp decline in unstructured socializing (Johnston et al., 2014; Patrick et al., 2011).

Unstructured socializing is often the setting for risk behaviors such as substance use.

unstructured socializing
socializing with friends without any specific goal or activity; includes behavior such as riding around in a car for fun, going to parties, visiting friends informally, and going out with friends

---

CRITICAL THINKING QUESTION

Besides unstructured socializing, what other factors might contribute to substance use in emerging adulthood?

Practice Quiz

1. Several interventions have been developed to reduce automobile injuries and fatalities for young drivers. Which of the following approaches has been shown to be most effective?
   a. Mandatory drivers' education
   b. Graduated driver licensing programs
   c. Increasing the minimum driving age
   d. Safe driving pledges

2. Across developed countries, the most serious threat to the lives and health of adolescents and emerging adults comes from _____.
   a. accidental overdoses
   b. automobile driving
   c. homicide
   d. suicide

3. Researchers who study young drivers have found that _____.
   a. as a result of campaigns to increase the use of seat belts, young people are now as likely as older drivers to wear seat belts
   b. rates of accidents and fatalities are low in the early months of driving, but increase steadily as new drivers gain confidence

   c. young drivers are no more likely to drive at excessive speeds compared to their older counterparts, but are more likely to report driving under the influence of alcohol
   d. young drivers are more likely than older drivers to believe their friends would approve of risky driving behavior, such as speeding

4. Data from the national Monitoring the Future study has shown that substance use of all kinds peaks in the _____.
   a. early teens
   b. mid-teens
   c. 20's
   d. 30's

5. The relation between unstructured socializing and deviance applies to _____.
   a. both genders
   b. substance abuse, but not other types of risk behavior
   c. only those in developed countries
   d. only those from European-American backgrounds

Summary: Physical Development

LO 9.1 Name the five developmental features distinctive to emerging adulthood.

The rise of emerging adulthood was due to four revolutions that began in the 1960s and '70s: the Technological Revolution, the Sexual Revolution, the Women's Movement, and the Youth Movement. Emerging adulthood is the age of identity explorations, the age of instability, the self-focused age, the age of feeling in-between, and the age of possibilities.

LO 9.2 Describe some of the ways emerging adulthood varies among cultures, with specific reference to European and Asian countries.

Emerging adulthood is longest in Europe, where education often lasts well into the 20s and the median age of entering marriage and parenthood is around 30. In Asian countries, emerging adults balance their identity explorations with a sense of obligation to family. They seek to become capable of supporting their parents, which is seen as a key marker of becoming an adult. Emerging adulthood is rare but growing in developing countries, especially in urban areas.

LO 9.3 Name the indicators that emerging adulthood is a period of peak physical functioning.

Emerging adulthood is a time of peak physical functioning as indicated in measures such as VO2 max and grip strength. However, many emerging adults feel less than optimally healthy and energetic due to lifestyle factors

such as poor nutrition and the strain of balancing school and work obligations.

LO 9.4 Summarize college students' sleep patterns and the main elements of sleep hygiene.

College students' sleep patterns are often irregular and disrupted, so that they accumulate a large sleep debt during the week and then try to compensate on weekends. Part of the problem is that they tend toward eveningness in their 20s, whereas the older adults who set emerging adults' work and class schedules tend toward morningness. Good sleep hygiene includes waking up at the same time each day, getting regular exercise, and limiting caffeine and alcohol consumption.

LO 9.5 Explain why young drivers have the highest rates of crashes, and name the most effective approach to reducing those rates.

Rates of automobile fatalities are high in adolescence and emerging adulthood due to a combination of inexperience and risky driving behaviors, but have been reduced substantially by GDL programs.

LO 9.6 Explain why rates of substance use peak in the early 20s and then decline.

Substance use rates peak in the early 20s primarily because this is when social control is lowest. The decline in substance use in the late 20s and beyond is primarily due to taking on new social roles such as spouse and parent, which provide new sources of social control.

Section 2 Cognitive Development

⌄ Learning Objectives

9.7 Describe how growing abilities of pragmatism allow emerging adults to become better at addressing real-life problems.

9.8 Outline the development of reflective judgment in Perry's theory.

9.9 Compare and contrast the tertiary education systems and college experiences in developed countries, and name the various long-term benefits of tertiary education.

9.10 Describe the transition from school to full-time work, and explain why unemployment rates among emerging adults are higher than for older adults.

COGNITIVE DEVELOPMENT:
Postformal Thinking

In Piaget's theory, formal operations is the culmination of cognitive development (see Chapter 8). Once formal operations is fully attained, by age 20 at the latest, cognitive maturation is complete. However, like many aspects of Piaget's theory of formal operations, this view has been altered by research. In fact, research indicates that cognitive development often continues in important ways during emerging adulthood. This research has inspired theories of cognitive development beyond formal operations, known as **postformal thinking** (Malott, 2011; Sinnott, 2014). Two of the most notable aspects of postformal thinking in emerging adulthood concern advances in pragmatism and reflective judgment.

Pragmatism

LO 9.7 **Describe how growing abilities of pragmatism allow emerging adults to become better at addressing real-life problems.**

Pragmatism involves adapting logical thinking to the practical constraints of real-life situations. Theories of postformal thought emphasizing pragmatism have been developed by several scholars (Basseches, 1984; Basseches, 1989; Labouvie-Vief, 1998; Labouvie-Vief, 2006; Labouvie-Vief & Diehl, 2002; Sinnott, 2014). The theories have in common an emphasis that the problems faced in normal adult life often contain complexities and inconsistencies that cannot be addressed with the logic of formal operations.

According to Gisela Labouvie-Vief (1982; 1990; 1998; 2006), cognitive development in emerging adulthood is distinguished from adolescent thinking by a greater recognition and incorporation of practical limitations to logical thinking. In this view, adolescents exaggerate the extent to which logical thinking will be effective in real life. In contrast, emerging adulthood brings a growing awareness of how social influences and factors specific to a given situation must be taken into account in approaching most of life's problems.

For example, in one study Labouvie-Vief (1990) presented adolescents and emerging adults with stories and asked them to predict what they thought would happen. One story described a man who was a heavy drinker, especially at parties. His wife had

postformal thinking

according to some theorists, the stage of cognitive development that follows formal operations and includes advances in pragmatism and reflective judgment

pragmatism

theory of cognitive development proposing that postformal thinking involves adapting logical thinking to the practical constraints of real-life situations

warned him that if he came home drunk one more time, she would leave him and take the children. Some time later he went to an office party and came home drunk. What would she do?

Labouvie-Vief found that adolescents tended to respond strictly in terms of the logic of formal operations: She said she would leave if he came home drunk once more, he came home drunk, therefore she will leave. In contrast, emerging adults considered many possible dimensions of the situation. Did he apologize and beg her not to leave? Did she really mean it when she said she would leave him? Has she considered the possible effects on the children? Rather than relying strictly on logic and assuming an outcome of definite wrong and right answers, the emerging adults tended to be postformal thinkers in the sense that they realized that the problems of real life often involve a great deal of complexity and ambiguity. However, Labouvie-Vief (2006) emphasizes that with postformal thinking, as with formal thinking, not everyone continues to move to higher levels of cognitive complexity, and many people continue to apply earlier, more concrete thinking in emerging adulthood and beyond.

A similar theory of cognitive development in emerging adulthood has been presented by Michael Basseches (1984; 1989). Like Labouvie-Vief, Basseches (1984) views cognitive development in emerging adulthood as involving a recognition that formal logic can rarely be applied to the problems most people face in their daily lives. **Dialectical thought** is Basseches's term for the kind of thinking that develops in emerging adulthood, involving a growing awareness that problems often have no clear solution and two opposing strategies or points of view may each have some merit (Basseches, 1984). For example, people may have to decide whether to quit a job they dislike without knowing whether their next job will be more satisfying.

Some cultures may promote dialectical thinking more than others. Chinese culture traditionally promotes dialectical thought, by advocating an approach to knowledge that strives to reconcile contradictions and combine opposing perspectives by seeking a middle ground (Peng & Nisbett, 1999). In contrast, the American approach tends to apply logic in a way that polarizes contradictory perspectives in an effort to determine which is correct.

To support this theory, one team of researchers conducted studies comparing Chinese and American college students (Peng & Nisbett, 1999). They found that the Chinese students were more likely than the Americans to prefer dialectical proverbs containing contradictions. In addition, when two apparently contradictory propositions were presented, the Americans tended to embrace one and reject the other, whereas the Chinese students were moderately accepting of both propositions, seeking to reconcile them.

dialectical thought

according to Basseches, a kind of thinking in emerging adulthood that involves a growing awareness that problems often have no clear solution and two opposing strategies or points of view may each have some merit

reflective judgment

capacity to evaluate the accuracy and logical coherence of evidence and arguments, theorized to develop during emerging adulthood

Reflective Judgment

LO 9.8 Outline the development of reflective judgment in Perry's theory.

Reflective judgment, another cognitive quality that has been found to develop in emerging adulthood, is the capacity to evaluate the accuracy and logical coherence of evidence and arguments. An influential theory of the development of reflective judgment in emerging adulthood was proposed by William Perry (1970; 1990), who based his theory on his studies of college students in their late teens and early 20s. According to Perry (1970; 1999), adolescents and first-year college students tend to engage in *dualistic thinking*, which means they often see situations and issues in polarized terms—an act is either right or wrong, with no in-between; a statement is either true or false, regardless of the nuances or the situation to which it is being applied. In this sense, they lack reflective judgment. However, reflective judgment begins to develop for most people around age 20. First a stage of *multiple thinking* begins, in which young people come to believe that there are two or more legitimate views of every issue, and that it can be difficult to justify one position as the only true or accurate one. In this stage people tend to value all points of view equally, even to the extent of asserting that it is impossible to make any judgments about whether one point of view is more valid than another.

Next, according to Perry, multiple thinking develops into *relativism*. Like people in the stage of multiple thinking, relativists are able to recognize the legitimacy of competing points of view. However, rather than denying that one view could be more persuasive than another, relativists attempt to evaluate the merits of competing views. Finally, by the end of their college years, many young people reach a stage of *commitment*, in which they commit themselves to a worldview they believe to be the most valid, while being open to reevaluating their views if new evidence is presented to them.

Research on reflective judgment indicates that significant gains may take place in emerging adulthood (King & Kitchener, 2015; Kitchener & King, 2006; Pascarella & Terenzini, 1991). However, the gains that take place in emerging adulthood appear to be due more to education than to maturation—that is, people who pursue a college education during emerging adulthood show greater advances in reflective judgment than people who do not. Also, Perry and his colleagues acknowledged that the development of reflective judgment is likely to be more common in a culture that values pluralism and whose educational system promotes tolerance of diverse points of view (Perry, 1970; Perry, 1999). However, thus far little cross-cultural research has taken place on reflective judgment.

Practice Quiz   ANSWERS AVAILABLE IN ANSWER KEY.

1. Two of the most notable aspects of _____ in emerging adulthood concern advances in pragmatism and reflective judgment.
   a. concrete thought
   b. postformal thought
   c. hypothetical and deductive reasoning
   d. metacognition

2. According to Labouvie-Vief, how would an adolescent who is in formal operations respond to the following scenario? "A man who was a heavy drinker, especially at parties, was warned by his wife that if he came home drunk one more time, she would leave him and take the children. Sometime later he went to an office party and came home drunk. What will she do?"
   a. "Did he apologize and beg her not to leave? Did she really mean it when she said she would leave him?"
   b. "She said she would leave if he came home drunk once more, he came home drunk, therefore she will leave."
   c. "Does she have some place to go?"
   d. "Does she really want to leave? It was most likely just a threat."

3. Bianca, a third-year college student, has developed a type of thinking that would be characterized as relativism. This means that she _____.

a. is able to perform mental operations on tangible problems, but lacks abstract thought
b. is able to understand the laws of relativity
c. is able to recognize the legitimacy of competing points of view
d. has meta-cognitive awareness

4. According to Perry, adolescents tend to engage in _____: an act is either right or wrong, with no in-between; a statement is either true or false, regardless of the nuances of the situation.
   a. concrete thinking
   b. relative hypothesis testing
   c. dualistic thinking
   d. rigid thinking

5. According to Perry, reflective judgment _____.
   a. refers to a type of dualistic thinking
   b. is more common when the educational system promotes tolerance of diverse points of view
   c. is less likely to develop in cultures that value pluralism
   d. is more characteristic of first-year college students than those in their senior year because first-year college students are more open to new ideas

COGNITIVE DEVELOPMENT:
Education and Work

As mentioned at the outset of the chapter, one of the changes of recent decades that has led to the development of a new life stage of emerging adulthood is increasing participation in higher education.

Tertiary Education: College, University, and Training Programs

LO 9.9 Compare and contrast the tertiary education systems and college experiences in developed countries and name the various long-term benefits of tertiary education.

As **Map 9.1** shows, a majority of emerging adults across a wide range of developed countries now obtain **tertiary education**, which includes any kind of education or training program beyond secondary school. This has been a remarkably rapid historical change. One hundred years ago, few young people—less than 10%—obtained tertiary education in any developed country; in fact, the majority did not even attend secondary school. Those who did attend college or university were mostly men. Historically, women were deemed to be cognitively inferior to men and therefore not worthy of higher education. A hundred years later, tertiary education is now a normative experience, and in most countries women are more likely than men to obtain it (Arnett, 2015).

Countries vary widely in how they structure tertiary education. Colleges in the United States, Canada, and Japan begin with 2 years of general education with no requirement of declaring a specialization or "major," which allows for the exploration of topics that may be unrelated to any occupational future. You may be a business major and nevertheless enjoy courses on literature or art or philosophy that lead you to explore a variety of ideas about what it means to be human. You may be a psychology major and yet find it engaging to explore ideas in courses on astronomy or chemistry.

Tertiary education is perhaps most relaxed and undemanding in Japan. You may find this surprising, because, as we have seen in Chapter 8, Japanese secondary

tertiary education

education or training beyond secondary school

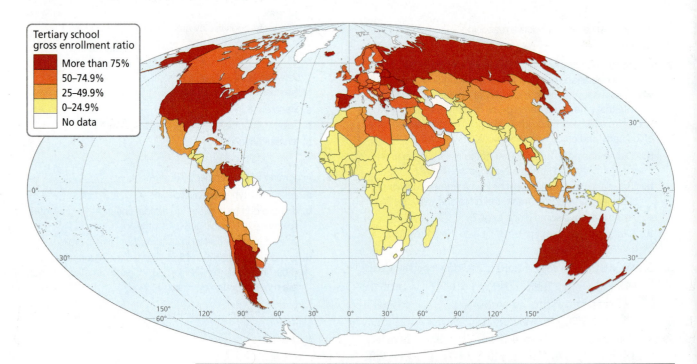

Map 9.1 Worldwide Enrollment in Tertiary Education

Which countries have the highest and lowest enrollment rates for higher education? How do these rates compare to the enrollment rates for secondary school (as shown in Map 8.1)? What economic and cultural factors might explain these variations?

SOURCE: Based on UNESCO (2013)

schools are exceptionally demanding and competition to get into the best universities is fierce (Fackler, 2007). Beyond college and university, the Japanese workplace is notoriously demanding as well, requiring long hours and mandatory after-hours socializing. For the Japanese, their time of leisure and fun comes during their college years. Once they enter college, grades matter little and standards for performance are relaxed. Instead, they have "four years of university-sanctioned leisure to think and explore" (Rohlen, 1983, p. 168; Fackler, 2007). Japanese college students spend a great deal of time walking around the city and hanging out together. Average homework time for Japanese college students is half the homework time of middle school or high school students (Takahashi & Takeuchi, 2006). For most Japanese, this brief period in emerging adulthood is the only time in their lives, from childhood until retirement, that they are allowed to enjoy extensive hours of leisure.

How is the European university system different from the American system? Cambridge University students in England are pictured here.

In Europe, the tertiary education system is structured quite differently than in the United States, Canada, and Japan. Rather than beginning with 2 years of general education, European students study in only one topic area from the time they enter university. Traditionally, university education in Europe often lasted 6 or more years because it culminated in a degree that was similar to American advanced degrees (master's or doctoral degree). However, the European system has changed recently to match the American system, with separate bachelor's, master's, and doctoral degrees. This was done to shorten the time European emerging adults spend in university, and to promote the development of coordinated programs between European and American universities. It also reflects the growing globalization of education.

For most young Americans, tertiary education takes longer now than it did two or three decades ago. Currently, it takes an average of 6 years for students to obtain a "4-year" degree. Furthermore, only 57% of students who enter a 4-year college or university have graduated 6 years later (National Center for Education Statistics, 2013).

A number of factors explain why it takes students longer to graduate and nearly half never graduate at all. Some students prefer to extend their college years to switch majors, add a minor field of study, or take advantage of internship programs or study-abroad programs. However, financial concerns are the main reason that a 4-year degree is so elusive for many emerging adults (Arnett & Schwab, 2012). Tuition rates have increased to a shocking extent and were over *four times higher* (even taking into account inflation) in 2013 than they were in 1982 in both public and private colleges and universities (NCES, 2014). Financial aid has also shifted markedly from grants to loans, which has led many students to work long hours while attending college in order to avoid accruing excessive debt before they graduate. African Americans especially struggle to fund their college educations, as **Figure 9.7** illustrates, and lack of money is one of the key reasons why they are less likely to obtain a college degree than Whites or Asian Americans are (McDonough & Calderone, 2006).

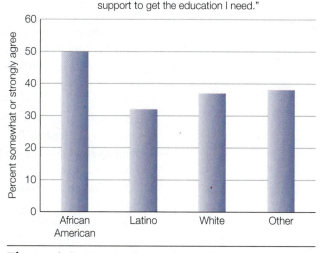

Figure 9.7 Ethnicity and College Affordability
SOURCE: Based on Arnett & Schwab (2012).

Cultural Focus: Post-Secondary Education Across Cultures

Tertiary education is becoming increasingly important around the world, as manufacturing becomes more mechanized and the new jobs created are mostly in areas such as health, education, and business, which require young people to gain knowledge and skills in these areas. In this video, emerging adults from various countries discuss their thoughts on higher education.

Watch POST-SECONDARY EDUCATION ACROSS CULTURES

Review Question:

Compare and contrast at least two of the individuals interviewed in this video regarding their views on higher education.

Is tertiary education worth the time and money it requires? It is certainly a substantial investment. Participation in tertiary education requires a great deal of money per year, paid mainly by emerging adults and their parents in the United States, and mainly by the government in other developed countries. Furthermore, the years in which emerging adults are focused on obtaining tertiary education are also years when most of them are not contributing to full-time economic activity. Not only are governments paying much or all of the costs of financing emerging adults' tertiary education, they are also losing the economic activity and tax revenue emerging adults would be contributing if their time and energy were devoted to working full time.

Nevertheless, the benefits of tertiary education are great. For societies, an educated population is a key to economic growth in a world economy that is increasingly based on information, technology, and services. This is why countries are willing to make such a large investment in the tertiary education of their emerging adults. For emerging adults themselves, the benefits are also clear. Emerging adults who obtain tertiary education tend to have considerably higher earnings, occupational status, and career attainment over the long run, compared to those who do not attend college (NCES, 2011; Pascarella, 2005; Pascarella, 2006; Schneider & Stevenson, 1999). Over a lifetime of working, Americans with a college degree or more make far more than those who only obtain a high school education or less, as **Figure 9.8** shows (Pew Research Center, 2014).

Tertiary education has multiple benefits in addition to increased earnings. Ernest Pascarella and Patrick Terenzini (1991; Pascarella, 2005; Pascarella, 2006) have conducted research in the United States on this topic for many years. They find a variety of intellectual benefits from attending college, in areas such as general verbal and quantitative

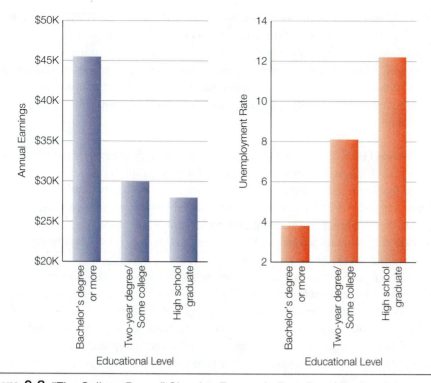

Figure 9.8 "The College Bonus" Showing Economic Benefits of Tertiary Education
SOURCE: Based on Pew Research Center (2014).

skills, oral and written communication skills, and critical thinking. These benefits hold up even after taking into account factors such as age, gender, precollege abilities, and family social class background. Pascarella and Terenzini also find that in the course of the college years students place less emphasis on college as a way to a better job and more emphasis on learning for the sake of enhancing their intellectual and personal growth.

In addition to the academic benefits, Pascarella and Terenzini describe a long list of nonacademic benefits. In the course of the college years, students develop clearer aesthetic and intellectual values. They gain a more distinct identity and become more confident socially. They become less dogmatic, less authoritarian, and less ethnocentric in their political and social views. Their self-concepts and psychological well-being improve. As with the academic benefits, these nonacademic benefits hold up even after taking into account characteristics such as age, gender, and family social class background.

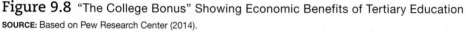

CRITICAL THINKING QUESTION

How does the way that a country structures its tertiary education system reflect its cultural values, if at all?

Finding Adult Work

LO 9.10 **Describe the transition from school to full-time work, and explain why unemployment rates among emerging adults are higher than for older adults.**

As we have seen in Chapter 8, some adolescents in developed countries work part time, but few of them see their part-time jobs as the beginning of the kind of work they expect to be doing as adults. The kinds of work adolescents do—waiting tables, washing dishes, mowing lawns, sales clerking, and the like—are generally viewed as temporary and transient, not as forming the basis of a long-term career (Mortimer, 2004; Mortimer, 2013). Most emerging adults, in contrast, are looking for a job that will turn into a career, something that will not only bring in a paycheck but provide personal fulfillment (Arnett, 2015; Taylor, 2005).

Work in emerging adulthood focuses on identity questions: What do I really want to *do*? What am I best at? What do I enjoy the most? How do my abilities and desires fit in with the kinds of opportunities that are available to me? In asking themselves what kind of work they want to do, emerging adults are also asking themselves what kind of person they are. In the course of emerging adulthood, as they try out various jobs, they begin to answer their identity questions, and they develop a better sense of what work suits them best.

THE TRANSITION TO WORK What career did you imagine for yourself when you were 15 years old? At 15 I thought I would probably go into law, then politics. I never imagined that I would become a psychologist and a writer. I knew nothing of psychology until my first year of college, and nothing about developmental psychology (my field) until after I graduated. I worked as a guitar player and singer for 2 years after college as I tried to decide what to do next, until I decided on developmental psychology for graduate school and set off on the path I am still on today.

Many adolescents have an idea, in high school, of what kind of career they want to go into (Schneider & Stevenson, 1999). Often that idea dissolves in the course of emerging adulthood, as they develop a clearer identity and discover that their high school aspiration does not align with it. In place of their high school notions many emerging adults seek *identity-based work*, something they enjoy and really want to do (Arnett, 2015; Vaughan, 2005). Watch the video *Looking for Identity-Based Work* for more information.

Watch LOOKING FOR IDENTITY-BASED WORK

For most American emerging adults the road to a stable, long-term job is long, with many brief, low-paying, dreary jobs along the way. The average American holds eight different jobs between the ages of 18 and 30 (U.S. Department of Labor, 2012).

Some emerging adults engage in systematic exploration as they look for a career path that they wish to settle into for the long term. They think about what they want to do, they try a job or a college major in that area to see if the fit is right, and if it is not they try another path until they find something they like better. But for many others, *exploration* is a bit too lofty a word to describe their work history during their late teens and early 20s. Often it is not nearly as systematic, organized, and focused as "exploration" implies. *Meandering* might be a more accurate word, or maybe *drifting* or even *floundering* (Hamilton & Hamilton, 2005). Many emerging adults express a sense that they did not really choose their current job, they just one day found themselves in it. In my interviews with emerging adults, "I just fell into it" is a frequently used phrase when they describe how they found their current job (Arnett, 2015). Yet even the meandering process of trying various jobs often serves the function of helping emerging adults sort out what kind of work they want to do. When you are in a dead-end job, at least you find out what you do *not* want to do. And there is also the possibility that as you drift through various jobs you may happen to drift into one you enjoy, one that unexpectedly clicks.

Although at least half of young people in developed countries now obtain tertiary education in some form, a substantial proportion of emerging adults finish their education after secondary school and enter the workplace. What are the work prospects like for these emerging adults, and how successfully are they able to make the transition from school to the workplace?

For the most part, they struggle to find work that pays enough to live on, much less the identity-based work that is the ideal for many emerging adults. Because the economy in developed countries has shifted from manufacturing to information, technology, and services over the past half century, tertiary education is more important than ever in obtaining jobs that pay well. Those who lack the training, knowledge, and credentials conferred by tertiary education are at a great disadvantage in the modern economy. In the last half of the 20th century, emerging adults with no tertiary education were "in a free-fall of declining earnings and diminished expectations" (Halpern, 1998, p. xii), and their prospects have not improved in the early years of the 21st century. Their rates of unemployment are about three times as high as for people who have obtained a college degree (OECD, 2014).

Is there anything that can be done about the dismal job prospects of emerging adults who have no tertiary education or training? Frank Levy (a scholar on education) and Richard Murnane (an economist) have researched the job skills needed by these emerging adults in order to succeed in the workplace (Levy & Murnane, 2004; Levy & Murnane, 2012; Murnane & Levy, 1997). Levy and Murnane conducted observations in a variety of factories and offices to gain information about the kinds of jobs now available to high school graduates and the kinds of skills required for those jobs. They focused not on routine jobs that require little skill and pay low wages but on the most promising new jobs available to high school graduates in the changing economy, jobs that offer the promise of career development and middle-class wages. They concluded that six basic skills are necessary for success at these new jobs:

1. reading at a 9th-grade level or higher;
2. doing math at a 9th-grade level or higher;
3. solving semistructured problems;
4. communicating orally and in writing;
5. using a computer for word processing and other tasks;
6. collaborating in diverse groups.

The good news is that all six of what Levy and Murnane call the *new basic skills* could be taught to adolescents by the time they leave high school. The bad news is that many American adolescents currently graduate from high school without learning them adequately. Levy and Murnane focused on reading and math skills because those are the skills on which the most data are available. They concluded that the data reveal a distressing picture: close to half of all 17-year-olds cannot read or do math at the level needed to succeed at the new jobs. The half who do have these skills are also the half who are most likely to go to college rather than seeking full-time work after high school. More recently, Levy and Murnane (2012) focused on the growing importance of computer skills, again concluding that high schools are failing to provide adolescents with the knowledge they need to succeed in the new economy.

Today, high-paying manufacturing jobs are scarce in developed countries.

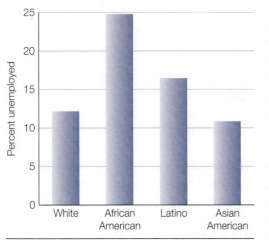

Figure 9.9 U.S. Unemployment Rates for Emerging Adults (Ages 16–24)

What explains the differences among ethnic groups?

SOURCE: Based on Bureau of Labor Statistics (2014)

unemployment

work status of adults who are not in school, are not working, and are looking for a job

Unemployment rates in emerging adulthood are especially high among African Americans and Latinos. Here, young African Americans seek opportunities at a job fair.

Of course, this does not mean that the current situation cannot be changed. There is certainly no reason that high schools could not be expected to require that students master the new basic skills by the time they graduate. The results of Levy and Murnane's research suggest that it may be wise for administrators of high schools and job-training programs to revise their curricula to fit the requirements of the new information- and technology-based economy.

UNEMPLOYMENT Although most young people in developed countries are able to find a job once they leave high school or college, this is not true for all of them. In both Europe and the United States, the unemployment rate for emerging adults is consistently *twice as high* as for adults beyond age 25 (OECD, 2014). In both Europe and the United States, unemployment has been found to be associated with higher risk for depression, especially for emerging adults who lack strong parental support (Bjarnason & Sigurdardottir, 2003; Hämäläinen et al., 2005; Mossakowski, 2009).

To say that someone is unemployed does not just mean that the person does not have a job. A large proportion of young people in their late teens and early 20s are attending high school or college, but they are not classified as unemployed because school is considered to be the focus of their efforts, not work. People whose time is mainly devoted to caring for their own children also would not be classified as unemployed. **Unemployment** applies only to people who are not in school, are not working, and are looking for a job.

This status applies to a substantial proportion of young people in the United States. **Figure 9.9** shows the unemployment rates for young people in their late teens and early 20s. As you can see from the figure, unemployment is especially concentrated among Black and Latino emerging adults. Also, unemployment is extremely high among young people who drop out of high school. *Over half* of high school dropouts ages 18 to 21 are unemployed (NCES, 2014).

What explains the high rates of unemployment among minority groups? This was not always the case. Consider that in 1954, the teenage unemployment rate for Blacks was only slightly higher than for Whites—16.5% for Blacks, lower than it is today, and 12% for Whites (Quillian, 2003). To a large extent, the explanation for the change lies in shifting employment patterns in the American economy. Over the past several decades, as the economy has become more strongly focused on information and technology rather than manufacturing, the number of jobs available to unskilled workers has diminished sharply (Levy & Murnane, 2012). The days are gone in the United States when stable, high-paying jobs were plentiful in settings such as automobile factories and steel mills. Today, most of the new jobs, and certainly the best jobs, require people to have at least a minimal level of information skills such as basic math knowledge and the ability to use a computer.

Those skills come from education, and young African Americans and Latinos tend to obtain less education than young Whites or Asian Americans (Hamilton & Hamilton, 2006; NCES, 2014). Without educational credentials, gaining access to jobs in the new economy is difficult.

Practice Quiz   ANSWERS AVAILABLE IN ANSWER KEY.

1. You are talking to a person from another country. She told you that when she was admitted to university in her native country, she studied in only one topic area, rather than taking courses in various disciplines as part of general education requirements. On which of the following continents is she most likely to have attended college?

a. South America
b. Europe
c. Asia
d. Africa

2. Why does it take much longer to complete an undergraduate degree now compared to a few decades ago?

a. Students are not academically prepared for university training and must take remedial coursework.
b. Financial concerns require that students also work, which increases the time to complete the degree.
c. Students lack focus and change their majors quite a few times, which adds time on to their academic programs.
d. More students transfer to different institutions that do not accept all of their previous credits.

3. Assuming they are all serious students, which of the following individuals would be most likely to describe their college

or university experience as a relatively relaxed time to think and explore?

a. A student from Canada
b. A student from England
c. A student from Japan
d. A student from China

4. Which of the following is one of the largest factors explaining the high rates of unemployment among minority groups?

a. A resurgence of growth in manufacturing jobs
b. Minority group members' unwillingness to look for jobs
c. Shifting employment patterns in the American economy
d. A strong allegiance to family that results in either not applying for the job or leaving it when it requires relocating

5. Which of the following individuals is most likely to be unemployed in emerging adulthood?

a. Simon, an African American
b. Liam, a European American
c. Jon, an Asian American
d. As a result of the struggling economy, rates of unemployment are equally high among all ethnic groups.

Summary: Cognitive Development

LO 9.7   Describe how growing abilities of pragmatism allow emerging adults to become better at addressing real-life problems.

In contrast to the thinking of formal operations, which emphasizes scientific approaches to problems, pragmatism recognizes that the problems people confront in their daily lives are often complex and ambiguous and do not submit to definite answers.

LO 9.8   Outline the development of reflective judgment in Perry's theory.

William Perry found that college students' reflective judgment develops through stages of dualistic thinking, multiple thinking, relativism, and commitment, but other research indicates this pattern is due more to education than to maturation.

LO 9.9   Compare and contrast the tertiary education systems and college experiences in developed countries, and name the various long-term benefits of tertiary education.

Participation in tertiary education has risen dramatically in recent decades. A majority of emerging adults now obtain tertiary education in most developed countries,

with women consistently attaining higher educational achievement than men. Countries vary greatly in their tertiary education systems, with Europe the most structured and Japan the least.

Tertiary education has been shown to have many benefits, occupationally and financially, as well as personally. Benefits include greater earnings and better verbal and quantitative skills, as well as nonacademic benefits such as developing a clearer identity and more definite values.

LO 9.10   Describe the transition from school to full-time work, and explain why unemployment rates among emerging adults are higher than for older adults.

Emerging adults tend to seek identity-based work that fits their abilities and interests. In developed countries the best jobs require tertiary education, and emerging adults often struggle in the job market because they lack basic skills as well as educational credentials. Across developed countries, unemployment peaks in emerging adulthood. In the United States, unemployment is especially high among African Americans and Latinos, because they are more likely to lack educational credentials.

Section 3 Emotional and Social Development

⌄ Learning Objectives

9.11 Describe the course of self-esteem from adolescence through emerging adulthood and explain the reasons for this pattern.

9.12 Describe the various forms identity development can take in emerging adulthood, and consider patterns of cultural and ethnic identity.

9.13 Summarize the changes in American gender beliefs in recent decades and include findings from research on gender stereotypes among college students.

9.14 Summarize Smith and Snell's description of the religious beliefs and practices of American emerging adults.

9.15 Explain why emerging adults have often been at the forefront of political movements, and contrast this with their involvement in conventional politics.

9.16 Describe patterns of home-leaving in the United States and Europe and how this transition influences relations with parents.

9.17 Describe the role of intimacy in emerging adults' friendships and the most common activities of emerging adult friends.

9.18 Explain how romantic relationships and sexual behavior change during emerging adulthood.

9.19 Explain how emerging adults use the Internet and mobile phones to maintain social contacts.

EMOTIONAL AND SOCIAL DEVELOPMENT: Emotional and Self-Development

Emerging adulthood is a period when emotional and self-development turn more favorable in a variety of ways. After declining in adolescence, self-esteem now rises steadily. Identity development advances and reaches fruition in some ways, as young people move toward making enduring choices in love and work. Gender issues are confronted in new ways as emerging adults enter the workplace and encounter occupational gender expectations and sometimes gender stereotypes.

Self-Esteem

LO 9.11 **Describe the course of self-esteem from adolescence through emerging adulthood and explain the reasons for this pattern.**

Think for a moment: how is your self-esteem today different from your self-esteem as an adolescent? As described in the previous chapter, self-esteem often declines during early adolescence. However, for most people it rises during emerging adulthood (Galambos et al., 2006; McLean & Breen, 2015). **Figure 9.10** shows this pattern.

There are a number of reasons why self-esteem increases during emerging adulthood. Physical appearance is important to adolescents' self-esteem, but by emerging adulthood most people have passed through the awkward changes of puberty and may be more comfortable with how they look. Also, feeling accepted and approved by parents contributes to self-esteem, and from adolescence to emerging adulthood, relationships with parents generally improve, while conflict diminishes (Arnett, 2015; Fingerman & Yahurin, 2015; Galambos et al., 2006). Peers and friends are also important to self-esteem, and entering emerging adulthood means leaving the social pressure cooker of secondary school, where peer evaluations are a part of daily life and can be harsh (Gavin & Furman, 1989; Pascoe, 2007).

Also, reaching emerging adulthood usually means having more control over the social contexts of everyday life, which makes it possible for emerging adults to seek out the contexts they prefer and avoid the contexts they find disagreeable, in a way that adolescents cannot. For example, adolescents who dislike school and do poorly have little choice but to attend school, where poor grades may repeatedly undermine their self-esteem. However, emerging adults can leave school and instead engage in full-time work that they may find more gratifying and enjoyable, thus enhancing their self-esteem.

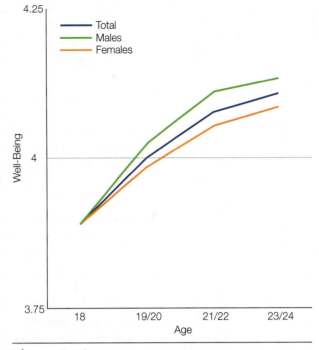

Figure 9.10 Changes in Self-Esteem

Why does self-esteem rise during the emerging adult years?
SOURCE: Monitoring the Future (2003)

Identity Development

LO 9.12 Describe the various forms identity development can take in emerging adulthood, and consider patterns of cultural and ethnic identity.

As noted earlier in the chapter, a key feature of emerging adulthood is that it is the age of identity explorations. Emerging adulthood is when most people move toward making definite, long-term choices in love and work. Making these choices often involves thinking about who you are, where you want your life to go, what you believe in, and how your life fits into the world around you. During this time, explorations are made into various aspects of identity, especially love and work, culminating in commitments that set the foundation for adult life.

It is now generally accepted among scholars that emerging adulthood is the life stage when many of the most important steps in identity development take place (Cote, 2006; Lyckyx, 2008; Schacter, 2005; Schwartz, 2015). However, for most of the history of research on identity, the focus was on adolescence. This focus was due mainly to Erik Erikson's influence, as I will explain shortly, but it is also because adolescence was formerly the life stage when the main choices in love and work were made. We'll first consider Erikson's theory and traditional research on identity development in adolescence and then discuss the more recent turn to identity development in emerging adulthood.

ERIK ERIKSON'S THEORY In Erik Erikson's (1950) theory of development (refer back to Chapter 1), each stage of life has a central crisis, and in adolescence the crisis is **identity versus identity confusion**. The healthy path in adolescence involves establishing a clear and definite sense of who you are and how you fit into the world around you. The unhealthy alternative is identity confusion, which is a failure to form a stable and secure identity. Identity formation involves reflecting on what your traits, abilities,

identity versus identity confusion

in Erikson's theory, the crisis of adolescence, with two alternative paths, establishing a clear and definite identity, or experiencing identity confusion, which is a failure to form a stable and secure identity

and interests are, then sifting through the range of life choices available in your culture, trying out various possibilities, and ultimately making commitments. The key areas in which identity is formed are love, work, and ideology (beliefs and values) (Erikson, 1968). In Erikson's view, a failure to establish commitments in these areas by the end of adolescence reflects identity confusion.

There are three elements essential to developing an identity according to Erikson. First, adolescents assess their own abilities and interests. By this age, most people have a growing sense of what their strengths and weaknesses are and what they most and least enjoy doing. Second, adolescents reflect on the *identifications* they have accumulated in childhood (Erikson, 1968). Children *identify* with their parents and other loved ones as they grow up—that is, children love and admire them and want to be like them. Thus, adolescents create an identity in part by modeling themselves after parents, friends, and others they have loved in childhood, not simply by imitating them but by integrating parts of their loved ones' behavior and attitudes into their own personality. Third, adolescents assess the opportunities available to them in their society. Many dream of a fabulous career in sports, music, or entertainment (Scheider, 2009), yet there are relatively few opportunities for people to make a living in these areas. Sometimes opportunities are restricted due to discrimination. Until fairly recently, women were discouraged or even barred from professions such as medicine and law. Today, ethnic minorities in many societies find that the doors to many professions are barred to them. In every society, adolescents need to take into account not only what they would like to do but what adults will allow them to do.

Erikson's most influential interpreter has been James Marcia (Marcia, 1966; Marcia, 1980; Marcia, 1989; Marcia, 1999; Marcia, 2010; Marcia & Carpendale, 2004). Marcia constructed a measure called the Identity Status Interview that classified adolescents into one of four identity statuses: *diffusion, moratorium, foreclosure*, or *achievement*. This system of four categories, known as the **identity status model**, has also been used by scholars who have constructed questionnaires to investigate identity development rather than using Marcia's interview (e.g., Adams, 1999; Benson et al., 1992; Grotevant & Adams, 1984; Kroger, 2007).

As shown in **Table 9.1**, each of these classifications involves a different combination of exploration and commitment. Erikson (1968) used the term *identity crisis* to describe the process through which young people construct their identity, but Marcia and other current scholars prefer the term *exploration* (Kroger, 2007; Marcia & Carpendale, 2004; Waterman, 2007). "Crisis" implies that the process inherently involves anguish and struggle, whereas "exploration" implies a more positive investigation of possibilities.

Diffusion is an identity status that combines no exploration with no commitment. For adolescents in a state of identity diffusion, no commitments have been made among the choices available to them. Furthermore, no exploration is taking place. The person in this status is not seriously attempting to sort through potential choices and make enduring commitments.

Moratorium involves exploration but no commitment. This is a status of actively trying out different personal, occupational, and ideological possibilities. Different possibilities are being sifted through, with some being discarded and some selected, in order for adolescents to be able to determine which of the available possibilities are best suited to them.

Adolescents who are in the *foreclosure* status have not experimented with a range of possibilities but have nevertheless committed themselves to certain choices—commitment, but no exploration. This is often a result of their parents' strong influence. Marcia and most other scholars tend to see exploration as a necessary part of forming a healthy identity, and therefore see foreclosure as unhealthy. This is an issue we will discuss further shortly.

Finally, the classification that combines exploration and commitment is *achievement*. Identity achievement is the status of young people

identity status model

model for researching Erikson's theory of identity development, classifying identity development into four categories: diffusion, foreclosure, moratorium, or achievement

Table 9.1 The Four Identity Statuses

		Commitment	
		Yes	No
Exploration	**Yes**	Achievement	Moratorium
	No	Foreclosure	Diffusion

who have made definite personal, occupational, and ideological choices. By definition, identity achievement is preceded by a period of identity moratorium in which exploration takes place. If commitment takes place without exploration, it is considered identity foreclosure rather than identity achievement.

Although Erikson designated adolescence as the stage of the identity crisis, and research using Marcia's model has mostly focused on adolescence, studies indicate that it takes longer than scholars had expected to reach identity achievement, and in fact for most young people this status is reached—if at all—in emerging adulthood or beyond rather than in adolescence. Studies that have compared adolescents from ages 12 through 18 have found that although the proportion of adolescents in the diffusion category decreases with age and the proportion of adolescents in the achievement category increases, even by early emerging adulthood less than half are classified as having reached identity achievement (van Hoof, 1999; Kroger, 2003; Meeus et al., 1999; Waterman, 1999).

Studies of college students find that progress toward identity achievement also takes place during the college years, but mainly in the specific area of occupational identity rather than for identity more generally (Waterman, 1992). Some studies indicate that identity achievement may come faster for emerging adults who do not attend college, perhaps because the college environment tends to be a place where young people's ideas about themselves are challenged and they are encouraged to question previously held ideas (Lytle et al., 1997; Munro & Adams, 1997). However, for non-college emerging adults as well, the majority have not reached identity achievement by age 21 (Kroger et al., 2010; Waterman, 1999).

Even 50 years ago, Erikson observed that identity formation was taking longer and longer for young people in developed countries. He commented on the "prolonged adolescence" that was becoming increasingly common in such countries and how this was leading to a prolonged period of identity formation, "during which the young adult through free role experimentation may find a niche in some section of his society" (1968, p. 156). Considering the changes that have taken place since he made this observation in the 1960s, including much later ages of marriage and parenthood and longer education, Erikson's observation applies to far more young people today than it did then (Schwartz et al., 2014). Indeed, the conception of emerging adulthood as a distinct period of life is based to a considerable extent on the fact that, over recent decades, the late teens and early 20s have become a period of "free role experimentation" for an increasing proportion of young people (Arnett, 2000; Arnett, 2004; Arnett, 2015). The achievement of an adult identity comes later, compared with earlier generations, as many emerging adults use the years of their late teens and 20s for identity explorations in love, work, and ideology.

In most cultures through history, young people have been expected to believe what their parents believe, not to decide on their own beliefs. Here, a young Israeli man prays.

CULTURE AND IDENTITY Most of the research inspired by Erikson's theory has taken place among White middle-class adolescents in the United States, Canada, and Europe (Schwartz et al., 2014). What can we say about identity development among adolescents and emerging adults in other cultures? One observation that can be made is that although Erikson sought to ground his theory in historical and cultural context (Erikson, 1950; Erikson, 1968; Kroger, 2002), his discussion of identity development nevertheless assumes an independent self that is allowed to make free choices in love, work, and ideology. The focus of Erikson's identity theory is on how young people develop an understanding of themselves as unique individuals. However, as we have discussed in earlier chapters, this conception of the self is distinctively Western and is historically recent (Markus & Kitiyama, 1991; Shweder et al., 2006;). In most cultures, until recently, the self has been understood as *interdependent*, defined in relation to others, rather than as independent. Even today, Erikson's assertions of the prominence of identity issues in adolescence may apply more to modern Western adolescents than to adolescents in other cultures. For example, explorations in love are clearly limited or even nonexistent in cultures where dating is not allowed and marriages are either arranged by parents or strongly influenced by them. Explorations in work are limited in cultures where the economy is simple and offers only a limited range of choices.

Limitations on explorations in both love and work tend to be narrower for girls in developing countries than they are for boys. With regard to love, some degree of sexual experimentation is encouraged for adolescent boys in most cultures, but for girls sexual experimentation is more likely to be restricted or forbidden (Schlegel, 2010). With regard to work, in most traditional cultures today and for most of human history in every culture, adolescent girls have been designated by their cultures for the roles of wife and mother, and these were essentially the only choices open to them.

In terms of ideology, too, a psychosocial moratorium has been the exception in human cultures rather than the standard. In most cultures, young people have been expected to grow up to believe what adults teach them to believe, without questioning it. It is only in recent history, and mainly in Western developed countries, that these expectations have changed, and that it has come to be seen as desirable for adolescents and emerging adults to think for themselves, decide on their own beliefs, and make their life choices independently (Bellah et al., 1985; Arnett, 1998).

Another identity issue that has important cultural dimensions is how globalization influences identity, especially for adolescents and emerging adults (Arnett, 2002; Arnett, 2011). Because of globalization, more young people around the world now develop a **bicultural identity**, with one part of their identity rooted in their local culture, while another part stems from an awareness of their relation to the global culture. For example, India has a growing, vigorous high-tech economic sector, led largely by young people. However, even the better-educated young people, who have become full-fledged members of the global economy, still mostly prefer to have an arranged marriage, in accordance with Indian tradition (Chaudhary & Sharma, 2012). They also generally expect to care for their parents in old age, again in accordance with Indian tradition. Thus they have one identity for participating in the global economy and succeeding in the fast-paced world of high technology, and another identity, rooted in Indian tradition, that they maintain with respect to their families and their personal lives.

ETHNIC IDENTITY In addition to the complex identity issues that arise as a consequence of globalization, many people experience the challenge of growing up as a member of an ethnic minority group. In fact, more people than ever experience this challenge, as worldwide immigration has climbed to unprecedented levels in recent decades (Berry et al., 2006; Phinney, 2006).

Like other identity issues, issues of ethnic identity come to the forefront in adolescence and continue to grow in importance into emerging adulthood (Pahl & Way, 2006; Syed & Mitchell, 2015). As part of their growing cognitive capacity for self-reflection, adolescents and emerging adults who are members of ethnic minorities are likely to have a sharpened awareness of what it means for them to be a member of their minority group. Bicultural identities such as *African American, Chinese Canadian*, and *Turkish Dutch* take on a new meaning, as adolescents and emerging adults can now think about what these terms mean and how the term for their ethnic group applies to themselves. Also, as a consequence of their growing capacity to think about what others think about them, adolescents and emerging adults become more acutely aware of the prejudices and stereotypes about their ethnic group that others may hold.

For emerging adults, ethnic identity issues are likely to take on a greater prominence as they enter new social contexts such as college and the workplace, and as they meet a broader range of people from different ethnic backgrounds (Phinney, 2006). As children and adolescents they may have been mostly around people of their own ethnic

bicultural identity

identity with two distinct facets, for example one for the local culture and one for the global culture, or one within one's ethnic group and one for others group, but emerging adulthood is likely to take them into new contexts with greater ethnic diversity, sharpening their awareness of their ethnic identity (Syed & Azmitia, 2010). For example, when you entered your college environment it is likely that you came into contact with persons from a greater variety of ethnic backgrounds than you had known previously.

Because adolescents and emerging adults who are members of ethnic minorities have to confront ethnic identity issues, their identity development is likely to be more complex than for those who are part of the majority culture (Phinney, 2000, 2006; Syed & Mitchell, 2015). Consider, for example, identity development in the area of love. Love—along with dating and sex—is an area where cultural conflicts are especially likely to come up for adolescents and emerging adults who are members of ethnic minorities. For example, part of identity development in the American majority culture means trying out different possibilities in love by forming emotionally intimate relationships with different people and gaining sexual experience. However, this model is in sharp conflict with the values of certain American ethnic minority groups. In most Asian American groups, for example, recreational dating is disapproved and sexual experimentation before marriage is taboo—especially for females (Qin, 2009; Talbani & Hasanali, 2000). Young people in Asian American ethnic groups face a challenge in reconciling the values of their ethnic group on such issues with the values of the majority culture, to which they are inevitably exposed through school, the media, and peers.

How, then, does identity development take place for young people who are members of minority groups within Western societies? To what extent do they develop an identity that reflects the values of the majority culture, and to what extent do they retain the values of their minority group? One scholar who has done extensive work on these questions among American minorities is Jean Phinney (Phinney, 1990; Phinney, 2000; Phinney, 2006; Phinney, 2010; Phinney & Devich-Navarro, 1997). On the basis of her research, Phinney has concluded that young people who are members of minority groups have four different ways of responding to their awareness of their ethnicity (see **Table 9.2**).

Assimilation is the option that involves leaving behind the ways of one's ethnic group and adopting the values and way of life of the majority culture. This is the path that is reflected in the idea that a society is a "melting pot" that blends people of diverse origins into one national culture. *Marginality* involves rejecting one's culture of origin but also feeling rejected by the majority culture. Some young people may feel little identification with the culture of their parents and grandparents, nor do they feel accepted and integrated into the larger society. *Separation* is the approach that involves associating only with members of one's own ethnic group and rejecting the ways of the majority culture. *Biculturalism* involves developing a dual identity, one based in the ethnic group of origin and one based in the majority culture. Being bicultural means moving back and forth between the ethnic culture and the majority culture, and alternating identities as appropriate to the situation.

Table 9.2 Four Ethnic Identity Statuses

		Identification with Ethnic Group	
		High	**Low**
Identification with Majority Culture	**High**	Bicultural	Assimilated
	Low	Separated	Marginal

Examples:

Assimilation: "I don't really think of myself as Asian American, just as American."

Separation: "I am not part of two cultures. I am just Black."

Marginality: "When I'm with my Indian friends, I feel White, and when I'm with my White friends, I feel Indian. I don't really feel like I belong with either of them."

Biculturalism: "Being both Mexican and American means having the best of both worlds. You have different strengths you can draw from in different situations."

SOURCE: Based on Phinney & Devich-Navarro (1997)

Biculturalism means developing a dual identity, one for the ethnic culture and one for the majority culture.

Which of these identity statuses is most common among ethnic minorities? Although ethnic identity is potentially most prominent in emerging adulthood (Phinney, 2006), most research thus far has taken place on adolescents. The bicultural status is the most common status among Mexican Americans and Asian Americans, as well as among some European minority groups such as Turkish adolescents in the Netherlands (Neto, 2002; Rotheram-Borus, 1990; Phinney, Dupont, et al., 1994; Verkuyten, 2002). However, separation is the most common ethnic identity status among African American adolescents, and marginality is pervasive among Native American adolescents. Of course, each ethnic group is diverse and contains adolescents with a variety of different ethnic identity statuses. Adolescents tend to be more aware of their ethnic identity when they are in a context where they are in the minority. For example, in one study, Latino adolescents attending a predominately non-Latino school reported significantly higher levels of ethnic identity than adolescents in a predominately Latino or a balanced Latino/non-Latino school (Umaña-Taylor, 2005).

Is ethnic identity related to other aspects of development in adolescence and emerging adulthood? Some studies have found that adolescents who are bicultural or assimilated have higher self-esteem (e.g., Farver et al., 2002). Furthermore, several studies have found that having a strong ethnic identity is related to a variety of other favorable aspects of development, such as overall well-being, academic achievement, and lower rates of risk behavior (Giang & Wittig, 2006; St. Louis & Liem, 2005; Syed & Mitchell, 2015; Yasui et al., 2005;).

Gender Development: Cultural Beliefs and Stereotypes

LO 9.13 Summarize the changes in American gender beliefs in recent decades and include findings from research on gender stereotypes among college students.

Emerging adulthood is an important time for gender development, because this is the life stage when many people become involved full time in the workplace. Consequently, they may encounter more vividly during this stage their society's beliefs about gender in relation to occupational roles and aspirations.

What sort of cultural beliefs about gender exist for adolescents and emerging adults currently growing up in American society? The results of the General Social Survey (GSS), an annual national survey of American adults, show a clear trend toward more egalitarian gender attitudes in recent decades, as **Figure 9.11** shows (Cotter et al., 2009). Compared to 1977, American adults today are less likely to believe men are better politicians, less likely to see women as the ones who should take care of the home, more likely to believe working mothers can have warm relationships with their children, and less likely to believe preschoolers would suffer if mothers work. However, the results of the GSS also show that a considerable proportion of Americans—from about one fourth to over one third, depending on the question—continue to harbor beliefs about gender roles not unlike the ones we have seen in traditional cultures: Men should hold the power and be out in the world doing things, and women should focus on caring for children and running the household.

Given the differential gender socialization that people in American society experience in childhood and adolescence, it should not be surprising to find that by the time

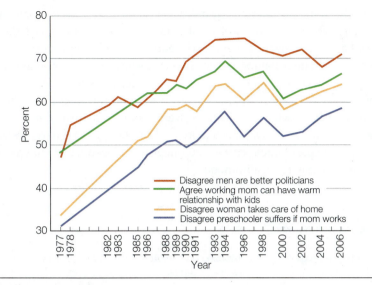

Figure 9.11 Change in American Gender Attitudes, 1977–2006

Over recent decades, views of gender roles have become less traditional.
SOURCE: General Social Survey (GSS), 1977–2006

they reach emerging adulthood, they have different expectations for males and females (Norona et al., 2015). Most research on gender expectations in adulthood has been conducted by social psychologists, and because social psychologists often use college undergraduates as their research participants, much of this research pertains to emerging adults' views of gender. Social psychologists have especially focused on gender stereotypes. A **stereotype** occurs when people believe others possess certain characteristics simply as a result of being a member of a particular group. Gender stereotypes, then, attribute certain characteristics to others on the basis of whether they are male or female (Kite et al., 2008).

One area of particular interest with regard to emerging adulthood is research on college students' gender stereotypes involving work. Generally, this research indicates that college students often evaluate women's work performance less favorably than men's. In one classic study, college women were asked to evaluate the quality of several articles supposedly written by professionals in a variety of fields (Goldberg, 1968). Some of the articles were in stereotypically female fields such as dietetics, some were in stereotypically male fields such as city planning, and some were in gender-neutral fields. There were two identical versions of each article, one supposedly written by, for example, "John McKay" and the other written by "Joan McKay." The results indicated that the women rated the articles more highly when they thought a man was the author. Even articles in the "female" fields were judged as better when written by a man. Other studies have found similar results with samples of both male and female college students (Cejka & Eagly, 1999; Paludi & Strayer, 1985). Recent studies have continued to find strong gender stereotypes related to work (Cabrera et al., 2009; Johnson et al., 2008; White & White, 2006). Although not all studies have found a tendency for men's work to be evaluated more favorably, when differences are found they tend to favor men.

One study reported that gender stereotypes can be especially harsh for persons who have high status in gender-incongruent occupations, for example a woman who has become head of an engineering department (Brescoll et al., 2010). College students were asked to read vignettes describing a leader's successful performance or mistakes in gender-congruent or gender-incongruent professions, then evaluate the leader's competence. Leaders who made mistakes in gender-incongruent professions were rated as lowest in competence.

stereotype

belief that others possess certain characteristics simply as a result of being a member of a particular group

Would you assume a female mechanic would be less competent than a male mechanic? Gender stereotypes related to work remain strong.

Gender-related evaluations may also depend on the age of the evaluator. One study compared males who were early adolescents, late adolescents, or college students (Lobel et al., 2004). Participants were given a description of either an average or outstanding male election candidate behaving gender-stereotypically or counter-stereotypically and were asked to indicate their personal election choice, to estimate the likelihood that others would choose each candidate, and to speculate how successful the candidate would be if he were elected. Adolescents were more likely than the emerging adult college students to favor the gender-stereotypical candidate. No differences were found between the two stages of adolescence. This suggests that gender stereotypes may wane from adolescence to emerging adulthood.

Practice Quiz   ANSWERS AVAILABLE IN ANSWER KEY.

1. What happens to self-esteem for most people during emerging adulthood?
   a. It remains at about the same level as it did in adolescence.
   b. It increases for females, but declines slightly for males.
   c. It increases.
   d. It declines gradually until rising again in middle adulthood.

2. According to Erikson's theory _____.
   a. identity develops in emerging adulthood
   b. failure to establish commitments in the key areas of identity results in identity confusion
   c. the search for identity is better described as exploration rather than crisis
   d. adolescents can be classified into one of four identity statuses based on an interview measure

3. Jacob, an only child, has been pressured by his father to take over the family car business. Reluctantly, Jacob has agreed to this because his father told him that he wanted to be able to pass on the fruits of his labor and Jacob doesn't think he can earn a better salary doing anything else. He has not explored his options, but has passively accepted the identity his father imposed on him. According to Marcia's model, Jacob would be described as _____.
   a. identity achieved
   b. diffused
   c. foreclosed
   d. in moratorium

4. Which of the following ethnic identity statuses is reflected in the idea of the American "melting pot?"
   a. Biculturalism
   b. Separation
   c. Assimilation
   d. Marginality

5. Shakira and Jerome are in an argument over childcare. Rather than put their two children in daycare, Jerome would like to be a stay-at-home father. Shakira thinks that because Jerome is a man, he will not be able to nurture and care for their two children as well as she would. Shakira is exhibiting concerns rooted in _____.
   a. gender stereotypes
   b. a separated identity status
   c. prejudice
   d. egocentrism

EMOTIONAL AND SOCIAL DEVELOPMENT: Cultural Beliefs

Children and adolescents learn the cultural beliefs distinctive to their culture, and by emerging adulthood they have developed a worldview composed of these beliefs. However, beliefs continue to develop during emerging adulthood and beyond. In emerging adulthood there are notable developments in religious and political beliefs and behavior.

Religious Development

LO 9.14 **Summarize Smith and Snell's description of the religious beliefs and practices of American emerging adults.**

A landmark study by Christian Smith and Patricia Snell went into greater depth and detail than previous studies on religious development among American emerging adults (Smith & Snell, 2010). The study included survey data on over 2,500 emerging adults (ages 18–23) in 37 states; 250 participants were interviewed. Most of the emerging adults in the study had been included in Smith's earlier study of adolescents' religious development 5 years earlier.

Overall, there was a decline in religiosity from adolescence to emerging adulthood, both in behavior and in beliefs. Only about 30% of emerging adults attended religious services at least once a month; over half attended only a few times a year or less. Beliefs were stronger than behavior; 44% reported that religious faith is "very" or "extremely" important in their lives, and 75% reported believing in God. Nevertheless, these percentages were lower than they had been in adolescence.

Just as in adolescence, in emerging adulthood religious beliefs were highly individualized. Few emerging adults accepted a standard religious doctrine; instead, they adopted a make-your-own approach to their religious beliefs, constructed partly from what they had learned from their parents but also from many other sources. Consequently, religious denomination did not hold much meaning for most of them. They could state they were "Catholic" or "Presbyterian" or "Jewish" without actually believing much of what is stated in the traditional doctrine of that faith and without participating in it. In fact, 38% of "Protestants" and 35% of "Catholics" reported that they *never* attend religious services. This individualized approach to religion led to great religious diversity in emerging adulthood, which can be classified into these four categories, listed here from least to most religious.

- Agnostics/atheists (40%): This includes emerging adults who do not believe in God (atheists) or who believe it is not possible to know if there is a God or not (agnostics), along with emerging adults who say they have no opinion on religion or do not think about it. Some are strongly anti-religious, but to most young people in this category religion is simply irrelevant to their lives.
- Deists (15%): Emerging adults in this category believe that there is "something out there," a God or spiritual force of some kind, but beyond this they are not sure what to believe.
- Liberal Believers (30%): When it comes to religion, these emerging adults take what they want and ignore the rest. That is, they believe only the parts of their denominational faith that appeal to them, and they often add other elements from sources including other religions and popular culture.
- Conservative Believers (15%): These are emerging adults who hold to a traditional, conservative faith.

Just as in adolescence, religious faith in emerging adulthood tends to be associated with a variety of positive characteristics. Smith and Snell (2010) found religious belief and participation among emerging adults to be related to higher well-being and lower rates of participation in a variety of types of risk behavior. Another study, comparing African American and White emerging adults, reported that African Americans were more likely to cope with stress by relying on their religious beliefs, and in turn they experienced fewer anxiety symptoms than White emerging adults did (Chapman & Steger, 2010). This is consistent with studies in other age periods showing that African Americans tend to be more religious than Whites are (Dilworth-Anderson et al., 2007).

Political Development

LO 9.15 **Explain why emerging adults have often been at the forefront of political movements, and contrast this with their involvement in conventional politics.**

In most countries, 18 is the age when people first receive the right to vote, so political development might be expected to be an important issue in emerging adulthood. However, political involvement tends to be very low among emerging adults (Núñez & Flanagan, 2015). In Europe, as well as in Canada and the United States, emerging adults' political participation is strikingly low by conventional measures such as voting rates and involvement in political parties (Barrio et al., 2007; Botcheva et al., 2007; Meeus, 2007; Sears et al., 2007). Emerging adults tend to have lower political participation not only in comparison to adults, but also in comparison to previous generations of young people. They tend to be skeptical of the motivations of politicians, and to see the activities of political parties as irrelevant to their lives. One study of young people in eight European countries found that low levels of trust in political authorities and political systems were consistent from adolescence through emerging adulthood (Hooghe & Wilkenfeld, 2008).

However, the rejection of conventional politics should not be construed as a lack of interest in improving the state of their communities, their societies, and the world. On the contrary, emerging adults in many countries are more likely than older adults to be involved in organizations devoted to particular issues, such as environmental protection and efforts against war and racism (Goossens & Luyckx, 2007; Meeus, 2007; Núñez & Flanagan, 2015). In one nationwide survey of college freshmen in the United States, only 28% said they were interested in politics, but 81% had done volunteer work, and 45% had participated in a political demonstration (Kellogg, 2001). Emerging adulthood is also the time when people in the United States are mostly likely to devote a year or two of their lives to volunteer programs such as the Peace Corps, Americorps, and Teach for America (Arnett, 2015). Often frustrated by conventional political processes, emerging adults choose instead to direct their energies toward specific areas of importance to them, where they believe they are more likely to see genuine progress.

Furthermore, emerging adults have often been involved in movements at the political extremes, including protests, revolutionary movements, and terrorism. The leaders of politically extreme groups are usually in midlife or later, but many of their most zealous followers are often emerging adults. There are many recent historical examples of this. The Cultural Revolution that took place in China from 1966 to 1975 and involved massive destruction and violence toward anyone deemed to be a threat to the "purity" of Chinese communism was instigated by Chairman Mao and his wife Jiang Ching, but it was carried out almost entirely by fervent Chinese emerging adults (MacFarquhar & Schoenhals, 2006). Terrorist attacks by Muslim extremists against Western (especially American) targets—most notably the attacks of September 11, 2001—have been planned by older men but executed almost entirely by young men in the 18–29 age range (Sen & Samad, 2007).

Emerging adults have often been at the forefront of political movements. Here, emerging adults participate in anti-government protests in Tahrir Square in Cairo, Egypt. Demonstrations such as this led to the peaceful overthrow of the government in 2011.

These examples involve destruction and violence, but emerging adults have also been prominent in peaceful political movements. For example, when the collapse of communism began in eastern Europe in 1989, it was initiated by emerging adults through strikes, demonstrations, and the formation of new youth-oriented political parties (Botcheva et al., 2007; Flanagan & Botcheva, 1999; Macek, 2006). Recent protests against governments in the Middle East have also involved emerging adults more than any other age group (Barber, 2013).

Why are emerging adults especially likely to be involved in extreme political movements? One reason is that they have fewer social ties and obligations than people in other age periods (Arnett, 2005). Children and adolescents can be restrained from involvement by their parents. Young, middle, and older adults can be deterred from involvement by their commitments to others who depend on them, especially a spouse and children. However, emerging adulthood is a time when social commitments and social control are at their low point. Emerging adults have more freedom than people at other age periods, and this freedom allows some of them to become involved in extreme political movements.

Another possibility is that their involvement is identity-related. As we have seen, one aspect of identity explorations is ideology or worldview (Arnett, 2015; Erikson, 1968). Emerging adulthood is a time when people are looking for an ideological framework for explaining the world, and some emerging adults may be attracted to the definite answers provided by extreme political movements. Embracing an extreme political ideology may relieve the discomfort that can accompany the uncertainty and doubt of ideological explorations. Still, these explanations raise the question, since only a small minority of emerging adults are involved in these extreme movements: why them and not the others?

Practice Quiz   ANSWERS AVAILABLE IN ANSWER KEY.

1. Doug refers to himself as a "cafeteria Catholic" because he believes in God and follows some of the practices of his religion, but ignores the rest. According to Smith and Snell (2010), Doug would be categorized as _____.

   a. an agnostic
   b. a deist
   c. a liberal believer
   d. a conservative believer

2. Research on the religious beliefs and practices of emerging adults has shown that _____.

   a. religious beliefs and practices are associated with lower rates of participation in a number of risk behaviors, as well as higher well-being
   b. most are categorized as agnostic or atheist
   c. White emerging adults are more likely than African Americans to cope with stress by relying on their religious beliefs
   d. virtually all individuals in this developmental period attend religious services at least once a month

3. Which of the following statements best describes political development during emerging adulthood?

   a. Emerging adults tend to have higher political participation in comparison to adults.
   b. This generation of emerging adults tends to have higher political participation compared to previous generations of young people.
   c. Emerging adults tend to be skeptical of the motivations of politicians.
   d. Emerging adults tend to be less likely than older adults to be involved in organizations devoted to particular issues, such as efforts against war and racism.

4. Which of the following is TRUE regarding political involvement in emerging adulthood?

   a. Emerging adults are especially likely to be involved in extreme political movements.
   b. Most emerging adults lack interest in improving the state of their communities because they are so self-focused at this time of life.
   c. Emerging adults tend to be most interested in conventional politics, rather than special topics.
   d. In Europe, as well as in Canada and the United States, voting rates and involvement in political parties is relatively high.

EMOTIONAL AND SOCIAL DEVELOPMENT: The Social and Cultural Contexts of Emerging Adulthood

Emerging adulthood is a life stage in which sociocultural contexts change in some profound and dramatic ways. After living within a family context from infancy through adolescence, emerging adults in many countries move out of their parents' household, diminishing their parents' influence and giving them more control over their daily lives. Friends are highly important, especially for emerging adults who are currently without a romantic relationship. Romantic relationships take on new importance, as intimacy deepens and emerging adults move toward making an enduring commitment to a love partner. Media remain a source of entertainment and enjoyment, especially new media such as the Internet and mobile phones.

Family Relationships

LO 9.16 **Describe patterns of home-leaving in the United States and Europe and how this transition influences relations with parents.**

In most Western majority cultures, most young people move out of their parents' home sometime during emerging adulthood. The most common reasons for leaving home stated by emerging adults are going to college, cohabiting with a partner, or simply the desire for independence (Goldscheider & Goldscheider, 1999; Seiffge-Krenke, 2009).

Typically, relationships between parents and emerging adults improve once the young person leaves home. In this case, at least, absence makes the heart grow fonder. Numerous studies have confirmed that emerging adults report greater closeness and fewer negative feelings toward their parents after moving out (Aquilino, 2006; Arnett & Schwab, 2012, 2013; Fingerman & Yahirun, 2015). Furthermore, emerging adults who move out tend to get along better with their parents than those who remain at home. For example, in one study of 21-year-olds, the emerging adults who had moved at least an hour away (by car) from their parents reported the highest levels of closeness to their parents and valued their parents' opinions most highly (Dubas & Petersen, 1996). Emerging adults who remained at home had the poorest relations with their parents, and those who had moved out but remained within an hour's drive were in between the other two groups.

What explains these patterns? Some scholars have suggested that leaving home leads young people to appreciate their parents more (Arnett, 2015; Katchadourian & Boli, 1985). Another factor may be that it is easier to be fond of someone you no longer live with. Once emerging adults move out, they no longer experience the day-to-day friction with their parents that inevitably results from living with others. They can now control the frequency and timing of their interactions with their parents in a way they could not when they were living with them. They can visit their parents for the weekend, for a holiday, or for dinner, enjoy the time together, and still maintain full control over their daily lives. As a 24-year-old woman in my research put it, "I don't have to talk to them when I don't want to, and when I want to, I can" (Arnett, 2004, p. 49).

In the United States, although most emerging adults move out of their parents' home in their late teens, a substantial proportion (over one third) stay home through their early 20s (Arnett & Schwab, 2012). Staying at home is more common among Latinos, Blacks, and Asian Americans than among White Americans. The reason for this is sometimes economic, especially for Latinos and African Americans, who have high rates of unemployment in emerging adulthood (U.S. Bureau of the Census, 2014). However, another important reason appears to be the greater emphasis on family closeness and interdependence in minority cultures, and less emphasis on being independent as a value in itself. For example, one emerging adult in my research (Arnett, 2004) lived with her Chinese American mother and Mexican American father throughout her college years at the University of California-Berkeley. She enjoyed the way staying home allowed her to remain in close contact with them. "I loved living at home. I respect my parents a lot, so being home with them was actually one of the things I liked to do most," she said. "Plus, it was free!" (Arnett, 2004, p. 54). For Latinos and Asian Americans, an additional reason for staying home is specific to young women, and concerns the high value placed on virginity before marriage.

About 40% of American emerging adults "return to the nest" to live at least once after they leave (Arnett & Schwab, 2012). There are many reasons why emerging adults sometimes move home again (Goldscheider & Goldscheider, 1999). For those who left home for college, moving back home may be a way of bridging their transition to post-college life after they graduate or drop out. It gives them a chance to decide what to do next, be it graduate school, a job near home, or a job farther away. For those who left home for independence, some may feel that the glow of independence dims after a while as the freedom of doing what they want when they want becomes outweighed by the burden of taking care of a household and paying all their own bills. An early divorce or a period of military service are other reasons emerging adults give for returning home (Goldscheider & Goldscheider, 1999). Under these circumstances, too, coming home may be attractive to young people as a transition period, a chance to get back on their feet before they venture again into the world.

There are a number of possible outcomes when emerging adults move back home (Arnett, 2015; Arnett & Schwab, 2013). For some, the return home is welcome and the transition is managed easily. A successful transition home is more likely if parents recognize the change in their children's maturity and treat them as adults rather than adolescents. For others, however, the return home is a bumpy transition. Parents may have come to enjoy having the nest all to themselves, without children to provide for and feel responsible for. Emerging adults may find it difficult to have parents monitoring them daily again, after a period when they had grown used to managing their own lives. In my research (Arnett, 2004), after Mary moved home she was dismayed to find that her mother would wait up for her when she went out with her boyfriend, just like it was high school all over again. They did not argue openly about it, but it made Mary feel "like she was sort of 'in my territory' or something" (p. 53). For many emerging adults, moving back home results in ambivalence. They are grateful for the support their parents provide, even as they resent returning to the subordinate role of a dependent child. Perhaps because of this ambivalence, the return home tends to be brief, with two-thirds of emerging adults moving out again within 1 year (Aquilino, 2006).

In European countries, emerging adults tend to live with their parents longer than in the United States, especially in southern and eastern Europe (Douglass, 2005, 2007; Kins et al., 2009). **Figure 9.12** shows the patterns in various European countries, as compared to the United States (Iacovov, 2011). There are a number of practical reasons why European emerging adults stay home longer. European university students are more likely than American students to continue to live at home while they attend university. European emerging adults who do not attend university may have difficulty finding or affording an apartment of their own. However, also important are European cultural values that emphasize mutual support within the family while also allowing young people substantial autonomy. Italy provides a good case in point (Chisholm & Hurrelman, 1995; Krause, 2005). Ninety-four percent of Italians aged 15 to 24 live with their parents, the highest percentage in the European Union (EU), and many of them continue to live with their parents even into their late 20s and early 30s (Bonino et al., 2012). However, only 8% of them view their living arrangements as a problem—the lowest percentage among EU countries. Many European emerging adults remain at home contentedly through their early 20s, by choice rather than necessity.

There is more to the changes in relationships with parents from adolescence to emerging adulthood than simply the effects of moving out, staying home, or moving back in. Emerging adults also grow in their ability to understand their parents (Arnett, 2015). Adolescence is in some ways an egocentric period, and adolescents often have difficulty taking their parents' perspectives. They sometimes evaluate their parents harshly, magnifying their deficiencies and becoming easily irritated by their imperfections. As emerging adults mature and begin to feel more adult themselves, they become more capable of understanding how their parents look at things. They come to see their parents as persons and begin to realize that their parents, like themselves, have a mix of qualities, merits as well as faults.

There has been little research on sibling relationships in emerging adulthood (Aquilino, 2006; Scharf & Schulman, 2015). However, one study of adolescents and emerging

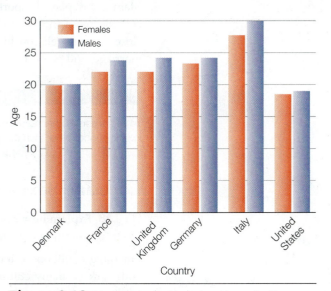

Figure 9.12 Median Age of Leaving Home in Europe Versus the United States

SOURCE: Based on Iacovov (2011)

adults in Israel found that emerging adults spent less time with their siblings than adolescents did but also felt more emotional closeness and warmth toward them (Scharf et al., 2005). Conflict and rivalry were also reported to be less intense by emerging adults than by adolescents. Qualitative analyses showed that emerging adults had a more mature perception of their relationship with their siblings than adolescents did, in the sense that they were better able to understand their siblings' needs and perspectives.

Friendships

LO 9.17 Describe the role of intimacy in emerging adults' friendships and the most common activities of emerging adult friends.

In a number of ways, friendships may be especially important in emerging adulthood (Barry et al., 2014). The majority of emerging adults move away from home and so lose the daily social support they may have received from their parents and siblings. Even for the ones who return home or remain home, they may rely less on their parents for social support as they strive toward becoming self-sufficient and making their own decisions (Arnett, 2015). Consequently, they may turn more to friends than to parents for companionship and support.

As we have seen, intimacy becomes more important to friendships in adolescence than it had been in middle childhood, and that trend may continue into emerging adulthood. In one study (Radmacher & Azmitia, 2006), early adolescents (ages 12–13) and emerging adults (ages 18–20) described a time when they felt especially close to a friend. Emerging adults' accounts contained more self-disclosure and fewer shared activities, compared to early adolescents. Among the emerging adults (but not the early adolescents) there was a gender difference. Self-disclosure promoted emotional closeness for young women, whereas for young men shared activities were usually the basis of feeling emotional closeness.

What kinds of things do emerging adults do with their friends? Much of their time together is unstructured socializing (described earlier in the chapter), in activities such as visiting each other informally and going out together. Some drink alcohol or use drugs together, and as we have seen earlier, unstructured socializing and substance use often take place together (Osgood, 2009). Emerging adults also participate in media-related activities together, such as watching TV or playing electronic games (Brown, 2006). Many enjoy playing sports or exercising together (Malebo et al., 2007). Overall, leisure activities with friends decline steadily in the course of the 20s as emerging adults form close romantic relationships and begin to enter adult responsibilities such as stable work, marriage, and parenthood (Osgood, 2009).

CRITICAL THINKING QUESTION

What are some other reasons why leisure activities with friends might decline in the course of emerging adulthood, other than those mentioned here?

Love and Sexuality

LO 9.18 Explain how romantic relationships and sexual behavior change during emerging adulthood.

Emerging adulthood is a time of gradually building the structure of an adult life in love and work. In many cultures, explorations in love are part of this process, as emerging adults experience a series of romantic and sexual relationships in the course of deciding on a long-term partner.

IN SEARCH OF A SOUL MATE: FINDING A ROMANTIC PARTNER A key part of emerging adulthood involves moving away from one's family, not just geographically but socially and emotionally, and toward a new love partner, in marriage or another long-term romantic partnership. Jennifer Tanner (Tanner, 2006; Tanner, 2015) calls this process "recentering." For children and adolescents, the center of their emotional lives is within their family, with their parents and siblings. For adults, the center of their emotional lives is usually with a new family constellation, mainly a romantic partner, and usually children as well. Emerging adulthood is when the change takes place, as the center of emotional life is transferred from the original family to a long-term romantic partner. Parents and siblings remain important, of course. As we have seen, relations with them even improve in many ways. But the center of emotional life usually moves to a romantic partner.

When they talk about what they are looking for in a romantic partner, emerging adults around the world mention a wide variety of ideal qualities (Gibbons & Stiles, 2004; Hatfield & Rapson, 2005). Sometimes these are qualities of the person, the individual: intelligent, attractive, or funny. But most often they mention interpersonal qualities, qualities a person brings to a relationship, such as kind, caring, loving, and trustworthy. Emerging adults hope to find someone who will treat them well and who will be capable of an intimate, mutually loving, durable relationship.

In romantic relationships as in friendships, intimacy becomes more important in emerging adulthood than it had been in adolescence (Shulman & Connolly, 2014). One study investigated views of the functions of love relationships among early adolescents (6th grade), late adolescents (11th grade), and college students (Roscoe et al., 1987). The early and late adolescents both considered recreation to be the most important function, followed by intimacy, and then status. In contrast, for the college students intimacy ranked highest, followed by companionship, with recreation a bit lower, and status much lower. A more recent study reported similar results (Montgomery, 2005).

In addition to looking for intimacy, emerging adults also seek a romantic partner who will be like themselves in many ways (Shulman & Connolly, 2015). Opposites rarely attract; on the contrary, birds of a feather flock together. A long line of studies has established that emerging adults, like people of other ages, tend to have romantic relationships with people who are similar to themselves in characteristics such as personality, intelligence, social class, ethnic background, religious beliefs, and physical attractiveness (Furman & Simon, 2008; Markey & Markey, 2007). Scholars attribute this to what they call *consensual validation*, which means that people like to find in others a match, or *consensus*, with their own characteristics. Finding this consensus reaffirms, or *validates*, their own way of looking at the world. The more similar your love partner is to you, the more likely you are to reaffirm each other, and the less likely you are to have conflicts that spring from having different views and preferences.

COHABITATION For many emerging adults in the West, the next step after forming an exclusive, enduring relationship with a romantic partner is not marriage but moving in together. In the United States and Canada, as well as in northern European countries, **cohabitation** before marriage is now experienced by at least two-thirds of emerging adults (Manning, 2013). The percentage is highest in the Scandinavian countries, where nearly all young people cohabit before marriage (Syltevik, 2010). Cohabitation tends to be brief and unstable for young Americans. One study found that half of cohabiting relationships lasted less than a year, and only 1 in 10 couples were together 5 years later (Bumpass & Liu, 2000). In contrast, cohabiting couples in European countries tend to stay together as long as married couples (Hacker, 2002; Hymowitz et al., 2013).

However, in Europe there are distinct differences in cohabitation between north and south (Kiernan, 2002, 2004). Emerging adults in southern Europe are considerably less

cohabitation
unmarried romantic partners living together

likely than their counterparts in the north to cohabit; most emerging adults in southern Europe live at home until marriage (Douglass, 2005), especially females. Perhaps due to the Catholic religious tradition in the south, cohabitation carries a moral stigma there that it does not have in the north. Cohabitation is also rare in Asian cultures, most of which have a long tradition of sexual conservatism and virginity at marriage.

Young people choose to cohabit sometimes for practical reasons—two together can live more cheaply than two separately—and sometimes because they wish to enhance the likelihood that when they marry, it will last. Indeed, in a national (American) survey of 20- to 29-year-olds, 62% agreed that "Living together with someone before marriage is a good way to avoid eventual divorce" (Popenoe & Whitehead, 2001). Emerging adults from divorced families are especially likely to cohabit, because they are especially determined to avoid their parents' fate (Cunningham & Thornton, 2007).

Although living together before marriage is motivated partly by the fear of divorce, the divorce rate is about the same for couples who cohabit and those who do not (Manning, 2013). This may be because cohabiting couples become used to living together while maintaining separate lives in many ways, especially financially, so that they are unprepared for the compromises required by marriage. Also, even before entering cohabitation, emerging adults who cohabit tend to be different from emerging adults who do not, in ways that are related to higher risk of divorce—less religious, more skeptical of the institution of marriage, and more accepting of divorce (Hymowitz et al., 2013). However, one analysis concluded that cohabitation itself increases the risk of divorce, because it leads some couples who are not compatible to marry anyway, out of "the inertia of cohabitation" (Stanley et al., 2006).

Premarital sex in emerging adulthood is accepted in some cultures and forbidden in others.

SEXUALITY In their sexual behavior as in other aspects of their lives, there is a great deal of diversity among emerging adults. The most common pattern among American 18- to 23-year-olds is to have had one partner in the past year (Lefkowitz, 2006; Regnerus & Uecker, 2011). However, emerging adults are more likely than adults in older age groups to have had either more or fewer sexual partners. About one third of 18- to 23-year-olds report having had two or more partners in the past year, but about one fourth report having had sex not at all in the past year (Regnerus & Uecker, 2011). At the beginning of emerging adulthood, age 18, about half of Americans have had intercourse at least once, and by age 25 nearly all emerging adults have had intercourse at least once, but those who have their first episode of intercourse relatively late tend to be "active abstainers" rather than "accidental abstainers" (Lefkowitz, 2006). That is, they remain virgins longer because they have chosen to wait rather than because they had no opportunity for sex. Common reasons for abstaining are fear of pregnancy, fear of sexually-transmitted infections (STIs), religious or moral beliefs, and the feeling one has not yet met the right person (Lefkowitz et al., 2004; Sprecher & Regan, 1996).

Sexual behavior in emerging adulthood most commonly takes place in the context of a close romantic relationship (Regnerus & Uecker, 2011). However, emerging adults are more likely than adults in older age groups to engage in recreational sex or "hooking up." Various studies indicate that about one fourth of sexual episodes among American emerging adults takes place outside of a romantic partnership (Claxton & van Dulmen, 2015). Within American ethnic groups, African American emerging adults are most likely to report casual sexual experiences, and Asian American emerging adults least likely

(Regnerus & Uecker, 2011). Male emerging adults are more likely than females to have sexual attitudes that favor recreational sex. They tend to be more likely than females to be willing to have intercourse with someone they have known for only a few hours, to have sex with two different partners in the same day, and to have sex with someone they do not love (Knox et al., 2001).

Frequently, episodes of hooking up are fueled by alcohol. In various studies, from one fourth to one half of emerging adults report having consumed alcohol before their most recent sexual encounter (Lefkowitz, 2006), and emerging adults who drink often are more likely than others to have had multiple sexual partners (Regnerus & Uecker, 2011). The college environment is especially conducive to hooking up since it brings together so many emerging adults in a common setting that includes frequent social events that involve alcohol use.

Most American emerging adults are quite responsible about contraceptive use, although certainly not all of them. Only about 10% of sexually active emerging adults report never using contraception, but an additional 35% of them report inconsistent or ineffective contraceptive use (Regnerus & Uecker, 2011). As a romantic relationship develops between emerging adults, they often move from condom use to oral contraceptives, because they believe sex feels better without a condom or because switching to oral contraceptives signifies a deeper level of trust and commitment (Hammer et al., 1996; Lefkowitz, 2006).

Surveys have been conducted in numerous countries that demonstrate the wide variability in cultural approaches to premarital sexuality around the world (Hatfield & Rapson, 2005). Rates of premarital sex are somewhat lower in the countries of South America, although the large differences in reported premarital sex by male and female adolescents in countries such as Brazil and Chile suggest that males exaggerate their sexual activity or females underreport theirs (or both). Finally, premarital sex is least common in Asian and Middle Eastern countries, where the emphasis on female virginity before marriage is still very strong (Davis & Davis, 2012).

SEXUALLY TRANSMITTED INFECTIONS Emerging adults in Western countries may view sex as a normal and enjoyable part of life, but that does not mean it is unproblematic. The long period between the initiation of sexual activity in adolescence and the entry into marriage in young adulthood typically includes sex with a series of romantic partners as well as occasional episodes of hooking up, and in the course of these years unintended pregnancies are not unusual. Although responsible contraceptive use is the norm among emerging adults, inconsistent and ineffective use of contraception is common enough to make emerging adulthood the age period when both abortion and nonmarital childbirth are most common, across many countries (Claxton & van Dulmen, 2015; Hymowitz et al., 2013).

Emerging adulthood is also the peak period for **sexually transmitted infections (STIs)**, which are infections transmitted through sexual contact, including chlamydia, human papilloma virus (HPV), herpes simplex virus 2 (HSV-2), and HIV/AIDS. One half of STIs in the United States occur in people who are ages 15–24 (CDC, 2013). Rates of STIs are higher in emerging adulthood than in any other life stage, in both the United States and Europe (Lehtinen et al., 2006).

Why are emerging adults particularly at risk for STIs? Although few emerging adults have sex with numerous partners, hooking up occasionally with a temporary partner is quite common (Claxton & van Dulmen, 2015). Even if sex takes place in a committed relationship, most youthful love relationships do not endure for long and partners eventually break up and move on. In this way, young people gain experience with love and sex and see what it is like to be involved with different people. Unfortunately, having sex with a variety of people, even within a series of relationships, carries with it a substantial risk for STIs.

The symptoms and consequences of STIs vary widely, from the merely annoying (pubic lice or "crabs") to the deadly (HIV/AIDS). Some STIs, such as chlamydia and

sexually transmitted infection (STI)

infection transmitted through sexual contact

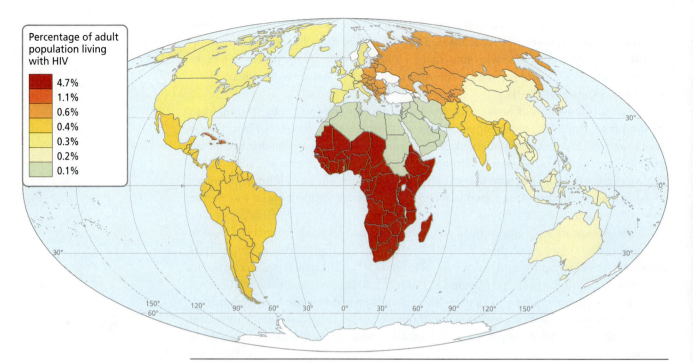

Map 9.2 HIV Population Worldwide, by Region

Which regions have the highest population of adults living with HIV? How might you explain these variations?

SOURCE: Based on UNAIDS, GAP Report (2014)

HPV, increase the risk of infertility for women (Mills et al., 2006). Fortunately, chlamydia can be treated effectively with antibiotics. Also, a vaccine for HPV is now available, and public health advocates in many Western countries are vigorously promoting that adolescents be vaccinated before they become sexually active (Kahn, 2007; Woodhall et al., 2007). Herpes simplex 2 cannot be cured, but medications can relieve the symptoms and speed up the healing process when an episode occurs (King, 2005).

One of the most deadly diseases, HIV/AIDS (see Chapter 2), has proven to be extremely difficult to treat, because the virus has the ability to change itself and thus render medications ineffective. AIDS has been most devastating in southern Africa, where 10 of every 11 new HIV infections worldwide take place (see **Map 9.2**). Incidence of new HIV infections has decreased among young people worldwide in the past decade, due to a decline in risky sexual practices such as having multiple sexual partners (UNAIDS, 2010).

In recent years effective drug treatments for slowing the progress of AIDS have been developed. The cost of these drug treatments was initially extremely high, but now the cost has declined and the drugs are widely available even in developing countries, mainly through international aid organizations (UNAIDS, 2010). Prevention programs to reduce HIV risk among emerging adults have now been conducted in many developing countries, and have been successful in changing young people's behavior to reduce their HIV risk (Ngongo et al., 2012).

Media Use

LO 9.19 Explain how emerging adults use the Internet and mobile phones to maintain social contacts.

Media are a big part of the lives of today's emerging adults. They have grown up in a time of extraordinary innovation in the way media products are delivered and consumed (Coyne et al., 2014). Educator and writer Marc Prensky (2010) calls them "digital natives," entirely at home in the digital world from infancy onward, in contrast to the "digital immigrants," their parents, many of whom never feel quite at home with all the new media

All together, American emerging adults are estimated to be engaged with media of some kind even more than adolescents are: 12 hours per day, or three-fourths of their waking hours (Coyne et al., 2014). Emerging adults' media use is diverse, from television and recorded music to electronic games, the Internet, and mobile phones—which are now not just phones but **digital devices** that can do everything from send text messages to record videos to surf the Internet (Hundley & Shyles, 2010). There is surprisingly little research on emerging adults' uses of television and music, perhaps because of an assumption that the effects of these media are more profound for children and adolescents. Instead, research has focused mainly on Internet use and mobile phones.

INTERNET USE Internet use is high worldwide among emerging adults. In a survey of Internet use among persons ages 18 and over in 13 countries in Europe, Asia, and the Americas, Internet use was over 80% among 18- to 24-year-olds in all countries but one (World Internet Project, 2012). Furthermore, in all countries Internet use was higher among emerging adults than in any other age group. An American study found that emerging adults spend about 3½ hours per day on the Internet (Padilla-Walker et al., 2010).

For what purposes do you use the Internet? The possibilities are as varied as the content of the Internet—virtually infinite, in other words—but most college students use the Internet as part of their education, to research topics they need to know about for courses (Selwyn, 2008). The Internet can be extremely valuable as a way to find information, but like other media forms, its effects can be negative at the extremes of use. One study of college students in the United Kingdom found a negative correlation between grade performance and hours per week spent online (Englander et al., 2010). Another study, of Chinese college students in eight universities, found that heavy Internet use (more than 15 hours a week) was related to poorer academic performance, as well as to symptoms of depression (Huang et al., 2009). The Internet is also sometimes misused for the purposes of academic cheating, for example downloading answers on a digital device during an exam (Mastin & Lilly, 2009; Stephens et al., 2007).

The use of the Internet for **social-networking web sites** such as Facebook is highly popular among emerging adults. Facebook was originally developed by and for college students, and college students and other emerging adults are still the main users, although it has rapidly become widely used by adolescents and adults as well (Baker & Moore, 2008; Raacke & Bonds-Raacke, 2008). Facebook is by far the most popular social-networking web site, surpassing one billion members worldwide in 2012. Among 18- to 29-year-olds in the United States, nearly 90% use social-networking web sites (as shown in **Figure 9.13**), the same rate as for teens and nearly twice the rate for persons age 30 and older (Duggan & Brenner, 2013).

Social-networking profiles are an arena for identity presentation and reflect the prominence of identity issues in emerging adulthood (Davis, 2010). That is, users make choices about how to present themselves on social networking web sites, and their choices reflect their perceptions of who they are and how they want others to perceive them. For adolescents as well as emerging adults, social networking web sites allow a space for "identity play," in which they try out different ways of presenting themselves in the course of deciding who they really are (Mazur & Kozarian, 2010).

digital device

electronic device that allows contact via phone and text message as well as access to the Internet, videos, television, and direct video conversations

social-networking web site

web site that allows people to establish and maintain electronic contact with a wide social group

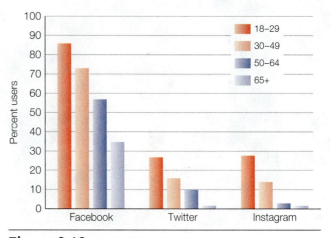

Figure 9.13 Social Media Use by Age
SOURCE: Based on Duggan & Brenner (2013).

Having a profile also allows users to maintain and expand their social networks. Emerging adults use the sites mainly to keep in touch with old friends and current friends and to make new ones (Ellison et al., 2007; Raacke & Bonds-Raacke, 2008). This function is especially important in emerging adulthood, because emerging adults often leave home and the network of friends they formed in secondary school. Furthermore, emerging adults frequently change educational settings, jobs, and residences. Social-networking web sites allow them to keep in contact with the friends they leave behind as they move through emerging adulthood, and to make new friends in each new place (Subrahmanyam et al., 2008).

Another common use of the Internet among emerging adults is to gain access to pornography. Although pornographic magazines and movies have existed for a long time, the invention of the Internet has made pornographic material much easier to obtain. In fact, of all the many uses of the Internet, the number-one use is accessing pornography, as measured by number of hits, number of web sites, or the amount of money spent (Young, 2008).

In the United States, use of the Internet for pornography is widespread among emerging adults. In a study of college students at six sites around the country, 87% of the young men and 31% of young women reported viewing Internet pornography (Carroll et al., 2008). Viewing pornography was related to risk behaviors, specifically to sexual risk behaviors and substance use, but of course this is a correlation rather than causation; it does not show that viewing pornography causes emerging adults to take sexual risks.

text messaging

form of communication on mobile phones that involves typing a message on the screen and sending it

Texting allows emerging adults to keep in contact with family and friends all day long.

A study of Swedish emerging adults found even higher rates of viewing Internet pornography among young men and women (Häggström-Nordin & Hanson, 2005). Ninety-eight percent of young men and 72% percent of young women in this study had ever viewed pornography. In a qualitative study by this research team (Häggström-Nordin et al., 2006), Swedish emerging adults expressed mixed feelings about pornography viewing. They described it as interesting and pleasurable to view, but also expressed concerns about the submissive and degrading ways women are depicted in pornography and the separation of sex from intimacy.

MOBILE PHONES Like the Internet, the pervasiveness and popularity of mobile phones has skyrocketed in the past decade, and like the Internet, mobile phones are especially popular among adolescents and emerging adults. For example, mobile phones are used by over 90% of 18- to 24-year-olds in Sweden (Axelsson, 2010). In the United States, 93% of 18- to 19-year-olds own a mobile phone, a higher rate than in any other age group (Lenhart, 2010). Mobile phones are used by young people not only for calling someone and talking the way other phones have long been used, but also for **text messaging**. A study of Japanese adolescents found that they used their mobile phones much more often for text messaging than for talking (Kamibeppu & Hitomi, 2005). More than half of those who owned a mobile phone sent at least 10 text messages a day to their friends. Similar results have been found in Western developed countries (Axelsson, 2010). One American study found that 18- to 29-year-olds report sending and receiving more texts per day than any older age group (Taylor & Keeter, 2010).

Mobile phones resemble e-mail and social-networking web sites as a way for adolescents and emerging adults to remain in contact with each other when they are apart, virtually all day long. The social worlds of young people are no longer neatly divided into time with family and time with friends or at school. Rather, the new media allow the world of friends to be a nearly constant presence in their lives. The limited evidence so far indicates that young people enjoy the way the new media allow them to keep in touch with their friends. In one study in Italy, adolescents reported many of their happiest moments took place while communicating with friends on the Internet or using their mobile phones (Bassi & Antonella, 2004). A study of emerging adults in Sweden reported that they were in contact with friends and family throughout the day via texting (Axelsson, 2010). In a national study of American 18- to 29-year-olds, 51% agreed that "I rely a lot on the support I get from family and friends through e-mail, texting, and social networking web sites" (Arnett & Schwab, 2012).

Emerging adults who have moved out of their parents' household often use their mobile phones to keep in contact with their parents. In one study of American college students, the students sent an average of 13 text messages a week to their parents (Hofer & Moore, 2010). Students valued texting as a way to keep in touch with their parents as they went about their busy days at school, allowing for parental support while also giving them room to run their own lives.

Cultural Focus: Media Use in Emerging Adulthood Across Cultures

All over the world, electronic media have become a big part of the daily lives of emerging adults. They use media to learn, to keep in contact with the people they care about, and to find new people who share their interests. In this video, emerging adults from various countries are interviewed about their media and technology use.

Watch   MEDIA USE IN EMERGING ADULTHOOD ACROSS CULTURES

Video

Review Question:

The U.S. emerging adult interviewed in this video mentions a heavy reliance on Facebook as a "tool" to stay connected. What are some other positive uses of Facebook and other social media? What are some negative aspects of social media use?

Practice Quiz ANSWERS AVAILABLE IN ANSWER KEY.

1. In the United States, _____ are LEAST LIKELY to be living at home with their parents in their early 20s.
   a. Latino Americans
   b. White Americans
   c. African Americans
   d. Asian Americans

2. Which of the following people would most likely willingly and happily live with his or her parents until his or her late 20s or early 30s?
   a. Brice, an emerging adult from the United States
   b. Antonio, an emerging adult from Italy
   c. Hector, an emerging adult from Canada
   d. Matthias, an emerging adult from Germany

3. When it comes to friendship in emerging adulthood, _____.
   a. there is a steady increase in the time spent in leisure activities in the twenties as these friendships become increasingly important
   b. much of their time together is spent in structured activities
   c. intimacy continues to be an important component
   d. both men and women reported that self-disclosure was what promoted the feeling of emotional closeness

4. Which of the following best illustrates the process of "recentering" as defined by Jennifer Tanner?
   a. There is a move from adolescent egocentrism to an inner self-focus during emerging adulthood.
   b. The center of emotional life is transferred from the original family to a long-term romantic partner.
   c. During infancy the center of development is located within an individual's genotype, but as time passes, environment plays a larger role, therefore moving the center of development.
   d. The center for physical development is located in the nucleus of all cells; however, cancer cells infiltrate and modify the nuclei of healthy cells, transferring the location of cellular development.

5. Of all the many uses of the Internet, the number one use is _____.
   a. accessing pornography
   b. using social media sites
   c. online shopping
   d. gambling

Summary: Emotional and Social Development

LO 9.11 Describe the course of self-esteem from adolescence through emerging adulthood and explain the reasons for this pattern.

Self-esteem often rises for emerging adults because they have moved beyond some of the difficult issues of adolescence and they have more control over their lives.

LO 9.12 Describe the various forms identity development can take in emerging adulthood, and consider patterns of cultural and ethnic identity.

In the identity status model, James Marcia proposed four categories of identity development: diffusion, moratorium, foreclosure, and achievement. Research indicates that for most people identity achievement is not reached until emerging adulthood or beyond. Cultures influence identity development by the extent to which they allow or restrict their young people's opportunities to make choices in love and work. Today, globalization often influences the cultural context of identity development, resulting in bicultural identities. For members of ethnic minorities, there are a variety of possible forms their ethnic identity may take, including assimilation, marginality, separation, and biculturalism.

LO 9.13 Summarize the changes in American gender beliefs in recent decades and include findings from research on gender stereotypes among college students.

Beliefs about gender roles have become less restrictive in American society over the last half century. However, gender stereotypes persist in occupational roles, in the expectations for men and women to perform different kinds of jobs, and in less favorable evaluations of women's work performance.

LO 9.14 Summarize Smith and Snell's description of the religious beliefs and practices of American emerging adults.

Religious beliefs and practices decline in emerging adulthood, reaching their lowest point in the life span. Emerging adults tend to hold highly individualized religious beliefs rather than adhering to a traditional doctrine.

LO 9.15 Explain why emerging adults have often been at the forefront of political movements, and contrast this with their involvement in conventional politics.

Political participation is low in emerging adulthood with respect to conventional measures such as voting. However, emerging adults are more likely than older adults to engage in volunteer work and to join extreme political movements, due to their ideological identity search and their lack of binding social commitments.

LO 9.16 **Describe patterns of home-leaving in the United States and Europe and how this transition influences relations with parents.**

Emerging adults in the United States and northern Europe usually move out of their parents' household at age 19 or 20 to live on their own or with a friend or romantic partner. In southern Europe, emerging adults usually remain at home for longer but enjoy doing so. Relations with parents often improve as emerging adults become better at taking their parents' perspectives.

LO 9.17 **Describe the role of intimacy in emerging adults' friendships and the most common activities of emerging adult friends.**

Friends are important to emerging adults, especially to those without a current romantic partner, and intimacy is more important to their friendships than it is in childhood or adolescence. Common activities among friends include unstructured socializing, which may involve alcohol use and media use. Activities with friends decline steadily during the 20s as emerging adults form stable romantic partnerships.

LO 9.18 **Explain how romantic relationships and sexual behavior change during emerging adulthood.**

Today's emerging adults often seek a "soul mate" who provides an ideal fit with their own identity. Cohabitation is now normative in most Western countries. In northern Europe cohabitation relationships are as enduring as marriages, but in the United States they typically dissolve within a year or two. Worldwide, emerging adults' premarital sexual behavior varies greatly across countries and cultures. STIs are more common in emerging adulthood than in any other age group, including chlamydia, HPV, herpes, and HIV/AIDS.

LO 9.19 **Explain how emerging adults use the Internet and mobile phones to maintain social contacts.**

Today's emerging adults are "digital natives," having grown up with the Internet, and they eagerly adopt new technologies such as mobile phones. Many emerging adults use the Internet for social networking and to access pornography. Mobile phones are most often used for text messaging.

Applying Your Knowledge as a Professional

The topics covered in this chapter apply to a wide variety of career professions. Watch these videos to learn how they apply to a director of career services, professor of sociology, director of a nonprofit for human trafficking victims, and a life science instructor.

Watch   CAREER FOCUS: DIRECTOR OF CAREER SERVICES

Jason Eckert
Director, Career Services
University of Dayton

Chapter Quiz

1. In emerging adulthood, _____.
   a. rates of residential change in American society are much higher at ages 18 to 29 than at any other period of life
   b. there is a sense of optimism about being able to "get where I want to be in life" among those from individualistic cultures, but not for those from collectivistic cultures
   c. the focus on self-exploration means that individuals are more egocentric than their adolescent counterparts
   d. the feeling "in-between" is unique to those in the United States and Canada because emerging adults in other cultures tend to remain at home, rather than moving out

2. Emerging adults who live in _____ would emphasize becoming capable of supporting parents financially as among the most important criteria for becoming an adult.
   a. Canada
   b. Japan
   c. the United States
   d. Europe

3. Which of the following is true of emerging adults' health?
   a. Most emerging adults experience an increased susceptibility to physical illness due to the increased stressors associated with this developmental period.
   b. For most sports, the peak age of performance comes during adolescence, and athletic abilities begin to decline in the early twenties.
   c. During emerging adulthood the immune system is weak.
   d. The heart is strong during emerging adulthood and reaction time is faster than at any other time of life.

4. Which of the following statements best summarizes the current research on sleep patterns of emerging adults?
   a. The research showing delayed sleep phase syndrome and sleep debt is based almost exclusively on low-income emerging adults who work full-time, rather than attending college.
   b. The preference of being a morning person versus a night person changes with age due to increased levels of cortisol.
   c. Sleep debt has negative consequences for both cognitive and emotional functioning.
   d. Students who stayed up all night before exams thought they did worse than their peers who got a full night's sleep.

5. Researchers who study young drivers have found that _____.
   a. increased parental monitoring does not reduce automobile accidents because adolescents spend so much time with their friends
   b. graduated driver licensing (GDL) is an excellent approach to reducing automobile accidents
   c. inexperience is the only factor found to be significantly correlated with accidents and fatalities

   d. the best way to reduce car accidents and fatalities is for parents to encourage their children to gain more experience driving with their friends who have taken driver's education and who will serve as role models for safe driving

6. Binge drinking _____.
   a. peaks in emerging adulthood in the United States, but not in Europe where adolescents are often allowed to drink alcohol with their meals
   b. has not been studied longitudinally because of the difficulty getting IRB approval to ask about alcohol use among high school students
   c. is highest among single mothers in their early twenties who do not go to college
   d. is more likely among emerging adults than those in other age groups because they spend more time in unstructured socializing

7. Dialectical thought _____.
   a. relies strictly on emotion in solving real-life problems
   b. has been found to characterize emerging adults in individualistic cultures more than those in collectivistic cultures
   c. refers to the need for explaining human actions in terms of logical principles
   d. involves the growing awareness that problems often have no clear-cut solutions

8. Reflective judgment _____.
   a. is a synonym for dualism
   b. increases over time for all emerging adults as a result of maturation, regardless of their educational background or the skills required in their job
   c. is more likely to characterize students in their first year of college than those in their senior year because first-year college students are more open to new ideas
   d. is more likely to develop in cultures that value pluralism

9. An emerging adult from _____ would be most likely to express the following sentiment upon first entering college: "In many ways, college is easier than high school; it's a relief to spend less time on homework and to have more time to explore my options."
   a. Canada
   b. Japan
   c. the United States
   d. Germany

10. Based on Murnane and Levy's research, which of the following is considered one of the six basic skills necessary for success at the most promising new jobs available to high school graduates in the changing economy?
    a. Reading at a sixth-grade level
    b. Solving totally unstructured problems
    c. Doing college-level math
    d. Collaborating in diverse groups

11. For most people, self-esteem _____.
   a. rises during emerging adulthood
   b. declines during emerging adulthood
   c. stays about the same as it was in adolescence
   d. declines during the first half of emerging adulthood and increases in later emerging adulthood

12. Which of the following ethnic identify statuses involves rejecting one's culture of origin but also feeling rejected by the majority culture?
   a. Assimilation
   b. Marginality
   c. Separation
   d. Biculturalism

13. Which of the following is true of gender-related evaluations of work?
   a. Generally, research indicates that college students often evaluate women's work performance more favorably than men's.
   b. College students evaluate work done by someone of their own gender higher than work done by someone of the opposite gender.
   c. Some studies have found that evaluations can be especially harsh when a person's behavior violates stereotypical gender expectations.
   d. Gender-related evaluations do not depend on characteristics of the evaluators, such as their age.

14. Which of the following best describes religious beliefs in emerging adulthood?
   a. There is an overall decline in religious behavior, but not religious beliefs from adolescence to emerging adulthood.
   b. Emerging adults are not tolerant of religious differences.
   c. In emerging adulthood, religious beliefs are highly individualized.
   d. Emerging adults place great emphasis on the religious doctrine of their faith.

15. Which of the following is true of emerging adults' political beliefs?
   a. Unlike their counterparts in Canada or Western Europe, emerging adults' political participation is very low in the United States.
   b. Emerging adults tend to see the activities of political parties as highly relevant to their lives.
   c. Emerging adults tend to be skeptical of the motivations of politicians.
   d. Emerging adults tend to have higher conventional political participation compared to previous generations of young people.

16. _____ are most likely to be living on their own rather than with their parents in their early twenties.
   a. Latinos
   b. African Americans
   c. White Americans
   d. Asian Americans

17. Leisure activities with friends _____.
   a. decline steadily in the course of the twenties
   b. decline for women, but not for men, in the course of the twenties
   c. increase slightly in the course of the twenties
   d. stay at about the same level in the course of the twenties as they were during adolescence

18. Male emerging adults are more likely than females to _____.
   a. have negative attitudes toward recreational sex
   b. suffer severe punishments if they have premarital sex
   c. be willing to have intercourse with someone they have known for only a few hours
   d. have sex only in the context of a close romantic relationship

19. Based on current research, which is a true statement about media use in emerging adulthood?
   a. In all countries, Internet use is higher among adolescents than among emerging adults because increased responsibilities among emerging adults reduce time they can spend online.
   b. Social networking profiles are a way for individuals to express their identity.
   c. Most emerging adults prefer face-to-face interactions to social contact via the Internet, and therefore the use of social networking has decreased in the past few years as the novelty has worn off.
   d. Cross-cultural research has shown that more women than men view pornography on the Internet.

Chapter 10
Young Adulthood

THERE ARE MANY WAYS OF REACHING YOUNG ADULTHOOD, AND MANY AGES AT WHICH THE ENTRANCE TO YOUNG ADULTHOOD CAN BE MARKED. A key reason for the cultural variations in age of reaching young adulthood is that some cultures have a period of emerging adulthood in between adolescence and young adulthood and some do not (see Chapter 9). Emerging adulthood exists in developed countries, where most people obtain tertiary education and the ages of entering marriage and parenthood are close to 30. However, emerging adulthood does not exist as a normative period of the life span in developing countries, especially in rural areas, where few young people continue education beyond secondary school and the median ages of entering marriage and parenthood are often in the late teens. Where there is no life stage of emerging adulthood, young people develop directly from adolescence to young adulthood in their late teens or very early 20s as they take on adult work and begin a new family.

A further complication is that the passage from emerging adulthood to young adulthood can be said to take place when a person meets culturally-accepted criteria for adult status—but these criteria vary widely among cultures.

For example, the Samburu of East Africa consider young men to have entered adulthood when they complete their 11-year warrior' training (young Samburu women enter adulthood earlier, when they reach menarche) (Gilmore, 1990). Rural cultures in developing countries consider full adulthood to be reached once a young couple has their first child (Delaney, 2000). And people in developed countries tend to view adulthood as occurring gradually, through the attainment of a variety of criteria that denote independence and self-sufficiency (Arnett, 2011).

Although the timing of the beginning of young adulthood has many cultural variations, most of this chapter will focus on the age period from the late 20s through the 30s. We begin with a look at the cultural variations in conceptions and criteria for entering adulthood and at the major physical changes and health issues associated with young adulthood. Next we'll focus on cognitive changes, including adult intelligence, expertise, and creativity. We'll close the chapter with a review of the emotional and social growth that occurs in young adulthood in the contexts of romantic relationships, becoming a parent, work, community involvement, and media use.

Watch   CHAPTER INTRODUCTION: YOUNG ADULTHOOD

Section 1   Physical Development

Learning Objectives

10.1 Compare and contrast criteria for adulthood according to young people across cultures.

10.2 Specify the signs of the beginning of physical aging and when they appear.

10.3 Explain how obesity is defined, its causes, its consequences, and the keys to prevention.

10.4 Explain the benefits of exercising in young adulthood.

PHYSICAL DEVELOPMENT:
The Transition to Adulthood

Every culture worldwide has a word signifying "adulthood" and a conception of what it means to become an adult. However, the criteria for adulthood vary widely among cultures, and reflect cultural values of individualism or collectivism.

What Makes an Adult?

LO 10.1   **Compare and contrast criteria for adulthood according to young people across cultures.**

Do you feel that you have reached adulthood? Yes, no—maybe? Depending on your age, this may or may not be a difficult question to answer. I remember when I first felt I had reached adulthood. I was in my early 30s, and I had just started what felt like my first "real job," as a junior professor at the University of Missouri. I was living with my girlfriend (now my wife), which was the first time I had ever lived with a romantic partner, and we had bought a house. Feeling adult for the first time made me wonder when other people felt that way, and what criteria were important to them in marking adulthood.

As noted in Chapter 1, for adult life stages there are no clear age divisions that mark the end of one stage and the beginning of the next. Marking the beginning of young adulthood is especially complex and challenging. If young adulthood could be said to begin with the transitions into stable adult work, marriage, and parenthood—which is one definition of adulthood commonly used in the social sciences—then young adulthood may begin as early as the late teens, especially in developing countries, or as late as the early 30s, especially in developed countries. But where does this definition of adulthood leave people who never marry or never become parents? And what if adulthood is not defined by adult work, marriage, and parenthood, but by entirely different criteria? What does it mean to reach full adult status, and how does a person know when the transition to adulthood is complete?

💬 Sometimes I feel like I've reached adulthood, and then I'll sit down and eat ice cream directly from the box, and I keep thinking, "I'll know I'm an adult when I don't eat ice cream right out of the box anymore." … But I guess in some ways I feel like I'm an adult. I'm a pretty responsible person. I mean, if I say I'm going to do something, I do it. Financially, I'm fairly responsible with my money. But there are still times where I think, "I can't believe I'm 25." A lot of times I don't really feel like an adult.

—Lisa, age 25 (Arnett, 2004, p. 14)

In the past two decades, many studies have examined what young people in various countries view as the key markers of the transition to adulthood. The results of the studies have been remarkably similar, in countries including the United States (Arnett, 1998a; Arnett, 2003; Nelson, 2003), Argentina (Facio & Micocci, 2003), Czech Republic (Macek, 2007), Romania (Nelson et al., 2008), Austria (Sirsch et al., 2009), the United Kingdom (Horowitz & Bromnick, 2008), Israel (Mayseless & Scharf, 2003), and China (Nelson et al., 2004). Across these studies young people from their early teens to their late 20s agreed that the most important markers of the transition to adulthood are:

1. *accepting responsibility for oneself,*
2. *making independent decisions*, and
3. *becoming financially independent.*

These three criteria rank highest not just across cultures and nations but across age groups, ethnic groups, and social classes (Arnett, 2001; Arnett, 2003; Arnett, 2011; Nelson & Luster, 2015).

Note the similarity among the top criteria: All three are characterized by *individualism;* that is, all three emphasize the importance of learning to stand alone as a self-sufficient person without relying on anyone else (Arnett, 1998). The criteria for adulthood favored by emerging adults in developed countries reflect the individualistic values of those societies (Douglass et al., 2005; Harkness et al., 2000).

In addition to the top three criteria for adulthood that have been found across cultures, studies have found distinctive cultural criteria as well (Nelson & Luster, 2015). Young Israelis view *completing military service* as important for becoming an adult, reflecting Israel's requirement of mandatory military service (Mayseless & Scharf, 2003). Young Argentines especially value being *able to support a family financially,* perhaps reflecting the economic upheavals Argentina has experienced for many years (Facio & Miccoci, 2003). Emerging adults in Korea and China view *being able to support their parents financially* as necessary for adulthood, reflecting the collectivistic value of obligation to parents found in Asian societies (Naito & Gielen, 2003; Nelson et al., 2004; Zhong & Arnett, 2014). In India, *emotional self-control* is one of the top criteria for adulthood (Nelson, 2011). This is consistent with the collectivistic emphasis in Indian culture on consideration of the well-being of others (Kakar & Kakar, 2007).

What about traditional cultures? Do they have different ideas about what marks the beginning of adulthood, compared to developed countries? The answer appears to be yes. Anthropologists have found that in virtually all traditional cultures, the transition to adulthood is clearly and explicitly marked by marriage (Schlegel, 2010). It is only after marriage that a person is considered to have attained adult status and is given adult privileges and responsibilities. In contrast, very few young people in developed countries consider marriage to be an important marker of the transition to adulthood. In fact, in developed countries marriage ranks near the bottom in surveys of possible criteria for adult status (Arnett, 2011).

What should we make of that contrast? One possible interpretation would be that traditional cultures elevate marriage as the key transition to adulthood because they prize the collectivistic value of *interdependence* (mutual obligations) more highly than the individualistic value of *independence,* and marriage signifies

Financial independence is an important criterion for adulthood in many cultures.

A newly married couple of the Maasai people of Kenya. Why is marriage important for adulthood in traditional cultures but not in the West?

that a person is taking on new interdependent relationships outside the family of origin (Arnett, 1995; Arnett, 1998; Shweder et al., 2006). Marriage is a social event rather than an individual, psychological process, and it represents the establishment of a new network of relationships with all the kin of one's marriage partner. This is especially true in traditional cultures, where family members are more likely than in the West to be close-knit and to have extensive daily contact with one another. Thus, cultures that value interdependence view marriage as the most important marker of entering adulthood because of the ways marriage confirms and strengthens interdependence.

Still, these conclusions about traditional cultures are based mainly on the observations of the anthropologists who have studied them. If you asked young people in these cultures directly about their own conceptions of what marks the beginning of adulthood, perhaps you would get a variety of answers other than marriage. For example, Susan Davis and Douglas Davis (2007) asked young Moroccans (ages 9 to 20), "How do you know you're grown up?" They found that the two most common types of responses were (1) those that emphasized chronological age or physical development, such as the beginning of facial hair among boys; and (2) those that emphasized character qualities, such as developing self-control. Few of the young people mentioned marriage, even though Davis and Davis (2007) stated that in Moroccan culture generally, "after marriage, one is considered an adult" (p. 59). This suggests that further investigation of young people's conceptions of the transition to adulthood in traditional cultures may prove enlightening, and that their views may not match the conceptions of adulthood held by adults.

Aging Begins

The first gray hairs appear in the 30s for most people.

LO 10.2 Specify the signs of the beginning of physical aging and when they appear.

As described in Chapter 9, emerging adulthood is the life stage of peak physical functioning in terms of strength, stamina, reaction time, and athletic performance. During young adulthood, physical functioning remains high. True, the peak of athletic performance has passed by the early 30s in most sports (Bruner et al., 2010). However, for ordinary people, little decline in physical functioning takes place through the 30s in most respects. Like emerging adulthood, young adulthood is a time when the immune system is strong and susceptibility to most infectious diseases is low. Furthermore, young adults are not as likely as emerging adults to engage in risky behaviors, such as excess substance use and unprotected sex with a series of partners (Claxton & van Dulmen, 2014; Johnston et al., 2014). Nor are young adults at risk yet for the types of diseases that occur in middle and later adulthood, such as cancer and heart disease. Altogether, young adulthood is time of healthy physical development for most people.

Even though most people detect little change in physical functioning in young adulthood, the aging process begins in many ways that become noticeable toward the end of this stage and the beginning of middle adulthood (see **Figure 10.1**). Perhaps the most obvious indicator that aging begins in young adulthood is graying hair. People vary widely in when their first gray hairs appear, but for most people this takes place in their 30s (Tobin, 2010). Young adulthood is also the life stage when the hair begins to thin, for both men and women, and the hairline begins to recede for many men, especially men with a European heritage. About half of men of European background experience substantial hair loss by age 40 (Ellis & Sinclair, 2008).

In cultures that value a youthful appearance, methods have been developed to conceal the physical changes in hair that accompany young adulthood.

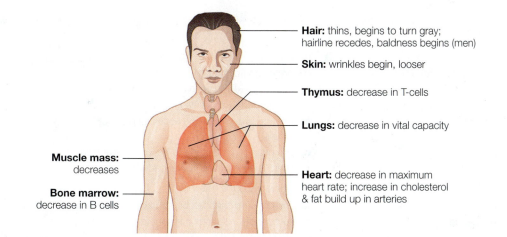

Figure 10.1 Aging in Young Adulthood

Inside figure:

Hair: thins, begins to turn gray; hairline recedes, baldness begins (men)

Skin: wrinkles begin, looser

Thymus: decrease in T-cells

Lungs: decrease in vital capacity

Muscle mass: decreases

Bone marrow: decrease in B cells

Heart: decrease in maximum heart rate; increase in cholesterol & fat build up in arteries

Women in many cultures color their hair, in part to conceal the gray hairs, and sometimes men do, too. It is estimated that one third to one half of adult women in the West and in Asia color their hair (Mendelsohn et al., 2009). Men who begin to go bald in young adulthood often believe it diminishes their physical attractiveness, and many seek hair replacement therapies and hairpieces (Cash, 2009).

Changes in skin and muscle tone also influence physical appearance. Levels of human growth hormone gradually decline in young adulthood and beyond, causing the skin to become looser and the amount of muscle mass to decrease. Other skin changes cause wrinkles to appear, especially around the eyes, forehead, and neck. People with white skin tend to exhibit skin aging earlier than people with darker skin tones, especially if their skin has been often exposed to direct sunlight in their younger years (Jackson & Aiken, 2006). Like the aging of hair, aging of skin is resisted by many people in cultures that value a youthful appearance, through methods such as plastic surgery or skin creams (McCullough & Kelly, 2009).

Most of the other physical changes that are part of aging are more subtle in young adulthood. The heart muscle starts to become more rigid, but this is not noticeable except during times of intense physical activity when there is a decrease in the maximum heart rate, which in turn decreases the amount of oxygen that the heart can deliver to the body (Haywood & Getchell, 2001). Deposits of cholesterol and fat begin to accumulate in the arteries of the cardiovascular system, especially in people whose diets are high in these substances, but there will be little risk for cardiovascular disease until middle adulthood (Daviglus et al., 2004).

Like the cardiovascular system, changes in the respiratory system are subtle and gradual in young adulthood. Rigidity gradually develops in the tendons and muscles of the lungs, chest, and ribs, which leads to a decrease in vital capacity (the maximum amount of air that can be contained in the lungs). Consequently, vital capacity decreases beginning at age 25, but only at about 10% per decade (Maharan et al., 1999). In young adulthood, this decline would be noticed only in strenuous physical exercise.

The immune system also shows signs of aging in young adulthood. As noted, it is strongest in emerging adulthood, and consequently rates of a wide range of illnesses and diseases are low. During young adulthood the immune system remains strong, but declines in ways that may not yet be detectable. The thymus, a gland in the upper part of the chest, gradually reduces its production of disease-fighting **T cells**, ceasing entirely by age 50 (Malaguarnera et al., 2001). Production of **B cells**, a type of immune cell that originates in bone marrow and produces antibodies to destroy bacteria and viruses, also declines (Issa, 2003). Also, it takes longer to recover from injuries in young adulthood than it did in emerging adulthood (Houglum, 2010).

T cells

immune cells produced by the thymus that fight disease in the body

B cells

immune cells that originate in bone marrow and produce antibodies that destroy bacteria and viruses

Practice Quiz

ANSWERS AVAILABLE IN ANSWER KEY.

1. The top three criteria that mark the transition to adult-hood across cultures and nations are characterized by _____.

   a. conformity   **c.** interdependence

   b. individualism   **d.** honesty

2. People from traditional cultures consider _____ as the key transition to adulthood.

   a. independent decision making

   b. marriage

   c. leaving the parents' house

   d. being able to sustain oneself independently

3. Skin becomes looser and muscle mass decreases during young adulthood and beyond because _____.

   a. there is a substantial decrease in iron and vitamin D

   b. there is a decrease in the production of vitamin K

   c. there is a decrease in growth hormones

   d. there is a decrease in calcium

4. Which of the following is TRUE regarding physical changes during young adulthood?

   a. Individuals with dark skin show skin aging earlier than their counterparts with white skin.

   b. The immune system increases its production of T cells and B cells.

   c. The heart muscle starts to become more rigid.

   d. There is an increase in vital capacity.

5. Vital capacity is the maximum _____.

   a. amount of air that can be contained in the lungs

   b. number of inhalations per minute of intense exercise

   c. target heart rate

   d. number of times the person's heart beats per minute

PHYSICAL DEVELOPMENT: Physical Health

In addition to showing the first signs of aging, young adults' bodies change in ways that make them likely to gain weight, even if their eating and exercise habits have not changed. Consequently, issues of fitness, diet, and obesity rise in importance during the young adult years.

Overweight and Obesity

LO 10.3   **Explain how obesity is defined, its causes, its consequences, and the keys to prevention.**

For nearly all of human history, obtaining enough food has been a problem. Today, people in many developed countries are facing a different kind of food problem: not too little food but too much, especially too much food that is loaded with fats and sugars. Perhaps our phylogenetic (species) history of being threatened with food scarcity or even starvation gave us a genetic legacy of finding satisfaction in foods laden with fats and sugars (Markham, 2009). Such foods were hard to come by until recently, and our bodies were ready to load up on them when the rare opportunity came along to consume them.

Today the risks of food scarcity and starvation are low in developed countries, yet the satisfaction we find in consuming fats and sugars remains, so many people in developed countries have a problem with *overweight* or *obesity*. As noted in Chapter 7, the medical definition of overweight or obesity is based on a person's body mass index (BMI), which is a ratio of height to weight (Centers for Disease Control and Prevention [CDC], 2009). To calculate your own BMI, go to http://www.cdc.gov/healthyweight/assessing/bmi/Index.html. For adults, the BMI thresholds for overweight and obesity are different than for children (see Chapter 7). An adult with a BMI of over 25 is classified as overweight, and an adult with a BMI over 30 is obese. For example, adults who are 5 feet 9 inches (175 cm) tall would be considered overweight if their weight exceeds 168 pounds and obese if they are over 202 pounds.

Research Focus: What Is "Overweight"? What Is "Obesity"?

One of the key issues in scientific research is how to measure the phenomenon being studied. In the case of obesity, researchers typically use body mass index (BMI) as the measure of whether someone is classified as "overweight" or "obese." BMI is a measure of the ratio of height to weight, and it's cheap, quick, and easy to calculate using this basic formula: weight (kilograms)/height (meters)^2

BMI is used as a measure of overweight and obesity because it is an indirect measure of body fat. That is, the higher a person's BMI, the more body fat they are likely to have in proportion to their height. Body fat is, in turn, related to a wide variety of health risks, from high blood pressure to diabetes to heart attacks and strokes, and even to some forms of cancer.

However, BMI is only an indirect measure of body fat. For most people it indicates body fat accurately, but there are exceptions. For example, women tend to have more body fat than men, and older people more body fat than younger people, even when their BMIs are equal. Also, some people have a BMI that is below the overweight range, but they nevertheless have high levels of abdominal fat—that is, a roll of fat right around the midsection—and abdominal fat is a predictor of health problems.

Another issue in the use of BMI as a measure of overweight and obesity is the cutoff points: 25 for overweight and 30 for obesity. There is, obviously, nothing magic about 25 or 30 that make them ideal cutoff points. A person with a BMI of 31 isn't notably more at risk for health problems than a person with a BMI of 29 is, even though the first is classified as "obese" and the second is not. But the classifications help adults to have a general idea of whether or not their current weight is within the healthy range.

Finally, there may be ethnic differences that should be taken into account. For example, Asians generally have higher proportions of body fat than non-Asians who have the same weight. For this reason, some researchers have proposed that the BMI overweight and obesity cutoffs should be lower for people of Asian backgrounds than for others. However, currently the 25 and 30 BMI cutoff points are used as the international standard.

Review Questions:

1. BMI is a direct measure of:
   a. The ratio of weight to height
   b. Body fat
   c. Heart attack risk
   d. Stroke risk

2. The BMI markers used by health authorities are _____ for overweight and _____ for obesity.
   a. 15; 20
   b. 20; 25
   c. 25; 30
   d. 30; 35

Watch   RESEARCH FOCUS: WHAT IS "OVERWEIGHT"? WHAT IS "OBESITY"?

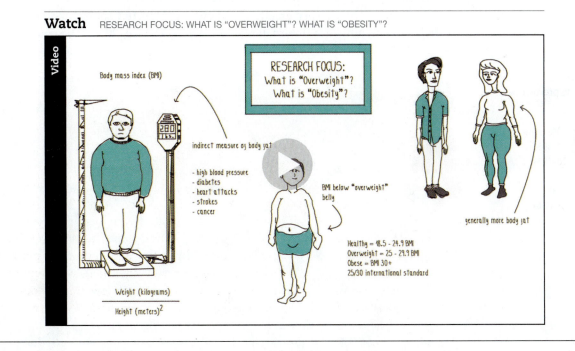

CAUSES OF OBESITY As we have seen in Chapter 7, obesity is a problem even for children in many countries. However, young adulthood is a crucial time for the development of obesity. An important physiological change takes place beginning at age 25 in the **basal metabolic rate (BMR)**, which is the amount of energy the body uses when at rest (Peitilainen et al., 2008). From age 25 to 50 the average person's BMR declines as a natural part of the aging process. This change makes it easier to accumulate weight, because

basal metabolic rate (BMR)

amount of energy the body uses when at rest

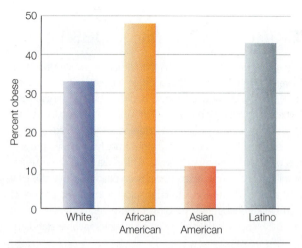

Figure 10.2 Obesity Rates by Ethnicity, Ages 24–32

SOURCE: Based on Ogden et al. (2013)

the body no longer burns as many calories when resting. Even to maintain the same weight from the late 20s through the 30s, a young adult would have to eat less or exercise more (or both) with each year.

Consequently, young adulthood is a stage when many people whose weight was in the healthy range become overweight or obese, and many of those who were already overweight become even heavier. A national American study involving thousands of adolescents, known as the National Study of Adolescent Health (see Chapter 8), followed them longitudinally from their teens to age 24–32 (Gordon-Larsen et al., 2010). Over that time obesity rates increased from 13% among the adolescents to 36% by the time they were young adults. There were substantial differences by gender and ethnic group, with obesity rates higher among females than among males (across age periods), and higher among Latinos and African Americans than among Whites and Asian Americans (see **Figure 10.2**). Rates of obesity in young adulthood were highest of all among African American women (55%).

Another biological contributor to weight is genetics. Even when eating the same diet, people will vary in how much weight they take on or off (Salbe et al., 2002). Studies of twins show that weights are more similar in monozygotic (MZ) twins than in dizygotic (DZ) twins, even when the twins grow up in different families (Collaku et al., 2004). Researchers have found that a specific protein, leptin, is involved in weight levels in both animals and humans (Zhang et al., 2006). Leptin is released by fat cells to signal that the body has had enough to eat, and it also influences BMR. Animals and humans with relatively low leptin levels become heavier, have a higher percentage of body fat, and lose weight more slowly following a reduction in food intake.

Rates of obesity vary greatly worldwide, as **Map 10.1** shows, and are strongly correlated with affluence (International Obesity Task Force, 2008). The countries with the

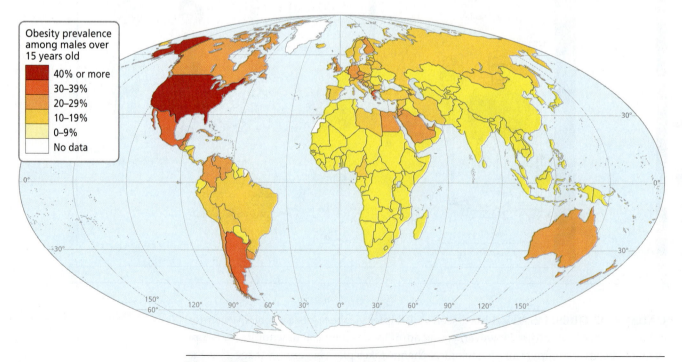

Map 10.1 Adult Obesity Rates Worldwide (Men)

Obesity rates tend to be higher in developed countries than in developing countries. What cultural and economic factors might influence obesity rates?

highest rates of obesity are also the wealthiest countries, the developed countries. Rates of obesity are lowest in Africa, the poorest region in the world. Obesity rates are increasing in some developing countries, such as China, along with economic growth (Caballero, 2007). Another contributor to obesity in developing countries is the adoption of Western foods containing unhealthy levels of fats and sugars (Bhargava, 2008). When I visited China a few years ago, in the urban areas there were Kentucky Fried Chicken outlets everywhere you looked—not exactly a source of healthy food.

Within developed countries, the opposite pattern often prevails: People in the lowest socioeconomic classes, with the least money, have the highest rates of obesity (Ball & Crawford, 2005). What explains this paradox? The main reason appears to be that in rich countries, unhealthy foods are cheap. Methods of food production and preparation are extremely efficient in developed countries, so it is possible for even relatively poor people in these countries to obtain high-calorie foods and meals at a low cost. A second important reason has to do with socioeconomic status (SES) differences in cultural beliefs and values. In developed countries, people at higher SES levels are the ones most likely to embrace values of a healthy lifestyle that includes eating organic and low-fat foods along with regular exercise (Bove & Olson, 2006; Caballero, 2007). The relation between SES and obesity is stronger for women than for men across developed countries, for unknown reasons (Ball & Crawford, 2010; Beydoun & Wang, 2010; Ogden et al., 2010).

Rates of obesity have risen dramatically in developed countries in recent decades, especially in the United States and Canada (CDC, 2010, 2014; Vanasse et al., 2006). There are many reasons for this increase. People began eating more. In one study that compared the diets of American adults in 1970 and 2000, women ate over 300 calories more per day in 2000 than in 1970, and men increased by more than 150 calories per day (National Center for Health Statistics [NCHS], 2004). A combination of more working single parents and more dual-career parents made the nightly home-cooked dinner less common (Shor, 2002). Consequently, more of what people ate over this time was "fast food" high in fats and sugars, such as hamburgers, hot dogs, pizza, and soft drinks (Critser, 2003). People have also engaged in less physical activity over recent decades (Donatelle, 2004). With a decrease in manufacturing jobs and an increase in jobs related to information and technology, more jobs involved sedentary work (Howley, 2001). Television became the main evening leisure activity, displacing more active pursuits such as gardening and sports (Proctor et al., 2003). Recent research indicates that the prevalence of obesity among American adults is continuing to rise (CDC, 2014).

People in developed countries frequently eat fast-food meals high in fats and sugars.

CRITICAL THINKING QUESTION

Given that the adoption of Western junk food is contributing to weight problems and dental problems in developing countries, do you think it is ethical for fast-food companies to market their products in these countries?

OBESITY CONSEQUENCES AND REMEDIES Obesity places people at risk for a variety of health problems in young adulthood and beyond. Common problems resulting from obesity in young adulthood are high blood pressure, diabetes, sleep disorders, and digestive problems (Calle et al., 2003; Gregg et al., 2007). There are social consequences as well. In the workplace, young adults who are obese may be the target of teasing, ridicule, and discrimination (Carr & Friedman, 2005). People who are obese have more difficulty than others in finding a romantic partner in young adulthood, and young adult women who are obese are more likely than other women to be depressed (Merten & Wickrama, 2008).

Are there effective ways for people to lose weight once they have become overweight or obese? Certainly there is no shortage of diet books, programs, foods, drinks, pills, and even surgeries promising an enthusiastic YES to this question. The reality, alas, is considerably less encouraging. No doubt some diet methods work for some people. Overall, however, most people who embrace a strategy to lose weight end up at their original weight or even heavier within 2 years (Vogels et al., 2005). Although there is a vast range of diet methods, research comparing methods has failed to show that one is more effective than the others (de Souza et al., 2012). There is no magic method for weight loss. The conclusion of research on how to lose weight is dauntingly simple (but at least it's free): eat less, eat healthier (fewer fats and sugars), and exercise more (Annunziato & Lowe, 2007; Bray & Champagne, 2004).

The Importance of Exercise

LO 10.4   **Explain the benefits of exercising in young adulthood.**

Because most people in developed countries spend their work days sitting down rather than planting and harvesting, or fetching water and firewood, or performing repetitive labor in a factory, they obtain little physical activity unless they seek it out. Children are more physically active than adolescents, and physical activity continues to drop through the 20s and 30s across developed countries (Gordon-Larsen et al., 2010; Weiss, 2004).

For young adults who do exercise regularly, there are many benefits, especially if it is **aerobic exercise** that substantially elevates the heart rate for at least 30 minutes (Shiraev & Barclay, 2012). Aerobic exercise includes activities such as running, swimming, and aerobic dancing, as well as a wide range of sports such as soccer and basketball. Aerobic exercise promotes a healthy weight, because it reduces body fat (Bray & Champagne, 2004). It also increases people's metabolic rate for several hours, which means that they continue to burn off calories long after they have stopped exercising (Janssen et al., 2004).

Exercise enhances health in other ways as well. Longitudinal studies have shown that regular exercise in young adulthood reduces the risk of a variety of illnesses and diseases in middle adulthood, including diabetes, cardiovascular disease, and several types of cancer (Bassuk & Manson, 2005; Tardon et al., 2005). A study that followed adults in Denmark over several decades showed that death rates were lower for those who maintained regular exercise in adulthood and for those who increased their levels of exercise from low to moderate or high (Schnohr et al., 2003).

There are also mental health benefits from exercising. It generates brain chemicals called **endorphins** that provide a pleasurable feeling and increase well-being (Corbin et al., 2005). People who exercise regularly have lower rates of anxiety and depression (Faulkner & Biddle, 2002). Exercise also enhances cognitive functioning (Padilla et al., 2014).

Despite these benefits, most adults in developed countries do not take part in regular exercise, especially in the United States (Sallis et al., 2009). Health authorities recommend aerobic exercise at a moderate-to-vigorous level for at least 2½ hours per week, along with muscle-strengthening exercise such as push-ups or lifting weights. About half of American adults meet the aerobic exercise guideline, but only 20% achieve both the aerobic and muscle-strengthening exercise standard (CDC, 2013). Adults at lower SES levels exercise less than those at higher SES levels, for a variety of reasons, including the facts that they have less access to health facilities (which usually cost money) and live in neighborhoods that are less safe (Wilson et al., 2004). Across SES groups, women exercise less than men.

aerobic exercise

exercise that involves vigorous movement that substantially elevates the heart rate for at least 30 minutes

endorphins

brain chemicals that provide a pleasurable feeling and increase well-being

What explains the low levels of participation in exercise, if it has so many benefits? A big part of the explanation is the busy pace of modern life, especially in young and middle adulthood (Artinian et al., 2010). Think about what daily life is like for a typical 35-year-old woman living in a developed country. She gets up early in the morning to go to work, and work involves sitting down most of the day. At the end of the workday, after driving through rush-hour traffic, she arrives home to experience what psychologist Reed Larson calls "the 6 o'clock crunch" (Larson & Richards, 1994). She greets her husband and children and catches up with them quickly, then it's time to make dinner. They make dinner and clean up, then the kids need help with their homework, or they need to be driven to music lessons or soccer practice or some other event. Then the kids need a bath, then she puts them to bed, which includes reading them a story. After they fall asleep, she and her husband drowsily watch a half hour of television in bed before falling asleep, exhausted.

Exactly when was she supposed to squeeze some exercise in there? Maybe she could have given up that half hour of television to jog around the block a few times, but you can hardly blame her if she didn't.

Now imagine that she's a single mom and has to deal with all the family and household responsibilities by herself. It is not surprising that daily exercising would be even less likely. This is part of the explanation for why exercising is less likely in low-SES groups. Single mothers are far more likely than married couples to have low incomes, for the obvious reason that they have only one income supporting the family, not two. Because single moms also bear all the household responsibilities, they have even less time for exercise than married young adults do.

Although dieting generally has poor results, the prevalence of obesity is inspiring intensive research efforts to develop medications that will prevent weight gain or promote weight loss. So far, none of them has proven to be very effective and they are not widely used (Bolen et al., 2010). It is also possible that new foods will be developed, possibly through genetic engineering, that will be just as tasty as high-fat, high-sugar foods but without causing obesity. However, there is no sign that such foods are likely to be developed any time soon.

Practice Quiz   ANSWERS AVAILABLE IN ANSWER KEY.

1. Amity is an adult with a BMI of 27. According to the Centers for Disease Control and Prevention, she would be classified as _____.

   a. average weight
   c. overweight
   b. underweight
   d. obese

2. Between the ages of 25 and 50, an individual's basal metabolic rate _____.

   a. increases steadily
   b. declines
   c. remains the same
   d. stays the same until the late 40's and then declines sharply

3. Based on a longitudinal study, the National Study of Adolescent Health, rates of obesity in young adulthood were highest among _____.

   a. African American men
   b. African American women
   c. European American men
   d. Asian men

4. Which of the following individuals is likely to spend the least amount of time exercising?

   a. Harrison who is of high SES and male
   b. Benita who is of low SES and female
   c. Ian who is of low SES and male
   d. Ramona who is of middle SES and female

5. Beyond reducing body fat, exercise has also been shown to _____.

   a. lower metabolic rate for several hours after exercise
   b. lower rates of schizophrenia and depression
   c. decrease white blood cells
   d. lower the death rate of those who maintain regular exercise in adulthood

Summary: Physical Development

LO 10.1 **Compare and contrast criteria for adulthood according to young people across cultures.**

Across developed countries, three common criteria for marking the attainment of adulthood are accepting responsibility for one's self, making independent decisions, and becoming financially independent.

Emerging adults in Asian cultures often value being able to support parents financially as a criterion for adulthood, and in many traditional cultures, marriage is the primary marker. There are also culturally-specific criteria such as, in Israel, completing mandatory military service.

LO 10.2 **Specify the signs of the beginning of physical aging and when they appear.**

Physical health is generally very good in young adulthood, but the aging process is evident in changes such as graying hair and a less effective immune system.

LO 10.3 **Explain how obesity is defined, its causes, its consequences, and the keys to prevention.**

Among adults, a BMI above 25 is classified as overweight and above 30 is considered obesity. Obesity increases sharply in prevalence during young adulthood in developed countries, partly due to a decrease in the basal metabolic rate but also due to sedentary work, little regular exercise, and eating too much food containing fats and sugars. Obesity places young adults at risk for a variety of health problems and social consequences. Although a vast range of diet programs have promised to reduce obesity, the only effective approach supported by research is to exercise more, eat less, and eat healthier foods.

LO 10.4 **Explain the benefits of exercising in young adulthood.**

Regular exercise promotes a healthy weight and reduces the risk of a variety of diseases. It also promotes mental health by increasing well-being and reducing anxiety and depression.

Section 2   Cognitive Development

∨   Learning Objectives

10.5   Summarize the extent to which IQ scores in childhood and adolescence predict career success in young adulthood.

10.6   Describe the different components that cultures include as part of their conceptions of intelligence.

10.7   Define expertise and explain why it is often first reached in young adulthood.

10.8   Explain how creativity is related to expertise and how it changes with age.

COGNITIVE DEVELOPMENT: Adult Intelligence

Although the focus of most research concerning cognitive development is on either advances in childhood or declines in old age, young adulthood is also a time of important changes. Various kinds of intelligence may advance and decline in different ways.

IQ Scores and Career Success

LO 10.5   **Summarize the extent to which IQ scores in childhood and adolescence predict career success in young adulthood.**

Intelligence tests administered in childhood and adolescence (see Chapter 7) are moderately correlated with school success, and they are often used in school settings to identify children and adolescents who have learning disabilities. IQ tests predict success in adulthood as well. One meta-analysis of longitudinal studies on intelligence found that scores on IQ tests in childhood were a powerful predictor of income and occupational status in adulthood (Strenze, 2007). Adults who score in the lowest 25% of the distribution on IQ tests are likely to have trouble performing most kinds of adult work successfully, especially work that involves the use of information and technology. Adults who score in the highest 25% of the IQ distribution often do well in their careers, in terms of income, advancement, and awards.

Longitudinal studies of children with high IQs show that IQ is a strong predictor of adult success (Benbow & Lubinski, 2009). For example, Louis Terman, one of the original developers of the Stanford Binet test, began a study in the 1920s of 1,500 children with exceptionally high IQ scores, of 140 or higher (the median IQ for the population as a whole is 100). The study followed these "Termites" (as they came to be called) for several decades into adulthood, along with a comparison group of children with average IQs. As a group, the Termites had a great deal of educational and occupational success, with dozens of patents, hundreds of books, and many other achievements to their credit (Terman & Oden, 1959). They were also less likely than the persons in the comparison group to have personal problems in adulthood, including alcoholism, divorce, and mental disorders. Since this classic study, other studies of children with exceptionally high

IQs have confirmed its findings (Benbow & Lubinski, 2009). Similarly, a low IQ in middle childhood is predictive of poor school performance and other difficulties in the present and future (McCartney & Berry, 2009).

Nevertheless, there is much about career success in adulthood that IQ scores do not predict (Labouvie-Vief, 2006; Rode et al., 2008). As we have seen in Chapter 9, the kinds of problems encountered by adults in their work—or their personal relationships—rarely have the kind of simple, definite solutions IQ tests reward. The problems adults confront are often complicated and require the ability to make decisions despite having insufficient or ambiguous information. Furthermore, different cultures emphasize different aspects of intelligence, as we will see next.

Cultural Conceptions of Intelligence

LO 10.6   **Describe the different components that cultures include as part of their conceptions of intelligence.**

Although the body of research showing a relation between IQ and adult career success is large, nearly all of it is concentrated in developed countries, and some scholars have asserted that people in non-Western cultures may have quite different ideas about what constitutes intelligence. Foremost among the scholars promoting a broader, more culturally based view of intelligence is Robert Sternberg, whose triarchic theory of intelligence we explored in Chapter 7 (Sternberg, 2004; Sternberg, 2007; Sternberg, 2010; Sternberg & Gringorenko, 2004; Sternberg & Gringorenko, 2005). Sternberg's review of intelligence as conceptualized across cultures finds a great deal of variety. Among Chinese adults, for example, intelligence includes features such as humility, self-knowledge, and freedom from conventional standards of judgment (Sternberg & Grigorenko, 2004).

Studies in various African cultures show a common theme that intelligence includes skills that help promote group harmony and social responsibilities. For example, adults in Zambia emphasize cooperativeness and obedience as qualities of intelligence (Serpell, 1996). In Kenya, adults include responsible participation in family and social life as important aspects of intelligence (Super & Harkness, 1993). In Zimbabwe, the word for intelligence, *ngware*, literally means to be prudent and cautious, especially in social relations (Sternberg & Grigorenko, 2004). In both Asian and African cultures, a common theme of conceptions of intelligence is that it includes social elements as well as cognitive elements such as knowledge (Sternberg, 2007).

According to Sternberg, knowledge of hunting and fishing is a component of intelligence in some cultures. Here, a Yup'ik hunter takes aim at a whale.

Sternberg (2004; 2010) has also argued that intelligence includes practical aspects, applied to the problems and challenges of everyday life. This was demonstrated among the Yup'ik, a Native Alaskan culture whose daily life is based mainly on hunting and fishing, in a study led by Sternberg's frequent collaborator, Elena Grigorenko. Grigorenko and colleagues (2004) began by interviewing adults and elders in Yup'ik culture about the knowledge required for performance in the situations encountered in everyday life among the Yup'ik. From these interviews the researchers developed a test of Yup'ik practical intelligence, covering topics such as how to hunt and fish, where to find edible berries, and knowledge of the weather. Adolescents in the study were given this test of practical intelligence as well as standard IQ tests. The researchers also interviewed adolescents, adults, and elders about the qualities most valued among the Yup'ik people, then asked the adults and elders to rate the adolescents on these qualities.

The results indicated that there was a correlation between the adolescents' performance on the test of practical intelligence and the likelihood that they would be nominated by the adults and elders for possessing the valued Yup'ik qualities. Furthermore, performance on the practical intelligence test was more likely than performance on the standard IQ test to predict which adolescents would be nominated. The researchers interpreted this finding as demonstrating that practical intelligence is a key component of intelligence that is culture-specific and is not adequately assessed by standard IQ tests.

In presenting the results, the researchers anticipated that others may object that their test of practical intelligence did not really measure intelligence. However, they responded:

> In terms of the kinds of knowledge and skills considered adaptive in the culture we have studied, we believe our measure was of intelligence in the sense in which the term most often has been used, namely, as a construct reflecting cultural adaptation. One could further argue that folk knowledge somehow should not "count." But it counts in the culture we studied and is the basis for everyday survival. And if intelligence is not about individual differences in everyday survival skills, what is it—or should it be—about?

Practice Quiz   ANSWERS AVAILABLE IN ANSWER KEY.

1. Longitudinal research on Terman's "Termites" has shown _____.

   a. that they had higher rates of alcoholism and divorce than a comparison group of individuals with average IQs
   b. they had a great deal of educational and occupational success
   c. that women achieved high levels of occupational success, but only a small percentage of the men did
   d. career success peaked in emerging adulthood, but there was a steep decline in the fourth decade of life as most of the sample experienced a mid-life crisis

2. IQ in childhood _____.

   a. has no relation to later occupational status
   b. correlates positively with later income, but not other measures of success
   c. is a powerful predictor of income and occupational status in adulthood
   d. has not been studied as a predictor of later adulthood outcomes because that would be considered unethical

3. Which of the following is the most accurate about Terman's research?

   a. Only the Termites who pursued careers in technology had more career success than the comparison group with average IQs.
   b. The price of a high IQ was a high risk of personal problems.
   c. The Termites were less likely to have personal problems such as alcoholism, divorce, and mental disorders.
   d. There is a correlation between childhood IQ and adult success, but it is weak.

4. In both Asian and _____ cultures, a common theme of conceptions of intelligence is that it includes social elements, as well as cognitive elements such as knowledge.

   a. French
   b. Italian
   c. African
   d. Irish

5. Cross-cultural research on intelligence _____.

   a. has not been conducted
   b. has shown that the most important qualities across cultures are analytical and verbal skills
   c. has shown that skills that allow individuals to adapt to their environment are considered a type of intelligence
   d. can only be conducted in cultures where individuals can read the questions on IQ tests

COGNITIVE DEVELOPMENT: Cognitive Changes in Young Adulthood

At what point in our life span is cognitive development fully complete? For Piaget, the culmination of cognitive maturation is the attainment of *formal operations* around age 15–20 (see Chapter 8). Other research indicates that cognitive development continues in important ways during emerging adulthood (see Chapter 9). Here, we look at two aspects of cognitive development that occur during the young adulthood years: the acquisition of expertise and creativity.

Expertise

LO 10.7 **Define expertise and explain why it is often first reached in young adulthood.**

One important way cognitive development changes from emerging adulthood to young adulthood is that the focus becomes more on gaining **expertise**, meaning *extensive knowledge and skills in a specific field* (Chi et al., 2014). According to scholars in this area, it takes about 10 years of study or practice in most fields to attain expertise (Feldhusen, 2005). Because most people begin steady work in a specific field sometime in their 20s, for most people expertise is first reached a decade later, during the young adult years, at some point in their 30s. Expertise continues to develop through middle adulthood, as we'll see in Chapter 11.

Gaining expertise allows people to address problems and tasks in their field more quickly and efficiently (Chi et al., 2014). They build a store of knowledge and experience in their field, and when confronted with a problem or task they are likely to know something about it and to have had experience with something similar. This allows them to form ideas quickly about how the new situation should be addressed. They know not only what has worked in the past but also what has not worked, so they waste less time than novices do in pursuing potential solutions that are unlikely to bear fruit (Masunaga & Horn, 2001). For example, someone who has gained expertise in running a business knows from experience what kinds of problems are likely to arise and may be able to anticipate and head them off before they develop. When problems do arise, the expertise of the business manager allows him or her to draw from a wide range of knowledge and experience with similar problems in the past in order to devise a solution that is likely to be effective.

Research in neuropsychology has begun to illuminate the ways that brain development underlies the development of expertise during young adulthood (Chi et al., 2014). As we have seen in Chapter 8, a burst of brain development takes place during adolescence, as dendritic connections between neurons multiply vastly (overproduction/exuberance) and are then pared down through synaptic pruning. The process of synaptic pruning continues into the 20s, but by the late 20s the brain is believed to reach adult maturity, in the sense that the period of overproduction/exuberance is long past and synaptic pruning is no longer taking place at a high rate. Researchers on neuropsychology especially note how the maturity of the frontal cortex during young adulthood reflects cognitive changes that underlie expertise (Eslinger & Biddle, 2008). The maturity of the frontal cortex promotes the kind of focused attention and goal-directed behavior that leads to expertise.

Creativity

LO 10.8 **Explain how creativity is related to expertise and how it changes with age.**

Another aspect of cognitive development that is especially important in young adulthood is **creativity**. A creative person is someone who is able to put ideas or materials together in new, culturally meaningful ways. A person who invents a new electronic device is exhibiting creativity, as is a person who composes a piece of music.

Creativity is easier to define than to measure. Because creativity involves coming up with something new, it is difficult to derive a test for it (Runco, 2014). Tests are scored for "right answers," and creativity involves coming up with answers than no one had thought of before. Assessments of creativity have focused instead on the number of works a person produces, or on the timing of a person's "best" works, as determined by experts in the area or by the works' influence. For example, creativity in musical composition could be judged by how much a work has been performed; creativity in academic

expertise
extensive knowledge and skills in a specific field

creativity
ability to put ideas or materials together in new, culturally meaningful ways

scholarship could be judged by how many times a work has been cited in publications by other scholars.

Using a variety of measures, young adulthood has been found to be an exceptionally creative life stage. A number of studies of persons with outstanding accomplishments have found that their creative achievements rise during young adulthood and peak in the late 30s and early 40s, then gradually decline through middle and later adulthood (Dennis, 1966; Dixon, 2003; Runco, 2014; Simonton, 1996; Simonton, 2000).

Why is young adulthood such a creative period? The answer may have something to do with the relation between creativity and expertise. As noted earlier, in any field it takes time to develop expertise, usually about 10 years. According to scholars of creativity, it is only after expertise is established in a field that people are capable of producing creative work (Feldman, 1999; Simonton, 2000). Most people choose a field sometime in their 20s, so their creativity flourishes during young adulthood, 10 years later. Gaining expertise enables people to move from *problem solving* to *problem finding,* as they use their acquired knowledge and skills to think in new ways (Arlin, 1989; Feldhusen, 2005; Hu et al., 2010). Young adulthood is the life stage when people are most likely to be able to combine expertise with other cognitive qualities that contribute to creativity: openness to new ideas, tolerance for ambiguity, and willingness to take intellectual risks (Lubart, 2003; Sternberg et al., 2002).

But why does creativity not continue to rise throughout life, since people continue to develop expertise in middle adulthood and beyond? Apparently because "familiarity breeds rigidity," as one early scholar of creativity put it (Mednick, 1963). At first, gaining expertise promotes creativity, because expertise provides the knowledge and skills that are the raw materials of creative work. Eventually, however, expertise becomes a liability. The problems, concepts, materials, and ideas people are working with are no longer fresh, and they have more difficulty seeing them in new ways. Their accumulated expertise now tends to steer them down the same paths they have trod many times before rather than forging new ones. Cognitive flexibility wanes, as people find it more difficult to give things a fresh look.

Young adulthood is often a life stage when creativity flourishes. Here, a young man in Indonesia paints a fabric in a traditional style known as batik.

Although young adulthood is often an exceptionally creative life stage, there are many variations and individual differences (Simonton, 2010). The peak of creativity varies across different fields. Artists, musicians, inventors, mathematicians, and physicists tend to be most creative in their 20s and 30s (Gardner, 1993; Runco, 2014). In contrast, novelists are often most creative in their 40s, 50s, and even 60s.

There are also many exceptions to the general rule that creativity peaks in young adulthood (Csikszentmihalyi & Nakamura, 2006). Beethoven completed his Ninth Symphony, often considered his best, at the age of 54. Picasso painted important works through his 70s and 80s. Sigmund Freud published *Civilization and Its Discontents,* one of his most influential works, in 1930, when he was 74. Joyce Carol Oates (b. 1938) is still writing powerful, popular, critically acclaimed novels in her 70s. Highly creative people are often creative throughout life, even if the peak of their creativity comes in young adulthood (Dixon, 2003; Feldhusen, 2005).

CRITICAL THINKING QUESTION

Think of some of the technological inventions of the past 20 years that have quickly spread around the world. Do the ages of the inventors fit the description here of the development of expertise and creativity?

Practice Quiz

1. Which of the following is TRUE about expertise?
   a. According to most researchers in the field, it takes about 25 years of study and practice in most fields to attain expertise.
   b. Expertise is associated with changes in the brain.
   c. Expertise tends to decline after young adulthood.
   d. Expertise is defined in terms of knowledge base, rather than problem solving, because it is difficult to measure problem solving skills.

2. Maturity of _____ reflects cognitive changes that underlie expertise.
   a. the synapses
   b. the frontal cortex
   c. the occipital lobe
   d. the hippocampus

3. A person who is high in _____ is able to put ideas or materials together in new, culturally meaningful ways.
   a. generativity
   b. kinesthetic intelligence
   c. creativity
   d. intrapersonal intelligence

4. Which statement about research on creativity is TRUE?
   a. Measures of creativity exist only in the fine arts.
   b. People reach a peak in creativity before attaining expertise in a particular domain and becoming set in their ways.
   c. Across various fields, the peak of creativity is in the 50's and early 60's.
   d. Highly creative people are often creative throughout life.

5. Which of the following, when combined with expertise, is most likely to contribute to creativity?
   a. Proficiency in computer skills
   b. Proficiency in math
   c. Tolerance for ambiguity
   d. Exceptional visual-spatial skills

Summary: Cognitive Development

LO 10.5 **Summarize the extent to which IQ scores in childhood and adolescence predict career success in young adulthood.**

Young adulthood is a period when many aspects of intelligence reach their peak. IQ scores in childhood and adolescence predict many aspects of young adult development with substantial accuracy, including income and occupational status.

LO 10.6 **Describe the different components that cultures include as part of their conceptions of intelligence.**

Many cultures include social skills and social responsibility in their conceptions of intelligence. According to Sternberg, intelligence also has a practical dimension that is culture-specific, reflecting knowledge of culturally important information and mastery of cultural skills.

LO 10.7 **Define expertise and explain why it is often first reached in young adulthood.**

Expertise is defined as extensive knowledge and skills in a specific field. It usually takes about 10 years to establish, so it often develops as emerging adults become young adults and stay in a stable line of work for an extended period of years.

LO 10.8 **Explain how creativity is related to expertise and how it changes with age.**

Expertise is usually required before a person knows enough about a field and has sufficient skills to produce a creative work. Consequently, creativity often peaks in young adulthood, although there are wide variations across fields and among individuals.

Section 3 Emotional and Social Development

 ## Learning Objectives

10.9 Describe Erikson's theory of emotional and psychosocial development in young adulthood.

10.10 Describe the three qualities in Sternberg's theory of love and how they change with age.

10.11 Compare and contrast different cultural traditions regarding marriage, and identify the factors that predict marital satisfaction in Western cultures.

10.12 Describe the most common causes of divorce in young adulthood, and explain why the United States has the highest divorce rate in the world.

10.13 Appraise common myths about single adults, and describe cultural and ethnic variations in singlehood.

10.14 Compare and contrast gay and lesbian partnerships with heterosexual partnerships, and describe how these partnerships have changed in recent years.

10.15 Explain why young adulthood tends to be a stage of peak sexual behavior, and identify gender differences in sexuality.

10.16 Summarize the social and emotional impact of becoming a parent, and describe the unique challenges faced by single parents.

10.17 List the stages of occupational development in Super's theory, and explain how personality and gender shape occupational goals.

10.18 Explain the relationship between community involvement and television use in the lives of young adults.

EMOTIONAL AND SOCIAL DEVELOPMENT: Emotional Development in Young Adulthood

Forming emotional relationships is an important part of human development at all life stages, but young adulthood is a key period in this respect. It is during young adulthood that most people make a commitment to a person who will be their main partner for the majority of their adult lives. The relationship with this partner will be at the center of the young adult's emotional life and will influence development in other contexts as well, including parenthood and work. Here we look at two theories of love. Later in the section we will look at other aspects of love and marriage.

Intimacy Versus Isolation: Erikson's Theory

LO 10.9 **Describe Erikson's theory of emotional and psychosocial development in young adulthood.**

In Erik Erikson's theory of the life span, **intimacy versus isolation** is the central emotional and psychosocial issue of young adulthood (see Chapter 1; Erikson, 1950). As we have seen in previous chapters, adolescence and emerging adulthood involve the challenge of forming an identity in love, work, and ideology. According to Erikson, establishing intimacy means uniting your newly formed identity with another person in an enduring, committed, intimate relationship. Healthy intimacy does not mean "losing yourself" in devotion to another person; on the contrary, it means having a strong enough identity to become emotionally close to someone without submerging yourself. The alternative is isolation, characterized by an inability to form an intimate relationship.

Some research supports Erikson's view that intimacy in young adulthood is built on a previous foundation of identity development (Beyers & Seiffge-Krenke, 2010; Kroger, 2002; Markstrom & Kalmanir, 2001). For example, in one study of adolescents and emerging adults (ages 12–24), at all ages identity development was a strong predictor of involvement in an intimate romantic relationship (Montgomery, 2005). In an analysis summarizing many studies of the relationship between identity and intimacy status, Annie Årseth and colleagues (2009) concluded that identity sometimes develops prior to intimacy, but they can also develop together and mutually reinforce each other. It should be noted that research on this topic has taken place only in the West, where intimacy is considered to be the ideal basis for romantic relationships and marriage. This is not true in all cultures, as we shall see shortly.

A substantial amount of the research on the relation between identity and intimacy has focused on gender differences. Most studies indicate that intimacy issues arise earlier for females than for males, so that females often accomplish intimacy before identity, or that developmental processes of identity and intimacy take place simultaneously for females, whereas males tend to achieve identity before intimacy (Årseth et al., 2009; Lytle et al., 1997). The relation between identity and intimacy tends to be more complex for young women than for young men, because they are more likely to take their intimate relationships into account in forming their personal identity goals, especially with respect to education and work (Frisén & Wängqvist, 2011).

Sternberg's Theory of Love

LO 10.10 **Describe the three qualities in Sternberg's theory of love and how they change with age.**

Another important theory that is relevant to the development of love in the lives of young adults is the **triangular theory of love** developed by Robert Sternberg (Sternberg, 1986; Sternberg, 1987; Sternberg, 1988; Sternberg, 2013; Sternberg & Weis, 2006). Sternberg proposed that different types of love involve combining three fundamental qualities in different ways. These three qualities are passion, intimacy, and commitment. *Passion* involves physical attraction and sexual desire. It is emotional as well as physical and may involve intense emotions such as anxiety, delight, anger, and jealousy. *Intimacy* is feelings of closeness and emotional attachment. It includes mutual understanding, mutual support, and open communication about issues not discussed with anyone else. *Commitment* is the pledge to love someone over the long run, through the ups and downs that are often part of love. Commitment is what sustains a long-term relationship through fluctuations in passion and intimacy.

intimacy versus isolation
in Erikson's life-span theory, the central emotional and psychosocial issue of young adulthood, in which the challenge is to unite the newly formed identity with another person in an enduring, committed, intimate relationship

triangular theory of love
Sternberg's theory that different types of love involve combining three fundamental qualities in different ways: passion, intimacy, and commitment

According to Erikson, intimacy versus isolation is the central issue of young adulthood.

These three qualities of love can be combined into seven different forms of love, as follows (**Figure 10.3**):

- *Liking* is intimacy alone, without passion or commitment. This is the type of love that characterizes most friendships. Friendships often involve some level of intimacy, but without passion and without an enduring commitment. Most people have many friendships that come and go in the course of their lives.
- *Infatuation* is passion alone, without intimacy or commitment. Infatuation involves a great deal of physiological and emotional arousal, and a heightened level of sexual desire, but without emotional closeness to the person or an enduring commitment.
- *Empty love* is commitment alone, without passion or intimacy. This might apply to a couple who have been married for many years and who have lost the passion and intimacy in their relationship but nevertheless remain together. It also could apply to the early stage of marriage in cultures where marriages are arranged and partners are selected by the parents rather than chosen by the young people themselves (Hatfield & Rapson, 2005; Schlegel, 2010). However, arranged marriages that begin as empty love may eventually develop passion and intimacy.
- *Romantic love* combines passion and intimacy, but without commitment. This is the kind of love people mean when they talk about being "in love." It is often experienced as intense and joyful, but it rarely lasts long.
- *Companionate love* combines intimacy and commitment, but without passion. It may be applied to married or long-term couples who have gradually decreased in their passion for each other but have maintained the other qualities of their love. It could also be applied to unusually close friendships, as well as to close family relationships.
- *Fatuous* (which means "silly" or "foolish") *love* involves passion and commitment without intimacy. This kind of love would apply to a "whirlwind" courtship where two people meet, fall passionately in love, and get married, all within a few weeks, before they even have time to know each other well.
- *Consummate love* integrates all three aspects of love into the ultimate love relationship. Of course, even if consummate love is reached in a relationship, over time passion may fade, or intimacy may falter, or commitment may be betrayed. But this is the kind of love that represents the ideal for many people.

Any of these types of love could occur in young adulthood. However, according to Sternberg (1986), the three qualities that form the different types of love follow predictable developmental patterns according to the duration of the relationship. As shown in **Figure 10.4**, passion tends to peak early in a relationship and then fade. This observation fits well with research finding that married couples often experience their highest levels of mutual happiness and marital satisfaction in the first year or two of their marriage (Cherlin, 2009). Passion is high, they feel deeply "in love," and they enjoy the afterglow from their wedding. However, passion fades fairly quickly in most relationships, as partners become used to each other and the stresses and conflicts of daily life accumulate. In contrast, intimacy and commitment begin lower than passion

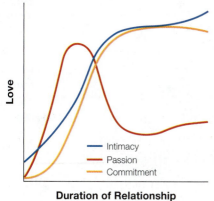

Figure 10.3 Sternberg's Triangular Theory of Love

Three components, intimacy, passion, and commitment, are combined in various ways to form seven different types of love.
SOURCE: Sternberg (1988), p. 122

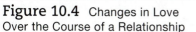

Figure 10.4 Changes in Love Over the Course of a Relationship

In Sternberg's theory, passion peaks early and then fades, whereas intimacy and commitment rise and then remain steady.
SOURCE: Based on Sternberg (1986)

and take longer to develop, but they also endure longer. Because most people first marry or form another type of long-term partnership in young adulthood, this is a life stage when people are most likely to feel a peak of passion in their romantic relationship, and also a stage when the feelings of intimacy and commitment in the relationship are gradually growing.

Practice Quiz   ANSWERS AVAILABLE IN ANSWER KEY.

1. Erik Erikson's notion of intimacy is best described as _____.
   a. when an individual develops the skills necessary for a relationship by modeling it after what he or she has observed from their environment
   b. uniting your newly formed identity with another person in an enduring, committed, emotionally close relationship
   c. when the ego works in conjunction with the superego to satisfy the desires of the id in a socially acceptable way
   d. a gratifying sexual relationship

2. Johanna is in her early 30's. According to Erik Erikson, she should be in the midst of the crisis of _____.
   a. identity versus role confusion
   b. intimacy versus isolation
   c. generativity versus stagnation
   d. autonomy versus shame and doubt

3. Erikson thought that intimacy was not possible until individuals _____.
   a. had established themselves in their career
   b. were capable of making independent decisions
   c. had a fairly stable sense of identity
   d. possessed formal operational thinking

4. Your friend's parents have been married for 25 years and have a relationship based on mutual understanding and support. You can tell that they care for each other, but the "romance" seems to be gone. According to Sternberg, what type of love do you think they are experiencing at this time?
   a. Consummate love   c. Compassionate love
   b. Companionate love   d. Empty

5. Sternberg's triangular theory of love includes three components: intimacy, passion, and _____.
   a. compassion   c. support
   b. commitment   d. similarity

EMOTIONAL AND SOCIAL DEVELOPMENT: The Social and Cultural Contexts of Young Adulthood

Young adulthood is a life stage when developing new family relationships is the central focus of social life for most people. Usually this means entering marriage and parenthood, but not always. Some people remain single, and some people become parents without becoming married. Work is another important social context in young adulthood, as most people try to settle into an occupation and develop a career. In addition to family and work, many young adults devote time to community activities, and most of them find time for media use, especially television.

Marriage in Young Adulthood

LO 10.11 **Compare and contrast different cultural traditions regarding marriage, and identify the factors that predict marital satisfaction in Western cultures.**

Marriage is a human universal. It is found in all cultures, and in all cultures it is an economic and sexual union that is expected to be more or less permanent (Ember et al., 2011). About 90% of people in most societies eventually marry or form another kind of long-term romantic partnership (King, 2005).

Why does marriage exist everywhere? A variety of explanations have been proposed (Thornton, 2009). All cultures have a division of labor and roles by gender, and marriage is a way of uniting people to serve complementary gender roles. Another explanation is that marriage reduces sexual competition and conflict, because it allows people to have socially-approved sexual relations on a regular basis. Perhaps the most compelling explanation is that marriage is necessary for a species like us that has such a long period of infant dependency, during which mother and infant would be highly vulnerable if they had no one to protect and provide for them (Buss, 2007). Among other animal species, too, stable mating pairs are most likely to exist in species where mothers are unable to feed both themselves and their young for an extended period following birth, and so require a mate who can bring back food or watch the young while she goes off to find food herself.

Although marriage is a human universal, it also varies immensely across and within cultures (Thornton, 2009). There are notable variations across cultures in the ways marriage partners are chosen, the economic transactions that accompany marriage, and the number of marriage partners a person may take.

CULTURAL VARIATIONS ON CHOOSING A MARRIAGE PARTNER In Chapter 9, we looked at how emerging adults choose a romantic partner, noting that intimacy and consensual validation combine to form the ideal of finding a "soul mate." But when it comes down to marriage, what determines how people choose a partner?

Psychologist David Buss (2003; Buss et al., 1990) carried out a massive study of over 10,000 young people in 37 countries on this question. The countries were from all over the world, including Africa, Asia, eastern and western Europe, and North and South America. The questionnaire had to be translated into 37 languages, with great care taken to make the meanings of words such as "love" as similar as possible in every country. In many of the countries, some of the young people were illiterate, so the questions had to be read aloud to them.

Despite all these challenges, the results showed impressive consistencies across countries and across genders (see **Table 10.1**). "Mutual attraction—love" ranked first among marriage criteria across countries, followed by "dependable character," "emotional stability and maturity," and "pleasing disposition." This cross-cultural consistency is somewhat surprising, given that there are many cultures where love is not the basis of marriage, as we will soon see. Similarity in religious and political background ranked very low, which is also surprising, given that (as noted in Chapter 9) people tend to marry others who are similar to them in these ways. "Good financial prospects" also ranked low.

Although the cross-cultural similarities were strong and striking, some cross-cultural differences were also notable. The sharpest cross-cultural division was on the issue of chastity (maintaining virginity until marriage). In Eastern cultures (e.g., China, India, Indonesia) and Middle Eastern cultures (Iran, Palestinian Arabs in Israel), chastity was rated as highly important in a marriage partner. However, in the West (e.g., Finland, France, Norway, Germany), chastity was generally considered unimportant. Also, even though "Mutual attraction—love" ranked highest overall, it did not rank highest in all countries. For example, Chinese women ranked it 8th, and South African men ranked it 10th.

Between men and women, too, there were notable differences despite their overall similarities, and these differences have been found in other surveys as well (Buunk, 2002; Cramer et al., 2003; Eagly & Wood, 2003). Although both sexes prize physical attractiveness, men prize it more highly than women (Perilloux et al., 2011). In contrast, women are more likely to value ambition and

Table 10.1 The Importance of Various Traits in Mate Selection Throughout the World

Men's Rankings	Women's Rankings
1. Mutual attraction—love	1. Mutual attraction—love
2. Dependable character	2. Dependable character
3. Emotional stability and maturity	3. Emotional stability and maturity
4. Pleasing disposition	4. Pleasing disposition
5. Good health	5. Education and intelligence
6. Education and intelligence	6. Sociability
7. Sociability	7. Good health
8. Desire for home and children	8. Desire for home and children
9. Refinement, neatness	9. Ambition and industriousness
10. Good looks	10. Refinement, neatness

SOURCE: Based on Hatfield & Rapson (2005)

In India and other cultures with arranged marriages, love is expected to develop after marriage, not before.

financial status in a prospective marriage partner (although both sexes rank these traits fairly low). In general, the more gender equality exists in a country, the more similar men and women are in their mate preferences (Toro-Morn & Sprecher, 2003). There are also generational differences, with younger men and women more similar than older men and women in the traits they value in a mate (Buss, 2003; Henry et al., 2013). This reflects growing gender equality in recent decades and less sharp division of gender roles.

One important variation on marriage outside the West is **polygyny**, the cultural custom in which men may have more than one wife. This form of marriage exists in several parts of the world, including parts of Asia and the Middle East. However, it is most common of all in sub-Saharan Africa. In one survey of 22 African countries, the median rate of polygynous marriages across countries was about 30% (Riley Bove, 2009). Polygyny was more common in rural areas than in urban areas, and the more education women had, the less likely they were to be in a polygynous marriage. Because polygyny is less likely with urban residence and education, it may be that as Africa continues to develop economically, the custom of polygyny will fade. However, for now polygyny is a major influence on adult development throughout Africa.

Another important area of cultural variability in marriage involves the question of who chooses the marriage partner. The idea that romantic love should be the basis of marriage is only about 300 years old in the West and is even newer in most of the rest of the world (Hatfield & Rapson, 2005). Marriage has more often been seen by cultures as an alliance between two *families,* rather than as the uniting of two individuals (Buunk et al., 2008). Parents and other adult kin have often held the power to arrange the marriages of their young people, sometimes with the young person's consent, sometimes without it. The most important considerations in an **arranged marriage** do not usually include the prospective bride and groom's love for one another—often they do not even know each other—or even their personal compatibility. Instead, the desirability of marriage between them is decided by each family on the basis of the other family's status, religion, and wealth. Economic considerations have often been of primary importance.

Arranged marriage is not the only way that marriage involves economic considerations. In about three-quarters of the cultures studied by anthropologists, some kind of explicit economic transaction takes place as part of marriage (Ember et al., 2011). These transactions take three forms: bride price, bride service, and dowry.

Bride price is the most common form of economic requirement for marriage, found in about half of the cultures that include economic factors as part of marriage (Ember et al., 2011). It involves a substantial gift of money or property (such as livestock or food) from the groom and his kin to the bride and her kin. For example, in many east African cultures, the bride price is in the form of cattle. Among Native Americans in North America, horses were traditionally the currency of bride price. In Nepal the bride price includes a live pig, several bags of rice, and a substantial amount of liquor (Hardman, 2000). With economic development around the world, money has become increasingly common for paying the bride price. The requirement of bride price is found in all world regions, but especially in African cultures (Esen, 2004).

polygyny
cultural tradition in which men have more than one wife

arranged marriage
marriage in which partners are chosen not by each other, but by their families, on the basis of family status, religion, and wealth

bride price
economic requirement for marriage that involves a substantial gift of money or property from the groom and his kin to the bride and her kin

Cultural Focus: Marriage and Love Relationships Across Cultures

Some cultures with a tradition of arranged marriage are beginning to change in their marriage expectations through the influence of globalization. India, for example, has a history of arranged marriage that has existed for 6,000 years (Prakasa & Rao, 1979). Today, however, nearly 40% of young Indians say they intend to choose their own mates (Chaudhary & Sharma, 2007; Netting, 2010). A similar pattern is taking place in many other cultures with a tradition of arranged marriage (Ahluwalia et al., 2009). Increasingly, young people in these cultures believe that they should be free to choose their mate or at least to have a significant role in whom their parents choose for them. Globalization has increased the extent to which young people value individual choice and the individual pursuit of happiness, and these values are difficult to reconcile with the tradition of arranged marriage.

Consequently, in many cultures the tradition of arranged marriage has become modified. Today in most Eastern cultures, the "semi-arranged marriage" is the most common practice (Ahluwalia et al., 2009; Netting, 2010). This means that parents influence the mate selection of their children but do not simply decide it without the children's consent. Parents may introduce a potential mate to their child. If the young person has a favorable impression of the potential mate, they date a few times. If they agree that they are compatible, they marry. Another variation of semi-arranged marriage is that young people meet a potential mate on their own but seek their parents' approval before proceeding to date the person or consider marriage.

In this video, a couple from Nepal discusses their arranged marriage. Other marriage variations are also discussed by young adults from various countries, including bride price in Botswana.

Watch   MARRIAGE AND LOVE RELATIONSHIPS ACROSS CULTURES

Review Question:

Compare and contrast marriage and love in two of the countries included in this video.

Why did the custom of bride price develop and become so common worldwide? In the majority of the world's cultures the married couple lives with or near the husband's family following marriage. Bride price compensates the bride's family for the expense of raising her and for the loss of her labor when she leaves to join the husband's family.

Another common type of economic transaction accompanying marriage is **bride service**, found in about 20% of the world's cultures (Ember et al., 2011). In bride service, the groom is obligated to work for the bride's family for a designated period before or after the marriage. In some cultures the service is brief; among some Inuit groups, the groom simply has to catch a seal for his wife's family after the marriage is arranged

bride service

marital arrangement in which the groom is obligated to work for the bride's family for a designated period before and/or after the marriage

(Condon, 1989). In others it is long and expensive, such as among the Subanun of the Philippines, who require 3 to 6 years of bride service. Sometimes the customs of bride price and bride service are combined, in that a groom can offer bride service to reduce the bride price required. Like bride price, bride service compensates the bride's family for raising her and for the loss of her labor in adulthood.

A third common economic transaction associated with marriage is **dowry**, found in about 10% of cultures that include an economic transaction as part of marriage (Ember et al., 2011). A dowry transfers money or property from the bride's family to the groom and his family upon marriage. Dowry is often found in cultures that emphasize the value and prestige of males over females (Rastoqi & Therly, 2006). Unlike bride price and bride service, which compensate the bride's family for the loss of her labor in adulthood, dowry adds an economic burden in addition to loss of labor in families that have girls, which reinforces a cultural preference and favoritism toward male children (Diamond-Smith et al., 2008).

Although dowry exists among only 10% of the world's cultures, one of them is India, which has a population of over a billion people. Dowry is illegal in India but the custom persists, sometimes leading to abuse or murder of young brides when their families fail to provide the promised dowry (Rastoqi & Therly, 2006). Dowry was also common in Europe among wealthy families until the 19th century (Anderson, 2003). The tradition that persists in Europe today (and in other countries populated by Europeans, such as the United States and Canada), of the bride's family paying the expenses of an elaborate wedding celebration, is the vestige of the dowry custom.

WESTERN MARITAL ROLES AND MARITAL SATISFACTION Although marriage in most of the world is structured according to the patterns just described, nearly all the research on marital roles and marital relations has taken place in the West, mostly with Americans. The current Western notion of marriage, with its search for a soul mate and its high expectations of intimacy and companionship, contrasts sharply with the historical and cultural framework for marriage in the rest of the world. Even in the West, marriage has traditionally been seen in pragmatic terms rather than as the uniting of soul mates (Cherlin, 2009).

It was not until the 20th century that this pragmatic view of marriage was replaced by an ideal of marriage in which couples devoted themselves to building a close emotional and sexual partnership. With marriage in the West now carrying such a weight of expectations, and with marriage partners hoping to find in each other a soul mate who is an ideal emotional, social, and sexual companion, it is perhaps not surprising that the early years of marriage typically entail a decline in marital satisfaction, as marriage partners adjust to the reality of living with each other and going through conflicts and compromises. For most American couples, marital satisfaction is higher in the first year than it ever will be again (Dew & Wilcox, 2011; Kurdek, 2005; Lavner & Bradbury, 2010). There is a steady decline in marital satisfaction in the first few years, followed by a plateau and then another decline after 9 or 10 years of marriage.

This is the overall pattern, but there is a great deal of variability among couples. What can a couple do to help make their marriage satisfying and enduring? There is an American saying that the key to a happy marriage can be summed up in 15 words: "I love you. You look great. Can I help? It's my fault. Let's eat out!"

Not bad advice, I'd say, after 25 years with my wife, but what does research say? According to abundant research, these factors especially predict marital satisfaction:

- *Realistic expectations.* Couples are happier with each other if they go into marriage with a realistic view of what will be involved and a minimum of myths about married life (Flanagan et al., 2001; McCarthy & McCarthy, 2004; Sharp & Ganong, 2000). Common myths to avoid include the belief that spouses should instinctively know how to make each other happy without being told, and the belief that biological

dowry
marriage custom that transfers money or property from the bride's family to the groom and his family

differences between men and women make it difficult or impossible for them to communicate with each other.

- *Shared interests.* Couples today in the West expect to be leisure companions, and marriages are happier if partners have many of their leisure interests in common (Stutzer & Frey, 2006).
- *Shared roles and responsibilities.* The old gender division of roles in marriage has faded, and most Western couples today are happier if they share responsibilities for family duties such as housework and child care (Carrere et al., 2000). Women's marital satisfaction is especially influenced by their spouses' contribution to family duties, because women often end up taking on more of these duties than their husbands do (Saginak & Saginak, 2005).
- *Shared power.* Spouses in Western marriages today expect to be equal partners, and marital satisfaction tends to be low if one partner attempts to dominate the other (Gottman & Silver, 1999). Couples with happy marriages are willing to compromise when they disagree and willing to admit when they are wrong and apologize (Lavner & Bradbury, 2010).

Other insights into what makes for a happy marriage come from research by Judith Wallerstein and Sandra Blakeslee (1995). Wallerstein had spent decades researching the causes and effects of divorce, then decided to investigate the basis of a good marriage by interviewing 50 couples who reported high levels of marital satisfaction. One interesting finding was that even these happy couples had had their ups and downs. Many of them reported having times over the years when they were dissatisfied and felt they had made a mistake in marrying their spouse. What kept them together was a fundamental enjoyment of each other's company and a commitment to solving their problems together. Many of the couples talked about the necessity of adjusting to each other over the years as each partner changed and as their lives met with different challenges and crises.

In Western countries, women's marital satisfaction often depends on how much their spouses contribute to family duties.

Divorce in Young Adulthood

LO 10.12 Describe the most common causes of divorce in young adulthood, and explain why the United States has the highest divorce rate in the world.

Partly as a consequence of the high expectations that people in the West have for marriage today, divorce has become more common in recent decades. The soul-mate marriage is often followed some years later by what sociologist Barbara Whitehead calls the **expressive divorce** (Whitehead, 2001). According to Whitehead, people in the West today expect marriage to fulfill their emotional needs for love and intimacy, and if it ceases to do so, they often seek to leave the marriage.

Rates of divorce vary widely across world regions. Even today it is rare in most parts of the world, including Asia, Africa, North Africa and the Middle East, Latin America, and southern Europe. It is highest in northern and eastern Europe, and in the United States, Canada, Australia, and New Zealand. The United States has the highest divorce rate in the world (Cherlin, 2009). However, the divorce rate is rising worldwide, a trend that researchers attribute to rising individualism (Abela et al., 2014).

Why is the rate of divorce especially high in the United States? According to Andrew Cherlin (2009), Americans believe more strongly in marriage than people in most other Western countries. For example, in one cross-national survey, only 10% of Americans agreed that "Marriage is an outdated institution," a lower percentage than in any European country (the highest percentage agreement was in France, 36%). However,

expressive divorce

according to Barbara Whitehead, the type of divorce common in the West today, in which people expect marriage to fulfill their emotional needs for love and intimacy, and they seek a divorce if it ceases to do so

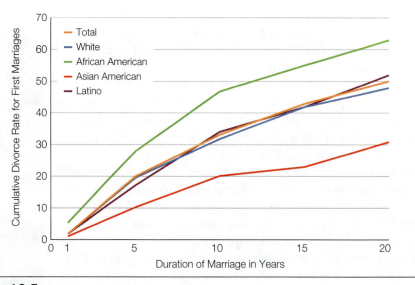

Figure 10.5 Divorce Peaks in Young Adulthood

Notice that the rise is steepest in the early years of marriage, reaching over 30% after 10 years, then continues at a less steep rate in the next 10 years to a cumulative risk of 50% after 20 years.
SOURCE: Based on Bramlett & Mosher (2001)

Americans also believe in expressive divorce; that is, they also believe that marriage should provide self-fulfillment, and if it does not, partners are not obligated to stay married. Only 25% of Americans believe that parents in an unhappy marriage should stay together for the sake of the children.

Because rates of divorce are so high in the United States, a great deal of American research has examined the causes and consequences of divorce. Some of the factors that are related to higher likelihood of divorce are young age at marriage (younger than 25), having divorced parents, and low religious involvement (Amato & Cheadle, 2005). Divorce risk peaks in young adulthood, 5–10 years after marriage, as **Figure 10.5** shows, which suggests that the strains of caring for young children may make maintaining marital intimacy more problematic (Cowan & Cowan, 2011; Dew & Wilcox, 2011).

Psychologist John Gottman has followed couples over many years to identify the predictors of divorce. In one study, he and his colleagues recruited a sample of young adult couples when the husbands were age 30 and the wives were age 28, on average (Gottman & Levenson, 2000). The study included questionnaires as well as observations of the couples' conversations about topics of conflict and events of the day. The researchers found they could predict whether or not couples would divorce with 93% accuracy, based on partners' responses to questionnaires about marital satisfaction and thoughts of leaving the marriage combined with researchers' ratings of the couples' positive and negative affect (emotional expression) during the observed conversations.

Socioeconomic status is also highly important as a risk factor for divorce. Among American partners who both have less than a high school degree, one third of marriages end in divorce within 5 years; when partners have a high school degree or some college, the 5-year divorce rate is one fourth; and for couples who both have 4-year college degrees, the 5-year divorce rate is just 13% (Cherlin, 2009). Conflict over financial issues is a predictor of divorce, so it may be that divorce is more common among less-educated couples because they make less money and consequently experience greater financial strains. Rates of divorce in the United States are especially high among African Americans—70%, compared to 47% among Whites (Cherlin, 2009)—in part because African American couples often have lower incomes.

Partners' behavior is also related to the likelihood of divorce. In one U.S. study, 2,000 married persons were interviewed and then followed up 3, 6, and 9 years later (Amato & Rogers, 1997). Divorce over this 9-year period was predicted most strongly by infidelity, disagreements over money, and excessive drinking or drug use. Also important was partners' ability to communicate effectively with each other around intimacy issues. Among couples who divorced, women often experienced anger, sadness, and bruised feelings, and felt their husbands did not show sufficient awareness and understanding of their feelings.

Most young adults build their social and personal lives around their marriage, so divorce is often a difficult adjustment (Amato, 2010; Hetherington & Kelly, 2002). For both men and women, divorce is followed by increased risk of psychological problems such as depression and anxiety disorders, as well as sleep disorders and increased substance use. Men usually leave the household in a divorce, and many miss the daily contact they had with their children before the divorce; women experience the strain of carrying out the household tasks and child care by themselves, and usually experience a steep loss of income. Overall, men experience a greater decline in functioning than women do following divorce, and take longer to recover, perhaps because women draw more on social support from family and friends (Hetherington & Kelly, 2002; Williams & Dunne-Bryant, 2006). For both men and women, the low point in functioning tends to come 1–2 years following the divorce, followed by a gradual recovery for most people. A key part of coming back from divorce for most people is finding a new partner (Coleman et al., 2006). Most Americans who divorce in young adulthood remarry within 5 years (Cherlin, 2009). More on remarriage will be presented in Chapter 11.

Single Adults

LO 10.13 **Appraise common myths about single adults, and describe cultural and ethnic variations in singlehood.**

Although marriage is the predominant form of social life in young adulthood across cultures, in most cultures there are also some people who do not marry in young adulthood. Some remain single through their young adult years; some even remain single their whole lives. Across countries, the proportion of young adults who have neither married nor had a long-term cohabiting relationship by age 40 is usually around 10% (Cherlin, 2009).

Marriage is widely believed to promote many positive aspects of development in young adulthood. Sociologists Linda Waite and Maggie Gallagher assert that research shows marriage to be the key to health, happiness, wealth, and an active sex life (Waite & Gallagher, 2000). In contrast, remaining single after age 30 predicts a variety of negative outcomes in comparison to married people, including mental health problems, physical health problems, and substance use (CDC, 2004).

However, psychologist Bella DePaulo (2006, 2012) has questioned these conclusions, claiming that among social scientists as well as in the general public, **singlism** is rampant, by which she means that "People who do not have a serious coupled relationship are stereotyped, discriminated against, and treated dismissively" (2006, p. 2). In a thorough analysis of the evidence comparing single and married people in young adulthood, she makes the case that the claims in favor of marriage and against remaining single have been overstated. It is true that people who are single rank slightly below married people on some measures of health and happiness, but young adults who have always remained single rank above those who married but later became separated, divorced, or widowed—and for *most* married people, one of these three fates awaits. Furthermore, in longitudinal studies, people's happiness levels blip upward in the year

singlism

negative stereotypes of single persons that lead to them being discriminated against and treated dismissively

after marriage but soon after sink down to the same level as before marriage, showing that marriage is not responsible for long-term happiness (Schmitt et al., 2007). Finally, although being *happily* married has many benefits, people who are in unhappy marriages are the lowest of all in overall happiness, even compared to people who are separated, divorced, or widowed.

Studies of young singles' views of their singlehood report that they see both advantages and disadvantages (Arnett & Schwab, 2014; Baumbusch, 2004; DePaulo, 2006; Lewis, 2000). They enjoy the freedom to make their own decisions and to do what they want when they want. On the other hand, they miss the companionship of being part of a couple, they become weary of changing romantic and sexual partners, and they sometimes feel out of step in a world where most young adults are part of a couple.

Within the United States there are ethnic differences in singlehood during young adulthood. At age 40, 41% of African Americans have never married, compared to one fourth of Latinos and 20% of Whites (Social Security Administration, 2014). However, African Americans have higher rates of cohabitation than the other two groups do, so rates of long-term partnerships among the groups are similar. Rates of remaining single are also high—and rising—in some Asian countries, especially in urban areas (Jones, 2010). In Tokyo, Japan, and Bangkok, Thailand, over one third of women ages 30–34 and over 20% of women ages 40–44 have never married. Furthermore, unlike in the West, cohabitation is rare in Asia; nearly all unmarried young adults continue to live at home, even into their 40s.

There are a number of reasons for this increase in singlehood among young adults in Asia, most notably the widening opportunities available to young women, who often prefer the excitement and freedom of their singlehood to the traditional obligations of female submission that still go along with marriage in most Asian countries (Rosenberg, 2007). In Japan, the derisive term *parasite singles* has been applied to young adults who remain single into their 30s, implying that they are selfish and immature (DePaulo, 2006). Nevertheless, single young adults are the happiest group in all of Japan—happier than older singles, and happier than married adults of any age group (Rosenberg, 2007).

African Americans have lower marriage rates than Latinos or Whites do but higher rates of cohabitation.

Gay and Lesbian Partnerships

LO 10.14 Compare and contrast gay and lesbian partnerships with heterosexual partnerships, and describe how these partnerships have changed in recent years.

Although most romantic partnerships in young adulthood are between a man and a woman, in nearly all cultures some persons have same-sex partners. Surveys across Western countries have found that 1–10% of adults identify as gay or lesbian, depending on the country and the survey question (Garnets & Kimmel, 2013). Consistently, more adults report same-sex desires and experiences than report identifying as gay or lesbian (National Survey of Sexual Health and Behavior, 2010).

Gay and lesbian couples are like heterosexual couples in most ways (Hyde & DeLamater, 2005; Kurdek, 2006; Peplau & Beals, 2004). Like heterosexuals, most gay and lesbian young adults seek a long-term relationship based on love, affection, and mutual respect. Like heterosexuals, they tend to seek out partners who are similar to themselves in many ways. Similar areas of conflict are common in heterosexual and homosexual relationships: money, sex, and household tasks.

Gay and lesbian couples also differ from heterosexual couples in some ways, and gay couples differ from lesbian couples. About half of gay couples have an "open relationship" that allows partners to have sexual episodes (but not loving relationships) with others, whereas lesbian and heterosexual couples nearly always place a high value on sexual fidelity (Bonello & Cross, 2010; Peplau & Beals, 2002; Peplau & Beals, 2004). The decision to have an open relationship is based partly on the desire for sexual variety but also on the goal of challenging the convention that monogamy is the only acceptable basis for a relationship (Anderson, 2012). Gay couples tend to have a higher frequency of sexual activity than heterosexual couples do, and lesbian couples have the lowest frequency (Michael et al., 1994).

In several Western countries, gay and lesbian couples can now marry.

Some differences that used to distinguish gay and lesbian couples from heterosexual couples are fading. The heterosexual majority in many cultures has persecuted and discriminated against homosexuals for many centuries. Discrimination remains today, but attitudes have grown dramatically more tolerant in recent decades (Garnets & Kimmel, 2013; Savin-Williams, 2005). Until recently, gay and lesbian couples were not allowed to marry, but gay and lesbian marriage is now legal in many American states and in several Western countries, including Belgium, Canada, Netherlands, and Spain. National "registered partnership" laws, providing many of the same legal benefits as marriage, now exist in Britain, Denmark, France, Germany, New Zealand, Norway, Switzerland, and Sweden (Cherlin, 2009). Sixty-six percent of Americans ages 18–30 support homosexual marriage, compared to only 35% of persons 65 and older, and rates of acceptance are rising across all age groups (Pew Research Center, 2013).

Sexuality in Young Adulthood

LO 10.15 **Explain why young adulthood tends to be a stage of peak sexual behavior, and identify gender differences in sexuality.**

Young adulthood is the life stage when sexual activity peaks in nearly all cultures. Adolescent sexual activity is forbidden in many cultures (Shlegel, 2010; Shlegel & Barry, 1991). Even where it is tolerated it takes place only occasionally, and adolescents go extended periods when they have no sexual partner. Where emerging adulthood exists, sexual activity may be discouraged (e.g., in Japan and South Korea and in southern Europe) or accepted (e.g., in northern Europe), but emerging adults, too, usually have periods when they have no partner. By middle adulthood, in some cultures sexual activity stops altogether, but even where it continues it takes place with less frequency than during young adulthood. It is during young adulthood that people are most likely to have a regular sexual partner, usually their marriage partner, and also during young adulthood that sexual activity is most likely to be supported and encouraged by cultural beliefs.

The primary reason for this in most cultures is not to promote the intimacy of the marital relationship, but rather to ensure that the young adult couple will have children. Producing children is typically considered an essential part of married life, and parents in most cultures want their children to have children, in order to continue the family into the next generation. Consequently, young adult couples are encouraged to have frequent sexual intercourse so that they will reproduce. For example, in India, adolescent sexuality is entirely forbidden and by middle adulthood sexual activity is expected to cease. However, young adulthood is considered to be the life stage of *jouvana,* a word that literally means sexually active; being sexually active is the very definition of the young adult life stage (Menon & Shweder, 1998). The more sexually active they are, the more likely they will soon produce children, and having children is considered to be the central meaning and purpose of marriage. Sexual activity is discouraged after young adulthood in India because it can no longer result in a new child once the wife has reached menopause and ceased to ovulate.

In the West, sexual activity in young adulthood is less focused on reproduction. Because most couples in the West will have only one or two children, relatively little of their sexual activity in young adulthood is intended to result in pregnancy. Instead, an active sex life is considered to be important for promoting the intimacy of the couple's relationship as well as their mutual enjoyment and pleasure. Research in the West reports that sexual enjoyment in young adult couples promotes as well as reflects emotional closeness in their relationship (Bancroft, 2002; Yeh et al., 2006).

The *Sex in America* study was a landmark study of sexual behavior conducted in the 1990s (Laumann et al., 1994; Michael et al., 1994). Although it is now more than 20 years old, it remains the most extensive study of young adults' sexual behavior. The research team interviewed a diverse sample of over 3,000 Americans ages 18–59. They found a great deal of stability in sexual behavior of young adults from the late 20s to the early 40s, with most people (about 75%) reporting one sexual partner in the past year, and relatively few reporting no sexual partner (about 10%) or more than one sexual partner (about 15%). Most people reported having intercourse from a few times per month to two to three times per week, with relatively few young adults reporting no episodes (8%) or having sex more than four times a week (6%). More recent studies have confirmed these results (Langer, 2004).

One interesting finding of the *Sex in America* study was that masturbation continues through the 30s and 40s. In fact, for women masturbation peaks in the 30s, with nearly 50% reporting masturbation "sometimes" or more, followed by a slight decline in the 40s and a steeper decline in the 50s (to about 20%). Men masturbate more than women at all ages, and for men the prevalence of masturbation peaks at a little over 70% "sometimes" or more in the late 20s, but is still over 60% in the 30s and 40s and just under 50% in the 50s. In adulthood as in adolescence, masturbation is correlated with other sexual activity, including frequency of intercourse. Masturbation is not a substitute for sex in young adulthood but a supplement to an active sex life.

Masturbation was just one of many areas where there were sharp gender differences in sexuality in the *Sex in America* study. There was a huge gender difference in frequency of orgasms, with 75% of men in their 30s and 40s reporting that they always experienced orgasm during sex with their primary partner, compared to only 30% of women. Men also reported more frequent sexual fantasies. In response to the question "How often do you think about sex?" over half of men responded "every day" or "several times a day," compared to just 19% of women. Similarly, men were much more likely to pursue sexual stimulation through X-rated movies and videos, nude dance clubs, and sexually-explicit magazines. This study took place prior to the Internet revolution, but recent studies have found that men are much more likely than women to view Internet pornography (Carroll et al., 2008).

Becoming a Parent

LO 10.16 Summarize the social and emotional impact of becoming a parent, and describe the unique challenges faced by single parents.

Until very recently in human history, most people spent nearly all their adult lives devoting a substantial proportion of their time and energy to their role as parents, caring for and providing for children from birth to maturity. They would marry around age 20 and have their first child about a year later, and continue to have children every few years until about age 40. They would have about eight children over the course of this 20-year period, and the last one would reach maturity when the parents were about age 60—and most people did not live beyond age 60. Today, all over the world, the combination of fewer children and longer life expectancy has transformed parenting young children from the central focus of adult life to an important but relatively small part of the entire life span, for most people. There remain sharp differences between urban and rural areas. In all world regions, people in urban areas live longer and have fewer children than people in rural areas (Population Reference Bureau [PRB], 2014).

PARENTING AND YOUNG ADULT ROLES Just as the majority of young adults get married, the majority of young adults become parents, in every country. In most countries about 90% of young adults have at least one child (Mascarenhas et al., 2012). There is some variation among developed countries. The proportion of women who have at least one child by age 40 is 70% in Germany, 80% in the United States, and 98% in Iceland. Among developing countries, the rates of becoming a parent by age 40 are over 90%, partly because they have less access to birth control and partly because their cultures place a much stronger value on having children.

For young adults in rural traditional cultures, becoming a parent is a highly important event in terms of their status in the community. Fertility is considered the main goal and function of young adult women, and women must have a child to be fully accepted by their husband's family. Women who are unable to bear children are objects of pity and scorn. For young men, having a child also means greater status and acceptance in the community. In many cultures, having a child is necessary in order to be considered fully adult. For example, among the Sambia of New Guinea, the passage to adulthood for young men takes place in a series of seven rituals over a period from middle childhood to young adulthood, and the final, crowning ritual takes place when the young man becomes a father for the first time (Herdt, 1986).

Although parenting young children is the main focus of young adulthood for women in traditional cultures, it is not a responsibility they bear alone (DeLoache & Gottlieb, 2000). Usually the mother-in-law is present, either in the household or nearby, and sometimes the young woman's mother as well. There may be aunts and cousins and neighbors nearby to share daily life with, not just to help with child care, but also food preparation, agricultural work, and other labor. Older children also help with child care and other tasks once they reach middle childhood. The father is not usually involved much in caring for young children but, as we have seen in earlier chapters, there are exceptions to this pattern.

For young adults in developed countries, and for many in urban areas of developing countries, becoming a parent is a conscious decision, something they can choose to do or choose not to do. Unlike young adults in rural traditional cultures, they have access to effective contraception that allows them to have an active sexual life without conceiving children. Also, unlike for their counterparts in rural traditional cultures, children are not an economic asset for urban couples. In a rural economy children can contribute from an early age and throughout childhood, helping to tend the fields, care for the livestock, and sell the goods the family produces.

In most countries, about 90% of young adults have at least one child.

Table 10.2 Views on Becoming a Parent: Advantages and Disadvantages

Advantages	Disadvantages
Giving and receiving love and affection	Loss of freedom, restrictions on choices
Greater meaning to life	Not enough time for both family and work
Becoming less selfish and learning to sacrifice	Less time with spouse or partner
Satisfaction of helping children learn and grow	Worries over children's health and safety
Greater acceptance as a responsible adult	Financial stress
Less fear of death, because children will carry on	Fear that children will turn out badly or be unhappy

SOURCE: Based on Cowan & Cowan (2000)

However, in developed countries children contribute little economically and cost a lot to bring up. Tally the food, clothes, school expenses, leisure expenses, and medical expenses parents expend on behalf of children, and the total spent over 18 to 25 years amounts to a lot of money. Furthermore, parents in developed countries are usually on their own, with little help from in-laws, other relatives, or neighbors. However, in some ethnic groups there is greater extended family support for young parents, for example among African Americans and Latinos (Oberlander et al., 2007).

Although there may be no economic benefits to having children, young adults see many rewards and advantages in becoming a parent. Philip Cowan and Carolyn Pape Cowan (2000) interviewed young American parents and found that they reported a wide range of rewards of becoming a parent, such as giving and receiving love and affection, becoming less selfish and learning to sacrifice, and the satisfaction of helping children grow. However, as **Table 10.2** shows, they perceived many disadvantages as well, such as loss of freedom, financial stress, and less time for their partner. The video *Challenges of Becoming a New Parent* examines this topic in more detail.

Watch   CHALLENGES OF BECOMING A NEW PARENT

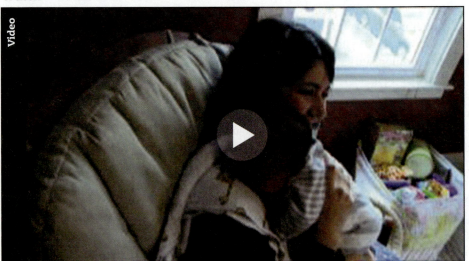

PARENTING AND THE MARITAL RELATIONSHIP IN YOUNG ADULTHOOD

In traditional cultures gender roles are distinct from early childhood onward, and women and men in young adult couples have different responsibilities. Her responsibility is to run the household, care for the children, and do other economic work such as tend crops or make items that can be sold. His responsibility is to provide economically for his wife and children. The roles of women and men do not overlap very much.

In contrast, gender roles today in developed countries, especially in the West, are less sharply defined, and in young adulthood couples often share many of the duties that traditionally fell to one gender or the other. Both men and women cook and clean, and both work outside the household to contribute to the family income. In the United States, most people now believe that marriages work best when both husband and wife have jobs and take responsibility for care of the house and children, a contrast to the pattern that prevailed historically (Russell, 2011).

Nevertheless, the traditional gender role divisions still exist in a modified form in developed countries. Both men and women may contribute to child care, but women contribute more, even in families where both husband and wife work full time. Both may do household tasks, but women consistently contribute more hours per week, across developed countries (Hook, 2010). Both work outside the home, but men work more hours than women do, and women are more likely to leave the workforce while the couple has young children (Voicu et al., 2009). Several studies have found that gender roles in developed countries become more traditional following the birth of the first child, in a variety of respects (Cowan & Cowan, 2000; Dew & Wilcox, 2011).

The arrival of the first child often changes the marital relationship in other ways as well. The "soul mate" ideal of marriage is difficult to sustain, as we have seen from the decline in marital satisfaction that takes place over the early years of marriage, and the birth of a child makes it even more challenging and elusive. The soul mate ideal is an ideal of intimacy, entailing a lot of time together as a couple, enjoying marital closeness and companionship—emotional as well as sexual. After the birth of the first child, this ideal often collides with the reality of caring for an infant. As we have seen, human infants are needy little creatures. They cannot care for themselves, and will not be able to do so for many years. Consequently, it becomes difficult for couples to find time and energy for quiet dinners, long walks, and sexual intimacy after they become parents. There is so much to do! The baby needs to be fed frequently, and taken for a walk, and diapers need to be changed, and now baby is crying again and needs to be soothed. Parents are awoken in the night repeatedly by a crying baby who needs to be fed, diapered, and soothed back to sleep, which also does not enhance their readiness for marital intimacy. The combination of increased household chores, financial strain, and fatigue puts a great strain on mothers and fathers and on their relationship (Meijer & van den Wittenboer, 2007). Also, parents in developed countries usually bear this responsibility with little or no help from others, in contrast to the more communal way children are cared for in traditional cultures (Rubin & Chung, 2006; Lamm & Keller, 2007).

As a result of all these changes following the birth of a child, marital satisfaction often declines (Lavner & Bradbury, 2010). It tends to decline more for women than for men, because women tend to take on more of the new responsibilities than men do, and women must simultaneously recover from the physical strain of childbirth (Dew & Wilcox, 2011; Lu, 2006).

However, marital satisfaction does not decline for all couples following the birth of the first child (Cowan & Cowan, 2011). For couples who already have a troubled marriage, their marital satisfaction tends to slip still further once they have the responsibilities of caring for a child

Marital satisfaction often declines following the birth of the first child, but not always.

(Feeney et al., 2001). In contrast, couples with a mutually supportive and satisfying relationship tend to maintain their marital happiness even under the strain of becoming parents (Driver et al., 2003). Of course, their marital relationship also changes in response to becoming parents; they, too, have less time and energy for emotional and sexual intimacy. However, they adjust to these changes by working together as a *coparenting team* to meet the challenges of child care, sharing the responsibilities more equally than less happy couples and providing support to each other (Feinberg et al., 2009; McHale & Rotman, 2007).

SINGLE PARENTS More than ever today in Western countries, parenthood is experienced not as part of a couple but as a single parent. Across countries, about 90% of single parents are single mothers (Breivik et al., 2006). When a single mother gives birth, she, rather than the father, is nearly always the person who then has primary care for the baby, and in cases of divorce, mothers receive custody in a high majority of cases (Dufur et al., 2010).

Rates of nonmarital births are especially high in Europe, Canada, and the United States, where over 40% of births are to single mothers (Haub, 2013). These rates are several times higher than 50 years ago, across countries. In the United States rates of single motherhood vary by state (see **Map 10.2**). Rates are about 70% among African Americans, but rates among Whites have risen dramatically in recent decades and are now over 40%. In addition to ethnic differences, in the United States there are large disparities in single motherhood by educational levels. According to the National Marriage Project, over half (54%) of babies born to the least-educated mothers are born to single mothers, as are 44% of babies of moderately educated mothers, but among highly educated mothers (four-year college degree or more), only 6% are single (Wilcox

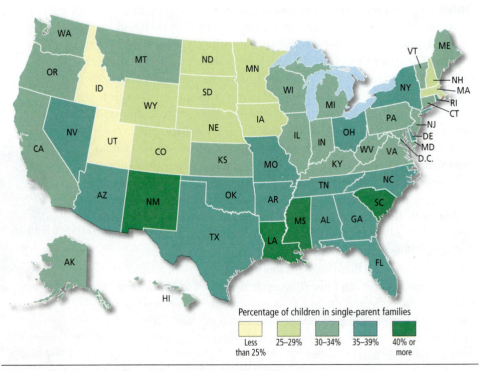

Percentage of children in single-parent families

Less than 25% | 25–29% | 30–34% | 35–39% | 40% or more

Map 10.2 Single-Parent Households in the United States

How do the rates of single-parent families vary across states? Which ethnicities have the highest and lowest rates? What impact do these rates have on income levels?

& Marquart, 2010). Low education often means low income, so rates of single motherhood vary widely by income group, as **Figure 10.6** shows.

Being a single mother does not necessarily mean having no partner to help in parenting. Patterns of single motherhood vary greatly among countries and cultures. In northern Europe, as we have seen, cohabitation is normative for many years before marriage, and children who are born to unmarried mothers usually have a father in the household as well; the partners are not legally married, but both are present and both are involved in the care of the child. In the United States, the rise in "single motherhood" since 1980 is due almost entirely to an increase in the proportion of children born to cohabiting parents (Cherlin, 2009). African American single mothers often receive assistance from their own mothers, and sometimes from male relatives and friends as well (Jayakody & Kalil, 2002; Woody & Woody, 2007).

Fathers are sometimes involved in caring for the child even if they do not live with the mother, and in the United States about 10% of children live with the unmarried father rather than with the mother (U.S. Bureau of the Census, 2010). As we have seen, it is increasingly common in some Western countries for gay or lesbian couples to adopt or conceive a child. Although these couples are often barred from legal marriage and so are classified as "single" parents, there are in fact two parents involved in caring for the child (Goldberg, 2011; Tasker, 2005).

For parents who are truly single parents, raising their children without assistance from another adult, the strains and stresses are considerable. Given the many challenges we have seen for couples in adjusting to and caring for a child, it is not hard to see how difficult it must be to handle these challenges alone. Single mothers often have relatively low incomes, partly because only one salary comes into the family instead of two, so the stress of handling parenting duties alone is compounded by financial stress (Cain & Combs-Orme, 2005). However, when single mothers receive social support from their own mothers or from friends and other family members, they experience less stress and are more patient and nurturing as parents (Kotchik et al., 2005).

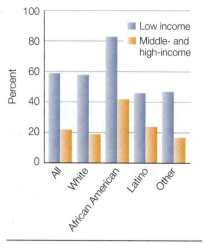

Figure 10.6 Percentage of Single-Parent Households in the United States, by Income and Race/Ethnicity

Work

LO 10.17   List the stages of occupational development in Super's theory, and explain how personality and gender shape occupational goals.

Although people almost everywhere start doing some kind of work prior to young adulthood, it is in young adulthood that people usually take on full adult responsibilities. The girl in a traditional rural village who has long taken care of her younger siblings and helped her mother with household duties now, in young adulthood, has a child and household of her own. The girl in a developed country who worked as a restaurant hostess during adolescence now, in young adulthood, takes a job as a hospital administrator. The boy in a traditional rural village who in childhood learned to navigate a boat and catch fish with his father now, in young adulthood, has a boat and catches fish of his own to sell. The adolescent boy in a developed country who worked at the counter in a clothing store now, in young adulthood, delivers packages for an overnight delivery company.

The path from child and adolescent work to adult work differs sharply between developing countries and developed countries. Adolescents in developing countries usually work alongside their parents—boys with their fathers and other men, girls with their mothers and other women—doing the kind of work adults do. Because the economies in such cultures are usually not diverse, there are few "occupations" to choose from. Boys learn to do what men do, whether it is hunting or farming or something else, and girls learn to do what women do, which is usually child care and running the household, and perhaps some gardening or other work. There is a certain security in this—you grow up knowing that you will have useful and important work to do as an adult, and you grow up gradually learning the skills required for it. On the other hand, there is a certain narrowness and limitation to it as well—if you are a boy, you must do the work that men do whether you care for it or not; and if you are a girl, your role is to learn child care and running a household regardless of what your individual preferences or talents might be.

Young people in developed countries face a different kind of trade-off. The economies of developed countries are astonishingly complex and diverse. This means that, as an adolescent or emerging adult, you have a tremendous range of possible occupations to choose from. However, every person has to find a place among all of that fabulous diversity of choice. And even once you make your choice, you have to hope that the occupation you decide you want will be achievable for you. More young people would like to be medical doctors, veterinarians, musicians, and professional athletes than is possible (Schneider & Stevenson, 1999).

Although there is great cultural variation in work paths during young adulthood, nearly all the research so far has taken place with young Americans. Let us take a look now at the developmental pattern in how Americans make occupational choices, and the various influences that play a part in their choices.

THE DEVELOPMENT OF OCCUPATIONAL GOALS Although children and adolescents may have occupational dreams—fantasies of being a famous basketball player, singer, or movie star—young adulthood is when more serious pursuit of occupational goals often begins (Arnett, 2015). For young adults, decisions must be made that will have potential long-term effects on their adult lives.

One influential theory of the development of occupational goals, by Donald Super (Super, 1967; Super, 1976; Super, 1980; Super, 1992; Tracey et al., 2005), begins with adolescence and continues through five stages into adulthood, as follows:

- *Crystallization*, ages 14 to 18. In this initial stage, adolescents begin to move beyond fantasizing and start to consider how their talents and interests match up with the occupational possibilities available to them. During this time, they may begin to seek out information about careers that are of interest to them, perhaps by talking over various possibilities with family and friends.
- *Specification*, ages 18 to 21. During this stage, occupational choices become more focused. For example, a young person who decided during the crystallization stage to seek an occupation that involves working with children may now decide whether that means being a child psychologist, a teacher, a daycare worker, or a pediatrician. Making this choice usually involves beginning to pursue the education or training required to obtain the desired occupation.
- *Implementation*, ages 21 to 24. This stage involves completing the education or training that began in the specification stage and entering the job itself. This may mean that young people must reconcile any discrepancy between what they would like to do and what is available in the work world. For example, you may have been educated to be a teacher but find out after graduation that there are more teachers than available jobs, so that you end up working in a social service agency or a business.
- *Stabilization*, ages 25 to 35. This is the stage in which young adults establish themselves in their careers. The initial period of getting their feet wet in a job comes to an end, and they become more stable and experienced in their work.
- *Consolidation*, age 35 and up. From this point onward, occupational development means continuing to gain expertise and seeking advancement into higher status positions as expertise grows.

Although this theory remains important in shaping the way scholars think about occupational development and the way career counselors provide advice to young people, not everyone fits the pattern prescribed by the theory, and certainly not according to these precise ages. It is less and less common for occupational development to follow the kind of linear path through the life course that is described in Super's theory. Increasingly, people have not just one career or occupation, but two or more in the course of their working lives. Most of today's young adults will change career directions at least once (Donahue, 2007). Also, for women and increasingly for men, balancing work and family goals may mean taking time off or at least working fewer hours during the young adult years when they have young children to care for (Cinamon, 2006; van der Lippe et al., 2006). Theories of career development that neglect this complexity do not fit the career paths that today's young adult women are likely to follow.

INFLUENCES ON OCCUPATIONAL GOALS Theories of occupational development provide a general outline of how young people may progress through their working lives. But how do young adults make choices among the great variety of occupations available to them? What sorts of influences go into their decisions? A great deal of research has been conducted on these questions, especially focusing on the influence of personality characteristics and gender.

One of the influences on occupational choice in cultures where people are allowed to choose from a wide range of possible occupations is the individual's judgment of how various occupations would be suited to his or her personality. People seek occupations that they judge to be consistent with their interests and talents. One influential theorist, John Holland (Holland, 1985; Holland, 1987; Holland, 1996; Gottfredson et al., 1993), investigated the kinds of personality characteristics that are typical of people who hold various jobs and of adolescents who aspire to those jobs. Holland's theory describes six personality categories to consider when matching a person with a prospective occupation (see **Table 10.3**).

You can probably see the potential for overlap in some of these categories. Obviously, they are not mutually exclusive. A person could have some Artistic qualities as well as some Social qualities, or some Intellectual qualities as well as some Enterprising qualities. Holland (1987) does not claim that all people fall neatly into clear types. However, he and others believe that most people will be happiest and most successful in their careers if they are able to find a match between their personality qualities and an occupation that allows them to express and develop those qualities (Vondracek & Porfelli, 2003). Holland's ideas have been used by career counselors to help adolescents gain insights into the types of fields that might be best for them to pursue. The widely used Strong-Campbell Vocational Interest Inventory is based on Holland's ideas.

Keep in mind the limitations of this approach to understanding occupational choice. Within any particular profession, you are likely to find persons with a considerable

Table 10.3 Holland's Theory

Category	Personality Characteristics	Best Occupations
Realistic	High physical strength, practical approach to problem solving, and low social understanding	Jobs that involve physical activity and practical application of knowledge, such as farming, truck driving, and construction
Intellectual	High on conceptual and theoretical thinking, low on social skills	Research in fields such as math and science
Social	High in verbal skills and social skills	Jobs working with people, such as teaching, social work, and counseling
Conventional	High on following directions carefully, dislike of unstructured activities	Jobs involve clear responsibilities but require little leadership, such as bank teller or secretary
Enterprising	High in verbal abilities, social skills, and leadership skills	Sales, politics, management, running a business
Artistic	Introspective, imaginative, sensitive, unconventional	Artistic occupations such as painting or writing fiction

Despite improvements in gender equality, there are still fewer women than men in STEM fields.

variety of personality traits. If you think of teachers you have known, for example, you will probably find that they varied a lot in their personalities, even if they may have had some characteristics in common. Their different personalities may have allowed them each to bring a different combination of strengths and weaknesses to the job. So, there probably is not just one personality type that is potentially well suited to a particular type of job.

In the same way, any one person's personality could probably fit well with many of the jobs available in a diverse economy. Because most people's personalities are too complex to fall neatly into one type or another, different occupations may bring out different combinations of strengths and weaknesses in a particular person. For this reason, assessing your personality traits may narrow somewhat the range of fields that you think of as being suitable for you, but for most people in developed countries, that would still leave a considerable number of possible occupations to choose from.

Gender also has a substantial influence on job choice. Although the proportion of young women who are employed has risen steeply in the 21st century, it remains true that some jobs are held mainly by men and some mainly by women (Porfelli et al., 2008; Vondracek & Porfelli, 2003). Jobs held mainly by women are concentrated in the service sector—for example, teacher, nurse, secretary, and child-care worker. Jobs held mainly by men include many scientific and technical fields: chemist, surgeon, and computer software designer. In general, "women's jobs" tend to be low paying and low status, whereas "men's jobs" tend to be high paying and high status. Women are especially underrepresented in the STEM fields (Science, Technology, Engineering, and Mathematics; Ceci & Williams, 2007).

These patterns have changed somewhat in recent years—for example, women are now nearly as likely as men to become lawyers and medical doctors. However, for many jobs the gender differences have proven to be remarkably stable (Ceci & Williams, 2007). Even within high-status professions, women tend to have the lower-status and lower-paying positions; for example, among physicians, women are more likely to be a family practice doctor than a surgeon.

Why do these gender differences in job choice persist, despite the fact that women now exceed men in terms of overall educational attainment? Gender socialization is certainly part of it. Children learn early on that some jobs are appropriate for either males or females, in the same way that they learn other aspects of gender roles (Maccoby, 2002; Porfelli et al., 2008). By the time young people reach the age when it is time for them to choose an occupational direction, their gender identities are well established and constitute a powerful influence on their job selection. One study of emerging adult women found that even mathematically-talented young women often avoid information technology (IT) fields because they view IT as male dominated, a perception that in turn perpetuates the male domination of IT (Messersmith et al., 2008). Similarly, a study in the Netherlands found that adolescent girls avoid going into computer science because they believe that others view women in computer science as sexually unattractive (Rommes et al., 2007).

Another important influence is that already in emerging adulthood, young women anticipate the difficulties they are likely to face in balancing their work and family roles, and this influences their job selection (Lips & Lawson, 2009). As we have seen earlier in the chapter, although men now do more of the child care than in previous generations, wives still do more housework than their husbands, even when both of them work full time (Gershury et al., 2005; Strandh & Nordenmark, 2006; van der Lippe et al., 2006).

Sociologists have called this the **second shift** (Hochschild, 1990; Hochschild, 1998), referring to the domestic work that women must perform after they complete their shift in the workplace.

In contrast to young women, it is extremely rare for young men to take time away from the workplace to raise young children. Even in European countries where the government pays up to 100% of a person's salary for up to a year for those who wish to leave the workplace temporarily while they have infant children, few young men take advantage of these policies (O'Brien & Moss, 2010; Plantin, 2007). However, this does not mean these patterns will never change. The period since women's entry into the workplace is still relatively brief in historical terms—less than 50 years. Many dramatic changes in gender roles have already taken place that could not have been anticipated a half century ago. The changes appear to be continuing. Young men now say they give time with family a higher priority than prestigious or high-paying work, more than older men and similar to young women (Arnett & Schwab, 2012). Furthermore, technologically driven changes in work that are likely to allow an increasing proportion of work to be done at home or in flexible shifts may make it easier for both men and women to balance successfully—and equally—the demands of work and family.

CRITICAL THINKING QUESTION

How would you explain the fact that wives usually end up doing most of the household work and child care even when they work as many hours as their husbands do? Do you think this is likely to change in the current generation of emerging adults?

....

Community Activities and Media Use

LO 10.18 **Explain the relationship between community involvement and television use in the lives of young adults.**

Family roles and work responsibilities are intense in young adulthood, as most people are bringing up young children in this life stage as well as striving for occupational progress. But what else is important in the lives of young adults? Two areas that many of them devote time to are community activities and media use. One of the distinctive features of the young adult stage of development is that it is a period of high involvement in community roles and activities. However, community involvement is lower in developed countries today than it used to be, and one of the key reasons is the appeal of watching television as a leisure activity.

COMMUNITY INVOLVEMENT In young adulthood, as family and work obligations are acquired, community involvement often increases (Gray et al., 2012; Putnam, 2000). When young couples have children, their involvement with their children and their concern for their children's future may lead them to become involved in civic organizations. A parent may become a Boy Scout or Girl Scout leader, or coach a child's sports team, or volunteer to help at special events at a child's school. Work ties may also lead to civic involvement. For example, a young adult may join a civic organization in order to enhance business contacts. Overall membership in civic associations rises in young adulthood in the United States, peaking in the early 40s (Barber et al., 2013; Putnam, 2000). However, it is notable that across age groups, civic involvement has decreased in recent decades.

second shift

term for the domestic work that women must perform after they complete their shift in the workplace

Having children often draws young adults into greater community involvement.

Watching TV is the most common leisure activity in young adulthood.

MEDIA USE Media influences have been studied intensively with respect to young children, as we have seen in previous chapters, and there is a large body of research on media use in adolescence as well (Arnett, 2007). However, media remain a major daily context in adulthood as well. Although many new media have been developed in recent decades, most notably the Internet and digital devices, television remains king. Of all evening leisure activities among American adults, watching TV is the most common, with 80% reporting that they watch TV "most weeknights after your evening meal and before bedtime"—a higher percentage than any other activity, including talk with family, shower or bathe, do chores, and walk the dog (Putnam, 2000). American adults ages 25–49 watch TV for about 30 hours a week, which works out to about 4 hours per day (Marketing Charts Staff, 2014).

Media are clearly part of young adults' daily lives, but do they *influence* adult development? A substantial amount of evidence indicates that the answer to this question is yes, especially with regard to community involvement (Kim et al., 2013). Hours watching TV in adulthood is negatively related to a wide range of civic and social activities among American adults, including attending a public meeting, volunteering, attending religious services, visiting friends, and attending parties (Putnam, 2000). True, these are correlations, and it is important to keep in mind here, as elsewhere, that correlation does not imply causation. However, it seems likely that before the invention of television, most adults used their free time more in all these other civic and social ways. Furthermore, according to the Canadian study described in Chapter 7, when television was first introduced to Notel, community activities of all kinds declined among adults, showing persuasive evidence of causation, not just correlation (MacBeth, 2007). Other studies have found that TV watching is associated with obesity in adulthood, as it is in childhood (Parsons et al., 2005).

What is it that makes television so attractive to adults as a leisure activity? Does it make them feel great? Does it bring them pleasure? Does it make them feel more fulfilled and engaged? Oddly, the answer to all these questions is a definite "no" (Putnam, 2000). On the contrary, Experience Sampling Method (ESM) studies of adults' moods during and after watching television show that TV makes viewers more passive and less alert (Kubey, 1994). Time diary studies show moods while watching TV to be about equal to moods while doing housework—low, that is, much lower than all other leisure activities, and lower than moods while working, too.

Why, then, do adults in developed countries devote so much of their leisure time to watching TV, when it is such an unsatisfying experience? Simply put, watching television is attractive because it is easy and requires so little out of us. As one research team observed, "Much of television's attraction is that it is ubiquitous and undemanding.…It requires no advance planning, costs next to nothing, requires no physical effort, seldom shocks or surprises, and can be done in the comfort of one's own home" (Robinson et al., 1999, p. 149).

Practice Quiz
ANSWERS AVAILABLE IN ANSWER KEY.

1. Research examining the importance of various traits in mate selection throughout the world found that the largest cross-cultural division was on the issue of _____.

   a. chastity

   b. desire for home and children

   c. education and intelligence

   d. mutual attraction-love

2. Bruce and Brenda are young adults who just got married. Based on the statistics, if they divorce, they are most likely to do so _____.

   a. 1 to 4 years after marriage

   b. 5 to 10 years after marriage

   c. 11 to 14 years after marriage

   d. 16 to 20 years after marriage

3. Which of the following statements about marriage is TRUE?

   a. People who are unhappily married are still happier than those who are single due to divorce.

   b. People who remain single after age 30 are more likely than their married counterparts to have mental health and physical health problems.

   c. Across countries, the proportion of young adults who have neither married nor had a long-term cohabiting relationship by age 40 is around 50%.

   d. By age 40, European Americans are more likely to have never married than their African American counterparts.

4. One difference between gay male couples and heterosexual couples is that gay male couples _____.

   a. have conflict in different areas

   b. tend to have a higher frequency of sexual activity

   c. seek out partners who are similar to themselves in many ways

   d. seek out long-term relationships based on love and mutual respect

5. Which of the following is the primary reason why many cultures encourage young wedded adults to have sex frequently?

   a. To produce children

   b. to ward off evil spirits

   c. To increase the chances that they will be happily married and stay together

   d. To increase intimacy in the marriage

6. Which of the following statements about becoming a parent is TRUE?

   a. In most countries, just below 50% of young adults have at least one child.

   b. In all world regions, people in urban areas have fewer children than people in rural areas.

   c. For couples who had a troubled marriage before the child was born, marital satisfaction increases after the baby arrives because it brings them closer together.

   d. Gender roles in developed countries become less traditional following the birth of a child.

7. Xavier is 23 years old and has recently graduated with his bachelor's degree in psychology. He is seeking employment and would like to find a job that leads to a promising career. Less than ideal, he applied for a position as an academic advisor at a community college, was offered a job, and accepted the position. Which stage of Donald Super's theory of occupational development is Xavier in?

   a. Implementation

   b. Crystallization

   c. Consolidation

   d. Stabilization

8. If Elle is typical of most American young adults, you would expect that she would spend her leisure time in the evening mostly on _____.

   a. taking walks and engaging in other low-impact physical activities

   b. communicating with friends via text messaging or social media, such as Facebook

   c. watching TV

   d. catching up with friends and/or family on the phone

Summary: Emotional and Social Development

LO 10.9 **Describe Erikson's theory of emotional and psychosocial development in young adulthood.**

In Erikson's theory, the primary crisis of young adulthood is intimacy versus isolation. Establishing intimacy involves uniting one's newly formed identity with another person in an enduring, committed, intimate relationship.

LO 10.10 **Describe the three qualities in Sternberg's theory of love and how they change with age.**

The three qualities of love are passion, intimacy, and commitment. In terms of Sternberg's theory, young adulthood is when passion reaches its peak and intimacy and commitment grow steadily.

LO 10.11 **Compare and contrast different cultural traditions regarding marriage, and identify the factors that predict marital satisfaction in Western cultures.**

Cross-national research indicates that there are broad similarities around the world in the criteria young people prize most in a marriage partner, with mutual attraction/love and dependable character at the top of the list. Chastity before marriage ranks very high in some cultures and very low in others. Outside the West, love is generally expected to develop after marriage, not before, and partners tend to have lower intimacy expectations for marriage than in the West. Arranged marriages have been common throughout history and remain common today, especially in Asia, although today they often take the form of semi-arranged marriages in which parents as well as young people are involved in the choice of a marriage partner. In many cultures the groom's family must pay a bride price or offer bride service to the bride's family to compensate them for the loss of her labor, but some cultures have a dowry custom in which the bride's family must pay the groom's. In American studies, marital satisfaction tends to be highest in the first year of marriage and then declines steadily, as the soul mate ideal collides with the demands and stresses of daily life.

LO 10.12 **Describe the most common causes of divorce in young adulthood, and explain why the United States has the highest divorce rate in the world.**

Factors related to higher likelihood of divorce include young age at marriage (younger than 25), having divorced parents, and low religious involvement. In the United States, divorce rates peak in young adulthood and are especially high among African Americans and young adults with low educational attainment. Young Americans believe in the value of marriage more than young people in most other Western countries, but they also believe that partners should not stay in a marriage that is unhappy.

LO 10.13 **Appraise common myths about single adults, and describe cultural and ethnic variations in singlehood.**

The majority of adults in all cultures marry, but about 10% remain single through young adulthood, across cultures. Single young adults rate lower on health and happiness than young adults who are happily married, but higher than those who are in unhappy marriages or who are separated, divorced, or widowed.

Rates of remaining single are exceptionally high in Asian cities such as Tokyo. Within the United States, African Americans are most likely to remain single, but they have higher rates of cohabitation, so their rates of long-term partnerships are about the same as for other ethnic groups.

LO 10.14 **Compare and contrast gay and lesbian partnerships with heterosexual partnerships, and describe how these partnerships have changed in recent years.**

Gay and lesbian partnerships in young adulthood are like heterosexual partnerships in most ways, although sexual frequency is relatively high among gay couples and relatively low among lesbian couples. In recent years, discrimination against gays and lesbians has diminished, especially on the part of the young, and some countries have allowed homosexuals to marry, but a substantial amount of discrimination remains.

LO 10.15 **Explain why young adulthood tends to be a stage of peak sexual behavior, and identify gender differences in sexuality.**

Across cultures, young adulthood tends to be the life stage when sexual activity reaches its peak; virtually all cultures encourage young adult sexual activity, most often in order to produce children, but in the West for promoting marital intimacy. According to an American survey, compared to young women, young men masturbate more frequently, reach orgasm during sex more consistently, and have more frequent sexual fantasies. Women masturbate more in their 30s than in any other decade of life.

LO 10.16 **Summarize the social and emotional impact of becoming a parent, and describe the unique challenges faced by single parents.**

Having a child is a stress to the intimacy of the marital relationship, but the relationships of couples with strong marriages tend to become stronger under the strain, whereas couples with marital problems prior to becoming parents tend to become even more unhappy with their marriage once a child is born. Single parents have lower family incomes because only one salary comes into the family, and they also have responsibility for parenting duties and household chores, but many of them receive assistance from relatives or friends.

LO 10.17 **List the stages of occupational development in Super's theory, and explain how personality and gender shape occupational goals.**

The stages of Super's theory are crystallization, specification, implementation, stabilization, and consolidation. Holland has proposed a theory to explain how occupations are chosen based on the fit with the individual's personality, but most personalities could fit a wide range of jobs, and most jobs include persons with a wide range of personalities. Gender is a major predictor of job choice, with many professions remaining sharply segregated by gender, although less now than in the past for professions such as law and medicine.

LO 10.18 **Explain the relationship between community involvement and television use in the lives of young adults.**

Community involvement often rises in young adulthood as adult roles are taken on, but community involvement has decreased in recent decades across age groups, primarily due to the rise and dominance of television. Watching television is the main leisure activity of young adults in developed countries, even though it is seldom an emotionally-satisfying experience.

Applying Your Knowledge as a Professional

The topics covered in this chapter apply to a wide variety of career professions. Watch these videos to learn how they apply to a counselor, the founder of a networking organization, and a community organizer.

Watch　CAREER FOCUS: COUNSELOR

Video

Dr. Judy Thornton
Clinical Director, Heart to Heart Counseling

Chapter Quiz

1. Marriage appears to be a very important marker of the transition to adulthood in _____.

   a. the West

   b. traditional cultures

   c. all cultures

   d. no cultures

2. Emerging adults in _____ view being able to support their parents financially as a necessary criterion for adulthood.

   a. the United States

   b. Canada

   c. China

   d. Israel

3. Which of the following changes occurs in the immune system during young adulthood?

   a. There are no changes in the immune system until late adulthood.

   b. There is a decline in the production of both B and T cells.

   c. The immune system increases its production of T cells and B cells.

   d. There is an increase in T cells and a decline in the production of B cells.

4. The countries with the highest obesity rates are _____.

   a. the wealthiest countries

   b. the poorest countries

   c. Asian countries

   d. traditional cultures

5. Which of the following statements about exercise is true?

   a. Nearly all adults in developed countries engage in regular exercise.

   b. Most adults in developed countries do not exercise regularly.

   c. Across SES groups, women exercise more than men.

   d. Adults at lower SES levels exercise more than adults at higher SES levels.

6. What happened to Terman's "Termites" when they became adults?

   a. They had higher rates of divorce.

   b. They suffered from emotional and psychological problems.

   c. They amassed great wealth, but were very unhappy.

   d. As a group, the Termites had a great deal of educational and occupational success.

7. In both Asian and African cultures, a common theme of conceptions of intelligence is that _____.

    a. it is based on educational level

    b. it can only be achieved by those with high SES

    c. it indicates social elements, as well as cognitive elements such as knowledge

    d. it is not achieved until you reach late adulthood

8. Recent research has shown that maturity of which brain structure during young adulthood reflects cognitive changes that underlie expertise?

    a. Temporal lobe

    b. Corpus callosum

    c. Frontal cortex

    d. Occipital lobe

9. How is creativity measured?

    a. It is assessed based on self-reports.

    b. Assessments of creativity have focused on the number of works a person produces, or on the timing of a person's "best" works, as determined by experts in the area or by the works' influence.

    c. No one has attempted to measure creativity.

    d. A standardized test has been developed that assesses both creativity and IQ.

10. Erikson thought that _____ was not possible until an individual had a fairly stable personal identity.

    a. marriage

    b. self-esteem

    c. intimacy

    d. trust

11. According to Sternberg, commitment, passion, and intimacy combine to form _____ love.

    a. romantic

    b. fatuous

    c. compassionate

    d. consummate

12. Today, the _____ marriage is the most common in most Eastern cultures.

    a. arranged

    b. semi-arranged

    c. romantic

    d. open

13. Which of the following is true regarding divorce rates?

    a. Rates of divorce are higher among Whites than among African Americans.

    b. Rates of divorce are higher among those with college degrees than those without because college graduates devote so much time to their careers.

    c. The United States has the highest divorce rate in the world.

    d. Divorce is common and rates are similar across all cultures.

14. Which of the following groups experiences the least overall happiness?

    a. People who are separated

    b. People who are widowed

    c. People in unhappy marriages

    d. People who are single

15. Which of the following best represents the research on gay and lesbian couples?

    a. Gay and lesbian adults often seek out romantic partners who are opposite from them in many ways.

    b. No differences have been identified between gay and lesbian couples.

    c. Gay and lesbian couples have different sources of conflict in their relationship than do heterosexual couples.

    d. Gay and lesbian couples are similar to heterosexual couples in most ways.

16. One of the findings from the most detailed study of sexual behavior among young adults in the United States was that _____.

    a. masturbation continues through the thirties and forties for most men

    b. women reported more frequent sexual fantasies than their male counterparts

    c. more than half of young adults from the late twenties to early forties reported more than one sexual partner in the past year

    d. there were no gender differences in the frequency of orgasm

17. Which of the following is true regarding research on couples after the birth of the first child in developed countries?

    a. Gender roles become more traditional and women are more likely to take an extended period of leave after the birth of a child.

    b. Marital satisfaction declines more for men than women after the birth of a child because men become jealous of the new baby.

    c. For couples who had a troubled marriage before the child was born, marital satisfaction increases after the baby arrives because it brings them closer together.

    d. Marital satisfaction improves for all couples following the birth of the first child.

18. According to Holland, people are likely to be unhappy if they _____.

    a. are not able to have a lot of social contacts on the job

    b. spend more time working the "second shift" than in their full-time workplace

    c. do not have a good fit between their personality and their job

    d. make less money than their spouse/romantic partner

19. Of the following evening leisure activities among American adults, the most common is _____.

    a. playing portable electronic devices

    b. using social media on the Internet

    c. watching television

    d. communicating with friends via text messaging on the phone

Chapter 11
Middle Adulthood

THE POPULAR AMERICAN VIEW OF THE AGE PERIOD from 40 to 60 is pretty dismal. Physical decline, sexual decline, and an agonizing "midlife crisis" is what supposedly awaits.

In contrast to this American view of the age period from 40–60, many cultures view this life stage not in terms of mental and physical decline, but rather in terms of changes in family relations and associated social responsibilities (Shweder, 1998). Becoming a grandparent is an especially important and welcome transition in many places, as we shall see. Furthermore, across cultural contexts, including in the United States, middle adulthood is most often experienced not as a time of misery and decline, but as the prime of life, the age when people reach the fulfillment of their expertise, their status and authority, and their enjoyment of life. Physical decline does occur with age, but usually the decline is mild before age 60,

and it is more than offset by the social and personal gains. Overall, midlife is a time when satisfaction with work and relationships peaks, for most people. In short, this may be the chapter in this book that surprises you the most.

In this chapter I will refer to ages 40–60 as "middle adulthood" or "midlife," but, as noted in Chapter 1, for adult life stages there is no precise age when they begin and end, only rough age ranges. Furthermore, it should be kept in mind that viewing this age period as the "middle" of life is a relatively recent development. As we have seen in previous chapters, until recently in human history, few people lived beyond age 60, so ages 40–60 were hardly the middle of the human life expectancy. However, with life expectancy now nearly 80 years in many parts of the world, it makes sense to conceptualize ages 40–60 as the middle period of adult development.

Watch   CHAPTER INTRODUCTION: MIDDLE ADULTHOOD

Video

Section 1   Physical Development

 Learning Objectives

11.1 Describe how vision and hearing decline in midlife, and explain the reasons for these declines.

11.2 Compare and contrast the reproductive changes in midlife for women and men.

11.3 Name the major health problems of middle adulthood, and identify the variations in their rates by gender, culture, and ethnicity.

11.4 Explain how midlife health predicts health through the rest of the life span.

PHYSICAL DEVELOPMENT:
Physical Changes in Middle Adulthood

When you look at a person for the first time, what are the signs that the person is in middle adulthood? That's easy for me—all I have to do is look in the mirror—but how about you? Gray hair is one obvious marker. As noted in Chapter 10, turning gray begins in young adulthood, but by middle adulthood most people have turned mostly or all gray (Tobin, 2010). Hair continues to thin from young to middle adulthood and baldness continues to increase, especially in men with a European background (Ellis & Sinclair, 2008). Skin tone continues to loosen as the three layers of our skin lose some of their fat content and adhere to each other less firmly, causing the skin to sag and wrinkle (Giacomoni & Rein, 2004). Obesity continues to rise in prevalence, partly due to a biological tendency toward increasing body fat and losing muscle mass in middle adulthood (Marcell, 2003; Ogden et al., 2013). These signs of aging were all covered in detail in Chapter 10, so our focus here will be on declines in sensory abilities and the aging of the reproductive system. The video *Physical Changes in Middle Adulthood* illustrates some of these changes.

Watch   PHYSICAL CHANGES IN MIDDLE ADULTHOOD

Changes in Sensory Abilities

LO 11.1 **Describe how vision and hearing decline in midlife, and explain the reasons for these declines.**

During middle age, the body's aging processes continue, and most people experience some changes in their sensory functioning. However, the declines are gradual, and people vary a great deal in how much change they experience, with some experiencing no decline at all and others experiencing substantial changes.

Overall, for most people, vision is the sense that declines most. The lens of the eye enlarges and becomes less flexible and less transparent, making it more difficult to perceive images in sharp focus and to see in dim light. The number of rods (light receptors) and cones (color receptors) in the eye diminishes to about half by age 60, further limiting vision (Bonnel et al., 2003).

The consequences of these changes are most evident in reading. Relatively few people need glasses for reading prior to middle adulthood, even if they needed visual assistance to perceive distant objects clearly, but by age 60 most people need reading glasses (Koopmans & Kooijman, 2006; Strenk et al., 2005).

Eyeglasses have been available for hundreds of years to correct vision, but recently other technologies have been developed. An operation known as Lasik can correct problems with distance vision (Kato et al., 2008). For reading vision, a type of Lasik called *monovision correction* can be used to reduce or eliminate the need for reading glasses (Braun et al., 2008). In monovision correction, one eye is corrected for near vision and one eye is corrected for distance vision. The brain automatically figures out which eye to rely on most, depending on whether near vision or distance vision is necessary. However, even with a monovision correction, most people need reading glasses by age 60 (Braun et al., 2008).

Hearing declines in midlife for about 13% of adults in developed countries, especially for high-pitched sounds (Gratton & Vasquez, 2003). Just like the hair on the head, the tiny hairs in the inner ear, known as *cilia*, which transmit sounds to the brain, thin out during middle adulthood (Wiley et al., 2005). The eardrum and other structures in the inner ear become less flexible, making them less sensitive to sounds, and the auditory cortex in the brain becomes less efficient in processing information from the inner ear.

Environmental factors also affect hearing in middle adulthood. Men generally experience greater hearing loss than women do in middle adulthood, in part because men are more likely to be employed in factory work and other jobs that include chronic exposure to loud noises (Heltzner et al., 2005). Rock stars fall into this category, too; performers such as Pete Townsend of the Who have lost most of their hearing by midlife, from years of performing in front of loud amplifiers. Studies of African tribal people in middle adulthood have found that they show less decline in hearing than people in developed countries do, evidently because they are exposed to less noise in their daily lives (Jarvis & van Heerden, 1967).

Hearing aids have been available for decades to compensate for hearing loss. However, recent technological advances have greatly improved the quality of hearing aids. The newest digital hearing aids are smaller as well as more effective (Chien & Lin, 2012; Kates, 2008).

By the end of middle adulthood, most people need glasses for reading.

CRITICAL THINKING QUESTION

Given the decline in vision that takes place in middle adulthood, should a vision test be required when renewing a driver's license beginning at age 50?

Changes in Reproductive Systems

LO 11.2 **Compare and contrast the reproductive changes in midlife for women and men.**

One of the most important physical changes of midlife occurs in the reproductive system as fertility declines, a change known as the **climacteric**. For women the climacteric is especially notable, because it culminates in **menopause**, the end of monthly ovulation and menstruation. In contrast, the climacteric for men is more gradual and steady, and men continue to produce sperm throughout life.

MENOPAUSE Menopause usually takes place in the late 40s or early 50s, but there is a wide range of individual variations, from the early 30s to the late 50s. The hormonal changes leading to menopause actually begin about 10 years earlier, as during this decade of *perimenopause,* the production of estrogen and progesterone steadily declines (Ortmann et al., 2011). When menopause occurs, production of these hormones drops further. Menopause tends to occur earlier among women if they smoke cigarettes or if they have never given birth (Rossi, 2005). It occurs later among women who exercise regularly (Santoro et al., 2007). The timing of menopause is also influenced by genetics, as shown by correlations among mothers and daughters and among identical twin women (Gosden, 2007).

All women experience hormonal declines and the end of menstruation in midlife, but women vary widely in how they experience the physiological and psychological effects of menopause and perimenopause. One common symptom is *hot flashes*, in which the woman suddenly sweats and feels very warm, and her skin reddens in the face and chest; afterward she feels chilled (Bastian et al., 2003). There is a vast range in the experience of hot flashes, from daily to not at all, but most women experience at least occasional hot flashes as part of menopause (Rossi, 2004). Other common symptoms of menopause include mood fluctuations, headaches, dizziness, and heart palpitations (Schwenkhagen, 2007). Women are also at increased risk for depression during perimenopause and menopause (Weber et al. 2014). Estrogen is crucial to memory, so menopause may also lead to disruptions in memory abilities, as the video *Estrogen and Memory* illustrates (Weber et al., 2014). Only about 10% of women experience symptoms of menopause extreme enough to cause severe distress, and many experience no symptoms at all (Grady, 2006; Rossi, 2004). Symptoms may be experienced during perimenopause but tend to be most severe around the time just before and just after menopause, when the drop in hormone levels is steepest.

climacteric

changes in the reproductive system that occur in middle adulthood; for women the cessation of ovulation and menstruation (menopause), and for men the gradual decline in the number and quality of sperm

menopause

the end of monthly ovulation and menstruation that occurs in women in midlife

Watch ESTROGEN AND MEMORY

Variations in how menopause is experienced take place not only within but between cultures (Melby et al., 2005). For example, hot flashes are reported by the majority of women in most world regions (with Africa highest at over 80%), but by only 15% of Japanese women (Obermeyer, 2000). Few women in India and few Mayan women in Mexico report hot flashes (Beyene & Martin, 2001; Menon, 2002). Among Indonesian women, 93% experience body and joint aches and only 5% report hot flashes (Haines et al., 2005). Within the United States, African American women are more likely than women in other American ethnic groups to report hot flashes, and Latino women are more likely to report heart palpitations (Fisher & Chervenak, 2013; Winterich, 2003).

One reason for fewer menopausal symptoms among Japanese women is that their diets are high in soybean-based foods, and soybeans contain plant estrogen, which compensates in part for the estrogen decline the women experience (Taku et al., 2012). Otherwise, the reasons for the cultural differences in menstrual symptoms are not clear.

HORMONE REPLACEMENT THERAPY For women who experience severe symptoms during menopause, *hormone replacement therapy (HRT)* is sometimes used to alleviate their distress (Ortmann et al., 2011; Schwenkhagen, 2007). On the face of it, this seems like a promising treatment. If women experience problems due to rapid declines in their estrogen and progesterone levels, perhaps replacing those hormones could alleviate their distress. However, the results of HRT have proven to be more complicated. The good news is that HRT is highly effective at reducing the symptoms of menopause, such as hot flashes (Roussouw et al., 2007). Furthermore, HRT has other beneficial health effects, such as strengthening the bones and reducing the risk of colon cancer (Schwenkhagen, 2007). There is even some evidence that it may have cognitive benefits (Erickson & Korol, 2009). The bad news is that HRT also increases the risks of stroke, heart attacks, and breast cancer (Bhavnani & Stricker, 2005).

The age of the woman receiving HRT appears to be crucial (Ploncyznski & Plonczynski, 2007). Women who receive HRT around the time of menopause, and for no more than 5 years, seem to obtain the benefits of it with few of the risks (LaCroix et al., 2011). However, women over 60 are now generally advised against HRT, especially if they have a family history of heart disease or breast cancer. Research is continuing on the effects of HRT, and new therapies are also being developed in an effort to address the problems some women experience during menopause but without HRT's risks. Various other approaches to reducing the symptoms of menopause are being investigated, including soy-based medicines, exercise, and acupuncture (Fischer & Chervenak, 2013). In the video *Menopause*, an American woman describes how menopause has impacted her life and shares her experience with hormone replacement therapy.

Watch MENOPAUSE

WOMEN'S RESPONSES TO MENOPAUSE Whatever their experience of the symptoms of menopause, women across cultures mainly welcome the end of their reproductive years (Melby et al., 2005). In cultures where most women give birth to only one or two children, such as in Europe and North America, menopause is welcomed by most women as the end of having to deal with monthly periods and the risk of an unintended pregnancy (Brim, 1999; Melby et al., 2005). In cultures where women give birth frequently and are pregnant or nursing for most of their reproductive years, menopause is often welcomed as the end of childbearing and the beginning of a new, less taxing period of life (Beyene & Martin, 2001).

Many traditional cultures have taboos associated with menstruation and restrict women's activities during their monthly period. As we have seen in previous chapters, these restrictions apply to many domains, including food preparation and consumption, social activities, religious practices, bathing, and sexual activities (Buckley & Gottlieb, 1988; Knight, 2013). In those cultures women welcome menopause because it marks the end of these restrictions (Avis et al., 2002; Menon, 1998).

REPRODUCTIVE CHANGES IN MEN Is there a male climacteric? Men certainly experience nothing comparable to menopause. Nevertheless, gradual changes take place in the male reproductive system during midlife. Testosterone levels decline by about 1% per year, and sperm quantity and quality gradually go down (Leonard, 2004). There is also an increase in problems related to sexual functioning, a topic we will explore in more detail later in the chapter.

Not only is there no male menopause, there is no menopause in other primate species. It is unique to human females. Why would this be so? Evolutionary biologist Jared Diamond (1992) proposes two reasons: the danger that childbirth poses to human mothers, and the danger that a mother's death poses to human children. In human evolutionary history, a mother with several children was risking her children's lives with every subsequent childbirth. Given the time and energy required in caring for human infants and children, if she died her children would have been highly vulnerable to neglect and early death. Natural selection (see Chapter 1) favored women who stopped menstruating at some point, because their children would have been more likely to survive than the children of women who continued bearing children and hence remained at risk for death from complications of childbirth. Men never evolved menopause because continuing to produce children throughout life carries no health risk for men.

Practice Quiz   ANSWERS AVAILABLE IN ANSWER KEY.

1. Which of the following is TRUE regarding visual changes in midlife?
   a. An operation can be performed to correct problems with distance vision.
   b. Vision changes are minor and very few middle adults require glasses.
   c. The number of rods and cones stays the same, but they function less effectively.
   d. The lens of the eye gets smaller and more transparent.

2. During midlife, _____.
   a. men generally experience less hearing loss than women
   b. the cilia thin out
   c. the eardrum becomes more flexible, making it more sensitive to sounds
   d. the only causes of hearing loss at this time in the life span are those that are genetic in nature

3. Your grandmother is experiencing very strong menopausal symptoms. She is 62 years old and is a breast cancer survivor. She has heard that hormone replacement therapy (HRT) can help with severe menopausal symptoms. Based on the research, what would you expect to be the advice she gets from her physician?
   a. She should try HRT cautiously and have frequent checkups.
   b. She should definitely use HRT; there are no reasons not to do so.
   c. She should definitely not use HRT because of the risks given her age and medical history.
   d. She should use HRT if she has other female relatives who have had success with this treatment.

4. In terms of American ethnic groups, women of _____ descent report the highest rate of hot flashes as a result of menopause.
   a. Asian
   b. African
   c. European
   d. Native American

5. Which of the following is TRUE?
   a. Menopause occurs later among women who smoke.
   b. There is no menopause in other primate species; it is unique to human females.
   c. Iron-rich foods compensate in part for the estrogen decline in women.
   d. The climacteric for men is more sudden than it is for women.

PHYSICAL DEVELOPMENT: Health and Disease

We have seen in the previous two chapters that emerging adulthood and young adulthood are exceptionally healthy stages of life. Many people remain healthy through midlife, but overall, maintaining good health becomes more of a challenge as the body ages. A variety of health issues become common that had been rare or nonexistent in previous life stages. Maintaining good health in midlife is important not only in the midlife years but afterward, because it is a strong predictor of later health and longevity. As in other life stages, regular exercise and a healthy diet are the keys to maintaining health and vigor in midlife, along with avoiding smoking and excess alcohol use.

Health Problems

LO 11.3 **Name the major health problems of middle adulthood, and identify the variations in their rates by gender, culture, and ethnicity.**

Most people maintain generally good health through middle adulthood, especially if they have adequate nutrition and access to modern medical care. Nevertheless, a number of health risks rise in middle adulthood, including sleep problems, osteoporosis, cardiovascular disease, and cancer.

SLEEP PROBLEMS Sleep problems become more common after age 40. Specifically, many people have more trouble sleeping through the night (Blumel et al., 2012). They wake up in the night and have trouble falling asleep again. Consequently, they are less likely to experience the deepest type of sleep and often do not feel fully rested in the morning (Abbot, 2003). Sleep problems in midlife are most common among people who have other physical and psychological problems as well, including obesity, cardiovascular disease, and depression (Foley et al., 2004). Even if they do not have sleep problems, many midlife adults do not get enough sleep. Medical authorities recommend 7–9 hours as optimal, but among midlife adults in the United States, more than one fourth report receiving less than 7 hours of sleep at least occasionally (Centers for Disease Control and Prevention [CDC], 2011).

OSTEOPOROSIS Bone mass begins to decline gradually in the late 30s for most people. Estrogen strengthens bones, so for women the decline in bone mass becomes steeper after the decline in estrogen levels that accompanies menopause. Sometimes the loss of bone mass is extreme enough to result in **osteoporosis**, a condition in which the bones become thin and brittle (Prentice et al., 2006). From middle adulthood onward, women lose about 50% of their bone mass, with over half of that loss coming in the decade following menopause (Alvarz-Leon et al., 2006). In one study of over 200,000 American women in middle adulthood who had passed menopause, 7% had osteoporosis and an additional 40% had lost enough bone mass to be at risk for it (Chestnut, 2001).

Estrogen loss after menopause places women at much higher risk for osteoporosis than men. In fact, about 80% of persons with osteoporosis are female (Lee et al., 2013; Whitehead et al., 2004). There is also a genetic contribution to the risk of osteoporosis, as shown in higher concordance rates among MZ than DZ twins (Notelovitz, 2002). People who are small and thin are at risk for osteoporosis because they start out

osteoporosis
condition common in women in midlife and beyond, in which the bones become thin and brittle as a result of rapid calcium depletion

Sleep problems become more common in middle adulthood.

with less bone mass than others. People of African origin have lower risk of osteoporosis than people of other groups because of their higher bone density.

Although biological factors contribute greatly to osteoporosis, lifestyle choices also make a difference. Factors increasing the risk of osteoporosis include the usual suspects: cigarette smoking, high alcohol consumption, poor diet (with little calcium), and low rates of physical activity (Whitehead et al., 2004). In contrast, osteoporosis can be prevented with a healthy lifestyle that includes calcium-rich foods (such as dairy products) and a regular program of exercise (Melton et al., 2004; Prentice et al., 2006). For women who are at especially high risk, medications are available that can prevent osteoporosis by building up bone mass and density (Fitzpatrick, 2003). Health authorities recommend that women over 50 have their bone density checked yearly, especially if they have a family history of osteoporosis.

CARDIOVASCULAR DISEASE Cardiovascular disease (or *coronary heart disease*) is the leading cause of death among adults worldwide (World Health Organization [WHO], 2014). It is rare prior to age 40, but the incidence rises sharply in middle adulthood (Safar & Smulyan, 2004). Risk for cardiovascular disease begins long before middle adulthood, and is the result of high-fat diets, smoking, and daily routines that include little physical activity (Blumenthal et al., 2005). Over the years, this lifestyle contributes to **atherosclerosis**, a condition where plaque builds up in the coronary arteries, causing the passage of blood through the arteries to become constricted. Atherosclerosis leads to high blood pressure and eventually to a heart attack when the arteries become so filled with plaque that they are closed off.

Rates of cardiovascular disease are highest in countries like Denmark, where a high-fat diet is common, and in countries like Russia that have high rates of smoking, which is extremely damaging to the cardiovascular system (De Meersman & Stein, 2007). Rates are lowest in countries like Japan, where a low-fat diet is common, and in countries like France that have the highest consumption of red wine, which protects against cardiovascular disease for people who drink a glass or two on a daily basis. Across countries, men are at much higher risk than women, apparently due mainly to higher rates of smoking (CDC, 2011; WHO, 2014). Within the United States, rates of cardiovascular disease are highest among African Americans and Native Americans, due to higher smoking rates and higher-fat diets (Warren-Findlow, 2006).

A classic study of Japanese men demonstrated vividly the influence of diet on the risk of cardiovascular disease (Ilola, 1990). Twelve thousand men of Japanese origin were studied, in two Japanese cities as well as in Honolulu, Hawaii, and San Francisco, California. Despite having a similar biological background, the men's rates of cardiovascular disease varied widely depending on where they lived. Men living in Japan consumed a low-fat diet of mainly fish and rice and had the lowest rates of cardiovascular problems. The men in San Francisco had the highest rates, mainly because their diets were 40% higher in fat. The men in Honolulu were midway between the other groups in both dietary fat and cardiovascular problems.

Stress is another factor that has been implicated in heart disease. Stress not only has direct effects on the functioning of the heart, it can also trigger coping behaviors such as smoking and overeating that also contribute to heart disease (Bekkouche et al., 2011). The relation between stress and heart disease is complex, but recent research indicates that stress is especially likely to contribute to heart disease in people who have a personality

atherosclerosis

condition where plaque builds up in coronary arteries, causing the passage of blood in arteries to become constricted

Smoking greatly increases the risk of cardiovascular disease.

that is especially prone to negative emotional states of anger, anxiety, and depression (Stanley & Burrows, 2008).

Recent research also shows that two different types of stress can contribute to cardiovascular disease, chronic stress (such as living in a dangerous neighborhood) or acute stress (experiencing a severely stressful event). In one study, women who had experienced a severely stressful event were screened for symptoms of *post-traumatic stress disorder (PTSD)*, then followed up 14 years later (Kubzansky et al., 2009). Women who exhibited five or more symptoms of PTSD at the screening were over three times as likely to have coronary heart disease at the 14-year follow-up screening.

In response to evidence of the relation between stress and heart disease, interventions have been developed to treat stress in order to reduce heart disease risk. In one study, 134 heart disease patients ages 40–84 were randomly divided into three groups, with one group receiving routine medical care, one group receiving routine care plus aerobic exercise training three times a week for 16 weeks, and one group receiving routine care plus stress management training once a week for 16 weeks (Blumenthal et al., 2005). Following the intervention, both the exercise and the stress-management groups exhibited better cardiovascular functioning as well as lower levels of distress and depression, compared to the routine care group.

Heart attacks are usually fatal, but if cardiovascular disease is diagnosed before it reaches that point it can be treated quite effectively using medications and surgery. In a common procedure known as *angioplasty*, the surgeon inserts a tube into the blocked artery and inflates a tiny balloon at the end, flattening the fatty deposits against the walls of the artery and allowing blood to flow more freely. The French obtain the same effect gradually through their custom of drinking red wine at meals, as wine inhibits the development of plaque and causes the arteries to expand. Other lifestyle practices that reduce cardiovascular risks include regular exercise, maintaining a healthy weight (and avoiding obesity), and taking a low-dose aspirin daily (American Heart Association, 2006). Most important of all, smoking and a high-fat diet should be avoided.

CANCER Like cardiovascular disease, cancer is relatively rare prior to middle adulthood. However, from young to middle adulthood the incidence of cancer grows 10 times higher (CDC, 2011). Worldwide, cancer is the second-leading cause of death among adults (WHO, 2014). Prostate cancer is the most common type of cancer among men, whereas breast cancer is the most common type among women (Jemal et al., 2006). For both men and women, the second and third most common types are lung cancer and colon cancer.

Cancer occurs when the body's usual cell production process goes awry in a particular part of the body, and abnormal cells begin to multiply rapidly and uncontrollably. Eventually, these abnormal cells form tumors that draw nutrients away from healthy parts of the body and disrupt the normal functioning of the tissues and organs where they are growing. It is not clear what initiates cancer, but some types, such as breast cancer, have a definite genetic basis, as shown in the correlation of breast cancer risk among biological relatives (Nkondjock & Ghadirian, 2004). A variety of environmental factors also raise the risk of cancer, including excessive exposure to sunlight, exposure to radiation, and exposure to hazardous chemicals or materials (such as asbestos). The lifestyle factor that raises cancer risk the most is smoking, which causes not only lung cancer but many other types of cancer as well (Moolgavkar et al., 2012; U.S. Department of Health and Human Services, 2005).

A massive amount of research on cancer treatments has taken place over the past 30 years, and advances have been made in treating and curing many types of cancer. One common type of treatment is *chemotherapy*, which involves subjecting the cancerous part of the body to toxic substances intended to poison the cancer cells. Another common treatment is *radiation therapy*, which attacks the tumor with focused radiation. Often, some combination of chemotherapy, radiation therapy, and surgery (cutting out the cancerous part) is used to treat cancer.

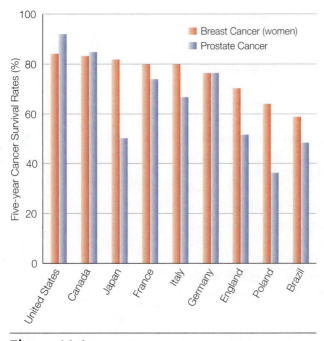

Figure 11.1 Survival Pattern for Breast Cancer and Prostate Cancer

Why do some countries have higher survival rates than others?
SOURCE: Based on Coleman et al. (2008)

These methods, along with early detection, have raised the 5-year survival rate for cancer from about 50% to 65% in the United States over the past 40 years (CDC, 2011). However, 5-year survival rates vary greatly depending on the type of cancer. Rates are over 65% for many cancer types, including prostate (96%), skin (92%), breast (85%), and rectal (67%) cancers. The lowest 5-year survival rates are for lung cancer (15%) and cancer of the pancreas (5%).

Rates of 5-year survival also vary considerably among countries. In a landmark study of over 2 million cancer patients in 31 developed countries, researchers examined variations in 5-year survival for cancer of the breast, prostate, colon, and rectum (Coleman et al., 2008). Five-year survival was generally highest for the wealthiest developed countries and lowest for the least wealthy. **Figure 11.1** shows the pattern for breast cancer and prostate cancer. The countries with the highest survival rates not only had more advanced technologies for treating cancer, but also a higher rate of persons who had received screening tests for early detection of cancers. For example, 84% of the American women in the study ages 50–64 reported receiving regular **mammograms**, which are X-rays that screen for breast cancer, compared to 63% of the British women, and the 5-year survival rate was correspondingly higher in the United States.

Despite substantial advances in treatment, the best way to avoid death from cancer remains prevention, including a healthy diet and avoiding the risk factors mentioned. Early detection is crucial to successful treatment, so it is important for men to have annual tests for prostate cancer once they reach middle adulthood. With regard to women and breast-cancer risk, experts differ in their recommendations about when to begin screening, but the Mayo Clinic in the United States recommends a three-pronged approach (Pruthi, 2011):

mammogram

X-ray procedure used to examine women for breast cancer

Annual mammograms are recommended for women over age 40.

- Breast health awareness, which includes a woman becoming familiar with her breasts during young adulthood in order to identify abnormalities or changes (and to inform her doctor of anything that may need further evaluation);
- Clinical breast exam performed by a health care provider, recommended annually beginning at age 40; and
- Annual mammogram beginning at age 40.

The issue of when women should begin receiving mammograms has been hotly debated, but two large recent studies conducted in northern Europe help clarify it. One study of over a million women in Sweden compared death rates from breast cancer in women who were screened during their 40s and those who were not, between 1986 and 2005 (Hellquist et al., 2011). The death rate from breast cancer was 29% lower for the women who received mammograms than for those who did not. The second study examined a national sample of women in Norway who did or did not receive a mammogram every 2 years after a program offering free mammograms was introduced (Kalager et al., 2010). In this study, the mammograms were found to reduce the death rate from breast cancer by 10%, less than in the Swedish study but still a notable amount.

Mammograms are not a perfect tool for screening for breast cancer. They can miss some cancers, and they can produce *false*

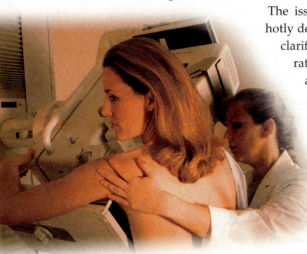

positives; that is, diagnoses of the disease that turn out to be false after further tests. For this reason, health experts recommend a yearly breast exam by a physician as well after age 40 (Berger, 2010).

Influences on Midlife Health and Later Development

LO 11.4 **Describe various influences on health and explain how midlife health predicts health through the rest of the life span.**

Health in midlife varies widely, with some people feeling healthier than ever, while others begin to experience serious problems or even early mortality. What influences the course of midlife health? In one sense, the answer to this question is simple and obvious: eat healthy foods, get regular exercise, and avoid health-damaging habits like excess eating, smoking, and alcohol abuse. However, attaining this healthy lifestyle is neither simple nor obvious; if it were, everyone would be doing it, and they most certainly are not.

The reasons for this are complex and involve cultural patterns of behavior, as well as access to healthy, affordable foods and adequate health care. In general, people who have limited economic resources have less access to good food and health care.

Overall, what aspects of midlife health are most important for predicting later physical and mental health? Research by George Vaillant (2002) provides an unusually detailed answer to that question for 21st-century Americans. Vaillant combined samples

Cultural Focus: Physical Health in Middle Adulthood Across Cultures

This video shows how cultural factors and individual circumstances affect health among individuals in developed as well as developing countries. The focus of these interviews is health and lifestyle during the middle adulthood years.

Watch PHYSICAL HEALTH IN MIDDLE ADULTHOOD ACROSS CULTURES

Review Question:

The standard pattern of work in the United States during the middle adult years typically interferes with maintaining a healthy lifestyle. List at least three ways that these adults could incorporate healthy habits into their busy lives.

from three studies: male Harvard graduates, boys from low-income urban families, and women with high IQs. Each of the studies began in the early decades of the 20th century and each was longitudinal, following their samples with assessments every year or two from childhood or emerging adulthood into late adulthood. The longitudinal design enabled Vaillant to identify the characteristics of midlife 50-year-olds that predicted health outcomes 25 to 30 years later.

By age 75–80 some of the participants had died, and Vaillant classified the health outcomes of the remaining participants into two categories, based on their emotional well-being and their physical health: *happy–well* and *sad–sick*. The characteristics of 50-year-olds that predicted later health most strongly were smoking habits, alcohol abuse, and being overweight. At age 50, heavy smokers, alcohol abusers, and people who were overweight were most likely to be dead 25–30 years later, and were most likely to be *sad–sick* if they still lived. In contrast, years of education and marriage stability were strong predictors of being *happy–well* in later adulthood. Several personality characteristics were also good midlife predictors of later *happy–well* status, including being thankful and forgiving, empathizing with others, sociability, and being future-oriented.

In another longitudinal study, the Americans' Changing Lives (ACL) study followed a nationally-representative sample of Americans ages 25 and older for 15 years beginning in 1986 and ending in 2001, assessing their physical health at four times during the 15-year period (House et al., 2005). The main findings of the study were that the relation between educational attainment and health was strong at all ages and became stronger from young adulthood to middle adulthood, then remained strong in the early part of late adulthood (the 60s and early 70s), before waning in the 80s. Specifically, people with high levels of educational attainment were less likely than others to die in middle adulthood or to experience chronic health problems in middle and late adulthood. People with low levels of educational attainment were at greater risk for early mortality and chronic health problems, mainly because in young and middle adulthood they experienced greater stress, less healthy work conditions, and were more likely to engage in unhealthy behaviors such as smoking. Education predicted health from middle to late adulthood more strongly than income did.

Practice Quiz   ANSWERS AVAILABLE IN ANSWER KEY.

1. Which of the following is associated with sleep problems in middle age?

 a. Living in a hot climate

 b. Being depressed

 c. Having a Type A personality

 d. Growing up in a large family where the environment was often noisy

2. Which of the following is a risk factor for osteoporosis?

 a. Too much high-impact exercise

 b. Having broken more than two bones during childhood

 c. Smoking

 d. Consuming a vegan diet high in soy-based foods

3. Among adults worldwide, what is the leading cause of death?

 a. Suicide

 b. Cardiovascular disease

 c. Breast cancer (for women); prostate cancer (for men)

 d. Homicide

4. Rates of cardiovascular disease are likely to be lowest for an individual living in _____.

 a. the United States   **c.** Denmark

 b. Japan   **d.** Russia

5. Which of the following is a finding that emerged from the Americans' Changing Lives study?

 a. People with high levels of educational attainment were less likely than others to die in middle adulthood or to experience chronic health problems in middle and late adulthood.

 b. People who had strong religious beliefs were less likely than others to die in middle adulthood or to experience chronic health problems in middle and late adulthood.

 c. People with extended family living with or near them were less likely than others to die in middle adulthood.

 d. People with larger social networks were more likely to experience chronic health problems in middle and late adulthood than those with smaller networks.

Summary: Physical Development

LO 11.1 Describe how vision and hearing decline in midlife, and explain the reasons for these declines.

In midlife, the lens of the eye becomes less flexible and transparent and the number of rods and cones declines, resulting in problems with vision and reading. Hearing declines are due to the thinning of hairs in the inner ear, the eardrum becoming less flexible, and environmental factors such as exposure to loud noises.

LO 11.2 Compare and contrast the reproductive changes in midlife for women and men.

Menopause takes place in middle adulthood for women, and is the culmination of hormonal declines over a decade of perimenopause. There are great variations in women's experience of menopause around the world, but in all cultures women welcome the end of monthly menstruation. Men experience slight declines in testosterone through middle adulthood but nothing comparable to menopause.

LO 11.3 Name the major health problems of middle adulthood, and identify the variations in their rates by gender, culture, and ethnicity.

Various health problems increase during middle adulthood, including sleep problems and, especially for women, osteoporosis. The two main causes of death in midlife are cardiovascular disease and cancer. Rates of cardiovascular disease are higher in countries with high-fat diets or high smoking rates. Effective treatments for both cancer and cardiovascular disease have been developed in recent years, but both can be best prevented by avoiding smoking and eating a low-fat diet.

LO 11.4 Explain how midlife health predicts health through the rest of the life span.

Midlife health habits such as smoking, alcohol abuse, and being overweight have a negative effect on later health. Other factors, including educational attainment, marriage stability, and personality characteristics such as sociability, can have a positive impact.

Section 2   Cognitive Development

⌄   Learning Objectives

11.5 Compare and contrast the changes in fluid and crystallized intelligence during midlife.

11.6 Explain why expertise tends to peak in midlife.

11.7 Summarize the positive and negative aspects of work situations in middle adulthood, and identify the impact of globalization on midlife workers.

11.8 Describe how perceptual speed declines during middle adulthood.

11.9 Compare and contrast how attention and memory change during middle adulthood.

COGNITIVE DEVELOPMENT:
Intelligence, Expertise, and Career Development

The pattern of midlife cognitive development is complex. On the one hand, people respond to information a bit slower than they did at younger ages. On the other hand, their overall store of information increases, as does their knowledge and skill in their areas of expertise. Work often reaches a peak of satisfaction and expertise in middle adulthood, but for those who lose their jobs the consequences can be severe.

Fluid and Crystallized Intelligence

LO 11.5   **Compare and contrast the changes in fluid and crystallized intelligence during midlife.**

Does intelligence decline during middle adulthood, or rise? Mostly it rises, but the answer depends on what kind of intelligence is being considered. Following the theory of Raymond Cattell (1963), scholars on intelligence have identified two general types, *fluid intelligence* and *crystallized intelligence.*

fluid intelligence

type of intelligence that involves information-processing abilities such as short-term memory, the ability to discern relations between visual stimuli, and the speed of synthesizing new information

    Fluid intelligence is the type of intelligence that involves information-processing abilities such as short-term memory, ability to discern relations between visual stimuli (such as the patterns in geometric shapes), and speed of synthesizing new information. In Cattell's theory, fluid intelligence is a biologically-based quality of the nervous system and cannot be trained or taught, although the ability could be developed. For example, people who are capable of learning to fly high-speed jets would have to have high fluid intelligence to begin with, but training would allow them to develop the specific skills necessary.

crystallized intelligence

accumulation of a person's culturally-based knowledge, language, and understanding of social conventions

    In contrast, **crystallized intelligence** represents the accumulation of a person's culturally-based knowledge, language, and understanding of social conventions. This includes vocabulary, cultural information stored in long-term memory, and logical reasoning abilities. For example, the knowledge accumulated by scholars in the course of a career of research in their field is crystallized intelligence. Although, according to Cattell, biologically-based abilities also contribute to crystallized intelligence, it depends more on learning and exposure to cultural knowledge than does fluid intelligence (McArdle & Hamagami, 2006).

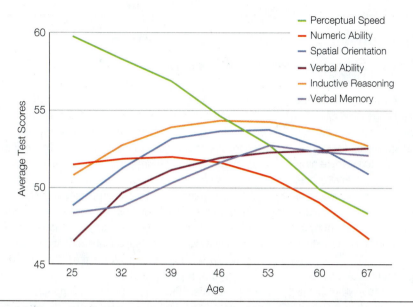

Figure 11.2 Seattle Longitudinal Study Scores on Intelligence Subtests

Perceptual speed declines in middle adulthood, but most aspects of intelligence rise.

SOURCE: Willis & Schaie (1998)

The best information on the course of fluid and crystallized intelligence through adulthood comes from the Seattle Longitudinal Study, which began with a sample of over 5,000 young and middle-aged adults in 1956 and continues to this day (Schaie, 1994; Schaie, 1996; Schaie, 1998; Schaie, 2005; 2012; McAardle et al., 2002). As **Figure 11.2** shows, scores on all three tests of crystallized intelligence—verbal ability, inductive reasoning, and verbal memory—increased in emerging and young adulthood and peaked in middle adulthood before declining in late adulthood. However, among the three tests of fluid intelligence, perceptual speed declined steeply through the adult years, numeric ability declined slightly during middle adulthood and then sharply in late adulthood, and spatial orientation rose until midlife and then declined.

All together, the results of the Seattle Longitudinal Study indicate that midlife is a period when many aspects of intelligence reach their peak, especially for crystallized intelligence (Willis & Schaie, 1999, Schaie 2012). Other studies have found a similar pattern using different methods, although the pattern varies somewhat depending on whether the study is cross-sectional or longitudinal, as detailed in the *Research Focus: Intelligence in Middle Adulthood: Two Research Approaches* feature on the next page. The peak of crystallized intelligence in midlife is also consistent with research on work showing that for most people their occupational achievements peak during this life stage, a topic we will explore further shortly.

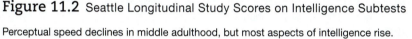

CRITICAL THINKING QUESTION

What jobs in midlife might especially require fluid intelligence?

The Peak of Expertise

LO 11.6   **Explain why expertise tends to peak in midlife.**

Have you noticed that when someone is chosen for a position of great responsibility and authority, such as heading a business or a political organization, it is almost always a person who is in middle adulthood? One key reason for this is that in many fields it takes

Research Focus: Intelligence in Middle Adulthood: Two Research Approaches

Our knowledge of how intelligence changes throughout the life span is based mainly on the Seattle Longitudinal Study, a study conducted over 60 years (and still continuing). Although there have been many other longitudinal studies of intelligence, none has lasted nearly as long as the Seattle study. There have also been many cross-sectional studies of adult intelligence. Unlike a longitudinal study, which follows a sample over time, a cross-sectional study takes place on one occasion. The Seattle Longitudinal Study started out as a cross-sectional study of adults ages 22–70, and the younger participants were then followed longitudinally.

For the most part, results from cross-sectional studies support the results of the Seattle Longitudinal Study, finding that crystallized intelligence rises from emerging adulthood through middle adulthood and then declines, whereas some types of fluid intelligence decline steadily throughout adulthood. However, on some tests of crystallized intelligence the cross-sectional data contrast strikingly with the longitudinal data.

Look at these two graphs, which show average test scores for inductive reasoning and spatial orientation. In each graph, both the longitudinal and the cross-sectional data are from the Seattle Longitudinal Study. As you can see, for spatial orientation and inductive reasoning, the longitudinal data show a peak in intelligence during middle adulthood followed by a mild decline, whereas the cross-sectional data show stability or decline from emerging adulthood to middle adulthood followed by a steep decline in late adulthood.

What explains these divergent findings? A cross-sectional study is not just a study of age differences but of different historical eras. In social science research, we say that they are members of different cohorts and the differences between them may

be due not only to the age, but also to cohort effects; that is, to the effects of growing up in different historical eras.

In the case of differences in intelligence, we know that cohort effects are likely to be substantial. For example, people in their 20s today in developed countries are extremely likely to have gone to secondary school, and most of them will have obtained at least some postsecondary education. In contrast, most people in their 80s today in developed countries never attended secondary school, and very few of them obtained any kind of postsecondary education. Consequently, one would expect that people in their 20s would have an advantage over people in their 80s in a test of something like inductive reasoning, because the younger cohort spent far more years in school, where (presumably) their reasoning skills were enhanced.

In any cross-sectional study, it is difficult to tell whether age differences are due to age or to cohort effects. For this reason, longitudinal studies are often viewed as methodologically preferable to cross-sectional studies, because they avoid the problem of cohort effects. However, longitudinal studies also have some limitations.

Typically, longitudinal studies experience attrition of the sample over time; that is, some people drop out due to illness, death, lack of interest, or other reasons. Consequently, after many years, the people who remain in the study are often more physically and psychologically healthy than the people who dropped out or the people in the general population. This may enhance their performance on tests of intellectual abilities.

Despite such limitations, longitudinal studies are generally considered more valid tests of age differences than cross-sectional studies, because they avoid cohort effects.

Watch RESEARCH FOCUS: INTELLIGENCE IN MIDDLE ADULTHOOD: TWO RESEARCH APPROACHES

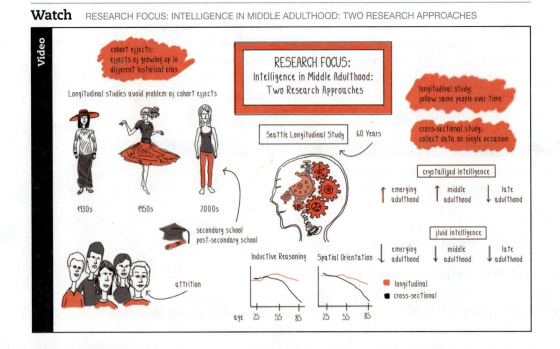

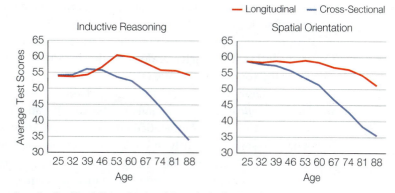

Longitudinal and Cross-Sectional Data from the Seattle Study
SOURCE: Schaie (1988)

Review Questions:

1. The longitudinal and cross-sectional results of the Seattle Longitudinal Study showed that from emerging adulthood to middle adulthood crystallized intelligence _____ and fluid intelligence _____.
   a. declined; increased
   b. declined; also declined
   c. increased; declined
   d. increased; also increased

2. Which study design involves the possibility of cohort effects?
   a. Cross-sectional
   b. Longitudinal
   c. Both cross-sectional and longitudinal
   d. Neither cross-sectional nor longitudinal

until middle adulthood to accumulate a high level of *expertise*, which is knowledge and experience in a specific domain (see Chapter 10) (Chi et al., 2014). For example, by middle adulthood a nurse has far more expertise than someone who has just completed nursing school, and so would be more likely to be selected to head a nursing staff in a hospital; a middle-aged school teacher has more expertise than a young adult teacher and so would be more likely to be selected to head a school. For me personally, I don't think I could have written this life span text you're reading when I was 20, 30, or even 40 years old. It took me until about age 50 to accumulate the necessary knowledge. Expertise is a form of crystallized intelligence, as it consists of accumulated knowledge and reasoning in a culturally-valued area.

Why does expertise peak in middle adulthood?

Cognitively, expertise allows people to process information more quickly and efficiently than novices can (Crawford & Channon, 2002). For middle-aged adults, their store of knowledge and experience means that when faced with a problem or issue, there is a good chance they will have faced something similar in the past. This allows them to focus on the aspects of a problem that are most likely to hold the solution and ignore irrelevant information. Think, for example, of how an experienced automobile mechanic analyzes the problem with your car when you bring it in because the brakes are making a strange noise. A novice might have to look in the owner's manual and perhaps try a wide range of different possible sources for the noise, but the experienced mechanic's expertise allows him to

focus quickly on the most likely explanation, because there is a good chance he has heard this kind of noise many times before.

With enough expertise, a substantial part of problem solving becomes automatic (Chi et al., 2014). The mechanic does not have to think through the various possible sources of the sounds in the brakes and decide among them; he hears the sound and immediately knows. Recall, too, the young chess experts described in Chapter 7, who could use this *automaticity* to remember chess configurations more effectively than adult novices could (Chi, 1978). Automaticity makes problem solving fast and efficient. Experts do not have to sort consciously through every alternative. Their experience allows them to solve problems based on intuition; the solution just seems right to them.

Experts are not only more automatic in their problem solving than novices are, they are also more flexible (Arts et al., 2006). If their first strategy is not successful, their experience allows them to think of alternative strategies.

Expertise is one reason why middle adulthood is the life stage when people rise to the top of their profession. The heads of companies, universities, governments, and other organizations are usually appointed in midlife because it takes until then to develop the expertise required. However, expertise does not apply only to the elite. In one study of expertise among food-services workers, expertise was defined in terms of knowledge (of menu items and food presentation); organizational skills (such as handling orders efficiently); and social skills (such as confidence in interacting with customers). Comparing young adult to middle adult workers, the study found that expertise increased in all these areas (Perlmutter et al., 1990).

Furthermore, expertise applies not only to occupational performance but also to leisure activities. In a study of players of the game *Go*, the ones who were more experienced were able to assess game situations faster and use their memories more efficiently than the less experienced players (Masunaga & Horn, 2000).

Work

LO 11.7　**Summarize the positive and negative aspects of work situations in middle adulthood, and identify the impact of globalization on midlife workers.**

Work situations in middle adulthood are highly diverse. For many, it is a time when job satisfaction peaks. Less commonly, it may be a time of changing occupational paths. For some women, it is a time of reentering the work force after a long period devoted to caring for children and running a household. For some women and some men, it is a time of leaving the work force, either involuntarily through losing a job or voluntarily through taking early retirement. Across all these situations, there are variations depending on social class and culture, and the workplace is changing rapidly worldwide due to globalization.

JOB PEAKS, JOB LOSSES A variety of American and European studies have found that job satisfaction peaks in middle adulthood, particularly in the 50s, for people in a wide variety of jobs, from executives to maintenance staff (Besen et al., 2013; Easterlin, 2006; Hochwarter et al., 2001). Pay increases with age, of course, in most jobs, but the main reasons given for enjoying work in midlife focus less on pay and promotions and more on enjoyment of the work itself. As people develop more expertise they get better at what they do, and there is satisfaction in doing a job well. They also gain more authority and become more involved in making the decisions that influence how their job is done. For example, someone who works as an administrative assistant might become an office manager in midlife and manage several other people. Another reason for greater satisfaction with work in midlife is that many people lower their goals and expectations for work (Tangri et al., 2003). Rather than striving for the highest achievements, and perhaps being frustrated at not reaching them, midlife workers tend to realize they have risen about as high as they are likely to go in their profession, and accept their achievements, however high or low they might be. High job satisfaction in midlife is reflected in lower absenteeism and fewer job changes compared to younger workers (Easterlin et al., 2006; Lachman, 2004).

However, not everyone is satisfied with their work in middle adulthood, and job changes sometimes do take place. Sometimes these changes take place in pursuit of new challenges and opportunities. For example, women working in large corporations are twice as likely as men to quit their jobs in midlife, often out of frustration with the **glass ceiling** that limits women's advancement due to gender discrimination (Barreto et al., 2009; Mergenhagen, 1996). The majority of these women go into business for themselves (rather than joining another corporation), with high rates of success (Ahuja, 2005). Other midlife adults quit their jobs because they become disillusioned, frustrated, and tired of their jobs, a phenomenon called **burnout**. People who quit due to burnout often complain of being overwhelmed by their work, and they are often in "helping professions" such as teaching, health care, or social services where the interpersonal stress of their work is high (Baker & Heuven, 2006; Taris et al., 2004; Zapf et al., 2001). Burnout is more common in the United States than in Western Europe, perhaps because European countries tend to have tighter legal regulations on work hours and work conditions, and all European countries legally require employers to give all workers a minimum number of weeks of vacation per year, as we will see later in the chapter.

Work satisfaction peaks in middle adulthood along with expertise and authority.

An especially difficult situation is faced by midlife adults who leave their jobs involuntarily and become unemployed. Despite their expertise, their low absenteeism, and their high productivity, midlife adults stay unemployed longer than younger adults do (U.S. Bureau of the Census, 2010). Midlife workers require higher wages than younger workers, and employers may see less of a long-term future for them (Lachman, 2004). Some midlife workers may lack the information-technology skills that are important for most jobs in developed countries, and employers may believe they are less likely than younger workers to learn such skills quickly (Czaja, 2006). When midlife workers do find a new job after being unemployed, it tends to have lower status and lower pay than the job they lost (Burgard et al., 2009). This puts added stress on them, as most have financial obligations that may include helping to support their emerging adult children, helping to support their parents, and trying to accumulate savings for retirement (Wrosch et al., 2000). Given these bleak circumstances, it is not surprising that people who become unemployed in middle adulthood experience more disruption to their functioning than younger adults do, including declines in both mental and physical health (Breslin & Mustard, 2003; Burgard et al., 2009).

GLOBALIZATION AND WORK IN MIDDLE ADULTHOOD The globalization of the world economy has had profound effects on the nature of work. The growing intensification of economic connections between various parts of the world has made work more unstable and unhealthy for some people, while opening up new opportunities for others.

With regard to middle adulthood, globalization has been a major influence in making the work path through the 40s and 50s much less linear and predictable than it used to be for many people. According to one view, there has been a major shift in recent decades from *organizational careers* to *protean careers* (Gubler et al., 2014; Hall & Mirvis, 1996). The organizational career developed as a common model in industrialized countries during the 19th century and expanded in the course of the 20th century. In this model, the employee stayed in the same field, and usually with the same employer, throughout his or her working life. Over the years, employees could work their way "up the ladder" within the organization, gaining increased responsibility, authority, and pay over time. By the mid-20th century, many workers following the path of the organizational career were members of unions that lobbied constantly to improve their working conditions and enhance their pay and benefits.

glass ceiling

unspoken limit on career advancement of women due to discrimination

burnout

state of becoming disillusioned, frustrated, and tired of one's job

By the end of the 20th century, the organizational career was fading and the protean career was becoming increasingly common. In contrast to the organizational career, the protean career is flexible, changeable, and idiosyncratic. Rather than remaining with one company, the person in the protean career path changes paths frequently in the course of working life—sometimes voluntarily, in pursuit of new opportunities, sometimes involuntarily, when laid off or "downsized." The protean career may involve changing not only jobs but fields, if the job the person has been doing ceases to be challenging and interesting—or if the person can no longer find a job in the original field.

For midlife adults with a high level of education and expertise, changing jobs and career paths may be attractive and rewarding. Workers with high levels of education are especially valuable in the global economy, because it is an economy that emphasizes information and technology and rewards those who can use them well (see Chapter 9). Such workers may be even more valuable and productive in middle adulthood than at younger ages, because of the expertise they have gained.

In contrast, for midlife adults with low levels of education, the protean career holds more peril than promise (Blustein, 2006). Workers with lower education are more likely to be doing work that involves simple, repetitive tasks, such as factory work. This work rarely pays well, and it is the kind of work that is most vulnerable to becoming automated or shifted to developing countries where labor is cheaper. As globalization increases, it is becoming possible even for work such as accounting and computer programming to be shifted around the globe to where it can be done most cheaply. This is good news for educated emerging adults and young adults in developing countries, who are getting the best jobs available as their economies expand, but bad news for many people in middle adulthood in developed countries, who are finding themselves out of work at an age when they still have substantial skills and would like—and perhaps need—to work longer.

It should be added that there remains a substantial proportion of the world, especially in Asia and Africa, where the work is mainly agricultural throughout life (see **Map 11.1**; ILO, 2011). Agricultural work is difficult at any age if it is manual and not

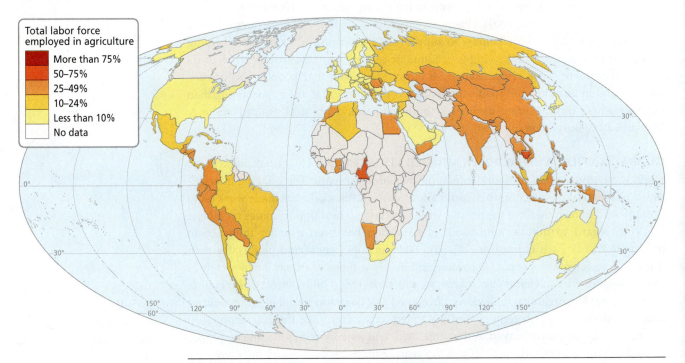

Total labor force employed in agriculture
- More than 75%
- 50–75%
- 25–49%
- 10–24%
- Less than 10%
- No data

Map 11.1 World Population Employed in Agricultural Labor

Which regions of the world have the highest percentage of their populations employed in agricultural work? What are the challenges of this kind of work for midlife adults?

SOURCE: Based on World Bank (2013)

mechanized, but it becomes more arduous in middle age, as strength and stamina decline and health problems such as arthritis become more common. For people in such jobs, there is neither the organizational career nor the protean career, but only the daily reality of having to do hard physical labor in order to survive.

Practice Quiz   ANSWERS AVAILABLE IN ANSWER KEY.

1. A person's vocabulary, cultural information stored in long-term memory, and logical reasoning abilities are known as what type of intelligence?

   a. Fluid intelligence

   b. Crystallized intelligence

   c. Performance intelligence

   d. Analytical intelligence

2. Crystallized and fluid intelligence were studied in the Seattle Longitudinal Study and it was found that perceptual speed _____.

   a. increased throughout the adult years

   b. followed the same pattern of change as crystallized intelligence

   c. leveled off in midlife and was maintained throughout the later adult years

   d. declined steeply throughout the adult years

3. Expertise would be considered a form of _____ intelligence.

   a. kinesthetic   **c.** crystallized

   b. fluid   **d.** perceptual

4. Developmentalists refer to knowledge and experience in a specific domain as _____.

   a. general intelligence

   b. expertise

   c. fluid intelligence

   d. automatic processing

5. In what way is Vladimir, a middle-age man, likely to be different from his 24-year-old co-worker who began working with him just under a year ago? Vladimir is _____.

   a. more likely to be satisfied with his job

   b. more likely to be absent

   c. more likely to have made several job changes in the last few years

   d. less likely to receive the "salesperson of the year" award, the highest achievement at his company

COGNITIVE DEVELOPMENT: Information Processing in Middle Adulthood

Although crystallized intelligence and expertise increase in midlife, in some ways cognitive abilities decline. A variety of information-processing abilities drop from young to middle adulthood, including processing speed, attention, and memory. However, not all aspects of memory decline.

Processing Speed

LO 11.8   **Describe how perceptual speed declines during middle adulthood.**

In the Seattle Longitudinal Study, the one test that showed an unmistakable decline from young to middle adulthood was the test of perceptual speed. This is the ability to respond quickly and accurately to sensory stimuli, for example, pressing a button in response to a sound, or pressing a button with the right hand when a blue light appears but with the left hand when a red light appears. Other studies have found similar evidence of decline in perceptual speed from young through middle adulthood, usually focusing on *reaction time*, the amount of time it takes the person to respond to the stimulus (Tun & Lachman, 2008). The reaction time of midlife adults is typically a few milliseconds longer than for young adults in laboratory tasks involving lights and sounds and pressing buttons (Deary & Der, 2005; Madden, 2001).

Does the decline in reaction time from young to middle adulthood have any real-life significance? Only for certain tasks and on rare occasions (Deary & Der, 2005; Salthouse, 2000). Few people in middle adulthood can compete successfully against foes from adolescence to young adulthood in electronic games that reward rapid reaction times (although there are cohort differences, too, because unlike their younger opponents, midlife adults did not grow up with the games). Midlife adults may also be slower than younger adults to respond to a driving situation that requires an immediate reaction, such as braking quickly when another driver stops unexpectedly (Tun & Lachman, 2008). However, few activities in the course of daily life require the kind of quick reaction times tested in psychology experiments.

Attention and Memory

LO 11.9 **Compare and contrast how attention and memory change during middle adulthood.**

Attention also declines in some respects in middle adulthood. A crucial aspect of cognitive functioning is the ability to focus attention on relevant information and ignore what is irrelevant, and laboratory tests of this ability indicate a decline from emerging to middle adulthood and further from middle to late adulthood (Mani et al., 2005). Specifically, with age people seem to become less able to inhibit a response to irrelevant information. For example, when shown a series of letters on a computer screen and told to press a bar only in response to certain letter combinations, midlife adults are more likely than younger adults to press the bar in response to the wrong combinations (Guerreiro et al., 2010; Hasher et al., 1999).

Another aspect of attention that appears to decline with age is the ability for *divided attention*, that is, the ability to maintain attention on two or more information sources simultaneously and switch back and forth between them. For example, in laboratory tasks that involve switching between assessing pairs of numbers as "odd or even" or as "more or less," emerging adults perform better than midlife adults (Radvansky et al., 2005; Verhaeghen et al., 2003). Here, too, there may be a cohort difference, as many of today's emerging adults have grown up in the presence of multiple media, which may have given them lifelong practice in juggling more than one information source— listening to music while reading, or talking on the phone while playing a computer game—that their middle adult elders may not have experienced.

The capacity for divided attention declines from emerging adulthood to middle adulthood. Is it an age difference or a cohort difference?

Declines in attention are likely to have important implications for real-life cognitive functioning. Certainly the ability to screen out irrelevant information is a crucial part of working productively, so any decline in this ability would seem to lead to a decline in productivity. Similarly, for many kinds of activity the ability to sustain divided attention would be valuable. Both work and leisure in the modern world often require and reward *multitasking*—answering e-mail messages during a meeting, for example, or making dinner while supervising a child's homework.

As for memory, this aspect of information processing appears to change little from young to middle adulthood. Some cross-sectional studies show a decline in short-term memory (Salthouse, 2000; Wang et al., 2011), for example when people are required to remember lists of words; but as we have seen, the Seattle Longitudinal Study actually showed an increase in verbal memory through middle adulthood (Schaie, 2005). Long-term memory stores continue to increase for most people through middle adulthood, as indicated in the Seattle Longitudinal Study on the vocabulary test and in other studies of *factual knowledge* (such as memory for historical events) and *procedural knowledge* (such as how to play a card game). Increases in factual knowledge and procedural knowledge contribute to the continued development of expertise.

Practice Quiz ANSWERS AVAILABLE IN ANSWER KEY.

1. A study that measures the time it takes a person to push a button once they hear a sound is focused on _____.
   a. divided attention
   c. reaction time
   b. procedural knowledge
   d. multitasking

2. Reaction time _____.
   a. decreases significantly enough during midlife that most activities of daily living are somewhat impaired
   b. is typically longer for midlife adults than it is for young adults in laboratory settings
   c. refers to the how people respond in emotionally charged situations
   d. of midlife adults is only significantly slower on tasks outside the lab setting

3. On which of the following tasks would midlife adults tend to do more poorly than their younger counterparts?
   a. Remembering historical events
   b. Remembering how to play a card game or a board game
   c. Switching between assessing pairs of numbers as "odd or even" or as "more or less"
   d. Knowing the meaning of vocabulary words

4. The ability to maintain attention on two or more information sources simultaneously and switch back and forth between them is known as _____.
   a. information processing
   b. divided attention
   c. automatization
   d. perceptual attention

5. The capacity for divided attention declines from emerging adulthood to middle adulthood and some researchers have argued that this is caused by _____.
   a. a cohort difference
   b. changes in the brain
   c. lack of sleep
   d. differences in diet

Summary: Cognitive Development

LO 11.5 **Compare and contrast the changes in fluid and crystallized intelligence during midlife.**

Fluid intelligence involves speed of responding to new information, whereas crystallized intelligence involves the accumulation of culturally-based knowledge. Fluid intelligence declines during middle adulthood in some respects, whereas crystallized intelligence increases.

LO 11.6 **Explain why expertise tends to peak in midlife.**

Expertise tends to peak in midlife because it takes many years to develop knowledge and experience in a given domain. Expertise is one reason middle adults are able to rise to the top of their professions.

LO 11.7 **Summarize the positive and negative aspects of work situations in middle adulthood, and identify the impact of globalization on midlife workers.**

Job satisfaction peaks in midlife, due to rising status, expertise, and authority in the workplace. Losing a job is

more difficult in midlife than at younger ages, and it may result in a longer period of unemployment, especially for those workers who lack the skills to compete in the global economy.

LO 11.8 **Describe how perceptual speed declines during middle adulthood.**

Perceptual speed declines during middle adulthood, most noticeably in tests of reaction time. The decline in perceptual speed has limited real-life significance, however.

LO 11.9 **Compare and contrast how attention and memory change during middle adulthood.**

Attention declines in some ways in midlife, including the ability to focus attention on relevant information, and also the ability to maintain divided attention. Memory changes little during middle adulthood.

Section 3   Emotional and Social Development

EMOTIONAL AND SOCIAL DEVELOPMENT: Emotional and Self-Development

Midlife is a time when the emotions cool for most people, partly for physiological reasons and partly because of the stability of their lives. In terms of self-development, midlife is notable as a time when life satisfaction rises to new heights and self-acceptance increases. However, for most people, middle adulthood is a time of focusing not just on the self but on how to contribute to the well-being of the young.

Changes in Self-Concept and Self-Acceptance

LO 11.10 **Identify the changes that occur in self-concept during middle adulthood, including cultural variations.**

A substantial amount of research from a variety of cultures indicates that middle adulthood is a period when contentment with the self is higher than in any previous life stage (Huang, 2010; Keyes et al., 2002). More than in earlier stages of life, most midlife adults appear to be at peace with themselves, no longer striving to be something different than they are. Unlike in later adulthood, most midlife adults have not yet had to confront the loss of meaningful roles or serious impairments in their physical health and functioning.

One area where the advances in self-development of middle adulthood are evident is in research on self-concept. Self-acceptance tends to be more favorable in middle adulthood than in earlier periods, resulting in a middle adulthood rise in psychological well-being and life satisfaction (Huang, 2010; Keyes et al., 2002). Unlike emerging adulthood, which was described in Chapter 9 as the "age of possibilities," middle adulthood is a life stage where possibilities are more limited but most people accept the life they have made and are trying to make the best of their roles and responsibilities. Asked about their goals, midlife adults tend to mention not lofty dreams of fame and fortune but fulfilling well the roles they currently have, such as parent, spouse, and friend (Bybee & Wells, 2003).

Another area where self-development ripens in middle adulthood is identity development. We have seen in earlier chapters that identity issues are important throughout the life span, but in some ways become most acute during emerging adulthood (Arnett, 2015). In middle adulthood, by contrast, the identity struggles that sometimes characterize adolescence and emerging adulthood have cooled for most people, and there is a heightened sense of self-understanding (Labouvie-Vief, 2003, 2006). In one longitudinal study of American women who were graduates of an elite college, "identity certainty" increased steadily with age through middle adulthood. Specifically, in middle adulthood, participants were less likely than they had been in young adulthood to agree with items such as feeling "excitement, turmoil, confusion about my impulses and potential" and more likely to agree with items such as "a sense of being my own person" and "feeling secure and committed" (Stewart et al., 2001).

A large cross-sectional study of Americans from their late teens to their 70s found similar enhancements in self-development in middle adulthood (Ryff, 1995). Specifically, three qualities of the self increased with age through the 50s before reaching a plateau.

- *Self-acceptance* increased, as midlife adults were more aware and accepting of having a mix of positive and negative qualities, and overall felt more positive about themselves and their lives than younger participants did.
- *Autonomy* increased, in the sense that midlife adults were less concerned with other's assessments than younger participants were, and more inclined to assess themselves according to self-defined standards.
- *Environmental mastery* increased, as midlife adults were more likely than younger participants to see themselves as being able to handle a variety of roles and responsibilities effectively.

Enhanced self-development is also evident in becoming more psychologically adaptive during middle adulthood. For example, in one large study of German adults in their 40s and 50s, most people reported a steady rise in what the researchers called "flexible goal adjustment," as defined by affirmative responses to items such as "I can adapt quite easily to changes in a situation" (Brandtstadter, 2006; Brandtstadter & Baltes-Götz, 1990; Brandtstadter & Greve, 1994).

It is not only in individualistic cultures that enhanced self-development is notable in middle adulthood. Narrative accounts of Japanese women in their 50s indicate that many devote themselves to cultivating one or more art forms, such as flower arranging, calligraphy, tea ceremony, poetry, or dance (Lock, 1998). The turn toward these contemplative arts is based on Buddhist philosophy. Specifically, the arts are seen as ways to remove one's self from the demands of everyday life while cultivating personal discipline and escaping the world of desire. This spiritual ideal in midlife and old age has a long tradition in Japan. It is not a somber and mournful turning away from life but a satisfying new sense of personal freedom. Middle-aged Japanese women often describe their current time of life with words like "boldness" or "nerve." As one researcher observed, "Because age brings experience, one can afford as one gets older to 'let go' and be playful" (Lock, 1998, p. 59).

Although middle adulthood appears to entail positive self-development in a variety of cultures, there are also notable differences between cultures. Midlife adults in some collectivistic cultures may emphasize self-development less and relations to others more.

In Korean culture, midlife adults derive fulfillment from their children's success.

For example, in a study comparing Americans and South Koreans in their 50s, Americans were higher in individualistic traits such as self-acceptance and autonomy (Keyes & Ryff, 1998). In contrast, the South Koreans placed more emphasis on close ties to others, especially family members. They remained in closer contact with their adult children, and based their sense of personal fulfillment less on their own success than on their children's success. Within cultures, enhanced self-development in middle adulthood is most likely among persons who maintain the best physical health and social relationships, including a strong marriage (Lachman & Firth, 2004; Lansford et al., 2005).

The Mostly Mythical Midlife Crisis

LO 11.11 Summarize the evidence on the question of whether the midlife crisis is a typical part of development in middle adulthood.

But wait a minute—if self-development is so favorable for most people in middle adulthood, what about the famous **midlife crisis**? Isn't middle adulthood a time of agonizing over the meaning of life and making radical and reckless changes in order to avoid living a life of quiet desperation any longer?

No doubt for some people it is, and this is certainly a popular theme in Hollywood films, but abundant research over the past several decades has shown the claims of a midlife crisis to be mostly mythical. The myth began in the 1930s, with claims by the Swiss psychologist Carl Jung (who coined the term) that the midlife crisis was a part of normal psychological development (Jung, 1930). He based this conclusion mainly on his own midlife struggles, which is usually not a good basis for generalizing to several billion other people. In the 1970s Jung's claim appeared to receive research support in the work of Daniel Levinson (1978), who claimed to have spotted a midlife crisis in three-quarters of the men he interviewed. He described the midlife crisis as including feelings of meaninglessness, turmoil, and confusion; dissatisfaction and disappointment with work and family life; and fear of aging and death. However, he only interviewed 40 men—most of them highly educated—so three-quarters of them amounted to just 30 people, which is still a dubious basis for generalizing to the rest of humanity. (He later interviewed a small sample of midlife women and claimed to find a normative crisis among them, too [Levinson & Levinson, 1996].) Like Jung, Levinson was inspired by his own midlife struggles.

Research since the 1970s has consistently refuted the claim by Jung and Levinson of a normative midlife crisis (Brim et al., 2004; Lachman, 2004; Lachman & Kranz, 2010). In one early test of the midlife crisis hypothesis, researchers developed a Midlife Crisis Scale based on Levinson's claims and administered it to a sample of men ages 30–60, but they found that none of the aspects of the midlife crisis were supported by a majority of the men (Costa & McCrae, 1978). Subsequent studies using interview methods similarly failed to find evidence that a crisis was experienced by most people, or even a substantial minority of people, in midlife (Farrell & Rosenberg, 1981; Whitbourne, 1986). More recently, a national study of over 3,000 Americans ages 25–72 found that not only were those in midlife (ages 40–60) *not* more likely to be experiencing a crisis than persons in other age groups, they were *less* likely to be nervous and worried than were young adults ages 25–39 (Brim, 1999). Furthermore, in this study as in many others, midlife was the time when positive characteristics often peaked, including sense of control at work, sense of financial security, and feelings of being able to handle multiple daily responsibilities. These are just a few examples among many studies, all of which point to the same conclusion, that the claim of a "universal" midlife crisis is false.

midlife crisis

state claimed to be common in middle adulthood, entailing anxiety, unhappiness, and a critical reappraisal of one's life, possibly provoking dramatic changes

This does not mean, of course, that midlife adults never experience a crisis. A feeling of crisis can be triggered by experiencing negative life events, such as losing a job, financial problems, divorce, or health problems (Lachman, 2004). However, in such cases it is not going through midlife that provokes the crisis but experiencing the negative life events, most of which can happen at any point in adult life (Lachman & Kranz, 2010; Wethington et al., 2004). Given the strengths in self-development during middle adulthood, it may be a life stage when people are especially well-equipped to handle crises that result from life events (Brim et al., 2004). It should also be mentioned that research on the midlife crisis has focused on the American experience, and there is no evidence that it is a common part of the life span in other cultures—in fact the opposite may be true, as we will see later in the chapter.

Generativity

LO 11.12 Define generativity and explain how it is expressed in middle adulthood.

Midlife is a good time of life for self-development, but it is also a time when many people turn their attention to how they can benefit others. As we have seen in previous chapters, Erik Erikson's (1950) theory of the life span proposed a distinctive crisis or challenge for each life stage. For middle adulthood, the crisis is **generativity versus stagnation**. By *generativity*, Erikson means the motivation to contribute to the well-being of the generations to come. According to Erikson, by midlife we realize our mortality more acutely than we did in earlier life stages. The sting of this awareness leads us to think about how we can "live on" in some sense after we have died, and this in turn leads to a desire to help those younger than ourselves so that the effects of our time on earth will still be evident when we are gone. The alternative path is stagnation, which means focusing on one's narrow self-interest without concern for the good of others now and in the future.

There are a variety of ways an adult can be generative (Erikson, 1950; McAdams, 2013; McAdams & Logan, 2004; Peterson, 2006). Perhaps the most common way is by being a parent and grandparent (An & Cooney, 2006). The role of parent often involves expending vast amounts of time and energy in helping children grow through infancy, childhood, adolescence, and into adulthood. Being a grandparent can also mean assisting the younger generations and supporting their healthy development. Especially in developing countries and in some Western minority groups such as African Americans and Latinos, the role of grandparent entails daily responsibilities of caring for grandchildren while the parents go about the duties of daily life (Kelch-Oliver, 2011; Villar et al., 2012). We'll explore the grandparent role in more detail later in the chapter.

Not only as grandparents but as parents, midlife adults in developing countries may be more likely than those in developed countries to express generativity through commitment to family obligations. Parents in developing countries often continue to have highly interdependent relations with their adult children. For example, as we have seen in previous chapters, in countries such as India and China the typical pattern, especially in rural areas, is for young married couples to move in with the husband's parents (Chaudhary & Sharma, 2007). With this living arrangement the midlife parents provide economic and social support to the young adult married couple, and assist with child care, too, once the young couple's first child is born. Often the generations are engaged in collective economic activity such as farming or running a small business. Generativity is expressed by midlife adults as they teach their children and grandchildren how to farm, fish, cook, build, sell, weave—or whatever the foundation of economic activity is in the culture.

generativity versus stagnation

in Erikson's theory, the central crisis of middle adulthood, characterized by two alternatives, the motivation to contribute to the well-being of the generations to come (generativity) or focusing on narrow self-interest without concern for the good of others (stagnation)

Most midlife adults in India live with extended family members.

Other midlife roles, such as mentor, teacher, or organization leader, can also involve generativity (McAdams & Logan, 2004). Midlife adults in leadership positions may use their knowledge, skills, and experience to help the young along the road they have already traveled. Involvement in community organizations that seek to change society for the better is also an indication of generativity (Pratt et al., 2001). In rare cases, generative contributions are made in the form of inventions or works of art (McAdams & Logan, 2004).

In general, studies of Americans and Canadians find an increase in generativity from young to middle adulthood. This increase has been found using a variety of methods, from self-described personality traits on questionnaires to interviews to life story narratives (Keyes & Ryff, 1998; McAdams, 2013; Peterson, 2006). It has also been found in both longitudinal and cross-sectional studies. In the longitudinal study mentioned earlier that followed graduates from an elite women's college from their college years through midlife, generativity increased from the 30s through the 50s (Stewart et al., 2001). Studies comparing African Americans and Whites have found especially high generativity among African Americans (Dillon & Wink, 2004; Hart et al., 2001). Among African Americans religious involvement tends to be high, and their generativity is often expressed in part through church involvement, as well as through the grandparent role (Hart et al., 2001; Kelch-Oliver, 2011).

Gender Issues in Midlife

LO 11.13 Explain why the status of women in some cultures increases at midlife, and describe cultural variations in gender equality.

Gender remains an important determinant of human experiences in middle adulthood across cultures, as it was in earlier life stages. In general, gender roles become less restrictive in midlife than they had been in previous stages of development. Growing gender equality worldwide is reflected in greater representation of midlife women in positions of political and economic power, although inequalities still remain.

ENHANCED STATUS OF MIDLIFE WOMEN In many cultures, for women in middle adulthood there is a rise in their freedom, authority, and well-being. For example, Usha Menon interviewed women in India ages 19–78 (Menon & Shweder, 1998; Menon, 2013). At all ages, women agreed that the best time of life is *prauda*, mature adulthood, lasting from about the late 30s through the 50s. They saw a variety of favorable qualities as peaking for women during this life stage, including status, control, responsibilities, capacity to reason, and life satisfaction.

According to Menon's research, young adulthood is not usually a happy time for a woman in India. She has many daily tasks to carry out, including cleaning, caring for the family cows, caring for her children, and cooking for her husband and his parents (who usually live in the same household). Furthermore, she is under the thumb of her mother-in-law and is required to obey her authority. She must perform daily rituals of respect to her husband's parents, including massaging their feet, eating only after they have eaten (and only off the plate her mother-in-law has just used), and drinking the water used in the ceremonial washing of her in-laws' feet before meals (yes, you read that correctly). She rarely leaves the household compound, and never unaccompanied.

In middle adulthood, however, a woman's status reverses dramatically. When her eldest son marries, he moves his bride into the family household, and now she becomes top dog, a mother-in-law with authority over a daughter-in-law. Her own mother-in-law is obliged to hand over the keys to the family stores of food and linen, signifying the transfer of authority from one generation to the next. Now the midlife woman has the power to run the household and assign responsibilities to others. Her authority in religious matters rises, too, as she becomes the one responsible for conducting rituals such as *sandhya*, a ceremony at sunset each day that keeps away evil spirits and invites Lakshmi, the goddess of wealth and good fortune, into the home.

Similar patterns of an increase in traits like assertiveness and self-confidence have been found in midlife for women in a variety of different cultures, including the Maya of Guatemala and the Druze of the Middle East, rural China, and the American middle class (Cruikshank, 2013; Fry, 1985; Gutmann & Huyck, 1994; James et al., 1995). In many cultures, women often flourish once they reach middle adulthood. However, the enhanced status and well-being of women in midlife is not universal and should not be overstated. In polygynous cultures such as the Gusii of Africa, in midlife men often take another, younger wife, leaving their first wives vulnerable and dependent on their children (Levine, 1998). Men in many cultures exalt the beauty of young women and regard women in midlife as no longer attractive, whereas a similar decline in physical attractiveness is not perceived for men. Even in India, where the status of women in middle adulthood is generally high, popular sayings portray physical appearance very differently by gender (Kakar, 1998). A woman by age 40 is called *teesi-kheesi*, meaning "her face caves in and her teeth jut out," signifying aging. In contrast, a man is *satha-patha* until age 60, that is, a "virile youth."

GREATER GENDER EQUALITY Even in cultures like India and China, where a woman in midlife may have a great deal of power within the household, she may have very little power outside of it. Cultures and countries vary widely in how much opportunity women have to achieve status and authority by midlife in the public arena. Every year the United Nations Human Development Programme calculates a Gender Empowerment Measure (GEM) for over 100 countries around the world, based on women's representation in positions of political power, the percentage of women in professional and technical occupations, and the ratio of females' to males' earned income. Some of the results are shown in **Map 11.2** (for full results see http://hdr.undp.org). European

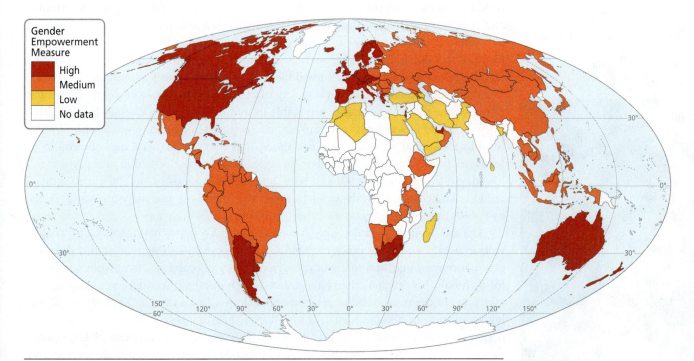

Map 11.2 Gender Empowerment Measure

The Gender Empowerment Measure (GEM) is based on women's representation in positions of political power, the percentage of women in professional and technical occupations, and the ratio of females' to males' earned income. Which countries have the highest and lowest GEM? To what extent is GEM related to economic factors?

countries are highest, and countries in Latin America also rank quite highly, along with Israel and South Africa. In general, GEM ratings are highest in countries with the highest economic development, but Japan and South Korea are relatively low on the GEM despite their high levels of wealth. In many countries in Asia and Africa a woman has never held the top position of political power (such as president or prime minister), and as of this writing that dubious distinction applies to the United States, Canada, and many European countries as well.

Although women's opportunities to achieve political and economic power by midlife are by no means equal to men's worldwide, they are certainly vastly higher than 50 years ago in most countries. In 1960 there were virtually no women who were political leaders, academic leaders, or CEOs anywhere in the world (Collins, 2010). Today, it is no longer a novelty in most countries for a woman to become prime minister or president of a university, or to lead a corporation. Almost always, these achievements come in middle adulthood.

However, for many women the achievements come at a cost. It is more difficult for a woman than a man to "have it all"; that is, to reach her goals in terms of work as well as family. Although gender roles have become much more egalitarian in many countries over the past half century, it remains true that an ambitious man is often married to a woman who is willing to serve a supportive, family-oriented role and take the main responsibility for caring for children and running the household, whereas it is rare for an ambitious woman to be a able to find a man who is willing to serve this kind of complementary role. Consequently, according to Sylvia Ann Hewlett (2003), high-achieving women often have to sacrifice their family goals as they pursue their work goals. At midlife (ages 40–55), 33% of the high-achieving women (in business, the arts, and academia) in Hewlett's national American study were childless and 40% were unmarried. The percentage with no children was especially high in the field of business: one half of the women business executives earning $100,000 or more per year were childless, compared to just 19% of comparable men. Few of the women Hewlett studied had chosen to be childless; on the contrary, most yearned to have children and had gone to great trouble and expense (through fertility treatments) in their 40s and early 50s to have one. Nearly all would also have preferred to be married by midlife rather than unmarried. However, they had focused on their career goals in their 20s and 30s, and often met with frustration and disappointment when they turned their focus to family goals in midlife.

Today, many women hold positions of authority in midlife. Chancellor of Germany Angela Merkel is pictured here.

What about men? Studies in a variety of cultures indicate that for men, too, gender roles become more flexible and permeable in midlife (Fry, 1985; Wiesner-Hanks, 2011). They no longer feel as much social pressure to appear strong and tough in order to conform to traditional gender role expectations, and they are allowed more license to be loving and emotionally sensitive. For example, an American longitudinal study that followed adults through their 50s and 60s found that women were initially more involved with grandchildren than men were, but men's involvement gradually increased so that by the 60s there were no gender differences (Kahn et al., 2011).

Overall, women's gender roles have changed a lot more than men's have. That is, women now have a wide range of occupational opportunities that were barely dreamed of a half century ago, and many of them have entered occupations that were previously for men only. Yet, even as they have entered the workplace, women have continued to take most of the responsibility for household duties. In Hewlett's (2003) study, 50% of high-achieving midlife women reported having primary responsibility for daily meal preparation; only 9% said their husbands did. Fifty-six percent had primary responsibility for doing the laundry; only 10% of their husbands did. Forty-five percent were mainly responsible for keeping the house clean, versus just 5% of their husbands. Other studies indicate that these patterns exist not just among high achievers. In the general population, too, even when marital partners both work full time, women consistently perform the bulk of the work for running the household (Strandh & Nordenmark, 2006; van der Lippe et al., 2006).

Practice Quiz ANSWERS AVAILABLE IN ANSWER KEY.

1. Which of the following would you most likely hear a midlife adult say?
   a. "I am going to be a well-known singer some day; if I dream it, I can become it."
   b. "I hope my kids remember me as a dedicated and loving parent."
   c. "I wish I were a better athlete."
   d. "I want to be the CEO of this company, rather than merely an employee."

2. When it comes to a midlife crisis, research evidence since the 1970's suggests _____.
   a. that the majority of the American population experiences it either in their 40's or 50's
   b. that the claim of a universal midlife crisis is false
   c. only those from ethnic minority backgrounds experience it because of more stress and discrimination than their counterparts from majority backgrounds
   d. that the majority of women experience this as a result of the empty nest, but it is much less likely to be experienced by men because they are more likely to work outside the home

3. What is the Eriksonian crisis in which individuals have the desire to "live on" after they have died and to help those younger than they so that the effects of their time on earth will be evident when they are gone?
   a. Autonomy vs. stagnation
   b. Generativity vs. stagnation
   c. Legacy vs. stagnation
   d. Integrity vs. despair

4. Clarisse loves to spend time with her grandchildren and makes every effort to help her daughter and son-in-law with babysitting and household chores while they focus on work. According to Erik Erikson, Clarisse's willingness to help and contribute to the generations after her means she will successfully resolve the _____ crisis.
   a. industry vs. inferiority
   b. generativity vs. despair
   c. generativity vs. stagnation
   d. integrity vs. despair

5. Which of the following is most accurate regarding the status of women?
   a. The Gender Empowerment Measure (GEM), a measure of women's opportunity to achieve status and authority, is highest in European countries.
   b. Across cultures, where women have a great deal of power within the household, they have a great deal of power outside of it as well.
   c. Research has shown that most high-achieving women choose to be childless.
   d. When both marital partners work full-time, men and women share the work of running the household equally.

EMOTIONAL AND SOCIAL DEVELOPMENT: The Social and Cultural Contexts of Middle Adulthood

Family ties remain at the heart of social life in middle adulthood, as they were in young adulthood, but the nature of those ties changes. As children grow into emerging and young adulthood, parents have less responsibility for them than at younger ages—although they may now have at least occasional responsibility for grandchildren. The midlife adult's own parents are now in late adulthood, and although some midlife adults obtain support from their parents, older adults need the help of their midlife children increasingly as they age. Divorce rates are generally low in middle adulthood, and when divorces occur they tend to be less acrimonious than in young adulthood, but midlife women who divorce often face financial difficulties. For couples who have stayed married into midlife, marital satisfaction tends to be high, but sexuality varies widely depending on cultural norms and physical health. Finally, most midlife adults have more leisure time than they did in young adulthood, and they use it for community involvement, vacations, and the ever-popular pastime of watching television.

Family Relationships

LO 11.14 Describe cultural variations in family relationships during midlife.

As we saw in Chapter 10, young adulthood is a time when parenting responsibilities are especially intense and demanding, as that is the time when most people have young children. In midlife, parenting responsibilities ease in some ways as children grow up. However, new family obligations soon arise, as grandchildren are born and as elderly parents need greater care from their midlife children.

These new family obligations are a relatively recent historical phenomenon. Until about a century ago, life expectancy was only around age 50, even in developed countries. This meant that few people in their 40s and 50s had parents who were still living. For example, in the United States in 1900 only 10% of persons in middle adulthood had at least one parent who was still alive; by 2000, 50% did (U.S. Bureau of the Census, 2006). Today in developing countries, life expectancies are increasing rapidly with advances in nutrition and health care, and more and more midlife adults have parents in late adulthood, as life expectancy in these countries steadily increases (Population Reference Bureau, 2014). The increase in life expectancy also means that children are more likely to have grandparents as part of their lives today than in the past, and for more years.

RELATIONS WITH ADULT CHILDREN Parenting in midlife may take many forms. Depending on how old the parents were when they had their children, in midlife their children may be anywhere from infancy to young adulthood. However, because most parents have their children during their 20s or 30s, midlife parents are most likely to have children who are in emerging or young adulthood.

A crucial determinant of relations with children who are in emerging and young adulthood is whether young people leave home or remain in their parents' household. As we have noted, the most common pattern historically in Asia, Africa, and South America has been that when a young couple marries, the son remains in his parents' household and his wife comes to live there as well. Where this system prevails, parents remain close to their sons throughout adulthood, as they all live in the same household; in contrast, daughters leave home upon marriage and parents may rarely or never see them again.

Today in many parts of the world, young people remain home through emerging adulthood, but under much different circumstances. Rather than bringing a spouse into the family household, they remain unmarried through most or all of their 20s but continue to live in their parents' household during this time (see Chapter 9). This pattern prevails today in southern Europe, as well as in Japan (Douglass, 2007; Moreno Mínguez et al., 2012; Rosenberg, 2007). Parents in these countries generally welcome their children's presence in the household through emerging adulthood. In fact, their view is that if a child leaves the home before marriage it is a sign of troubled family relations. Parents generally have harmonious relations with their children, and when the children reach emerging adulthood the parents let them live their own lives and do not feel responsible for monitoring them or providing for them, so the previous responsibilities they experienced as parents are diminished (Douglass, 2005; Fingerman & Yahurin, 2015).

In northern Europe, and in countries such as the United States, the United Kingdom, and Canada, the dominant cultural pattern is that children leave home when they reach emerging adulthood (Douglass, 2007; Iacovou, 2011). These cultures place a strong value on independence, and this includes the belief that children should be capable of leaving home and living on their own by age 18 or 19 (Arnett, 1998; Arnett, 2015). Contrary to claims of an "empty nest syndrome," parents generally experience the departure of their emerging adult children with a blend of loss and liberation. Many parents miss the love and companionship of their emerging adult children, and deeply feel the loss of their daily presence (Arnett & Schwab, 2013). This response is especially common among mothers who have devoted themselves to the maternal role while their children were growing up and do not have a strong dedication to working outside the home (Crowley et al., 2003; Dennerstein et al., 2002). However, parents also experience a new burst of freedom when their children leave home (Arnett & Schwab, 2013; Morfei et al., 2004). They no longer have to coordinate their own schedules with their children's. They can devote the time and energy previously allotted to parenting to their own occupational and recreational interests. Married couples can revive or enhance the intimacy of their marriage, now that they have more time for each other. There is less child-related stress from anxieties such as waiting late at night for a child to come home.

As noted in Chapter 9, about 40% of American emerging adults return home after moving out, usually for a transitional period of no more than a year. When their emerging adults stay home or return home, most American parents are remarkably favorable toward it (Aquilino, 2006; Mitchell, 2006). In a national study of parents of 18- to 29-year-olds, 61% of parents with a child living at home said their response to the living situation was "mostly positive," and only 6% "mostly negative" (Arnett & Schwab, 2013). However, some parents also named negative consequences, such as "more financial stress" (40%) and "less time for myself" (29%).

Even after their children leave home, many midlife parents continue to provide a variety of kinds of support as their children pass through emerging and young adulthood (Fingerman & Yahurin, 2015). Sometimes this is financial support; through their 20s, many emerging adults receive money from their parents while they are pursuing their education, or in-between jobs, or need money for a crisis such as a major car repair (Swartz, 2009). In the United States, two-thirds of emerging adults in their early 20s and two-fifths in their late 20s receive some level of financial support from parents (Arnett & Schwab, 2013). In Europe as well as in the United States, the higher the parents' income, the more money they provide to their children during emerging adulthood (Swartz & O'Brien, 2009). Sometimes parents provide emotional support, for example when a hoped-for job fails to come through or a romantic relationship breaks up (Murry et al., 2006). Support from parents generally declines through the 20s, and by age 30 most emerging adults have a more equal relationship with their parents (Arnett, 2015). Parents of emerging adults are generally willing to provide some degree of support if they see it as reasonable assistance in helping their children make the transition to a stable adult life. However, some midlife parents have problems of their own, either economic or personal, that make them less likely to provide support to their emerging adults (Fingerman & Yahurin, 2015).

Children often make the transition from emerging to young adulthood during their parents' middle adulthood, by entering stable adult roles in love and work. The impact of the transition to marriage on the parent–child relationship depends a great deal on how well the parents get along with their child's partner. When parents object to their child's partner for some reason, or when there is a lack of compatibility between the parents and the partner, relations between the parents and the child also suffer (Murry et al., 2006). In most cases, however, relations with parents improve over the years, as intimacy grows and conflict declines, across a range of cultures (Akiyama & Antonucci, 1999; Fingerman & Yahurin, 2015).

RELATIONS WITH PARENTS Like relations which children, relations with parents in middle adulthood are highly variable depending on cultural customs. In many traditional cultures, midlife married couples continue to live in the same household as the husband's parents, although most of the authority and responsibility for running the household is transferred to the midlife couple. In Asian countries, midlife adults typically accept caring for their aging parents as one of the duties of this time of life (Ho et al., 2003; Maehara & Takmura, 2007). Specifically, daughters-in-law are expected to devote themselves to caring for the husband's parents (Shuey & Hardy, 2003). However, it is becoming increasingly common in Asian countries for elderly parents to live in their own household or in a government-run care facility (Zhan et al., 2008; Zhang, 2004). Often parents, as well as their midlife children, prefer to live in separate

In Asian countries, midlife adults are traditionally expected to care for their aging parents, as this woman in Beijing, China, cares for her elderly mother. Why is this custom beginning to change?

households in order to have greater freedom and independence. There is also less conflict when parents and children live separately (Sherrell et al., 2001).

Having parents live in the household is relatively rare for midlife adults in most Western countries. In a survey of Americans ages 42–61, 8% reported that a parent was living in their household (Fetterman, 2008). Most of the households with an elderly parent had a cultural background such as Asian or Latino that includes this cultural tradition. In Europe, there are differences between north and south in the prevalence of living with elderly parents. One study comparing 11 European countries found that in the more individualistic north, care for elderly parents was provided mainly by the government, and it was rare for elderly parents to be living in the household of their midlife children (Haberkern & Szydlik, 2010). In the countries of the more collectivistic south, care for elderly parents was viewed as a family rather than a government responsibility, and parents more often lived with their midlife children.

Relations with parents in midlife tend to be mutually supportive (Kahn et al., 2011; Vincent et al., 2006). That is, sometimes midlife adults help their parents, and sometimes their parents help them. The direction of support may depend on who has the most resources and what the current circumstances are in each person's life (Hoyer & Roodin, 2003). If parents in late adulthood are affluent, they may provide financial assistance to a child in middle adulthood who is having financial trouble; if the midlife child is the one with more money, the child may provide assistance to the parents. If a midlife adult experiences a negative event such as losing a job or becoming divorced, perhaps parents help out; if the parents experience events such as losing a spouse or having health problems, perhaps the midlife adult helps out. The history of their relationship matters, too. When midlife adults recall their parents as having spent time with them when they were young and as helping them out financially through their young adulthood, they are generally willing to provide financial and social support to their parents through late adulthood (Silverstein et al., 2002). In Asian families, one reason midlife adults are devoted to caring for their parents is that they believe their parents made many sacrifices for them when they were children (Kim & Lee, 2003).

Relations with parents in midlife depend especially on how healthy the parents are. When parents remain healthy in late adulthood it is possible for parent–child relationships to be mutually supportive, but if parents suffer health problems, then the support mostly goes from the children to the parents. Overall, the balance of help shifts with the years toward the parents, whose needs usually increase as they age (Kunemund et al., 2005).

This is not easy for either side. In Western countries, where independence is valued, people in late adulthood generally do not want to live with their children and do not want to rely on them financially (Stuifbergen et al., 2010). They may feel guilty and ashamed at having to rely on their children to help them as their abilities to care for themselves diminish.

As for the midlife adults, the responsibility for caring for elderly parents is piled on top of their many other responsibilities at work, in the community, in their marital relationship, and with their own children (Grundy & Henretta, 2006; Riley & Bowen, 2005). This is highly stressful, particularly because the need for care often occurs in sudden crises such as a heart attack, stroke, or injury, and because the duration of the care that will be required is unpredictable. Midlife adults who are highly involved in a parent's care experience high rates of exhaustion and depression (Killian et al., 2005). Their job performance is disrupted because they must leave work in order to deal with the latest crisis, and some quit their jobs because they feel they cannot handle the dual strain of working and caring for a parent (Takamura & Williams, 2002). However, those who remain working often find that they experience the workplace as a refuge, boosting their mood and giving them somewhere else to direct their attention and energy (Stephens & Franks, 1999).

The strain of caring for an ill, elderly parent is experienced even when the midlife adults have cultural expectations that they will care for their elderly parents. One study compared midlife adults in Korea, which has a strong tradition of caring for elderly parents, Korean American midlife adults, and White midlife adults, all of whom had the responsibility for caring for elderly parents with mental disabilities (Youn et al., 1999). Korean and Korean American midlife adults reported higher rates of anxiety and depression than the White Americans, perhaps because they felt greater responsibility for their parents' well-being.

In some affluent developed countries, such as Denmark, Sweden, and Japan, a government agency provides trained personnel who visit the homes of elderly persons with disabilities (Kim & Antanopolous, 2011). Some American states provide similar services for a small fee (Weiner, 2010). These services help reduce the strain of care on midlife adults and also help older adults remain independent for as long as possible, as nearly all of them would prefer to do.

Another way midlife adults reduce the strain of caring for elderly parents is by sharing the responsibility among siblings. A study of care for elderly parents in rural China found that siblings rotated meals and residences for their parents, taking turns hosting them for meals and having the parents live with each of them in turn (Zhang & Wang, 2010). In Western countries, too, siblings often rotate responsibility for parents' care, with each of them taking responsibility for a certain time period, or each of them taking responsibility for a different area (e.g., finances, social visits; Fontaine et al., 2009). However, across cultures, female siblings usually end up taking the majority of the responsibility for parents' care (Kahn et al., 2011).

Generally, contact with siblings is lower in young adulthood and middle adulthood than it is at either earlier or later life stages (White, 2001). However, for midlife adults who are not married and have no children living nearby, siblings may be relied upon more for support and companionship (Cicirelli, 1996; Van Volkom, 2006). Of course, this reliance requires that siblings get along reasonably well, which we've seen in previous chapters is often not the case. In one German study of midlife siblings, the quality of sibling relationships was mixed, but it was generally better if siblings perceived themselves to be treated equally by their parents and worse if they perceived each other as receiving parental favoritism (Boll et al., 2005). Even in midlife, sibling rivalry for parents' recognition and resources was still apparent.

BECOMING A GRANDPARENT In addition to maintaining their relationships with children and parents, most people add a new family role in middle adulthood: grandparent. In developing countries, where most women have their first child around age 20, their parents usually become grandparents around age 40 (Population Reference Bureau, 2014). In developed countries, where most women have their first child in their late 20s or early 30s, their parents usually become grandparents in their 50s.

African Americans are frequently involved in care of grandchildren during middle adulthood.

The grandparent role varies greatly around the world, depending especially on whether the grandparent is involved in the daily care of the grandchildren. In the multigenerational households that are common in Asia, Africa, and Latin America, grandparents are often involved in the daily household responsibilities, including child care (Ice et al., 2008; Maehara & Takamura, 2007). Grandmothers are far more likely than grandfathers to be involved in daily care of their grandchildren (DeLoache & Gottlieb, 2000). In urban areas of these regions, when mothers work outside the home, grandmothers often care for the children during work hours (Parker & Short, 2009).

Grandparents are sometimes involved in daily child care in developed countries as well, especially in families headed by a single mother. For example, in African American families nearly 70% of children are born to single mothers, and in these families grandmothers are frequently involved in daily child

Cultural Focus: Family Relationships in Middle Adulthood Across Cultures

Middle adulthood is a time of peak responsibilities for most people, in work as well as in their relationships. Midlife adults are sometimes referred to as the "sandwich generation" because most of them have responsibilities for their not-quite-adult children as well for their aging parents. Within the United States, midlife adults who are members of ethnic minorities are especially likely to feel this squeeze, due to strong cultural traditions of providing care to elderly parents (Cravey & Mltra,

2011). Worldwide, in developing countries, care for elderly parents is often required from midlife adults, because of cultural traditions, and also because older adults usually lack the financial resources to care for themselves even if they would like to (UNDP, 2014).

In this video, middle adults from various countries are interviewed about their relationships with both their parents and children.

Watch FAMILY RELATIONSHIPS IN MIDDLE ADULTHOOD ACROSS CULTURES

Video

Review Question:

The idea of adults caring for their aging parents while still caring for their children is typically known as the "sandwich generation." To what extent are there cultural differences in experiencing this, as shown here in Botswana, Mexico, and the United States?

care (Kelch-Oliver, 2011; Stevenson et al., 2007). Although the birth rate among African Americans is similar to the birth rate among Whites in the United States, African Americans are more likely to have their first child in their teens or early 20s, as single mothers, and these teen mothers are in great need of the support of their own mothers in order to handle the duties involved in caring for a child. Often this care is provided in a multigenerational household including the grandmother, her daughter, the daughter's children, and perhaps others (Oberlander et al., 2007). African American cultural beliefs support the value and importance of the grandmother's role, so many grandmothers expect to be highly involved in their grandchildren's care (Baydar & Brooks-Gunn, 1998; Stevenson et al., 2007).

The degree of grandparents' involvement also depends partly on how close the grandparents live to their grandchildren. In developed countries where residential mobility is high, grandparents often live long distances from their grandchildren and may see them only occasionally (Hurme et al., 2010). However, even when visits are rare, grandchildren often regard grandparents as important persons in their lives, and grandparents often value their relations to their grandchildren. Today, grandparents who live far from their grandchildren can maintain frequent electronic contact via e-mail, texting, phones, and social networking web sites (Tee et al., 2009). But even in the most mobile developed countries, most grandparents live close enough to at least one grandchild to see them several times a year or more (Hurme et al., 2010). The video *Grandparenting* provides some examples of the relationships between grandparents and their grandchildren.

Watch GRANDPARENTING

Another important influence on grandparents' involvement is how well they get along with their children and sons- and daughters-in-law. Relations with daughters-in-law appear to be especially important (Fingerman, 2004). Grandparents typically have contact with their grandchildren via the children's parents, so if relations between parents and grandparents are strained, visits with grandchildren are likely to be limited. When parents divorce, grandparents on the father's side often find their visits reduced or cut off due to conflict between the mother and father (Smith & Drew, 2002). In contrast, the involvement of grandparents on the mother's side often increases, as the now-single mother experiences a greater need for their assistance (Ganong & Coleman, 2006).

The gender of the grandparent is also highly important in most countries. In developed countries as in developing countries, grandmothers tend to be more involved with their grandchildren than grandfathers are, just as mothers tend to be more involved with their children than fathers are (Brown & Rodin, 2004). Grandmothers participate more in recreational, religious, and family activities with their grandchildren than grandfathers do, and they are emotionally closer to them as well (Monserud, 2010; Silverstein & Marenco, 2001). Grandmothers also tend to enjoy the grandparent role more (Smith & Drew, 2002). Grandmother–granddaughter relationships are often especially close, across many countries (Brown & Rodin, 2004).

In developed countries, and in urban areas of developing countries, grandparents' involvement with their grandchildren is based more on choice than on duty. Consequently, some grandparents choose not be involved, or to be involved only minimally (Mueller et al., 2002). They may be busy with their own work and leisure activities, or have distant or conflicted relations with their children, or perhaps they find young children stressful to be around. Under these circumstances midlife adults may prefer a distant and remote grandparent role. However, more often, grandparents would prefer to be closer emotionally to their grandchildren than they are, and to see them more often than they do (Brussoni & Boone, 1998). Both grandmothers and grandfathers generally derive great enjoyment and meaning from their roles as grandparents, for reasons including (AARP, 2002; Hebblethwaite & Norris, 2011; Mueller et al., 2002):

1. *Passing on family history.* Grandparents are often sources of stories and details of the family's history across several generations;
2. *Minimum responsibilities, maximum fun.* Grandparents are often able to enjoy being with their grandchildren and providing special gifts and experiences to them, without the "heavy lifting" of parenting, such as disciplining;
3. *The wise grandparent.* Grandparents enjoy feeling they are viewed as someone who has good judgment based on long life experience;
4. *Reduced fear of death.* Witnessing the development of their children's children assures grandparents that some aspects of themselves will live on after their death.

Note how the enjoyment of the grandparenting role includes elements of generativity, in passing on family history and imparting wisdom.

CRITICAL THINKING QUESTION

What might the list of reasons for enjoying the grandparent role look like if based on grandparenting in developing countries? How might it be similar and different?

Love and Sexuality

LO 11.15 Describe the typical patterns of marital satisfaction and divorce in midlife, and identify some challenges to maintaining an active sex life in middle adulthood.

Marriage in midlife often reaches a state of quiet harmony, as couples have more time for each other once the main duties of caring for children have passed. Sexuality in middle age varies greatly depending on cultural expectations and to some extent on physiological changes.

MARRIAGE IN MIDLIFE Now that life expectancy is close to 80 in developed countries and rising rapidly in developing countries, marriages last for longer than ever before—at least potentially. People who marry in their 20s or early 30s may be done with direct parenting, for the most part, by the time they reach age 50, and have decades of married life remaining—if they stay healthy, and if they stay married.

This has never happened before in human history, as a normative pattern of life. How is this new experiment in marriage working out? For the most part, the news is good. Decades of research have shown that marital satisfaction follows a U-shaped pattern (as illustrated in **Figure 11.3**). Satisfaction is high in the first year of marriage, declining in the second year, reaching a low point when caring for young children, and remaining relatively low until midlife. Once the children grow into emerging adulthood and beyond, marital satisfaction rises steeply and steadily thereafter to its highest level of the life span. The relation between marriage and good mental health grows stronger with time and is especially high in the later part of middle adulthood (Lansford et al., 2005; Marks et al., 2004).

Some scholars have argued that this pattern is misleading (Umbertson et al., 2005; VanLaningham et al., 2001). After all, the unhappiest married people get divorced by midlife, which suggests that the U-shaped pattern does not indicate that marital quality improves in midlife for most people, only that the people with the worst marital quality do not stay married, making overall marital quality look higher at later ages. Furthermore, as we saw in Chapter 10,

Marital satisfaction tends to be high in middle adulthood.

research on people who remain single indicates clearly that happily married people are happier than single or divorced people in young and middle adulthood—but unhappily married people are the unhappiest of all (DePaulo, 2006, 2012).

Nevertheless, these considerations do not explain the rise in marital satisfaction in middle adulthood, once most children leave home. Most divorces take place before midlife, as we saw in Chapter 10. Other research on marriage also supports the conclusion that marital satisfaction grows in middle adulthood. By midlife, most marriage partners have greater financial security, fewer stresses from the daily responsibilities of child care, less time spent on household chores, and more leisure time to spend as a couple (Marks et al., 2004). Many reach a state of *companionate love*, in Sternberg's theory (see Chapter 10), in which passion may have ebbed but intimacy and commitment are high (Cherlin, 2009; Sternberg, 1986). In an American study involving over 2,000 midlife adults ages 40–59, nearly three-fourths described their marriage as "excellent" or "very good" (Brim, 1999). Other studies have shown that midlife married couples often describe their spouse as their "best friend," and most feel their spouse has become more interesting, not less, in the course of married life (Levenson et al., 1993).

In cultures where emotional intimacy is less expected as a part of marriage, marriage in midlife often entails partners developing their own separate activities and interests. As noted earlier in the chapter, women in India often enjoy their new status as head of the household, which includes supervising a daughter-in-law and helping care for grandchildren (Kakar, 1998; Menon, 2013). Some women in Japan devote themselves to the grandmother role, whereas others seek to develop their artistic abilities (Lock, 1998). Midlife men in most traditional cultures generally prefer to spend their leisure time with other men, talking, playing games, and perhaps drinking alcohol, rather than with their wives (Davis & Davis, 2007; Gilmore, 1990).

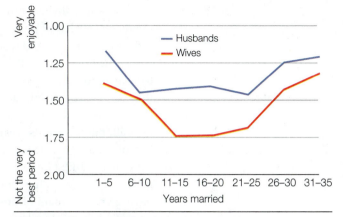

Figure 11.3 Marital Satisfaction and Years Married

For most couples, marital satisfaction rises once their children grow into emerging adulthood and beyond.

SOURCE: Vaillant & Vaillant (1993)

DIVORCE AND REMARRIAGE Most divorces take place within the first 10 years of marriage, but about 25% of divorces in the United States and Canada occur after 20 or more years, often timed with children leaving the nest. It used to be that divorce after 20-plus years together was rare, but in recent decades rates have risen sharply. A 2012 study found that while the overall divorce rate in the United States has declined since 1990, for those over 50 it has doubled (Brown & Lin, 2012). Among the reasons given for the increase: longer lives mean less willingness to spend post-parenting decades with an incompatible spouse; less social stigma about splitting up; and more women working and some out-earning their spouses.

How does divorce in midlife differ from divorce in young adulthood? Although most research has focused on divorces that take place in young adulthood, two large studies in the United States have included divorces that take place in midlife. One study followed a sample of married couples over a 14-year period and charted the divorces that took place in young and middle adulthood (Gottman & Levenson, 2000). Divorces in young adulthood tended to be full of anger and conflict, with each partner bitterly blaming the other for the failure of the marriage. In contrast, the midlife divorces tended to be between couples whose love had gone cold. They no longer enjoyed each other's company and tended to avoid being together. In terms of Sternberg's theory, these couples often fit the profile of "empty love," with little passion, little intimacy, and ultimately, no more commitment.

A study of over 1,000 American adults ages 40–79 who had divorced sometime in their 40s, 50s, or 60s found diverse motivations for divorce (AARP, 2004). Men most often mentioned "fell out of love" (17%) or "different values/lifestyles" (14%), reasons that suggest empty love; another 14% mentioned infidelity. Women, in contrast, most often mentioned verbal or physical abuse (23%) or alcohol/drug abuse (18%); 17% mentioned infidelity. Both men and women tended to state that they felt the marriage was over long before the divorce, and they had stayed together until midlife only because they wanted to wait until their children had left home. Three-fourths of both men and women felt they had made the right decision by divorcing.

Just as at younger ages, the effects of divorce in midlife are complex and varied. Overall, midlife adults weather the stress of divorce better than young adults, showing less of a decline in well-being and less risk of depression following divorce (Birditt & Antonucci, 2012; Gottman & Levenson, 2000; Marks & Lambert, 1998). In some ways, midlife divorces are harder on women. They are more vulnerable financially, since many have given up years of employment when they were caring for young children, and many find themselves having to reenter the work world in midlife without the skills and experience necessary to obtain a good job (Hilton & Anderson, 2009; Williams & Dunne-Bryant, 2006). In the study of over 1,000 divorced adults mentioned in the previous paragraph, 44% of the women mentioned having financial problems, compared to only 11% of the men (AARP, 2004). Also, only one third of women who divorce after age 40 remarry, whereas most men are already involved with a new partner at the time of the divorce and nearly all remarry (Rokach et al., 2004). However, many women find their midlife divorce to be a release from the daily unhappiness of their marriage, and some say it inspires positive changes of greater self-reliance and personal growth (Amato & Previti, 2003; Baum et al., 2005).

OTHER PATHS: GAYS, LESBIANS, AND SINGLE ADULTS IN MIDLIFE Although most people in most cultures are married during midlife, many are not. Some divorce and do not remarry, and some remain single through young and middle adulthood. For gays and lesbians, even though there are now some places where they are allowed to marry, for the most part they are unmarried at midlife.

Lesbians and gays at midlife face a variety of challenges different from those faced by heterosexuals (Whitman, 2010). They live in societies where the transition from one adult life stage to the next is usually marked by events that are normative in the lives of heterosexuals, such as entering marriage, entering parenthood, and children leaving home, yet most of them do not experience these events. Being different in this way can sometimes lead to a sense of being marginalized, but for some it can give them a sense of freedom and flexibility (Kimmel & Sang, 2003). For example, gays and lesbians are often less restricted by gender-role scripts than heterosexuals are, because they learned in earlier life stages how to cross traditional gender boundaries. Lesbians are less likely than heterosexual women to interpret menopause as a passage that marks a decline in their physical attractiveness and their sexual pleasure (Whitman, 2010).

Midlife can also be the life stage when gays and lesbians come out for the first time (Hammack & Cohler, 2009). Because tolerance of homosexual orientations has increased in Western societies in the past 20 years, there are many gays and lesbians who did not come out in their youth due to the fear of stigma but come out in midlife now that the stigma has waned. Coming out in midlife can result in feelings of living a more authentic life and finding one's true identity. However, it can also be difficult, because by midlife the complex structure of a heterosexual life may have been built over many years (Barker et al., 2006). Changing it in midlife can result in a loss of status and power at work and in disruptions in relations with family, friends, and children. Even though the stigma against homosexuality has diminished considerably in Western countries over the past 20 years, it is still substantial in most countries.

Single adults at midlife are a diverse group. Some are divorced, some never married, some are in long-term cohabiting relationships, and some are gays and lesbians who have had a marriage-like relationship for years but have been legally prohibited from marrying. In most societies there are considerably more women than men who are single at midlife, because fewer women marry following divorce and because more men die in midlife (Brim et al., 2004).

Many single persons in middle adulthood would like to be married and are actively looking for a partner, often electronically. Midlife adults are more likely than adults in any other age group to use dating web sites to meet new partners (Fitzpatrick et al., 2009). For the most part, however, single adults in middle adulthood are happy with their lives (DePaulo, 2006, 2012). They enjoy the freedom and independence of being single. For some, this freedom has allowed them to focus on their careers and reach high achievements (Hewlett, 2003).

Single adults are more likely than other adults to have close friendships in midlife (Adams & Ueno, 2006; Rose, 2007). For most adults, the demands of family obligations take up most of their time outside of work, and consequently middle adulthood is the life stage when people are least likely to have close friendships, at least in the Western countries where this topic has been studied (Blieszner & Roberto, 2007). However, single adults more often have time to devote to friendships, and they often rely on friends for social support (Mulbauer & Chrisler, 2007).

SEXUALITY IN MIDDLE ADULTHOOD: MAYBE, MAYBE NOT As we saw in Chapter 10, young adulthood is a life stage in which sexual activity is acceptable in all cultures and usually strongly encouraged. After all, no culture would last long that forbade sexual activity during the main reproductive years. In some cultures young adult sexuality is viewed mainly in terms of reproduction, in others it is viewed as promoting the intimacy and harmony of the married couple as well, but in all cultures young adult sexuality is seen as a good and necessary part of life.

What about sexuality in middle adulthood? By middle adulthood, sexual behavior no longer has much reproductive purpose; some people do have babies in middle adulthood, but it is rare. Consequently, one might expect to find middle adulthood sexuality encouraged most in cultures where intimacy in the marital bond is highly valued. Sexuality in middle adulthood would be one way of continuing and enhancing marital intimacy. Or, it could be that many cultures would encourage or at least condone sexual activity in middle adulthood because sex is pleasurable and there is no particular reason why people should not be allowed this pleasure.

An interesting cultural contrast in views of sexuality in middle adulthood can be found in comparing India and the United States. In the traditional Hindu life stage model, midlife is the stage of becoming a "forest dweller" (see Chapter 1; Kakar, 1998; Menon, 2013). This stage is reached, for a man, when his first grandson is born, which for most Indians takes place in their 40s. As a forest dweller, a person is supposed to begin relinquishing attachments to the things of this world and gradually turn to religious life and the pursuit of spiritual purity. For Indians, this search for a higher spiritual life includes renunciation of sexuality. In fact, even before the first grandson is born, middle adulthood sexuality ceases if the oldest child is a son, because Hindus believe it is wrong for parents and children to be having sexual relations within the same household and sons typically bring their new wives to their parents' home to live (Menon & Shweder, 1998).

In the United States, there are few who would find renunciation of sexuality in middle adulthood a worthy ideal. To Americans, sexuality throughout adulthood is desirable as a way of enhancing the emotional intimacy of marriage and providing mutual pleasure (Lamont, 1997). According to the *Sex in America* study described in Chapter 10, a national study of sexuality among 18- to 59-year-olds, most Americans remain sexually active in their 40s and 50s, although the frequency of their sexual activity declines compared to during emerging and young adulthood (Michael et al., 1995). The decline takes place for homosexuals as well as heterosexuals.

Frequency of sexual activity varies widely in midlife, depending especially on gender and on having an available partner. The *Sex in America* study found that among women in their 50s, over half reported having sex only "a few times per year" or less in the past year; 30% reported "not at all" (Michael et al., 1995). In contrast, one third of men reported having sex "a few times a year" or less, with only 10% reporting "not at all." This gender difference is due partly to more men dying in their 50s (leaving some of the remaining women with no partner) and partly to some men in their 50s being married (or remarried) to younger women. Another national study in the United States found 88% of women in their 50s who had a partner present were sexually active within the past 6 months, compared to only 37% of women who were neither married nor cohabiting (Brim, 1999).

Whatever their culture, midlife adults who wish to continue enjoying sexuality as part of their lives often find they undergo various physical changes that make the experience of sexual pleasure more challenging. For women, one consequence of the midlife estrogen decline mentioned earlier in the chapter is that the genitals are less easily aroused and the vagina takes longer to become lubricated during sexual relations. The vagina actually shrinks at menopause, including the entrance to it; in combination with the lack of lubrication, this may make intercourse painful. Over one third of American women in their 40s and 50s report some kind of difficulty in sexual functioning (Walsh & Berman, 2004).

For men, the main sexual complaint in midlife is impotence or **erectile dysfunction**. An erection involves the flow of blood to the penis, and by midlife physiological changes result in a reduction in this flow. Consequently, erections usually require more stimulation to achieve and can be harder to maintain. About half of men report erectile problems by age 60 (Vissamsetti & Pearce, 2011). Risk of erectile dysfunction is highest among men who have the poorest physical health, due to smoking, diabetes, hypertension, or other medical conditions (Montorsi, 2005; Shiri et al., 2003). Most men also experience a gradual decline in their sexual desire in the course of middle adulthood, as their testosterone levels decline (Gooren, 2003; Hyde & DeLamater, 2004).

For both men and women, there are remedies for most of these sexual problems. Women can use a variety of creams and gels to increase the lubrication of the vagina. Men can now use a variety of medications to stimulate erections. These drugs work by increasing the blood flow to the penis, and they are highly effective, with success rates of 60–80% (Kim & Park, 2006; Morales, 2003). There appear to be few side effects from the medications for most men (although about 1 in 10 men experiences headaches and about 1 in 30 experiences temporary vision problems), and—so far—no long-term negative effects have been observed (Vissamsetti & Pearce, 2011).

Community and Leisure Activities

LO 11.16 Describe community and leisure activities associated with middle adulthood, and identify their impact on physical and cognitive functioning.

In addition to time devoted to family relationships, romantic partnerships, and work in middle adulthood, most people devote some time to community and leisure activities. In the same way that people gain status in the workplace in middle adulthood, they may seek or be asked to fill positions of responsibility and influence in the community. More time for leisure may appear for many people as the daily responsibilities of caring for children wane.

COMMUNITY INVOLVEMENT In the United States, membership in community organizations rises from the mid-teens onward and peaks in the 30s, as described in Chapter 10, but it remains fairly high through the 40s and 50s. This includes involvement in social organizations, volunteer organizations, and political advocacy groups (Smith & Snell, 2009). According to one analysis of civic engagement across 12 indicators (such as "attended a public meeting" and "signed a petition"), among Americans ages 18 and older, the peak in civic engagement was from age 30 to 59, when 42% reported at least one of the 12 forms of civic engagement in the past year, a higher prevalence than at lower or higher ages (Putnam, 2000).

erectile dysfunction

inability to achieve and maintain an erection consistently during sexual contact

Is community involvement in middle adulthood a reflection of the generativity described earlier in the chapter? Some of this involvement may be part of an attempt to preserve or improve the quality of life for the next generation—for example, working to prevent climate change even though the effects of climate change are likely to be apparent only many decades from now. However, some of it may be simply for the adult's own enjoyment—for example, joining an outdoor recreation club or a reading group. Even working for social or political causes may be motivated by wanting to improve the state of the world while we are still here—perhaps in addition to the motive of caring about the world we will leave to the generations to come (Hart et al., 2003; McAdams, 2013).

LEISURE IN MIDDLE ADULTHOOD The idea of leisure as a regular part of life is a new one. There have always been festivals, in all human cultures, that allowed an occasional break from work and daily routine, but these events have usually been infrequent, maybe a few times a year at most. Otherwise, people worked daily to survive and to keep their animals alive. Once industrialization arose, the hours were long. Factory work often meant 12-hour workdays, 6 days a week. It was not until the 20th century in developed countries that a combination of legal regulations and labor unions restricted the number of hours that employers could ask the employees to work, and not until the middle of the 20th century that the "40-hour week" became typical. In developing countries, even now, working in industrial settings often means long hours, 6 days a week, with little leisure time (Chang, 2008).

Today, most developed countries restrict the number of hours employers can demand per week and require employers to pay higher "overtime" rates to employees who work more than 40 hours a week. Increasingly, by the time they reach their 50s, people in developed countries work fewer than 40 hours a week. For example, in a survey across developed countries among employed persons ages 50–54, two-thirds worked 40 or more hours a week and one third worked fewer hours (Organization for Economic Co-operation and Development [OECD], 2010). There was also great variation among developed countries. In the United States, Canada, and Turkey, about 80% of 50- to 54-year-olds worked 40 or more hours per week, but only one half did in Germany, only one third in France, and just 18% in Norway.

What do people do with their leisure time in middle adulthood? As we saw in Chapter 10, around the world the most popular leisure activity in both young and middle adulthood is watching television. Countries vary, but 2–3 hours of television a day is typical in middle adulthood (Gripsrud, 2007). Other common leisure activities in middle adulthood include exercise and sports, going out to dinner, having dinner with friends, other media use (e.g., books, the Internet, DVDs), and socializing (mainly with family members) (Lindstrom et al., 2005; Putnam, 2000).

In developed countries, leisure includes periods of vacation (or "holiday") several weeks a year. Like the 40-hour work week, vacation is an invention of modern times. In agricultural economies vacations are rare—there is always something to be done during the growing season, and in the months between there are still animals to be taken care of daily. In the early decades of industrialization there were no vacations from factory work. It was only in the 20th century that a combination of government legal requirements and union demands led to the widespread practice of granting employees a specified number of weeks of paid vacation each year. Today all developed countries except the United States guarantee workers a minimum number of weeks of paid vacation per year, as **Figure 11.4** shows. Across Europe, workers receive at least 4 weeks of holiday per year (International Labor Organization [ILO], 2011).

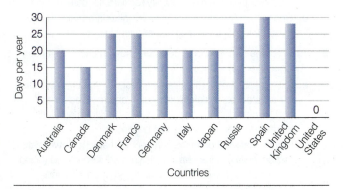

Figure 11.4 Guaranteed Vacation Time in Developed Countries

SOURCE: Based on ILO (2011).

What do people do with their vacation time in middle adulthood? For some, there is simply more of what they do in their other leisure time—television and other media use, exercise and sports, and socializing (Hall, 2007). In the middle class and above, traveling for vacations is common (Plagnol & Easterlin, 2008). Midlife adults often use vacation time as an opportunity to visit their children and grandchildren.

Research indicates that vacation time enhances cognitive and physical functioning. Productivity and work satisfaction are greater among workers who receive vacation time than among those who do not (Kuhnel & Sonnentag, 2011). Vacation time helps midlife workers avoid burnout (Westman & Etzion, 2001). Physical health is also better among those who take vacations (Stern & Konno, 2009). In one study of over 12,000 men ages 35–57, vacation time was assessed over a 5-year period, then medical records were tracked for the next 9 years (Gump & Matthews, 2000). Men who took annual vacations during the 5-year assessment period were one third less likely to die from coronary heart disease over the next 9 years than men who never vacationed.

Taking vacations enhances physical health and helps midlife adults avoid burnout.

Practice Quiz   ANSWERS AVAILABLE IN ANSWER KEY.

1. The most common pattern historically in Asia, Africa, and South America has been that when a woman and man marry,

_____.

a. the son's wife has most of the decision-making power

b. the son remains in his parents' household and his wife moves in

c. the son remains in the same town as his parents, especially if they are over age 65

d. they both move out of their parents' home

2. Which of the following statements about family relations is TRUE?

a. In Western countries, people in late adulthood usually want to live with their adult children.

b. Midlife adults who are highly involved in a parent's care experience high rates of exhaustion and depression.

c. Across cultures, the oldest sibling usually ends up taking the majority of the responsibility for parents' care.

d. Generally, contact with siblings is higher in middle adulthood than it is at either earlier or later life stages.

3. Which of the following best describes how marital satisfaction changes over the life span?

a. High satisfaction for the first few years of marriage, increasing satisfaction while children are in emerging adulthood and young adulthood, and then plummeting to an all-time low satisfaction for midlife and beyond

b. Highest satisfaction in the first year of marriage, lower satisfaction while children are in emerging adulthood and young adulthood, and even lower satisfaction for midlife and beyond

c. High satisfaction in the first few years of marriage, reaching a low point while caring for young children and remaining low until the children enter emerging adulthood, then a steep and steady rise in satisfaction at midlife and beyond

d. Low satisfaction for the first few years of marriage, higher satisfaction while children are in emerging adulthood and young adulthood, and the highest satisfaction for midlife and beyond

4. Research on marriage in the United States has shown that

_____.

a. most divorces take place during midlife

b. nearly three-fourths of midlife adults describe their marriage as "okay" or "acceptable"

c. midlife married couples often describe their spouse as their best friend

d. only those who report high levels of passion maintain high marital satisfaction in midlife

5. Which of the following statements about work and leisure is most accurate?

a. All developed countries except the United States guarantee workers a minimum number of weeks of paid vacation per year.

b. Among middle adults across the world, the most popular leisure activity is spending time with friends.

c. Among middle adults across the world, the most popular leisure activity is spending time with immediate and extended family.

d. Work satisfaction is higher among those who receive vacation time, but productivity is much lower.

Summary: Emotional and Social Development

LO 11.10 **Identify the changes that occur in self-concept during middle adulthood, including cultural variations.**

Self-development matures in many ways in middle adulthood, as many people lower their ambitions and focus on making the most of the life they have. Identity struggles lessen as people reach a mature self-knowledge and self-acceptance. Midlife adults in collectivistic cultures may emphasize relations with others rather than self-development, although some Japanese women focus on individual arts.

LO 11.11 **Summarize the evidence on the question of whether the midlife crisis is a typical part of development in middle adulthood.**

Claims of a normative midlife crisis have been shown to be false. On the contrary, midlife is more likely to be a period of stability and high life satisfaction.

LO 11.12 **Define generativity and explain how it is expressed in middle adulthood.**

Generativity is the motivation to contribute to the well-being of the generations to come. It may be expressed through being a parent or grandparent, or through roles such as mentor or teacher.

LO 11.13 **Explain why the status of women in some cultures increases at midlife, and describe cultural variations in gender equality.**

In many cultures, midlife is a time of new freedoms and new authority within the household for women. Gender equality tends to be greatest in countries with the highest economic development, although Japan and South Korea are exceptions. However, even in developed countries, women often face many obstacles to reaching the top echelon of occupational achievement in midlife and find they have to relinquish their family goals in order to reach their goals in the workplace.

LO 11.14 **Describe cultural variations in family relationships during midlife.**

Relations with parents often improve from young to middle adulthood. Midlife adults sometimes receive support of various kinds from their parents, but over time the direction of support shifts steadily toward parents, especially once they have health problems. Cultures vary in expectations for whether elderly parents will live with their children and how long midlife parents will have children in their household. Parents are generally willing to support their children to some degree through emerging adulthood and young adulthood, provided that the parents have sufficient resources themselves. Relations with grandchildren tend to be close and meaningful across cultures, although grandparents often have less contact with their grandchildren in developed countries.

LO 11.15 **Describe the typical patterns of marital satisfaction and divorce in midlife, and identify some challenges to maintaining an active sex life in middle adulthood.**

Marriage quality generally improves in midlife, as couples have fewer stresses from caring for small children and from financial concerns. Divorce in this life stage is often a result of love gone cold rather than anger and conflict. While many middle adults enjoy an active sex life, there are biological changes associated with the female and male climacteric that influence sexuality, specifically slower sexual arousal in women and erectile dysfunction in men.

LO 11.16 **Describe community and leisure activities associated with middle adulthood, and identify their impact on physical and cognitive functioning.**

Community involvement is relatively high in midlife in the United States, although not quite as high as in young adulthood. For people in developed countries, leisure time in middle adulthood is often spent watching TV, socializing with family members, or spending time with friends. Vacations are devoted to similar activities, along with visiting children and grandchildren.

Applying Your Knowledge as a Professional

The topics covered in this chapter apply to a wide variety of career professions. Watch these videos to learn how they apply to the head of community development for a bank and a life coach.

Watch CAREER FOCUS: HEAD OF COMMUNITY DEVELOPMENT FOR A BANK

Stacey Thompson
VP, KeyBank
Community Development Banking

Chapter Quiz

1. The aspect of hearing that declines most significantly in midlife is the ability to _____.

   a. interpret a whisper
   b. hear high-pitched tones
   c. follow a conversation
   d. hear a voice over the telephone

2. Which of the following statements about menopause is true?

   a. Women's hormone levels remain unchanged until menopause, at which point they drop dramatically.
   b. After menopause, estrogen levels rise.
   c. Menopause tends to occur later among women who smoke or who have not given birth.
   d. Japanese woman experience less extreme menopausal symptoms than those in other ethnic groups.

3. _____ is/are the leading cause(s) of death worldwide.

   a. Breast cancer for women and prostate cancer for men
   b. Diabetes
   c. Cardiovascular disease
   d. Lung cancer

4. Which of the following is most accurate regarding research on predictors of health in middle adulthood and later adulthood?

   a. There has been no longitudinal research to address this question; therefore researchers have been unable to draw any definitive conclusions.
   b. Education predicted health from middle to late adulthood more strongly than did income.
   c. Alcohol use, but not smoking, has been shown to correlate with later health and mortality.
   d. Health habits have little relation to later physical and mental health.

5. Crystallized intelligence represents a person's _____.

   a. pure ability
   b. adaptability
   c. decision-making power
   d. culturally-based knowledge

6. Experts _____.

   a. are more creative, but less flexible, than are novices

   b. process information more slowly than novices because they are more systematic in their reasoning

   c. tend to reach the top of their field due to increases in physical strength and skill compared to their younger counterparts

   d. are more automatic in their problem-solving than are novices

7. Midlife adults _____.

   a. stay unemployed longer than young adults after experiencing a job loss

   b. tend to get a job of higher status and higher pay when they get a new job after being unemployed

   c. have higher absenteeism rates than young adults due to a weakened immune system with advancing age

   d. are less satisfied with their jobs than are younger adults

8. The one test in the Seattle Longitudinal Study that showed a clear decline from young to middle adulthood was _____.

   a. procedural memory

   b. expertise

   c. verbal memory

   d. perceptual speed

9. Which of the following decreases for most people through middle adulthood?

   a. Long-term memory stores

   b. Procedural knowledge

   c. Ability for divided attention

   d. Factual knowledge

10. Which of the following is most accurate regarding research on self-development in middle adulthood?

   a. Self-acceptance, autonomy, and environmental mastery all increase during middle adulthood.

   b. There is no evidence of self-development among middle-aged people living in collectivistic cultures.

   c. Across cultures during middle adulthood, contentment with the self shows a small, but significant, decline as people confront a number of physiological changes.

   d. Middle-aged adults' enhanced self-development makes them less likely to adapt to new situations or to be flexible in their goals.

11. One of the weaknesses of the research of Daniel Levinson, who studied the midlife crisis in the 1970s, is that his initial observations were based on a(n) _____.

   a. questionnaire survey of 400 men

   b. intensive study of only 40 men

   c. cross-sectional questionnaire study of men and women in several age groups

   d. study of poorly educated men from three different countries

12. Research on generativity _____.

   a. has focused almost exclusively on Asian countries

   b. has shown that significantly more women than men achieve a sense of generativity during midlife

   c. has shown that there are a variety of ways an adult can be generative

   d. has shown a peak during emerging adulthood, followed by a plateau in middle adulthood among Americans and Canadians

13. During middle adulthood, women in India _____.

   a. gain the authority that once belonged to their mother-in-law

   b. generally experience a decrease in happiness as a result of the many tasks they have to carry out

   c. experience a sharp increase in divorce

   d. experience an increase in psychological disorders because of the cumulative trauma they have faced in their subordinate position within the family

14. Which of the following is true of grandparents in developed countries?

   a. Grandfathers participate more than grandmothers in recreational and family activities.

   b. European American grandmothers are more likely to be involved in the daily care of their grandchildren compared to other ethnic groups because they have the resources to do so.

   c. Grandparents' involvement with their grandchildren depends partly on their relationship with their children and sons- and daughters-in-law.

   d. Grandparents' involvement with their grandchildren is usually based on a sense of duty or obligation.

15. Research on marriage in the United States has shown that by midlife _____.

   a. most marriage partners have less time to spend as a couple than they did earlier in their marriage because of increased job demands

   b. the correlation between marriage and mental health is weaker than it was earlier in the life span

   c. nearly three-fourths of American adults describe their marriage as "excellent" or "very good"

   d. marital satisfaction stays relatively low until the early seventies when most people are retired

16. Research indicates that vacation time _____.

   a. lowers worker productivity

   b. is positively correlated with cognitive decline

   c. is less beneficial for men than women

   d. increases cognitive and physical functioning

Chapter 12
Late Adulthood

NELSON MANDELA MISSED OUT ON MIDDLE ADULTHOOD. In 1964, at the age of 46, he was imprisoned by the government of South Africa for leading resistance to the White regime that ruled the country. Although the population of South Africa was 80% Black Africans, the apartheid government was run by the White minority.

Mandela's imprisonment lasted for the next *26 years.* Finally, in 1990, at the age of 72, he was released by the South African president, Frederik Willem de Klerk, who had concluded that the White-dominated government that had ruled South Africa for nearly a century could not be sustained any longer. In 1993, Mandela received the Nobel Peace Prize (along with de Klerk). As the leader of the African National Congress, Mandela negotiated with de Klerk over the transition to democracy, and in 1994, at the age of 75, Mandela was elected the first Black president of South Africa. He served one 5-year term and, after leaving office at age 80, he remained active, raising money for his Mandela Foundation to build schools and medical clinics in rural South Africa and serving as a mediator to resolve armed conflicts in other African countries. He was also involved in the fight against AIDS, which killed his son in 2005. He died in 2013 at the age of 95.

Nelson Mandela's late adulthood was unusual—in fact, extraordinary. Nevertheless, he represents well the way that late adulthood has changed in recent history. First, more people reach this stage in life than ever before. Life expectancies are now close to age 80 in developed countries and are rapidly rising in developing countries. Second, people in late adulthood are generally healthier and more active today than in the past, in part due to more effective medical treatments and in part due to greater awareness of the importance of exercise, diet, and cognitive activity for maintaining health. Of course, aging still does take place, and physical and cognitive problems become more prevalent in late adulthood than at earlier stages of life, as we will see in this chapter. Nevertheless, many people in late adulthood maintain an active life, and life satisfaction in late adulthood is often high, especially for people who maintain good health.

In this chapter we examine the consequences of physical and cognitive aging in late adulthood, as well as the variability in functioning and ways to enhance the likelihood of remaining healthy. We also explore the social and cultural contexts that continue to be important in late adulthood, including family relationships, love and sexuality, and work, among others. We will see that late adulthood is in many ways the most diverse life stage, when some people experience decline but others sustain a high level of functioning into their 80s and beyond.

Watch   CHAPTER INTRODUCTION: LATE ADULTHOOD

Section 1   Physical Development

∨   Learning Objectives

12.1 Compare cultural views toward older adults, and distinguish between the three substages of late adulthood.

12.2 Define the old-age dependency ratio, and explain its impact on developed countries.

12.3 Identify the signs of physical aging in late adulthood, and differentiate the impact of primary and secondary aging on appearance.

12.4 Describe the changes in vision, hearing, taste, and smell in late adulthood.

12.5 Describe the changes in sleep patterns that occur during late adulthood.

12.6 Identify the major health problems associated with late adulthood, and list some treatment options.

12.7 Identify three lifestyle practices that have a positive influence on health.

PHYSICAL DEVELOPMENT: Cultural Beliefs About Late Adulthood

If late adulthood begins at about age 65, it can be a long life stage, given that many people in developed countries today live into their 80s, 90s, and beyond. Although people in their late 60s often function differently from those who are past 80, there is a great deal of variability in any age group in late adulthood, based on physical and mental health. Worldwide, the proportion of older adults in the population is steadily growing as birthrates decline and life expectancy increases.

How Old Is "Old"?

LO 12.1   **Compare cultural views toward older adults, and distinguish between the three substages of late adulthood.**

In many cultures there are traditions of respect for people in late adulthood, and in the West the portrayal of late adulthood is growing more favorable in some ways. Because late adulthood may last for many years, it has been conceptualized as containing three substages.

CULTURAL VARIATIONS IN CONCEPTIONS OF LATE ADULTHOOD In the history of Western cultures, the portrayal of late adulthood has often been bleak and grim (Schott, 2009; Whitebourne, 2009). As described in Chapter 1, the Greek philosopher Solon (638–558 BCE) laid out a stage theory of human development with each stage lasting 7 years. In the last stage, ages 63–70, the central task was to "make preparations for a not untimely death." In the 12th century the Italian poet Dante described four life stages, the last of which was "senility," from age 70 onward. Shakespeare, in the 16th century, offered one of the most caustic views of all, through his character Jaques in *As You Like It,* who depicted seven life stages, culminating in old age: "Last scene of all,/That ends this strange eventful history,/Is second childishness, and mere oblivion,/Sans teeth, sans eyes, sans taste, sans everything." (*Sans* is French for "without.")

Perhaps this history still influences our perceptions of late adulthood, despite the more positive recent reality. Many studies in Western countries have found that older adults often encounter **ageism**, which is prejudice and discrimination based on age (Rosenthal, 2014). Attitudes toward older adults are generally more negative than toward younger adults in a variety of respects, from competence at work-related tasks to physical attractiveness. Older adults applying for jobs are often assumed to be on the decline, and lacking in cognitive sharpness and physical stamina (Hedge at al., 2006; Rupp et al., 2006). Social psychology studies that present participants with a hypothetical situation involving cognitive functioning—misplacing an object, for example—find that when the person in the scenario is described as young, participants assume the mistake is due to a temporary state ("He had a lot on his mind"), whereas when the person is old the mistake is assumed to be due to irreversible decline ("He's going senile") (Nelson, 2004). Other studies have found that older adults often experience being ignored or patronized (referred to as "honey" or "baby") and are assumed to have difficulty hearing or understanding simple instructions (Palmore, 2001; Whitbourne & Sneed, 2004).

Although ageism and a negative view of late adulthood is widespread today, there are also cultural variations in how this life stage is viewed. In many Asian, African, and Latin American cultures the view of late adulthood is quite favorable. For example, in Japan there is an annual Respect for the Aged Day, which is a national holiday (Coulmas et al., 2008). Also, the transition from middle to late adulthood is marked with a ritual called *kanreki,* usually held around the person's 60th birthday. The ritual symbolizes the person's freedom from previous responsibilities of child care and household duties, and elevation to a new and respected status as an elder in the family and in society. In other Asian cultures, the tradition of filial piety continues through late adulthood. This means that no matter how old children are, they owe obedience and respect to their parents.

In most traditional cultures worldwide, status is based in part on age: The older people become, the more authority and respect they have. Older people are also more likely to have high status in cultures where they control important family or community resources and where extended family households are common (Menon, 2013; Sangree, 1989).

Even in the West the depiction of late adulthood is becoming more favorable in some ways. An analysis of American television advertisements containing older adults found that 78% presented them in positive ways, such as the "adventurous golden ager" (active, social, and fun loving), the "perfect grandparent" (loving, generous, and family-oriented), or the "productive golden ager" (intelligent, independent, and successful) (Miller et al., 2004). This positive depiction of older adults in advertisements may be due to their increasing economic power (Simcock, 2012). Prior to 50 years ago, older adults were often the poorest segment of society in developed countries, because they had stopped working but had a meager pension and had to pay for their own escalating health care expenses (Pew Social Trends Staff, 2010). However, increased social welfare and health entitlements in the 1960s and 1970s have now made older adults the wealthiest segment of developed countries, and advertisers who depict them negatively may risk alienating them and losing their business.

ageism

prejudice and discrimination based on age

Today, older adults are often shown positively in advertisements out of respect for their economic power.

Are there any rituals marking late adulthood in your culture? If you were going to design one, what might a ritual include?

SUBSTAGES OF LATE ADULTHOOD Before we proceed any further, some attention should be given to the substages of late adulthood. If late adulthood is the life stage from age 65 onward, for some people (mainly in developing countries) it may last for only a few years, but for others (mainly in developed countries) it may last several decades. When a life stage lasts several decades, a great deal of change can take place over the course of it, so the early part of late adulthood may differ considerably from the later part. Consequently, developmental psychologists and demographers have divided the period of late adulthood into three substages: the *young-old* are persons ages 65–74; the *old-old* are ages 75–84; and the *oldest-old* are ages 85 and up (Baltes & Smith, 2003).

This is an important distinction because the three groups vary widely in their functioning, especially the oldest-old compared to the other two groups. As we will see in the course of the chapter, declines in functioning are fairly mild in the first two age groups, but much steeper among the oldest-old. People who are among the oldest-old are at higher risk for a wide range of problems, including physical and cognitive disabilities; social isolation; and psychological disorders, especially depression. They are far more likely than the two younger groups to have difficulties performing **activities of daily living (ADLs)** such as bathing, dressing, food preparation and eating, housekeeping, and paying bills (U.S. Dept. of Health & Human Services, 2005).

Nevertheless, even among the oldest-old there is substantial variability. Fewer than half of Americans ages 85–89 have a disability (Siegler et al., 2003). Only one fourth of Americans over 85 are impaired enough in their ADL capacities to be in a nursing home or other facility that provides professional care (Roberts et al., 1994). And it is not only the oldest-old who may be impaired; some people among the old-old or even the young-old have disabilities and ADL difficulties. Consequently, **gerontologists** (researchers on

activities of daily living (ADLs)

daily requirements of life for adults, such as bathing, dressing, food preparation and eating, housekeeping, and paying bills

gerontologist

researcher on aging

Late adulthood spans three substages: the young-old, the old-old, and the oldest-old.

aging) have proposed the concept of **functional age** to signify the actual competence and performance of older adults (Neugarten & Neugarten, 1987; Starc et al., 2012). Although chronological age and functional age are correlated, some 90-year-olds may have a younger functional age than some 65-year-olds because the older adults' physical, cognitive, and social functioning is better. The video *Successful Aging* has more information on how older adults can maintain an active and independent lifestyle.

Watch   SUCCESSFUL AGING

Global Aging Patterns: The Worldwide Boom in Older Adults

LO 12.2   **Define the old-age dependency ratio, and explain its impact on developed countries.**

One thing is certain about older adults: There will be a lot more of them in the future than there are now. As we have seen in previous chapters, nearly all developed countries have birth rates below 2.1 children per woman, and consequently these countries are likely to see their total populations decline in the course of the 21st century. However, even as their total populations decline, the proportion of the population age 65 and over will continue to grow. In developing countries, too, populations are aging as birth rates decline and older adults live longer. Worldwide, in 2050, the number of adults over age 60 will surpass the number of children under age 15 for the first time in human history.

Especially important in terms of how late adulthood is likely to change in the decades to come is the ratio of adults age 65 and over to younger adults, which is called the **old-age dependency ratio (OADR)**. The ratio is typically represented as a percentage and is calculated as follows:

$$\frac{\text{Number of Persons Age 65 or Older}}{\text{Number of Persons Age 20 to 64}} \times 100$$

In nearly every country, most persons ages 20–64 are in the work force, generating economic activity and paying taxes into the government systems that provide social services, including old-age pensions and medical care for older adults. Most persons age

functional age

age that indicates the actual competence and performance of older adults; may be higher or lower than chronological age

old-age dependency ratio (OADR)

in a population, the ratio of persons age 65 and over to persons age 20–64

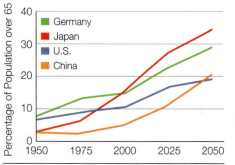

Figure 12.1 Rising Proportions of Older Adults in Developed Countries

SOURCE: Population Division, DESA, United Nations

65 and older are not in the work force, and in many countries they receive a pension and health care provided by the government. Consequently, as populations decline due to fertility rates below 2.1, the number of persons in the work force gradually falls while the number of persons in pension and health care programs gradually rises as life expectancy increases.

Developed countries are faced with difficult challenges in the decades ahead due to the rising OADR. Most serious are the challenges facing countries with especially low fertility rates, such as Japan, South Korea, Spain, Italy, and Greece, all of which have had birthrates around 1.1–1.3 for several decades. The United States and Canada, in contrast, have a less immediate problem because their total populations are still growing due to immigration and are expected to continue to grow in the 21st century.

The country with the most serious problem of all is Japan, which has an OADR of 36% (UNdata, 2014). This means that for every three Japanese ages 20–64, there is one who is age 65 or over. By the year 2050, Japan's OADR is projected to more than double to 74%, as the working-age population continues to decrease and the 65-and-over population continues to grow. Overall, by 2050, about 35% of Japanese people will be age 65 and over (see **Figure 12.1**), by far the highest proportion in the world. Japan has been slow to respond to its demographic problem in some respects. Many companies still require their employees to retire by age 60, even though this means that most will have at least 20 years of retirement, and some may have much more. However, some changes are beginning to occur. A "New Old People's Movement" has sprung up to promote a more active, engaged way of life for the elderly, including remaining in the work force (Yasuko & Megumi, 2010).

Medical care for older adults is likely to become even more advanced in the decades to come because vast sums of research funding are being spent on aging research. Even now, life expectancy at age 65 is 15–25 years in developed countries (Organization for Economic Co-operation and Development [OECD], 2014). That is, people who make it to age 65 can expect to live to be at least 80 to 85 years old (see **Map 12.1**). However, there are gender differences in life expectancy that become more pronounced with age. Worldwide, at age 65, women have a longer life expectancy than men, usually by about 5 years; and women especially outnumber men among the oldest-old. For example, in the United States, among 65- to 69-year-olds there are 115 women for every 100 men, but past age 85 there are 226 women for every 100 men (U.S. Dept. of Health & Human Services, 2005). This gender difference is due partly to behavior—globally, men are more likely than women to smoke cigarettes and drink alcohol excessively. But mainly the gender difference is due to genetics, because it exists among many animal species, from rats to dogs (Shock, 1977).

Within the United States, there are substantial variations in patterns of life expectancy by ethnic group (Kochanek et al., 2013). Overall, Whites have a life expectancy that is about 5 years longer than for African Americans. In both ethnic groups, life expectancy has risen over the past 40 years, but it has risen faster for African Americans than for Whites, so the gap between the ethnic groups is growing smaller. Life expectancy among Latinos and Asian Americans is higher than for either Whites or African Americans (Centers for Disease Control, 2013).

Traditionally, in all societies, most elderly people have been poor, because once they stopped working their income stopped, too; there was no pension system for older adults until very recently in human history. However, the second half of the 20th century was a great success story for relieving poverty in old age in developed countries, through pension and health care programs. For example, in the United States, poverty among persons age 65 and over fell from 35% in 1959 to 9% in 2006; in Canada, elderly poverty fell from 37% in 1971 to 6% in 2004 (Center for American Progress, 2011;

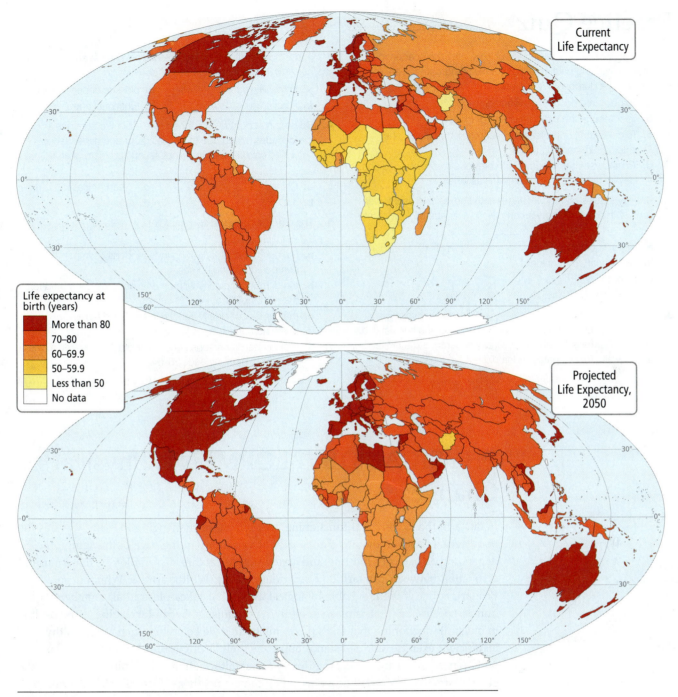

Map 12.1 Current and Projected Life Expectancy Worldwide

How is life expectancy projected to change between now and 2050? How do the rates vary between developed and developing countries?

Conference Board of Canada, 2011). Nevertheless, some older people do experience poverty in developed countries. African Americans and Latinos over age 65 are twice as likely to live in poverty as White Americans are (Center for American Progress, 2011). Across developed countries, women are more likely than men to be in poverty in late adulthood (Zaidi et al., 2006). Most developing countries have no pension system for older adults, and consequently they are economically dependent on their children and grandchildren.

Practice Quiz ANSWERS AVAILABLE IN ANSWER KEY.

1. Your co-worker was talking about how, after the academic year, he is going back to Japan for his grandmother's kanreki. What is the purpose of this ritual?

  a. To celebrate her 50th anniversary

  b. To celebrate the birth of her first grandson

  c. To celebrate her professional accomplishments as she enters retirement

  d. To celebrate her freedom from previous responsibilities and elevate her to a respected status as elder

2. Dr. Hoy studies memory changes with age, as well as interventions to improve memory among those over age 65. It is most likely that Dr. Hoy is a(n) _____.

  a. biopsychologist

  b. evolutionary psychologist

  c. gerontologist

  d. psychologist of ageism

3. Bertha has a higher _____ than her younger sister, Edna. Despite the fact that Bertha is 89 and her sister is only 72, Bertha is still able to live independently and even takes a daily walk. Unfortunately, Edna did not live a healthy lifestyle and is now confined to a wheelchair and needs an aide to help her with many of her activities of daily living.

  a. actual lifespan

  b. chronological lifespan

  c. old-age dependency ratio

  d. functional age

4. Developing countries are faced with difficult challenges in the decades ahead due to the rising old-age dependency ratio. The country with the most serious problem of all is _____.

  a. China

  b. Japan

  c. South Africa

  d. Australia

5. The old-age dependency ratio (OADR) refers to _____.

  a. the number of elderly living independently compared to the number in nursing homes

  b. the number of elderly with chronic illnesses compared to the number without any illnesses

  c. the number of elderly living with extended family compared to the number living with just a spouse

  d. the number of persons aged 65 or older compared to the number of persons ages 20-64

PHYSICAL DEVELOPMENT: Physical Changes

In late adulthood, physical functioning becomes more challenging in many ways as the body ages. However, there is a great deal of variability in the pace of the aging process, depending on heredity, lifestyle, and access to medical care. Gerontologists make a useful distinction between primary and secondary aging (Whitbourne & Whitbourne, 2010). **Primary aging** is the inevitable biological aging that takes place in all members of the human species, as it takes place in all living organisms. **Secondary aging** is the decline in physical functioning that takes place due to lifestyle behaviors such as unhealthy diet, insufficient exercise, and substance abuse, as well as environmental influences such as pollution. All of us are subject to primary aging (although in many cultures people make great efforts to conceal it). Secondary aging can be mostly avoided or at least minimized, as we will see.

Changes in Appearance

LO 12.3 **Identify the signs of physical aging in late adulthood, and differentiate the impact of primary and secondary aging on appearance.**

In some ways, the signs of physical aging that develop in late adulthood are a continuation of the changes that began in middle adulthood or even earlier. The hair continues to become grayer and thinner in both men and women. Actually, it is not that hair "turns gray" or white, but that it loses the pigments that had previously made it appear to be other colors. The skin continues to wrinkle and sag. Bones continue to thin, especially in women, and the thinning of the bones contributes to a stooped posture.

In addition, new signs of aging first appear in late adulthood. As hair becomes thinner on the head, it may sprout for the first time in surprising (and not especially welcome)

primary aging
inevitable biological aging that takes place in all living organisms

secondary aging
decline in physical functioning that takes place due to lifestyle behaviors such as unhealthy diet, insufficient exercise, and substance abuse, as well as environmental influences such as pollution

places, such as the ears and (on women) the chin. On the skin, many people develop "age spots," pools of dark pigment. Age spots are due to the accumulation of decades of exposure to the sun, and are most likely to develop on light-skinned persons and on the parts of the bodies that receive the most sun exposure: the face, arms, and hands. More moles develop on the skin, and veins become more visible as the fat layer in the skin begins to thin, again especially in light-skinned persons. Height slowly declines, about 1½ inches for men and 2 inches for women after age 60, due to the loss of bone mass in the spinal column (Pfirrmann et al., 2006). Loss of bone mass in the jaw makes the face look thinner. Body weight declines from its middle adulthood peak, mainly because people eat less due to changes in the hormones that regulate hunger (Di Francesco et al., 2007). Teeth become yellower due to loss of enamel from their surface along with the accumulated effects of food, tea, coffee, and tobacco. Prior to recent advances in dental care, most people lost some or all of their teeth by late adulthood; even today about 20% of Americans over age 65 have lost all their natural teeth (Pleis & Lethbridge-Cejku, 2006).

In late adulthood as in middle adulthood, many people in developed countries take steps to conceal or reverse the effects of aging on physical appearance. They dye their hair, rub creams on their skin, and put in dentures in place of teeth that fell out. But the best way to slow the appearance of aging is regular exercise and a healthy diet, as we'll see in more detail soon.

Changes in the Senses

LO 12.4 **Describe the changes in vision, hearing, taste, and smell in late adulthood.**

The functioning of all the senses declines in late adulthood, especially among the oldest old. For some of these declines, treatments and remedies are available, with varying degrees of effectiveness. However, these methods are mainly available in developed countries. For a look at how some older adults respond to the challenges of declining sensory abilities in Thailand, a developing country, watch the video *Getting Older in Thailand.*

Watch GETTING OLDER IN THAILAND

CHANGES IN VISION Declines take place in late adulthood in the functioning of all the main parts of the visual system: cornea, lens, retina, and optic nerve (see **Figure 12.2** on the next page). The cornea (the surface of the eye) becomes hazier, leading to lower visual acuity and higher sensitivity to bright lights (Dugdale, 2010). The lens becomes

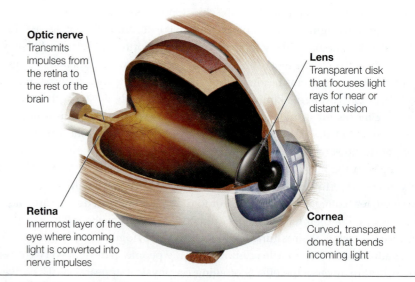

Optic nerve
Transmits impulses from the retina to the rest of the brain

Lens
Transparent disk that focuses light rays for near or distant vision

Retina
Innermost layer of the eye where incoming light is converted into nerve impulses

Cornea
Curved, transparent dome that bends incoming light

Figure 12.2 Parts of the Eye Affected by Aging

thicker and yellower, continuing a process that began in middle adulthood. Frequently, older people develop **cataracts**, a progressive thickening of the lens causing vision to become cloudy and distorted. Cataracts are the most common visual impairment in late adulthood, affecting 25% of persons in their 70s and 50% in their 80s (Fujikado et al., 2004). Biological aging is the main reason cataracts develop, but smoking and sun exposure increase the risk (Klein et al., 2003). There is no remedy for the decline in the functioning of the cornea, but the lens can now be replaced with an artificial lens in a simple operation—at least for those in developed countries (Stifter et al., 2004; Walker et al., 2006). People in developing countries rarely have access to this operation and, consequently, for them cataracts are the number one cause of blindness in late adulthood (Resnikoff et al., 2004).

In the retina, aging especially affects the *macula*, the center of the retina where vision is normally clearest. As the cells in this region deteriorate, older adults may develop **macular degeneration**, the loss of clarity in the center of the visual field. This disease affects about 4% of persons ages 65–74 and 15% of those 75 and over (Chopdar et al., 2003). Once again, primary aging is the main cause, but smoking increases the risk, and eating a healthy diet that includes fish and green leafy vegetables lowers it (Johnson & Schaefer, 2006; Rattner & Nathans, 2006). If detected early it can be treated with laser surgery or medications, but if untreated it leads to blindness (Lim et al., 2012).

Finally, the optic nerve gradually transmits visual information to the brain less efficiently with age (Gawande, 2007). Furthermore, in about 10% of persons over age 90, fluid builds up in the eye and the pressure damages the optic nerve, leading to **glaucoma**, which causes loss of peripheral vision. It can be treated with medicated eye drops, but if untreated it leads eventually to blindness. Because older adults are at high risk for cataracts, macular degeneration, and glaucoma, it is important for them to have regular eye examinations.

Vision is crucial to most human activities, so the decline in vision during late adulthood has pervasive effects on older adults' lives. The loss of visual acuity (clarity) makes it more difficult for them to carry out daily activities such as driving a car; automobile accidents rise sharply after age 80, partly due to vision problems. Housekeeping, meal preparation, and personal grooming may become more laborious and prone to error (Marsiske et al., 1997). Reading may become more difficult and may require large-print books or an especially large font on the computer screen. Leisure activities such as watching television or going to a theater may be less enjoyable with impaired vision. Nevertheless, due to effective treatments for some of the most common vision problems,

cataracts
progressive thickening of the lens of the eye that causes vision to become cloudy, opaque, and distorted

macular degeneration
loss of clarity in the center of the visual field, due to aging of the visual system

glaucoma
loss of peripheral vision due to buildup of fluid that damages the optic nerve

even among persons over 85 years old, only 30% report that their visual problems are serious enough to interfere with their daily lives (Crews & Campbell, 2004). This figure applies to the United States and may apply to other developed countries as well, but rates in developing countries are likely to be substantially higher because older adults in those countries rarely have access to medical treatments for vision problems.

Hearing aids can help compensate for hearing loss in late adulthood, but most older adults are reluctant to wear them.

CHANGES IN HEARING Hearing declines in the course of late adulthood for most people, and by the late 70s about 75% of persons report some degree of hearing impairment (Crews & Campbell, 2004). As noted in Chapter 11, hairs in the inner ear that transmit sound, called cilia, thin out with age. The structures of the inner ear become less flexible and less efficient. The auditory nerve that transmits information from the ear to the brain begins to deteriorate. Hearing acuity diminishes first for high-pitched sounds, then for detecting differences in sound patterns (Hietanen et al., 2004). Some older persons have **tinnitus**, which involves hearing a ringing or buzzing sound with no external source (Meikle et al., 2012). Most hearing impairment is due simply to primary aging, but smoking (again) increases the risk, and hearing loss sometimes takes place in response to health problems (such as diabetes) or as a side effect of medications (Helzner et al., 2005).

Like declines in vision, declines in hearing have multiple effects on daily functioning in late adulthood, especially social functioning. Not being able to hear clearly makes it difficult to carry on even a simple conversation, especially if there is considerable background noise (Murphy et al., 2006). Sometimes hearing loss leads to social withdrawal, as older adults begin to avoid contacts with others because conversations are strenuous and stressful. Hearing loss is associated with loneliness and depression (Kramer et al., 2002). Impaired hearing has also been associated with cognitive decline. When older adults have difficulty hearing, their cognitive resources must be focused on perceiving what others are saying and are thus diverted from understanding and remembering what is said (Wingfield et al., 2005).

Hearing aids are sometimes used to compensate for declines in hearing abilities. However, most older adults with hearing losses are unwilling to wear them (Lesner, 2003). Some resist because hearing aids magnify all sounds, not just the sounds they wish to hear, which still makes it difficult to follow a conversation. Others resist because they fear that wearing a hearing aid will make them appear "old" and will cause others to regard them with contempt or pity (Meister & von Wedel, 2003). However, recent advances have made hearing aids less outwardly visible, which may lessen the stigma associated with them (Whitbourne & Whitbourne, 2010).

CHANGES IN TASTE AND SMELL Taste and smell also decline in late adulthood (Dugdale, 2010). After age 60 the number of taste buds on the tongue declines, the cells in the smell receptors of the nose diminish, and the olfactory bulbs in the brain (which process smells) start to shrivel. In addition to primary aging, taste and smell diminish in late adulthood due to smoking (again!) and as a side effect of certain diseases and medications (Rawson, 2006). About one fourth of adults over age 65 report some degree of impairment in taste and smell, but the prevalence of impairment rises to over 60% in adults over age 80 (Murphy et al., 2002).

Declines in taste and smell make eating less enjoyable, as older adults find their food less appetizing and often miss the tastes they used to enjoy (Seiberling & Conley 2004).

tinnitus

problem in the auditory system that entails hearing a ringing or buzzing sound with no external source

Impairments in taste and smell sometimes lead to malnutrition in older adults who eat too little because they no longer enjoy their food as they did before (DiMaria-Ghalili et al., 2008; Savina et al., 2003). There is also increased risk of harm in situations where older adults are unable to detect a smell that signifies danger, such as gas fumes or smoke from a household fire.

Changes in Sleep Patterns

LO 12.5   **Describe the changes in sleep patterns that occur during late adulthood.**

The prevalence of sleep problems begins to increase around age 40, as we saw in Chapter 11, but increases substantially again after age 60 (Crowley, 2011). The amount of sleep people need declines only slightly from middle adulthood to late adulthood (Ancoli-Israel & Cooke, 2005). However, in late adulthood many people take longer to fall asleep and wake up more often during the night. Furthermore, most people sleep less deeply with age. The amount of time spent in Stage 1, the lightest sleep, increases, and time spent in the deepest sleep of Stage 4 and REM sleep decreases (Kamel & Gammack, 2006).

Changes also take place in people's patterns of sleep and waking hours from middle to late adulthood. With age, most people come to prefer an earlier bedtime as well as an earlier wake-up time—in the terminology introduced in Chapter 9, they develop an increasing preference for *morningness* over *eveningness*. In one study comparing adults over age 65 to younger adults, most of the older adults, and virtually none of the younger adults, described themselves as feeling healthiest and most alert "definitely mornings" or "mostly mornings"; whereas most of the younger adults, and virtually none of the older adults, described themselves as "mostly" or "definitely" feeling best during the evening hours (Hasher et al., 2005).

One especially common sleep problem of late adulthood, affecting over half of persons over age 65, is **sleep apnea**, which is a sleep-related respiratory disorder (Crowley, 2011). In people with sleep apnea, breathing actually stops for 10 seconds or more numerous times in the course of a typical night, as the air passage to the lungs closes, resulting in a sudden loud snore as the airway opens again and the sleeper awakens. Sleep apnea is especially common among older adults who are obese or who drink alcohol heavily, and it is substantially more common among men than among women (Ye et al., 2009). The most common treatment for sleep apnea is *continuous positive airway pressure (CPAP)*, in which a ventilation device blows a gentle stream of air into the nose during sleep to keep the airway open (Roux & Kyger, 2010). This treatment is usually highly effective, but some people dislike the feeling of pressure and so resist wearing the device. Attempts to develop an effective medication for sleep apnea have been ineffective so far (Hedner et al., 2008).

Changes in sleep in late adulthood are due partly to primary aging but also to psychological and medical conditions (Riedel & Lichstein, 2000). Psychological problems such as depression or anxiety can disrupt sleep, and so can medical conditions such as arthritis and osteoporosis. Several aspects of aging in late adulthood contribute to sleep disturbances, including "restless legs," which entail involuntary leg movements during sleep due to muscle tension and reduced blood circulation. Also, part of primary aging is a steadily shrinking bladder, as well as (in men) enlargement of the prostate gland, and these changes lead to more frequent urination during both day and night.

sleep apnea

sleep-related respiratory disorder in which breathing stops for 10 seconds or more numerous times in the course of a typical night, as the air passage to the lungs closes, resulting in a sudden loud snore as the airway opens again and the sleeper awakens

The most common treatment for sleep apnea is for adults to use a CPAP device.

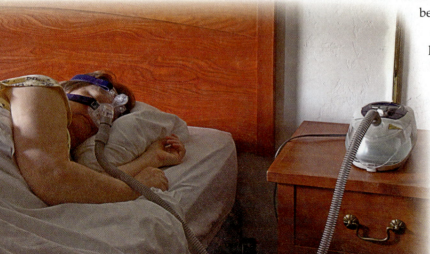

To address sleep problems, specialists recommend a regular time of sleeping and waking, and avoiding alcohol or caffeine in the hours before bedtime (Crowley, 2011). Regular exercise during the daylight hours enhances sleep at night for many people (Van Someren et al., 1997). Daytime naps should be avoided, as they increase the difficulty of falling asleep at night (Foley et al., 2007). Many medications are available for sleep disorders, and older adults receive them more often than any other age group (Feinsilver, 2003). Formerly, such medications often made sleep problems worse rather than better in the long run by increasing the severity of sleep apnea symptoms, but the newest medications appear to be more effective with fewer side effects (Salzman, 2008).

Practice Quiz   ANSWERS AVAILABLE IN ANSWER KEY.

1. During late adulthood _____.
  a. veins become less visible as a result of the increase in fat layers of the skin
  b. height slowly declines for women, but not for men
  c. body weight increases from middle adulthood because few older adults exercise
  d. loss of bone mass in the jaw makes the face look thinner

2. Your mother has quite a bit of gray hair. She told you that she first started getting gray hair when she was 32 and it keeps getting grayer each year. Which of the following explains why your mother's hair keeps on graying?
  a. People who gray prematurely experience more graying than others who gray later in life.
  b. Gray pigments occur more frequently in older adults.
  c. Gray pigments are more concentrated in fair-skinned older adults.
  d. As we age, there is a loss of pigment that provides color to hair.

3. Which of the following is an example of primary aging?
  a. Cardiovascular disease
  b. Alzheimer's disease
  c. Wrinkled skin caused by years of sun tanning
  d. Graying and thinning of the hair

4. After your mother's operation, she was relieved that all the colors on the TV seem more vivid and the headlights on cars now look white again rather than cloudy. She most likely had surgery for _____.
  a. macular degeneration   **c.** glaucoma
  b. cataracts   **d.** tinnitus

5. Kareem's father complains about having to wear a continuous positive airway pressure (CPAP) device at night, because it makes it hard for him to sleep. He most likely has _____.
  a. insomnia
  b. a REM sleep-related disorder
  c. tinnitus
  d. sleep apnea

PHYSICAL DEVELOPMENT: Health in Late Adulthood

Although many people maintain good health into late adulthood, this is also a life stage where rates of a variety of health problems increase. Here we examine some of the most common health problems of late adulthood. Then we look at health care and health promotion for older adults, coming back to the themes of the importance of diet and exercise and the importance of avoiding smoking and heavy drinking.

Chronic Health Problems

LO 12.6   Identify the major health problems associated with late adulthood, and list some treatment options.

A wide variety of health problems are prevalent in late adulthood, due to a combination of primary and secondary aging. Three of the most common chronic health problems of late adulthood are arthritis, osteoporosis, and hypertension. For all three, research has taken place almost entirely in developed countries, where research resources are greatest.

Most women in late adulthood have osteoporosis.

arthritis
disease of the joints that especially affects the hips, knees, neck, hands, and lower back

hypertension
high blood pressure, often due to a combination of primary and secondary aging

ARTHRITIS One common chronic health problem of late adulthood is **arthritis**, a disease of the joints that especially affects the hips, knees, neck, hands, and lower back. About half of adults over age 65 in developed countries report symptoms of arthritis, with women more often affected than men for unknown reasons (Bolen et al., 2010). Most arthritis is due simply to decades of using the joints, which eventually wears out the cartilage that cushions joint movement. The fluid in the joints that acts as a shock absorber also diminishes as part of primary aging. The result is stiffness and pain, and greater difficulty carrying out daily activities such as opening a jar or turning a key.

There is no cure for arthritis, so treatment involves managing and reducing the pain, mainly through medications. For pain from arthritis that is especially acute in one part of the body, such as a hip or a knee, surgery to insert an artificial joint is common in developed countries (Davenport, 2004). New treatments are being developed that inject a synthetic fluid to replace the fluid lost to primary aging, but at present this approach is in the experimental phase.

Exercise can also help relieve the symptoms of arthritis. In one study, older adults with arthritis were divided into three groups (Suomi & Collier, 2003). Two of the groups participated in an 8-week exercise program, one involving aquatic exercise and one involving land exercise; the third group was the control group. At the end of the 8-week period, participants in the two exercise programs were more likely than members of the control group to perform a variety of daily activities without discomfort, such as walking, bending, lifting, and climbing stairs.

OSTEOPOROSIS As noted in Chapter 11, the risk of osteoporosis rises sharply for women in midlife, as a consequence of the steep drop in estrogen that takes place at menopause. Although the decline in bone mass is steepest in the decade following menopause, the process continues in late adulthood and the risk of osteoporosis continues to rise. Beyond age 60 about two-thirds of women in developed countries are affected by osteoporosis (International Osteoporosis Foundation [IOF], 2011). Osteoporosis places older women at higher risk for broken bones and subsequent mortality; about 15% of women over age 65 who experience a major bone fracture die within a year (Reginster & Burlet, 2006). Health authorities recommend that women receive regular bone density checks after menopause, because osteoporosis can be delayed or even reversed with a combination of regular bone-strengthening exercise (such as weightlifting) and a calcium-rich diet (Dolan et al., 2004). Men can get osteoporosis, too, but their rates are about one fifth the rates for women (IOF, 2011).

HYPERTENSION A third common health problem of late adulthood is **hypertension**, also known as high blood pressure. In the United States, 70% of adults over age 65 have hypertension (Centers for Disease Control and Prevention [CDC], 2014), and rates are similar in other developed countries. In part, rising rates of hypertension in late adulthood are due to primary aging, as the heart muscle becomes stiffer and pumps less efficiently over time. However, secondary aging also contributes to hypertension. The walls of the arteries become more rigid and accumulate plaque due to consumption of foods high in cholesterol and fat. Stress elevates blood pressure, and people in poverty are at high risk for hypertension due to a combination of high-fat diets and chronic stress (Almeida et al., 2005).

There are no direct symptoms of hypertension. However, over time hypertension weakens the circulatory system by putting it under constant strain. The heart is forced to work harder, and the arteries develop areas of weakness and inflammation. In middle adulthood, and even more in late adulthood, persons with hypertension are at high risk for death due to cardiovascular disease (Bowman et al., 2006). Fortunately, effective medications are now available for treating hypertension (Ruppar, 2010). However, the lack of symptoms makes it easy to forget to take medications for hypertension, and the medications may have side effects such as fatigue, diarrhea, and dizziness that also lead people to stop taking them (Viswanathan & Lambert, 2005).

Health Care and Health Promotion

LO 12.7 **Identify three lifestyle practices that have a positive influence on health.**

Fortunately, there are medical interventions for nearly all the most common health problems of late adulthood that can eliminate or at least reduce them. Across developed countries, older adults consume far more medical care resources than any other age group in the population, as **Figure 12.3** illustrates (OECD, 2009, p. 169).

Every developed country has a government program that provides health care for adults over age 65. In contrast, most older adults in developing countries are unlikely to have access to even simple and inexpensive medical interventions that could relieve their suffering and extend their lives. The vast difference in life expectancy between developed and developing countries is due primarily to differences in infant/child mortality and access to health care in late adulthood (Mahfuz, 2008).

However, nearly all developed countries are facing serious financial challenges in the 21st century in their funding of health care programs for older adults. Every year new advances in medical care allow older adults to live healthier, longer lives. This is wonderful, yes, but every one of those new advances costs money and adds more to the overall cost of health care for older adults. Furthermore, as we saw earlier, the OADR is rising rapidly in every developed country, meaning that with each decade there is a lower proportion of adults age 20–64 paying taxes into the system that funds health care for adults age 65 and over.

As fabulous as the new medical interventions are that have extended life expectancy and allowed people to restore their health and reduce their pain and disability, the best ways to maintain good health in late adulthood are simple and require no medical intervention: eat a healthy diet, exercise regularly, and avoid unhealthy practices such as cigarette smoking and excess alcohol consumption. Although the health value of these principles has been known for a long time, recent research has demonstrated how they work and the extent of their effects.

HEALTH EFFECTS OF DIET Eating a balanced diet that is low in fats and sugars enhances health at all ages. However, eating a good diet is even more important in late adulthood than at earlier ages because it slows down primary aging and enhances the immune system at a time when risks of a variety of illnesses and diseases increase. Healthy foods contain specific micronutrients that enhance health, such as calcium, zinc, and vitamins A, B6, B12, C, D, and E. Usually a good diet provides a sufficient quantity of micronutrients, but some studies have found that taking a daily supplement of Vitamin D results in a steep drop in the number and severity of illnesses in late adulthood (Hewison, 2012).

In contrast, a poor diet high in fats and sugars places people at risk for a wide range of illnesses and diseases, with the risks increasing with age (Blumenthal et al., 2005). Poor diet makes obesity more likely, and in turn obesity raises the risk of disease and death, especially in middle and late adulthood. Cardiovascular disease is the leading cause of death in adulthood

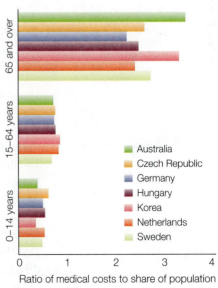

Figure 12.3 Use of Medical Resources by Age Group

Persons age 65 and over consume far more medical resources than persons in other age groups.

SOURCE: OECD (2009)

Cultural Focus: Physical Health in Late Adulthood Across Cultures

Developing countries have a lower OADR than developed countries do, because relatively few of their people live into late adulthood and they have higher birth rates. However, their challenge is to provide even basic medical care to their population, because such care is expensive and these countries lack the financial resources to build a medical system with the latest treatments and technologies.

This video shows a variety of interviews with individuals in developed as well as developing countries. The focus of these interviews is health and treatment during the late adulthood years. Notice especially the difficulties of the man in Mexico in obtaining treatment for his physical ailments, and his response to those difficulties.

Watch PHYSICAL HEALTH IN LATE ADULTHOOD ACROSS CULTURES

Video

Review Question:

Analyze the attitudes and lifestyles of the American couple and the man from the Mexican village. What do you feel are the major differences? Can you find any similarities?

worldwide (WHO, 2014), and risk of cardiovascular disease is higher in adults who are obese (Ajani et al., 2006). Rates are especially high in countries where consumption of red meat is highest, such as Russia, Romania, and Poland (Rosamond et al., 2007). Cancer is the second leading cause of death in developed countries, and obesity raises the risk of a wide range of cancers by over 50%, including cancer of the colon, liver, pancreas, and kidney, as well as (in women) breast and cervical cancers (Calle et al., 2003). Some specific foods are related to specific types of cancer. For example, stomach cancer is highest in Japan, Korea, and parts of eastern Europe, apparently due to high consumption of foods that are smoked, salted, or pickled (Tsugane, 2005).

The social context of late adulthood sometimes makes it difficult to follow a healthy diet. Older adults in developed countries are more likely than persons in younger age groups to live alone, and shopping and preparing a meal may seem more daunting and less pleasurable when it is done alone. For these reasons, many developed countries have social services that bring healthy hot meals to the homes of older adults on a regular basis, for a small fee or free of charge (Tinetti et al., 2002).

HEALTH EFFECTS OF EXERCISE Like healthy eating, regular exercise is an important part of good health at all ages but becomes increasingly important in late adulthood because it slows the effects of primary aging. Specifically, it improves motor coordination and the functioning of the cardiovascular and digestive systems (Ferrera, 2004; Marcus et al., 2006). Regular exercise increases muscle and bone mass and reduces the likelihood of bone fractures (Karlsson, 2004). It lowers the risk of a variety of diseases, such as cardiovascular disease, stroke, and osteoporosis, and reduces the symptoms of diseases such as arthritis and diabetes (Singh, 2004). According to one estimate, regular light exercise reduces the risk of heart attacks by one fourth and regular vigorous exercise reduces the risk by one half (Lovasi et al., 2007).

Regular exercise in late adulthood slows primary aging and lowers the risk of disease.

Studies have delineated the link between specific types of exercise and specific health outcomes. *Aerobic exercise,* such as walking at a rapid pace, jogging, or pedaling a stationary bike, enhances the functioning of the respiratory, cardiovascular, and digestive systems. For example, in one study that randomly assigned adults in their late 60s to either an aerobic exercise group, a yoga group, or a control group, only the aerobic group showed improvements 16 weeks later in the functioning of their lungs and heart, as well as a drop in their cholesterol levels (Blumenthal et al., 1989). Aerobic exercise also enhances cognitive functioning in late adulthood, as we will see later in the chapter. *Strength training,* which usually involves lifting weights, builds muscle and bone mass and promotes the functioning of the circulatory system (deJong & Franklin, 2004; Seguin & Nelson, 2003). In addition, it can ease the performance of a variety of tasks of daily life, from carrying a shopping bag to opening a "child-proof" cap.

Despite the many benefits of regular exercise, participation in exercise decreases with age throughout adulthood and is lowest in late adulthood. In the United States, about 85% of older adults age 65–74 never engage in vigorous exercise, rising to 95% for those 75 and over (Pleis & Lethbridge-Cejku, 2006). As with nutrition, with exercise there are certain obstacles that are specific to late adulthood (Singh, 2004). Exercise may enhance physical functioning, but people whose physical functioning has already declined considerably may find exercising more difficult and less gratifying. For example, arthritis may make it more painful to make the kinds of movements that exercise requires. Back pain may make aerobic exercise difficult or impossible. Exercise may enhance feelings of energy in the long run, but it takes a certain amount of energy to begin exercising in the first place.

AUTOMOBILE DRIVING IN LATE ADULTHOOD My extended family gathers in New Hampshire every year for a vacation, and on one of those vacations a few years ago I found myself driving in a car behind my dad, who was 80 years old at the time. I was stunned and terrified to find that driving behind him was like driving behind a person who was intoxicated. He changed speeds abruptly, and he swerved out of his lane several times. I told him what I had observed afterward and strongly urged him to stop driving. He ended his highway driving after that, but he continued to drive around town to do errands, despite my protests and my blunt warnings. He only finally stopped driving 5 years later, when a health crisis resulted in his transition to an assisted living situation.

Automobile crashes are a major threat to older adults' health in developed countries. In the United States, which keeps especially detailed statistics on automobile crashes, adults over age 75 have automobile fatality rates nearly as high as for 16- to 20-year-olds (National Highway Traffic Safety Administration [NHTSA], 2014). Older adults have fewer crashes than 16- to 20-year-olds, but crashes are more likely to be fatal for older adults because their bodies are not as strong and resilient.

We have seen in this chapter that several sensory abilities related to driving decline in late adulthood, including vision and hearing. Studies of driving behavior also show that some specific driving abilities decline with age such as responses to the behavior of other drivers (Waard et al., 2009). Nevertheless, older drivers tend to assess their abilities as better than they actually are. In one study, drivers age 65 and older assigned high ratings to their driving performance even when laboratory driving simulations showed that they made many mistakes that raised their crash risk (Freund et al., 2005).

Driving is often difficult for older adults to give up. To give up driving means that they also give up a substantial amount of their independence (Ralston et al., 2001). They may have to stop driving because of declining health, but driving cessation may itself lead to a decline in health. In one study that had assessed the physical health of older adults, they were assessed again 1, 2, 3, and 5 years later, and many of them had ceased to drive at some point during that period (Edwards et al., 2009). Driving cessation predicted a decline in physical and social functioning. In another longitudinal study, driving cessation predicted symptoms of depression (Fonda et al., 2001). Driving cessation among older adults can also be difficult for those who care for them, because older adults who have stopped driving usually rely on family and friends to take them places rather than using public transportation or other local transportation services for the elderly (Taylor & Tripodes, 2001).

It is important to add that many older adults remain excellent drivers. The skills related to driving decline at different rates for different people. Older adults who remain in good health and whose senses remain sharp do not decline in their driving skills (Ball, 2003). Also, in the course of late adulthood many people compensate for declines in their driving skills by modifying their driving behavior, for example driving less, driving only in daytime, and sticking to familiar routes (Donorfio et al., 2008). Few countries have laws restricting the driving of older adults, because opponents of restrictions argue that even though the risk of crashes increases with age in late adulthood, at every age there are many whose skills remain strong (Griffith, 2007).

WHAT NOT TO DO: THE DAMAGE FROM SMOKING AND HEAVY DRINKING If good nutrition and regular exercise are the keys to a healthy life in late adulthood, what practices should be avoided? Of all the behaviors that a person should avoid in order to live to a long and healthy late adulthood, smoking is undoubtedly number one. Most people today are aware that smoking causes lung cancer, which is responsible for more deaths than any other type of cancer and is among the cancers least susceptible to treatment and cure (American Cancer Society, 2007). However, smoking is the source of an astonishing range of other damaging health effects (CDC, 2014). It causes cancer not only of the lungs but also of the mouth, throat, esophagus, larynx, bladder, kidney, cervix, pancreas, and stomach. It causes cardiovascular disease and leads to heart attacks, because it damages the heart and the arteries. It also causes strokes. As noted earlier in the chapter, it causes vision, hearing, taste, and smell to decline more quickly. In men, it also contributes to erectile dysfunction (Chew et al., 2009).

Fortunately, rates of cigarette smoking are decreasing in developed countries. In the United States, where the public health campaign against smoking has been especially strong, the proportion of smokers in the adult population has decreased from about 50% in the 1960s to just 18% today (CDC, 2014; Roeseler & Burns, 2010). However, rates of smoking are rising in developing countries as tobacco companies' marketing and promotion efforts focus on that emerging market (see **Map 12.2**).

Alcohol can also be damaging to health, but its health effects are more complex. Moderate alcohol consumption of one to two glasses of beer or wine per day actually enhances the functioning of the cardiovascular system and reduces the risk of

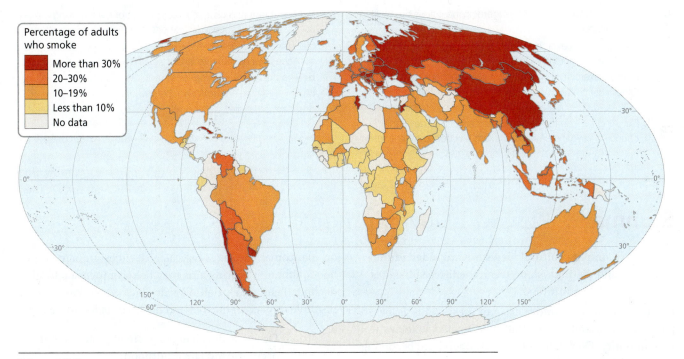

Map 12.2 Smoking Rates Worldwide

Which countries have the highest smoking rates? What cultural factors might explain these variations? What impact might the higher rates have on the overall health of these countries' populations?

cardiovascular disease and strokes (see Chapter 11; Byles et al., 2006). However, beyond this level alcohol begins to have damaging effects, increasing the risk of strokes and causing harm to the liver and kidneys (Reynolds et al., 2003).

Together, a lifestyle that includes a healthy diet, regular exercise, and avoiding health-damaging behavior not only lengthens life expectancy but extends people's **active life span**, the number of years their physical functioning is favorable enough for them to enjoy their lives and perform most of their daily activities without impairment. Active life span has increased in the past 50 years along with life expectancy in developed countries (WHO, 2009). The portrait is quite different in developing countries, where active life span is below age 50 in the most troubled countries, such as Afghanistan, Haiti, and Rwanda.

active life span

number of years of physical functioning favorable enough for people to enjoy their lives and perform most of their daily activities without impairment

Practice Quiz   ANSWERS AVAILABLE IN ANSWER KEY.

1. Eloise has been studying the aging process in her health class. She is dreading getting _____, a common chronic health problem of late adulthood for which there is no cure, because her grandparents both had it and seemed to be in a lot of pain all the time.

    a. osteoporosis

    b. hypertension

    c. colon cancer

    d. arthritis

2. Your grandmother is 78 and just found out that her osteoporosis has gotten much worse. For her birthday you thought you would get her a gift to help improve her bone density. What gift should you give her?

    a. Weights to carry with her on her walk

    b. A gift certificate to the organic meat market

    c. A yoga mat and a video with stretching exercises

    d. A gift certificate for zumba classes

3. Arthritis _____.

    a. is caused by a steep drop in estrogen

    b. affects more men than women

    c. is caused by excess exercise in previous decades

    d. has no cure

4. Which of the following is TRUE regarding influences on health in late adulthood?

a. Participation in exercise increases slightly after age 65 as people have more leisure time.

b. Aerobic exercise enhances cognitive functioning.

c. Older adults have more automobile crashes than 16-to 20-year-olds, but their crashes are less likely to be fatal.

d. Smoking rates in the United States and other developing countries have increased in the last few decades as a result of more aggressive marketing campaigns.

5. Beyond infant and child mortality, which of the following makes up the vast difference in life expectancy between developed and developing countries?

a. Access to health care in late adulthood

b. The degree of physical labor required of jobs

c. Carcinogens and toxins in the environment

d. The type of diet

Summary: Physical Development

LO 12.1   **Compare cultural views toward older adults, and distinguish between the three substages of late adulthood.**

In many Asian and traditional cultures, status is based partly on age, and older adults are treated with respect and authority. Depictions of late adulthood are becoming more positive in the West as well, as shown in advertisements. Developmental psychologists divide late adulthood into three substages: young-old (age 65–74); old-old (age 75–84); and oldest-old (age 85 and up). Adults in these substages may differ based on how they perform activities of daily living (ADLs), so gerontologists today often refer to the concept of functional age.

LO 12.2   **Define the old-age dependency ratio, and explain its impact on developed countries.**

The old-age dependency ratio (OADR) is calculated by dividing the number of persons age 65 or older by the number of persons age 20–64 and multiplying by 100. The OADR in developed countries is rising because of decreasing fertility rates and increased life expectancy, due largely to medical interventions. Countries such as Japan face strains on their social welfare systems due to the rising OADR.

LO 12.3   **Identify the signs of physical aging in late adulthood, and differentiate the impact of primary and secondary aging on appearance.**

Signs of physical aging include graying and thinning hair, age spots, decrease in body weight, and possible loss of teeth. Many of these changes are due to primary aging, although secondary aging influences such as sun exposure and diet have an effect as well.

LO 12.4   **Describe the changes in vision, hearing, taste, and smell in late adulthood.**

Changes to the cornea, lens, retina, and optic nerve in late adulthood may lead to cataracts, macular degeneration, or glaucoma. Hearing typically declines in late adulthood, although hearing aids may help compensate for this decline. Taste and smell also decline, which can have a negative impact on the diet and health of older adults.

LO 12.5   **Describe the changes in sleep patterns that occur during late adulthood.**

In late adulthood many people take longer to fall asleep, wake up more often during the night, and sleep less deeply. Many older adults also experience sleep apnea. Changes in sleep patterns are due both to normal aging and to psychological and medical conditions.

LO 12.6   **Identify the major health problems associated with late adulthood, and list some treatment options.**

One common chronic health problem of late adulthood is arthritis, a disease of the joints that especially affects the hips, knees, neck, hands, and lower back. There is no cure, but medication and surgery can be used to treat the pain. Loss of bone mass continues in late adulthood, causing the risk of osteoporosis to rise, mostly for women. Osteoporosis can be delayed or even reversed with a combination of regular bone-strengthening exercise (such as weightlifting) and a calcium-rich diet. Rates of hypertension, or high blood pressure, rise in late adulthood due to primary and secondary aging.

LO 12.7   **Identify three lifestyle practices that have a positive influence on health.**

Eating a healthy diet, exercising regularly, and avoiding unhealthy practices, such as cigarette smoking and excess alcohol consumption, all have a positive effect on health in late adulthood.

Section 2   Cognitive Development

∨ Learning Objectives

12.8 Describe how attention and memory change during late adulthood.

12.9 Explain how the brain changes during late adulthood, and identify the symptoms and risk factors for Alzheimer's disease.

12.10 Define wisdom, and summarize research on the impact of age and culture on wisdom.

12.11 Describe the effect of intervention studies on cognitive decline, and explain how older adults adapt to physical and cognitive changes.

COGNITIVE DEVELOPMENT:
Cognitive Changes and Decline

Like physical development, cognitive development declines in the course of late adulthood, especially after age 85. However, there are ways to slow the aging process and stay sharper for longer, through a healthy diet, exercise, and maintaining a high level of cognitive activity.

Changes in Attention and Memory

LO 12.8   **Describe how attention and memory change during late adulthood.**

The information processing abilities of attention and memory decline to some degree in late adulthood. However, there is a great deal of individual variation in the extent and pace of decline. The degree of decline also varies depending on the type of task involved.

ATTENTION With regard to attention, the declines that began from young adulthood to middle adulthood continue into late adulthood. Several different types of attention decline, including selective attention, divided attention, and sustained attention. As noted in Chapter 11, people experience age-related declines in *selective attention*, which requires the ability to tune out irrelevant information. This is shown in a classic psychology experiment called the Stroop test, in which people are asked to indicate the color of a word flashing on a screen, but the word itself presents contrary information. So, for example, the word "blue" is flashed in red. Older adults have more difficulty with this task than younger adults do, because it requires them to focus on the relevant information (that the color of the word is in red) and ignore irrelevant information (the word itself is "blue") (Brink & McDowd, 1999; Hogan, 2003).

Divided attention, the ability to keep track of more than one information source simultaneously, also declines with age. For example, in laboratory tasks where people are required to perform two tasks at once, such as a simulated driving task where a person navigates on a monitor while carrying on a conversation, older adults perform worse than younger adults do (Verhaeghen et al., 2003).

Sustained attention, in which people are required to concentrate on a task for an extended period of time, also declines. In laboratory tests of sustained attention, participants are presented with a series of stimuli (for example letters) and required to press a key only when they see a particular pattern (for example an *A* followed by an *X*). Older

sustained attention

ability to concentrate on a task for an extended period of time

adults respond more slowly and make more errors than younger adults do on this kind of task (Rush et al., 2006).

MEMORY A great deal of research has been conducted on memory in late adulthood, and the results show that the degree and pace of decline depends in part on the type of memory involved. There is relatively little decline in *procedural memory*, which is memory for how to perform tasks or activities involving motor skills, such as playing a musical instrument, typing on a keyboard, or sewing a button. This appears to be true even for recently-learned tasks. In one study, persons ages 18–95 were taught a task that involved sliding a small nut off a rod, with the goal of performing it as rapidly as possible. The oldest adults were able to perform the task 2 years after they were taught it, with no decline in their performance (Smith et al., 2005). *Semantic memory*, involving the meaning of words and memory for factual information, also shows little decline with age (Wiggs et al., 2006). This kind of memory can be seen as an aspect of crystallized intelligence, which, as we saw in Chapter 11, does not decline as much in late adulthood as fluid intelligence does.

Other kinds of memory show steeper declines in late adulthood. *Working memory*, which is memory for information currently the focus of your attention, declines (Chaytor & Schmitter-Edgecombe, 2004). So does long-term memory, making late adulthood a time of more frequently experiencing the "tip-of-the-tongue phenomenon," feeling that the information (such as a person's name) is in there somewhere but being unable to retrieve it (O'Hanlon et al., 2005). Although older adults often believe that they can remember events of long ago with special clarity, research has shown substantial declines in *episodic memory* in late adulthood, for recent information such as important events within the past year, as well as for more distant information such as events shown on television years ago (Davis et al., 2001; Parker et al., 2004). A related line of research, on *autobiographical memory*, shows that people tend to remember past events

Memory for factual information remains relatively strong in late adulthood.

in a way that maintains a positive self-image, recalling pleasant events (the award you received) but forgetting unpleasant ones (the job promotion you wanted but did not get) (Berntsen & Rubin, 2002; Loftus, 2003; Piolino et al., 2006). Research in this area also shows that in late adulthood there is *reminiscence bump* for ages 10 to 30 (Scherman, 2013). That is, people recall autobiographical events from age 10 to 30 more vividly and with more detail than they recall the period from age 30 to 50 (Rubin, 2000; Schroots et al., 2004). The age 10 to 30 period may be especially vivid because so many important life events take place during those years for many people, such as reaching puberty, first romantic and sexual experiences, first jobs, leaving home, and entering marriage and parenthood. But even public events that took place during this age period—who won a major sports event, who was elected to a high political office—are more likely to be recalled (Rubin et al., 1998; Scherman, 2013).

One especially interesting aspect of memory decline in late adulthood is *source memory*, which is memory for where a piece of information was acquired. In the course of late adulthood people have increasing difficulty remembering where they learned something or when an item was used first (Thomas & Bulevish, 2006). This memory difficulty can lead older adults to "remember" things that never actually happened (Dodson et al., 2007). For example, in one experiment participants of various ages were shown a list of related items (e.g., candy, cookie, honey), then later shown another list and asked which of the items on the new list had been on the original list. Older participants were more likely than younger participants to state that they had seen a word (e.g., "sweet") that applied to the category of items but was not actually one of the words shown (Jacoby & Rhodes, 2006). However, some researchers have found that when the information has personal relevance, older adults make no more mistakes in source memory than younger adults do (Hasher, 2003).

Brain Changes and Brain Diseases: Dementia and Alzheimer's Disease

LO 12.9   **Explain how the brain changes during late adulthood, and identify the symptoms and risk factors for Alzheimer's disease.**

A variety of changes take place in the brain in late adulthood that lead to the declines in cognitive ability just described. Most of these changes are due to primary aging, but they are influenced by secondary aging as well, especially smoking (for the worse), exercise (for the better), and cognitive stimulation (also for the better). For many people, neurological changes eventually result in brain deterioration that severely affects not only cognitive functioning but all aspects of living.

CHANGES IN THE BRAIN   In late adulthood the brain actually shrinks and total brain mass declines. This process begins around age 30 but accelerates around age 60, so that by age 80 most people have lost 5–10% of their peak brain mass (Raz et al., 2007). The amount of space between brain and skull doubles from age 30 to 70, and spaces within the brain enlarge as well. Certain brain structures are especially affected, most notably the hippocampus (which influences the transfer of information to long-term memory), the cerebellum (involved in balance and coordination), and the frontal lobes (responsible for planning and judgment). The decline in brain mass is due to the death of neurons and insufficient replacement with new neurons, and to a decrease in myelination of the neurons (Raz, 2005). Neurons are dying and being generated anew throughout life, but in late adulthood the ratio shifts as more die than are replaced (Manev & Manev, 2005). However, there is a great deal of variability in late adulthood in how much brain mass is lost, and staying physically and cognitively active lessens the decline and preserves brain functioning (Colcombe et al., 2006; Raz et al., 2007). The video *Exercise Your Brain* describes how aerobic exercise can help improve your cognitive functioning.

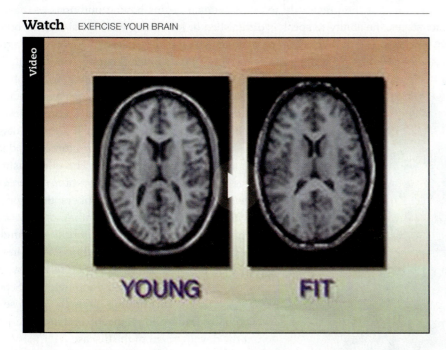

Watch   EXERCISE YOUR BRAIN

Video

YOUNG   FIT

Declines also take place in certain neurotransmitters in late adulthood, most notably *acetylcholine,* which is especially involved in the functioning of memory (Descarries et al., 2004). There is also a reduction in *dopamine,* which influences movement and motor coordination. Late adulthood is a period of increased risk for Parkinson's disease, which involves an extreme reduction in dopamine levels, leading to severe difficulties in motor control (Erickson et al., 2012; Murre et al., 2013).

DIAGNOSIS OF ALZHEIMER'S DISEASE In the course of late adulthood the risk rises for experiencing **dementia**, a condition that entails losses in cognitive functioning severe enough to interfere with daily life. Across developed countries, only 1–2% of persons in their 60s are afflicted with dementia, but the prevalence rises steeply after age 75 and reaches over 50% beyond age 85 (Beers, 20061). In developing countries, few people in India or Africa are affected by dementia because relatively few people live into late adulthood, but in Asian and Latin American countries rates are around 5% for persons over age 65 and are increasing as life expectancy increases (Kalaria et al., 2008).

Over 70 different kinds of dementia have been identified, but the most common type by far is **Alzheimer's disease**, which is a distinctive pattern of structural decline in the brain that accounts for over half of cases of dementia in late adulthood (Matthews & Brayne, 2005). Because of its prevalence, Alzheimer's disease has been studied far more than other types of dementia.

The earliest symptom of Alzheimer's disease is a loss of memory for recent events and familiar names and tasks. Of course, as we have seen, memory decline takes place across late adulthood as part of primary aging, but the loss of memory in Alzheimer's disease is more striking and severe—inability to remember a grandchild's name, for example, or forgetting the route to the grocery store taken many, many times before. Memory for recent events is affected first, but gradually earlier events and persons are forgotten as well. Ultimately, even awareness of the people, places, events, and facts most familiar and most valued is lost. This decline into unawareness, *sans everything,* is what makes Alzheimer's disease such a frightening prospect to many people (Frazier, 2002).

Other symptoms also develop in the course of the disease. Personality is often affected for the worse, including higher anxiety and aggression, lower interest in others, and lower interest in previously-enjoyed activities. As the frontal lobe is increasingly affected, its role in inhibiting socially undesirable behavior is undermined, resulting in behavior that may shock and dismay others—the previously polite man suddenly begins using foul language at high volume, or the previously reserved woman begins having outbursts of rage. In the later stages, the ability to speak is diminished or lost, along with the ability to control bodily functions. The disease is eventually fatal, with the life expectancy following diagnosis of Alzheimer's about 5 years for men and 6 years for women (Wattmo et al., 2014).

The pattern of structural decline in the brain that distinguishes Alzheimer's disease has two main features. One is that there is an accumulation in the brain of *amyloid plaques,* which are deposits of the protein *amyloid* along with clumps of dead neurons (Galvan et al., 2006). The other distinctive feature is the development of *neurofibrillary tangles,* bundles of twisted fibers that appear within the neurons (Blumenthal, 2004). Both amyloid plaques and neurofibrillary tangles begin to form in middle adulthood, early in the disease process, many years before any symptoms of Alzheimer's disease are evident (Scheff & Price, 2006). This finding holds the promise of eventually leading to medications that could prevent the development of the disease.

The diagnosis of Alzheimer's disease is based on changes in cognitive and behavioral functioning, especially severe memory loss, that cannot be explained

dementia

neurological condition that entails losses in cognitive functioning severe enough to interfere with daily life

Alzheimer's disease

type of dementia that has a distinctive pattern of structural decline in the brain involving the accumulation of amyloid plaques and the development of neurofibrillary tangles

People with Alzheimer's disease lose their memory for familiar names and tasks.

by other causes. However, it is not possible to make a definite diagnosis of Alzheimer's until after death, when an autopsy can reveal the presence of amyloid plaques and neurofibrillary tangles (Wattmo et al., 2014). New diagnostic methods are currently being researched that may make it possible to identify the development of the disease through tests of the blood, urine, or spinal fluid, or through functional magnetic resonance imaging (fMRI) of brain activity.

FACTORS INFLUENCING ALZHEIMER'S What causes Alzheimer's disease? There is an early-onset form of Alzheimer's, occurring before age 65, which clearly has a genetic basis, as it runs very strongly in families. In fact, researchers have identified specific genes that produce the excess amyloid that results in amyloid plaques. However, this kind of Alzheimer's accounts for only about 5% of cases (Harman, 2006).

The majority of Alzheimer's cases also appear to have a partly genetic basis, but not as strongly as early-onset cases do. A specific gene known as the *ApoE* gene that signals high risk for Alzheimer's disease has been identified. Even in middle adulthood, years before the onset of the first symptoms of Alzheimer's, the fMRIs of people with the *ApoE* gene look different when recalling information, compared to people without the gene (Thomas & Fenech, 2007).

The *ApoE* gene indicates risk for Alzheimer's disease, but not everyone with the gene develops the disease. One cross-cultural study provided an excellent example of the interaction between genes and environment for Alzheimer's disease. The study compared an African American sample to a sample of the Yoruba tribe in Nigeria (Gureje et al., 2006; Lahiri et al., 2007). African Americans have higher rates of Alzheimer's disease than any other American ethnic group, and this study found that African Americans with the *ApoE* gene were especially likely to develop the disease. However, among the Yoruba sample rates of Alzheimer's were very low, even when they possessed the *ApoE* gene. Apparently the key difference lay in their diets. The African Americans ate a diet high in fats and sugars, apparently triggering the vulnerability indicated by the *ApoE* gene, while the Yoruba ate a low-fat diet of mostly vegetables, fruits, and occasional meat, so that the *ApoE* gene was never expressed.

Other studies also show that diet is an important factor in the development of Alzheimer's disease (Hall et al., 2006). Although diets high in fats and sugars increase the risk of developing the disease, the risk is lowered by the "Mediterranean diet" common in the cultures surrounding the Mediterranean sea, featuring tomatoes, fish, olive oil, and red wine (Panza et al., 2004; Scarmeas et al., 2006). Regular physical activity also lowers the risk of Alzheimer's disease (Podewils et al., 2005). For example, in a study of persons ages 71–93, those who walked at least 2 miles a day were only half as likely to develop Alzheimer's disease as those who walked less than a quarter of a mile a day (Abbott et al., 2004).

Maintaining a high level of cognitive activity appears to be another protective factor against developing Alzheimer's disease (Wattmo et al., 2014). There is a strong negative association between education and Alzheimer's risk, with people who have attained a university degree only half as likely to develop the disease as people who have not (Qui et al., 2001). High levels of cognitive engagement in late adulthood, through work or leisure activities, continue to lower the risk of Alzheimer's disease (Wilson et al., 2002). Cognitive activity in late adulthood appears to act as a kind of brain exercise, creating new dendritic connections and a *cognitive reserve* that can enable the brain to keep functioning well even as primary aging of the brain takes place (Briones, 2006).

Eating a "Mediterranean diet" helps lower the risk of Alzheimer's disease.

TREATMENT AND CARE FOR THOSE WITH ALZHEIMER'S There is no cure for Alzheimer's disease at this time, and medications to alleviate the symptoms have limited effectiveness. Most current medications seek to limit the loss of acetylcholine, the neurotransmitter that is involved in memory and that declines sharply in people who have Alzheimer's (Salomone et al., 2012). However, the most effective of these medications works on only about half of Alzheimer's patients, and even then relief of symptoms is only temporary. Other recent approaches focus on removing amyloid plaques, and there is also an attempt to develop a vaccine against plaque formation (Dasilva et al., 2006; Rafii & Aisen, 2009). However, so far these efforts have not yielded success (Salomone et al., 2012).

For now, the progression of Alzheimer's disease is difficult to thwart as it gradually undermines the person's cognitive, physical, and emotional functioning. This decline places a great strain on the people responsible for caring for the person with Alzheimer's, usually the person's spouse and/or children (Gaugler et al., 2003). People with Alzheimer's eventually require constant care as they become unable to feed and clothe themselves and they lose control over their bladder and bowel movements. They cease to recognize even those they have loved most and become increasingly volatile emotionally (Kozmala & Kloszewska, 2004). Caregivers for Alzheimer's experience high rates of depression as they become physically and psychologically exhausted (Gaugler et al., 2003; Thomas et al., 2006). The caregivers' burden can be lessened by providing them with knowledge of the disease, training in how to cope with the symptoms, and an occasional respite from constant care responsibilities (Callahan et al., 2006).

Practice Quiz   ANSWERS AVAILABLE IN ANSWER KEY.

1. Memory for where a piece of information is acquired is known as _____.

   a. semantic memory
   b. working memory
   c. procedural memory
   d. source memory

2. Which of the following would you expect a late adult to do best?

   a. Tune out irrelevant information
   b. Keep track of more than one information source simultaneously
   c. Concentrate on a task for an extended period of time
   d. Remember factual information

3. When you are reminiscing with your grandfather, you notice that he tends to remember more events from ages _____, probably because so many important life events take place during those years.

   a. 5–15
   b. 10–30
   c. 25–40
   d. 40–60

4. _____ are especially at risk for developing Alzheimer's disease.

   a. Highly educated people
   b. African Americans
   c. Those with a history of high blood pressure
   d. Individuals who eat a lot of fish and olive oil

5. Which of the following about Alzheimer's disease is TRUE?

   a. Life expectancy following diagnosis of Alzheimer's is about 10 years for men and 15 years for women.
   b. Eating a Mediterranean diet increases the risk of developing Alzheimer's because of an associated protein deficiency.
   c. There is no evidence of a genetic basis of Alzheimer's disease.
   d. There is no cure for Alzheimer's

COGNITIVE DEVELOPMENT:
Alternative Views of Cognitive Changes

Cognitive changes in late adulthood are not only in the direction of decline. In many cultures old age is viewed as a time when wisdom ripens (although the research on this topic is more ambiguous, as we will see shortly). For people who have experienced cognitive decline, there are a variety of ways to adapt so that valued activities can be continued. Learning still occurs in late adulthood, and in fact late-life learning helps to keep cognitive functioning sharp.

Wisdom

LO 12.10 **Define wisdom, and summarize research on the impact of age and culture on wisdom.**

Although cognitive development in late adulthood often involves declines in specific abilities, old age is also associated with wisdom in the lore of many cultures. For example, in Asian cultures age is associated with respect and authority, and the higher the age, the higher the respect and authority the person merits (Chadha, 2004). In many African cultures, an elderly man is called a "big man" and an elderly woman a "big woman," signifying their status and wisdom, not the size of their waistline. Throughout the world, positions of authority that require wisdom are often filled by persons in late adulthood—from tribal leader and shaman to prime minister, CEO, and supreme court justice. In one study that asked adults of various ages to name public figures high in wisdom, most selected older adults, with a median age of 64 (Baltes et al., 1995).

But what *is* wisdom, exactly? Writings about wisdom have existed for many millennia. For several decades, social scientists have been investigating the nature of wisdom and its relation to age, led by German psychologist Paul Baltes (2005). After reviewing conceptions of wisdom across many cultures and many historical epochs, Baltes concluded that **wisdom** can be defined as "expertise in the conduct and meaning of life" (Baltes & Staudinger, 2000, p. 124). Specifically, this may include deep *insight* into human nature and the human condition; *knowledge* of human social relations and emotions; *strategies* for applying this insight and knowledge to everyday problems and life decisions; a concern with promoting the highest human *values*; and an *awareness* that human problems often involve multiple considerations and no easy answer (Staudinger, 2013; Staudinger et al., 2005).

Research using Baltes's model has generally taken the approach of presenting people with hypothetical situations and rating their responses on the dimensions of wisdom just described. The hypothetical situations involve problems such as receiving a phone call from a friend contemplating suicide, or deciding what advice to give a 14-year-old girl who wants to move out of her parents' household. Studies using this approach in research on adults of all ages have found that only a small proportion of responses are classified as "wise," usually less than 10% (Baltes & Staudinger, 2000; Smith & Baltes, 1990; Staudinger & Baltes, 1996; Staudinger et al., 2005). Furthermore, wisdom is generally unrelated to age; emerging adults and young adults are as likely as middle and older adults to be high in wisdom. Wisdom is positively correlated with educational levels, and people who hold leadership positions are more likely than others to score high in wisdom (Kramer, 2003; Staudinger, 2013).

Research with Baltes's model provides a fascinating beginning to investigating the nature of wisdom and its relation to age, but it leaves many questions unanswered. Are responses to hypothetical situations a valid measure of people's wisdom? Also—crucially—is wisdom viewed the same across cultures, or is it culturally variable? Most of the research using Baltes's model has been on German samples. Is German wisdom the same as Chinese wisdom, or Nigerian wisdom, or Peruvian wisdom, or Egyptian wisdom?

A related question is whether the wisdom of elders might be valued differently depending on a culture's rate of social change. That is, the wisdom accumulated by late adulthood may be more valuable in a culture where social change is slow than in a culture where change is rapid. Writing nearly 100 years ago, toward the beginning of a century of remarkable social change in many parts of the world, anthropologist Margaret Mead (1928) observed that when the pace of change is slow, young people learn mostly from older adults and the status of older adults is high; but as the pace of change increases, young people learn more from each other and the status of older adults declines as their knowledge becomes less relevant to contemporary problems. Mead's

wisdom
expertise in the conduct and meaning of life

observations seem prophetic now, in a time when young people who wish to learn how to download music or make a web page are more likely to ask a peer than a grandparent. Does this explain in part why the status of older adults seems to be lower in Western countries than it is in more traditional societies (Degnen, 2007; Ryan et al., 2004)? Or is the wisdom of late adulthood something that should be relevant to human problems that persist across history and across cultures, regardless of the pace of social and technological change? Perhaps research on wisdom will illuminate the answers to these questions in the years to come.

CRITICAL THINKING QUESTION

Would age patterns in wisdom look different if people were interviewed about their own real-life responses to problems rather than with the hypothetical situations used in Baltes's model?

Responding to Cognitive Decline

LO 12.11 Describe the effect of intervention studies on cognitive decline, and explain how older adults adapt to physical and cognitive changes.

As we have seen, some of the decline in cognitive functioning that takes place in late adulthood is due to primary aging, including the shrinking of the brain and the decline in levels of the neurotransmitter acetylcholine. But not only do persons in late adulthood have older brains than younger persons do, the level of their daily cognitive tasks and challenges also is usually different. In developed countries most people have retired from work by the time they reach late adulthood (although there is increasing variability in the timing of retirement, as we will see later in the chapter). This means that they do not receive the daily cognitive stimulation that is part of performing most work tasks.

So, how much of the cognitive changes in late adulthood is due to primary aging, and how much is due to secondary aging—specifically the decline in cognitive stimulation that often accompanies late adulthood? In recent decades several major intervention studies have taken place seeking to stem or reverse cognitive decline in late adulthood, and they show surprising and promising results (Stine-Morrow & Basak, 2011).

Continued learning in late adulthood slows the cognitive decline of primary aging.

LATE-LIFE LEARNING One intervention project was conducted by leading aging researchers Sherry Willis and Warner Schaie and involved participants in the Seattle Longitudinal Study described in Chapter 11. Having longitudinal data was of key importance to the study design, because it enabled researchers to compare participants' current performance on cognitive tasks to their performance years earlier. The participants, all age 65 and older, received five 1-hour training sessions in spatial orientation and reasoning skills. Following this intervention, two-thirds of the participants improved their performance significantly, and 40% matched the level of performance they had shown on the tasks 14 years earlier (Schaie, 2005). Furthermore, when assessed 7 years later, participants in the intervention still out-performed age-mates who had not received the intervention, although scores had declined for both groups.

In another study by Willis, participants ages 65–84 were randomly assigned to an intervention group or a control group, and those in the intervention group received ten 1-hour training sessions to enhance memory skills, reasoning skills, and processing speed (Willis et al., 2006). Intervention participants also received four "booster" sessions at 1 and 3 years after the original intervention sessions. Once again, the results of the intervention were both substantial and durable. Five years after the study began, intervention participants were 75% better at memory tasks, 40% better on reasoning tasks, and 300% better on processing-speed tasks, compared to the control group. This study also examined the effects of the intervention on everyday tasks such as looking up a phone number or preparing a meal, and found that participants in the intervention were more confident in their ability to complete these tasks than control group participants were.

These studies are the most widely known, but numerous other intervention studies on cognitive functioning in late adulthood have shown similar results (Stine-Morrow & Basak, 2011). It seems clear that in the same way regular physical exercise enhances physical functioning and slows primary aging in late adulthood, regular mental exercise enhances mental abilities and slows cognitive decline. Mental exercise could include activities such as crossword puzzles, playing card games, watching educational television, and reading books. The video *Longitudinal Study of Aging Well* provides more on this topic.

Watch   LONGITUDINAL STUDY OF AGING WELL

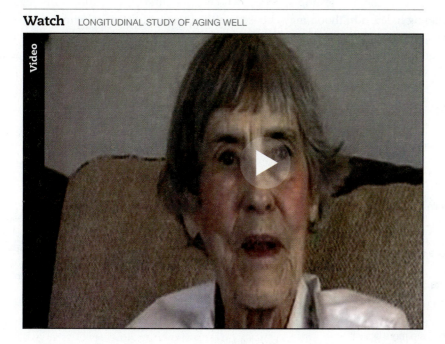

SELECTIVE OPTIMIZATION WITH COMPENSATION Although keeping mentally and physically active slows the aging process, declines eventually take place due to primary aging for both physical and cognitive abilities. How do older adults adapt to these declines, and how can they make the most of their physical and cognitive resources? One influential model has been proposed by Paul Baltes and his colleagues (Baltes, 2003; Baltes & Baltes, 1990; Freund & Baltes, 2002; Hahn & Lachmann, 2014). According to Baltes and colleagues, the most successful adaptation to declining physical and cognitive abilities in late adulthood involves **selective optimization with compensation (SOC).** That is, successful aging involves *selecting* valued activities that can still be done well enough to be enjoyed, and dropping activities that have become too strenuous. By reducing the range of activities in this way, *optimizing* performance in the remaining activities becomes more likely because all the person's energy and attention can be focused

selective optimization with compensation (SOC)

response to aging that entails *selecting* valued activities and dropping others; *optimizing* performance in the remaining activities; and *compensating* for physical and cognitive declines, by developing new strategies or by using technology

on them. Older adults can also find ways of *compensating* for physical and cognitive declines, by developing new strategies or by using technology.

To illustrate the SOC model, Baltes and colleagues described the approach used by renowned pianist Arthur Rubinstein when he performed in late adulthood (Baltes & Baltes, 1990). Asked how he managed to maintain a reputation as one of the world's top concert pianists even into his 70s and 80s, he explained that he had reduced the range of pieces he played in his concerts (selection); he practiced each of the remaining pieces more (optimization); and he had learned to play very slowly just before beginning a fast passage, to make the contrast more effective since he could not play as fast as when he was younger (compensation).

Few older adults face the challenges of performing before large audiences, but the SOC model also applies to the activities of everyday life. A person who has always enjoyed cooking may decide in late adulthood to have fewer elaborate dinner parties because they require so much time and energy and instead focus on making simpler dishes (selection) that can be made well without too many steps (optimization), and perhaps buy materials (such as prepared sauces) that cut the number of steps further (compensation). A person who begins to find reading long historical novels overwhelming in late adulthood may choose to read fewer of them (selection), read fewer pages at a time (optimization), and skip parts that are too detailed (compensation). SOC can also apply to social cognition. For example, people who begin to find large family gatherings overwhelming in late adulthood may choose to attend fewer of them (selection), so that they can enjoy the occasions more (optimization), and they may be sure to get extra rest before a gathering occurs (compensation). The key to successful aging, in the SOC model, is to know your limits and find ways to enjoy life within those limits.

Practice Quiz   ANSWERS AVAILABLE IN ANSWER KEY.

1. Which of the following has been found in research about wisdom?
    a. Wisdom correlates strongly with brain size.
    b. Wisdom is negatively correlated with educational levels.
    c. People who hold leadership positions are more likely to score lower in wisdom.
    d. Wisdom is generally unrelated to age.

2. Which of the following is TRUE regarding research on wisdom?
    a. People who hold leadership positions are more likely than others to score high on measures of wisdom.
    b. There has been no empirical research conducted on wisdom because researchers disagree about how it should be measured.
    c. The construct of wisdom has only been studied in the United States.
    d. Wisdom increases as people get older, but it increases more for men than for women.

3. Which of the following did Baltes define as "expertise in the conduct and meaning of life"?
    a. Enlightenment
    b. Dialectical thinking
    c. Post-formal thinking
    d. Wisdom

4. When renowned pianist Arthur Rubinstein was asked how he managed to maintain a reputation as one of the world's top concert pianists well into late adulthood, he explained that he had reduced the range of pieces he played, practiced each of the remaining pieces more, and learned to play very slowly just before beginning a fast passage, to make the contrast more effective since he could not play as fast as when he was younger. Arthur Rubinstein's behaviors are an illustration of
    _____.
    a. improved procedural memory with age
    b. selective optimization with compensation
    c. habituation
    d. dishabituation

5. Interventions to determine whether cognitive decline can be prevented or even reversed _____.
    a. have only been conducted with cross-sectional studies
    b. found that only men show significant improvement
    c. found that only men and women from Asian American backgrounds show improvement
    d. resulted in significant improvement for a substantial proportion of individuals

Summary: Cognitive Development

LO 12.8 **Describe how attention and memory change during late adulthood.**

Several different types of attention decline in late adulthood, including selective, divided, and sustained attention. Memory declines vary based on the type of memory involved. There is relatively little decline in procedural memory and semantic memory, but declines are steeper in working memory, long-term memory, episodic memory, and source memory.

LO 12.9 **Explain how the brain changes during late adulthood, and identify the symptoms and risk factors for Alzheimer's disease.**

In late adulthood the brain actually shrinks and total brain mass declines. Declines also take place in certain neurotransmitters, such as acetylcholine and dopamine. The earliest symptom of Alzheimer's disease is a loss of memory for recent events and familiar names and tasks. Personality is often negatively affected, along with the ability to control bodily functions. A specific gene known as the *ApoE* gene indicates risk for Alzheimer's disease, but not everyone with the gene develops the disease. Diets high in fats and sugars increase the risk of developing the disease, and maintaining a high level of cognitive activity appears to be a protective factor against it.

LO 12.10 **Define wisdom, and summarize research on the impact of age and culture on wisdom.**

Wisdom is defined by Baltes as "expertise in the conduct and meaning of life," and wisdom research has focused on rating responses to hypothetical questions. Research on responses to hypothetical situations has found that wisdom is as likely to be found among the young as among the old. Wisdom accumulated by late adulthood may be more valuable in a culture where social change is slow than in a culture where change is rapid, because if it is slow, the life experiences of elders may be more relevant to the current experiences of people of younger ages.

LO 12.11 **Describe the effect of intervention studies on cognitive decline, and explain how older adults adapt to physical and cognitive changes.**

Intervention studies show that regular mental exercise enhances mental abilities and slows the cognitive decline that takes place with primary aging. This could include activities such as crossword puzzles, playing card games, watching educational television, and reading books. The most successful adaptation to declining physical and cognitive abilities in late adulthood involves selective optimization with compensation (SOC).

Section **3** Emotional and Social Development

⌄	# Learning Objectives

12.12 Explain why late adulthood is a time of positive emotions and high self-esteem.

12.13 Distinguish between Erikson's theory and Carstensen's socioemotional selectivity theory of late adulthood.

12.14 Describe how relations with children, grandchildren, and great-grandchildren change during late adulthood.

12.15 Compare cultural differences in living situations during late adulthood.

12.16 Explain how romantic relationships and sexuality change during late adulthood.

12.17 Describe variations in retirement, and identify the impact of retirement on older adults.

12.18 Describe how leisure activities, community involvement, religious involvement, and media use change in late adulthood.

EMOTIONAL AND SOCIAL DEVELOPMENT: Emotional and Self-Development

So far in this chapter we have seen that late adulthood is a time of challenges and difficulties for many people. For nearly everyone, physical functioning declines in the course of late adulthood, and chronic physical ailments increase. For many people, cognitive functioning declines as well, especially for people who do not receive much in the way of cognitive stimulation in the course of their daily lives.

You might expect, then, that emotional and self-development would follow physical and cognitive development downward in the course of late adulthood. Difficulties in physical and cognitive functioning surely make it harder to be happy and more likely that people will feel low. However, despite these challenges, numerous studies indicate that late adulthood is a time of exceptionally favorable emotional and self-development.

Positive Emotions and Self-Concept

LO 12.12 **Explain why late adulthood is a time of positive emotions and high self-esteem.**

Far from being a time when despondency is common, late adulthood is more often a time of contentment and peace. For example, one study of over 2,700 Americans age 25–74 assessed their emotional status over the past 30 days with regard to six positive and six negative indicators (Mroczek, 2001; Mroczek & Kolarz, 1998). The indicators of positive affect included "cheerful, "calm and peaceful," and "in good spirits." Negative affect indicators included "nervous," "hopeless," and "worthless." For each item, participants indicated how often they had felt that way in the past 30 days using ratings from 1 (none of the time) to 5 (all of the time). Ratings were then converted into a total affect score, which ranged from 6 to 30. Positive emotions were stable from emerging adulthood through middle adulthood and then increased sharply in late adulthood, while negative emotions declined steadily across the age range.

Other studies have shown similar results. A large study of Americans from their 20s through their 80s using the Experience Sampling Method (see Chapter 8), in which people record their emotions when beeped at random times during the day, found that reports of positive emotional states increased steadily with age, through the 80s (Carstensen et al., 2011). An analysis combining results from numerous studies around the world involving a total of over 300,000 people, using a simple one-item measure of self-esteem, found a rise in self-esteem from the 40s through the 70s, followed by a sharp decline in the 80s (Robins et al., 2002).

Studies of self-development across adulthood indicate that older adults tend to be more accepting of their past and present selves than young adults or middle adults are, whereas young and middle adults tend to be more optimistic about their future selves (Ryff, 1991). Nevertheless, a longitudinal German study of people from age 70 to 103 found that over a 4-year period, most of the participants continued to imagine possible selves and to plan on achieving their goals for self-development, especially with regard to the quality of their health and their social relationships (Smith & Freund, 2002).

Not only are positive emotions and self-evaluations more common in late adulthood than at earlier ages, but depressive symptoms are lower, including periods of enduring sadness, guilt, and suicidal thoughts (Amore et al., 2007). One national American study of adults age 18 and over found that adults over age 55 were less likely than any younger age group to report symptoms that fit the diagnosis of major depressive disorder (Office of Applied Studies, 2006). For both self-esteem and depressive symptoms, studies have consistently found that the gender differences that exist in earlier development—girls and women lower in self-esteem and higher in depression than boys and men—diminish or disappear by late adulthood (Barefoot et al., 2001; Robins et al., 2002).

Late adulthood is often a time of high emotional well-being.

Theories on Emotions in Late Adulthood

LO 12.13   **Distinguish between Erikson's theory and Carstensen's socioemotional selectivity theory of late adulthood.**

Why is emotional and self-development so favorable in late adulthood? Two major theories on late adulthood address this issue. Erik Erikson's theory proposes that late adulthood is a time to reflect on one's life, and socioemotional selectivity theory proposes that satisfaction with life depends on limiting one's emotional and social contacts to those that are enjoyed the most.

ERIKSON'S THEORY Erik Erikson, in his theory of the life span, proposed that late adulthood is when the central challenge is **ego integrity versus despair** (Erikson, 1950). Ego integrity means looking back on one's life and accepting the outcome of it—including the choices that turned out well along with the mistakes and disappointments—and concluding that overall it was a life well lived. In contrast, despair in late adulthood entails regrets about the course of one's life, and the bitter conclusion that it has not gone well and now cannot be changed.

In a classic study, Bernice Neugarten (1972, 1977) interviewed Americans in late adulthood and found a variety of different paths of self-development, but the most common

ego integrity versus despair in Erikson's life span theory, the central crisis of late adulthood, with alternatives of ego integrity, which means looking back on one's life and accepting it for better and worse, or despair, which entails regrets and bitterness about the course of one's life

was what she termed the *integrated personality*, the person who accepts becoming older and looks at the past, present, and future with contentment. This sounds close to Erikson's idea of ego integrity, and the high prevalence of the integrated personality in Neugarten's research, along with the many studies finding high well-being in this life stage, suggests that ego integrity may be a common outcome of self-development in late adulthood.

Of course, not all people achieve such a state of peace and contentment in late adulthood, as Neugarten and others have found. The physical and cognitive problems that become more common in the course of late adulthood often contribute to lower emotional states and lower self-esteem (Hybels & Blazer, 2004). People who experience hearing or visual problems in late adulthood are also more likely to report depressive symptoms (Lupsakko et al., 2002). Arthritis is an additional risk factor for depression (Oslin et al., 2002). When physical disabilities are severe enough to make self-care tasks difficult or impossible (such as dressing or preparing a meal), self-esteem declines and the risk of depression rises (Yang, 2006). Rates of depression are twice as high among older adults who live in nursing homes or other long-term care settings (Sneed et al., 2006). Depressive symptoms can also be side effects of medications older adults take to cope with physical problems (Delano-Wood & Abeles, 2005).

Cognitively, depression is high in the early stages of dementia, as older adults realize the worsening and incurable nature of their condition (Chodosh et al., 2007; Hybels & Blazer, 2004). Caring for an ailing spouse also increases the risk of depression in older adults (Fultz et al., 2005). The death of a spouse is most commonly experienced in late adulthood, and this, too, makes depression more likely (Bruce, 2002). Given all these risk factors for depression in late adulthood, it is all the more remarkable that late adulthood is, for most, a time of high emotional well-being and low rates of depression.

SOCIOEMOTIONAL SELECTIVITY THEORY An alternative theory of emotional development has been proposed more recently, by Laura Carstensen (Carstensen, 1995; Carstensen, 1998; Carstensen et al., 2003; Carstensen et al., 2011). According to Carstensen's **socioemotional selectivity theory**, older adults maximize their emotional well-being by becoming increasingly selective in their social contacts. As we have seen in previous chapters, emerging, young, and middle adulthood are all life stages when people have many social connections. Emerging adults have elaborate friendship networks, close ties to family, and additional ties to romantic partners, coworkers, fellow students, and perhaps roommates; young adults usually have a spouse and children as well as community ties and relationships with neighbors and coworkers; and midlife adults have all the ties young adults have and perhaps grandchildren as well. However, by late adulthood children have long moved on to make their own lives, coworkers are no longer present after retirement, and community involvement gradually declines.

Consequently, from the late 60s onward the number of social partners steadily declines, especially for relationships that are not close (Lang et al., 1998). Rather than having a wide variety of social contacts, older adults prefer to withdraw from relationships that are not emotionally rewarding and focus on the relationships that mean the most to them.

According to Carstensen and her colleagues (2011), one key reason for increasing socioemotional selectivity in late adulthood is that there are changes in the goals people have for their relationships (see **Figure 12.4**). At younger ages, the goals that people have for their social relationships are often *knowledge-based*. You have relationships with your employer and coworkers because you work on projects together that all of you want to accomplish successfully. You have relationships with neighbors because

socioemotional selectivity theory

Carstensen's theory that older adults maximize their emotional well-being by becoming increasingly selective in their social contacts

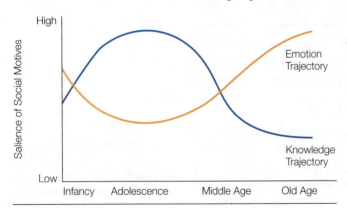

Figure 12.4 Changes in Relationship Goals with Age

Older adults pursue emotional goals rather than knowledge goals in their relationships.

SOURCE: Carstensen et al. (1999)

you provide each other with information about the quality of local schools and where to get the best price on a used car. However, in late adulthood these goals fade in importance as people leave the workplace and no longer have daily responsibilities as coworkers and parents. Instead, relationship goals become more *emotion-based*. Older adults seek to maintain and develop relationships that are low in conflict and high in mutual enjoyment, and drop the rest. For most of them, it works: Although they have smaller social networks than adults in earlier life stages, their relationships are higher in happiness and lower in conflict (Fingerman & Birditt, 2003).

Practice Quiz   ANSWERS AVAILABLE IN ANSWER KEY.

1. _____ are more common in late adulthood than at earlier ages.
   a. Sex differences in gender roles
   b. Sex differences in self-esteem
   c. Positive emotions
   d. Negative emotions

2. Perry grew up in a small town and has gone to every high school reunion, despite moving across the country. Based on the research, at which reunion would he be the least self-conscious and more accepting of his past and present selves?
   a. His 5th year reunion
   b. His 10th year reunion
   c. His 30th year reunion
   d. His 50th year reunion

3. Drawing upon research conducted in the United States, which of the following individuals is LEAST likely to report symptoms of major depressive disorder?
   a. Carmen, a 14-year-old
   b. Roberta, a 23-year-old
   c. Maren, a 48-year-old
   d. Charlotte, a 68-year-old

4. According to socioemotional selectivity theory _____.
   a. people experience more negative emotions as they get older
   b. shrinking social networks in adulthood are by choice
   c. the elderly tend to withdraw from society due to increased rates of depression in late adulthood
   d. the older we get, the more important it becomes to acquire knowledge and become less emotional

5. Older adults maximize their emotional well-being by becoming increasingly selective in their _____.
   a. career choices
   b. choice of cognitive activities
   c. physical activities
   d. social contacts

EMOTIONAL AND SOCIAL DEVELOPMENT: The Social and Cultural Contexts of Late Adulthood

Family relationships remain central to social life in late adulthood across cultures, and most people have grandchildren during this life stage and perhaps even great-grandchildren. In married couples rates of divorce are very low in late adulthood but becoming widowed is common, and for many people there is a late-life remarriage. Some older adults continue to work through their 60s and even into their 70s and 80s, although for most people in developed countries, late adulthood is a time mainly of retirement and leisure. In some cultures religious participation rises substantially, and in most cultures television use is more prevalent during late adulthood than in any previous life stage.

Family Relationships

LO 12.14 **Describe how relations with children, grandchildren, and great-grandchildren change during late adulthood.**

Relationships with children often shift in late adulthood, as parents gradually go from caring for to being cared for, and from supporting to being supported. Most older adults have grandchildren, and these relationships tend to be a source of uncomplicated joy and mutual affection. For older adults who live long enough, there may be great-grandchildren as well, but these relationships are usually not as close as relationships with grandchildren.

RELATIONS WITH ADULT CHILDREN In late adulthood few people have parents who are still living, but most continue to have close relationships with their children. In most of the world, parents and at least some of their children continue to live in the same household through adult life. In contrast, the dominant tradition in Western cultures is that parents and children live in separate households once children reach adulthood. However, even in Western cultures contact with children continues to be frequent through late adulthood. In a national American study, 58% of older adults reported seeing at least one child several times a week (Ward, 2008). In European countries, older adults' contact with children is even more frequent, as family members move less often and tend to live closer to one another than in the United States, especially in southern Europe. In one study that compared contact with elderly parents in four European countries, contact was more frequent in Italy than in three northern European countries (Tomassini et al., 2004). The video *Successful Aging: Extended Family: Maria, Age 68* highlights an older adult from Italy living with her daughter's American family.

Watch   SUCCESSFUL AGING: EXTENDED FAMILY: MARIA, AGE 68

In most parts of the world, there are cultural beliefs that parents are obligated to provide for their children while the children are growing up, but in the course of adulthood the balance of obligation gradually shifts. By late adulthood, the direction of the obligation has reversed and children take care of their parents. In many Asian cultures, as we have seen in earlier chapters, the cultural belief in *filial piety* is central to structuring family relations. Children have a strong obligation to respect and obey the authority of their parents. When parents reach late adulthood, filial piety requires children to care for their parents and provide for them, just as their parents cared for them and provided for them when they were young (Zhan et al., 2008; Zhong & Arnett, 2014). This includes having the parents live in the household of one of their children. Most African and Latin American cultures, too, place a high value on adult children caring for their elderly parents as parents cared for them when they were young (Flores et al., 2009).

In the West, too, there is something of a role reversal between parents and children when the parents reach late adulthood, but with variations depending on the type of assistance provided. According to a national study in the United States, parents in late adulthood reported that their children provided mainly emotional support, but one third had also received assistance with daily tasks within the past month (Shapiro, 2004). In contrast, financial assistance is provided mainly from parents to children, even in late adulthood (Van Gaalen & Dykstra, 2006).

Parents in the United States and other Western countries generally seek to minimize their requests to children even as they need more help in the course of late adulthood, because they do not wish to be dependent on their children or a burden to them (Spitze & Gallant, 2004). When children urge parents to accept help the parents do not need or want, the parents often feel resentful and diminished (Liang et al., 2001). However, as parents reach their 80s and beyond, they often need increasing assistance from their children due to health issues, requiring both sides to adapt to a new balance of dependency in their relationship (Ron, 2000). This is especially likely after one of the parents dies and the one who remains no longer has a spouse to provide mutual assistance (Silverstein et al., 2006).

Many cultures have a belief that adult children should take care of their elderly parents. Here, a Chinese woman cooks a meal for her mother.

There are some notable gender differences between the West and the East in the care of elderly parents. In Eastern countries such as China, Japan, and India, the tradition is that older parents live with the eldest son, who provides for them financially while his wife provides for their other needs. In contrast, research in Western countries indicates consistently that daughters are more likely than sons to provide care for elderly parents (An & Cooney, 2006). However, in China, there is evidence that daughters are becoming the main source of support to their older parents, perhaps indicating a cultural change away from the traditional pattern (Chou, 2011; Ji-liang et al., 2003). This is due in part to China's one-child policy of recent decades, which has resulted in many families that have a daughter as their only child.

RELATIONS WITH GRANDCHILDREN AND GREAT-GRANDCHILDREN Most people become grandparents for the first time in middle adulthood, but in late adulthood relations with grandchildren may change as the children grow into adolescence and emerging and young adulthood. In developed countries, about half of adults over age 65 have at least one grandchild who is at least 18 years old (AARP, 2002). Older adults generally report their ties with adult grandchildren to be highly positive (Scharf, 2015).

Although they often see each other less over time, as the grandchildren become busy with the tasks of adult life, feelings of closeness and affection established earlier remain strong for most. Now that the grandchildren are older, grandparents tell them more about family history, traditions, and customs (Wiscott & Kopera-Frye, 2000). Gender differences established earlier endure, with most grandchildren feeling closer to their grandmothers (especially on the mother's side) than to their grandfathers (Chan & Elder, 2000; Lavers-Preston et al., 2003). Sometimes a relationship with one particular grandchild becomes especially important, due to more frequent contact or to similarities of interests or personalities (Fingerman, 1998).

As they reach their 70s and 80s and beyond, older adults may become great-grandparents. Within the United States, African Americans are more likely than people in other ethnic groups to have great-grandchildren, because they tend to have their children at younger ages (Baird et al., 2000). Relations with great-grandchildren tend to be less close than with grandchildren, and contact is less frequent (Roberto & Skoglund, 1996). Nevertheless, most older adults regard the arrival of great-grandchildren favorably as a sign of the endurance of the family into another generation, and they tend to serve as a source of family history for the great-grandchildren as they did for their grandchildren (Harris, 2002).

Living Arrangements in Late Adulthood

LO 12.15 **Compare cultural differences in living situations during late adulthood.**

Where do older adults typically live and how do their living arrangements influence their quality of life? As noted earlier in the chapter, a century ago, before government pension and health care programs, the elderly were the poorest segment of the population and had no choice in late adulthood except to live with their children or other relatives because they generally could not afford to live on their own (Pew Social Trends Staff, 2010). In developed countries, due to the social welfare programs instituted in the course of the 20th century, persons over age 65 are now the most affluent segment of the population, so they usually are not forced to live with their children out of economic necessity.

In Western countries, most people in late adulthood would prefer to live independently rather than with their children (Beswick et al., 2008). However, living independently becomes increasingly difficult during the 80s and beyond, if health problems accumulate. Generally, if older adults cannot live on their own they would prefer to live with one of their children. In one European study of older adults and their children in 10 countries, about 30% of adults age 60 and over lived with an adult child and an additional 50% lived within 25 kilometers of a child (Hank, 2011). However, there were substantial differences between northern and southern Europe, a pattern we have seen repeatedly in the course of this book. In the countries of northern Europe (Denmark, Netherlands, Sweden), only about 5% of older adults lived with a child, although an additional 70% lived within 25 kilometers of a child. In contrast, coresidence of older adults and adult children was common in southern European countries (Greece, Italy, Spain), at a rate of about 45%, and an additional 45% of older adults lived within 25 kilometers of a child.

Some older adults who cannot live on their own receive institutional care.

If older adults can neither live on their own nor with a child, there is a variety of other possible living arrangements. In the West, many different kinds of living facilities for older adults have sprung up in the past half century as life expectancies have increased. *Assisted living* facilities have separate apartments for each person, but residents are provided with meals in a common dining area, housekeeping services, transportation for shopping and medical appointments, and social activities. *Nursing homes* provide all of these services as well as extensive medical care, and most residents are afflicted with dementia or other serious health problems (Aguero-Torres et al., 2001). Rates of institutional care in assisted living, nursing homes, or similar facilities are higher in the United States, Canada, and northern Europe than in the rest of the world. There are also differences within countries, as older adults who are members of minorities with Asian, Latino, or African cultural backgrounds are less likely to be in institutional care (Yaffe et al., 2002).

Institutional care is expensive, and the elderly proportion of the population is increasing steadily in every developed country as life expectancies increase, so many countries have instituted programs to provide services to older adults in their homes in order to allow them to live independently longer. These services may include hot meals, laundry, and cleaning, as well as health services such as physical therapy (Tinetti et al., 2002). In Denmark, a program to provide home services and an assisted living option to older adults resulted in a 30% decline in nursing home placements over 15 years (Stuart & Weinrich, 2001).

For older adults who do enter nursing homes, the quality of their lives varies widely depending on the quality of care they receive. One key ingredient is the amount of personal control they have over their daily lives (Logsdon, 2000). In a classic study, researchers randomly assigned nursing home residents into two groups, with one group allowed to make decisions about their daily activities while the other group was given no choices and encouraged to let the nursing home staff take care of them (Langer & Rodin, 1979). Eighteen months later, the results were unambiguous: 30% of the low-choice group had died, compared to only 15% of the high-choice group.

In Asian countries, there are few nursing homes or assisted living facilities for older adults. Traditionally, to have a parent live in such a place, cared for by strangers, would be a serious violation of filial piety, and Asians regard it as something shameful to be avoided if possible (Ng et al., 2002). In a study comparing living arrangements of older adults in 43 countries, rates of living with children were highest in Asia (Bongaarts & Zimmer, 2002).

However, this pattern may be shifting as Asian societies change. According to one study, institutional arrangements in late adulthood are growing more common in China because parents often have only one child and that child may have migrated to an urban area a long distance from the parents (Silverstein et al., 2006). Growing individualism may also be eroding the filial piety that obligates adult children to take care of elderly parents (Ng et al., 2002). In recent years, the government of China has developed a formal Family Support Agreement (FSA)—a voluntary but legal contract in which adult children pledge to support their parents—and, according to a large national study, about 6% of elders and their children have signed one (Chou, 2011). The FSA would not be necessary if the tradition of filial piety were not beginning to wane. Nevertheless, in most Chinese families older adults still either live with an adult child or receive children's frequent assistance with the tasks of daily living (Sereny, 2011; Zhang & Wang, 2010; Zhao & Qian, 2008). Furthermore, most adult children contribute financial support to their parents—a reversal of the Western pattern—in part because China does not have an old-age pension system as Western countries do (Silverstein et al., 2006; Sun, 2002).

Love and Sexuality

LO 12.16 **Explain how romantic relationships and sexuality change during late adulthood.**

Will and Ariel Durant married in 1913, when he was 28 years old and she was just 15; she had been a student at a school where he taught history. In the course of nearly 70 years together they raised two children, a boy and a girl, and worked side by side, principally on a grand 11-volume work entitled *The Story of Civilization* that encompassed 2,500 years of Western history. It became the most popular work of history ever written. After 66 years of marriage they died within 2 weeks of each other in 1981, when he was 96 and she was 83.

Theirs was a great love story, and a rare one. For most older adults, love takes a bumpier path in late adulthood, and many of them, especially women, spend the final years of their life without a partner.

MARRIAGE, WIDOWHOOD, AND REMARRIAGE In most cultures, marriage has typically been considered a life-long bond, "'til death do us part," but as we have seen in previous chapters, until recent decades death parted most couples long before late adulthood, because relatively few people lived past the age of 60 or 65. It is only in the past century, with advances in medical care and increases in life expectancy, that many marriages have endured into late adulthood.

In general, marital satisfaction increases from middle adulthood to late adulthood and reaches its highest point of the entire life span (Cherlin, 2009; Jose & Alfons, 2007). There are several reasons for this pattern. First, the most troubled marriages have ended in divorce (in cultures that allow divorce) long before late adulthood, and it is mostly the stronger, happier marriages that remain. Even in high-divorce countries like the United States and Canada, only about 1% of divorces take place after age 65 (Kreider, 2005). Second, older couples tend to have fewer major daily responsibilities that cause stress and inspire conflict between marital partners, such as caring for young children and working in demanding jobs (Kemp & Kemp, 2002). Third, because most people have retired or cut back on work by late adulthood, older couples have more time to enjoy joint leisure activities that strengthen the marital bond (Henry et al., 2005). Fourth, older couples are more likely to solve their disagreements calmly, without becoming angry (Hatch & Bulcroft, 2004). This is consistent with the growth in emotional maturity discussed earlier.

Few couples have the timing of Will and Ariel Durant to die nearly in the same breath, so the longer people survive into late adulthood, the more likely they are to experience widowhood. Because women have longer life expectancies all over the world and tend to marry men who are older than they are (by about 2 years on average, worldwide), they are more likely to become widows than men are to become widowers. Across developed countries, about half of women over age 65 are widows, but only 15% of men over 65 are widowers; past age 85 about 80% of women are widows and only about one third of men are widowers (OECD, 2009).

Losing a spouse is a painful and difficult transition for most (Lund & Caserta, 2004). By late adulthood a marriage may have lasted 30, 40, or even 50 years or more, and it is jarring and disorienting to face the absence of the person who had been a close companion through so much of life. Social life changes, not only because the spouse is no longer there as a companion but because socializing with other married couples may now seem awkward (van den Hoonard, 1994). Whatever daily tasks the deceased spouse had been responsible for must now be taken on by the remaining spouse (Hanson & Hayslip, 2000).

Grief in the aftermath of the spouse's death may endure as depressive symptoms that last for years afterward (Galatzer-Levy & Bonanno, 2012). For several years after the death of a spouse the risk of death is higher for the remaining spouse than for peers because the emotional trauma of the loss has effects on physical functioning (Manzoli et al., 2007). Men take the loss of a spouse especially hard. They are more likely than women to become depressed after a spouse dies, and they take more years to recover to previous levels of mental health, especially if they do not remarry (Galatzer-Levy & Bonanno, 2012). They have fewer friends than women do and fewer close family relations, so they have less social support to rely on when their spouse dies (Bennett et al., 2005). The risk of death after the loss of a spouse is greater for men than for women (Stimpson et al., 2007).

Loneliness is common in the years following the death of a spouse, even after depression fades (Lund & Caserta, 2004). One way many widows and widowers cope with their loneliness is to continue to have "conversations" with their deceased spouse. In one study, more than half of older adults who had lost a spouse within the past 5 years said they talked to their spouse at least several times a month (Carnelly et al., 2006). Even those who had lost their spouses 35 years ago continued to talk to them occasionally. But even as they continue to remember the loved one they lost, most widows and widowers move on within a few years after their loss, by seeking to maintain and strengthen their remaining social relationships with friends and family (Utz et al., 2002).

One way they may move on is by remarrying. However, rates of remarriage in late adulthood are relatively low, in part because the gender disparity is so great. Because there are so many more widows than widowers, men are

Marital satisfaction is highest of all in late adulthood.

far more likely than women to remarry in late adulthood (Bookwala, 2012). Remarriages tend to be more successful in late adulthood than at earlier life stages, in terms of lower likelihood of divorce and higher marital satisfaction (Moorman et al., 2006). However, many couples in late adulthood choose to cohabit or maintain a long-term relationship rather than marrying, because of potentially negative financial consequences or resistance from children, or simply because they prefer their independence (King & Scott, 2005). In the video *Falling in Love Again,* an older adult couple discuss their relationship.

Watch   FALLING IN LOVE AGAIN

SEXUALITY IN LATE ADULTHOOD In late adulthood as in middle adulthood, there are wide cultural variations in views of the acceptability and appropriateness of sexual activity. One analysis of 106 tribal cultures found that sex in old age was expected in most and was common among those who still had a marriage partner (Winn & Newton, 1982). In contrast, as we saw in Chapter 11, India and some East Asian cultures view sexual activity in middle and late adulthood as inappropriate and spiritually contaminating. In the modern West there is a pervasive stereotype that old people have little sexual desire and that sex between old people is disgusting or laughable (Hillman, 2000). However, there is no strong cultural ban on sex in late adulthood, and many older adults continue to be sexually active.

Sexual activity in late adulthood depends not only on the availability of a partner but on physical health (Gott & Hinchliff, 2003). As noted earlier in the chapter, physical ailments and disabilities become more common in the course of late adulthood, and rates of sexual activity are much lower among those who rate their health as poor (Bancroft, 2007).

There are also physical changes specific to sexuality in late adulthood. In women, the decline in vaginal lubrication that began in middle adulthood continues into late adulthood, making intercourse more painful and less pleasurable (National Institute on Aging [NIA], 2008). In men, testosterone levels decline by about one third from the 40s to the 70s, and one consequence is that erections take longer to achieve and are more difficult to maintain. In a national American survey of men ages 57–85, 90% of men reported occasional erectile problems and about one third reported chronic erectile dysfunction (Lindau et al., 2007). Lubricants are available for women, and highly effective medications for erectile dysfunction have been developed for men (see Chapter 11; Hooyman & Kiyak, 2011).

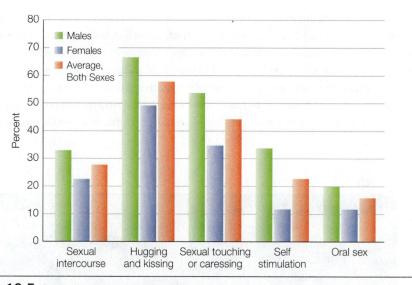

Figure 12.5 Sexuality in Middle and Late Adulthood

In American society, many adults age 45 and over take part in a variety of sexual activities. This figure shows the percentage of adults engaging in sexual activities once a week or more often within the past 6 months.
SOURCE: Based on AARP (2009)

It is important to remember that there is more to sexuality than sexual intercourse. In a national American study of sexuality in middle and late adulthood (persons age 45 and over), participants were polled on how often they engaged in various sexual activities within the past 6 months. Rates of kissing, hugging, and sexual touching or caressing were higher than rates of intercourse, as **Figure 12.5** shows (AARP, 2009). Although sexual desire often declines in late adulthood, the desire persists in the majority of persons over age 65 in American national surveys (Lindau et al., 2007).

CRITICAL THINKING QUESTION

If a person in late adulthood reports a loss of sexual desire to a physician, should it be viewed as a disorder in need of treatment or simply as a normal part of aging? Would the answer depend on the person's culture, or not?

Work and Retirement

LO 12.17 Describe variations in retirement, and identify the impact of retirement on older adults.

For nearly all of human history, people have worked until they could simply work no longer. As we have seen, life expectancy was relatively low, and few people lived into what we now call "late adulthood." Those who did live into their 60s and 70s and beyond had to keep working to survive, or they had to depend on children or other relatives who would provide for them once they could no longer provide for themselves.

In the early 20th century, developed countries began to establish national pension programs—first the Western European countries, in the first 2 decades of the 20th century, then Canada in 1927 and the United States in 1935. In the course of the 20th century, additional programs for the elderly were added to the welfare states in developed countries, most notably health care programs. At the same time, life expectancy steadily increased.

By the early 21st century, most people in developed countries experienced a period of retirement of at least a decade, during which they were no longer employed and supported themselves through a combination of national pension programs, employer pension programs, and their personal savings and investments.

Today the median retirement age is 60–63 across developed countries, and life expectancies range from the mid-70s to the mid-80s. However, there is also considerable variation among developed countries in the percentage of people who work past age 65, from 2% in France and 6% in Germany to 13% in Canada, 19% in the United States, and 21% in Japan (OECD, 2014). As populations age, these percentages may rise along with the retirement age. In several developed countries, including the United States, the age at which a person can receive a government retirement pension (Social Security in the United States) has been raised to 67, and the pressure to increase it further will intensify as new medical interventions allow people to live still longer than they do now.

THE DECISION TO RETIRE The decision about precisely when to retire is based on a variety of factors, especially financial considerations, physical health, and job satisfaction (or lack of it) (Rix, 2008). Once they retire, financial security and physical health are also major determinants of how well people adjust (Whitbourne & Whitbourne, 2010). Not surprisingly, people enjoy retirement more if they feel they have ample money to live on and if their physical health is good. Retirement satisfaction tends to be especially high for well-educated people who had held high-status jobs, not only because they have greater financial resources but because they are generally more successful than others at finding stimulating, enjoyable retirement activities (Kim & Moen, 2002; Szinovacz & Davey, 2004). For couples, retirement is one of the reasons marital satisfaction tends to be high in late adulthood, because they have less stress in their lives and more time to enjoy leisure activities together (Smith & Moen, 2004).

Cultural Focus: Work and Retirement Across Cultures

Even as recently as a century ago, retirement was rare. About three-fourths of men age 65 and over in developed countries were still employed. In the United States, for example, the average "retirement age" was 74—but of course hardly anyone lived long enough to experience it (Hooyman & Kiyak, 2011). Only the very wealthy could afford to stop working once they reached old age.

Today, retirement is typical in developed countries beginning in the early 60s. However, retirement remains rare in developing countries, and never occurs for most people. In this video, older adults from various countries are interviewed about their work lives in late adulthood.

Watch WORK AND RETIREMENT ACROSS CULTURES

Review Question:

How do people in these different countries adapt their work lives to accommodate the fact that they are growing older?

Although most older adults welcome retirement and adjust well to it, about one fourth have adjustment problems of one kind or another (Prisuta, 2004). Older adults who were forced into retirement due to their company shrinking or closing are less happy with retirement than those who retired because they wanted to (Warr et al., 2004). People who choose to retire typically experience improvements in their physical and mental health following the transition, whereas people who retired involuntarily tend to decline (Rix, 2008).

WORKING PART TIME Increasingly, retirement is not a single event where a person goes from working full time to not working at all, but rather a years-long process of gradually reducing work hours or moving from full-time work to a series of part-time jobs, punctuated by periods of not working. Many people now pass through a period of semi-retirement in late adulthood in which they have a "bridge job," that is, they reduce their work hours but remain in the labor force, or they take another job that is less demanding and involves fewer hours per week (Hardy, 2006). About 60% of Americans take a bridge job prior to full retirement, compared to just 14% of Europeans (Brunello & Langella, 2013). This is consistent with research at other life stages showing that Americans work more hours than Europeans do and take fewer vacations. Most older Americans say they would prefer to enter retirement gradually, through bridge jobs that do not require full-time hours (Harvard/MetLife, 2004).

Money is an obvious reason for working beyond the traditional "retirement age," but for most older adults it is not the main reason. In one national American survey, only 33% of workers age 55 and older said the only reason they continued to work was for the money (AARP, 2006). The main benefits of continuing to work, according to older adults, are that it allows them to remain active, socialize, and learn new things (Calvo, 2006; Holden, 2008).

What are the benefits of continuing to work in late adulthood?

Women are especially likely to see working in late adulthood as a way to promote further career development and personal growth, perhaps because they were more likely than men to have spent years out of the labor force in young adulthood while they were caring for young children (Piktialis, 2008).

Although there are many benefits to working in late adulthood, there are notable barriers and problems as well. Stereotypes about late adulthood often make employers reluctant to hire older workers, because of the assumption that they will be less productive and less mentally acute than younger workers (Hooyman & Kiyak, 2011). Potential employers also have legitimate concerns that compared to younger workers, older workers may need more training in new technology, incur higher health care costs, and are not likely to remain in the labor force as long (Hardy, 2006). In part due to these barriers, older adults are more likely than younger adults to be self-employed (Wan et al., 2005).

Life Outside Work and Home: Leisure, Community, Religion, and Media Use

LO 12.18 Describe how leisure activities, community involvement, religious involvement, and media use change in late adulthood.

After retirement, older adults have more time for leisure such as travel. Many devote some of their time to community activities and religious involvement. On a daily basis, the most time of all in late adulthood is devoted to media use, mainly television.

LEISURE ACTIVITIES As the amount of time spent working declines in late adulthood, people have a lot more time to devote to leisure activities. Sometimes people take up activities they have never done before, such as painting. However, more often their leisure activities in late adulthood are a continuation of things they had enjoyed earlier in life and now have more time for. The person who had always enjoyed golf now has a chance to play three times a week instead of one; the person who had always enjoyed gardening now spends time on it almost every day in the warmer months instead of fitting it in occasionally among a whirl of other daily obligations.

Because older people have a longer average retirement period than ever before, and because as a group they now have more money than ever before, a vast industry has sprung up over the past half century to provide them with leisure opportunities (Moody, 2004-05). Many colleges and universities have developed courses specifically for older adults, where they can learn everything from culinary skills to foreign languages (Manheimer, 2008).

Travel is one common form of leisure among older adults. In the United States, a popular program called *Exploritas* combines older adults' desire to learn with their desire to travel. Exploritas sponsors "learning adventures" throughout the world, in which older adults travel to an attractive location and enjoy the sights while also spending time on a college campus learning more about the sights they are seeing. Some examples of Exploritas adventures are studying architecture in London, seals in Antarctica, monkeys in Belize, or ancient art in Greece. The programs are offered in 90 countries and have involved 1,500 academic institutions (Elderhostel, 2007). Recently Exploritas has begun offering more physically challenging programs, involving activities such as hiking, to attract more early retirees and young-old participants.

Cognitively-challenging leisure activities such as Exploritas programs have a variety of benefits for older adults' physical, cognitive, and social functioning (Cohen, 2005). However, not all older adults have the money or the inclination to engage in such challenging and strenuous leisure activities. Most of older adults' leisure time is spent on activities that are far less demanding, such as watching television, reading, and visiting family and friends (Hooyman & Kiyak, 2011). Older adults also spend more time than younger adults do on routine activities such as personal care, shopping, and cooking (Johnson & Schaner, 2005). For many of them, these everyday activities become a form of leisure, something they take their time doing and take satisfaction in being able to do for themselves. In the course of late adulthood, leisure activities become steadily less strenuous and more sedentary, as physical energy diminishes (Hooyman & Kiyak, 2011).

COMMUNITY SERVICE AND CIVIC ENGAGEMENT Although most adults withdraw from the workplace in the course of late adulthood, some remain engaged in community and religious activities. Religious organizations are the main setting for volunteer work in the United States, especially in late adulthood (Hooyman & Kiyak, 2011). These organizations provide services such as clothes and meals for the poor, visiting the sick, and youth groups for children and adolescents. Other organizations with volunteer opportunities for older adults are hospitals and environmental groups.

Rates of volunteering in the United States peak in middle adulthood and remain high among people in their 60s, at about 40% (per year), before declining among the old-old and oldest-old to about 10% (Hooyman & Kiyak, 2011). However, number of hours volunteered per person rises from middle adulthood to late adulthood and does not decline until the late 70s (Hendricks & Cutler, 2004). This may be because people have more time available for volunteering in late adulthood than they did at younger ages due to reduced family and work obligations, but rates of volunteering are actually higher among older adults who are still employed than among those

Older adults have more leisure time than persons at other ages.

who have retired (Hooyman & Kiyak 2011). African American elders volunteer at higher rates than older adults in other ethnic groups, mainly because they are more religious and hence more involved in service groups through their churches (Taylor et al., 2004).

High rates of volunteering in late adulthood show how generativity extends into late adulthood for many people (Klieber & Nimrod, 2008). Community service organizations contribute to the common good and often involve efforts to enhance the well-being of the generations to come. However, older adults also benefit from the community service they provide. Studies show that they obtain a variety of psychological benefits from volunteering, including higher life satisfaction, a sense of meaning and accomplishment, and cognitive challenge and stimulation (Corporation for National and Community Service, 2007; Wilson & Harlow-Rosentraub, 2008). There are even physical benefits from volunteering, including higher self-rated health, lower rates of disability, and lower risk of mortality (Greenfield & Marks, 2007). The effects likely run in both directions, with healthier and happier older adults being more likely to volunteer (Morrow-Howell et al., 2009).

Late adulthood is also a time of being highly involved in civic organizations of various kinds, from book clubs to garden clubs to religious congregations to political action groups (Martinson & Minkler, 2006). This is mainly an American phenomenon, as the United States has a long tradition of civic organizations that is stronger than in any other developed country (Putnam, 2000). Involvement in these groups may be due partly to older adults having more time and fewer family and work obligations than younger adults do, but this is not the whole story. There is also a cohort effect here, as the current generation of older adults is exceptional in the extent of their civic involvement. In a historical analysis, Robert Putnam (2000, 2002, 2004) showed that civic involvement was relatively low at the beginning of the 20th century, then rose sharply after World War II, when the current generation of older adults was in young adulthood. They created a vast number of new groups when they were young adults, from youth organizations to business clubs to political action groups, and joined them in large numbers. Civic involvement waned steadily with each cohort in the late 20th century, but among this exceptional generation, civic involvement has remained high even into late adulthood (Putnam, 2004).

Older adults today are more likely than adults in younger age groups to take part not only in civic organizations but in civic activities that promote their political beliefs, including voting, contributing to a political candidate, and writing a letter to a local newspaper (Putnam, 2004). This pattern exists not just in the United States but across developed countries, where older adults consistently have the highest rates of voting in elections and emerging and young adults the lowest (Esser & de Vreese, 2007).

Across countries, adults over age 65 are the age group most likely to vote.

RELIGIOUS INVOLVEMENT Religious participation is the most common type of civic engagement for Americans in late adulthood. Various surveys report that 40–50% of Americans over age 65 attend religious services weekly, and an additional 25% attend at least occasionally (Smith & Snell, 2009). Attendance tends to decline after age 80, for reasons of health and transportation rather than waning beliefs (Idler, 2006; Wink & Dillon, 2002). In Europe, religious attendance and beliefs tend to be lower than in other parts of the world; this is especially true in northern Europe. But in Europe, too, older adults are more religious than persons in younger groups (Halman & Draulans, 2006).

Not only religious participation but participation in a wide range of religious beliefs and practices

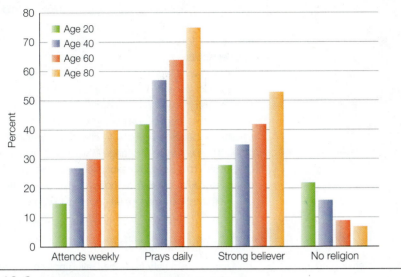

Figure 12.6 Age and Religiosity in the United States

The older Americans are, the more religious they are.
BASED ON: Smith & Snell (2009)

is highest in late adulthood (see **Figure 12.6**). In a national U.S. survey, over 70% of persons over age 60 stated that religion was "very important" to them, the highest level of any age group; emerging adults (age 18–29) were lowest, at under 50% (Pew Research Center, 2010). Older Americans are also more likely than persons in other age groups to pray, to rely on their faith to cope with personal problems, and to watch religious TV programs (Smith & Snell, 2009). Their higher religiosity may be partly a cohort effect—part of their more general civic involvement as a generation—but it is also an age effect, as we'll see in the *Research Focus: Do People Become More Religious with Age?* feature.

Research Focus: Do People Become More Religious with Age?

Many studies have found that older adults in the United States are more religious than any younger age group, in both beliefs and practices. But what does this mean?

For any research finding that involves age differences, there are two possible interpretations: (1) An *age effect*. People vary on the characteristic depending on their age. In this case, an age effect would mean that as people become older they become more religious. If this interpretation is correct, today's emerging, young, and middle adults will also become more religious as they grow into late adulthood.

(2) A *cohort effect*. People of one historical period are different from people of another historical period. In this case, a cohort effect would mean that people who are in late adulthood today are part of an especially religious generation or *cohort,* and American society has become steadily less religious in each of the cohorts that has followed them. If this interpretation is correct, today's emerging, young, and middle adults will be less religious in late adulthood than today's older adults are, because they are part of less religious cohorts.

So, which interpretation is the most plausible explanation for age differences in religiosity in the United States? It takes longitudinal data to answer this question, following the same cohorts over time to see how they change with age. Fortunately these data are available because the Gallup organization has been conducting national surveys of religious beliefs and practices in the United States for over 60 years.

To address the question of whether changes in religiosity with age are an age effect or a cohort effect, Gallup data over more than 60 years can be organized by cohort/generation: Greatest (born before 1928); Silent (born 1928–45); Boomers (born 1946–64); Generation X (born 1965–80); and Millennials (born 1981 or later). For the most part, the Gallup data support the interpretation that the greater religiosity of older adults is an age effect more than a cohort effect.

For example, with regard to beliefs, in the late 1970s, 56% of Silents (then age 30–47) indicated that their religious beliefs were "very important" to them. Thirty years later, 67% of the same generation (now age 60–77) responded that their religious beliefs were "very important" to them (see the figure on the next page). The same pattern of a rise with age was found in the other cohorts.

But wait—a third interpretation is possible. Religiosity is positively related to healthy physical functioning in a variety of ways—and to lower risk of mortality. This means that the higher religiosity of people in late adulthood could be a *selection effect,*

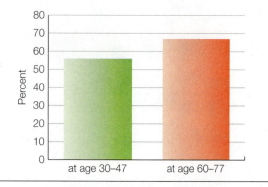

Importance of Religion to Silent Generation

Percentage of people stating that their religious beliefs are "very important" to them.
SOURCE: Schaie (1988)

which occurs when people with certain characteristics are more likely to remain part of the sample than people who have other characteristics. In this case, it means that people who are high in religiosity are more likely to survive into late adulthood than the people who are low in religiosity. Consequently, late adulthood appears to be a more religious time of life than younger age periods, not only because some people become more religious

with age but because people who are highly religious are the ones who are most likely to be alive. It appears that both age effects and selection effects are involved in the higher religiosity of older adults.

However, it would be a mistake to rule out cohort effects entirely. Just because cohort effects on religiosity do not appear to be strong in cohorts studied over the late 20th century does not mean that there will be no cohort effects in the 21st century, because societies are constantly changing and the United States of the 21st century may change in ways that influence the religiosity of its inhabitants. The exceptionally low religiosity of today's emerging adults makes the possibility of cohort effects in this area well worth studying in the decades to come.

Review Question:

1. Data on religiosity from the Gallup polls over several decades indicate that the increase in religiosity with age is due mainly to:
   a. An age effect
   b. A cohort effect
   c. A prediction effect
   d. None of the above

Watch   RESEARCH FOCUS: DO PEOPLE BECOME MORE RELIGIOUS WITH AGE?

Religiosity has long been high among African Americans, especially in late adulthood. Their Christian faith has deep historical roots, dating back to the days of slavery, when they drew comfort from Bible stories that seemed to match their own difficult plight, such as the captivity of the ancient Jews under the Egyptians, and they hoped for a similar happy ending of freedom and triumph (Taylor et al., 2004). Church became an institution where they could support each other and gain strength to face the struggles of daily life, and it remains so today (Roff et al., 2006). Many African American churches provide a wide variety of social services to older adults, including meals, household help, transportation, and links to government service agencies (Idler, 2006). For older African Americans, church has long been a place where they could attain a level of status, authority, and respect that was denied to them in the larger society (Mattis & Jagers, 2001).

Across cultures and countries, women are more religious than men, in both beliefs and practices (Idler, 2006). However, older men usually dominate positions of religious leadership, in most faiths. It is nearly always older men who are the highest-ranking priests, ministers, rabbis, and imams, and women are often excluded entirely from religious leadership. In the Catholic church, for example, in recent centuries most popes have been elected in late adulthood, and women are not allowed to be popes, cardinals, bishops, or priests.

It is not only in the West that late adulthood is a time of heightened religiosity, but in the East as well. In the Confucian philosophy that has been so influential throughout Asia for 2,500 years, duty and obligation are supposed to be the primary values for most of life, but at age 70 older adults are encouraged to leave the things of this world behind and turn their attention to spiritual contemplation (Lock, 1998; Ryff et al., 2015). Similarly, in Buddhism, the most influential religion in most of Asia throughout history, late adulthood is a time for withdrawal from the world and contemplation of the next life to come (following reincarnation). In Hinduism, the dominant religion for a billion persons in India, late adulthood is the period when one should become a *sanyasa*, who renounces the world and seeks spiritual purity while waiting patiently for death (Kakar, 1998).

There has been a considerable amount of research on how religiosity affects the lives of older Americans, and the results are consistently positive for both mental and physical health. Religiosity in late adulthood promotes self-esteem, life satisfaction, overall happiness, and a sense of meaning (Roff et al., 2006). The more religious older Americans are, the less likely they are to become depressed, and the more quickly they recover if they do become depressed (Idler, 2006). Religious beliefs make older adults feel less lonely and less afraid of dying (Koenig, 2007). Higher religiosity in late adulthood is related to better functioning of the immune system and lower blood pressure (Atchley, 2009). Religious involvement in late adulthood lowers the likelihood of physical disability and extends life expectancy (Hill, 2008; Roff et al., 2006). This wide range of positive effects from religion appears to be due to the psychological benefits of religion, in providing hope, meaning, and a sense of control, and the social benefits, in providing direct assistance and social support (Bosworth et al., 2003; Smith et al., 2003). The positive effects of religiosity grow steadily stronger throughout the course of late adulthood (Idler, 2006).

However, it is worth noting that Europeans in late adulthood do not appear to suffer from their low religiosity. In fact, throughout adulthood Europeans report higher average levels of happiness than people in any other part of the world. For older Europeans, affluence, strong family ties, and a generous social welfare system may provide the resources that Americans find in religious beliefs and practices (Rifkin, 2004).

MEDIA USE In his late adulthood, my dad was the person I would always go to for the story of how the football or basketball game ended the night before—the one I didn't get a chance to watch because I was playing cards with my family or putting the kids to bed or grading papers or writing my human development textbook. He was also a great source of movie reviews, because he saw almost every movie that came out, several a week. My dad's patterns reflect the general pattern. Older adults spend a lot of time on media because most of them have a lot of leisure time to spend; they no longer have work, child care, or other daily responsibilities that demand their time (Bowman, 2009).

According to one estimate, Americans age 65 and over spend about 40% of their leisure time watching television, listening to music, reading, and going to the movies (Robinson et al., 2004). Television is by far the most-used media form in late adulthood. In fact, watching television is the most frequently reported daily activity in late adulthood, and older adults watch more TV than any other age group, an average of over 5 hours a day (Wadsworth & Johnson, 2008). Among older adults, women watch more TV than men, and African Americans watch more than Whites, a pattern that carries over from younger ages (Bowman, 2009).

How does the introduction of television to a culture change the social status of older adults? Here, a family gathers around a television in Vietnam.

Older adults especially like news programs, but they also enjoy dramas (especially women), sports (especially men), and game shows (both sexes) (Robinson et al., 2004). Older adults use media for entertainment, but also to find out what is going on in the world, through news programs. They also learn about health topics and medical treatments, although what they learn may not be complete and accurate (Wadsworth & Johnson, 2008).

Older adults are big TV-watchers even though there are not many older adults shown in American TV programs. Analyses of program content report that both fictional and real television characters tend to be young, and older adults are the least likely to be shown of any age group (Signorielli, 2004). Television programs and advertisements that do feature older adults tend to reflect cultural beliefs. One study compared TV advertisements in the United States and China and found that the American ads emphasized the independence of older adults, whereas the Chinese ads more often showed themes of filial piety and family obligation (Lin, 2001).

Television has been asserted to be a major force in globalization, and there is evidence that this is as true among older adults as it is at younger ages. A study by Rukmalie Jayakody (2008) provides a compelling example. Jayakody studied a Vietnamese village where television had just been introduced. The effects on social life were immediate, especially for the village elders. Traditionally, filial piety was strong and elders were highly respected. However, this began to change with television. The villagers have no written language, and elders have long had an important role as storytellers, but now the young are more attracted to the stories they follow on TV. Similarly, elders have previously been viewed as a source of knowledge, but now TV is considered superior. For example, TV programs about how to increase crop yields and use pesticides are prized over the elders' memories of their farming experiences.

The elders also believed that TV affected them through its influence on the young. Their adult children, inspired by television to pursue a better lifestyle and more opportunities, were migrating to the cities and leaving the elders to care for their grandchildren. The grandchildren's values were becoming more individualistic and less collectivistic, as they were introduced to the individualistic values of the television characters they followed. Vietnam is rapidly urbanizing and developing economically, and change was probably coming to the villages in any case, but TV appears to have accelerated the process.

One other type of media use among older adults that should be mentioned is Internet use. Older adults are the least likely to use the Internet of any age group, perhaps because widespread Internet use came along late in life for them and it may not have been necessary to learn to use it for their work or their social lives (Pew Research Center, 2010; Reisenwitz et al., 2007). However, there is abundant evidence that they can learn to use the Internet in a variety of ways that enhance their health and their quality of life. Medical practitioners in a variety of developed countries are now advocating **e-health**, the use of the Internet and electronic devices to enhance communication between health providers and patients, especially older adults (Mair et al., 2012; Naveh-Deutsch et al., 2007; Tse et al., 2008). Internet use can also enhance older adults' social lives, allowing them to keep in regular contact with children, grandchildren, and friends who may live far away (Arazi, 2009). One study in Israel found that in a sample of older adults in a nursing home (mean age of 80), those who participated in a course on computer skills and Internet browsing showed positive results, in contrast to a comparison group, on measures including life satisfaction, depression, and loneliness (Shapira et al., 2007).

e-health

use of the Internet and electronic devices to enhance communication between health providers and patients, especially older adults

Practice Quiz ANSWERS AVAILABLE IN ANSWER KEY.

1. Mrs. Bourdeau is an American woman living in the United States who is widowed, and has a married son and a married daughter. If she becomes ill, she is likely to be cared for by _____.

a. her best friend, who is also a widow

b. her oldest child

c. her son and daughter equally

d. her daughter or daughter-in-law

2. Jane recently moved her mother into a(n) _____ and was relieved that her mother was actually enjoying it there. Each person there has a separate apartment, but residents are provided with meals in a common dining area. She has transportation for shopping and medical appointments, but Jane has been able to arrange her schedule so that she can take her mother to her doctors' appointments.

a. nursing home   **c.** group home

b. assisted living facility   **d.** hospice care center

3. Which of the following best describes late adulthood relationships in Western culture?

a. Marital satisfaction is almost as high as it was in middle adulthood.

b. Women are more likely than men to become depressed after a spouse dies.

c. Rates of remarriage in late adulthood are higher than in middle adulthood because children are less likely to be living in the same household.

d. The risk of death after the loss of a spouse is greater for men than for women.

4. Retirement satisfaction tends to be especially high for _____.

a. women

b. men

c. well-educated people who had high-status jobs

d. people who have children who live nearby

5. Older Americans _____.

a. who are higher in religious practices are more likely to have mental health problems

b. who are higher in religious practices are more likely to have physical health problems

c. report higher religious beliefs and practices if they are male than if they are female

d. are more religious than their younger counterparts

Summary: Emotional and Social Development

LO 12.12 Explain why late adulthood is a time of positive emotions and high self-esteem.

Positive emotions and self-esteem rise during late adulthood, because older adults tend to be more accepting of their past and present selves than young or middle adults are. Gender differences in self-esteem diminish or disappear by late adulthood.

LO 12.13 Distinguish between Erikson's theory and Carstensen's socioemotional selectivity theory of late adulthood.

Erikson proposed that late adulthood is a period when the central challenge is ego integrity versus despair. Ego integrity means looking back on one's life and accepting the outcome of it, whereas despair entails regrets and bitterness about the course of one's life, and a conclusion that it has not gone well and now cannot be changed. Carstensen's socioemotional selectivity theory states that older adults maximize their emotional well-being by becoming increasingly selective in their social contacts. Carstensen argues that in late adulthood, knowledge-based goals fade in importance as people leave the workplace and no longer have daily responsibilities as coworkers and parents, causing relationship goals to become more emotion-based.

LO 12.14 Describe how relations with children, grandchildren, and great-grandchildren change during late adulthood.

Across cultures, contact with children continues to be frequent through late adulthood, and there may be a role reversal between parents and children, with parents now depending on their children for care and support. Although grandparents and grandchildren often decrease their frequency of contact as the grandchildren become busy with the tasks of adult life, feelings of closeness and affection established earlier remain strong for most. Relations with great-grandchildren tend to be less close than with grandchildren, and contact is less frequent.

LO 12.15 Compare cultural differences in living situations during late adulthood.

There is great variety in living situations for older adults: Some live independently, others live with children, and still others live in assisted living facilities or nursing homes. In Asian cultures, where filial piety is strong, older adults have traditionally lived with their children, although this pattern may be changing.

LO 12.16 **Explain how romantic relationships and sexuality change during late adulthood.**

Marital satisfaction increases from middle adulthood to late adulthood and reaches its highest point of the entire life span. Many people, especially women, lose their spouse during late adulthood, a painful and difficult transition for most. Rates of remarriage are low but tend to be more successful in late adulthood than at earlier ages. There are wide cultural variations in views of the acceptability and appropriateness of sexual activity in late adulthood. Sexual activity depends crucially on physical health. A U.S. study reported that frequencies of kissing, hugging, and sexual touching and caressing were higher than rates of intercourse in late adulthood.

LO 12.17 **Describe variations in retirement, and identify the impact of retirement on older adults.**

The decision about precisely when to retire is based on a variety of factors, especially financial considerations, physical health, and job satisfaction. Many older Americans enter retirement gradually, through bridge jobs that do not require full-time hours. Most older adults adjust well to retirement, but adults who were forced into retirement are less happy with retirement than those who retired by choice. People who choose to retire generally experience improvements in their physical and mental health following the transition, whereas people who retired involuntarily tend to decline.

LO 12.18 **Describe how leisure activities, community involvement, religious involvement, and media use change in late adulthood.**

Leisure activities in late adulthood tend to be a continuation of things adults had enjoyed earlier in life. Many older adults travel, but most of older adults' leisure time is spent watching television, reading, and visiting family and friends. Volunteering, involvement in civic organizations, and religious participation are high during late adulthood. Television use is also high, and Internet use can enhance the health care and social lives of older adults.

Applying Your Knowledge as a Professional

The topics covered in this chapter apply to a wide variety of career professions. Watch these videos to learn how they apply to an advertising executive, a senior care worker, and a board member at a senior center.

Watch CAREER FOCUS: SENIOR CARE WORKER

Video

Lissette Cardona-Lynch
Assisted Living/Senior Care Worker

Chapter Quiz

1. Older adults in developed countries _____.
   a. are the group most likely to be receiving public assistance
   b. are the wealthiest segment of the population
   c. are now more likely to be living in extended-family households than in the past
   d. usually perform a ritual celebrating the person's freedom from previous responsibilities

2. The old-age dependency ratio _____.
   a. is not a problem for countries with low fertility rates
   b. is lowest in Japan where individuals retire in their 70s
   c. is not an immediate problem in the United States because its population is growing due to immigration
   d. is highest in developing countries, particularly in Africa

3. During late adulthood _____.

   a. bones thicken in women

   b. body weight increases from middle adulthood because few older adults exercise

   c. many people develop age spots

   d. veins become less visible as skin thickens

4. Which is the most common visual impairment in late adulthood?

   a. Macular degeneration

   b. Cataracts

   c. Tinnitus

   d. Glaucoma

5. Which of the following best describes how sleep patterns change during late adulthood?

   a. Women in late adulthood often experience sleep apnea, but the disorder is rare among men.

   b. People experience changes in sleep, but these changes are not correlated with psychological problems, such as depression, as they were in earlier parts of the life span.

   c. People have fewer sleep problems than they did earlier in their lives because they no longer have the daily stress associated with work and children.

   d. People sleep less deeply than they did when they were younger.

6. Arthritis is usually caused by _____.

   a. a steep drop in estrogen

   b. a sedentary lifestyle

   c. longtime use of the joints

   d. a diet low in protein

7. Which statement best describes exercise habits in late adulthood?

   a. Older adults exercise more often than midlife adults because they have fewer family obligations.

   b. Eighty-five to ninety-five percent of adults over age 65 never engage in vigorous exercise.

   c. Doctors don't recommend exercise for this age group.

   d. Aerobic exercise is not advised because it increases the risk of a heart attack.

8. _____ shows relatively little decline in late adulthood.

   a. Procedural memory

   b. Working memory

   c. Selective attention

   d. Divided attention

9. _____ is a protective factor against developing Alzheimer's disease.

   a. Being of African heritage

   b. Regular physical activity

   c. Abstaining from all alcohol

   d. Having the ApoE gene

10. How is wisdom related to age, according to research?

   a. Wisdom is at its peak during the college years.

   b. Wisdom is only attained when you reach late adulthood.

   c. Wisdom is generally unrelated to age.

   d. Wisdom declines after early adulthood.

11. Mary has always loved to sew but at age 80, she now sews only a few items of clothing per year, follows simple patterns, and she now uses a machine instead of stitching by hand. This is an example of _____.

   a. improved procedural memory with age

   b. better divided attention among experts

   c. selective optimization with compensation

   d. faster reaction times of older experts compared to their younger counterparts

12. Which best describes emotions during late adulthood?.

   a. Emotions during this period fluctuate greatly depending on the time of year.

   b. Late adults are often severely depressed and isolated.

   c. Negative emotions are high due to health issues.

   d. Positive emotions are more common in late adulthood than at earlier ages.

13. According to _____, shrinking social networks in adulthood are by choice.

   a. selective optimization with compensation

   b. primary aging theory

   c. Erikson's theory

   d. socioemotional selectivity theory

14. Mrs. Chang is a Chinese woman in her 80s, who is no longer able to live independently. With whom is she most likely to live?

   a. her niece

   b. her eldest daughter

   c. her eldest son

   d. her son or daughter, whomever lives closest to her

15. J.M. is a 92-year-old woman living in Canada. She would be most likely to be living in a nursing home if she has a(n) _____ cultural background.

   a. Asian   **c.** African

   b. European   **d.** Latino

16. Which of the following is true regarding the loss of a spouse?

   a. The risk of death after the loss of a spouse is greater for men than for women.

   b. The risk of death after the loss of a spouse is greater for women than for men.

   c. Women are more likely than men to become depressed after a spouse dies.

   d. Depressive symptoms are not common and if they occur, they typically disappear within a month after the death.

17. Which of the following is true regarding work and retirement?

   a. Retirement satisfaction tends to be higher among those in lower-status jobs because they feel a sense of relief to no longer have to go to work every day.

   b. Most older Americans say they would prefer to enter retirement gradually.

   c. For most older adults, the main reason they work past the traditional "retirement age" is that they need the money.

   d. Younger adults are more likely to be self-employed than their older counterparts.

18. In late adulthood, religious beliefs are _____.

   a. weaker than in middle adulthood because many older adults have become disillusioned with organized religion

   b. strongest among Europeans

   c. positively correlated with both mental and physical health

   d. strong among Christians, but weak among followers of Eastern religions such as Buddhism

Chapter 13

Death and Afterlife Beliefs

IN THIS CHAPTER WE EXAMINE A VARIETY OF AS-PECTS OF DEATH, BEGINNING WITH AN EXAMINA-TION OF THE TWO MAJOR WAYS THAT PEOPLE DIE IN DEVELOPED COUNTRIES, HEART DISEASE AND CANCER, AND A LOOK AT RECENT ATTEMPTS TO DEVELOP WAYS OF POSTPONING DEATH AND EX-TENDING THE HUMAN LIFE SPAN. Then we look at the sociocultural contexts of death, in an age when advanced medical technology draws out the process of death much longer than in the past and raises challenging social and ethical questions. We'll also explore the emotional side of death, bereavement and grief. An important feature of human development with regard to death is that most people in most cultures believe in some kind of existence beyond death. We close the chapter with an examination of afterlife beliefs and mourning rituals in the major religions, including a discussion of how people around the world honor the dead in their daily lives.

Watch   CHAPTER INTRODUCTION: DEATH AND AFTERLIFE BELIEFS

Video

Section 1   Physical Aspects of Death

∨   Learning Objectives

13.1   Describe how causes of death have changed throughout history and identify the two major causes of death today.

13.2   Describe the role that telomeres and free radicals play in aging, and review efforts to delay the aging process.

13.3   Compare and contrast the benefits and drawbacks of dying at home versus in a hospital.

13.4   Summarize the options and controversies that exist regarding end-of-life care and death.

PHYSICAL ASPECTS OF DEATH:
The Biological Processes of Death and Aging

This chapter appears at the very end of your textbook on human development, after the chapter on late adulthood, but of course this does not mean that late adulthood is always when death arrives. Although most people today live into late adulthood, for most of history death was distributed throughout the life span and occurred mainly due to infectious diseases. Today in developed countries, death is due mainly to accidents at younger ages and to heart disease and cancer in middle and late adulthood. There is also an increased understanding of the biological process of aging, which is leading to efforts to extend the human life span.

Major Causes of Death

LO 13.1   **Describe how causes of death have changed throughout history and identify the two major causes of death today.**

Until the past century, infancy was the life stage with the highest mortality rates across cultures, and toddlerhood and early childhood were also times of high risk, due to young children's susceptibility to infectious diseases (Floud et al., 2011). Young women frequently died in childbirth; young men frequently died in wars (Diamond, 1991). Beyond young adulthood, people became increasingly vulnerable with age to death from a wide variety of infectious diseases, such as typhus, diphtheria, tuberculosis, and smallpox.

Most of the topics in this book have been researched only for a few decades at the most, but causes of death have been recorded systematically for at least 150 years in many developed countries. These records show that infectious diseases were the dominant cause of death until the early 20th century. Then, in the course of the 20th century, medical advances, including vaccines and antibiotics, coupled with better sanitation, resulted in a dramatic decline in deaths from infectious diseases. Over half of all deaths in the middle of the 19th century were due to infectious diseases; by the early 21st century, the rate was just 5% (Floud et al., 2011). As infectious diseases declined, life expectancy increased steadily over the course of the past century. Once people lived longer, they began to die more commonly from causes that had been rare before, especially

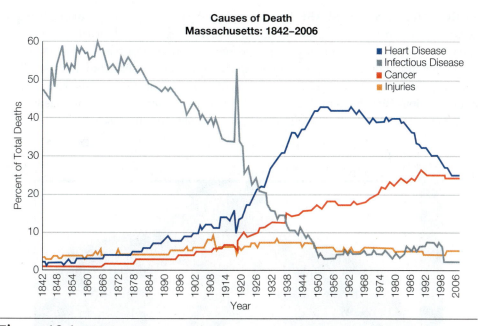

Figure 13.1 Causes of Death in Massachusetts from the 1840s to the Present

As infectious diseases were effectively prevented and treated, deaths due to heart disease and cancer increased.

SOURCE: Massachusetts Department of Public Health (2008).

heart disease and cancer. People rarely died from heart disease or cancer prior to the 20th century, because most people died of infectious diseases long before they reached middle or late adulthood, when susceptibility to heart disease and cancer increases. **Figure 13.1** illustrates the changes in causes of death from the 1840s to the present, using data from the state of Massachusetts, where reliable records have been kept throughout that period (Caceres, 2008).

Today, the most common causes of death vary greatly with age and by country. Infectious diseases remain the primary cause of death in some developing countries, especially for children under age 5 and especially in Africa, as we have seen in earlier chapters. However, in developed countries deaths under age 5 are rare and occur most often due to accidents, mainly automobile accidents (World Health Organization [WHO], 2014). Death in middle childhood is even rarer than in the earlier years in developed countries, and again accidents are the primary cause. In adolescence, emerging adulthood, and young adulthood, the most common causes of death in developed countries are automobile accidents, homicide, and suicide.

Mortality rates are substantially higher in middle adulthood and late adulthood than earlier in the life span in developed countries. Furthermore, the main sources of death change in the later stages of the life span; the common causes are no longer accidents, homicide, and suicide, but cardiovascular disease and cancer. Let us now examine these two main causes of death in greater detail, followed by suicide, which is a common cause of death in some countries and some age groups.

In developing countries, automobile accidents are the leading cause of death among young people.

CORONARY HEART DISEASE Heart disease is the number one cause of death among adults in developed countries (WHO, 2014). In heart disease, the arteries that carry blood from the heart become gradually narrower due to a buildup of plaque (*atherosclerosis*), until the buildup becomes severe enough to cut off the flow of blood to the heart. Diets high in fat increase plaque formation, and regular exercise decreases it, as we have seen in the previous two chapters. The video *Coronary Heart Disease* gives an overview of the symptoms, risk factors, and various statistics associated with this disease.

Watch CORONARY HEART DISEASE

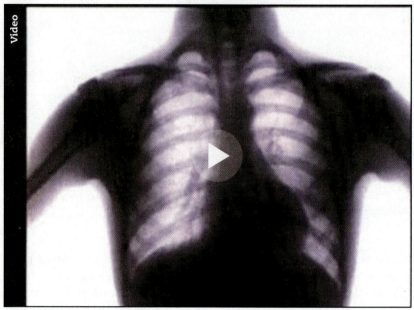

As atherosclerosis becomes more severe, a person may experience *angina pectoris*, involving severe pain in the chest, neck, and left arm. Further constriction of the arteries to the heart eventually blocks them entirely, leading to a heart attack. A heart attack indicates that heart tissue has died due to lack of blood supply. Symptoms include acute pain, weakness, dizziness, confusion, and shortness of breath. Sometimes the symptoms are mild, so people may not realize they are experiencing a heart attack. Even in developed countries, about half of all people who experience a heart attack die before reaching the hospital, and an additional 30% die within a year (Hooyman & Kiyak, 2011).

Death from heart disease is rare before middle adulthood, then rises substantially after age 45. However, rates are highest of all in late adulthood. People age 65 and over are nearly 10 times as likely to die of heart disease as people ages 45–64 (American Heart Association, 2005).

Men have higher rates of death from heart disease than women do in both middle and late adulthood, across countries. Within the United States, rates are highest among African Americans and lowest among Latinos and Asian Americans (CDC, 2014). There are also variations among developed countries, with the highest rates in eastern European countries such as Russia and Hungary and the lowest rates in Japan and in southern European countries such as Spain and Italy.

These cultural and national differences can be explained in part by diet. African Americans and eastern Europeans have relatively high rates of heart disease because they tend to consume diets that are high in fats and sugars; southern Europeans, Asian Americans, and Japanese have relatively low rates of heart disease because they tend to have low-fat, low-sugar diets and also eat a lot of fish (De Meersman & Stein, 2007).

Another important factor in group differences in heart disease is cigarette smoking. As we have seen in previous chapters, smoking is extremely damaging to physical health in multiple ways, and this includes damage to the functioning of the heart. The contribution of smoking to heart disease can be seen in the steep drop in death rates of the disease that has taken place in the United States since 1950. The drop has been dramatic—rates of death from heart disease are only about one third today what they were in 1950 (Weintraub, 2010). The decline in death rates from heart disease has continued into the 21st century, across ethnic groups, as shown in **Figure 13.2**. This decline is all the more remarkable when you consider that some of the risk factors for heart disease have actually grown worse, not better, over this period. Most notably, as described in several of the previous chapters, rates of obesity have climbed alarmingly in the past several decades, and obesity is one of the top risk factors for heart disease (Jacob & Johnson, 2001). Diets have become worse, as people have relied more on fast foods. Yet declines in smoking have had more effect than the rise in obesity; only 18% of American adults smoke today, compared to about 50% in the 1960s (CDC, 2014; Roeseler & Burns, 2010). The effects of public smoking bans also attest to the importance of smoking in heart disease. Numerous studies have shown that when a state or country bans smoking in public places, rates of heart attacks drop by over half within the first year (Weintraub, 2010). Better medicines for controlling blood pressure and reducing cholesterol have also contributed to the decline in heart disease, but the drop in smoking has been the key factor.

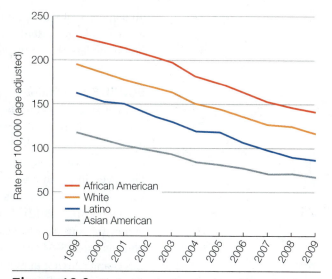

Figure 13.2 Reduction in Deaths from Heart Disease

Deaths from heart disease have fallen across all ethnic groups. The decline is due mostly to a corresponding decline in smoking rates.
SOURCE: Based on U.S. Dept. of Health and Human Services (2014).

CANCER Like heart disease, cancer occurs more commonly in middle adulthood than in earlier life stages, but it occurs most commonly of all in late adulthood. What is it about late adulthood that generates high rates of cancer? All throughout life the body is replacing cells that have died. Beyond the 20s this process of cell replacement becomes steadily less efficient and accurate, and by late adulthood the rate of mistakes becomes high in three kinds of genes: *stability genes* that repair mistakes in DNA replication during cell replacement; *oncogenes* that had previously functioned normally but now produce abnormal cell duplication; and *tumor suppressor genes* that functioned to suppress the activity of oncogenes (Campisi, 2005; Vogelstein & Kinzler, 2004).

Once cancer begins, cancer cells in the affected part of the body multiply at an extreme rate. Eventually, the cells form tumors. The tumors deplete the resources of healthy cells and gradually impair the functioning of the affected body part and then the entire body system, culminating in death.

Symptoms of cancer depend on the specific cancer, but common symptoms across types include weight loss, fatigue, and weakness (Hooyman & Kiyak, 2011). However, these symptoms are often inaccurately interpreted as indications of depression, dementia, or simply primary aging, so the person experiencing them may not be examined for cancer. In most developed countries, screening tests are available to detect cancers, and medical authorities recommend that persons in late adulthood have yearly exams for cancer and other potential health problems.

About 70% of cancer deaths occur in persons who are age 65 and older (Christ, 2009). Overall, cancer is more common among men than among women, in part because men are more likely to be smokers (WHO, 2014). Incidence of cancer is highest in the developed countries where smoking is highest, such as Japan and Russia, because smoking causes not only lung cancer but a variety of other types.

In addition to smoking, other risk factors for developing cancer include poor diet, excessive alcohol use, and chronic exposure to sunlight. However, other than smoking, environmental factors are not as strongly related to cancer as they are for heart disease.

To some extent susceptibility to cancer is genetic, especially when it occurs at younger ages. To a larger extent, cancer is simply a consequence of growing old and of the body becoming less able to duplicate cells as effectively as it once did.

SUICIDE In addition to the diseases described in this section, people also die as a consequence of taking their own lives. Suicide is a major cause of death in developed countries, although it is relatively uncommon in developing countries. In most developed countries, suicide is most common among the elderly, especially among those who are over 80 years old and experiencing declining quality of life due to aging or illness. However, in Japan and South Korea, suicide is the leading cause of death among persons age 15 to 39, and it is more prevalent in this age group than in any older age group (Cabinet Office, 2012). For decades in the United States, suicide was most prevalent among persons over 80 years old, but in recent years it has become most common among persons ages 45–64 (American Foundation for Suicide Prevention, 2014). The reasons for this change are not known.

In nearly all countries, there are distinct gender differences: women are more likely than men to attempt suicide, but men are more likely than women to complete the suicide (Suicide.org, 2014). This appears to be due mainly to the fact that women usually choose methods such as an overdose of medications, whereas men are more likely to choose more lethal methods such as firearms.

Within the United States, there are notable ethnic differences in suicide patterns. Among Whites, suicide rates rise with age and are highest in middle and late adulthood. Suicide rates are highest of all among elderly White males. However, among African American males, suicide rates are highest in the 20s and decline in middle and late adulthood. In contrast, African American females have the lowest suicide rates of any gender/ethnic group in American society. Rates are also relatively low among Asian Americans and Latinos, both males and females (American Foundation for Suicide Prevention, 2014).

Beyond Death? Attempts to Extend the Human Life Span

LO 13.2 Describe the role that telomeres and free radicals play in aging, and review efforts to delay the aging process.

"In this world nothing can be said to be certain except death and taxes." So Benjamin Franklin observed some 200 years ago. Taxes are unlikely to go away anytime soon, but what about death? Must we inevitably die? Aging is a biological process we all experience, and eventually it leads to death. But is it possible that by understanding this biological process we could learn to delay it or even to reverse it?

Much has been learned in recent decades about the biological process of aging. Several important contributors to aging have been identified. First let us examine two of the key contributors and how they might be altered to extend the life span. Then we will look at two other strategies for extending life.

cellular clock

intrinsic limit to the number of times cells can replicate themselves

Hayflick limit

limit of 50 times that cells can replicate themselves

THE SOURCES OF AGING: CELLULAR CLOCKS AND FREE RADICALS One important factor in aging is that the cells of the body appear to have a **cellular clock** that limits the number of times they can replicate themselves. Throughout the human life span new cells are being created through cell replication to replace the ones that wear out and die. However, after about 50 times cells lose their ability to replicate. First discovered by the biologist Leonard Hayflick (1965, 1998, 2004), this principle is known as the **Hayflick limit**.

The source of the Hayflick limit appears to lie in a part of the cell DNA at the end of chromosomes called **telomeres** (Thoms et al., 2007). With each cell replication telomeres become slightly shorter, and eventually they become so short that no more replication can occur. This shortening provides an advantage in the short term, as it helps prevent the mutations that might otherwise take place in the course of many cell replications (Shay & Wright, 2004). However, in the long term, the cell stops replicating when the Hayflick limit is reached and the telomeres become too short. Shortened telomeres have been found to be associated with a wide range of diseases such as cancer (Chung et al., 2007). A study of healthy centenarians (people who have lived to be at least 100 years old)—that is, centenarians who did not have heart disease, cancer, stroke, or diabetes— found them to have significantly longer telomeres than their centenarian peers who had two or more of these conditions (Effros, 2009a). Watch the video *Centenarian* to see an interview with a remarkably healthy 102-year-old woman.

Watch   CENTENARIAN

Video

telomere

portion of cell DNA at the end of chromosomes that become slightly shorter with each cell replication and that eventually becomes so short that replication can no longer occur

free radicals

unstable molecules that cause damage to the DNA and other structures required by the cell to function

Antioxidants, found naturally in many fruits and vegetables, combat the cell damage caused by free radicals.

CRITICAL THINKING QUESTION

Would you want to live to be 200 years old if it were possible to remain reasonably healthy for that long? What if it meant you had to work until you were 170?

Is there a way to regrow telomeres so that the Hayflick limit can be exceeded? Recent research provides clues. An enzyme called *telomerase* has been identified that regulates the length of telomeres. In laboratory studies, scientists have succeeded in increasing telomerase functioning in some types of animals and thereby preventing the shortening of telomeres (Effros, 2009b; Nandakumar & Cech, 2013). Other studies are focusing on discovering which genes control telomerase activity and regulating the length of telomeres through those genes, but this research is in the early phases (Effros, 2009a; Sahin & DePinho, 2012). Recent studies also suggest the possibility that telomeres can grow again after shortening, as described in the *Research Focus: Growing Telomeres* feature on the next page.

Another major contributor to primary aging is the accumulation of cell-damaging **free radicals** (Thavanati et al., 2008). Our cells need

oxygen to survive, but in the course of metabolizing oxygen, unstable molecules are created that contain an unpaired electron; these molecules are the free radicals. As they drift about the cell in their unstable state, free radicals cause damage to the DNA and other structures the cell needs in order to function. Free radicals are believed to contribute to many of the fatal diseases that occur most commonly in late adulthood, including cancer, heart disease, and Alzheimer's disease (Sierra, 2006).

Is there a way to prevent the development of free radicals? There is substantial evidence that the activity of free radicals is muted by the presence of **antioxidants**, which absorb the extra electrons in the free radicals and thereby prevent them from damaging the cell. Antioxidants such as beta carotene and vitamins E and C occur naturally in many foods, especially fruits and vegetables, which is why eating a good diet that includes fruits and vegetables promotes health and longevity (Troen, 2003). Animal studies have shown that high doses of antioxidant drugs can enhance physical functioning, and in worms can even extend the life span by 50% (Hooyman & Kiyak, 2011). However, studies of humans show little gain from ingesting extra quantities of antioxidant medications (Kedziora-Kornatowski et al., 2007). In fact, some studies indicate that supplements of antioxidants such as vitamin E may actually be damaging to health (Miller et al., 2009). Research is now occurring to see if it may be possible to insert a gene in some cells that will produce enzymes that serve as antioxidants.

antioxidants

substances, present in many fruits and vegetables, that absorb the extra electron in free radicals, thereby preventing them from damaging the cell

Research Focus: Growing Telomeres

It is now known that the gradual shrinking of telomeres is a key part of aging. Each time a cell replicates, the telomeres at the end of the chromosomes shorten, until they reach the point where they are too short to replicate any longer and the cell dies. But what if it were possible to reverse the shortening of the telomeres? What if telomeres could be induced to grow so that they would not become too short to replicate?

New research offers potentially important evidence that these questions may not be merely speculative. In one study, researchers took biological samples from 31 women with cervical cancer who had been randomized to one of two groups, those who received six counseling sessions by telephone and those who received usual care without counseling (Beigler et al., 2011).

The six sessions focused on managing stress and emotions, enhancing health and wellness, and addressing relational and sexual concerns. At the beginning of the study and after 4 months, the researchers investigated changes over time to see if the counseling had any effects.

The results indicated positive psychological effects of counseling. Women in the counseling group reported more improved quality of life over the 4-month period than women in the control group. They also showed improvements in their immune systems. These findings, while welcome, were not surprising, as they had been reported many times before in other studies.

The real surprise of the study involved the telomeres. In the course of examining the full range of data on the two groups

Watch   RESEARCH FOCUS: GROWING TELOMERES

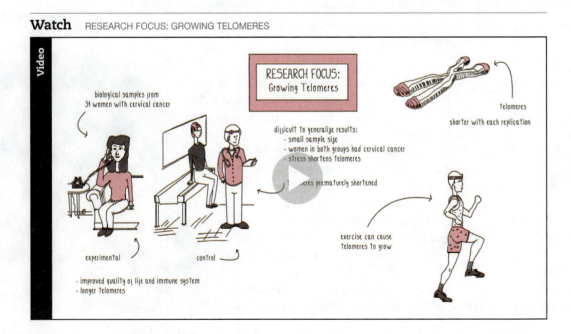

of women, the researchers discovered unexpectedly that the women in the counseling group had longer telomeres at the end of the 4-month period than they did at the beginning. The counseling appeared to have caused their telomeres to grow, thus lengthening the life of their cells.

This study, while groundbreaking, must be interpreted with caution. Can you see why it might be difficult to generalize from this study to the general population? First, the sample was very small; only 15 women were in the group that received the counseling and showed telomere growth. Second, the women all had cervical cancer. It has been known for some time that stress can cause premature shortening of the telomeres, and a diagnosis of cervical cancer certainly qualifies as a stressful condition. Consequently, it may be that reversing the shrinkage of telomeres would be possible only in people whose telomeres had shortened prematurely due to stress, and not in people whose telomeres shortened only as a part of normal aging.

Nevertheless, the study established the crucial principle that the shortening of the telomeres is not irreversible and may not be inevitable. Another recent study provided additional support for this principle, reporting that exercise, too, can cause telomeres to grow in people for whom stress had caused their telomeres to shorten prematurely (Jin et al., 2011). Future research is likely to provide further information about what causes telomeres to shorten and how this process may be reversed in order to slow aging and increase longevity.

Review Questions:

1. Research described here showed that telomeres:
   a. Shrink with age regardless of what people experience.
   b. Can be lengthened if people's experiences change.
   c. Can slow in the rate at which they change if people are given certain medications.
   d. Increase with age and can become cancerous.

2. Which of the following is a limitation of the study?
   a. The sample was small.
   b. There were no men in the sample.
   c. The participants were under unusual stress.
   d. All of the above.

CAN AGING BE REVERSED? HORMONE REPLACEMENT AND CALORIE RESTRICTION Two other approaches to slowing or reversing the aging process are hormone replacement and calorie restriction. The two hormones that have been the focus of this research are growth hormone and DHEA.

Growth hormone is a key part of physical growth in the early decades of life, but its steady decline after the mid-20s contributes to primary aging. Experimental studies in which animals and humans receive supplements of growth hormone have yielded sometimes dramatic results, including increased muscle mass and bone density, reduced fat, and increased activity levels (Hooyman & Kiyak, 2011). However, these effects have not been permanent, and regular use of growth hormones has been found to have some unpleasant side effects, including growth of excess hair; liver damage; and abnormal growth of the hands, feet, and facial bones.

DHEA is a hormone involved in muscle growth, bone density, and the functioning of the cardiovascular system. It is produced by the adrenal glands, then converted into the sex hormones, estrogen and testosterone. DHEA production increases until about age 30 and then declines until age 80, when the body contains only about 5% of the DHEA it had at age 30. In mice, injections of DHEA result in increased activity levels and learning speed. In humans, experimental studies have failed to demonstrate clear benefits from DHEA supplements for older adults, but research is continuing (Nair et al., 2006; Naqvi et al., 2013).

Another approach to extending life is calorie restriction. In a wide variety of animal species, decreasing caloric intake by 30–50% results in an increase in life span of up to 50% (Martini et al., 2008). For example, rats put on caloric restriction live 30% longer than other rats and have higher levels of muscle mass and physical activity (Hooyman & Kiyak, 2011). In rhesus monkeys, over a 6-year period, those who were subject to 30% calorie restriction lived longer and had higher activity levels, less body fat, and higher DHEA levels than other monkeys (Messaoudi et al., 2006). There are few studies of calorie restriction among humans—this

growth hormone

hormone that is a crucial contributor to physical growth in the early decades of life; its steady decline after the mid-20s contributes to primary aging

DHEA

hormone involved in muscle growth, bone density, and the functioning of the cardiovascular system

Calorie restriction over an extended time may lengthen life. Would you be willing to try it?

is not the kind of study for which volunteers are plentiful—but one study of 18 midlife adults who reduced their calorie intake for 6 years reported a variety of health benefits, including better cardiovascular functioning and lower blood pressure (Fontana et al., 2004). Research is now occurring into ways to allow people to benefit from the effects of calorie restriction without requiring them to be perpetually hungry (Chung et al., 2013; Ingram et al., 2007).

Practice Quiz   ANSWERS AVAILABLE IN ANSWER KEY.

1. In developed countries, _____ were the dominant cause of death until the early 20th century.
   a. chronic illnesses
   b. infectious diseases
   c. suicides
   d. injuries

2. Wyatt is a two-year-old from the Northeastern part of the United States. His main risk of early death is from _____.
   a. pediatric cancer
   b. Lou Gehrig's disease
   c. complications from an accident
   d. homicide

3. Within the United States, _____ have the highest rates of death from heart disease.
   a. Whites
   b. Asian Americans
   c. Latinos
   d. African Americans

4. Manuel eats a healthy diet full of fruits and vegetables, hoping to benefit from their naturally occurring _____, which promote longevity.
   a. antibiotics
   b. free radicals
   c. telomeres
   d. antioxidants

5. Edna is a healthy, active 103-year-old. Considering the findings in a recent study on healthy centenarians, Edna likely has longer _____ than her centenarian peers who have heart disease, cancer, stroke, or diabetes.
   a. dendrites
   b. synaptic gaps
   c. immune responses
   d. telomeres

PHYSICAL ASPECTS OF DEATH:
The Sociocultural Contexts of Death

We have examined many differences between developed countries and developing countries in the course of this book, and death is one of the areas where the difference is largest. Most people in developing countries today die as people have always done through human history—at home among family, or through accidents or wars. In contrast, death in developed countries today is usually a highly technological event, because it typically takes place in the context of the advanced medical technologies used to try to keep the dying person alive. We first examine homes and hospitals as sociocultural contexts for death, then look at the hospice approach as an alternative that is rising in acceptance. Next we look at the difficult questions raised by the use of medical methods not to keep people alive, but to ease them into death. Finally we consider the increasing use of written plans to direct others in what steps to take if the dying person is incapacitated.

Where We Die: Homes and Hospitals

LO 13.3   **Compare and contrast the benefits and drawbacks of dying at home versus in a hospital.**

For most of human history, death has most commonly occurred at home. Most people died of infectious diseases, and they experienced a relatively short period of illness before their death, ranging from a few days to a few weeks. Today, most people in developing countries die at home because they rarely have access to medical care in a hospital or clinic setting (World Health Organization, 2014). Even in developed countries, surveys indicate that 80–90% of people would prefer to die at home (National Hospice and Palliative Care Organization [NHPCO], 2008). Actually, however, only about 20% die at home. Most people in developed countries die in hospitals, about 60%, and another 20% die in nursing homes (Grunier et al., 2007).

The prospect of dying at home appeals to many people because they imagine facing the uncertainty and pain of death in the context of the security and comfort of home, cared for by the familiar people they know and love (Germino, 2003; NHPCO, 2008). However, the reality of dying at home is considerably more challenging and difficult, especially for the caregivers. Because the major causes of death in developed countries are not infectious diseases but heart disease and cancer, and because modern medications and technology make it possible to keep people alive long past when they would have died in previous eras, dying often takes place slowly and gradually over a period of many months or even years. During this time, as the dying person's health declines, the home caregivers are often required to help them with daily activities of eating, using the toilet, bathing, and taking medications (Singer et al., 2005).

This is often a tremendous physical and psychological strain on the caregivers, and even nearly a year after a home death, family caregivers report higher levels of stress than persons whose family member died in a hospital (Addington-Hall, 2000). The strain is reduced if caregivers have support from health care professionals, but even then most homes are not suited to providing well for the physical and medical needs of a dying person (Perrault et al., 2004). Most older adults anticipate the difficulty of home care, and even though they would prefer to die at home, they realize the burden this would place on their family members (Gott et al., 2004).

Hospitals can provide the necessary medical care when a person is dying, but hospitals also have their drawbacks as a setting for death (O'Connor, 2003). Dying people and their families often complain that hospital care is impersonal and dehumanizing, because the focus of medical personnel is on the technology and medications intended to keep the person alive rather than on emotional and social needs (Open Society Institute, 2003). A large American study of seriously ill and dying hospital patients found that most physicians and their patients did not discuss the prospect of the patient's death or make plans for end-of-life care (Christopher, 2003). Dying in a hospital often means experiencing loneliness, fear, and untreated pain (Grunier et al., 2007; Weitzen et al., 2003).

Options and Decisions Regarding the End of Life

LO 13.4 **Summarize the options and controversies that exist regarding end-of-life care and death.**

Now that people in developed countries live so much longer than in the past, societies have had to create ways of addressing the issues that arise when older adults are near the end of their lives and in declining health. Hospice care provides a humane setting that allows terminally ill people to live the final chapter of their lives with dignity. Euthanasia is sometimes considered when death is near and there is no possibility of recovery, although it is highly controversial. Many older adults in developed countries now record instructions for their end-of-life care long before they become ill, so that their loved ones will not be faced with making difficult choices on their behalf.

THE HOSPICE APPROACH TO CARE OF THE DYING In response to widespread dissatisfaction with end-of-life hospital care, the **hospice** approach has become increasingly popular in developed countries. Hospice care aims to address not just medical

hospice
alternative to hospital care at the end of life that emphasizes the physical, emotional, social, and spiritual needs of dying persons and their families

issues but the physical, emotional, social, and spiritual needs of dying persons and their families (NHPCO, 2008). The hospice approach only begins when medical interventions to extend life have ceased and the person is considered to have 6 months or less to live. The focus of medical efforts is on **palliative care**, that is, on relieving the patient's pain and suffering and providing care in a way that allows the person to die with dignity.

Sometimes the hospice approach is implemented at a separate institution devoted to hospice care, but more often the hospice approach is applied in the home or hospital setting or in a nursing home. Hospice care takes place at home more commonly than in any other setting, making it possible for people to die among family members as they prefer (Centers for Medicare and Medicaid Services, 2009; Muramatsu et al., 2008). Family members who care for the dying person with hospice support have better psychological functioning two years later, compared to family members without hospice support (Ragow-O'Brien et al., 2000).

Hospice care attends not only to medical issues of a terminally ill person, but to emotional, social, and spiritual issues.

In addition to palliative care, the hospice approach has the following features (NHPCO, 2008):

- Interdisciplinary care team including medical personnel, counselors, and volunteers;
- Psychological and spiritual counseling available for patients and family members;
- For family members providing home hospice care, housekeeping support and periodic relief from care for a few hours;
- Psychological support and comfort for the dying person, sometimes including music therapy and celebrations of special events such as birthdays and holidays;
- Bereavement care for family and friends after the patient dies.

Hospice care has expanded greatly in recent years in developed countries, in part because research has shown that dying persons and their families respond much more favorably to it than to standard hospital care (Muramatsu et al., 2008; Tang et al., 2004). Another key reason for the expansion of hospice care is that it is much less expensive than standard hospital care (Morrison et al., 2008). With medical costs escalating and nearly every developed country facing the prospect of a rapidly aging population in the decades to come, hospice care is likely to grow further.

Despite the evidence of the advantages of the hospice approach, currently only about 40% of deaths in the United States involve a hospice program (NHPCO, 2008). Furthermore, hospice care tends to be applied only at the very end of life, with a median length of just 20 days. There are also sharp ethnic differences within the United States in hospice care, with the majority of Whites receiving such care at the end of life but just 10% of African Americans (Cohen, 2008).

There are a variety of reasons why the prevalence of hospice care is limited so far. Physicians are trained to heal people and keep them alive, and some tend to be optimistic about recovery prospects and reluctant to cease medical interventions even when the patient has a terminal illness (Hooyman & Kiyak, 2011). Many patients and their families are reluctant to accept hospice care because it means giving up the hope of a cure and acknowledging that death is imminent (Waldrop, 2006). African American families tend to be more likely to prefer aggressive medical treatments rather than accepting end-of-life palliative care, in part because they often believe that the more aggressive approach shows respect and love for elders and leaves the decision of the timing of death in God's hands (Dula et al., 2005). In response to such concerns,

palliative care

for terminally ill persons, a type of care that focuses on relieving the patient's pain and suffering and allows the person to die with dignity some hospice service providers are instituting "open access" policies that combine the hospice approach with continued cure efforts such as chemotherapy and dialysis (Wright & Katz, 2007).

EUTHANASIA There are few objections to the hospice approach, as it seems to offer a humane, compassionate, dignified way of reaching the end of life. However, some related approaches are regarded with far more ambivalence and ethical objections. **Euthanasia**, which means "good death," is the term for the practice of ending the life of a person who is suffering from an incurable disease or a severe disability. There are two types of euthanasia.

- *Passive euthanasia* involves ceasing medical interventions that would prolong a person's life. For example, this would include ending chemotherapy for a person who had been receiving this treatment for cancer, or removing the respirator from a person whose brain activity had ceased but whose lungs were continuing to function with medical assistance. Passive euthanasia allows death to take place but does not cause it.
- *Active euthanasia* involves not just ceasing treatment but taking steps to hasten death. It may take place when medical personnel provide a dying person with the medical means to die without pain, for example when a physician provides a terminally ill person with a prescription for a drug that will end life, at the person's request. This is also known as *assisted suicide*. Or, medical personnel or persons close to the dying person may take deliberate steps to end life, for example by administering a lethal injection.

These seem to be two quite different types of euthanasia. However, in practice the distinctions between them may be harder to draw. Take this hypothetical example. A 92-year-old woman is in the last stages of colon cancer. She was diagnosed when the cancer was far advanced, and her doctor told her she probably had only 3 months to live. For 2 months, at her request, the doctor tries chemotherapy and radiation, but the treatments make her feel miserable and do little to reverse the progress of the cancer, so she requests an end to them. She leaves the hospital and returns home, where her son, taking a leave from work, moves in with her and cares for her with the help of visits by health workers and others providing assistance. In the weeks to come her condition deteriorates further, and early one morning she wakes up crying in pain and begging her son to relieve her pain, telling him she is ready to die. He calls her doctor, who sends over a nurse with a bottle of morphine and prescribes a heavy dosage. The nurse administers the morphine and tells the son how to administer another dosage if the pain continues. The patient falls deeply asleep in response to the morphine, but wakes up later in the day, groggy and disoriented but still complaining desperately of the pain. Her son administers another dosage of the morphine, and that night she dies.

So, what happened? Was this passive euthanasia, because the treatment for the terminal condition was ended and the patient subsequently died in about the expected interval? Or was it active euthanasia, because the physician provided a prescription for a dose of morphine strong enough to end her life and because the administration of morphine probably ended the patient's life more quickly than if she had not received it?

Perhaps because the types of euthanasia are difficult to distinguish in real-life cases, surveys of people in developed countries indicate broad public support for both passive and active euthanasia. A survey on attitudes toward active euthanasia in five developed countries showed strong support (at least 70%) across all five (World Federation of Right to Die Societies, 2006). However, when "assisted suicide" is surveyed it receives lower support, slightly less than 50% (DiCamillo & Field, 2006; Pew Research Center, 2006). This may be due to the visceral response to the word *suicide*. When the survey question asks if physicians should be allowed to provide life-ending prescriptions at the request of terminally-ill persons but does not use

euthanasia
practice of ending the life of a person who is suffering from an incurable disease or severe disability

the term *assisted suicide*, support rises to three-fourths of respondents (Journal of Pain and Palliative Care Pharmacotherapy, 2006).

In the legal arena as in the real world, the distinction between the different types of euthanasia appears at first to be clear but then turns out not to be. In virtually all countries, passive euthanasia is legal but active euthanasia is not (Gupta & Naskar, 2013). Major medical societies such as the American and Canadian Medical Associations support passive euthanasia but oppose active euthanasia. However, courts generally accept the judgment of physicians in providing medications to relieve the pain of dying persons, even to the point of "terminal sedation" (Hooyman & Kiyak, 2011). Providing drugs to ease pain is legally acceptable and providing drugs with the intent to cause death is not, but in practice it is nearly impossible to tell where the easing of pain ends and the hastening of death occurs. Consequently, end-of-life decisions made between physicians and patients and patients' families are rarely questioned by the courts.

Only one developed country explicitly allows active euthanasia, the Netherlands, where these procedures have been legal for several decades. There are several conditions that must be followed under the law: the patient has clearly indicated a desire to die; the patient's physical and/or mental suffering is severe and unlikely to improve; all other options for care have been attempted or refused by the patient; and a second doctor has been consulted to ensure that these conditions have been met (Dees et al., 2010).

How well is the law succeeding in practice? Over half of Dutch doctors report performing active euthanasia, usually with terminally ill cancer patients (Rurup et al., 2005). However, in an anonymous survey, many physicians admitted that the conditions specified by the law are frequently ignored, especially the requirement of consulting a second doctor (Onwuteaka-Philipsen et al., 2005). Some physicians also admit to providing assisted suicide to elderly persons who are not terminally ill but simply "weary of life" (Rurup et al., 2005). This finding has provided fuel to critics who fear that laws allowing active euthanasia send society down a slippery slope that may lead to elderly ill persons feeling an obligation to die sooner rather than later (Jost, 2005).

Another place where active euthanasia is legal is the state of Oregon, where it has been allowed since 1997 for persons who are terminally ill and are diagnosed as having less than 6 months to live. Despite their legality, these procedures remain rare in Oregon, accounting for only one tenth of one percent of deaths (Niemeyer, 2006). Notably, 10 times as many people initiate the process of approval for assisted suicide as carry it through to the end. The law is not controversial in Oregon, where residents generally approve of the law and appreciate having the option of active euthanasia even if they do not intend to make use of it (National Journal, 2011). Washington and Vermont now have laws similar to Oregon's.

advance directive

person's written and oral instructions concerning end-of-life care

Do Not Resuscitate (DNR)

provision in a living will indicating that medical personnel are not to attempt to prolong life if the heart stops or the person stops breathing

Many older adults prepare an advance directive in case they become incapacitated, but physicians often ignore them.

EASING THE EXIT: ADVANCE DIRECTIVES Perhaps the most controversial part of euthanasia involves cases where the dying person is incapacitated and therefore unable to make the decision about which medical treatments should—or should not—be provided. In such cases it is often left to medical personnel and family members to decide, and they may have conflicting views as to what the person would have wanted.

One increasingly prevalent method for avoiding this dilemma is the use of an **advance directive**, a person's written and oral instructions concerning end-of-life care (Mitty et al., 2008). Advance directives may include a *living will*, which is a document specifying the treatments the person does or does not want in case of terminal illness, coma, or brain death. Living wills may include a **Do Not Resuscitate (DNR)** provision, indicating that medical personnel are not to attempt to prolong life if the heart stops or the person stops breathing (Scott & Caughlin, 2012). Advanced directives also may specify a *health care proxy*, which is a person (usually a family member) designated to make treatment decisions on behalf of the dying person in the event of incapacitation.

Although advance directives have been legally approved in most developed countries and are recommended by medical authorities, they do not solve all end-of-life dilemmas. One study found that even when patients had an advance directive, fewer than half the physicians overseeing their care were aware it existed (Kass-Bartelmes & Hughes, 2003). Other research has found that even when physicians have been informed of the patient's advance directive, they are often reluctant to follow it, partly from fear of legal vulnerability and partly because they have been trained to do all they can to save patients, not to let them die (Gorman et al., 2005; McArdle, 2002).

Practice Quiz   ANSWERS AVAILABLE IN ANSWER KEY.

1. In developed countries today, most people die
_____.

    a. at home
    b. in a privately funded hospice home
    c. in nursing homes or assisted living facilities
    d. in a hospital

2. Which of the following is TRUE?

    a. Even nearly a year after a home death, family caregivers report that it was relatively easy to not have to be in an institutional setting.
    b. Dying in a hospital usually means that pain will be treated and the person is less likely to be fearful.
    c. Research on patients who died in hospitals and their families has found that they were amazed and appreciative of the focus on the emotional needs of the patient.
    d. Most people prefer to die at home.

3. Research on hospice has found that _____.

    a. it is more expensive than standard hospital care
    b. family members who provide for the dying person with hospice support have better psychological functioning two years later, compared to family members without hospice support

    c. it is more common among African Americans, who tend to be higher than other groups in spirituality
    d. families of the dying find it to be more stressful than those who do not rely on hospice care because they feel a loss of control

4. Kathy was taking care of her husband who has been battling colon cancer for five years and had resisted the recommendation of family members to contact hospice. Based on research, what is the most likely reason she would not accept this help?

    a. She is a trained medical professional and feels competent managing on her own.
    b. She is an introvert and is shy about having people come into her home.
    c. She is concerned that this approach goes against her religious beliefs.
    d. It means acknowledging that death is imminent.

5. Ending chemotherapy treatment for a cancer patient is an example of _____.

    a. passive euthanasia
    b. assisted suicide
    c. active euthanasia
    d. a DNR provision

Summary: Physical Aspects of Death

LO 13.1 **Describe how causes of death have changed throughout history and identify the two major causes of death today.**

Until the past century, many deaths occurred during infancy, toddlerhood, and early childhood due to young children's susceptibility to infectious diseases. During the 20th century, causes of death such as cancer and heart disease became more common in developed countries as death occurs later in the life span.

Cardiovascular disease is the number one cause of death among adults in developed countries. Symptoms of a heart attack include acute pain, weakness, dizziness, confusion, and shortness of breath. Men and African

Americans have higher rates of heart disease. Symptoms of cancer depend on the type but may include weight loss, fatigue, and weakness. Cancer is most common in late adulthood and has a partly genetic origin, but smoking, poor diet, excessive alcohol use, and chronic exposure to sunlight can increase the risk of developing the disease.

LO 13.2 **Describe the role that telomeres and free radicals play in aging, and review efforts to delay the aging process.**

When the Hayflick limit is reached, the telomeres become too short and cells stop replicating. Shortened telomeres have been found to be associated with a wide range of diseases such as cancer. Some studies have reported that under certain conditions there can be an increase in an enzyme called telomerase, which regulates the length of telomeres. Free radicals cause damage to the DNA and other structures that cells need to function. The activity of free radicals is muted by the presence of antioxidants, which absorb the extra electron in the free radicals and thereby prevent them from damaging the cell. Antioxidants are found naturally in many foods, especially fruits and vegetables, yet research shows there are more risks than benefits from ingesting antioxidant medications and supplements.

Experimental studies in which animals and humans receive supplements of growth hormone have yielded sometimes dramatic results, but these effects have not been permanent, and regular use of growth hormones has been found to have some unpleasant side effects. Studies on DHEA supplements have so far failed to show benefits. In a wide variety of animal species, decreasing caloric intake by 30–50% results in an increase in life span of up to 50%, but few studies have been done on humans.

LO 13.3   Compare and contrast the benefits and drawbacks of dying at home versus in a hospital.

Most people would prefer to die at home, yet few do in developed countries. Dying at home often takes place slowly and gradually, leaving caregivers under the strain of helping the dying person with daily activities. Hospitals offer advanced medical care but are often seen as impersonal and dehumanizing.

LO 13.4   Summarize the options and controversies that exist regarding end-of-life care and death.

Hospice care provides a humane setting that allows terminally ill people to live the final chapter of their lives with dignity. Euthanasia, which involves either ceasing medical interventions or taking steps to bring about death, is sometimes considered when death is near and there is no possibility of recovery, although it is highly controversial. Many older adults in developed countries now create advance directives before they become ill so that their loved ones will not be faced with making difficult choices on their behalf.

Section 2 Emotional Responses to Death

⌄ Learning Objectives

13.5 Describe how the emotional responses associated with grief change over time.

13.6 Describe variations in the grieving process, and identify factors that influence these variations.

13.7 Summarize Kübler-Ross's theory of death and dying.

13.8 Identify some limitations of Kübler-Ross's theory, and describe some other responses to death and dying.

EMOTIONAL RESPONSES TO DEATH: Bereavement and Grief

In the course of our lives, nearly all of us experience the death of people we love and value. *Bereavement* is the experience of losing a loved one, and *grief* is the psychological response that often accompanies bereavement. Grief is perhaps the most intense and complex psychological process we experience throughout the course of a human lifetime, and there is no simple or easy way to characterize it. With this in mind, first let us look at the general pattern of the grief process, then at some of the major sources of variability.

The Emotional Arc of Grief

LO 13.5 **Describe how the emotional responses associated with grief change over time.**

In the initial hours, days, and perhaps weeks following bereavement, grief often involves shock, numbness, and disbelief. At first we find it hard to believe that the person we loved could really be gone forever. This is often accompanied by an intense yearning to see and hear the person again. Watch the video *Grieving a Loss, Part 1* on the next page to see how one family grieves over the loss of their daughter and sister.

As the initial shock fades, it is frequently succeeded by a cascade of powerful, unsettling, and shifting emotions, possibly including sadness, anger, anxiety, loneliness, guilt, and helplessness (Scannell-Desch, 2003). These intense emotional states may alternate with states that resemble the symptoms of depression: lethargy, aimlessness, confusion, and disorganization (Hensley, 2006). Simply getting out of bed in the morning and going through the tasks of the day may seem overwhelming. There may be difficulty sleeping and a loss of interest in eating.

After some time has passed—perhaps weeks later, perhaps months—the intense emotions of grief begin to subside, and the bereaved person is able to resume previous daily activities and social relationships (Lotterman et al., 2014). New activities may be taken up, as part of the reorganization of life now that the loved person is gone. New relationships may be formed, to provide support and companionship that had been missed as a consequence of the loved one's death. The survivor's identity may change, too, to incorporate the recognition of the death. For example, a woman who has lost her spouse may now think of herself as a widow rather than as a wife. After my mom died,

Watch GRIEVING A LOSS, PART 1

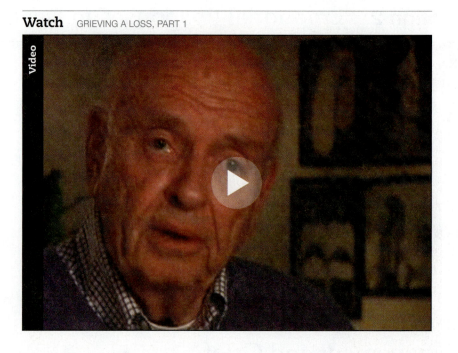

my dad continued to wear his wedding ring for several years afterward. When he finally took it off, it symbolized his acceptance that his identity had changed and he was now a widower.

Grief subsides for most people over time, but when there was a close attachment to the person who died, the feelings of loss and yearning may never entirely fade (Worden, 2009). Survivors may not so much recover from their loss as learn to live with it (Levin, 2004). They may also maintain a persistent sense of the dead person's psychological presence. As noted in Chapter 12, widows and widowers may continue to "talk with" their deceased spouse, even years after the death (Carnelly et al., 2006; Stroebe & Stroebe, 1991).

Variations in Grieving

LO 13.6 **Describe variations in the grieving process, and identify factors that influence these variations.**

Within the general pattern of grieving just described, there is a substantial amount of variability. The variations in forms and patterns of grieving depend on *who* has died and *how* the death occurred.

Regarding the question of who died, the more intense the attachment had been to the person, the more intense the grief is likely to be (Bonanno, 2004). In general, the deaths that provoke the most grief are of parents, children, and spouses. Children who experience the death of a parent tend to be deeply affected, even years later (Dowdney, 2000; Lotterman et al., 2014). Their grief depends in part on how old they are when the parent dies and how much support they receive from others, but in general the death of a parent places them at risk for emotional difficulties, especially depression, in both the near term and the long term (Shear, 2009). Similarly, parents who experience the death of a child tend to have a severe and enduring reaction (Dent & Stewart, 2004). They tend to report high levels of distress even years later, and the death also places them at high risk for divorce (Kreicbergs et al., 2004).

Death of a spouse has profound effects on the widowed, but these effects are complex and vary by gender. Among older adults, a wide variety of psychological problems are nearly 10 times higher among the newly bereaved as among their married peers, including depression, anxiety, substance use, and cognitive difficulties with memory and concentration (Hooyman & Kiyak, 2011). In the first year following the death of a spouse, the risk of mortality for the bereaved person is 7 times as high as among married peers (Subramanian et al., 2008). The video *Death of a Spouse* details how one woman is coping with the death of her husband.

Watch   DEATH OF A SPOUSE

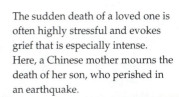

Because men tend to be older than the women they marry and women tend to live longer than men do, over 80% of wives outlive their husbands (Hooyman & Kiyak, 2011; OECD, 2009). This pattern is consistent across cultures, nations, and historical periods. Widows often struggle financially after their husbands die, and if widowed in late adulthood they are unlikely to remarry (Angel et al., 2003; Schulz et al., 2006). However, they often show considerable resilience as they strengthen their relations with children and friends and build new lives for themselves (Cheng, 2006; Rossi et al., 2007). In contrast, men are more likely to experience physical and mental health problems following their bereavement, and they recover their emotional equilibrium more slowly (Berg et al., 2009). Widowers are 7 times more likely than widows to remarry late in life, in part because there are so many more women available than men but also because men feel less able than women to face the challenges of life on their own, without a spouse (Ajrouch et al., 2005; Bookwala, 2012).

The sudden death of a loved one is often highly stressful and evokes grief that is especially intense. Here, a Chinese mother mourns the death of her son, who perished in an earthquake.

CRITICAL THINKING QUESTION

Why do you think men experience greater difficulties during bereavement and recover more slowly than women do? What else have you learned in the course of this book that could help explain this pattern?

The *how* of death also affects the course of grief, specifically how expected or unexpected the death is. Sudden death tends to evoke grief that is especially intense. In one study, the experience adults ages 18–45 rated as most stressful was the sudden death of a loved one (Breslau et al., 1998). A sudden death often shatters the survivors' assumptions

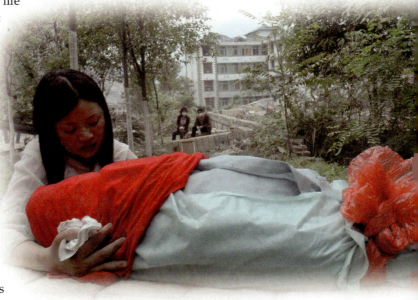

that the world is benevolent, just, and predictable, and the psychological effects are evident for years afterward (Burton et al., 2006). Suicide is especially devastating, as it frequently arouses feelings not only of sorrow but of guilt and shame (Dunne & Dunne-Maxim, 2004).

In contrast, when death is expected because it takes place after a long illness or when the person is very old, the survivors are able to prepare themselves through *anticipatory grief*, as they accept that death is inevitable and begin to adapt to it emotionally. Especially for family members who have attended to a dying loved one through a long illness, grief may be combined with relief at being able to return to their own lives (Keene & Prokos, 2008).

Grief is complicated and various, and there is no one "best way" to grieve (Wortman, 2008). Because grief is so emotionally challenging, cultures around the world have developed mourning rituals to structure it and make it comprehensible and bearable, as we will see later in the chapter.

Practice Quiz ANSWERS AVAILABLE IN ANSWER KEY.

1. Research on grief has shown that _____.
   a. talking to the deceased spouse was found only among those who had psychological disorders before the loss
   b. survivors who experience a change in their identity to incorporate the recognition of the death are the ones most at risk of suicide
   c. after the initial shock fades, people who were not depressed before the loss will not be depressed after it because of their innate resiliency
   d. after the initial shock fades, most bereaved people resume their daily activities, but it may take weeks or months

2. After experiencing the death of a loved one, it is not uncommon for intense emotional states to alternate with states that resemble the symptoms of _____.
   a. Tourette's syndrome
   b. dissociative identity disorder
   c. obsessive-compulsive disorder
   d. depression

3. When individuals die, there is a period of grief. The most grief is experienced with the loss of parents, spouses, and _____.
   a. close friends, especially those from early in childhood
   b. siblings
   c. grandparents
   d. children

4. Following the death of a spouse _____.
   a. women are more likely than men to experience mental health problems because they are less likely to get remarried
   b. men are more likely than women to experience physical and mental health problems.
   c. the risk of mortality is about the same as among married peers because widows and widowers are often given a lot of social support
   d. older adults tend to grieve similarly regardless of how their spouse died because of deeply engrained beliefs of what is "appropriate"

5. When death is expected, such as a death that occurs after a long illness, _____.
   a. the survivors are able to prepare themselves through antipcatory grief
   b. the grief experienced by survivors is especially intense
   c. family members often take longer to adapt to it emotionally than if it were sudden death
   d. it usually causes long-term physical and mental health problems

EMOTIONAL RESPONSES TO DEATH: Confronting Death

In addition to coping with the death of those we love, we also have to cope with the prospect of our own death. In fact, one of our most distinctive qualities as a species is that we are aware that one day we will die, because of our unique capacity for anticipating the future (Becker, 2007). For people afflicted with a terminal illness, this awareness becomes especially acute.

Stage Theory of Death

LO 13.7 **Summarize Kübler-Ross's theory of death and dying.**

One person who has been influential in describing people's psychological responses to awareness of a fatal illness is Elizabeth Kübler-Ross (1969, 1982). Based on her interviews with 200 terminally ill patients, she proposed that people go through a series of five stages in their responses to imminent death.

1. *Denial.* Many people with a diagnosis of terminal illness initially refuse to believe it. *No, it can't be true,* they might think. *There must be some mistake. Perhaps my test results got mixed up with someone else's.* Kübler-Ross advised family members and health professionals not to encourage denial, because doing so would prevent the person from going ahead with making arrangements to prepare for death. However, other therapists have framed denial more positively, as a way of protecting the ego while the person adjusts to the psychological blow of a terminal diagnosis (Schacter, 2009).

2. *Anger.* After denial fades, anger is next. *It's not fair,* the person may reason. *I'm a good person. Look at all the people who are much worse than me and yet they're still healthy.* The anger may be felt toward family members, medical personnel, God, or healthy people generally.

3. *Bargaining.* Anger, too, eventually fades, and now the terminally ill person tries to bargain for extra time. Usually the bargaining is directed toward God or the fates or some vague spiritual entity. *Just let me live, and I promise I'll dedicate my life to healing others. Just give me one more year, so I can see my child get married. Please, let me live to celebrate one more holiday with my family.*

4. *Depression.* After bargaining, depression often sets in. Despite the attempts to bargain, the terminally ill person's condition steadily worsens. Invasive medical procedures are painful and result in a loss of dignity. The person realizes that death is growing nearer and there is little that can be done.

5. *Acceptance.* Finally, the person comes to accept death. There may be a feeling of peace as resistance to death is abandoned, or there may be little feeling at all, but rather a sense of disengagement and a desire to be with only the few people most valued.

Kübler-Ross's theory had an enormous impact on the care of terminally ill patients. Many health care professionals found it to be useful in understanding and caring for their patients. However, it has not held up well in subsequent research, as we will see next.

Other Methods of Confronting Death

LO 13.8 **Identify some limitations of Kübler-Ross's theory, and describe some other responses to death and dying.**

Few people go through the five stages in a sequence as Kübler-Ross claimed, and many people experience few or none of the stages. The theory also oddly overlooks fear as a response to a diagnosis of terminal illness, which research shows is very common (Krikorian et al., 2012; Langner, 2002). And of course it overlooks cultural context entirely, whereas other studies show that people often interpret impending death through a framework of cultural beliefs (Hooyman & Kiyak, 2011). As noted in earlier chapters, nearly all cultures have some form of religious beliefs, and religions nearly always include some kind of explanation for what happens when we die, usually including the promise of some kind of afterlife, as we will see later in the chapter.

In Chinese culture, the grieving process often focuses on how death will change relationships with others.

Despite its lack of validity, Kübler-Ross's theory has been influential not only in the care of terminally ill patients but in American cultural views of death. According to Ruth Konigsberg (2011), the theory is invoked to explain everything from how we will recover from the death of a loved one, to responses to a sudden environmental catastrophe, and even to the trading away of a favorite basketball star, even though abundant research contradicts it.

As Konigsberg describes, responses to terminal illness are highly variable, and there is no common series of stages and no one healthy way to respond. Konigsberg also presents examples of how people in other cultures respond to terminal illness and grief, noting, for example, how in Chinese culture the focus is on the ways the prospect of death will change relationships with others, rather than being focused on the individual's emotions.

Practice Quiz   ANSWERS AVAILABLE IN ANSWER KEY.

1. According to Elisabeth Kübler-Ross, which of the following is the correct order of emotions that people go through as a response to death?
   a. Denial, anger, bargaining, depression, and acceptance
   b. Depression, anger, denial, bargaining, and acceptance
   c. Bargaining, anger, depression, denial, and acceptance
   d. Anger, denial, depression, bargaining, and acceptance

2. Elijah was recently given the news that his cancer has spread rapidly, and he does not have much longer to live. After a brief period of disbelief, he now says things like, "I'm a good person, why does that guy get to live and I have to die?" and, "That lady has been smoking for 30 years and she's fine. Why am I the one who has to get sick?" Elijah is clearly in Kübler-Ross's _____ stage, the second stage of her five proposed stages of responses to imminent death.
   a. acceptance
   b. depression
   c. bargaining
   d. anger

3. Which of the following is a critique of Kübler-Ross's theory?
   a. The number of stages is insufficient to capture the complexity of responding to imminent death.
   b. It has not been influential in the care of terminally ill patients in this country.
   c. She did not collect any data to inform her theory.
   d. It overlooks the cultural context.

4. One critique of Kübler-Ross's theory is that it overlooks _____ as a response to a diagnosis of terminal illness.
   a. relief   c. anger
   b. fear   d. depression

5. Some research has shown that a person from _____ would be most likely to respond to terminal illness and grief by focusing on the ways the prospect of death will change relationships with others.
   a. Canada   c. New Zealand
   b. the United States   d. China

Summary: Emotional Responses to Death

LO 13.5 Describe how the emotional responses associated with grief change over time.

The early responses to grief often entail shock, numbness, and disbelief, followed by a period of intense emotions alternating with states that resemble the symptoms of depression. Grief gradually subsides and the bereaved person is able to resume previous daily activities and social relationships, although feelings of loss and yearning may never entirely fade.

LO 13.6 Describe variations in the grieving process, and identify factors that influence these variations.

There are variations in grieving depending on *who* has died and *how* the death occurred, with the most intense grief experienced for deaths of a parent, child, or spouse, and for deaths that occurred suddenly. Men and women

generally deal with the death of a spouse differently, with men more likely to experience physical and mental health problems.

LO 13.7 Summarize Kübler-Ross's theory of death and dying.

Kübler-Ross proposed that people go through a series of five stages in their responses to imminent death: denial, anger, bargaining, depression, and acceptance.

LO 13.8 Identify some limitations of Kübler-Ross's theory and describe some other responses to death and dying.

Her theory has been influential but has not held up well in subsequent research. Few people go through the five stages in this sequence, and many people experience few or none of the stages.

Section 3 Beliefs About Death and the Afterlife

⌄ Learning Objective

13.9 Describe how children's understanding of death changes from childhood to adolescence.

13.10 Describe how beliefs and fears about death change throughout adulthood.

13.11 Explain how individual beliefs about the afterlife vary across countries and within the United States.

13.12 Compare and contrast the mourning rituals of Hinduism, Buddhism, Judaism, Christianity, and Islam.

13.13 Describe the rituals and traditions used by various religions to remember and honor the dead.

BELIEFS ABOUT DEATH AND THE AFTERLIFE: Beliefs About Death Throughout the Life Span

We are, so far as we know, the only animal who anticipates death. That unusually large cerebral cortex of ours, which is built so well for anticipating future events, allows us to realize that among those future events will be our own death. But how do thoughts and beliefs about death change in the course of human development? Let us examine changes in *awareness* of death and *anxiety* about death with age. As we will see, awareness and anxiety about death do not always go hand in hand.

Beliefs About Death in Childhood and Adolescence

LO 13.9 **Describe how children's understanding of death changes from childhood to adolescence.**

By the age of 3 or 4, most children have some experience with death. They may know of a family member or neighbor or family friend who died. They have almost certainly seen dead animals, perhaps a family pet, or a dead bird, or at least a dead bug. But do they really understand what it means to be dead?

In some ways they do, and in some ways they do not (Irish et al., 2014; Kenyon, 2001). Even in early childhood, most children understand that death is *permanent.* They realize the dead bug is not going to get up and walk away. However, for most children it is not until middle childhood that they realize that death is *inevitable.* It is not just bugs and bad people who die, but every living thing, including "me." Watch the video *Children's Perceptions of Death* on the next page to learn more about how young children understand death.

One reason for children's limited understanding of death is that most cultures have customs of using euphemisms to refer to death and withholding the full truth

Watch   CHILDREN'S PERCEPTIONS OF DEATH

Video

Even in early childhood most children have some experience with death, but do they really understand what death is?

about death from children, in an effort to protect them from the fear of death and the pain of losing a loved one (Cicirelli, 2006; Wass, 2004). Thus adults might tell children "Grandma has passed on" or the family pet has "gone to sleep," rather than being told bluntly of their death. Furthermore, as we will see later in the chapter, nearly all cultures have beliefs about life after death. Nearly always, these beliefs make death seem neither permanent nor inevitable, and children learn the afterlife beliefs of their culture early (Wass, 2004).

In adolescence, beliefs about death become more abstract and complex, reflecting adolescents' gains in cognitive development. When describing their thoughts about death, adolescents often use abstractions such as "eternal light" and "nothingness," whereas children usually do not (Brent et al., 1996; Irish et al., 2014; Wenestam & Wass, 1987). Adolescents are also more likely than children to discuss religious concepts of death, such as reincarnation, heaven and hell, and the existence of a soul that endures after death (Mearns, 2000; Noppe & Noppe, 1997; Yang & Chen, 2002).

Adolescents understand death better than children in some ways, but do they really understand the reality of their own death? This question is more difficult to answer. As we saw in Chapter 8, adolescence is the life stage of the *personal fable*, the belief that they are unique and special and that bad things will not happen to them. Some adolescents who are diagnosed with a terminal illness have a personal fable so resilient that they refuse to believe they really will die soon (Blumberg et al., 1984).

Beliefs About Death in Adulthood

LO 13.10 **Describe how beliefs and fears about death change throughout adulthood.**

You might think that the older people are, the closer they are to death, and so the more they fear dying. However, research shows that the pattern in adulthood is just the opposite. Death anxiety is highest in emerging adulthood, then declines with age, and is lowest in late adulthood (Russac et al., 2007).

Greater fear of death at the younger life stages appears to be due mainly to having plans and goals that remain to be accomplished. By late adulthood, especially among persons beyond age 80, most people feel they are nearing the end of their life span and they no longer feel they need to stay alive in order to reach the goals they had set out for themselves (Cicirelli, 2006). For many people late adulthood is a time of what psychologist Robert Butler calls **life review**, thinking about the life they have lived and coming to an acceptance of it, both the lows and the highs (Butler, 2002). As described in the previous chapter, Erikson (1950) proposed that the main crisis of late adulthood is *ego integrity versus despair,* and research indicates that most people reach a state of ego integrity, accepting what their life has been for better and worse. Although they may not fear death itself, older adults often do have some fears associated with death, such as suffering and pain, loss of self-control, and the effects of their death on loved ones (Kwak et al., 2008; Irish et al., 2014).

Within each life stage, death anxiety is lowest in people who have the strongest religious faith, because they are more likely than others to be confident that there is a pleasant life after death awaiting them (Irish et al., 2014). Death anxiety is highest not in atheists and agnostics but in people who are unsure believers and inconsistent participants in religious activities (Cicirelli, 2006). Apparently their involvement in religion is enough to make them contemplate death but not enough to provide consolation. Death anxiety is also consistently higher among women than among men, across cultures, but why this is so is not clear (Russac et al., 2007; Tomer et al., 2000).

In addition to changes in death anxiety, thoughts about death change in other ways in the course of adulthood (Cicirelli, 2006). In young adulthood, fears of death tend to be focused on fear for one's children, both the fear of the children dying and the fear that the children would be vulnerable if their parents died. In middle adulthood, as noted in Chapter 11, people often become aware that they have passed the halfway point and have fewer years remaining than they have lived so far. For some, this sharpens their awareness of death and makes them reexamine their lives to see if they need to make changes in order to make the most of the years they have left.

In late adulthood, people become more familiar with death because this is where death is concentrated, especially in developed countries. In the course of late adulthood, the longer they live the more likely they are to witness the deaths of parents, friends, and siblings. This experience, combined with their own closer proximity to death, leads them to think and talk more about death than younger people do (Hayslip & Hansson, 2003; Irish et al., 2014). Talking about death helps them cope effectively with it, using mutual consolation and sometimes humor. It also enables them to address practical concerns such as making a will and arranging for the distribution of their personal possessions (Kastenbaum, 2007).

life review

according to Robert Butler, the process in late adulthood when people reflect on the life they have lived and come to an acceptance of it

Practice Quiz   ANSWERS AVAILABLE IN ANSWER KEY.

1. Lianna, a teenager, and her sister, who is only 8 years old, recently lost their grandmother. Lianna is more likely than her sister to _____.
   a. cry over the loss
   b. understand that the death is permanent
   c. grieve
   d. discuss religious concepts surrounding the death

2. Your niece is 4 years old, and her grandfather recently died. When adults in your family speak to her about her grandfather's death, they will probably tell her that her grandfather _____ to avoid being blunt and upsetting her.
   a. has passed on
   b. is dead
   c. will be back soon
   d. died in a car accident

3. Kyle is 80 years old and is likely to conduct a _____, thinking back on his life and accepting both the good and the bad.
   a. personal fable
   b. life review
   c. euphamism
   d. living will

4. Research on death anxiety has shown that _____.

   a. strength of religious faith is unrelated to level of death anxiety

   b. younger people talk more about death than older people do because they see it as less of a threat because it is further away

   c. older adults are more afraid of death than younger age groups because they've witnessed the death of friends and family members

   d. death anxiety is higher among women than men

5. Research has shown that anxiety about death is highest among those who _____.

   a. maintain strong religious faith

   b. are atheist or agnostic

   c. are unsure believers or inconsistent participants in religious activities

   d. believe that they are sinners

BELIEFS ABOUT DEATH AND THE AFTERLIFE: Afterlife Beliefs and Mourning Rituals

This book has been devoted to explaining what happens in the course of human development, from beginning to end, from womb to tomb, from lust to dust. But one remarkable feature of the human species, at least since the Neolithic revolution 40,000 years ago, is that we are the only creature that believes that death is not the end, that part of us—the soul, the spirit, some disembodied essence of ourselves—goes on. Here we examine what people in a variety of countries believe about life after death. Then we look at how the mourning rituals and remembrance practices of the major religions reflect afterlife beliefs and assist the mourners in carrying on with life.

What Do Individuals Believe About Life After Death?

LO 13.11 **Explain how individual beliefs about the afterlife vary across countries and within the United States.**

Over the past several thousand years, vast changes have taken place in how people live; yet over that same time, how people explain death has been surprisingly enduring and stable. The early Egyptian and Greek beliefs about life after death, developed thousands of years ago, are still evident in several major religions. Most notable is the belief that death is a moral event. Both ancient civilizations came to believe that upon death we are judged for our moral conduct, and our destination in the afterlife depends on the outcome of that judgment. The afterlife beliefs of the major religions are quite diverse, but all of them have this belief in common. Many of the beliefs of the major religions today date from around 3,500 to 2,000 years ago; even the most recent major religion, Islam, is about 1,500 years old. Afterlife beliefs are part of all the major religious traditions, including Hinduism, Buddhism, Judaism, Christianity, and Islam.

There are some striking similarities across these beliefs. First, in every religion death is not the end. In some religions the body continues on in some way after death and in some it does not, but in all religions there is a belief in a soul that remains in existence. Second, in every religion the determination of the soul's destiny in the afterlife depends on the kind of moral life the person has lived. Good people are rewarded after death, either with a higher reincarnation status (Hinduism and Buddhism) or with entry into heaven (Christianity and Islam). Bad people are punished, either with a lower reincarnation status (Hinduism and Buddhism) or the torments of hell (Judaism, Christianity, and Islam). Christianity may seem to be an exception to this rule, because it holds that faith is ultimately the most important criterion for an afterlife reward, but even in Christianity

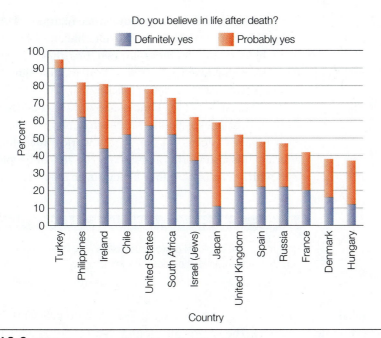

Figure 13.3 ISSP Survey on Belief in Life After Death
SOURCE: ISSP (2012)

faith and works are supposed to go together. That is, an essential part of following the faith is leading a good moral life.

But what do individual people actually believe about the afterlife? After all, each of these religions (except Judaism) has hundreds of millions of adherents, so there must be some variability of afterlife beliefs with each faith. Next, we take a closer look at what people around the world have reported about their afterlife beliefs.

AFTERLIFE BELIEFS AROUND THE WORLD Several times over the past 20 years, the International Social Survey Program (http://www.issp.org/) has surveyed people in 32 countries around the world about a wide range of topics, including their afterlife beliefs. According to this survey, as shown in **Figure 13.3**, for the question "Do you believe in life after death?" the proportion of "definitely yes" responses ranged from 12% in Hungary to 90% in Turkey. Adding "probably yes" and "definitely yes" together, the frequencies ranged from 37% in Hungary to 95% in Turkey.

Some other patterns can be seen in the responses across countries. "Yes" responses were highest in the two least economically developed countries in the survey, Turkey and the Philippines, as well as in the United States, which has long been found to be more religious than most other developed countries and which has a large population of Latinos (13%), who tend to be more religious than the general population (Pew Forum on Religion and Public Life, 2008). "No" responses were highest in the countries of eastern Europe such as Russia and Hungary, in which religious observances were suppressed when atheism was the official state policy during their decades under Communist rule in the 20th century. "No" responses were also high in the prosperous northern European countries of France and Denmark. In these countries, participation in organized religion has faded substantially in the course of the past century and few people participate actively in religious institutions today (Zuckerman, 2008).

AFTERLIFE BELIEFS IN THE UNITED STATES More detailed information about afterlife beliefs is available for the United States in the surveys by the Pew Forum on Religion and Public Life (2008). Because the United States has immigrants from many countries, the Pew survey provides information about afterlife beliefs among adherents of many different religions.

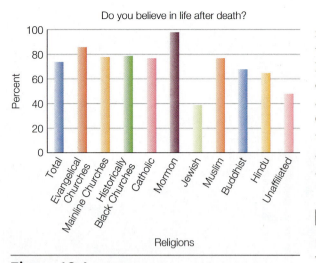

Do you believe in life after death?

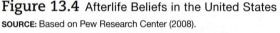

Religions

Figure 13.4 Afterlife Beliefs in the United States
SOURCE: Based on Pew Research Center (2008).

As **Figure 13.4** shows, about three-quarters of Americans in the Pew survey said they believe in life after. Afterlife beliefs were highest among those in two branches of Christianity, Protestants (the average of Evangelical and Mainline Protestant churches was 82%) and Catholics (77%), but were also high among Muslims (77%), Hindus (65%), and Buddhists (68%). Only 39% of Jews expressed a belief in an afterlife, consistent with Judaism's focus on life in this world rather than on the afterlife. It is also worth noting that even 48% of people unaffiliated with a religion said they believe in an afterlife.

CRITICAL THINKING QUESTION

How might one's cultural or religious beliefs about the afterlife affect the way that person views the death of a loved one?

Across religious groups, people were somewhat less likely to believe in hell (59%) than to believe in heaven (74%). The survey also found that 61% of Hindus believe in **reincarnation** (being born again into the world after death) and 62% of Buddhists believe in *nirvana* (release from the cycle of death and rebirth).

Perhaps because there so many different religious groups living together in the United States, Americans are generally tolerant of different views about religion and the afterlife. The Pew survey found that in all faiths a majority of respondents agreed that "many religions can lead to eternal life." This view is in direct contradiction to the traditional doctrine of both Christianity and Islam, which emphasize belief in their faith as a requirement for being rewarded in the afterlife.

Mourning Rituals of the Major Religions

LO 13.12 Compare and contrast the mourning rituals of Hinduism, Buddhism, Judaism, Christianity, and Islam.

Each of the major religions has mourning rituals that help survivors adjust to the death of a loved one. As you read about the mourning rituals, keep in mind that in each religion there are local and regional variations and the rituals described here may not match precisely how they are performed in each specific place.

HINDUISM In Hinduism, reincarnation is the central afterlife belief. When a person dies, the body no longer functions but the soul returns to the earth in a new form, perhaps again as a human, perhaps in animal form, depending on the overall moral balance of good and evil that has accumulated in the person's life. However, before the soul returns to earth there is a period when its bodily destination in the next life is still to be determined. It is here that Hindu mourning rituals are crucial, because the devotion of the survivors to performing these rituals is a key influence on what the soul's status will be in the next life (Hockey & Katz, 2001). The rituals are highly elaborate, so only a brief version is described here.

Most Hindus die at home. When death is imminent, family members keep a vigil all day and night, singing hymns, praying, and reading Hindu scriptures. Holy ashes are applied to the forehead, and a few drops of milk or holy water may be trickled into the mouth.

Upon death, a lamp is lit and incense is burned continually. The thumbs are tied together, as are the big toes. Religious pictures are turned to the wall, and mirrors may be covered to signify that mourners should not be thinking of themselves during this

reincarnation

belief that after death the soul returns again to earth in another bodily form

time. Extended kin are called together to bid farewell to the deceased and sing sacred songs beside the body.

Next the body is taken to be **cremated**; that is, burned to ashes. Sometimes this is done on an open fire, but increasingly it occurs at a place designated for the purpose, called a *crematorium*. Only men go to the site of the cremation, regardless of the gender of the deceased. All of them bathe upon returning to the home, to wash themselves of the spiritual impurity associated with death.

About 12 hours after cremation, the family men return to collect the ashes. The ashes are then scattered in a holy body of water, ideally the holy Ganges River, along with flowers. In the days that follow, family members are not to visit each others' homes, attend festivals or temple, or make wedding arrangements. Pictures remain turned to the wall, and all religious icons are covered with white cloths. About a week after the death, family members gather to share a meal of the deceased's favorite foods. A portion is offered before a photo of the deceased.

A memorial service is held 31 days after the death. Afterward, all join in cleaning the house and the period of spiritual impurity is considered to be over. Although some families observe the prohibitions just described for up to a year, Hindu tradition generally discourages prolonged mourning and encourages the survivors to move on with life after the 31st day.

Reincarnation is a key part of Hindu beliefs.

BUDDHISM Like Hinduism, Buddhism includes belief in reincarnation and, as in Hinduism, cremation is the prescribed practice upon death. Furthermore, in both religions it is believed that the period immediately following death is of special importance, and mourning rituals must be followed scrupulously to lessen the soul's suffering during the interim period between death and rebirth and to ensure the soul as favorable a reincarnation as possible. In Buddhism as in Hinduism, there are differences in mourning rituals by region and sect, so the information that follows describes the general pattern (Wilson, 2009).

In Buddhist mourning rituals, monks play a prominent role. They arrive at the home when death is near to comfort the dying person and the family. At this time the monks begin chanting verses about the brevity of life and the inevitability of death. After death, there is a bathing ceremony in which relatives and friends pour water over one hand of the deceased. The body is then placed in a coffin and flowers, candles, and incense are placed alongside it, perhaps along with a picture of the deceased.

Cremation usually takes place within 3 days. Each day monks come to the house to chant prayers for the soul of the deceased. Food is offered to the monks by the family. Neighbors and family also arrive each day to feast, share fellowship, and observe the prayers offered by the monks.

On the day of cremation, the monks lead a prayer service at the home and then lead the procession of mourners to the temple, where the cremation takes place. More prayers are chanted, and then mourners approach the coffin with lighted torches of wood, incense, and candles and toss them beneath to begin the cremation process. Later the ashes will be collected and kept in an urn.

cremated

after death, burning the body to ashes

In Buddhist mourning rituals, an important role is played by monks, such as the Cambodian monks shown here.

In Judaism, when a family member dies the surviving family members recite the Kaddish prayer every day for 11 months.

On the evening of the cremation ritual one last feast is held. Now instead of prayers there is music, and the feast is intended to banish sorrow and fear of the spirits of the dead through fellowship among the survivors. In some Buddhist traditions prayers for the deceased continue to be chanted every 7 days for 49 days; in others, every 10 days for 100 days. As long as the rituals continue they are believed to benefit the soul of the deceased.

JUDAISM In Judaism, upon death the eyes are closed, the body is covered and laid on the floor, and candles are lit nearby (Wahlhaus, 2005). The body is not to be left alone, so various family members remain beside it at all times. Eating and drinking are forbidden in the same room as the body, as this would mock the deceased who is no longer able to enjoy these pleasures. For the same reason flowers are not present at the funeral, nor are they sent to the family. The body is buried in a grave, not cremated. Following the burial there is usually a "meal of condolence" consisting of eggs and bread (symbolizing life), for family members only. Visitors may come to offer condolences following the meal.

Although Judaism emphasizes life after death less than any other major religion, its mourning rituals after death are among the most highly ritualized. Upon hearing of the death of a family member or close friend, the tradition is to express grief by tearing one's clothing (although today often a black ribbon is worn instead). After the burial, family members enter an intense 7-day period called sitting *shiva* (meaning "seven"). During this time they sit only on low stools or on the floor, and they do not work, bathe, shave, cut their hair, wear cosmetics, have sexual relations, or change their clothes. Mirrors in the house are covered. Prayer services are held that include family and friends.

Following shiva, another period of restrictions lasts until 30 days after burial, called *schloshim* (meaning "thirty"). Mourners may not shave or cut their hair, attend parties, or listen to music. A further period, lasting until a year after death, is observed for parents' death only. Children of the deceased parent are not to attend parties, theater performances, or concerts during this time. Furthermore, they must recite a prayer called the *Kaddish* every day for 11 months.

CHRISTIANITY Christianity has more adherents worldwide (about 2 billion) than any other religion, and the mourning rituals of Christianity often take local forms. However, there are two main general types of mourning rituals in Christianity: Catholic and Protestant (Hunter, 2007).

In the Catholic church, when a person is ill and near death there is a traditional ritual called *Anointing of the Sick*. The purpose of this ritual is to bring comfort to the sick person and family members who may be anguished over the impending death, to forgive any sins the sick person may not have repented, and to prepare the person's soul for passing over to eternal life. It can take place in a home, hospital, or church. The rite is administered by a priest, who begins by reading a Bible verse, then places his hands on the dying person's head, then blesses the oil and applies it to the forehead of the dying person.

After the person dies, a *vigil* (also called a *wake*) is held in the home or the church. Family members and friends gather to share food and drink, pray for the deceased person, remember the person's life, and comfort one another. The deceased is in a coffin, which is usually open, and often there are candles, flowers, and a crucifix. In some cultures, mirrors are covered or turned to the wall if the vigil takes place at home. The vigil can last from a few hours to 2 days.

The day following the end of the vigil, a *Requiem Mass* is held. After the Mass is over, the coffin is immediately taken to the cemetery to be buried. At the gravesite the priest sprinkles holy water on the coffin and on the grave. Special prayers are said, asking that the soul rest in peace and receive God's mercy. After the burial it is customary to gather again at the home of the deceased for food, drink, remembrance, and consolation.

The Protestant funeral service resembles the Catholic service in some ways, but is much less standardized and ritualized, and much more variable. Typical elements include prayers, music, and reading of scripture, led by a minister. One common element of Protestant funeral services that is unique is that there is often a *eulogy,* which is a special sermon on the life of the deceased, usually performed by the minister. Following the funeral service the mourners proceed to the grave if the body is to be buried, where there may be a short prayer and scripture reading as the coffin is lowered into the grave. If the body has been cremated, this part of the service may involve the scattering of the ashes.

ISLAM When a Muslim is near death, loved ones gather near the deathbed and recite verses from the Koran (Gatrad, 1994). They try to make the dying person comfortable, and encourage the person to recite words of remembrance and prayer.

Burial takes place within a short time after death, because Islam does not allow embalming or otherwise disturbing the body after death. Cremation is forbidden, because Muslims believe that there will be a Day of Judgment in which their bodies will be raised from the dead.

The body is taken to the cemetery, where funeral prayers are recited. Then the body is laid in the grave in only a cloth shroud, no coffin (unless required by local law). It is placed on its right side, facing Mecca, the holiest site in Islam. More prayers are recited, asking for Allah's forgiveness of the deceased. Only a simple grave marker is planted, because lavish displays are discouraged in Islam.

Loved ones observe a 3-day mourning period, during which they are to pray, receive visitors and condolences, and avoid decorative clothing and jewelry. Widows are committed to a mourning period of 4 months and 10 days. During this period they are not to marry, move from their homes, or wear jewelry.

Across traditions, there are common themes. The body of the deceased person is treated with great care. Normal life comes to a stop, as the survivors show their love and respect for the deceased by altering their daily activities and avoiding earthly pleasures. Prayers for the dead are offered. Mourning often takes place for a prescribed period, and the end of the mourning period is often marked by a special meal. Beyond the mourning period, there are also common themes in the way people of various cultures remember and honor their deceased loved ones, as we will see next.

Remembering and Honoring the Dead

LO 13.13 Describe the rituals and traditions used by various religions to remember and honor the dead.

When someone we love dies, we grieve and we mourn their passing, and we miss them. After the mourning rituals and the prescribed periods of mourning are over we resume our daily lives, but we never forget those who have died. In all human cultures, there are customs for remembering and honoring the dead.

Ritual honoring of the dead is an important part of life for Hindus (Knipe, 2008). Each year, on the anniversary of a family member's death, a meal is prepared of dishes the deceased person enjoyed in life, and the food is served as an offering in a ritual ceremony led by a male, usually the oldest son. A special dish called *pinda* (rice balls) is prepared for the occasion and set out for the spirit of the ancestor on the roof of the family home. If a crow comes and devours the rice balls the offering is believed to be accepted, as crows are believed to be messengers of Yama, the god of the dead. In addition, every year there is a 16-day period called *Fortnight of the Ancestors* that is devoted to honoring the dead.

Buddhist rituals honoring the dead are blended with traditions of ancestor worship that have existed for millennia. In China, for example, ceremonies worshiping the ancestors are held several times a year, including on Chinese New Year and seasonal festivals in autumn, winter, and spring (Chung & Wegars, 2009). On these occasions, offerings of food and other gifts are made to the ancestors, gratitude is expressed for past favors granted, and appeals are made for the protection of the family from misfortunes and disasters, as well as for good fortune and prosperity in the future. These practices honoring deceased ancestors are one reflection of the Chinese value of filial piety. Parents and other elders are to be obeyed and honored not only during their lifetimes but for generations after their deaths.

In addition to the many occasions each year when the living pay their respects to the dead, there is a period each year during which the souls of the dead are believed to visit the living. This period is called the Ghost Month, and during this month the gates of the underworld are said to be opened up and ghosts are free to roam the earth, where they seek food and entertainment (Zhang, 2009). Families pray to their ancestors and prepare elaborate meals as an offering to them. They also burn, as an offering to the ancestors, paper fashioned into valued items such as money, cars, houses, and televisions. Historians believe that this is an echo of a previous custom in which valuable objects were actually buried with the dead.

In the Jewish tradition, the death of parents, siblings, spouses, or children is commemorated each year on the anniversary of death, a custom called the *Yahrzeit* (Marcus, 2004). A special Yahrzeit candle is lit and burns for 24 hours. The Kaddish prayer recited at funerals is now recited three times (evening of the previous day, morning, and afternoon), and many attend synagogue on this day. Some people observe a custom of fasting on the day of the Yahrzeit, or at least refraining from meat and wine. Many synagogues will have lights on a special memorial plaque on one of the synagogue's walls, with names of synagogue members who have died. Each of these lights will be lit for individuals on their Yahrzeit.

In Christian tradition, the dead are especially remembered and honored during a 3-day period beginning on the last night in October. This tradition began many centuries ago in Ireland, where it was believed that this is a time when the boundary between the spirit world and the earthly world is at its thinnest and spirits are most likely to be roaming the earth. Fires and pumpkin lanterns were lit to frighten away witches and ghosts.

On the Day of the Dead in Mexico, families sometimes have a picnic at the gravesite of the loved one.

Eventually this night became known as *All Hallows' Eve* (*hallows* means "spirits"), or Halloween. November 1, the day after Halloween, is All Saints' Day, when the lives of saints and martyrs are remembered and praised. The next day, November 2, is All Souls' Day, when people pray for all their loved ones who have died.

A distinctive form of the Christian observance of All Souls' Day takes place in Mexico, where it is known as *Día de los Muertos,* the Day of the Dead (Beatty, 2009). Friends and family gather to pray for and remember the dead, but the Day of the Dead is a time of celebration when eating and parties are common. Families may build small shrines or altars in their homes on this occasion. Sometimes families go to the cemetery to be with the soul of the deceased. There, they clean and decorate the grave, and perhaps present the favorite food and drink of the dead as an offering. Celebrants may recall humorous events and stories from the life of the deceased. In some parts of Mexico the family picnics at the gravesite, and in others the family may stay beside the grave all night long. A common symbol of the holiday is the skull, a tradition believed to have originated in the pre-Christian past, when it was common to display skulls to symbolize death and rebirth. Today the skulls are often made of sugar or chocolate and inscribed with the name of the loved one who has passed away.

Muslims are encouraged to visit the graves of their loved ones, to show their respect and to remind them of the afterlife to come. Prayers should be offered at home before going to the cemetery. Shoes are to be taken off before entering the graveyard, and prayers are recited at the grave. The death anniversaries of saints are observed as religious days, when believers are obliged to gather, recite the Koran, and do charitable works.

In sum, the major religions have different ways of remembering and honoring the dead, but across religions these customs allow the survivors to maintain a sense of psychological contact with the dead. The death of someone we love is among the most difficult human experiences, and ritual ways of remembering those we have lost provide consolation and a mode of expression for the feelings that still exist even though the person who was the object of those feelings is with us no longer.

Cultural Focus: Remembering and Honoring the Dead Across Cultures

Cultural beliefs regarding death and afterlife beliefs represent one of the most remarkable examples of human cultural creativity. Around the world, people believe that we face a divine moral judgment when we die, or that our destiny after death depends on which religious faith we believe, or that we return again and again to life in different forms. In many cultures, there are especially strong beliefs about loved ones who have recently died and how to honor them. In this video, a variety of people from various countries are interviewed about how they honor their ancestors.

Watch   REMEMBERING AND HONORING THE DEAD ACROSS CULTURES

Review Question:

What is one common tribute that all of the individuals interviewed in this video do to honor their ancestors?

Practice Quiz   ANSWERS AVAILABLE IN ANSWER KEY.

1. Which of the following statements best reflects the results of the Pew survey on afterlife beliefs within the United States?

  a. Only a small percentage of Americans believe in life after death.

  b. Afterlife beliefs were high among Christians, but quite low among other religions such as Muslims and Hindus.

  c. Most Americans are tolerant of different views about religion and the afterlife, believing that many religions can lead to eternal life.

  d. Across religious groups, people are somewhat more likely to believe in hell than to believe in heaven.

2. One of your friends tells you that her mother died and they will be sitting shiva. In addition, she must recite a prayer called the Kaddish every day for 11 months. Your friend most likely follows which religion?

  a. Protestant   **c.** Hinduism

  b. Judaism   **d.** Buddhism

3. During the Chinese period of the Ghost Month, _____.

  a. ghosts are free to roam the earth seeking food and entertainment

  b. families fast to ward away ghosts and evil spirits.

  c. families build shrines to their ancestors.

  d. children receive gifts in honor of the deceased.

4. What is the Day of the Dead?

  a. Another name for All Hallows' Eve, originating in England.

  b. In Germany, it is the day when all who have died that winter finally get buried.

  c. Part of the period of the Buddhist religion called Ghost Month.

  d. A joyful celebration in Mexico, remembering all who have died.

Summary: Beliefs About Death and the Afterlife

LO 13.9   **Describe how children's understanding of death changes from childhood to adolescence.**

Children realize that death is permanent, but not until middle childhood do they realize that death is inevitable. In adolescence, beliefs about death become more abstract and more complex, reflecting adolescents' more general gains in cognitive development

LO 13.10   **Describe how beliefs and fears about death change throughout adulthood.**

Death anxiety is highest in emerging adulthood, then declines with age, and is lowest in late adulthood, as many adults undergo a life review and come to accept the life they have lived. Death is also more familiar to those in late adulthood, so they spend more time talking about it and planning for it than younger adults do.

LO 13.11   **Explain how individual beliefs about the afterlife vary across countries and within the United States.**

Belief in life after death varies by country, but the majority of people in most countries believe in some kind of afterlife. Americans are more likely than people in other developed countries to believe in life after death, although fewer than half of American Jews hold this belief.

LO 13.12   **Compare and contrast the mourning rituals of Hinduism, Buddhism, Judaism, Christianity, and Islam.**

Mourning rituals are important to Hindus and Buddhists, as they believe that these rituals will help influence what a soul's status will be in the next life. Both religions practice cremation. Jewish mourning rituals after death are among the most highly ritualized, and include sitting shiva with the deceased. Christian rituals may include the anointing of the sick, vigils, and a mass. Muslim burial takes place within a short time after death, because Islam does not allow embalming or otherwise disturbing the body after death. Prayers are recited outdoors and the body is laid to rest in a grave facing Mecca.

LO 13.13   **Describe the rituals and traditions used by various religions to remember and honor the dead.**

Rituals and traditions for remembering and honoring the dead exist in all traditions. They vary greatly, but many include leaving an offering such as food for the deceased, lighting candles in remembrance, saying prayers, and visiting the grave.

Applying Your Knowledge as a Professional

The topics covered in this chapter apply to a wide variety of career professions. Watch these videos to learn how they apply to a minister and nurses at a hospice center.

Watch   CAREER FOCUS: HOSPICE WORKERS

Debra Johnson
Clinical Director, Horizon Hospice

Chapter Quiz

1. _____ is/are the dominant cause of death in developing countries today.

   a. Suicide

   b. Infectious diseases

   c. Heart disease

   d. Chronic conditions such as cancer

2. Within the United States, this ethnic group has the LOWEST rates of death from heart disease.

   a. Asian Americans

   b. African Americans

   c. White Americans

   d. Native Americans

3. Researchers comparing telomeres of healthy centenarians to a comparison group of their peers with two or more chronic health conditions found that the telomeres of those who were healthy were _____.

   a. thicker

   b. thinner and more brittle

   c. longer

   d. shorter

4. _____ has/have sometimes yielded dramatic results in slowing the aging process, but with some unpleasant side effects including growth of excess hair, liver damage, and abnormal growth of facial bones.

   a. DHEA supplements

   b. Antioxidant supplements

   c. Calorie restriction for over a year

   d. Regular use of growth hormone

5. In developed countries today, what percent of people die at home?

   a. There are no records on where people die.

   b. About 20%

   c. About 60%

   d. Less than 5%

6. The focus of hospice care is _____.

   a. to offer more intensive medical treatments to help cure life-threatening diseases

   b. to euthanize patients who are in severe pain

   c. to provide emotional support to family members without interacting directly with the patient

   d. to relieve a patient's pain and suffering and provide care that allows the patient to die with dignity

7. In the initial period following bereavement, grief _____.

   a. subsides and the person begins to resume daily activities

   b. often involves shock, numbness, and disbelief

   c. manifests itself in anger and aggressive behavior

   d. follows a predictable sequence of stages

8. Parents who experience the death of a child _____.

   a. have double the risk of cancer

   b. experience great distress, but recover from it quickly

   c. are at a higher risk of divorce

   d. form a deeper bond with each other and have a stronger marriage as a result

9. Which of the following is NOT considered a critique of the theory of Kübler-Ross?

   a. It overlooks the cultural context.

   b. It overlooks fear as a response.

   c. Many people don't go through all five stages.

   d. It places too much emphasis on cultural and spiritual beliefs.

10. When Lia's grandmother died, her parents told her "Grandma has passed on." This is an example of

   a. ego integrity versus despair.

   b. a life review.

   c. a personal fable.

   d. a euphemism.

11. For many people, late adulthood is a time of _____.

   a. thinking about the life they have lived and coming to an acceptance of it

   b. high anxiety about death

   c. distress over the goals they never accomplished

   d. high death anxiety, but only for men

12. Which statement best describes the results of the International Social Survey Program survey on afterlife beliefs?

   a. Only a small percentage of Americans believe in life after death.

   b. There was great similarity in afterlife beliefs around the world.

   c. There was great variability in the proportion of adults responding "definitely yes" to a belief in life after death.

   d. Afterlife beliefs were strongest in European countries.

13. In which religion is cremation forbidden?

   a. Islam

   b. Protestant

   c. Hinduism

   d. Buddhism

14. Carlo's sister Angela is very ill and near death. She has asked that a Catholic priest come to her bedside in order to perform what ritual?

   a. Recite a kaddish prayer

   b. A requiem mass

   c. Anointing of the sick

   d. Perform a vigil

Epilogue

And so, my fellow frogs, we reach the end of a long journey. How does human development look to you now, from the top of the well? Reflect for a moment on all you have learned about the human experience in the course of this book. Now you know that infants in many cultures are held or carried all day long and sleep next to their mothers at night. Now you know that toddlerhood is considered the "terrible twos" only in cultures where they have already learned by that age that individual expressiveness is encouraged rather than impeded. Now you know that many girls in middle childhood have daily responsibilities of caring for their younger siblings. Now you know that there is a life stage called "emerging adulthood" that has arisen in developed countries between adolescence and young adulthood, and that it is rapidly spreading to developing countries as well. Now you know that in India the sex life of married couples typically ends by middle adulthood, but that this stage of life is nevertheless regarded as a positive time of new opportunities for personal growth. Now you know that filial piety is a core value of Asian cultures, and that one reflection of it is the obligation to care for parents in their old age. And so much more.

Perhaps most important of all, you have learned that culture is profoundly important in shaping the path that each of us takes through life. All of us are made from the same basic biological material—46 human chromosomes—yet how we live and how we experience each life stage is vastly different depending on where we happened to be born. In the course of this book, we have seen many examples of the importance of biological influences in human development. Yet, in the end, culture usually trumps biology, because culture takes the raw material of human potential and shapes it toward a certain way of life, including beliefs about what is most important and what values we should live by.

The power of culture over biology can be seen in recent human history, in how all of us have been influenced by globalization. Human biology has not altered over the past century. It takes many, many centuries of evolution before biological changes are established in the human species. Yet globalization, and the spread of information and technology it brings, has changed all of us with astonishing speed. These changes are especially felt by people in developing countries, who are undergoing in a period of a few decades the economic and cultural modernization that developed countries experienced gradually, over the course of centuries. Young children today in developing countries are sure to experience a future entirely different from the lives their grandparents knew, for better or worse.

A few years ago, I traveled for the first time to India, where I had been invited to visit colleagues at a university there. One day we drove to a rural village where the university's human development department had established a preschool. Life in the village was, in many ways, unchanged from its traditional patterns. The homes were mostly simple and without electricity. Young women brought their families' dirty clothes to the edge of the lake, where they scrubbed and pounded and washed them by hand. Young men walked by, carrying bundles of sticks on their shoulders. We came across one home where a matriarch and her daughters and daughters-in-law were chatting as they squatted together in a courtyard over a small fire, making the midday meal for their husbands, who were out in the fields. All of them wore astonishingly beautiful handmade saris (see accompanying photo). They offered us a piece of the bread they had made.

It's a scene that might have been taken from any time in the past several thousand years, you might think, and in a way this is true. Yet in the distance, visible from the village, were two gleaming towers: the office buildings of a Swedish company that was expanding its business in India and had recently bought up part of the village land. In the village itself, not all the dwellings were simple huts anymore; some were brick apartment buildings with automobiles in front. Talking to the villagers, we learned that many of their family members and neighbors had migrated to the cities in search of jobs and the comforts and opportunities of city life; meanwhile, city dwellers were moving into the brick apartment buildings in the village, seeking a cheap place to live, away from the discomforts and stress of city life.

The conclusion seemed inescapable that the traditional life of the village was doomed. The women washing at the lake, the men with their bundles, the matriarch and her daughters squatting by their cooking fire—none of it could possibly survive the wave of economic development, urbanization, and globalization that was already cresting a short distance away. And this village is a microcosm of what is happening all around the world. Traditional village life is declining as previously poor countries develop economically, and more and more people—especially young people—migrate from the villages to the cities. As noted in Chapter 1, in 2010, for the first time in human history, more people lived in cities than in rural areas, and this is a trend that will surely continue.

Visiting the village, I felt a sense of loss, even as I tried hard not to romanticize the lives of the villagers. I am sure their daily lives are difficult and physically strenuous in ways I can only imagine. We can hardly begrudge them the refrigerators, stoves, electric lighting, television, medical care, automobiles, mobile phones, and computers that add comfort, ease, and enjoyment to our lives. Yet there will be something lost, too, if globalization continues in a way that gradually reduces the scope of human cultural variation and we all, increasingly, live in similar ways and have similar beliefs about the nature of human life and death, all over the world.

There is, of course, no way to know what the future of the human species will hold a hundred, a thousand, or a million years from now. Certainly right now, at this moment in human history, cultural variation remains immense and extraordinary, as you have seen in the course of this text. Perhaps we can have faith that, given the amazing creativity that our species has shown in the past 40,000 years in devising and constantly revising its ways of life, no amount of globalization will ever extinguish the human capacity for cultural innovation.

Glossary

accommodation cognitive process of changing a scheme to adapt to new information

active genotype → environment effects in the theory of genotype → environment effects, the type that results when people seek out environments that correspond to their genotypic characteristics

active life span number of years of physical functioning favorable enough for people to enjoy their lives and perform most of their daily activities without impairment

activities of daily living (ADLs) daily requirements of life for adults, such as bathing, dressing, food preparation and eating, housekeeping, and paying bills

actual self person's perception of the self as it is, contrasted with the possible self

adolescence period of the life span between the time puberty begins and the time adult status is approached, when young people are preparing to take on the roles and responsibilities of adulthood in their culture

adolescent egocentrism type of egocentrism in which adolescents have difficulty distinguishing their thinking about their own thoughts from their thinking about the thoughts of others

adolescent-limited delinquent (ALD) delinquent who shows no evidence of problems prior to adolescence and whose delinquent behavior in adolescence is temporary

advance directive person's written and oral instructions concerning end-of-life care

aerobic exercise exercise that involves vigorous movement that substantially elevates the heart rate for at least 30 minutes

age graded social organization based on grouping persons of similar ages

ageism prejudice and discrimination based on age

AIDS (acquired immune deficiency syndrome) sexually transmitted infection caused by HIV, resulting in damage to the immune system

allele on a pair of chromosomes, each of two forms of a gene

Alzheimer's disease type of dementia that has a distinctive pattern of structural decline in the brain involving the accumulation of amyloid plaques and the development of neurofibrillary tangles

ambivalence emotional state of experiencing two contradictory emotions at once

amniocentesis prenatal procedure in which a needle is used to withdraw amniotic fluid containing fetal cells from the placenta, allowing possible prenatal problems to be detected

amnion fluid-filled membrane that surrounds and protects the developing organism in the womb

androgens sex hormones that have especially high levels in males from puberty onward and are mostly responsible for male primary and secondary sex characteristics

anemia dietary deficiency of iron that causes problems such as fatigue, irritability, and attention difficulties

animism tendency to attribute human thoughts and feelings to inanimate objects and forces

anorexia nervosa eating disorder characterized by intentional self-starvation

anoxia deprivation of oxygen during birth process and soon after that can result in serious neurological damage within minutes

antioxidants substances, present in many fruits and vegetables, that absorb the extra electron in free radicals, thereby preventing them from damaging the cell

Apgar scale neonatal assessment scale with five subtests: Appearance (color), Pulse (heart rate), Grimace (reflex irritability), Activity (muscle tone), and Respiration (breathing)

apprenticeship an arrangement, common in Europe, in which an adolescent "novice" serves under contract to a "master" who has substantial experience in a profession, and through working under the master, learns the skills required to enter the profession

arranged marriage marriage in which partners are chosen not by each other, but by their families, on the basis of family status, religion, and wealth

arthritis disease of the joints that especially affects the hips, knees, neck, hands, and lower back

artificial insemination procedure of injecting sperm directly into the uterus

assimilation cognitive process of altering new information to fit an existing scheme

assisted reproductive technologies (ART) methods for overcoming infertility that include artificial insemination, fertility drugs, and IVF

asthma chronic illness of the lungs characterized by wheezing, coughing, and shortness of breath

atherosclerosis condition where plaque builds up in coronary arteries, causing the passage of blood in arteries to become constricted

attachment theory Bowlby's theory of emotional and social development, focusing on the crucial importance of the infant's relationship with the primary caregiver

attention-deficit/hyperactivity disorder (ADHD) diagnosis that includes problems of inattention, hyperactivity, and impulsiveness

authoritarian parents in classifications of parenting styles, parents who are high in demandingness but low in responsiveness

authoritative parents in classifications of parenting styles, parents who are high in demandingness and high in responsiveness

autism developmental disorder marked by a lack of interest in social relations, abnormal language development, and repetitive behavior

autonomy quality of being independent and self-sufficient, capable of thinking for one's self

axon part of a neuron that transmits electric impulses and releases neurotransmitters

babbling repetitive prelanguage consonant–vowel combinations such as "ba-ba-ba" or "do-do-do-do," made by infants universally beginning at about 6 months old

basal metabolic rate (BMR) amount of energy the body uses when at rest

Bayley Scales of Infant Development widely used assessment of infant development from age 3 months to 3½ years

B cells immune cells that originate in bone marrow and produce antibodies that destroy bacteria and viruses

behavior genetics field in the study of human development that aims to identify the extent to which genes influence behavior, primarily by comparing persons who share different amounts of their genes

bicultural identity identity with two distinct facets, for example one for the local culture and one for the global culture, or one within one's ethnic group and one for others

bilingual capable of using two languages

binge drinking consuming five or more drinks in a row for men, four in a row for women

binocular vision ability to combine the images of the two eyes into one image

blastocyst ball of about 100 cells formed by about 1 week following conception

body mass index (BMI) measure of the ratio of weight to height

bonding concept that in humans the first few minutes and hours after birth are critical to mother–infant relationships

Brazelton Neonatal Behavioral Assessment Scale (NBAS) 27-item scale of neonatal functioning with overall ratings "worrisome," "normal," and "superior"

breech presentation positioning of the fetus so that feet or buttocks, rather than the head, are positioned to come first out of the birth canal

bride price economic requirement for marriage that involves a substantial gift of money or property from the groom and his kin to the bride and her kin

bride service marital arrangement in which the groom is obligated to work for the bride's family for a designated period before and/or after the marriage

Broca's area portion of the left frontal lobe of the human brain that is specialized for language production

bulimia eating disorder characterized by episodes of binge eating followed by purging (self-induced vomiting)

bullying pattern of maltreatment of peers, including aggression; repetition; and power imbalance

burnout state of becoming disillusioned, frustrated, and tired of one's job

cardiac output quantity of blood flow from the heart

cataracts progressive thickening of the lens of the eye that causes vision to become cloudy, opaque, and distorted

cellular clock intrinsic limit to the number of times cells can replicate themselves

centration Piaget's term for young children's thinking as being centered, or focused, on one noticeable aspect of a cognitive problem to the exclusion of other important aspects

cephalocaudal principle principle of biological development that growth tends to begin at the top, with the head, and then proceeds downward to the rest of the body

cerebellum structure at the base of the brain involved in balance and motor movements

cerebral cortex outer portion of the brain, containing four regions with distinct functions

cesarean delivery, or c-section type of birth in which mother's abdomen is cut open and fetus is retrieved directly from the uterus

child maltreatment abuse or neglect of children, including physical, emotional, or sexual abuse

chorionic villus sampling (CVS) prenatal technique for diagnosing genetic problems, involving taking a sample of cells at 5–10 weeks gestation by inserting a tube into the uterus

chromosome sausage-shaped structure in the nucleus of cells, containing genes, which are paired, except in reproductive cells

civilization form of human social life, beginning about 5,000 years ago, that includes cities, writing, occupational specialization, and states

classification ability to understand that objects can be part of more than one cognitive group, for example an object can be classified with red objects as well as with round objects

climacteric changes in the reproductive system that occur in middle adulthood; for women the cessation of ovulation and menstruation (menopause), and for men the gradual decline in the number and quality of sperm

clique small group of friends who know each other well, do things together, and form a regular social group

coercive cycle pattern in relations between parents and children in which children's disobedient behavior evokes harsh responses from parents, which in turn makes children even more resistant to parental control, evoking even harsher responses

cognitive-developmental approach focus on how cognitive abilities change with age in stage sequence of development, pioneered by Piaget and since taken up by other researchers

cohabitation unmarried romantic partners living together

cohort effect in scientific research, an explanation of group differences among people of different ages based on the fact that they grew up in different *cohorts* or historical periods

colic infant crying pattern in which the crying goes on for more than 3 hours a day over more than 3 days at a time for more than 3 weeks

collectivistic cultural values such as obedience and group harmony

colostrum thick, yellowish liquid produced by mammalian mothers during the first days following birth, extremely rich in protein and antibodies that strengthen the baby's immune system

coming out for homosexuals, the process of acknowledging their homosexuality and then disclosing the truth to their friends, family, and others

concordance rate degree of similarity in phenotype among pairs of family members, expressed as a percentage

concrete operations in Piaget's theory, the cognitive stage in which children become capable of using mental operations

conservation mental ability to understand that the quantity of a substance or material remains the same even if its appearance changes

contexts settings and circumstances that contribute to variations in pathways of human development, including SES, gender, and ethnicity, as well as family, school, community, media, and culture

conventional reasoning second level in Kohlberg's theory of moral development, in which moral reasoning is based on the expectations of others

cooing prelanguage "oo-ing" and "ah-ing," and gurgling sounds babies make beginning at about 2 months old

coregulation relationship between parents and children in which parents provide broad guidelines for behavior but children are capable of a substantial amount of independent, self-directed behavior

corporal punishment physical punishment of children

corpus callosum band of neural fibers connecting the two hemispheres of the brain

correlation statistical relationship between two variables such that knowing one of the variables makes it possible to predict the other

cosleeping cultural practice in which infants and sometimes older children sleep with one or both parents

creativity ability to put ideas or materials together in new, culturally meaningful ways

cremated after death, burning the body to ashes

crossing over   at the outset of meiosis, the exchange of genetic material between paired chromosomes

cross-sectional research   research design that involves collecting on a single occasion

crowd   large, reputation-based group of adolescents

crystallized intelligence   accumulation of a person's culturally-based knowledge, language, and understanding of social convention

cultural models   cognitive structures pertaining to common cultural activities

culture   total pattern of a group's customs, beliefs, art, and technology

custom complex   distinctive cultural pattern of behavior that reflects underlying cultural beliefs

cyberbullying   bullying via electronic means, mainly through the Internet

cytoplasm   in an ovum, fluid that provides nutrients for the first 2 weeks of growth if the ovum is fertilized, until it reaches the uterus and begins drawing nutrients from the mother

deferred imitation   ability to repeat actions observed at an earlier time

delivery   second stage of the birth process, during which the fetus is pushed out of the cervix and through the birth canal

demandingness   degree to which parents set down rules and expectations for behavior and require their children to comply with them

dementia   neurological condition that entails losses in cognitive functioning severe enough to interfere with daily life

dendrite   part of the neuron that receives neurotransmitters

dependent variable   in an experiment, the outcome that is measured to calculate the results of the experiment by comparing the experimental group to the control group

depressed mood   enduring period of sadness, without any other related symptoms of depression

depth perception   ability to discern the relative distance of objects in the environment

developed countries   world's most economically developed and affluent countries, with the highest median levels of income and education

developing countries   countries that have lower levels of income and education than developed countries but are experiencing rapid economic growth

developmental quotient (DQ)   in assessments of infant development, the overall score indicating developmental progress

DHEA   hormone involved in muscle growth, bone density, and the functioning of the cardiovascular system

dialectical thought   according to Basseches, a kind of thinking in emerging adulthood that involves a growing awareness that problems often have no clear solution and two opposing strategies or points of view may each have some merit

digital device   electronic device that allows contact via phone and text message as well as access to the Internet, videos, television, and direct video conversations

disengaged parents   in classifications of parenting styles, parents who are low in both demandingness and responsiveness

dishabituation   following habituation, the revival of attention when a new stimulus is presented

disorganized–disoriented attachment   classification of parent–child attachment in which the child seems dazed and detached, with

possible outbursts of anger, when the parent leaves the room, and exhibits fear upon parent's return

displacement effect   in media research, term for how media use occupies time that may have been spent on other activities

divided attention   ability to focus on more than one task at a time

divorce mediation   arrangement in which a professional mediator meets with divorcing parents to help them negotiate an agreement that both will find acceptable

dizygotic (DZ) twins   twins that result when two ova are released by a female instead of one, and both are fertilized by sperm; also called fraternal twins

DNA (deoxyribonucleic acid)   long strand of cell material that stores and transfers genetic information in all life forms

dominant–recessive inheritance   pattern of inheritance in which a pair of chromosomes contains one dominant and one recessive gene, but only the dominant gene is expressed in the phenotype

Do Not Resuscitate (DNR)   provision in a living will indicating that medical personnel are not to attempt to prolong life if the heart stops or the person stops breathing

Down syndrome   genetic disorder due to carrying an extra chromosome on the 21st pair

dowry   marriage custom that transfers money or property from the bride's family to the groom and his family

dyslexia   learning disability that includes difficulty sounding out letters, difficulty learning to spell words, and a tendency to misperceive the order of letters in words

early intervention program   program directed at young children who are at risk for later problems, intended to prevent problems from developing

ecological theory   Bronfenbrenner's theory that human development is shaped by five interrelated systems in the social environment

ectoderm   in the embryonic period, the outer layer of cells, which will eventually become the skin, hair, nails, sensory organs, and nervous system (brain and spinal cord)

EEG (electroencephalogram)   device that measures the electrical activity of the cerebral cortex, allowing researchers to measure overall activity of the cerebral cortex as well as activation of specific parts of it

egocentrism   cognitive inability to distinguish between one's own perspective and another person's perspective

ego integrity versus despair   in Erikson's life span theory, the central crisis of late adulthood, with alternatives of ego integrity, which means looking back on one's life and accepting it for better and worse, or despair, which entails regrets and bitterness about the course of one's life

e-health   use of the Internet and electronic devices to enhance communication between health providers and patients, especially older adults

elaboration   mnemonic that involves transforming bits of information in a way that connects them and hence makes them easier to remember

electronic fetal monitoring (EFM)   method that tracks the fetus's heartbeat, either externally through the mother's abdomen or directly by running a wire through the cervix and placing a sensor on the fetus's scalp

embryonic disk   in the blastocyst, the inner layer of cells, which will go on to form the embryo

embryonic period   weeks 3–8 of prenatal development

emerging adulthood   new life stage in developed countries, lasting from the late teens through the twenties, in which people are gradually making their way toward taking on adult responsibilities in love and work

emotional contagion in infants, crying in response to hearing another infant cry, evident beginning at just a few days old

emotional self-regulation ability to exercise control over one's emotions

empathy ability to understand and respond helpfully to another person's distress

endoderm in the embryonic period, the inner layer of cells, which will become the digestive system and the respiratory system

endorphins brain chemicals that provide a pleasurable feeling and increase well-being

epidural during birth process, injection of an anesthetic drug into the spinal fluid to help the mother manage the pain while also remaining alert

epigenesis in development, the continuous bidirectional interactions between genes and environment

episiotomy incision to make the vaginal opening larger during birth process

erectile dysfunction inability to achieve and maintain an erection consistently during sexual contact

estradiol the estrogen most important in pubertal development among girls

estrogens sex hormones that have especially high levels in females from puberty onward and are mostly responsible for female primary and secondary sex characteristics

ethnicity group identity that may include components such as cultural origin, cultural traditions, race, religion, and language

ethnographic research research method that involves spending extensive time among the people being studied

ethology study of animal behavior

euthanasia practice of ending the life of a person who is suffering from an incurable disease or severe disability

eveningness preference for going to bed late and waking up late

evocative genotype → environment effects in the theory of genotype → environment effects, the type that results when a person's inherited characteristics evoke responses from others in the environment

evolutionary psychology branch of psychology that examines how patterns of human functioning and behavior have resulted from adaptations to evolutionary conditions

Experience Sampling Method (ESM) research method that involves having people wear beepers, usually for a period of 1 week; when they are beeped at random times during the day, they record a variety of characteristics of their experience at that moment

experimental research method research method that entails comparing an *experimental group* that receives a treatment of some kind to a *control group* that receives no treatment

expertise extensive knowledge and skills in a specific field

expressive divorce according to Barbara Whitehead, the type of divorce common in the West today, in which people expect marriage to fulfill their emotional needs for love and intimacy, and they seek a divorce if it ceases to do so

externalizing problems problems that involve others, such as aggression

extremely low birth weight term for neonates who weigh less than 2.2 pounds (1,000 grams) at birth

false self self a person may present to others while realizing that it does not represent what he or she is actually thinking and feeling

familismo cultural belief among Latinos that emphasizes the love, closeness, and mutual obligations among family members

family process quality of the relationships between family members

fast mapping learning and remembering a word for an object after just one time of being told what the object is called

feared self person one imagines it is possible to become but dreads becoming

fetal alcohol spectrum disorder (FASD) set of problems that occur as a consequence of high maternal alcohol use during pregnancy, including facial deformities, heart problems, misshapen limbs, and a variety of cognitive problems

fetal period in prenatal development, the period from Week 9 until birth

filial piety belief that children should respect, obey, and revere their parents throughout life; common in Asian cultures

fine motor development development of motor abilities involving finely tuned movements of the hands such as grasping and manipulating objects

fluid intelligence type of intelligence that involves information-processing abilities such as short-term memory, the ability to discern relations between visual stimuli, and the speed of synthesizing new information

Flynn effect steep rise in the median IQ score in Western countries during the 20th century, named after James Flynn, who first identified it

fMRI (functional magnetic resonance imaging) method of monitoring brain activity in which a person lies inside a machine that uses a magnetic field to record changes in blood flow and oxygen use in the brain in response to different kinds of stimulation

follicle during the female reproductive cycle, the ovum plus other cells that surround the ovum and provide nutrients

fontanels soft spots on the skull between loosely joined pieces of the skull that shift during the birth process to assist passage through the birth canal

forceps pair of tongs used to extract the baby's head from the womb during delivery

formal operations in Piaget's theory, cognitive stage beginning at age 11 in which people learn to think systematically about possibilities and hypotheses

foster care for maltreated children, approach in which adults approved by a state agency take over the care of the child

free radicals unstable molecules that cause damage to the DNA and other structures required by the cell to function

functional age age that indicates the actual competence and performance of older adults; may be higher or lower than chronological age

gametes cells, distinctive to each sex, that are involved in reproduction (egg cells in the ovaries of the female and sperm in the testes of the male)

gender cultural categories of "male" and "female"

gender constancy understanding that maleness and femaleness are biological and cannot change

gender identity awareness of one's self as male or female

gender-intensification hypothesis hypothesis that psychological and behavioral differences between males and females become more pronounced at adolescence because of intensified socialization pressures to conform to culturally prescribed gender roles

gender roles cultural expectations for appearance and behavior specific to males or females

gender schema gender-based cognitive structure for organizing and processing information, comprising expectations for males' and females' appearance and behavior

gene   segment of DNA containing coded instructions for the growth and functioning of the organism

generativity versus stagnation   in Erikson's theory, the central crisis of middle adulthood, characterized by two alternatives, the motivation to contribute to the well-being of the generations to come (generativity) or focusing on narrow self-interest without concern for the good of others (stagnation)

genome   entire store of an organism's hereditary information

genotype   organism's unique genetic inheritance

germinal period   first 2 weeks after conception

gerontologist   researcher on aging

gestation   in prenatal development, elapsed time since conception

gifted   in IQ test performance, persons who score 130 or above

glass ceiling   unspoken limit on career advancement of women due to discrimination

glaucoma   loss of peripheral vision due to buildup of fluid that damages the optic nerve

globalization   increasing connections between different parts of the world in trade, travel, migration, and communication

goodness-of-fit   theoretical principle that children develop best if there is a good fit between the temperament of the child and environmental demands

graduated driver licensing (GDL)   government program in which young people obtain driving privileges gradually, contingent on a safe driving record, rather than all at once

grammar   a language's distinctive system of rules

gross motor development   development of motor abilities including balance and posture as well as whole-body movements such as crawling

growth hormone   hormone that is a crucial contributor to physical growth in the early decades of life; its steady decline after the mid-20s contributes to primary aging

guided participation   teaching interaction between two people (often an adult and a child) as they participate in a culturally valued activity

habituation   gradual decrease in attention to a stimulus after repeated presentations

handedness   preference for using either the right or left hand in gross and fine motor activities

Hayflick limit   limit of 50 times that cells can replicate themselves

heritability   statistical estimate of the extent to which genes are responsible for the differences among persons within a specific population, with values ranging from 0 to 1.00

hippocampus   structure involved in transfer of information from short-term to long-term memory

holophrase   single word that is used to represent a whole sentence

hominid   evolutionary line that led to modern humans

homophobia   fear and hatred of homosexuals

Homo sapiens   species of modern humans

hospice   alternative to hospital care at the end of life that emphasizes the physical, emotional, social, and spiritual needs of dying persons and their families

hostile aggression   type of aggression that entails signs of anger and intent to inflict pain or harm on others

human development   ways people grow and change across the life span; includes people's biological, cognitive, psychological, and social functioning

hunter-gatherer   social and economic system in which economic life is based on hunting (mostly by males) and gathering edible plants (mostly by females)

hypertension   high blood pressure, often due to a combination of primary and secondary aging

hypothesis   in the scientific process, a researcher's idea about one possible answer to the question proposed for investigation

hypothetical-deductive reasoning   Piaget's term for the process of applying scientific thinking to cognitive tasks

ideal self   person one would like to be

identity status model   model for researching Erikson's theory of identity development, classifying identity development into four categories: diffusion, foreclosure, moratorium, or achievement

identity versus identity confusion   in Erikson's theory, the crisis of adolescence, with two alternative paths, establishing a clear and definite identity, or experiencing identity confusion, which is a failure to form a stable and secure identity

imaginary audience   belief that others are acutely aware of and attentive to one's appearance and behavior

imprinting   instant and enduring bond to the first moving object seen after birth; common in birds

incomplete dominance   form of dominant–recessive inheritance in which the phenotype is influenced primarily by the dominant gene but also to some extent by the recessive gene

independent variable   in an experiment, the variable that is different for the experimental group than for the control group

individualistic   cultural values such as independence and self-expression

industry versus inferiority   Erikson's middle childhood stage, in which the alternatives are to learn to work effectively with cultural materials or, if adults are too critical, develop a sense of being incapable of working effectively

infant-directed (ID) speech   special form of speech that adults in many cultures direct toward infants, in which the pitch of the voice becomes higher than in normal speech, the intonation is exaggerated, and words and phrases are repeated

infantile amnesia   inability to remember anything that happened prior to age 2

infertility   inability to attain pregnancy after at least a year of regular sexual intercourse

infinite generativity   ability to take the word symbols of a language and combine them in a virtually infinite number of new ways

information processing approach   approach to understanding cognitive functioning that focuses on cognitive processes that exist at all ages, rather than on viewing cognitive developing in terms of discontinuous stages

informed consent   standard procedure in social scientific studies that entails informing potential participants of what their participation would involve, including any possible risks, and giving them the opportunity to agree to participate or not

initiative vs. guilt   in Erikson's lifespan theory, the early childhood stage in which the alternatives are learning to plan activities in a purposeful way, or being afflicted with excess guilt that undermines initiative

insecure–avoidant attachment   classification of parent–child attachment in which there is relatively little interaction between them and the child shows little response to the parent's absence and may resist being picked up when the parent returns

insecure–resistant attachment   classification of parent–child attachment in which the child shows little exploratory behavior when the parent is present, great distress when the parent leaves the room, and ambivalence upon the parent's return

instrumental aggression type of aggression when a child wants something and uses aggressive behavior or words to get it

intellectual disability level of cognitive abilities of persons who score 70 or below on IQ tests

intelligence capacity for acquiring knowledge, reasoning, and solving problems

intelligence quotient (IQ) score of mental ability as assessed by intelligence tests, calculated relative to the performance of other people the same age

intermodal perception integration and coordination of information from the various senses

internalizing problems problems that entail turning distress inward, toward the self, such as depression and anxiety

intervention program intended to change the attitudes or behavior of the participants

intimacy degree to which two people share personal knowledge, thoughts, and feelings

intimacy versus isolation in Erikson's life-span theory, the central emotional and psychosocial issue of young adulthood, in which the challenge is to unite the newly formed identity with another person in an enduring, committed, intimate relationship

in vitro fertilization (IVF) form of infertility treatment that involves using drugs to stimulate the growth of multiple follicles in the ovaries, removing the follicles and combining them with sperm, then transferring the most promising zygotes to the uterus

kangaroo care recommended care for preterm and low-birth-weight neonates, in which mothers or fathers are advised to place the baby skin-to-skin on their chests for 2–3 hours a day for the early weeks of life

kwashiorkor protein deficiency in childhood, leading to symptoms such as lethargy, irritability, thinning hair, and swollen body, which may be fatal if not treated

labor first stage of the birth process, in which the cervix dilates and the muscles of the uterus contract to push the fetus into the vagina toward the cervix

language acquisition device (LAD) according to Chomsky, innate feature of the brain that enables children to perceive and grasp quickly the grammatical rules in the language around them

lateralization specialization of functions in the two hemispheres of the brain

learning disability cognitive disorder that impedes the development of learning a specific skill such as reading or math

let-down reflex in females, a reflex that causes milk to be released to the tip of the nipples in response to the sound of an infant's cry, seeing its open mouth, or even thinking about breast-feeding

life-course-persistent delinquent (LCPD) delinquent who shows a pattern of problems from birth onward and whose problems continue into adulthood

life review according to Robert Butler, the process in late adulthood when people reflect on the life they have lived and come to an acceptance of it

longitudinal research research design in which the same persons are followed over time and data are collected on two or more occasions

low birth weight term for neonates weighing less than 5 pounds (2,500 grams)

macular degeneration loss of clarity in the center of the visual field, due to aging of the visual system

major depressive disorder clinical diagnosis that includes a range of specific symptoms such as depressed mood, appetite disturbances, sleeping disturbances, and fatigue

majority culture within a country, the cultural group that sets most of the norms and standards and holds most of the positions of political, economic, intellectual, and media power

mammary glands in females, the glands that produce milk to nourish babies

mammogram X-ray procedure used to examine women for breast cancer

marasmus disease in which the body wastes away from lack of nutrients

maturation concept that an innate, biologically based program is the driving force behind development

media multitasking simultaneous use of more than one media form, such as playing an electronic game while watching TV

median in a distribution of data, the score that is precisely in the middle, with half the distribution lying above and half below

meiosis process by which gametes are generated, through separation and duplication of chromosome pairs, ending in four new gametes from the original cell, each with half the number of chromosomes of the original cell

menarche first menstrual period

menopause the end of monthly ovulation and menstruation that occurs in women in midlife

mental representations Piaget's final stage of sensorimotor development in which toddlers first think about the range of possibilities and then select the action most likely to achieve the desired outcome

mental structure in Piaget's theory of cognitive development, the cognitive systems that organize thinking into coherent patterns so that all thinking takes place on the same level of cognitive functioning

mesoderm in the embryonic period, the middle of the three cell layers, which will become the muscles, bones, reproductive system, and circulatory system

metacognition capacity to think about thinking

metalinguistic skills in the understanding of language, skills that reflect awareness of the underlying structure of language

metamemory understanding of how memory works

micronutrients dietary ingredients essential to optimal physical growth, including iodine, iron, zinc, and vitamins A, B12, C, and D

midlife crisis state claimed to be common in middle adulthood, entailing anxiety, unhappiness, and a critical reappraisal of one's life, possibly provoking dramatic changes

midwife person who assists in pregnant women's prenatal care and the birth process

mitosis process of cell replication in which the chromosomes duplicate themselves and the cell divides into two cells, each with the same number of chromosomes as the original cell

mnemonics memory strategies, such as rehearsal, organization, and elaboration

monozygotic (MZ) twins twins who have exactly the same genotype; also called identical twins

morningness preference for going to bed early and waking up early

Moro reflex reflex in response to a sensation of falling backward or to a loud sound, in which the neonate arches its back, flings out its arms, and then brings its arms quickly together in an embrace

multilingual capable of using three or more languages

myelination process of the growth of the myelin sheath around the axon of a neuron

myopia visual condition of being unable to see distant objects clearly; also known as being nearsighted

natural childbirth   approach to childbirth that avoids medical technologies and interventions

natural experiment   situation that exists naturally but provides interesting scientific information

nature–nurture debate   debate among scholars as to whether human development is influenced mainly by genes (nature) or environment (nurture)

Neolithic period   era of human history from 10,000 to 5,000 years ago, when animals and plants were first domesticated

neonatal jaundice   yellowish pallor common in the first few days of life due to immaturity of the liver

neonate   newborn baby, up to 4 weeks old

neural tube   in the embryonic period, the part of the ectoderm that will become the spinal cord and brain

neuron   cell of the nervous system

neurotransmitter   chemical that enables neurons to communicate across synapses

natural selection   evolutionary process in which the offspring best adapted to their environment survive to produce offspring of their own

normal distribution   typical distribution of characteristics of a population, resembling a bell curve in which most cases fall near the middle and the proportions decrease at the low and high extremes

numeracy   understanding of the meaning of numbers

obese   in children, defined as having a BMI exceeding 21

object permanence   awareness that objects (including people) continue to exist even when we are not in direct sensory or motor contact with them

obstetrics   field of medicine that focuses on prenatal care and birth

old-age dependency ratio (OADR)   in a population, the ratio of persons age 65 and over to persons age 20–64

only child   child who has no siblings

ontogenetic   characteristic pattern of individual development in a species

opposable thumb   position of the thumb apart from the fingers, unique to humans, that makes possible fine motor movements

oral rehydration therapy (ORT)   treatment for infant diarrhea that involves drinking a solution of salt and glucose mixed with clean water

organization   mnemonic that involves placing things mentally into meaningful categories

osteoporosis   condition common in women in midlife and beyond, in which the bones become thin and brittle as a result of rapid calcium depletion

overcontrol   trait of having excessive emotional self-regulation

overextension   use of a single word to represent a variety of related objects

overproduction/exuberance   burst in the production of dendritic connections between neurons

overregularization   applying grammatical rules even to words that are the exception to the rule

overweight   in children, defined as having a BMI exceeding 18

ovum   mature egg that develops in ovaries, about every 28 days in human females

oxytocin   hormone released by pituitary gland that causes labor to begin

palliative care   for terminally ill persons, a type of care that focuses on relieving the patient's pain and suffering and allows the person to die with dignity

parenting styles   practices that parents exhibit in relation to their children and their beliefs about those practices

passive genotype → environment effects   in the theory of genotype → environment effects, the type that results from the fact that in a biological family, parents provide both genes and environment to their children

peer-review   in scientific research, the system of having other scientists review a manuscript to judge its merits and worthiness for publication

peers   persons who share some aspect of their status in common, such as age

permissive culture   culture that encourages and expects sexual activity from their adolescents

permissive parents   in classifications of parenting styles, parents who are low in demandingness and high in responsiveness

personal fable   belief in one's personal uniqueness, often including a sense of invulnerability to the consequences of taking risks

phenotype   organism's actual characteristics, derived from its genotype

phonics approach   method of teaching reading that advocates breaking down words into their component sounds, called phonics, then putting the phonics together into words

phylogenetic   pertaining to the development of a species

placenta   in the womb, gatekeeper between mother and fetus, protecting the fetus from bacteria and wastes in the mother's blood, and producing hormones that maintain the blood in the uterine lining and cause the mother's breasts to produce milk

plasticity   degree to which development can be influenced by environmental circumstances

polygenic inheritance   expression of phenotypic characteristics due to the interaction of multiple genes

polygyny   cultural tradition in which men have more than one wife

population   in research, the entire category of people represented by a sample

possible self   person's conceptions of the self as it potentially may be; may include both an ideal self and a feared self

postconventional reasoning   third level in Kohlberg's theory of moral development, in which moral reasoning is based on the individual's own independent judgments rather than on what others view as wrong or right

postformal thinking   according to some theorists, the stage of cognitive development that follows formal operations and includes advances in pragmatism and reflective judgment

postpartum depression   in parents with a new baby, feelings of sadness and anxiety so intense as to interfere with the ability to carry out simple daily tasks

pragmatics   social and cultural context of language that guides people as to what is appropriate to say and not to say in a given social situation

pragmatism   theory of cognitive development proposing that postformal thinking involves adapting logical thinking to the practical constraints of real-life situations

preconventional reasoning   first level in Kohlberg's theory of moral development, in which moral reasoning is based on perceptions of the likelihood of external rewards and punishments

preoperational stage   cognitive stage from age 2 to 7 during which the child becomes capable of representing the world symbolically—for example, through the use of language—but is still very limited in ability to use mental operations

preterm babies born at 37 weeks gestation or less

primary aging inevitable biological aging that takes place in all living organisms

primary attachment figure person who is sought out when a child experiences some kind of distress or threat in the environment

primary emotions most basic emotions, such as anger, sadness, fear, disgust, surprise, and happiness

primary sex characteristics production of eggs (ova) and sperm and the development of the sex organs

private speech in Vygotsky's theory, self-guiding and self-directing comments children make to themselves as they learn in the zone of proximal development and have conversations with those guiding them; first spoken aloud, then internally

procedure the way a study is conducted and the data are collected

prosocial behavior positive behavior toward others, including kindness, friendliness, and sharing

protective factors characteristics of young people that are related to lower likelihood of problems despite experiencing high-risk circumstances

proximodistal principle principle of biological development that growth proceeds from the middle of the body outward

psychological control parenting strategy that uses shame and withdrawal of love to influence children's behavior

psychosexual theory Freud's theory proposing that sexual desire is the driving force behind human development

psychosocial theory Erikson's theory that human development is driven by the need to become integrated into the social and cultural environment

puberty changes in physiology, anatomy, and physical functioning that develop a person into a mature adult biologically and prepare the body for sexual reproduction

puberty ritual formal custom developed in many cultures to mark the departure from childhood and the entrance into adolescence

qualitative data that is collected in nonnumerical form

quantitative data that is collected in numerical form

rapid eye movement (REM) sleep phase of the sleep cycle in which a person's eyes move back and forth rapidly under the eyelids; persons in REM sleep experience other physiological changes as well

reaction range range of possible developmental paths established by genes; environment determines where development takes place within that range

reciprocal or bidirectional effects in relations between two persons, the principle that each of them affects the other

reflective judgment capacity to evaluate the accuracy and logical coherence of evidence and arguments, theorized to develop during emerging adulthood

reflex automatic response to certain kinds of stimulation

rehearsal mnemonic that involves repeating the same information over and over

reincarnation belief that after death the soul returns again to earth in another bodily form

relational aggression type of aggression that involves damaging another person's reputation among peers through social exclusion and malicious gossip

reliability in scientific research, the consistency of measurements across different occasions

research design plan for when and how to collect the data for a study

research method in the scientific process, the approach to investigating the hypothesis

resilience overcoming adverse environmental circumstances and achieving healthy development despite those circumstances

responsiveness degree to which parents are sensitive to their children's needs and express love, warmth, and concern for them

restrictive culture culture that places strong prohibitions on adolescent sexual activity before marriage

reticular formation part of the lower brain, involved in attention

reversibility ability to reverse an action mentally

rooting reflex reflex that causes the neonate to turn its head and open its mouth when it is touched on the cheek or the side of the mouth; helps the neonate find the breast

rote learning learning by memorization and repetition

ruminate to think persistently about bad feelings and experiences

sample subset of a population for which data are collected in a scientific study

scaffolding degree of assistance provided to the learner in the zone of proximal development, gradually decreasing as the learner's skills develop

schemes cognitive structures for processing, organizing, and interpreting information

scientific method process of scientific investigation, involving a series of steps from identifying a research question through forming a hypothesis, selecting research methods and designs, collecting and analyzing data, and drawing conclusions

secondary aging decline in physical functioning that takes place due to lifestyle behaviors such as unhealthy diet, insufficient exercise, and substance use, as well as environmental influences such as pollution

secondary emotions emotions that require social learning, such as embarrassment, shame, and guilt; also called sociomoral emotions

secondary school school attended during adolescence, after primary school

secondary sex characteristics bodily changes of puberty not directly related to reproduction

secondhand smoke smoke from a cigarette inhaled by those near the smoker

second shift term for the domestic work that women must perform after they complete their shift in the workplace

secular based on nonreligious beliefs and values

secular trend change in the characteristics of a population over time

secure attachment healthiest classification of parent–child attachment, in which the child uses the parent as a secure base from which to explore, protests when separated from parent, and is happy when the parent returns

secure base role of primary attachment figure, allows child to explore world while seeking comfort when threats arise

selective association in social relations, the principle that people tend to prefer being around others who are like themselves

selective attention ability to focus attention on relevant information and disregard what is irrelevant

selective optimization with compensation (SOC) response to aging that entails *selecting* valued activities and dropping others; *optimizing* performance in the remaining activities; and *compensating* for physical and cognitive declines, by developing new strategies or by using technology

self-concept person's perception and evaluation of him- or herself

self-esteem person's overall sense of worth and well-being

self-medication use of substances to relieve unpleasant emotional states

self-recognition   ability to recognize one's image in the mirror as one's self

self-reflection   capacity to think about one's self as one would think about other persons and objects

self-socialization   process by which people seek to maintain consistency between their gender schemas and their behavior

semirestrictive culture   culture that has prohibitions on premarital adolescent sex, but the prohibitions are not strongly enforced and are easily evaded

sensitive period   in the course of development, a period when the capacity for learning in a specific area is especially pronounced

sensorimotor stage   in Piaget's theory, the first 2 years of cognitive development, which involves learning how to coordinate the activities of the senses with motor activities

seriation   ability to arrange things in a logical order, such as shortest to longest, thinnest to thickest, or lightest to darkest

sex   biological status of being male or female

sex chromosomes   chromosomes that determine whether an organism is male (XY) or female (XX)

sexually transmitted infection (STI)   infection transmitted through sexual contact

sexual orientation   a person's tendencies of sexual attraction

singlism   negative stereotypes of single persons that lead to them being discriminated against and treated dismissively

sleep apnea   sleep-related respiratory disorder in which breathing stops for 10 seconds or more numerous times in the course of a typical night, as the air passage to the lungs closes, resulting in a sudden loud snore as the airway opens again and the sleeper awakens

small for date   term applied to neonates who weigh less than 90% of other neonates who were born at the same gestational age

social comparison   how persons view themselves in relation to others with regard to status, abilities, or achievements

social control   restraints on behavior imposed by social obligations and relationships

social information processing (SIP)   in social encounters, evaluations of others' intentions, motivations, and behavior

social-networking web site   web site that allows people to establish and maintain electronic contact with a wide social group

social referencing   term for process of becoming more adept at observing others' emotional responses to ambiguous and uncertain situations, and using that information to shape one's own emotional responses

social skills   behaviors that include being friendly, helpful, cooperative, and considerate

social smile   expression of happiness in response to interacting with others, first appearing at age 2–3 months

social status   within a group, the degree of power, authority, and influence that each person has in the view of the others

socioeconomic status (SES)   person's social class, including educational level, income level, and occupational status

socioemotional selectivity theory   Carstensen's theory that older adults maximize their emotional well-being by becoming increasingly selective in their social contacts

sociomoral emotions   emotions evoked based on learned, culturally based standards of right and wrong; also called *secondary emotions*

sound localization   perceptual ability for telling where a sound is coming from

spermarche   beginning of development of sperm in boys' testicles at puberty

state   centralized political system that is an essential feature of a civilization

stereotype   belief that others possess certain characteristics simply as a result of being a member of a particular group

stranger anxiety   fear in response to unfamiliar persons, usually evident in infants by age 6 months

Strange Situation   laboratory assessment of attachment entailing a series of introductions, separations, and reunions involving the child, the mother, and an unfamiliar person

sudden infant death syndrome (SIDS)   death within the first year of life due to unknown reasons, with no apparent illness or disorder

surfactant   substance in lungs that promotes breathing and keeps the air sacs in the lungs from collapsing

sustained attention   ability to concentrate on a task for an extended period of time

swaddling   practice of infant care that involves wrapping an infant tightly in cloths or blankets

synaptic density   density of synapses among neurons in the brain; peaks around age 3

synaptic pruning   process in brain development in which dendritic connections that are used become stronger and faster and those that are unused whither away

T cells   immune cells produced by the thymus that fight disease in the body

teething   period of discomfort and pain experienced by infants as their new teeth break through their gums

telegraphic speech   two-word phrases that strip away connecting words, such as *the* and *and*

telomere   portion of cell DNA at the end of chromosomes that become slightly shorter with each cell replication and that eventually becomes so short that replication can no longer occur

temperament   innate responses to the physical and social environment, including qualities of activity level, irritability, soothability, emotional reactivity, and sociability

teratogen   behavior, environment, or bodily condition that can have damaging influence on prenatal development

tertiary education   education or training beyond secondary school

testosterone   the androgen most important in pubertal development among boys

text messaging   form of communication on mobile phones that involves typing a message on the screen and sending it

theory   framework that presents a set of interconnected ideas in an original way and inspires further research

theory of genotype → environment effects   theory proposing that genes influence the kind of environment we experience

theory of mind   ability to understand thinking processes in one's self and others

theory of multiple intelligences   Gardner's theory that there are eight distinct types of intelligence

time out   disciplinary strategy in which the child is required to sit still in a designated place for a brief period

tinnitus   problem in the auditory system that entails hearing a ringing or buzzing sound with no external source

total fertility rate (TFR)   in a population, the number of births per woman

traditional culture   in developing countries, a rural culture that adheres more closely to cultural traditions than people in urban areas do

triangular theory of love Sternberg's theory that different types of love involve combining three fundamental qualities in different ways: passion, intimacy, and commitment

triarchic theory of intelligence Sternberg's theory that there are three distinct but related forms of intelligence

trimester one of the three 3-month periods of prenatal development

trophoblast in the blastocyst, the outer layer of cells, which will go on to form structures that provide protection and nourishment to the embryo

trust-versus-mistrust in Erikson's psychosocial theory, the first stage of development, during infancy, in which the central crisis is the need to establish a stable attachment to a loving and nurturing caregiver

ultrasound machine that uses sound waves to produce images of the fetus during pregnancy

umbilical cord structure connecting the placenta to the mother's uterus

undercontrol trait of having inadequate emotional self-regulation

underextension applying a general word to a specific object

unemployment work status of adults who are not in school, are not working, and are looking for a job

unstructured socializing socializing with friends without any specific goal or activity; includes behavior such as riding around in a car for fun, going to parties, visiting friends informally, and going out with friends

Upper Paleolithic period period of human history from 40,000 to 10,000 years ago, when distinct human cultures first developed

validity in scientific research, the extent to which a research method measures what it claims to measure

vernix at birth, babies are covered with this oily, cheesy substance, which protects their skin from chapping in the womb

very low birth weight term for neonates who weigh less than 3.3 pounds (1,500 grams) at birth

VO2 max ability of the body to take in oxygen and transport it to various organs; also called maximum oxygen update

weaning cessation of breast-feeding

Wernicke's area portion of the left temporal lobe of the human brain that is specialized for language comprehension

wet nursing cultural practice, common in human history, of hiring a lactating woman other than the mother to feed the infant

whole-language approach method of teaching reading in which the emphasis is on the meaning of written language in whole passages, rather than breaking down words into their smallest components

wisdom expertise in the conduct and meaning of life

worldview set of cultural beliefs that explain what it means to be human, how human relations should be conducted, and how human problems should be addressed

X-linked inheritance pattern of inheritance in which a recessive characteristic is expressed because it is carried on the male's X chromosome

zone of proximal development difference between skills or tasks that children can accomplish alone and those they are capable of performing if guided by an adult or a more competent peer

zygote following fertilization, the new cell formed from the union of sperm and ovum

References

AAP Task Force on Sudden Infant Death Syndrome (2011). SIDS and other sleep-related infant deaths: Expansion of recommendations for a safe infant sleeping environment. *Pediatrics, 128*, e1341–e1367.

AARP (2002). *The Grandparent Study 2002 report.* Washington, DC: Author.

AARP (2009). *The divorce experience: A study of divorce at midlife and beyond.* Washington, DC: Author.

AARP (2006). *Boomers turning 60.* Washington, DC: AARP.

A man's world? Good news. The education gap between men and women is narrowing. (2007, November 3). *The Economist,* 75.

A special report on the human genome. (2010). *The Economist.* Retrieved from http://www.economist.com/node/16349358

Abela, A., Walker, J., Amato, P. R., & Boyd, L. M. (2014). *Children and divorce in worldwide perspective.* New York, NY: Wiley.

Abbott, A. (2003). Restless nights, listless days. *Nature, 425,* 896–898.

Abbott, R. D., White, L. R., Ross, G. W., Masaki, K. M., Cub, J. D., & Petrovich, H. (2004). Walking and dementia in physically capable elderly men. *JAMA: Journal of the American Medical Association, 292,* 1147–1153.

Abbott, S. (1992). Holding on and pushing away: Comparative perspectives on an eastern Kentucky child-rearing practice. *Ethos, 20,* 33–65.

Abrejo, F. G., Shaikh, B. T., & Rizvi, N. (2009). And they kill me, only because I am a girl…a review of sex-selective abortions in South Asia. *European Journal of Contraception and Reproductive Health Care, 14,* 10–16.

Ackerman, P. L. (2000). Domain-specific knowledge as the "dark matter" of adult intelligence: Personality and interest correlates. *Journal of Gerontology, 55B,* P69–P84.

Adams, G. R. (1999). *The objective measure of ego identity status: A manual on test theory and construction.* Guelph, Ontario, Canada: Author.

Adams, R. G., & Ueno, K. (2006). Middle-aged and older adult men's friendships. In V. H. Bedford & T. B. Formaniak (Eds.), *Men in relationships: A new look from a life course perspective* (pp. 103–124). New York, NY: Springer.

Adamson, L., & Frick, J. (2003). The still face: A history of a shared experimental paradigm. *Infancy, 4,* 451–473.

Addington-Hall, J. (2000). Do home deaths increase distress in bereavement? *Palliative Medicine, 14,* 161–162.

Adolph, K. E., & Berger, S. E. (2005). Physical and motor development. In M. H. Bornstein & M. E. Lamb (Eds.), *Developmental science: An advanced textbook* (5th ed., pp. 223–281). Mahwah, NJ: Lawrence Erlbaum.

Adolph, K. E., & Berger, S. E. (2006). Motor development. In W. Damon & R. Lerner (Series Eds.), & D. Kuhn & R. Sieglery (Vol. Eds.), *Handbook of child psychology: Vol. 2. Cognition, perception and language* (6th ed., pp. 161–213). New York, NY: Wiley.

Adolph, K. E., Karasik, L. B., & Tamis-Lemonda, C. S. (2010). Motor skill. In M. H. Bornstein (Ed.), *Handbook of cultural developmental science* (pp. 61–88). New York, NY: Psychology Press.

Agüero-Torres, H., von Strauss, E., Viitanen, M., Winblad, B., & Fratiglioni, L. (2001). Institutionalization in the elderly: The role of chronic diseases and dementia. Cross-sectional and longitudinal data from a population-based study. *Journal of Clinical Epidemiology, 54,* 795–801.

Ahluwalia, M. K., Suzuki, L. A., & Mir, M. (2009). Dating, partnerships, and arranged marriages. In N. Tewari & A. N. Alvarez, *Asian American psychology: Current perspectives* (pp. 273–294).

Ahmed, R. A. (2010). North Africa and the Middle East. In M. H. Bornstein, *Handbook of cultural developmental science* (pp. 359–381). New York, NY: Psychology Press.

Ahuja, J. (2005). *Women's entrepreneurship in the United States.* Kansas City, MO: Kauffman Center for Entrepreneurial Leadership, Clearinghouse on Entrepreneurship Education. Retrieved from www.celcee.edu

Aikat, D. (2007). Violence, extent and responses to. In J. J. Arnett (Ed.), *Encyclopedia of children, adolescents, and the media* (Vol. 2, pp. 852–854). Thousand Oaks, CA: Sage.

Ainsworth, M. D. S., & Bell, S. M. (1969). Some contemporary patterns of mother–infant interaction in the feeding situation. In A. Ambrose (Ed.), *Stimulation in early infancy* (pp. 133–170). London, UK: Academic Press.

Ainsworth, M. D. S., Behar, M. C., Waters, E., & Wall, S. (1978). *Patterns of attachment: A psychological study of the strange situation.* Oxford, UK: Erlbaum.

Ainsworth, M. S. (1977). Infant development and mother–infant interaction among Ganda and American families. In P. H. Leiderman, S. R. Tulkin, & A. Rosenfeld (Eds.), *Culture and infancy: Variations in the human experience* (pp. 119–149). New York, NY: Academic Press.

Ajani, U. A., Ford, E. S., & McGuire, L. C. (2006). Distribution of lifestyle and emerging risk factors by 10-year risk for coronary heart disease. *European Journal of Cardiovascular Prevention and Rehabilitation, 13,* 745–752.

Ajrouch, K., Blandon, A., & Antonucci, T. (2005). Social networks among men and women: The effects of age and socioeconomic status. *Journal of Gerontology: Social Sciences, 60B,* S311–S317.

Akhtar, N. (2005). Is joint attention necessary for early language learning? In B. D. Homer & C. S. Tamis-LeMonda (Eds.), *The development of social cognition and communication* (pp. 165–179). Mahwah, NJ: Lawrence Erlbaum.

Akhtar, N., & Tomasello, M. (2000). The social nature of words and word learning. In R. M. Golinkoff, K. Hirsh-Pasek, L. Bloom, L. B. Smith, A. L. Woodward, & N. Akhtar (Eds.), *Becoming a word learner: A debate on lexical acquisition* (pp. 115–135). New York, NY: Oxford University Press.

Akimoto, S. A., & Sanbonmatsu, D. M. (1999). Differences in self-effacing behavior between European and Japanese Americans: Effect on competence evaluations. *Journal of Cross-Cultural Psychology, 30,* 159–177.

Akinbami, L. J., & Schoendorf, K. C. (2002). Trends in childhood asthma: Prevalence, health care utilization, and mortality. *Pediatrics, 110,* 315–22.

Akiyama, H., & Antonucci, T. C. (1999). *Mother–daughter dynamics over the life course.* Paper presented at the meeting of the Gerentological Association of America, San Francisco.

Akshoomoff, N. A., Feroleto, C. C., Doyle, R. E., & Stiles, J. (2002). The impact of early unilateral brain injury on perceptual organization and visual memory. *Neuropsychologia, 40,* 539–561.

Alaggia, R., & Vine, C. (Eds.). (2006). *Cruel but not unusual: Violence in Canadian families.* Waterloo, Ontario, Canada: Wilfrid Laurier University Press.

Alan Guttmacher Institute (AGI) (2001). *Teenage sexual and reproductive behavior in developed countries: Can more progress be made?* New York, NY: Author. Available: www.agi-usa.org.

Alberts, A., Elkind, D., & Ginsberg, S. (2007). The personal fable and risk-taking in early adolescence. *Journal of Youth and Adolescence, 36,* 71–76.

Aldridge, M. A., Stillman, R. D., & Bower, T. G. R. (2001). Newborn categorization of vowel-like sounds. *Developmental Science, 4,* 220–232.

Aldwin, C. M., & Spiro, A. III (2006). *Health, behavior, and optimal aging: A life span developmental perspective.* San Diego, CA: Academic Press.

Alexander, B. (2001, June). Radical idea serves youth, saves money. *Youth Today,* pp. 1, 42–44.

Alexander, G. M., & Hines, M. (2002). Sex differences in response to children's toys in nonhuman primates. *Evolution and Human Behavior, 23,* 467–479.

Alink, L. R. A., Mesman, J., van Zeijl, J., Stolk, M. N., Juffer, F., Koot, H. M.,…van IJzendoorn, M. H. (2006). The early childhood aggression curve: Development of physical aggression in 10- to 50-month-old children. *Child Development, 77,* 954–966.

Almeida, D. M., Neupert, S. D., Banks, S. R., & Serido, J. (2005). Do daily stress processes account for socioeconomic health disparities? *Journal of Gerontology, 60B,* 34–39.

Alsaker, F. D., & Flammer, A. (1999). *The adolescent experience: European and American adolescents in the 1990s.* Mahwah, NJ: Erlbaum.

Alsaker, F. D., & Flammer, A. (2006). Pubertal maturation. In S. Jackson & L. Goossens (Eds.), *Handbook of adolescent development* (pp. 30–50). New York, NY: Psychology Press.

Alvarez, M. (2004). Caregiving and early infant crying in a Danish community. *Journal of Developmental and Behavioral Pediatrics, 25,* 91–98.

Alvarez-Leon, E. E., Roman-Vinas, B., & Serra-Majem, L. (2006). Dairy products and health: A review of the epidemiological evidence. *British Journal of Nutrition, 96,*(Suppl.), S94–S99.

Alwin, D. F. (1988). From obedience to autonomy: Changes in traits desired in children, 1928–1978. *Public Opinion Quarterly, 52,* 33–52.

Alzheimer's Association. (2004, May 28). Standard prescriptions for Alzheimer's. Retrieved from http://www.alz.org/AboutAD/Treatment/Standard.asp

Al-Mateen, C. S., & Afzal, A. (2004). The Muslim child, adolescent, and family. *Child and Adolescent Psychiatry Clinics of North America, 13,* 183–200.

Amato, P. (2004). To have and have not: Marriage and divorce in the United States. In M. Coleman & L. Ganong (Eds.), *Handbook of contemporary families* (pp. 265–281). Thousand Oaks, CA: Sage.

Amato, P. (2010). Research on divorce: Continuing trends and new developments. *Journal of Marriage and the Family, 72,* 650–666.

Amato, P. R. (2000). Diversity within single-parent families. In D. H. Demo, K. R. Allen, & M. A. Fine (Eds.), *Handbook of family diversity* (pp. 149–172). New York, NY: Oxford University Press.

Amato, P. R., & Anthony, C. J. (2014). Estimating the effects of parental divorce and death with fixed effects models. *Journal of Marriage and Family, 76*(2), 370–386.

Amato, P. R., & Boyd, L. M. (2013). Children and divorce in world perspective. Contemporary Issues in Family Studies: *Global Perspectives on Partnerships, Parenting and Support in a Changing World, 227–243.*

Amato, P. R., & Cheadle, J. (2005). Divorce and child well-being across three generations. *Journal of Marriage and Family, 67,* 191–206.

Amato, P. R., & Fowler, F. (2002). Parenting practices, child adjustment, and family diversity. *Journal of Marriage and the Family, 64,* 703–716.

Amato, P. R., & Rogers, S. J. (1997). A longitudinal study of marital problems and subsequent divorce. *Journal of Marriage and the Family, 59,* 612–624. American Academy of Pediatrics (2001). *Toilet training.* Available: www.aap.org/family./toil.htm/

Amato, P., & Previti, D. (2003). People's reasons for divorcing: Gender, social class, the life course, and adjustment. *Journal of Family Issues, 24,* 602–626.

American Academy of Pediatrics Committee on Public Education. (2001). Children, adolescents, and television. *Pediatrics, 107,* 423–426.

American Academy of Pediatrics Task Force on Infant Positioning and SIDS (AAPTFIPS). (2000). Changing concepts of sudden infant death syndrome. *Pediatrics, 105,* 650–656.

American Academy of Pediatrics, Subcommittee on Attention-Deficit Hyperactivity Disorder (2005). Treatment of attention-deficit hyperactivity disorder. *Pediatrics, 115,* e749–e757.

American Academy of Pediatrics. (2004). *Sports programs.* Retrieved from http://www.medem.com/medlb/article_detaillb_for_printer. cfm?article_ID=ZZZD2QD5M7C&sub_cat=405/

American Academy of Pediatrics. (2005). Breastfeeding and the use of human milk: Policy statement. *Pediatrics, 115,* 496–506.

American Academy of Pediatrics. (2011). *AAP issues new guidelines for identifying and managing newborn jaundice.* Retrieved from http://www. aap.org/family/jaundicefeature.htm

American Cancer Society (2007). *Cancer facts and figures 2007.* Atlanta, GA: Author.

American Heart Association. (2005). *Heart disease and stroke statistics 2005 update.* Dallas, TX: American Heart Association.

American Heart Association. (2006). *Heart disease and stroke statistics: 2006 update.* Dallas, TX: Author.

American Pregnancy Association. (2011). *In-vitro fertilization (IVF).* Retrieved from http://www.americanpregnancy.org/infertility/ivf.html/

American Psychiatric Association. (1994). *Diagnostic and statistical manual of mental disorders* (4th ed.). Washington, DC: Author.

American Psychiatric Association (2013). *Diagnostic and statistical manual of mental disorders* (5th ed.). Arlington, VA: American Psychiatric Association.

Ammaniti, M. A. S. S. I. M. O., Speranza, A. M., & Fedele, S. I. L. V. I. A. (2005). Attachment in infancy and in early and late childhood. *Attachment in middle childhood, 115–136.*

Amore, M., Tagariello, P., Laterza, C., & Savoia, E. M. (2007). Beyond nosography of depression in elderly. *Archives of Gerontology and Geriatrics, 44*(Suppl. 1), 13–22.

Amsterlaw, J., & Wellman, H. (2006). Theories of mind in transition: A microgenetic study of the development of false belief understanding. *Journal of Cognition and Development, 7,* 139–172.

An, J. S., & Cooney, T. M. (2006). Psychological well-being in mid to late life: The role of generativity development in parent–child relationships across the lifespan. *International Journal of Behavioral Development, 30,* 410–421.

Anand, S., & Krosnick, J. A. (2005). Demographic predictors of media use among infants, toddlers, and preschoolers. *American Behavioral Scientist, 48*(5), 539–561.

Ancoli-Israel, S., & Cooke, J. R. (2005). Prevalence and comorbidity of insomnia and effect on functioning in elderly populations. *Journal of the American Geriatrics Society, 53,* S264–271.

Anders, T. F., & Taylor, T. (1994). Babies and their sleep environment. *Children's Environments, 11,* 123–134.

Anderson, C. A. (2004). An update on the effects of playing violent video games. *Journal of Adolescence, 27,* 113–122.

Anderson, C. A., Gentile, D. A., & Buckley, K. E. (2007). *Violent video game effects on children and adolescents: Theory, research, and public policy.* New York, NY: Oxford University Press.

Anderson, C. M. (2000). The persistence of polygyny as an adaptive response to poverty and oppression in apartheid South Africa. *Cross-cultural research, 34,* 99–112.

Anderson, C., & Ford, C. M. (1987). Affect of the game player: Short-term effects of highly and mildly aggressive video games. *Personality and Social Psychology Bulletin, 12,* 390–402.

Anderson, D. R., Huston, A. C., Schmitt, K., Linebarger, D. L., & Wright, J. C. (2001). Early childhood viewing and adolescent behavior: The recontact study. *Monographs of the Society for Research in Child Development, 66*(1, Serial No. 264).

Anderson, E. (2000). Exploring register knowledge: The value of "controlled improvisation." In L. Menn & N. B. Ratner (Eds.), *Methods for studying language production* (pp. 225–248). Mahwah, NJ: Erlbaum.

Anderson, E. (2012). *The monogamy gap: Men, love, and the reality of cheating.* Oxford University Press.

Anderson, P., & Butcher, K. (2006). Childhood obesity: Trends and potential causes. *The Future of Children, 16,* 19–45.

Anderson, S. (2003). Why dowry payments declined with modernization in Europe but are rising in India. *Journal of Political Economy, 111,* 269–279.

Anderson, V., & Jacobs, R. (Eds.). (2008). *Executive functions and the frontal lobes: A lifespan perspective.* Philadelphia, PA: Taylor & Francis.

Ando, M., Asakura, T., & Simons-Morton, B. (2005). Psychosocial influences in physical, verbal and indirect bullying among Japanese early adolescents. *Journal of Early Adolescence, 25,* 268–297.

Andrews, G., Halford, G., & Bunch, K. (2003). Theory of mind and relational complexity. *Child Development, 74,* 1476–1499.

Angel, J. L., Douglas, N., & Angel, R. J. (2003). Gender, widowhood, and long-term care in the older Mexican population. *Journal of Women and Aging, 15,* 89–105.

Anglin, J. M. (1993). Vocabulary development: A morphological analysis. *Monographs of the Society for Research in Child Development, 58*(10, Serial No. 238).

Annunziato, R., & Lowe, M. (2007). Taking action to lose weight: Toward an understanding of individual differences. *Eating Behaviors, 8,* 185–194.

Appoh, L. Y. (2004). Consequences of early malnutrition for subsequent social and emotional behaviour of children in Ghana. *Journal of Psychology in Africa; South of the Sahara, the Caribbean, and Afro-Latin America, 14,* 87–94.

Appoh, L. Y., & Krekling, S. (2004). Effects of early childhood malnutrition on cognitive performance of Ghanaian children. *Journal of Psychology in Africa; South of the Sahara, the Caribbean, and Afro-Latin America, 14,* 1–7.

Apter, T. (1990). *Altered loves: Mothers and daughters during adolescence.* New York, NY: St. Martin's.

Aquilino, W. S. (2006). Family relationships and support systems in emerging adulthood. In J. J. Arnett & J. Tanner (Eds.), *Coming of age in the 21st century: The lives and contexts of emerging adults* (pp. 193–218). Washington, DC: American Psychological Association.

Arazi, B. (2009). Enhancing elderly utilization of social networks. *International Journal of Disability and Human Development, 8,* 199–206.

Arcangeli, T., Thilaganathan, B., Hooper, R., Khan, K. S., & Bhide, A. (2012). Neurodevelopmental delay in small babies at term: A systematic review. *Ultrasound in Obstetrics & Gynecology, 40,* 267–275.

Archer, S. L. (2002). Commentary on "Feminist perspectives on Erikson's theory: Their relevance for contemporary identity development research." *Identity, 2,* 267–270.

Archibald, A. B., Graber, J. A., & Brooks-Gunn, J. (2003). Pubertal processes and physiological growth in adolescence. In G. Adams & M. Berzonsky (Eds.), *Blackwell handbook of adolescence.* Malden, MA: Blackwell.

Arditi-Babchuk, H., Eidelman, A. I., & Feldman, R. (2009). Rapid eye movement (REM) in premature neonates and developmental outcome at 6 months. *Infant Behavior & Development, 32,* 27–32.

Arlin, P. K. (1989). Problem solving and problem finding in young artists and young scientists. In M. L. Commons, J. D. Sinnott, F. A. Richards, & C. Armon (Eds.), *Adult development, Vol. 1: Comparisons and applications of development models* (pp. 197–216). New York, NY: Praeger.

Arnett, J. (1994). Are college students adults? Their conceptions of the transition to adulthood. *Journal of Adult Development, 1,* 154–168.

Arnett, J. J. (1995). Broad and narrow socialization: The family in the context of a cultural theory. *Journal of Marriage and the Family, 57,* 617–628.

Arnett, J. J. (1996). *Metalheads: Heavy metal music and adolescent alienation.* Boulder, CO: Westview Press.

Arnett, J. J. (1997). Young people's conceptions of the transition to adulthood. *Youth & Society, 29,* 1–23.

Arnett, J. J. (1998). Learning to stand alone: The contemporary American transition to adulthood in cultural and historical context. *Human Development, 41,* 295–315.

Arnett, J. J. (1999). Adolescent storm and stress, reconsidered. *American Psychologist, 54,* 317–326.

Arnett, J. J. (2000). Emerging adulthood: A theory of development from the late teens through the twenties. *American Psychologist, 55,* 469–480.

Arnett, J. J. (2001). Conceptions of the transition to adulthood: Perspectives from adolescence to midlife. *Journal of Adult Development, 8,* 133–143.

Arnett, J. J. (2002). Adolescents in Western countries in the 21st century: Vast opportunities—for all? In B. B. Brown, R. W. Larson, & T. S. Saraswathi (Eds.), *The world's youth: Adolescence in eight regions of the globe* (pp. 307–343). New York, NY: Cambridge University Press.

Arnett, J. J. (2002). The psychology of globalization. *American Psychologist, 57,* 774–483.

Arnett, J. J. (2003). Conceptions of the transition to adulthood among emerging adults in American ethnic groups. *New Directions in Child and Adolescent Development, 100,* 63–75.

Arnett, J. J. (2004). *Emerging adulthood: The winding road from the late teens through the twenties.* New York: Oxford University Press.

Arnett, J. J. (2005a). The Vitality Criterion: A new standard of publication for *Journal of Adolescent Research. Journal of Adolescent Research, 20,* 3–7.

Arnett, J. J. (2005b). The developmental context of substance use in emerging adulthood. *Journal of Drug Issues, 35,* 235–253.

Arnett, J. J. (2006). G. Stanley Hall's adolescence: Brilliance and nonsense. *History of Psychology, 9,* 186–197.

Arnett, J. J. (2007). Introduction. In J. J. Arnett (Ed.), *Encyclopedia of children, adolescents, and the media, Volume 1: A-K* (pp. xxxv-xxxvi). Thousand Oaks, CA: Sage.

Arnett, J. J. (2007). The long and leisurely route: Coming of age in Europe today. *Current History, 106,* 130–136.

Arnett, J. J. (2008). The neglected 95%: Why American psychology needs to become less American. *American Psychologist, 63,* 602–614.

Arnett, J. J. (2011). Emerging adulthood(s): The cultural psychology of a new life stage. In L. A. Jensen (Ed.), *Bridging cultural and developmental psychology: New syntheses in theory, research, and policy.* New York, NY: Oxford University Press.

Arnett, J. J. (2015). *Emerging adulthood: The winding road from the late teens through the twenties* (2nd ed.). New York, NY: Oxford University Press.

Arnett, J. J. (2015). The cultural psychology of emerging adulthood. In L. A. Jensen (Ed.), *Oxford handbook of human development and culture.* New York, NY: Oxford University Press.

Arnett, J. J., & Jensen, L. A. (2002). A congregation of one: Individualized religious beliefs among emerging adults. *Journal of Adolescent Research,17,* 451–467.

Arnett, J. J., & Schwab, J. (2012). *The Clark University Poll of Emerging Adults: Thriving, struggling, and hopeful.* Worcester,

MA: Clark University. Retrieved from http://www.clarku.edu/clark-poll-emerging-adults/

Arnett, J. J., & Schwab, J. (2013). *Parents and their grown kids: Harmony, support, and (occasional) conflict.* Worcester, MA: Clark University. Retrieved from http://www.clarku.edu/clark-poll-emerging-adults/

Arnett, J. J., & Schwab, J. (2014). *Beyond emerging adulthood: The Clark University Poll of Established Adults.* Worcester, MA: Clark University. Retrieved from http://www.clarku.edu/clark-poll-emerging-adults/

Arnett, J. J., & Tanner, J. L. (2009). Toward a cultural-developmental stage theory of the life course. In K. McCartney & R. Weisberg (Eds.), *Development and experience: A festschrift in honor of Sandra Wood Scarr* (pp. 17–38). New York, NY: Taylor & Francis.

Arnett, J. J., Ramos, K. D., & Jensen, L. A. (2001). Ideologies in emerging adulthood: Balancing the ethics of autonomy and community. *Journal of Adult Development, 8,* 69–79.

Aronson, P. J., Mortimer, J. T., Zierman, C., & Hacker, M. (1996). Adolescents, work, and family: *An intergenerational developmental analyses. Understanding families, 6,* 25–62.

Årseth, A. K., Kroger, J., & Martinussen, M. (2009). Meta-analytic studies of identity status and the relational issues of attachment and intimacy. *Identity: An International Journal of Theory and Research, 9,* 1–32.

Artinian, N. T., Fletcher, G. F., Mozaffarian, D., Kris-Etherton, P., Van Horn, L., Lichtenstein, A. H., ... & Burke, L. E. (2010). Interventions to promote physical activity and dietary lifestyle changes for cardiovascular risk factor reduction in adults: A scientific statement from the American Heart Association. *Circulation,122*(4), 406–441.

Arts, J. A. R., Gijselaers, W. H., & Bohuizen, H. P. A. (2006). Understanding managerial problem-solving, knowledge use and information processing: Investigating stages from school to the workplace. *Contemporary Educational Psychology, 31,* 387–410.

Asawa, L. E., Hansen, D. J., & Flood, M. F. (2008). Early childhood intervention programs: Opportunities and challenges for preventing child maltreatment. *Education and Treatment of Children, 31,* 73–110.

Ashcraft, M. H. (2009). *Cognition.* Upper Saddle River, NJ: Prentice Hall.

Asher, S. R., & Rose, A. J. (1997). Promoting children's social–emotional adjustment with peers. In P. Salovey & D. J. Sluyter (Eds.), *Emotional development and emotional intelligence* (pp. 193–195). New York, NY: Basic Books.

Aslin, R. N., Jusczyk, P. W., & Pisoni, D. B. (1998). Speech and auditory processing during infancy: Constraints on and precursors to language. In W. Damon (Ed.), *Handbook of child psychology* (5th ed., Vol. 2). New York, NY: Wiley.

Atchley, R. C. (2009). *Spirituality and aging.* Baltimore, MD: John Hopkins University Press.

Atella, L. D., DiPietro, J., Smith, B. A., & St. James-Roberts, I. (2003). More than meets the eye: Parental and infant contributors to maternal and paternal reports of early infant difficultness. *Parenting: Science and Practice, 3,* 265–284.

Atkinson, J. (2000). *The developing visual brain.* Oxford, UK: Oxford University Press.

Atkinson, L., & Goldberg, S. (Eds.). (2004). *Attachment issues in psychopathology and intervention.* Mahwah, NJ: Erlbaum.

Atkinson, L., Chisholm, V. C., Scott, B., Goldberg, S., Vaughn, B. E., Blackwell, J., Dickens, S., & Tam, F. (1999). Maternal sensitivity, child functional level, and attachment in Down syndrome. *Monographs of the Society for Research in Child Development, 64,* 45–66.

Aunio, P., Aubrey, C., Godfrey, R., Pan, Y., & Liu, Y. (2008). Children's early numeracy in England, Finland and People's Republic of China. *International Journal of Early Years Education, 16,* 203–221.

Aunola, K., & Nurmi, J.-E. (2004). Maternal affection moderates the impact of psychological control on a child's mathematical performance. *Developmental Psychology, 40,* 965–978.

Avery, L., & Lazdane, G. (2008). What do we know about sexual and reproductive health among adolescents in Europe? *European Journal of Contraception and Reproductive Health, 13,* 58–70.

Avis, N. E., Crawford, S., & Johannes, C. B. (2002). Menopause. In G. M. Wingood & R. J. DeClemente (Eds.), *Handbook of women's sexual and reproductive health* (pp. 367–391). New York, NY: Kluwer.

Axelsson, A.-S. (2010). Perpetual and personal: Swedish youth adults and their use of mobile phones. *New Media & Society, 12,* 35–54.

Azmitia, M., Kamprath, N., & Linnet, J. (1998). Intimacy and conflict: The dynamics of boys' and girls' friendships during middle childhood and early adolescence. In L. Meyer, H. Park, M. Gront-Scheyer, I. Schwartz, & B. Harry (Eds.), *Making friends: The influences of culture and development* (pp. 171–189). Baltimore, MD: Brookes Publishing.

Axia, G., Bonichini, S., & Benini, F. (1999). Attention and reaction to distress in infancy: A longitudinal study. *Developmental Psychology, 35,* 500–504.

Bachman, J. G., O'Malley, P. M., Schulenberg, J. E., Johnston, L. D., Freedman-Doan, P., & Messersmith, E. E. (2008). *The education-drug use connection: How successes and failures in school relate to adolescent smoking, drinking, drug use, and delinquency.* New York, NY: Lawrence Erlbaum.

Bachman, J. G., Safron, D. J., Sy, S. R., & Schulenberg, J. E. (2003). Wishing to work: New perspectives on how adolescents' part-time work intensity is linked to educational engagement, substance use, and other problem behaviors. *International Journal of Behavioral Development, 27,* 301–315.

Badrinath, C. (2003). The householder, grhastha in the Mahabharata. In M. Pernau, I. Ahmad, & H. Reifeld (Eds.), *Family and gender: Changing values in Germany and India* (pp. 113–139). New Delhi, India: Sage.

Baer, J. S., Sampson, P. D., Barr, H. M., Connor, P. D., & Streissguth, A. P. (2003). A 21-year longitudinal analysis of the effects of prenatal alcohol exposure on young adult drinking. *Archives of General Psychiatry, 60,* 377–385.

Bagwell, C. L., & Schmidt, M. E. (2013). Friendships in childhood and adolescence. Guilford Press.

Baildum, E. M., Hillier, V. F., Menon, S., Bamford, F. N., Moore, W. M. O., & Ward, B. S. (2000). Attention to infants in the first year. *Child: Care, Health and Development, 26,* 199–216.

Baillargeon, R. (2008). Innate ideas revisited: For a principle of persistence in infants' physical reasoning. *Perspectives on Psychological Science, 3*(Special issue: From philosophical thinking to psychological empiricism), 2–13.

Baird, A., John, R., & Hayslip, B., Jr. (2000). Custodial grandparenting among African Americans: A focus group perspective. In B. Hayslip, Jr. & R. Goldberg-Glen (Eds.), *Grandparents raising grandchildren: Theoretical, empirical, and clinical perspectives.* New York, NY: Springer.

Bakker, A. B., & Heuven, E. (2006). Emotional dissonance, burnout, and in-role performance among nurses and police officers. *International Journal of Stress Management, 13,* 423–440.

Baker, C. (2011). *Foundations of bilingual education and bilingualism* (5th ed.). New York, NY: Multilingual Matters.

Baker, J. M. (2002). *How homophobia hurts children: Nurturing diversity at home, at school, and in the community.* New York, NY: Haworth Press.

Bakker, M. P., Ormel, J., Verhulst, F. C., & Oldehinkel, A. J. (2010). Peer stressors and gender differences in adolescents' mental health: the TRAILS study. *Journal of Adolescent Health, 46*(5), 444–450.

Baker, J. R., & Moore, S. M. (2008). Distress, coping and blogging: Comparing new MySpace users by their intention to blog. *CyberPsychology & Behavior, 11*, 81–85.

Bakermans-Kranenburg, M. J., van Uzendoorn, M. H., Bokhorst, C. L., & Schuengel, C. (2004). The importance of shared environment in infant–father attachment: A behavioral genetic study of the attachment q-sort. *Journal of Family Psychology, 18*, 545–549.

Baldry, A. C., & Farrington, D. P. (2004). Evaluation of an intervention program for the reduction of bullying and victimization in schools. *Aggressive Behavior, 30*, 1–15.

Balen, F. v., & Inhorn, M. C. (2002). Interpreting infertility: A view from the social sciences. In M. C. Inhorn & F. v. Balen, *Infertility around the globe: New thinking on childlessness, gender, and reproductive technologies* (pp. 3–32). Berkeley, CA: University of California Press.

Ball, K., & Crawford, D. (2005). Socioeconomic status and weight change in adults: A review. *Social Science & Medicine, 60*, 1987–2010.

Balodis, I. M., Wynne-Edwards, K. E., & Olmstead, M. C. (2011). The stress-response-dampening effects of placebo. *Hormones and Behavior, 59*, 465–472.

Baltes, P. B. (2003). On the incomplete architecture of human ontogeny: Selection, optimization, and compensation as foundation for developmental theory. In U. M. Staudinger & U. Lindenberger (Eds.), *Understanding human development: Dialogues with lifespan psychology* (pp. 17–44). Boston, MA: Kluwer.

Baltes, P. B., & Baltes, M. M. (1990). Psychological perspectives on successful aging: The model of selective optimization with compensation. In P. B. Baltes & M. M. Baltes (Eds.), *Successful aging: Perspectives from the behavioral sciences* (pp. 1–34). New York, NY: Cambridge University Press.

Baltes, P. B., & Smith, J. (2003). New frontiers in the future of aging: From successful aging of the young old to the dilemmas of the fourth age. *Gerontology, 49*, 123–135.

Baltes, P. B., & Staudinger, U. M. (2000). Wisdom. *American Psychologist, 55*, 122–136.

Baltes, P. B., Lindenberger, U., & Staudinger, U. M. (2006). Life span theory in developmental psychology. In W. Damon & R. M. Lerner (Eds.), *Handbook of child psychology* (Vol. 1., pp. 569–664). New York, NY: Wiley.

Baltes, P. B., Staudinger, U. M., Maercker, A., & Smith, J. (1995). People nominated as wise: A comparative study of wisdom-related knowledge. *Psychology and Aging, 10*, 155–166.

Bancroft, J. (2002). The medicalization of female sexual dysfunction: The need for caution. *Archives of Sexual Behavior, 31*, 451–455.

Bancroft, J. (2007). Sex and aging. *The New England Journal of Medicine, 357*, 820–822.

Bandura, A. (1977). *Social learning theory*. Englewood Cliffs, NJ: Prentice-Hall.

Bandura, A. (2002). Social cognitive theory in cultural context. *Applied Psychology: An International Review, 51*(Special Issue), 269–290.

Bandura, A., & Bussey, K. (2004). On broadening the cognitive, motivational, and sociostructural scope of theorizing about gender development and functioning: Comments on Martin, Buble and Szkrybalo (2002). *Psychological Bulletin, 130*, 691–701.

Bandura, A., Ross, D., & Ross, S. A. (1961). The transmission of aggression through imitation of aggressive models. *Journal of Abnormal and Social Psychology, 63*, 575–582.

Banerjee, R. (2005). Gender identity and the development of gender roles. In S. Ding & K. Littleton (Eds.), *Children's personal and social development* (pp. 142–179). Malden, MA: Blackwell.

Banks, M. S. (2005). The benefits and costs of combining information between and within the senses. In J. J. Reiser, J. J. Lockman, & C. A. Nelson (Eds.), *Action as an organizer of learning and development* (pp. 161–198). Mahwah, NJ: Erlbaum.

Barajas, R. G., Martin, A., Brooks-Gunn, J., & Hale, L. (2011). Mother-child bed-sharing in toddlerhood and cognitive and behavioral outcomes. *Pediatrics,128*(2), e339–e347.

Barber, B. K. (Ed.). (2002). *Intrusive parenting: How psychological control affects children and adolescents*. Washington, D.C: American Psychological Association.

Barber, B. K. (2013). Annual Research Review: The experience of youth with political conflict–challenging notions of resilience and encouraging research refinement. *Journal of Child Psychology and Psychiatry, 54*(4), 461–473.

Barber, B. K., Stolz, H. E., & Olsen, J. A. (2005). Parental support, psychological control, and behavioral control: Assessing relevance across time, culture, and method: IV. Assessing relevance across time: U.S. analyses and results. *Monographs of the Society for Research in Child Development, 70*(4).

Barber, C., Mueller, C. T., & Ogata, S. (2013). Volunteerism as purpose: Examining the long-term predictors of continued community engagement. *Educational Psychology, 33*(3), 314–333.

Barefoot, J. C., Mortensen, E. L., Helms, M. J., Avlund, K., & Schroll, M. (2001). A longitudinal study of gender differences in depressive symptoms from age 50 to 80. *Psychology and Aging, 16*, 342–345.

Barker, J. C., de Vries, B., & Herdt, G. (2006). Social support in the lives of lesbians and gay men at midlife and later. *Sexuality Research & Social Policy: A Journal of the NSRC, 3*, 1–23.

Barkley, R. A. (2002). Major life activity and health outcomes associated with attention-deficit/hyperactivity disorder. *Journal of Clinical Psychiatry, 63*, 10–15.

Barling, J., & Kelloway, E. K. (1999). *Young workers: Varieties of experience*. Washington, DC: American Psychological Association.

Barnett, D., Ganiban, J., & Cicchetti, D. (1999). Maltreatment, negative expressivity, and the development of type D attachments from 12 to 24 months of age. *Monographs of the Society for Research in Child Development, 64*, 97–118.

Barnett, W. S., & Hustedt, J. T. (2005). Head Start's lasting benefits. *Infants and Young Children, 18*, 16–24.

Baron, E. M., & Denmark, F. L. (2006). An exploration of female genital mutilation. In F. L. Denmark, H. H. Krauss, E. Halpern, & J. A. Sechzer (Eds.), *Violence and exploitation against women and girls* (pp. 339–355). Malden, MA: Blackwell.

Barone, J. G., Jasutkar, N., & Schneider, D. (2009). Later toilet training is associated with urge incontinence in children. *Journal of pediatric urology, 5*(6), 458–461.

Barr, H. M., & Streissguth, A. P. (2001). Identifying maternal self-reported alcohol use associated with Fetal Alcohol Spectrum Disorders. *Alcoholism: Clinical and Experimental Research, 25*, 283–287.

Barr, R. G. (2009). The phenomena of early infant crying and colic. Paper presented at the Centre for Community and Child Health, Melbourne, Australia, March 2.

Barr, R. G., & Gunnar, M. (2000). Colic: The "transient responsivity" hypothesis. In R. G. Barr, B. Hopkins, & J. A. Green (Eds.), *Crying as a sign, a symptom, and a signal* (pp. 41–66). Cambridge, UK: Cambridge University Press.

Barr, R., & Hayne, H. (2003). It's not what you know, it's who you know: Older siblings facilitate imitation during infancy. *Child Development, 70*, 1067–1081.

Barr, R., Marrott, H., & Rovee-Collier, C. (2003). The role of sensory preconditioning in memory retrieval by preverbal infants. *Learning and Behavior, 31*, 111–123.

Barreto, M., Ryan, M. K., & Schmitt, M. T. (Eds.). (2009). *The glass ceiling in the 21st century: Understanding barriers to gender equality*. Washington, DC: American Psychological Association.

Barrett, D. E., & Frank, D. A. (1987). *The effects of undernutrition on children's behavior*. New York, NY: Gordon & Breach.

Barrett, K. C., & Nelson-Goens, G. C. (1997). Emotion communication and the development of the social emotions. *New Directions for Child Development, 77,* 69–88.

Barrio, C., Morena, A., & Linaza, J. L. (2007). Spain. In J. J. Arnett, R. Ahmed, B. Nsamenang, T. S. Saraswathi, & R. Silbereisen (Eds.), *International encyclopedia of adolescence.* New York, NY: Routledge.

Barry, C.M., Madsen, S.D., & Grace, A. (2015). Friendships in emerging adulthood. In J. J. Arnett (Ed.), *Oxford Handbook of Emerging Adulthood.* New York, NY: Oxford University Press.

Barry, H. III, Bacon, M. K., & Child I. L. (1957). A cross-cultural survey of some sex differences in socialization. *Journal of Abnormal Social Psychology, 55,* 327–332.

Bartoshuk, L. M., & Beauchamp, G. K. (1994). Chemical senses. *Annual Review of Psychology, 45,* 419–449.

Basow, S. A., & Rubin, L. R. (1999). Gender influences on adolescent development. In N. G. Johnson & M. C. Roberts (Eds.), *Beyond appearance: A new look at adolescent girls* (pp. 25–52). Washington, DC: American Psychological Association.

Basseches, M. (1984). *Dialectical thinking and adult development.* Norwood, NJ: Ablex.

Basseches, M. (1989). Dialectical thinking as an organized whole: Comments on Irwin and Kramer. In M. L. Commons, J. D. Sinnott, F. A. Richards, & C. Armon (Eds.), *Adult development, Vol. 1: Comparisons and applications of developmental models* (pp. 161–178). New York, NY: Praeger.

Bassi, M., & Antonella, D. F. (2004). Adolescence and the changing context of optimal experience in time: Italy 1986–2000. *Journal of Happiness Studies, 5,* 155–179.

Bassuk, S. S., & Manson, J. E. (2005). Epidemiological evidence for the role of physical activity in reducing risk of type 2 diabetes and cardiovascular disease. *Journal of Applied Physiology, 99,* 1193–1204.

Bastian, L. A., Smith, C. M., & Nanda, K. (2003). Is this woman perimenopausal? *JAMA: Journal of the American Medical Association, 289,* 895–902.

Basu, A. K., & Chau, N. H. (2007). An exploration of the worst forms of child labor: Is redemption a viable option? In K. A. Appiah & M. Bunzl (Eds.), *Buying freedom: The ethics of economics of slave redemption* (pp. 37–76). Princeton, NJ: Princeton University Press.

Bates, B., & Turner, A. N. (2003). Imagery and symbolism in the birth practices of traditional cultures. In L. Dundes (Ed.), *The manner born: Birth rites in cross-cultural perspective* (pp. 85–97). Walnut Creek, CA: AltaMira Press.

Batzer, F. R., & Ravitsky, V. (2009). Preimplantation genetic diagnosis: Ethical considerations. In V. Ravitsky, A. Fiester, & A. L. Caplan (Eds.), *The Penn Center guide to bioethics* (pp. 339–354). New York, NY: Springer.

Bauer, P. J. (2006). Event memory. In W. Damon & R. Lerner (Eds.), *Handbook of child psychology: Vol. 2. Cognition, perception and language* (6th ed., pp. 373–425). New York, NY: Wiley.

Bauer, P. J., San Souci, P., & Pathman, T. (2010). Infant memory. *Wiley Interdisciplinary Reviews: Cognitive Science, 1,* 267–277.

Bauer, P. J., Wenner, J. A., Dropik, P. I., & Wewerka, S. S. (2000). Parameters of remembering and forgetting in the transition from infancy to early childhood. *Monographs of the Society for Research in Child Development, 65,* 1–204.

Bauer, P. J., Wiebe, S. A., Carver, L. J., Waters, J. M., & Nelson, C. A. (2003). Developments in long-term explicit memory late in the first year of life: Behavioral and electrophysiological indices. *Psychological Science, 14,* 629–635.

Bauer, P. J., Wiebe, S. A., Waters, J. M., & Banston, S. K. (2001). Reexposure breeds recall: Effects of experience on 9-month olds' ordered recall. *Journal of Experimental Child Psychology, 80,* 174–200.

Bauer, P. M., Hanson, J. L., Pierson, R. K., Davidson, R. J., & Pollak, S. D. (2009). Cerebellar volume and cognitive functioning in children who experienced early deprivation. *Biological Psychiatry, 66,* 1100–1106.

Baum, N., Rahav, G., & Sharon, D. (2005). Changes in the self-concepts of divorced women. *Journal of Divorce and Remarriage, 43,* 47–67.

Baumbusch, J. L. (2004). Unclaimed treasures: Older women's reflections on lifelong singlehood. *Journal of Women and Aging, 16,* 105–121.

Bauminger, N., Finzi-Dottan, R., Chason, S., & Har-Even, D. (2008). Intimacy in adolescent friendship: The roles of attachment, coherence, and self-disclosure. *Journal of Social and Personal Relationships, 25,* 409–428.

Baumrind, D. (1968). Authoritative vs. authoritarian parental control. *Adolescence, 3,* 255–272.

Baumrind, D. (1971). Current patterns of parental authority. *Developmental Psychology Monograph, 4* (No. 1, Pt. 2).

Baumrind, D. (1991a). Effective parenting during the early adolescent transition. In P. A. Cowan & E. M. Hetherington (Ed.), *Advances in family research* (Vol. 2, pp. 111–163). Hillsdale, NJ: Erlbaum.

Baumrind, D. (1991b). The influence of parenting style on adolescent competence and drug use. *Journal of Early Adolescence, 11,* 56–95.

Baumrind, D. (1993). The average expectable environment is not enough: A response to Scarr. *Child Development, 64,* 1299–1317.

Baydar, N., & Brooks-Gunn, J. (1998). Profiles of grandmothers who help care for their grandchildren in the United States. *Family Relations, 47,* 385–393.

Bayley, N. (2005). *Bayley Scales of Infant and Toddler Development, Third Edition* (Bayley-III). San Antonio, TX: Harcourt Assessment.

Beatty, A., & Brandes, S. (2009). Skulls to the living, bread to the dead: The Day of the Dead in Mexico and beyond. *Journal of the Royal Anthropological Institute, 15,* 209–211.

Beck, C. T. (2002). Theoretical perspectives on postpartum depression and their treatment implications. *American Journal of Maternal/Child Nursing, 27,* 282–287.

Becker, A. E. (2004). Television, disordered eating, and young women in Fiji: Negotiating body image and identity during rapid social change. *Culture, Medicine, and Psychiatry, 28,* 533–559.

Becker, A. E., Fay, K., Gilman, S. E., & Striegel-Moore, R. (2007). Facets of acculturation and their diverse relations to body shape concern in Fiji. *International Journal of Eating Disorders, 40,* 42–50.

Becker, E. (2007). *The denial of death.* Simon and Schuster.

Becker, O. A., Salzburger, V., Lois, N., & Nauck, B. (2013). What narrows the stepgap? Closeness between parents and adult (step) children in Germany. *Journal of Marriage and Family, 75*(5), 1130–1148.

Beckett, C., Maughan, B., Rutter, M., Castle, J., Colvert, E., Groothues, C.,…Sonuga-Barke, E. J. S. (2006). Do the effects of early severe deprivation on cognition persist into early adolescence? Findings from the English and Romanian adoptees study. *Child Development, 77,* 696–711.

Beck, I. L., & Beck, M. E. (2013). *Making sense of phonics: The hows and whys.* New York, NY: Guildford.

Beentjes, J. W. L., Koolstra, C. M., Marseille, N., & van der Voort, T. H. A. (2001). Children's use of different media: For how long and why? In S. M. Livingstone & M. Bovill (Eds.), *Children and their changing media environment: A European comparative study* (pp. 85–112). Hillsdale, NJ: Lawrence Erlbaum.

Beers, M. H. (2006). Dementia. In M. H. Beers & T. V. Jones (Eds.), *Merck manual of geriatrics.* Whitehouse Station, NJ: Merck & Co. Retrieved from www.merck.com/mrkshared/mmg/sec5/ch40/ch40a.jsp

Bekkouche, N. S., Holmes, S., Whitttaker, K. S., & Krantz, D. (2011). Stress and the heart: Psychosocial stress and coronary heart disease. In R. J. Contrada & A. Baum, *The handbook of stress science:*

Biology, psychology, and health (pp. 385–398). New York, NY: Springer.

Bell, M. A. (1998). Frontal lobe function during infancy: Implications for the development of cognition and attention. In J. E. Richards (Ed.), *Cognitive neuroscience of attention: A developmental perspective* (pp. 327–362). Mahwah, NJ: Erlbaum.

Bel, A., & Bel, B. (2007). Birth attendants: Between the devil and the deep blue sea. In B. Bel, J. Brouwer, B. T. Das, V. Parthasarathi, & G. Poitevin (Eds.), *Communication processes 2: The social and the symbolic* (pp. 353–385). Thousand Oaks, CA: Sage.

Bell, M. A., & Wolfe, C. D. (2007). The cognitive neuroscience of early socioemotional development. In C. A. Brownell & C. B. Kopp (Eds.), *Socioemotional development in the toddler years: Transitions and transformations* (pp. 345–369). New York, NY: Guilford Press.

Bell, S. M., & Ainsworth, M. D. S. (1972). Infant crying and maternal responsiveness. *Child Development, 43,* 1171–1190.

Bellah, R. N., Madsen, R., Sullivan, W. M., Swidler, A., & Tipton, S. M. (1985). *Habits of the heart: Individualism and commitment in American life.* New York, NY: Harper & Row.

Bellamy, C. (2005). *The state of the world's children: 2005.* New York, NY: UNICEF.

Belsky, J. (2006). Early child care and early child development: Major findings from the NICHD Study of Early Child Care. *European Journal of Developmental Psychology, 3,* 95–110.

Belleville, S., Gilbert, B., Fontaine, F., Gagnon, L., Menard, E., & Gauthier, S. (2006). Improvement of episodic memory in persons with mild cognitive impairment and healthy older adults: Evidence from a cognitive intervention program. *Dementia and Geriatric Cognitive Disorders, 22,* 486–499.

Bem, S. L. (1981). Gender schema theory: A cognitive account of sex-typing. *Psychological Review, 88,* 354–364.

Benbow, C. P., & Lubinski, D. (2009). Extending Sandra Scarr's ideas about development to the longitudinal study of intellectually precocious youth. In K. McCartney & R. A. Weinberg (Eds.), *Experience and development: A festschrift in honor of Sandra Wood Scarr* (pp. 231–252). New York, NY: Psychology Press.

Bender, H. L., Allen, J. P., McElhaney, K. B., Antonishak, J., Moore, C. M., Kelly, H. O., & Davis, S. M. (2007). Use of harsh physical discipline and developmental outcomes in adolescence. *Development and Psychopathology, 19,* 227–242.

Bennett, K. M., Smith, P. T., & Hughes, G. M. (2005). Coping, depressive feelings and gender differences in late life widowhood. *Aging and Mental Health, 9,* 348–353.

Bennik, E. C., Nederhof, E., Ormel, J., & Oldehinkel, A. J. (2013). Anhedonia and depressed mood in adolescence: Course, stability, and reciprocal relation in the TRAILS study. *European Child & Adolescent Psychiatry,* 1–8.

Benson, M., Harris, P., & Rogers, C. (1992). Identity consequences of attachment to mothers and fathers among late adolescents. *Journal of Research on Adolescents, 2,* 187–204.

Berch, D., & Mazzocco, M. (2007). Why is math so hard for some children? *The nature and origins of mathematical learning difficulties and disabilities.* Baltimore, MD: Paul H. Brookes.

Berg, A. I., Hoffman, L., Hassing, L. B., McClearn, G. E., & Johansson, B. (2009). What matters, and what matters most, for change in life satisfaction in the oldest-old? A study of over 6 years among individuals 80+, *Aging & Mental Health, 13,* 191–201.

Berger, E. (2010). *Mammograms reduce breast cancer deaths, studies show.* Retrieved from http://www.cancer.org/Cancer/news/News/mammograms-reduce-breast-cancer-deaths-studies-show

Berger, K. S. (2007). Update on bullying at school: Science forgotten? *Developmental Review, 27,* 90–126.

Berger, S. E., Adolph, K. E., & Lobo, S. A. (2005). Out of the toolbox: Toddlers differentiate wobbly and wooden handrails. *Child Development, 76,* 1294–1307.

Bergstrom, A. (2007a). Food advertising, international. In J. J. Arnett (Ed.), *Encyclopedia of children, adolescents, and the media* (pp. 347–348). Thousand Oaks, CA: Sage.

Bergstrom, A. (2007b). Cartoons, educational. In J. J. Arnett (Ed.), *Encyclopedia of children, adolescents, and the media* (pp. 137–140). Thousand Oaks, CA: Sage.

Bergström, L., Richards, L., Morse, J. M., & Roberts, J. (2010). How caregivers manage pain and distress in second-stage labor. *Journal of Midwifery & Women's Health, 55,* 38–45.

Bergström, M., Kieler, H., & Waldenström, U. (2009). Effects of natural childbirth preparation versus standard antenatal education on epidural rates, experience of childbirth and parental stress in mothers and fathers: A randomised controlled multicentre trial. *BJOG: An International Journal of Obstetrics & Gynaecology 116,* 1167–1176.

Berkman, D. S., Lescano, A. G., Gilman, R. H., Lopez, L., & Black, M. M. (2002). Effects of Stunting, diarrhoeal disease, and parasitic infection during infancy on cognition in late Childhood: A follow-up study. *The Lancet, 359,* 564–571.

Berkman, N. D., Lohr, K. N., & Bulik, C. M. (2007). Outcomes of eating disorders: A systematic review of the literature. *International Journal of Eating Disorders, 40,* 293–309.

Berko, J. (1958). The child's learning of English morphology. *Word, 14,* 150–177.

Berndt, T. J. (1996). Transitions in friendship and friends' influence. In J. A. Graber, J. Brooks-Gunn, & A. C. Petersen (Eds.), *Transitions through adolescence: Interpersonal domains and context* (pp. 57–84). Mahwah, NJ: Erlbaum.

Berndt, T. J., & Mekos, D. (1995). Adolescents' perceptions of the stressful and desirable aspects of the transition to junior high school. *Journal of Research on Adolescence, 5*(1), 123–142.

Berney, T. (2009). Ageing in Down Syndrome. In G. O'Brien, & L. Rosenbloom (Eds.), *Developmental disability and ageing* (pp. 31–38). London, UK: Mac Keith Press.

Berninger, V. W., Abbott, R. D., Jones, J., Wolf, B. J., Gould, L., Anderson-Youngstrom, M.,…Apel, K. (2006). Early development of language by hand: Composing, reading, listening, and speaking connections; three letter-writing modes; and fast mapping in spelling. *Developmental Neuropsychology, 29* (Special issue on writing), 61–92.

Berninger, V. W., Vermeulen, K., Abbott, R. D., McCutchen, D., Cotton, S., & Cude, J. (2003). Naming speed and phonological awareness as predictors of reading development. *Journal of Educational Psychology, 95,* 452–464.

Bernsten, D., & Rubin, D. C. (2002). Emotionally charged autobiography memories across the life span: The recall of happy, sad, traumatic and involuntary memories. *Psychology and Aging, 17,* 636–652.

Berry, J. W., Phinney, J. S., Sam, D. L., & Vedder, P. (Eds.). (2006). *Immigrant youth in cultural transition: Acculturation, identity, and adaptation across national contexts.* Mahwah, NJ: Lawrence Erlbaum.

Berry, R. J., Li, Z., Erickson, J. D., Li, S., Moore, C. A., Wang, H.,…Correa, A. (1999). Prevention of neural-tube defects with folic acid in China. *New England Journal of Medicine, 341,* 1485–1490.

Berthier, N. E., & Carrico, R. L. (2010). Visual information and object size in infant reaching. *Infant Behavior and Development, 33,* 555–566.

Besen, E., Matz-Costa, C., Brown, M., Smyer, M. A., & Pitt-Catsouphes, M. (2013). Job characteristics, core self-evaluations, and job satisfaction: What's age got to do with it? *The International Journal of Aging and Human Development, 76*(4), 269–295.

Best, D. L. (2001). Gender concepts: Convergence in cross-cultural research and methodologies. *Cross-cultural Research: The Journal of Comparative Social Science, 35,* 23–43.

Beswick, A. D., Rees, K., Dieppe, P., Ayis, S., Gooberman-Hill, R., Horwood, J., & Ebrahim, S. (2008). Complex interventions to improve physical function and maintain independent living in elderly people: A systematic review and meta-analysis. *The Lancet, 371,* 725–735.

Beydoun, M. A., & Wang, Y. (2010). Pathways linking socioeconomic status to obesity through depression and lifestyle factors among young U.S. adults. *Journal of Affective Disorders, 123,* 52–63.

Beyene, Y., & Martin, M. C. (2001). Menopausal experiences and bone density of Mayan women in Yucatan, Mexico. *American Journal of Human Biology, 13,* 47–71.

Beyers, W., & Seiffge-Krenke, I. (2010). Does identity precede intimacy? Testing Erikson's theory of romantic development in emerging adults of the 21st century. *Journal of Adolescent Research, 25,* 387–415.

Bhargava, A. (2008). *Food, economics, and health.* New York, NY: Oxford University Press.

Bhargava, S., & Mendiratta, A. (2006). Understanding language patterns of multilingual children (8–10 years) belonging to high socio-economic class. *Social Science International, 22,* 148–158.

Bhavnani, B. R., & Strickler, R. C. (2005). Menopausal hormone therapy. *Journal of Obstetrics and Gynaecology Canada, 27,* 137–162.

Bialystok, E. (1993). Metalinguistic awareness: The development of children's representations in language. In C. Pratt & A. Garton (Eds.), *Systems of representation in children* (pp. 211–233). London, UK: Wiley.

Bialystok, E. (1997). Effects of bilingualism and biliteracy on children's emerging concepts of print. *Developmental Psychology, 33,* 429–440.

Bialystok, E. (1999). Cognitive complexity and attentional control in the bilingual mind. *Child Development, 70,* 636–644.

Bialystok, E. (2001). *Bilingualism in development: Language, literacy, and cognition.* New York, NY: Cambridge University Press.

Bibok, M. B., Müller, U., & Carpendale, J. I. M. (2009). Childhood. In U. Müller, J. I. M. Carpendale, & L. Smith (Eds.), *The Cambridge companion to Piaget* (pp. 229–254). New York, NY: Cambridge University Press.

Biegler, K. A., Nelson, E., Osann, K., Hsieh, S., & Wenzel, L. (2011, April). *Longitudinal associations between telomere length, chronic stress, and immune system stance in cervical cancer survivors.* Poster presented at the annual meeting of the American Association for Cancer Research, Orlando, FL.

Biehl, M. C., Natsuaki, M. N., & Ge, X. (2007). The influence of pubertal timing on alcohol use and heavy drinking trajectories. *Journal of Youth and Adolescence, 36,* 153–167.

Bina, M., Graziano, F., & Bonino, S. (2006). Risky driving and lifestyles in adolescence. *Accident Analysis & Prevention, 38,* 472–481.

Birch, L. L., Fisher, J. O., & Davison, K. K. (2003). Learning to overeat: Maternal use of restrictive feeding practices promotes girls' eating in the absence of hunger. *American Journal of Clinical Nutrition, 78,* 215–220.

Birditt, K. S., & Antonucci, T. C. (2012). Till death do us part: Contexts and implications of marriage, divorce, and remarriage across adulthood. *Research in Human Development, 9*(2), 103–105.

Birdsong, D. (2006). Age and second language acquisition and processing: A selective overview. *Language Learning, 56* (Suppl. s1), 9–49.

Birren, J. E., & Svensson, C. M. (2005). Wisdom in history. In R. J. Sternberg & J. Jordan (Eds.), *A handbook of wisdom: Psychological perspectives* (pp. 3–28). New York, NY: Cambridge University Press.

Bjarnason, T., & Sigurdardottir, T. J. (2003). Psychological distress during unemployment and beyond: Social support and material deprivation among youth in six Northern European counties. *Social Science & Medicine, 56,* 973–985.

Black, R. E., Williams, S. M., Jones, I. E., & Goulding, A. (2002). Children who avoid drinking cow milk have lower dietary calcium intakes and poor bone health. *American Journal of Clinical Nutrition, 76,* 675–680.

Blair, J. M., Hanson, D. L., Jones, H., & Dwokin, M. S. (2004). Trends in pregnancy rates among women with human immunodeficiency virus. *Obstetrics and Gynecology, 103,* 663–668.

Blakemore, J. E. O. (2003). Children's beliefs about violating gender norms: Boys shouldn't look like girls, and girls shouldn't act like boys. *Sex Roles, 48,* 411–419.

Blieszner, R., & Roberto, K. A. (2007). Friendship across the life span: Reciprocity in individual and relationship development In F. R. Lang & K. L. Fingerman (Eds.), *Growing together: Personal relationships across the life span* (pp. 159–182). Cambridge, UK: Cambridge University Press.

Bloch, M., Klein, E., Koren, D., & Rotenberg, N. (2006). Risk factors for early postpartum depressive symptoms. *General Hospital Psychiatry, 28,* 3–8.

Blomberg, S., Edebalk, P. G., & Petersson, J. (2000). The withdrawal of the welfare state: Elderly care in Sweden in the 1990s. *European Journal of Social Work, 3,* 151–163.

Bloom, L. (1998). Language acquisition in its developmental context. In W. Damon (Ed.), & D. Kuhn & R. S. Siegler (Vol. Eds.), *Handbook of Child Psychology* (5th ed.): *Vol. 2. Cognition, perception and language* (pp. 309–370). New York, NY: Wiley.

Bloom, L., Lifter, K., & Broughton, J. (1985). The convergence of early cognition and language in the second year of life: Problems in conceptualization and measurement. In M. Barrett (Ed.), *Single word speech* (pp. 149–181). New York, NY: Wiley.

Bloom, P. (2000). *How children learn the meanings of words.* Cambridge, MA: MIT Press.

Bluestone, C. D., & Klein, J. O. (2007). *Otitis media in infants and children.* New York, NY: Decker.

Bluestone, C., & Tamis-LeMonda, C. S. (1999). Correlates of parenting styles in predominately working- and middle-class African American mothers. *Journal of Marriage and the Family, 61,* 881–893.

Blum, N. J., Taubman, B., & Nemeth, N. (2004). Why is toilet training occurring at older ages? A study of factors associated with later training. *Journal of Pediatrics, 145,* 107–111.

Blumberg, B. D., Lewis, M. J., & Susman, E. J. (1984). Adolescence: A time of transition. In M. G. Eisenberg, L. C. Sutkin, & M. A. Jansen (Eds.), *Chronic illness and disability through the life span: Effects on self and family* (pp. 133–149). New York, NY: Springer.

Blümel, J. E., Cano, A., Mezones-Holguín, E., Barón, G., Bencosme, A., Benítez, Z., ... & Chedraui, P. (2012). A multinational study of sleep disorders during female mid-life. *Maturitas, 72*(4), 359–366.

Blumenthal, J. A., Emery, C. F., Madden, D. J., George, L. K., Coleman, R. E., Riddle, M. W., ... Williams, R. S. (1989). Cardiovascular and behavioral effects of aerobic exercise training in healthy older men and women. *Journals of Gerontology A: Biological Sciences and Medical Sciences, 44,* M147–M157.

Blumenthal, J., Jeffries, N. O., Castellanos, F. X., Liu, H., Zidjdenbos, A., Paus, T., ... Giedd, J. N. (1999). Brain development during childhood and adolescence: A longitudinal MRI study. *Nature Neuroscience, 10,* 861–863.

Blumenthal, J. A., Sherwood, A., Babyak, M. A., Watkins, L. L., Waugh, R., Georgiades, A., ... Hinderliter, A. (2005). Effects of exercise and stress management training on markers of cardiovascular risk in patients with ischemic heart disease: A randomized controlled trial. *JAMA: Journal of the American Medical Association, 293,* 1626–1634.

Blustein, D. L. (2006). *The psychology of working: A new perspective for career development, counseling, and public policy.* Mahwah, NJ: Erlbaum.

Bochner, S., & Jones, J. (2003). Augmentative and alternative forms of communication as stepping stones to speech. *Child Language Development: Learning to Talk, Second Edition,* 143–156.

Boden, J. M., Horwood, L. J., & Fergusson, D. M. (2007). Exposure to childhood sexual and physical abuse and subsequent educational achievement outcomes. *Child Abuse and Neglect, 31,* 1101–1114.

Boer, F., Goedhardt, A. W., & Treffers, P. D. A. (2013). Siblings and their parents. In F. Boer, J. Dunn, & J. F. Dunn (Eds.), *Children's sibling relationships: Developmental and clinical issues* (pp. 41–54). New York, NY: Wiley.

Bois-Reymond, M., & Ravesloot, J. (1996). The roles of parents and peers in the sexual and relational socialization of adolescents. In K. Hurrelmann & S. Hamilton (Eds.), *Social problems and social contexts in adolescence: Perspectives across boundaries* (pp. 175–197). Hawthorne, NY: Aldine de Gruyter.

Bokhorst, C. L., Sumpter, S. R., & Westenberg, P. M. (2010). Social support from parents, friends, classmates, and teachers in children and adolescents aged 9 to 18 years: Who is perceived as most supportive. *Social Development 19*(2), 417–426. doi: 10.1111/j.1467-9507.2009.00540.x

Bolen, J., et al. (2010). Differences in the prevalence and impact of arthritis among racial/ethnic groups in the United States. *Prevention of Chronic Disease, 7,* A64.

Boll, T., Ferring, D., & Filipp, S. H. (2005). Effects of parental differential treatment on relationship quality with siblings and parents: Justice evaluations as mediators. *Social Justice Research, 18,* 155–182.

Bolen, S. D., Clark, J. M., Richards, T. M., Shore, A. D., Goodwin, S. M., & Weiner, J. P. (2010). Trends in and patterns of obesity reduction medication use in an insured cohort. *Obesity, 18,* 206–209.

Bolzani, L. H., Messinger, D. S., Yale, M., & Dondi, M. (2002). Smiling in infancy. In M. H. Abel (Ed.), *An empirical reflection on the smile* (pp. 111–136). Lewiston, NY: Edwin Mellen Press.

Bonanno, G. A. (2004). Loss, trauma, and human resilience: Have we underestimated the human capacity to thrive after extremely aversive events? *American Psychologist, 59,* 20–28.

Bonello, K., & Cross, M. C. (2010). Gay monogamy: I love you but I can't have sex with only you. *Journal of Homosexuality, 57,* 117–139.

Bong, C. L., Hilliard, J., & Seefelder, C. (2008). Severe methemoglobinemia from topical benzocaine 7.5%(baby orajel) use for teething pain in a toddler. *Clinical pediatrics.*

Bongaarts, J., & Zimmer, Z. (2002). Living arrangements of older adults in the developing world: An analysis of demographic and health survey household surveys. *Journals of Gerontology B: Psychological Sciences and Social Sciences, 57,* S145–S157.

Bonino, S., & Cattelino, E. (2012). Italy. In J. J. Arnett (Ed.), *Adolescent psychology around the world.* New York, NY: Taylor & Francis.

Bonnanno, G., Boerner, K., & Wortman, C. B. (2008). Trajectories of grieving. In M. S. Stroebe, R. O. Hansson, W. Stroebe, & H. Schut (Eds.), *Handbook of bereavement research and practice* (pp. 287–307). Washington, DC: American Psychological Association.

Bonnel, S., Mohand-Said, S., & Sahel, J.-A. (2003). The aging of the retina. *Experimental Gerontology, 38,* 825–831.

Bookwala, J. (2012). Marriage and other partnered relationships in middle and late adulthood. In R. Blieszner & V. H. Bedford (Eds.), *Handbook of Families and Aging.* New York, NY: ABC-CLIO.

Bookwala, J., & Jacobs, J. (2004). Age, marital processes, and depressed affect. *The Gerontologist, 44,* 328–338.

Booth, D. A., Higgs, S., Schneider, J., & Klinkenberg, I. (2010). Learned liking versus inborn delight: Can sweetness give sensual pleasure or is it just motivating? *Psychological Science, 21,* 1656–1663.

Booth, M. (2002). Arab adolescents facing the future: Enduring ideals and pressures for change. In B. B. Brown, R. Larson, & T. S. Saraswathi (Eds.), *The world's youth: Adolescence in eight regions of the globe* (pp. 207–242). New York, NY: Cambridge University Press.

Borduin, C. M., Schaeffer, C. M., & Ronis, S. T. (2003). Multisystemic treatment of serious antisocial behavior in adolescents. In C. A. Essau (Ed.), *Conduct and oppositional defiant disorders: Epidemiology, risk factors, and treatment* (pp. 299–318). Mahwah, NJ: Lawrence Erlbaum.

Borgaonkar, D. S. (1997). Chromosomal variation in man: A catalog of chromosomal variants and anomalies (8th ed.). New York, NY: Wiley.

Bornstein, M. H. (2006). Parenting science and practice. In W. Damon & R. Lerner (Eds.), & K. A. Renninger & L. E. Sigel (Vol. Eds.), *Handbook of child psychology: Vol. 4. Child psychology in practice* (6th ed., pp. 893–949). New York, NY: Wiley.

Bornstein, M. H., & Arterberry, M. E. (2010). The development of object categorization in young children: Hierarchical inclusiveness, age, perceptual attribute, and group versus individual analyses. *Developmental Psychology, 46,* 350–365. doi: 10.1037/a0018411

Bornstein, M. H., & Bradley, R. H. (2014). *Socioeconomic status, parenting, and child development.* New York, NY: Routledge.

Bornstein, M. H., Slater, A., Brown, E., Robers, E., & Barrett, J. (1997). Stability of mental development from infancy to later childhood: Three "waves" of research. In G. Bremner, A. Slater, & G. Butterworth (Eds.), *Infant development: Recent advances* (pp. 191–215). East Sussex, UK: Psychology Press.

Bortolus, R., Parazzini, F., Chatenoud, L., Benzi, G., Bianchi, M. M., & Marini, A. (1999). The epidemiology of multiple births. *Human Reproduction Update, 5,* 179–187.

Boschi-Pinto, C., Lanata, C. F., & Black, R. E. (2009). The global burden of childhood diarrhea. *Maternal and Child Health, 3,* 225–243.

Bosse, Y., & Hudson, T. J. (2007). Toward a comprehensive set of asthma susceptibility genes. *Annual Review of Medicine, 58,* 171–184.

Bostic, J. Q., Rubin, D. H., Prince, J., & Schlozman, S. (2005). Treatment of depression in children and adolescents. *Journal of Psychiatric Practice, 11,* 141–154.

Bosworth, H., Park, K., McQuoid, D., Hays, J., & Steffens, D. (2003). The impact of religious practice and religious coping on geriatric depression. *International Journal of Geriatric Psychiatry, 18,* 905–914.

Botcheva, L., Kalchev, P., & Ledierman, P. H. (2007). Bulgaria. In J. J. Arnett, R. Ahmed, B. Nsamenang, T. S. Saraswathi, & R. Silbereisen (Eds.), *International encyclopedia of adolescence.* New York, NY: Routledge.

Bottenberg, P., Van Melkebeke, L., Louckx, F., & Vandenplas, Y. (2008). Knowledge of Flemish paediatricians about children's oral health—Results of a survey. *Acta Paediatrica, 97,* 959–963.

Bouchard, T. J., & McGue, M. (2003). Genetic and environmental influences on human psychological differences. *Journal of Neurobiology, 54,* 4–45.

Bousquet, J., Dahl, R., & Khaltaev, N. (2007). Global alliance against chronic respiratory diseases. *Allergy, 62,* 216–223.

Bove, C., & Olson, C. (2006). Obesity in low-income rural women: Qualitative insights about physical activity and eating patterns. *Women & Health, 44,* 57–78.

Bove, R., & Valeggia, C. (2009). Polygyny and women's health in sub-Saharan Africa. *Social Science & Medicine, 68,* 21–29.

Bower, B. (1985). The left hand of math and verbal talent. *Science News, 127,* 263.

Bowers, W. A., Evans, K., LeGrange, D., & Andersen, A. E. (2003). Treatment of adolescent eating disorders. In M. A. Reinecke & F. M. Dattilio (Eds.), *Cognitive therapy with children and adolescents: A casebook for clinical practice* (2nd ed., pp. 247–280). New York, NY: Guilford Press.

Bowlby, J. (1969/1982). *Attachment and loss: Vol. 1. Attachment.* (2nd ed.). New York, NY: Basic Books.

Bowlby, J. (1980). *Attachment and loss: Vol. 3. Loss: Sadness and depression.* New York, NY: Basic Books.

Bowman, S. A. (2009). Socioeconomic characteristics, dietary and lifestyle patterns, and health and weight status of older adults in NHANES, 1999–2002: A comparison of Caucasians and African Americans. *Journal of Nutrition for the Elderly, 28,* 30–46.

Bowman, T. S., Sesso, H. D., & Gaziano, J. M. (2006). Effect of age on blood pressure parameters and risk of cardiovascular death in men. *American Journal of Hypertension, 19*, 47–52.

Boyle, P. (2001). Why are Dutch teens so sexually safe? *Youth Today, 10*, 1, 34.

Braine, L. G., Schauble, L., Kugelmass, S., & Winter, A. (1993). Representation of depth by children: Spatial strategies and lateral biases. *Developmental Psychology, 29*, 466–479.

Brake, D. (2006). Electronic games, effects. In J. J. Arnett (Ed.), *Encyclopedia of children, adolescents, and the media.* Thousand Oaks, CA: Sage.

Brambati, B., & Tului, L. (2005). Chronic villus sampling and amniocentesis. *Current Opinion in Obstetrics and Gynecology, 17*, 197–201.

Brame, B., Nagin, D. S., & Tremblay, R. E. (2001). Developmental trajectories of physical aggression from school entry to late adolescence. *Journal of Child Psychology and Psychiatry, 42*, 503–512.

Brandtstädter, J. (2006). Adaptive resources in later life: Tenacious goal pursuit and flexible goal adjustment. In M. Csikszentmihalyi & I. S. Csikszentmihalyi, (Eds.), *A life worth living: Contributions to positive psychology* (pp. 143–164). New York, NY: Oxford University Press.

Brandtstadter, J., & Baltes-Gotz, B. (1990). Personal control over development and quality of perspectives in adulthood. In P. Baltes & M. M. Baltes (Eds.), *Successful aging* (pp. 197–224). Cambridge, UK: Cambridge University Press.

Brandtstadter, J., & Greve, W. (1994). The aging self: Stabilizing and protective processes. *Developmental Review, 14*, 52–80.

Brant, A. M., Haberstick, B. C., Corley, R. P., Wadsworth, S. J., DeFries, J. C., & Hewitt, J. K. (2009). The development etiology of high IQ. *Behavior Genetics, 39*, 393–405.

Braun, E. H. P., Lee, J., & Steinert, R. F. (2008). Monovision in LASIK. *Ophthalmology, 115*, 1196–1202.

Braveman, P., Egerter, S., & Williams, D. R. (2011). The social determinants of health: Coming of age. *Annual Review of Public Health, 32*, 381–398.

Bray, G. A., & Champagne, C. M. (2004). Obesity and the metabolic syndrome. *Journal of the American Dietetic Association, 104*, 86–89.

Bray, J. H. (1999). From marriage to remarriage and beyond: Findings from the Developmental Issues in Stepfamilies Research Project. In E. M. Hetherington (Ed.), *Coping with divorce, single parenting, and remarriage: A risk and resiliency perspective* (pp. 295–319). Mahwah, NJ: Erlbaum.

Brazelton, T. B., & Sparrow, J. D. (2004). *Toilet training the Brazelton way.* Cambridge, MA: deCapo Press.

Brazelton, T. B., Koslowski, B., & Tronick, E. (1976). Neonatal behavior among urban Zambians and Americans. *Journal of the American Academy of Child Psychiatry, 15*, 97–107.

Breger, L. (2000). *Freud: Darkness in the midst of vision.* New York, NY: Wiley & Sons.

Breivik, K., & Olweus, D. (2006). Adolescents' adjustment in four post–divorce family structures: Single mother, stepfather, joint physical custody and single father families. *Journal of Divorce & Remarriage, 44*, 99–124.

Brent, D. A. (2004). Antidepressants and pediatric depression: The risk of doing nothing. *New England Journal of Medicine, 35*, 1598–1601.

Brent, S. B., Speece, M. W., Lin, C., Dong, Q., & Yang, C. (1996). The development of the concept of death among Chinese and U.S. children 3–17 years of age: From binary to "fuzzy" concepts? *Omega, 33*, 67–83.

Brescoll, V. L., Dawson, E., & Uhlmann, E. L. (2010). Hard won and easily lost: The fragile status of leaders in gender-stereotype-incongruent occupations. *Psychological Science, 21*, 1640–1642.

Breslau, N., Kessler, R. C., Chilcoat, H. D., Schultz, L. R., Davis, G. C., & Andreski, P. (1998). Trauma and posttraumatic stress disorder in the community: The 1996 Detroit Area Survey of Trauma. *Archives of General Psychiatry, 55*, 626–632.

Breslin, F. C., & Mustard, C. (2003). Factors influencing the impact of unemployment on mental health among young and older adults in a longitudinal, population-based survey. *Scandinavian Journal of Work, Environment, and Health, 29*, 5–14.

Bretherton, I., & Munholland, K. (1999). Internal working models in attachment relationships: A construct revisited. In J. Cassidy & P. R. Shaver (Eds.), *Handbook of attachment: Theory, research, and clinical applications* (pp. 89–111). New York, NY: Guilford Press.

Bridge, J. A., Yengar, S., Salary, C. B., et al. (2007). Clinical response and risk for reported suicidal ideation and suicide attempts in pediatric antidepressant treatment: A meta-analysis of randomized controlled trials. *JAMA, 63*, 332–339.

Bridges, L., & Moore, K. (2002). Religious involvement and children's well-being: What research tells us (and what it doesn't). *Child Trends Research Brief.* Washington, DC: Author. Available: www.childtrends.org

Brim, O. (1999). *The MacArthur Foundation study of midlife development.* Vero Beach, FL: MacArthur Foundation.

Brim, O. G., Ryff, C. D., & Kessler, R. (Eds.). (2004). *How healthy are we: A national study of well-being in midlife.* Chicago, IL: University of Chicago Press.

Brink, J. M., & McDowd, J. M. (1999). Aging and selective attention: An issue of complexity or multiple mechanisms? *Journal of Gerontology: Psychological Sciences, 54B*, P30–P33.

Briones, T. L. (2006). Environment, physical activity, and neurogenesis: Implications for prevention and treatment of Alzheimer's disease. *Current Alzheimer Research, 3*, 49–54.

Brody, G. (2004). Siblings' direct and indirect contributions to child development. *Current Directions in Psychological Science, 13*, 124–126.

Brody, G. H., & Flor, D. L. (1998). Maternal resources, parenting practices, and child competence in rural, single-parent African American families. *Child Development, 69*, 803–816.

Brody, G. H., Kim, S., Murry, V. M., & Brown, A. C. (2003). Longitudinal direct and indirect pathways linking older sibling competence to the development of young sibling competence. *Developmental Psychology, 39*, 618–628.

Bronfenbrenner, U. (1980). *The ecology of human development.* Cambridge, MA: Harvard University Press.

Bronfenbrenner, U. (2000). Ecological theory: In A. Kazdin (Ed.), *Encyclopedia of psychology.* Washington, DC: American Psychological Association.

Bronfenbrenner, U. (Ed.). (2005). *Making human beings human: Bioecological perspectives on human development.* Thousand Oaks, CA: Sage.

Bronfenbrenner, U., & Morris, P. A. (1998). The ecology of developmental processes. In W. Damon (Series Ed.) and R. Lerner (Vol. Ed.), *Handbook of child psychology, Vol. 1: Theoretical models of human development* (pp. 993–1028). New York, NY: Wiley.

Brooks, R., & Meltzoff, A. N. (2005). The development of gaze following and its relation to language. *Developmental Science, 8*, 535–543.

Brooks-Gunn, J. (2003). Do you believe in magic? What we can expect from early childhood intervention programs. *Social Policy Report of the Society for Research in Child Development, 17*, 3–14.

Brotanek, J. M., Gosz, J., & Weitzman, M. (2007). Iron deficiency in early childhood in the United States: Risk factors and racial/ethnic disparities. *Pediatrics, 120*, 568–575.

Brown, A. M., & Miracle, J. A. (2003). Early binocular vision in human infants: Limitations on the generality of the Superposition Hypothesis. *Vision Research, 43*, 1563–1574.

Brown, A. S., & Susser, E. S. (2002). In utero infection and adult schizophrenia. *Mental Retardation and Developmental Disabilities Research Reviews, 8*, 51–57.

Brown, B. B., & Braun, M. T. (2013). Peer relations. In *Research, Applications, and Interventions for Children and Adolescents* (pp. 149–164). Netherlands: Springer.

Brown, B. B., & Klute, C. (2003). Friendships, cliques, and crowds. In R. G. Adams & D. M. Berzonsky (Eds.), *Blackwell handbook of adolescence* (pp. 330–348). Malden, MA: Blackwell.

Brown, B. B., Herman, M., Hamm, J. V., & Heck, D. K. (2008). Ethnicity and image: Correlates of crowd affiliation among ethnic minority youth. *Child Development, 79*, 529–546.

Brown, J. D. (2006). Emerging adults in a media-saturated world. In J. J. Arnett & J. Tanner (Eds.), *Coming of age in the 21st century: The lives and contexts of emerging adults* (pp. 279–299). Washington, DC: American Psychological Association.

Brown, J. D., Steele, J., & Walsh-Childers, K. (Eds.). (2002). *Sexual teens, sexual media*. Mahwah, NJ: Erlbaum.

Brown, L. H., & Rodin, P. A. (2004). Grandparent–grandchild relationships and the life course perspective. In J. Demick & C. Andreoletti (Eds.), *Handbook of adult development* (pp. 459–474). New York, NY: Springer.

Brown, R. (1973). *A first language: The early stages*. Cambridge, MA: Harvard University Press.

Brown, S. H., & Lin, I. (2012). *The gray divorce revolution: Rising divorce rates among middle-ages and older adults, 1990–2009*. Bowling Green, OH: National Center for Family & Marriage Research.

Brownell, C. A., & Kopp, C. B. (2007). *Socioemotional development in the toddler years*. New York, NY: Guilford.

Bruce, M. L. (2002). Psychosocial risk factors for depressive disorders in late life. *Biological Psychiatry, 52*, 175–184.

Brumberg, J. J. (1997). *The body project: An intimate history of American girls*. New York, NY: Random House.

Brunello, G., & Langella, M. (2013). Bridge jobs in Europe. *IZA Journal of Labor Policy, 2:11*.

Bruner, M. W., Erickson, K., Wilson, B., & Côté, J. (2010). An appraisal of athlete development models through citation network analysis. *Psychology of Sport and Exercise, 11*, 133–139.

Brussoni, M. J., & Boon, S. D. (1998). Grandparental impact in young adults' relationships with their closest grandparents: The role of relationship strength and emotional closeness. *International Journal of Aging and Human Development, 45*, 267–286.

Bryant, B. E. (2014). Sibling relationships in middle childhood. In M. E. Lamb & B. Sutton-Smith (Eds.), *Sibling relationships: Their nature and significance across the lifespan* (pp. 87–122). London, England: Routledge.

Bryant, G. A., & Barrett, H. C. (2007). Recognizing intentions in infant-directed speech: Evidence for universals. *Psychological Science, 18*, 746–751.

Bryder, L. (2009). From breast to bottle: a history of modern infant feeding. *Endeavour 33*, 54–59.

Buboltz, W. C., Soper, B., Brown, F., & Jenkins, S. (2002). Treatment approaches for sleep difficulties in college students. *Counseling Psychology Quarterly, 15*, 229–237.

Buchanan, C. M., Eccles, J. S., & Becker, J. B. (1992). Are adolescents the victims of raging hormones? Evidence for activational effects of hormones on moods and behavior at adolescence. *Psychological Bulletin, 111*, 62–107.

Buckley, T., & Gottlieb, A. (1988). *Blood magic: The anthropology of menstruation*. Berkeley, CA: University of California Press.

Budd, K. (1999). The facts of life: Everything you wanted to know about sex (after 50). *Modern Maturity, 42*, 78.

Bugental, D. B., & Grusec, J. E. (2006). Socialization processes. In N. Eisenberg, W. Damon, & R. M. Lerner (Eds.), *Handbook of child psychology: Vol. 3. Social, emotional, and personality development* (6th ed., pp. 366–428, xxiv, 1128). Hoboken, NJ: John Wiley & Sons.

Bugental, D. B., & Happaney, K. (2004). Predicting infant maltreatment in low-income families: The interactive effects of maternal attributions and child status at birth. *Developmental Psychology, 40*, 234–243.

Bugg, J. M., DeLosh, E. L., & Clegg, B. A. (2006). Physical activity moderates time-of-day differences in older adults' working memory performance. *Experimental Aging Research, 32*, 431–446.

Buhrmester, D. (2013). The developmental courses of sibling and peer relationships. In F. Boer, J. Dunn, & J. F. Dunn (Eds.), *Children's sibling relationships: Developmental and clinical issues* (pp. 19–40). New York, NY: Wiley.

Buhs, E. S., & Ladd, G. W. (2001). Peer rejection as antecedent of young children's school adjustment: An examination of mediating processes. *Developmental Psychology, 37*, 550–560.

Bulik, C. M., Berkman, N. D., Brownley, K. A., Sedway, L. A., & Lohr, K. N. (2007). Anorexia nervosa treatment: A systematic review of randomized controlled trials. *International Journal of Eating Disorders, 40*, 310–320.

Bullough, V. L. (1981). Comments on Mosher's "Three dimensions of depth involvement in human sexual response." *Journal of Sex Research, 17*, 177–178.

Bumpass, L., & Liu, H. H. (2000, March). Trends in cohabitation and implications for children's family contexts in the United States. *Population Studies, 54*, 29–41.

Burgard, S. A., Brand, J. E., & House, J. S. (2009). Perceived job insecurity and worker health in the United States. *Social Science & Medicine, 69*, 777–785.

Burgess, K. B., & Rubin, K. H. (2000). Middle childhood: Social and emotional development. In A. Kazdin (Ed.), *Encyclopedia of psychology* (Vol. 5, pp. 234–239). Washington, DC: American Psychological Association.

Burnett, A. L. (2004). The impact of sildenafil on molecular science and sexual health. *European Urology, 46*, 9–14.

Burnham, M., Goodlin-Jones, B., & Gaylor, E. (2002). Nighttime sleep–wake patterns and self–soothing from birth to one year of age: A longitudinal intervention study. *Journal of Child Psychology & Psychiatry & Allied Disciplines, 43*, 713–725.

Burton, A., Hayley, W., & Small, B. (2006). Bereavement after caregiving or unexpected death: Effects on elderly spouses. *Aging & Mental Health, 10*, 319–326.

Bushman, B. J., & Chandler, J. J. (2007). Violence, effects of. In J. J. Arnett (Ed.), *Encyclopedia of children, adolescents, and the media* (Vol. 2, pp. 847–850). Thousand Oaks, CA: Sage.

Bushman, B. J., & Huesmann, L. R. (2001). Effects of televised violence on aggression. In D. G. Singer & J. L. Singer (Eds.), *Handbook of children and the media* (pp. 223–254). Thousand Oaks, CA: Sage.

Buss, A. H. (1995). *Personality, temperament, social behavior, and the self*. Boston, MA: Allyn & Bacon.

Buss, D. M. (2003). *The evolution of desire: Strategies of human mating* (Revised Ed.). New York, NY: Basic Books.

Buss, D. M. (2007). The evolution of human mating. *Acta Psychologica Sinica, 39 (Special issue: Evolutionary psychology)*, 502–512.

Buss, D. M., Abbott, M., Angleitner, A., Asherian, A., Biaggio, A., Bianco-Villasenor, et al. (1990). International preferences in selecting mates: A study of cultures. *Journal of Cross-Cultural Psychology, 21*, 5–47.

Buss, K. A., & Goldsmith, H. H. (1998). Fear and anger regulation in infancy: Effects on the temporal dynamics of affective expression. *Child Development, 69*, 359–374.

Buss, K. A., & Plomin, R. (1984). *Temperament: Early developing personality traits*. Hillsdale, NJ: Erlbaum.

Bussey, K. (1992). Lying and truthfulness: Children's definitions, standards, and evaluative reactions. *Child Development, 63*, 129–137.

Bussey, K., & Bandura, A. (2004). Social cognitive theory of gender development and functioning. In A. H. Eagly, A. Beall, & R. Sternberg (Eds.), *The psychology of gender* (2nd ed., pp. 92–119). New York, NY: Guilford.

Butler, R. N. (2002). The life review. *Journal of Geriatric Psychiatry, 35,* 7–10.

Buunk, A. P., Park, J. H., & Dubbs, S. L. (2008). Parent–offspring conflict in mate preferences. *Review of General Psychology, 12,* 47–62.

Buunk, B. P. (2002). Age and gender differences in mate selection criteria for various involvement levels. *Personal Relationships, 9,* 271–278.

Bybee, J. A., & Wells, Y. V. (2003). The development of possible selves during adulthood. In J. Demick & C. Adnreoletti (Eds.), *Handbook of adult development* (pp. 257–270). New York, NY: Springer.

Byles, J., Young, A., Furuya, H., & Parkinson, L. (2006). A drink to healthy aging: The association between older women's use of alcohol and their health-related quality of life. *Journal of the American Geriatric Society, 54,* 1341–1347.

Byrd, C. M. (2012). The measurement of racial/ethnic identity in children a critical review. *Journal of Black Psychology, 38*(1), 3–31.

Caballero, B. (2007). The global epidemic of obesity: An overview. *Epidemiology Review, 29,* 1–5.

Cabrera, N. J., & Garcia-Coll, C. (2004). Latino fathers: Uncharted territory in need of much exploration. In M. E. Lamb (Ed.), *The role of the father in child development* (4th ed., pp. 98–120). Hoboken, NJ: Wiley.

Cabrera, S. F., Sauer, S. J., & Thomas-Hunt, M. C. (2009). The evolving manager stereotype: The effects of industry gender typing on performance expectations for leaders and their teams. *Psychology of Women Quarterly, 33,* 419–428.

Cáceres, I. A. (2008). Massachusetts deaths 2006. *Massachusetts Department of Public Health Bureau of Health Information, Statistics, Research, and Evaluation.* Retrieved from http://www.mass.gov/Eeohhs2/docs/dph/research_epi/death_report_08.pdf

Caetano, R., Ramisetty-Mikler, S., Floyd, L. R., & McGrath, C. (2006). The epidemiology of drinking among women of child-bearing age. *Alcoholism: Clinical and Experimental Research, 30,* 1023–1030.

Cain, D. S., & Combs-Orme, T. (2005). Family structure effects on parenting stress and practices in the African-American family. *Journal of Sociology and Social Welfare, XXXII,* 19–40.

Calkins, S. (2012). Caregiving as coregulation: Psychobiological processes and child functioning. In A. Booth, S. M. McHale, & N. Landale (Eds.), *Biosocial foundations of family processes* (pp. 49–59). New York, NY: Springer.

Calkins, S. D. (2002). Does aversive behavior during toddlerhood matter? The effects of difficult temperament on maternal perceptions and behavior. *Child Development, 67,* 523–540.

Call, J. (2001). Object permanence in orangutans, chimpanzees, and children. *Journal of Comparative Psychology, 115,* 159–171.

Callahan, C. M., Boustani, M. A., Unverzagt, F. W., Austrom, M. G., Damush, T. M., Perkins, et al. (2006). Effectiveness of collaborative care for older adults with Alzheimer disease in primary care: A randomized controlled trial. *JAMA: Journal of the American Medical Association, 295,* 2148–2157.

Calle, E. E., Rodriguez, C., Walker-Thurmond, K., & Thun, M. J. (2003). Overweight, obesity, and mortality from cancer in a prospectively studied cohort of U.S. adults. *New England Journal of Medicine, 348,* 1625–1638.

Calvo, E. (2006). *Does working longer make people healthier and happier?* Retrieved from http://www.bc.edu/centers/crr/issues/wob_2.pdf

Cameron, J. L. (2001). Effects of sex hormones on brain development. In C. A. Nelson & M. Luciana (Eds.), *Handbook of developmental cognitive neuroscience* (pp. 59–78).

Campbell, A., Shirley, L., & Candy, J. (2004). A longitudinal study of gender-related cognition and behavior. *Developmental Science, 7,* 1–9.

Campbell, E., Ramey, C., & Pungello, E. (2002). Early childhood education: Young adult outcomes from the Abecedarian Project. *Applied Developmental Science, 6,* 42–57.

Campbell, J. (1959). *The masks of god, I: Primitive mythology.* New York, NY: Viking.

Campione-Barr, N., & Smetana, J. G. (2010). "Who said you could wear my sweater?" Adolescent siblings' conflicts and associations with relationship quality. *Child Development, 81,* 464–471.

Campisi, J. (2005). Aging, tumor suppression and cancer: High-wire act. *Mechanics of Aging and Development, 126,* 51–58.

Campos, J. J., Langer, A., & Krowitz, A. (1970). Cardiac responses on the visual cliff in prelocomotor human infants. *Science, 170,* 196–197.

Camras, L. A., Lambrecht, L., & Michel, G. F. (1996). Infant "surprise" expressions as coordinative motor structures. *Journal of Nonverbal Behavior, 20,* 183–195.

Canda, E., Nakashama, M., & Furman, L. (2004). Ethical considerations about spirituality in social work: Insights from a national qualitative survey. *Families in Society, 85,* 27–35.

Canadian Fitness and Lifestyle Research Institute. (2002). *Physical activity monitor 2002.* Retrieved from www.cflri.ca

Caravita, S., & Cillessen, A. H. (2012). Agentic or communal? Associations between interpersonal goals, popularity, and bullying in middle childhood and early adolescence. *Social development, 21* (2), 376–395.

Carlson, S. M. (2003). Executive function in context: Development, measurement, theory and experience. *Monographs of the Society for Research in Child Development,68*(3, Serial No. 274), 138–151.

Carnelly, K. B., Wortman, C. B., Bolger, N., & Burke, C. T. (2006). The time course of grief reactions to spousal loss: Evidence from a national probability sample. *Journal of Personality and Social Psychology, 91,* 476–492.

Carr, D., & Friedman, M. A. (2005). Is obesity stigmatizing? Body weight, perceived discrimination, and psychological well-being in the United States. *Journal of Health and Social Behavior, 46,* 244–259.

Carr, J. (2002). Down syndrome. In P. Howlin & O. Udwin (Eds.), *Outcomes in neurodevelopmental and genetic disorders* (pp. 169–197). New York, NY: Cambridge University Press.

Carrere, S., Buehlman, K. T., Gottman, J. M., Coan, J. A., & Ruckstuhl, L. (2000). Predicting marital stability and divorce in newlywed couples. *Journal of Family Psychology, 14,* 42–58.

Carroll, J. L., & Wolpe, P. R. (2005). *Sexuality now: Embracing diversity:* Belmont, CA: Wadsworth.

Carroll, J. S., Padilla-Walker, L. M., Nelson, L. J., Olson, C. D., Barry, C. M., & Madsen, S. D. (2008). Generation XXX: Pornography acceptance and use among emerging adults. *Journal of Adolescent Research, 23,* 6–30.

Carstensen, L. L. (1995). Evidence for a life-span theory of socioemotional selectivity. *Current Directions in Psychological Science, 5,* 151–156.

Carstensen, L. L. (1998). A life-span approach to social motivation. In J. Heckhausen & C. Dweck (Eds.), *Motivation and self-regulation across the life span* (pp. 341–364). New York, NY: Cambridge University Press.

Carstensen, L. L., et al. (2011). Emotional experience improves with age: Evidence based on over 10 years of experience sampling. *Psychology and Aging, 26,* 21–33.

Carstensen, L. L., Fung, H. H., & Charles, S. T. (2003). Socioeconomic selectivity theory and the regulation of emotion in the second half of life. *Motivation and Emotion, 27,* 103–123.

Carstensen, L. L., Isaacowitz, D. M., & Charles, S. T. (1999). Taking time seriously: A theory of socioemotional selectivity. *American Psychologist, 54,* 165–181.

Carter, K. C., & Carter, B. R. (2005). *Childbed fever. A scientific biography of Ignaz Semmelweis.* Edison, NJ: Transaction.

Carter-Saltzman, L. (1980). Biological and sociocultural effects on handedness: Comparison between biological and adoptive families. *Science, 209,* 1263–1265.

Carver, K., Joyner, K., & Udry, J. R. (2003). National estimates of adolescent romantic relationships. In P. Florsheim (Ed.), *Adolescent romantic relations and sexual behavior: Theory, research, and practical implications* (pp. 23–56). Mahwah, NJ: Lawrence Erlbaum.

Case, R. (1999). Conceptual development in the child and the field: A personal view of the Piagetian legacy. In E. K. Skolnick, K. Nelson, S. A. Gelman, & P. H. Miller (Eds.), *Conceptual Development.* Mahwah, NJ: Erlbaum.

Case, R., & Okamato, Y. (Eds.). (1996). The role of central conceptual structures in the development of children's thought. *Monographs of the Society for Research in Child Development, 61* (1–2, Serial No. 246).

Casey Foundation (2010). *2010 Kids Count data book.* Baltimore, MD: Annie E. Casey Foundation.

Casey, B. J., Getz, S., & Galvan, A. (2008). The adolescent brain. *Developmental Review, 28,* 62–77.

Casey, B. M., McIntire, D. D., & Leveno, K. J. (2001). The continuing value of Apgar score for the assessment of the newborn infants. *New England Journal of Medicine, 344,* 467–471.

Cash, T. F. (2009). Attitudes, behaviors, and expectations of men seeking medical treatment for male pattern hair loss: Results of multinational survey. *Current Medical Research and Opinion, 25,* 1811–1820.

Cassidy, K. W., Werner, R. S., Rourke, M., Zubernis, L. S., & Balaraman, G. (2003). The relationship between psychological understanding and positive social behaviors. *Social Development, 12,* 198–221.

Cassidy, J., & Shaver, P. R. (2008). *Handbook of attachment: Theory, research, and clinical applications.* New York, NY: Guilford.

Cassidy, T. (2006). *Birth: The surprising history of how we are born.* New York, NY: Atlantic Monthly Press.

Cassidy, T. (2008). *Taking Great Pains: An Abridged History of Pain Relief in Childbirth.* Retrieved from http://wondertime.go.com/learning/article/ childbirth-pain-relief.html

Castellanos, F. X., Sharp, W. S., Gottesman, R. F., Greenstein, D. K., Giedd, J. N., & Rapoport, J. L. (2003). Anatomic brain abnormalities in monozygotic twins discordant for attention-deficit hyperactivity disorder. *American Journal of Psychiatry, 160,* 1693–1695.

Cattell, R.B. (1963). Theory of fluid and crystallized intelligence: A critical experiment. *Journal of Educational Psychology, 54,* 1–22.

Cavallini, A., Fazzi, E., & Viviani, V. (2002). Visual acuity in the first two years of life in healthy term newborns: An experience with the Teller Acuity Cards. *Functional Neurology: New Trends in Adaptive & Behavioral Disorders, 17,* 87–92.

Ceci, S. J., & Williams, W. M. (Eds.). (2007). *Why aren't more women in science? Top researchers debate the evidence.* Washington, DC: American Psychological Association.

Cejka, M. A., & Eagly, A. H. (1999). Gender-stereotypic images of occupations correspond to the sex segregation of employment. *Personality and Social Psychology Bulletin, 25,* 413–423.

Center for Disease Control (2008). Breastfeeding in the United States: Findings from the National Health and Nutrition Examination Surveys, 1999–2006. *NCHS Data Brief, No. 5.*

Centers for Disease Control (CDC). (2010). *Neonatal mortality rates, by race and Hispanic origin of mother, and state: United States, average annual 1989–1991, 2001–2003, and 2004–2006.* Retrieved from http://www.cdc.gov/nchs/data/hus/2010/019.pdf

Centers for Disease Control (CDC). (2010). *U.S. Obesity Trends: Trends by State 1985–2009.* Atlanta, GA: Author.

Centers for Disease Control (CDC). (2011). *Spina bifida fact sheet.* Retrieved from http://www.cdc.gov/ncbddd/spinabifida/documents/spina–bifida- fact-sheet1209.pdf

Centers for Disease Control (CDC) (2011). Heart disease is the number one cause of death. Retrieved from http://www.cdc.gov/features/heartmonth/

Centers for Disease Control and Prevention (2004). *Married adults are healthiest, new CDC report shows.* News release, National Center for Health Statistics. Hyattsville, MD, December 15, 2004.

Centers for Disease Control and Prevention (2007). Trends in health and aging. Retrieved from http://www.cdc.gov/nchs/agingact.htm

Centers for Disease Control and Prevention (2009). Defining overweight and obesity. Retrieved from http://www.cdc.gov/obesity/defining.html

Centers for Disease Control and Prevention (2010). *Sudden Infant Death Syndrome (SIDS) and infant vaccines.* Retrieved from http://www.cdc.gov/vaccinesafety/Concerns/sids_faq.html

Centers for Disease Control and Prevention (2013). *FastStats: Exercise or physical activity.* Atlanta, GA: Author. Retrieved from http://www.cdc.gov/nchs/fastats/exercise.htm

Centers for Disease Control and Prevention (2013). Progress in increasing breastfeeding and reducing racial/ethnic differences. *MMWR, 62(5),* 77–80.

Centers for Disease Control and Prevention (2013). *Sexually Transmitted Disease Surveillance 2012.* Atlanta, GA: U.S. Department of Health and Human Services.

Centers for Disease Control and Prevention (2014). *Adult obesity facts.* Atlanta, GA: Author. Retrieved from http://www.cdc.gov/obesity/data/adult.html#Socioeconomic

Centers for Disease Control and Prevention (2014). *Fact sheet: Adult cigarette smoking in the United States: Current estimates.* Retrieved from http://www.cdc.gov/tobacco/data_statistics/fact_sheets/adult_data/cig_smoking/

Centers for Disease Control and Prevention (2014). *Health, United States, 2013: Table 64.* Atlanta, GA: Author.

Centers for Disease Control and Prevention (2014). *Health, United States, 2013.* Atlanta, GA: Author.

Centers for Disease Control and Prevention (2014). *Breastfeeding report card.* Retrieved from http://www.cdc.gov/breastfeeding/pdf/2013breastfeedingreportcard.pdf

Centers for Disease Control and Prevention (2014). Prevalence of autism spectrum disorder among children aged 8 years. *MMWR, 63,* 1–21.

Centers for Disease Control and Prevention (2014). Tobacco-related mortality. Retrieved from http://www.cdc.gov/tobacco/data_statistics/fact_sheets/health_effects/tobacco_related_mortality/

Centers for Disease Control and Prevention (CDC). (2011). *Autism spectrum disorders (ASDs).* Retrieved from http://www.cdc.gov/ncbddd/autism/ data.html

Centers for Disease Control and Prevention (CDC) (2011). Sleep and sleep disorders. Retrieved from http://www.cdc.gov/sleep/

Centers for Disease Control and Prevention (CDC) (2002). Infant mortality and low birth weight among Black and White infants: United States, 1980–2000. *Morbidity & Mortality Weekly Report, 51,* 589–592.

Centers for Disease Control and Prevention (CDC) (2006). School health policies and programs study (SHPPS). *Journal of School Health.* 2007; 27(8).

Centers for Disease Control and Prevention (CDC) (2006). Vaccine preventable deaths and the global immunization vision and strategy, 2006–15. *Mortality and Morbidity Weekly Report, 55,* 511–515.

Centers for Medicare and Medicaid Services. (2009). Hospice payment system. Retrieved from http://www.cms.hhs.gov/mlnproducts/downloads/ hospice_pay_sys_fs.pdf

Chadha, N. K. (2004). Understanding intergenerational relationships of India. In E. Larkin, D. Friedlander, S. Newman, & R. Goff (Eds.), *Intergenerational relationships: Conversations on practice and research across cultures* (pp. 63–73). New York, NY: Haworth Press.

Chalk, L. M., Meara, N. M., Day, J. D., & Davis, K. L. (2005). Occupational possible selves: Fears and aspirations of college women. *Journal of Career Assessment, 13,* 188–203.

Chambers, M. L., Hewitt, J. K., Schmitz, S., Corley, R. P., & Fulker, D. W. (2001). Height, weight, and body mass index. In R. N. Emde & J. K. Hewitt (Eds.), *Infancy to early childhood: Genetic and environmental influences on developmental change* (pp. 292–306). New York, NY: Oxford University Press.

Champion, K. M., Vernberg, E. M., & Shipman, K. (2003). Non-bullying victims of bullies: Aggression, social skills, and friendship characteristics. *Journal of Applied Developmental Psychology, 24,* 535–551.

Chapman, L. K., & Steger, M. F. (2010). Race and religion: Differential prediction of anxiety symptoms by religious coping in African American and European American young adults. *Depression and Anxiety, 27*(3), 316–322.

Chan, C. G., & Elder, G. H., Jr. (2000). Matrilineal advantage in grand-child–grandparent relations. *Gerontologist, 40,* 179–190.

Chang, L. (2008). *Factory girls: From village to city in a changing China.* New York, NY: Spiegel & Grau.

Chao, R., & Tseng, V. (2002). Parenting of Asians. In M. H. Bornstein (Ed.), *Handbook of parenting, Vol. 4: Social conditions and applied parenting* (pp. 59–93). Mahwah, NJ: Erlbaum.

Charles, S. T., & Carstensen, L. L. (2004). A life-span view of emotional functioning in adulthood and old age. In P. Costa & I. C. Siegler (Eds.), *Advances in cell aging and gerontology series* (Vol. 15, pp. 133–162). New York, NY: Elsevier.

Charpak, N., Ruiz-Pelaez, J. G., & Figueroa, Z. (2005). Influence of feeding patterns and other factors on early somatic growth of healthy, preterm infants in home-based kangaroo mother care: A cohort study. *Journal of Pediatric Gastroenterology and Nutrition, 41,* 430–437.

Chatters, L. M., Taylor, R. J., Bullard, K. M., & Jackson, J. S. (2008). Spirituality and subjective religiosity among African Americans, Caribbean Blacks, and non-Hispanic Whites. *Journal for the Scientific Study of Religion,* 725–737.

Chaudhary, N., & Sharma, N. (2007). India. In J. J. Arnett (Ed.), *International encyclopedia of adolescence* (pp. 442–459). New York, NY: Routledge.

Chaudhary, N., & Sharma, P. (2012). India. In J. J. Arnett (Ed.), *Adolescent psychology around the world.* New York, NY: Taylor & Francis.

Chaytor, N., & Scmitter-Edgecombe, M. (2004). Working memory and aging: A cross-sectional and longitudinal analysis using a self-ordered pointing task. *Journal of the International Neuropsychological Society, 10,* 489–503.

Chen, X. (2011). Culture, peer relationships, and human development. In L. A. Jensen (Ed.), *Bridging cultural and developmental approaches to psychology* (pp. 92–111). New York, NY: Oxford University Press.

Chen, X.,, K. H., & Li, Z. (1995). Social functioning and adjustment in Chinese children: A longitudinal study. *Developmental Psychology, 31,* 531–539.

Chen, X., Cen, G., Li, D., & He, Y. (2005). Social functioning and adjustment in Chinese children: The imprint of historical time. *Child Development, 76,* 182–195.

Chen, X., Wang, L., & DeSouza, A. (2007). Temperament, socioemotional functioning, and peer relationships in Chinese and North American children. In X. Chen, D. C. French, & B. H. Schneider

(Eds.), *Peer relationships in cultural context* (pp. 123–146). New York, NY: Cambridge University Press.

Cheng, C. (2006). Living alone: The choice and health of older women. *Journal of Gerontological Nursing, 32,* 24–25.

Cherlin, A. J. (2009). *The marriage-go-round: The State of marriage and the family in American today.* New York, NY: Knopf.

Chess, S., & Thomas, A. (1984). *Origins and evolution of behavior disorders.* New York, NY: Brunner/Mazel.

Chestnut, C. H., III. (2001). Osteoporosis, an underdiagnosed disease. *JAMA: Journal of the American Medical Association, 286,* 2865–2866.

Cheung, A. H., Emslie, G. J., & Mayes, T. (2005). Review of the efficacy and safety of antidepressants in youth depression. *Journal of Child Psychology & Psychiatry,* 735–754.

Chew, K.-K., Bremner, A., Stuckey, B., Earle, C., & Jamrozik, K. (2009). Is the relationship between cigarette smoking and male erectile dysfunction independent of cardiovascular disease? Findings from a population-based cross-sectional study. *Journal of Sexual Medicine, 6,* 222–231.

Chibber, R., El-saleh, E., & El harmi, J. (2011). Female circumcision: Obstetrical and psychological sequelae continues unabated in the 21st century. *Journal of Maternal-Fetal and Neonatal Medicine 24*(6), 833–836.

Children's Defense Fund (2005). *State of America's children.* Washington, DC: Author.

Chi, D. L., Momany, E. T., Neff, J., Jones, M. P., Warren, J. J., Slayton, R. L.,…Damiano, P. C. (2011). Impact of chronic condition status and the severity on the time of first dental visit for newly Medicaid-enrolled children in Iowa. *Health Services Research, 46,* 572–595.

Chi, M. T. (1978). Knowledge structures and memory development. In R. S. Siegler (Ed.), *Children's thinking: What develops?* (pp. 73–96). Hillsdale, NJ: Erlbaum.

Chi, M. T., Glaser, R., & Farr, M. J. (Eds.) (2014). *The nature of expertise.* New York, NY: Psychology Press.

Chien, W., & Lin, F. R. (2012). Prevalence of hearing aid use among older adults in the United States. *Archives of Internal Medicine, 172*(3), 292–293.

Child Trends (2014). *Low and very low birth weight infants.* Child Trends Data Bank. Retrieved from http://www.childtrends.org/?indicators=low-and-very-low-birthweight-infants

Child Welfare Information Gateway (2013). *Foster care statistics.* Retrieved from https://www.childwelfare.gov/pubs/factsheets/foster.pdf#page=1&view=Key Findings

Chinas, L. (1992). *The Isthmus Zapotecs: A matrifocal culture of Mexico.* New York, NY: Harcourt Brace Jovanovich College Publishers.

Chisholm, L., & Hurrelmann, K. (1995). Adolescence in modern Europe: Pluralized transition patterns and their implications for personal and social risks. *Journal of Adolescence, 18,* 129–158.

Chodosh, J., Kado, D. M., Seeman, T. E., & Karlamangla, A. S. (2007). Depressive symptoms as a predictor of cognitive decline: MacArthur Studies of Successful Aging. *American Journal of Geriatric Psychiatry, 15,* 406–415.

Chopdar, A., Chakravarthy, U., & Verma, D. (2003). Age related macular degeneration. *British Journal of Medicine, 326,* 485–488.

Chou, R. J. (2011). Perceived need and actual usage of the Family Support Agreement in rural China: Results from a nationally representative survey. *The Gerontologist, 51,* 295–309. doi: 10.1093/geront/gnq062

Christ, G. (2008). *Chronic illness and aging: Cancer as a chronic life threatening condition.* Council on Social Work Education, Section 4.

Christopher, M. J. (2003). The new place of end-of-life issues on the policy agenda. *Public Policy and Aging Report, 13,* 23–26.

Chuang, M. E., Lamb, C. P., & Hwang, C. P. (2004). Internal reliability, temporal stability, and correlates of individual differences in parental involvement: A 15-year longitudinal study in Sweden. In

R. D. Day & M. E. Lamb (Eds.), *Conceptualizing and measuring father involvement* (pp. 129–148). Mahwah, NJ: Erlbaum.

Chung, K. W., et al. (2013). Recent advances in calorie restriction research on aging. *Experimental Gerontology, 48,* 1049–1053.

Chung, S. A., Wei, A. Q., Connor, D. E., Webb, G. C., Molloy, T., Pajic, M., & Diwan, A. D. (2007). Nucleus pulposus cellular longevity by telomerase gene therapy. *Spine, 15,* 1188–1196.

Chung, S. F., & Wegars, P. (Eds.). (2009). *Chinese American death rituals: Respecting the ancestors.* New York, NY: AltaMira Press.

CIA (2014). Country comparisons, people living with HIV/AIDS. Retrieved from https://www.cia.gov/library/publications/the-world-factbook/rankorder/2156rank.html#

Cicchetti, D. (2001). How a child builds a brain. In W. W. Hartup & R. A. Weinberg (Eds.), *Child psychology in retrospect and prospect* (pp. 23–71) Mahwah, NJ: Erlbaum.

Cicchetti, D., & Toth, S. L. (1998). Perspectives on research and practice in developmental psychology. In W. Damon (Series Ed.) & I. E. Sigel & K. A. Renninger (Vol. Eds.), *Handbook of child psychology* (Vol. 4) (pp. 479–583). New York, NY: Wiley.

Cicirelli, V. G. (1996). Sibling relationships in middle and old age. In G. H. Brody (Ed.), *Sibling relationships: Their causes and consequences* (pp. 47–73). Westport, CT: Ablex.

Cicirelli, V. G. (2006). Fear of death in mid-old age. *Journal of Gerontology: Psychological Sciences, 61B,* P75–P81.

Cillessen, A. H. N., & Mayeux, L. (2004). From censure to reinforcement: Developmental changes in the association between aggression and social status. *Child Development, 75,* 147–163.

Cinamon, R. H. (2006). Anticipated work–family conflict: Effects of gender, self-efficacy, and family background. *Career Development Quarterly, 54,* 202–215.

Cipriano, E. A., & Stifter, C. A. (2010). Predicting preschool effortful control from toddler temperament and parenting behaviour. *Journal of Applied Developmental Psychology, 31,* 221–230.

Clapp, J. D., Johnson, M., Voas, R. B., Lange, J. E., Shillington, A., & Russell, C. (2005). Reducing DUI among U.S. college students: Results of an environmental prevention trial. *Addiction, 100,* 327–334.

Clark, E. V. (1995). The lexicon and syntax. In J. L. Miller & P. D. Eimas (Eds.), *Speech, language, and communication* (pp. 303–337). San Diego, CA: Academic Press.

Clark, J. J. (2010). Life as a source of theory: Erik Erikson's contributions, boundaries, and marginalities. In T. W. Miller (Ed.), *Handbook of stressful transitions across the lifespan* (pp. 59–83). New York, NY: Springer.

Clark, K.B., & Clark, M.P. (1947). Racial Identification and Preference in Negro Children. *Readings in Social Psychology,* 602–611.

Clarke-Stewart, A., & Brentano, C. (2006). *Divorce: Causes and consequences.* New Haven, CT: Yale University Press.

Clarke-Stewart, K., & Allhusen, V. (2002). Nonparental caregiving. In M. Born- stein (Ed.), *Handbook of parenting: Vol. 3: Being and becoming a parent* (2nd ed., pp. 215–252). Mahwah, NJ: Lawrence Erlbaum Associates.

Clarke-Stewart, K., Fitzpatrick, M., Allhusen, V., & Goldberg, W. (2000). Measuring difficult temperament the easy way. *Developmental and Behavioral Pediatrics, 21,* 207–223.

Claxton, S.E., & van Dulmen, M.H. (2015). Casual sexual relationships and experiences. In J.J. Arnett (Ed.), *Oxford Handbook of Emerging Adulthood.* New York: Oxford University Press.

Clay, E. C. & Seehusen, D. A. (2004). A review of postpartum depression for the primary care physician. *Southern Medical Journal, 97,* 157–162.

Coghill, D., Spiel, G., Baldursson, G., Döpfner, M., Lorenzo, M. J., Ralston, S. J., & Rothenberger, A., & ADORE Study Group (2006). Which factors impact on clinician-rated impairment in children

with ADHD? *European Child & Adolescent Psychiatry, 15* (Suppl. 1), I30–I37.

Cohan, C. L., & Kleinbaum, S. (2002). Toward a greater understanding of the cohabitation effect: Premarital cohabitation and marital communication. *Journal of Marriage & the Family, 64,* 180–192.

Cohen, D., Gerardin, P., Mazet, P., Purper-Ouakil, D., & Flament, M. F. (2004). Pharmacological treatment of adolescent major depression. *Journal of Child and Adolescent Psychopharmacology, 14,* 19–31.

Cohen, G. D. (2005). *The mature mind: The positive power of the aging brain.* New York, NY: Avon Books.

Cohen, L. L. (2008). Racial/ethnic disparities in hospice care: A systematic review. *Journal of Palliative Medicine, 11,* 763–768.

Cohn, J. F., & Tronick, E. Z. (1983). Three-month-old infants' reaction to stimulated maternal depression. *Child Development, 23,* 185–193.

Coie, J. (2004). The impact of negative social experiences on the development of antisocial behavior. In J. B. Kupersmidt & K. A. Dodge (Eds.), *Children's peer relations: From the development to intervention.* Washington, DC: American Psychological Association.

Colby, A., Kohlberg, L., Gibbs, J., & Lieberman, M. (1983). A longitudinal study of moral judgment. *Monographs of the Society for Research in Child Development, 48*(1–2).

Colcombe, S. J., Erickson, K. I., Scalf, P. E., Kim, J. S., Prakash, R., McAuley, E., et al. (2006). Aerobic exercise training increases brain volume in aging humans. *Journal of Gerontology, A. Biological Sciences and Medical Sciences, 61,* 1166–1170.

Cole, A., & Kerns, K. A. (2001). Perceptions of sibling qualities and activities in early adolescents. *Journal of Early Adolescence, 21,* 204–226.

Cole, M. (1996). *Cultural psychology: A once and future discipline.* Cambridge, MA: Harvard University Press.

Cole, P. M., Teti, L. O., & Zahn-Waxler, C. (2003). Mutual emotion regulation and the stability of conduct problems between preschool and early school age. *Development and Psychopathology, 15,* 1–18.

Cole, T. J., Bellizzi, M. C., Flegal, K. M., & Dietz, W. H. (2000). Establishing a standard definition for child overweight and obesity worldwide: International survey. *British Medical Journal, 320,* 1240–1243.

Coleman, M., Ganong, L., & Fine, M. (2000). Reinvestigating remarriage: Another decade of progress. *Journal of Marriage and the Family, 62,* 1288–1307.

Coleman, M., Ganong, L. H., & Rothrauff, T. C. (2006). Racial and ethnic similarities and differences in beliefs about intergenerational assistance to older adults after divorce and remarriage. *Family Relations, 55,* 576–587.

Coleman, M. P., Quaresma, M., Berrino, F., Lutz, J. M., De Angelis, R., Capocaccia, R.,...CONCORD Working Group (2008). Cancer survival in five countries: A worldwide population–based study (CONCORD). *Lancet Oncology, 9,* 730–756.

Colen, C.G., & Ramey, D.M. (2014). Is breast truly best? Estimating the effects of breastfeeding on long-term child health and well-being in the United States using sibling comparisons. *Social Science Medicine, 109,* 55–65.

Collaku, A., Rankinen, T., Rice, T., Leon, A. S., Rao, D. C., Skinner, J. S., Wilmore, J. H., & Bouchard, C. (2004). A genome-wide linkage scan for dietary energy and nutrient intakes. *American Journal of Clinical Nutrition, 79,* 881–886.

Collier-Baker, E., & Suddendorf, T. (2006). Do chimpanzees and 2-year-old children understand double invisible displacement? *Journal of Comparative Psychology, 120,* 89–97.

Collins, G. (2010). *When everything changed: The amazing journey of American women from 1960 to the present.* New York, NY: Back Bay Books.

Collins, W. A., & Laursen, B. (2004). Parent–adolescent relationships and influences. In R. M. Lerner & L. Steinberg (Eds.), *Handbook of adolescent psychology* (2nd ed., pp. 331–361).

Collins, W. A., Maccoby, E. E., Steinberg, L., Hetherington, E. M., & Bornstein, M. H. (2000). Contemporary research on parenting: The case for nature and nurture. *American Psychologist, 55,* 218–232.

Collins, W. A., Madsen, S. D., & Susman-Stillman, A. (2002). Parenting during middle childhood. In M. H. Bornstein (Ed.), *Handbook of parenting: Vol. 1* (2nd ed., pp. 73–101). Mahwah, NJ: Erlbaum.

Colombo, J., & Mitchell, D. W. (2009). Infant visual habituation. *Neurobiology of Learning and Memory, 92,* 225–234.

Combs-Ronto, L. A., Olson, S. L., Lunkenheimer, E. S., & Sameroff, A. J. (2009). Interactions between maternal parenting and children's early disruptive behaviour: Bidirectional associations across the transition from preschool to school entry. *Journal of Abnormal Child Psychology, 37,* 1151–1163.

Compas, B. E., Ey, S., & Grant, K. E. (1993). Taxonomy, assessment, and diagnosis of depression during adolescence. *Psychological Bulletin, 114,* 323–344.

Condon, R. G. (1987). *Inuit youth: Growth and change in the Canadian Arctic.* New Brunswick, NJ: Rutgers University Press.

Conference Board of Canada. (2011). *Society: Elderly poverty.* Retrieved from http://www.conferenceboard.ca/hcp/details/society/elderly-poverty.aspx/

Connolly, J., & McIsaac, C. (2011). Romantic relationships in adolescence. In M. K. Underwood & J. H. Rosen (Eds.), *Social development: Relationships in infancy, childhood, and adolescence,* 180–206. New York, NY: Guilford.

Connolly, K. J., & Dalgleish, M. (1989). The emergence of a tool-using skill in infancy. *Developmental Psychology, 25,* 894–912.

Connolly, M., & Sullivan, D. (2004). *The essential c-section guide: Pain control, healing at home, getting your body back, and everything else you need to know about a cesarean birth.* New York, NY: Broadway Books.

Connor, R. (1992). *Cracking the over-50 job market.* New York, NY: Penguin Books.

Conway, C. C., Rancourt, D., Adelman, C. B., Burk, W. J., & Prinstein, M. J. (2011). Depression socialization within friendship groups at the transition to adolescence: the roles of gender and group centrality as moderators of peer influence. *Journal of abnormal psychology, 120*(4), 857.

Coovadia, H. M., & Wittenberg, D. F. (Eds.) (2004). *Pediatrics and child health: A manual for health professionals in developing countries.* (5th ed.). New York, NY: Oxford University Press.

Coplan, R. J., Prakash, K., O'Neil, K., & Arner, M. (2004). Do you "want" to play? Distinguishing between conflicted shyness and social disinterest in early childhood. *Developmental Psychology, 40,* 244–258.

Corbin, C. B., Welk, G. J., Corbin, W. R., & Welk, K. A. (2005). *Concepts of physical fitness* (12th ed.). New York, NY: McGraw-Hill.

Corbin, W. R., & Fromme, K. (2002). Alcohol use and serial monogamy as risks for sexually transmitted diseases in young adults. *Health Psychology, 21,* 229–236.

Core Institute (2013). Executive summary, Core Alcohol and Drug Survey-Long Form. Retrieved from http://core.siu.edu/_common/documents/report0911.pdf

Cornelius, M. D., Day, N. L., De Genna, N. M., Goldschmidt, L., Leech, S. L., & Willford, J. A. (2011). Effects of prenatal cigarette smoke exposure on neurobehavioral outcomes in 10-year-old children of adolescent mothers. *Neurotoxicology and Teratology, 33,* 137–144.

Corporation for National and Community Service, Office of Research and Policy Development. (2007). *The health benefits of volunteering: A review of recent research.* Washington, DC: Author.

Cosminsky, S. (2003). Cross-cultural perspectives on midwifery. In L. Dundes (Ed.), *The manner born: Birth rites in cross-cultural perspective* (pp. 69–84). Walnut Creek, CA: AltaMira Press.

Costa, P. T. J., & McCrae, R. R. (1978). Objective personality assessment. In M. Storandt, I. C. Spiegler, & M. F. Elias (Eds.), *The clinical psychology of aging* (pp. 119–143). New York, NY: Plenum.

Costello, D. M., Swendsen, J., Rose, J. S., & Dierker, L. C. (2008). Risk and protective factors associated with trajectories of depressed mood from adolescence to early adulthood. *Journal of Consulting and Clinical Psychology, 76,* 173–183.

Coté, J. (1994). *Adolescent storm and stress: An evaluation of the Mead-Freeman controversy.* Hillsdale, NJ: Erlbaum.

Côté, J. (2000). *Arrested adulthood: The changing nature of maturity and identity in the late modern world.* New York, NY: New York University Press.

Côté, J. (2005). Editor's introduction. *Identity, 5,* 95–96.

Côté, J. (2006). Emerging adulthood as an institutionalized moratorium: Risks and benefits to identity formation. In J. J. Arnett & J. L. Tanner (Eds.), *Emerging adults in America: Coming of age in the 21st century* (pp. 85–116). Washington, DC: American Psychological Association Press.

Cotter, D., Hermsen, J. M., & Vanneman, R. (2011). The End of the Gender Revolution? Gender Role Attitudes from 1977 to 20081. *American Journal of Sociology, 117*(1), 259–289.

Coughlin, C. R. (2009). Prenatal choices: Genetic counseling for variable genetic diseases. In V. Ravitsky, A. Fiester, A. L. Caplan (Eds.), *The Penn Center guide to bioethics* (pp. 415–424). New York, NY: Springer.

Coulmas, F. (2007). *Population decline and ageing in Japan-the social consequences.* Routledge.

Courage, M. L., Howe, M. L., & Squires, S. E. (2004). Individual differences in 3.5 month olds' visual attention: What do they predict at 1 year? *Infant Behavior and Development, 127,* 19–30.

Courage, M., & Cowan, N. (Eds.). (2009). *The development of memory in infancy and childhood* (2nd ed.). New York, NY: Psychology Press.

Courage, M. L., & Setliff, A. E. (2009). Debating the impact of television and video material on very young children: Attention, learning, and the developing brain. *Child Development Perspectives, 3*(1), 72–78.

Cowan, C. P., & Cowan, P. A. (2000). Working with couples during stressful transitions. In S. Dreman (Ed.), *The family on the threshold of the 21st century* (pp. 17–47). Mahwah, NJ: Erlbaum.

Cowan, P. A., & Cowan, C. P. (2011). After the baby: Keeping the couple relationship alive. *NCFR Newsletter, 49,* 1–2, 5.

Coyne, S. (2007). Violence, longitudinal studies of. In J. J. Arnett (Ed.), *Encyclopedia of children, adolescents, and the media* (Vol. 2, pp. 859–860). Thousand Oaks, CA: Sage.

Craig, J. M., & Piquero, A. R. (2014). Crime and punishment in emerging adulthood. In J. J. Arnett (Ed.), *Oxford handbook of emerging adulthood.* New York, NY: Oxford University Press.

Crain, W. (2000). *Theories of development: Concepts and applications.* Upper Saddle River, NJ: Prentice Hall.

Cramer, R. E., Schaefer, J. T., & Reid, S. (2003). More evidence for male–female convergence. In N. J. Pallone (Ed.), *Love, romance, sexual interaction: Research perspectives from current psychology* (pp. 61–73). New Brunswick, NJ: Transaction.

Cratty, B. J. (1986). *Perceptual and motor development in infants and children* (3rd ed.). Englewood Cliffs, NJ: Prentice-Hall.

Cravey, T., & Mitra, A. (2011). Demographics of the sandwich generation by race and ethnicity in the United States. *The Journal of Socio-Economics, 40*(3), 306–311.

Crawford, C., & Krebs, D. (2008). *Foundations of evolutionary psychology.* New York, NY: Lawrence Erlbaum.

Crawford, M., & Popp, D. (2003). Sexual double standards: A review and methodological critique of two decades of research. *Journal of Sex Research, 40,* 13–26.

Crawford, S., & Channon, S. (2002). Dissociation between performance on abstract tests of executive function and problem solving in real-life type situations in normal aging. *Aging and Mental Health, 6,* 12–21.

Crews, J. E., & Campbell, V. A. (2004). Vision impairment and hearing loss among community-dwelling older Americans: Implications for health and functioning. *American Journal of Public Health, 94,* 823–829.

Crick, N. R., Ostrov, J. M., Burr, J. E., Cullerton-Sen, C., Jansen-Yeh, E., & Ralston, P. (2006). A longitudinal study of relational and physical aggression in preschool. *Journal of Applied Developmental Psychology, 27,* 254–268.

Critser, G. (2003). *Fat land.* Boston, MA: Houghton Mifflin.

Crncec, R., Matthey, S., & Nemeth, D. (2010). Infant sleep problems and emotional health: A review of two behavioural approaches. *Journal of Reproductive and Infant Psychology, 28,* 44–54.

Cross, S. E., & Gore, J. S. (2003). Cultural models of the self. In E. S. Cross, S. J. Gore, & R. M. Leary (Eds.), *Handbook of self and identity* (pp. 536–564). New York, NY: Guilford Press.

Crouter, A. C., Manke, B. A., & McHale, S. M. (1995). The family context of gender intensification in early adolescence. *Child Development, 66,* 317–329.

Crow, J. F. (2003). There's something curious about parental–age effects. *Science, 301,* 606–607.

Crowley, B., Hayslip, B., & Hobdy, J. (2003). Psychological hardiness and adjustment to life events in adulthood. *Journal of Adult Development, 10,* 237–248.

Crowley, K. (2011). Sleep and sleep disorders in older adults. *Neuropsychology Review, 21,* 41–53.

Crowther, M., & Rodriguez, R. (2003). A stress and coping model of custodial grandparenting among African Americans. In B. Hayslip & I. Patrick (Eds.), *Working with custodial grandparents* (pp. 145–162). New York, NY: Springer.

Cruikshank, M. (2013). *Learning to be old: Gender, culture, and aging.* London, England: Rowman & Littlefield.

Crum, W. (2010). Foster parent parenting characteristics that lead to increased placement stability or disruption. *Children and Youth Services Review, 32,* 185–190.

Crumbley, D. H. (2006). "Power in the blood": Menstrual taboos and women's power in an African Instituted Church. In R. M. Griffith & B. D. Savage, *Women and religion in the African diaspora: Knowledge, power, and performance* (pp. 81–97). Baltimore, MD: Johns Hopkins University Press.

Csibra, G., Davis, G., Spratling, M. W., & Johnson, M. H. (2000). Gamma oscillations and object processing in the infant brain. *Science, 290,* 1582–1585.

Csikszentmihalyi, M., & Larson, R. W. (1984). *Being adolescent: Conflict and growth in the teenage years.* New York, NY: Basic Books.

Csikszentmihalyi, M., & Nakamura, J. (2005). The role of emotions in the development of wisdom. In R. J. Sternberg & J. Jordan (Eds.), *A handbook of wisdom: Psychological perspectives* (pp. 220–242). New York, NY: Cambridge University Press.

Cuddy, A. J. C., & Fiske, S. T. (2004). Doddering but dear: Process, content, and function in stereotyping of older persons. In T. Nelson (Ed.), *Ageism: Stereotyping and prejudice against older persons.* Cambridge, MA: MIT Press.

Cuevas, K., & Bell, M. A. (2014). Infant attention and early childhood executive function. *Child Development, 85,* 397–404. doi: 10.1111/cdev.12126

Cummings, E. M., George, M. R., & Kouros, C. D. (2010). Emotional development. In I. B. Weiner & W. B. Craighead (Eds.), *Corsini encyclopedia of psychology* (pp. 1–2). New York, NY: Wiley.

Cummings, K. M. (2002). Marketing to America's youth: Evidence from corporate documents. *Tobacco Control, 11* (Suppl. 1), i5–i17.

Cunningham, M., & Thorton, A. (2007). Direct and indirect influences of parents' marital instability on children's attitudes toward cohabitation in young adulthood. *Journal of Divorce & Remarriage, 46,* 125–143.

Curnow, T. (2008). Introduction: Sophia's world: Episodes from the history of wisdom. In M. Ferrari & G. Potworowski (Eds.), *Teaching for wisdom: Cross–cultural perspectives on fostering wisdom* (pp. 1–19). New York, NY: Springer.

Curran, K., DuCette, J., Eisenstein, J., & Hyman, I. A. (2001, August). *Statistical analysis of the cross-cultural data: The third year.* Paper presented at the meeting of the American Psychological Association, San Francisco, CA.

Czaja, S. J. (2006). Employment and the baby boomers: What can we expect in the future? In S. K. Whitbourne & S. L. Willis (Eds.), *The baby boomers grow up: Contemporary perspectives on midlife* (pp. 283–298).

D'Andrade, R. (1987). A folk model of the mind. In D. Holland & N. Quinn (Eds.), *Cultural models in language and thought* (pp. 112–148). New York, NY: Cambridge University Press.

da Motta, C. C. L., Naziri, D., & Rinne, C. (2006). The Influence of emotional support during childbirth: A clinical study. *Journal of Prenatal & Perinatal Psychology & Health, 20,* 325–341.

Daddis, C., & Smetana, J. (2005). Middle-class African American families' expectations for adolescents' behavioural autonomy. *International Journal of Behavioral Development, 29,* 371–381.

Dale, P. S., & Goodman, J. C. (2005). Commonality and individual differences in vocabulary growth. In M. Tomasello & D. I. Slobin (Eds.), *Beyond nature–nurture: Essays in honor of Elizabeth Bates* (pp. 41–78). Mahwah, NJ: Erlbaum.

Damon, W. (1983). *Social and personality development.* New York, NY: Norton.

Daniels, P., Godfrey, F. N., & Mayberry, R. (2006). Barriers to prenatal care among Black women of low socioeconomic status. *American Journal of Health Behavior, 30,* 188–198.

Darwin, C. (1859). *On the origin of species.* London, UK: John Murray.

Darwin, C. (1872). *The expression of the emotions in man and animals.* New York, NY: D. Appleton.

Dasen, P., Inhelder, B., Lavalle, M., & Retschitzki, J. (1978). *Naissance de l'intelligence chez l'enfant Baoule de Cote d'Ivorie.* Berne: Hans Huber.

Dasilva, K. A., Aubert, I., & McLaurin, J. (2006). Vaccine development for Alzheimer's disease. *Current Pharmaceutical Design, 12,* 4283–4293.

Daum, M. M., Prinz, W., & Aschersleben, G. (2011). Perception and production of object-related grasping in 6-month-olds. *Journal of experimental child psychology, 108*(4), 810–818.

Davenport, G. (2004). Rheumatology and musculoskeletal medicine. *British Journal of General Practice, 54,* 457–464.

David, B., Grace, D., & Ryan, M. K. (2004). The gender wars: A self-categorization perspective on the development of gender identity. In M. Bennett & S. Fabio (Eds.), *The development of the social self* (pp. 135–157). East Sussex, England: Psychology Press.

Davies, P. T., Harold, G. T., Goeke-Morey, M. C., & Cummings, E. M. (2002). Child emotional security and interparental conflict. *Monography of the Society for Research in Child Development, 67*(3, Serial No. 270).

Davies, R. (2004). New understandings of parental grief. *Journal of Advanced Nursing, 46,* 506–513.

Daviglus, M. L., Stamler, J., Pirzada, A., Yan, L. L., Garside, D. B., & Liu, K. (2004). Favorable cardiovascular risk profile in young women and long-term risk of cardiovascular and all-cause mortality. *JAMA: Journal of the American Medical Association, 292,* 1588–1592.

Davis, D. W. (2003). Cognitive outcomes in school-age children born prematurely. *Neonatal Network, 22,* 27–38.

Davis, H. P., Trussell, L. H., & Klebe, K. J. (2001). A ten-year longitudinal examination of repetition priming, incidental recall, free recall, and recognition in young and elderly. *Brain and Cognition, 46,* 99–104.

Davis, K. (2010). Coming of age online: The developmental underpinnings of girls' blogs. *Journal of Adolescent Research, 25,* 145–171.

Davis, K. F., Parker, K. P., & Montgomery, G. L. (2004). Sleep in infants and young children. Part I: Normal sleep. *Journal of Pediatric Health Care, 18,* 65–71.

Davis, S. S., & Davis, D. A. (2007). Morocco. In J. J. Arnett, R. Ahmed, B. Nsamenang, T. S. Saraswathi, & R. Silbereisen (Eds.), *International encyclopedia of adolescence* (pp. 645–655). New York, NY: Routledge.

Davis, S., & Davis, D. (2012). Morocco. In J. J. Arnett (Ed.), *Adolescent Psychology Around the World.* New York, NY: Taylor & Francis.

Dawson, G., Meltzoff, A. N., Osterling, J., Rinaldi, J., & Brown, E. (1998). Children with autism fail to orient to naturally occurring social stimuli. *Journal of Autism & Developmental Disorders, 28,* 479–485.

Day, R. D., & Lamb, M. E. (Eds.). (2004). *Conceptualizing and measuring father involvement.* Mahwah, NJ: Erlbaum.

de Haan, M., & Johnson, M. H. (2003). Mechanisms and theories of brain development. In M. de Haan & M. H. Johnson (Eds.), *The cognitive neuroscience of development* (pp. 1–18). Hove, UK: Psychology Press.

De Leon, M. J., Desanti, S., Zinkowski, R., Mehta, P. D., Pratico, D., & Segal, S. (2004). MRI and CSF studies in the early diagnosis of Alzheimer's disease. *Journal of Internal Medicine, 256,* 205–223.

De Marco, A. C., & Berzin, S. C. (2008). The influence of family economic status on home-leaving patterns during emerging adulthood. *Families in Society, 89,* 208–218.

De Meersman, R., & Stein, P. (February). Vagal modulation and aging. *Biological Psychology, 74,* 165–173.

de Munck, V. C., & Korotayev, A. V. (2007). Wife–husband intimacy and female status in cross-cultural perspective. *Cross-Cultural Research: The Journal of Comparative Social Science, 41,* 307–335.

de Villarreal, L. E. M., Arredondo, P., Hernández, R., & Villarreal, J. Z. (2006). Weekly administration of folic acid and epidemiology of neural tube defects. *Maternal and Child Health Journal, 10,* 397–401.

de Villiers, P. A., & de Villiers, J. G. (1978). *Language acquisition.* Cambridge, MA: Harvard University Press.

de Vonderweid, U., & Leonessa, M. (2009). Family centered neonatal care. *Early Human Development, 85,* S37–S38.

de Waal, F. (2005). *Our inner ape.* New York, NY: Penguin Group.

De Weerd, A. W., & van den Bossche, A. S. (2003). The development of sleep during the first months of life. *Sleep Medicine Reviews, 7,* 179–191.

Deakin, M. B. (2004, May 9). The (new) parent trap. *Boston Globe Magazine,* pp.18–21, 28–33.

Deary, I. J., & Der, G. (2005). Reaction time, age, and cognitive ability: Longitudinal findings from age 16 to 63 years in representative population samples. *Aging, Neuropsychology, and Cognition, 12,* 187–215.

DeCasper, A. J., & Spence, M. J. (1986). Prenatal maternal speech influences newborns' perception of speech sounds. *Infant Behavior and Development, 9,* 133–150.

Dees, M., Dekkers, W., van Weel, C., & Vernooij–Dassen, M. (2010). Review unbearable suffering of patients with a request for euthanasia or physician–assisted suicide: An integrative review. *Psycho-Oncology, 19,* 339–352.

Degnen, C. (2007). Minding the gap: The construction of old age and oldness amongst peers. *Journal of Aging Studies, 21,* 69–80.

DeHart, T., Pelham, B., & Tennen, H. (2006). What lies beneath: Parenting style and implicit self–esteem. *Journal of Experimental Social Psychology, 42,* 1–17.

Deihl, L. M., Vicary, J. R., & Deike, R. C. (1997). Longitudinal trajectories of self-esteem from early to middle adolescence and related psychosocial variables among rural adolescents. *Journal of Research on Adolescence, 7,* 393–411.

DeJong, A., & Franklin, B. A. (2004). Prescribing exercise for the elderly: Current research and recommendations. *Current Sports Medicine Reports, 3,* 337–343.

DeKosky, S. T., & Marck, K. (2003). Looking backward to move forward: Early detection of neurodegenerative disorders. *Science, 302,* 830–834.

Delaney, C. (2000). Making babies in a Turkish village. In J. DeLoache & A. Gottlieb (Eds.), *A world of babies: Imagined childcare guides for seven societies* (pp. 117–144). New York, NY: Cambridge University Press.

Delano-Wood, L., & Abeles, N. (2005). Late-life depression: Detection, risk reduction, and somatic intervention. *Clinical Psychology: Science and Practice, 12,* 207–217.

DeLoache, J. S., Chiong, C., Sherman, K., Islam, N., Vanderborght, M., Troseth, G. L.,…O'Doherty, K. (2010). Do babies learn from baby media? *Psychological Science, 21,* 1570–1574.

DeLoache, J., & Gottlieb, A. (2000). *A world of babies: Imagined childcare guides for seven societies.* New York, NY: Cambridge University Press.

DeMarie, D., Abshier, D. W., & Ferron, J. (2001, April). *Longitudinal study of predictors of memory improvement over the elementary school years: Capacity, strategies, and metamemory revisited.* Paper presented at the meeting of the Society for Research in Child Development, Minneapolis, MN.

DeMeo, J. (2006). *Saharasia: The 4000 bce origins of child abuse, sex-repression, warfare and social violence, in the deserts of the old world* (Revised 2nd ed.). El Cerrito, CA: Natural Energy Works.

Demetriou, A., & Raftopoulos, A. (Eds.). (2004). *Cognitive developmental change: Theories, models and measurement.* New York, NY: Cambridge University Press.

Dennerstein, L., Dudley, E., & Guthrie, J. (2002). Empty nest or revolving door? A prospective study of women's quality of life in midlife during the phase of children leaving and re-entering the home. *Psychological Medicine, 32,* 545–550.

Dennett, D. C. (1996). *Darwin's dangerous idea: Evolution and the meanings of life.* New York, NY: Simon & Schuster.

Dennis, C. L. (2004). Can we identify mothers at risk for postpartum depression in the immediate postpartum period using the Edinburgh Postnatal Depression Scale? *Journal of Affective Disorders, 78,* 163–169.

Dennis, W. (1966). Age and creative productivity. *Journal of Gerontology, 21,* 1–8.

Dent, A., & Stewart, A. (2004). *Sudden death in childhood: Support for the bereaved family.* London, UK: Butterworth-Heinemann.

DeParle, J. (2010, June 27). A world on the move. *The New York Times,* pp. WK1, 4.

DePaulo, B. (2006). *Singled out: How singles are stereotyped, stigmatized, and ignored, and still live happily ever after.* New York, NY: St. Martin's.

DePaulo, B. M. (2012). *Single people.* New York, NY: Oxford University Press.

Dermody, J., Hanmer-Lloyd, S., & Scullion, R. (2010). Young people and voting behaviour: Alienated youth and (or) an interested and critical citizenry? *European Journal of Marketing, 44,* 421–435.

Derom, C., Thiery, E., Vlientinck, R., Loos, R., & Derom, R. (1996). Handedness in twins according to zygosity and chorion type: A preliminary report. *Behavior Genetics, 26,* 407–408.

DeRosier, M. E., & Thomas, J. M. (2003). Strengthening sociometric prediction: Scientific advances in the assessment of children's peer relations. *Child Development, 75,* 1379–1392.

Descarries, L., Mechawar, N., Anavour, N., & Watkins, K. C. (2004). Structural determinants of the roles of acetylcholine in the cerebral cortex. *Progress in Brain Research, 145,* 45–58.

DeSena, A. D., Murphy, R. A., Douglas-Palumberi, H., Blau, G., Kelly, B., Horwitz, S. M., & Kaufman, J. (2005). SAFE homes: Is it worth the cost? An evaluation of a group home permanency planning program for children who first enter out-of-home care. *Child Abuse and Neglect, 29,* 627–643.

Desmairis, S., & Curtis, J. (1999). Gender differences in employment and income experiences among young people. In J. Barling & E. K. Kelloway (Eds.), *Youth workers: Varieties of experience* (pp. 59–88). Washington, DC: American Psychological Association.

de Souza, R. J., Bray, G. A., Carey, V. J., Hall, K. D., LeBoff, M. S., Loria, C. M.,…& Smith, S. R. (2012). Effects of 4 weight-loss diets differing in fat, protein, and carbohydrate on fat mass, lean mass, visceral adipose tissue, and hepatic fat: Results from the POUNDS LOST trial. *The American Journal of Clinical Nutrition, 95*(3), 614–625.

Dew, J., & Wilcox, W. B. (2011). If Momma ain't happy: Explaining declines in marital satisfaction among new mothers. *Journal of Marriage & the Family, 73,* 1–12.

Dewar, G. (2010). What the scientific evidence reveals about the timing of toilet training. Retrieved from http://www.parentingscience.com/science- of-toilet-training.html

Dey, A. N., & Bloom, B. (2005). Summary health statistics for U.S. children: National Health Interview Survey, 2003. *Vital Health Statistics, 21,* 217–227.

Dey, E. L., & Hurtado, S. (1999). Students, colleges, and society: Considering the interconnections. In P. G. Altbach, R. O. Berndahl, & P. J. Gumport (Eds.), *American higher education in the twenty-first century: Social, political, and economic challenges* (pp. 298–322). Baltimore, MD: Johns Hopkins University Press.

Diamond, A. (2004). Normal development of prefrontal cortex from birth to young adulthood: Cognitive functions, anatomy, and biochemistry. In D. T. Stuff & R. T. Knight (Eds.), *Principles of frontal lobe function* (pp. 466–503). New York, NY: Oxford University Press.

Diamond, A. D. (1985). Development of the ability to use recall to guide action, as indicated by infants' performance on AB. *Child Development, 56,* 868–883.

Diamond, J. (1992). *The third chimpanzee: The evolution and future of the human animal.* New York, NY: Harper Perennial.

Diamond-Smith, N., Luke, N., & McGarvey, S. (2008). "Too many girls, too much dowry": Son preference and daughter aversion in rural Tamil Nadu, India. *Culture, Health & Sexuality, 10,* 697–708.

DiCamillo, M., & Field, M. (2006). *Continued support for doctor-assisted suicide. Most would want their physician to assist them if they were incurably ill and wanted to die.* San Francisco, CA: Field Research Corporation.

Dick, F., Dronkers, N. F., Pizzamiglio, L., Saygin, A. P., Small, S. L., & Wilson, S. (2004). Language and the brain. In M. Tomasello & D. I. Slobin (Eds.), *Beyond nature–nurture: Essays in honor of Elizabeth Bates* (pp. 237–260). Mahwah, NH: Erlbaum.

Diener, M. (2000). Gifts from gods: A Balinese guide to early child rearing. In J. DeLoache & A. Gottlieb (Eds.), *A world of babies: Imagined childcare guides for seven societies* (pp. 91–116). New York, NY: Cambridge University Press.

Dieter, J. N., Field, T., Hernandez-Reif, M., Emory, E. K., & Redzepi, M. (2003). Stable preterm infants gain more weight and sleep less after five days of massage therapy. *Journal of Pediatric Psychology, 28*(6), 403–411.

Dietz, W. H. (2004). Overweight in childhood and adolescence. *New England Journal of Medicine, 350,* 855–857.

DiFrancesco, V., Fantin, F., Omizzolo, F., Residon, L., Bissoli, L., Bosello, L., & Zamboni, M. (2007). The anorexia of aging. *Digestive Diseases, 25,* 129–137.

Dijkstra, J. K., Lidenberg, S., & Veenstra, R. (2008). Beyond the class norm: Bullying behavior of popular adolescents and its relation to peer acceptance and rejection. *Journal of Abnormal Child Psychology, 36,* 1289–1299.

Dillon, M., & Wink, P. (2004). American religion, generativity, and the therapeutic culture. In E. de St. Aubin, D. P. McAdams, & T. C. Kim (Eds.), *The generative society: Caring for future generations* (pp. 153–174). Washington, DC: American Psychological Association.

Dilworth-Anderson, Boswell, G., & Cohen, M. D. (2007). Spiritual and religious coping values and beliefs among African American caregivers: A qualitative study. *Journal of Applied Gerontology, 26,* 355–369.

DiMaria-Ghalili, R. A. (2008). Nutrition. In E. Capezuti, D. Zwicker, M. Mezey, T. T. Fulmer, D. Gray-Miceli, & M. Kluger (Eds.), *Evidence-based geriatric nursing protocols for best practice* (3rd ed., pp. 353–367). New York, NY: Springer.

DiPietro, J., Hilton, S., Hawkins, M., Costigan, K., & Pressman, E. (2002). Maternal stress and affect influence fetal neurobehavioral development. *Developmental Psychology, 38,* 659–668.

Dishion, T. J., & Dodge, K. A. (2005). Peer contagion in interventions for children and adolescents: Moving towards an understanding of the ecology and dynamics of change. *Journal of Abnormal Child Psychology, 33,* 395–400.

Dishion, T. J., McCord, J., & Poulin, F. (1999). When interventions harm: Groups and problem behavior. *American Psychologist, 54,* 755–764.

Dixon, R. A. (2003). Themes in the aging of intelligence: Robust decline with intriguing possibilities. In R. J. Sternberg, J. Lautrey, & T. I. Lubart (Eds.), *Models of intelligence: International perspectives* (pp. 151–167). Washington, DC: American Psychological Association.

Dixon Jr, W. E., Salley, B. J., & Clements, A. D. (2006). Temperament, distraction, and learning in toddlerhood. *Infant Behavior and Development, 29*(3), 342–357.

Dodge, K. A. (2007). The nature–nurture debate and public policy. In G. W. Ladd (Ed.), *Appraising the human developmental sciences: Essays in honor of Merrill-Palmer Quarterly* (pp. 262–271). Detroit, MI: Wayne State University Press.

Dodge, K. A. (2008). Framing public policy and prevention of chronic violence in American youths. *American Psychologist, 63,* 573–590.

Dodge, K. A., Coie, J.D., & Lynam, D. (2006). Aggression and anti-social behavior in youth. In W. Damon & R. Lerner (Eds.), & N. Eisenberg (Vol. Ed.), *Handbook of child psychology: Vol. 3. Social, emotional and personality development* (6th ed., pp. 719–788). New York, NY: Wiley.

Dodson, C. S., Bawa, S., & Slotnick, S. D. (2007). Aging, source memory, and misrecollections. *Journal of Experimental Psychology: Learning, Memory, and Cognition, 33,* 169–181.

Doheny, K. (2009). Obese women more likely to have babies with birth defects, study shows. *WebMD Health News.* Retrieved from http://www.webmd. com/baby/news/20090210/obesity-carries-pregnancy-risks

Doherty, I., & Landells, J. (2006). Literacy and numeracy. In J. Clegg & J. Ginsborg (Eds.), *Language and social disadvantage: Theory into practice* (pp. 44–58). Hoboken, NJ: John Wiley & Sons.

Dolan, A. L., Koshy, E., Waker, M., & Goble, C. M. (2004). Access to bone densitometry increase general practitioners' prescribing for osteoporosis in steroid treated patients. *Annals of Rheumatoid Diseases, 63,* 183–186.

Dolphin, T., & Lanning, T. (Eds.) (2011). *Rethinking apprenticeships*. London, England: Institute for Public Policy Research.

Domsch, H., Lohaus, A., & Thomas, H. (2010). Infant attention, heart rate, and looking time during habituation/dishabituation. *Infant Behavior & Development, 33*, 321–329.

Donat, D. (2006). Reading their way: A balanced approach that increases achievement. *Reading & Writing Quarterly: Overcoming Learning Difficulties, 22*, 305–323.

Donatelle, R. (2004). *Health: The basics* (6th ed.). San Francisco, CA: Benjamin Cummings.

Donini, L. M., Savina, C., & Cannella, C. (2003). Eating habits and appetite control in the elderly: The anorexia of aging. *International Psychogeriatrics, 15*, 73–87.

Donohue, R. (2007). Examining career persistence and career change intent using the career attitudes and strategies inventory. *Journal of Vocational Behavior, 70*, 259–276.

Donorfio, L. K. M., D'Ambrosio, L. A., Coughlin, J. F., & Mohyde, M. (2008). Health, safety, self-regulation, and the older driver: It's not just a matter of age. *Journal of Safety Research, 39*, 555–561.

Donovan, J., & Zucker, C. (2010, October). Autism's first child. *The Atlantic*, pp. 78–90.

Dooley, D., Prause, J., & Ham-Rowbottom, K. A. (2000). Underemployment and depression: Longitudinal relationships. *Journal of Health and Social Behavior, 41*, 421–436.

Dorjee, T., Baig, N., & Ting-Toomey, S. (2013). A social ecological perspective on understanding "honor killing": An intercultural moral dilemma. *Journal of Intercultural Communication Research, 42*(1), 1–21.

Douglass, C. B. (2005). *Barren states: The population "implosion" in Europe*. New York, NY: Berg.

Douglass, C. B. (2007). From duty to desire: Emerging adulthood in Europe and its consequences. *Child Development Perspectives, 1*, 101–108.

Dowdney, L. (2000). Annotation: Childhood bereavement following parental death. *Journal of Child Psychology and Psychiatry and Allied Disciplines, 41*, 819–830.

Doyle, L. W., Faber, B., Callanan, C., Ford, G. W., & Davis, N. M. (2004). Extremely low birth weight and body size in early adulthood. *Archives of Disorders in Childhood, 89*, 347–350.

Doyle, L. W., Faber, B., Callanan, C., Ford, G. W., & Davis, N. M. (2004). Extremely low birth weight and body size in early adulthood. *Archives of Disorders in Childhood, 89*, 347–350.

Driessen, R., Leyendecker, B., Schölmerich, A., & Harwood, R. (2010). Everyday experiences of 18- to 36-month-old children from migrant families: The influence of host culture and migration experience. *Early Child Development and Care, 180*, 1143–1163.

Driver, J., Tabares, A., & Shapiro, A. (2003). Interactional patterns in marital success and failure: Gottman laboratory studies. In F. Walsh (Ed.), *Normal family processes: Growing diversity and complexity* (3rd ed.). New York, NY: Guilford.

Dubas, J. S., & Petersen, A. (1991). A longitudinal investigation of adolescents' changing perceptions of pubertal timing. *Developmental Psychology, 27*, 580–586.

DuBois, D., Felner, R., Brand, S., Phillip, R., & Lease, A. (1996). Early adolescent self-esteem: A developmental–ecological framework and assessment strategy. *Journal of Research on Adolescence, 6*, 543–579.

Due, P., Holstein, B. E., Lunch, J., Diderichsen, F., Gabhain, S. N., Scheidt, P., & Currie, C. (2005). The health behavior in school-aged children bullying working group. *European Journal of Public Health, 15*, 128–132.

Dufur, M. J., Howell, N. C., Downey, D. B., Ainsworth, J. W., & Lapray, A. J. (2010). Sex differences in parenting behaviors in single–mother and single–father households. *Journal of Marriage and Family, 72*, 1092–1106.

Dugdale, D. C. (2010). Aging changes in the senses. *Medline Plus*.

Duggan, M., & Brenner, J. (2013). *The demographics of social media users*. Washington, DC: Pew Research Center.

Dula, A., & Williams, S. (2005). When race matters. *Clinical Geriatric Medicine, 21*, 239–253.

Dunlosky, J., Kubat-Silman, A. K., & Hertzog, C. (2003). Training monitoring skills improves older adults' self-paced associative learning. *Psychology and Aging, 18*, 340–345.

Dunn, D. M., Culhane, S. E., & Taussig, H. N. (2010). Children's appraisals of their experiences in out-of-home care. *Children and Youth Services Reviews, 32*, 1324–1330.

Dunn, J. (1988). *The beginnings of social understanding*. Cambridge, MA: Harvard University Press.

Dunn, J. (2002). The adjustment of children in stepfamilies: Lessons from community studies. *Child and Adolescent Mental Health, 7*, 154–161.

Dunn, J. (2004). Sibling relationships. In P. K. Smith & C. H. Hart (Eds.), *Handbook of childhood social development* (pp. 223–237). Malden, MA: Blackwell.

Dunn, J., & Kendrick, C. (1982). *Siblings: Love, envy, and understanding*. London, UK: Grant McIntyre.

Dunn, J., & Munn, P. (1985). Becoming a family member: Family conflict and the development of social understanding in the second year. *Child Development, 56*, 480–492.

Dunn, J., Cheng, H., O'Connor, T. G., & Bridges, L. (2004). Children's perspectives on their relationships with their nonresident fathers: Influences, outcomes and implications. *Journal of Child Psychology and Psychiatry, 45*, 553–566.

Dunne, E. J., & Dunne-Maxim, K. (2004). Working with families in the aftermath of suicide. In F. Walsh & M. McGoldrick (Eds.), *Living beyond loss: Death in the family* (2nd ed., pp. 272–284). New York, NY: Norton.

Durston, S., Pol, H. E. H., Schnack, H. G., Buitelaar, J. K., Steenhuis, M. P., & Minderaa, R. B. (2004). Magnetic resonance imaging of boys with attention-deficit/hyperactivity disorder and their unaffected siblings. *Journal of the American Academy of Child and Adolescent Psychiatry, 43*, 332–340.

Dustmann, C., & Schoenberg, U. (2008). Why does the German apprenticeship system work? In K. U. Mayer & H. Solga (Eds.), *Skill information: Interdisciplinary and cross-national perspective* (p. 85–108). New York, NY: Cambridge University Press.

Dworkin, J. B., & Larson, R. (2001). Age trends in the experience of family discord in single-mother families across adolescence. *Journal of Adolescence, 24*, 529–534.

Dyer, S., & Moneta, G. (2006). Frequency of parallel, associative and cooperative play in British children of different socioeconomic status. *Social Behavior and Personality, 34*, 587–592.

Eagly, A. H., & Wood, W. (2003). The origins of sex differences in human behavior: Evolved dispositions versus social roles. In C. B. Travis, *Evolution, gender and rape* (pp. 265–304). Cambridge, MA: MIT Press.

Easterlin, R. A. (2006). Life cycle happiness and its sources: Intersections of psychology, economics, and demography. *Journal of Economic Psychology, 27*, 463–482.

Eberhart-Phillips, J. E., Frederick, P. D., & Baron, R. C. (1993). Measles in pregnancy: A descriptive study of 58 cases. *Obstetrics and Gynecology, 82*, 797–801.

Eckenrode, J., Zielinski, D., Smith, E., Marcynyszyn, L. A., Henderson, C. R., Jr., & Kitzman, H. (2001). Child maltreatment and the early onset of problem behaviors: Can a program of nurse home visitation break the link? *Development and Psychopathology, 13*, 873–890.

Eder, D. (1995). *School talk: Gender and adolescent culture*. New Brunswick, NJ: Rutgers University Press.

Edmonds, L. (2011). Telegraphic speech. In J. Kreutzer, J. DeLuca, & B. Kaplan (Eds.), *Encyclopedia of clinical neuropsychology.* New York, NY: Springer.

Edwards, C. P. (2000). Children's play in cross-cultural perspective: A new look at the Six Cultures study. *Cross-Cultural Research: The Journal of Comparative Social Science, 34,* 318–338.

Edwards, C. P. (2005). Children's play in cross-cultural perspective: A new look at the "six cultures" study. In F. F. McMahon, D. E. Lytle, & B. Sutton-Smith (Eds.), *Play: An interdisciplinary synthesis* (pp. 81–96). Lanham, MD: University Press of America.

Edwards, C. P., Ren, L., & Brown, J. (2015). Early contexts of learning: Family and community socialization during infancy and toddlerhood. In L. A. Jensen (Ed.), *Oxford handbook of human development and culture.* New York, NY: Oxford University Press.

Edwards, J. D., Lunsman, M., Perkins, M., Rebok, G. W., & Roth, D. L. (2009). Driving cessation and health trajectories in older adults. *Journals of Gerontology: Series A: Biological Sciences and Medical Sciences, 64A,* 1290–1295.

Effros, R. B. (2009a). The immunological theory of aging revisited. In V. L. Bengtson, D. Gans, N. M. Putney, & M. Silverstein (Eds.), *Handbook of theories and aging* (2nd ed., pp. 163–178). New York, NY: Springer.

Effros, R. B. (2009b). Kleemeier award lecture 2008: The canary in the coal mine: Telomeres and human healthspan. Journal of Gerontology: Biological Sciences, 64A, 511–515.

Egeland, B., & Carlson, B. (2004). Attachment and psychopathology. In L. Atkinson & S. Goldberg (Eds.), *Attachment issues in psychopathology and intervention* (pp. 27–48). Mahwah, NJ: Erlbaum.

Ehrenberg, H. M., Dierker, L., Milluzzi, C., & Mercer, B. M. (2003). Low maternal weight, failure to thrive in pregnancy, and adverse pregnancy outcomes. *American Journal of Obstetrics and Gynecology, 189,* 1726–1730.

Ehrenreich, B. (2010). *Witches, midwives, and nurses: A history of women healers.* New York, NY: Feminist Press.

Eiden, R. D., & Reifman, A. (1996). Effects of Brazelton demonstrations on later parenting: A meta-analysis. *Journal of Pediatric Psychology, 21,* 857–868.

Einon, D., & Potegal, M. (1994). Temper tantrums. In M. Potegal & J. F. Knutson (Eds.), *The dynamics of aggression: Biological and social processes in dyads and groups* (pp. 157–194). Hillsdale, NJ: Erlbaum.

Eisenberg, N., & Fabes, R. A. (2006). Emotion regulation and children's socioemotional competence. In L. Balter & C. S. Tamis-LeMonda (Eds.), *Child psychology: A handbook of contemporary issues* (2nd ed., pp. 357–381). New York, NY: Psychology Press.

Eisenberg, N. & Valiente, C. (2004). Empathy-related responding: Moral, social and socialization correlates. In A. G. Miller (Ed.), *Social psychology of good and evil.* New York, NY: Guilford Press.

Eisenberg, N., Hofer, C., & Vaughan, J. (2007). Effortful control and its socioemotional consequences. In J. J. Gross (Ed.), *Handbook of emotional regulation* (pp. 287–306). New York, NY: Guilford.

Eisenberg, N., Zhou, Q, Liew, J., Champion, C., & Pidada, S. U. (2006). Emotion, emotion-regulated regulation, and social functioning. In X. Chen, D. C. French, & B. H. Schneider (Eds.), *Peer relationships in cultural context* (pp. 170–199). New York, NY: Cambridge University Press.

Ekman, P. (2003). *Emotions revealed.* New York, NY: Times Books.

Elderhostel (2005). *Adventures in lifelong learning.* Retrieved from http://www.elderhostel.org

Eldin, A. S. (2009). Female mutilation. In P. S. Chandra, H. Herrman, J. Fisher, M. Kastrup, U. Niaz, M. B. Rondón, & A. Okasha (Eds.), *Contemporary topics in women's mental health: Global perspectives in a changing society* (pp. 485–498). Hoboken, NJ: Wiley & Sons.

Elkind, D. (1967). Egocentrism in adolescence. *Child Development, 38,* 1025–1034.

Elkind, D. (1978). Understanding the young adolescent. *Adolescence, 13,* 127–134.

Elkind, D. (1985). Egocentrism redux. *Developmental Review, 5,* 218–226.

Elliott, G. C., Cunningham, S. M., Linder, M., Colangelo, M., & Gross, M. (2005). Child physical abuse and self-perceived social isolation among adolescents. *Journal of Interpersonal Violence, 20,* 1663–1684.

Ellis, J. A., & Sinclair, R. D. (2008). Male pattern baldness: Current treatments, future prospects. *Drug Discovery Today, 13,* 791–797.

Ellison, N. C., Steinfield, C., & Lampe, C. (2007). The benefits of Facebook "friends": Social capital and college students' use of online social network sites. *Journal of Computer-Mediated Communication, 12,* 1143–1168.

Ember, C. R. (2011). What we know and what we don't know about variation in social organization: Melvin Ember's approach to the study of kinship. *Cross–Cultural Research, 45,* 16–36.

Ember, C. R., Ember, M., & Peregrine, P. N. (2011). *Anthropology* (13th edition). New York, NY: Pearson.

Ember, M., Ember, C. R., & Low, B. S. (2007). Comparing explanations of polygyny. *Cross–Cultural Research, 41,* 428–440.

Emery, R. E., Sbarra, D., & Grover, T. (2005). Divorce mediation: Research and reflections. *Family Court Review, 43,* 22–37.

Engelmann, J. B., Moore, S., Capra, C. M., & Berns, G. S. (2012). Differential neurobiological effects of expert advice on risky choice in adolescents and adults. *Social cognitive and affective neuroscience, 7*(5), 557–567.

Englander, F., Terregrossa, R. A., & Wang, Z. (2010). Internet use among college students: Tool or toy? *Educational Review, 62,* 85–96.

Engle, P. I., & Breaux, C. (1998). Fathers' involvement with children: Perspectives from developing countries. *Social Policy Report, XII(1),* 1–21.

Engler, A. J., Ludington-Hoe, S. M., Cusson, R. M., Adams, R., Bahnsen, M., Brumbaugh, E.,…Williams, D. (2002). Kangaroo care: National survey of practice, knowledge, barriers, and perceptions. *American Journal of Maternal/Child Nursing, 27,* 146–153.

Eppig, C., Fincher, C. L., & Thornhill, R. (2010). Parasite prevalence and the worldwide distribution of cognitive ability. *Proceedings of the Royal Society B, 277,* 3801–3808.

Erickson, K. I., Miller, D. L., Weinstein, A. M., Akl, S. L., & Banducci, S. (2012). Physical activity and brain plasticity in late adulthood: a conceptual and comprehensive review. *Ageing Research, 3*(1), e6.

Ericsson, K. A. (1990). Peak performance and age: An examination of peak performance in sports. In P. Baltes & M. M. Baltes (Eds.), *Successful aging* (pp. 164–196). Cambridge, MA: Cambridge University Press.

Erikson, E. H. (1950). *Childhood and society.* New York, NY: Norton.

Erikson, E. H. (1968). *Identity: Youth and crisis.* New York, NY: Norton.

Eriksson, C., Hamberg, K., & Salander, P. (2007). Men's experiences of intense fear related to childbirth investigated in a Swedish qualitative study. *Journal of Men's Health & Gender, 4,* 409–418.

Erickson, K. I., & Korol, D. L. (2009). The effects of hormone replacement therapy on the brains of postmenopausal women: A review of human neuro-imaging studies. In W. J. Chodzko-Zajko, A. F. Kramer, & L. Poon (Eds.), *Enhancing cognitive functioning and brain plasticity (aging, exercise, and cognition)* (pp. 133–158). Champaign, IL: Human Kinetics.

Erlandsson, K., & Lindgren, H. (2009). From belonging to belonging through a blessed moment of love for a child—The birth of a child from the fathers' perspective. *Journal of Men's Health, 338–344.*

Esen, U. (2004). African women, bride price, and AIDS. *The Lancet, 363,* 1734–1734.

Eslea, M., Menesini, E., Morita, Y., O'Moore, M., Mora-Nerchan, J. A., Pereira, B., & Smith, P. K. (2004). Friendship and loneliness among bullies and victims: Data from seven countries. *Aggressive Behavior, 30,* 71–83.

Eslinger, P. J., & Biddle, K. R. (2008). Prefrontal cortex and the maturation of executive functions, cognitive expertise, and social adaptation. In V. Anderson, R. Jacobs, & P. J. Anderson (Eds.), *Executive functions and the frontal lobes: A lifespan perspective* (pp. 299–316). Philadelphia, PA: Taylor & Francis.

Espelage, D. L., & Swearer, S. M. (2004). *Bullying in American schools.* Mahwah, NJ: Lawrence Erlbaum.

Esser, F., & de Vreese, C. H. (2007). Comparing young voters' political engagement in the United States and Europe. *American Behavioral Scientist, 50*, 1195–1213.

Espy, K. A., Fang, H., Johnson, C., Stopp, C., Wiebe, S. A., & Respass, J. (2011). Prenatal tobacco exposure: Developmental outcomes in the neonatal period. *Developmental Psychology, 47*, 153–169.

Eveleth, P. B., & Tanner, J. M. (1990). *Worldwide variation in human growth.* Cambridge, MA: Cambridge University Press.

Everett, G. E., Olmi, D. J., Edwards, R. P., Tingstrom, D. H., Sterling-Turner, H. E. & Christ, T. J. (2007). An empirical investigation of time-out with and without escape extinction to treat escape-maintained noncompliance. *Behavior Modification, 31*, 412–434.

Fabes, R. A., Martin, C. L., & Hanish, L. D. (2003). Young children's play qualities in same-, other-, and mixed-sex peer groups. *Child Development, 74*, 921–932.

Fabiano, G. A., Pelham, Jr., W. E., Manos, M. J., Gnagy, E. M., Chronis, A. M., Onvango, A. N.,…Swain, S. (2004). An evaluation of three time-out procedures for children with attention deficit/hyperactivity disorder. *Behavior Therapy, 35*, 449–469.

Facio, A., & Micocci, F. (2003). Emerging adulthood in Argentina. In J. J. Arnett & N. Galabmos (Eds.), *New Directions in Child and Adolescent Development, 100*, 21–31.

Fackler, M. (2007, June 22). As Japan ages, universities struggle to fill classrooms. *The New York Times*, p. A3.

Fagan, J. F., Holland, C. R., & Wheeler, K. (2007). The prediction, from infancy, of adult IQ and achievement. *Intelligence, 35*, 225–231.

Fajardo, M., & Di Cesare, P. E. (2005). Disease-modifying therapies for osteoarthritis. *Drugs and Aging, 22*, 141–161.

Falk, C. F., Heine, S. J., Yuki, M., & Takemura, K. (2009). Why do Westerners self–enhance more than East Asians? European Journal of Personality, 23 (Special issue: Personality and culture), 183–203.

Farrell, M. P., & Rosenberg, S. D. (1981). *Men at midlife.* Boston, MA: Auburn House.

Farver, J. A., Bhadha, B. R., & Narang, S. K. (2002). Acculturation and psychological functioning in Asian Indian adolescents. *Social Development, 11*, 11–29.

Faulkner, G., & Biddle, S. (2002). Mental health nursing and the promotion of physical activity. *Journal of Psychiatric and Mental Health Nursing, 9*, 659–665.

Fearon, P., O'Connell, P., Frangou, S., Aquino, P., Nosarti, C., Allin, M.,…Murray, R. (2004). Brain volumes in adult survivors of very low birth weight: A sibling–controlled study. Q *Pediatrics, 114*, 367–371.

Federico, M. J., & Liu, A. H. (2003). Overcoming childhood asthma disparities of the inner-city poor. *Pediatric Clinics of North America, 50*, 655–675.

Feeney, J. A., Hohaus, L., Noller, P., & Alexander, R. P. (2001). *Becoming parents: Exploring the bonds between mothers, fathers, and their infants.* New York, NY: Cambridge University Press.

Feigenbaum, P. (2002). Private speech: Cornerstone of Vygotsky's theory of the development of higher psychological processes. Voices within Vygotsky's non-classical psychology: Past, present, future, 161–174.

Feinberg, M. E., Kan, M. L., Goslin, M. C. (2009). Enhancing coparenting, parenting, and child self-regulation: Effects of family foundations 1 year after birth. *Prevention Science, 10*, 276–285.

Feinsilver, S. H. (2003). Sleep in the elderly: What is normal? *Clinical Geriatric Medicine, 19*, 177–188.

Fekkes, M., Pijpers, F. I., & Verloove-Vanhorick, S. P. (2004). Bullying behavior and associations with psychosomatic complaints and depression in victims. *Journal of Pediatrics, 144*, 17–22.

Feldhusen, J. F. (2005). Giftedness, talent, expertise, and creative achievement. In R. J. Sternberg & J. E. Davidson (Eds.), *Conceptions of giftedness* (2nd ed., pp. 64–79). New York, NY: Cambridge University Press.

Feldkamper, M., & Schaeffel, F. (2003). Interactions of genes and environment in myopia. *Developmental Opthalmology, 37*, 34–49.

Feldman, R., & Eidelman, A. I. (2003). Skin-to-skin contact (kangaroo care) accelerates autonomic and neurobehavioral maturation in preterm infants. *Developmental Medicine and Child Neurology, 45*, 274–281.

Feldman, R., Weller, A., Sirota, L., & Eidelman, A. I. (2003). Testing a family intervention hypothesis: The contribution of mother–infant skin-to-skin (kangaroo care) to family interaction, proximity, and touch. *Journal of Family Psychology, 17*, 94–107.

Feldman-Salverlsberg, P. (2002). Is infertility an unrecognized public health and population problem? The view from the Cameroon grassfields. In M. C. Inhorn & F. van Balen (Eds.), *Infertility around the globe: New thinking on childlessness, gender, and reproductive technologies* (pp. 215–231). Berkeley: University of California Press.

Female genital mutilation: Is it crime or culture? (1999, February 11). *The Economist.* Retrieved from http://www.economist.com/node/185966

Ferber, S. G., & Makhoul, I. R. (2004). The effect of skin-to-skin contact (kangaroo care) shortly after birth on the neurobehavioral responses of the term newborn: A randomized, controlled trial. *Pediatrics, 113*, 858–865.

Ferber, S. G., Kuint, J., Weller, A., Feldman, S. D., Arbel, E., & Kohelet, D. (2002). Massage therapy by mothers and trained professionals enhances weight gain in preterm infants. *Early Human Development, 67*, 37–45.

Ferguson, C. J. (2013). Spanking, corporal punishment and negative long-term outcomes: *A meta-analytic review of longitudinal studies. Clinical Psychology Review, 33*(1), 196–208.

Ferguson, G. M., Hafen, C. A., & Laursen, B. (2010). Adolescent psychological and academic adjustment as a function of discrepancies between actual and ideal self-perceptions. *Journal of Youth and Adolescence, 39*, 1485–1497.

Ferguson, S. A., Teoh, E. R., & McCartt, A. T. (2007). Progress in teenage crash risk during the last decade. *Journal of Safety Research, 38*, 137–145.

Fergusson, D. M., Boden, J. M., & Horwood, L. J. (2008). Exposure to childhood sexual and physical abuse and adjustment in early adulthood. *Child Abuse and Neglect, 32*, 607–619.

Fernald, A., & O'Neill, D. K. (1993). Peekaboo across cultures: How mothers and infants play with voices, faces, and expectations. In K. MacDonald (Ed.), *Parent–child play* (pp. 259–285). Albany: State University of New York Press.

Fernald, A., Perfors, A., & Marchman, V. A. (2006). Picking up speed in understanding: Speech processing efficiency and vocabulary growth across the 2nd year. *Developmental Psychology, 42*, 98–116.

Ferrara, N. (2004). The aging heart and exercise training. *Archives of Gerontology and Geriatrics, 35*(Suppl.), 145–156.

Fetterman, M. (2008). *Becoming "parent of your parent" an emotionally wrenching process.* USA Today.

Field, M. J., & Behrman, R. E. (Eds.) (2002). *When children die.* Washington, DC: National Academies Press.

Field, T. (2010). Pregnancy and labor massage. *Expert Reviews in Obstetrics & Gynecology, 5*, 177–181.

Field, T. M. (1998). Massage therapy effects. *American Psychologist, 53*, 1270–1281.

Field, T. M. (2001). Massage therapy facilitates weight gain in preterm infants. *Current Directions in Psychological Science, 10,* 51–55.

Field, T. M. (2004). Massage therapy effects on depressed pregnant women. *Journal of Psychosomatic Obstetrics and Gynaecology, 25,*115–122.

Field, T., Diego, M., & Hernandez-Reif, M. (2010). Preterm infant massage therapy: A review. *Infant Behavior and Development, 33,* 115–124.

Field, T., Hernandez-Reif, M., & Diego, M. (2006). Newborns of depressed mothers who received moderate versus light pressure massage during therapy. *Infant Behavior and Development, 29,* 54–58.

Figley, C. R. (1973). Child density and the marital relationship. *Journal of Marriage and the Family, 35,* 272–282.

Fildes, V. (1995). The culture and biology of breastfeeding: An historical review of Western Europe. In P. Stuart-Macadam & K. A. Dettwyler (Eds.), *Breastfeeding: Biocultural perspectives* (pp. 101–131). Hawthorne, NY: Aldein de Gruyter.

Filipek, P. A., Accardo, P. J., Ashwal, S., Baranek, G. T., Cook, E. H., Dawson, G.,… Volkmar, F. R. (2000). Practice parameter: Screening and diagnosis of autism: Report of the Quality Standards Subcommittee of the American Academy of Neurology and the Child Neurology Society. *Neurology, 55,* 468–479.

Fingerman, K. L. (1998). The good, the bad, and the worrisome: Emotional complexities in grandparents' experiences with individual grandchildren. *Family Relations, 47,* 403–414.

Fingerman, K. L. (2004). The role of offspring and in-laws in grandparents' ties to their grandchildren. *Journal of Family Issues, 25,* 1026–1049.

Fingerman, K. L., & Birditt, K. S. (2003). Do we get better at picking our battles? Age group differences in descriptions of behavioral reactions to interpersonal tensions. *Journal of Gerontology, 60B,* P121–P128.

Fingerman, K.L., & Yahirun, J.J. (2015). Family relationships. In J.J. Arnett (Ed.), *Oxford Handbook of Emerging Adulthood.* New York: Oxford University Press.

Finkel, M. (2007). Bedlam in the blood: Malaria. *National Geographic,* July, 32–67.

Finkel, M. (2007). Stopping a global killer. *National Geographic Magazine.* Retrieved from http://ngm.nationalgeographic.com/2007/07/malaria/finkel-text

Finley, G. E., & Schwartz, S. J. (2010). The divided world of the child: Divorce and long-term psychosocial adjustment. *Family Court Review, 48,* 516–527.

Finn, C. A. (2001). Reproductive ageing and the menopause. *International Journal of Developmental Biology, 45,* 613–617.

Fisch, H., Hyun, G., Golden, R., Hensle, T. W., Olsson, C. A., & Liberson, G. L. (2003). The influence of paternal age on Down syndrome. *Journal of Urology, 169,* 2275–2278.

Fischer, K. W., & Bidell, T. R. (1998). Dynamic development of psychological structures in action and thought. In W. Damon (Ed.), & R. M. Lerner (Vol. Ed.), *Handbook of child psychology: Vol. 1. Theoretical models of human development* (5th ed., pp. 467–561). New York, NY: Wiley.

Fisher, C. B. (2003). A goodness–of–fit ethic for child assent to nonbeneficial research. *The American Journal of Bioethics, 3,* 27–28.

Fisher, T. E., & Chervenak, J. L. (2012). Lifestyle alterations for the amelioration of hot flashes. *Maturitas, 71*(3), 217–220.

Fitneva, S. A. (2015). The emergence and development of language across cultures. In L. A. Jensen (Ed.), *Oxford handbook of human development and culture.* New York, NY: Oxford University Press.

Fitneva, S., & Matsui, T. (2015). The emergence and development of language across cultures. In L. A. Jensen (Ed.), *Oxford handbook of human development and culture: An interdisciplinary perspective.* New York, NY: Oxford University Press.

Fitzpatrick, J., Reifman, A., & Sharp, E. A. (2009). Midlife singles' willingness to date partners with heterogeneous characteristics. *Family Relations, 58,* 121–133.

Fitzpatrick, L. A. (2003). Phytoestrogens: Mechanism of action and effect on bone mineral density. *Endocrinology and Metabolism Clinics of North America, 32,* 233–252.

Flammer, A., & Alsaker, F. D. (2006). Adolescents in school. In S. Jackson & L. Goossens (Eds.), *Handbook of adolescent development: European perspectives* (pp. 223–245). Hove, UK: Psychology Press.

Flammer, A., Alsaker, F. D., & Noack, P. (1999). Time use by adolescents in international perspective: The case of leisure activities. In F. D. Alsaker & A. Flammer (Eds.), *The adolescent experience: European and American adolescents in the 1990s* (pp. 33–60). Mahwah, NJ: Erlbaum.

Flanagan, C., & Botcheva, L. (1999). Adolescents' preference for their homeland and other countries. In F. D. Alsaker & A. Flammer (Eds.), *The adolescent experience: European and American adolescents in the 1990s* (pp. 131–144). Mahwah, NJ: Erlbaum.

Flanagan, K. M., Clements, M. L., Whitton, S. W., Portney, M. J., Randall, D. W., & Markman, H. J. (2001). Retrospect and prospect in the psychological study of marital and couple relationships. In J. P. McHale & W. S. Grolnick, (Eds.), *Retrospect and prospect in the psychological study of families* (99–132). Mahwah, NJ: Erlbaum.

Flannery, K. A., & Liederman, J. (1995). Is there really a syndrome involving the co-occurrence of neurodevelopmental disorder, talent, non–right handedness and immune disorder among children? *Cortex, 31,* 503–515.

Flavell, J. H., Beach, D. R., & Chinsky, J. M. (1966). Spontaneous verbal rehearsal in a memory task as a function of age. *Child Development, 37,* 283–299.

Flavell, J. H., Friedrichs, A., & Hoyt, J. (1970). Developmental changes in memorization process. *Cognitive Psychology, 1,* 324–340.

Flavell, J. H., Miller, P. H., & Miller, S. A. (2002). *Cognitive development* (4th ed.). Upper Saddle River, NJ: Prentice Hall.

Fleming, T. P. (2006). The periconceptional and embryonic period. In P. Gluckman, & M. Hanson (Eds.), *Developmental origins of health and disease* (pp. 51–61). New York, NY: Cambridge University Press.

Flores, Y. G., Hinton, L., Barker, J. C., Franz, C. E., & Velasquez, A. (2009). Beyond familism: A case study of the ethics of care of a Latina caregiver of an elderly parent with dementia. *Health Care for Women International, 30,* 1055–1072.

Floud, R., Fogel, R. W., Harris, B., & Hong, S. C. (2011). *The changing body: Health, nutrition, and human development in the Western world since 1700.* New York, NY: Cambridge University Press.

Flowers, P., & Buston, K. (2001). "I was terrified of being different": Exploring gay men's accounts of growing up in a heterosexist society. *Journal of Adolescence, 24,* 51–66.

Floyd, F., & Bakeman, R. (2006). Coming-out across the life course: Implications of age and historical context. *Archives of Sexual Behavior, 35,* 287–297.

Flynn, J. R. (1999). The discovery of IQ gains over time. *American Psychologist, 54,* 5–20.

Flynn, J. R. (2003). Movies about intelligence: The limitations of g. *Current Directions in Psychological Science, 12,* 95–99.

Foehr, U. (2007). Computer use, age differences in. In J. J. Arnett (Ed.), *Encyclopedia of children, adolescents, and the media, Vol. 1* (pp. 202–204). Thousand Oaks, CA: Sage.

Fogel, A., Hsu, H., Nelson-Goens, G. C., Shapiro, A. F., & Secrist, C. (2006). Effects of normal and perturbed social play on the duration and amplitude of different types of infant smiles. *Developmental Psychology, 42,* 459–473.

Foley, D. J., Vitiello, M. V., Bliwise, D. L., Ancoli-Israel, S., Monjan, A. A., & Walsh, J. K. (2007). Frequent napping is associated with excessive daytime sleepiness, depression, pain, and nocturia in older adults: Findings from the National Sleep Foundation "2003 Sleep in America" Poll. *American Journal of Geriatric Psychology, 15,* 344–350.

Foley, D., Ancoli-Israel, S., Britz, P., & Walsh, J. (2004). Sleep disturbances and chronic disease in older adults: Results of the 2003 National Sleep Foundation Sleep in America survey. *Journal of Psychosomatic Research, 56,* 497–502.

Fomon, S. J., & Nelson, S. E. (2002). Body composition of the male and female reference infants. *Annual Review of Nutrition, 22,* 1–17.

Fonda, S. J., Wallace, R. B., & Herzog, A R. (2001). Changes in driving patterns and worsening depressive symptoms among older adults. *Journals of Gerontology: Series B: Psychological Sciences and Social Sciences, 56B,* S343–S351.

Fong, V. L. (2002). China's one-child policy and the empowerment of urban daughters. *American Anthropologist, 104,* 1098–1109.

Fontaine, R., Gramain, A., & Wittwer, J. (2009). Providing care for an elderly parent: Interactions among siblings. *Health Economics, 18,* 1011–1029.

Fontana, L., Meyer, T. E., Klein, S., & Holloszy, J. O. (2004). Long-term calorie restriction is highly effective in reducing the risk of atherosclerosis in humans. *Proceedings of the National Academy of Sciences of the United States of America, 101,* 6659–6663.

Fontanel, B., & d'Harcourt, C. (1997). *Babies: History, art and folklore.* New York, NY: Harry N. Abrams.

Ford, C. S. (1945). *A comparative study of human reproduction.* New Haven, CT: Yale University Press.

Ford, C., & Beach, F. (1951). *Patterns of sexual behavior.* New York, NY: Harper & Row.

Foss, R. D. (2007). Improving graduated driver licensing systems: A conceptual approach and its implications. *Journal of Safety Research, 38,* 185–192.

Foureur, M., Ryan, C. L., Nicholl, M., & Homer, C. (2010). Inconsistent evidence: Analysis of six national guidelines for vaginal birth after cesarean section. *Birth: Issues in Perinatal Care, 37,* 3–10.

Fox, M. K., Pac, S., Devaney, B., & Jankowski, L. (2004). Feeding infants and toddlers study: What foods are infants and toddlers eating? *American Dietetic Association Journal, 104* (Suppl.), S22–S30.

Fraley, R. C., Roisman, G. I., Booth-LaForce, C., Owen, M. T., & Holland, A. S. (2013). Interpersonal and genetic origins of adult attachment styles: A longitudinal study from infancy to early adulthood. *Journal of Personality and Social Psychology, 104,* 817–838. doi: 10.1037/a0031435

Frankenburg, W. K., Dodds, J., Archer, P., Shapiro, H., & Bresnick, B. (1992). The Denver II: A major revision and restandardization of the Denver Developmental Screening Test. *Pediatrics, 89,* 91–97.

Frankman, E. A., Wang, L., Bunker, C. H., & Lowder, J. L. (2009). Episiotomy in the United States: Has anything changed? *American Journal of Obstetrics and Gynecology, 537,* e1-e7.

Fransen, M., Meertens, R., & Schrander-Stumpel, C. (2006). Communication and risk presentation in genetic counseling: Development of a checklist. *Patient Education and Counseling, 61,* 126–133.

Frawley, T. J. (2008). Gender schema and prejudicial recall: How children misremember, fabricate, and distort gendered picture book information. *Journal of Research in Childhood Education, 22,* 291–303.

Frayling, T. M., Timpson, N. J., Weedon, M. N., Zeggini, E., Freathy, R. M., Lindgren, C. M.,…McCarthy, M. I. (2007). A common variant in the *FTO* gene is associated with body mass index and predisposes children and adult obesity. *Science, 316,* 889–894.

Frazier, L. D. (2002). Perceptions of control over health: Implications for sense of self in healthy and ill older adults. In S. P. Shohov (Ed.), *Advances in psychology research* (Vol. 10, pp. 145–163). Huntington, NY: Nova Scotia.

Freedman, D. S., Khan, L. K., Serdula, M. K., Ogden, C. L., & Dietz, W. H. (2006). Racial and ethnic differences in secular trends for childhood BMI, weight, and height. *Obesity,* 301–308.

French, D. (2015). Cultural templates of adolescent friendships. In L. A. Jensen (Ed.), *Oxford handbook of human development and culture: An interdisciplinary perspective.* New York, NY: Oxford University Press.

French, D. C., Eisenberg, N., Vaughan, J., Purwono, U., & Suryanti, T. A. (2008). Religious involvement and the social competence and adjustment of Indonesian Muslim adolescents. *Developmental Psychology, 44,* 597–611.

French, D. C., Rianasari, J. M., Piadada, S., Nelwan, P., & Buhrmester, D. (2001). Social support of Indonesian and U.S. children and adolescents by family members and friends. *Merrill-Palmer Quarterly, 47,* 377–394.

Frenkel, D., Dori, M., & Solomon, B. (2004). Generation of anti-beta-amyloid antibodies via phage display technology. *Vaccine, 22,* 2505–2508.

Freud, S. (1940/64). *An outline of psychoanalysis: Standard edition of the works of Sigmund Freud.* London, UK: Hogarth Press.

Freund, A. M., & Baltes, P. B. (2002). Life-management strategies of selection, optimization, and compensation: Measurement by self-report and construct validity. *Journal of Personality and Social Psychology, 82,* 642–662.

Freund, B., Colgrove, L. A., Burke, B. L., & McLeod, R. (2005). Self-rated performance among elderly drivers referred for driving evaluation. *Accident Analysis and Prevention, 37,* 613–618.

Frick, P. J., & Kimonis, E. R. (2005). Externalizing disorders of childhood and adolescence. In E. J. Maddux & A. B. Winstead (Eds.), *Psychopathology: Foundations for a contemporary understanding* (pp. 325–351). Mahwah, NJ: Lawrence.

Friedlmeier, W., Corapci, F., & Benga, O. (2015). Early emotional development in cultural perspective. In L. A. Jensen (Ed.), *Oxford handbook of human development and culture: An interdisciplinary perspective.* New York, NY: Oxford University Press.

Friedman, H. S., & Martin, L. R. (2011). *The longevity project.* New York, NY: Penguin.

Frisén A., & Wängqvist, M. (2011). Emerging adults in Sweden: Identity formation in the light of love, work, and family. *Journal of Adolescent Research, 26,* 200–221.

Fritz, G., & Rockney, R. (2004). Summary of the practice parameter for the assessment and treatment of children and adolescents with enuresis. *Work Group on Quality Issues: Journal of the American Academy of Child & Adolescent Psychiatry, 43,* 123–125.

Fryar, C. D., Carroll, M. D., & Ogden, C. L. (2012). Prevalence of obesity among children and adolescents: United States, Trends 1963-1965 Through 2009-2010. Prevention. Retrieved from http://www.cdc.gov/nchs/data/hestat/obesity_child_09_10/obesity_child_09_10.pdf

Frydenberg, E., & Lodge, J. (2007). Australia. In J.J. Arnett (Ed.), *International encyclopedia of adolescence.* New York, NY: Routledge.

Fry, C. L. (1985). Culture, behavior, and aging in the comparative perspective. In J. E. Birren & K. W. Schaie (Eds.), *Handbook of the psychology of aging* (2nd ed., pp. 216–244). New York, NY: Van Nostrand Reinhold.

Fujikado, T., Kuroa, T., Maeda, N., Ninomiya, S., Goto, H., Tano, Y.,…Mihashi, T. (2004). Light scattering and optical aberrations as objective parameters to predict visual deterioration in eyes with cataracts. *Journal of Cataract and Refractive Surgery, 30,* 1198–1208.

Fuligni, A. J. (2011). Social identity, motivation, and well being among adolescents from Asian and Latin American backgrounds. In G. Carlo, L. J. Crockett, & M. A. Carranza (Eds.), *Health disparities in youth and families: Research and applications* (pp. 97–120). New York, NY: Springer.

Fuligni, A. J., Witkow, M. (2004). The postsecondary educational progress of youth from immigrant families. *Journal of Research on Adolescence, 14,* 159–183.

Fuligni, A., Tseng, V., & Lam, M. (1999). Attitudes toward family obligation among American adolescents with Asian, Latin American, and European backgrounds. *Child Development, 70,* 1030–1044.

Fuller, A., Beck, V., & Unwin, L. (2005). The gendered nature of apprenticeship: Employers' and young peoples' perspectives. *Education & Training, 47,* 298–311.

Fultz, N. H., Jenkins, K. R., Ostbye, T., Taylor, D. H. J., Kabeto, M. U., & Langa, K. M. (2005). The impact of own and spouse's urinary incontinence on depressive symptoms. *Social Science and Medicine, 60,* 2537–2548.

Fung, H. H., & Cartensen, L. L. (2004). Motivational changes in response to blocked goals and foreshortened time: Testing alternatives to socioemotional selectivity theory. *Psychology and Aging, 19,* 68–78.

Funk, J. B. (2003). Violent video games: Who's at risk? In D. Ravitch & J. P. Viteritti (Eds.), *Kid stuff: Marketing sex and violence to America's children* (pp. 168–192). Baltimore, MD: Johns Hopkins University Press.

Funk, J. B. (2005). Children's exposure to violent video games and desensitization to violence. *Child & Adolescent Psychiatric Clinics of North America, 14,* 387–404.

Funk, J. B., Flores, B., Buchman, D. D., & Germann, J. N. (1999). Rating electronic video games: Violence is in the eye of the beholder. *Youth & Society, 30,* 283–312.

Funk, J. B., Hagan, J., Schimming, J., Bullock, W. A., Buchman, D. D., & Myers, M. (2002). Aggression an psychopathology in adolescents with a preference for violent electronic games. *Aggressive Behavior, 28,* 134–144.

Furman, W., & Hand, L. S. (2006). The slippery nature of romantic relationships: Issues in definition and differentiation. In A. C. Crouter & A. Booth (Eds.), *Romance and sex in adolescence and emerging adulthood: Risks and opportunities* (pp. 171–178). The Penn State University family issues symposia series. Mahwah, NJ: Lawrence Erlbaum.

Furman, W., & Simon, V. A. (2008). Homophily in adolescent romantic relationships. In M. J. Prinstein & K. A. Dodge (Eds.), *Understanding peer influence in children and adolescents* (pp. 203–224). New York, NY: Guilford.

Futagi, Y., Toribe, Y., & Suzuki, Y. (2009). Neurological assessment of early infants. *Current Pediatric Reviews, 5,* 65–70.

Fyfe, K. (2006). Wolves in sheep's clothing: A content analysis of children's television. Retrieved from http://wwww.parentstelevision.org/

Galambos, N. L. (2004). Gender and gender role development in adolescence. In R. Lerner & L. Steinberg (Eds.), *Handbook of adolescent psychology.* New York, NY: Wiley.

Galambos, N. L., Barker, E. T., & Krahn, H. J. (2006). Depression, anger, and self-esteem in emerging adulthood: Seven-year trajectories. *Developmental Psychology, 42,* 350–365.

Galambos, N., Almeida, D., & Petersen, A. (1990). Masculinity, femininity, and sex role attitudes in early adolescence: Exploring gender intensification. *Child Development, 61,* 1905–1914.

Galatzer-Levy, I. R., & Bonanno, G. A. (2012). Beyond normality in the study of bereavement: Heterogeneity in depression outcomes following loss in older adults. *Social Science & Medicine, 74*(12), 1987–1994.

Gale, C. R., Godfrey, K. M., Law, C. M., Martyn, C. N., & O'Callaghan, F. J. (2004). Critical periods of brain growth and cognitive function in children. *Brain: A Journal of Neurology, 127,* 321–329.

Gall, S. (Ed.). (1996). *Multiple pregnancy and delivery.* St. Louis, MO: Mosby.

Gallagher, D. (2004). Overweight and obesity BMI cut-offs and their relation to metabolic disorders in Koreans/Asians. *Obesity Research, 12,* 440–441.

Galler, J. R., Bryce, C. P., Waber, D., Hock, R. S., Exner, N., Eaglesfield, D.,…Harrison, R. (2010). Early childhood malnutrition predicts depressive symptoms at ages 11–17. *Journal of Child Psychology and Psychiatry, 51,* 789–798.

Galler, J. R., Waber, D., Harrison, R., & Ramsey, F. (2005). Behavioral effects of childhood malnutrition. *The American Journal of Psychiatry, 162,* 1760–1761.

Gallup Poll. (2002). Poll topics and trends: Religion. Retrieved from http://www.gallup.com/poll/topics/religion2.asp/

Gallup Poll. (2006). *Religion most important to Blacks, women, and older Americans.* Retrieved from http://www.gallup.com/poll/topics/

Galston, W. A., & Lopez, M. H. (2006). Civic Engagement in the United States. In S. P. Simson & L. Wilson (Eds.), *Civic engagement and the baby boomer generation: Research, policy, and practice perspectives* (pp. 3–19). New York, NY: Haworth Press.

Galvan, V., Gorostiza, O. F., Banwait, S., Ataie, M., Logvinova, A. V., Sitaraman, S., et al. (2006). Reversal of Alzheimer's-like pathology and behavior in human APP transgenic mice by mutation of *Asp664. Proceedings of the National Academies of Sciences of the United States of America, 103,* 7130–7135.

Ganger, J., & Brent, M. R. (2004). Reexamining the vocabulary spurt. *Developmental Psychology, 40,* 621–632.

Ganong, L., & Coleman, M. (2006). Patterns of exchange and intergenerational responsibilities after divorce and remarriage. *Journal of Aging Studies, 20,* 265–278.

Gans, J. (1990). *America's adolescents: How healthy are they?* Chicago, IL: American Medical Association.

Gardiner, H. W. (2001). Child and adolescent development: Cross-cultural perspectives. In L. L. Adler & U. P. Gielen (Eds.), *Cross-cultural topics in psychology* (pp. 63–79). Westport, CT: Praeger.

Gardner, H. (1983). *Frames of mind.* New York, NY: Basic Books.

Gardner, H. (1993). *Multiple intelligences: The theory in practice.* New York, NY: Basic Books.

Gardner, H. (1999). Who owns intelligence? *Atlantic Monthly, 283,* 67–76.

Gardner, H. (2004). *Frames of mind: The theory of multiple intelligences.* New York, NY: Basic Books.

Gardner, H. (2011). Multiple intelligences: The first thirty years. *Harvard Graduate School of Education.*

Gardner, T. W., Dishion, T. J., & Connell, A. M. (2008). Adolescent self-regulation as resilience: Resistance to antisocial behavior within the deviant peer context. *Journal of Abnormal Child Psychology, 36,* 273–284.

Garnets, L., & Kimmel, D. C. (Eds.). (2013). *Psychological perspectives on lesbian, gay, and bisexual experiences.* New York, NY: Columbia University Press.

Garrison, M. M., & Christakis, D. A. (2005). *A teacher in the living room? Educational media for babies, toddlers and preschoolers.* Menlo Park, CA: The Henry J. Kaiser Family Foundation.

Gartstein, M. A., Gonzalez, C., Carranza, J. A., Ahadi, S. A., Ye, R., Rothbart, M. K., & Yang, S. W. (2006). Studying cross-cultural differences in the development of infant temperament: People's Republic of China, the United States of America, and Spain. *Child Psychiatry and Human Development, 37,* 145–161.

Gaskins, S. (2000). Children's daily activities in a Mayan village: A culturally grounded description. *Cross-Cultural Research, 34,* 375–389.

Gaskins, S. (2015). Childhood practices across cultures: Play and household work. In L. A. Jensen (Ed.), *Oxford handbook of human development and culture: An interdisciplinary perspective.* New York, NY: Oxford University Press.

Gatrad, A. R. (1994). Muslim customs surrounding death, bereavement, postmortem examinations, and organ transplants. *BMJ, 309,* 521.

Gaugler, J. E., Zarit, S. H., & Perlin, L. (2003). The onset of dementia caregiving and its longitudinal implications. *Psychology and Aging, 18,* 171–180.

Gauvain, M., & Nicolaides, C. (2015). Cognition in childhood across cultures. In L. A. Jensen (Ed.), *Oxford handbook of human development and culture: An interdisciplinary perspective.* New York, NY: Oxford University Press.

Gavin, A. R., Hill, K. G., Hawkins, J. D., & Maas, C. (2011). The role of maternal early-life and later-life risk factors on offspring low birth weight: Findings from a three-generational study. *Journal of Adolescent Health, 49,* 166–171.

Gavin, L., & Furman, W. (1989). Age differences in adolescents' perceptions of their peer groups. *Developmental Psychology, 25,* 827–834.

Gawande, A. (2007, April 30). The way we age now. *The New Yorker,* 49–59.

Gazzaniga, M. (2008). *Human: The science behind what makes us unique.* New York, NY: Ecco.

Ge, X., Natsuaki, M. N., Neiderhiser, J. M., & Reiss, D. (2007). Genetic and environmental influences on pubertal timing: Results from two national sibling studies. *Journal of Research on Adolescence, 17,* 767–788.

Geangu, E., Benga, O., Stahl, D., & Striano, T. (2010). Contagious crying beyond the first days of life. *Infant Behavior & Development, 33,* 279–288.

Geary, D. C. (2010). *Male, female: The evolution of human sex differences* (2nd ed.). Washington, DC: American Psychological Association.

Geeraert, L., Van den Noortgate, W., Grietens, H., & Onghena, P. (2004). The effects of early prevention programs for families with young children at risk for physical child abuse and neglect: A meta-analysis. *Child Maltreatment, 9,* 277–291.

Geldhof, G. J., Little, T. D., & Columbo, J. (2010). Self-regulation across the lifespan. *Handbook of Lifespan Development.* New York, NY: Wiley.

Gelman, R. (1969). Conservation acquisition: A problem of learning to attend to relevant attributes. *Journal of Experimental Child Psychology, 7,* 67–87.

Gelman, S. A., Taylor, M. G., & Nguyen, S. P. (2004). Mother–child conversations about gender. *Monographs of the Society for Research in Child Development, 69*(Serial No. 275), pp. 1–127.

Genesoni, L., & Tallandini, M. A. (2009). Men's psychological transition to fatherhood: An analysis of the literature, 1989–2008. *Birth: Issues in Perinatal Care, 36,* 305–318.

Gentile, D. (2011). The multiple dimensions of violent video game effects. *Child Development Perspectives 5,* 75–81. doi: 10.1111/j.1750-8606.2011.00159.x

George, C., & Solomon, J. (1999). Attachment and caregiving: The caregiving behavioural system. In J. Cassidy & P. R. Shaver (Eds.), *Handbook of attachment: Theory, research, and clinical applications* (pp. 649–670). New York, NY: Guilford Press.

Gergen, K. (2011). The acculturated brain. *Theory and Psychology, 20,* 1–20.

Germino, B. B. (2003). Dying at home. In I. Corless, B. B. Germino, & M. A. Pittman (Eds.), *Dying, death, and bereavement: A challenge for the living* (pp. 105–116). New York, NY: Springer.

Gershoff, E. T. (2002). Corporal punishment by parents and associated child behaviors and experiences: A meta-analytic and theoretical review. *Psychological Bulletin, 128,* 539–579.

Gershuny, J., Bittman, M., & Brice, J. (2005). Exit, voice, and suffering: Do couples adapt to changing employment patterns? *Journal of Marriage and Family. 67,* 656–665.

Gesell, A. (1946). The ontogenesis of infant behaviour. In L. Carmichael (Ed.), *Manual of child psychology* (pp. 295–331). Hoboken, NJ: Wiley.

Gesell, A. L. (1934). *Infancy and human growth.* New York, NY: Macmillan.

Gewirtz, J. (1977). Maternal responding and the conditioning of infant crying: Directions of influence within the attachment–acquisition process. In B. C. Etzel, J. M. LeBlanc, & D. M. Baer (Eds.), *New developments in behavioral research* (pp. 31–57). Hillsdale, NJ: Lawrence Erlbaum.

Giacomoni, P. U., & Rein, G. (2004). A mechanistic model for the aging of human skin. *Micron, 35,* 179–184.

Giang, M. T., & Wittig, M. A. (2006). Implications of adolescents' acculturation strategies for personal and collective self-esteem. *Cultural Diversity and Ethnic Minority Psychology, 12,* 725–739.

Gibbons, J. L., & Stiles, D. A. (2004). *The thoughts of youth: An international perspective on adolescents' ideal persons.* Greenwich, CT: IAP Information Age.

Gibbs, J. C. (2003). *Moral development and reality: Beyond the theories of Kohlberg and Hoffman.* Thousand Oaks, CA: Sage.

Gibbs, J. C., Basinger, K. S., Grime, R. L., & Snarey, J. R. (2007). Moral judgment development across cultures: Revisiting Kohlberg's universality claims. *Developmental Review, 27,* 443–500.

Gibson, E. J., & Walk, R. D. (1960). The "visual cliff." *Scientific American, 202,* 64–71.

Gibson, J. H., Harries, M., Mitchell, A., Godfrey, R., Lunt, M., & Reeve, J. (2000). Determinants of bone density and prevalence of osteopenia among female runners in their second to seventh decades of age. *Bone, 26,* 591–598.

Giddens, A. (2000). *Runaway world: How globalization is reshaping our lives.* New York, NY: Routledge.

Giedd, J. N. (2008). The teen brain: Insights from neuroimaging. *Journal of Adolescent Health, 42,* 335–343.

Giedd, J. N., Raznahan, A., Mills, K. L., & Lenroot, R. K. (2012). Review: magnetic resonance imaging of male/female differences in human adolescent brain anatomy. *Biol Sex Differ, 3*(1), 19.

Giedd, J. N., Stockman, M., Weddle, C., Liverpool, M., Alexander-Bloch, A., et al. (2010). Anatomic magnetic resonance imaging of the developing child and adolescent brain: The effects of genetic variation. *Neuropsychology Review, 20,* 349–361.

Giles-Sims, J., & Lockhart, C. (2005). Culturally shaped patterns of disciplining children. *Journal of Family Issues, 26,* 196–218.

Gilmore, D. (1990). *Manhood in the making: Cultural concepts of masculinity.* New Haven, CT: Yale University Press.

Gini, G., Albierto, P., Benelli, B., & Altoe, G. (2008). Determinants of adolescents' active defending and passive bystanding behavior in bullying. *Journal of Adolescence, 31,* 93–105.

Ginsburg, H. P., & Opper, S. (1979). *Piaget's theory of intellectual development.* Englewood Cliffs, NJ: Prentice Hall.

Giscombé, C. L., & Lobel, M. (2005). Explaining disproportionately high rates of adverse birth outcomes among African Americans: The impact of stress, racism, and related factors in pregnancy. *Psychological Bulletin, 131,* 662–683.

Gladwell, M. (1998, February 2). The Pima paradox. *The New Yorker,* pp. 44–57.

Glassman, T. J., Dodd, V., Miller, E. M., & Braun, R. E. (2010). Preventing high-risk drinking among college students: A social marketing case study. *Social Marketing Quarterly, 16,* 92–110.

Glauber, J. H., Farber, H. J., & Homer, C. J. (2001). Asthma clinical pathways: Toward what end? *Pediatrics, 107,* 590–592.

Godfrey, J. R., & Meyers, D. (2009). Toward optimal health: Maternal benefits on breastfeeding. *Journal of Women's Health, 18,* 1307–1310.

Goldbaum, S., Craig, W. M., Pepler, D., & Connolly, J. (2003). Developmental trajectories of victimization: Identifying risk and protective factors. *Journal of Applied School Psychology, 19,* 139–156.

Goldberg, A. E. (2010). *Lesbian and gay parents and their children.* Washington, DC: American Psychological Association.

Goldberg, M. C., Maurer, D., & Lewis, T. L. (2001). Developmental changes in attention: The effects of endogenous cueing and of distracters. *Developmental Science, 4,* 209–219.

Goldberg, P. H. (1968). Are women prejudiced against women? *Transaction, 5,* 28–30.

Goldfield, B. A., & Reznick, J. S. (1990). Early lexical acquisition: Rate, content and the vocabulary spurt. *Journal of Child Language, 17,* 171–183.

Goldin-Meadow, S. (2009). Using the hands to study how children learn language. In J. Colombo, L. Freund, & P. McCardle (Eds.), *Infant pathways to language: Methods, models, and research disorders* (pp. 195–210). New York, NY: Psychology Press.

Goldman, B. D., & Buysse, V. (2007). Friendships in very young children. In *Contemporary perspectives on socialization and social development in early childhood education,* 165–192. New York: IAP.

Goldscheider, F., & Goldscheider, C. (1999). *The changing transition to adulthood: Leaving and returning home.* Thousand Oaks, CA: Sage.

Goldsmith, H. H. (2009). Genetics of emotional development. In R. J. Davidson, K. R. Scherer, & H. H. Goldsmith (Eds.), *Handbook of affective sciences* (pp. 300–319). New York, NY: Oxford University Press.

Goldstein, T. R., & Winner, E. (2012). Enhancing empathy and theory of mind. *Journal of Cognition and Development, 13*(1), 19–37.

Goleman, D. (1997). *Emotional intelligence.* New York, NY: Bantam.

Gosden, R. G. (2007). Menopause. In J. E. Birren, *Encyclopedia of gerontology: Age, aging, and the aged* (2nd ed., pp. 151–158). San Diego, CA: Academic Press.

Goode, E. (1999, May 20). Study finds TV trims Fiji girls' body image and eating habits. *The New York Times,* p. A1.

Goodwin, C. J. (2009). *Research in psychology: Methods and design.* New York, NY: Wiley.

Gooren, L. J. (2003). Androgen deficiency in the aging male: Benefits and risks of androgen supplementation. *Journal of Steroid Biochemistry and Molecular Biology, 85,* 349–355.

Goossens, L., & Luyckx, K. (2007). Belgium. In J. J. Arnett, U. Gielen, R. Ahmed, B. Nsamenang, T. S. Saraswathi, & R. Silbereisen (Eds.), *International encyclopedia of adolescence* (pp. 64–76). New York, NY: Routledge.

Gopnik, A., & Astington, J. W. (1998). Children's understanding of representational change and its relation to the understanding of false belief and the appearance–reality distinction. *Child Development, 59,* 26–37.

Gopnik, A., Meltzoff, A. N., & Kuhl, P. K. (1999). *The scientist in the crib: Minds, brains, and how children learn.* New York, NY: William Morrow.

Gordon-Larsen, P., Nelson, M. C., & Popkin, B. M. (2004). Longitudinal physical activity and sedentary behavior trends: Adolescence to adulthood. *American Journal of Preventative Medicine, 27,* 277–283.

Gorman, T. E., Ahern, S. P., Wiseman, J., & Skrobik, Y. (2005). Residents' end-of-life decision making with adult hospitalized patients: A review of the literature. *Academic Medicine, 80,* 622–633.

Gott, M., & Hinchliff, S. (2003). How important is sex in later life? The views of older people. *Social Science and Medicine, 56,* 1617–1628.

Gott, M., Seymour, J., Bellamy, G., Clark, D., & Ahmedzai, S. (2004). Older people's views about home as a place of care at the end of life. *Palliative Medicine, 18,* 460–467.

Gottesman, I. I. (1994). *Schizophrenia genetics: The origins of madness.* New York, NY: Freeman.

Gottesman, I. I. (2004). Postscript: Eyewitness to maturation. In L. E. DiLalla (Ed.), *Behavior genetics principles.* Washington, DC: American Psychological Association.

Gottfredson, G. D., Jones, E. M., & Holland, J. L. (1993). Personality and vocational interests: The relation of Holland's six interest dimensions to five robust dimensions of personality. *Journal of Counseling Psychology, 40,* 518–524.

Gottfredson, M., & Hirschi, T. (1990). *A general theory of crime.* Stanford, CA: Stanford University Press.

Gottlieb, A. (2000). Luring your child into this life: A Beng path for infant care. In J. DeLoache & A. Gottlieb (Eds.), *A world of babies: Imagined childcare guides for seven societies* (pp. 55–89). New York, NY: Cambridge University Press.

Gottlieb, G. (2004). Normally occurring environmental and behavioral influences on gene activity. In C. G. Coll, E. L. Bearer, & R. M. Lerner (Eds.), *Nature and nature: The complex interplay of genetic and environmental influences on human behavior and development* (pp. 85–106). Mahwah, NJ: Erlbaum.

Gottlieb, G., & Lickliter, R. (2007) Probabilistic epigenesis. *Developmental Science, 10,* 1–11.

Gottman, J. M., & Levenson, R. W. (2000). The timing of divorce: Predicting when a couple will divorce over a 14-year period. *Journal of Marriage and the Family, 62,* 737–745.

Gottman, J. M., & Silver, N. (1999). *The seven principles for making marriages work.* New York, NY: Crown.

Gould, S. J. (1981). *The mismeasure of man.* New York, NY: Norton.

Grabe, S., Hyde, J. S., & Lindberg, S. M. (2007). Body objectification and depression in adolescents: The role of gender, shame, and rumination. *Psychology of Women Quarterly, 31,* 164–175.

Graber, J. A., Lewinsohn, P. M., Seeley, J. R., & Brooks-Gunn, J. (1997). Is psychopathology associated with the timing of pubertal development? *Journal of the American Academy of Child and Adolescent Psychiatry, 36,* 1768–1776.

Graber, J. A., Seeley, J. R., Brooks-Gunn, J., & Lewinsohn, P. M. (2004). Is pubertal timing associated with psychopathology in young adulthood? *Journal of the American Academy of Child & Adolescent Psychiatry, 43,* 718–726.

Grady, D. (2006). Management of menopausal symptoms. *New England Journal of Medicine, 355,* 2338–2347.

Graham, M. J., Larsen, U., & Xu, X. (1999). Secular trend in age of menarche in China: A case study of two rural counties in Anhui province. *Journal of Biosocial Science, 31,* 257–267.

Gralinski, J. H., & Kopp, C. B. (1993). Everyday rules for behavior: Mothers' requests to young children. *Developmental Psychology, 29,* 573–584.

Granic, I., Dishion, T. J., & Hollerstein, T. (2003). The family ecology of adolescence: A dynamic systems perspective on normative development. In G. R. Adams & M. D. Berzonsky (Eds.), *Blackwell handbook of adolescence* (pp. 60–91). Malden, MA: Blackwell.

Gratton, M. A., & Vasquez, A. E. (2003). Age-related hearing loss: Current research. *Current Opinion in Otolaryngology—Head and Neck Surgery, 11,* 367–371.

Gray, C., Ferguson, J., Behan, S., Dunbar, C., Dunn, J., & Mitchell, D. (2007). Developing young readers through the linguistic phonics approach. *International Journal of Early Years Education, 15,* 15–33.

Gray, E., Khoo, S. E., & Reimondos, A. (2012). Participation in different types of volunteering at young, middle and older adulthood. *Journal of Population Research, 29*(4), 373–398.

Gray, W. N., Simon, S. L., Janicke, D. M., & Dumont-Driscoll, M. (2011). Moderators of weight-based stigmatization among youth who are overweight and non-overweight: The role of gender, race, and body dissatisfaction. *Journal of Developmental & Behavioral Pediatrics, 32*(2), 110–116.

Graziano, A. M., & Hamblen, J. L. (1996). Subabusive violence in child rearing in middle-class American families. *Pediatrics, 98,* 845–848.

Green, E. G. T., Deschamps, J.-C., & Paez, D. (2005). Variation of individualism and collectivism within and between 20 countries:

A typological analysis. *Journal of Cross-Cultural Psychology, 36,* 321–339.

Greenberger, E., & Steinberg, L. (1986). *When teenagers work: The psychological social costs of adolescent employment.* New York, NY: Basic Books.

Greenfield, E., & Marks, N. (2007). Continuous participation in voluntary groups as a protective factor for the psychological well-being of adults who develop functional limitations: Evidence from the National Survey of Families and Households. *Journal of Gerontology: Social Sciences, 62B,* S60–S68.

Greenfield, P. M. (2005). Paradigms of cultural thought. In K. J. Holyoak, & R. G. Morrison (Eds.), *The Cambridge Handbook of Thinking and Reasoning* (pp. 663–682). New York, NY: Cambridge University Press.

Greenwood, V. (2011). Why are asthma rates soaring? *Scientific American,* March 22. Retrieved from http://www.scientificameri-can.com/article/why-are-asthma-rates-soaring/

Gregg, E. W., Cheng, Y. J., Narayan, K. M. V., Thompson, T. J., & Williamson, D. F. (2007). The relative contributions of different levels of overweight and obesity to the increased prevalence of diabetes in the United States: 1976–2004. *Preventative Medicine: An International Journal Devoted to Practice and Theory, 45,* 348–352.

Greve, T. (2003). Norway: The breastfeeding top of the world. *Midwifery Today International, 67,* 57–59.

Griffith, G. (2007). *Older drivers: A review of licensing requirements and research findings.* Retrieved from http://www.parliament.nsw.gov.au/prod/parlment/publications.nsf/0/EFE9D4AB5C456905CA257376000D7777/$File/Older%20drivers%20final%20&%20INDEX.pdf

Grigorenko, E. (2003). Intraindividual fluctuations in intellectual functioning: Selected links between nutrition and the mind. In R. Sternberg & J. Lautrey (Eds.), *Models of intelligence: International perspectives.* Washington, DC: American Psychological Association.

Grigorenko, E. L., Lipka, J., Meier, E., Mohatt, G., Sternberg, R. J., & Yanez, E. (2004). Academic and practical intelligence: A case study of the Yup'ik in Alaska. *Learning and Individual Differences, 14,* 183–207.

Grigorenko, E. L., & O'Keefe, P. A. (2004). What do children do when they cannot go to school? In R. J. Sternberg & E. L. Grigorenko (Eds.), *Culture and competence: Contexts of life success* (pp. 23–53). Washington, DC: American Psychological Association.

Grilo, C. M., & Mitchell, J. E. (Eds.). (2010). *The treatment of eating disorders: A clinical handbook.* New York, NY: Guilford.

Grimshaw, G. S., & Wilson, M. S. (2013). A sinister plot? Facts, beliefs, and stereotypes about the left-handed personality. *Laterality: Asymmetries of Body, Brain and Cognition, 18,* 135–151.

Grimsley, K. D. (2000, April 3). Family a priority for young workers: Survey finds change in men's thinking. *The Washington Post,* pp. E1–2.

Gripsrud, J. (2007). Television and the European public sphere. *European Journal of Communication, 22,* 479–492.

Grolnick, W. S., McMenamy, J. M., & Kurowski, C. O. (2006). Emotional self-regulation in infancy and toddlerhood. In L. Balter & C. S. Tamis-Lamonda (Eds.), *Child psychology: A book of contemporary issues* (pp. 3–25). New York, NY: Psychology Press.

Gross, D. (2008). *Infancy (3rd ed.)* Upper Saddle River, NJ: Prentice Hall.

Grossman, K. E., Grossman, K., and Waters, E. (Eds.). (2005). *Attachment from infancy to adulthood: The major longitudinal studies.* New York, NY: Guilford.

Grotevant, H. D., & Adams, G. R. (1984). Development of an objective measure to assess ego identity in adolescence: Validation and replication. *Journal of Youth and Adolescence, 13,* 419–438.

Grunbaum, A. (2006). Is Sigmund Freud's psychoanalytic edifice relevant to the 21st century? *Psychoanalytic Psychology, 23,* 257–284.

Grundy, E., & Henretta, J. (2006). Between elderly parents and adult children: A new look at the intergenerational care provided by the "sandwich generation." *Ageing & Society, 26,* 707–722.

Grünebaum, A., et al. (2013). Apgar score of 0 at 5 minutes and neonatal seizures or serious neurologic dysfunction in relation to birth setting. *American Journal of Obstetrics and Gynecology, 323,* e1-e6.

Grünebaum, A., et al. (2014). Early and total neonatal mortality in relation to birth setting in the United States, 2006-09. *American Journal of Obstetrics and Gynecology, 324.* doi: 10.1016/j.ajog.2014.03.047

Grunier, A., Vincent, M., Weitzen, S., Truchil, R., Teno, J., & Roy, J. (2007). Where people die: A multilevel approach to understanding influence on site of death in America. *Medical Care Research & Review, 64,* 351–378.

Gu, D., Reynolds, K., Wu, N., Chen, J., Duan, X., Reynolds, R. F., et al. (InterASIA Collaborative Group) (2005). Prevalence of the metabolic syndrome and overweight among adults in China. *Lancet, 365,* 1398–1405.

Guasti, M. T. (2000). An excursion into interrogatives in early English and Italian. In M. A. Friedemann & L. Rizzi (Eds.), *The acquisition of syntax* (pp. 105–128). Harlow, England: Longman.

Guay, F., Chanal, J., Ratelle, C. F., Marsh, H. W., Larose, S., & Boivin, M. (2010). Intrinsic, identified, and controlled types of motivation for school subjects in young elementary school children. *British Journal of Educational Psychology, 80,* 711–735.

Gubler, M., Arnold, J., & Coombs, C. (2014). Reassessing the protean career concept: Empirical findings, conceptual components, and measurement. *Journal of Organizational Behavior, 35,* S23-S40.

Guernsey, L. (2007). *Into the minds of babes: How screen time affects children from birth to age 5.* New York, NY: Perseus.

Guerreiro, M. J. S., Murphy, D. R., & Van Gerven, P. W. M. (2010). The role of sensory modality in age-related distraction: A critical review and a renewed view. *Psychological Bulletin, 136,* 975–1022.

Guest, A. M. (2007). Cultures of childhood and psychosocial characteristics: Self-esteem and social comparison in two distinct communities. *Ethos, 35,* 1–32.

Guillaume, M., & Lissau, I. (2002). Epidemiology. In W. Burniat, T. Cole, I. Lissau, & E. M. E. Poskitt (Eds.), *Child and adolescent obesity: Causes and consequences, prevention and management* (pp. 28–49). Cambridge, MA: Cambridge University Press.

Guise, J. M. F., & Gill, J. S. (2007). "Binge drinking? It's good, it's harmless fun": A discourse analysis of female undergraduate drinking in Scotland. *Health Education Research, 22,* 895–906.

Gump, B., & Matthews, K. (2000, March). *Annual vacations, health, and death.* Paper presented at the meeting of American Psychosomatic Society, Savannah, GA.

Gunnoe, M. L., & Mariner, C. L. (1997). Toward a developmental–contextual model of the effects of parental spanking on children's aggression. *Archives of Pediatrics and Adolescent Medicine, 151,* 768–775.

Gupta, S., & Naskar, A. (2013). Euthanasia: An Indian and international perspective. *ZENITH International Journal of Multidisciplinary Research, 3(7),* 15–24.

Gureje, O., Ogunniyi, A., Baiyewu, O., Price, B., Unverzagt, F. W., & Evans, R. M. (2006). APOE epsilon4 is not associated with Alzheimer's disease in elderly Nigerians. *Annals of Neurology, 59,* 182–185.

Gutmann, D. L., & Huych, M. H. (1994). Development and psychology in post-parental men: A community study. In E. Thompson, Jr. (Ed.), *Older men's lives* (pp. 65–84). Thousand Oaks, CA: Sage.

Guyer, B. (2000). *ADHD.* Boston, MA: Allyn & Bacon.

Haan, M. d., & Matheson, A. (2009). The development and neural bases of processing emotion in faces and voices. In M. d. H. & M. R. Gunnar, *Handbook of developmental social neuroscience* (pp. 107–121). New York, NY: Guilford.

Haberkern, K., & Szydlik, M. (2010). State care provision, societal opinion and children's care of older parents in 11 European countries. *Ageing & Society, 30,* 299–323.

Hack, M., Taylor, G., Drotar, D., Schluchter, M., Cartar, L., Wilson-Costello, D.,…Morrow, M. (2005). Poor predictive validity of the Bayley Scales of Infant Development for cognitive function of extremely low birth weight children at school age. *Pediatrics, 116,* 333–341.

Hacker, J. (2002). *The divided welfare state: The battle over public and private social benefits in the United States.* New York, NY: Cambridge University Press.

Hadjikhani, N., Chabris, C. F., Joseph, R. M., Clark, J., McGrath, L., Aharon, L.,…Harris, G. J. (2004). Early visual cortex organization in autism: An fMRI study. *Neuroreport: For Rapid Communication of Neuroscience Research, 15,* 267–270.

Haffner, W. H. J. (2007). Development before birth. In M. L. Batshaw, L. Pellegrino, & N. J. Roizen (Eds.), *Children with disabilities* (pp. 23–33). Baltimore, MD: Paul H Brookes.

Hagen, J., & Hale, G. (1973). The development of attention in children. In A. Pick (Ed.), *Minnesota symposium on child psychology* (Vol. 7, pp. 117–140). Minneapolis, MN: University of Minnesota Press.

Häggström-Nordin, E., Hanson, U., & Tyden, T. (2006). Associations between pornography consumption and sexual practices among adolescents in Sweden. *International Journal of STD & AIDS, 16,* 102–107.

Hahn, B., Ross, T. J., Wolkenberg, F. A., Shakleya, D. M., Huestis, M. A., & Stein, E. A. (2009). Performance effects of nicotine during selective attention, divided attention, and simple stimulus detection: An fMRI study. *Cerebral Cortex, 19,* 1990–2000.

Hahn, E. A., & Lachman, M. E. (2014). Everyday experiences of memory problems and control: the adaptive role of selective optimization with compensation in the context of memory decline. *Aging, Neuropsychology, and Cognition,* 1–17.

Haidt, J., Koller, S. H., & Dias, M. G. (1993). Affect, culture, and morality, or is it wrong to eat your dog? *Journal of Personality and Social Psychology, 65,* 613–628.

Haines, C. J., Xing, S-M., Park, K-H., Holinka, C. F., & Ausmanas, M. K. (2005). Prevalence of menopausal symptoms in different ethnic groups of Asian women and responsiveness to therapy with three doses of conjugated estrogens/medroxyprogesterone acetate: The Pan-Asia menopause (PAM) study. *Maturitas, 52,* 264–276.

Hakuta, K. (1999). The debate on bilingual education. *Developmental and Behavioral Pediatrics, 20,* 36–37.

Hale, C. M., & Tager-Flusberg, H. (2005). Social communication with children with autism: The relationship between theory of mind and discourse development. *Autism, 9,* 157–178.

Halford, G. S. (2005). Development of thinking. In K. J. Holyoak & Robert G. Morrison (Eds.), *The Cambridge handbook of thinking and reasoning* (pp. 529–558). New York, NY: Cambridge University Press.

Halgunseth, L. C., Ispa, J. M., & Rudy, D. (2006). Parental control in Latino families: An integrated review of the literature. *Child Development, 77,* 1282–1297.

Hall, D. T., & Mirvis, P. H. (1996). The new protean career: Psychological success and the path with a heart. In D. T. Hall (Ed.), *The career is dead—Long live the career: A relational approach to the career* (pp. 15–45). San Francisco, CA: Jossey-Bass.

Hall, K., Murrell, J., Ogunniyi, A., Deeg, M., Baiyewu, O., & Gao, S. (2006). Cholesterol, *APOE* genotype, and Alzheimer disease: An epidemiologic study of Nigerian Yoruba. *Neurology, 66,* 223–227.

Hall, R. L. (2007). On the move: Exercise, leisure activities, and midlife women. In V. Muhlbauer & J. C. Chrisler (Eds.), *Women over 50: Psychological perspectives* (pp. 79–94). New York, NY: Springer.

Halpern, D. F. (2000). Sex differences in cognitive abilities (3rd ed.)., Mahwah, NJ: Lawrence Erlbaum.

Halman, L., & Draulans, V. (2006). How secular is Europe? *British Journal of Sociology, 57,* 264–288.

Halpern, S. (1998). *The forgotten half revisited: American youth and young families, 1988–2008.* Washington, DC: American Youth Policy Forum.

Hämäläinen, J., Poikolainen, K., Isometsa, E., Kaprio, J., Heikkinen, M., Lindermman, S., & Aro, H. (2005). Major depressive episode related to long unemployment and frequent alcohol intoxication. *Nordic Journal of Psychiatry, 59,* 486–491.

Hamilton, S. F., & Hamilton, M. A. (2000). Research, intervention, and social change: Improving adolescents' career opportunities. In L. J. Crockett & R. K. Silbereisen (Eds.), *Negotiating adolescence in times of social change* (pp. 267–283). New York, NY: Cambridge University Press.

Hamilton, S., & Hamilton, M. A. (2006). School, work, and emerging adulthood. In J. J. Arnett & J. L. Tanner (Eds.), *Coming of age in the 21st century: The lives and contexts of emerging adults* (pp. 257–277). Washington, DC: American Psychological Association.

Hammack, P., & Cohler, B. (2009). *The story of sexual identity: Narrative perspectives on the gay and lesbian life course.* New York, NY: Oxford University Press.

Hammer, J. C., Fisher, J. D., Fitzgerald, P., & Fisher, W. A. (1996). When two heads aren't better than one: AIDS risk behavior in college-age couples. *Journal of Applied Social Psychology, 26,* 375–397.

Han, C. (2011). Embitterment in Asia: Losing face, inequality, and alienation under historical and modern perspectives. In M. Linden & A. Maercker (Eds.), *Embitterment: Societal, psychological, and clinical perspectives* (pp. 168–176). New York, NY: Springer.

Haninger, K., & Thompson, K. M. (2004). Content and ratings of teen rated video games. *JAMA: Journal of the American Medical Association, 291,* 856–865.

Hank, K. (2011). Societal determinants of productive aging: A multilevel analysis across 11 European countries. *European sociological review, 27*(4), 526–541.

Hannon, T. S., Rao, G., & Arslanian, S. A. (2005). Childhood obesity and Type 2 diabetes mellitus. *Pediatrics, 116,* 473–480.

Hanson, R., & Hayslip, B. (2000). Widowhood in later life. In J. Harvey & E. Miller (Eds.), *Loss and trauma: General and close relationship perspectives.* New York, NY: Brunner-Routledge.

Harden, K. P., & Mendle, J. (2012). Gene-environment interplay in the association between pubertal timing and delinquency in adolescent girls. *Journal of Abnormal Psychology, 121*(1), 73.

Hardman, C. E. (2000). *Other worlds: Notions of self and emotion among the Lohorung Rai.* New York, NY: Berg.

Hardy, M. (2006). Older workers. In R. Binstock & L. George (Eds.), *Handbook of aging and the social sciences* (6th ed., pp. 201–218). New York, NY: Academic Press.

Harkness, S., Mavridis, C. J., Liu, J. J., & Super, C. (2015). Parental ethnotheories and the development of family relationships in early and middle childhood. In L. A. Jensen (Ed.), *Oxford handbook of human development and culture: An interdisciplinary perspective.* New York, NY: Oxford University Press.

Harkness, S., Super, C. M., & van Tijen, N. (2000). Individualism and the "Western mind" reconsidered: American and Dutch parents' ethnotheories of the child. In S. Harkness & C. Raeff (Eds.), *Variability in the social construction of the child* (pp. 23–39). San Francisco, CA: Jossey-Bass.

Harlow, H. F. (1958). The nature of love. *American Psychologist, 13,* 673–685.

Harman, D. (2006). Alzheimer's disease pathogenesis: Role of aging. *Annals of the New York Academy of Sciences, 1067,* 454–460.

Harnad, S. (2012). *Lateralization in the nervous system.* New York, NY: Academic Press.

Harris, G. (2002). *Grandparenting: How to meet its responsibilities.* Los Angeles: The Americas Group.

Hart, B., & Risley, T. R. (1999). *The social world of children learning to talk*. Baltimore, MD: Paul H. Brookes.

Hart, C. H., Burts, D. C., Durland, M. A., Charlesworth, R., DeWolf, M., & Fleege, P. O. (1998). Stress behaviors and activity type participation of preschoolers in more and less developmentally appropriate classrooms: SES and sex differences. *Journal of Research in Childhood Education, 12,* 176–196.

Hart, C. H., Newell, L. D., & Olsen, S. F. (2003). Parenting skills and social-communicative competence in childhood. In J. O. Greene & B. R. Burleson (Eds.), *Handbook of communication and social interaction skills* (pp. 753–797). Mahwah, NJ: Erlbaum.

Hart, D., & Atkins, R. (2004). Religious participation and the development of moral identity in adolescence. In T. A. Thorkildsen & H. J. Walberg (Eds.), *Nurturing morality* (pp. 157–172). New York, NY: Kluwer.

Hart, D., Southerland, N., & Atkins, R. (2003). Community service and adult development. In J. Demick & C. Andreoletti (Eds.), *Handbook of adult development* (pp. 585–597). New York, NY: Kluwer.

Hart, H. M., McAdams, D. P., Hirsch, B. J., & Bauer, J. J. (2001). Generativity and social involvement among African Americans and White adults. *Journal of Research in Personality, 35,* 208–230.

Harter, S. (1990a). Processes underlying adolescent self-concept formation. In R. Montemayor, G. R. Adams, & T. P. Gullotta (Eds.), *From childhood to adolescence: A transitional period?* Newbury Park, CA: Sage.

Harter, S. (1990b). Self and identity development. In S. S. Feldman & G. R. Elliott (Eds.), *At the threshold: The developing adolescent* (pp. 352–387). Cambridge, MA: Harvard University Press.

Harter, S. (1999). *The construction of the self: A developmental perspective.* New York, NY: Guilford.

Harter, S. (2003). The development of self-representations during childhood and adolescence. In M. R. Leary & J. P. Tangney (Eds.), *Handbook of self and identity* (pp. 610–642). New York, NY: Guilford.

Harter, S. (2006a). The development of self-esteem. In M. H. Kernis (Ed.), *Self-esteem issues and answers: A sourcebook of current perspectives* (pp. 144–150). New York, NY: Psychology Press.

Harter, S. (2006b). The self. In W. Damon & R. Lerner (Eds.), & N. Eisenberg (Vol. Ed.), *Handbook of child psychology: Vol. 3. Social, emotional and personality development* (6th ed., pp. 505–570). New York, NY: Wiley.

Harter, S. (2012). The construction of the self: *Developmental and sociocultural foundations.* New York: Guilford.

Harter, S., Waters, P. L., & Whitesell, N. R. (1997). Lack of voice as a manifestation of false-self behavior among adolescents: The school setting as a stage upon which the drama of authenticity is enacted. *Educational Psychologist, 32,* 153–173.

Hartos, J. L., Simons-Morton, B. G., Beck, K. H., & Leaf, W. A. (2005). Parent-imposed limits on high-risk adolescent driving: Are they stricter with graduated driver licensing? *Accident Analysis & Prevention, 37,* 557–562.

Hartup, W. W. (1996). The company they keep: Friendships and their developmental significance. *Child Development, 67,* 1–13.

Hartup, W. W., & Abecassis, M. (2004). Friends and enemies. In P. K. Smith & C. H. Hart (Eds.), *Blackwell handbook of childhood social development* (pp. 285–306). Malden, MA: Blackwell.

Harvard School of Public Health/MetLife Foundation. (2004). *Reinventing aging: Baby boomers and civic engagement.* Cambridge, MA: Harvard School of Public Health, Center for Health Communication.

Harvard Mental Health Letter (HMHL) (2005). The treatment of attention deficit disorder: New evidence. *Harvard Mental Health Letter, 21,* 6.

Harvey, J. H., & Fine, M. A. (2004). *Children of divorce: Stories of loss and growth.* Mahwah, NJ: Lawrence Erlbaum Associates.

Harvey, J., & Weber, A. (2002). *Odyssey of the heart: Close relationships in the 21st century* (2nd ed.). Mahwah, NJ: Lawrence Erlbaum.

Harwood, J. (2001). Comparing grandchildren's and grandparents' stake in their relationship. *International Journal of Aging and Human Development, 53,* 195–210.

Harwood, R., Leyendecker, B., Carlson, V., Asencio, M., & Miller, A. (2002). Parenting among Latino families in the U.S. In M. H. Bornstein (Ed.), *Handbook of parenting, Vol. 4. Social conditions and applied parenting* (2nd ed., pp. 21–46). Mahwah, NJ: Erlbaum.

Hasebrink, U. (2007a). Computer use, international. In J. J. Arnett (Ed.), *Encyclopedia of children, adolescents, and the media* (pp. 207–210). Thousand Oaks, CA: Sage.

Hasebrink, U. (2007b). Television, international viewing patterns and. In J. J. Arnett (Ed.), *Encyclopedia of children, adolescents, and the media* (pp. 808–810). Thousand Oaks, CA: Sage.

Hasher, L. (2003, February 28). Commentary in "The wisdom of the wizened." *Science, 299,* 1300–1302.

Hasher, L., Goldstein, F., & May, C. (2005). It's about time: Circadian rhythms, memory, and aging. In C. Izawa & N. Ohta (Eds.), *Human learning and memory: Advances in theory and application* (Vol. 18, pp. 179–186). Mahwah, NJ: Lawrence Erlbaum Associates.

Hasher, L., Zachs, R. T., & May, C. P. (1999). Inhibitory control, circadian arousal, and age. In D. Gopher & A. Koriat (Eds.), *Attention and performance* (Vol. 17, pp. 653–675).

Hassett, J. M., Siebert, E. R., & Wallen, K. (2008). Sex differences in rhesus monkey toy preference parallel those of children. *Hormones and Behavior, 54,* 359–364.

Hassold, T. J., & Patterson, D. (Eds.) (1999). *Down syndrome: A promising future, together.* New York, NY: Wiley-Liss.

Hastings, P. D., McShane, K. E., Parker, R., & Ladha, F. (2007). Ready to make nice: Parental socialization of young sons' and daughters' prosocial behaviors with peers. *The Journal of Genetic Psychology: Research and Theory on Human Development, 168,* 177–200.

Hatch, L. R., & Bulcroft, K. (2004). Does long-term marriage bring less frequent disagreements? *Journal of Family Issues, 25,* 465–495.

Hatfield, E., & Rapson, R. L. (2005). *Love and sex: Cross-cultural perspectives* (2nd edition). Boston, MA: Allyn & Bacon.

Hatfield, E., & Rapson, R. L. (1996). *Love and sex: Cross-cultural perspectives.* Boston, MA: Allyn & Bacon.

Haub, C. (2013). *Rising trend of births outside marriage.* Washington, DC: Population Reference Bureau. Retrieved from http://www.prb.org/Publications/Articles/2013/nonmarital-births.aspx

Haugaard, J. L., & Hazan, C. (2004). Recognizing and treating uncommon behavioral and emotional disorders in children and adolescents who have been severely maltreated: Reactive attachment disorder. *Child Maltreatment, 9,* 154–160.

Hautala, L. A., Junnila, J., Helenius, H., Vaananen, A.-M., Liuksila, P.-R., Raiha, H., et al. (2008). Towards understanding gender differences in disordered eating among adolescents. *Journal of Clinical Nursing, 17,* 1803–1813.

Hawkins, A. J., Lovejoy, K. R., Holmes, E. K., Blanchard, V. L., & Fawcett, E. (2008). Increasing fathers' involvement in child care with a couple–focused intervention during the transition to parenthood. *Family Relations, 57,* 49–59.

Hawkins, D. L., Pepler, D. J., & Craig, W. M. (2001). Naturalistic observations of peer intervention in bullying. *Social Development, 10,* 512–527.

Hay, D., Payne, A., & Chadwick, A. (2004). Peer relations in childhood. *Journal of Child Psychology & Psychiatry & Allied Disciplines, 45,* 84–108.

Hayashi, A., Karasawa, M., & Tobin, J. (2009). The Japanese preschool's pedagogy of feeling: Cultural strategies for supporting young children's emotional development. *Ethos, 37,* 32–49.

Hayflick, L. (1965). The limited in vitro lifetime of human diploid cell strains. *Experimental Cell Research, 37,* 614–636.

Hayflick, L. (1998). How and why we age. *Experimental Gerontology, 33*, 639–653.

Hayflick, L. (2004). Anti-aging is an oxymoron. *Journal of Gerontology: Biological Sciences, 59A*, B573–B578.

Haynie, D. L., & Osgood, D. W. (2005). Reconsidering peers and delinquency: How do peers matter? *Social Forces, 84*, 1109–1130.

Hayslip, B., & Hansson, R. (2003). Death awareness and adjustment across the life span. In C. D. Bryant (Ed.), *Handbook of death and dying* (pp. 437–447). Thousand Oaks, CA: Sage.

Haywood, K. M., & Getchell, N. (2001). *Life span motor development* (3rd ed.). Champaign, IL: Human Kinetics.

Hebblethwaite, S., & Norris, J. (2011). Expressions of generativity through family leisure: Experiences of grandparents and adult grandchildren. *Family Relations: An Interdisciplinary Journal of Applied Family Studies, 60*, 121–133.

Heckhausen, J., & Tomasik, M. J. (2002). Get an apprenticeship before school is out: How German adolescents adjust vocational aspirations when getting close to a developmental deadline. *Journal of Vocational Behavior, 60*, 199–219.

Hedberg, K., Hopkins, D., & Kohn, M. (2003). Five years of legal physician-assisted suicide in Oregon. *New England Journal of Medicine, 348*, 961–964.

Hedge, J. W., Borman, W. C., & Lammlein, S. E. (2006). *The aging workforce: Realities, myths, and implications for organizations.* Washington, DC: American Psychological Association.

Hedlund, J., & Compton, R. (2005). Graduated driver licensing research in 2004 and 2005. *Journal of Safety Research, 36*, 109–119.

Hedner, J., Grote, L., & Zou, D. (2008). Pharmacological treatment of sleep apnea: Current situation and future. *Sleep Medicine Reviews, 12*, 33–47.

Hein, K. (1988). *Issues in adolescent health: An overview.* Washington, DC: Carnegie Council on Adolescent Development.

Heine, S. H., Lehman, D. R., Markus, H. R., & Kitayama, S. (1999). Is there a universal need for positive self-regard? *Psychological Review, 106*, 766–794.

Helgeson, V. (2002). *The psychology of gender.* Upper Saddle River, NJ: Prentice Hall.

Helson, R., Jones, C. J., & Kwan, V. S. Y. (2002). Personality change over 40 years of adulthood: Hierarchical linear modeling analyses of two longitudinal samples. *Journal of Personality and Social Psychology, 83*, 752–766.

Helwig, C. C. (2008). The moral judgment of the child reevaluated: Heteronomy, early morality, and reasoning about social justice and inequalities. In C. Wainryb, J. G. Smetana, & E. Turiel (Eds.), *Social development, social inequalities, and social justice* (pp. 27–51). New York, NY: Taylor & Francis Group.

Helzner, E. P., Cauley, J. A., Pratt, S. R., Wisniewski, S. R., Zmuda, J. M., Talbott,…Newman, A. B. (2005). Race and sex differences in age-related hearing loss: The Health, Aging, and Body Composition Study. *Journal of the American Geriatrics Society, 53*, 2119–2127.

Hellquist, B. N., Duffy, S. W., Abdsaleh, S., Björneld, L., Bordás, P., Tabár, L.,…Jonsson, H. (2011). Effectiveness of population-based service screening with mammography for women ages 40 to 49 years. *Cancer, 117*, 714–722.

Hendricks, J., & Cutler, S. J. (2004). Volunteerism and socioemotional selectivity in later life. *Journal of Gerontology, 59B*, S251–S257.

Henggeler, S. W. (2011). Efficacy studies to large-scale transport: The development and validation of multisystemic therapy programs. *Annual Review of Clinical Psychology 7*, 351–381.

Henggeler, S. W., Sheidow, A. J., & Lee, T. (2007). Multisystemic treatment of serious clinical problems in youths and their families. In D. W. Springer & A. R. Roberts (Eds.), *Handbook of forensic mental health with victims and offenders: Assessment, treatments, and research* (pp. 315–345). New York, NY: Springer.

Henrichs, J., Schenk, J. J., Barendregt, C. S., Schmidt, H. G., Steegers, E. A. P., Hofman, A.,…Tiemeier, H. (2010). Fetal growth from mid- to late pregnancy is associated with infant development: The Generation R study. *Developmental Medicine & Child Neurology, 52*, 644–651.

Henry, J., Helm, H. W., Jr., & Cruz, N. (2013). Mate selection: Gender and generational differences. *North American Journal of Psychology, 15* (1).

Henry, R., Miller, R., & Giarrusso, R. (2005). Difficulties, disagreements, and disappointments in late-life marriages. *International Journal of Aging & Human Development, 61*, 243–264.

Hensler, B. A., Schatschneider, C., Taylor, J., & Wagner, R. K. (2010). Behavioral genetic approach to the study of dyslexia. *Journal of Developmental and Behavioral Pediatrics, 31*(Special Issue: The genetics and genomics of childhood neurodevelopmental disorders: An update), 525–532.

Hensley, P. (2006). Treatment of bereavement-related depression and traumatic grief. *Journal of Affective Disorders, 92*, 117–124.

Hepper, P. G., Wells, D. L., & Lynch, C. (2005). Prenatal thumb sucking is related to postnatal handedness. *Neuropsychologia, 43*, 313–315.

Herdt, G. (1987). *The Sambia: Ritual and gender in New Guinea.* New York, NY: Holt, Rinehart & Winston.

Herman-Giddens, M., Slora, E., Wasserman, R., Bourdony, C., Bhapkar, M., Koch, G., & Hasemeier, C. (1997). Secondary sexual characteristics and menses in young girls seen in office practice: A study from the Pediatric Research in Office Settings Network. *Pediatrics, 88*, 505–512.

Herman-Giddens, M., Wang, L., & Koch, G. (2001). Secondary sexual characteristics in boys. *Archives of Pediatrics and Adolescent Medicine, 155*, 1022–1028.

Hermans, H. (2015). Human development in today's globalizing world: Implications for self and identity. In L. A. Jensen (Ed.), *Oxford handbook of human development and culture.* New York, NY: Oxford University Press.

Herpetz-Dahlmann, B., Wille, N., Holling, J., Vloet, T. D., Ravens-Sieberer, U. [BELLA study group (Germany)]. (2008). Disordered eating behavior and attitudes, associated psychopathology and health-related quality of life: Results of the BELLA study. *European Child & Adolescent Psychiatry, 17*(Suppl. 1), 82–91.

Herrenkohl, T. I., Mason, W. A., Kosterman, R., Lengua, L. J., Hawkins, J. D., & Abbott, R. D. (2004). Pathways from physical childhood abuse to partner violence in young adulthood. *Violence and Victims, 19*, 123–136.

Herrera, E., Reissland, N., & Shepherd, J. (2004). Maternal touch and maternal child-directed speech: Effects of depressed mood in the postnatal period. *Journal of Affective Disorders, 81*, 29–39.

Heslop, A., & Gorman, M. (2002). *Chronic poverty and older people in the developing world.* Manchester, UK: Chronic Poverty Research Centre.

Hetherington, E. M., & Kelly, J. (2002) *For better or worse: Divorce reconsidered.* New York, NY: Norton.

Hetherington, E. M., & Stanley-Hagan, M. (2002). Parenting in divorced and remarried families. In M. H. Bornstein (Ed.), *Handbook of parenting* (pp. 287–299). Mahwah, NJ: Erlbaum.

Hetherington, E. M., Henderson, S., & Reiss, D. (1999). Adolescent siblings in stepfamilies: Family functioning and adolescent adjustment. *Monographs of the Society for Research in Child Development, 64*(4).

Heuveline, P. (2002). An international comparison of adolescent and young adult morality. *Annals of the American Academy of Political Social Science, 580*, 172–200.

Hewison, M. (2012). An update on vitamin D and human immunity. *Clinical endocrinology, 76*(3), 315–325.

Hewlett, B. S. (2004). Fathers in forager, farmer and pastoral cultures. In M. E. Lamb (Ed.), *The role of the father in child development* (94th ed., pp. 182–195). New York, NY: Wiley.

Hewlett, B. S., & Roulette, J. W. (2014). Cosleeping beyond infancy: Culture, ecology, and evolutionary biology of bed-sharing among Aka foragers and Ngandu farmers in central Africa. In D. Narvaez et al., (Eds.), *Ancestral landscapes in human evolution: Culture, childrearing, and social well-being.* New York, NY: Oxford University Press.

Hewlett, S. (2003). *Creating a life: What every women needs to know about having a baby and a career.* New York, NY: Miramax.

Heyman, G. D., & Legare, C. H. (2004). Children's beliefs about gender differences in the academic and social domains. *Sex Roles, 50,* 227–239.

Hietanen, A., Era, P., Sorri, M., & Heikkinen, E. (2004). Changes in hearing in 80-year-old people: A 10-year follow-up study. *International Journal of Audiology, 43,* 126–135.

Hildreth, K., Sweeney, B., & Rovee-Collier, C. (2003). Differential memory-preserving effects of reminders at 6 months. *Journal of Experimental Child Psychology, 84,* 41–62.

Hildyard, K. L., & Wolfe, D. A. (2002). Child neglect: Developmental issues and outcomes. *Child Abuse and Neglect, 26,* 679–695.

Hill, J., Inder, T., Neil, J., Dierker, D., Harwell, J., & Van Essen, D. (2010). Similar patterns of cortical expansion during human development and evolution. *Proceedings of the National Academy of Sciences, 107,* 13135–13140.

Hill, J., & Lynch, M. (1983). The intensification of gender-related role expectations during early adolescence. In J. Brooks-Gunn & A. Petersen (Eds.), *Girls at puberty: Biological and psychosocial perspectives* (pp. 201–228). New York, NY: Plenum.

Hill, T. D. (2008). Religious involvement and healthy cognitive aging: Patterns, explanations, and future directions. *Journal of Gerontology: Psychological Sciences, 63A,* P478–479.

Hillman, J. L. (2000). *Clinical perspectives on elderly sexuality.* New York, NY: Kluwer Academic.

Hilton, J. M., & Anderson, T. L. (2009). Characteristics of women with children who divorce in midlife compared to those who remain married. *Journal of Divorce & Remarriage, 50,* 309–329.

Hinduja, S., & Patchin, J. W. (2008). Personal information of adolescents on the Internet: A quantitative content analysis of MySpace. *Journal of Adolescence, 31,* 125–146.

Hines, M., Brook, C., & Conway, G. S. (2004). Androgen and psychosexual development: Core gender identity, sexual orientation, and recalled childhood gender role behavior in women and men with congenital adrenal hyperplasia (CAH). *Journal of sex research, 41(1),* 75–81.

Hinojosa, T., Sheu, C.-F., & Michael, G. F. (2003). Infant hand-use preference for grasping objects contributes to the development of a hand-use preference for manipulating objects. *Developmental Psychobiology, 43,* 328–334.

Hirschi, T. (2002). *Causes of delinquency.* Piscataway, NJ: Transaction.

Hiscock, H., & Jordan, B. (2004). Problem crying in infancy. *Medical Journal of Australia, 181,* 507–512.

Hjelmsedt, A., Andersson, L., Skoog-Svanberg, A., Bergh, T., Boivin, J., & Collins, A. (1999). Gender differences in psychological reactions to infertility among couples seeking IVF- and ICSI-treatment. *Acta Obstet Gynecol Scand, 78,* 42–48.

Ho, B., Friedland, J., Rappolt, S., & Noh, S. (2003). Caregiving for relatives with Alzheimer's disease: Feelings of Chinese-Canadian women. *Journal of Aging Studies, 17,* 301–321.

Ho, D. Y. F. (1987). Fatherhood in Chinese culture. In M. E. Lamb (Ed.), *The father's role: Cross-cultural perspectives* (pp. 227–245). Hillsdale, NJ: Erlbaum.

Hochschild, A. R. (1990). *The second shift.* New York, NY: William Morrow.

Hochschild, A. R. (1998). *The time bind: When work becomes home and home becomes work.* New York, NY: Henry Holt.

Hochwarter, W. A., Ferris, G. R., Perrewe, P. L., Witt, L. A., & Kiewitz, C. (2001). A note on the nonlinearity of age–job satisfaction relationship. *Journal of Applied Social Psychology, 31,* 1223–1237.

Hockey, J. L., & Katz, J. (2001). *Grief, mourning and death rituals.* London, UK: McGraw Hill.

Hodapp, R. M., Burke, M. M., & Urdano, R. C. (2012). What's age got to do with it? Implications of maternal age on families of offspring with Down syndrome. In R. M. Hodapp (Ed.), *International review of research in developmental disabilities* (pp. 111–143). New York, NY: Academic Press.

Hodnett, E. D., Gates, S., Hofneyr, G. J., & Sakala, C. (2007). Continuous support for women during childbirth. *Cochrane Database of Systematic Reviews, 3.*

Hofer, K., & Moore, A. S. (2010). *The iconnected parent: Staying close to your kids in college (and beyond) while letting them grow up.* New York, NY: Free Press.

Hoff, E. (2004). The specificity of environmental influence: Socioeconomic status affects early vocabulary development via maternal speech. *Child Development, 74,* 1368–1378.

Hoff, E. (2009). *Language development.* Belmont, CA: Wadsworth.

Hoffman, M. (2007). The origins of empathic morality in toddlerhood. In C. A. Brownell & C. B. Kopp (Eds.), *Socioemotional development in the toddler years* (pp. 132–145). New York, NY: Guilford.

Hoffman, M. L. (2000). *Empathy and moral development.* New York, NY: Cambridge University Press.

Hofman, P. L., Regan, F., Jackson, W. E., Jefferies, C., Knight, D. B., Robinson, E. M., & Cutfield, W. S. (2004). Premature birth and later insulin resistance. *New England Journal of Medicine, 351,* 2179–2186.

Hofmeyr, G. J. (2002). Interventions to help external cephalic version for breech presentation at term. *Cochrane Database of Systematic Reviews, 2,* CD000184.

Hogan, M. C., Foreman, K. J., Naghavi, M., Ahn, S. Y., Wang, M., Makela, S. M.,...Murray, C. J. L. (2010). Maternal mortality for 181 countries, 1980–2008: A systematic analysis of progress toward Millennium Development Goal 5. *The Lancet, 375,* 1–15.

Hogan, M. J. (2003). Divided attention in older but not younger adults is impaired by anxiety. *Experimental Aging Research, 29,* 111–136.

Hogben M., & Williams S. P. (2001). Exploring the context of women's relationship perceptions, sexual behavior, and contraceptive strategies. *Journal of Psychology and Human Sexuality, 13,* 1–20.

Hoge, D. R., Johnson, B., & Luidens, D. A. (1993). Determinants of church involvement of young adults who grew up in the Presbyterian churches. *Journal for the Scientific Study of Religion, 32,* 242–255.

Hoh, J., & Ott, J. (2003). Mathematical multi-locus approaches to localizing complex human trait genes. *Nature Reviews Genetics, 4,* 701–709.

Hokoda, A., Lu, H.-H., A., & Angeles, M. (2006). School bullying in Taiwanese adolescents. *Journal of Emotional Abuse, 64,* 69–90.

Holden, K. C. (2008). The boomers and their economic prospects. In R. B. Hudson (Ed.), *Boomer bust? Economic and political issues of the graying society* (Vol. 1., pp. 63–76). Westport, CT: Praeger.

Holland, J. (1985). *Making vocational choice: A theory of careers* (2nd ed.). Englewood Cliffs, NJ: Prentice Hall.

Holland, J. L. (1987). Current status of Holland's theory of careers: Another perspective. *Career Development Quarterly, 36,* 24–30.

Holland, J. L. (1996). Exploring careers with a typology: What we have learned and some new directions. *American Psychologist, 51,* 397–406.

Holodynski, M. (2009). Milestones and mechanisms of emotional development. *In Emotions as bio-cultural processes* (pp. 139–163). Springer US.

Holsti, L., & Grunau, R. E. (2010). Considerations for using sucrose to reduce procedural pain in preterm infants. *Pediatrics, 125,* 1042–1049.

Holtzen, D. W. (2000). Handedness and professional tennis. *International Journal of Neuroscience, 105,* 101–119.

Honein, M. A., Paulozzi, L. J., Mathews, T. J., Erickson, J. D., & Wong, L. C. (2001). Impact of folic acid fortification of the U.S. food supply on the occurrence of neural tube defects. *The Journal of American Medical Association, 285,* 2981–2986.

Hong, Z.-R., Veach, P. M., & Lawrenz, F. (2003). An investigation of the gender stereotyped thinking of Taiwanese secondary school boys and girls. *Sex Roles, 48,* 495–504.

Hood, B., Cole-Davies, V., & Dias, M. (2003). Looking and search measures of object knowledge in preschool children. *Developmental Psychology, 39,* 61–70.

Hooghe, M., & Wilkenfeld, B. (2008). The stability of political attitudes and behaviors across adolescence and early adulthood: A comparison of survey data on adolescents and young adults in eight countries. *Journal of Youth and Adolescence, 37,* 155–167.

Hook, J. L. (2010). Gender inequality in the welfare state: Sex segregation in housework, 1965–2003. *American Journal of Sociology, 115,* 1480–1523.

Hooyman, N. R., & Kiyak, H. A. (2008). *Social gerontology: A multidisciplinary perspective* (8th ed.). Boston, MA: Pearson.

Hooyman, N. R., & Kiyak, H. A. (2011). *Social gerontology: A multidisciplinary perspective* (9th ed.). Boston, MA: Pearson.

Horowitz, A. D., & Bromnick, R. D. (2007). "Contestable adulthood": Variability and disparity in markers for negotiating the transition to adulthood. *Youth & Society, 39,* 209–231.

Hopkins, B., & Westra, T. (1990). Motor development, maternal expectations and the role of handling. *Infant Behavior and Development, 13,* 117–122.

Hopkins-Golightly, T., Raz, S., & Sander, C. (2003). Influence of slight to moderate risk for birth hypoxia on acquisition of cognitive and language function in the preterm infant: A cross-sectional comparison with preterm-birth controls. *Neuropsychology, 17,* 3–13.

Horn, I. B., Brenner, R., Rao, M., & Cheng, T. L. (2006). Beliefs about the appropriate age for initiating toilet training: are there racial and socioeconomic differences?. *The Journal of pediatrics, 149*(2), 165–168.

Horn, K., Dino, G., Kalsekar, I., & Mody, R. (2005). The impact of *Not on Tobacco* on teen smoking cessation: End-program evaluation results, 1998–2003. *Journal of Adolescent Research, 20,* 640–661.

Horn, S. (2003). Adolescents' reasoning about exclusion from social groups. *Developmental Psychology, 39,* 71–84.

Hornblower, M. (1997, June 9). Great Xpectations. *Time,* 58–68.

Horne, J. (2014). Sleep hygiene: Exercise and other "do's and don'ts." *Sleep Medicine.*

Horton, D. M. (2001). The disappearing bell curve. *Journal of Secondary Gifted Education, 12,* 185–188.

Houglum, P. A. (2010). *Therapeutic exercise for musculoskeletal injuries.* Champaign, IL: Human Kinetics.

House, J. S., Lantz, P. M., & Herd, P. (2005). Continuity and change in the social stratification of aging and health over the life course: Evidence from a nationally representative longitudinal study from 1986 to 2001/2002 (Americans' Changing Lives Study). *Journal of Gerontology, 60B*(Special Issue II), 15–26.

Howard, A. (1998). Youth in Rotuma, then and now. In G. Herdt & S. C. Leavitt (Eds.), *Adolescence in Pacific island societies* (pp. 148–172). Pittsburgh, PA: University of Pittsburgh Press.

Howard, K. S., Carothers, S. S., Smith, L. E., & Akai, C. E. (2007). Overcoming the odds: Protective factors in the lives of children. In J. G. Borkowski, J. R. Farris, T. L. Whitman, S. S. Carothers, K.

Weed, & D. A. Keogh (Eds.), *Risk and resilience: Adolescent mothers and their children grow up* (pp. 205–232). Mahwah, NJ: Lawrence Erlbaum.

Howard, R. W. (2001). Searching the real world for signs of rising population intelligence. *Personality & Individual Differences, 30,* 1039–1058.

Howe, M. L., Courage, M. L., Rooksby, M. (2009). The genesis and development of autobiographical memory. In M. L. Courage & N. Cowan (Eds.), *The development of memory in infancy and childhood* (2nd ed., pp. 177–196). New York, NY: Psychology Press.

Howe, N., & Recchia, H. (2009). Individual differences in sibling teaching in early and middle childhood. *Early Education and Development, 20,* 174–197.

Howe, N., Aquan-Assee, J., & Bukowski, W. M. (2001). Predicting sibling relations over time: Synchrony between maternal management styles and sibling relationship quality. *Merrill-Palmer Quarterly, 47,* 121–141.

Howes, C. (1985). Sharing fantasy: Social pretend play in toddlers. *Child Development, 56,* 1253–1258.

Howes, C. (1996). The earliest friendships. In W. M. Bukowski, A. F. Newcomb, & W. W. Hartup (Eds.), *The company they keep: Friendship in childhood and adolescence* (pp. 66–86). Boston, MA: Cambridge University Press.

Howley, E. T. (2001). Type of activity: Resistance, aerobic and leisure versus occupational physical activity. *Medical Science and Sports Exercise, 33*(Suppl.), S364–369.

Hoyer, W. J., & Roodin, P. A. (2003). *Adult development and aging* (5th ed.). New York, NY: McGraw Hill.

Hoza, B., Kaiser, N., & Hurt, E. S. (2008). Evidence-based treatments for attention-deficit/hyperactivity disorder (ADHD). In G. Ric, T. D. Elkin, & M. C. Robers (Eds.), *Handbook of evidence-based therapies for children and adolescents: Bridging science and practice. Issues in clinical child psychology* (pp. 197–219). New York, NY: Springer.

Hsu, F. L. K. (1985). The self in cross-cultural perspective. In A. J. Marsella, G. DeVos, & F. L. K. Hsu (Eds.), *Culture and self: Asian and Western perspectives* (pp. 24–55). London, UK: Tavistock.

Huang, C. (2010). Mean-level change in self-esteem from childhood through adulthood: Meta-analysis of longitudinal studies. *Review of General Psychology, 14,* 251–260. doi: 10.1037/a0020543

Hu, W., Shi, Q. Z., Han, Q., Wang, X., & Adey, P. (2010). Creative scientific problem finding and its developmental trend. *Creativity Research Journal, 22*(1), 46–52.

Huang, K.-Y., Caughy, M. O., Lee, L.-C., Miller, T., & Genevro, J. (2009). Stability of maternal discipline practices and the quality of mother–child interaction during toddlerhood. *Journal of Applied Developmental Psychology, 30,* 431–441.

Huang, R. L., Lu, Z., Liu, J. J., You, Y. M., Pan, Z. Q., Wei, Z.,...Wang, Z. Z. (2009). Features and predictors of problematic Internet use in Chinese college students. *Behaviour & Information Technology, 28,* 485–490.

Huesmann, L. R., Eron, L. D., Lefkowitz, M. M., & Walder, L. O. (1984). Stability of aggression over time and generations. *Developmental Psychology, 20,* 1120–1134.

Huesmann, L. R., Moise-Titus, J., Podolski, C., & Eron, L. D. (2003). Longitudinal relations between children's exposure to TV violence and their aggressiveness in young adulthood, 1977–1992. *Developmental Psychology, 39,* 201–221.

Huffman, L. R., & Speer, P. W. (2000). Academic performance among at-risk children: The role of developmentally appropriate practices. *Early Childhood Research Quarterly, 15,* 167–184.

Hughes, C., & Dunn, J. (2007). Children's relationships with other children. In C. A. Brownell & C. B. Kopp (Eds.), *Socioemotional development in the toddler years* (pp. 177–200). New York, NY: Guilford.

Hulei, E., Zevenbergen, A., & Jacobs, S. (2006). Discipline behaviors of Chinese American and European American mothers. *Journal of Psychology: Interdisciplinary and Appeal, 140,* 459–475.

Hundley, H. L., & Shyles, L. (2010). U.S. teenagers' perceptions and awareness of digital technology: A focus group approach. *New Media & Society, 12,* 417–433.

Hunnius, S., de Wit, T. C. J., Vrins, S., & von Hofsten, C. (2011). Facing threat: Infants' and adults' visual scanning of faces with neutral, happy, sad, angry, and fearful emotional expressions. *Cognition and Emotion, 25,* 193–205.

Hunt, E. (1989). Cognitive science: Definition, status, and questions. *Annual Review of Psychology, 40,* 603–629.

Hunter, J. (2007). Bereavement: An incomplete rite of passage. *OMEGA—Journal of Death and Dying, 56,* 153–173.

Hunziker, U. A., & Barr, R. G. (1986). Increased carrying reduces infant crying: A randomized controlled trial. *Pediatrics, 77,* 641–648.

Hurme, H., Westerback, S., & Quadrello, T. (2010). Traditional and new forms of contact between grandparents and grandchildren. *Journal of Intergenerational Relationships, 8*(Special issue: Grandparenting in Europe), 264–280.

Hurrelmann, K. (1996). The social world of adolescents: A sociological perspective. In K. Hurrelmann & S. Hamilton (Eds.), *Social problems and social contexts in adolescence: Perspectives across boundaries* (pp. 39–62). Hawthorne, NY: Aldine de Gruyter.

Hursti, U. K. (1999). Factors influencing children's food choice. *Annals of Medicine, 31,* 26–32.

Huttenlocher, P. R. (2002). *Neural plasticity: The effects of environment on the development of the cerebral cortex.* Cambridge, MA: Harvard University Press.

Huyck, M. H. (1998). Gender roles and gender identity in midlife. In S. L. Willis & J. D. Reid (Eds.), *Life in the middle* (pp. 209–232). San Diego, CA: Academic Press.

Hybels, C. F., & Blazer, D. G. (2004). Epidemiology of the late-life mental disorders. *Clinical Geriatric Medicine, 19,* 663–696.

Hyde, J. S., & DeLamater, J. D. (2004). *Understanding human sexuality* (9th ed.). Boston, MA: McGraw Hill.

Hyde, J. S., & DeLamater, J. D. (2005). *Understanding human sexuality* (8th ed., Rev.).

Hyder, A. A., & Lunnen, J. (2009). Reduction of childhood mortality through millennium, development goal 4. *BMJ, 342.*

Hyder, A. A., & Lunnen, J. (2011). Reduction of childhood mortality through millennium development goal 4. *BMJ, 342:*d357.

Hymel, S., McDougall, P., & Renshaw, P. (2004). Peer acceptance/rejection. In P. K. Smith & C. H. Hart (Eds.), *Blackwell handbook of childhood social development* (pp. 265–284). Malden, MA: Blackwell.

Hymowitz, K., Carroll, J. S., Wilcox, W. B., & Kaye, K. (2013). *Knot yet: The benefits and costs of delayed marriage in America.* Charlottesville, VA: National Marriage Project.

Iacovou, M. (2002). Regional differences in the transition to adulthood. *Annals of the American Academy of Political Science Studies, 580,* 40–69.

Iacovou, M. (2011). *Leaving home: Independence, togetherness, and income in Europe.* New York, NY: United Nations Population Division. Retrieved from http://www.un.org/en/development/desa/population/publications/pdf/expert/2011-10_Iacovou_Expert-paper.pdf

Iannelli, V. I. (2007). *Tummy time: Infants.* About.com Guide. Retrieved from http://pediatrics.about.com/od/infants/a/0607_tummy_time.htm

Ice, G. H., Zidron, A., & Juma, E. (2008). Health and health perceptions among Kenyan grandparents. *Journal of Cross-Cultural Gerontology, 23*(Special issue: Aging and social change in Africa), 111–129.

Idler, E. L. (2006). Religion and aging. In R. Binstock & L. K. George (Eds.), *Handbook of aging and the social sciences* (6th ed., pp. 277–300). New York, NY: Academic Press.

Iglowstein, I., Jenni, O. G., Molinari, L., & Largo, R. H. (2003). Sleep duration from infancy to adolescence: Reference values and generational trends. *Pediatrics, 111,* 302–307.

Iles, J., Slade, P., & Spiby, H. (2011). Posttraumatic stress symptoms and postpartum depression in couples after childbirth: The role of partner support and attachment. *Journal of Anxiety Disorders, 25,* 520–530.

Ilich, J. Z., & Brownbill, R. A. (2010). Nutrition through the life span: Needs and health concerns in critical periods. In T. W. Miller (Ed.), *Handbook of stressful transitions across the lifespan* (pp. 625–641). New York, NY: Springer.

ILO (2002). *A future without child labour.* New York, NY: Author.

ILO (2004). *Investing in every child: An economic study of the costs and benefits of eliminating child labour.* New York, NY: Author.

Ilola, L. M. (1990). *Culture and health.* In R. W. Brislin (Ed.), *Applied cross-cultural psychology* (pp. 278–301). Newbury Park, CA: Sage.

Ingram, D. K., Young, J., & Mattison, J. A. (2007). Calorie restriction in nonhuman primates: Assessing effects on brain and behavioral aging. *Neuroscience, 14,* 1359–1364.

Inhelder, B., & Piaget, J. (1958). *The growth of logical thinking from childhood to adolescence.* New York, NY: Basic Books.

Inhorn, M. C., & van Balen, F. (2002). *Infertility around the globe: New thinking on childlessness, gender, and reproductive technologies.* Berkeley: University of California Press.

Insel, T. (2010). Rethinking schizophrenia. *Nature, 468,* 187–193.

Institute of Medicine of the National Academies (2005). *Preventing childhood obesity: Health in the balance.* Washington, DC.

International Genome Sequencing Consortium. (2004). Finishing euchromatic sequence of the human genome. *Nature, 431,* 931–945.

International Labour Organization (ILO) (2002). *A future without child labour.* New York, NY: Author.

International Labour Organization (ILO) (2004). *Investing in every child. An economic study of the costs and benefits of eliminating child labour.* New York, NY: Author.

International Labor Organization (ILO) (2006). *The end of child labour: Within reach.* Geneva, Switzerland: International Labour Office.

International Labour Organization (ILO) (2011). *Global employment trends 2011.* Geneva, Switzerland: Author.

International Labour Organization (ILO) (2013). *Marking progress against child labour: Global estimates and trends 2000-2012.* Geneva, Switzerland: Author.

International Obesity Taskforce (2008). *Global prevalence of adult obesity.* Retrieved from http://www.iotf.org/database/documents/GlobalPreva-lenceofAdultObesity16December08.pdf

International Labor Organization (ILO) (2008, June 12). *World day against child labour 2008—Education: The right response to child labour.* Retrieved from http://www.ilo.org/ipec/Campaignandadvocacy/WDACL/2008/lang–en/index.htm

International Osteoporosis Foundation (IOF) (2011). *Facts and statistics about osteoporosis and its impact.* Retrieved from http://www.iof-bonehealth.org/facts-and-statistics.html#factsheet-category-14

International Social Survey Programme (ISSP) (2012). *Religion III, variable report.* Unter Sachsenhausen, Germany: Leibniz. Institute for Social Sciences.

Ip, S., Chung, M., Raman, G., Chew, P., Magula, N., DeVine, D.,…Lau, J. (2007). *Breastfeeding and maternal and infant health outcomes in developed countries. Evidence Report/Technology Assessment No. 153.* Rockville, MD. Agency for Healthcare Research and Quality.

Ireland, J. L., & Archer, N. (2004). Association between measures of aggression and bullying among juvenile young offenders. *Aggressive Behavior, 30,* 29–42.

Irish, D. P., Lundquist, K. F., & Nelsen, V. J. (Eds.). (2014). *Ethnic variations in dying, death and grief: Diversity in universality.* New York: Taylor & Francis.

Ishihara, N. (2014). Is it rude language? Children learning pragmatics through visual narrative. *TESL Canada Journal, 30*(7), 135.

Issa, J. P. (2003). Age-related epigenetic changes and the immune system. *Clinical Immunology, 109,* 103–108.

Ispa, J. M., & Halgunseth, L. C. (2004). Talking about corporal punishment: Nine low-income African American mothers' perspectives. *Early Childhood Research Quarterly, 19,* 463–484.

Israel, E. (2005). Introduction: The rise of the age of individualism—variability in the pathobiology, response to treatment, and treatment outcomes in asthma. *Journal of Allergy and Clinical Immunology, 115,* S525.

Iverson, R., Kuhl, P. K., Akahane-Yamada, R., Diesch, E., Tohkura, Y., & Kettermann, A. (2003). A perceptual interference account of acquisition difficulties for non-native phonemes. *Cognition, 87,* B47–B57.

Izard, C. E., & Ackerman, B. P. (2000). Motivational, organizational, and regulatory functions of discrete emotions. In M. Lewis & J. M. Haviland-Jones (Eds.), *Handbook of emotions,* (2nd ed., pp. 253–264). New York, NY: Guilford.

Jaakkola, J. J., & Gissler, M. (2004). Maternal smoking in pregnancy, fetal development, and childhood asthma. *American Journal of Public Health, 94,* 136–140.

Jackson, K. M., & Aiken, L. S. (2006). Evaluation of a multicomponent appearance-based sun-protective intervention for young women: Uncovering the mechanisms of program efficacy. *Health Psychology, 25,* 34–46.

Jackson, L. M., Pratt, M. W., Hunsberger, B., & Pancer, S. M. (2005). Optimism as a mediator of the relation between perceived parental authoritativeness and adjustment among adolescents: Finding the sunny side of the street. *Social Development, 14,* 273–304.

Jacob, T., & Johnson, S. L. (2001). Sequential interactions in the parent–child communications of depressed fathers and depressed mothers. *Journal of Family Psychology, 15,* 38–52.

Jacobson, J. (1998). *Islam in transition: Religion and identity among British Pakistani youth.* London, UK: Taylor & Francis.

Jacoby, L. L., & Rhodes, M. G. (2006). False remembering in the aged. *Current Directions in Psychological Science, 15,* 49–53.

Jaeger, S. (1985). The origin of the diary method in developmental psychology. In G. Eckardt, W. G. Bringmann, & L. Sprung (Eds.), *Contributions to a history of developmental psychology* (pp. 63–74). New York, NY: Mouton.

Jaffee, S. R., Caspi, A., Moffitt, T. E., Polo-Tomas, M., Price, T. S., & Taylor, A. (2004). The limits of child effects: Evidence for genetically mediated child effects on corporal punishment but not on physical maltreatment. *Developmental Psychology, 40,* 1047–1058.

Jagust, W., Gitcho, A., Sun, F., Kuczynski, B., Mungas, D., & Haan, M. (2006). Brain imaging evidence of preclinical Alzheimer's disease in normal aging. *Annals of Neurology, 59,* 673–681.

Jahromi, L. B., Putnam, S. P., & Stifter, C. A. (2004). Maternal regulation of infant reactivity from 2 to 6 months. *Developmental Psychology, 40,* 477–487.

Jain, A. (2002). Influences of vitamins and trace-elements on the incidence of respiratory infection in the elderly. *Nutrition Research, 22,* 85–87.

Jalonick, M. C. (2010, December 13). Obama signs historic school lunch nutrition bill. Retrieved from http://www.salon.com/food/feature/2010/12/13/us_obama_child_nutrition

James, C., Hadley, D. W., Holtzman, N. A., & Winkelstein, J. A. (2006). How does the mode of inheritance of a genetic condition influence families? A study of guilt, blame, stigma, and understanding of inheritance and reproductive risks in families with X-linked and autosomal recessive diseases. *Genetics in Medicine, 8,* 234–242.

James, D. K. (2010). Fetal learning: A critical review. *Infant and Child Development, 19,* 45–54.

James, J. B., Lewkowicz, C., Libhaber, J., & Lachman, M. (1995). Rethinking the gender identity crossover hypothesis: A test of a new model. *Sex Roles, 32,* 185–207.

Jankowiak, W., Sudakov, M., & Wilreker, B. C. (2005). Co-wife conflict and cooperation. *Ethnology, 44,* 81–98.

Jankowiak, W. R., & Fischer, E. F. (1992). A cross-cultural perspective on romantic love. *Ethology, 31,* 149–155.

Janssen, I., Katzmarzyk, P. T., Ross, R., Leon, A. S., Skinner, J. S., Rao, D. C., Wilmore, J. H.,…Bouchard, C. (2004). Fitness alters the associations of BMI and waist circumference with total and abdominal fat. *Obesity Research, 12,* 525–537.

Janssen, M., et al. (2014). A short physical activity break from cognitive tasks increases selective attention in primary school children aged 10-11. *Mental Health and Physical Activity, 7,* 129–134.

Jarvis, J. F., & van Heerden, H. G. (1967). The acuity of hearing in the Kalahari Bushman: A pilot study. *Journal of Laryngology and Otology, 81,* 63–68.

Jayakody, R., & Kalil, A. (2002). Social fathering in low-income, African-American families with preschool children. *Journal of Marriage and Family, 64,* 504–516.

Jayakody, R. (2008). The aging experience, social change, and television. In K. W. Schaie & R. P. Abeles (Eds.), *Social structures and aging individuals: Continuing challenges* (pp. 285–301). New York, NY: Springer.

Jeffrey, J. (2004, November). Parents often blind to their kids' weight. *British Medical Journal Online.* Retrieved from content.health.msn.com/content/article/97/104292.htm

Jemal, A., Siegel, R., Ward, E., Murray, T., Xu, J., Smigal, C., & Thun, M. J. (2006). Cancer statistics, 2006. *CA: A Cancer Journal for Clinicians, 56,* 106–130.

Jenkins, J. M., Rabash, J., & O'Connor, T. G. (2003). The role of the shared family context in differential parenting. *Developmental Psychology, 39,* 99–113.

Jennings, N. (2007). Advertising, viewer age and. In J. J. Arnett (Ed.), *Encyclopedia of children, adolescents, and the media* (pp. 55–57). Thousand Oaks, CA: Sage.

Jennings, W. G., & Reingle, J. M. (2012). On the number and shape of developmental/life-course violence, aggression, and delinquency trajectories: A state-of-the-art review. *Journal of Criminal Justice, 40,* 472–489.

Jensen, L. A. (1995). Habits of the heart revisited: Autonomy, community, and divinity in adults' moral language. *Qualitative Sociology, 18,* 71–86.

Jensen, L. A. (1997a). Culture wars: American moral divisions across the adult life span. *Journal of Adult Development, 4,* 107–121.

Jensen, L. A. (1997b). Different worldviews, different morals: America's culture war divide. *Human Development, 40,* 325–344.

Jensen, L. A. (2008). Coming of age in a multicultural world: Globalization and adolescent cultural identity formation. In D. L. Browning (Ed.), *Adolescent identities: A collection of readings* (pp. 3–17). Relational perspectives book series. New York, NY: Analytic Press.

Jensen, L. A. (Ed.). (2011). *Bridging cultural and developmental psychology.* New York, NY: Oxford University Press.

Jensen, L. A. (2015). Cultural-developmental scholarship for a global world: An introduction. In L. A. Jensen (Ed.), *Oxford handbook of human development and culture.* New York, NY: Oxford University Press.

Jensen, L. A. (2015). *Moral development in a global world: Research from a cultural-developmental perspective.* New York, NY: Cambridge University Press.

Jensen, L. A. (2015). Moral reasoning: Developmental emergence and life course pathways among cultures. In L. A. Jensen (Ed.), *Oxford handbook of human development and culture: An interdisciplinary perspective.* New York, NY: Oxford University Press.

Jensen, L. A., Arnett, J. J., & McKenzie, J. (2012). Globalization and cultural identity development in adolescence and emerging adulthood. In S. J. Schwartz, K. Luyckx, & V. L. Vignoles (Eds.), *Handbook of identity theory and research* (pp. 285–301). New York, NY: Springer Publishing Company.

Jequier, A. (2011). *Male infertility: A clinical guide.* New York, NY: Cambridge University Press.

Jessor, R., Colby, A., & Shweder, R. A. (1996). *Ethnography and human development: Context and meaning in social inquiry.* Chicago, IL: University of Chicago Press.

Jeynes, W. (2007). The impact of parental remarriage on children: A metaanalysis. *Marriage & Family Review, 40,* 75–102.

Jiao, S., Ji, G., & Jing, Q. (1996). Cognitive development of Chinese urban only children and children with siblings. *Child Development, 67,* 387–395.

Ji-liang, S., Li-qing, Z., & Yan, T. (2003). The impact of intergenerational social support and filial expectation on the loneliness of elder parents. *Chinese Journal of Clinical Psychology, 11,* 167–169.

Jochman, K. A., & Fromme, K. (2010). Maturing out of substance use: The other side of etiology. In L. Scheier (Ed.), *Handbook of drug use etiology: Theory, methods, and empirical findings* (pp. 565–578). Washington, DC: American Psychological Association.

Johnson, D. J., Jaeger, E., Randolph, S. M., Cauce, A. M., Ward, J. & National Institute of Child Health and Human Development: Early Child Care Research Network. (2003). Studying the effects of early child care experiences on the development of children of color in the United States: Toward a more inclusive research agenda. *Child Development, 74,* 1227–1244.

Johnson, D. M. (2005). Mind, brain, and the upper Paleolithic. In C. E. Erneling & D. M. Johnson (Eds.), *The mind as a scientific object: Between brain and culture* (pp. 499–510). New York, NY: Oxford University Press.

Johnson, E. J., & Schaefer, E. J. (2006). Potential role of dietary n-3 fatty acids in the prevention of dementia and macular degeneration. *American Journal of Clinical Nutrition, 83,* 1494S–1498.

Johnson, J. G., Cohen, P., Kasen, S., & Brook, J. S. (2002). Eating disorders during adolescence and the risk for physical and mental disorders during early adulthood. *Archives of General Psychiatry, 59,* 545–552.

Johnson, J. S., & Newport, E. L. (1991). Critical period effects on universal properties of language: The status of subjacency in the acquisition of a second language. *Cognition, 39,* 215–258.

Johnson, M. C. (2000). The view from the Wuro: A guide to child rearing for Fulani parents. In J. DeLoache & A. Gottlieb (Eds.), *A world of babies: Imagined childcare guides for seven societies* (pp. 171–198). New York, NY: Cambridge University Press.

Johnson, M. D. (2008). *Human biology: Concepts and current issues.* Upper Saddle River, NJ: Prentice Hall.

Johnson, M. H. (2001). Functional brain development in humans. *Nature Reviews Neuroscience, 2,* 475–483.

Johnson, R. W., & Schaner, S. G. (2005). *Value of unpaid activities by older Americans tops $160 billion per year.* Retrieved from http://www.urban.org/UploadedPDF/311227_older_americans.pdf

Johnson, S. K., Murphy, S. R., Zewdie, S., & Reichard, R. J. (2008). The strong, sensitive type: Effects of gender stereotypes and leadership prototypes on the evaluation of male and female leaders. *Organizational Behavior and Human Decision Processes, 106,* 39–60.

Johnson, W., te Nijenhuis, J., & Bouchard, T. J., Jr. (2008). Still just 1 g: Consistent results from five tests batteries. *Intelligence, 36,* 81–95.

Johnston, L. D., O'Malley, P. M., Bachman, J. G., Schulenberg, J. E. & Miech, R. A. (2014). Monitoring the Future national survey results on drug use, 1975–2013: Volume 2, College students and adults ages 19–55. Ann Arbor, MI: Institute for Social Research, The University of Michigan.

Johnston, L. D., O'Malley, P. M., Miech, R. A., Bachman, J. G., & Schulenberg, J. E. (2014). *Monitoring the future national results on drug use: 1975-2013: Overview, key findings on adolescent drug use.* Ann Arbor, MI: Institute for Social Research, The University of Michigan.

Jones, E., & Kay, M. A. (2003). The cultural anthropology of the placenta. In L. Dundes (Ed.), *The manner born: Birth rites in cross-cultural perspective* (pp. 101–116). Walnut Creek, CA: AltaMira Press.

Jones, F. (2003). *Religious commitment in Canada, 1997 to 2000. Religious Commitment Monograph No. 3.* Ottawa, Ontario, Canada: Christian Commitment Research Institute.

Jones, G. W. (2010). Changing marriage patterns in Asia. Asia Research Institute. Retrieved from http://www.ari.nus.edu.sg/docs/wps/wps10_131.pdf

Jones, G. W., & Ramdas, K. (2004). *(Un)tying the knot: Ideal and reality in Asian marriage.* Singapore: Asia Research Institute.

Jones, R. E. (2006). *Human reproductive biology.* New York, NY: Academic Press.

Jones, R. K., Darroch, J. E., & Henshaw, S. K. (2002). Contraceptive use among U.S. women having abortions in 2000–2001. *Perspectives on Sexual and Reproductive Health, 34,* 294–303.

Jordan, B. (1993). *Birth in four cultures: A cross-cultural investigation of childbirth in Yucatan, Holland, Sweden, and the United States.* Long Grove, Illinois: Waveland.

Jordan, B. (1994). *Birth in four cultures.* Long Grove, IL: Westland.

Jose, O., & Alfons, V. (2007). Do demographics affect marital satisfaction? *Journal of Sex and Marital Therapy, 33,* 73–85.

Jose, P. E., & Brown, I. (2008). When does the gender difference in rumination begin? Gender and age differences in the use of rumination by adolescents. *Journal of Youth and Adolescence, 37*(2), 180–192.

Josselyn, S. A., & Frankland, P. W. (2012). Infantile amnesia: a neurogenic hypothesis. *Learning & Memory, 19*(9), 423–433.

Jost, K. (2005). Right to die. *The CQ Researcher,* 423–438.

Journal of Pain and Palliative Care Pharmacotherapy. (2006). News and innovations: Physicians and general public support for physician-assisted suicide. *Journal of Pain and Palliative Care, 20,* 100.

Joyce, D. (2010). *Essentials of temperament assessment.* Hoboken, NJ: John Wiley and Sons.

Jung, C. G. (1930). The stages of life. In C. G. Jung (author), W. S. Dell & C. F. Baynes (Trans.), *Modern man in search of a soul* (pp. 95–114). New York, NY: Harvest Books.

Kabir, M. (2008). Determinants of life expectancy in developing countries. *Journal of Developing Areas, 41,* 185–204.

Kagan, J. (1994). *Galen's prophecy: Temperament in human nature.* New York, NY: Basic Books.

Kagan, J. (1998). Biology and the child. In N. Eisenberg (Ed.), *Handbook of child psychology: Vol. 3. Social, emotional, and personality development* (5th ed., pp. 177–236). New York, NY: Wiley.

Kagan, J. (2000). Temperament. In A. Kazdin (Ed.), *Encyclopedia of psychology* (Vol. 8, pp. 34–37). Washington, DC: American Psychological Association.

Kagan, J. (2003). Behavioral inhibition as a temperamental category. In R. J. Davidson, K. R. Scherer, & H. H. Goldsmith (Eds.), *Handbook of affective science* (pp. 320–331). New York, NY: Oxford University Press.

Kagan, J., & Fox, N. A. (2006). Biology, culture, and temperamental biases. In W. Damon & R. Lerner (Eds.), & N. Eisenberg (Vol. Ed.), *Handbook of child psychology: Vol. 3. Social, emotional, and personality development* (6th ed., pp. 167–225). New York, NY: Wiley.

Kagan, J., & Herschkowitz, E. C. (2005). *Young mind in a growing brain.* Mahwah, NJ: Erlbaum.

Kağitçibaşi, C., & Yalin, C. (2015). Family in adolescence: Relatedness and cutonomy across cultures. In L. A. Jensen (Ed.), *Oxford handbook of human development and culture: An interdisciplinary perspective.* New York, NY: Oxford University Press.

Kahana-Kalman, R., & Walker-Andrews, A. S. (2001). The role of person familiarity in young infants' perception of emotional expressions. *Child Development, 72,* 352–369.

Kahn, J. A. (2007). Maximizing the potential public health impact of HPV vaccines: A focus on parents. *Journal of Adolescent Health, 20,* 101–103.

Kahn, J. R., McGill, B. S., & Bianchi, S. M. (2011). Help to family and friends: Are there gender differences at older ages? *Journal of Marriage and Family, 73,* 77–92.

Kail, R. V. (2003). Information processing and memory. In M. H. Bornstein, L. Davidson, C. L. M. Keyes, K. A. Moore, and the Center for Child Well-Being (Eds.), *Well-being: Positive development across the life course* (pp. 269–280). Mahwah, NJ: Erlbaum.

Kail, R., & Park, Y. (1992). Global developmental change in processing time. *Merrill-Palmer Quarterly, 38,* 525–541.

Kainz, G., Eliasson, M., & von Post, I. (2010). The child's father, an important person for the mother's well-being during the childbirth: A hermeneutic study. *Health Care for Women International, 31,* 621–635.

Kaiser Family Foundation (2013). *Distribution of U.S. population by race and ethnicity, 2010 and 2050.* Retrieved from http://kaiserfamily-foundation.files.wordpress.com/2013/03/distribution-of-u-s-population-by-raceethnicity-2010-and-2050-disparities.png

Kaiser Family Foundation (2014). The global HIV/AIDS epidemic. Retrieved from http://kff.org/global-health-policy/fact-sheet/the-global-hivaids-epidemic/#endnote_link_UNAIDSSlides

Kakar, S. (1998). The search for the middle age in India. In R. A. Shweder (Ed.), *Welcome to middle age! (and other cultural fictions)* (pp. 75–98). Chicago, IL: University of Chicago Press.

Kakar, S., & Kakar, K. (2007). *The Indians: Portrait of a people.* New York, NY: Penguin.

Kalager, M., Zelen, M., Langmark, F., & Adami, H-O. (2010). Effect of screening mammography on breast-cancer mortality in Norway. *New England Journal of Medicine, 363,* 1203–1210.

Kalaria, R. N., Maestre, G. E., Arizaga, R., Friedland, R. P., Galasko, D., Hall, K., & World Federation of Neurology Dementia Research group (2008). Alzheimer's disease and vascular dementia in developing countries: prevalence, management, and risk factors. *Lancet Neurology, 7,* 812–826.

Kalb, C., & McCormick, J. (1998, September 21). Bellying up to the bar. *Newsweek,* 89.

Kamel, N. S., & Gammack, J. K. (2006). Insomnia in the elderly: Cause, approach, and treatment. *American Journal of Medicine, 119,* 463–469.

Kamibeppu, K., & Sugiura, H. (2005). Impact of the mobile phone on junior high-school students' friendsltips in the Tokyo metropolitan area. *Cyber Psychology & Behavior, 8,* 121–130.

Kane, P., & Garber, J. (2004). The relations among depression in fathers, children's psychopathology, and father–child conflict: A meta-analysis. *Child Psychology Review, 24,* 339–360.

Kanetsuna, T., Smith, P., & Morita, Y. (2006). Coping with bullying at school: Children's recommended strategies and attitudes to school-based intervention in England and Japan. *Aggressive Behavior, 32,* 570–580.

Kapadia, S., & Bhangaokar, R. (2015). An Indian moral worldview: Developmental patterns in adolescents and adults. In L. A. Jensen (Ed.), *Moral development in a global world: Research from a cultural-developmental perspective.* New York, NY: Cambridge University Press.

Kapadia, S., & Gala, J. (2015). Gender across cultures: Sex and socialization in childhood. In L. A. Jensen (Ed.), *Oxford handbook of human development and culture: An interdisciplinary perspective.* New York, NY: Oxford University Press.

Kaplan, B. J., Crawford, S. G., Field, C. J., Simpson, J., & Steven, A. (2007). Vitamins, minerals, and mood. *Psychological Bulletin, 133,* 747–760.

Kaplan, H., & Dove, H. (1987). Infant development among the Ache of Eastern Paraguay. *Developmental Psychology, 23,* 190–198.

Kaplan, S., Heiligenstein, J., West, S., Busner, J., Hardor, D., Dittmann, R., . . . Wernicke, J. E. (2004). Efficacy and safety of atomoxetine in childhood attention deficit/hyperactivity disorder with comorbidity oppositional defiant disorder. *Journal of Attention Disorders, 8,* 45–52.

Karlsson, J. L. (2006). Specific genes for intelligence. In L. V. Wesley (Ed.), *Intelligence: New research* (pp. 23–46). Hauppauge, NY: Nova Science.

Karlsson, M. (2004). Has exercise an antifracture efficacy in women? *Scandinavian Journal of Medical Science and Sports, 14,* 2–15.

Karney, B. R., & Bradbury, T. N. (2005). Contextual influences on marriage. *Current Directions in Psychological Science, 14,* 171–174.

Kass-Bartelemes, B. L., Hughes, R., & Rutherford, M. K. (2003). *Advance care planning: Preferences for care at the end of life.* Rockville, MD: Agency for Healthcare Research and Quality.

Kastenbaum, R. (2007). *Death, society, and human experience* (9th ed.). Boston, MA: Allyn & Bacon.

Katchadourian, H., & Boli, J. (1985). *Careerism and intellectualism among college students.* San Francisco, CA: Jossey-Bass.

Kates, J. L. (2008). *Digital hearing aids.* Cambridge, UK: Cambridge University Press.

Kato, N., Toda, I., Hori-Komai, Y., Sakai, C., & Tsubota, K. (2008). Five-year outcome of LASIK for myopia. *Ophthalmology, 115,* 839–844.

Katz, L. F., & Windecker-Nelson, B. (2004). Parental meta-emotion philosophy in families with conduct-problem children: Links with peer relations. *Journal of Abnormal Child Psychology, 32,* 385–398.

Kaufman, A. S. (2001). WAIS-III IQs, Horn's theory, and generational changes from young adulthood to old age. *Intelligence, 29,* 131–167.

Kavšek, M. (2003). Development of depth and object perception in infancy. In G. Schwarzer & H. Leder (Eds.), *The development of face processing* (pp. 35–52). Ashland, OH: Hogrefe & Huber.

Kavšek, M. (2004). Predicting later IQ from infant visual habituation and dishabituation: A meta-analysis. *Journal of Applied Developmental Psychology, 25,* 369–393.

Kavšek, M., & Bornstein, M. H. (2010). Visual habituation and dishabituation in preterm infants: A review and meta-analysis. *Research in Developmental Disabilities, 31,* 951–975.

Kazdin, A. E., & Benjet, C. (2003). Spanking children: Evidence and issues. *Current Directions in Psychological Science, 12,* 99–103.

Keating, D. (1990). Adolescent thinking. In S. Feldman & G. Elliott (Eds.), *At the threshold: The developing adolescent* (pp. 54–89). Cambridge, MA: Harvard University Press.

Keating, D. (2004). Cognitive and brain development. In L. Steinberg & R. M. Lerner (Eds.), *Handbook of adolescent psychology* (2nd ed., pp. 45–84). New York, NY: Wiley.

Kedziora-Kornatowski, K., Szewczyk-Golec, K., Czuczejko, J., van Marke de Lumen, K., Pawluk, H., Motyl, J.,…Kedziora, J. (2007). Effect of melatonin on the oxidative stress in erythrocytes of healthy young and elderly subjects. *Journal of Pineal Research, 42,* 153–158.

Keegan, R. T., & Gruber, H. E. (1985). Charles Darwin's unpublished "Diary of an infant": An early phase in his psychological work. In G. Eckardt, W. G. Bringmann, & L. Sprung (Eds.), *Contributions to a history of developmental psychology* (pp. 127–145). New York, NY: Mouton.

Keen, R. (2005). Using perceptual representations to guide reaching and looking. In J. J. Reiser, J. J. Lockman, & C. A. Nelson (Eds.), *Action as an organizer of learning and development: Minnesota Symposia on Child Psychology* (Vol. 33, pp. 301–322). Mahwah, NJ: Erlbaum.

Keene, J. R., & Prokos, A. H. (2008). Widowhood and the end of spousal caregiving: Relief or wear and tear? *Aging & Society, 28,* 551–570.

Keller, M. A., & Goldberg, W. A. (2004). Co–sleeping: Help or hindrance for young children's independence? *Infant and Child Development, 13,* 369–388.

Kellman, P. J., & Arterberry, M. E. (2006). Infant visual perception. In W. Damon & R. Lerner (Eds.), & D. Kuhn & R. Siegler (Vol. Eds.), *Handbook of child psychology: Vol. 2. Cognition, perception, and language* (6th ed., pp. 109–160). New York, NY: Wiley.

Kellogg, A. (2001, January). Looking inward, freshmen care less about politics and more about money. *Chronicle of Higher Education,* A47–A49.

Kelly, B., Halford, J. C. G., Boyland, E. J., Chapman, K., Bautista-Castaño, I., Berg, C., et al. (2010). Television food advertising to children: A global perspective. *American Journal of Public Health, 100,* 1730–1736.

Kelly, J. B. (2003). Changing perspectives on children's adjustment following divorce: A view from the United States. *Childhood: A Global Journal of Child Research, 10,* 237–254.

Kelly, J. B., & Emery, R. E. (2003). Children's adjustment following divorce: Risk and resilience perspectives. *Family Relations, 52,* 352–362.

Kelly, Y., Nazroo, J., Sacker, A., & Schoon, I. (2006). Ethnic differences in achievement of developmental milestones by 9 months of age: The Millennium Cohort Study. *Developmental Medicine & Child Neurology, 48,* 825–830.

Kelch-Oliver, K. (2011). The experiences of African American grandmothers in grandparent–headed families. *The Family Journal, 19,* 73–82.

Kember, D., & Watkins, D. (2010). Approaches to learning and teaching by the Chinese. In M. Harris (Ed.), *The Oxford handbook of Chinese psychology* (pp. 169–185). New York, NY: Oxford University Press.

Kemp, E. A., & Kemp, J. E. (2002). *Older couples: New romances.* Berkeley, CA: Celestial Arts.

Kenneally, C. (2007). *The first words: The search for the origins of language.* New York, NY: Viking.

Kent, M. M., & Haub, C. (2005). Global demographic divide. *Population Bulletin, 60,* 1–24.

Kenyon, B. L. (2001). Current research in children's conceptions of death: A critical review. *Omega, 43,* 63–91.

Kerber, L. K. (1997). *Toward an intellectual history of women.* Chapel Hill: University of North Carolina Press.

Kerestes, M., Youniss, J., & Metz, E. (2004). Longitudinal patterns of religious perspective and civic integration. *Applied Developmental Science, 8,* 39–46.

Kesson, A. M. (2007). Respiratory virus infections. *Paediatric Respiratory Reviews, 8,* 240–248.

Keyes, C. L. M., & Ryff, C. D. (1998). Generativity and adult lives: Social structural contours and quality of life consequences. In D. P. McAdams & E. de St. Aubin (Eds.), *Generativity and adult development: How and why we care for the next generation* (pp. 227–263). Washington, DC: American Psychological Association.

Keyes, C. L. M., Shmotkin, D., & Ryff, C. D. (2002). Optimizing well-being: The empirical encounter of two traditions. *Journal of Personality and Social Psychology, 82,* 1007–1022.

Kiang, L., Moreno, A. J., & Robinson, J. L. (2004). Maternal preconceptions about parenting predict child temperament, maternal sensitivity, and children's empathy. *Developmental Psychology, 40,* 1081–1092.

Kiernan, K. (2002). Cohabitation in Western Europe: Trends, issues, and implications. In A. Booth & A. C. Crouter (Eds.), *Just living together: Implications of cohabitation on families, children, and social policy* (pp. 3–31). Mahwah, NJ: Lawrence Erlbaum.

Kiernan, K. (2004). Cohabitation and divorce across nations and generations. In P. L. Chase-Lansdale, K. Kiernan, & R. J. Friedman (Eds.), *Human development across lives and generations: The potential for change* (pp. 139–170). New York, NY: Cambridge University Press.

Killen, M., & Wainryb, C. (2000). Independence and interdependence in diverse cultural contexts. In S. Harkness, C. Raeff, & C. M. Super (Eds.), *Variability in the social construction of the child* (pp. 5–21). San Francisco, CA: Jossey-Bass.

Killian, T., Turner, J., & Cain, R. (2005). Depressive symptoms of caregiving women in midlife: The role of physical health. *Journal of Women and Aging, 17,* 115–127.

Kim, J. E., & Moen, P. (2002). Is retirement good or bad for subjective well-being? *Current Directions in Psychological Science, 10,* 83–86.

Kim, J.-S., & Lee, E.-H. (2003). Cultural and noncultural predictors of health outcomes in Korean daughter and daughter-in-law caregivers. *Public Health Nursing, 20,* 111–119.

Kim, K., & Antonopolous, R. (2011). *Unpaid and paid care: The effects of child care and elder care on the standard of living.* New York, NY: Levy Economics Institute.

Kim, M., McGregor, K. K., & Thompson, C. K. (2000). Early lexical development in English- and Korean-speaking children: Language-general and language-specific patterns. *Journal of Child Language, 27,* 225–254.

Kim, S., & Park, H. (2006). Five years after the launch of Viagra in Korea: Changes in perceptions of erectile dysfunction treatment by physicians, patients, and the patients' spouses. *Journal of Sexual Medicine, 3,* 132–137.

Kim, Y., Hsu, S. H., & de Zúñiga, H. G. (2013). Influence of social media use on discussion network heterogeneity and civic engagement: The moderating role of personality traits. *Journal of Communication, 63*(3), 498–516.

Kimmel, D. C., & Sang, B. E. (2003). Lesbians and gay men in midlife. In L. D. Garnets & D. C. Kimmel (Eds.), *Psychological perspectives on lesbian, gay, and bisexual experiences* (2nd ed., pp. 602–628). New York, NY: Columbia University Press.

King, B. M. (2005). *Human sexuality today* (5th ed.). Upper Saddle River, NJ: Prentice Hall.

King, P. E., Furrow, J. L., & Roth, N. (2002). The influence of families and peers on adolescent religiousness. *Journal of Psychology and Christianity, 21,* 109–120.

King, P. M., & Kitchener, K. S. (2002). The reflective judgment model: Twenty years of research on epistemic cognition. In B. K. Hofner & P. R. Pintrich (Eds.), *Personal epistemology: The psychology of beliefs about knowledge and knowing* (pp. 37–61). Mahwah, NJ: Erlbaum.

King, P. M., & Kitchener, K. S. (2004). Reflective judgment: Theory and research on the development of epistemic judgment through adulthood. *Educational Psychologist, 39,* 5–18.

King, P. M., & Kitchener, K. S. (2015). Cognitive development in the emerging adult: The emergence of complex cognitive skills. In J. J. Arnett (Ed.), *Oxford handbook of emerging adulthood.* New York, NY: Oxford University Press.

King, V., & Scott, M. E. (2005). A comparison of cohabiting relationships among older and younger adults. *Journal of Marriage and the Family, 67,* 271–285.

Kingsberg, S. A. (2002). The impact of aging on sexual function in women and their partners. *Archives of Sexual Behavior, 31,* 431–437.

Kinnally, W. (2007). Music listening, age effects on. In J. J. Arnett (Ed.), *Encyclopedia of children, adolescents, and the media* (pp. 585–586). Thousand Oaks, CA: Sage.

Kinney, H. C., & Thach, B. T. (2009). Medical progress: The sudden infant death syndrome. *The New England Journal of Medicine, 361,* 795–805.

Kins, E., Beyers, W., Soenens, B., & Vansteenkiste, M. (2009). Patterns of home leaving and subjective well-being in emerging adulthood: The role of motivational processes and parental autonomy support. *Developmental Psychology, 45,* 1416–1429.

Kirchner, G. (2000). *Children's games from around the world.* Boston, MA: Allyn & Bacon.

Kirkorian, H. L., Wartella, E. A., & Anderson, D. R. (2008). Media and young children's learning. *The Future of Children, 18*(1), 39–61.

Kisilevsky, B. S., Hains, S. M., Lee, K., Xic, X., Huang, H., Ye, H. H., Zhang, K. & Wang, Z. (2003). Effects of experience on fetal voice recognition. *Psychological Science, 14,* 220–224.

Kitchener, K. S., King, P. M., & DeLuca, S. (2006). Development of reflective judgment in adulthood. In C. Hoare (Ed), *Handbook of adult development and learning* (pp. 73–98). New York, NY: Oxford University Press.

Kitchener, K. S., Lynch, C. L., Fischer, K. W., & Wood, P. K. (1993). Developmental range of reflective judgment: The effect of contextual support and practice on developmental stage. *Developmental Psychology, 29,* 893–906.

Kite, M. E., Deaux, K., & Hines, E. (2008). Gender stereotypes. In F. L. Denmark & M. A. Paludi (Eds.), *Psychology of women: A handbook of issues and theories* (2nd ed., pp. 205–236). Westport, CT: Praeger.

Kitsao-Wekulo, P., Holding, P., Taylor, G. H., Abubakar, A., Kvalsvig, J., & Connolly, K. (2013). Nutrition as an important mediator of the impact of background variables on outcomes in middle childhood. *Frontiers in Human Neuroscience, 7,* 713.

Kitzmann, K. M., Cohen, R., & Lockwood, R. L. (2002). Are only children missing out? Comparison of the peer-related social competence of only children and siblings. *Journal of Social and Personal Relationships, 19,* 299–316.

Klahr, D., & MacWhinney, B. (1998). Information processing. In D. Kuhn & R. S. Siegler (Eds.), *Handbook of child psychology: Vol. 2. Cognition, perception, and language* (5th ed., pp. 631–678). New York, NY: Wiley.

Klass, C. S. (2008). *The home visitor's guidebook: Promoting optimal parent and child development* (3rd ed.). Baltimore, MD: Paul H. Brookes.

Klaus, M. H., & Kennell, J. H. (1976). *Maternal–infant bonding: The impact of early separation or loss on family development.* St. Louis, MO: Mosby.

Kleiber, D., & Nimrod, G. (2008). Expressions of generativity and civic engagement in a "learning in retirement" group. *Journal of Adult Development, 15,* 76–86.

Klein, B. E., Klein, R., Lee, K. E., & Meuer, S. M. (2003). Socioeconomic and lifestyle factors and the 10-year incidence of age-related cataracts. *American Journal of Ophthalmology, 136,* 506–512.

Klerman, E. B., Duffy, J. F., Dijk, D. J., & Czeisler, C. A. (2001). Circadian phase resetting in older people by ocular bright light exposure. *Journal of Investigative Medicine, 49,* 30–40.

Klomek, A. B., Marrocco, F., Kleinman, M., Schonfeld, I. S., & Gould, M. S. (2007). Bullying, depression, and suicidality in adolescents. *Journal of the American Academy of Child & Adolescent Psychiatry, 46,* 40–49.

Klomsten, A. T., Skaalvik, E. M., & Espnes, G. A. (2004). Physical self-concept and sports: Do gender differences exist? *Sex Roles, 50,* 119–127.

Knecht, S., Drager, B., Deppe, M., Bobe, L., Lohmann, H., Floel, A.,…Henningsen, H. (2000). Handedness and hemispheric language dominance in healthy humans. *Brain, 135,* 2512–2518.

Knect, S., Jansen, A., Frank, A., van Randenborgh, J., Sommer, J., Kanowski, M., & Heinze, H. J. (2003). How atypical is atypical language dominance? *Neuroimage, 18,* 917–927.

Knickmeyer, C.R., & Baron-Cohen, S. (2006). Fetal testosterone and sex differences. *Early human development, 82*(12), 755–760.

Knight, C. (2013). *Blood relations: Menstruation and the origins of culture.* New Haven, CT: Yale University Press.

Knipe, D. M. (2008). Make that sesame on rice, please! Appetites of the dead in Hinduism. *Indian Folklore Research Journal, 5,* 27–45.

Knox, D., Sturdivant, L., & Zusman, M. E. (2001). College student attitudes toward sexual intimacy. *College Student Journal, 35,* 241–243.

Kochanek, K. D., Murphy, S. I., Anderson, R. B., & Scott, C. (2004). Deaths: Final data for 2002. *National Vital Statistics Report, 53,* 1–116.

Kochanska, G. (2002). Mutually responsive orientation between mothers and their young children: A context for the early development of conscience. *Current Directions in Psychological Science, 11,* 191–195.

Kochenderfer-Ladd, B. (2003). Identification of aggressive and asocial victims and the stability of their peer victimization. *Merrill-Palmer Quarterly, 49,* 401–425.

Koenig, H. G. (2007). *Spirituality in patient care* (2nd ed.). Philadelphia, PA: Templeton Foundation Press.

Kohlberg, L. (1958). *The development of modes of moral thinking and choice in the years 10 to 16.* Unpublished doctoral dissertation. University of Chicago.

Kohlberg, L. (1986). A current statement on some theoretical issues. In S. Modgit & C. Modgl (Eds.), *Lawrence Kohlberg.* Philadelphia, PA: Falmer.

Konigsberg, R. D. (2011). *The truth about grief: The myth of its five stages and the new science of loss.* New York, NY: Simon & Schuster.

Koopmans, S., & Kooijman, A. (2006). Prebyopia correction and accommodative intraocular lenses. *Gerentechnology, 5,* 222–230.

Kopp, C. B. (1989). Regulation of distress and negative emotions: A developmental view. *Developmental Psychology, 25,* 343–354.

Kopp, C. B. (2003). *Baby steps: A guide to your child's social, physical, mental, and emotional development in the first two years.* New York, NY: Owl.

Korkman, M., Kettunen, S., & Autti-Rämö, I. (2003). Neurocognitive impairment in early adolescence following prenatal alcohol exposure of varying duration. *Child Neuropsy chology, 9*(2), 117–128.

Kornhaber, M. L. (2004). Using multiple intelligences to overcome cultural barriers to identifications for gifted education. In D. Boothe & J. C. Stanley. (Eds.), *In the eyes of the beholder: Critical issues for diversity in gifted education* (pp. 215–225). Waco, TX: Prufrock Press.

Kosmala, K., & Kloszweska, I. (2004). The burden of providing care for Alzheimer's disease patients in Poland. *International Journal of Geriatric Psychiatry, 19,* 191–193.

Kostandy, R. R., Ludington-Hoe, S. M., Cong, X., Abouelfettoh, A., Bronson, C., Stankus, A., & Jarrell, J. R. (2008). Kangaroo care (skin contact) reduces crying response to pain in preterm neonates: Pilot results. *Pain Management Nursing, 9,* 55–65.

Kotchick, B. A., Dorsey, S., & Heller, L. (2005). Predictors of parenting among African American single mothers: Personal and contextual factors. *Journal of Marriage and Family, 67,* 448–460.

Kotkin, J. (2010). *The next hundred million: America in 2050.* New York, NY: Penguin.

Kotler, J. (2007). Television, prosocial content and. In J. J. Arnett (Ed.), *Encyclopedia of children, adolescents, and the media, Vol. 2* (pp. 817–819). Thousand Oaks, CA: Sage.

Kostovic, I., & Vasung, L. (2009). Insights from in vitro magnetic resonance imaging of cerebral development. *Seminars in Perinatology, 33,* 220–233.

Kouvonen, A., & Kivivuori, J. (2001). Part-time jobs, delinquency and victimization among Finnish adolescents. *Journal of Scandinavian Studies in Criminology and Crime Prevention, 2*(2), 191–212.

Kowalski, R. M., Limber, S., Limber, S. P., & Agatston, P. W. (2012). *Cyberbullying: Bullying in the digital age.* New York, NY: John Wiley & Sons.

Kowalski, R. M., & Limber, S. P. (2007). Electronic bullying among middle school students. *Journal of Adolescent Health, 41,* S22–S30.

Kramer, D. A. (2003). The ontogeny of wisdom in its variations. In J. Demick & C. Andreoletti (Eds.), *Handbook of adult development* (pp. 131–151). New York, NY: Springer.

Kramer, L., & Kowal, A. K. (2005). Sibling relationship quality from birth to adolescence: The enduring contributions of friends. *Journal of Family Psychology, 19*(Special issue: Sibling Relationship Contributions to Individual and Family Well-Being), 503–511.

Kramer, L., Perozynski, L., & Chung, T. (1999). Parental responses to sibling conflict: The effects of development and parent gender. *Child Development, 70,* 1401–1414.

Kramer, M. S., Aboud, F., Mironova, E., Vanilovich, I., Platt, R. W., Matush, L.,...Promotion of Breastfeeding Intervention Trial (PROBIT) Study Group (2008). Breastfeeding and child cognitive development: New evidence from a large randomized trial. *Archives of General Psychiatry, 65,* 578–584.

Kramer, M. S., Lidia, M., Vanilovich, I., Platt, R. W., & Bogdanovich, N. (2009). A randomized breast-feeding promotion intervention did not reduce child obesity in Belarus. *Journal of Nutrition, 139,* 417S–421S.

Kramer, S. E., Kapteyn, T. S., Kuik, D. J., & Deeng, D. J. (2002). The association of hearing impairment and chronic diseases with psychosocial health status in older age. *Journal of Aging and Health, 14,* 122–137.

Kraus, E. L. (2005). "Toys and perfumes": Imploding Italy's population paradox and motherly myths. In C. B. Douglass (Ed.), *Barren states: The population "implosion" in Europe* (pp. 159–182). New York, NY: Berg.

Kreicbergs, U., Valdimarsdottir, U., Onelov, E., Henter, J.-I., & Steineck, G. (2004). Anxiety and depression in parents 4–9 years after the loss of a child owing to a malignancy: A population-based follow-up. *Psychological Medicine, 34,* 1431–1441.

Kreider, R. M. (2005). *Number, timing, and duration of marriages: 2001.* Washington, DC: U.S. Bureau of the Census.

Kreutzer, M., Leonard, C., & Flavell, J. H. (1975). An interview study of children's knowledge about memory. *Monographs of the Society for Research in Child Development, 40*(1, Serial No. 159).

Krikorian, A., Limonero, J. T., & Maté, J. (2012). Suffering and distress at the end-of-life. *Psycho-Oncology, 21*(8), 799–808.

Kroger, J. (2002). Commentary on "Feminist perspectives on Erikson's theory: Their relevance for contemporary identity development research." *Identity, 2,* 257–266.

Kroger, J. (2003). Identity development during adolescence. In G. Adams & M. Berzonsky (Eds.), *Blackwell handbook of adolescence* (pp. 205–225). Malden, MA: Blackwell.

Kroger, J. (2007). *Identity development: Adolescence through adulthood* (2nd ed.). Thousand Oaks, CA: Sage.

Kroger, J., Martinussen, M., & Marcia, J. E. (2010). Identity status change during adolescence and young adulthood: A meta-analysis. *Journal of Adolescence, 33,* 683–698.

Kubey, R. (1994). Media implications for the quality of family life. In D. Zillmann, J. Bryant, & A. C. Huston (Eds.), *Media, children, and the family: Social scientific, psychodynamic, and clinical perspectives* (pp. 61–69). Hillsdale, NJ: Lawrence Erlbaum.

Kubisch, S. (2007). Electronic games, age and. In J. J. Arnett (Ed.), *Encyclopedia of children, adolescents, and the media* (pp. 264–265). Thousand Oaks, CA: Sage.

Kübler-Ross, E. (1969). *On death and dying.* New York, NY: Macmillan.

Kübler-Ross, E. (1982). *Working it through.* New York, NY: Macmillan.

Kubzansky, L. D., Koenen, K. C., Jones, C., & Eaton, W. W. (2009). A prospective study of posttraumatic stress disorder symptoms and coronary heart disease in women. *Health Psychology, 28,* 125–130.

Kuhl, P. K. (2004). Early language acquisition: Cracking the speech code. *Nature Reviews Neuroscience, 5,* 831–843.

Kuhn, D. (2008). Formal operations from a twenty-first century perspective. *Human Development, 51*(Special issue: Celebrating a Legacy of Theory with New Directions for Research on Human Development), 48–55.

Kuhn, G. (Ed.). *Sober living for the revolution: Hardcore punk, straight-edge, and radical politics.* Oakland, CA: PM Press.

Kühnel, J., & Sonnentag, S. (2011). How long do you benefit from vacation? A closer look at the fade-out of vacation effects. *Journal of Organizational Behavior, 32,* 125–143.

Künemund, H., Motel-Klingebiel, A., & Kohli, M. (2005). Do private intergenerational transfers increase social inequality in middle adulthood? Evidence from the German Aging Survey. *Journal of Gerontology: Social Sciences, 60B,* S30–S36.

Kuntsche, E., Rehm, J., & Gmel, G. (2004). Characteristics of binge drinkers in Europe. *Social Science & Medicine, 59,* 113–127.

Kunzmann, U., & Baltes, P. B. (2005). The psychology of wisdom: Theoretical and empirical challenges. In R. J. Sternberg & J. Jordan (Eds.), Handbook of wisdom: *Psychological perspectives* (pp. 110–135). New York, NY: Cambridge University Press.

Kurdek, L. A. (1999). The nature and predictors of the trajectory of change in marital quality for husbands and wives over the first 10 years of marriage. *Developmental Psychology, 35,* 1283–1296.

Kurdek, L. A. (2006). Differences between partners from heterosexual, gay, and lesbian cohabiting couples. *Journal of Marriage and Family, 68,* 509–528.

Kuttler, A. F., La Greca, A. M., & Prinstein, M. J. (1999). Friendship qualities and social-emotional functioning of adolescents with close, cross-sex friendships. *Journal of Research on Adolescence, 9,* 339–366.

Kvavilashvili, L., & Ford, R. M. (2014). Metamemory prediction accuracy for simple prospective and retrospective memory tasks in 5-year-old children. *Journal of Experimental Psychology.*

Kwak, J., Haley, W. E., & Chiraboga, D. A. (2008). Racial differences in hospice use and in-hospital death among Medicare and Medicaid dual-eligible nursing home residents. *The Gerontologist, 48,* 32–41.

Labouvie-Vief, G. (1982). Dynamic development and mature autonomy: A theoretical prologue. *Human Development, 25,* 161–191.

Labouvie-Vief, G. (1990). Modes of knowledge and the organization of development. In M. L. Commons, J. D. Sinnott, F. A. Richards, & C. Armon (Eds.), *Models and methods in the study of adolescent and adult thought* (pp. 43–62). New York, NY: Praeger.

Labouvie-Vief, G. (1998). Cognitive-emotional integration in adulthood. In K. W. Schaie & M. P. Lawton (Eds.), *Annual review of gerontology and geriatrics, Vol. 17: Focus on emotion and adult development* (pp. 206–237). New York, NY: Springer.

Labouvie-Vief, G. (2003). Dynamic integration: Affect, cognition, and the self in adulthood. *Current Directions in Psychological Science, 12,* 201–206.

Labouvie-Vief, G. (2006). Emerging structures of adult thought. In J. J. Arnett & J. Tanner (Eds.), *Emerging adults in America: Coming of age in the 21st century* (pp. 59–84). Washington, DC: American Psychological Association.

Labouvie-Vief, G., & Diehl, M. (2002). Cognitive complexity and cognitive-affective integration: Related or separate domains of adult development? *Psychology and Aging, 15,* 490–594.

Lachman, M. E. (2004). Development in midlife. *Annual Review of Psychology, 55,* 305–331.

Lachman, M. E., & Firth, K. (2004). The adaptive value of feeling in control during midlife. In G. Brim, C. D. Ryff, & R. Kessler (Eds.), *How healthy we are: A national study of well-being in midlife.* Chicago, IL: University of Chicago Press.

Lachman, M. E., & Kranz, E. M. (2010). Midlife crisis. *Corsini Encyclopedia of Psychology.* New York, NY: Wiley.

Lachman, M. E., Neupert, S. D., Bertrand, R., & Jette, A. M. (2006). The effects of strength training on memory in older adults. *Journal of Aging and Physical Activity, 14,* 59–73.

LaCroix, A. Z., Chlebowski, R. T., Manson, J. E., & Aragaki, A. K. (2011). Health outcomes after stopping conjugated equine estrogens among postmenopausal women with prior hysterectomy: A randomized controlled trial. *JAMA: Journal of the American Medical Association, 305,* 1305–1314.

Ladd, G. W., Buhs, E., & Troop, W. (2004). School adjustment and social skills training. In P. K. Smith & C. H. Hart (Eds.), *Blackwell handbook of childhood social development* (pp. 394–416). Malden, MA: Blackwell.

Laflamme, D., Pomerleau, A., & Malcuit, G. (2002). A comparison of fathers' and mothers' involvement in childcare and stimulation behaviors during free-play with their infants at 9 and 15 months. *Sex Roles, 47,* 507–518.

LaFromboise, T. D., Hoyt, D. R., Oliver, L., & Whitbeck, L. B. (2006). Family, community, and school influences on resilience among American Indian adolescents in the upper Midwest. *Journal of Community Psychology, 34,* 193–209.

Lahiri, D. K., Maloney, B., Basha, M. R., Ge, Y. W., & Zawia, N. H. (2007). How and when environmental agents and dietary factors affect the course of Alzheimer's disease: The "LEARn" model (latent early-life associated regulation) may explain the triggering of AD. *Current Alzheimer Research, 4,* 219–228.

Laible, D. (2004). Mother–child discourse in two contexts: Links with child temperament, attachment security and socioemotional competence. *Developmental Psychology, 40,* 979–992.

Lakatta, E. G. (1990). Heart and circulation. In E. L. Schneider & J. W. Rowe (Eds.), *Handbook of the biology of aging* (3rd ed., pp. 181–217). San Diego, CA: Academic Press.

Lamb, M. E. (1994). Infant care practices and the application of knowledge. In C. B. Fisher & R. M. Lerner (Eds.), *Applied developmental psychology* (pp. 23–45). New York, NY: McGraw-Hill.

Lamb, M. E. (2000). The history of research on father involvement: An overview. In H. E. Peters, G. W. Peterson, S. K. Steinmetz, & R. D. Day (Eds.), *Fatherhood: Research, interventions, and policies* (pp. 23–42). New York, NY: Haworth Press.

Lamb, M. E. (2010). *The role of the father in child development.* New York, NY: Wiley.

Lamb, M. E., Chuang, S. S., & Hwang, C. P. (2004). Internal reliability, temporal stability, and correlates of individual differences in parental involvement: A 15-year longitudinal study in Sweden. In R. D. Day & M. E. Lamb (Eds.), *Conceptualizing and measuring father involvement* (pp. 111–128). Mahwah, NJ: Erlbaum.

Lamb, M. E., & Lewis, C. (2005). The role of parent–child relationships in child development. In M. H. Bornstein & M. E. Lamb (Eds.),

Developmental psychology (5th ed., pp. 429–468). Mahwah, NJ: Erlbaum.

Lamb, M. E., & Lewis, C. (2010). The role and significance of father-child relationships in two-parent families. In M. E. Lamb (Ed.), *The role of the father in child development* (pp. 94–153). New York, NY: Wiley.

Lamberti, L. M., Walker, C. L. F., Noiman, A., Victora, C., & Black, R. E. (2011). Breastfeeding and the risk for diarrhea morbidity and mortality. *BMC public health, 11*(Suppl 3), S15.

Lamm, B., & Keller, H. (2007). Understanding cultural models of parenting: The role of intracultural variation and response style. *Journal of Cross-Cultural Psychology, 38,* 50–57.

Lamont, J. A. (1997). Sexuality. In D. E. Stewart & G. E. Robinson (Eds.), *A clinician's guide to menopause. Clinical practice* (pp. 63–75). Washington, DC: Health Press International.

Lampl, M., Johnson, M. L., & Frongillo, E. A., Jr. (2001). Mixed distribution analysis identifies saltation and stasis growth. *Annals of Human Biology, 28,* 403–411.

Lander, E. S., Linton, L. M., & Birren, B. (2001). Initial sequencing and analysis of the human genome. *Nature, 409,* 860–921.

Landgren, B. M., Collins, A., Csemiczky, G., Burger, H. G., Baksheev, L., & Robertson, D. M. (2004). Menopause transition. *Journal of Clinical and Endocrinological Metabolism, 89,* 2763–2769.

Lane, B. (2009). *Epidural rates in the U.S. and around the world: How many mothers choose to use an epidural to provide pain relief?* Retrieved from http://www.suite101.com/content/epidural-for-labor-a168170

Lang, F. R., Staudinger, U. M., & Cerstensen, L. L. (1998). Perspectives on socioemotional selectivity in late life: How personality and social context do (and do not) make a difference. *Journal of Gerontology, 53B,* P21–P30.

Langer, G. (2004). *ABC new prime time live poll: The American sex survey.* Retrieved from abcnews.go.com/Primetime/News/story?id=174461&page=1

Langner, T. S. (2002). *Choices for living: Coping with fear of dying.* New York, NY: Kluwer Academic.

Langer, E., & Rodin, J. (1976). The effects of choice and enhanced personal responsibility for the aged: A field experiment in an institutional setting. *Journal of Personality and Social Psychology, 34,* 191–198.

Lansford, J. E., Antonucci, T. C., Akiyama, H., & Takahashi, K. (2005). A quantitative and qualitative approach to social relationships and well-being in the United States and Japan. *Journal of Comparative Family Studies, 36,* 1–22.

Lansford, J. E., Deater-Deckard, K., Dodge, K. A., Bates, J. E., & Pettit, G. S. (2004). Ethnic differences in the link between physical discipline and later adolescent externalizing behaviors. *Journal of Child Psychology and Psychiatry, 45,* 801–812.

Lansford, J. E., Malone, P. S., Dodge, K. A., Crozier, J. C., Pettit, G. S., & Bates, J. E. (2006). A 12-year prospective study of patterns of social information processing problems and externalizing behaviors. *Journal of Abnormal Child Psychology, 34,* 715–724.

Lapsley, D., & Woodbury, R. D. (2015). Social cognitive development in emerging adulthood. In J. J. Arnett (Ed.), *Oxford handbook of emerging adulthood.* New York, NY: Oxford University Press.

Larson, E. B., Shadlen, M. F., Wang, L., McCormick, W. C., Bowen, J. D., Teri, L., & Kukull, W. A. (2004). Survival after initial diagnosis of Alzheimer disease. *Annals of Internal Medicine, 140,* 501–509.

Larson, R., & Csikszentmihalyi, M. (2014). The Experience Sampling Method. In M. Csikszentmihalyi, *Flow and Positive Psychology* (pp. 21–34). New York, NY: Springer.

Larson, R. W., Csikszentmihalyi, M., & Graef, R. (1980). Mood variability and the psycho-social adjustment of adolescents. *Journal of Youth & Adolescence, 9,* 469–490.

Larson, R. W., Moneta, G., Richards, M. H., & Wilson, S. (2002). Continuity, stability, and change in daily emotional experience across adolescence. *Child Development, 73,* 1151–1165.

Larson, R. W., Wilson, S., & Rickman, A. (2010). Globalization, societal change, and adolescence across the world. In R. Lerner & L. Steinberg (Eds.), *Handbook of adolescent psychology* (3rd ed., pp. 590–622). Hoboken, NJ: John Wiley & Sons.

Larson, R., & Richards, M. H. (1994). *Divergent realities: The emotional lives of mothers, fathers, and adolescents.* New York, NY: Basic Books.

Larson, R., Verman, S., & Dwokin, J. (2000, March). Adolescence without family disengagement: The daily family lives of Indian middle-class teenagers. Paper presented at the biennial meeting of the Society for Research on Adolescence, Chicago, IL.

Latzer, Y., Merrick, J., & Stein, D. (2011). *Understanding Eating Disorders: Integrating Culture, Psychology and Biology.* Nova Science.

Lauer, J. C., & Lauer, R. H. (1999). *How to survive and thrive in an empty nest.* Oakland, CA: New Harbinger.

Lauersen, N. H., & Bouchez, C. (2000). *Getting pregnant: What you need to know right now.* New York, NY: Fireside.

Laumann, E. O., Gagnon, J. H., Michael, R. T., & Michaels, S. (1994). *The social organization of sexuality.* Chicago, IL: University of Chicago Press.

Laursen, B., Coy, K. C., & Collins, W. A. (1998). Reconsidering changes in parent–child conflict across adolescence: A meta-analysis. *Child Development, 69,* 817–832.

Lavers-Preston, C., & Sonuga-Barke, E. (2003). An intergenerational perspective on parent–child relationships: The reciprocal effects of trigenerational grandparent–parent–child relationships. In R. Gupta & D. Parry-Gupta (Eds.), *Children and parents: Clinical issues for psychologists and psychiatrists.* London, UK: Whurr Publishers.

Lavner, J. A., & Bradbury, T. N. (2010). Patterns of change in marital satisfaction over the newlywed years. *Journal of Marriage and the Family, 72,* 1171–1187.

Lavzer, J. L., & Goodson, B. D. (2006). The "quality" of early care and education settings: Definitional and measurement issues. *Evaluation Review, 30,* 556–576.

Lawson, A. E., & Wollman, W. T. (2003). Encouraging the transition from concrete to formal operations: An experiment. *Journal of Research in Science Teaching, 40*(Suppl.), S33–S50.

Layton, E., Dollahite, D. C., & Hardy, S. A. (2011). Anchors of religious commitment in adolescents. *Journal of Adolescent Research, 26,* 381–413.

Le, H. N. (2000). Never leave your little one alone: Raising an Ifaluk child. In J. DeLoache & A. Gottlieb (Eds.), *A world of babies: Imagined childcare guides for seven societies* (pp. 199–222). New York, NY: Cambridge University Press.

Leakey, R. (1994). *The origins of humankind.* New York, NY: Basic Books.

Leaper, C., & Smith, T. E. (2004). A meta-analytic review of gender variations in children's language use: Talkativeness, affiliative speech, and assertive speech. *Developmental Psychology, 40,* 993–1027.

Leapfrog Group (2014). *Fact sheet: Maternity care.* New York, NY: Author.

Leathers, H. D., & Foster, P. (2004). *The world food problem: Tackling causes of undernutrition in the third world.* Boulder, CO: Lynne Rienner Publishers.

Leavitt, S. C. (1998). The Bikhet mystique: Masculine identity and patterns of rebellion among Bumbita adolescent males. In G. Herdt & S. C. Leavitt (Eds.), *Adolescence in Pacific island societies* (pp. 173–194). Pittsburgh, PA: University of Pittsburgh Press.

Lee, H. M., Bhat, A., Scholz, J. P., & Galloway, J. C. (2008). Toy-oriented changes during early arm movements: IV: Shoulder-elbow coordination. *Infant Behavior and Development, 31,* 447–469.

Lee, J., Lee, S., Jang, S., & Ryu, O. H. (2013). Age-related changes in the prevalence of osteoporosis according to gender and skeletal site: The Korea National Health and Nutrition Examination Survey 2008-2010. *Endocrinology and Metabolism, 28*(3), 180–191.

Lee, J. C., & Staff, J. (2007). When work matters: The varying impact of work intensity on high school dropouts. *Sociology of Education, 80,* 158–178.

Lee, M. M. C., Chang, K. S. F., & Chan, M. M. C. (1963). Sexual maturation of Chinese girls in Hong Kong. *Pediatrics, 32,* 389–398.

Lee, S. A. S., Davis, B., & MacNeilage, P. (2010). Universal production patterns and ambient language influences in babbling: A cross-linguistic study of Korean- and English-learning infants. *Journal of Child Language, 37,* 293–318.

Lee, V. E., & Burkam, D. T. (2002). *Inequality at the starting gate.* Washington, DC: Economic Policy Institute.

Lefkowitz, E. S., & Gillen, M. M. (2006). "Sex is just a normal part of life": Sexuality in emerging adulthood. In J. J. Arnett & J. L. Tanner (Eds.), *Emerging adults in America: Coming of age in the 21st century* (pp. 235–255). Washington, DC: American Psychological Association.

Lefkowitz, E. S., Gillen, M. M., Shearer, C. L., & Boone, T. L. (2004). Religiosity, sexual behaviors, and sexual attitudes during emerging adulthood. *Journal of Sex Research, 41,* 150–159.

Lehr, U., Seiler, E., & Thomae, H. (2000). Aging in a cross-cultural perspective. In A. L. Comunian & U. P. Gielen (Eds.), *International perspectives on human development* (pp. 571–589). Lengerich, Germany: Pabst Science.

Lehtinen, M., Paavonen, J., & Apter, D. (2006). Preventing common sexually transmitted infections in adolescents: Time for rethinking. *The European Journal of Contraception and Reproductive Health Care, 11,* 247–249.

Lemish, D. (2007). *Children and television: A global perspective.* Oxford, UK: Blackwell.

Lempers, J. D., & Clark-Lempers, D. S. (1993). A functional comparison of same-sex and opposite-sex friendship during adolescence. *Journal of Adolescent Research, 8,* 89–108.

Lenhart, A., Purcell, K., Smith, A., & Zickuhr, K. (2010). *Social media and mobile Internet use among teens and young adults.* Washington, DC: Pew Research Center.

Leon, K. (2003). Risk and protective factors in young children's adjustment to parental divorce: A review of the research. *Family Relations, 52,* 258–270.

Leonard, B. (2004). Women's conditions occurring in men: Breast cancer, osteoporosis, male menopause, and eating disorders. *Nursing Clinics of North America, 39,* 379–393.

Leonard, L. (2002). Problematizing fertility: "Scientific" accounts and Chadian women's narratives. In M. C. Inhorn & F. van Balen (Eds.), *Infertility around the globe: New thinking on childlessness, gender, and reproductive technologies* (pp. 193–213). Berkeley, CA: University of California Press.

Lerner, R. M. (2006). Developmental science, developmental systems, and contemporary theories of human development. In W. Damon & R. M. Lerner (Eds.), *Handbook of child psychology, Vol. 1: Theoretical models of human development* (5th ed., pp. 1–17). New York, NY: Wiley.

Lerner, R. M., Theokas, C., & Jelicic, H. (2005). Youth as active agents in their own positive development: A developmental systems perspective. In W. Greve, L. Rothermund, & D. Wentura, *The adaptive self: Personal continuity and intentional self-development* (pp. 31–47). Göttingen, Germany: Hogrefe & Huber.

Lessinger, J. (2002). Asian Indian marriages: Arranged, semi-arranged, or based on love? In N. V. Benokraitis (Ed.), *Contemporary ethnic families in the United States: Characteristics, variations, and dynamics* (pp. 101–104). Englewood Cliffs, NJ: Prentice.

Lesner, S. (2003). Candidacy and management of assistive listening devices: Special needs of the elderly. *International Journal of Audiology, 42,* 2S68–2S76.

Lessow-Hurley, J. (2005). *The foundations of dual language instruction* (4th ed.). Boston, MA: Allyn & Bacon.

Lestaeghe, R., & Moors, G. (2000). Recent trends in fertility and household formation in the industrialized world. *Review of Population and Social Policy, 9,* 121–170.

Levenson, R. W., Carstensen, L. L., & Gottman, J. M. (1993). Long-term marriage: Age, gender, and satisfaction. *Psychology and Aging, 8,* 301–313.

Levin, B. G. (2004). Coping with traumatic loss. *International Journal of Emergency Mental Health, 6,* 25–31.

Levinson, D. (1997). *The seasons of a woman's life.* New York, NY: Ballantine.

LeVine, D. N. (1966). The concept of masculinity in Ethiopian culture. *International Journal of Social Psychiatry, 12,* 17–23.

LeVine, R. A. (1977). Child rearing as cultural adaptation. In P. H. Leiderman, S. R. Tulkin, & A. Rosenfeld (Eds.), *Culture and infancy: Variations in the human experience* (pp. 15–27). New York, NY: Academic Press.

LeVine, R. A. (1994). *Child care and culture.* Cambridge, UK: Cambridge University Press.

LeVine, R. A., & LeVine, S. (1998). Fertility and maturity in Africa: Gusii parents in middle adulthood. In R.A. Shweder (Ed.), *Welcome to middle age* (pp. 189–205). Chicago: University of Chicago Press.

LeVine, R. A., & New, R. S. (Eds.). (2008). *Anthropology and child development: A cross-cultural reader.* Malden, MA: Blackwell.

LeVine, R. A., Dixon, S., LeVine, S. E., Richman, A., Keefer, C., Liederman, P. H., & Brazelton, T. B. (2008). The comparative study of parenting. In R. A. LeVine & R. S. New, *Anthropology and child development: A cross–cultural reader* (pp. 55–65). Malden, MA: Blackwell Publishing.

LeVine, R. A., Dixon, S., LeVine, S., Richman, A., Leiderman, P. H., Keefer, C. H., & Brazelton, T. B. (1994). *Childcare and culture: Lessons from Africa.* New York, NY: Cambridge University Press.

LeVine, R. A., New, R. S. (Eds.) (2008). *Anthropology and child development: A cross-cultural reader.* Malden, MA: Blackwell Publishing.

Levinson, D. J. (1978). *The seasons of a man's life.* New York, NY: Knopf.

Levitin, D. (2007). *This is your brain on music.* New York, NY: Plume.

Levy, B. R., Jennings, P., & Langer, E. J. (2001). Improving attention in old age. *Journal of Adult Development, 8,* 189–192.

Levy, F., & Murnane, R. (2012). *The new division of labor: How computers are creating the next job market.* Princeton, NJ: Princeton University Press.

Lewin, T. (2008, December 3). Higher education may soon be unaffordable for most Americans, report says. *The New York Times,* p. A17.

Lewis, M. (2000). The emergence of human emotions. In M. Lewis & J. M. Haviland-Jones (Eds.), *Handbook of emotions* (2nd ed., pp. 265–280). New York, NY: Guilford Press.

Lewis, M. (2002). Early emotional development. In A. Slater & M. Lewis (Eds.), *Introduction to infant development* (pp. 216–232). New York, NY: Oxford University Press.

Lewis, M. (2008). The emergence of human emotions. In L. F. Barrett, J. M. Haviland-Jones, & M. Lewis (Eds.), *Handbook of emotions* (3rd ed., pp. 304–319). New York, NY: Guilford Press.

Lewis, M. (2010). The development of anger. In M. Potegal, G. Stemmler, & C. Spielberger (Eds.), *International handbook of anger: Constituent and concomitant biological, psychological, and social processes* (pp. 177–191). New York, NY: Springer.

Lewis, M., & Brooks-Gunn, J. (1979). *Social cognition and the acquisition of self.* New York, NY: Plenum.

Lewis, M., & Ramsay, D. S. (1999). Effect of maternal soothing and infant stress response. *Child Development, 70,* 11–20.

Lewis, M., & Ramsay, D. S. (2004). Development of self-recognition, personal pronoun use, and pretend play during the 2nd year. *Child Development, 75,* 1821–1831.

Lewis, M., Feiring, C., & Rosenthal, S. (2000). Attachment over time. *Child Development, 71,* 707–720.

Lewis, R. (2005). *Human genetics* (6th ed.). New York, NY: McGraw-Hill.

Lewis, S. N., West, A. F., Stein, A., Malmberg, L.-E., Bethell, K., Barnes, J., & Leach, P. (2009). A comparison of father–infant interaction between primary and non-primary care giving fathers. *Child Care, Health, and Development, 35,* 199–207.

Lewkowitz, D. J., & Lickliter, R. (2013). *The development of intersensory perception.* New York, NY: Psychology Press.

Li, F., Godinet, M. T., & Arnsberger, P. (2010). Protective factors among families with children at risk of maltreatment: Follow up to early school years. *Children and Youth Services Review, 33,* 139–148.

Li, J., Fraser, M. W., & Wike, T. L. (2013). Promoting social competence and preventing childhood aggression: A framework for applying social information processing theory in intervention research. *Aggression and Violent Behavior, 18*(3), 357–364.

Liang, J., Krause, N. M., & Bennett, J. M. (2001). Social exchange and well-being: Is giving better than receiving? *Psychology and Aging, 16,* 511–523.

Liben, L. S., & Bigler, R. S. (2002). The developmental course of gender differentiation: Conceptualizing, measuring, and evaluating constructs and pathways. *Monographs of the Society for Research in Child Development, 6*(4, Series. No. 271).

Liben, L. S., Bigler, R. S., & Hilliard, L. J. (2013). Gender Development. Societal Contexts of Child Development: *Pathways of Influence and Implications for Practice and Policy, 3.*

Liben, L. S., & Signorella, M. L. (1993). Gender-schematic processing in children: The role of initial interpretation of stimuli. *Developmental Psychology, 29,* 141–149.

Liben, L. S., Bigler, R. S., & Krogh, H. R. (2001). Pink and blue collar jobs: Children's adjustments of job status and job aspirations in relation to sex of worker. *Journal of Experimental Child Psychology, 79,* 346–363.

Lichter, D. T., Turner, R. N., & Sassler, S. (2010). National estimates of the rise of serial cohabitation. *Social Science Research, 39,* 754–765.

Lieber, E., Nihira, K., & Mink, I. T. (2004). Filial piety, modernization, and the challenges of raising children for Chinese immigrants: Quantitative and qualitative evidence. *Ethos, 32,* 324–347.

Lillard, A. S. (2007). Pretend play in toddlers. In C. A. Brownell & C. B. Kopp (Eds.), *Socioemotional development in the toddler years* (pp. 149–176). New York, NY: Guilford.

Lillard, A. S. (2008). *Montessori: The science behind the genius.* New York, NY: Oxford University Press.

Lillard, A. S. & Else-Quest, N. (2006). Evaluating Montessori education. *Science, 313,* 1893–1894.

Lim, L. S., Mitchell, P., Seddon, J. M., Holz, F. G., & Wong, T. Y. (2012). Age-related macular degeneration. *The Lancet, 379*(9827), 1728–1738.

Lin, C. A. (2001). Cultural values reflected in Chinese and American television advertising. *Journal of Advertising, 30,* 83–94.

Lindau, S. T., Schumm, P., Laumann, E., Levinson, W., Muircheartaigh, C., & Waite, L. (2007). A study of sexuality and health among older adults in the United States. *The New England Journal of Medicine, 357,* 762–774.

Lindsay, L. A., & Miescher, S. F. (Eds.). (2003). *Men and masculinities in modern Africa.* Portsmouth, NH: Heinemann.

Lindsey, E., & Colwell, M. (2003). Preschooler's emotional competence: Links to pretend and physical play. *Child Study Journal, 33,* 39–52.

Lindstrom, H. A., Fritsch, T., Petot, G., Smyth, K. A., Chen, C. H., Debanne, S. M.,…Friedland, R. P. (2005). The relationships between television viewing in midlife and the development of

Alzheimer's disease in a case-control study. *Brain and Cognition, 58,* 157–165.

Linebarger, D. L., & Walker, D. (2005). Infants' and toddlers' television viewing and language outcomes. *American Behavioral Scientist, 48*(5), 624–645.

Linver, M. R., Brooks-Gunn, J., & Kohen, D. E. (2002). Family processes as pathways from income to young children's development. *Developmental Psychology, 38,* 719–734.

Lipman, E. L., Boyle, M. H., Dooley, M. D., & Offord, D. R. (2002). Child well-being in single-mother families. *Journal of the American Academy of Child and Adolescent Psychiatry, 41,* 75–82.

Lips, H., & Lawson, K. (2009). Work values, gender, and expectations about work commitment and pay: Laying the groundwork for the "motherhood penalty"? *Sex Roles, 61,* 667–676.

Lipsitt, L. P. (2003). Crib death: A biobehavioral phenomenon? *Psychological Science, 12,* 164–170.

Liston, C., & Kagan, J. (2002). Brain development: Memory enhancement in early childhood. *Nature, 419*(6910), 896–896.

Litovsky, R. Y., & Ashmead, D. H. (1997). Development of binatural and spatial hearing in infants and children. In R. H. Gilkey & T. R. Anderson (Eds.), *Binaural and spatial hearing in real and virtual environments* (pp. 571–592). Mahwah, NJ: Erlbaum.

Liu, J., Raine, A., Venables, P. H., Dalais, C., & Mednick, S. A. (2003). Malnutrition at age 3 years and lower cognitive ability at age 11 years. *Archives of Paediatric and Adolescent Medicine, 157,* 593–600.

Lloyd, C. B., Grant, M., & Ritchie, A. (2008). Gender differences in time use among adolescents in developing countries: Implications of rising school enrollment rates. *Journal of Research on Adolescence, 18,* 99–120.

Lloyd, C. (Ed.). (2005). *Growing up global: The changing transitions to adulthood in developing countries.* Washington, DC: National Research Council and Institute of Medicine.

Lobel, T. E., Nov-Krispin, N., Schiller, D., Lobel, O., & Feldman, A. (2004). Perceptions of social status, sexual orientation, and value dissimilarity. Gender discriminatory behavior during adolescence and young adulthood: A developmental analysis. *Journal of Youth & Adolescence, 33,* 535–546.

Lock, M. (1998). Deconstructing the change: Female maturation in Japan and North America. In R. A. Shweder (Ed.), *Welcome to middle age! (and Other Cultural Fictions)* (pp. 45–74). Chicago, IL: University of Chicago Press.

Loeb, S., Fuller, B., Kagan, S. L., & Carrol, B. (2004). Child care in poor communities: Early learning effects on type, quality, and stability. *Child Development, 75,* 47–65.

Loeber, R., & Burke, J. D. (2011). Developmental pathways in juvenile externalizing and internalizing problems. *Journal of Research on Adolescence, 21,* 34–46.

Loeber, R., Lacourse, E., & Homish, D. L. (2005). Homicide, violence, and developmental trajectories. In R. E. Tremblay, W. W. Hartup, & J. Archer (Eds.), *Developmental origins of aggression* (pp. 202–222). New York, NY: Guilford Press.

Loehlin, J. C., Horn, J. M., & Willerman, L. (1997). Heredity, environment, and IQ in the Texas Adoption Project. In R. J. Sternberg & E. L. Grigrenko (Eds.), *Intelligence, heredity, and environment* (pp. 105–125). New York, NY: Cambridge University Press.

Loftus, E. F. (2003, November). Make-believe memories. *American Psychologist,* 867–873.

Logsdon, R. G. (2000). *Enhancing quality of life in long term care: A comprehensive guide.* New York, NY: Hatherleigh Press.

Lohaus, A., Keller, H., Ball, J., Voelker, S., & Elben, C. (2004). Maternal sensitivity in interactions with three- and 12-month-old infants: Stability, structural composition, and developmental consequences. *Infant and Child Development, 13,* 235–252.

Longest, K. C., & Shanahan, M. J. (2007). Adolescent work intensity and substance use: The meditational and moderational roles of parenting. *Journal of Marriage & Family, 69,* 703–720.

Lord, C., & Bishop, S. L. (2010). Autism spectrum disorders. *Social Policy Report, 24*(2), 3–16.

Lorenz, J. M., Wooliever, D. E., Jetton, J. R., & Paneth, N. (1998). A quantitative review of mortality and developmental disability in extremely premature newborns. *Archives of Pediatric Medicine, 152,* 425–435.

Lorenz, K. (1957). Companionship in bird life. In C. Scholler (Ed.), *Instinctive behavior: The development of a modern concept* (pp. 83–128). New York, NY: International Universities Press.

Lorenz, K. Z. (1965). *Evolution and the modification of behavior.* Chicago, IL: University of Chicago Press.

Lotterman, J. H., Bonanno, G. A., & Galatzer-Levy, I. (2014). The heterogeneity of long-term grief reactions. *Journal of Affective Disorders.*

Lourenco, O. (2003). Making sense of Turiel's dispute with Kohlberg: The case of the child's moral competence. *New Ideas in Psychology, 21,* 43–68.

Lovas, G. S. (2011). Gender and patterns of language development in mother-toddler and father-toddler dyads. *First language, 31*(1), 83–108.

Lovasi, G. S., Lemaitre, R. N., Siscovick, D. S., Dublin, S., Bis, J. C., Lumley, T.,...Psaty, B. M. (2007). Amount of leisure-time physical activity and risk of nonfatal myocardial infarction. *Annuals of Epidemiology, 17,* 410–416.

Love, J. M., Chazan-Cohen, R., Raikes, H., & Brooks-Gunn, J. (2013). What makes a difference: Early Head Start evaluation findings in a developmental context. *Monographs of the Society for Research in Child Development, 78*(1), vii–viii.

Lu, L. (2006). The transition to parenthood: Stress, resources, and gender differences in a Chinese society. *Journal of Community Psychology, 34,* 471–488.

Lubart, T. I. (2003). In search of creative intelligence. In R. J. Sternberg, J. Lautrey, & T. I. Lubart (Eds.), *Models of intelligence: International perspectives* (pp. 279–292). Washington, DC: American Psychological Association.

Lucas, R. E., Clark, A. E., Georgellis, Y., & Diener, E. (2003). Reexamining adaptation and the set point model of happiness: Reactions to changes in marital status. *Journal of Personality and Social Psychology, 84,* 527–539.

Luckie, M. (2010). School year around the world. Retrieved from http://californiawatch.org/k-12/how-long-school-year-compare-california-world

Ludington-Hoe, S. M. (2013). Kangaroo care as neonatal therapy. *Newborn and Infant Nursing Reviews, 13,* 73. doi: 10.1053/j.nainr.2013.03.004

Lund, D. A., & Caserta, M. S. (2004). Facing life alone: Loss of a significant other in later life. In D. Doda (Ed.), *Living with grief: Loss in later life* (pp. 207–223). Washington, DC: Hospice Foundation of America.

Lung, F.-W., Chiang, T.-L., Lin, S.-J., Feng, J.-Y., Chen, P.-F., Shu, B.-C. (2011). Gender differences of children's developmental trajectory from 6 to 60 months in the Taiwan Birth Cohort Pilot Study. *Research in Developmental Disabilities, 32,* 100–106.

Lupsakko, T., Mantyjarvi, M., Kautiainen, H., & Sulkava, R. (2002). Combined hearing and visual impairment and depression in a population aged 75 years and older. *International Journal of Geriatric Psychiatry, 17,* 808–813.

Lyckyx, K. (2006). *Identity formation in emerging adulthood: Developmental trajectories, antecedents, and consequences.* Dissertation, Catholic University, Leuven, Belgium.

Lynch, A., Lee, H. M., Bhat, A., & Galloway, J. C. (2008). No stable arm preference during the pre-reaching period: A comparison of right and left hand kinematics with and without a toy present. *Developmental Psychobiology, 50,* 390–398.

Lynch, M. E. (1991). Gender intensification. In R. M. Lerner, A. C. Petersen, & J. Brooks-Gunn (Eds.), *Encyclopedia of adolescence* (Vol. 1). New York, NY: Garland.

Lynn, R., & Mikk, J. (2007). National differences in intelligence and educational attainment. *Intelligence, 35,* 115–121.

Lynne, S. D., Graber, J. A., Nichols, T. R., Brooks-Gunn, J., & Botvin, G. J. (2007). Links between pubertal timing, peer influences, and externalizing behaviors among urban students followed through middle school. *Journal of Adolescent Health, 40,* e7–e13.

Lyon, E. (2007). *The big book of birth.* New York, NY: Plume.

Lyon, T. D., & Flavell, J. H. (1993). Young children's understanding of forgetting over time. *Child Development, 64,* 789–800.

Lyons-Ruth, K. (1996). Attachment relationships among children with aggressive behavior problems: The role of disorganized early attachment patterns. *Journal of Consulting and Clinical Psychology, 64,* 64–73.

Lyons-Ruth, K., Bronfman, E., Parsons, E. (1999). Maternal frightened, frightening, or atypical behavior and disorganized infant attachment patterns. *Monographs of the Society for Research in Child Development, 64*(3, Serial No. 258), 67–96.

Lyons-Ruth, K., Easterbrooks, A., & Cibelli, C. (1997). Infant attachment strategies, infant mental lag, and maternal depressive symptoms: Predictors of internalizing and externalizing problems at age 7. *Developmental Psychology, 33,* 681–692.

Lytle, L. J., Bakken, L, & Romig, C. (1997). Adolescent female identity development. *Sex Roles, 37,* 175–185.

Ma, J., Betts, N. M., Horacek, T., Georgiou, C., White, A., & Nitzke, S. (2002). The importance of decisional balance and self-efficacy in relation to stages of change for fruit and vegetable intakes by young adults. *American Journal of Health Promotion, 16,* 157–166.

MacBeth, T. M. (2007). Violence, natural experiments and. In J. J. Arnett (Ed.), *Encyclopedia of children, adolescents, and the media* (Vol. 2, pp. 864–867). Thousand Oaks, CA: Sage.

Maccoby, E. E. (1984). Socialization and developmental change. *Child Development, 55,* 317–328.

Maccoby, E. E. (2002). Gender and group process: A developmental perspective. *Current Directions in Psychological Science, 11,* 54–57.

Maccoby, E. E., & Lewis, C. C. (2003). Less day care or different day care? *Child Development, 76,* 1069–1075.

Maccoby, E., & Martin, J. (1983). Socialization in the context of the family: Parent–child interaction. In P. H. Mussen (Ed.) & E. M. Hetherington (Vol. Ed.), *Handbook of child psychology. Vol. 4: Socialization, personality, and social development* (4th ed., pp. 1–101). New York, NY: Wiley.

MacDorman, M. F., Menacker, F., & Declercq, E. (2010). Trends and characteristics of home and other out-of-hospital births in the United States, 1990–2006. *National Vital Statistics Reports, 58,* 1–14, 16.

Macek, P. (2007). Czech Republic. In J. J. Arnett (Ed.), *International encyclopedia of adolescence* (pp. 206–219). New York, NY: Routledge.

Macek, P., Bejcek, J., & Vanickova, J. (2007). Contemporary Czech emerging adults: Generation growing up in the period of social changes. *Journal of Adolescent Research, 22,* 444–475.

MacFarquhar, R., & Schoenhals, J. (2006). *Mao's last revolution.* Cambridge, MA: Harvard University Press.

Macfie, J., Cicchetti, D., & Toth, S. L. (2001). The development of dissociation in maltreated preschool-aged children, *Development and Psychopathology, 13,* 233–254.

Machado, A., & Silva, F. J. (2007). Toward a richer view of the scientific method: The role of conceptual analysis. *American Psychologist, 62,* 671–681.

MacKenzie, P. J. (2009). Mother tongue first multilingual education among the tribal communities in India. *International Journal of Bilingual Education and Bilingualism, 12,* 369–385.

Maddell, D., & Muncer, S. (2004). Back from the beach but hanging on the telephone? English adolescents' attitudes and experiences of mobile phones and the Internet. *CyberPsychology & Behavior, 73,* 359–367.

Madden, D. J. (2001). Speed and timing of behavioral processes. In J. E. Birren & K. W. Schaie (Eds.), *Handbook of the psychology of aging* (5th ed., pp. 288–312). San Diego, CA: Academic Press.

Madhavan, S. (2002). Best of friends and worst of enemies: Competition and collaboration in polygyny. *Ethnology, 41,* 69–84.

Madlon-Kay, D. J. (2002). Maternal assessment of neonatal jaundice after hospital discharge. *The Journal of Family Practice, 51,* 445–448.

Maehara, T., & Takemura, A. (2007). The norms of filial piety and grandmother roles as perceived by grandmothers and their grandchildren in Japan and South Korea. *International Journal of Behavioral Development, 31,* 585–593.

Magnuson, M. J., & Dundes, L. (2008). Gender differences in "social portraits" reflected in MySpace profiles. *CyberPsychology & Behavior, 11,* 239–241.

Mahanran, L. G., Bauman, P. A., Kalman, D., Skolnik, H., & Pele, S. M. (1999). Master athletes: Factors affecting performance. *Sports Medicine, 28,* 273–285.

Maheshwari, A., Hamilton, M., & Bhattacharya, S. (2008). Effect of female age on the diagnostic categories of infertility. *Human Reproduction, 23,* 538–542.

Mahfuz, K. (2008). Determinants of life expectancy in developing countries. *Journal of Developing Areas, 41,* 185–204.

Mahn, H. (2003). Periods in child development: Vygotsky's perspective. In A. Kozulin, & B. Gindis (Eds.), *Vygotsky's educational theory in cultural context* (pp. 119–137). New York, NY: Cambridge University Press.

Maimon, D., & Browning, C. R. (2010). Unstructured socializing, collective efficacy, and violent behavior among urban youth. *Criminology: An Interdisciplinary Journal, 48,* 443–474.

Mair, F. S., May, C., et al. (2012). Factors that promote or inhibit the implementation of e-health systems: An explanatory systematic review. *Bulletin of the World Health Organization, 90,* 357–364.

Malaguarnera, L., Ferlito, L., Imbesi, R. M., Gulizia, G. S., Di Mauro, S., Maugeri, D.,…Messina, A. (2001). Immunosenescence: A review. *Archives of Gerontology and Geriatrics, 32,* 1–14.

Malebo, A., van Eeden, C., & Wissing, M. P. (2007). Sport participation, psychological well-being, and psychosocial development in a group of young black adults. *South African Journal of Psychology, 37,* 188–206.

Males, M. (2009). Does the adolescent brain make risk-taking inevitable? A skeptical appraisal. *Journal of Adolescent Research, 24,* 3–20.

Males, M. (2010). Is jumping off the roof always a bad idea? A rejoinder on risk taking and the adolescent brain. *Journal of Adolescent Research, 25,* 48–63.

Malina, R. M., Bouchard, C., & Bar-Or, O. (2004). *Growth, maturation and physical activity* (2nd ed.). Champaign, IL: Human Kinetics.

Malott, C. S. (2011). What is postformal psychology? Toward a theory of critical complexity. In C. S. Malott (Ed.), *Critical pedagogy and cognition* (pp. 97–111). Netherlands: Springer.

Mandel, D. R., Lusczyk, P. W., & Pisoni, D. B. (1995). Infants' recognition of the sound patterns of their own names. *Psychological Science, 6,* 314–317.

Manev, R., & Manev, H. (2005). The meaning of mammalian adult neurogenesis and the function of newly added neurons: The "small world" network. *Medical Hypotheses, 64,* 114–117.

Mange, E. J., & Mange, A. P. (1998). *Basic human genetics* (2nd ed.). Sunderland, MA: Sinauer Associates.

Manheimer, R. J. (2008). Gearing up for the big show: Lifelong learning programs are coming of age. In R. B. Hudson (Ed.), *Boomer bust? Economic and political issues of the graying society* (Vol. 2, pp. 99–112). Westport, CT: Praeger.

Mani, T. M., Bedwell, J. S., & Miller, L. S. (2005). Age-related decrements in performance on a brief continuous performance task. *Archives of Clinical Neuropsychology, 20,* 575–586.

Manning, M. L. (1998). Play development from ages eight to twelve. In D. P. Fromberg & D. Bergen, *Play from birth to twelve and beyond* (pp. 154–161). London, UK: Garland Publishing.

Manning, W.D. (2013). *Trends in cohabitation: Over twenty years of change, 1987–2010.* (FP-13-12). National Center for Family & Marriage Research. Retrieved from http://ncfmr.bgsu.edu/pdf/family_profiles/file130944.pdf

Manzoli, L., Villari, P. M., Pirone, G., & Boccia, A. (2007). Marital status and mortality in the elderly: A systematic review and meta-analysis. *Social Science & Medicine, 64,* 77–94.

Maratsos, M. (1998). The acquisition of grammar. In W. Damon (Ed.), & D. Kuhn & R. S. Siegler (Vol. Eds.), *Handbook of child psychology* (5th ed.): *Vol. 2.Cognition, perception and language* (pp. 421–466). New York, NY: Wiley.

Marcell, J. J. (2003). Sarcopenia: Causes, consequences, and preventions. *Journals of Gerontology A: Biological and Medical Sciences, 58,* M911–M916.

Marcia, J. (1966). Development and validation of ego identity status. *Journal of Personality and Social Psychology, 3,* 551–558.

Marcia, J. E., & Carpendale, J. I. (2004). Identity: Does thinking make it so? *Changing conceptions of psychological life,* 113–126.

Marcia, J. (1980). Identity in adolescence. In J. Adelson (Ed.), *Handbook of adolescent Psychology* (pp. 159–187). New York, NY: Wiley.

Marcia, J. (1989). Identity and intervention. *Journal of Adolescence, 12,* 401–410.

Marcia, J. E. (1999). Representational thought in ego identity, psychotherapy, and psychosocial developmental theory. In I. E. Siegel (Ed.), *Development of mental representation: Theories and applications* (pp. 391–414). Mahwah, NJ: Erlbaum.

Marcia, J. E. (2010). Life transitions and stress in the context of psychosocial development. In T. W. Miller (Ed.), *Handbook of stressful transitions across the lifespan* (pp. 19–34). New York, NY: Springer.

Marcon, R. A. (1999). Positive relationships between parent–school involvement and public school inner-city preschoolers' development and academic performance. *School Psychology Review, 28,* 395–412.

Marcotte, D., Fortin, L., Potvin, P., & Papillon, M. (2002). Gender differences in depressive symptoms during adolescence: Role of gender-typed characteristics, self-esteem, body image, stressful life events, and pubertal status. *Journal of Emotional and Behavioral Disorders, 10,* 29–42.

Marcovitch, S., Zelazo, P., & Schmuckler, M. (2003). The effect of the number of A trials on performance on the A-not-B task. *Infancy, 3,* 519–529.

Marcus, B. H., Williams, D. M., Dubbert, P. M., Sallis, J. F., King, A. C., Yancey, A. K., et al. (2006). Physical activity intervention studies: What we know and what we need to know: A scientific statement from the American Heart Association Council on nutrition, physical activity, and metabolism (Subcommittee on Physical Activity); Council on Cardiovascular Disease in the Young; and the Interdisciplinary Working Group on Quality of Care and Outcomes Research. *Circulation, 114,* 2739–2752.

Marcus, I. G. (2004). *The Jewish life cycle: Rites of passage from biblical to modern times.* Seattle, WA: University of Washington Press.

Marhsall, M. (1979). *Weekend warriors.* Palo Alto, CA: Mayfield.

MarketingCharts Staff (2014). *Are young people watching less TV?* Retrieved from http://www.marketingcharts.com/television/are-young-people-watching-less-tv-24817/

Markey, P. M., & Markey, C. N. (2007). Romantic ideals, romantic obtainment, and relationship experiences: The complementary of interpersonal traits among romantic partners. *Journal of Social and Personal Relationships, 24,* 517–533.

Markman, E. M., & Jaswal, V. K. (2004). Acquiring and using a grammatical form class: Lessons from the proper-count distinction. *Weaving a lexicon,* 371–409.

Marks, N. (1995). Midlife marital status differences in social support relationships with adult children and psychological well-being. *Journal of Family Issues, 16,* 5–28.

Marks, N. F. (1996). Caregiving across the lifespan: National prevalence and predictors. *Family Relations, 45,* 27–36.

Marks, N. F., & Lambert, J. D. (1998). Marital status continuity and change among young and midlife adults. *Journal of Family Issues, 19,* 652–686.

Marks, N. F., Bumpass, L. L., & Jun, H. (2004). Family roles and well-being during the middle life course. In O. G. Brim, C. D. Ryff, & R. C. Kessler (Eds.), *How healthy are we? A national study of well-being at midlife* (pp. 514–549).

Markstrom, C. A., & Kalmanir, H. M. (2001). Linkages between the psychosocial stages of identity and intimacy and the ego strengths of fidelity and love. *Identity, 1,* 179–196.

Markus, H. R., & Kitayama, S. (2003). Culture, self, and the reality of the social. *Psychological Inquiry, 14,* 277–283.

Markus, H., & Kitayama, S. (1991). Culture and the self: Implications for cognition, emotion, and motivation. *Psychological Review, 98,* 224–253.

Markus, H. R., & Kitayama, S. (2010). Cultures and Selves A Cycle of Mutual Constitution. *Perspectives on Psychological Science, 5*(4), 420–430.

Markus, H., & Nurius, R. (1986). Possible selves. *American Psychologist, 41,* 954–969.

Marlier, L, Schaal, B., & Soussignan, R. (1998). Neonatal responsiveness to the odor of amniotic and lacteal fluids: A test of perinatal chemosensory continuity. *Child Development, 69,* 611–623.

Marlow, N., Wolke, D., Bracewell, M. A., & Samara, M. (2005). Neurologic and developmental disability at six years of age after extremely preterm births. *New England Journal of Medicine, 352,* 9–19.

Marsh, H. W., & Ayotte, V. (2003). Do multiple dimensions of self concept become more differentiated with age? The differential distinctiveness hypothesis. *Journal of Educational Psychology, 95,* 687–706.

Marsh, H., & Kleitman, S. (2005). Consequences of employment during high school: Character building, subversion of academic goals, or a threshold? *American Educational Research Journal, 42,* 331–369.

Marsh, M., & Ronner, W. (1996). *The empty cradle: Infertility in America from colonial times to the present.* Baltimore, MD: Johns Hopkins University Press.

Marshall, W. (1978). *Puberty.* In F. Falkner & J. Tanner (Eds.), *Human growth* (Vol. 2). New York, NY: Plenum.

Marsiske, M., Klumb, P. L., & Baltes, M. M. (1997). Everyday activity patterns and sensory functioning in old age. *Psychology and Aging, 12,* 444–457.

Marti, E., & Rodriguez, C. (Eds.) (2012). *After Piaget.* New York, NY: Transaction Publishers.

Martin, A., Brooks-Gunn, J., Klebanov, P., Buka, S., & McCormick, M. (2008). Long-term maternal effects of early childhood intervention: Findings from the Infant Health and Development Program (IHDP). *Journal of Applied Developmental Psychology, 29,* 101–117.

Martin, C. K., & Fabes, R. A. (2001). The stability and consequences of young children's same-sex peer interactions. *Developmental Psychology, 37*, 431–446.

Martin, C. L., & Rubie, D. (2004). Children's search for gender cues: Cognitive perspectives on gender development. *Current Directions in Psychological Science, 13*, 67–70.

Martin, J., & Sokol, B. (2011). Generalized others and imaginary audiences: A neo-Meadian approach to adolescent egocentrism. *New Ideas in Psychology, 29*(3), 364–375.

Martin, J. A., Hamilton, B. E., Sutton, P. D., Ventura, S. J., Menacker, F., & Munson, M. L (2005). Births: Final data for 2003. *National Vital Statistics Reports, 54*, 1–116.

Martin, J. A., Park, M. M., & Sutton, P. D. (2002). Births: Preliminary data for 2001. *National Vital Statistics Reports, 50*(10). Hyattsville, MD: National Center for Health Statistics.

Martin, J. L, & Ross, H. S. (2005). Sibling aggression: Sex differences and parents' reactions. *International Journal of Behavioral Development, 29*, 129–138.

Martin, P., & Midgley, E. (2010). *Immigration in America, 2010.* Washington, DC: Population Reference Bureau.

Martini, C., Pallottini, V., DeMarinis, E., Marino, M., Cavallini, G., Donati, A., …Trentalance, A. (2008). Omega-3 as well as caloric restriction prevent the age-related modifications of cholesterol metabolism. *Mechanisms of Ageing and Development, 129*, 722–727.

Martini, M. (1996). "What's new?" at the dinner table: Family dynamics during mealtimes in two cultural groups in Hawaii. *Early Development and Parenting, 5*, 23–24.

Martins, C., & Gaffan, E. A. (2000). Effects of maternal depression on patterns of infant–mother attachment: A meta-analytic investigation. *Journal of Child Psychology and Psychiatry, 41*, 737–746.

Martinson, M., & Minkler, M. (2006). Civic engagement and older adults: A critical perspective. *The Gerontologist, 46*, 318–324.

Martlew, M., & Connolly, K. J. (1996). Human figure drawings by schooled and unschooled children in Papua New Guinea. *Child Development, 67*, 2743–2762.

Marván, M. L., & Trujillo, P. (2010). Menstrual socialization, beliefs, and attitudes concerning menstruation in rural and urban Mexican women. *Health Care for Women International, 31*, 53–67.

Mascarenhas, M. N., Flaxman, S. R., Boerma, T., Vanderpoels, S., & Stevens, G. A. (2012). National, regional, and global trends in infertility prevalence since 1990: A systematic analysis of 277 health surveys. *PLOS Medicine, 9*, 1–12.

Mascolo, M. F., & Fischer, K. W. (2007). The codevelopment of self and sociomoral emotions during the toddler years. In C. A. Brownell & C. B. Kopp (Eds.), *Socioemotional development in the toddler years* (pp. 66–99). New York, NY: Guilford.

Maslach, C., Schaufeli, W. B., & Leiter, M. P. (2001). Job burnout. *Annual Review of Psychology, 52*, 397–422.

Masten, A. S. (2007). Competence, resilience, and development in adolescence: Clues for prevention science. In D. Romer & E. F. Walker (Eds.), *Adolescent psychopathology and the developing brain: Integrating brain and prevention science* (pp. 31–52). New York, NY: Oxford University Press.

Masten, A. S. (2014). Global perspectives on resilience in children and youth. *Child Development, 85*(1), 6–20.

Masten, A. S., Obradovic, J., & Burt, K. B. (2006). Resilience in embracing emerging adulthood: Developmental perspectives on continuity and transformation. In J. J. Arnett & J. L. Tanner (Eds.), *Emerging adults in America: Coming of age in the 21st century* (pp. 173–190). Washington, DC: American Psychological Association.

Mastin, D. F., Peszka, J., & Lilly, D. R. (2009). Online academic integrity. *Teaching of Psychology, 36*, 174–178.

Masunaga, H., & Horn, J. (2000). Characterizing mature human intelligence: Expertise development. *Learning & Individual Differences, 12*, 5–33.

Masunaga, H., & Horn, J. (2001). Expertise and age-related changes in components of intelligence. *Psychology and Aging, 16*, 293–311.

Matlin, M. W. (2004). *The psychology of women* (5th ed.). Belmont, CA: Wadsworth.

Matsumoto, D., & Yoo, S. H. (2006). Toward a new generation of cross-cultural research. *Perspectives on Psychological Science, 1*, 234–250.

Matthews, F., & Brayne, C. (2005). The incidence of dementia in England and Wales: Findings from the five identical sites of the MRC and CFA Study. *PLoS Medicine, 2*, e193.mmg/sec5/ch40/ch40a.jsp

Mattis, J., & Jagers, M. (2001). A relational framework for the study of religiosity and spirituality in the lives of African Americans. *Journal of Community Psychology, 29*, 519–539.

Mattson, S. N., Roesch, S. C., Fagerlund, Å., Autti-Rämö, I., Jones, K. L., May, P. A., Adnams, C. M., Konovalova, V., Riley, E. P., & CIFASD. (2010). Toward a neurobehavioral profile of fetal alcohol spectrum disorders. *Alcoholism: Clinical and Experimental Research, 34*, 1640–1650.

Matusov, E., & Hayes, R. (2000). Sociocultural critique of Piaget and Vygotsky. *New Ideas in Psychology, 18*, 215–239.

Maynard, A. E. (2008). What we thought we knew and how we came to know it: Four decades of cross-cultural research from a Piagetian point of view. *Human Development, 51* (Special issue: Celebrating a legacy of theory with new directions for research on human development), 56–65.

Maynard, A. E., & Greenfield, P. M. (2003). Implicit cognitive development in cultural tools and children: Lessons from Maya Mexico. *Cognitive Development, 18*(Special Issue: The sociocultural construction of implicit knowledge), 485–510.

Maynard, A. E., & Martini, M. I. (Eds.). (2005). *Learning in cultural context: Family, peers, and school.* New York, NY: Kluwer.

Mayo Clinic Staff (2011). *Stages of Labor: Baby, it's time!* Retrieved from http://www.mayoclinic.com/health/stages-of-labor/PR00106/NSECTIONGROUP=2

Mayseless, O., & Scharf, M. (2003). What does it mean to be an adult? The Israeli experience. In J. J. Arnett & N. Galambos (Eds.), *New directions in child and adolescent development* (Vol. 100, pp. 5–20). San Francisco, CA: Jossey-Bass.

Mazuka, R., Kondo, T., & Hayashi, A. (2008). Japanese mothers' use of specialized vocabulary in infant-directed speech: Infant–directed vocabulary in Japanese. In N. Masataka (Ed.), *The origins of language: Unraveling evolutionary forces* (pp. 39–58). New York, NY: Springer.

Mazur, E., & Kozarian, L. (2010). Self-presentation and interaction in blogs of adolescents and young emerging adults. *Journal of Adolescent Research, 25*, 124–144.

McAdams, D. P. (2013). The positive psychology of adult generativity: Caring for the next generation and constructing a redemptive life. In *Positive Psychology* (pp. 191–205). New York, NY: Springer.

McAdams, D. P., & Logan, R. L. (2004). What is generativity? In D. P. McAdams & E. de St. Aubin (Eds.), *The generative society: Caring for future generations* (pp. 15–31). Washington, DC: American Psychological Association.

McAlister, A., & Peterson, C. (2007). A longitudinal study of child siblings and theory of mind development. *Cognitive Development, 22*, 258–270.

McArdle, E. F. (2002). New York's Do-Not-Resuscitate law: Groundbreaking protection of patient autonomy or a physician's right to make medical futility determinations? *DePaul Journal of Health Care Law, 8*, 55–82.

McArdle, J. J., & Hamagami, F. (2006). Longitudinal tests of dynamic hypotheses on intellectual abilities measured over sixty years. In C. S. Bergeman & S. M. Boker (Eds.), *Methodological issues in aging research* (pp. 43–98). Mahwah, NJ: Lawrence Erlbaum.

McArdle, J. J., Ferrer-Caja, E., Hamagami, F., & Woodcock, R. W. (2002). Comparative longitudinal structural analyses of the growth and decline of multiple intellectual abilities over the life span. *Developmental Psychology, 38,* 115–142.

McCarthy, B., & McCarthy, E. J. (2004). *Getting it right the first time: Creating a healthy marriage.* New York, NY: Brunner-Routledge.

McCarthy, G., & Maughan, B. (2010). Negative childhood experiences and adult love relationships: The role of internal working models of attachment. *Attachment & human development, 12*(5), 445–461.

McCartney, K., & Berry, D. (2009). Whether the environment matters more for children in poverty. In K. McCartney and R. A. Weinberg (Eds.), *Experience and development: A festschrift in honor of Sandra Wood Scarr* (pp. 99–124). New York, NY: Psychology Press.

McCarty, M. E., Clifton, R. K., & Collard, R. R. (2001). The beginnings of tool use by infants and toddlers. *Infancy, 2*(2), 233–256.

McClure, V. S. (2000). *Infant massage—Revised Edition: A handbook for loving parents.* New York, NY: Bantam.

McCullough, J. L., & Kelly, K. M. (2006). Prevention and treatment of skin aging. *Annals of the New York Academy of Sciences, 1067,* 323–331.

McDade, T. W., & Worthman, C. M. (2004). Socialization ambiguity in Samoan adolescents: A model for human development and stress in the context for culture change. *Journal of Research on Adolescence, 14,* 49–72.

McDonough, P. M., & Calderone, S. (2006). The meaning of money: Perceptual differences between college counselors and low-income families about college costs and financial aid. *American Behavioral Scientist, 49,* 1703–1718.

McDowell, M. A., Brody, D. J., & Hughes, J. P. (2007). Has age at menarche changed? Results from the National Health and Nutrition Examination Survey (NHANES) 1999–2004. *Journal of Adolescent Health, 40,* 227–231.

McFalls, J. A. (2007). Population: A lively introduction. *Population Bulletin, 62,* 1–31.

McGue, M., & Christensen, K. (2002). The heritability of level and rate-of-change in cognitive functioning in Danish twins aged 70 years and older. *Experimental Aging Research, 28,* 435–451.

McGuire, S., Manke, B., Eftekhari, A., & Dunn, J. (2000). Children's perceptions of sibling conflict during middle childhood: Issues and sibling (Dis)similarity. *Social Development, 9,* 173–190.

McHale, J. P., & Rotman, T. (2007). Is seeing believing? Expectant parents' outlooks on coparenting and later coparenting solidarity. *Infant Behavior & Development, 30,* 63–81.

McHale, S. M., Crouter, A. C., Tucker, C. J. (2001). Free-time activities in middle childhood: Links with adjustment in early adolescence. *Child Development, 72,* 1764–1778.

McHale, S., Dariotis, J., & Kauh, T. (2003). Social development and social relationships in middle childhood. In R. Lerner & M. Easterbrooks (Eds.), *Handbook of psychology: Developmental psychology* (Vol. 6., pp. 241–265). New York, NY: John Wiley & Sons.

McKenna, J. J., & McDade, T. (2005). Why babies should never sleep alone: A review of the co-sleeping controversy in relation to SIDS, bedsharing, and breastfeeding. *Paediatric Respiratory Reviews, 6,* 134–152.

McKinsey Global Institute (2010). *Lions on the move: The progress and potential of Africa's economies.* Washington, DC: Author.

McKnight Investigators (2003). Risk factors for the onset of eating disorders in adolescent girls: Results on the McKnight longitudinal risk factor study. *American Journal of Psychiatry, 160,* 248–254.

McKnight, A. J., & Peck, R. C. (2002). Graduated licensing: What works? *Injury Prevention, 8*(Suppl. 2), ii32–ii38.

McLean, K. C., & Breen, A. V. (2015). Selves in a world of stories during emerging adulthood. In J. J. Arnett (Ed.), *Oxford handbook of emerging adulthood.* New York, NY: Oxford University Press.

McLoyd, V. C., & Smith, J. (2002). Physical discipline and behavior problems in African-American, European-American, and Hispanic children: Emotional support as a moderator. *Journal of Marriage and the Family, 64,* 40–53.

McLuhan, M. (1960). *The Gutenberg galaxy.* Toronto, Canada: University of Toronto Press.

McNamara, F., & Sullivan, C. E. (2000). Obstructive sleep apnea in infants. *Journal of Pediatrics, 136,* 318–323.

Mead, G. H. (1934). *Mind, self, and society.* Chicago, IL: University of Chicago Press.

Mead, M. (1928/1978). *Culture and commitment.* Garden City, NY: Anchor.

Mead, M. (1930/2001). *Growing up in New Guinea.* New York, NY: Anchor.

Mearns, S. (2000). The impact of loss on adolescents: Developing appropriate support. *International Journal of Palliative Nursing, 6,* 12–17.

Mechling, J. (2008). Toilet training. In *Encyclopedia of children and childhood in history and society.* Retrieved from http://www.faqs.org/childhood/Th-W/Toilet-Training.html

Medina, J., Ojeda-Aciego, M., & Ruiz-Calviño, J. (2009). Formal concept analysis via multi-adjoint concept lattices. *Fuzzy Sets and Systems, 160*(2), 130–144.

Medline (2008). Kwashiorkor. *Medline Plus medical encyclopedia.* Available: http://www.nlm.nih.gov/MEDLINEPLUS/ency/article/001604.htm

Mednick, S. A. (1963). Research creativity in psychology graduate students. *Journal of Consulting Psychology, 27,* 265–266.

Meeus, W. (2007). Netherlands. In J. J. Arnett, R. Ahmed, B. Nsamenang, T. S. Saraswathi, & R. Silbereisen (Eds.), *International encyclopedia of adolescence* (pp. 666–680). New York, NY: Routledge.

Meeus, W., Iedema, J., Helsen, M., & Vollebergh, W. (1999). Patterns of adolescent identity development: Review of literature and longitudinal analysis. *Developmental Review, 19,* 419–461.

Meijer, A. M., & van den Wittenboer, G. L. H. (2007). Contribution of infants' sleep and crying to marital relationship of first-time parent couples in the first year after childbirth. *Journal of Family Psychology, 21,* 49–57.

Meikle, M. B., Henry, J. A., Griest, S. E., Stewart, B. J., Abrams, H. B., McArdle, R.,…& Vernon, J. A. (2012). The tinnitus functional index: development of a new clinical measure for chronic, intrusive tinnitus. *Ear and hearing, 33*(2), 153–176.

Meister, H., & von Wedel, H. (2003). Demands on hearing aid features—special signal processing for elderly users? *International Journal of Audiology, 42,* 2S58–2S62.

Melby, M. K. (2005). Factor analysis of climacteric symptoms in Japan. *Maturitas, 52,* 205–222.

Melby, M. K., Lock, M., & Kaufert, P. (2005). Culture and symptom reporting at menopause. *Human Reproduction Update, 11,* 495–512.

Melton, L. J., Johnell, O., Lau, E., Mautalen, C. A., & Seeman, E. (2004). Osteoporosis and the global competition for health care resources. *Journal of Bone and Mineral Resources, 19,* 1055–1058.

Meltzoff, A. N., & Moore, M. K. (1994). Imitation, memory, and the representation of persons. *Infant Behavior and Development, 17,* 83–99.

Mendelsohn, J. B., Li, Q-Z., Ji, B-T., Shu, X-O., Yang, G., Li, H. L.,…Chow, W. H. (2009). Personal use of hair dye and cancer risk in a prospective cohort of Chinese women. *Cancer Science, 100,* 1088–1091.

Mendle, J., & Ferrero, J. (2012). Detrimental psychological outcomes associated with pubertal timing in adolescent boys. *Developmental Review, 32*(1), 49–66.

Menella, J. (2000, June). The psychology of eating. Paper presented at the annual meeting of the American Psychological Society, Miami, FL.

Menon, U. (2002). Middle adulthood in cultural perspective: The imagined and the experienced in three cultures. In M. E. Lachman (Ed.), *Handbook of midlife development* (pp. 40–74). New York, NY: Wiley.

Menon, U. (2013). The Hindu concept of self-refinement: Implicit yet meaningful. *Psychology & Developing Societies, 25*(1), 195–222.

Menyuk, P., Liebergott, J., & Schultz, M. (1995). *Early language development in full-term and premature infants.* Hillsdale, NJ: Erlbaum.

Merewood, A., Mehta, S. D., Chamberlain, L. B., Phillipp, B. L., & Bauchner, H. (2005). Breastfeeding rates in U.S. baby-friendly hospitals: Results of a national survey. *Pediatrics, 116,* 628–634.

Mergenhagen, P. (1996). Her own boss. *American Demographics, 18,* 36–41.

Merten, M. J., Wickrama, K. A. S., & Williams, A. L. (2008). Adolescent obesity and young adult psychosocial outcomes: Gender and racial differences. *Journal of Youth and Adolescence, 37,* 1111–1122.

Merten, S., Dratva, J., & Achermann-Liebrich, U. (2005). Do baby-friendly hospitals influence breastfeeding duration on a national level? *Pediatrics, 116,* c702–c708.

Merz, E., & Abramowicz, J. (2012). 3D/4D ultrasound in prenatal diagnosis: Is it time for routine use? *Clinical Obstetrics & Gynecology, 55,* 336–351.

Meskel, L. (2001). The Egyptian ways of death. *Archeological Papers of the American Anthropological Association, 10,* 27–40.

Mesman, J., van IJzendoorn, M. H., Bakermans-Kranenburg, M. J. (2009). The many faces of the Still-Face Paradigm: A review and meta-analysis. *Developmental Review, 29,* 120–162.

Messaoudi, I., Warner, J., Fischer, M., Park, B., Hill, B., Mattison, J.,…Nikolich-Zugich, J. (2006). Delay of T cell senescence by caloric restriction in aged long-lived nonhuman primates. *Proceedings of the National Academy of Sciences, 103,* 19448–19453.

Messersmith, E. E., Garrett, J. L., Davis-Kean, P. E., Malanchuk, O., & Eccles, J. S. (2008). Career development from adolescence through emerging adulthood: Insights from information technology occupations. *Journal of Adolescent Research, 23,* 206–227.

Messinger, D. S., & Lester, B. M. (2008). Prenatal substance exposure and human development. In A. Fogel, B. J. King, & S. G. Shanker (Eds.), *Human development in the 21st century: Visionary policy ideas from systems scientists* (pp. 225–232). Bethesda, MD: Council on Human Development.

Meyers, C., Adam, R., Dungan, J., & Prenger, V. (1997). Aneuploidy in twin gestations: When is maternal age advanced? *Obstetrics and Gynecology, 89,* 248–251.

Michael, R. T., Gagnon, J. H., Laumann, E. O., & Kolata, G. (1995). *Sex in America: A definitive study.* New York, NY: Warner Books.

Milan, S., Snow, S., & Belay, S. (2007). The context of preschool children's sleep: Racial/ethnic differences in sleep locations, routines, and concerns. *Journal of Family Psychology, 21*(Special issue: *Carpe noctem:* Sleep and family processes), 20–28.

Miller, D. W., Leyell, T. S., & Mazachek, J. (2004). Stereotypes of the elderly in U.S. television commercials from the 1950s to the 1990s. *International Journal of Aging and Human Development, 58,* 315–340.

Miller, J. B. (1991). The development of women's sense of self. In J. V. Jordan, A. G. Kaplan, J. B. Miller, I. P. Stiver, & J. L. Surrey (Eds.), *Women and growth in connection: Writings from the stone center* (pp. 11–26). New York, NY: Guilford.

Miller, J. G. (2004). The cultural deep structure of psychological theories of social development. In R. J. Sternberg & E. L. Grigorenko (Eds.), *Culture and competence: Contexts of life success* (pp. 111–138). Washington, DC: American Psychological Association.

Miller, P. E., Vasey, J. J., Short, P. F., & Hartman, T. J. (2009, January). Dietary supplement use in adult cancer survivors. In *Oncology nursing forum* (Vol. 36, No. 1, pp. 61–68). Oncology Nursing Society.

Miller, P. J. (2014). Placing discursive practices front and center: A sociocultural approach to the study of early socialization. In C. Wainryb & H. E. Recchia (Eds.), *Talking about right and wrong: Parent-child conversations as contexts for moral development* (pp. 416–447). New York, NY: Cambridge University Press.

Miller, P. J., Wiley, A. R., Fung, H., & Liang, C.-H. (1997). Personal storytelling as a medium of socialization in Chinese and American families. *Child Development, 68,* 557–568.

Miller, T. R., Finkelstein, A. E., Zaloshnja, E., & Hendrie, D. (2012). The cost of child and adolescent injuries and savings from prevention. In K. Liller (Ed.), *Injury prevention for children and adolescents* (pp. 21–81). Washington, DC: American Public Health Association.

Miller-Day, M. A. (2004). *Communication among grandmothers, mothers, and adult daughters.* Mahwah, NJ: Erlbaum.

Miller-Johnson, S., Costanzo, P. R., Cole, J. D., Rose, M. R., & Browne, D. C. (2003). Peer social structure and risk-taking behaviour among African American early adolescents. *Journal of Youth & Adolescence, 32,* 375–384.

Millman, R. P. (2005). Excessive sleepiness in adolescents and young adults: Causes, consequences, and treatment strategies. *Pediatrics, 115,* 1774–1786.

Mills, N., Daker-White, G., Graham, A., Campbell, R., & The Chlamydia Screening Studies (ClaSS) Group. (2006). Population screening for *Chlamydia trachomatis* infection in the UK: A qualitative study of the experiences of those screened. *Family Practice, 23,* 550–557.

Minami, M., & McCabe, A. (1995). Rice balls and bear hunts: Japanese and North American family narrative patterns. *Journal of Child Language, 22,* 423–445.

Mindell, J. A., Sadeh, A., Kohyama, J., & How, T. H. (2010). Parental behaviors and sleep outcomes in infants and toddlers: A cross-cultural comparison. *Sleep Medicine, 11,* 393–399.

Mintz, T. H. (2005). Linguistic and conceptual influences on adjective acquisition in 24- and 36-month-olds. *Developmental Psychology, 41,* 17–29.

Mireault, G. C., et al. (2014). Social looking, social referencing, and humor perception in 6- and 12-month-old infants. *Infant Behavior and Development, 37,* 536–545.

Mishna, F., Newman, P. A., Daley, A., & Solomon, S. (2009). Bullying of lesbian and gay youth: A qualitative investigation. *British Journal of Social Work, 39,* 1598–1614.

Mistry, J., & Saraswathi, T. (2003). The cultural context of child development. In R. Lerner & M. Easterbrooks (Eds.), *Handbook of psychology: Developmental psychology* (Vol. 6, pp. 267–291). New York, NY: John Wiley & Sons.

Mitchell, A., & Boss, B. J. (2002). Adverse effects of pain on the nervous systems of newborns and young children: A review of the literature. *Journal of Neuroscience and Nursing, 34,* 228–235.

Mitchell, B. A. (2006). *The boomerang age: Transitions to adulthood in families.* New Brunswick, NJ: Aldine Transaction.

Mitty, E. L., & Ramsey, G. (2008). Advance directives. In E. Capezuti, D. Zwicker, & T. Fulmer (Eds.), *Evidence-based geriatric nursing protocols for best practice* (3rd ed., pp. 539–563). New York, NY: Springer.

Modell, J. (1989). *Into one's own: From youth to adulthood in the United States, 1920–1975.* Berkeley: University of California Press.

Moffitt, T. E. (2003). Life-course-persistent and adolescence-limited antisocial behavior: A 10-year research review and a research agenda. In B. B. Lahey & T. E. Moffitt (Eds.), *Causes of conduct disorder and juvenile delinquency* (pp. 49–75). New York, NY: Guilford.

Moffitt, T. E. (2007). A review of research on the taxonomy of life-course persistent versus adolescence-limited antisocial behavior. In D. J. Flannery, A. T. Vazsonyi, & I. D. Waldman (Eds.), *The Cambridge handbook of violent behavior and aggression* (pp. 49–74). New York, NY: Cambridge University Press.

Moffitt, T. E., (2006). Life–course–persistent versus adolescence–limited antisocial behavior. In D. J. Cohen & D. Cicchetti (Eds.), *Developmental psychopathology, Vol. 3: Risk, order, and adaption* (2nd ed., pp. 570–598). Hoboken, NJ: Wiley.

Money, J. (1980). *Love and love sickness: The science of sex, gender difference, and pair-bonding.* Baltimore, MD: Johns Hopkins University Press.

Monitoring the Future. (2003). *ISR study finds drinking and drug use decline after college.* Ann Arbor, MI: Author. Available: www.umich.edu/newsinfo/releases/2002/Jan02/r013002a.html

Monserud, M. A. (2010). Continuity and change in grandchildren's closeness to grandparents: Consequences of changing intergenerational ties. *Marriage & Family Review, 46,* 366–388.

Montessori, M. (1964). *The Montessori method.* New York, NY: Schocken.

Montgomery, M. J. (2005). Psychosocial intimacy and identity: From early adolescence to emerging adulthood. *Journal of Adolescent Research, 20,* 346–374.

Montorsi, F. (2005). Assessment, diagnosis, and investigation of erectile dysfunction. *Clinical Cornerstone, 7,* 29–35.

Moody, H. R. (2004–2005). Silver industries and the new aging enterprise. *Generations, 28,* 75–78.

Moolgavkar, S. H., Holford, T. R., Levy, D. T., Kong, C. Y., Foy, M., Clarke, L.,... & Feuer, E. J. (2012). Impact of reduced tobacco smoking on lung cancer mortality in the United States during 1975–2000. *Journal of the National Cancer Institute, 104*(7), 541–548.

Moon, R. Y., Kington, M., Oden, R., Iglesias, J., & Hauck, F. R. (2007). Physician recommendations regarding SIDS risk reduction: A national survey of pediatricians and family physicians. *Clinical Pediatrics, 46,* 791–800.

Moore, D. (2001). *The dependent gene.* New York, NY: W. H. Freeman.

Moore, G. A., Cohn, J. F., & Campbell, S. B. (1997). Mothers' affective behavior with infant siblings: Stability and change. *Developmental Psychology, 33,* 856–860.

Moore, J. L. (2010). The neuropsychological functioning of prisoners of war following repatriation. In C. H. Kennedy & J. L. Moore (Eds.), *Military neuropsychology* (pp. 267–295). New York, NY: Springer.

Moore, K. A., Chalk, R., Scarpa, J., & Vandivere, S. (2002, August). Family strengths: Often overlooked, but real. *Child Trends Research Brief,* 1–8.

Moore, K. L., & Persaud, T. V. N. (2003). *Before we are born* (6th ed.). Philadelphia, PA: Saunders.

Moore, S., & Rosenthal, D. (2006). *Sexuality in adolescence: Current trends.* New York, NY: Routledge.

Moorman, S. M., Booth, A., & Fingerman, K. L. (2006). Women's romantic relationships after widowhood. *Journal of Family Issues, 27,* 1281–1304.

Morales, A. (2003). Erectile dysfunction: An overview. *Clinical Geriatric Medicine, 19,* 529–538.

Morawska, A., & Sanders, M. (2011). Parental use of time out revisited: A useful or harmful parenting strategy? *Journal of Child and Family Studies, 20,* 1–8.

Morelli, G. (2015). The evolution of attachment theory and cultures of human attachment in infancy and early childhood. In L. A. Jensen (Ed.), *Oxford handbook of human development and culture.* New York, NY: Oxford University Press.

Morelli, G., Rogoff, B., Oppenheim, D., & Goldsmith, D. (1992). Cultural variation in infants' sleeping arrangements: Question of independence. *Developmental Psychology, 39,* 604–613.

Morelli, G., & Rothbaum, F. (2007). Situating the child in context: Attachment relationships and self-regulation in different cultures. In S. Kitayama & D. Cohen (Eds.), *Handbook of cultural psychology* (pp. 500–527). New York, NY: Guilford Press.

Moreno Mínguez, A., López Peláez, A., & Sánchez-Cabezudo, S. S. (2012). *The transition to adulthood in Spain: Economic crisis and late emancipation.* Barcelona, Spain: La Caixa Foundation.

Moretti, M. M., & Wiebe, V. J. (1999). Self-discrepancy in adolescence: Own and parental standpoints on the self. *Merrill-Palmer Quarterly, 45,* 624–649.

Morfei, M. Z., Hooker, K., Carpenter, J., Blakeley, E., & Mix, C. (2004). Agentic and communal generative behavior in four areas of adult life: Implications for psychological well-being. *Journal of Adult Development, 11,* 55–58.

Morgan, M. A., Cragan, J. D., Goldenberg, R. L., Rasmussen, S. A., & Schulkin, J. (2010). Management of prescription and nonprescription drug use during pregnancy. *Journal of Maternal–Fetal and Neonatal Medicine, 23,* 813–819.

Morra, S., Gobbo, C., Marini, Z., & Sheese, R. (2008). *Cognitive development: Neo–Piagetian perspectives.* New York, NY: Taylor & Francis.

Morrison, R. S., Penrod, J. D., Cassel, J. B., Caust-Ellenbogen, M., Litke, A., Spragens, L.,...Meier, D. E. (2008). Cost savings associated with U.S. hospital palliative care consultation programs. *Archives of Internal Medicine, 168,* 1784–1790.

Morrongiello, B. A., Fenwick, K. D., Hillier, L., & Chance, G. (1994). Sound localization in newborn human infants. *Developmental Psychobiology, 27,* 519–538.

Morrow-Howell, N., Hong, S. I., & Tang, F. (2009). Who benefits from volunteering? Variations in perceived benefits. *The Gerontologist, 49,* 91–102.

Mortimer, J. (2013). Work and its positive and negative effects on youth's psychosocial development. *Health and Safety of Young Workers,* 66–79.

Mortimer, J. T. (2004). *Working and growing up in America.* Cambridge, MA: Harvard University Press.

Mortimer, J. T., Vuolo, M., Staff, J., Wakefield, S., & Xie, W. (2008). Tracing the timing of "career" acquisition in a contemporary youth cohort. *Work and Occupations, 35,* 44–84.

Mortimer, J. T., Zimmer-Gembeck, M. J., Holmes, M., & Shanahan, M. J. (2002). The process of occupational decision making: Patterns during the transition to adulthood. *Journal of Vocational Behavior, 61,* 439–465.

Mosby, L., Rawls, A. W., Meehan, A. J., Mays, E., & Pettinari, C. J. (1999). Troubles in interracial talk about discipline: An examination of African American child rearing narratives. *Journal of Comparative Family Studies, 30,* 489–521.

Mossakowski, K. N. (2009). The influence of past unemployment duration on symptoms of depression among young women and men in the United States. *American Journal of Public Health, 99* (10), 1826–1832.

Motola, M., Sinisalo, P., & Guichard, J. (1998). Social habitus and future plans. In J. Nurmi (Ed.), *Adolescents, cultures, and conflicts* (pp. 43–73). New York, NY: Garland.

Mroczek, D. K. (2001). Age and emotion in adulthood. *Current Directions in Psychological Science, 10,* 87–90.

Mroczek, D. K., & Kolarz, C. M. (1998). The effect of age on positive and negative affect: A developmental perspective on happiness. *Journal of Personality and Social Psychology, 75,* 1333–1349.

Mueller, M., Wilhelm, B., & Elder, G. (2002). Variations in grandparenting. *Research on Aging, 24*, 360–388.

Mugford, M. (2006). Cost effectiveness of prevention and treatment of neonatal respiratory distress (RDS) with exogenous surfactant: What has changed in the last three decades? *Early Human Development, 82*, 105–115.

Muhlbauer, V., & Chrisler, J. C. (2007). *Women over 50: Psychological perspectives*. New York, NY: Springer.

Muller, F., Rebiff, M., Taillandier, A., Qury, J. F., & Mornet, E. (2000). Parental origin of the extra chromosome in prenatally diagnosed fetal trisomy. *Human Genetics, 106*, 340–344.

Munro, G., & Adams, G. R. (1977). Ego-identity formation in college students and working youth. *Developmental Psychology, 13*, 523–524.

Muramatsu, N., Hoyem, R. L., Yin, H., & Campbell, R. T. (2008). Place of death among older Americans: Does state spending on home and community-based services promote home death? *Medical Care, 46*, 829–838.

Muret-Wagstaff, S., & Moore, S. G. (1989). The Hmong in America: Infant behavior and rearing practices. In J. K. Nugent, B. M. Lester, & T. B. Brazelton (Eds.), *Biology, culture, and development* (Vol. 1, pp. 319–339). Norwood, NJ: Ablex.

Murkoff, H. (2011). *What to expect the second year*. New York, NY: Workman.

Murkoff, H. E., Eisenberg, A., Mazel, S., & Hathaway, S. E. (2003). *What to expect the first year* (2nd ed.). New York, NY: Workman.

Murkoff, H., & Mazel, S. (2008). *What to expect when you're expecting*. New York, NY: Workman.

Murkoff, H., Eisenberg, A., & Hathaway, S. (2009). *What to expect the first year*. New York, NY: Workman.

Murnane, R. J., & Levy, F. (1997). *Teaching the new basic skills: Principles for educating children to thrive in a changing economy*. New York, NY: Free Press.

Murphy, C., Schubert, C. R., Cruickshanks, K. J., Klein, B. E., Klein, R., & Nondahl, D. M. (2002). Prevalence of olfactory impairment in older adults. *JAMA: Journal of the American Medical Association, 288*, 2307–2312.

Murphy, D. R., Daneman, M., & Schneider, B.A. (2006). Why do older adults have difficulty following conversations? *Psychology and Aging, 21*, 49–61.

Murray-Close, D., Ostrov, J., & Crick, N. (2007). A short-term longitudinal study of growth and relational aggression during middle childhood: Associations with gender, friendship, intimacy, and internalizing problems. *Development and Psychopathology, 19*, 187–203.

Murre, J. M., Janssen, S. M., Rouw, R., & Meeter, M. (2013). The rise and fall of immediate and delayed memory for verbal and visuospatial information from late childhood to late adulthood. *Acta psychologica, 142*(1), 96–107.

Murry, V. M., Hurt, T. R., Kogan, S. M., & Luo, Z. (2006). Contextual processes of romantic relationships: Plausible explanations for gender and race effects. In A. C. Crouter & A. Booth (Eds.), *Romance and sex in adolescence and emerging adulthood: Risks and opportunities* (pp. 151–160). Mahwah, NJ: Lawrence Erlbaum.

Mustillo, S., Worthman, C., Erkanli, A., Keeler, G., Angold, A., Costello, E. J. (2003). Obesity and psychiatric disorder: Developmental trajectories. *Pediatrics, 111*, 851–859.

Mutti, D. O., Mitchell, G. L., Moeschberger, M. L., Jones, L. A., & Zadnik, K. (2002). Parental myopia, near work, school achievement, and children's refractive error. *Investigative Ophthalmology and Visual Science, 43*, 3633–3640.

Nair, K. S., Rizza, R. A., O'Brien, P., Dhatariay, K. K., Short, K. R., Nehra, A.,...Jensen, M. D. (2006). DHEA in elderly women and DHEA or testosterone in elderly men. *New England Journal of Medicine, 355*, 1647–1659.

Naito, T., & Gielen, U. P. (2003). The changing Japanese family: A psychological portrait. In J. L. Roopnarine & U. P. Gielen (Eds.), *Families in global perspective* (pp. 63–84). Boston, MA: Allyn & Bacon.

Nakano, H., & Blumstein, S. E. (2004). Deficits in thematic processes in Broca's and Wernicke's aphasia. *Brain and Language, 88*, 96–107.

Nandakumar, J., & Cech, T. R. (2013). Finding the end: Recruitment of telomerase to telomeres. *Nature Reviews: Molecular Cell Biology, 14*, 69–82. doi:10.1038/nrm3505

Napier, K., & Meister, K. (2000). *Growing healthy kids: A parents' guide to infant and child nutrition*. New York, NY: American Council on Science and Heath.

Naqvi, R., et al. (2013). Preventing cognitive decline in healthy older adults. *CMAJ*. doi:10.1503/cmaj.121448

Narayanan, U., & Warren, S. T. (2006). Neurobiology of related disorders: Fragile X syndrome. In S. O. Moldin & J. L. R. Rubenstein, *Understanding autism: From basic neuroscience to treatment* (pp. 113–131). Washington, DC: Taylor Francis.

National Center for Education in Maternal and Child Health. (2002). *Bright futures in practice: Nutrition pocket guide*. Washington, DC: Georgetown University.

National Center for Education Statistics (2009). *The condition of education, 2009*. Washington, DC: U. S. Department of Education. Available: www.nces.gov

National Center for Health Statistics (2000). *Health United States, 1999*. Atlanta, GA: Prevention.

National Center for Health Statistics (2004). *Health United States, 2003*. Atlanta, GA: Prevention.

National Center for Health Statistics (2005). *Health, United States, 2005. With chartbook on trends in the health of Americans*. Hyattsville, MD: Author.

National Center for Health Statistics (2009). *Health, United States, 2009*. Hyattsville, MD: Prevention.

National Council of Youth Sports. (2002). *Report on trends and participation in youth sports*. Stuart, FL: Author.

National Highway Traffic Safety Administration (2011). *Traffic safety facts*. Washington, DC: U.S. Department of Transportation.

National Hospice and Palliative Care Organization and Research Department. (2008). *Hospice facts and figures*. Retrieved from http://www.nhpco.org/files/public/Statistics_Research/NHPCO_facts-and-figures_2008.pdf

National Institute of Child Health and Development (NICHD) (2004). Follow-up care of high-risk infants. *Pediatrics, 114*, 1377–1397.

National Institute of Drug Abuse (2001). *Marijuana*. Washington, DC: National Institutes of Health.

National Institute on Aging (NIA). (2008). *Age page: Menopause*. Washington, DC: NIA. Retrieved from http://www.nia.nih.gov/HealthInformation/Publication/menopause.htm

National Institute on Aging. (2005). *Progress report of Alzheimer's disease 2004–2005: New discoveries, new insights*. Bethesda, MD: Author.

National Journal (2011). *Living Well at the End of Life Poll: Topline results*. Retrieved from http://syndication.nationaljournal.com/communications/NationalJournalRegenceSeattleToplines.pdf

National Resource Center on ADHD (2014). *Statistical prevalence of ADHD*. Retrieved from http://www.help4adhd.org/about/statistics

National Sudden and Unexpected Infant/Child Death & Pregnancy Loss Resource Center (2010). *Statistics overview*. Retrieved from http://sidcenter.org/Statistics.html

National Survey of Sexual Health and Behavior (NSSHB) (2010). Findings from the National Survey of Sexual Health and Behavior, Centre for Sexual Health Promotion, Indiana University. *Journal of Sexual Medicine*, Vol. 7, Supplement 5.

National Women's Health Information Center. (2011). *Infertility.* Retrieved from http://www.womenshealth.gov/faq/infertility.cfm#f

Natsopoulos, D., Kiosseoglou, G., Xeroxmeritou, A., & Alevriadou, A. (1998). Do the hands talk on the mind's behalf? Differences in language between left- and right-handed children. *Brain and Language, 64,* 182–214.

Natsuaki, M. N., Ge, X., Reiss, D., & Neiderhiser, J. M. (2009). Aggressive behavior between siblings and the development of externalizing problems: Evidence from a genetically sensitive study. *Developmental Psychology, 45,* 1009–1018.

Naveh-Deutsch, N., Ish-Shalom, S., Rozen, G. S., & Bitterman, N. (2007). Interactive computer nutrition for elderly. *Gerontechnology, 6,* 236–240.

Neberich, W., Penke, L., Lenhart, J., & Asendorph, J. B. (2010). Family of origin, age at menarche, and reproductive strategies: A test of four evolutionary–developmental models. *European Journal of Developmental Psychology, 7,* 153–177.

Nelson, C. A. (1997). The neurobiological basis of early memory development. In N. Cowan (Ed.), *The development of memory in childhood* (pp. 41–82). Hove, UK: Psychology Press.

Nelson, D. A., Robinson, C. C., & Hart, C. H. (2005). Relational and physical aggression of preschool-age children: Peer status linkages across informants. *Early Education and Development, 16,* 115–139.

Nelson, L. J. (2003). Rites of passage in emerging adulthood: Perspectives of young Mormons. *New Directions in Child and Adolescent Development,100,* 33–50.

Nelson, L. J., & Chen, X. (2007). Emerging adulthood in China: The role of social and cultural factors. *Child Development Perspectives, 1,* 86–91.

Nelson, L. J., & Luster, S. S. (2015). "Adulthood" by whose definition? The complexity of emerging adults' conceptions of adulthood. In J. J. Arnett (Ed.), *Oxford handbook of emerging adulthood.* New York, NY: Oxford University Press.

Nelson, L. J., Badger, S., & Wu, B. (2004). The influence of culture in emerging adulthood: Perspectives of Chinese college students. *International Journal of Behavioral Development, 28,* 26–36.

Nelson, T. (2004). *Ageism: Stereotyping and prejudice against older persons.* Cambridge, MA: MIT Press.

Nelson-Becker, H., Nakashima, M., & Canda, E. (2006). Spirituality in professional helping interventions. In B. Berkman (Ed.), *Handbook of social work in health and aging* (pp. 797–808). New York, NY: Oxford Press.

Nesbitt, R. E. (2009). *Intelligence and how to get it: Why schools and cultures matter.* New York, NY: Norton.

Neto, F. (2002). Acculturation strategies among adolescents from immigrant families in Portugal. *International Journal of Intercultural Relations, 26,* 17–38.

Netting, N. (2010). Marital ideoscapes in 21st-century India: Creative combinations of love and responsibility. *Journal of Family Issues, 31,* 707–726.

Neugarten, B. L. (1972). Personality and the aging process. *The Gerontologist, 12,* 9–15.

Neugarten, B. L. (1977). Personality and aging. In J. E. Birren & K. W. Schaie (Eds.), *Handbook for the psychology of aging* (pp. 626–649). New York, NY: Van Nostrand Reinhold.

Neugarten, B., & Neugarten, D. (1987, May). The changing meanings of age. *Psychology Today, 21(5),* 29–33.

Newcombe, N. S., Lloyd, M. E., & Ratliff, K. R. (2007). Development of episodic and autobiographical memory: A cognitive neuroscience perspective. In R. V. Kail (Ed.), *Advances in child development and behavior* (Vol. 35, pp. 37–85). San Diego, CA: Elsevier Academic Press.

Newcombe, N., & Huttenlocher, J. (2006). Development of spatial cognition. In W. Damon & R. Lerner (Eds.), & D. Kuhn & R. Siegler (Vol. Eds.), *Handbook of child psychology: Vol. 2. Cognition, perception and language* (6th ed., pp. 734–776). New York, NY: Wiley.

Newton, N., & Newton, M. (2003). Childbirth in cross–cultural perspective. In L. Dundes (Ed.), *The manner born: Birth rites in cross–cultural perspective* (pp. 9–32). Walnut Creek, CA: AltaMira.

Ng, M., et al. (2014). Global, regional, and national prevalence of overweight and obesity in children and adults during 1980-2013: A systematic analysis of the Global Burden of Disease Study 2013. *The Lancet 309.* doi: 10.1016/S0140-6736(14)60460-8

Ng, S. (2002). Will families support their elders? Answers from across cultures. In T. Nelson (Ed.), *Ageism: Stereotyping and prejudice against older persons* (pp. 295–309). Cambridge, MA: MIT Press.

Ngongo, P. B., Priddy, F., Park, H., Becker, J., Bender, B., Fast, P.,... & Mebrahtu, T. (2012). Developing standards of care for HIV prevention research in developing countries—A case study of 10 research centers in Eastern and Southern Africa. *AIDS Care, 24(10),* 1277–1289.

NICHD (National Institute of Child Health and Human Development) Early Child Care Research Network. (1997). The effects of infant child care on infant–mother attachment security: Results of the NICHD Study of Early Child Care. *Child Development, 68,* 860–879.

NICHD Early Child Care Research Network. (2000). Factors associated with fathers' caregiving activities and sensitivity with young children. *Developmental Psychology, 14,* 200–219.

NICHD Early Child Care Research Network (2004). Trajectories of physical aggression from toddlerhood to middle childhood. *Monographs of the Society for Research in Child Development, 69* (Serial No. 278), vii–129.

NICHD Early Child Care Research Network (2006). Infant-mother attachment classification: Risk and protection in relation to changing maternal caregiving quality. *Developmental Psychology, 42,* 38–58.

NICHD Early Child Care Research Network (2006). *Child care and child development: Results from the NICHD study of early child care and youth development.* New York, NY: Guilford.

Nicholson, J. M., Sanders, M. R., Halford, W. K., Phillips, M., & Whitton, S. W. (2008). The prevention and treatment of children's adjustment problems in stepfamilies. In J. Pryor (Ed.), *The international handbook of stepfamilies: Policy and practice in legal, research, and clinical environments* (pp. 485–521). Hoboken, NJ: John Wiley & Sons.

Nichter, M. (2001). *Fat talk: What girls and their parents say about dieting.* Cambridge, MA: Harvard University Press.

Nickerson, A. B., & Nagle, R. J. (2005). Parent and peer attachment in late childhood and early adolescence. *Journal of Early Adolescence, 25,* 223–249.

Nielsen, S. J., Siega-Riz, A. M., & Popkin, B. M. (2002). Trends in energy intake between 1977 and 1986: Similar shifts seen across age groups. *Obesity Research, 10,* 370–378.

Niemeyer, D. (2006). *Eighth annual report on Oregon's Death with Dignity Act.* Portland, OR: Oregon Department of Human Services.

Nihart, M. A. (1993). Growth and development of the brain. *Journal of Child and Adolescent Psychiatric and Mental Health Nursing, 6,* 39–40.

Nkondjock, A., & Ghadirian, P. (2004). Epidemiology of breast cancer among BRCA mutation carriers: An overview. *Cancer Letters, 205,* 1–8.

Noam, E., Groebel, J., & Gerbarg, D. (2004). *Internet television.* Mahwah, NJ: Lawrence Erlbaum.

Noia, G., Cesari, E., Ligato, M. S., Visconti, D., Tintoni, M., Mappa, I.,...Caruso, A. (2008). Pain in the fetus. *Neonatal Pain, 2,* 45–55.

Nolan, K., Schell, L. M., Stark, A. D., & Gomez, M. I. (2002). Longitudinal study of energy and nutrient intakes for infants from low-income, urban families. *Public Health Nutrition, 5,* 405–412.

Noller, P. (2005). Sibling relationships in adolescence: Learning and growing together. *Personal Relationships, 12,* 1–22.

Nolen-Hoeksema, S., Wisco, B. E., & Lyubomirsky, S. (2008). Rethinking rumination. *Perspectives on psychological science, 3*(5), 400–424.

Noppe, I. C., & Noppe, L. D. (1997). Evolving meanings of death during early, middle, and later adolescence. *Death Studies, 21,* 253–275.

Norona, J. C., Preddy, T. M., & Welsh, D. P. (2015). How gender shapes emerging adulthood. In J. J. Arnett (Ed.), *Oxford handbook of emerging adulthood.* New York, NY: Oxford University Press.

Notelovitz, M. (2002). Overview of bone mineral density in postmenopausal women. *Journal of Reproductive Medicine, 47*(Suppl.), 71–81.

Novik, T. S., Hervas, A., Ralston, S. J., Dalsgaard, S., Rodrigues Pereira, R., Lorenzo, M. J., & ADORE Study Group. (2006). Influence of gender on attention deficit/hyperactivity disorder in Europe—ADORE. *European Child & Adolescent Psychiatry, 15*(Suppl. 1), 5–24.

Nsamengnang, B. A. (1992). Perceptions of parenting among the Nso of Cameroon. *Father–child relations: Cultural and biosocial contexts* (pp. 321–344). New York, NY: De Gruyter.

Nugent, K. J., Petrauskas, B. J., & Brazelton, T. B. (Eds.). (2009). *The newborn as a person: Enabling healthy infant development worldwide.* Hoboken, NJ: John Wiley & Sons.

Nugent, K., & Brazelton, T. B. (2000). Preventive infant mental health: Uses of the Brazelton scale. In J. D. Osofsky & H. E. Fitzgerald (Eds.), *WAIMH Handbook of infant mental health* (Vol. 2). New York, NY: Wiley.

Nuland, S. B. (2003). *The doctor's plague: Germs, childbed fever, and the strange story of Ignac Semmelweis.* New York, NY: Norton.

Núñez, J., & Flanagan, C. (2015). Political beliefs and civic engagement in emerging adulthood. In J. J. Arnett (Ed.), *Oxford handbook of emerging adulthood.* New York, NY: Oxford University Press.

Nwokah, E. E., Hsu, H., Davies, P., & Fogel, A. (1999). The integration of laughter and speech in vocal communication: A dynamic systems perspective. *Journal of Speech and Hearing Research, 42,* 880–894.

Nylen, K., Moran, T., Franklin, C., & O'Hara, M. (2006). Maternal depression: A review of relevant treatment approaches for mothers and infants. *Infant Mental Health Journal, 27,* 327–343.

O'Brien, M., & Moss, P. (2010). Fathers, work, and family policies in Europe. In M. E. Lamb (Ed.), *The role of the father in child development* (5th ed., pp. 551–577). Hoboken, NJ: John Wiley & Sons.

O'Connor, P. (2003). Dying in the hospital. In I. Corless, B. B. Germino, & M. A. Pitman (Eds.), *Dying, death, and bereavement: A challenge for the living* (2nd ed., pp. 87–103). New York, NY: Springer.

O'Connor, T. G., & Croft, C. M. (2001). A twin study of attachment in preschool children. *Child Development, 72,* 1501–1511.

O'Connor, T. G., Rutter, M., Beckett, C., Keaveney, L., Dreppner, J. M., & the English and Romanian Adoptees Study Team. (2000). The effects of global severe privation on cognitive competence: Extension and longitudinal follow-up. *Child Development, 71,* 376–390.

O'Hanlon, L., Kemper, S., Wilcox, K. A. (2005). Aging, encoding, and word retrieval: Distinguishing phonological and memory processes. *Experimental Aging Research, 31,* 149–171.

O'Malley, P., & Bachman, J. (1983). Self-esteem: Change and stability between ages 13 and 23. *Developmental Psychology, 19,* 257–268.

Oates, M. R., Cox, J. L., Neema, S., Asten, P., Glangeaud-Freudenthal, N., Figueiredo, B.,...TCS–PND Group. (2004). Postnatal depression across countries and cultures: A qualitative study. *British Journal of Psychiatry, 184,* s10–s16.

Oberlander, S. E., Black, M. M., & Starr, R. H., Jr. (2007). African American adolescent mothers and grandmothers: A multigenerational approach to parenting. *American Journal of Community Psychology, 39,* 37–46.

Obermeyer, C. M. (2000). Menopause across cultures: A review of the evidence. *Menopause, 7,* 184–192.

Odeku, K., Rembe, S., & Anwo, J. (2009). Female genital mutilation: A human rights perspective. *Journal of Psychology in Africa, 19*(Special issue: Violence against children in Africa), 55–62.

OECD (2009). *Health at a glance 2009: OECD indicators.* Author.

OECD (2010). Incidence of employment by usual weekly hours worked. *StatExtracts.* Retrieved from http://stats.oecd.org/Index.aspx?DataSetCode%20%09=USLHRS_I

OECD (2013). *Education at a glance: Indicators and annexes.* Retrieved from http://www.oecd.org/edu/educationataglance2013-indicatorsandannexes.htm#ChapterC

OECD (2014). *Health at a glance 2014: OECD indicators.* Paris, France: Author.

OECD (2014). Infant mortality. Family database, Social Policy Division. Retrieved from www.oecd.org/social/family/database

OECD (2014). Life expectancy at age 65, males/females. Retrieved from http://www.oecd-ilibrary.org/social-issues-migration-health/life-expectancy-at-age-65-males_lifeexp65men-table-en, http://www.oecd-ilibrary.org/social-issues-migration-health/life-expectancy-at-age-65-females_lifeexp65women-table-en

OECD (2014). *OECD Statextracts: Labor Force Statistics by sex and age.* Retrieved from http://stats.oecd.org/Index.aspx?DatasetCode=LFS_SEXAGE_I_R

Office of Applied Studies. (2006). Suicidal thoughts, suicide attempts, major depressive episodes, and substance use among adults. Substance Abuse and Mental Health Services Administration. Results from the 2005 National Survey on Drug Use and Health: National findings. Rockville, MD. Retrieved from http://oas.samhsa.gov/2k6/suicide/suicide.pdf

Ogbu, J. U. (2002). Cultural amplifiers of intelligence: IQ and minority status in cross-cultural perspective. In J. M. Fish (Ed.), *Race and intelligence: Separating science from myth* (pp. 241–278). Mahwah, NJ: Erlbaum.

Ogden, C. L., Carroll, M. D., Kit, B. K., & Flegal, K. M. (2014). Prevalence of childhood and adult obesity. *JAMA 311,* 806–814.

Ogden, C. L., Carroll, M. D., Kit, B. K., & Flegal, K. M. (2013). Prevalence of obesity among adults. *NCHS Data Brief, Number 131.* Atlanta, GA: Prevention. Retrieved from http://www.cdc.gov/nchs/data/databriefs/db131.pdf

Ogden, C. L., Kuczmarski, R. J., Flegal, K. M., Mei, Z., Guo, S., Wei, R.,...Johnson, C. L. (2002). Prevention 2000 growth charts for the United States: Improvements to the 1977 National Center for Health Statistics version. *Pediatrics, 109,* 45–60.

Ogden, C. L., Lamb, M. M., Carroll, M. D., & Flegal, K. M. (2010). Obesity and socioeconomic status in adults: United States, 2005-2008. *NCHS Data Brief, Number 50.* Atlanta, GA: Prevention. Retrieved from http://www.cdc.gov/nchs/data/databriefs/db50.pdf

Ogden, T., & Amlund-Hagen, K. (2006). Multisystemic treatment of serious behavior problems in youth: Sustainability of therapy effectiveness two years after intake. *Child and Adolescent Mental Health, 11,* 142–149.

Ogletree, S. M., Martinez, C. N., Turner, T. R., & Mason, M. (2004). Pokémon: Exploring the role of gender. *Sex Roles, 50*(11–12), 851–859.

Ohgi, S., Arisawa, K., Takahashi, T., Kusomoto, T., Goto, Y. & Saito, A .T. (2003). Neonatal behavioral assessment scale as a predictor of later developmental disabilities of low birth-weight and/or premature infants. *Brain Development, 25,* 313–321.

Oken, E., & Lightdale, J. R. (2000). Updates in pediatric nutrition. *Current Opinion in Pediatrics, 12,* 282–290.

Okie, S. (2002, April 10). Study cites alcohol link in campus deaths. *The Washington Post,* p. A2.

Olds, D. L. (2010). The nurse–family partnership: From trials to practice. In A. J. Reynolds, A. J. Rolnick, M. M. Englund, & J. A. Temple (Eds.), *Childhood programs and practices in the first decade of life: A human capital integration* (pp. 49–75). New York, NY: Cambridge University Press.

Ollendick, T. H., Shortt, A. L., & Sander, J. B. (2008). Internalizing disorders in children and adolescents. In J. E. Maddux & B. A. Winstead (Eds.), *Psychopathology: Foundations for a contemporary understanding* (2nd ed., pp. 375–399). New York, NY: Routledge.

Oller, D. K., Eilers, R. E., Urbano, R., & Cobo-Lewis, A. B. (1997). Development of precursors to speech in infants exposed to two languages. *Journal of Child Language, 24,* 407–425.

Olson, C. K., Kutner, L. A., & Warner, D. E. (2008). The role of violent video game content in adolescent development: Boys' perspectives. *Journal of Adolescent Research, 23,* 55–75.

Olson, C. K., Kutner, L. A., Warner, D. E., Almerigi, J., Baer, L., Nicholi, A. M., & Beresin, E. V. (2007). Factors correlated with violent video game use by adolescent boys and girls. *Journal of Adolescent Health, 41,* 77–83.

Olweus, D. (2000). Bullying. In A. E. Kazdin (Ed.), *Encyclopedia of psychology* (Vol. 1, pp. 487–489). Washington, DC: American Psychological Association.

Onwuteaka-Philipsen, B. D., van der Heide, A., Muller, M. T., Rurup, M., Rietjens, J. A. C., & Georges, J.-J. (2005). Dutch experience of monitoring euthanasia. *British Medical Journal, 331,* 691–693.

Open Society Institute. (2003). *Project on death in America.* New York, NY: Author.

Oren, D. L. (1981). Cognitive advantages of bilingual children related to labeling ability. *The Journal of Educational Research,* 163–169.

Ortmann, O., Doren, M., & Windler, E. (2011). Hormone therapy in perimenopause and postmenopause (HT). *Archives of Gynecology and Obstetrics, 284,* 343–355.

Osgood, D. W. (2009). Illegal behavior: A presentation to the Committee on the Science of Adolescence of the National Academies. Washington, DC.

Osgood, D. W., Anderson, A. L., & Shaffer, J. N. (2005). Unstructured leisure in the afterschool hours. In L. J. Mahoney, R. W. Larson, & J. S. Eccles (Eds.), *Organized activities as contexts of development: Extracurricular activities, after-school and community programs* (pp. 45–64). Mahwah, NJ: Lawrence Erlbaum.

Osgood, D. W., Wilson, J. K., Bachman, J. G., O'Malley, P. M., & Johnston, L. D. (1996). Routine activities and individual deviant behavior. *American Sociological Review, 61,* 635–655.

Oslin, D. W., Datto, C. J., Kallan, M. J., Katz, I. R., Edell, W. S., & TenHave, T. (2002). Association between medical comorbidity and treatment outcomes in late-life depression. *Journal of the American Geriatrics Society, 50,* 823–828.

Oster, H., Hegley, D., & Nagel, L. (1992). Adult judgments and fine-grained analysis of infant facial expressions: Testing the validity of a priori coding formulas. *Developmental Psychology, 28,* 1115–1131.

Out, D., Pieper, S., Bakermans-Kranenburg, M. J., Zeskind, P. S., & van IJzendoorn, M. H. (2010). Intended sensitive and harsh caregiving responses to infant crying: The role of cry pitch and perceived urgency in an adult twin sample. *Child Abuse & Neglect, 34,* 863–873.

Overpeck, M. D., Brenner, R. A., Trumble, A. C., Smith, G. S., MacDorman, M. F., & Berendes, H. W. (1999). Infant injury deaths with unknown intent: What else do we know? *Injury Prevention, 5,* 272–275.

Owen, C. G., Whincup, P. H., Odoki, K., Gilg, J. A. & Cook, D. G. (2002). Infant feeding and blood cholesterol: A study in adolescents and a systematic review. *Pediatrics, 110,* 597–608.

Owens, J. A. (2004). Sleep in children: Cross-cultural perspectives. *Sleep and Biological Rhythms, 2*(3), 165–173.

Oyserman, D., & Fryberg, S. (2006). The possible selves of diverse adolescents: Content and function across gender, race and national origin. In C. Dunkel & J. Kerpelman (Eds.), *Possible selves: Theory, research and applications* (pp. 17–39). Hauppauge, NY: Nova Science.

Pacella, R., McLellan, M., Grice, K., Del Bono, E. A., Wiggs, J. L., & Gwiazda, J. E. (1999). Role of genetic factors in the etiology of juvenile-onset myopia based on the longitudinal study of refractive error. *Optometry and Vision Science, 76,* 381–386.

Padilla, C., Pérez, L., & Andrés, P. (2014). Chronic exercise keeps working memory and inhibitory capacities fit. *Frontiers in behavioral neuroscience, 8.*

Padilla-Walker, L. M., Nelson, L. J., Carroll, J. S., & Jensen, A. C. (2010). More than a just a game: Video game and Internet use during emerging adulthood. *Journal of Youth and Adolescence, 39,* 103–113.

Padrón, E., Carlson, E. A., & Sroufe, L. A. (2014). Frightened versus not frightened disorganized infant attachment: Newborn characteristics and maternal caregiving. *American Journal of Orthopsychiatry, 84,* 201–208.

Pahl, K. (2005). Longitudinal trajectories of ethnic identity among urban low-income ethnic and racial minority adolescents. *Dissertation Abstracts International, 65,* Retrieved from EBSCO*host.*

Pahl, K., & Way, N. (2006). Longitudinal trajectories of ethnic identity among urban Black and Latino adolescents. *Child Development, 77,* 1403–1415.

Pahl, K., Greene, M., & Way, N. (2000, April). *Self-esteem trajectories among urban, low-income, ethnic minority high school students.* Poster presented at the biennial meeting of the Society for Research on Adolescence, Chicago, IL.

Palmore, E. (2001). The ageism survey: First findings. *Gerontologist, 41,* 572–575.

Paludi, M. A., & Strayer, L. A. (1985). What's in an author's name? Differential evaluations of performance as a function of author's name. *Sex Roles, 12,* 353–362.

Pan, B. A., & Snow, C. E. (1999). The development of conversation and discourse skills. In M. Barrett (Ed.), *The development of language* (pp. 229–249). Hove, UK: Psychology Press.

Pan, S. Y., Desmueles, M., Morrison, H., Semenciw, R., Ugnat, A.-M., Thompson, W., & Mao, Y. (2007). Adolescent injury deaths and hospitalization in Canada: Magnitude and temporal trends (1979–2003). *Journal of Adolescent Health, 41,* 84–92.

Pankow, L. J. (2008). Genetic theory. In B. A. Thyer, K. M. Sowers, & C. N. Dulmus (Eds.), *Comprehensive handbook of social work and social welfare: Vol. 2. Human behavior in the social environment* (pp. 327–353). Hoboken, NJ: John Wiley & Sons.

Panza, F., Solfrizzi, V., Colacicco, A. M., D'Introno, A., Capruso, C., & Torres, F. (2004). Mediterranean diet and cognitive decline. *Public Health Nutrition, 7,* 959–963.

Papadakis, A. A., Prince, R. P., Jones, N. P., & Strauman, T. J. (2006). Self-regulation, rumination, and vulnerability to depression in adolescent girls. *Development and Psychopathology, 18,* 815–829.

Paquette, D. (2004). Theorizing the father–child relationship: Mechanisms and developmental outcomes. *Human Development, 47,* 193–219.

Parameswaran, G. (2003). Age, gender, and training in children's performance of Piaget's horizontality task. *Educational Studies, 29,* 307–319.

Park, S. H., Shim, Y. K., Kim, H. S., & Eun, B. L. (1999). Age and seasonal distribution of menarche in Korean girls. *Journal of Adolescent Health, 25,* 97.

Parke, R. D. (2004). Development in the family. *Annual Review of Psychology, 55,* 363–399.

Parke, R. D., & Buriel, R. (2006). Socialization in the family: Ethnic and ecological perspectives. In W. Damon & R. Lerner (Eds.), & N. Eisenberg (Vol. Ed.), *Handbook of child psychology: Vol. 3. Social, emotional and personality development* (6th ed., pp. 429–504). New York, NY: Wiley.

Parker, E. D., Schmitz, K. H., Jacobs, D. R., Jr., Dengel, D. R., & Schreiner, P. J. (2007). Physical activity in young adults and incident hypertension over 15 years of follow-up: The CARDIA study. *American Journal of Public Health, 97,* 703–709.

Parker, E. M., & Short, S. E. (2009). Grandmother coresidence, maternal orphans, and school enrollment in Sub-Saharan Africa. *Journal of Family Issues, 30,* 813–836.

Parker, E. S., Landau, S. M., Whipple, S. C., & Schwartz, B. L. (2004). Aging, recall, and recognition: A study on the sensitivity of the University of Southern California Repeatable Episodic Memory Test (USC-REMT). *Journal of Clinical and Experimental Neuropsychology, 26,* 428–440.

Parsons, T. J., Power, C., & Manor, O. (2005). Physical activity, television viewing and body mass index: A cross sectional analysis from childhood to adulthood in the 1958 British cohort. *International Journal of Obesity, 29,* 1212–1221.

Parten, M. (1932). Social play among preschool children. *Journal of Abnormal Social Psychology, 27,* 243–269.

Pascalis, O., & Kelly, D. J. (2009). The origins of face processing in humans: Phylogeny and ontogeny. *Perspectives on Psychological Science, 4,* 200–209.

Pascarella, E. T. (2005). Cognitive impacts of the first year of college. In R. S. Feldman (Ed.), *Improving the first year of college: Research and practice* (pp. 111–140). Mahwah, NJ: Lawrence Erlbaum.

Pascarella, E. T. (2006). How college affects students: Ten directions for future research. *Journal of College Student Development, 47,* 508–520.

Pascarella, E., & Terenzini, P. (1991). *How college affects students: Findings and insights from twenty years of research.* San Francisco, CA: Jossey-Bass.

Pascoe, C. J. (2007). *Dude, you're a fag: Masculinity and sexuality in high school.* Berkeley, CA: University of California Press.

Pashigian, M. J. (2002). Conceiving the happy family: Infertility and marital politics in northern Vietnam. In M.C. Inhorn & F. van Balen (Eds.), *Infertility around the globe: New thinking on childlessness, gender, and reproductive technologies* (pp. 134–150). Berkeley, CA: University of California Press.

Patel, Z. P., & Niederberger, C. S. (2011). Male Factor Assessment in Infertility. *Medical Clinics of North America, 95,* 223–234.

Patrick, M. E., Schulenberg, J. E., O'malley, P. M., Johnston, L. D., & Bachman, J. G. (2011). Adolescents' reported reasons for alcohol and marijuana use as predictors of substance use and problems in adulthood. *Journal of studies on alcohol and drugs, 72*(1), 106.

Patterson, G. R. (2002). The early development of coercive family process. In J. B Reid, G. R. Patterson, & J. Snyder (Eds.), *Antisocial behavior in children and adolescents: A developmental analysis and model for intervention* (pp. 25–44). Washington, DC: American Psychological Association.

Patterson, M. L., & Werker, J. F. (2002). Infants' ability to match dynamic phonetic and gender information in the face and voice. *Journal of Experimental Child Psychology, 81,* 93–115.

Patton, G. C., Coffey, C., et al. (2009). Global patterns of mortality in young people: A systematic analysis of population health data. *Lancet, 374,* 881–892.

Paul, E. L., McManus, B., & Hayes, A. (2000). "Hookups": Characteristics and correlates of college students' spontaneous and anonymous sexual experiences. *The Journal of Sex Research, 37,* 76–88.

Paus, T., Zijdenbos, A., Worsley, K., Collins, D. L., Blumental, J., Gledd, J. N.,…Evans, A. C. (1999). Structural maturation of neural pathways in children and adolescents: In vivo study. *Science, 19,* 1908–1911.

Pearlman, D., Zierler, S., Meersman, S., Kim, H., Viner-Brown, S., & Caron, C. (2006). Race disparities in childhood asthma: Does where you live matter? *Journal of the National Medical Association, 98,* 239–247.

Peirano, P., Algarin, C., & Uauy, R. (2003). Sleep–wake states and their regulatory mechanism throughout early human development. *Journal of Pediatrics, 143*(Suppl.), S70–S79.

Peitilainen, K. H., Kaprio, J., Borg, P., Plasqui, G., Yki-Järvinen, H., Kujala, U. M.,…Rissanen, A. (2008). Physical inactivity and obesity: A vicious circle. *Obesity, 16,* 409–414.

Pelaez, M., Field, T., Pickens, J. N., & Hart, S. (2008). Disengaged and authoritarian parenting behavior of depressed mothers with their toddlers. *Infant Behavior and Development, 31,* 145–148.

Peng, K., & Nisbett, R. E. (1999). Culture, dialectics, and reasoning about contradiction. *American Psychologist, 54,* 741–754.

Pennington, B. F., Moon, J., Edgin, J., Stedron, J., & Nadel, L. (2003). The neuropsychology of Down syndrome: Evidence for hippocampal dysfunction. *Child Development, 74,* 75–93.

Peplau, L. A., & Beals, K. P. (2002). Lesbians, gay men, and bisexuals in relationships. In J. Worell (Ed.), *Encyclopedia of women and gender* (pp. 657–666). San Diego, CA: Academic Press.

Peplau, L. A., & Beals, K. P. (2004). The family lives of lesbians and gay men. In A.L. Vangelisti (Ed.), *Handbook of family communication* (pp. 233–248). Mahwah, NJ: Erlbaum.

Pepler, D. J., Craig, W. M., Connolly, J. A., Yuile, A., McMaster, L., & Jiang, D. (2006). A developmental perspective on bullying. *Aggressive Behavior, 32,* 376–384.

Pepler, D. J., Jiang, D., Craig, W. M., & Connolly, J. A. (2008). Developmental trajectories of bullying and associated factors. *Child Development, 79,* 325–338.

Pepler, D., Craig, W., Yuile, A., & Connolly, J. (2004). Girls who bully: A developmental and relational perspective. In M. Putallaz & K. L. Bierman (Eds.), *Aggression, antisocial behavior, and violence among girls: A developmental perspective* (pp. 90–109). New York, NY: Guilford.

Perilloux, C., Fleischman, D. S., & Buss, D. M. (2011). Meet the parents: Parent-offspring convergence and divergence in mate preferences. *Personality and Individual Differences, 50,* 253–258.

Perlmutter, M., Kaplan, M., & Nyquist, L. (1990). Development of adaptive competence in adulthood. *Human Development, 33,* 185–197.

Perrault, A., Fothergill-Bourbonnais, F., & Fiset, V. (2004). The experience of family members caring for a dying loved one. *International Journal of Palliative Nursing, 10,* 133–143.

Perry, W. G. (1970/1999). *Forms of ethical and intellectual development in the college years: A scheme.* San Francisco, CA: Jossey-Bass.

Peterson, B. (2006). Generativity and successful parenting: An analysis of young adult outcomes. *Journal of Personality, 74,* 847–869.

Peterson, C., & Whalen, N. (2001). Five years later: Children's memory for medical emergencies. *Applied Cognitive Psychology, 15*(Special issue: Trauma, stress, and autobiographical memory), S7–S24.

Peterson, D. M., Marcia, J. E., & Carpendale, J. I. M. (2004). Identity: Does thinking make it so? In C. Lightfood & M. Chandler (Eds.), *Changing conceptions of psychological life* (pp. 113–126). Mahwah, NJ: Erlbaum.

Pew Commission on Children in Foster Care (2004). *Safety, permanence and well-being for children in foster care.* Retrieved from: http://pewfostercare.org/research/docs/FinalReport.pdf

Pew Forum on Religion & Public Life (2008). *U.S. religious landscape survey.* Washington, DC: Author.

Pew Research Center. (2006). *Strong public support for right to die.* Retrieved from http://people-press.org/reports

Pew Research Center (2007). *As marriage and parenthood drift apart, public is concerned about the social impact.* Retrieved from http://pewsocialtrends.org/2007/07/01/as-marriage-and-parenthood-drift-apart-public- is-concerned-about-social-impact/

Pew Research Center (2010). *Millennials: A report on Generation Next.* Washington, DC: Author.

Pew Research Center (2010). *Religion Among the Millennials.* Washington, DC: Author.

Pew Research Center (2013). *Gay marriage: Key data points from Pew research.* Retrieved from http://www.pewresearch.org/key-data-points/gay-marriage-key-data-points-from-pew-research/

Pew Social Trends Staff. (2010). *The return of the multi-generational family household.* Retrieved from http://pewsocialtrends.org/2010/03/18/the-return-of-the-multi-generational-family-household/

Pfirrmann, C. W., Metzdorf, A., Elfering, A., Hodler, J., & Boos, N. (2006). Effect of aging and degeneration on disc volume and shape: A quantitative study in asymptomatic volunteers. *Journal of Orthopedics Research, 24,* 1086–1094.

Phelan, T. W. (2010). *1-2-3 magic: Effective discipline for children 2-12.* New York, NY: Child Management.

Phinney, J. S. (1990). Ethnic identity in adolescents and adults: A review of research. *Psychological Bulletin, 108,* 499–514.

Phinney, J. S. (2000, March). *Identity formation among U.S. ethnic adolescents from collectivist cultures.* Paper presented at the biennial meeting of the Society of Research on Adolescence, Chicago, IL.

Phinney, J. S. (2006). Ethnic identity in emerging adulthood. In J. J. Arnett & J. L. Tanner (Eds.), *Emerging adults in America: Coming of age in the 21st century* (pp. 117–134). Washington, DC: American Psychological Association.

Phinney, J. S., & Baldelomar, O. A. (2011). Identity development in multiple cultural contexts. In L. A. Jensen (Ed.), *Bridging cultural and developmental psychology: New syntheses in theory, research and policy* (pp. 161–186). New York, NY: Oxford University Press.

Phinney, J. S., & Devich-Navarro, M. (1997). Variation in bicultural identification among African American and Mexican American adolescents. *Journal of Research on Adolescence, 7,* 3–32.

Phinney, J. S., & Ong, A. D. (2002). Adolescent–parent disagreement and life satisfaction in families from Vietnamese and European American backgrounds. *International Journal of Behavioral Development, 26,* 556–561.

Phinney, J. S., & Rosenthal, D. A. (1992). Ethnic identity in adolescence: Process, context, and outcome. In G. R. Adams, T. P. Gullotta, & R. Montemayor (Eds.), *Adolescent identity formation* (pp. 145–172). Newbury Park, CA: Sage.

Phinney, J. S., DuPont, S., Espinosa, A., Revill, J., & Sanders, K. (1994). Ethnic identity and American identification among ethnic minority adolescents. In A. M. Bouvy, F. J. R. van de Vijver, P. Boski, & P. Schmitz (Eds.), *Journeys into cross-cultural psychology* (pp. 167–183). Amsterdam: Swets & Zeitlinger.

Phinney, J. S., Kim-Jo, T., Osorio, S., & Vilhjalmsdottir, P. (2005). Autonomy and relatedness in adolescent-parent disagreements: Ethnic and developmental factors. *Journal of Adolescent Research, 20,* 8–39.

Piaget, J. (1936/1952). *The origins of intelligence in children.* New York, NY: Norton.

Piaget, J. (1954). *The construction of reality in the child.* New York, NY: Basic Books.

Piaget, J. (1965). *The moral judgment of the child.* New York, NY: Free Press. (Original work published 1932).

Piaget, J. (1967). *Six psychological studies.* New York, NY: Random House.

Piaget, J. (1972). Intellectual evolution from adolescence to adulthood. *Human Development, 15,* 1–12.

Piaget, J. (2002). The epigenetic system and the development of cognitive functions. In R. O. Gilmore, Mark H. Johnson, & Yuko Munakata (Eds.), *Brain development and cognition: A reader* (2nd ed., pp. 29–35). Malden: Blackwell.

Piaget, J., & Inhelder, B. (1969). *The child's conception of space* (F. J. Langdon & J. L. Lunger, Trans.). New York, NY: W. W. Norton.

Pickett, K. E., Luo, Y., & Lauderdale, D. S. (2005). Widening social inequalities in risk for sudden infant death syndrome. *American Journal of Public Health, 95*(11), 1976.

Piek, J. P., Dawson, L., Smith, L., & Gasson, N. (2008). The role of early fine and gross motor development on later motor and cognitive ability. *Human Movement Science, 27,* 668–681.

Pierroutsakos, S. L. (2000). Infants of the dreaming. In J. DeLoache & A. Gottlieb (Eds.), *A world of babies: Imagined childcare guides for seven societies* (pp. 145–170). New York, NY: Cambridge University Press.

Pierroutsakos, S. L., & Troseth, G. L. (2003). Video verite: Infants' manual investigation of objects on video. *Infant Behavior & Development, 26,* 183–199.

Pike, A., Coldwell, J., & Dunn, J. F. (2005). Sibling relationships in early/middle childhood: Links with individual adjustment. *Journal of Family Psychology, 19,* 523–532.

Piktialis, D. S. (2008). Redesigning work for an aging labor force: Employer and employee perspectives. In R. B. Hudson (Ed.), *Boomer bust? Economic and political issues of the graying society* (Vol. 2, pp. 17–32). Westport, CT: Praeger.

Pilcher, J. J., & Walters, A. S. (1997). How sleep deprivation affects psychological variables related to college students' cognitive performance. *Journal of American College Health, 46,* 121–126.

Pinilla, F. G. (2006). The impact of diet and exercise on brain plasticity and disease. *Nutrition and Health, 18,* 277–284.

Pinker, S. (1994). *The language instinct.* New York, NY: Williams Morrow.

Pinker, S. (2004). *The blank slate: The modern denial of human nature.* New York, NY: Penguin.

Piolino, P., Desgranges, B., Clarys, D., Guillery-Girard, B., Taconnat, L., Isingrini, M., & Eustache, F. (2006). Autobiographical memory, autonoetic consciousness, and self-perspective in aging. *Psychology and Aging, 21,* 510–525.

Pipp, S., Fischer, K. W., & Jennings, S. (1987). Acquisition of self- and mother knowledge in infancy. *Developmental Psychology, 23,* 86–96.

Pirttilae-Backman, A. M., & Kajanne, A. (2001). The development of implicit epistemologies during early adulthood. *Journal of Adult Development, 8,* 81–97.

Pisetsky, E. M., Chao, Y. M., Dierker, L. C., May, A. M., & Striegel-Moore, R. H. (2008). Disordered eating and substance use in high school students: Results from the Youth Risk Behavior Surveillance System. *International Journal of Eating Disorders, 41,* 464–470.

Pizzamiglio, A. P., Saygin, S. L., Small, S., & Wilson, S. (2005). Language and the brain. In M. Tomasello & D. A. Slobin (Eds.), *Beyond nature-nurture* (pp. 237–260). Mahwah, NJ: Erlbaum.

Plagnol, A. C., & Easterlin, R. A. (2008). Aspirations, attainments, and satisfaction: Life cycle differences between American women and men. *Journal of Happiness Studies, 9,* 601–619.

Plant, M., Miller, P., Plant, M., Gmel, G., Kuntsche, S., Bergmark, K., . . . Vidal, A. (2010). The social consequences of binge drinking among 24- to 32-year-olds in six European countries. *Substance Use & Misuse, 45,* 528–542.

Plant, R. W., & Siegel, L. (2008). Children in foster care: Prevention and treatment of mental health problems. In T. P. Gullotta & G. M. Blau (Eds.), *Family influences on childhood behavior and development: Evidence-based prevention and treatment approaches* (pp. 209–230).

Plantin, L. (2007). Different classes, different fathers?: On fatherhood, economic conditions and class in Sweden. *Community, Work & Family, 10*, 93–110.

Pleck, J. H. (2010). Paternal involvement: Revised conceptualization and theoretical linkages to child outcomes. In M. E. Lamb (Ed.), *The role of the father in child development* (pp. 58–93). New York, NY: Wiley.

Pleck, J. H., & Masciadrelli, B. P. (2004). Paternal involvement by U.S. residential fathers: Levels, sources and consequences. In M. E. Lamb (Ed.), *The role of the father in child development* (4th ed., pp. 272–306). New York, NY: Wiley.

Pleis, J. R., & Lethbridge-Cejku, M. (2006). Summary health statistics for U.S. adults: National Health Interview Survey, 2005, *10*(232).

Ploeg, J., Campbell, L., Denton, M., Joshi, A., & Davies, S. (2004). Helping to build and rebuild secure lives and futures: Financial transfers from parents to adult children and grandchildren. *Canadian Journal on Aging, 23*, S131–S143.

Plomin, R. (2009). The nature of nurture. In K. McCartney and R. A. Weinberg (Eds.), *Experience and development: A festschrift in honor of Sandra Wood Scarr* (pp. 61–80). New York, NY: Psychology Press.

Plonczynski, D. J., & Plonczynski, K. J. (2007). Hormone therapy in perimenopausal and postmenopausal women: Examining the evidence on cardiovascular disease risks. *Journal of Gerentological Nursing, 33*, 48–55.

Plotkin, S. A., Katz, M., & Cordero, J. F. (1999). The eradication of rubella. *JAMA: Journal of the American Medical Association, 306*, 343–450.

Podewils, L. J., Fuallar, E., Kuller, L. H., Fried, L. P., Lopez, O. L., Carlson, M., & Lyketsos, C. G. (2005). Physical activity, *APOE* genotype, and dementia risk: Findings from the Cardiovascular Health Cognition Study. *American Journal of Epidemiology, 161*, 639–651.

Pollitt, E., Golub, M., Gorman, K., Gratham-McGregor, S., Levitsky, D., Schurch, B.,…Wachs, T. (1996). A reconceptualization of the effects of undernutrition on children's biological, psychosocial, and behavioral development. *Social Policy Report, 10*, 1–28.

Pons, F., Lawson, J., Harris, P. L., & de Rosnay, M. (2003). Individual differences in children's emotion understanding: Effects of age and language. *Scandinavian Journal of Psychology, 44*, 347–353.

Pool, M. M., Koolstra, C. M., & van der Voort, T. H. A. (2003). The impact of background radio and television on high school students' homework performance. *Journal of Communication, 53*, 74–87.

Popenoe, D., & Whitehead, B. D. (2001). *The state of our unions, 2001: The social health of marriage in America.* Report of the National Marriage Project, Rutgers, New Brunswick, NJ. Available: http://marriage.rutgers.edu

Popkin, B. M. (2010). Recent dynamics suggest selected countries catching up to US obesity. *The American journal of clinical nutrition, 91*(1), 284S–288S.

Popp, D., Lauren, B., Kerr, M., Stattin, H., & Burk, W. K. (2008). Modeling homophily over time with an actor–partner independence model. *Developmental Psychology, 44*, 1028–1039.

Popp, M. S. (2005). *Teaching language and literacy in elementary classrooms.* Mahwah, NJ: Erlbaum.

Population Reference Bureau (PRB) (2000). *The world's youth 2000.* Washington, DC: Author.

Population Reference Bureau (PRB) (2009). *2009 World Population Data Sheet.* Washington, DC: Author.

Population Reference Bureau (PRB) (2010). *World population data sheet.* Washington, DC.

Population Reference Bureau (2014). *World population data sheet, 2014.* Washington, DC: Author.

Porath, M., Korp, L., Wendrich, D., Dlugay, V., Roth, B., & Kribs, A. (2011). Surfactant in spontaneous breathing with nCPAP: Neurodevelopmental outcome at early school age of infants = 27 weeks. *Acta Paediatrica, 100*, 352–359.

Porfelli, E. J., Hartung, P. J., & Vondracek, F. W. (2008). Children's vocational development: A research rationale. *Career Development Quarterly, 57*, 25–37.

Porges, S. W., & Lispitt, L. P. (1993). Neonatal responsivity to gustatory stimulation: The gustatory–vagal hypothesis. *Infant Behavior & Development, 16*, 487–494.

Porter, R. H., & Rieser, J. J. (2005). Retention of olfactory memories by newborn infants. In R. T. Mason, P. M. LeMaster, & D. Müller-Schwarze (Eds.), *Chemical Signals in Vertebrates* (pp. 300–307). New York, NY: Springer.

Portes, P. R., Dunham, R., & Castillo, K. D. (2000). Identity formation and status across cultures: Exploring the cultural validity of Eriksonian theory. In A. Comunian & U. P. Gielen (Eds.), *International perspectives on human development* (pp. 449–459). Lengerich, Germany: Pabst Science.

Posada, G., Gao, Y., Wu, F., Posada, R., Tascon, M., Schoelmerich, A.,…Synnevaag, B. (1995). The secure-base phenomenon across cultures: Children's behavior, mothers' preferences, and experts' concepts. *Monographs of the Society for Research in Child Development, 60*, 27–48.

Posner, M. I., & Rothbart, M. K. (2007). Numeracy. In M. I. Posner & M. K. Rothbart, *Educating the human brain* (pp. 173–187). Washington, DC: American Psychological Association.

Posner, R. B. (2006). Early menarche: A review of research on trends in timing, racial differences, etiology and psychosocial consequences. *Sex Roles, 54*, 315–322.

Potegal, M., & Davison, R. J. (2003). Temper tantrums in young children, 1: Behavioral composition. *Journal of Developmental & Behavioral Pediatrics, 24*, 140–147.

Powls, A., Botting, N., Cooke, R. W. I., & Marlow, N. (1996). Handedness in very-low birth-weight (VLBW) children at 12 years of age: Relation to perinatal and outcome variables. *Developmental Medicine and Child Neurology, 38*, 594–602.

Prakasa, V. V., & Rao, V. N. (1979). Arranged marriages: An assessment of the attitudes of college students in India. In G. Kurian (Ed.), *Cross-cultural perspectives on mate selection and marriage* (pp. 11–31). Westport, CT: Greenwood Press.

Prasad, V., Brogan, E., Mulvaney, C., Grainge, M., Stanton, W., & Sayal, K. (2013). How effective are drug treatments for children with ADHD at improving on-task behaviour and academic achievement in the school classroom? A systematic review and meta-analysis. *European child & adolescent psychiatry, 22*(4), 203–216.

Pratt, M. W., Danso, H. A., Arnold, M. L., Norris, J. E., & Filyer, R. (2001). Adult generativity and the socialization of adolescents: Relations to mothers' and fathers' parenting beliefs, styles, and practices. *Journal of Personality, 69*, 89–120.

Prentice, A., Schoenmakers, I., Laskey, M. A., de Bono, S., Ginty, F., & Goldberg, G. R. (2006). Nutrition and bone growth and development. *Proceedings of the Nutritional Society, 65*, 348–360.

Pressley, M., Wharton-McDonald, R., Raphael, L. M., Bogner, K., & Roehrig, A. (2002). Exemplary first-grade teaching. In B. M. Taylor & P. D. Pearson (Eds.), *Teaching reading: Effective schools, accomplished teachers* (pp. 73–88). Mahwah, NJ: Erlbaum.

Pretorius, E., Naude, H., & Van Vuuren, C. J. (2002). Can cultural behavior have a negative impact on the development of visual integration pathways? *Early Child Development and Care, 123*, 173–181.

Preuss, U., Ralston, S. J., Baldursson, G., Falissard, B., Lorenzo, M. J., Rodrigues Pereira, R.,…ADORE Study Group. (2006). Study design, baseline patient characteristics and intervention in a cross-cultural framework: Results from the ADORE study. *European Child & Adolescent Psychiatry, 15*(Suppl. 1), 4–19.

Preusser, D. F., & Tison, J. (2007). GDL then and now. *Journal of Safety Research, 38,* 159–163.

Price Waterhouse Coopers (2011). The accelerating shift of global economic power: Challenges and opportunities. Retrieved from http://www.pwc.com/en_GX/gx/world-2050/pdf/world-in-2050-jan-2011.pdf

Priess, H. A., & Lindberg, S. A. (2014). Gender intensification. In R. Levesque (Ed.), *Encyclopedia of Adolescence* (pp. 1135–1142). New York, NY: Springer.

Prisuta, R. (2004). Enhancing volunteerism among aging boomers. Harvard School of Public Health and MetLife. *Reinventing aging: Baby boomers and civic engagement.* Boston, MA: Harvard School of Public Health, Center for Health Communication.

Proctor, M. H., Moore, L. L., Gao, D., Cupples, L. A., Bradlee, M. L., Hood, M. Y., & Ellison, R. C. (2003). Television viewing and change in body fat from preschool to early adolescence: The Framingham Children's Study. *International Journal of Obesity, 27,* 827–833.

Provins, K. A. (1997). Handedness and speech: A critical reappraisal of the role of genetic and environmental factors in the cerebral lateralization of function. *Psychological Review, 104,* 554–571.

Pruthi, S. (2011). *Mammogram guidelines: What are they?* Retrieved from http://www.mayoclinic.com/health/mammogram-guidelines/AN02052

Puhl, R. M., Heuer, C. A., & Brownell, K. D. (2010). Stigma and social consequences of obesity. In P.G. Kopelman, I.D. Caterson, & W.H. Dietz (Eds.), *Clinical obesity in adults and children* (pp. 25–40). New York: Wiley.

Purdie, N., Carroll, A., & Roche, L. (2004). Parenting and adolescent self-regulation. *Journal of Adolescence, 27,* 663–676.

Putnam, R. (2000). *Bowling alone: The collapse and revival of American community.* New York, NY: Simon & Schuster.

Putnam, R. (2002). Bowling together. *The American Prospect, 13,* 20–22. Putnam, R. (2004). *Democracies in flux.* New York, NY: Oxford University Press.

Qin, D. B. (2009). Being "good" or being "popular": Gender and ethnic identity negotiations of Chinese immigrant adolescents. *Journal of Adolescent Research, 24,* 37–66.

Qiu, C., Backman, L., Winblad, B., Aguero-Torres, H., & Fratiglioni, L. (2001). The influence of education on clinically diagnosed dementia incidence and mortality data from the Kungsholmen Project. *Archives of Neurology, 58,* 2034–2039.

Quillian, L. (2003). The decline of male employment in low income Black neighborhoods, 1950–1990. *Social Science Research, 32,* 220–250.

Quinn, C. T., Rogers, Z. R., & Buchanan, G. R. (2004). Survival of children with sickle cell disease. *Blood, 103,* 4023–4027.

Quinn, P. C., Eimas, P. D., & Rosenkranz, S. L. (1993). Evidence for representations of perceptually similar natural categories by 3-month-old and 4-month-old infants. *Perception, 22,* 463–475.

Quinnell, T. G., & Smith, I. E. (2004). Obstructive sleep apnea in the elderly: Recognition and management considerations. *Drugs and Aging, 21,* 307–322.

Raacke, J., & Bonds-Raacke, J. (2008). MySpace and Facebook: Applying the uses and gratifications theory to exploring friend-networking sites. *CyberPsychology & Behavior, 11,* 169–174.

Raag, T. (2003). Racism, gender identities and young children: Social relations in a multi-ethnic, inner-city primary school. *Archives of Sexual Behavior, 32,* 392–393.

Radmacher, K., & Azmitia, M. (2006). Are there gendered pathways to intimacy in early adolescents' and emerging adults' friendships? *Journal of Adolescent Research, 21,* 415–448.

Radvansky, G. A., Zacks, R. T., & Hasher, L. (2005). Age and inhibition: The retrieval situation models. *Journal of Gerontology, 60B,* P276–P278.

Rafaelli, M., & Iturbide, M. (2015). Adolescence risks and resiliences across cultures. In L. A. Jensen (Ed.), *Oxford handbook of human development and culture: An interdisciplinary perspective.* New York, NY: Oxford University Press.

Rafii, M. S., & Aisen, P. S. (2009). Recent developments in Alzheimer's disease therapeutics. *BMC Medicine, 7,* 1741–1751.

Ragow-O'Brien, D., Hayslip, B., Jr., & Guarnaccia, C. A. (2000). The impact of hospice on attitudes toward funerals and subsequent bereavement adjustment. *Omega, 41,* 291–305.

Raikes, H. H., Chazan-Cohen, R., Love, J. M., & Brooks-Gunn, J. (2010). Early Head Start impacts at age 3 and a description of the age 5 follow-up study. In A. J. Reynolds, A. J. Rolnick, & M. M. Englund (Eds.), *Childhood programs and practices in the first decade of life: A human capital integration* (pp. 99–118). New York, NY: Cambridge University Press.

Rajaratnam, J. K., Marcus, J. R., Flaxman, A. D., Wang, H., Levin-Rector, A., Dwyer, L.,…Murray, C. J. L. (2003). Neonatal, post-neonatal, childhood, and under–5 mortality for 187 countries, 1970–2010: A systematic analysis of progress towards Millennium Development Goal 4. *Pediatrics, 111,* e61–e66.

Ralph, K., Harrington, K., & Pandha, H. (2004). Recent developments and current status of gene therapy using viral vectors in the United Kingdom. *British Medical Journal, 329,* 839–842.

Ralston, L. S., Bell, S. L., Mote, J. K., Rainey, T. B., Brayman, S., & Shotwell, M. (2001). Giving up the car keys: Perceptions of well elders and families. *Physical & Occupational Therapy in Geriatrics, 19,* 59–70.

Ramchandani, P., Stein, A., Evans, J., O'Connor, T. G., & the ALSPAC Study Team. (2005). Paternal depression in the postnatal period and child development: A prospective population study. *Lancet, 365,* 2201–2205.

Ramos, D. (2010). *Japanese elderly look for meaning.* Retrieved from: http://www.projo.com/opinion/contributors/content/CT_ramos22_04-22-10_NGI4PV9_v9.4056148.html

Ramos, M. C., Guerin, D. W., Gottfried, A. W., Bathurst, K., & Oliver, P. H. (2005). Family conflict and children's behavior problems: The moderating role of child temperament. *Structural Equation Modeling, 12,* 278–298.

Randell, A. C., & Peterson, C. C. (2009). Affective qualities of sibling disputes, mothers' conflict attitudes, and children's theory of mind development. *Social Development, 18,* 857–874.

Rao, R., & Georgieff, M. K. (2001). Neonatal iron nutrition. *Seminars in Neonatology, 6,* 425–435.

Rapp, M., Krampe, R., & Balles, P. (2006). Adaptive task prioritization in aging: Selective resource allocation to postural control is preserved in Alzheimer disease. *American Journal of Geriatric Psychiatry, 14,* 52–61.

Rasmussen, E. R., Neuman, R. J., Heath, A. C., Levy, F., Hay, D. A., & Todd, R. D. (2004). Familial clustering of latent class and DSM-IV defined attention-deficit hyperactivity disorder (ADHD) subtypes. *Journal of Child Psychology and Psychiatry, 45,* 589–598.

Rastogi, M., & Therly, P. (2006). Dowry and its link to violence against women in India: Feminist psychological perspectives. *Trauma, Violence, & Abuse, 7,* 66–77.

Ratanachu-Ek, S. (2003). Effects of multivitamin and folic acid supplementation in malnourished children. *Journal of the Medical Association of Thailand, 4,* 86–91.

Rattner, A., & Nathans, J. (2006). Macular degeneration: Recent advances and therapeutic opportunities. *Nature Reviews Neuroscience, 7,* 860–872.

Raudsepp, L., & Liblik, R. (2002). Relationship of perceived and actual motor competence in children. *Perception and Motor Skills, 94,* 1059–1070.

Rauscher, F. H. (2003). Can music instruction affect children's cognitive development? *ERIC Digest, EDO-PS-03-12.*

Rauscher, F. H., Shaw, G. L., & Ky, K. N. (1993). Listening to Mozart enhances spatial-temporal reasoning: Towards a neurophysiological basis. *Neuroscience Letters, 185,* 44–47.

Ravn, M. N. (2005). A matter of free choice? Some structural and cultural influences on the decision to have or not to have children in Norway. In C. B. Douglas (Ed.), *Barren states: The population "implosion" in Europe* (pp. 29–47). New York, NY: Berg.

Rawson, N. E. (2006). Olfactory loss in aging. *Science Aging Knowledge Environment, 5,* 6–10.

Raymo, J. M., Liang, J., Sugisawa, H., Kobayashi, E., & Sugihara, Y. (2004). Work at older ages in Japan: Variation by gender and employment status. *Journals of Gerontology B: Psychological Sciences and Social Sciences, 59,* S154–S163.

Rayner, K., Foorman, B. R., Perfetti, C. A., Pesetsky, D., & Seidenberg, M. S. (2002). How should reading be taught? *Scientific American, 286,* 84–91.

Reynolds, K., Lewis, L. B., Nolen, J. D. L., Kinney, G. L., Sathya, B., & He, J. (2003). Alcohol consumption and risk of stroke: A meta-analysis. *Journal of the American Medical Association, 289,* 579–588.

Raz, N. (2005). The aging brain observed in vivo: Differential changes and their modifiers. In R. Cabeza, L. Nyberg, & D. Park (Eds.), *Cognitive neuroscience of aging: Linking cognitive and cerebral aging* (pp. 19–57). New York, NY: Oxford University Press.

Raz, N., Rodrigue, K., Kennedy, K., & Acker, J. (2007, March). Vascular health and longitudinal changes in brain and cognition in middle-aged and older adults. *Neuropsychology, 21,* 149–157.

Reday-Mulvey, G. (2000). Gradual retirement in Europe. *Journal of Aging and Social Policy, 11,* 49–60.

Redcay, E., Haist, F., & Courchesne, E. (2008). Functional neuroimaging of speech perception during a pivotal period in language acquisition. *Developmental science, 11*(2), 237–252.

Reddy, U. M., & Mennuti, M. T. (2006). Incorporating first-trimester Down syndrome studies into prenatal screening. *Obstetrics and Gynecology, 107,* 167–173.

Redshaw, M. E. (1997). Mothers of babies requiring special care: Attitudes and experiences. *Journal of Reproductive & Infant Psychology, 15,* 109–120.

Reese, D. (2000). A parenting manual, with words of advice for Puritan mothers. In J. DeLoache & A. Gottlieb (Eds.), *A world of babies: Imagined childcare guides for seven societies* (pp. 29–54). New York, NY: Cambridge University Press.

Reeves, G., & Schweitzer, J. (2004). Pharmacological management of attention deficit hyperactivity disorder. *Expert Opinions in Pharmacotherapy, 5,* 1313–1320.

Regan, P. C., Durvasula, R., Howell, L., Ureno, O., & Rea, M. (2004). Gender, ethnicity, and the developmental timing of the first sexual and romantic experiences. *Social Behavior & Personality, 32,* 667–676.

Regestein, Q., Natarajan, V., Pavlova, M., Kawasaki, S., Gleason, R., & Koff, E. (2010). Sleep debt and depression in female college students. *Psychiatry research, 176*(1), 34–39.

Reginster, J. Y., & Burlet, N. (2006). Osteoporosis: A still increasing prevalence. *Bone, 38,* 4–9.

Regnerus, M., & Uecker, J. (2011). *Premarital sex in America: How young Americans meet, mate, and think about marrying.* New York, NY: Oxford University Press.

Reid, C. (2004). Kangaroo care. *Neonatal Network, 23,* 53.

Reifman, A., Arnett, J. J., & Colwell, M. J. (2006). Emerging adulthood: Theory, assessment, and application. *Journal of Youth Development, 1,* 1–12.

Reimuller, A., Shadur, J., & Hussong, A. M. (2011). Parental social support as a moderator of self-medication in adolescents. *Addictive Behaviors, 36,* 203–208.

Reisenwitz, T., Iyer, R., Kuhlmeier, D. B., & Eastman, J. K. (2007). The elderly's Internet usage: An updated look. *Journal of Consumer Marketing, 24,* 406–418.

Reiss, D., Neiderhiser, J., Hetherington, E. M., & Plomin, R. (2000). The relationship code: Deciphering genetic and social influences on adolescent development. Cambridge, MA: Harvard University Press.

Resnick, G. (2010). Project Head Start: Quality and links to child outcomes. In A. J. Reynolds, A. J. Rolnick, M. M. Englund, & J. A. Temple (Eds.), *Childhood programs and practices in the first decade of life: A human capital integration* (pp. 121–156). New York, NY: Cambridge University Press.

Resnikoff, S., Pascolini, D., Etya'ale, D., Kocur, I., Pararajasegaram, R., Pokharel, G. P., Mariotti, S. P. (2004). Global data on visual impairment in the year 2004. *Bulletin of the World Health Organization, 82,* 844–851.

Rey-López, J. P., and the HELENA Study Group (2010). Sedentary patterns and media availability in European adolescents: The HELENA study. *Preventive Medicine 51,* 50–55.

Reznick, J. S., Corley, R., & Robinson, J. (1997). A longitudinal study of intelligence in the second year. *Monographs of the Society for Research in Child Development, 62,* 1–154.

Rhodes, J. R., & DuBois, D. L. (2008). Mentoring relationships and programs for youth. *Current Directions in Psychological Science, 17,* 254–258.

Ricciuti, H. N. (2004). Single parenthood, achievement, and problem behavior in White, Black, and Hispanic children. *Journal of Educational Research, 97,* 196–206.

Richards, M. H., Crowe, P. A., Larson, R., & Swarr, A. (2002). Developmental patterns and gender differences in the experience of peer companionship in adolescence. *Child Development, 69,* 154–163.

Richman, A. L., Miller, P. M., & LeVine, R. A. (2010). Cultural and educational variations in maternal responsiveness. In R. A. LeVine (Ed.), *Psychological anthropology: A reader on self in culture* (pp. 181–192). Malden, MA: Wiley-Blackwell.

Rideout, V. (2013). *Zero to eight: Children's use of media in America, 2013.* Washington, DC: Common Sense Media.

Rideout, V. J., & Hamel, E. (2006). *The media family: Electronic media in the lives of infants, toddlers, preschoolers, and their parents.* Menlo Park, CA: The Henry J. Kaiser Family Foundation.

Rideout, V. J., Vandewater, E. A., & Wartella, E. A. (2003). *Zero to six: Electronic media in the lives of infants, toddlers and preschoolers.* Menlo Park, CA: The Henry J. Kaiser Family Foundation.

Ridley, M. (2010). *The rational optimist: How prosperity evolves.* New York, NY: Harper.

Riedel, B. W., Robinson, L. A., Klesges, R. C., & McLain-Allen, B. (2003). Ethnic differences in smoking withdrawal effects among adolescents. *Addictive Behaviors, 28,* 129–140.

Riedel, B., & Lichstein, K. (2000). Insomnia in older adults. In S. K. Whitbourne (Ed.), *Psychopathology in later life* (pp. 299–322). New York, NY: Wiley.

Rifkin, J. (2004). *The European dream.* New York, NY: Tarcher.

Rigby, K. (2004). Bullying in childhood. In P. K. Smith & C. H. Hart (Eds.), *Blackwell handbook of childhood social development.* Malden, MA: Blackwell.

Righetti, P. L., Dell'Avanzo, M., Grigio, M., & Nicolini, U. (2005). Maternal/paternal antenatal attachment and fourth–dimensional ultrasound technique: A preliminary report. *British Journal of Psychology, 96,* 129–137.

Righetti-Veltema, M., Conne-Perreard, E., Bousquest, A., & Manzano, J. (2002). Postpartum depression and mother–infant relationship at 3 months old. *Journal of Affective Disorders, 70*, 291–306.

Riley, A. W., Lyman, L. M., Spiel, G., Döpfner, M., Lorenzo, M. J., Ralston, S. J., & ADORE Study Group. (2006). The Family Strain Index (FSI). Reliability, validity, and factor structure of a brief questionnaire for families of children with ADHD. *European Child & Adolescent Psychiatry, 15*(Suppl. 1), 72–78.

Riley Bove, C. V. (2009). Polygyny and women's health in sub-Saharan Africa. *Social Science & Medicine, 68*, 21–29.

Riley, L. D., & Bowen, C. P. (2005). The sandwich generation: Challenges and coping strategies of multigenerational families. *Counseling and Therapy for Couples and Families, 13*, 52–58.

Rix, S. E. (2008). Will the boomers revolutionize work and retirement? In R. Hudson (Ed.), *Boomer bust? Economic and political issues of the graying society* (Vol. 1, pp. 77–94). Westport, CT: Praeger.

Roberto, C. A., Steinglass, J., Mayer, L. E. S., Attia, E., & Walsh, B. T. (2008). The clinical significance of amenorrhea as a diagnostic criterion for anorexia nervosa. *International Journal of Eating Disorders, 41*, 559–563.

Roberto, K. A., & Skoglund, R. R. (1996). Interactions with grandparents and great-grandparents: A comparison of activities, influences, and relationships. *International Journal of Aging and Human Development, 43*, 107–117.

Roberts, B. L., Dunkle, R., & Haug, M. (1994). Physical, psychological, and social resources as moderators of stress to mental health of the very old. *Journal of Gerontology, 49*, S35–S43.

Roberts, B. W., Caspi, A., & Moffitt, T. E. (2001). The kids are alright: Growth and stability in personality development from adolescence to adulthood. *Journal of Personality and Social Psychology, 81*, 670–683.

Roberts, D. F., Foehr, U. G., & Rideout, V. (2005). *Generation M: Media in the lives of 8–18 year-olds*. Washington, DC: The Henry J. Kaiser Family Foundation.

Roberts, R. G., Deutchman, M., King, V. J., Fryer, G. E., & Miyoshi, T. J. (2007). Changing policies on vaginal birth after cesarean: Impact on access. *Birth: Issues in Perinatal Care, 34*, 316–322.

Robertson, J. (2008). Stepfathers in families. In J. Pryor (Ed.), *The international handbook of stepfamilies: Policy and practice in legal, research, and clinical environments* (pp. 125–150). Hoboken, NJ: John Wiley & Sons.

Robins, R. W., Gosling, S. D. & Craik, K. H. (1999). An empirical analysis of trends in psychology. *American Psychologist, 54*, 117–128.

Robins, R. W., & Trzesniewski, K. H. (2005). Self-esteem development across the lifespan. *Current Directions in Psychological Science, 14*, 158–162.

Robins, R. W., Trzesniewski, K. H., Tracey, J. L., Potter, J., & Gosling, S. D. (2002). Age differences in self-esteem from age 9 to 90. *Psychology and Aging, 17*, 423–434.

Robinson, C. C., Anderson, G. T., Porter, C. L., Hart, C. H., & Wouden-Miller, M. (2003). Sequential transition patterns of preschoolers' social interactions during child-initiated play: Is parallel-aware play a bi-directional bridge to other play states? *Early Childhood Research Quarterly, 18*, 3–21.

Robinson, G. (2020. Cross-cultural perspectives on menopause. In A. Hunter & C. Forden (Eds.), *Readings in the psychology of gender: Exploring our differences and commonalities*. Needham Heights, MA: Allyn & Bacon.

Robinson, J. D., Skill, T., & Turner, J. W. (2004). Media usage patterns and portrayals of seniors. In J. F. Nussbaum & J. Coupland (Eds.), *Handbook of communication and aging research* (2nd ed., 423–446). Mahwah, NJ: Lawrence Erlbaum.

Robinson, J. L., Klute, M. M., Faldowski, R., Pan, B., Staerkel, F., Summers, J. A., & Wall, S. (2009). Mixed approach programs in the Early Head Start Research and Evaluation Project: An in-depth view. *Early Education and Development, 20*, 893–919.

Robinson, J. P., Godbey, G., & Putnam, R. D. (1999). *Time for life: The surprising ways Americans use their time*. State College, PA: Pennsylvania State University Press.

Rochat, P., & Hespos, S. J. (1997). Differential rooting responses by neonates: Evidence for an early sense of self. *Early Development and Parenting, 6*, 105–112.

Rode, J. C., Arthaud-Day, M. L., Mooney, C. H., Near, J. P., & Baldwin, T. T. (2008). Ability and personality predictors of salary, perceived job success, and perceived career success in the initial career stage. *International Journal of Selection and Assessment, 16*, 292–299.

Rodgers, J. L., & Wanstrom, L. (2007). Identification of a Flynn Effect in the NLSY: Moving from the center to the boundaries. *Intelligence, 35*, 187–196.

Rodier, P. M. (2009). *Science under attack: Vaccines and autism*. Berkeley, CA: University of California Press.

Roeder, M. B., Mahone, E. M., Larson, J. G., Mostofsky, S., Cutting, L. E., Goldberg, M. C., & Denckla, M. B. (2008). Left–right differences on timed motor examination in children. *Child Neuropsychology, 14*, 249–262.

Roenneberg, T., Kuehnle, T., Juda, M., Kantermann, T., Allebrandt, K., Gordijn, M., & Merrow, M. (2007). Epidemiology of the human circadian clock. *Sleep Medicine Reviews, 11*, 429–438.

Roeseler, A., & Burns, D. (2010). The quarter that changed the world. *Tob Control, 19* (Suppl. 1), i3–i15.

Roff, L. L., Klemmack, D. L., Simon, C., Cho, G. W., Parker, M. W., Koenig, H. G.,…Allman, R. M. (2006). Functional limitations and religious service attendance among African American and White older adults. *Health and Social Work, 31*, 246–255.

Rogoff, B. (1990). Apprenticeship in thinking: *Cognitive development in social context*. New York, NY: Oxford University Press.

Rogoff, B. (1995). Observing sociocultural activities on three planes: Participatory appropriation, guided participation, and apprenticeship. In J. V. Wertsch, P. del Rio, & A. Alvarez (Eds.), *Sociocultural studies of the mind* (pp. 273–294). New York, NY: Cambridge University Press.

Rogoff, B. (1998). Cognition as a collaborative process. In D. Kuhn & R. S. Siegler (Eds.), *Handbook of child psychology: Vol. 2. Cognition, perception, and language* (5th ed., pp. 679–744). New York, NY: Wiley.

Rogoff, B. (2003). *The cultural nature of human development*. New York, NY: Oxford University Press.

Rogoff, B., Correa-Chávez, M., & Cotuc, M. N. (2005). A cultural / historical view of schooling in human development. In D. B. Pillemer & S. H. White (Eds.), *Developmental psychology and social change: Research, history and policy* (pp. 225–263). New York, NY: Cambridge University Press.

Rogoff, B., Paradise, R., Arauz, R. M., Correa-Chavez, M., & Angelillo, C. (2003). Firsthand learning through intent participation. *Annual Review of Psychology, 54*, 175–203.

Rohlen, T. P. (1983). *Japan's high schools*. Berkeley, CA: University of California Press.

Roizen, N. J., & Patterson, D. (2003). Down's syndrome. *Lancet, 361*, 1281–1289.

Rokach, R., Cohen, O., & Dreman, S. (2004). Who pulls the trigger? Who initiates divorce among 45-year-olds. *Journal of Divorce and Remarriage, 42*, 61–83.

Rolls, E. T. (2000). Memory systems in the brain. *Annual review of psychology, 51*(1), 599–630.

Roméo, F., Gramain, A., & Wittwer, J. (2009). Providing care for an elderly parent: Interactions among siblings? *Health Economics, 18*, 1011–1029.

Ron, P. (2006). Care giving offspring to aging parents: How it affects their marital relations, parenting, and mental health. *Illness, Crisis, & Loss, 14,* 1–21.

Rommes, E., Overbeek, G., Scholte, R., Engels, R., & de Kamp, R. (2007). "I'm not interested in computers.": Gender-biased occupational choices of adolescents. *Information, Communication & Society, 10,* 299–319.

Rooney, M. (2003, March 19). Fewer college students graduate in 4 years, survey finds. *Chronicle of Higher Education: Today's news* (pp. 1–2). Retrieved from http://chronicle.com/daily/2003/03/2003031901n.htm

Roopnarine, J. L., Hossain, Z., Gill, P., & Brophy, H. (1994). Play in the East Indian context. In J. L. Roopnarine, J. E. Johnson, & F. H. Hooper (Eds.), *Children's play in diverse cultures* (pp. 9–30). Albany, NY: State University of New York Press.

Rosamond, W., Flegal, K., Friday, F., Furie, K., Go, A., Greenlund, K.,…Hong, Y. (2007). Heart disease, and stroke statistics–2007 update: A report from the American Heart Association Statistics Committee and Stroke Statistics Subcommittee. *Circulation, 115,* E69–E171.

Roscoe, B., Dian, M. S., & Brooks, R. H. (1987). Early, middle, and late adolescents' views on dating and factors influencing partner selection. *Adolescence, 22,* 59–68.

Rose, A. J., & Asher, S. R. (1999). Children's goals and strategies in response to conflicts within a friendship. *Developmental Psychology, 35,* 69–79.

Rose, P. (2004). The forest dweller and the beggar. *American Scholar, 73,* 5–11.

Rose, S. A., Feldman, J. F., Jankowski, J. J., & Van Rossem, R. (2005). Pathways from prematurity and infant abilities to later cognition. *Child Development, 76,* 1172–1184.

Rose, S. M. (2007). Enjoying the returns: Women's friendships after 50. In J. C. Chrisler & V. Muhlbauer (Eds.), *Women over 50: Psychological perspectives* (pp. 112–130). New York, NY: Springer.

Rosenberg, M. (1979). *Conceiving the self.* New York, NY: Basic Books.

Rosenberger, N. (2007). Rethinking emerging adulthood in Japan: Perspectives from long–term single women. *Child Development Perspectives, 1,* 92–95.

Rosenbloom, S. R., & Way, N. (2004). Experiences of discrimination among African American, Asian American, and Latino adolescents in an urban high school. *Youth & Society, 35,* 420–451.

Rosenthal, C. J., & Gladstone, J. (2000). *Grandparenthood in Canada.* Ottawa, Ontario, Canada: Vanier Institute of the Family.

Rosenthal, E. R. (2014). *Women, aging, and ageism.* London, England: Routledge.

Rosnow, R. L., & Rosenthal, R. L. (2005). *Beginning behavioral research* (5th ed.). Upper Saddle River, NJ: Prentice Hall.

Ross, H. S., & Lollis, S. P. (1989). A social relations analysis of toddler peer relationships. *Child Development, 60,* 1082–1091.

Rossi, A. S. (2005). The menopausal transition and aging processes. In O. G. Brim, C. D. Ryff, & R. C. Kessler (Eds.), *How healthy are we? A national study of well-being at midlife* (pp. 153–201). Chicago, IL: University of Chicago Press.

Rossi, G. (1997). The nestling. Why young adults stay at home longer: The Italian case. *Journal of Family Issues, 18,* 627–644.

Rossi, N. E., Bisconti, T. L., & Bergeman, C. S. (2007). The role of dispositional resilience in regaining life satisfaction after the loss of a spouse. *Death Studies, 31,* 863–883.

Rossouw, J. E., Prentice, R. L., Manson, J. E., Wu, L., Barad, D., Barnabei, V. M.,…Stefanick, M. L. (2007). Postmenopausal hormone therapy and risk of cardiovascular disease by age and years since menopause. *JAMA: Journal of the American Medical Association, 297,* 1465–1477.

Rothbart, M. K. (2004). Emotion-related regulation: Sharpening the definition. *Child Development, 75,* 334–339.

Rothbart, M. K., & Bates, J. E. (2006). Temperament. In W. Damon & R. Lerner (Series Eds.), & N. Eisenberg (Vol. Ed.), *Handbook of child psychology: Vol. 3. Social, emotional, and personality development* (6th ed., pp. 99–166). New York, NY: Wiley.

Rothbart, M. K., Ahadi, S. A., & Evans, D. E. (2000). Temperament and personality: Origins and outcome. *Journal of Personality and Social Psychology, 78,* 122–135.

Rothbaum, F., Kakinuma, M., Nagaoka, R., & Azuma, H. (2007). Attachment and *amae*: Parent–child closeness in the United States & Japan. *Journal of Cross-Cultural Psychology, 38,* 465–486.

Rothbaum, F., & Morelli, G. (2005). Attachment and culture: Bridging relativism and universalism. In W. Friedlmeier, P. Chakkarath, & B. Schwarz (Eds.), Culture and human development: *The importance of cross-cultural research to the social sciences* (pp. 99–124). Lisse, The Netherlands: Swets & Zeitlinger.

Rothbaum, F., Weisz, J., Pott, M., Miyake, K., & Morelli, G. (2000). Attachment and culture: Security in the United States and Japan. *American Psychologist, 55,* 1093–1104.

Rothbaum, F., Weisz, J., Pott, M., Miyake, K., & Morelli, G. (2001). Deeper into attachment and culture. *American Psychologist, 56,* 827–829.

Rothenberger, A., Coghill, D., Dopfner, M., Falissard, B., & Stenhausen, H. C. (2006). Naturalistic observational studies in the framework of ADHD health care. *European Child and Adolescent Psychiatry, 15*(Suppl. 1), 1–3.

Rotheram-Borus, M. J. (1990). Adolescents' reference group choices, self-esteem, and adjustment. *Journal of Personality and Social Psychology, 59,* 1075–1081.

Roux, F. J., & Kryger, M. H. (2010). Medication effects on sleep. *Clinics in chest medicine, 31*(2), 397–405.

Rovee-Collier, C. K. (1999). The development of infant memory. *Current Directions in Psychological Science, 8,* 80–85.

Rowley, S. J., Kurtz-Costes, B., Mistry, R., & Feagans, L. (2007). Social status as a predictor of race and gender stereotypes in late childhood and early adolescence. *Social Development, 16,* 150–168.

Rox, F. J., & Kryger, M. H. (2010). Therapeutics for sleep–disordered breathing. *Sleep Medicine Clinics, 5,* 647–657.

Roy, A., & Wisnivesky, J. P. (2010). Comprehensive use of environmental control practices among adults with asthma. *Allergy and Asthma Proceedings, 31,* 72–77.

Rozario, P. A. (2006–2007). Volunteering among current cohorts of older adults and baby boomers. *Generations, 30,* 31–36.

Rozin, P. (2006). Domain denigration and process preference in academic psychology. *Perspectives on Psychological Science, 1,* 365–376.

Rubin, D. C. (2000). The distribution of early childhood memories. *Memory, 8*(4), 265–269.

Rubin, D. C., Rahhal, T. A., & Poon, L. W. (1998). Things learned in early adulthood are remembered best. *Memory and Cognition, 26,* 3–19.

Rubin, K. H., & Chung, O. B. (Eds.). (2006). *Parenting beliefs, behaviors, and parent–child relations: A cross-cultural perspective.* New York, NY: Psychology Press.

Rubin, K. H., Coplan, R. J., Fox, N. A., & Calkins, S. D. (1995). Emotionality, emotion regulation, and preschoolers' social adaptation. *Development and Psychopathology, 7,* 49–62.

Rubin, K. H., & Coplan, R. J. (Eds.). (2010). *The development of shyness and social withdrawal.* New York, NY: Guilford Press.

Rubin, K. H., Bukowski, W., & Parker, J. G. (2006). Peer interactions, relationships and groups. In W. Damon & R. Lerner (Eds.), & N. Eisenberg (Vol. Ed.), *Handbook of child psychology: Vol. 3. Social, emotional and personality development* (6th ed., pp. 571–645). New York, NY: Wiley.

Rubin, K. H., Burgess, K. B., & Hastings, P. D. (2002). Stability and social-behavioral consequences of toddlers' inhibited temperament and parenting behaviors. *Child Development, 73*, 483–495.

Rubin, K. H., Coplan, J., Chen, X., Buskirk, A. A., & Wojslawowicz, J. C. (2005). Peer relationships in childhood. In M. H. Bornstein & M. E. Lamb (Eds.), *Developmental science: An advanced textbook* (pp. 469–512). Mahwah, NJ: Erlbaum.

Rubin, K. H., & Pepler, D. J. (Eds.). (2013). The development and treatment of childhood aggression. Psychology Press.

Rubin, K., Fredstrom, B., & Bowker, J. (2008). Future directions in friendship in childhood and early adolescence. *Social Development, 17*, 1085–1096.

Ruble, D. N., Martin, C. L., & Berenbaum, S. (2006). Gender development. In W. Damon & R. M. Lerner (Series Eds.), & N. Eisenberg (Vol. Ed.), *Handbook of child psychology: Vol. 3. Social, emotional and personality development* (6th ed., pp. 858–932). Hoboken, NJ: Wiley.

Rucker, J. H., & McGuffin, P. (2010). Polygenic heterogeneity: A complex model of genetic inheritance in psychiatric disorders. *Biological Psychiatry, 68*, 312–313.

Rückinger, S., Beyerlein, A., Jacobsen, G., von Kries, R., & Vik, T. (2010). Growth in utero and body mass index at age 5 years in children of smoking and non-smoking mothers. *Early Human Development, 86*, 773–777.

Rückinger, S., et al. (2010). Prenatal and postnatal tobacco exposure and behavioral problems in 10-year-old children: Results from the GINI-plus Prospective Birth Cohort Study. *Environmental Health Perspectives, 118*, 150–154.

Rudy, D., & Grusec, J. (2006). Authoritarian parenting in individualist and collectivist groups: Associations with maternal emotion and cognition and children's self esteem. *Journal of Family Psychology, 43*, 302–319.

Ruggeri, K., & Bird, C. E. (2014). *Single parents and employment in Europe.* Cambridge, England: Rand Europe.

Ruiz, S. A., & Silverstein, M. (2007). Relationships with grandparents and the emotional well-being of late adolescent and young adult grandchildren. *Journal of Social Issues, 63*, 793–808.

Runco, M. A. (2014). *Creativity: Theories and themes: Research, development, and practice.* London, England: Elsevier.

Rupp, D., Vodanovich, S., & Crede, M. (2006, June). Age bias in the workplace: The impact of ageism and causal attributions. *Journal of Applied Social Psychology, 36*, 1337–1364.

Ruppar, T. M. (2010). Randomized pilot study of a behavioral feedback intervention to improve medication adherence in older adults with hypertension. *Journal of Cardiovascular Nursing, 25*, 470–479.

Rurup, M. L., Muller, M. T., Onwuteaka-Philipsen, B. D., van der Heide, A., van der Wal, G., & van der Maas, P. J. (2005). Requests for euthanasia or physician-assisted suicide from older persons who do not have a severe disease: An interview study. *Psychological Medicine, 35*, 665–671.

Rusconi, A. (2004). Different pathways out of the parental home: A comparison of West Germany and Italy. *Journal of Comparative Family Studies, 35*, 627–649.

Rush, B. K., Barch, D. M., & Braver, T. S. (2006). Accounting for cognitive aging: Context processing, inhibition or processing speed? *Aging, Neuropsychology, and Cognition, 13*, 588–610.

Russac, R. J., Gatliff, C., Reece, M., & Spottswood, D. (2007). Death anxiety across the adult years: An examination of age and gender effects. *Death Studies, 31*, 549–561.

Russell, A., Hart, C. H., Robinson, C. C., & Olsen, S. F. (2003). Children's sociable and aggressive behavior with peers: A comparison of the U.S. and Australian, and contributions of temperament and parenting styles. *International Journal of Behavioral Development, 27*, 74–86.

Russell, J. (May 8, 2011). Equal time. *The Boston Globe, Sunday Magazine*, pp. 14–19.

Rutter, M. (1996). Maternal deprivation. In M. H. Bornstein (Ed.), *Handbook of parenting: Vol. 4. Applied and practical parenting* (pp. 3–31). Mahwah, NJ: Erlbaum.

Rutter, M., O'Connor, T. G., and the English and Romanian Adoptees Study Team. (2004). Are there biological programming effects for psychological development? Findings from a study of Romanian adoptees. *Developmental Psychology, 40*, 81–94.

Ryan, A. S., Zhou, W., & Arensberg, M. B. (2006). The effects of employment status on breastfeeding in the United States. *Women's Health Issues, 16*, 243–251.

Ryan, C., Huebner, D., Diaz, R. M., & Sanchez, J. (2009). Family rejection as a predictor of negative health outcomes in white and Latino lesbian, gay and bisexual young adults. *Pediatrics, 123*, 346–352.

Ryan, E. B., Jin, Y., Anas, A. P., & Luh, J. J. (2004). Communication beliefs about young and old age in Asia and Canada. *Journal of Cross-Cultural Gerontology, 19*, 343–360.

Rychlak, J. F. (2003). The self takes over. In J. F. Rychlak, *The human image in postmodern America* (pp. 69–82). Washington, DC: American Psychological Association.

Ryff, C., et al. (2015). Adult development in Japan and the United States: Comparing theories and findings about growth, maturity, and well-being. In L. A. Jensen (Ed.), *Oxford handbook of human development and culture: An interdisciplinary perspective.* New York, NY: Oxford University Press.

Ryff, C. D. (1991). Possible selves in adulthood and old age: A tale of shifting horizons. *Psychology and Aging, 6*, 286–295.

Ryff, C. D. (1995). Psychological well-being in adult life. *Current Directions in Psychological Science, 4*, 99–104.

Ryff, C. D., Singer, B. H., & Seltzer, M. M. (2002). Pathways through challenge: Implications for well-being and health. In L. Pulkkinen & A. Caspi (Eds.), *Paths to successful development* (pp. 302–328). Cambridge, UK: Cambridge University Press.

Saarni, C. (1999). *The development of emotional competence.* New York, NY: Guilford.

Sachs, B. P., Kobelin, C., Castro, M. A., & Frigoletto, F. (1999). The risks of lowering the cesarean–delivery rate. *New England Journal of Medicine, 340*, 54–57.

Sadker, M., & Sadker, D. (1994). *Failing at fairness: How America's schools cheat girls.* New York, NY: Scribner.

Safar, M. E., & Smulyan, H. (2004). Hypertension in women. *American Journal of Hypertension, 17*, 82–87.

Safe Kids Worldwide. (2002). Childhood injury worldwide: Meeting the challenge. Retrieved from http://www.safekidsworldwide.org

Safe Kids Worldwide. (2009). *News and facts.* Retrieved from www.safekids.org

Safe Kids Worldwide (2013). *Unintentional childhood injury-related deaths.* Retrieved from http://www.safekidsgainesvillehall.org/unintentional-childhood-injury-related-deaths

Saffran, J. R., Werker, J. F., & Werner, L. A. (2006). The infant's auditory world: Hearing, speech and the beginnings of language. In W. Damon & R. Lerner (Eds.), & D. Kuhn & R. Siegler (Vol. Eds.), *Handbook of child psychology: Vol. 2. Cognition, perception, and language* (6th ed., pp. 58–108). New York, NY: Wiley.

Sagan, C., & Druyan, A. (1992). *Shadows of forgotten ancestors.* New York, NY: Ballantine.

Saginak, K. A., & Saginak, M. A. (2005). Balancing work and family: Equity, gender, and marital satisfaction. *Counseling and Therapy for Couples and Families, 13*, 162–166.

Saha, C., Riner, M. E., & Liu, G. (2005). Individual and neighborhood-level factors in predicting asthma. *Archives of Pediatrics and Adolescent Medicine, 159*, 759–763.

Sahin, E., & DePinho, R. A. (2012). Axis of ageing: Telomeres, p53, and mitochondria. *Nature Reviews: Molecular Cell Biology, 13,* 397-404. doi:10.1038/nrm3352

Saigal, S., den Ouden, L., Wolke, D., Hoult, L., Paneth, N., Streiner, D. L., Whitaker, A., & Pinto-Martin, J. (2003). School–age outcomes in children who were extremely low birth weight from four international population–based cohorts. *Pediatrics, 112,* 943–950.

Salbe, A. D., Weyer, C., Lindsay, R. S., Ravussin, E., & Tataranni, P. A. (2002). Assessing risk factors for obesity between childhood and adolescence: I. Birth weight, childhood adiposity, parental obesity, insulin, and leptin. *Pediatrics, 110,* 299–306.

Saldana, L., & Henggeler, S. W. (2006). Multisystemic therapy in the treatment of adolescent conduct disorder. In W. M. Nelson, III, A. J. Finch, Jr., & K. L. Hart (Eds.), *Conduct disorders: A practitioner's guide to comparative treatments* (pp. 217–258). New York, NY: Springer.

Salkind, N. (2011). *Exploring research.* Upper Saddle River, NJ: Pearson.

Salkind, N. J. (2009). *Exploring research.* Upper Saddle River, NJ: Prentice Hall.

Sallis, J. F., Bowles, H. R., Bauman, A., Ainsworth, B. E., Bull, F. C., Craig, C. L.,…De Bourdeaudhuij, I. (2009). Neighborhood environments and physical activity among adults in 11 countries. *American Journal of Preventive Medicine, 36,* 484–490.

Salmela-Aro, K., Nurmi, J.-E., Saisto, T., & Halmesmaki, E. (2001). Goal reconstruction and depressive symptoms during the transition to motherhood: Evidence from two cross-lagged longitudinal studies. *Journal of Personality and Social Psychology, 81,* 1144–1159.

Salmivalli, C., & Voeten, M. (2004). Connections between attitudes, group norms, and behaviour in bullying situations. *International Journal of Behavioral Development, 28,* 246–258.

Salomone, S., Caraci, F., Leggio, G. M., Fedotova, J., & Drago, F. (2011). New pharmacological strategies for treatment of Alzheimer's disease: Focus on disease-modifying drugs. *British Journal of Clinical Pharmacology, 73,* 504–517.

Salthouse, T. A. (2000). Aging and measures of processing speed. *Biological Psychology, 54,* 35–54.

Salthouse, T. A., Atkinson, T. M., & Berish, D. E. (2003). Executive functioning as a potential mediator of age-related cognitive decline in normal adults. *Journal of Experimental Psychology, General, 132,* 566–594.

Salzman, C. (2008). Pharmacologic treatment of disturbed sleep in the elderly. *Harvard Review of Psychiatry, 16,* 271–278.

Sameroff, A. J., & Haith, M. M. (1996). *The five to seven year shift: The age of reason and responsibility.* Chicago, IL: University of Chicago Press.

Samuels, H. R. (1980). The effect of an older sibling on infant locomotor exploration of a new environment, *Child Development, 51,* 607–609.

Sandberg, D. E., Ehrhardt, A. A., Ince, S. E., & Meyer-Bahlburg, H. (1991). Gender differences in children's and adolescents' career aspirations: A follow-up study. *Journal of Adolescent Research, 6,* 371–386.

Sandberg, J. F., & Hofferth, S. L. (2001). Changes in children's time with parents: United States, 1981–1997. *Demography, 38,* 423–436.

Sandhya, S. (2009). The social context of marital happiness in urban Indian couples: Interplay of intimacy and conflict. *Journal of Marital and Family Therapy, 35,* 74–96.

Sandstrom, M. J., & Zakriski, A. L. (2004). Understanding the experience of peer rejection. In J. B. Kupersmidt & K. A. Dodge (Eds.), *Children's peer relations: From development to intervention.* Washington, DC: American Psychological Association.

Sang, B., Miao, X., & Deng, C. (2002). The development of gifted and nongifted young children in metamemory knowledge. *Psychological Science (China), 25,* 406–424.

Sangree, W. H. (1989). Age and power: Life-course trajectories and age structuring of power relation in East and West Africa. In D. J. Kertzer & K. W. Schaie (Eds.), *Age structuring in comparative perspective* (pp. 23–46). Hillsdale, NJ: Erlbaum.

Sansavani, A., Bertoncini, J., & Giovanelli, G. (1997). Newborns discriminate the rhythm of multisyllabic stressed words. *Developmental Psychology, 33,* 3–11.

Santoro, N., Brockwell, S., Johnston, J., Crawford, S. L., Gold, E. B., Harlow, S. D., ... & Sutton-Tyrrell, K. (2007). Helping midlife women predict the onset of the final menses: SWAN, the Study of Women's Health Across the Nation. *Menopause, 14*(3), 415–424.

Saraswathi, T. S. (1999). Adult–child continuity in India: Is adolescence a myth or an emerging reality? In T. S. Saraswathi (Ed.), *Culture, socialization, and human development: Theory, research, and applications in India* (pp. 213–232). Thousand Oaks, CA: Sage.

Sarrell, E. M., Horev, Z., Cohen, Z., & Cohen, H. A. (2005). Parents' and medical personnel's beliefs about infant teething. *Patient Education and Counseling, 57,* 122–125.

Sassler, S., Ciambrone, D., & Benway, G. (2008). Are they really mama's boys/ daddy's girls? The negotiation of adulthood upon returning to the parental home. *Sociological Forum, 23,* 670–698.

Saudino, K. J. (2003). Parent ratings of infant temperament: Lessons from twin studies. *Infant Behavior and Development, 26,* 100–107.

Savin-Williams, R. (2001). *Mom, Dad, I'm gay.* Washington, DC: American Psychological Association.

Savin-Williams, R. C., & Joyner, K. (2014). The dubious assessment of gay, lesbian, and bisexual adolescents of Add Health. *Archives of Sexual Behavior 43*(3), 413–422.

Saw, S. M., Carkeet, A., Chia, K. S., Stone, R. A., & Tan, D. T. (2002). Component dependent risk factors for ocular parameters in Singapore Chinese children. *Ophthalmology, 109,* 2065–2071.

Sawnani, H., Jackson, T., Murphy, T., Beckerman, R., & Simakajornboon, N. (2004). The effect of maternal smoking on respiratory and arousal patterns in preterm infants during sleep. *American Journal of Respiratory and Critical Care Medicine, 169,* 733–738.

Sax, L., & Kautz, K. J. (2003). Who first suggests the diagnosis of attention deficit/hyperactivity disorder? *Annals of Family Medicine, 1,* 171–174.

Saxe, G. B. (1994). Studying cognitive development in sociocultural contexts: The development of practice-based approaches. *Mind, Culture, and Activity, 1,* 135–157.

Saxe, G. B. (2002). Candy selling and math learning. In C. Desforges & R. Fox (Eds.), *Teaching and learning: The essential readings* (pp. 86–106). Malden, MA: Blackwell.

Sbarra, D. A., & Emery, R. E. (2008). Deeper into divorce: Using actor–partner analyses to explore systemic differences in coparenting conflict following custody dispute resolution. *Journal of Family Psychology, 22,* 144–152.

Scannell-Desch, E. (2003). Women's adjustment to widowhood: Theory, research, and methods. *Journal of Psychosocial Nursing and Mental Health Services, 41,* 28–36.

Scantlin, R. (2007). Educational television, effects of. In J. J. Arnett (Ed.), *Encyclopedia of children, adolescents, and the media* (pp. 255–258). Thousand Oaks, CA: Sage.

Scarmeas, N., Stern, Y., Mayeux, R., & Luchsinger, J. A. (2006). Mediterranean diet, Alzheimer disease, and vascular mediation. *Archives of Neurology, 63,* 1709–1717.

Scarr, S. (1993). Biological and cultural diversity: The legacy of Darwin for development. *Child Development, 54,* 424–435.

Scarr, S., & McCartney, K. (1983). How people make their own environments: A theory of genotype environment effects. *Child Development, 54,* 424–435.

Schaal, B., Marlier, L., & Soussignan, R. (2000). Human fetuses learn odours from their pregnant mother's diet. *Chemical Senses, 25,* 729–737.

Schachter, E. P. (2005). Erikson meets the postmodern: Can classic identity theory rise to the challenge? *Identity, 5,* 137–160.

Schachter, S. C., & Ransil, B. J. (1996). Handedness distributions in nine professional groups. *Perceptual and Motor Skills, 82,* 51–63.

Schachter, S. R. (2009). Cancer patients facing death: Is the patient who focuses on living in denial of his/her death? In M. K. Bartalos (Ed.), *Speaking of death: America's new sense of mortality* (pp. 42–77). Westport, CT: Praeger.

Schaeffer, C., Petras, H., & Ialongo, B. (2003). Modeling growth in boys' aggressive behavior across elementary school: Links to later criminal involvement, conduct disorder, and antisocial personality disorder. *Developmental Psychology, 39,* 1020–1035.

Schaie, K. W. (1994). The course of adult intellectual development. *American Psychologist, 49,* 304–313.

Schaie, K. W. (1996). *Intellectual development in adulthood: The Seattle Longitudinal Study.* New York, NY: Cambridge University Press.

Schaie, K. W. (1998). The Seattle Longitudinal Studies of Adult Intelligence. In M. P. Lawton & T. A. Salthouse (Eds.), *Essential papers on the psychology of aging* (pp. 263–271). New York, NY: New York University Press.

Schaie, K. W. (2005). *Developmental influences on adult intelligence: The Seattle Longitudinal Study.* New York, NY: Oxford University Press.

Schaie, K. W. (2012). *Developmental influences on adult intelligence: The Seattle Longitudinal Study.* New York, NY: Oxford University Press.

Scharf, M., Shulman, S., & Avigad-Spitz, L. (2005). Sibling relationships in emerging adulthood and in adolescence. *Journal of Adolescent Research, 20,* 64–90.

Scheff, S. W., & Price, D. A. (2006). Alzheimer's disease-related alterations in synaptic density: Neocortex and hippocampus. *Journal of Alzheimer's Disease, 9,* 101–115.

Scheibe, C. (2007). Advertising on children's programs. In J. J. Arnett (Ed.), *Encyclopedia of children, adolescents, and the media* (pp. 59–60). Thousand Oaks, CA: Sage.

Scheiber, R. A., & Sacks, J. J. (2001). Measuring community bicycle helmet use among children. *Public Health Reports, 116,* 113–121.

Scheidel, D. G., & Marcia, J. E. (1985). Ego identity, intimacy, sex role orientation, and gender. *Developmental Psychology, 21,* 149–160.

Scheiwe, K., & Willekins, H. (2009). *Childcare and preschool development in Europe.* New York, NY: Palgrave MacMillan.

Scher, A., Epstein, R., & Tirosh, E. (2004). Stability and changes in sleep regulation: A longitudinal study from 3 months to 3 years. *International Journal of Behavioral Development, 28,* 268–274.

Scherman, A. Z. (2013). Cultural life script theory and the reminiscence bump: A reanalysis of seven studies across cultures. *Nordic Psychology, 65,* 103–119.

Scherzer, A. L. (2009). Experience in Cambodia with the use of a culturally relevant developmental milestone chart for children in low- and middle-income countries. *Journal of Policy and Practice in Intellectual Disabilities, 6,* 287–292.

Schieffelin, B. B. (1986). The acquisition of Kaluli. In D. Slobin (Ed.), *The cross-linguistic study of language acquisition* (pp. 525–593). Hillsdale, NJ: Erlbaum.

Schieffelin, B. B. (1990). *The give and take of everyday life: Language socialization of Kaluli children.* New York, NY: Cambridge University Press.

Schlegel, A. (2010). Adolescent ties to adult communities: The intersection of culture and development. In L. Jensen (Ed.), *Bridging cultural and developmental approaches to psychology* (pp. 138–159). New York, NY: Oxford University Press.

Schlegel, A., & Barry, H. (1991). *Adolescence: An anthropological inquiry.* New York, NY: Free Press.

Schlegel, A., & Barry III, H. (2015). The nature and meaning of adolescent transition rituals. In L. A. Jensen (Ed.), *Oxford handbook of human development and culture: An interdisciplinary perspective.* New York, NY: Oxford University Press.

Schmidt, L., Holstein, B., Christensen, U., & Boivin, J. (2005). Does infertility cause marital benefit? An epidemiological study of 2250 men and women in fertility treatment. *Patient Education and Counseling, 59,* 244–251.

Schmitow, C., & Stenberg, G. (2013). Social referencing in 10-month-old infants. *European Journal of Developmental Psychology, 10,* 533–545. doi: 10.1080/17405629.2013.763473

Schmitt, M., Kliegel, M., & Shapiro, A. (2007). Marital interaction in middle and old age: A predictor of marital satisfaction? *The International Journal of Aging & Human Development, 65,* 283–300.

Schneider, B. (2006). In the moment: The benefits of the Experience Sampling Method. In M. Pitt-Catsouphes, E. E. Kossek, & S. Sweet (Eds.), *The work and family handbook: Multi-disciplinary perspectives, methods, and approaches* (pp. 469–488). Mahwah, NJ: Erlbaum.

Schneider, B. (2009). Challenges of transitioning into adulthood. In I. Schoon & R. K. Silbereisen (Eds.), *Transitions from school to work: Globalization, individualization, and patterns of diversity* (pp. 265–290). New York, NY: Cambridge University Press.

Schneider, B., & Stevenson, D. (1999). *The ambitious generation: America's teenagers, motivated but directionless.* New Haven, CT: Yale University Press.

Schneider, W. (2002). Memory development in childhood. In U. Goswami (Ed.), *Blackwell handbook of childhood cognitive development* (pp. 236–256). Malden, MA: Blackwell.

Schneider, W. (2010). Metacognition and memory development in childhood and adolescence. In H. S. Waters & W. Schneider (Eds.), *Metacognition, strategy use, and instruction* (pp. 54–81). New York, NY: Guilford.

Schneider, W., & Bjorklund, D. F. (1992). Expertise, aptitude, and strategic remembering. *Child Development, 63,* 461–473.

Schneider, W., & Pressley, M. (1997). *Memory development between two and twenty* (2nd ed.). Mahwah, NJ: Erlbaum.

Schnohr, P., Scharling, H., & Jensen, J. S. (2003). Changes in leisure-time physical activity and risk of death: An observational study of 7,000 men and women. *American Journal of Epidemiology, 158,* 639–644.

Schoeni, R., & Ross, K. (2005). Material assistance received from families during the transition to adulthood. In R. A. Settersten, Jr., F. F. Furstenberg, Jr., & R. G. Rumbaut (Eds.), *On the frontier of adulthood: Theory, research and public policy* (pp. 396–416). Chicago, IL: University of Chicago Press.

Schoenwald, S. K., Heiblum, N., Saldana, L., & Henggeler, S. W. (2008). The international implementation of multisystemic therapy. *Evaluation & the Health Professions, 31,* 211–225.

Schoolcraft, W. (2010). *If at first you don't conceive: A complete guide to infertility from one of the nation's leading clinics.* New York, NY: Rodale Books.

Schott, B. (2009, October 19). On the division of our three score and ten. *The New York Times* blog post. Retrieved from http://www.nytimes.com/interactive/2009/09/08/opinion/20091019opart.html

Schott, J. M., & Rossor, M. N. (2003). The grasp and other primitive reflexes. *Journal of Neurology and Neurosurgical Psychiatry, 74,* 558–560.

Schroeder, D. H., & Salthouse, T. A. (2004). Age-related effects on cognition between 20 and 50 years of age. *Personality and Individual Differences, 36,* 393–404.

Schroots, J. J. F., van Dijkum, C., & Assink, M. H. J. (2004). Autobiographical memory from a life span perspective. *International Journal of Aging and Human Development, 58,* 69–85.

Schulenberg, J. (2000, April). *College students get drunk, so what? National panel data on binge drinking trajectories before, during and after college.* Paper presented at the biennial meeting of the Society for Research on Adolescence, Chicago, IL.

Schulenberg, J. E., & Zarrett, N. R. (2006). Mental health during emerging adulthood: Continuity and discontinuity in courses, causes, and functions. In J. J. Arnett & J. L. Tanner (Eds.), *Emerging adults in America: Coming of age in the 21st century* (pp. 135–172). Washington, DC: American Psychological Association.

Schulenberg, J., & Maggs, J. L. (2000). *A developmental perspective on alcohol use and heavy drinking behavior during adolescence and the transition to adulthood.* Washington, DC: National Institute on Alcohol Abuse and Alcoholism.

Schulz, R., Boerner, K., Shear, K., Zhang, S., & Gitlin, L. N. (2006). Predictors of complicated grief among dementia caregivers: A prospective study of bereavement. *American Journal of Geriatric Psychiatry, 14,* 650.

Schulz, R., & Curnow, C. (1988). Peak performance and age among superathletes: track and field, swimming, baseball, tennis, and golf. *Journal of Gerontology, 43*(5), P113-P120.

Schulze, P. A., & Carlisle, S. A. (2010). What research does and doesn't say about breastfeeding: A critical review. *Early Child Development and Care, 180,* 703–718.

Schum, T. R., McAuliffe, T. L., Simms, M. D., Walter, J. A., Lewis, M., & Pupp, R. (2001). Factors associated with toilet training in the 1990s. *Ambulatory Pediatrics, 1,* 79–86.

Schwalb, D. W., Nakawaza, J., Yamamoto, T., & Hyun, J.-H. (2004). Fathering in Japanese, Chinese, and Korean cultures: A review of the research literature. In M. E. Lamb (Ed.), *The role of the father in child development* (4th ed., pp. 146–181). Hoboken, NJ: Wiley.

Schwalb, D. W., & Schwalb, B. J. (2015). Fathering diversity within societies. In L. A. Jensen (Ed.), *Oxford handbook of human development and culture.* New York, NY: Oxford University Press.

Schwartz, D., Proctor, L. J., & Chien, D. H. (2001). The aggressive victim of bullying: Emotional and behavioral dysregulation as a pathway to victimization by peers. In J. Juonen & S. Graham (Eds.), *Peer harassment in school: The plight of the vulnerable and victimized* (pp. 147–174). New York, NY: Guilford.

Schwartz, M., Share, D. L., Leikin, M., & Kozminsky, E. (2008). On the benefits of bi-literacy: Just a head start in reading or specific orthographic insights? *Reading and Writing, 21,* 905–927.

Schwartz, S. J. (2005). A new identity for identity research: Recommendations for expanding and refocusing the identity literature. *Journal of Adolescent Research, 20,* 293–308.

Schwartz, S. J. (2015). Identity development in emerging adulthood. In J. J. Arnett (Ed.), *Oxford handbook of emerging adulthood.* New York, NY: Oxford University Press.

Schwartz, S. J., & Pantin, H. (2006). Identity development in adolescence and emerging adulthood: The interface of self, context, and culture. In A. P. Prescott (Ed.), *The concept of self in psychology* (pp. 45–85). Hauppauge, NY: Nova Science Publishers.

Schwartz, S. J., Zamboanga, B. L., Weisskirch, R. S., & Wang, S. C. (2010). The relationships of personal and cultural identity to adaptive and maladaptive psychosocial functioning in emerging adults. *The Journal of Social Psychology, 150,* 1–31.

Schweinle, A. & Wilcox, T. (2004). Intermodal perception and physical reasoning in young infants. *Infant Behavior & Development, 27,* 246–265.

Schwenkhagen, A. (2007). Hormonal changes in menopause and implications on sexual health. *The Journal of Sexual Medicine, 4*(Suppl.), 220–226.

Schweinhart, L. J., Montie, J., Xiang, Z., Barnett, W. S., & Belfield, C. R. (2004). *Lifetime effects: The High/Scope Perry Preschool Study through age 40.* Boston, MA: Strategies for Children. Retrieved from www.highscope.org/Research/PerryProject/perrymain.htm

Schwimmer, J. B., Burwinkle, T. M., & Varni, J. W. (2003). Health-related quality of life of severely obese children and adolescents. *JAMA: Journal of the American Medical Association, 289,* 1813–1819.

Scott, A. M., & Caughlin, J. P. (2012). Managing multiple goals in family discourse about end-of-life health decisions. *Research on Aging, 34*(6), 670–691.

Scott, E., & Panksepp, J. (2003). Rough-and-tumble play in human children. *Aggressive Behavior, 29,* 539–551.

Seach, K. A., Dharmage, S. C., Lowe, A. J., & Dixon, J. B. (2010). Delayed introduction of solid feeding reduces child overweight and obesity at 10 years. *International Journal of Obesity, 34,* 1475–1479.

Sears, H. (2007). Canada. In J. J. Arnett (Ed.), *International encyclopedia of adolescence.* New York, NY: Routledge.

Sears, H. (2012). Canada. In J. J. Arnett (Ed.), *Adolescent psychology around the world.* New York, NY: Taylor & Francis.

Segal, A. F. (2004). *Life after death: A history of the afterlife in Western religion.* New York, NY: Doubleday.

Segall, M. H., Dasen, P. R., Berry, J. W., & Poortinga, Y. H. (1999). *Human behavior in global perspective: An introduction to cross-cultural psychology.* Boston, MA: Allyn & Bacon.

Seguin, R., & Nelson, M. E. (2003). The benefits of strength training for older adults. *American Journal of Preventive Medicine, 25* (Suppl. 2), 141–149.

Seiberling, K. A., & Conley, D. B. (2004). Aging and olfactory and taste function. *Otolaryngologic Clinics of North America, 37,* 1209–1228.

Selander, J. (2011). *Cultural beliefs honor placenta.* Retrieved from http://placentabenefits.info/culture.asp

Sellen, D. W. (2001). Comparison of infant feeding patterns reported for nonindustrial populations with current recommendations. *Journal of Nutrition, 131,* 2707–2715.

Selwyn, N. (2008). An investigation of differences in undergraduates' academic use of the Internet. *Active Learning in Higher Education, 9,* 11–22.

Sembuya, R. (2010). Mother or nothing: The agony of infertility. *Bulletin of the World Health Organization, 88,* 881–882.

Sen, K., & Samad, A. Y. (Eds.). (2007). *Islam in the European Union: Transnationalism, youth, and the war on terror.* New York, NY: Oxford University Press.

Sepa, A., Frodi, A., & Ludvigsson, J. (2004). Psychosocial correlates of parenting stress, lack of support and lack of confidence/security. *Scandinavian Journal of Psychology, 45,* 169–179.

Sereny, M. (2011). Living arrangements of older adults in China: The interplay among preferences, realities, and health. *Research on Aging, 33,* 172–204.

Serpell, R. (1996). Cultural models of childhood in indigenous socialization and formal schooling in Zambia. In C. P. Hwang, M. E. Lamb, & I. E. Sigel (Eds.), *Images of childhood* (pp. 129–142). Hillsdale, NJ: Lawrence Erlbaum.

Shalatin, S., & Phillip, M. (2003). The role of obesity and leptin in the pubertal process and pubertal growth: A review. *International Journal of Obesity and Related Metabolic Disorders, 27,* 869–874.

Shanahan, L., McHale, S. M., Osgood, D. W., & Crouter, A. C. (2007). Conflict frequency with mothers and fathers from middle childhood to late adolescence: Within- and between-families comparisons. *Developmental Psychology, 43,* 539–550.

Shapira, N., Barak, A., & Gal, I. (2007). Promoting older adults' well-being through Internet training and use. *Aging & Mental Health, 11,* 477–484.

Shapiro, A. (2004). Revisiting the generation gap: Exploring the relationships of parent/adult-child dyads. *International Journal of Aging and Human Development, 58,* 127–146.

Shapiro, A. E., Gottman, J. M., & Carrere, S. (2000). The baby and the marriage: Identifying factors that buffer against the decline of marital satisfaction after the first baby arrives. *Journal of Family Psychology, 14,* 59–70.

Shapiro, L. J., & Azuma, H. (2004). Intellectual, attitudinal, and interpersonal aspects of competence in the United States and Japan. In R. J. Sternberg & E. L. Grigorenko (Eds.), *Culture and competence: Contexts of life success* (pp. 187–206). Washington, DC: American Psychological Association.

Shapka, J. D., & Keating, D. P. (2005). Structure and change in self-concept during adolescence. *Canadian Journal of Behavioural Science, 37,* 83–96.

Sharp, E. A., & Ganong, L. H. (2000). Awareness about expectations: Are unrealistic beliefs changed by integrative teaching? *Family Relations, 49,* 71–76.

Shaughnessy, J., Zechmeister, E., & Zechmeister, J. (2011). *Research methods in psychology* (11th ed.). New York, NY: McGraw-Hill.

Shaw, P., Greenstein, D., Lerch, J., Clasen, L., Lenroot, R., Gogtay, N., & Evans, A. (2006). Intellectual ability and cortical development in children and adolescents. *Nature, 440,* 676–679.

Shay, J. W., & Wright, W. E. (2004). Telomeres are double-strand DNA breaks hidden from DNA damage responses. *Molecular Cell, 14,* 420–421.

Shaywitz, B. A., Shaywitz, S. E., Blachman, B. A., Pugh, K. R., Fulbright, R. K., Skudlarski, P., …Gore, J. C. (2004). Development of left occipitotemporal systems for skilled reading in children after a phonologically-based intervention. *Biological Psychiatry, 55,* 926–933.

Shear, M. K. (2009). Grief and depression: Treatment decisions for bereaved children and adults. *American Journal of Psychiatry, 166,* 746–748.

Shen, V. (2008). Wisdom and learning to be wise in Chinese Mahayana Buddhism. In M. Ferrari & G. Potworowski (Eds.), *Teaching for wisdom: Cross–cultural perspectives on fostering wisdom* (pp. 113–133). New York, NY: Springer.

Sherrell, K., Buckwalter, K. C., & Morhardt, D. (2001). Negotiating family relationships: Dementia care as a midlife developmental task. Families in Society: *The Journal of Contemporary Social Services, 82*(4), 383–392.

Shields, L., Mamun, A. A., O'Callaghan, M., Williams, G. M., & Najman, J. M. (2010). Breastfeeding and obesity at 21 years: A cohort study. *Journal of Clinical Nursing, 19,* 1612–1617.

Shih, R. A., Miles, J. N., Tucker, J. S., Zhou, A. J., & D'Amico, E. J. (2010). Racial/ethnic differences in adolescent substance use: Mediation by individual, family, and school factors. *Journal of Studies on Alcohol and Drugs, 71*(5), 640.

Shipman, K. L., Zeman, J., Nesin, A. E., & Fitzgerald, M. (2003). Children's strategies for displaying anger and sadness: What works with whom? *Merrill-Palmer Quarterly, 49,* 100–122.

Shiraev, T., & Barclay, G. (2012). Evidence based exercise: Clinical benefits of high intensity interval training. *Australian Family Physician, 41*(12), 960.

Shiri, R., Koskimaki, J., Hakam, M., Hakkinen, J., Tammela, T. L., Huhtala, H., & Auvinen, A. (2003). Effect of chronic diseases on incidence of erectile dysfunction. *Urology, 62,* 1097–1102.

Shirtcliff, E. A., Dahl, R E., & Pollak, S. D. (2009). Pubertal development: Correspondence between hormonal and physical development. *Child Development, 80,* 327–337.

Shock, N. W. (1977). Biological theories of aging. In J. E. Birren & K. W. Schaie (Eds.), *Handbook of the psychology of aging* (pp. 103–115). New York, NY: Van Nostrand Reinhold.

Shonkoff, J. P., & Phillips, D. A. (Eds.). (2000). *From neurons to neighborhoods: The science of early childhood development.* Washington, DC: National Academy Press.

Shope, J. T. (2002). Discussion paper. *Injury Prevention, 8*(Suppl. 2), ii14–ii16.

Shope, J. T. (2007). Graduated driver licensing: Review of evaluation results since 2002. *Journal of Safety Research, 38,* 165–175.

Shope, J. T., & Bingham, C. R. (2008). Teen driving: Motor-vehicle crashes and factors that contribute. *American Journal of Preventative Medicine, 35*(3, Suppl. 1), S261–S271.

Shorten, A. (2010). Bridging the gap between mothers and medicine: "New insights" from the NIH Consensus Conference on VBAC. *Birth: Issues in Perinatal Care, Vol. 3,* 181–183.

Shreeve, J. (2010, July). The evolutionary road. *National Geographic,* 34–50.

Shuey, K., & Hardy, M. A. (2003). Assistance to aging parents and parents-in-law: Does lineage affect family allocation decisions? *Journal of Marriage and Family, 65,* 418–431.

Shulman, S., & Connolly, J. (2015). Romantic relationships in emerging adulthood. In J. J. Arnett (Ed.), *Oxford handbook of emerging adulthood.* New York, NY: Oxford University Press.

Shulman, S., Laursen, B., Kalman, Z., & Karpovsky, S. (1997). Adolescent intimacy revisited. *Journal of Youth & Adolescence, 26,* 597–617.

Shumaker, D. M., Miller, C., Ortiz, C., & Deutsch, R. (2011). The forgotten bonds: The assessment and contemplation of sibling attachment in divorce and parental separation. *Family Court Review, 49*(1), 46–58.

Shweder, R. A. (1998). Introduction: Welcome to middle age! In R. A. Shweder (Ed.), *Welcome to middle age! (and other cultural fictions)* (pp. ix–xvii). Chicago, IL: University of Chicago Press.

Shweder, R. A. (2003). *Why do men barbecue? Recipes for cultural psychology.* Cambridge, MA: Harvard University Press.

Shweder, R. A. (Ed.) (2009). *The child: An encyclopedic companion.* Chicago, IL: The University of Chicago Press.

Shweder, R. A., Goodnow, J. J., Hatano, G., LeVine, R. A., Markus, H. R., & Miller, P. J. (2006). The cultural psychology of development: One mind, many mentalities. In W. Damon & R. Lerner (Eds.), & R. M. Lerner (Vol. Eds.), *Handbook of child psychology: Vol. 1. Theoretical models of human development* (6th ed., pp. 716–792). New York, NY: Wiley.

Shweder, R. A., Goodnow, J., Hatano, G., Levine, R. A., Markus, H., & Miller, P. (2011). The cultural psychology of development: One mind, many mentalities. In W. Damon (Ed.), *Handbook of child development* (6th ed.). New York, NY: Wiley.

Shweder, R. A., Jensen, L., & Goldstein, W. A. (1995). Who sleeps by whom revisited: A method for extracting the moral goods implicit in practice. In J. J. Goodnow, P. J. Miller, & F. Kessel (Eds.), *Cultural practices as contexts for development* (Vol. 67, pp. 21–39). San Francisco, CA: Jossey-Bass Publishers.

Shweder, R. A., Mahapatra, M., & Miller, J. G. (1990). Culture and moral development. In J. W. Stigler, R. A. Shweder, & G. Herdt (Eds.), *Cultural psychology* (pp. 130–204). New York, NY: Cambridge University Press.

Shweder, R. A., Much, N. C., Mahapatra, M., & Park, L. (1997). The "big three" of morality (autonomy, community, divinity) and the "big three" explanations of suffering. In A. Brandt & D. Rozin (Eds.), *Morality and health* (pp. 119–169). New York, NY: Routledge.

Sidorowicz, L. S., & Lunney, G. S. (1980). Baby X revisited. *Sex Roles, 6,* 67–73.

Siegler, I. C., Bosworth, H. B., & Poon, L. W. (2003). Disease, health, and aging. In R. M. Lerner, M. A. Easterbrooks, J. Mistry, & I. B. Weiner (Eds.), *Handbook of psychology: Health psychology* (Vol. 9, pp. 487–510). Hoboken, NJ: Wiley.

Sierra, F. (2006). Is (your cellular response to) stress killing you? *Journals of Gerontology: Series A: Biological Sciences and Medical Sciences, 61*, 557–561.

Sigman, M. (1999). Developmental deficits in children with Down syndrome. In H. Tager-Flusberg (Ed.), *Neurodevelopmental disorders: Developmental cognitive neuroscience* (pp. 179–195). Cambridge, MA: MIT Press.

Sigman, M., Cohen, S., & Beckwith, L. (2000). Why does infant attention predict adolescent intelligence? In D. Muir & A. Slater (Eds.), *Infant development: The essential readings* (pp. 239–253). Malden, MA: Blackwell.

Signorielli, N. (2004). Aging on television: Messages relating to gender, race and occupation in prime time. *Journal of Broadcasting & Electronic Media, 48*, 279–301.

Silk, J. S., Morris, A. S., Kanaya, T., & Steinberg, L. (2003). Psychological control and autonomy granting: Opposite ends of a continuum or distinct constructs? *Journal of Research on Adolescence, 13*, 113–128.

Silva, C., & Martins, M. (2003). Relations between children's invented spelling and the development of phonological awareness. *Educational Psychology, 23*, 3–16.

Silverstein, M., & Marenco, A. (2001). How Americans enact the grandparent role across the family life course. *Journal of Family Issues, 22*, 493–522.

Silverstein, M., Conroy, S., Wang, H., Giarrusso, R., & Bengtson, V. I. (2002). Reciprocity in parent–child relations over the adult life course. *Journal of Marriage and the Family, 60*, 912–923.

Silverstein, M., Gans, D., & Yang, F. M. (2006). Intergenerational support to aging parents: The role of norms and needs. *Journal of Family Issues, 27*, 1068–1084.

Simcock, P. (2012). Seeing ourselves as the adman sees us? The representation and portrayal of older people in advertising. In A. Hetsroni (Ed.), *Advertising and reality: A global study of representation and content* (pp. 129–142). New York, NY: Bloomsbury.

Simkin, P. (2007). *The birth partner, Third edition: A complete guide to childbirth for dads, doulas, and all other labor companions.* Boston, MA: Harvard Common Press.

Simmons, C. A. (2014). Playing with popular culture–an ethnography of children's sociodramatic play in the classroom. *Ethnography and Education*, 1–14.

Simons, L. G., Simons, R. L., & Su, X. (2013). Consequences of corporal punishment among African Americans: The importance of context and outcome. *Journal of youth and adolescence, 42*(8), 1273–1285.

Simons, S. H. P., van Dijk, M., Anand, K. S., Roofhooft, D., van Lingen, R., & Tibboel, D. (2003). Do we still hurt newborn babies: A prospective study of procedural pain and analgesia in neonates. *Archives of Pediatrics & Adolescent Medicine, 157*, 1058–1064.

Simons-Morton, B. (2007). Parent involvement in novice teen driving: Rationale, evidence of effects, and potential for enhancing graduated driver licensing effectiveness. *Journal of Safety Research, 38*, 192–202.

Simons-Morton, B. G., Hartos, J. L., & Leaf, W. A. (2002). Promoting parental management of teen driving. *Injury Prevention, 8*(Suppl. 2), ii24–ii31.

Simons-Morton, B. G., Hartos, J. L., Leaf, W. A., & Preusser, D. F. (2006). Increasing parent limits on novice young drivers: Cognitive mediation of the effect of persuasive messages. *Journal of Adolescent Research, 21*, 83–105.

Simons-Morton, B. G., Ouimet, M. C., & Catalano, R. F. (2008). Parenting and the young driver problem. *American Journal of Preventative Medicine, 35*(3, Suppl. 1), S294–S303.

Simonton, D. K. (1996). Creativity. In J. E. Birren (Ed.), *Encyclopedia of gerontology* (pp. 341–351). San Diego, CA: Academic Press.

Simonton, D. K. (2000). Creativity: Cognitive, personal, developmental, and social aspects. *American Psychologist, 55*, 151–158.

Simonton, D. K. (2010). Creativity in highly eminent individuals. In J. C. Kaufman & R. J. Sternberg (Eds.), *The Cambridge handbook of creativity* (pp. 174–188). New York, NY: Cambridge University Press.

Singer, J. L., & Singer, D. G. (1998). *Barney & Friends* as entertainment and education: Evaluating the quality and effectiveness of a television series for preschool children. In J. K. Asamen & G. L. Berry (Eds.), *Research paradigms, television and social behavior* (pp. 305–367). Thousand Oaks, CA: Sage.

Singer, Y., Bachner, Y. G., Shvartzman, P., & Carmel, S. (2005). Home death—the caregivers' experiences. *Journal of Pain and Symptom Management, 30*, 70–74.

Singerman, J., & Lee, L. (2008). Consistency of the Babinski reflex and its variants. *European Journal of Neurology, 15*, 960–964.

Singh, L., Nestor, S., Parikh, C., & Yull, A. (2009). Influences of infant-directed speech on early word recognition. *Infancy, 14*, 654–666.

Singh, M. A. F. (2004). Exercise and aging. *Clinical Geriatric Medicine, 20*, 201–221.

Singh, S., Darroch, J. E., & Frost, J. J. (2001). Socioeconomic disadvantage and adolescent women's sexual and reproductive behavior: The case of five developed countries. *Perspectives on Sexual and Reproductive Health, 33*, 251–258 & 289.

Sinha, S. P., & Goel, Y. (2012). Impulsivity and selective attention among adolescents. *Journal of Psychosocial Research, 7*(1).

Sinnott, J. D. (2014). *Adult development: Cognitive aspects of thriving close relationships.* New York, NY: Oxford University Press.

Sippola, L. K., Buchanan, C. M., & Kehoe, S. (2007). Correlates of false self in adolescent romantic relationships. *Journal of Clinical Child and Adolescent Psychology, 36*, 515–521.

Sirsch, U., Dreher, E., Mayr, E., & Willinger, U. (2009). What does it take to be an adult in Austria? Views on adulthood in Austrian adolescents, emerging adults, and adults. *Journal of Adolescent Research, 24*, 275–292.

Sirsch, U., Dreher, E., Mayr, E., & Willinger, U. (2009). What does it take to be an adult in Austria?: Views of adulthood in Austrian adolescents, emerging adults, and adults. *Journal of Adolescent Research, 24*, 275–292.

Slater, A., Field, T., & Hernandez-Reif, M. (2002). The development of the senses. In A. Slater & M. Lewis (Eds.), *Introduction to infant development.* New York, NY: Oxford University Press.

Slater, M. D., Henry, K. L., Swaim, R. C., & Anderson, L. L. (2003). Violent media content and aggressiveness in adolescents: A downward spiral model. *Communication Research, 30*, 713–736.

Slobin, D. (1972, July). Children and language: They learn the same way around the world. *Psychology Today*, 71–76.

Slobin, D. I. (2014). The universal, the typological, and the particular in acquisition. In D. I. Slobin (Ed.), *The cross-linguistic study of language acquisition* (Vol. 5, pp. 1–40). New York, NY: Psychology Press.

Slonje, R., & Smith, P. K. (2008). Cyberbullying: Another main type of bullying? *Scandinavian Journal of Psychology, 49*, 147–154.

Small, M. (2001). *Kids: How biology and culture shape the way we raise young children.* New York, NY: Anchor.

Small, M. F. (1998). *Our babies, ourselves: How biology and culture shape the way we parent.* New York, NY: Anchor.

Small, M. F. (2005). The natural history of children. In Sharna Olfman (Ed.), *Childhood lost: How American culture is failing our kids* (pp. 3–17). Westport, CT: Praeger.

Small, N. (2001). Theories of grief: A critical review. In J. Hockney, J. Katz, & N. Small (Eds.), *Grief, mourning, and death ritual* (pp. 19–48). Buckingham, England: Open University Press.

Smetana, J. G. (2005). Adolescent–parent conflict: Resistance and subversion as developmental processes. In L. Nucci (Ed.), *Conflict, contradiction, and contrarian elements in moral development and education* (pp. 69–91). Mahwah, NJ: Erlbaum.

Smink, F. R. E., van Hoeken, D., & Hoek, H. W. (2012). Epidemiology of eating disorders: Incidence, prevalence, and mortality rates. *Current Psychiatry Report, 14*, 404–414.

Smith, C. D., Walton, A., Loveland, A. D., Umberger, G. H., Kryscio, R. J., & Gash, D. M. (2005). Memories that last in old age: Motor skill learning and memory preservation. *Neurobiology of Aging, 26*, 883–890.

Smith, C., & Denton, M. L. (2005). *Soul searching: The religious and spiritual lives of American teenagers.* New York, NY: Oxford University Press.

Smith, C., & Snell, P. (2010). *Souls in transition: The religious lives of emerging adults in America.* New York, NY: Oxford University Press.

Smith, D. B., & Moen, P. (2004). Retirement satisfaction for retirees and their spouses: Do gender and the retirement decision-making process matter? *Journal of Family Issues, 25*, 262–285.

Smith, J., & Baltes, P. B. (1990). Wisdom-related knowledge: Age-cohort differences in responses to life-planning problems. *Developmental Psychology, 26*, 494–505.

Smith, J., & Freund, A. M. (2002). The dynamics of possible selves in old age. *Journal of Gerontology, 57B*, P492–P500.

Smith, K., Downs, B., & O'Connell, M. (2001). Maternity leave and employment patterns: 1961–1995. *Current Population Reports P70(79)* (pp. 1–21). Washington, DC: U.S. Bureau of the Census.

Smith, P. K., & Drew, L. M. (2002). Grandparenthood. In M. H. Bornstein (Ed.), *Handbook of parenting, Vol. 3* (2nd ed., pp. 141–172). Mahwah, NJ: Erlbaum.

Smith, T. B., McCullough, M. E., & Poll, J. (2003). Religiousness and depression: Evidence for a main effect and the moderating influence of stressful life events. *Psychological Bulletin, 129*, 614–636.

Smith, W. B. (2011). *Youth leaving foster care: A developmental, relationship-based approach to practice.* New York, NY: Oxford University Press.

Snarey, J. R. (1985). Cross-cultural universality of social moral development: A review of Kohlbergian research. *Psychological Bulletin, 97*, 202–232.

Sneed, J. R., Kasen, S., & Cohen, P. (2007). Early-life risk factors for late-onset depression. *International Journal of Geriatric Psychiatry, 22*, 663–667.

Sneeding, T. M., & Phillips, K. R. (2002). Cross-national differences in employment and economic sufficiency. *Annals of the American Academy of Political Social Science, 580*, 103–133.

Snowling, M. J. (2004). Reading development and dyslexia. In U. Goswami (Ed.), *Blackwell handbook of childhood cognitive development.* Malden, MA: Blackwell.

Snyder, J., Cramer, A., & Afrank, J. (2005). The contributions of ineffective discipline and parental hostile attributions of child misbehavior to the development of conduct problems at home and school. *Developmental Psychology, 41*, 30–41.

Social Security Administration (2014). Research summary: Marriage trends and women's benefits, differences by race-ethnicity. Retrieved from http://www.ssa.gov/retirementpolicy/research/marriage-trends-race-ethnicity.html

Society for Assisted Reproductive Technology (SART) (2014). *Clinic summary report.* Retrieved from https://www.sartcorsonline.com/rptCSR_PublicMultYear.aspx?ClinicPKID=0

Soderstrom, M. (2007). Beyond babytalk: Re-evaluating the nature and content of speech input to preverbal infants. *Developmental Review, 27*, 501–532.

Soken, N. H., & Pick, A. D. (1992). Intermodal perception of happy and angry expressive behaviors by seven-month-old infants. *Child Development, 63*, 787–795.

Sokol, R. J., Delaney-Black, V., & Nordstrom, B. (2003). Fetal alcohol spectrum disorder. *JAMA: Journal of the American Medical Association, 290*, 2996–2999.

Sørensen, K., Mouritsen, A., Aksglaede, L., Hagen, C. P., & Morgensen, S. S. (2012). Recent secular trends in pubertal timing: Implications for evaluation and diagnosis of precocious puberty. *Hormone research in pediatrics 77(3)*, 137–145.

Sowell, E. R., Thompson, P. M., Holmes, C. J., Jernigan, T. I., & Toga, A. W. (1999). In vivo evidence for post-adolescence brain maturation in frontal and striatal regions. *Nature Neuroscience, 2*, 859–861.

Sowell, E., Trauner, D., Ganst, A., & Jernigan, T. (2002). Development of cortical and subcortical brain structures in childhood and adolescence: A structural MRI study. *Developmental Medicine and Child Neurology, 44*, 4–16.

Spafford, C. S., & Grosser, G. S. (2005). *Dyslexia and reading difficulties* (2nd ed.). Boston, MA: Allyn & Bacon.

Spelke, E. S. (1979). Perceiving bimodally specified events in infancy. *Developmental Psychology, 5*, 626–636.

Spence, M. J., & DeCasper, A. J. (1987). Prenatal experience with low-frequency maternal voice sounds influences neonatal perception of maternal voice samples. *Infant Behavior and Development, 10*, 133–142.

Spencer, J. P., Verejiken, B., Diedrich, F. J., & Thelen, E. (2000). Posture and the emergence of manual skills. *Developmental Science, 3*, 216–233.

Spera, C. (2005). A review of the relationship among parenting practices, parenting styles, and adolescent school achievement. *Educational Psychology Review, 17*, 125–146.

Sperber, M. (2000). Beer and circus: How big-time college sports is crippling undergraduate education. New York, NY: Henry Holt.

Spitz, R. (1945). Hospitalism: An inquiry into the genesis of psychiatric conditions in early childhood. In A. Freud, H. Hartmann, & E. Kris (Eds.), *The psychoanalytic study of the child* (pp. 53–74). New York, NY: International Universities Press.

Spitze, G., & Gallant, M. P. (2004). "The bitter with the sweet": Older adults' strategies for handling ambivalence in relations with their adult children. *Research on Aging, 26*, 387–412.

Spock, B. (1966). *Baby and child care.* New York, NY: Pocket Books.

Spock, B., & Needlman, R. (2004). *Dr. Spock's baby and child care* (8th ed.). New York, NY: Pocket.

Sprecher, S., & Regan, P. C. (1996). College virgins: How men and women perceive their sexual status. *Journal of Sex Research, 33*, 3–15.

Stafford, L. (2004). Communication competencies and sociocultural priorities of middle childhood. *Handbook of family communication*, 311–332.

Stanley, S. M., Rhoades, G. K., & Markman, H. J. (2006). Sliding versus deciding: Inertia and the premarital cohabitation effect. *Family Relations, 55*, 499–509.

Stanley, S. M., Whitton, S. W., & Markman, H. J. (2004). May I do: Interpersonal commitment levels and premarital or non-marital cohabitation. *Journal of Family Issues, 25*, 496–519.

Starc, V., Leban, M., Šinigoj, P., Vrhovec, M., Potočnik, N., Fernlund, E.,... & Center, P. C. (2012). Can functional cardiac age be predicted from the ECG in a normal healthy population. *Computing in Cardiology, 39*, 101–104.

Statistic Brain (2014). Youth sports statistics. Retrieved from http://www.statisticbrain.com/youth-sports-statistics/

Staudinger, U. M. (2013). The need to distinguish personal from general wisdom: A short history and empirical evidence. In *The scientific study of personal wisdom* (pp. 3–19). Springer Netherlands.

Sternberg, R. J. (2007). *Wisdom, intelligence, and creativity synthesized.* New York, NY: Cambridge University Press.

Sroufe, L. A., Carlson, E., & Schulman, S. (1993). Individuals in relationships: Development from infancy through adolescence. In D. C. Funder, R. D. Parke, C. Tomlinson-Keasey, & K. Widaman (Eds.), *Studying lives through time: Personality and development* (pp. 51–60). Norwood, NJ: Ablex.

Srouge, L. A., Egeland, B., Carlson, E. A., & Collins, W. A. (2005). *The development of the person: The Minnesota study of risk and adaptation from birth to adulthood.* New York, NY: Guilford.

Sternberg, R. J. (2010). Assessment of gifted students for identification purposes: New techniques for a new millennium. *Learning and Individual Differences, 20,* 327–336.

Sternberg, R. S. (2013). Searching for love. *The Psychologist, 26,* 98–101.

Sternberg, R. S., & Weis, K. (Eds.) (2006). *The new psychology of love.* New Haven, CT: Yale University Press.

St. James-Roberts, I., & Plewis, I. (1996). Individual differences, daily fluctuations, and developmental changes in amounts of infant waking, fussing, crying, feeding, and sleeping. *Child Development, 67,* 2527–2540.

St. James-Roberts, I., Bargn, J. G., Peter, B., Adams, D., & Hunt, S. (2003). Individual differences in responsivity to a neurobehavioural examination predict crying patterns of 1-week-old infants at home. *Developmental Medicine & Child Neurology, 45,* 400–407.

St. Louis, G. R., & Liem, J. H. (2005). Ego identity, ethnic identity, and psychosocial well-being of ethnic minority and majority college students. *Identity, 5,* 227–246.

Staff, J., Mortimer, J. T., & Uggen, C. (2004). Work and leisure in adolescence. In R. M. Lerner & L. Steinberg (Eds.), *Handbook of adolescent psychology* (2nd ed., pp. 429–450). Hoboken, NJ: John Wiley & Sons.

Stanley, R. O., & Burrows, G. D. (2008). Psychogenic heart disease–Stress and the heart: A historical perspective. *Journal of the International Society for the Investigation of Stress, 24* (Special issue: Stress and the heart), 181–187.

Staudinger, L. (1996). Wisdom and the social-interactive foundation of the mind. In P. B. Baltes & U. M. Staudinger (Eds.), *Interactive minds: Lifespan perspectives on the social foundations of cognition* (pp. 276–315). New York, NY: Cambridge University Press.

Staudinger, U. M. (2008). A psychology of wisdom: History and recent developments. *Research in Human Development, 5* (Special issue: Lifespan psychology: The legacy of Paul Baltes), 107–120.

Staudinger, U. M., & Baltes, P. B. (1996). Interactive minds: A facilitative setting for wisdom-related performance? *Journal of Personality and Social Psychology, 71,* 746–762.

Staudinger, U. M., Dorner, J., & Mickler, C. (2005). In R. J. Sternberg & J. Jordan (Eds.), *A handbook of wisdom: Psychological perspectives* (pp. 191–219). New York, NY: Cambridge University Press.

Steele, J. (2006). Media practice model. In J. J. Arnett (Ed.), *Encyclopedia of children, adolescents, and the media.* Thousand Oaks, CA: Sage.

Steele, R. G., Nesbitt-Daly, J. S., Daniel, R. C., & Forehand, R. (2005). Factor structure of the Parenting Scale in a low-income African American sample. *Journal of Child and Family Studies, 14,* 535–549.

Steinberg, L. (2000, April). *We know some things: Parent–adolescent relations in retrospect and prospect.* [Presidential Address]. Presented at the biennial meeting of the Society for Research on Adolescence, Chicago, IL.

Steinberg, L., & Levine, A. (1997). *You and your adolescent: A parents' guide for ages 10 to 20* (rev. ed.). New York, NY: HarperCollins.

Steinhausen, H.-C., Boyadjieva, S., Griogoroiu-Serbanescue, M., & Neumarker, K.-J. (2003). The outcome of adolescent eating disorders: Findings from an international collaborative study. *European Child & Adolescent Psychiatry, 12,* i91–i98.

Stenberg, C. R., Campos, J. J., & Emde, R. N. (1983). The facial expression of anger in seven-month-old infants. *Child Development,* 178–184.

Stephens, J. M., Young, M. F., & Calabrese, T. (2007). Does moral judgment go offline when students are online? A comparative analysis of undergraduates' belief of behaviors relates to conventional and digital cheating. *Ethics & Behavior, 17* (Special issue: Academic dishonesty), 233–254.

Stephens, M. A. P., & Franks, M. M. (1999). Parent care in the context of women's multiple roles. *Current Directions in Psychological Science, 8,* 149–152.

Steptoe, A., & Wardle, J. (2001). Health behavior, risk awareness, and emotional well-being in students from Eastern and Western Europe. *Social Science and Medicine, 53,* 1621–1630.

Stern, C., & Konno, R. (2009). Physical leisure activities and their role in preventing dementia: A systematic review. *International Journal of Evidence–Based Healthcare, 7,* 270–282.

Stern, S. (2002). Sexual selves on the World Wide Web: Adolescent girls' home pages as sites for sexual self-expression. In J. D. Brown, J. R. Steele, & K. Walsh-Childers (Eds.), *Sexual teens, sexual media: Investigating media's influence on adolescent sexuality* (pp. 265–285). Mahwah, NJ: Erlbaum.

Sternberg, R. (1983). Components of human intelligence. *Cognition, 15,* 1–48.

Sternberg, R. (1988). *The triarchic mind: A new theory of human intelligence.* New York, NY: Viking Penguin.

Sternberg, R. J. (1986). Triangular theory of love. *Psychological Review, 93,* 119–135.

Sternberg, R. J. (1987). Liking versus loving: A comparative evaluation of theories. *Psychological Bulletin, 102,* 331–345.

Sternberg, R. J. (1988). Triangulating love. In R. J. Sternberg & M. L. Barnes (Eds.), *The psychology of love* (pp. 119–138). New Haven, CT: Yale University Press.

Sternberg, R. J. (2002). Intelligence is not just inside the head: The theory of successful intelligence. In J. Aronson (Ed.), *Improving academic achievement* (pp. 227–244). San Diego, CA: Academic Press.

Sternberg, R. J. (2003). Our research program validating the triarchic theory of successful intelligence: Reply to Gottfredson. *Intelligence, 31,* 399–413.

Sternberg, R. J. (2004). Cultural and intelligence. *American Psychologist, 59,* 325–338.

Sternberg, R. J. (2005). The triarchic theory of successful intelligence. In D. P. Flanagan & P. L. Harrison (Eds.), *Contemporary Intellectual Assessment: Theories, Tests and Issues* (pp. 103–119). New York, NY: Guilford Press.

Sternberg, R. J. (2007). Intelligence and culture. In S. Kitayama & D. Cohen (Eds.), *Handbook of cultural psychology* (pp. 547–568). New York, NY: Guilford.

Sternberg, R. J., & Grigorenko, E. L. (Eds.). (2004). *Culture and competence.* Washington, DC: American Psychological Association.

Sternberg, R. J., Kaufman, J. C., & Pretz, J. E. (2002). *The creativity conundrum: A propulsion model of creative contributions.* Philadelphia, PA: Psychology Press.

Sternberg, R. J., & Weis, K. (Eds.). (2006). *The new psychology of love.* Yale University Press.

Sterns, H. L., & Huyck, M. H. (2001). The role of work in midlife. In M. E. Lachman (Ed.), *Handbook of midlife development* (pp. 447–486). New York, NY: Wiley.

Steur, F. B., Applefield, J. M., & Smith, R. (1971). Televised aggression and interpersonal aggression of preschool children. *Journal of Experimental Child Psychology, 11,* 442–447.

Stevenson, H. W., Lee, S., & Mu, X. (2000). Successful achievement in mathematics: China and the United States. In C. F. M. van Lieshout & P. G. Heymans (Eds.), *Developing talent across the lifespan* (pp. 167–183). Philadelphia, PA: Psychology Press.

Stevenson, M., & Henderson, T., & Baugh, E. (2007). Vital defenses: Social support appraisals of Black grandmothers parenting grandchildren. *Journal of Family Issues, 28,* 182–211.

Stevens-Watkins, D., & Rostosky, S. (2010). Binge drinking in African American males from adolescence to young adulthood: The protective influence of religiosity, family connectedness, and close friends' substance use. *Substance Use & Misuse, 45,* 1435–1451.

Stewart, A. J., Ostrove, J. M., & Helson, R. (2001). Middle aging in women: Patterns of personality change from the 30s to the 50s. *Journal of Adult Development, 8,* 23–37.

Stewart, A. L., Verboncoeur, C. J., McLellan, B. Y., Gillis, D. E., Rush, S., & Mills, K. M. (2001). Physical activity promotion program for older adults. *Journal of Gerontology, 56A,* M465–M470.

Stifter, E., Sacu, S., Weghaupt, H., Konig, F., Richter-Muksch, S., Thaler, A.,…Radner, W. (2004). Reading performance depending on the type of cataract and its predictability on the visual outcome. *Journal of Cataract and Refractive Surgery, 30,* 1259–1267.

Stimpson, J. P., Kuo, Y. F., Ray, L. A., Raji, M. A., & Peek, M. K. (2007). Risk of morality related to widowhood in older Mexican Americans. *Annals of Epidemiology, 17,* 313–319.

Stine-Morrow, E. A. L., & Basak, C. (2011). Cognitive interventions. In W. Schaie & S. Willis (Eds.), *Handbook of Aging* (pp. 153–170). New York, NY: Academic Press.

Stipek, D. J., Gralinski, J. H., Kopp, C. B. (1990). Self-concept development in toddler years. *Developmental Psychology, 26,* 972–977.

Stolar, A., & Goldfarb, J. (2006). HIV/AIDS among neonates and infants. In F. Fernandez, & P. Ruiz (Eds.), *Psychiatric aspects of HIV/AIDS* (pp. 250–258). Philadelphia, PA: Lippincott Williams & Wilkins.

Stoll, B., Hansen, N. I., Adams-Chapman, I., Fanaroff, A. A., Hintz, S. R., Vohr, B.,…Human Development Neonatal Research Network (2004). Neurodevelopmental and growth impairment among extremely low-birth-weight infants with neonatal infection. *JAMA: Journal of the American Medical Association, 292,* 2357–2365.

Stones, M. J., & Kozma, A. (1996). Activity, exercise, and behavior. In J. E. Birren & K. W. Schaie (Eds.), *Handbook of psychology and aging* (4th ed., pp. 338–352). San Diego, CA: Academic Press.

Stotland, N. E., Gilbert, P., Bogetz, A., Harper, C. C., Abrams, B., & Gerbert, B. (2010). Excessive weight gain in pregnancy: How do prenatal care providers approach counseling? *Journal of Women's Health, 19,* 807–814.

Strandh, M., & Nordenmark, M. (2006). The interference of paid work with household demands in different social policy contests: Perceived work-household conflict in Sweden, the UK, the Netherlands, Hungary & the Czech Republic. *British Journal of Sociology, 57,* 597–617.

Strang-Karlsson, S., Räikkönen, K., Pesonen, A.-K., Kajantie, E., Paavonen, J., Lahti, J.,…Andersson, S. (2008). Very low birth weight and behavioral symptoms of Attention Deficit Hyperactivity Disorder in young adulthood: The Helsinki Study of very-low-birth-weight adults. *American Journal of Psychiatry, 165,* 1345–1353.

Strauch, B. (2005). *The primal teen: What the new discoveries about the teenage brain tell us about our kids.* New York, NY: Anchor.

Straus, M. A., & Donnelly, D. A. (1994). *Beating the devil out of them: Corporal punishment in American families.* New York, NY: Lexington Books.

Strauss, R. S., & Pollack, H. A. (2003). Social marginalization of overweight children. *Archives of Pediatric and Adolescent Medicine, 157,* 746–752.

Strenk, S. A., Strenk, L. M., & Koretz, J. F. (2005). The mechanism of presbyopia. *Progress in Retinal and Eye Research, 24,* 379–393.

Strenze, T. (2007). Intelligence and socioeconomic success: A meta-analytic review of longitudinal research. *Intelligence, 35,* 401–426.

Striegel-Moore, R. H., & Franko, D. L. (2006). Adolescent eating disorders. In C. A. Essau (Ed.), *Child and adolescent psychopathology: Theoretical and clinical implications* (pp. 160–183). New York, NY: Routledge.

Striegel-Moore, R. H., Seeley, J. R., & Lewinsohn, P. M. (2003). Psychosocial adjustment in young adulthood of women who experienced an eating disorder in adolescence. *Journal of the American Academy of Child & Adolescent Psychiatry, 42,* 587–593.

Stroebe, M., & Stroebe, W. (1991). Does "grief work" work? *Journal of Consulting and Clinical Psychology, 59,* 57–65.

Stromquist, N. P. (2007). Gender equity education globally. In S. S. Klein, B. Richardson, D. A. Grayson, L. H. Fox, C. Kramarae, D. S. Pollard, & C. A. Dwyer (Eds.), *Handbook for achieving gender equity through education* (2nd ed., pp. 33–42). Mahwah, NJ: Lawrence Erlbaum.

Stuart, M., & Weinrich, M. (2001). Home- and community-based long-term care: Lessons from Denmark. *Gerontologist, 41,* 474–480.

Stuifbergen, M. C., Dykstra, P. A., Lanting, K. N., & van Delden, J. J. M. (2010). Autonomy in an ascribed relationship: The case of adult children and elderly parents. *Journal of Aging Studies, 24,* 257–265.

Stutzer, A., & Frey, B. (2006). Does marriage make people happy, or do happy people get married? *The Journal of Socio-Economics, 35,* 326–347.

Suarez-Orozco, C. (2015). Migration within and between countries: Implications for families and acculturation. In L. A. Jensen (Ed.), *Oxford handbook of human development and culture.* New York, NY: Oxford University Press.

Suarez-Orozco, C., & Suarez-Orozco, M. (1996). *Transformations: Migration, family life and achievement motivation among Latino adolescents.* Palo Alto, CA: Stanford University Press.

Subrahmanyam, K., Reich, S. M., Waechter, N., & Espinoza, G. (2008). Online and offline social networks: Use of social networking sites by emerging adults. *Journal of Applied Developmental Psychology, 29,* 420–433.

Subramanian, S. V., Elwert, F., & Christakis, N. (2008). Widowhood and mortality among the elderly: The modifying role of neighborhood concentration of widowed individuals. *Social Science & Medicine, 66,* 873–884.

Sullivan, C., & Cottone, R. R. (2010). Emergent characteristics of effective cross-cultural research: A review of the literature. *Journal of Counseling and Development, 88,* 357–362.

Sullivan, J. L. (2003). Prevention to mother-to-child transmission of HIV—what next? *Journal of Acquired Immune Deficiency Syndrome* (Suppl. 1), *34,* S67–S72.

Sun, J., Dunne, M. P., Hou, X. Y., & Xu, A. Q. (2013). Educational stress among Chinese adolescents: Individual, family, school and peer influences. *Educational Review, 65*(3), 284–302.

Sun, R. (2002). Old age support in contemporary urban China from both parents' and children's perspectives. *Research on Aging, 24,* 337–359.

Suomi, R., & Collier, D. (2003). Effects of arthritis exercise programs on functional fitness and perceived activities of daily living measures in older adults with arthritis. *Archives of Physical Medicine and Rehabilitation, 84,* 1589–1594.

Super, C. M., & Harkness, S. (1986). The developmental niche: A conceptualization at the interface of child and culture. *International Journal of Behavior Development, 9,* 545–569.

Super, C. M., & Harkness, S. (1993). The developmental niche: A conceptualization at the interface of child and culture. In R. A. Pierce & M. A. Black (Eds.), *Life-span development: A diversity reader* (pp. 61–77). Dubuque, IA: Kendall/Hunt.

Super, C. M., & Harkness, S. (2009). The developmental niche of the newborn in rural Kenya. In K. J. Nugent, B. J. Petrauskas, & T. B. Brazelton (Eds.), *The newborn as a person: Enabling healthy infant development worldwide* (pp. 85–97). Hoboken, NJ: John Wiley & Sons.

Super, C. M., Harkness, S., van Tijen, N., van der Vlugt, E., Fintelman, M., & Dijkstra, J. (1996). The three R's of Dutch childrearing and the socialization of infant arousal. In S. Harkness & C. M. Super (Eds.), *Parents' cultural belief systems: Their origins, expressions and consequences* (pp. 447–466). New York, NY: Guilford Press.

Super, D. (1992). Toward a comprehensive study of career development. In D. H. Montross & C. J. Shinkman (Eds.), *Career development: Theory and practice* (pp. 35–64). Springfield, IL: Charles C. Thomas.

Super, D. E. (1967). *The psychology of careers.* New York, NY: Harper & Row.

Super, D. E. (1976). *Career education and the meanings of work.* Washington, DC: U.S. Office of Education.

Super, D. E. (1980). A life-span life-space approach to career development. *Journal of Vocational Behavior, 16,* 282–298.

Surrey, J. L. (1991). The self-in-relation: A theory of women's development. In J. V. Jordan, A. G. Kaplan, J. B. Miller, L. R. Stiver, & J. L. Surrey (Eds.), *Women and growth in connection* (pp. 51–66). New York, NY: Guilford.

Susman, E. J., & Rogol, A. (2004). Puberty and psychological development. In R. M. Lerner & L. Steinberg (Eds.), *Handbook of adolescent psychology* (2nd ed., pp. 15–44). Hoboken, NJ: Wiley & Sons.

Sussman, S., Pokhrel, P., Ashmore, R. D., & Brown, B. B. (2007). Adolescent peer group identification and characteristics: A review of the literature. *Addictive Behaviors, 32,* 1602–1627.

Suzman, R. M., Harris, T., Hadley, E. C., Kovar, M. G., & Weindruch, R. (1992). The robust oldest old: Optimistic perspectives for increasing healthy life expectancy. In R. M. Suzman, D. P. Willis, & K. G. Manton (Eds.), *The oldest old* (pp. 341–358). New York, NY: Oxford University Press.

Svetlova, M., Nichols, S. R., & Brownell, C. A. (2010). Toddlers' prosocial behavior: From instrumental to empathic to altruistic helping. *Child development, 81*(6), 1814–1827.

Swanson, H., Saez, L., & Gerber, M. (2004). Literacy and cognitive functioning in bilingual and nonbilingual children at or not at risk for reading disabilities. *Journal of Educational Psychology, 96,* 3–18.

Swanson, S. A., Crow, S. J., Le Grange, D., Swendsen, J., & Merikangas, K. R. (2011). Prevalence and correlates of eating disorders in adolescents: Results from the National Comorbidity Survey Replication—Adolescent Supplement. *Archives of General Psychiatry 68*(7), 714–723. doi:10.1001/archgenpsychiatry.2011.22.

Swartz, T. T. (2009). Intergenerational family relations in adulthood: Patterns, variations, and implications in the contemporary United States. *Annual Review of Sociology, 35,* 191–212.

Swartz, T. T., & O'Brien, K. B. (2009). Intergenerational support during the transition to adulthood. In A. Furlong (Ed.), *Handbook of youth and young adulthood: New perspectives and agendas* (pp. 217–225). London, UK: Routledge.

Swenson, C. C., Henggeler, S. W., Taylor, I. S., & Addison, O. W. (2005). *Multisystemic therapy and neighborhood partnerships: Reducing adolescent violence and substance abuse.* New York, NY: Guilford.

Swinbourne, J. M., & Touyz, S. W. (2007). The comorbidity of eating disorders and anxiety disorders: A review. *European Eating Disorders Review, 15,* 253–274.

Swingley, D. (2010). Fast mapping and slow mapping in children's word learning. *Language Learning and Development, 6,* 179–183.

Syed, M., & Azmitia, M. (2010). Narrative and ethnic identity exploration: A longitudinal account of emerging adults' ethnicity–related experiences. *Developmental Psychology, 46,* 208–219.

Syed, M., & Mitchell, L. J. (2015). How race and ethnicity shape emerging adulthood. In J. J. Arnett (Ed.), *Oxford handbook of emerging adulthood.* New York, NY: Oxford University Press.

Syltevik, L. J. (2010). Sense and sensibility: Cohabitation in "cohabitation land." *The Sociological Review, 58,* 444–462.

Symons, D. K. (2001). A dyad-oriented approach to distress and mother–child relationship outcomes in the first 24 months. *Parenting: Science and Practice, 1,* 101–122.

Szinovac, M. E., & Davey, A. (2004). Honeymoons and joint lunches: Effects of retirement and spouse's employment on depressive symptoms. *Journal of Gerontology: Social Sciences, 59B,* P233–P245.

Taber-Thomas, B., & Perez-Edgar, K. (2015). Emerging adulthood brain development. In J. J. Arnett (Ed.), *Oxford handbook of emerging adulthood.* New York, NY: Oxford University Press.

Taga, K. A., Markey, C. N., & Friedman, H. S. (2006). A longitudinal investigation of associations between boys' pubertal timing and adult behavioral health and well-being. *Journal of Youth and Adolescence, 35,* 401–411.

Takahashi, K., & Takeuchi, K. (2007). Japan. In J. J. Arnett (Ed.), *International encyclopedia of adolescence* (525-539.New York, NY: Routledge.

Takahashi, M. (2000). Toward a culturally inclusive understanding of wisdom: Historical roots in the East and West. *International Journal of Aging and Human Development, 51,* 217–230.

Takahashi, M., & Overton, W. F. (2005). Cultural foundations of wisdom: An integrated developmental approach. In R. J. Sternberg & J. Jordan (Eds.), *A handbook of wisdom: Psychological perspectives* (pp. 32–60). New York, NY: Cambridge University Press.

Takamura, J., & Williams, B. (2002). *Informal caregiving: Compassion in action.* Arlington, TX: Arc of the United States.

Taku, K., Melby, M. K., Kronenberg, F., Kurzer, M. S., & Messina, M. (2012). Extracted or synthesized soybean isoflavones reduce menopausal hot flash frequency and severity: Systematic review and meta-analysis of randomized controlled trials. *Menopause, 19*(7), 776–790.

Talbani, A., & Hasanali, P. (2000). Adolescent females between tradition and modernity: Gender role socialization in south Asian immigrant families. *Journal of Adolescence, 23,* 615–627.

Tamaru, S., Kikuchi, A., Takagi, K., Wakamatsu, M., Ono, K., Horikoshi, T., Kihara, H., & Nakamura, T. (2011). Neurodevelopmental outcomes of very low birth weight and extremely low birth weight infants at 18 months of corrected age associated with prenatal risk factors. *Early Human Development, 87,* 55–59.

Tamay, Z., Akcay, A., Ones, U., Guler, N., Kilie, G., & Zencir, M. (2007). Prevalence and risk factors for allergic rhinitis in primary school children. *International Journal of Pediatric Otorhinolaryngology, 71,* 463–471.

Tamis-LeMonda, C. S., Bornstein, M. H., & Baumwell, L. (2001). Maternal responsiveness and children's achievement of language milestones. *Child Development, 72,* 749–767.

Tamis-LeMonda, C. S., Way, N., Hughes, D., Yoshikawa, H., Kalman, R. K., & Niwa, E. Y. (2008). Parents' goals for children: The dynamic coexistence of individualism and collectivism in cultures and individuals. *Social Development, 17,* 183–209.

Tanaka, H., & Seals, D. R. (2003). Dynamic exercise performance in master athletes: Insight into the effects of primary human aging on physiological functional capacity. *Journal of Applied Physiology, 95,* 2152–2162.

Tang, W. R., Aaronson, L. S., & Forbes, S. A. (2004). Quality of life in hospice patients with terminal illnesses. *Western Journal of Nursing Research, 26,* 113–128.

Tangri, S., Thomas, V., & Mednick, M. (2003). Predictors of satisfaction among college-educated African American women in midlife. *Journal of Adult Development, 10,* 113–125.

Tanner, J. L. (2006). Recentering during emerging adulthood: A critical turning point in life span human development. In J. J. Arnett & J. L. Tanner (Eds.), *Emerging adults in America: Coming of age in the*

21st century (pp. 21–55). Washington, DC: American Psychological Association.

Tanner, J. L. (2015). Mental health in emerging adulthood. In J. J. Arnett (Ed.), *Oxford handbook of emerging adulthood*. New York, NY: Oxford University Press.

Tanon, F. (1994). *A cultural view on planning: The case of weaving in Ivory Coast*. Tilburg, Netherlands: Tilburg University Press.

Tardif, T., Wellman, H. M., & Cheung, K. M. (2004). False belief understanding in Cantonese-speaking children. *Journal of Child Language, 31*, 779–800.

Tardon, A., Lee, W. J., Delgado-Rodriguez, M., Dosemeci, M., Albanese, D., Hoover, R., & Blair, A. (2005). Leisure-time physical activity and lung cancer: A meta-analysis. *Cancer Causes and Control, 16*, 389–397.

Taris, T., van Horn, J., & Schaufeli, W. (2004). Inequity, burnout and psychological withdrawal among teachers: A dynamic exchange model. *Anxiety, Stress & Coping: An International Journal, 17*, 103–122.

Tasker, F. (2005). Lesbian mothers, gay fathers, and their children: A review. *Developmental and Behavioral Pediatrics, 26*, 224–240.

Taylor, A. (2005). It's for the rest of your life: The pragmatics of youth career decision making. *Youth & Society, 36*, 471–503.

Taylor, B. D., & Tipodes, S. (2001). The effects of driving cessation on the elderly with dementia and their caregivers. *Accident Analysis and Prevention, 33*, 519–528.

Taylor, H. G., Klein, N., & Hack, M. (2000). School-age consequences of >750 g birth weight: A review and update. *Developmental Neuropsychology, 17*, 289–321.

Taylor, H. G., Klein, N., Minich, N. M., & Hack, M. (2000). Middle-school-age outcomes with very low birth weight. *Child Development, 71*, 1495–1511.

Taylor, M. J. (2006). Neural Bases of Cognitive Development. In E. Bialystok & F. I. M. Craik (Eds.), *Lifespan cognition: Mechanisms of change* (pp. 15–26.) New York, NY: Oxford University Press.

Taylor, P., & Keeter, S. (2010). *Millennials: Confident. Connected. Open to Change*. Retrieved from http://www.pewsocialtrends.org/files/2010/10/millennials-confident-connected-open-to-change.pdf

Taylor, R., Chatters, L., & Levin, J. (2004). *Religion in the lives of African Americans*. Thousand Oaks, CA: Sage.

Tedeschi, A., & Airaghi, L. (2006). Is affluence a risk factor for bronchial asthma and type 1 diabetes? *Pediatric Allergy and Immunology, 17*, 533–537.

Tee, K., Brush, A. J., Bernheim, I., & Kori, M. (2009). Exploring communication and sharing between extended families. *International Journal of Human–Computer Studies, 67*, 128–138.

Teitler, J. O. (2002). Trends in youth sexual initiation and fertility in developed counties: 1960–1995. *Annals of the American Academy of Political Science Studies, 580*, 134–152.

Telama, R., Yang, X., Viikari, J., Välimäki, I., Wanne, O., & Raitakari, O. (2005). Physical activity from childhood to adulthood: A 21-year tracking study. *American Journal of Preventative Medicine, 28*, 267–273.

Terman, L. M., & Oden, M. H. (1959). *The gifted group at mid-life: Thirty-five years follow-up of the superior child*. Stanford, CA: Stanford University Press.

Terry, W. S. (2003). *Learning and memory* (2nd ed.). Boston, MA: Allyn & Bacon.

Teti, D. M., Sakin, K., Kucera, E., Corns, K. M., & Eiden, R.D. (1996). And baby makes four: Predictors of attachment security among preschool-aged first-borns during the transition to sibling-hood. *Child Development, 68*, 579–596.

Thach, B. T. (2009). Does swaddling decrease or increase the risk for Sudden Infant Death syndrome? *Journal of Pediatrics, 155*, 461–462.

Thacher, P. V. (2008). University students and the "all nighter": Correlates and patterns of students' engagement in a single night of total sleep deprivation. *Behavioral Sleep Medicine, 6*, 16–31.

Thacher, T. D., & Clarke, B. L. (2011, January). Vitamin D insufficiency. In Mayo Clinic Proceedings (Vol. 86, No. 1, pp. 50–60). Elsevier.

Thacker, S. B., & Stroup, D. E. (2003). Revisiting the use of the electronic fetal monitor. *Lancet, 361*, 445–446.

Thapar, A., Collishaw, S., Pine, D. S., & Thapar, A. K. (2012). Depression in adolescence. *The Lancet, 379*(9820), 1056–1067.

Tharpe, A. M., & Ashmead, D. H. (2001). A longitudinal investigation of infant auditory sensitivity. *AJA: American Journal of Audiology, 10*, 104–112.

Thavanati, P. K. R., Kanala, K. R., deDios, A. E., & Garza, J. M. C. (2008). Age-related correlation between antioxidant enzymes and DNA damage with smoking and body mass index. *Journal of Gerontology: Biological Sciences, 63A*, 360–364.

Thelen, E. (2001). Dynamic mechanisms of change in early perceptual-motor development. In J. L. McClelland & R. S. Siegler (Eds.), *Mechanisms of cognitive development: Behavioral and neural perspectives* (pp. 161–184). Mahwah, NJ: Erlbaum.

Thiessen, E. D., Hill, E. A., & Saffran, J. R. (2005). Infant-directed speech facilitates word segmentation. *Infancy, 7*, 53–71.

Thomas, A. K., & Bulevich, J. B. (2006). Effective cue utilization reduces memory errors in older adults. *Psychology and Aging, 21*, 379–389.

Thomas, A., & Chess, S. (1977). *Temperament and development*. New York, NY: Brunner/Mazel.

Thomas, A., Chess, S., & Birch, H. G. (1968). *Temperament and behavior disorders in children*. New York, NY: New York University Press.

Thomas, P., & Fenech, M. (2007). A review of genome maturation and Alzheimer's disease. *Mutagenesis, 22*, 15–33.

Thomas, P., Lalloue, F., Preux, P., Hazif-Thomas, C., Pariel, S., Inscale, R., et al. (2006, January). Dementia patients caregivers quality of life: The PIXEL study. *International Journal of Geriatric Psychiatry, 21*, 50–56.

Thompson, C. J. (2005). Consumer risk perceptions in a community of reflexive doubt. *The Journal of Consumer Research, 32*, 235–248.

Thompson, P. M., Giedd, J. N., Woods, R. P., MacDonald, D., Evans, A. C. & Toga, A. W. (2000). Growth patterns in the developing brain detected by using continuum mechanical tensor maps. *Nature, 404*, 190–193.

Thompson, R. A. (1998). Early sociopersonality development. In W. Damon (Editor-in-Chief), & N. Eisenberg (Vol. Ed.), *Handbook of child psychology: Vol. 3. Social, emotional and personality development* (5th ed., pp. 25–104). New York, NY: Wiley.

Thompson, R. A. (2006). The development of the person: Social understanding, relationships, conscience, self. In W. Damon & R. Lerner (Eds.), & N. Eisenberg (Vol. Ed.), *Handbook of child psychology: Vol. 3. Social, emotional and personality development* (6th ed., pp. 24–98). New York, NY: Wiley.

Thompson, R. A., & Goodvin, R. (2007). Taming the tempest in the teapot: Emotional regulation in toddlers. In C. A. Brownell & C. B. Kopp (Eds.), *Socioemotional development in the toddler years* (pp. 320–341). New York, NY: Guilford.

Thompson, R. A., & Nelson, C. A. (2001). Developmental science and the media. *American Psychologist, 56*, 5–15.

Thompson, R. A., & Raikes, H. A. (2003). Toward the next quarter-century: Conceptual and methodological challenges for attachment theory. *Development and Psychopathology, 15*, 691–718.

Thoms, K. M., Kuschal, C., & Emmert, S. (2007). Lessons learned from DNA repair defective syndromes. *Experimental Dermatology, 16*, 532–544.

Thorne, A. (1995). Developmental truths in memories of childhood and adolescence. *Journal of Personality, 63*(2), 139–163.

Thornton, A. (2009). Historical and cross-cultural perspectives on marriage. In H. E. Peters & C. M. Kamp Dush, *Marriage and family: Complexities and perspectives* (pp. 3–32). New York, NY: Columbia University Press.

Tierra, L., & Tierra, M. (1998). *Chinese traditional herbal medicine.* Twin Lakes, WI: Lotus Light.

Tiggemann, M., & Anesbury, T. (2000). Negative stereotyping of obesity in children: The role of controllability beliefs. *Journal of Applied Social Psychology, 30,* 1977–1993.

Tinetti, M. E., Baker, D., Gallo, W. T., Nanda, A., Charpentier, P., & O'Leary, J. (2002). Evaluation of restorative care vs. usual care for older adults receiving an acute episode of home care. *JAMA: Journal of the American Medical Association, 287,* 2098–2105.

Tobach, E. (2004). Development of sex and gender: Biochemistry, physiology, and experience. In A. M. Paludi (Ed.), *Praeger guide to the psychology of gender* (pp. 240–270). Westport, CT: Praeger.

Tobin, D. D., Menon, M., Menon, M., Spatta, B. C., Hodges, E. V. E., & Perry, D. G. (2010). The intrapsychics of gender: A model of self-socialization. *Psychological Review, 117,* 601–622.

Tobin, D. J. (2010). *Gerontobiology of the hair follicle.* New York, NY: Springer.

Tobin, J., Hsueh, Y., & Karasawa, M. (2009). *Preschool in three cultures revisited: China, Japan, and the United States.* Chicago, IL: University of Chicago Press.

Tomasello, M., & Rakoczy, H. (2003). What makes human cognition unique? From individual to shared to collective intentionality. *Mind and Language, 18,* 121–147.

Tomassini, C., Kalogirou, S., Grundy, E., Fokkema, T., Martikainen, P., van Groenou, M. B., & Karisto, A. (2004). Contacts between elderly parents and their children in four European countries: Current patterns and future prospects. *European Journal of Ageing, 1,* 54–63.

Toro-Morn, M., & Sprecher, S. (2003). A cross-cultural comparison of mate preferences among university students: The United States vs. the People's Republic of China (PRC). *Journal of Comparative Family Studies, 34,* 151–170.

Tough, S., Clarke, M., & Cook, J. (2007). Fetal alcohol spectrum disorder prevention approaches among Canadian physicians by proportion of native/aboriginal patients: Practices during the preconception and prenatal periods. *Maternal and Child Health Journal, 11,* 385–393.

Tracey, T. J. G., Robbins, S. B., & Hofsess, C. D. (2005). Stability and change in interests: A longitudinal study of adolescents from grades 8 through 12. *Journal of Vocational Behavior, 66,* 1–25.

Trainor, L. J., Austin, C. M., & Desjardins, R. N. (2000). Is infant-directed speech prosody a result of the vocal expression of emotion? *Psychological Science, 11,* 188–195.

Trajanovska, M., Manias, E., Cranswick, N., & Johnston, L. (2010). Parental management of childhood complaints: Over-the-counter medicine use and advice-seeking behaviours. *Journal of Clinical Nursing, 19,* 2065–2075.

Travis, L. L., & Sigman, M. D. (2000). A developmental approach to autism. In A. J. Sameroff, M. Lewis, & S. M. Miller (Eds.), *Handbook of developmental psychopathology* (2nd ed., pp. 641–655). New York, NY: Plenum.

Treatment for Adolescents with Depression Study (TADS) team, U.S. (2004). Fluoxetine, cognitive-behavioral therapy, and their combination for adolescents with depression: Treatment for Adolescents with Depression Study (TADS) randomized controlled trial. *JAMA: Journal of the American Medical Association, 29,* 807–820.

Treatment for Adolescents with Depression Study Team (2007). Long-term effectiveness and safety outcomes. *Archives of General Psychiatry, 64,* 1132–1143.

Trehub, S. E. (2001). Musical predispositions in infancy. *Annals of the New York Academy of Sciences, 930,* 1–16.

Trehub, S. E., Thorpe, L. A., & Morrongiello, B. A. (1985). Infants' perception of melodies: Changes in a single tone. *Infant Behavior and Development, 8,* 213–223.

Tremblay, R. E. (2000). The development of aggressive behaviour during childhood: What have we learned in the past century? *International Journal of Behavioral Development, 24,* 129–141.

Tremblay, R. E. (2002). Prevention of injury by early socialization of aggressive behavior. *Injury Prevention, 8*(Suppl. IV), 17–21.

Tremblay, R. E., & Nagin, D. S. (2005). Developmental origins of physical aggression in humans. In R. E. Tremblay, W. W. Hartup, & J. Archer (Eds.), *Developmental origins of aggression* (pp. 83–106). New York, NY: Guilford Press.

Tremblay, T., Monetta, L., & Joanette, Y. (2004). Phonological processing of words in right- and left-handers. *Brain and Cognition, 55,* 427–432.

Triandis, H. C. (1995). *Individualism and collectivism.* Boulder, CO: Westview Press.

Troen, B. R. (2003). The biology of aging. *Mt. Sinai Journal of Medicine, 70,* 3–22.

Tronick, E. (2007). *The neurobehavioral and social-emotional development of infants and children.* New York, NY: W. W. Norton.

Trost, K. (2012). Norway. In J. J. Arnett (Ed.), *Adolescent psychology around the world.* New York, NY: Taylor & Francis.

Truglio, R. T. (2007). Sesame Workshop. In J. J. Arnett (Ed.), *Encyclopedia of children, adolescents, and the media* (pp. 749–750). Thousand Oaks, CA: Sage.

Tse, M. M. Y., Choi, K. C. Y., & Leung, R. S. W. (2008). E–health for older people: The use of technology in health promotion. *CyberPsychology & Behavior, 11,* 475–479.

Tseng, V. (2004). Family interdependence and academic adjustments in college: Youth from immigrant and U.S.-born families. *Child Development, 75,* 966–983.

Tsugane, S. (2005). Salt, salted food intake, and risk of gastric cancer: Epidemiologic evidence. *Cancer Science, 96,* 1–6.

Tudge, J. R. H., & Scrimsher, S. (2002). Lev S. Vygotsky on education. In B. J. Zimmerman & D. H. Schunk (Eds.), *Educational psychology.* Mahwah, NJ: Erlbaum.

Tudge, J. R. H., Doucet, F., Odero, D., Sperb, T. M., Piccinini, C. A., & Lopes, R. S. (2006). A window into different cultural worlds: Young children's everyday activities in the United States, Brazil, and Kenya. *Child Development, 77,* 1446–1469.

Tun, P. A., & Lachman, M. E. (2008). Age differences in reaction time and attention in a national telephone sample of adults: Education, sex, and task complexity matter. *Developmental Psychology, 44,* 1421–1429.

Turkheimer, E., Harden, K. P., D'Onofrio, B., & Gottesman, I. I. (2009). The Scarr-Rowe interaction between measured socioeconomic status and the heritability of cognitive ability. In K. McCartney & R. A. Weinberg (Eds.), *Experience and development: A festschrift in honor of Sandra Wood Scarr* (pp. 81–98). New York, NY: Psychology Press.

Twenge, J. M., & Crocker, J. (2002). Race and self-esteem: Meta-analyses comparing Whites, Blacks, Hispanics, Asians, and America Indians and comment on Gray-Little and Hafdahl (2000). *Psychological Bulletin, 128,* 371–408.

Twenge, J. M. (2006). *Generation me: Why today's young Americans are more confident, assertive, entitled—and more miserable than ever before.* New York, NY: Free Press.

Twisk, D. A. M., & Stacey, C. (2007). Trends in young driver risk and countermeasures in European countries. *Journal of Safety Research, 38,* 245–257.

Tyano, S., Keren, M., Herrman, H., & Cox, J. (2010). *The competent fetus.* New York, NY: Wiley.

U.S. Bureau of the Census (2006). *Statistical abstracts of the United States.* Washington, DC: U.S. Government Printing Office.

U.S. Bureau of the Census (2009). *Statistical abstracts of the United States*. Washington, DC: U.S. Government Printing Office.

U.S. Bureau of the Census (2010). *Statistical abstracts of the United States*. Washington, DC: U.S. Government Printing Office.

U.S. Bureau of the Census (2010). *Statistical abstract of the United States*. Washington, DC: Author.

U.S. Bureau of the Census (2011). *Current population survey and annual social and economic supplements*. Washington, DC: U.S. Bureau of the Census.

U.S. Bureau of the Census (2011). *Statistical abstract of the United States*. Washington, DC: Author.

U.S. Department of Health and Human Services (2004). *Trends in the well-being of America's children and youth, 2003* (No. 017–022–01571–4). Washington, DC: U.S. Government Printing Office.

U. S. Department of Health and Human Services. (2005). *Profile of older Americans 2004*. Retrieved from www.aoa.dhhs.gov/aoa/stats/profile/2004/default

U.S. Department of Health and Human Services (2005). *CDC acute injury care research agenda: Guiding research for the future*. Atlanta, GA: National Center for Injury Prevention and Control.

U.S. Department of Health and Human Services (2005). *Health, United States, with chartbook on trends in the health of Americans*. Hyattsville, MD: National Center for Health Statistics.

U.S. Department of Health and Human Services (2014). *Healthy people 2020: Heart disease and stroke*. Retrieved from http://www.healthypeople.gov/2020/topicsobjectives2020/nationalsnapshot.aspx?topicId=21

U. S. Department of Labor (1932). *Infant care*. Children's Bureau, Publication 8.

U.S. Department of Labor (2012). Number of jobs held, labor market activity, and earnings growth among the youngest Baby Boomers: Results from a longitudinal survey summary. Economic News Release, Table 1. Retrieved from http://www.bls.gov/news.release/nlsoy.nro.htm

U.S. Department of Transportation (1995). *The economic costs of motor vehicle crashes, Technical report 1994*. Washington, DC: National Highway Traffic Safety Administration.

Umaña-Taylor, A. J. (2005). Self-esteem and ethnic identity among Latino adolescents. *Directions in Rehabilitation Counseling, 16,* 9–18.

Umberson, D., Williams, K., Powers, D., Chen, M., & Campbell, A. (2005). As good as it gets? A life course perspective on marital quality. *Social Forces, 81,* 493–511.

Umrigar, A., Banijee, M., & Tsien, F. (2014). Down syndrome (Trisomy 21). LSUHSC School of Medicine. Retrieved from http://www.medschool.lsuhsc.edu/genetics/down_syndrome.aspx

UNAIDS (2010). UNAIDS report on the global AIDS epidemic. Available: http://www.unaids.org/globalreport/documents/20101123_GlobalReport_full_en.pdf

UNdata (2014). Elderly-dependency ratio: Japan. Retrieved from https://data.un.org/Data.aspx?d=PopDiv&f=variableID%3A44

Under threat of change, slowly but surely, universities in France—and all across Europe—are reforming. (2008, June 7). *The Economist*, 62.

Underwood, M. (2003). *Social-aggression among girls*. New York, NY: Guilford Press.

UNESCO (2006). EFA global monitoring report: Strong foundations: Early childhood care and education. Paris, France: Author.

UNESCO (2014). Education: Total net enrollment, lower secondary school. Retrieved from http://data.uis.unesco.org/?ReportId=167.#

UNICEF (2004). *Low birth weight: Country, regional, and global estimates*. New York, NY: Author.

UNICEF (2004). *The state of the world's children 2002*. Geneva, Switzerland: Author.

UNICEF (2008). *State of the world's children*. New York, NY: Author.

UNICEF (2009). *State of the world's children, 2009*. New York, NY: Author.

UNICEF (2011). *Breastfeeding Initiatives Exchange*. Retrieved from http://www.unicef.org/programme/breastfeeding/

UNICEF (2013). *Progress toward global immunization goals, 2012: Summary presentation of key indicators*. Retrieved from http://www.who.int/immunization/monitoring_surveillance/SlidesGlobalImmunization.pdf?ua=1

UNICEF (2014). Four out of five unattended births worldwide take place in sub-Saharan Africa and South Asia. Retrieved from http://data.unicef.org/maternal-health/delivery-care

UNICEF (2014). *The state of the world's children in numbers*. New York, NY: Author.

United Nations Development Programme (2006). *Human development report*. New York, NY: Author.

United Nations Development Programme (2008). *Human development report*. New York, NY: Author.

United Nations Development Programme (2010). *Human development report*. New York, NY: Author.

United Nations Development Programme (2011). *Human development report*. New York, NY: Author.

United Nations Development Programme (UNDP) (2014). *Human development report*. New York, NY: Author.

United Nations Population Division. (2002). *World population ageing: 1950–2050*. New York, NY: United Nations.

Unsworth, G., Devilly, G. J., & Ward, T. (2007). The effect of playing violent video games on adolescents: Should parents be quaking in their boots? *Psychology, Crime, & Law, 13,* 383–394.

Updegraff, K. A., McHale, S. M., & Crouter, A. (2002). Adolescents' sibling relationship and friendship experiences: Developmental patterns and relationship linkages. *Social Development, 11,* 182–204.

Updegraff, K. A., Thayer, S. M., Whiteman, S. D., Denning, D. J., & McHale, S. M. (2005). Relational aggression in adolescents' sibling relationships: Links to sibling and parent–adolescent relationship quality. *Family Relations, 54,* 373–385.

Utter, J., Neumark-Sztainer, D., Wall, M., & Story, M. (2003). Reading magazine articles about dieting and associated weight control behaviors among adolescents. *Journal of Adolescent Health, 32,* 78–82.

Utz, R. L., Carr, D., Nesse, R., & Wortman, C. B. (2002). The effect of widowhood on older adults' social participation: An evaluation of activity, disengagement, and continuity theories. *Gerontologist, 42,* 522–533.

Vaillancourt, T., & Hymel, S. (2006). Aggression and social status: The moderating roles of sex and peer-values characteristics. *Aggressive Behavior, 32,* 396–408.

Vaillancourt, T., Brendgen, M., Boivin, M., & Tremblay, R. E. (2003). A longitudinal confirmatory factor analysis of indirect and physical aggression: Evidence of two factors over time? *Child Development, 74,* 1628–1638.

Vaillant, C. O. & Vaillant, G. E., Is the U-curve of marital satisfaction an illusion? A 40-year study of marriage. *Journal of Marriage and the Family, 55,* 230–239.

Vaillant, G. E. (2002). *Aging well*. Boston, MA: Little, Brown.

Vainio, A. (2015). Finnish moral landscapes: A comparison of nonreligious, liberal religious, and conservative religious adolescents. In L. A. Jensen (Ed.), *Moral development in a global world: Research from a cultural-developmental perspective*. New York, NY: Cambridge University Press.

Valencia-Martín, J. L., Galan, I., & Rodríguez-Artalejo, F. (2007). Binge drinking in Madrid, Spain. *Alcoholism: Clinical and Experimental Research, 31,* 1723–1730.

Valentine, D., Williams, M., & Young, R. K. (2013). *Age-related factors in driving safety*. Austin, TX: Center for Transportation Research.

Valkenburg, P. M., & Buijzen, M. (2007). Advertising, purchase requests and. In J. J. Arnett (Ed.), *Encyclopedia of children, adolescents, and the media* (pp. 47–48). Thousand Oaks, CA: Sage.

Valkenberg, P. M., & Peter, J. (2011). Online communication among adolescents: An integrated model of its attractions, opportunities, and risks. *Journal of Adolescent Health 48*(2), 121–127.

Vallejo, M. C., Ramesh, V., Phelps, A. L., & Sah, N. (2007). Epidural labor analgesia: Continuous infusion versus patient–controlled epidural analgesia with background infusion versus without a background infusion. *The Journal of Pain, 8*, 970–975.

Vanasse, A., Demers, M., Hemiari, A., & Courteau, J. (2006). Obesity in Canada: Where and how many? *International Journal of Obesity, 30*, 677–683.

van Beinum, F. J. (2008). Frames and babbling in hearing and deaf infants. In B. L. Davis & K. Zajdó (Eds.), *The syllable in speech production* (pp. 225–241). New York, NY: Lawrence Erlbaum.

Van de Poel, E. V., Hosseinpoor, A. R., Speybroek, N., Van Ourti, T., & Vega, J. (2008). Socioeconomic inequality in malnutrition in developing countries. *Bulletin of the World Health Organization, 86*, 282–291.

Van den Hoonaard, D. K. (1994). Paradise lost: Widowhood in a Florida retirement community. *Journal of Aging Studies, 8*, 121–132.

van der Lippe, T., Jager, A., & Kops, Y. (2006). Combination pressure: The paid work-family balance of men and women in European countries. *Acta Sociologica, 49*, 303–319.

Van Evra, J. (2007). School-age children, impact of media on. In J. J. Arnett (Ed.), *Encyclopedia of children, adolescents, and the media* (pp. 739–742). Thousand Oaks, CA: Sage.

Van Gaalen, R. I., & Dykstra, P. A. (2006). Solidarity and conflict between adult children and parents: A latent class analysis. *Journal of Marriage and the Family, 68*, 947–960.

Van Hecke, A. V., Mundy, P. C., Acra, C. F., Block, J. J., Delgado, C. E. F., Parlade, M. V.,...Pomares, Y. B. (2007). Infant joint attention, temperament, and social competence in preschool children. *Child Development, 78*, 53–69.

Van Hoof, A. (1999). The identity status approach: In need of fundamental revision and qualitative change. *Developmental Review, 19*, 622–647.

Van Horn, K. R., & Cunegatto, M. J. (2000). Interpersonal relationships in Brazilian adolescents. *International Journal of Behavioral Development, 24*, 199–203.

van IJzendoorn, M. H., & Hubbard, F. O. A. (2000). Are infant crying and maternal responsiveness during the first year related to infant–mother attachment at 15 months? *Attachment and Human Development, 2*, 371–391.

van IJzendoorn, M. H., & Kroonenberg, P. M. (1988). Cross-cultural patterns of attachment: A meta-analysis of the Strange Situation. *Child Development, 59*, 147–156.

Van Ijzendoorn, M. H., & Sagi-Schwartz, A. (2008). Cross-cultural patterns of attachment: Universal and contextual dimensions. In J. Cassidy, Jude & P. Shaver (Eds.), *Handbook of attachment: Theory, research, and clinical applications (2nd ed.)* (pp. 880–905). New York: Guilford Press.

van IJzendoorn, M. H., Schuengel, C., & Bakermans-Kranenburg, M. J. (1999). Disorganized attachment in early childhood: Meta-analysis of precursors, concomitants and sequelae. *Development and Pscyhopathology, 11*, 225–249.

van IJzendoorn, M. H., Vereijken, C. M. J. L., Bakermans-Kraneburg, M. J., & Riksen-Walraven, J. M. (2004). Assessing attachment security with the Attachment Q Sort: Meta-analytic evidence for the validity of the Observer AQS. *Child Development, 75*, 1188–1213.

van Sleuwen, B. E., Engelberts, A. C., Boere-Boonekamp, M. M., Kuis, W., Schulpen, T. W. J., & L'Hoir, M. P. (2007). Swaddling: A systematic review. *Pediatrics, 120*, e1097–e1106.

Van Someren, E. J., Lijzenga, C., Mirmiran, M., & Swaab, D. F. (1997). Long-term fitness training improves the circadian rest–activity rhythm in healthy elderly males. *Journal of Biological Rhythms, 12*, 146–156.

Van Volkom, M. (2006). Sibling relationships in middle and older adulthood: A review of the literature. *Marriage & Family Review, 40*, 151–170.

Vandell, D. L. (2004). Early child-care: The known and the unknown. *Merrill-Palmer Quarterly, 50* (Special Issue: The maturing of human developmental sciences: Appraising past, present and prospective agendas), 387–414.

Vandell, D. L., Burchinal, M. R., Belsky, J., Owen, M. T., Friedman, S. L., Clarke-Stewart, A.,...Weinraub, M. (2005). Early child care and children's development in the primary grades: Follow-up results from the NICHD Study of Early Child Care. Paper presented at the biennial meeting of the Society for Research in Child Development, Atlanta, GA.

Vandereycken, W., & Van Deth, R. (1994). *From fasting saints to anorexic girls: The history of self-starvation*. New York, NY: New York University Press.

Vanier Institute of the Family. (2004). *Profiling Canada's families III*. Retrieved from www.vifamily.ca/profiling/3d.htm

VanLaningham, J., Johnson, D., & Amato, P. (2001). Marital happiness, marital duration, and the U-shaped curve: Evidence from the five-wave panel study. *Social Forces, 78*, 1313–1341.

Varendi, H., Christensson, K., Porter, R. H., & Wineberg, J. (1998). Soothing effect of amniotic fluid smell in newborn infants. *Early Human Development, 51*, 47–55.

Vaughan, K. (2005). The pathways framework meets consumer culture: Young people, careers, and commitment. *Journal of Youth Studies, 8*, 173–186.

Vazsonyi, A. T., & Snider, J. B. (2008). Mentoring, competencies, and adjustment in adolescents: American part-time employment and European apprenticeships. *International Journal of Behavioral Development, 32*, 46–55.

Verhaeghen, P., Steitz, D. W., Sliwinski, M. J., & Cerella, J. (2003). Aging and dual-task performance: A meta-analysis. *Psychology and Aging, 18*, 443–460.

Verkuyten, M. (2002). Multiculturalism among minority and majority adolescents in the Netherlands. *International Journal of Intercultural Relations, 26*, 91–108.

Verma, R. P., Shibli, S., Fang, H., & Komaroff, E. (2009). Clinical determinants and the utility of early postnatal maximum weight loss in fluid management of extremely low birth weight infants. *Early Human Development, 85*, 59–64.

Verma, S., & Larson, R. (1999). Are adolescents more emotional? A study of daily emotions of middle class Indian adolescents. *Psychology and Developing Societies, 11*, 179–194.

Verma, S., & Saraswathi, T. S. (2002). Adolescents in India: Street urchins or Silicon Valley millionaires? In B. B. Brown, R. Larson, & T. S. Saraswathi (Eds.), *The world's youth: Adolescence in eight regions of the globe* (pp. 105–140). New York, NY: Cambridge University Press.

Vidyasagar, T. R. (2004). Neural underpinnings of dyslexia as a disorder of visuospatial attention. *Clinical and Experimental Optometry, 87*, 4–10.

Vig, S., Chinitz, S., & Shulman, L. (2005). Young children in foster care: Multiple vulnerabilities and complex service needs. *Infants and Young Children, 18*, 147–160.

Vilette, B. (2002). Do young children grasp the inverse relationship between addition and subtraction? Evidence against early arithmetic. *Cognitive Development, 17*, 1365–1383.

Vilhjalmsson, R., & Kristjansdottir, G. (2003). Gender differences in physical activity in older children and adolescents: The central role of organized sport. *Social Science Medicine, 56,* 363–374.

Villar, F., Celdrán, M., & Triadó, C. (2012). Grandmothers offering regular auxiliary care for their grandchildren: An expression of generativity in later life? *Journal of Women & Aging, 24*(4), 292–312.

Vinanen, A., Munhbayarlah, S., Zevgee, T., Narantsetseg, L., Naidansuren, T. S., Koskenvuo, M.,...Terho, E. O. (2007). The protective effect of rural living against atopy in Mongolia. *Allergy, 62,* 272–280.

Vincent, J. A., Phillipson, C. R., & Downs, M. (2006). *The futures of old age.* Thousand Oaks, CA: Sage.

Vincent, L. (2008). "Boys will be boys": Traditional Xhosa male circumcision, HIV and sexual socialization in contemporary South Africa. *Culture, Health, and Sexuality, 10,* 431–446.

Vinden, P. G. (1996). Junin Quechua children's understanding of mind. *Child Development, 67,* 1707–1716.

Visher, E. B., Visher, J. S., & Pasley, K. (2003). Remarriage families and step-parenting. In F. Walsh (Ed.), *Normal family processes* (pp. 153–175). New York, NY: Guilford.

Vissamsetti, B., & Pearce, I. (2011). Erectile dysfunction. *Midlife & Beyond,* 467–471.

Viswanathan, H., & Lambert, B. L. (2005). An inquiry into medication meanings, illness, medication use, and the transformative potential of chronic illness among African Americans with hypertension. *Research in Social & Administrative Pharmacy, 1,* 21–39.

Vlaardingerbroek, J., van Goudoever, J. B., & van den Akker, C. H. P. (2009). Initial nutritional management of the preterm infant. *Early Human Development, 85,* 691–695.

Voeller, K. K. (2004). Attention-deficit hyperactivity disorder. *Journal of Child Neurology, 19,* 798–814.

Vogels, N., Diepvens, K., & Westerterp-Plantenga, M. S. (2005). Predictors of long-term weight maintenance. *Obesity Research, 13,* 2162–2168.

Vogelstein, B., & Kinzler, K. (2004). Cancer genes and the pathways they control. *Nature Medicine, 10,* 789–799.

Voicu, M., Voicu, B., & Strapcova, K. (2009). Housework and gender inequality in European countries. *European Sociological Review, 25,* 365–377.

Volk, A., Craif, W., Bryce, W., & King, M. (2006). Adolescent risk correlates of bullying and different types of victimization. *International Journal of Adolescent Medicine and Health, 18,* 575–586.

Volling, B. L. (2003). Sibling relationships. In M. H. Bornstein, L. Davidson, C. L. M. Keyes, & K. A. Moore (Eds.), *Well-being: Positive development across the life course* (pp. 205–220). Mahwah, NJ: Erlbaum.

Vondra, J. L., & Barnett, D. (Eds.). (1999). Atypical attachment in infancy and early childhood among children at developmental risk. *Monographs of the Society for Research in Child Development, 64*(3, Serial No. 258).

Vondracek, F. W., & Porfelli, E. J. (2003). The world of work and careers. In G. R. Adams & M. D. Berzonsky (Eds.), *Blackwell handbook of adolescence: Blackwell handbooks of developmental psychology* (pp. 109–128). Malden, MA: Blackwell.

Vouloumanos, A., & Werker, J. F. (2004). Tuned to the signal: The privileged status of speech for young infants. *Developmental Science, 7,* 270–276.

Vouloumanos, A., Hauser, M. D., Werker, J. F., & Martin, A. (2010). The tuning of human neonates' preference for speech. *Child Development, 81,* 517–527.

Waard, D., Dijksterhuis, C., & Brookhuis, K. A. (2009). Merging into heavy motorway traffic by young and elderly drivers. *Accident Analysis and Prevention, 41,* 588–497.

Wadsworth, L. A., & Johnson, C. P. (2008). Mass media and healthy aging. *Journal of Nutrition for the Elderly, 27,* 319–331.

Wagner, C. L., & Greer, F. R. (2008). Prevention of rickets and vitamin D deficiency in infants, children, and adolescents. *Pediatrics, 122*(5), 1142–1152.

Wahlbeck, K., Forsén, T., Osmond, C., Barker, D. J. P., & Eriksson, J. G. (2001). Association of schizophrenia with low maternal body mass index, small size at birth, and thinness during childhood. *Archives of General Psychiatry, 58,* 48–52.

Wahlhaus, E. (2005). The psychological benefits of the traditional Jewish mourning rituals: Have the changes instituted by the Progressive movement enhanced or diminished them? *European Judaism, 38,* 95–109.

Waite, L. J., & Gallagher, M. (2000). *The case for marriage: Why married people are happier, healthier, and better off financially.* New York, NY: Doubleday.

Walcott, D. D., Pratt, H. D., & Patel, D. R. (2003). Adolescents and eating disorders: Gender, racial, ethnic, sociocultural and socioeconomic issues. *Journal of Adolescent Research, 18,* 223–243.

Waldrop, D. P. (2006). At the eleventh hour: Psychosocial dynamics in short hospice stays. *The Gerontologist, 46,* 106–114.

Walker, J., Anstey, K., & Lord, S. (2006). Psychological distress and visual functioning in relation to vision-related disability in older individuals with cataracts. *British Journal of Health Psychology, 11,* 303–317.

Wallace, J. M., & Williams, D. R. (1997). Religion and adolescent health-compromising behavior. In J. Schulenberg, J. L. Maggs, & K. Hurrelmann (Eds.), *Health risks and developmental transitions during adolescence* (pp. 444–468). New York, NY: Cambridge University Press.

Wallace, J. M., Yamaguchi, R., Bachman, J. G., O'Malley, P. M., Schulenberg, J. E., & Johnston, L. D. (2007). Religiosity and adolescent substance use: The role of individual and contextual influences. *Social Problems, 54,* 308–327.

Wallerstein, J. S., & Blakeslee, S. (1995). *The good marriage.* Boston, MA: Houghton Mifflin.

Wallerstein, J. S., & Johnson-Reitz, K. (2004). Communication in divorced and single parent families. In A. L. Vangelisti (Ed.), *Handbook of family communication* (pp. 197–214). Mahwah, NJ: Erlbaum.

Walsh, K. E., & Berman, J. R. (2004). Sexual dysfunction in the older woman: An overview of the current understanding and management. *Therapy in Practice, 21,* 655–675.

Walshaw, C.A. (2010). Are we getting the best from breastfeeding? *Acta Paediatria, 99,* 1292–1297.

Wan, H., Sengupta, M., Velkoff, V., & DeBarros, K. (2005). U.S. Census Bureau, *Current Population Reports, P23-209, 65+ in the United States: 2005.* Washington, DC: U.S. Government Printing Office.

Wang, M., Gamo, N. J., Yang, Y., Jin, L. E., Wang, X. J., Laubach, M.,...& Arnsten, A. F. (2011). Neuronal basis of age-related working memory decline. *Nature, 476*(7359), 210-213.

Wang, S., & Tamis-LeMonda, C. (2003). Do childrearing values in Taiwan and the United States reflect cultural values of collectivism and individualism? *Journal of Cross-Cultural Psychology, 34,* 629–642.

Wang, S., Baillargeon, R., & Paterson, S. (2005). Detecting continuity violations in infancy: A new account and new evidence from covering and tube events. *Cognition, 95,* 129–173.

Wang, Y., & Fong, V. L. (2009). Little emperors and the 4:2:1 generation: China's singletons. *Journal of the American Academy of Child & Adolescent Psychiatry, 48,* 1137–1139.

Wang, Y., & Lobstein, T. (2006). Worldwide trends in childhood overweight and obesity. *International Journal of Pediatric Obesity, 1,* 11–25.

Wang, Y., Wang, X., Kong, Y., Zhang, J. H., & Zeng, Q. (2010). The Great Chinese Famine leads to shorter and overweight females in Chongqing Chinese population after 50 years. *Obesity, 18*, 588–592.

Wannamethee, S. G., Shaper, A. G., Walker, M., & Ebrahim, S. (1998). Lifestyle and 15-year survival free of heart attack, stroke, and diabetes in middle-aged British men. *Archives of Internal Medicine, 158*, 2433–2440.

Ward, R. A. (2008). Multiple parent–adult child relations and well-being in middle and later life. *The Journals of Gerontology, 63*, S239–S47.

Warnock, F. F., Castral, T. C., Brant, R., Sekilian, M., Leite, A. M., De La Presa Owens, S., & Schochi, C. G. S. (2010). Brief report: Maternal Kangaroo Care for neonatal pain relief: A systematic narrative review. *Journal of Pediatric Psychology, 35*, 975–984.

Warnock, F., & Sandrin, D. (2004). Comprehensive description of newborn distress behavior in response to acute pain (newborn male circumcision). *Pain, 107*, 242–255.

Warr, P. B. (1992). Age and occupational well-being. *Psychology and Aging, 7*, 37–45.

Warr, P. B. (1994). Age and employment. In M. D. Dunnette, L. Hough, & H. Triandis (Eds.), *Handbook of industrial and organizational psychology* (pp. 485–550). Palo Alto, CA: Consulting Psychologists Press.

Warr, P., Butcher, V., Robertson, I., & Callinan, M. (2004). Older people's well-being as a function of employment, retirement, environmental characteristics, and role preference. *British Journal of Psychology, 95*, 297–324.

Warren-Findlow, J. (2006). Weathering: Stress and heart disease in African American women living in Chicago. *Qualitative Health Research, 16*, 221–237.

Warren, R. (2007). Electronic media, children's use of. In J. J. Arnett (Ed.), *Encyclopedia of children, adolescents, and the media* (Vol. 1, pp. 286–288). Thousand Oaks, CA: Sage.

Warren, S. L., & Simmens, S. J. (2005). Predicting toddler anxiety/depressive symptoms: Effects of caregiver sensitivity of temperamentally vulnerable children. *Infant of Medical Health Journal, 26*, 40–55.

Wass, H. (2004). A perspective on the current state of death education. *Death Studies, 28*, 289–308.

Waterman, A. S. (1992). Identity as an aspect of optimal functioning. In G. R. Adams, T. P. Gullotta, & R. Montemayor (Eds.), *Adolescent identity formation* (Vol. 4, pp. 50–72). Newbury Park, CA: Sage.

Waterman, A. S. (1999). Issues of identity formation revisited: United States and the Netherlands. *Developmental Review, 19*, 462–479.

Waterman, A. S. (2007). Doing well: The relationship of identity status to three conceptions of well-being. *Identity, 7*, 289–307.

Waters, E., Weinfield, N. S., & Hamilton, C. E. (2000). The stability of attachment security from infancy to adolescence and early adulthood: General discussion. *Child Development, 71*, 703–706.

Watkin, P. M. (2011). The value of the neonatal hearing screen. *Paediatrics and Child Health, 21*, 37–41.

Watson, P. (2014). *The age of atheists: How we have sought to live since the death of God.* New York, NY: Simon and Schuster.

Wattmo, C., Londos, E., & Minthon, L. (2014). Risk factors that affect life expectancy in Alzheimer's disease: A 15-year follow-up. *Dementia and Geriatric Cognitive Disorders, 38*, 286–299.

Waxman, S. R. (2003). Links between object categorization and naming: Origins and emergence in human infants. In D. H. Rakison & L. M. Oakes (Eds.), *Early category and concept development: Making sense of the blooming, buzzing confusion* (pp. 193–209). New York, NY: Oxford University Press.

Waxman, S. R., & Lidz, J. L. (2006). Early word learning. In W. Damon & R. Lerner (Eds.), & D. Kuhn & R. Siegler (Vol. Eds.), *Handbook of child psychology: Vol. 2. Cognition, perception and language* (6th ed., pp. 299–335). New York, NY: Wiley.

Way, N. (2004). Intimacy, desire, and distrust in the friendships of adolescent boys. In N. Way & J. Y. Chu (Eds.), *Adolescent boys: Exploring diverse cultures of boyhood* (pp. 167–196). New York, NY: New York University Press.

Way, N., Reddy, R., & Rhodes, J. (2007). Students' perceptions of school climate during the middle school years: Associations with trajectories of psychological and behavioral adjustment. *American Journal of Community Psychology, 40*, 194–213.

Weaver, R. F. (2005). *Molecular Biology* (3rd ed.). New York, NY: McGraw-Hill.

Weaver, S. E., & Coleman, M. (2010). Caught in the middle mothers in step-families. *Journal of Social and Personal Relationships, 27*, 305–326.

Weber, D. (2006). Media use by infants and toddlers: *A potential for play.* Oxford University Press, New York.

Weber, M. T., Maki, P. M., & McDermott, M. P. (2014). Cognition and mood in perimenopause: A systematic review and meta-analysis. *Journal of Steroid Biochemistry and Molecular Biology, 142*, 90–98.

WebMD (2011). *Vaginal birth after cesarean (VBAC)—Risks of VBAC and cesarean deliveries.* Retrieved from http://www.webmd.com/baby/tc/vaginal-birth-after-cesarean-vbac-risks-of-vbac-and-cesarean-deliveries

Wechsler, H., & Nelson, T. F. (2001). Binge drinking and the American college student: What's the five drinks? *Psychology of Addictive Behaviors, 15*, 287–291.

Weekley, A. (2007). *Placentophagia: Benefits of eating the placenta.* Retrieved from http://www.associatedcontent.com/article/289824/placentophagia_benefits_of_eating_the.html?cat=51

Weichold, K., Silbereisen, R. K., & Schmitt-Rodermund, E. (2003). Short-term and long-term consequences of early vs. late physical maturation in adolescents. In C. Haywood (Ed.), *Puberty and psychopathology* (pp. 241–276). Cambridge, MA: Cambridge University Press.

Weinberg, R. A. (2004). The infant and the family in the twenty-first century. *Journal of the American Academy of Child & Adolescent Psychiatry, 43*, 115–116.

Weiner, I. B. (1992). *Psychological disturbance in adolescence* (2nd ed.). New York, NY: Wiley.

Weinfeld, N. S., Whaley, G. J. L., & Egeland, B. (2004). Continuity, discontinuity, and coherence in attachment from infancy to late adolescence: Sequelae of organization and disorganization. *Attachment and Human Development, 6*, 73–97.

Weinfield, N. S., Sroufe, L. A., & Egeland, B. (2000). Attachment from infancy to early adulthood in a high-risk sample: Continuity, discontinuity, and their correlates. *Child Development, 71*, 695–702.

Weintraub, W. S. (2010). Do more cardiac rehabilitation visits reduce events compared with fewer visits? *Circulation, 121*(1), 8–9.

Weir, K. F., & Jose, P. E. (2010). The perception of false self scale for adolescents: Reliability, validity, and longitudinal relationships with depressive and anxious symptoms. *British Journal of Developmental Psychology, 28*, 393–411.

Weisgram, E. S., Bigler, R. S., & Liben, L. S. (2010). Gender, values, and occupational interests among children, adolescents, and adults. *Child Development, 81*(3), 778–796.

Weisleder, A., & Fernald, A. (2013). Talking to children matters early language experience strengthens processing and builds vocabulary. *Psychological science, 24*(11), 2143–2152.

Weisner, T. S. (1996). The 5 to 7 transition as an ecocultural project. In A. J. Sameroff & M. M. Haith, *The five to seven year shift: The age of reason and responsibility* (pp. 295–326). Chicago, IL: University of Chicago Press.

Weiss, M. R. (Ed.). (2004). *Developmental sport and exercise psychology: A lifespan perspective.* Morgantown, WV: Fitness Information Technology.

Weissman, M. M., Warner, V., Wickramaratne, P. J., & Kandel, D. B. (1999). Maternal smoking during pregnancy and psychopathology in offspring followed to adulthood. *Journal of the American Academy of Child & Adolescent Psychiatry, 38,* 892–899.

Weitzen, S., Teno, J., Fennell, M., & Mor, V. (2003). Factors associated with site of death: A national study of where people die. *Medical Care, 41,* 323–335.

Welti, C. (2002). Adolescents in Latin America: Facing the future with skepticism. In B. Brown, R. Larson, & T. S. Saraswathi (Eds.), *The world's youth: Adolescence in eight regions of the globe* (pp. 276–306). New York, NY: Cambridge University Press.

Wendland-Carro, J., Piccinini, C. A., & Millar, W. S. (1999). The role of an early intervention on enhancing the quality of mother–infant interaction. *Child Development, 70,* 713–731.

Wenestam, C. G., & Wass, H. (1987). Swedish and U.S. children's thinking about death: A qualitative study and cross-cultural comparison. *Death Studies, 11,* 99–121.

Wentzel, K. R. (2003). Sociometric status and adjustment in middle school: A longitudinal study. *The Journal of Early Adolescence, 23,* 5–38.

Werker, J. F., & Fennell, C. T. (2009). Infant speech perception and later language acquisition: Methodological underpinnings. In J. Colombo, P. McCardle, & L. Freund (Eds.), *Infant pathways to language: Methods, models, and research disorders* (pp. 85–98). New York, NY: Psychology Press.

Werner, E. E., & Smith, R. S. (1982). *Vulnerable but invincible: A study of resilient children.* New York, NY: McGraw-Hill.

Werner, E. E., & Smith, R. S. (1992). *Overcoming the odds: High-risk children from birth to adulthood.* Ithaca, NY: Cornell University Press.

Werner, E. E., & Smith, R. S. (2001). *Journeys from childhood to midlife: Risk, resilience, and recovery.* Ithaca, NY: Cornell University Press.

Werner, E., Dawson, G., Osterling, J., & Dinno, N. (2000). Recognition of autism spectrum disorder before one year of age. A retrospective study based on home videotapes. *Journal of Autism & Developmental Disorders, 30,* 157–162.

Werner, L. A., & Marean, G. C. (1996). *Human auditory development.* Boulder, CO: Westview Press.

Werner, L. A., & Marean, G. C. (1996). *Human auditory development.* Madison, WI: Brown & Benchmark.

Westfall, R. E., & Benoit, C. (2004). The rhetoric of "natural" in natural childbirth: Childbearing women's perspectives on prolonged pregnancy and induction of labour. *Social Science & Medicine, 59,* 1397–1408.

Westling, E., Andrews, J. A., Hampson, S. E., & Peterson, M. (2008). Pubertal timing and substance use: The effects of gender, parental monitoring and deviant peers. *Journal of Adolescent Health, 42,* 555–563.

Westman, M., & Etzion, D. (2001). The impact of vacation and job stress on burnout and absenteeism. *Psychology & Health, 16* (Special issue: Burnout and health), 595–606.

Westoff, C. F. (2003). *Trends in marriage and early childbearing in developing countries.* DHS Comparative Reports No. 5. Calverton, MD: ORC Macro.

Wethington, E., Kessler, R., & Pixley, J. (2004). Turning points in adulthood. In G. Brim, C. D. Ryff, & R. Kessler (Eds.), *How healthy are we?: A national study of well-being at midlife.* Chicago, IL: University of Chicago Press.

Whalen, C. K. (2000). Attention deficit hyperactivity disorder. In A. Kazdin (Ed.), *Encyclopedia of psychology.* Washington, DC: American Psychological Association.

Whaley, D. E. (2007). A life span developmental approach to studying sport and exercise behavior. In G. Tenenbaum & R. C. Eklund (Eds.), *Handbook of sport psychology* (3rd ed., pp. 645–661).

Whitaker, R. C., Wright, J. A., Pepe, M. S., Seidel, K. D., & Dietz, W. H. (1997). Predicting obesity in young adulthood from childhood and parental obesity. *The New England Journal of Medicine, 337,* 869–873.

Whitbourne, S. K. (1986). *The me I know: A study of adult identity.* New York, NY: Springer-Verlag.

Whitbourne, S. K. (2008). *The search for fulfillment: Life paths in adulthood.* New York, NY: Ballantine Books.

Whitbourne, S. K. (2009, November). Fulfillment at any age. *Psychology Today* blog post. Retrieved from http://www.psychologytoday.com/blog/fulfillment-anyage/200911/rewriting-shakespeares-view-later-life-no-longer-sans-everything

Whitbourne, S. K., & Sneed, J. R. (2004). The paradox of well-being, identity processes, and stereotype threat: Ageism and its potential relationships to the self in later life. In T. Nelson (Ed.), *Ageism: Stereotyping and prejudice against older persons* (pp. 247–276). Cambridge, MA: MIT Press.

Whitbourne, S. K., & Whitbourne, S. B. (2010). *Adult development and aging: Biopsychosocial perspectives.* New York: John Wiley & Sons.

White, L. (2001). Sibling relationships over the life course: A panel analysis. *Journal of Marriage and Family, 63,* 555–568.

White, M. J., & White, G. B. (2006). Implicit and explicit occupational gender stereotypes. *Sex Roles, 55,* 259–266.

White, N. R. (2002). "Not under my roof!" Young people's experience of home. *Youth and Society, 34,* 214–231.

Whitehead, B. (2001). How we mate. In M. Magnet (Ed.), *Modern sex: Liberation and its discontents* (pp. 5–26). Chicago, IL: Ivan R Dee.

Whitehead, D., Keast, J., Montgomery, V., & Hayman, S. (2004). A preventive health education program for osteoporosis. *Journal of Advanced Nursing, 47,* 15–24.

Whiting, B. B., & Edwards, C. P. (1988). *Children of different worlds: The formation of social behavior.* Cambridge, MA: Harvard University Press. Whitman, J. S. (2010). Lesbians and gay men at midlife. In M. H. Guindon (Ed.), *Self-esteem across the lifespan: Issues and interventions* (pp. 235–248). New York, NY: Routledge.

Whitty, M. (2002). Possible selves: An exploration of utility of a narrative approach. *Identity, 2,* 211–228.

Wichstrom, L. (1999). The emergence of gender difference in depressed mood during adolescence: The role of intensified gender socialization. *Developmental Psychology, 35,* 232–245.

Wiesner-Hanks, M. E. (2011). *Gender in history: Global perspectives.* New York, NY: Wiley.

Wigfield, A., Eccles, J. S., Yoon, K. S., Harold, R. D., Arbreton, A. J., Freedman-Doan, C., & Blumenfeld, P. C. (1997). Changes in children's competence beliefs and subjective task values across the elementary school years: A three-year study. *Journal of Educational Psychology, 89,* 451–469.

Wiggins, M., & Uwaydat, S. (2006). Age-related macular degeneration: Options for earlier detection and improved treatment. *The Journal of Family Practice, 55,* 22–27.

Wiggs, C. L., Weisberg, J., & Martin, A. (2006). Repetition priming across the adult lifespan—The long and short of it. *Aging, Neuropsychology, and Cognition, 13,* 308–325.

Wilcox, A. J., Weinberg, C. R., & Baird, D. D. (1995). Timing of sexual intercourse in relation to ovulation: Effects on the probability of conception, survival of the pregnancy, and sex of the baby. *New England Journal of Medicine, 333,* 1517–1519.

Wilcox, S., Evenson, K. R., Aragaki, A., Wassertheil Smoller, S., Mouton, C. P., & Loevinger, B. L. (2003). The effects of widowhood on physical and mental health, health behaviors, and health outcomes: The Women's Health Initiative. *Health Psychology, 22,* 513–522.

Wilcox, W. B. (2008). Focused on their families: Religion, parenting, and child well-being. In K. K. Kline (Ed.), *Authoritative communities:*

The scientific case for nurturing the whole child (pp. 227–244). The Search Institute series on developmentally attentive community and society. New York, NY: Springer.

Wilcox, W. B., & Marquart, E. (2010). *The state of our unions: Marriage in America, 2010.* Charlottesville, VA: National Marriage Project.

Wild, K., & Cotrell, V. (2003). Identifying driving impairment in Alzheimer disease: A comparison of self and observer reports versus driving evaluation. *Alzheimer Disease and Associated Disorders, 17,* 27–34.

Wiley, T. L., Nondahl, D. M., Cruickshanks, K. J., & Tweed, T. S. (2005). Five-year changes in middle ear function for older adults. *Journal of the American Academy of Audiology, 16,* 129–139.

Willford, Jennifer A., et al. (2004). Verbal and visuospatial learning and memory function in children with moderate prenatal alcohol exposure. Alcoholism: *Clinical and Experimental Research, 28*(3), 497–507.

Williams, A. F., & Ferguson, S. A. (2002). Rationale for graduated licensing and the risks it should address. *Injury Prevention, 8* (Suppl. II), ii9–ii16.

Williams, A. F., Tefft, B. C., & Grabowski, J. G. (2012). Graduated driver licensing research, 2010-present. *Journal of Safety Research, 43*(3), 195–203.

Williams, A. L., Khattak, A. Z., Garza, C. N., & Lasky, R. E. (2009). The behavioral pain response to heelstick in preterm neonates studied longitudinally: Description, development, determinants, and components. *Early Human Development, 85,* 369–374.

Williams, D. R. (2005). The health of U.S. racial and ethnic populations. *Journals of Gerontology, 60B*(Special Issue II), 53–62.

Williams, J. M., & Dunlop, L. C. (1999). Pubertal timing and self-reported delinquency among male adolescents. *Journal of Adolescence, 22,* 157–171.

Williams, K., & Dunne-Bryant, A. (2006). Divorce and adult psychological well-being: Clarifying the role of gender and child age. *Journal of Marriage and Family, 68,* 1178–1196.

Williams, L. R., Degnan, K. A., Perez-Edgar, K. E., Henderson, H. A., Rubin, K. H., Pine, D. S., et al. (2009). Impact of behavioral inhibition and parenting style on internalizing and externalizing problems from early childhood through adolescence. *Journal of Abnormal Child Psychology, 37,* 1063–1075.

Williams, M. H. (2005). *Nutrition for health, fitness, and sport* (7th ed.). New York, NY: McGraw-Hill.

Willinger, M., Ko, C.-W., Hoffman, J. J., Kessler, R. C., & Corwin, M. J. (2003). Trends in infant bed sharing in the United States. *Archives of Pediatrics and Adolescent Medicine, 157,* 43–49.

Willis, S. L., & Schaie, K. W. (1999). Intellectual functioning in midlife. In S. L. Willis & J. D. Reid (Eds.), *Life in the middle* (pp. 105–146). San Diego, CA: Academic Press.

Willis, S., Tennstedt, S., Marsiske, M., Ball, K., Elias, J., Koepke, K.,...Wright, E. (2006). Long-term effects of cognitive training on everyday functional outcomes in older adults. *JAMA: Journal of the American Medical Association, 296,* 2805–2814.

Wilson, D. K., Kirtland, K. A., Ainsworth, B. E., & Addy, C. L. (2004). Socioeconomic status and perceptions of access and safety for physical activity. *Annals of Behavioral Medicine, 28,* 20–28.

Wilson, E. O. (2012). *The social conquest of earth.* New York, NY: W.W. Norton.

Wilson, J. (2009). *Mourning the unborn dead: A Buddhist ritual comes to America.* New York, NY: Oxford University Press.

Wilson, J. Q., & Herrnstein, R. J. (1985). *Crime and human nature.* New York, NY: Simon and Schuster.

Wilson, L. B., & Harlow-Rosentraub, K. (2008). Providing new opportunities for volunteerism and civic engagement for boomers: Chaos theory redefined. In R. B. Hudson (Ed.), *Boomer bust? Economic and political issues of the graying society* (Vol. 2, pp. 79–98). Westport, CT: Praeger.

Wilson, R. S., Mendes De Leon, C. F., Barnes, L. L, Schneider, J. A., Bienias, J. L., Evans, D. A., & Bennett, D. A. (2002). Participation in cognitively stimulating activities and risk of incident Alzheimer disease. *JAMA: Journal of the American Medical Association, 287,* 742–748.

Wilson, W. J. (1996). *When work disappears: The world of the new urban poor.* New York, NY: Knopf.

Wilson, W. J. (2006). *Social theory and the concept "underclass."* In D. B. Grusky & R. Kanbur (Eds.), *Poverty and inequality: Studies in social inequality* (pp. 103–116). Stanford, CA: Stanford University Press.

Wingfield, A., Tun, P. A., & McCoy, S. L. (2005). Hearing loss in older adulthood: What it is and how it interacts with cognitive performance. *Current Directions in Psychological Science, 14,* 144–147.

Wink, P., & Dillon, M. (2003). Religiousness, spirituality, and psychosocial functioning in late adulthood: Findings from a longitudinal study. *Psychology and Aging, 18,* 916–924.

Winsler, A., Fernyhough, C., & Montero, I. (Eds.). (2009). Private speech, executive functioning, and the development of verbal self-regulation. Cambridge: Cambridge University Press.

Winn, R., & Newton, N. (1982). Sexual activity in aging: A study of 106 cultures. *Archives of Sexual Behavior, 11,* 283–298.

Winterich, J. (2003). Sex, menopause, and culture: Sexual orientation and the meaning of menopause for women's sex lives. *Gender & Society, 17,* 627–642.

Wiscott, R., & Kopera-Frye, K. (2000). Sharing of culture: Adult grandchildren's perceptions of intergenerational relations. *International Journal of Aging and Human Development, 5,* 199–215.

Witherington, D. C., Campos, J. J., Anderson, D. I., Lejeune, L., & Seah, E. (2005). Avoidance of heights on the Visual Cliff in newly walking infants. *Infancy, 7,* 285–298.

Wolak, J., Mitchell, K. J., & Finkelhor, D. (2007). Does online harassment constitute bullying? An exploration of online harassment by known peers and online-only contacts. *Journal of Adolescent Health, 41*(Suppl. 6), S51–S58.

Wolbers, M. H. J. (2007). Patterns of labor market entry: A comparative perspective on school-to-work transitions in 11 European countries. *Acta Sociologica, 50,* 189–210.

Wolf, J. B. (2007). Is breast really best? Risk and total motherhood in the national breastfeeding awareness campaign. *Journal of Health Politics, Policy and Law, 32,* 595–63.

Wong, C. A. (1997, April). *What does it mean to be African-American or European-American growing up in a multi-ethnic community?* Paper presented at the biennial meeting of the Society for Research in Child Development, Washington, DC.

Wong, S., Chan, K., Wong, V., & Wong, W. (2002). Use of chopsticks in Chinese children. *Child: Care, Health, & Development, 28,* 157–161.

Wood, A. G., Harvey, A. S., Wellard, R. M., Abbott, D. F., Anderson, V., Kean, M.,...Jackson, G. D. (2004). Language cortex activation in normal children. *Neurology, 63,* 1035–1044.

Wood, E., Desmarais, S., & Gugula, S. (2002). The impact of parenting experience on gender stereotyped toy play of children. *Sex Roles, 47,* 39–49.

Wood, R. M., & Gustafson, G. E. (2001). Infant crying and adults' anticipated caregiving responses: Acoustic and contextual influences. *Child Development, 72,* 1287–1300.

Woodhall, S. C., Lehtinen, M., Verho, T., Huhtala, H., Hokkanen, M., & Kosunen, E. (2007). Anticipated acceptance of HPV vaccination at the baseline of implementation: A survey of parental and adolescent knowledge and attitudes in Finland. *Journal of Adolescent Health, 40,* 466–469.

Woodward, A. L., & Markman, E. M. (1998). Early word learning. In W. Damon (Ed.), & D. Kuhn & R. S. Siegler (Vol. Eds.), *Handbook of child psychology: Vol. 2. Cognition, perception and language* (5th ed., pp. 371–420). New York, NY: Wiley.

Woodward, E. H., & Gridina, N. (2000). *Media in the home, 2000: The fifth annual survey of parents and children*. Philadelphia, PA: The Annenberg Public Policy Center of the University of Pennsylvania. Available: http://www.appcpenn.org/mediainhome/survey/survey7.pdf

Woodward, L., & Fergusson, D. (1999). Early conduct problems and later risk of teenage pregnancy in girls. *Development and Psychopathology, 11,* 127–142.

Woodward, L., Fergusson, D. M., & Belsky, J. (2000). Timing of parental separation and attachment to parents in adolescence: Results of a prospective study from birth to age 16. *Journal of Marriage & the Family, 62,* 162–174.

Woody, D., III, & Woody, D. J. (2007). The significance of social support on parenting among a group of single, low-income, African American mothers. *Journal of Human Behavior in the Social Environment, 15,* 183–198.

Worden, W. J. (2009). *Grief counseling and grief therapy: A handbook for the mental health practitioner* (4th ed.). New York, NY: Springer.

World Bank (2011). India's undernourished children: A call for action. Retrieved from http://web.worldbank.org/WBSITE/EXTERNAL/COUNTRIES/SOUTHASIAEXT/0,,contentMDK:20916955~pagePK:146736~piPK:146830~theSitePK:223547,00.html

World Education Services. (2005). World education database. Retrieved from www.wes.org

World Federation of Right to Die Soçieties. (2006). Public opinion. Retrieved from www.worldrtd.net

World Health Organization (WHO) (1999). *Death rates from coronary heart disease*. Geneva, Switzerland: Author.

World Health Organization (WHO) (2000). *Healthy life expectancy rankings*. Geneva, Switzerland: Author.

World Health Organization (WHO) (2000). WHO Global Data Bank on Breastfeeding. Available: http://www.who.int/nut/db_bfd.htm.

World Health Organization (WHO) (2001). *The World Health Report 2001. Mental health: New understanding, new hope*. Retrieved from http://www.who.int/whr2001/2001/main/en/index.htm

World Health Organization (WHO) (2002). Micronutrient deficiencies. Retrieved from http://www.who.int/nut/#mic

World Health Organization (WHO) (2004). *Infecundity, infertility, and childlessness in developing countries. Demographic and Health Surveys (DHS) Comparative reports No. 9*. Geneva, Switzerland: Author.

World Health Organization (WHO) (2008). *Inequalities in young people's health: Health behavior in school-aged children*. Retrieved from http://www.hbsc.org/

World Health Organization (WHO) (2008). Significant caries index: Data for some selected countries. Retrieved from www.whocollab.od.mah.se/sicdata.html

World Health Organization (WHO) (2008). *World report on child injury prevention*. Retrieved from http://whqlibdoc.who.int/publications/2008/9789241563574_eng.pdf?ua=1

World Health Organization (WHO) (2008). *Worldwide prevalence of anaemia*. Geneva, Switzerland: Author.

World Health Organization (WHO) (2009). *Department of making pregnancy safer: Annual report*. Geneva, Switzerland: Author.

World Health Organization (WHO) (2010). Method of delivery and pregnancy outcomes in Asia: The WHO global survey on maternal and perinatal health, 2007–2008. *The Lancet, 375,* 490–499.

World Health Organization (WHO) (2009). *Monitoring emergency obstetric care: A handbook*. Geneva, Switzerland: Author.

World Health Organization (WHO) (2010). *Towards universal access: Scaling up priority HIV/AIDS interventions in the health sector*. Geneva, Switzerland: Author.

World Health Organization (WHO) (2010). *World Health Statistics 2010*. Geneva, Switzerland: Author.

World Health Organization (WHO) (2010). WHO vaccine-preventable diseases: Monitoring system—2010 global summary. Geneva, Switzerland: Author.

World Health Organization (WHO) (2011). Cigarette consumption. Retrieved February 21, 2011, from http://www.who.int/tobacco/en/atlas8.pdf

World Health Organization (WHO) (2011). *Vacuum extraction versus forceps for assisted vaginal delivery*. Retrieved from http://apps.who.int/rhl/pregnancy_childbirth/childbirth/2nd_stage/facom/en/

World Health Organization (WHO) (2012). *Social determinants of health and well-being among young people: Health behavior in school-aged children*. Retrieved from http://www.euro.who.int/__data/assets/pdf_file/0003/163857/Social-determinants-of-health-and-well-being-among-young-people.pdf?ua=1

World Health Organization (WHO) (2013). *World malaria report*. Geneva, Switzerland: Author.

World Health Organization (WHO) (2014). *Fact sheet: Top 10 causes of death*. Geneva, Switzerland: Author. Retrieved from http://www.who.int/mediacentre/factsheets/fs310/en/

World Health Organization (WHO) (2014). *World health statistics*. Geneva, Switzerland: Author.

World Health Organization, Multicentre Growth Reference Study Group (2006). *WHO child growth standards: Length/height-for-age, weight-for-age, weight-for-length, weight-for-height and body mass index-for-age*. Geneva, Switzerland: World Health Organization. Retrieved from http://www.who.int/childgrowth/standards/en/

World Internet Project (2008). Center for the digital future at USC Annenberg with 13 partner countries release the first World Internet Project report. Retrieved from http://www.worldinternetproject.net

Worthman, C. M. (1987). Interactions of physical maturation and cultural practice in ontogeny: Kikuyu adolescents. *Cultural Anthropology, 2,* 29–38.

Wrangham, R. (2009). *Catching fire: How cooking made us human*. New York, NY: Basic Books.

Wright, A. A., & Katz, I. T. (2007). Letting go of the rope: Aggressive treatment, hospice care, and open access. *New England Journal of Medicine, 357,* 324–327.

Wright, V. C., Schieve, L. A., Reynolds, M. A., Jeng, G., & Kissin, D. (2004). Assisted reproductive technology surveillance—United States 2001. *Morbidity and Mortality Weekly Report, 53,* 1–20.

Wrosch, C., Heckhausen, J., & Lachman, M. E. (2000). Primary and secondary control strategies for managing health and financial stress across adulthood. *Psychology and Aging, 15,* 387–399.

Wrotniak, B. H., Epstein, L. H., Raluch, R. A., & Roemmich, J. N. (2004). Parent weight change as a predictor of child weight change in family-based behavioral obesity treatment. *Archives of Pediatric and Adolescent Medicine, 158,* 342–347.

Wu, L., Schlenger, W., & Galvin, D. (2003). The relationship between employment and substance abuse among students aged 12 to 17. *Journal of Adolescent Health, 32,* 5–15.

Wu, Z. (1999). Premarital cohabitation and the timing of first marriage. *Canadian Review of Sociology and Anthropology, 36,* 109–127.

Xue, Y., & Meisels, S. J. (2004). Early literacy instruction and learning in kindergarten: Evidence from the early childhood longitudinal study—kindergarten classes of 1998–1999. *American Educational Research Journal, 41,* 191–229.

Yaffe, K., Fox, P., Newcomer, R., Sands, L., Lindquist, K., Dane, K., & Covinsky, K. E. (2002). Patient and caregiver characteristics and nursing home placement in patients with dementia. *JAMA: Journal of the American Medical Association, 287,* 2090–2097.

Yang, B., Ollendick, T. H., Dong, Q., Xia, Y., & Lin, L. (1995). Only children and children with siblings in the People's Republic of China: Levels of fear, anxiety, and depression. *Child Development, 66,* 1301–1311.

Yang, S. C., & Chen, S.-F. (2002). A phenomenographic approach to the meaning of death: A Chinese perspective. *Death Studies, 26,* 143–175.

Yang, Y. (2006). How does functional disability affect depressive symptoms in late life? The role of perceived social support and psychological resources. *Journal of Health and Social Behavior, 47,* 355–372.

Yasui, M., Dorham, C. L., & Dishion, T. J. (2004). Ethnic identity and psychological adjustment: A validity analysis for European American and African American adolescents. *Journal of Adolescent Research, 19,* 807–825.

Yasuko, S., & Megumi, F. (2010). *Living to a grand old age in Japan.* Retrieved from http://generalhealthtopics.com/living-grand-old-age-japan-352.html

Ye, L., Pien, G. W., & Weaver, T. E. (2009). Gender differences in the clinical manifestation of obstructive sleep apnea. *Sleep Medicine, 10,* 1075–1084.

Yeh, H.-C., Lorenz, F. O., Wickrama, K. A. S., Cogner, R. D., & Elder, G. H., Jr. (2006). Relationships among sexual satisfaction, marital quality, and marital instability at midlife. *Journal of Family Psychology, 20,* 339–343.

Yeung, D. Y. L., & Tang, C. S.-K., & Lee, A. (2005). Psychosocial and cultural factors influencing expectations of menarche: A study on Chinese premenarcheal teenage girls. *Journal of Adolescent Research, 20,* 118–135.

Yoos, H. L., Kitzman, H., Halterman, J. S., Henderson, C., Sidora-Arcoleo, K., & McMullen, A. (2006). Treatment regimens and health care utilization in children with persistent asthma symptoms. *Journal of Asthma, 43,* 385–391.

Youn, G., Knight, B. G., Jeon, H., & Benton, D. (1999). Differences in familism values among Korean, Korean American, and White American dementia caregivers. *Psychology and Aging, 14,* 355–364.

Young, K. S. (2008). Internet sex addiction risk factors, stages of development, and treatment. *American Behavioral Scientist, 52,* 21–37.

Young-Hyman, D., Schlundt, D. G., Herman-Wenderoth, L., & Bozylinski, K. (2003). Obesity, appearance, and psychosocial adaptation in young African American children. *Journal of Pediatric Psychology, 28,* 463–472.

Youniss, J., & Smollar, J. (1985). *Adolescent relations with mothers, fathers, and friends.* Chicago, IL: University of Chicago Press.

Youniss, J., McLellan, J. A., & Yates, M. (1999). Religion, community service, and identity in American youth. *Journal of Adolescence, 22,* 243–253.

Zach, T., Pramanik, A., & Ford, S. P. (2001). Multiple births. *eMedicine.* Retrieved from www.mypage.direct.ca/csamson/multiples/2twinningrates.html

Zachrisson, H. D., Dearing, E., Lekhal, R., & Toppelberg, C. O. (2013). Little evidence that time in child care causes externalizing problems during early childhood in Norway. *Child Development, 84,* 1152–1170.

Zaidi, A., Mattia, M., Fuchs, M., Lipszyc, B., Lelkes, M. R., Marin, B., & de Vos, K. (2006). *Poverty of elderly people in EU25.* Report submitted to the European Commission. Vienna, Austria: European Centre for Social Welfare Policy and Research.

Zald, D. H. (2003). The human amygdala and the emotional evaluation of sensory stimuli. *Brain Research Review, 41,* 88–123.

Zapf, D., Seifert, C., Schmutte, B., Mertini, H., & Hotz, M. (2001). Emotion work and job stressors and their effects on burnout. *Psychology and Health, 16,* 527–545.

Zarit, S. H., & Eggebeen, D. J. (2002). Parent–child relationships in adulthood and later years. In M. H. Bornstein (Ed.), *Handbook of parenting, Vol. 1* (2nd ed., pp. 135–161). Mahwah, NJ: Erlbaum.

Zehle, K., Wen, L. M., Orr, N., & Rissel, C. (2007). "It's not an issue at the moment": A qualitative study of mothers about childhood obesity. *MCN: The American Journal of Maternal/Child Nursing, 32,* 36–41.

Zeijl, E., te Poel, Y., de Bois-Reymond, M., Ravesloot, J., & Meulmann, J. J. (2000). The role of parents and peers in the leisure activities of young adolescents. *Journal of Leisure Research, 32,* 281–302.

Zeserson, J. M. (2001). Chi no michi as metaphor: Conversations with Japanese women about menopause. *Anthropology & Medicine, 8,* 177–199.

Zeskind, P. S., & Lester, B. M. (2001). Analysis of infant crying. In L. T. Singer & P. S. Zeskind (Eds.), *Biobehavioral assessment of the infant* (pp. 149–166). New York, NY: Guilford.

Zeskind, P. S., Klein, L., & Marshall, T. R. (1992). Adults' perceptions of experimental modifications of durations and expiratory sounds in infant crying. *Developmental Psychology, 28,* 1153–1162.

Zhan, H. J., Feng, X., & Luo, B. (2008). Placing elderly parents in institutions in urban China: A reinterpretation of filial piety. *Research on Aging, 30,* 543–571.

Zhang, Q. F. (2004). Economic transition and new patterns of parent–child coresidence in urban China. *Journal of Marriage and Family, 66,* 1231–1245.

Zhang, W. (2009). How do we think about death?—A cultural glance of superstitious ideas from Chinese and Western ghost festivals. *International Education Studies, 2,* 68–71.

Zhang, W., & Fuligni, A. J. (2006). Authority, autonomy, and family relationships among adolescents in urban and rural China. *Journal of Research on Adolescence, 16,* 527–537.

Zhang, W., & Wang, Y. (2010). Meal and residence rotation of elderly parents in contemporary rural Northern China. *Journal of Cross–Cultural Gerontology, 25,* 217–237.

Zhang, Y., & Scarpace, P. J. (2006). The role of leptin in leptin resistance and obesity. *Physiology & Behavior, 88,* 249–256.

Zhao, S., Grasmuck, S., & Martin, J. (2008). Identity construction on Facebook: Digital empowerment in anchored relationships. *Computers in Human Behavior, 24,* 1816–1836.

Zhong, J., & Arnett, J. J. (2014). Conceptions of adulthood among migrant women workers in China. *International Journal of Behavioral Development, 38,* 255–265.

Zielinski, D. S. (2009). Child maltreatment and adult socioeconomic well-being. *Child Abuse and Neglect, 33,* 666–678.

Zigler, E., & Styfco, S. J. (Eds.). (2004). *The Head Start debates.* Baltimore, MD: Brookes.

Zimmerman, M. A., Copeland, L. A., Shope, J. T., & Dielman, T. E. (1997). A longitudinal study of self-esteem: Implications for adolescent development. *Journal of Youth and Adolescence, 26,* 117–141.

Zimmermann, M. B., Pieter, L. J., & Chandrakant, S. P. (2008). Iodine-deficiency disorders. *The Lancet, 372,* 1251–1262.

Zuckerman, P. (2008). *Society without God: What the least religious nations can tell us about contentment.* New York: New York University Press.

Zumwalt, M. (2008). Effects of the menstrual cycle on the acquisition of peak bone mass. In J. J. Robert-McComb, R. Norman, & M. Zumwalt (Eds.), *The active female: Health issues throughout the lifespan* (pp. 141–151). Totowa, NJ: Humana Press.

Zuzanek, J. (2000). *The effects of time use and time pressure on child–parent relationships.* Waterloo, Ontario, Canada: Otium.

Answers

Chapter 1

Practice Quiz (p. 10)

1. d; 2. b; 3. a; 4. a; 5. a

Practice Quiz (p. 16)

1. b; 2. b; 3. c; 4. c; 5. a

Practice Quiz (p. 21)

1. b; 2. c; 3. b

Practice Quiz (p. 28)

1. c; 2. b; 3. d; 4. c; 5. a

Practice Quiz (p. 33)

1. d; 2. b; 3. c; 4. c; 5. c

Research Focus (p. 37)

1. c; 2. a

Practice Quiz (p. 41)

1. b; 2. b; 3. c; 4. c; 5. a

Chapter Quiz (pp. 42–43)

1. b; 2. a; 3. d; 4. c;
5. c; 6. c; 7. b; 8. b;
9. c; 10. d; 11. a; 12. b;
13. a; 14. c; 15. d

Chapter 2

Practice Quiz (p. 51)

1. b; 2. b; 3. c; 4. c; 5. a

Research Focus (p. 56)

1. d; 2. c

Practice Quiz (p. 56)

1. b; 2. a; 3. c; 4. c; 5. d

Practice Quiz (p. 59)

1. d; 2. c; 3. c; 4. b; 5. a

Practice Quiz (p. 64)

1. a; 2. a; 3. c; 4. c; 5. c

Practice Quiz (p. 71)

1. d; 2. b; 3. a; 4. b; 5. a

Practice Quiz (p. 75)

1. d; 2. c; 3. c; 4. c; 5. a

Practice Quiz (p. 78)

1. b; 2. a; 3. c; 4. c

Chapter Quiz (pp. 80–81)

1. b; 2. b; 3. a; 4. c;
5. a; 6. d; 7. d; 8. b;
9. d; 10. c; 11. c; 12. b;

13. b; 14. b; 15. d; 16. c;
17. d; 18. d

Chapter 3

Practice Quiz (p. 88)

1. b; 2. a; 3. d; 4. b; 5. d

Practice Quiz (p. 98)

1. b; 2. a; 3. d; 4. d; 5. b

Practice Quiz (p. 104)

1. c; 2. a; 3. b; 4. d; 5. d

Practice Quiz (p. 110)

1. a; 2. d; 3. d; 4. d; 5. b

Research Focus (p. 117)

1. b; 2. c

Practice Quiz (p. 118)

1. c; 2. d; 3. a; 4. d; 5. c

Practice Quiz (p. 124)

1. d; 2. a; 3. c; 4. c; 5. a

Chapter Quiz (pp. 125–127)

1. c; 2. a; 3. c; 4. a;
5. d; 6. c; 7. b; 8. a;
9. b; 10. c; 11. b; 12. c;
13. a; 14. d; 15. d; 16. b

Chapter 4

Practice Quiz (p. 138)

1. d; 2. a; 3. d; 4. c; 5. c

Practice Quiz (p. 143)

1. c; 2. b; 3. a; 4. b; 5. d

Practice Quiz (p. 148)

1. c; 2. a; 3. c; 4. c; 5. c

Practice Quiz (p. 155)

1. c; 2. a; 3. a; 4. c; 5. a

Practice Quiz (p. 158)

1. b; 2. a; 3. c; 4. b; 5. a

Practice Quiz (p. 161)

1. b; 2. a; 3. d; 4. c

Practice Quiz (p. 165)

1. b; 2. c; 3. c; 4. c; 5. b

Research Focus (p. 169)

1. d; 2. b

Practice Quiz (p. 170)

1. c; 2. a; 3. a; 4. c; 5. a

Practice Quiz (p. 174)

1. c; 2. b; 3. b; 4. c; 5. d

Practice Quiz (p. 177)

1. d; 2. a; 3. c; 4. d; 5. b

Chapter Quiz (pp. 178–179)

1. b; 2. b; 3. b; 4. a;
5. c; 6. b; 7. b; 8. d;
9. c; 10. a; 11. c; 12. a;
13. c; 14. a; 15. c; 16. d;
17. a; 18. c; 19. c; 20. b;
21. b; 22. d; 23. b

Chapter 5

Practice Quiz (p. 188)

1. c; 2. a; 3. d; 4. c; 5. a

Practice Quiz (p. 191)

1. c; 2. b; 3. a; 4. d; 5. a

Practice Quiz (p. 197)

1. d; 2. a; 3. b; 4. c; 5. a

Practice Quiz (p. 205)

1. b; 2. a; 3. c; 4. d; 5. a

Research Focus (p. 218)

1. b; 2. d

Practice Quiz (p. 212)

1. b; 2. c; 3. c; 4. c; 5. c

Practice Quiz (p. 221)

1. b; 2. a; 3. c; 4. a; 5. b

Practice Quiz (p. 228)

1. d; 2. b; 3. c; 4. b; 5. d

Chapter Quiz (pp. 230–231)

1. d; 2. b; 3. a; 4. b;
5. d; 6. a; 7. b; 8. a;
9. c; 10. c; 11. a; 12. b;
13. d; 14. b; 15. c; 16. c;
17. b; 18. d; 19. b; 20. b;
21. c

Chapter 6

Practice Quiz (p. 239)

1. d; 2. a; 3. b; 4. c; 5. a

Practice Quiz (p. 242)

1. d; 2. a; 3. c; 4. a; 5. a

Practice Quiz (p. 250)

1. d; 2. a; 3. d; 4. a; 5. a

Practice Quiz (p. 254)

1. b; 2. a; 3. d; 4. a; 5. c

Practice Quiz (p. 257)

1. b; 2. a; 3. d; 4. c

Practice Quiz (p. 265)

1. c; 2. a; 3. c; 4. c; 5. d

Practice Quiz (p. 273)

1. c; 2. a; 3. c; 4. a; 5. a

Research Focus (p. 279)

1. c

Practice Quiz (p. 283)

1. a; 2. a; 3. c; 4. b; 5. a

Chapter Quiz (pp. 285–287)

1. a; 2. d; 3. c; 4. d;
5. a; 6. b; 7. c; 8. a;
9. c; 10. b; 11. a; 12. c;
13. d; 14. a; 15. c; 16. c;
17. c; 18. b; 19. b; 20. c;
21. a; 22. b

Chapter 7

Practice Quiz (p. 294)

1. b; 2. b; 3. c; 4. c; 5. a

Practice Quiz (p. 298)

1. d; 2. a; 3. c; 4. c; 5. a

Practice Quiz (p. 311)

1. d; 2. c; 3. c; 4. c; 5. a

Practice Quiz (p. 314)

1. c; 2. a; 3. b; 4. c

Practice Quiz (p. 320)

1. d; 2. a; 3. d; 4. a; 5. a

Practice Quiz (p. 328)

1. c; 2. a; 3. c; 4. c; 5. a

Practice Quiz (p. 343)

1. a; 2. a; 3. c; 4. c; 5. a

Research Focus (p. 343)

1. b

Chapter Quiz (pp. 345–347)

1. b; 2. a; 3. a; 4. b;
5. a; 6. b; 7. c; 8. a;
9. d; 10. c; 11. b; 12. a;
13. a; 14. c; 15. a; 16. b;
17. b; 18. a; 19. c

Chapter 8

Practice Quiz (p. 357)

1. b; 2. c; 3. c; 4. b; 5. a

Practice Quiz (p. 362)

1. b; 2. a; 3. c; 4. a; 5. a

Practice Quiz (p. 369)

1. b; 2. b; 3. c; 4. c; 5. a

Practice Quiz (p. 375)

1. b; 2. c; 3. b; 4. c; 5. a

Practice Quiz (p. 381)

1. b; 2. d; 3. a; 4. c; 5. a; 6. b

Practice Quiz (p. 385)

1. b; 2. b; 3. c; 4. c

Research Focus (p. 388)

1. b

Practice Quiz (pp. 397–398)

1. c; 2. a; 3. c; 4. b; 5. c

Practice Quiz (p. 402)

1. a; 2. a; 3. c; 4. c; 5. d

Chapter Quiz (pp. 404–405)

1. b; 2. b; 3. c; 4. a;
5. b; 6. a; 7. d; 8. b;
9. a; 10. c; 11. c; 12. d;
13. b; 14. b; 15. c; 16. a;
17. b; 18. c; 19. a; 20. c;
21. d; 22. d; 23. c; 24. b

Chapter 9

Practice Quiz (p. 414)

1. b; 2. a; 3. d; 4. c; 5. a

Practice Quiz (p. 417)

1. b; 2. b; 3. c; 4. c; 5. b

Research Focus (p. 420)

1. b; 2. c

Practice Quiz (p. 422)

1. b; 2. b; 3. d; 4. c; 5. a

Practice Quiz (p. 425)

1. b; 2. b; 3. c; 4. c; 5. b

Practice Quiz (p. 433)

1. b; 2. b; 3. c; 4. c; 5. a

Practice Quiz (p. 442)

1. c; 2. b; 3. c; 4. c; 5. a

Practice Quiz (p. 445)

1. c; 2. a; 3. c; 4. a

Practice Quiz (p. 456)

1. b; 2. b; 3. c; 4. b; 5. a

Chapter Quiz (pp. 458–459)

1. a; 2. b; 3. d; 4. c;
5. b; 6. d; 7. d; 8. d;
9. b; 10. d; 11. a; 12. b;
13. c; 14. c; 15. c; 16. c;
17. a; 18. c; 19. b

Chapter 10

Practice Quiz (p. 466)

1. b; 2. b; 3. c; 4. c; 5. a

Research Focus (p. 467)

1. a; 2. c

Practice Quiz (p. 471)

1. c; 2. b; 3. b; 4. b; 5. d

Practice Quiz (p. 475)

1. b; 2. c; 3. c; 4. c; 5. c

Practice Quiz (p. 478)

1. b; 2. b; 3. c; 4. d; 5. c

Practice Quiz (p. 482)

1. b; 2. b; 3. c; 4. b; 5. b

Practice Quiz (p. 503)

1. a; 2. b; 3. b; 4. b; 5. a;
6. b; 7. a; 8. c

Chapter Quiz (pp. 505–507)

1. b; 2. c; 3. b; 4. a;
5. b; 6. d; 7. c; 8. c;
9. b; 10. c; 11. d; 12. b;
13. c; 14. c; 15. d; 16. a;
17. a; 18. c; 19. c

Chapter 11

Practice Quiz (p. 514)

1. a; 2. b; 3. c; 4. b; 5. b

Practice Quiz (p. 520)

1. b; 2. c; 3. b; 4. b; 5. a

Research Focus (p. 525)

1. c; 2. a

Practice Quiz (p. 529)

1. b; 2. d; 3. c; 4. b; 5. a

Practice Quiz (p. 531)

1. c; 2. b; 3. c; 4. b; 5. a

Practice Quiz (p. 539)

1. b; 2. b; 3. b; 4. c; 5. a

Practice Quiz (p. 552)

1. b; 2. b; 3. c; 4. c; 5. a

Chapter Quiz (pp. 554–555)

1. b; 2. d; 3. c; 4. b;
5. d; 6. d; 7. a; 8. d;
9. c; 10. a; 11. b; 12. c;
13. a; 14. c; 15. c; 16. d

Chapter 12

Practice Quiz (p. 564)

1. d; 2. c; 3. d; 4. b; 5. d

Practice Quiz (p. 569)

1. d; 2. d; 3. d; 4. b; 5. d

Practice Quiz (p. 575)

1. d; 2. a; 3. d; 4. b; 5. a

Practice Quiz (p. 582)

1. d; 2. d; 3. b; 4. b; 5. d

Practice Quiz (p. 586)

1. d; 2. a; 3. d; 4. b; 5. d

Practice Quiz (p. 591)

1. c; 2. d; 3. d; 4. b; 5. d

Research Focus (p. 604)

1. a

Practice Quiz (p. 607)

1. d; 2. b; 3. d; 4. c; 5. d

Chapter Quiz (pp. 608–609)

1. b; 2. c; 3. c; 4. b;
5. d; 6. c; 7. b; 8. a;
9. b; 10. c; 11. c; 12. d;
13. d; 14. c; 15. b; 16. a;
17. b; 18. c

Chapter 13

Research Focus (p. 619)

1. b; 2. d

Practice Quiz (p. 620)

1. b; 2. c; 3. d; 4. d; 5. d

Practice Quiz (p. 625)

1. d; 2. d; 3. b; 4. d; 5. a

Practice Quiz (p. 630)

1. d; 2. d; 3. d; 4. b; 5. a

Practice Quiz (p. 632)

1. a; 2. d; 3. d; 4. b; 5. d

Practice Quiz (p. 635)

1. d; 2. a; 3. b; 4. d; 5. c

Practice Quiz (p. 644)

1. c; 2. b; 3. a; 4. d

Chapter Quiz (pp. 645–646)

1. b; 2. a; 3. c; 4. d;
5. b; 6. d; 7. b; 8. c;
9. d; 10. d; 11. a; 12. c;
13. a; 14. c

Credits

Text and Art

Chapter 1   **Figure 1.1, p. 5:** Source: Data from Ember, M. Ember, C.R. & Low, B.S. (2007). Comparing explanations of polygyny. Cross-Cultural Research, 41, 428–440; **Figure 1.4, p. 13:** Source: © Pearson Education, Inc. **Research Focus, p. 36–37:** Darwin, Charles. 1859. The Origin of the Species. London: John Murray.

Chapter 2   **Figure 2.8, p. 68:** Source: Moore, 1974; **Figure 2.9, p. 73:** Source: Reproductive Medicine Associates of New Jersey, 2002; **Figure 2.10, p. 76:** babycenter.com (2014). http://www.babycenter.com/0_chart-the-effect-of-age-on-fertility_6155.bc; **Extract, p. 76, "The womb must be…":** Source: Marsh, M., & Ronner, W. (1996). The empty cradle: Infertility in America from colonial times to the present. Baltimore, MD: Johns Hopkins University Press, p. 15

Chapter 3   **Extract, p. 88, "Attempting a vaginal birth…":** Source: WedMD(2011). Vaginal birth after cesarean (VBAC)-Risks of VBAC and cesarean deliveries. Retrieved from http://www.webmd.com/baby/tc/vaginal-birth-after-cesaran -vbac-risks-of-vbac-and-cesarean-deliveries. p. 2; **Extract, p. 89, "No one does more harm…":** Source: Cassidy, T. (2006). Birth: The surprising history of how we are born. New York, NY: Atlantic Monthly Press; **Extract, p. 95, "Rock in a rocking chair…":** Source: Mayo Clinic Staff(2011). Stages of Labor: Baby, it's time! Retrieved from; **Table 3.1, p. 100:** Source: Based on Apgar (1953); **Extract, p. 116, "should not infer…":** Source: IP, S., Chung, M., Rmana, G., Chew, P., Maguka, N., DeVine, D.,…Lau, J.(2007). Breastfeeding and maternal and infant health outcomes in developed countries. Evidence report/Technology Assessment No. 153. Rockville, MD. Agency for Healthcare Reseach and Quality; **Extract, p. 118, "Fussing: This is a kind of warm-up cry…":** Source: Wood, R.M., & Gustafson, G.E. (2001). Infant crying and adults' anticipated caregiving responses: Acoustic and contextual influences. Child Development, 72, 1287–1300; **Figure 3.2, p. 119:** Source: Barr, R.G. (2009) The phenomena of early infant crying and colic, Paper presented at the Centre for Community and Child Health, Melbourne Australia, March 2; **Table 3.3, p. 119:** Source: Barr, R.G. (2009) The phenomena of early infant crying and colic, Paper presented at the Centre for Community and Child Health, Melbourne Australia, March 2. [see http://www.purplecrying.info/sections/index.php?sct=1&]; **Extract, p. 120 "Lifting baby up…":** Source: Data from Eisenberg et al., 2011; **Extract, p. 120 "rule of threes":** Source: Barr, R.G. (2009) The phenomena of early infant crying and colic, Paper presented at the Centre for Community and Child Health, Melbourne Australia, March 2

Chapter 4   **Figure 4.4, p. 135:** Source: Based on Beckett, C., Maughan, B., Rutter, M., Castle, J., Colvert, E., Groothus, C, Sonuga-Barke, W.J.S. (2006) "Do the effects of early severe deprivation on cognition persist into early adolescence? Findings from the English and Romanian adoptees study", Child Development, 77, 696–711; **Extract, p. 137 "a form of child neglect…":** Source: DeLoache, J.S., & Gottlied, A. (2000). A world of babies: Imagined childcare guides for seven societies. New York, NY: Cambridge University Press; **Extract, p. 151 "two sides of the same cognitive coin":** Source: Flavell. J. H., Miller, P.H., & Miller, S. A.(2002). Congnitive development(4th ed.). Upper Saddle, NY: Prentice Hall. P. 5; **Table 4.3, p. 168:** Source: Based on Buss, K.A., & Plomin, R. (1984). Temperament: Early developing personality traits. Hillsdale, NJ: Erlbaum; Rithbart, M.K., Ahadi, S.A., & Evans, D. E. (2000), Temperament and personality: Origins and outcome. Journals of personality and Social Psychology, 78, 122–135; Thomas, A., Chess, S.(1977). Temperment and development. New York, NY: Brunner/Mazel.

Chapter 5   **Figure 5.1, p. 183:** Source: Based on National Center for Health Statistics; **Figure 5.2, p. 185:** Source: Data from THE POSTNATAL DEVELOPMENT OF THE HUMAN CEREBRAL CORTEX, VOLUMES I-VII, by J. LeRoy Conel, Cambridge, Mass: Harvard University Press; **Table 5.1, p. 187:** Source: Based on Adolph, K.E., & Berger, S. E.(2006). Motor development. In W. Damon & R. Lerner (Series Eds.), & D. Kuhn & R. Sieglery (Vol. Eds.), Handbook of child psychology: Vol 2. Cognition Perception and language (6th ed., pp. 161–213) New York, NY: Wiley; Bayley, N. (2005) Baylay scales of infant and toddler development, Third edition (Bayley-III. San Antonio, TX: Harcourt Assessment; Coovadia, H.M., & Writtenberg, D. F.(Eds.) (2004) Pediatrics and child health: A manual for health professionals in developing countries. (5th ed) New York: NY: Oxford University Press; Frankenburg, W. K., Dodds, J., Ancher, P., Sharpiro, H., & Bresnick, B. (1992). The Denver II: A major revision and restandardization of the Denver Development Screening Test. Pediatrics, 89, 91–97; Murkoff et al. (2006); **Table 5.2, p. 188:** Source: Based on Adolph, K.E., & Berger, S. E.(2006). Motor development. In W. Damon & R. Lerner (Series Eds.), & D. Kuhn & R. Sieglery (Vol. Eds.), Handbook of child psychology: Vol 2. Cognition Perception and language (6th ed., pp. 161–213) New York, NY: Wiley; Bayley, N. (2005) Baylay scales of infant and toddler development, Third edition (Bayley-III. San Antonio, TX: Harcourt Assessment; Coovadia, H.M., & Writtenberg, D. F.(Eds.)(2004) Pediatrics and child health: A manual for health professionals in developing countries. (5th ed) New York: NY: Oxford University Press; Frankenburg, W. K., Dodds, J., Ancher, P., Sharpiro, H., & Bresnick, B. (1992). The Denver II: A major revision and restandardization of the Denver Development Screening Test. Pediatrics, 89, 91–97; Murkoff et al. (2006); **Extract, p. 197 "the direction offered…":** Source: Rogoff, B. (1995). Observing sociocultural activities on three planes: Perticipatory appropriation, guided participation, and apprenticeship. In J. V. Wertsch, P. del Rio, & A. Alvarez(Eds.) Sociocultural studies of the mind (pp. 273–294). New York: NY: Cambridge University Press. p. 142; **Extract, p. 197–198 "Only language could have broken…":** Source: Leakey, R. (1994). The origins of human kind. New York, NY: Basic Books. p. 119; **Extract, p. 207 "Tantrums are a fact of toddler life…":** Source: Murkoff, H. E., Eisenberg, A., Mazel, S., & Hathway, S.E. (2003). What to expect the first year(2nd ed) New York, NY: Workman; **Figure 5.4, p. 220:** Source: van IJzendoorn, M. H., & Kroonenberg, P. M. (1988). Cross-cultural patterns of attachment: A meta-analysis of the Strange Situation. Child Development, 59, 147–156; **Extract, p. 220 "a remarkable increase…":** Source: Aisworth, M. S. (1977). Infant development and mother-infant interaction among Ganda and American families. In P.H. Leiderman, S. R. Tulkin, & A. Rosenfeld(Eds.), Culture and infancy: Variations in the human experience (pp. 119–149). New York, NY: Academic Press. p. 143; **Extract, p. 225 "no apparent affection…":** Source: Donovan, J., & Zucker, C. (2010, October). Austim's first child. The Atlantic, pp. 78–90. p. 85

Chapter 6   **Figure 6.4, p. 254:** Chart: Major Findings of the High Scope Preschool Study. High Scope participants showed better academic performance, IQ scores, and earning potential and were less likely to be arrested later in life than other children; Author: L.J. Schweinhart, Author: J. Montie, Author: Z. Xiang, Author: W.S. Barnett, Author: C. R. Belfield, Author: M. Nores, in source: Schweinhart, L.J., Montie, J., Xiang, Z., Barnett, W.S., Belfield, C.R., & Nores, M., (2004) Lifetime Effects: The High/Scope Perry Preschool Study Through Age 40. Ypsilanti; MI: HighScope Press. Retrieved from www.highscope.org/Research/PerryProject/perrymain.htm; **Figure 6.5, p. 255:** Source: Adapted from Berko, J. (1958) "The child's learning of English morphology," Word, 14 pp. 150–177; **Extract, p. 265 "cultural myths**

become…": Source: Bem, S. L. (1981). Gender schema theory: A cognitive account of sex-typing. Psychological Review, 88, 354–364. p. 355

Chapter 7   Figure 7.2, p. 295: Source: Ogden, C.L., Carroll, M.D., Kit, B.K., & Flegal, K.M. (2014). Prevalence of childhood and adult obesity. JAMA, 311, 806–814; **Figure 7.3, p. 295:** Source: Data taken from Table 1 of http://www.cdc.gov/nchs/data/hestat/obesity_child_09_10/obesity_child_09_10.pdf; **Extract, p. 300 "Piaget: Are there more girls or more children?…":** Source: Piaget, J.(1965) The moral judgement of the child. New York, NY: Free Press (Original work published 1932) p. 167; **Extract, p. 300 "Piaget: Which would make a bigger bunch…":** Source: Adapted from Ginsburg. H.P. & Opper, S (1979) Piaget's Theory of Intellectual Development. Eaglewood cliffs, NJ: Prentice Hall. P. 123; **Figure 7.5, p. 307:** Source: Data from Brant, A.M., Haberstick, B.C., Corley, R.P., Wadsworth, S.J., DeFries, J.C. & Hewitt, J.K. (2009) "The development etiology of high IQ" Behavior Genetics 39, pp. 393–405; **Figure 7.6, p. 308:** Source: Flynn, J.R. (1999) "The discovery of IQ gains over time" American Psychologist 54 (1999) pp. 5–20; **Figure 7.7, p. 309:** Eppig, C., Fincher, C.L., and Thornhill, R.(2010). Parasite prevalence and the worldwide distribution of cognitive ability. Proceedings of the Royal Society B, 277, 3801–3808; **Figure 7.8, p. 315:** Source: Based on UNICEF (2014). State of the world's children. New York: Author; **Table 7.3, p. 316:** Source: Based on Rogoff, B., Correa-Chavez, M. & Cotus, M.N. (2005) "A cultural/historical view of schooling in human development" in Developmental Psychology and Social Change: Research, History and Policy (pp 225–263) Cambridge University Press; **Extract, p. 323 "quite enjoyable lives…":** Source: Larson, R., & Richards, M. H. (1994, p. 85). Divergent realities: The emotional lives of mothers, fathers, and adolescents. New York, NY: Basic Books. **Figure 7.9, p. 340:** Data Source: Rideout (2013).

Chapter 8   Figure 8.1, p. 351: Source: Nottelman, Sussman et al. (1987 "Gonadal and Adrenal Hormone Correlates of Adjustment in Early Adolescence" in Lerner & Fochs (eds) Biological Psychosicial Interactions in Early Adolescence; **Figure 8.2, p. 352:** Source: Based on Goldstein (1976); Chumlea et al. (2003); **Figure 8.3, p. 354:** Source: Eveleth, P. B., & Tanner, J. M. (1990). Worldwide variation in human growth. Cambridge, MA: Cambridge University Press; **Figure 8.4, p. 361:** Source: World Health Organization (WHO) (2008) "Inequalities in young people's health: Health behavior in school-aged children; **Figure 8.6, p. 370:** Source: Based on NCES (2014); **Figure 8.7, p. 372:** Source: Based on NCES, 2014; **Figure 8.8, p. 377:** Source: Larson, R.W., Moneta, G., Richards, M.H. & Wilson, S. (2002) "Continuity, stability and change in daily emotional experiences across adolescence" Child Development 73, pp. 1151–1165; **Figure 8.9, p. 383:** Source: Based on Based on Jensen, L.A. (2008) "Coming of age in a multicultural world: Globalization and adolescent cultural identity formation" in D.L. Browning (ed) Adolescent Identities: A Collection of Readings (pp. 3–17). Relational perspective book series. New York, NY: Analytic Press; **Table 8.1, p. 383:** Source: Based on Smith, C. & Denton, M.L. (2005) Soul Searching: The Religious and Spiritual Lives of American Teenagers (Oxford University Press); **Figure 8.10, p. 386:** Source: Granic, I., Dishion, T. J., & Hollerstein, T. (2003). The family ecology of adolescence: A dynamic systems perspective on normative development. In G. R. Adams & M. D. Berzonsky (Eds.), Blackwell handbook of adolescence (pp. 60–91). Malden, MA: Blackwell; **Figure 8.11, p. 395:** Source: Based on: WHO (2010); **Figure 8.12, p. 397:** Brown, J.D., Steele, J. & Walsh-Childrers, K. (eds). (2002) Sexual Teens, Sexual Media, Mahwah, NJ: Erlbaum p. 9; **Figure 8.13, p. 399:** Source: Gottfredson .M., & Hirschi, T (1990) A general theory of crime. Standford, CA: Standford University Press p. 125; Osgood, D. W (2009) Illegal behaviour: A presentation to the committee on the science of the adolescence of the National Academics. Washington, DC; **Figure 8.14, p. 400:** Source: Data from Alexander, B. (2001, June), Radical idea serves youth, saves money. Youth today, pp. 1, 42–44 p. 42.

Chapter 9   Figure 9.1, p. 409: Source: Based on U.S. Bureau of the Census (2004, 2010); **Figure 9.3, p. 410:** Source: U.S. Bureau of the Census (2011)**Figure 9.4, p. 411:** Source: Based on Arnett (2015); **Extract, p. 411 "I am confident…":** Source: Arnett, J.J., & Schwab, J. (2012).

The Clark University Poll of Emerging Adults: Thriving, struggling, and hopeful. Worcester, MA: Clark University. Retrieved from http://www.clarku.edu/clark-poll-emerging-adults/"; **Extract, p. 416 "waking at the same time…":** Source: Brown, A. S., & Susser, E. S. (2002). In utero infection and adult schizophrenia. Mental Retardation and Developmental Disabilities Research Reviews, 8, 51–57; **Figure 9.5, p. 418:** Source: Based on NHTSA (2014) 418 09 "Source: Arnett, J. J. (1996). Metalheads: Heavy metal music and adolescent alienation. Boulder, CO: Westview Press. P.79; **Figure 9.5, p. 420:** Source: Johnson, S. K., Murphy, S. R., Zewdie, S., & Reichard, R. J. (2008). The strong, sensitive type: Effects of gender stereotypes and leadership prototypes on the evaluation of male and female leaders. Organizational Behavior and Human Decision Processes, 106, 39–60; **Extract, p. 427 "four years of…":** Source: Rohlen, T. P. (1983). Japan's high schools. Berkeley: University of California Press; **Figure 9.8, p. 427:** Source: Based on Arnett, J.J., & Schwab, J. (2012). The Clark University Poll of Emerging Adults: Thriving, struggling, and hopeful. Worcester, MA: Clark University. Retrieved from http://www.clarku.edu/clark-poll-emerging-adults/; **Figure 9.9, p. 429:** Source: Based on Pew Research Center (2014); **Extract, p. 427 "in a free fall…":** Source: Halpern, S. (1998). The forgotten half revisited: American youth and young families, 1988–2008. Washington, DC: American Youth Policy Forum. p. xii; **Figure 9.10, p. 432:** Source: Based on Bureau of Labor Statistics, http://www.bls.gov/news.release/youth.t02.htm; **Figure 9.11, p. 435:** Source: Monitoring the Future. (2003). ISR study finds drinking and drug use decline after college. Ann Arbor, MI: Author. Available: www.umich.edu/newsinfo/releases/2002/Jan02/r013002a.html; **Extract, p. 437 "during which the young adult…":** Source: Erikson, E. H. (1968). Identity: Youth and crisis. New York, NY: Norton. P.156; **Table 9.2, p. 439:** Source: Based on Phinney, J. S., & Devich-Navarro, M. (1997). Variation in bicultural identification among African American and Mexican American adolescents. Journal of Research on Adolescence, 7, 3–32; **Figure 9.12, p. 441:** Source: David A. Cotter, et al., "The End of the Gender Revolution? Gender Role Attitudes from 1977 to 2006," General Social Survey (GSS), 1977–2006, November 2008; **Extract, p. 446 "I don't have to talk to them…":** Source Source: Arnett, J. J. (2004). Emerging adulthood: The winding road from the late teens through the twenties. New York: Oxford University Press. P.49; **Extract, p. 446–447 "I loved living at home…":** Source: Arnett, J. J. (2004). Emerging adulthood: The winding road from the late teens through the twenties. New York: Oxford University Press. P.54, 53; **Figure 9.13, p. 447:** Source: Data from Iacovou, M. (2011). Leaving home: Independence, togetherness, and income in Europe. New York: United Nations Population Division. Re-trieved from http://www.un.org/en/development/desa/population/publications/pdf/expert/2011-10_Iacovou_Expert-paper.pdf; **Extract, p. 450 "Living together with someone before marriage…":** Source: Popenoe, D., & Whitehead, B. D. (2001). The state of our unions, 2001: The social health of marriage in America. Report of the National Marriage Project, Rutgers, New Brunswick, NJ. Available: http://marriage.rutgers.edu; **Figure 9.14, p. 453:** Source: Based on Duggan, M., & Brenner, J. (2013). The demographics of social media users. Washington, DC: Pew Research Center; **Extract, p. 455 "I rely a lot on the support…":** Source: Arnett, J.J., & Schwab, J. (2012). The Clark University Poll of Emerging Adults: Thriving, struggling, and hopeful. Worcester, MA: Clark University. Retrieved from http://www.clarku.edu/clark-poll-emerging-adults/

Chapter 10   Extract, p. 462–463 "Sometimes I feel like I've reached…": Source: Arnett, J. J. (2004). Emerging adulthood: The winding road from the late teens through the twenties. New York: Oxford University Press; **Extract, p. 464 "after marriage…":** Source: Davis, S. S., & Davis, D. A. (2007). Morocco. In J. J. Arnett, R. Ahmed, B. Nsamenang, T. S. Saraswathi, & R. Silbereisen (Eds.), International encyclopedia of adolescence (pp. 645–655). New York, NY: Routledge. p. 59; **Figure 10.2, p. 468:** Source: Data fom Ogden, C.L., Carroll, M.D., Kit, B.D., & Flegal, K.M. (2013). Prevalence of obesity among adults. NCHS Data Brief, Number 131. Atlanta, GA: Centers for Disease Control and Prevention. Retrieved from http://www.cdc.gov/nchs/data/databriefs/db131.pdf; **Figure 10.3, p. 480:** Source: Sternberg, R. (1988).

The triarchic mind: A new theory of human intelligence. New York, NY: Viking Penguin. P.122; **Figure 10.4, p. 481:** Source: Based on Sternberg, R. J. (1986). Triangular theory of love. Psychological Review, 93, 119–135; **Table 10.1, p. 483:** Source: Based on Hatfield, E., & Rapson, R. L. (2005). Love and sex: Cross-cultural perspectives (2nd edition). Boston, MA: Allyn & Bacon; **Figure 10.5, p. 488:** Source: Based on Bramlett & Mosher (2001); **Extract, p. 489 "People who do not have…":** Source: DePaulo, B. (2006). Singled out: How singles are stereotyped, stigmatized, and ignored, and still live happily ever after. New York, NY: St. Martin's. p.2; **Table 10.1, p. 494:** Source: Based on Cowan, C. P., & Cowan, P. A. (2000). Working with couples during stressful transitions. In S. Dreman (Ed.), The family on the threshold of the 21st century (pp. 17–47). Mahwah, NJ: Erlbaum; **Extract, p. 502 "most week-nights…":** Source: Putnam, R. (2000). Bowling alone: The collapse and revival of American community. New York, NY: Simon & Schuster; **Extract, p. 502 "Much of television's attraction…":** Source: Robinson, J. P., Godbey, G., & Putnam, R. D. (1999). Time for life: The surprising ways Americans use their time. State College, PA: Pennsylvania State University Press. p. 149

Chapter 11 Figure 11.1, p. 518: Source: Based on Coleman, M. P., Quaresma, M., Berrino, F., Lutz, J. M., De Angelis, R., Ca-pocaccia, R.,…CONCORD Working Group (2008). Cancer survival in five countries: A worldwide population–based study (CONCORD). Lancet Oncology, 9, 730–756; **Figure 11.2, p. 523:** Source: Willis, S. L., & Schaie, K. W. (1999). Intellectual functioning in midlife. In S. L. Willis & J. D. Reid (Eds.), Life in the middle (pp. 105–146). San Diego, CA: Academic Press; **Unnumbered figure 11.1, p. 525:** Source: Schaie, K. W. (1998). The Seattle Longitudinal Studies of Adult Intelligence. In M. P. Lawton & T. A. Salthouse (Eds.), Essential papers on the psychology of aging (pp. 263–271). New York: New York University Press; **Extract, p. 533 "Excitement, turmoil, confusion…":** Source: Stewart, A. J., Ostrove, J. M., & Helson, R. (2001). Middle aging in women: Patterns of personality change from the 30s to the 50s. Journal of Adult Development, 8, 23–37; **Extract, p. 533 "flexible goal adjustment…":** Source: Brandtstädter, J. (2006). Adaptive resources in later life: Tenacious goal pursuit and flexible goal adjustment. In M. Csikszentmihalyi & I. S. Csik-szentmihalyi, (Eds.), A life worth living: Contributions to positive psychology (pp. 143–164). New York, NY: Oxford University Press; **Extract, p. 533 "Because age brings experience…":** Source: Lock, M. (1998). Deconstructing the change: Female maturation in Japan and North America. In R.A. Shweder (Ed.), Welcome to middle age! (and Other Cultural Fictions) (pp. 45–74). Chicago, IL: University of Chicago Press. p. 59; **Extract, p. 546 "Passing on family history…":** Source: AARP (2002). The Grandparent Study 2002 report. Washington, DC: Author; Hebblethwaite, S., & Norris, J. (2011). Expressions of generativity through family leisure: Experiences of grandparents and adult grandchildren. Family Relations: An Interdisciplinary Journal of Applied Family Studies, 60, 121–133; Mueller, M., Wilhelm, B., & Elder, G. (2002). Variations in grandparenting. Research on Aging, 24, 360–388."; **Figure 11.3, p. 547:** Source: Vaillant, C.O. & Vaillant, G.E., Is the U-curve of marital satisfaction an illusion? A 40-year study of marriage. Journal of Marriage and the Family, 55, 230–239; **Figure 11.4, p. 551:** Source: Based on International Labor Organization (ILO) (2011). Global employment trends 2011. Geneva, Switzerland: Author.

Chapter 12 Extract, p. 559 "Last scene of all…": Source: William Shakespeare, As You Like It, Act II, Scene VII [All the world's a stage]; **Figure 12.1, p. 562:** Source: Population Division, DESA, United Nations; **Figure 12.2, p. 571:** Source: Based on OECD (2009). Health at a glance 2009: OECD indicators. Author; **Extract, p. 583 "expertise in the conduct…":** Source: Baltes, P. B., & Staudinger, U. M. (2000, p. 124). Wisdom. American Psychologist, 55, 122–136; **Figure 12.4, p. 590:** Source: Carstensen, L.L., Isaacowitz, D.M., & Charles, S.T. (1999). Taking time seriously: A theory of socioemotional selectivity. American Psychologist, 54, 165–181; **Figure 12.5, p. 598:** Source: Based on AARP (2009). The divorce experience: A study of divorce at midlife and beyond. Washington, DC: Author; **Figure 12.6, p. 603:** Source: Based on Smith & Snell (2009).

Chapter 13 Figure 13.1, p. 613: Source: Massachusetts Department of Public Health; **Figure 13.2, p. 615:** Source: http://www.healthypeople.gov/2020/topicsobjectives2020/nationalsnapshot.aspx?topicId=21; **Extract, p. 616 "In this world nothing can be said…":** Source: Benjamin Franklin, Quoted in Letter to Jean-Baptiste Leroy (13 November 1789); reported in Bartlett's Familiar Quotations, 10th ed. (1919); **Extract, p. 622 "Interdisciplinary care team…":** Source: National Hospice and Palliative Care Organization and Research Department. (2008). Hospice facts and figures. Retrieved from http://www.nhpco.org/files/public/Statistics_Research/NHPCO_facts-and-figures_2008.pdf; **Extract, p. 624 "terminal sedation…":** Source: Hooyman, N. R., & Kiyak, H. A. (2011). Social gerontology: A multidisciplinary perspective (9th ed.). Boston, MA: Pearson; **Extract, p. 624 "weary of life":** Source: Rurup, M. L., Muller, M. T., Onwuteaka-Philipsen, B. D., van der Heide, A., van der Wal, G., & van der Maas, P. J. (2005). Requests for euthanasia or physician-assisted suicide from older persons who do not have a severe disease: An interview study. Psychological Medicine, 35, 665–671; **Figure 13.3, p. 637:** Source: Based on ISSP (International Social Survey Programme) survey (1998); **Figure 13.4, p. 638:** Source: Based on U.S. Religious Landscape Survey, Pew Center's Forum on Religion & Public Life, © 2008, Pew Research Center. http://religions.pewforum.org/

Photographs

Chapter 1 p. 6: Pavel Gospodinov/Alamy; **p. 8:** Aldo Pavan/Horizons WWP/Alamy; **p. 10:** Robin Laurance/Alamy; **p. 12:** Publiphoto/Science Source; **p. 13:** Daniel Maurer/AP Images; **p. 13:** Herbert Kraft/akg-images/Newscom; **p. 20:** Pierre Roussel/Ethno Images, Inc./Alamy; **p. 23:** PHOTOEDIT/PhotoEdit; **p. 26:** Vladimir Melnik/Shutterstock; **p. 27:** David R. Frazier Photolibrary, Inc./Alamy; **p. 31:** Véronique Burger/Science Source; **p. 34:** Richard T. Nowitz/Science Source; **p. 35:** Bettmann/CORBIS; **p. 37:** Jeff Greenberg 5 of 6/Alamy; **p. 40:** CK Archive; **p. 40:** CK Archive; **p. 40:** CK Archive; **p. 40:** CK Archive; **p. 13:** Igor Strukov/Fotolia; **p. 13:** Nikreates/Alamy; **p. 13:** 300dpi/Shutterstock; **p. 13:** Gianni Dagli Orti/The Art Archive at Art Resource, NY; **p. 24:** Chubykin Arkady/Shutterstock; **p. 24:** Felix Mizioznikov/Shutterstock; **p. 24:** Monkey Business Images/Shutterstock; **p. 24:** mamahoohooba/Shutterstock; **p. 24:** Monkey Business Images/Shutterstock; **p. 24:** Stephen Coburn/Shutterstock; **p. 24:** Noam/Fotolia; **p. 24:** szefei/Shutterstock; **p. 647:** Jeff Arnett

Chapter 2 p. 47: SPL/Science Source; **p. 52:** Thinkstock Images/Stockbyte/Getty Images; **p. 53:** dbtravel/dbimages/Alamy; **p. 54:** SerrNovik/Fotolia; **p. 59:** Sashkin/Fotolia; **p. 61:** BSIP/Newscom; **p. 61:** kage-mikrofotografie/doc-stock/Alamy; **p. 61:** Dr. M.A. Ansary/Science Source; **p. 61:** Steve Allen/Alamy; **p. 61:** Neil Bromhall/Science Source; **p. 61:** Science Source; **p. 62:** R. Rawlins PhD/Custom Medical Stock Photo/Newscom; **p. 67:** Anna Omelchenko/Shutterstock; **p. 69:** Sue Cunningham Photographic/Alamy; **p. 70:** Gideon Mendel/Corbis News/Corbis for UNICEF; **p. 72:** Alex Segre/Alamy; **p. 74:** Keith Brofsky/Photodisc/Getty Images; **p. 77:** Машков Юрий/ITAR-TASS/Newscom

Chapter 3 p. 85: Tyler Olson/Shutterstock; **p. 90:** Emilio Ereza/Alamy; **p. 90:** Bush/Stringer/Hulton Archive/Getty Images; **p. 91:** Angela Hampton Picture Library/Alamy; **p. 94:** Borderlands/Alamy; **p. 99:** Buddy Mays/Alamy; **p. 103:** Jake Lyell/Alamy; **p. 104:** Hypermania/Alamy; **p. 105:** Rohit Seth/Shutterstock; **p. 107:** Picture Partners/Alamy; **p. 109:** Kathleen Nelson/Alamy; **p. 113:** Henri Roger/Roger-Viollet/The Image Works; **p. 114:** Lindsay Hebberd/Corbis; **p. 120:** BananaStock/Getty Images; **p. 120:** Gale Zucker/Aurora Photos/Alamy; **p. 122:** Nina Leen/Time Life Pictures/Getty Images; **p. 123:** Voisin/Phanie/Science Source

Chapter 4 p. 131: Red Images, LLC/Alamy; **p. 132:** Gelpi/Shutterstock; **p. 134:** Mike Abrahams/Alamy; **p. 137:** Stanislav Fridkin/Shutterstock; **p. 140:** Paul Almasy/CORBIS; **p. 141:** Joerg Boethling/Alamy; **p. 142:** infocusphotos.com/Alamy; **p. 144:** dbimages/Alamy; **p. 146:** Dave Spataro/LuckyPix/Corbis; **p. 147:** Mark

Name Index

Subject Index

Note: Boldface terms and page numbers are key terms; page numbers followed by f indicate figures; those followed by t indicate tables.